W9-AOU-507

PRENTICE HALL
LITERATURE

GRADE 8

COMMON CORE EDITION ©

Upper Saddle River, New Jersey

Boston, Massachusetts

Chandler, Arizona

Glenview, Illinois

ISBN-13: 978-0-13-319554-5
ISBN-10:   0-13-319554-6
8 9 10 V063 15 14 13

Contributing Authors

The contributing authors guided the direction and philosophy of Pearson Prentice Hall Literature. *Working with the development team, they helped to build the pedagogical integrity of the program and to ensure its relevance for today's teachers and students.*

Grant Wiggins, Ed.D., is the President of Authentic Education in Hopewell, New Jersey. He earned his Ed.D. from Harvard University and his B.A. from St. John's College in Annapolis. Grant consults with schools, districts, and state education departments on a variety of reform matters; organizes conferences and workshops; and develops print materials and Web resources on curricular change. He is the coauthor, with Jay McTighe, of *Understanding by Design* and *The Understanding by Design Handbook,* the award-winning and highly successful materials on curriculum published by ASCD. His work has been supported by the Pew Charitable Trusts, the Geraldine R. Dodge Foundation, and the National Science Foundation. *The Association for Supervision of Curriculum Development (ASCD), publisher of the "Understanding by Design Handbook" co-authored by Grant Wiggins and registered owner of the trademark "Understanding by Design," has not authorized, approved, or sponsored this work and is in no way affiliated with Pearson or its products.*

Jeff Anderson has worked with  struggling writers and readers for almost 20 years. Anderson's specialty is the integration of grammar and editing instruction into the processes of reading and writing. He has published two books, *Mechanically Inclined: Building Grammar, Usage, and Style into Writer's Workshop* and *Everyday Editing: Inviting Students to Develop Skill and Craft in Writer's Workshop,* as well as a DVD, *The Craft of Grammar.* Anderson's work has appeared in *English Journal.* Anderson won the NCTE Paul and Kate Farmer Award for his *English Journal* article on teaching grammar in context.

Arnetha F. Ball, Ph.D., is a  Professor at Stanford University. Her areas of expertise include language and literacy studies of diverse student populations, research on writing instruction, and teacher preparation for working with diverse populations. She is the author of *African American Literacies Unleashed* with Dr. Ted Lardner, and *Multicultural Strategies for Education and Social Change.*

Sheridan Blau is Professor of  Education and English at the University of California, Santa Barbara, where he directs the South Coast Writing Project and the Literature Institute for Teachers. He has served in senior advisory roles for such groups as the National Board for Professional Teaching Standards, the College Board, and the American Board for Teacher Education. Blau served for twenty years on the National Writing Project Advisory Board and Task Force, and is a former president of NCTE. Blau is the author of *The Literature Workshop: Teaching Texts and Their Readers,* which was named by the Conference on English Education as the 2004 Richard Meade Award winner for outstanding research in English education.

William G. Brozo, Ph.D., is a Professor of Literacy at George Mason University in Fairfax, Virginia. He has taught reading and language arts in junior and senior high school and is the author of numerous texts on literacy development. Dr. Brozo's work focuses on building capacity among teacher leaders, enriching the literate culture of schools, enhancing the literate lives of boys, and making teaching more responsive to the needs of all students. His recent publications include *Bright Beginnings for Boys: Engaging Young Boys in Active Literacy* and the *Adolescent Literacy Inventory.*

Doug Buehl is a teacher, author, and  national literacy consultant. He is the author of *Classroom Strategies for Interactive Learning* and coauthor of *Reading and the High School Student: Strategies to Enhance Literacy;* and *Strategies to Enhance Literacy and Learning in Middle School Content Area Classrooms.*

Jim Cummins, Ph.D, is a profes-  sor in the Modern Language Centre at the University of Toronto. He is the author of numerous publications, including *Negotiating Identities: Education for Empowerment in a Diverse Society.* Cummins coined the acronyms BICS and CAPT to help differentiate the type of language ability students need for success.

Harvey Daniels, Ph.D., has been  a classroom teacher, writing project director, author, and university professor. "Smokey" serves as an international consultant to schools, districts, and educational agencies. He is known for his work on student-led book clubs, as recounted in *Literature Circles: Voice and Choice in Book Clubs & Reading Groups* and *Mini Lessons for Literature Circles.* Recent works include *Subjects Matter: Every Teacher's Guide to Content-Area Reading* and *Content Area Writing: Every Teacher's Guide.*

Jane Feber taught language arts in  Jacksonville, Florida, for 36 years. Her innovative approach to instruction has earned her several awards, including the NMSA Distinguished Educator Award, the NCTE Edwin A. Hoey Award, the Gladys Prior Award for Teaching Excellence, and the Florida Council of Teachers of English Teacher of the Year Award. She is a National Board Certified Teacher, past president of the Florida Council of Teachers of English and is the author of *Creative Book Reports* and *Active Word Play*.

Danling Fu, Ph.D., is Professor  of Language and Culture in the College of Education at the University of Florida. She researches and provides inservice to public schools nationally, focusing on literacy instruction for new immigrant students. Fu's books include *My Trouble is My English* and *An Island of English* addressing English language learners in the secondary schools. She has authored chapters in the *Handbook of Adolescent Literacy Research* and in *Adolescent Literacy: Turning Promise to Practice*.

Kelly Gallagher is a full-time English  teacher at Magnolia High School in Anaheim, California. He is the former co-director of the South Basin Writing Project at California State University, Long Beach. Gallagher wrote *Reading Reasons: Motivational Mini-Lessons for the Middle and High School, Deeper Reading: Comprehending Challenging Texts 4-12,* and *Teaching Adolescent Writers.* Gallagher won the Secondary Award of Classroom Excellence from the California Association of Teachers of English—the state's top English teacher honor.

Sharroky Hollie, Ph.D., is an  assistant professor at California State University, Dominguez Hills, and an urban literacy visiting professor at Webster University, St. Louis. Hollie's work focuses on professional development, African American education, and second language methodology. He is a contributing author in two texts on culturally and linguistically responsive teaching. He is the Executive Director of the Center for Culturally Responsive Teaching and Learning and the co-founding director of the Culture and Language Academy of Success, an independent charter school in Los Angeles.

Dr. Donald J. Leu, Ph.D., teaches  at the University of Connecticut and holds a joint appointment in Curriculum and Instruction and in Educational Psychology. He directs the New Literacies Research Lab and is a member of the Board of Directors of the International Reading Association. Leu studies the skills required to read, write, and learn with Internet technologies. His research has been funded by groups including the U.S. Department of Education, the National Science Foundation, and the Bill & Melinda Gates Foundation.

Jon Scieszka founded GUYS READ,  a nonprofit literacy initiative for boys, to call attention to the problem of getting boys connected with reading. In 2008, he was named the first U.S. National Ambassador for Young People's Literature by the Library of Congress. Scieszka taught from first grade to eighth grade for ten years in New York City, drawing inspiration from his students to write *The True Story of the 3 Little Pigs!, The Stinky Cheese Man*, the *Time Warp Trio* series of chapter books, and the *Trucktown* series of books for beginning readers.

Sharon Vaughn, Ph.D., teaches  at the University of Texas at Austin. She is the previous Editor-in-Chief of the *Journal of Learning Disabilities* and the co-editor of *Learning Disabilities Research and Practice*. She is the recipient of the American Education Research Association SIG Award for Outstanding Researcher. Vaughn's work focuses on effective practices for enhancing reading outcomes for students with reading difficulties. She is the author of more than 100 articles and numerous books designed to improve research-based practices in the classroom.

Karen K. Wixson is Dean of the  School of Education at the University of North Carolina, Greensboro. She has published widely in the areas of literacy curriculum, instruction, and assessment. Wixson has been an advisor to the National Research Council and helped develop the National Assessment of Educational Progress (NAEP) reading tests. She is a past member of the IRA Board of Directors and co-chair of the IRA Commission on RTI. Recently, Wixson served on the English Language Arts Work Team that was part of the Common Core State Standards Initiative.

Each unit addresses a BIG Question to enrich exploration of literary concepts and reading strategies.

Is *truth* the same for everyone?

INFORMATIONAL TEXT HIGHLIGHTED

Skills at a Glance

This page provides a quick look at the skills you will learn and practice in Unit 1.

Reading Skills

Make Predictions
  Make and Support Predictions
  Read Ahead to Confirm or Modify Predictions
Author's Purpose
  Recognize Details Indicating Author's Purpose
  Evaluate Whether the Author
    Achieves His or Her Purpose

Reading for Information

Use Information to Solve a Problem
Identify Central Idea and Details

Literary Analysis

Theme
Central Idea
Plot
Conflict and Resolution
Comparing Narrative Structure
Mood
Author's Style
Comparing Characters of Different Eras

Vocabulary

Big Question Vocabulary
Roots: *-scope-, -trib-, -limin-, -judex-,*
  -lum-, -duc-, -sol-, -equi-
Using a Dictionary and Thesaurus

Conventions

Common and Proper Nouns
Plural Nouns
Using Concrete, Abstract, and Possessive Nouns
Personal Pronouns
Reflexive Pronouns
Revising for Pronoun-Antecedent Agreement

Writing

Writing About the Big Question
New Ending
Letter
Personal Narrative
Observation Journal
Timed Writing
Writing Workshop: Explanatory Text:
  Description of a Person
Writing Workshop: Narrative Text:
  Autobiographical Essay

Speaking and Listening

Radio Broadcast
Role Play
Effective Listening and Note-Taking

Research and Technology

Research Report
Brochure

Common Core State Standards
Addressed in This Unit

Reading Literature RL.8.1, RL.8.2, RL.8.3, RL.8.4, RL.8.5, RL.8.10

Reading Informational Text RI.8.2, RI.8.3, RI.8.4, RI.8.5, RI.8.10

Writing W.8.2, W.8.2.c, W.8.2.d, W.8.2.f, W.8.3, W.8.3.a, W.8.3.b, W.8.3.c, W.8.3.d, W.8.3.e, W.8.5, W.8.6, W.8.7, W.8.8

Speaking and Listening SL.8.1, SL.8.1.d, SL.8.2, SL.8.3, SL.8.6

Language L.8.1, L.8.2, L.8.3, L.8.4, L.8.4.b, L.8.4.c, L.8.4.d, L.8.6

[For the full wording of the standards, see the standards chart in the front of your textbook.]

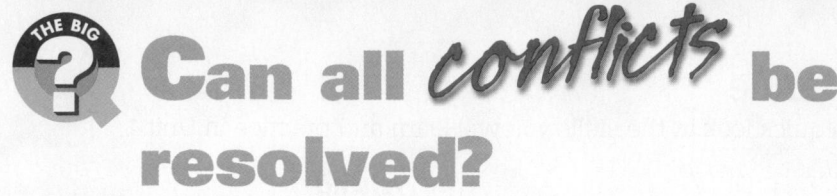

Can all *conflicts* be resolved?

INFORMATIONAL TEXT HIGHLIGHTED

PHLit Online!
www.PHLitOnline.com
Interactive resources provide
personalized instruction and
activities online.

Skills at a Glance

This page provides a quick look at the skills you will learn and practice in Unit 2.

Reading Skills

Compare and Contrast

  Ask Questions to Compare and Contrast

  Compare Characters' Perspectives

Make Inferences

  Use Details to Make Inferences

  Identify Connections to Make Inferences

Reading for Information

Compare Summaries to an Original Text

Evaluate Persuasive Appeals

Literary Analysis

Character and Plot

Theme

Setting

Character Traits

Comparing Types of Narratives

Point of View

Theme

Comparing Symbols

Vocabulary

Big Question Vocabulary

Prefixes: *de-, mis-, per-*

Suffixes: *-ee, -ity*

Roots: *-nounc-* or *-nunc-, -spec-*

Word Origins

Conventions

Action and Linking Verbs

Principal Parts of Regular Verbs

Revising Verb Phrases for Mood

Simple Tenses of Verbs

Tense and Mood of Verbs

Revising for Subject-Verb Agreement

Writing

Writing About the Big Question

Description

Character Profile

Dialogue

Personal Essay

Timed Writing

Writing Workshop: Argument: Critical Review

Writing Workshop: Narrative Text: Short Story

Speaking and Listening

Oral Response

Panel Discussion

Conducting Interviews

Research and Technology

Oral Report

Summary of an Article

 Common Core State Standards Addressed in This Unit

Reading Literature RL.8.1, RL.8.2, RL.8.3, RL.8.4, RL.8.6, RL.8.10

Reading Informational Text RI.8.1, RI.8.2, RI.8.10

Writing W.8.1.a, W.8.1.b, W.8.2, W.8.2.b, W.8.3, W.8.3.a, W.8.3.b, W.8.3.d, W.8.4, W.8.5, W.8.9

Speaking and Listening SL.8.1, SL.8.1.a, SL.8.1.b, SL.8.1.c, SL.8.1.d, SL.8.4, SL.8.6

Language L.8.1, L.8.1.b, L.8.1.c, L.8.2.c, L.8.3.a, L.8.4, L.8.4.a, L.8.4.b, L.8.4.c, L.8.5, L.8.6

[For the full wording of the standards, see the standards chart in the front of your textbook.]

How much *information* is enough?

Point of View and Purpose
Organizational Structure
Word Choice and Tone

Main Idea
Narrative Essay

Main Idea
Biography and
Autobiography

INFORMATIONAL TEXT HIGHLIGHTED

PHLit Online!
www.PHLitOnline.com
Interactive resources provide personalized instruction and activities online.

Skills at a Glance

This page provides a quick look at the skills you will learn and practice in Unit 3.

Reading Skills

Main Idea
  Identify the Implied Main Idea
  Make Connections
Fact and Opinion
  Use Clue Words to Distinguish
    Fact From Opinion
  Ask Questions to Evaluate Support

Reading for Information

Analyze Treatment, Scope, and
  Organization of Ideas
Analyze Proposition and Support

Literary Analysis

Point of View and Purpose
Organizational Structure
Word Choice and Tone
Narrative Essay
Biography and Autobiography
Comparing Types of Organization
Persuasive Techniques
Word Choice
Comparing Tone

Vocabulary

Big Question Vocabulary
Suffixes: *-ance, -ly*
Roots: *-nym-, -val-, -vad-, -bellum-,*
  -pass-, -tract-
Words With Multiple Meanings

Conventions

Adjectives and Articles
Adverbs
Revising to Correct Comparative
  and Superlative Forms
Conjunctions

Prepositions
Revising Sentences by Combining
  With Conjunctions

Writing

Writing About the Big Question
Biographical Sketch
Reflective Essay
Evaluation of Persuasive Argument
Response
Timed Writing
Writing Workshop: Informative Text:
  How-to Essay
Writing Workshop: Argument: Editorial

Speaking and Listening

Skit
Speech
Evaluating an Oral Presentation

Research and Technology

Multimedia Presentation
Snapshot of Arguments

**Ⓒ Common Core State Standards
Addressed in This Unit**

Reading Literature RL.8.10
Reading Informational Text RI.8.2, RI.8.3, RI.8.4,
RI.8.5, RI.8.8, RI.8.9, RI.8.10
Writing W.8.1, W.8.1.a, W.8.1.b, W.8.1.c, W.8.1.d,
W.8.1.e, W.8.2, W.8.2.b, W.8.2.c, W.8.6, W.8.7, W.8.9,
W.8.9.b
Speaking and Listening SL.8.1, SL.8.2, SL.8.3,
SL.8.4, SL.8.5, SL.8.6
Language L.8.1, L.8.4, L.8.4.a, L.8.4.b, L.8.4.c., L.8.5.c,
L.8.6
[For the full wording of the standards, see the standards
chart in the front of your textbook.]

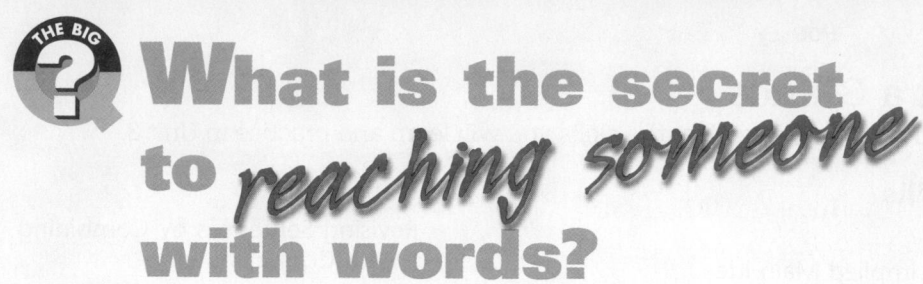

What is the secret to *reaching someone* with words?

INFORMATIONAL TEXT HIGHLIGHTED

Compare and Contrast Features of Consumer Materials

Comparing Poetry and Prose

Paraphrase Forms of Poetry

Paraphrase Imagery

Contents **xxi**

Skills at a Glance

This page provides a quick look at the skills you will learn and practice in Unit 4.

Reading Skills

Context Clues
  Preview to Identify Unfamiliar Words
  Reread and Read Ahead to Confirm Meaning
Paraphrase
  Reread to Clarify Meaning
  Read Aloud Fluently According to Punctuation

Reading for Information

Compare and Contrast Features
  of Consumer Materials
Analyze Technical Directions

Literary Analysis

Connotative Meanings
Simile; Metaphor
Allusion
Sound Devices
Figurative Language
Comparing Poetry and Prose
Forms of Poetry
Imagery
Comparing Types of Description

Vocabulary

Big Question Vocabulary
Prefixes: *im-, in-, trans-*
Suffixes: *-ous, -ive*
Roots: *-cede-, -ceed-, -vert-*
Idioms

Conventions

Subject Complements
Direct and Indirect Objects
Choosing Between Active and Passive Voice
Prepositional Phrases

Infinitive Phrases
Revising to Vary Sentence Patterns

Writing

Writing About the Big Question
Poem
Study for a Poem
Writing Workshop: Argument:
  Problem-and-Solution Essay
Lyric or Narrative Poem
Review
Timed Writing
Writing Workshop: Informative Text:
  Comparison-and-Contrast Essay

Speaking and Listening

Poetry Recitation
Evaluation Form
Evaluating Media Messages

Research and Technology

Mini-Anthology
Poet's Profile

 Common Core State Standards Addressed in This Unit

Reading Literature RL.8.1, RL.8.2, RL.8.4, RL.8.5, RL.8.10

Reading Informational Text RI.8.4, RI.8.5, RI.8.7, RI.8.10

Writing W.8.1, W.8.2, W.8.2.a, W.8.2.b, W.8.3, W.8.4, W.8.8, W.8.9

Speaking and Listening SL.8.1, SL.8.2, L.8.5.b, SL.8.6

Language L.8.1, L.8.2.c, L.8.4.a, L.8.4.b, L.8.5, L.8.5.a, L.8.5.b, L.8.6

[For the full wording of the standards, see the standards chart in the front of your textbook.]

Is it our *differences* or our *similarities* that matter most?

INFORMATIONAL TEXT HIGHLIGHTED

Skills at a Glance

This page provides a quick look at the skills you will learn and practice in Unit 5.

Reading Skill

Draw Conclusions
  Make Connections

Cause and Effect
  Use Background Information to
    Link Historical Causes With Effects
  Ask Questions to Analyze
    Cause-and-Effect Relationships

Reading for Information

Compare and Contrast Features
  and Elements

Evaluate Unity and Coherence

Literary Analysis

Character

Conflict

Elements of Drama

Setting and Character

Comparing Adaptations to Originals

Dialogue

Character's Motivation

Comparing Sources With
  a Dramatization

Vocabulary

Amazing Words:
  Big Question Vocabulary

Prefixes: *in-*

Suffixes: *-ory, -ist*

Borrowed and Foreign Words

Conventions

Participial Phrases

Revising to Combine Sentences
  Using Gerunds and Participles

Dangling and Misplaced Modifiers

Clauses

Revising to Combine Sentences
  Using Clauses

Writing

Writing About the Big Question

Public Service Announcement

Writing Workshop: Informative Text:
  Business Letter

Diary Entries

Film Review

Timed Writing

Writing Workshop: Informative Text:
  Research Report

Speaking and Listening

Debate

Guided Tour

Delivering a Narrative
  Presentation

Research and Technology

Bulletin Board Display

**Ⓒ Common Core State Standards
Addressed in This Unit**

Reading Literature RL.8.1, RL.8.3, RL.8.4, RL.8.5,
RL.8.6, RL.8.7, RL.8.9, RL.8.10

Reading Informational Text RI.8.5, RI.8.6, RI.8.10

Writing W.8.1, W.8.2, W.8.2.a, W.8.3, W.8.4, W.8.7,
W.8.8, W.8.9, W.8.10

Speaking and Listening SL.8.1, SL.8.4, SL.8.6

Language L.8.1, L.8.1.a, L.8.2.b, L.8.4.b, L.8.6

[For the full wording of the standards, see the standards
chart in the front of your textbook.]

Are yesterday's *heroes* important today?

Skills at a Glance

This page provides a quick look at the skills you will learn and practice in Unit 6.

Reading Skill

Summarize
  Reread to Identify Main Events or Ideas
  Use Graphics to Organize Main Events
Purpose for Reading
  Ask Questions to Set a Purpose for Reading
  Adjust Your Reading Rate According to Purpose

Reading for Information

Evaluate Structural Patterns
Evaluate the Treatment, Scope, and Organization of Ideas

Literary Analysis

Social and Cultural Context
Theme
Mythology
Oral Tradition
Comparing Heroic Characters
Cultural Context
Author's Influences
Comparing Works on a Similar Theme

Vocabulary

Big Question Vocabulary
Roots: -sacr-, -grat-, -nat-, -her-, -aud-
Dialect
Suffixes: -ful, -eer
Figurative Language

Conventions

Sentence Structure
Commas
Using Language to Maintain Interest
Semicolons and Colons
Capitalization
Revising Run-on Sentences and Sentence Fragments

Writing

Writing About the Big Question
Myth
Critical Analysis
Writing Workshop: Informative Text: Multimedia Report
Research Proposal
Persuasive Speech
Timed Writing
Writing Workshop: Explanatory Text: Cause-and-Effect Essay

Speaking and Listening

Oral Presentation
Storytelling Workshop
Delivering a Persuasive Speech Using Multimedia

Research and Technology

Letter
Newspaper Article

 Common Core State Standards Addressed in This Unit

Reading Literature RL.8.2, RL.8.3, RL.8.4, RL.8.5, RL.8.7, RL.8.9, RL.8.10
Reading Informational Text RI.8.3, RI.8.7, RI.8.10
Writing W.8.1, W.8.2, W.8.3, W.8.3.b, W.8.3.e, W.8.5, W.8.7, W.8.10
Speaking and Listening SL.8.1, SL.8.5, SL.8.6
Language L.8.1, L.8.2, L.8.4.b, L.8.5, L.8.6
[For the full wording of the standards, see the standards chart in the front of your textbook.]

Literature

▶ Poetry

Informational Text—Literary Nonfiction

▶ Functional Text

▶ Literature in Context—Reading in the Content Areas

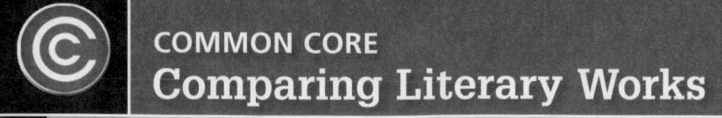

▶ Writing Workshops

▶ Vocabulary Workshops

▶ Communications Workshops

The **Common Core State Standards** will prepare you to succeed in college and your future career. They are separated into four sections—Reading (Literature and Informational Text), Writing, Speaking and Listening, and Language. Beginning each section, the College and Career Readiness Anchor Standards define what you need to achieve by the end of high school. The grade-specific standards that follow define what you need to know by the end of your current grade level.

© Common Core Reading Standards

College and Career Readiness Anchor Standards

Key Ideas and Details

1. Read closely to determine what the text says explicitly and to make logical inferences from it; cite specific textual evidence when writing or speaking to support conclusions drawn from the text.

2. Determine central ideas or themes of a text and analyze their development; summarize the key supporting details and ideas.

3. Analyze how and why individuals, events, and ideas develop and interact over the course of a text.

Craft and Structure

4. Interpret words and phrases as they are used in a text, including determining technical, connotative, and figurative meanings, and analyze how specific word choices shape meaning or tone.

5. Analyze the structure of texts, including how specific sentences, paragraphs, and larger portions of the text (e.g., a section, chapter, scene, or stanza) relate to each other and the whole.

6. Assess how point of view or purpose shapes the content and style of a text.

Integration of Knowledge and Ideas

7. Integrate and evaluate content presented in diverse formats and media, including visually and quantitatively, as well as in words.

8. Delineate and evaluate the argument and specific claims in a text, including the validity of the reasoning as well as the relevance and sufficiency of the evidence.

9. Analyze how two or more texts address similar themes or topics in order to build knowledge or to compare the approaches the authors take.

Range of Reading and Level of Text Complexity

10. Read and comprehend complex literary and informational texts independently and proficiently.

Grade 8 Reading Standards for Literature

Key Ideas and Details

1. Cite the textual evidence that most strongly supports an analysis of what the text says explicitly as well as inferences drawn from the text.

2. Determine a theme or central idea of a text and analyze its development over the course of the text, including its relationship to the characters, setting, and plot; provide an objective summary of the text.

3. Analyze how particular lines of dialogue or incidents in a story or drama propel the action, reveal aspects of a character, or provoke a decision.

Craft and Structure

4. Determine the meaning of words and phrases as they are used in a text, including figurative and connotative meanings; analyze the impact of specific word choices on meaning and tone, including analogies or allusions to other texts.

5. Compare and contrast the structure of two or more texts and analyze how the differing structure of each text contributes to its meaning and style.

6. Analyze how differences in the points of view of the characters and the audience or reader (e.g., created through the use of dramatic irony) create such effects as suspense or humor.

Integration of Knowledge and Ideas

7. Analyze the extent to which a filmed or live production of a story or drama stays faithful to or departs from the text or script, evaluating the choices made by the director or actors.

8. (Not applicable to literature)

9. Analyze how a modern work of fiction draws on themes, patterns of events, or character types from myths, traditional stories, or religious works such as the Bible, including describing how the material is rendered new.

Range of Reading and Level of Text Complexity

10. By the end of the year, read and comprehend literature, including stories, dramas, and poems, at the high end of grades 6–8 text complexity band independently and proficiently.

Grade 8 Reading Standards for Informational Text

Key Ideas and Details

1. Cite the textual evidence that most strongly supports an analysis of what the text says explicitly as well as inferences drawn from the text.

2. Determine a central idea of a text and analyze its development over the course of the text, including its relationship to supporting ideas; provide an objective summary of the text.

3. Analyze how a text makes connections among and distinctions between individuals, ideas, or events (e.g., through comparisons, analogies, or categories).

Craft and Structure

4. Determine the meaning of words and phrases as they are used in a text, including figurative, connotative, and technical meanings; analyze the impact of specific word choices on meaning and tone, including analogies or allusions to other texts.

5. Analyze in detail the structure of a specific paragraph in a text, including the role of particular sentences in developing and refining a key concept.

6. Determine an author's point of view or purpose in a text and analyze how the author acknowledges and responds to conflicting evidence or viewpoints.

Integration of Knowledge and Ideas

7. Evaluate the advantages and disadvantages of using different mediums (e.g., print or digital text, video, multimedia) to present a particular topic or idea.

8. Delineate and evaluate the argument and specific claims in a text, assessing whether the reasoning is sound and the evidence is relevant and sufficient; recognize when irrelevant evidence is introduced.

9. Analyze a case in which two or more texts provide conflicting information on the same topic and identify where the texts disagree on matters of fact or interpretation.

Range of Reading and Level of Text Complexity

10. By the end of the year, read and comprehend literary nonfiction at the high end of the grades 6–8 text complexity band independently and proficiently.

© Common Core Writing Standards

College and Career Readiness Anchor Standards

Text Types and Purposes

1. Write arguments to support claims in an analysis of substantive topics or texts, using valid reasoning and relevant and sufficient evidence.

2. Write informative/explanatory texts to examine and convey complex ideas and information clearly and accurately through the effective selection, organization, and analysis of content.

3. Write narratives to develop real or imagined experiences or events using effective technique, well-chosen details, and well-structured event sequences.

Production and Distribution of Writing

4. Produce clear and coherent writing in which the development, organization, and style are appropriate to task, purpose, and audience.

5. Develop and strengthen writing as needed by planning, revising, editing, rewriting, or trying a new approach.

6. Use technology, including the Internet, to produce and publish writing and to interact and collaborate with others.

Research to Build and Present Knowledge

7. Conduct short as well as more sustained research projects based on focused questions, demonstrating understanding of the subject under investigation.

8. Gather relevant information from multiple print and digital sources, assess the credibility and accuracy of each source, and integrate the information while avoiding plagiarism.

9. Draw evidence from literary or informational texts to support analysis, reflection, and research.

Range of Writing

10. Write routinely over extended time frames (time for research, reflection, and revision) and shorter time frames (a single sitting or a day or two) for a range of tasks, purposes, and audiences.

Grade 8 Writing Standards

Text Types and Purposes

1. Write arguments to support claims with clear reasons and relevant evidence.
   a. Introduce claim(s), acknowledge and distinguish the claim(s) from alternate or opposing claims, and organize the reasons and evidence logically.
   b. Support claim(s) with logical reasoning and relevant evidence, using accurate, credible sources and demonstrating an understanding of the topic or text.
   c. Use words, phrases, and clauses to create cohesion and clarify the relationships among claim(s), counterclaims, reasons, and evidence.
   d. Establish and maintain a formal style.
   e. Provide a concluding statement or section that follows from and supports the argument presented.

2. Write informative/explanatory texts to examine a topic and convey ideas, concepts, and information through the selection, organization, and analysis of relevant content.
   a. Introduce a topic clearly, previewing what is to follow; organize ideas, concepts, and information into broader categories; include formatting (e.g., headings), graphics (e.g., charts, tables), and multimedia when useful to aiding comprehension.
   b. Develop the topic with relevant, well-chosen facts, definitions, concrete details, quotations, or other information and examples.
   c. Use appropriate and varied transitions to create cohesion and clarify the relationships among ideas and concepts.
   d. Use precise language and domain-specific vocabulary to inform about or explain the topic.
   e. Establish and maintain a formal style.
   f. Provide a concluding statement or section that follows from and supports the information or explanation presented.

3. Write narratives to develop real or imagined experiences or events using effective technique, relevant descriptive details, and well-structured event sequences.
   a. Engage and orient the reader by establishing a context and point of view and introducing a narrator and/or characters; organize an event sequence that unfolds naturally and logically.
   b. Use narrative techniques, such as dialogue, pacing, description, and reflection, to develop experiences, events, and/or characters.
   c. Use a variety of transition words, phrases, and clauses to convey sequence, signal shifts from one time frame or setting to another, and show the relationships among experiences and events.
   d. Use precise words and phrases, relevant descriptive details, and sensory language to capture the action and convey experiences and events.
   e. Provide a conclusion that follows from and reflects on the narrated experiences or events.

Production and Distribution of Writing

4. Produce clear and coherent writing in which the development, organization, and style are appropriate to task, purpose, and audience.

5. With some guidance and support from peers and adults, develop and strengthen writing as needed by planning, revising, editing, rewriting, or trying a new approach, focusing on how well purpose and audience have been addressed.

6. Use technology, including the Internet, to produce and publish writing and present the relationships between information and ideas efficiently as well as to interact and collaborate with others.

Research to Build and Present Knowledge

7. Conduct short research projects to answer a question (including a self-generated question), drawing on several sources and generating additional related, focused questions that allow for multiple avenues of exploration.

8. Gather relevant information from multiple print and digital sources, using search terms effectively; assess the credibility and accuracy of each source; and quote or paraphrase the data and conclusions of others while avoiding plagiarism and following a standard format for citation.

9. Draw evidence from literary or informational texts to support analysis, reflection, and research.

   a. Apply *grade 8 Reading standards* to literature (e.g., "Analyze how a modern work of fiction draws on themes, patterns of events, or character types from myths, traditional stories, or religious works such as the Bible, including describing how the material is rendered new").

   b. Apply *grade 8 Reading standards* to literary nonfiction (e.g., "Delineate and evaluate the argument and specific claims in a text, assessing whether the reasoning is sound and the evidence is relevant and sufficient; recognize when irrelevant evidence is introduced").

Range of Writing

10. Write routinely over extended time frames (time for research, reflection, and revision) and shorter time frames (a single sitting or a day or two) for a range of discipline-specific tasks, purposes, and audiences.

Common Core
Speaking and Listening Standards

College and Career Readiness Anchor Standards

Comprehension and Collaboration

1. Prepare for and participate effectively in a range of conversations and collaborations with diverse partners, building on others' ideas and expressing their own clearly and persuasively.

2. Integrate and evaluate information presented in diverse media and formats, including visually, quantitatively, and orally.

3. Evaluate a speaker's point of view, reasoning, and use of evidence and rhetoric.

Presentation of Knowledge and Ideas

4. Present information, findings, and supporting evidence such that listeners can follow the line of reasoning and the organization, development, and style are appropriate to task, purpose, and audience.

5. Make strategic use of digital media and visual displays of data to express information and enhance understanding of presentations.

6. Adapt speech to a variety of contexts and communicative tasks, demonstrating command of formal English when indicated or appropriate.

Grade 8 Speaking and Listening Standards

Comprehension and Collaboration

1. Engage effectively in a range of collaborative discussions (one-on-one, in groups, and teacher-led) with diverse partners on *grade 8 topics, texts, and issues,* building on others' ideas and expressing their own clearly.

   a. Come to discussions prepared, having read or researched material under study; explicitly draw on that preparation by referring to evidence on the topic, text, or issue to probe and reflect on ideas under discussion.

   b. Follow rules for collegial discussions and decision-making, track progress toward specific goals and deadlines, and define individual roles as needed.

   c. Pose questions that connect the ideas of several speakers and respond to others' questions and comments with relevant evidence, observations, and ideas.

   d. Acknowledge new information expressed by others, and, when warranted, qualify or justify their own views in light of the evidence presented.

2. Analyze the purpose of information presented in diverse media and formats (e.g., visually, quantitatively, orally) and evaluate the motives (e.g., social, commercial, political) behind its presentation.

3. Delineate a speaker's argument and specific claims, evaluating the soundness of the reasoning and relevance and sufficiency of the evidence and identifying when irrelevant evidence is introduced.

Presentation of Knowledge and Ideas

4. Present claims and findings, emphasizing salient points in a focused, coherent manner with relevant evidence, sound valid reasoning, and well-chosen details; use appropriate eye contact, adequate volume, and clear pronunciation.

5. Integrate multimedia and visual displays into presentations to clarify information, strengthen claims and evidence, and add interest.

6. Adapt speech to a variety of contexts and tasks, demonstrating command of formal English when indicated or appropriate. (See grade 8 Language standards 1 and 3 for specific expectations.)

© Common Core Language Standards

College and Career Readiness Anchor Standards

Conventions of Standard English

1. Demonstrate command of the conventions of standard English grammar and usage when writing or speaking.

2. Demonstrate command of the conventions of standard English capitalization, punctuation, and spelling when writing.

Knowledge of Language

3. Apply knowledge of language to understand how language functions in different contexts, to make effective choices for meaning or style, and to comprehend more fully when reading or listening.

Vocabulary Acquisition and Use

4. Determine or clarify the meaning of unknown and multiple-meaning words and phrases by using context clues, analyzing meaningful word parts, and consulting general and specialized reference materials, as appropriate.

5. Demonstrate understanding of figurative language, word relationships, and nuances in word meanings.

6. Acquire and use accurately a range of general academic and domain-specific words and phrases sufficient for reading, writing, speaking, and listening at the college and career readiness level; demonstrate independence in gathering vocabulary knowledge when considering a word or phrase important to comprehension or expression.

Grade 8 Language Standards

Conventions of Standard English

1. Demonstrate command of the conventions of standard English grammar and usage when writing or speaking.
   a. Explain the function of verbals (gerunds, participles, infinitives) in general and their function in particular sentences.
   b. Form and use verbs in the active and passive voice.
   c. Form and use verbs in the indicative, imperative, interrogative, conditional, and subjunctive mood.
   d. Recognize and correct inappropriate shifts in verb voice and mood.

2. Demonstrate command of the conventions of standard English capitalization, punctuation, and spelling when writing.

   a. Use punctuation (comma, ellipsis, dash) to indicate a pause or break.

   b. Use an ellipsis to indicate an omission.

   c. Spell correctly.

Knowledge of Language

3. Use knowledge of language and its conventions when writing, speaking, reading, or listening.

   a. Use verbs in the active and passive voice and in the conditional and subjunctive mood to achieve particular effects (e.g., emphasizing the actor or the action; expressing uncertainty or describing a state contrary to fact).

Vocabulary Acquisition and Use

4. Determine or clarify the meaning of unknown and multiple-meaning words and phrases based on *grade 8 reading and content*, choosing flexibly from a range of strategies.

   a. Use context (e.g., the overall meaning of a sentence or paragraph; a word's position or function in a sentence) as a clue to the meaning of a word or phrase.

   b. Use common, grade-appropriate Greek or Latin affixes and roots as clues to the meaning of a word (e.g., *precede, recede, secede*).

   c. Consult general and specialized reference materials (e.g., dictionaries, glossaries, thesauruses), both print and digital, to find the pronunciation of a word or determine or clarify its precise meaning or its part of speech.

   d. Verify the preliminary determination of the meaning of a word or phrase (e.g., by checking the inferred meaning in context or in a dictionary).

5. Demonstrate understanding of figurative language, word relationships, and nuances in word meanings.

   a. Interpret figures of speech (e.g. verbal irony, puns) in context.

   b. Use the relationship between particular words to better understand each of the words.

   c. Distinguish among the connotations (associations) of words with similar denotations (definitions) (e.g., *bullheaded, willful, firm, persistent, resolute*).

6. Acquire and use accurately grade-appropriate general academic and domain-specific words and phrases; gather vocabulary knowledge when considering a word or phrase important to comprehension or expression.

Introductory Unit

© COMMON CORE
Workshops

Building Academic Vocabulary

Writing an Objective Summary

Comprehending Complex Texts

Analyzing Arguments

© Common Core State Standards

Reading Literature 2, 10
Reading Informational Text 2, 8
Writing 1.a, 1.b, 1.e
Language 6

Building Academic Vocabulary

Academic vocabulary is the language you encounter in textbooks and on standardized tests and other assessments. Understanding these words and using them in your classroom discussions and writing will help you communicate your ideas clearly and effectively.

There are two basic types of academic vocabulary: general and domain-specific. **General academic vocabulary** includes words that are not specific to any single course of study. For example, the general academic vocabulary word *analyze* is used in language arts, math, social studies, art, and so on. **Domain-specific academic vocabulary** includes words that are usually encountered in the study of a specific discipline. For example, the words *factor* and *remainder* are most often used in mathematics classrooms and texts.

**Common Core
State Standards**

Language 6. Acquire and use accurately grade-appropriate general academic and domain-specific words and phrases; gather vocabulary knowledge when considering a word or phrase important to comprehension or expression.

General Academic Vocabulary

Word	Definition	Related Words	Word in Context
accumulate (uh KYOO myuh layt) *v.*	collect or gather	accumulation accumulating	Dust began to accumulate on the tables and chairs in the empty classroom.
argument (AHR gyuh muhnt) *n.*	claim; persuasive reasoning	argue argumentative	The argument in the essay is well supported.
aspects (AS pehkts) *n.*	ways in which an idea or a problem may be viewed or seen		I needed to consider all the aspects of his argument before replying.
assumption (uh SUHMP shuhn) *n.*	act of taking for granted	assume assuming	My assumption was based on insufficient evidence.
benefit (BEHN uh fiht) *n.*	advantage or positive result	beneficial beneficiary	The benefit of studying geometry is clear for certain careers such as architecture and engineering.
bias (BY uhs) *n.*	tendency to see things from a slanted or prejudiced viewpoint	biased	In the past, accusations of bias have been hurled at the media during political campaigns.

Word	Definition	Related Words	Word in Context
challenge (CHAL uhnj) v.	call into question; demand proof	challenging challenged	The teacher asked his students to challenge accepted points of view and to be distrustful of opinions that are not well supported by facts.
class (klas) n.	group of people or objects	classification	They studied how the differences between the nobility and the merchant class contributed to the French Revolution.
confirm (kuhn FURM) v.	prove or establish as true	confirmation confirming	He asked them to confirm their answers one more time before submitting their tests.
connection (kuh NEHK shuhn) n.	tie; link	connect connected	It was easy to find a connection between the character's motives and his actions.
contradict (kon truh DIHKT) v.	deny; present an opposing viewpoint	contradictory contradiction	He was afraid to contradict the expert on nutrition, even though he was familiar with research that undermined her position.
cultural (KUHL chuhr uhl) adj.	related to the customs and beliefs of a group or community	culture culturally	The museum exhibit explored the cultural achievements of the Aztecs.
decision (dih SIHZH uhn) n.	choice; act of making up one's mind	decisively decide	Once she had made her decision about which political candidate to support, no argument could change her mind.
development (dih VEHL uhp muhnt) n.	event or happening; outcome	develop developer	The law professor asked his class to follow every development in an important Supreme Court case about job discrimination.

Ordinary Language: The two characters **disagree with** each other constantly.

Academic Language: The two characters **contradict** each other constantly.

Word	Definition	Related Words	Word in Context
discriminate (dihs KRIHM uh nayt) *v.*	see differences between; tell apart	discriminatory discrimination	The food critic was able to discriminate between two dishes that had been prepared in slightly different ways.
discrimination (dihs krihm uh NAY shuhn) *n.*	unfair treatment of a person or group	discriminate discriminatory	Housing regulations outlaw discrimination against buyers or renters based on race or nationality.
distinguish (dihs TIHNG gwihsh) *v.*	mark as different; set apart	distinguishing distinction	Paints come in so many colors that it can be difficult to distinguish between various shades of the same basic color.
divide (duh VYD) *v.*	separate	divisive division	The teacher asked the students to divide into small groups to discuss the reading.
doubtful (DOWT fuhl) *adj.*	not likely; open to challenge	doubtfully doubt	The historian made the doubtful claim that the royal family had survived the revolution, when their deaths had already been well documented.
emphasize (EHM fuh syz) *v.*	stress; show the importance of	emphasis emphatically	In her classes, she decided to emphasize reasoning and analysis over memorizing facts.
endure (ehn DUR) *v.*	hold up under; last	enduring durable	Sarah had to endure a twenty-minute lecture from her older sister every time she made a minor mistake.
evidence (EHV uh duhns) *n.*	proof	evidently evidentiary	He gave evidence from his own experience, as well as from the reading, to support his central points.
exaggerate (ehg ZAJ uh rayt) *v.*	make too much of; overstate	exaggeration exaggeratedly	Writers of tall tales exaggerate the abilities of their heroes by making them bigger, stronger, faster, and smarter than most main characters.
explanation (ehks pluh NAY shuhn) *n.*	act of giving meaning to, or clarifying, an idea or a concept	explanatory explain	A good explanation leaves no confusion in the mind of the reader.

Word	Definition	Related Words	Word in Context
factor (FAK tuhr) *n.*	any of the circumstances or conditions that lead to a result	factoring factory	One major factor in his decision to skip the prom was that he was embarrassed about his dancing skills.
factual (FAK choo uhl) *adj.*	based on or limited to fact	fact factually	Her opposition had no factual basis; it was based purely on emotion.
global (GLOH buhl) *adj.*	complete, covering a large class of cases	globally globe	He favored a global approach to the community's problems—addressing each problem in isolation was just not going to work.
identify (y DEHN tuh fy) *v.*	classify; name	identification identity	She could identify many different species of trees by examining their leaves and bark.
illogical (ih LOJ uh kuhl) *adj.*	contrary or opposed to fact	illogically logic	He held the illogical belief that everything he said was correct simply because he stated it was so.
imitate (IHM uh tayt) *v.*	copy or follow the example of	imitation imitative	The assignment asked the students to imitate the style of Mark Twain in a five-page story.
individuality (ihn duh VIHJ oo AL uh tee) *n.*	way in which a person or thing stands apart or is different	individualize individually	Emily Dickinson expressed her individuality through her short, unpredictable poems.
influence (IHN floo uhns) *v.*	sway or affect	influential	He tried to influence the crowd to vote for him based on his eight-year record as a governor.
insecurity (ihn sih KYUR uh tee) *n.*	lack of confidence; self-doubt	insecure security	His insecurity about his mathematical abilities surfaced whenever the teacher asked a question in algebra class and he hid from view.

Ordinary Language:
The writer's argument doesn't make sense.

Academic Language:
The writer's argument is illogical.

Word	Definition	Related Words	Word in Context
interact (ihn tuhr AKT) v.	deal with or work with someone or something	interaction interactive	Being lab partners forced them to interact, even though they disliked each other.
investigate (ihn VEHS tuh gayt) v.	search; look into	investigative investigation	The reporter was sent to investigate a banking scandal.
judge (juhj) v.	form an opinion about	judgmental adjudicate	It is wise to collect facts before you judge someone's actions.
objective (uhb JEHK tihv) adj.	open-minded; not influenced by personal feelings or prejudice	objectively	Reporters try to remain objective about the subjects of their articles, letting their readers form their own opinions based on the facts presented.
observation (ob zuhr VAY shuhn) n.	statement; point of view	observe observing	His observation that the economy often goes through boom and bust cycles was obvious to anyone who knew economic history.
opinion (uh PIHN yuhn) n.	personal view or attitude	opinionated opine	He formed his opinion about the issue based on articles he read on Web sites and in newspapers.
oppose (uh POHZ) v.	go against; stand in the way of	opposition opposite	They decided to oppose the dam project because they feared a negative effect on local fish populations.
persuade (puhr SWAYD) v.	convince; bring around to one's way of thinking	persuasion persuasively	It is difficult to persuade people to change their minds when their opinions are based purely on emotion.
prove (proov) v.	show or demonstrate	proof proving	Prove your case by showing me persuasive evidence.
quality (KWOL uh tee) n.	characteristic or feature	qualitative qualify	The main character had a mischievous quality that proved popular with young readers.
quantity (KWON tuh tee) n.	amount	quantitative quantify	The quantity of caffeine is different in coffee, tea, and soda.
reaction (ree AK shuhn) n.	response to an influence, action, or statement	react reactive	What was their reaction to the announcement that the performance was being cancelled?
relevant (REHL uh vuhnt) adj.	to the point; relating to the matter at hand	relevance irrelevant	Her argument that a new playground was unnecessary was not relevant to a discussion of child safety.

Ordinary Language:
The subplot about the two workers did not seem to matter.

Academic Language:
The subplot about the two workers did not seem relevant.

Practice

Examples of various kinds of domain-specific academic vocabulary appear in the charts below. Some chart rows are not filled in. Look up the definitions of the remaining words, provide one or two related words, and use each word in context on a separate piece of paper.

Social Studies: Domain-Specific Academic Vocabulary

Word	Definition	Related Words	Word in Context
federalism (FED er uh liz uhm) *n.*	support for a strong federal (or national) government	federal federalist	Alexander Hamilton believed strongly in federalism.
founder (FOUN der) *n.*	a person who founds or establishes something	founded	The Pilgrims were the founders of the Plymouth colony.
framer (FRAYM er) *n.*	a person who helps design or build a document, policy, or movement	frame framing	Benjamin Franklin was a framer of the U.S. Constitution.
hierarchy (HY uh rahr kee) *n.*	an organized system in which people or things are ranked one above another	hierarchical	The people at the top of a hierarchy have more power than those below them.
recession (ri SESH uhn) *n.*	in economics, a period of economic downturn	recede	Many people lost money and jobs in the recession of 2008.
commerce (KOM ers) *n.*			
congressional (kuhn GRESH uh nl) *adj.*			
constitutional (kon sti TOO shuh nl) *adj.*			
exchange (eks CHAYNJ) *v., n.*			
nationalism (NASH uh nl iz uhm) *n.*			

Mathematics: Domain-Specific Academic Vocabulary

Word	Definition	Related Words	Word in Context
array (uh REY) *n.*	an arrangement of a series of terms in rows and columns according to value	arrays	We were told to arrange the numbers in an array from smallest to largest.
complementary angles (kom pluh MEN tuh ree ANG guhlz) *n.*	two angles that, when added together, produce an angle of 90 degrees	complement	An angle of 30 degrees and an angle of 60 degrees are complementary angles.
corresponding angles (kawr uh SPON ding ANG guhlz) *n.*	two angles that are formed in corresponding positions on two parallel lines that are crossed by a third line	correspond	I created corresponding angles by drawing a line that crossed two parallel lines.
supplementary angles (suhp luh MEN tuh ree ANG guhlz) *n.*	two angles that, when added together, produce an angle of 180 degrees	supplement	Two 90 degree angles are supplementary angles.
transversal (trans VUR suhl) *n.*	a line that intersects two or more other lines	transverse	The transversal intersected two parallel lines.
infinite (IN fuh nit) *adj.*			
intercept (IN ter sept) *v.*			
nonlinear (nahn LIN ee er) *adj.*			
symmetry (SIM i tree) *n.*			
vertex (VUR teks) *n.*			

Science: Domain-Specific Academic Vocabulary

Word	Definition	Related Words	Word in Context
electron (ih LEK tron) *n.*	an elementary particle having a negative charge	electric electrical	A hydrogen atom has one electron.
inertia (in UR shuh) *n.*	the property of matter by which it maintains its state of rest or uniform motion	inert	The lab we completed tested the inertia of matter.
mutualism (MYOO choo uh liz uhm) *n.*	a relationship that benefits two interacting organisms	mutual	The bees and the flowers benefited from mutualism.
neutron (NOO tron) *n.*	an elementary particle that has no charge	neutral	Except for hydrogen, all atoms have neutrons.
reactant (ree AK tuhnt) *n.*	a substance that undergoes a chemical change in a reaction	react reaction	One reactant in the experiment was oxygen.

Science: Domain-Specific Academic Vocabulary (*continued*)

Word	Definition	Related Words	Word in Context
acid (AS id) *n.*			
compound (KOM pound) *n.*			
density (DEN si tee) *n.*			
element (EL uh muhnt) *n.*			
immunity (ih MYOO ni tee) *n.*			

Art: Domain-Specific Academic Vocabulary

Word	Definition	Related Words	Word in Context
contour line (KON toor lyn) *n.*	a line that shows the important interior ridges and edges (or contours) of an object	contoured contouring	The first step to drawing the bowl is to make contour lines.
primary color (PRY mere ee KUHL er) *n.*	red, yellow, and blue; colors that can be mixed to make all other colors	primarily	The teacher told us to use primary colors to make the colors we wanted.
rhythm (RITH uhm) *n.*	the visual tempo or beat created by placing repeated elements in a work of art	rhythmic	The muralist placed buildings and cars repeatedly in his work to create a lively rhythm.
secondary color (SEK uhn der ee KUHL er) *n.*	orange, green, and violet; colors made by mixing two primary colors in equal amounts	second	I mixed red and yellow to make the secondary color of orange.
tertiary color (TUR shee er ee KUHL er) *n.*	color produced by mixing two secondary colors	third	The artist used two secondary colors to make the tertiary color of brown.
balance (BAL uhns) *n., v.*			
cool color (kool KUHL er) *n.*			
shape (sheyp) *n.*			
style (styl) *n.*			
warm color (wawrm KUHL er) *n.*			

Technology: Domain-Specific Academic Vocabulary

Word	Definition	Related Words	Word in Context
cursor (KUR ser) *n.*	a movable, blinking symbol that shows the position of the next character that will be entered from the keyboard	cursory	I placed the cursor where I wanted to insert a new paragraph.
home row (hohm rohw) *n.*	the row on a computer keyboard that contains the home keys: *A, S, D,* and *F* on the left and *J, K, L,* and the semicolon on the right	home row	You can type faster and more accurately by placing your hands correctly on the home row.
spreadsheet (SPRED sheet) *n.*	a worksheet that contains columns and rows for data	spreadsheets	We kept our budget in a spreadsheet to track what we spent.
storyboard (STOHR ee bawrd) *n.*	a series of illustrated panels that show the action planned for a film, video, or animation	boards story	Our group made a storyboard to show the sequence of events in our film.
telecommunications (tel i ku myoo ni KEY shuhnz) *n.*	technology that enables the sending of information over great distances	communicate communications telephone	The telecommunications industry drastically changed after the invention of cell phones.
chat room (chat room) *n.*			
file folder (fyl FOHL der) *n.*			
home page (hohm payj) *n.*			
import (IM pohrt) *n., v.*			
menu bar (MEN yoo bahr) *n.*			

Increasing Your Word Knowledge

Increase your word knowledge and chances of success by taking an active role in developing your vocabulary. Here are some tips for you.

To own a word, follow these steps:

Steps to Follow	Model
1. Learn to identify the word and its basic meaning.	The word *examine* means "to look at closely."
2. Take note of the word's spelling.	*Examine* begins and ends with an *e*.
3. Practice pronouncing the word so that you can use it in conversation.	The *e* on the end of the word *examine* is silent. Its second syllable gets the most stress.
4. Visualize the word and illustrate its key meaning.	When I think of the word *examine*, I visualize a doctor checking a patient's health.
5. Learn the various forms of the word and its related words.	*Examination* and *exam* are forms of the word *examine*.
6. Compare the word with similar words.	*Examine, peruse,* and *study* are synonyms.
7. Contrast the word with similar words.	*Examine* suggests a more detailed study than *read* or *look at*.
8. Use the word in various contexts.	"I'd like to *examine* the footprints more closely." "I will *examine* the use of imagery in this poem."

Building Your Speaking Vocabulary

Language gives us the ability to express ourselves. The more words you know, the better able you will be to get your points across. There are two main aspects of language: reading and speaking. Using the steps above will help you acquire a rich vocabulary. Follow these steps to help you learn to use this rich vocabulary in discussions, speeches, and conversations:

Steps to Follow	Tip
1. Practice pronouncing the word.	Become familiar with pronunciation guides to allow you to sound out unfamiliar words. Listening to audio books as you read the text will help you learn pronunciations of words.
2. Learn word forms.	Dictionaries often list forms of words following the main word entry. Practice saying word families aloud: "generate," "generated," "generation," "regenerate," "generator."
3. Translate your thoughts.	Restate your own thoughts and ideas in a variety of ways, to inject formality or to change your tone, for example.
4. Hold discussions.	With a classmate, practice using academic vocabulary words in discussions about the text. Choose one term to practice at a time, and see how many statements you can create using that term.
5. Tape-record yourself.	Analyze your word choices by listening to yourself objectively. Note places your word choice could be strengthened or changed.

Writing an Objective Summary

The ability to summarize a text effectively will lead to success in school as well as in many careers. When you write an effective objective summary, you identify the key ideas of a text and show your overall understanding of the original text.

What Is an Objective Summary?

An effective objective summary is a concise, complete, accurate, and objective overview of a text. Effective objective summaries have the following characteristics:

- The summary should contain reference to the original text's title and author.

- If the original text is a narrative, the summary should include key plot events that lead to the story's conclusion.

- If the text is informational, the summary should include specific, relevant details that support that theme or central idea.

What to Avoid in an Objective Summary

- Do not include sentences or paragraphs copied from the original source.

- Do not include every event, detail, or point in the original text.

- Do not include evaluative comments, such as your overall opinion of or reaction to the selection.

- Do not include your interpretation or a critical analysis of the text.

 Common Core State Standards

Reading Literature 2. Determine a theme or central idea of a text and analyze its development over the course of the text, including its relationship to the characters, setting, and plot; provide an objective summary of the text.

Reading Informational Text 2. Determine a central idea of a text and analyze its development over the course of the text, including its relationship to supporting ideas; provide an objective summary of the text.

INFORMATIONAL TEXT

Model Objective Summary

Review the elements of an effective objective summary, called out in the sidenotes. Then, write an objective summary of a text you have recently read. Review your summary. Delete any unnecessary details, opinions, or evaluations.

Summary of "Ribbons" by Laurence Yep

"Ribbons" by Laurence Yep tells the story of Stacy, a Chinese American girl adjusting to the changes she must make when her Paw-paw, or maternal Chinese grandmother, comes from Hong Kong to live with the family in San Francisco. ~~This story is one of the best I have read this year.~~

First of all, Stacy must give her room to her grandmother and share a room with her younger brother Ian. Also, Stacy must give up her ballet lessons, which she loves, to pay for her grandmother's transportation from Hong Kong.

When Paw-paw arrives, Stacy notices that she is unsteady on her feet; she uses two canes. Although Stacy is curious about her grandmother's feet, she respects her mother's wishes and doesn't ask her grandmother about them.

As days go by, there are more changes in the household to accommodate Grandmother. It is also becoming apparent to Stacy that Ian has become Grandmother's favorite. ~~Ian looks like his Chinese grandmother; Stacy looks like her Caucasian father.~~ Stacy is hurt, but she decides to try to get to know her grandmother better. Stacy feels that one way to get to know someone better is to share something you love. So Stacy decides to dance for Grandmother.

As Stacy puts on her toe shoes, the ribbons on one of her shoes fall off. Stacy, ~~remembering that her grandmother is an excellent seamstress,~~ brings the ribbons to her and asks her to sew them back on. At the sight of the ribbons, Grandmother gets furious, first at Stacy, and then at Stacy's mom. When Stacy asks her mom about her grandmother's anger, her mother says that the ribbons remind Paw-paw of something awful that happened to her a long time ago.

A still-angry Stacy decides to ignore her grandmother, and tension in the house grows. Quite by accident, Stacy walks into the bathroom and sees her grandmother soaking her misshapen feet. It is after that that Stacy's mother explains that at one time in China young girls had their feet bent and then bound with ribbons, which was horribly painful and disfiguring. Grandmother had mistakenly thought that Stacy's mother was going to bind Stacy's feet. Once that misunderstanding is cleared up, Stacy and Grandmother begin to get to know each other better.

A one-sentence synopsis highlighting the central idea of the story can be an effective start to a summary.

This sentence is an opinion and should be deleted.

Relating the development of the text in chronological order makes a summary of a narrative easy to follow.

Eliminate unnecessary details, such as these.

Comprehending Complex Texts

Common Core State Standards

Reading Literature 10. By the end of the year, read and comprehend literature, including stories, dramas, and poems, at the high end of the grades 6–8 text complexity band independently and proficiently.

During this year and in high school, you will be required to read increasingly complex texts to prepare for college and the workplace. A complex text contains challenging vocabulary; long, complex sentences; figurative language; multiple levels of meaning; or unfamiliar settings and situations.

The selections in this textbook include a range of readings, from short stories to autobiographies, poetry, drama, myths, and even science and social studies texts. You will be able to read some of these texts easily; others may be more challenging.

Strategy 1: Multidraft Reading

Good readers develop the habit of rereading texts in order to comprehend them completely. Just as you might listen to a new song over and over again to understand the lyrics, good readers return to texts to more fully enjoy and comprehend them. To fully understand a text, try this multidraft reading strategy:

1st Reading

The first time you read a text, read to gain its basic meaning. If you are reading a narrative text, look for story basics: what happened, to whom, and why. If the text is nonfiction, look for its main ideas. If you are reading poetry, read first to get an overall sense of the poem and its speaker. Also take note of its mood or setting.

2nd Reading

During your second reading of a text, focus on the artistry or effectiveness of the writing. Look for text structures, and think about why the author chose those organizational patterns. Then, examine the author's creative uses of language and the effects of that language. For example, has the author used alliteration? Rhythms? Hyperbole? Parallelism? If so, to what end?

3rd Reading

Once you have completed your third reading, begin to synthesize your ideas. To do so, compare and contrast the text with others of its kind you have read. Also think about the message the work conveys and whether or not that message is original and/or valid. Then, evaluate the text's overall effectiveness and whether or not it has broadened your understanding.

Independent Practice

As you read this poem, practice the multidraft reading strategy by completing a chart like the one below.

"Migrant Birds" by Moumin Manzoor Quazi

Swept by invisible brooms,

black birds, like words on a page,

specks of spilt ground

pepper blown in the wind,

much bigger though,

tightly—not randomly—

change course all

together at the same,

exact moment.

So-called "junk" birds

swim the skies, come north

for a while to make a life.

Ready now, they once again

become fluid spice, do their

instinctual dance, moved

not by whim, but fancy anyway,

and the hot pepper blows home to southern climes,

seasoning skies elsewhere for a time.

Multidraft Reading Chart

	My Understanding
1st Reading Look for key ideas and details that unlock basic meaning.	
2nd Reading Read for deeper meanings. Look for ways in which the author used text structures and language to create effects.	
3rd Reading Read to integrate your knowledge and ideas. Connect the text to others of its kind and to your own experience.	

Strategy 2: Close Read the Text

Complex texts require close reading, a careful analysis of the words, phrases, and sentences. When you close read, use the following tips to comprehend the text:

Tips for Close Reading
1. Break down long sentences into parts. Look for the subject of the sentence and its verb. Then identify which parts of the sentence modify, or give more information about, its subject.
2. Reread passages. When reading complex texts, be sure to reread dense passages to confirm their meaning.

3. Look for context clues, such as the following:
 	
  a. Restatements of ideas within text. For example, in this sentence, "completely destroyed" restates the verb *devastated*.
 	
    The earthquake and tsunami **devastated,** or <u>completely destroyed</u>, the small fishing village.
 	
  b. Examples of concepts and topics. In the following sentence, the fact that we know that bobsledding and skiing are winter sports indicates that luge must also be a winter sport.
 	
    The United States athletes won medals in <u>bobsledding, skiing, and **luge**</u>.
 	
  c. Comparisons of ideas and topics.
 	
    The **dulcet** tones of the singer were as <u>sweet and soothing as a mother's lullaby</u>.
 	
  d. Contrasts of ideas and topics.
 	
    Criticism, <u>unlike praise</u>, can be hurtful.

4. Identify pronoun antecedents. If long sentences contain pronouns, reread the text to make sure you know to what the pronouns refer. The pronoun *its* in the following sentence refers to the Quiet Room, not the company.   The Quiet Room was set aside by the company for employees to enjoy **its** peaceful comfort.
5. Look for conjunctions, such as *and, but,* and *yet,* to understand relationships between ideas.
6. Paraphrase, or restate in your own words, passages of difficult text in order to check your understanding. Remember that a paraphrase is a word-for-word rephrasing of an original text; it is not a summary.

INFORMATIONAL TEXT

Close-Read Model

As you read this document, take note of the sidenotes that model ways to unlock meaning in the text.

from *On Duty* by Cicero

. . . Now, those who care for the interests of a part of the citizens and neglect another part, introduce into the civil service a dangerous element — dissension and party strife. . . As a result of this party spirit bitter strife arose at Athens, and in our own country not only dissensions but also disastrous civil wars broke out. All this the citizen who is patriotic, brave, and worthy of a leading place in the state will shun with abhorrence; he will dedicate himself unreservedly to his country, without aiming at influence or power for himself; and he will devote himself to the state in its entirety in such a way as to further the interests of all. . .

A most wretched custom, assuredly, is our electioneering and scrambling for office. Concerning this also we find a fine thought in Plato: "Those who compete against one another," he says, "to see which of two candidates shall administer the government, are like sailors quarrelling as to which one of them shall do the steering." And he likewise lays down the rule that we should regard only those as adversaries who take up arms against the state, not those who strive to have the government administered according to their convictions. . .

Neither must we listen to those who think that one should indulge in violent anger against one's political enemies and imagine that such is the attitude of a great-spirited, brave man. For nothing is more commendable, nothing more becoming in a pre-eminently great man than courtesy and forbearance. Indeed, in a free people, where all enjoy equal rights before the law, we must school ourselves to affability and what is called "mental poise"; for if we are irritated when people intrude upon us at unseasonable hours or make unreasonable requests, we shall develop a sour, churlish temper, prejudicial to ourselves and offensive to others. And yet gentleness of spirit and forbearance are to be commended only with the understanding that strictness may be exercised for the good of the state; for without that, the government cannot be well administered. On the other hand, if punishment or correction must be administered, it need not be insulting; it ought to have regard to the welfare of the state, not to the personal satisfaction of the man who administers the punishment or reproof...

Search for context clues. The words in blue are context clues that help you figure out the meaning of the word *dissension*.

Look for antecedents. In this sentence, the noun phrase *the citizen who is patriotic . . .* is replaced by the pronoun *he*.

This sentence is inverted: its subject comes last. A paraphrase of this sentence might be "Desperately trying to get elected has become commonplace."

Search for context clues. The words in green are comparison context clues that hint at the meaning of "affability." The words in light blue provide contrasting context clues that describe what an affable person is *not*.

The antecedent for the pronoun *it* in this sentence is *punishment or correction*.

Strategy 3: Ask Questions

Be an attentive reader by asking questions as you read. Each selection in this textbook is followed by questions for you to answer. These questions are sorted into three basic categories that build in sophistication and lead you to a deeper understanding of the texts you read. Here is an example from this text:

Some questions are about **Key Ideas and Details** in the text. To answer these questions, you will need to locate and cite explicit information in the text or draw inferences from what you have read.

Some questions are about **Craft and Structure** in the text. To answer these questions, you will need to analyze how the author developed and structured the text. You will also look for ways in which the author artfully used language and how those word choices impacted the meaning and tone of the work.

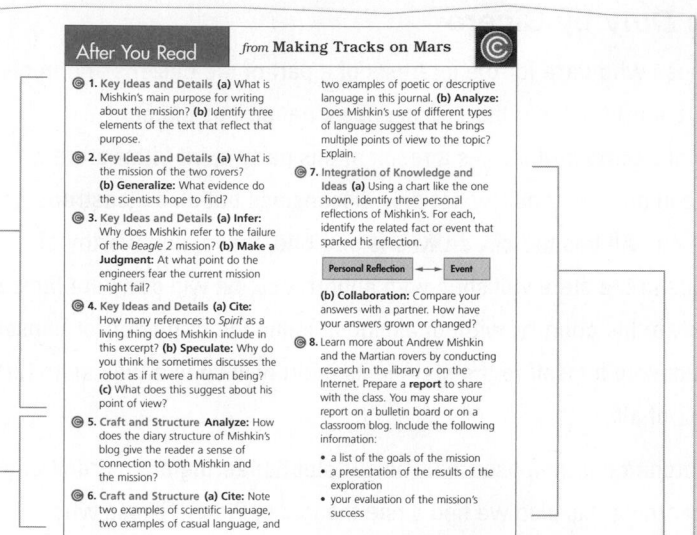

After You Read   *from* **Making Tracks on Mars**

1. **Key Ideas and Details (a)** What is Mishkin's main purpose for writing about the mission? **(b)** Identify three elements of the text that reflect that purpose.

2. **Key Ideas and Details (a)** What is the mission of the two rovers? **(b) Generalize:** What evidence do the scientists hope to find?

3. **Key Ideas and Details (a) Infer:** Why does Mishkin refer to the failure of the *Beagle 2* mission? **(b) Make a Judgment:** At what point do the engineers fear the current mission might fail?

4. **Key Ideas and Details (a) Cite:** How many references to *Spirit* as a living thing does Mishkin include in this excerpt? **(b) Speculate:** Why do you think he sometimes discusses the robot as if it were a human being? **(c)** What does this suggest about his point of view?

5. **Craft and Structure Analyze:** How does the diary structure of Mishkin's blog give the reader a sense of connection to both Mishkin and the mission?

6. **Craft and Structure (a) Cite:** Note two examples of scientific language, two examples of casual language, and

two examples of poetic or descriptive language in this journal. **(b) Analyze:** Does Mishkin's use of different types of language suggest that he brings multiple points of view to the topic? Explain.

7. **Integration of Knowledge and Ideas (a)** Using a chart like the one shown, identify three personal reflections of Mishkin's. For each, identify the related fact or event that sparked his reflection.

| Personal Reflection | ⟷ | Event |

(b) Collaboration: Compare your answers with a partner. How have your answers grown or changed?

8. Learn more about Andrew Mishkin and the Martian rovers by conducting research in the library or on the Internet. Prepare a **report** to share with the class. You may share your report on a bulletin board or on a classroom blog. Include the following information:

- a list of the goals of the mission
- a presentation of the results of the exploration
- your evaluation of the mission's success

Some questions are about the **Integration of Knowledge and Ideas** in the text. These questions ask you to evaluate a text in many different ways, such as comparing texts, analyzing arguments in the text, and using many other methods of thinking critically about a text's ideas.

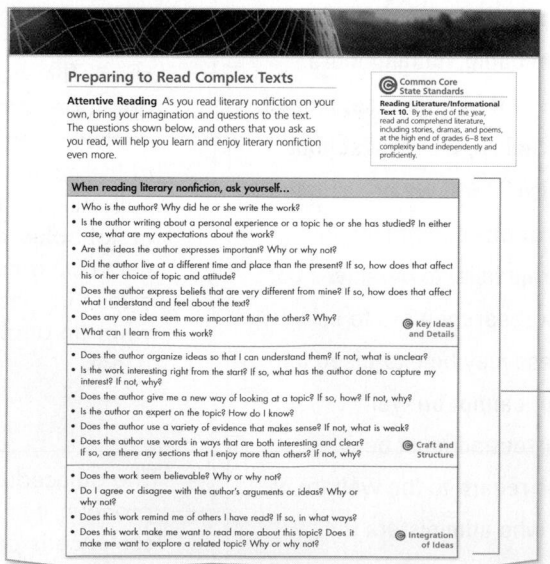

Preparing to Read Complex Texts

Attentive Reading As you read literary nonfiction on your own, bring your imagination and questions to the text. The questions shown below, and others that you ask as you read, will help you learn and enjoy literary nonfiction even more.

Common Core State Standards

Reading Literature/Informational Text 10. By the end of the year, read and comprehend literature, including stories, dramas, and poems, at the high end of grades 6–8 text complexity band independently and proficiently.

When reading literary nonfiction, ask yourself...

- Who is the author? Why did he or she write the work?
- Is the author writing about a personal experience or a topic he or she has studied? In either case, what are my expectations about the work?
- Are the ideas the author expresses important? Why or why not?
- Did the author live at a different time and place than the present? If so, how does that affect his or her choice of topic and attitude?
- Does the author express beliefs that are very different from mine? If so, how does that affect what I understand and feel about the text?
- Does any one idea seem more important than the others? Why?
- What can I learn from this work?

Key Ideas and Details

- Does the author organize ideas so that I can understand them? If not, what is unclear?
- Is the work interesting right from the start? If so, what has the author done to capture my interest? If not, why?
- Does the author give me a new way of looking at a topic? If so, how? If not, why?
- Is the author an expert on the topic? How do I know?
- Does the author use a variety of evidence that makes sense? If not, what is weak?
- Does the author use words in ways that are both interesting and clear? If so, are there any sections that I enjoy more than others? If not, why?

Craft and Structure

- Does the work seem believable? Why or why not?
- Do I agree or disagree with the author's arguments or ideas? Why or why not?
- Does this work remind me of others I have read? If so, in what ways?
- Does this work make me want to read more about this topic? Does it make me want to explore a related topic? Why or why not?

Integration of Ideas

As you read independently, ask similar types of questions to ensure that you fully enjoy and comprehend texts you read for school and for pleasure. We have provided sets of questions for you on the Independent Reading pages at the end of each unit.

INFORMATIONAL TEXT

Model

Following is an example of a complex text. The sidenotes show sample questions that an attentive reader might ask while reading.

from "The Funeral Oration of Pericles" retold by Thucydides

A speech given in 431 B.C. to honor Athenian soldiers and praise Athenian democracy:

Our constitution is called a democracy because power is in the hands not of a minority but of the whole people. When it is a question of settling private disputes, everyone is equal before the law; when it is a question of putting one person before another in positions of public responsibility, what counts is not membership of a particular class, but the actual ability which the man possesses. No one, so long as he has it in him to be of service to the state, is kept in political obscurity because of poverty. And, just as our political life is free and open, so is our day-to-day life in our relations with each other. . . . We are free and tolerant in our private lives; but in public affairs we keep to the law. This is because it commands our deep respect.

Sample questions:

Key Ideas and Details Who is the *Our* in this sentence?

Craft and Structure Why might Thucydides have chosen to use repetition in this passage?

Integration of Knowledge and Ideas If you were to make a digital presentation display of advantages of life in Athens, what would your bullet points be?

Independent Practice

Write three to five questions you might ask yourself as you continue reading "The Funeral Oration of Pericles."

We give our obedience to those whom we put in positions of authority, and we obey the laws themselves, especially those which are for the protection of the oppressed, and those unwritten laws which it is an acknowledged shame to break. . . . Here each individual is interested not only in his own affairs but in the affairs of the state as well: even those who are mostly occupied with their own business are extremely well-informed on general politics—this is a peculiarity of ours: we do not say that a man who takes no interest in politics is a man who minds his own business; we say that he has no business here at all. We Athenians, in our own persons, take our decisions on policy or submit them to proper discussions: for we do not think that there is an incompatibility between words and deeds; the worst thing is to rush into action before the consequences have been properly debated. . . . Taking everything together then, I declare that our city is an education to Greece. . .you have only to consider the power which our city possesses and which has been won by those very qualities which I have mentioned.

Analyzing Arguments

The ability to evaluate an argument, as well as to make one, is an important skill for success in college and in the workplace.

What Is an Argument?

Informally speaking, an *argument* is disagreement between people. This type of argument involves trading opinions and evidence in a conversation. A formal written argument, however, presents one side of a controversial or debatable issue. An effective argument is supported by reasoning and evidence.

Purposes of Argument

There are three main purposes for writing a formal argument:

- to change the reader's mind about a controversial issue
- to convince the reader to accept your ideas
- to motivate the reader to take action

Elements of Argument

Claim (assertion)—what the writer is trying to prove
Example: Students in the United States need to be more competitive to keep up with students in other countries.

Grounds (evidence)—the support used to convince the reader
Example: American students scored lower on math and science tests than children in many other countries.

Justification—the link between the grounds and the claim; why the grounds are credible
Example: Longer school days and year-round school would help students in the United States perform better on assessments.

Evaluating Claims

When reading or listening to a formal argument, critically assess the claims that are made. Which claims are based on fact or can be proved true? Also evaluate evidence that supports the claims. To evaluate an argument, ask questions such as these:

- What specific claims are presented?
- Are the claims logically presented?
- Is there enough evidence to support the stated claims?
- Does the evidence directly support the claims, or is any evidence irrelevant?
- Can the evidence be proved to be true?

Common Core State Standards

Reading Informational Text 8. Delineate and evaluate the argument and specific claims in a text, assessing whether the reasoning is sound and the evidence is relevant and sufficient; recognize when irrelevant evidence is introduced.

Language 6. Acquire and use accurately grade-appropriate general academic and domain-specific words and phrases; gather vocabulary knowledge when considering a word or phrase important to comprehension or expression.

INFORMATIONAL TEXT

Model Argument

This excerpt from a speech by President John F. Kennedy is an example of an argument.

from "We Choose to Go to the Moon" by John F. Kennedy

...Despite the striking fact that most of the scientists that the world has ever known are alive and working today, despite the fact that this Nation's own scientific manpower is doubling every 12 years in a rate of growth more than three times that of our population as a whole, despite that, the vast stretches of the unknown and the unanswered and the unfinished still far outstrip our collective comprehension. . . .

This is a breathtaking pace, and such a pace cannot help but create new ills as it dispels old, new ignorance, new problems, new dangers. Surely the opening vistas of space promise high costs and hardships, as well as high reward.

So it is not surprising that some would have us stay where we are a little longer to rest, to wait. But this. . .country of the United States was not built by those who waited and rested and wished to look behind them. This country was conquered by those who moved forward—and so will space. . . .

If this capsule history of our progress teaches us anything, it is that man, in his quest for knowledge and progress, is determined and cannot be deterred. The exploration of space will go ahead, whether we join in it or not, and it is one of the great adventures of all time, and no nation which expects to be the leader of other nations can expect to stay behind in this race for space. Those who came before us made certain that this country rode the first waves of the industrial revolution, the first waves of modern invention, and the first wave of nuclear power, and this generation does not intend to founder in the backwash of the coming age of space. We mean to be a part of it—we mean to lead it. For the eyes of the world now look into space, to the moon and to the planets beyond, and we have vowed that we shall not see it governed by a hostile flag of conquest, but by a banner of freedom and peace. We have vowed that we shall not see space filled with weapons of mass destruction, but with instruments of knowledge and understanding. . . .

We choose to go to the moon. We choose to go to the moon in this decade and do the other things, not because they are easy, but because they are hard, because that goal will serve to organize and measure the best of energies and skills, because that challenge is one that we are willing to accept, one we are unwilling to postpone, and one which we intend to win. . . .

Claim: Despite advances in science, there is much we still do not know.

An opposing argument is acknowledged and refuted.

Justification: The United States must be the leader in space exploration if we are to be the leader of other nations.

Grounds: The U.S. has led the world in industry, invention, and nuclear power.

Grounds: Space should be governed in freedom and peace, not by a hostile government.

Grounds: Going to the moon will bring out the best of our country's energies and skills.

A strong conclusion does more than simply restate the claim.

The Art of Argument: Rhetorical Devices and Persuasive Techniques

Rhetorical Devices

Rhetoric is the art of using language in order to make a point or to persuade listeners. Rhetorical devices such as the ones listed below are accepted elements of argument. Their use does not invalidate or weaken an argument. Rather, the use of rhetorical devices is regarded as a key part of an effective argument.

Rhetorical Devices	Examples
Repetition The repeated use of certain words, phrases, or sentences	Let's go! Let's fight! Let's win!
Parallelism The repeated use of similar grammatical structures	Reading is reflective. Writing is expressive.
Rhetorical Question Calling attention to the issue by implying an obvious answer	Should we sit and watch while the rest of the world acts?
Sound Devices The use of alliteration, rhyme, or rhythm	We the people must be powerful and purposeful.
Simile and Metaphor Comparing two unlike things or asserting that one thing is another	The Iron Curtain has fallen, separating democratic nations from communist countries.

Persuasive Techniques

The persuasive techniques below are often found in advertisements and in other forms of informal persuasion. Although techniques like the ones below are sometimes found in formal arguments, these techniques are usually avoided.

Persuasive Techniques	Examples
Bandwagon Approach/Anti-Bandwagon Approach Appeals to a person's desire to belong/Encourages or celebrates individuality	Nine out of ten Americans want to go "green."
Emotional Appeal Capitalizes on people's fear, anger, or desire	To protect your child, serve organic foods.
Endorsement/Testimony Employs a well-known person to promote a product or idea	Attending Middletown University was my stepping stone to success.
Loaded Language Uses words charged with emotion	These poor, tired, and desperate citizens have been forsaken by our government.
"Plain Folks" Appeal Shows a connection to everyday, ordinary people	I, like you, have worked in the fields, tilling the soil.
Hyperbole Exaggerates to make a point	This is a once-in-a-lifetime chance to vote your heart!

INFORMATIONAL TEXT

Model Speech

The excerpted speech below includes examples of rhetorical devices and persuasive techniques.

"A Tribute to the Dog" by George Graham Vest

Gentlemen of the Jury: The best friend a man has in the world may turn against him and become his enemy. His son or daughter that he has reared with loving care may prove ungrateful. Those who are nearest and dearest to us, those whom we trust with our happiness and our good name may become traitors to their faith. The money that a man has, he may lose. It flies away from him, perhaps when he needs it most. A man's reputation may be sacrificed in a moment of ill-considered action. The people who are prone to fall on their knees to do us honor when success is with us, may be the first to throw the stone of malice when failure settles its cloud upon our heads.

The one absolutely unselfish friend that man can have in this selfish world, the one that never deserts him, the one that never proves ungrateful or treacherous is his dog. A man's dog stands by him in prosperity and in poverty, in health and in sickness. He will sleep on the cold ground, where the wintry winds blow and the snow drives fiercely, if only he may be near his master's side. He will kiss the hand that has no food to offer; he will lick the wounds and sores that come in encounters with the roughness of the world. He guards the sleep of his pauper master as if he were a prince. When all other friends desert, he remains. When riches take wings, and reputation falls to pieces, he is as constant in his love as the sun in its journey through the heavens.

If fortune drives the master forth an outcast in the world, friendless and homeless, the faithful dog asks no higher privilege than that of accompanying him, to guard him against danger, to fight against his enemies. And when the last scene of all comes, and death takes his master in its embrace and his body is laid away in the cold ground, no matter if all other friends pursue their way, there by the graveside will the noble dog be found, his head between his paws, his eyes sad, but open in alert watchfulness, faithful and true even in death.

The parallelism created by repeated grammatical structures gives the speech rhythm.

Sound devices, such as alliteration, can be used to emphasize a phrase.

Figurative language helps the speaker make his point.

The speaker uses words with strong positive connotations.

Composing an Argument

 Common Core State Standards

Writing 1.a. Introduce claim(s), acknowledge and distinguish the claim(s) from alternate or opposing claims, and organize the reasons and evidence logically.
1.b. Support claim(s) with logical reasoning and relevant evidence, using accurate, credible sources and demonstrating an understanding of the topic or text.
1.e. Provide a concluding statement or section that follows from and supports the argument presented.

Choosing a Topic

When choosing a topic for an argumentative essay, brainstorm topics you would like to write about; then, choose the topic that most interests you. Once you have chosen a topic, check to be sure you can make an arguable claim. Ask yourself:

1. What is my argument? What ideas about my argument do I need to convey?

2. What people might disagree with my claim? What opinions might they have?

3. What evidence supports my claim? Is my evidence sufficient and relevant?

If you are able to put into words what you want to prove and answered "yes" to questions 2 and 3, you have an arguable claim.

Introducing the Claim and Establishing Its Significance

Before you begin writing, think about your audience and how much you think they already know about your chosen topic. Then, provide background information, as necessary. Once you have provided context for your argument, you should clearly state your claim, or thesis. A written argument's claim often, but not always, appears in the first paragraph.

Developing Your Claim with Reasoning and Evidence

Now that you have made your claim, support it with evidence that proves it to be true. A good argument should have at least three solid pieces of evidence to support each claim. Evidence can range from personal experience to researched data or expert opinion. Knowing your audience's knowledge level, concerns, values, and possible biases can help inform your decision on what kind of evidence will have the strongest impact. Make sure your evidence is up to date and comes from a reliable source that you credit.

You should also address the opposing points of view within the body of your argument. Consider points you have made or evidence you have provided that a person might challenge. Acknowledge the validity of counterclaims, even as you make the case that your argument is stronger.

Writing a Concluding Statement or Section

Once you have developed your argument, restate your claim in the conclusion. Then synthesize, or pull together, the evidence you have provided. Your conclusion should be powerful and memorable.

Practice

Complete a graphic organizer like the one below to help you plan your own argument.

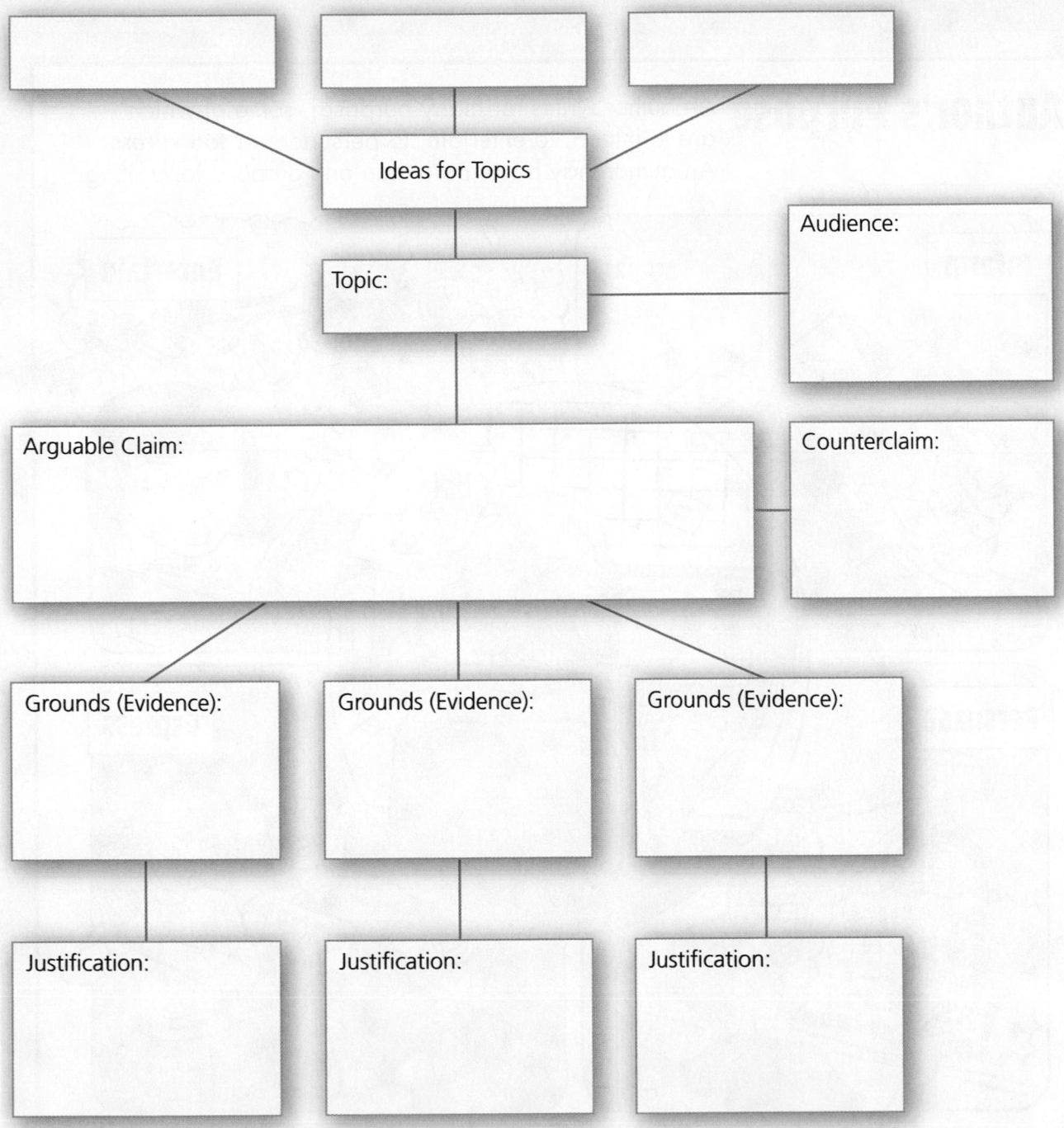

PICTURE IT!
A Comprehension Handbook

Author's Purpose

An author writes for many purposes, some of which are to inform, to entertain, to persuade, or to express. An author may have more than one purpose for writing.

Inform

Entertain

Persuade

Express

Cause and Effect

An effect is something that happens. A cause is why that thing happens. An effect sometimes has more than one cause. A cause sometimes has more than one effect. Clue words such as *because*, *as a result*, *therefore*, and *so that* can signal causes and effects.

Cause

Effect

Draw Conclusions

When we draw conclusions, we make sensible decisions or form reasonable opinions after thinking about the facts and details in what we are reading.

Fact and Opinion

A fact is something that can be proved. Facts are based on evidence. Opinions express ideas and are based on interpretation of evidence.

Main Idea and Details

Main idea is the most important idea about a topic.

Details are smaller pieces of information that support the main idea.

Making Predictions

To make predictions, use text, graphics, and prior knowledge to predict what might happen in a story or what you might learn from a text. As you read, new information can lead to new or revised predictions.

Making Inferences

When we make inferences, or infer something, we come to a conclusion based on a detail an author provides in the text.

Paraphrasing

Paraphrasing is restating a sentence or an idea in your own words. Paraphrasing can lead to a better understanding of what we read.

Setting a Purpose for Reading

When we set a purpose for reading, we approach a text with a specific goal or question that we would like answered. Setting a purpose for reading guides comprehension by focusing our attention on specific information.

Summarizing

To summarize, we restate the main ideas of a text or the main events of a plot. In a summary, we leave out the supporting details.

Media Literacy Handbook

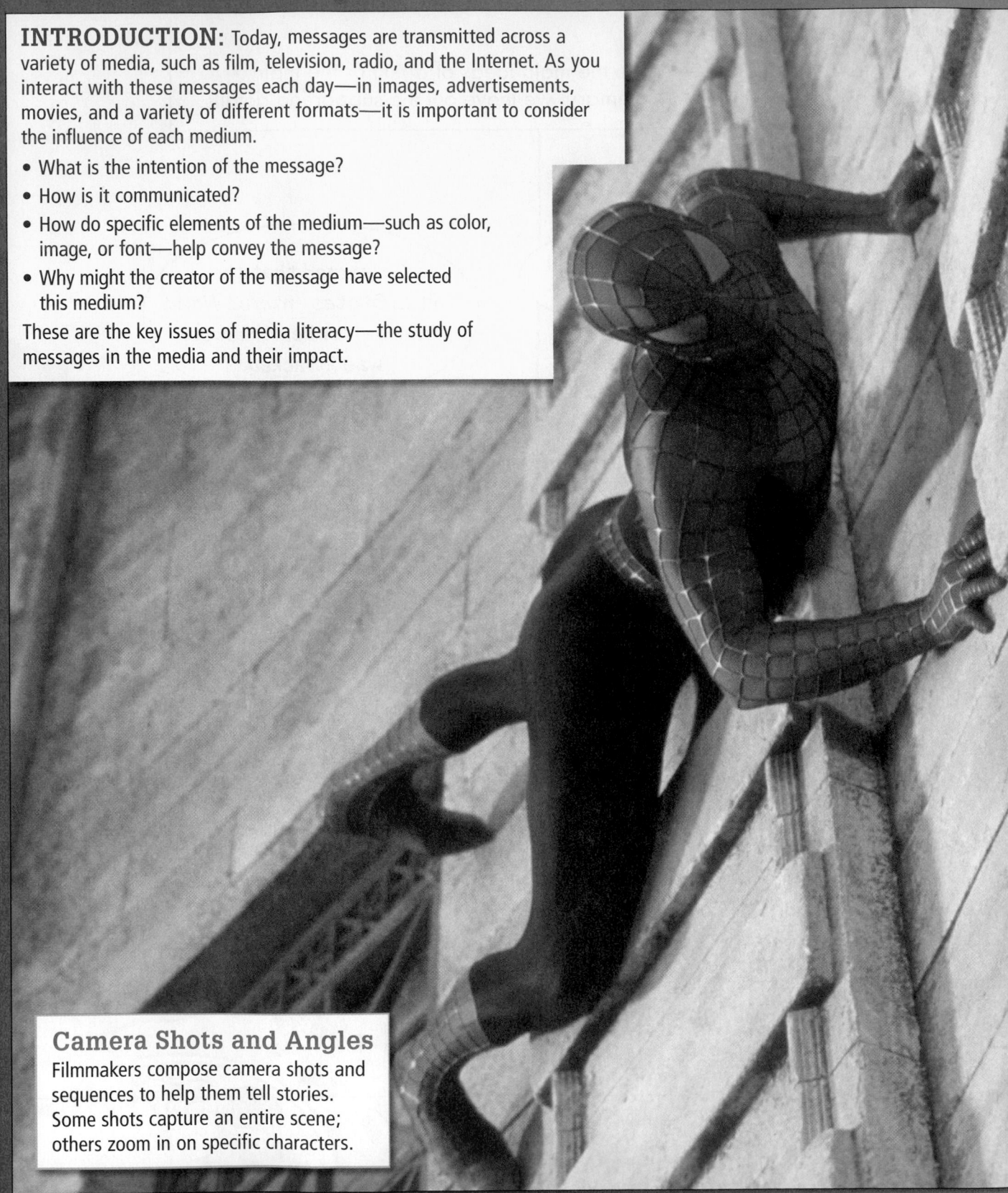

INTRODUCTION: Today, messages are transmitted across a variety of media, such as film, television, radio, and the Internet. As you interact with these messages each day—in images, advertisements, movies, and a variety of different formats—it is important to consider the influence of each medium.

- What is the intention of the message?
- How is it communicated?
- How do specific elements of the medium—such as color, image, or font—help convey the message?
- Why might the creator of the message have selected this medium?

These are the key issues of media literacy—the study of messages in the media and their impact.

Camera Shots and Angles
Filmmakers compose camera shots and sequences to help them tell stories. Some shots capture an entire scene; others zoom in on specific characters.

Special Effects

Filmmakers use special effects to create on-screen illusions that bring the imagination to life.

▌ Questions About Film Techniques

- What effect is created by the choice of camera angle shown in the image at left? Choose another camera angle and explain how that shot might convey a different impression than the one shown here.

- Study the images above. In what way does the use of special effects make the film better for viewers?

Media Literacy Handbook

Focus and Framing
A sharp focus captures all the details in a photographic image. A softer focus decreases the amount of detail that can be seen. The framing of elements within a photograph directs the eye toward a portion of the image.

Lighting and Shadow
Lighting techniques are used in photography to enhance mood and direct the viewer's focus.

Special Techniques

Most images you see today have been manipulated or changed in some way. Even a small change—such as an added graphic element or a difference in shading—can alter the mood of an image.

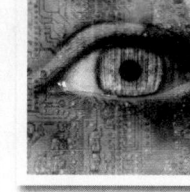

Questions About Graphics and Photos

- What would be the effect if the alligator image used a sharp focus instead of a combination of a sharp and soft focus?

- In what way does the use of color and light create mood in the riverboat photo?

- What special techniques were applied to the original photograph shown above right? What effect does the use of special techniques create?

New York feeds all of us in its own way.
Now it's time for us to help City Harvest feed
the hungry of New York.

Persuasive Techniques
Advertisements use carefully selected visual elements and specific language to appeal to the viewer's emotions.

WILL WORK FOR FOOD

CITY HARVEST

When you support City Harvest, your dollars help rescue and deliver food for working families, seniors and children. More than one million New Yorkers don't know where their next meal is coming from. You can help them by making a generous donation today.

To donate by credit card please call or visit us online:

1 800 77-HARVEST • www.cityharvest.org

Text and Graphics

Newspaper and magazine layouts are constructed to capture the eye and quickly convey the important ideas of a story. The use of type fonts, imagery, and blank space on the page directs the eye to portions of the printed page.

Questions About Print Media

• What image or graphic dominates the advertisement at left? In what way does the use of language in the ad enhance its message?

• What grabs your attention on the magazine cover? Explain.

• What do you notice first on the newspaper's front page? What overall effect does the use of type size and fonts create?

How is this book organized?

- There are six units, each focusing on a specific genre.
- Each unit has a **Big Question** to get you thinking about important ideas and to guide your reading.
- A **Literary Analysis Workshop** begins each unit, providing instruction and practice for essential skills.

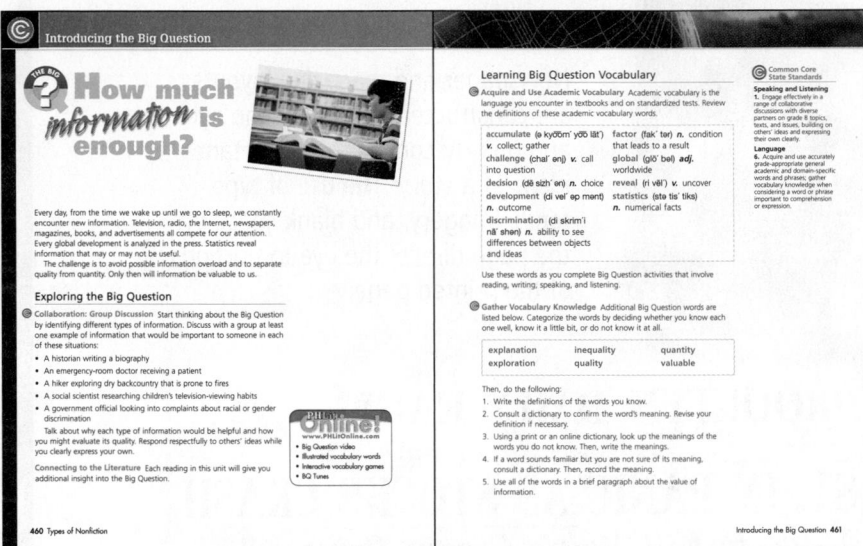

◀ At the beginning of the unit, **Introducing the Big Question** provides a reading focus for the entire unit. Use **academic vocabulary** to think, talk, and write about this question.

A **Literary Analysis Workshop** provides an overview of the unit genre, an in-depth exploration of Common Core State Standards, as well as models and practice opportunities. ▶

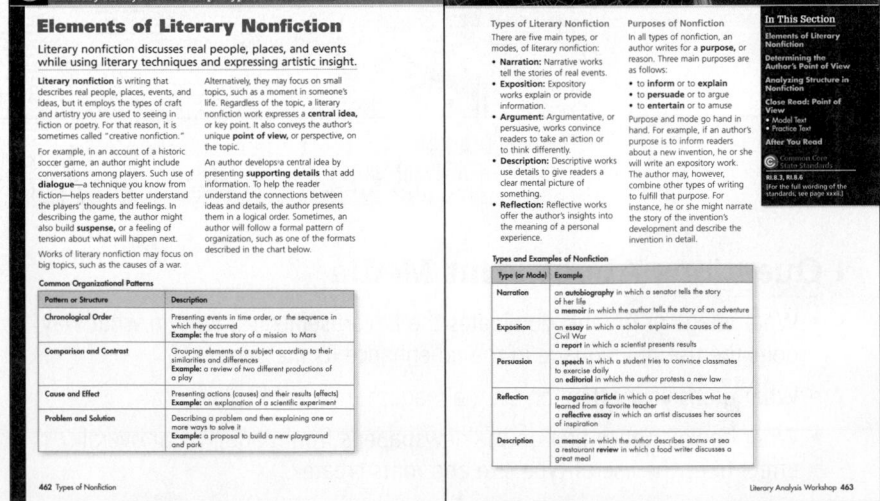

How are the literary selections organized?

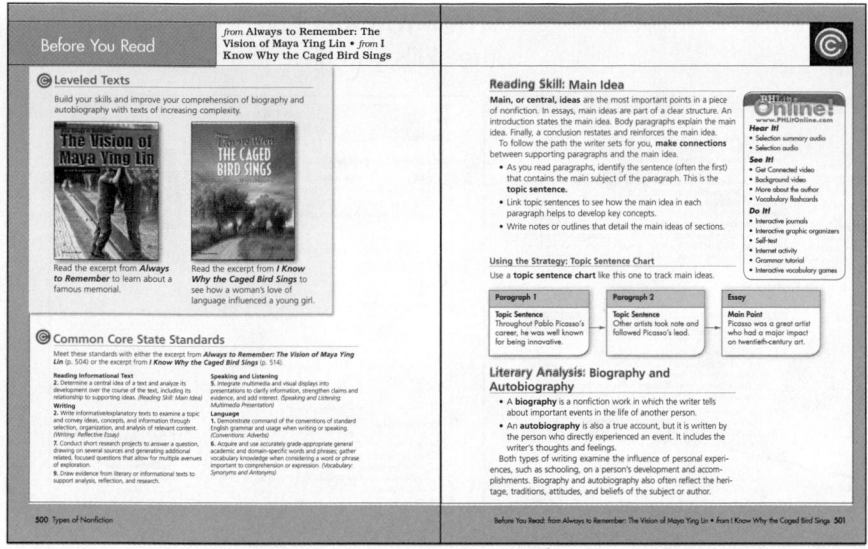

◀ **Before You Read** introduces two selection choices that both teach the same skills. Your teacher will help you choose the selection that is right for you.

Writing About the Big Question is a quick-writing activity that helps you connect the Big Question to the selection you are about to read.

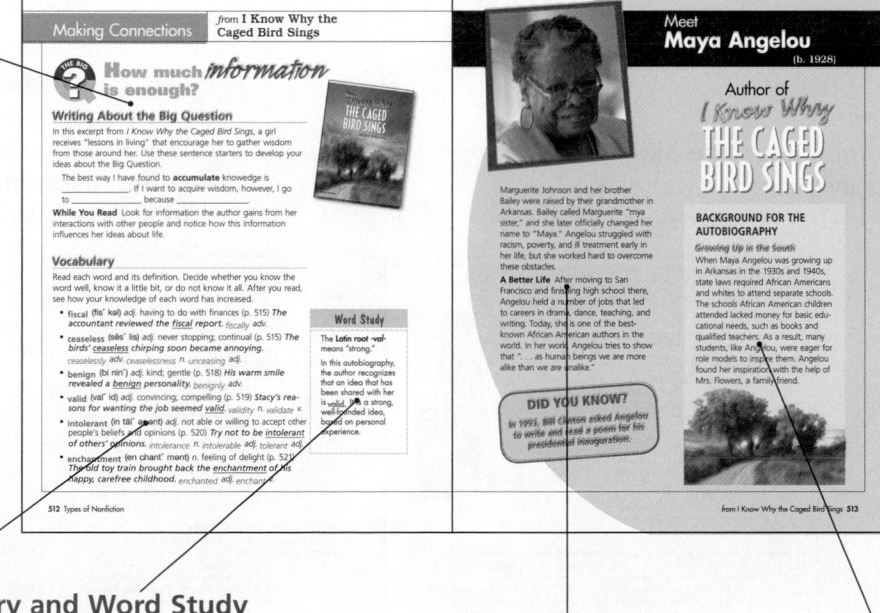

Vocabulary and Word Study introduce important selection vocabulary words and teach you about prefixes, suffixes, and roots.

Meet the Author and Background teach you about the author's life and provide information that will help you understand the selection.

How are the literary selections organized? *(continued)*

After You Read helps you practice the skills you have learned. ▼

Critical Thinking questions help you reflect on what you have read and apply the Big Question to the selection.

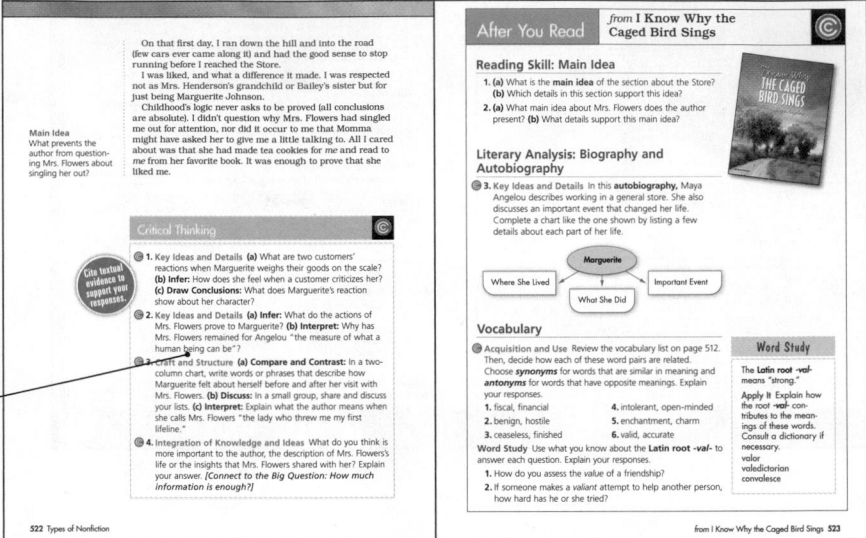

Integrated Language Skills provides instruction and practice for important grammar skills.

Projects and activities help you deepen your understanding of the selection while strengthening your **writing, listening, speaking, and research skills.**

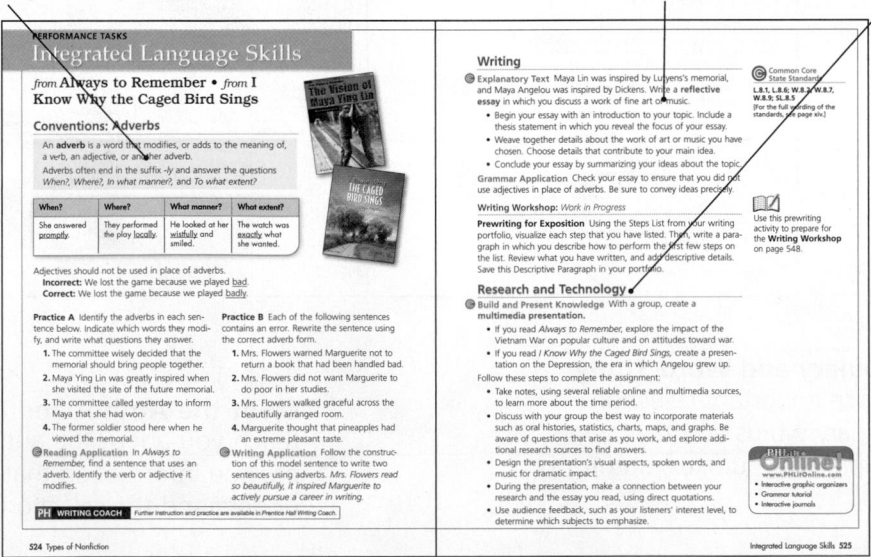

What special features will I find in this book?

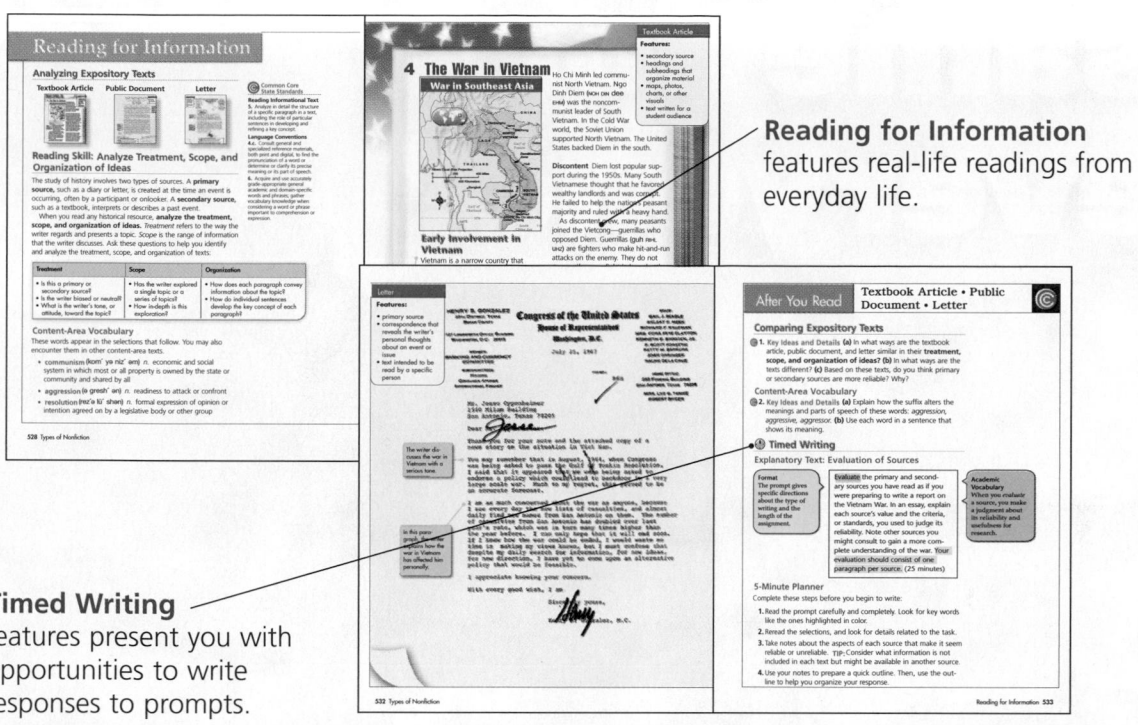

Reading for Information features real-life readings from everyday life.

Timed Writing features present you with opportunities to write responses to prompts.

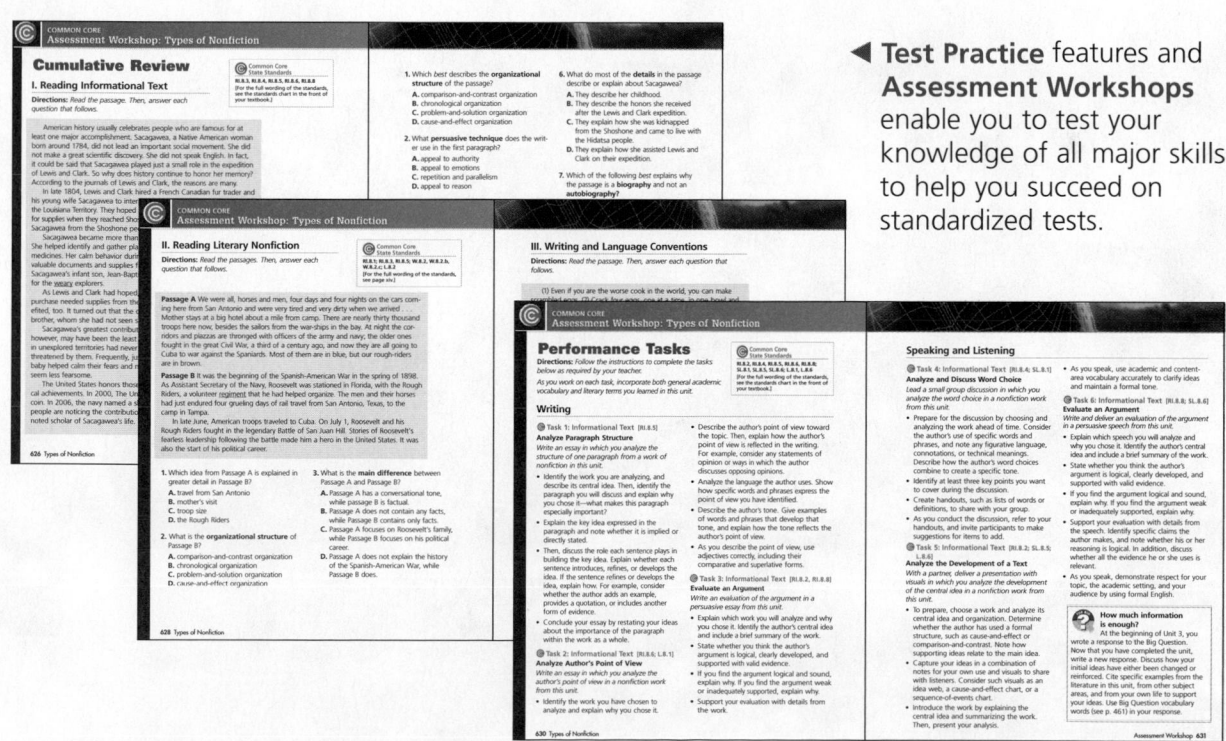

◀ **Test Practice** features and **Assessment Workshops** enable you to test your knowledge of all major skills to help you succeed on standardized tests.

THE BIG ? Is *truth* the same for everyone?

Fiction and Nonfiction

PHLit
Online!
www.PHLitOnline.com

Hear It!
- Selection summary audio
- Selection audio
- BQ Tunes

See It!
- Author videos
- Big Question video
- Get Connected videos
- Background videos
- More about the authors
- Illustrated vocabulary words
- Vocabulary flashcards

Do It!
- Interactive journals
- Interactive graphic organizers
- Grammar tutorials
- Interactive vocabulary games
- Test practice

Is *truth* the same for everyone?

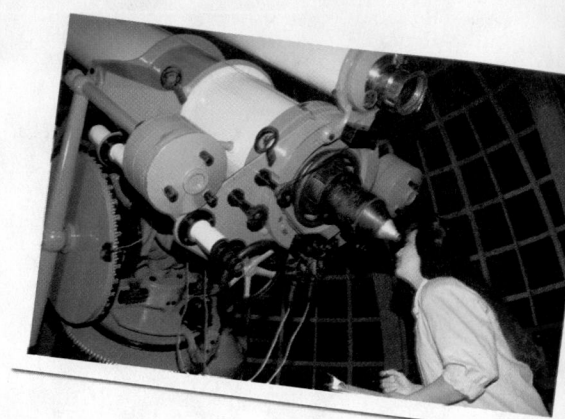

People search for **truth** in different ways. Scientists use observation to investigate and uncover truths about the natural world. They use experimental results as evidence to prove or contradict theories. Reporters research all sides of a story to capture an objective truth—a truth that does not reveal a one-sided bias. Poets, essayists, and short-story writers search for insights that will inspire a reader to say, "I never thought of it that way before!" or simply, "How true!"

Exploring the Big Question

Collaboration: One-on-One Discussion Start thinking about the Big Question by making a list of situations you have experienced or heard about in which it may have been difficult to determine the truth. Describe one specific example of each of the following situations:

- Conflicting accounts about who caused an accident or a fight
- Stories, books, or movies that blend **fantasy** with reality
- Crime dramas in which lawyers try to **persuade** a jury
- A reporter who covers a controversial topic
- A scientist who investigates the outbreak of a deadly disease
- A singer who writes a breakup song

Talk with a partner about the challenges that must be faced when you are trying to determine the truth. Use the Big Question vocabulary in your discussion.

Connecting to the Literature The selections in this unit will help you think about how people's views of what is true may differ, stay the same, or change over time. Each reading in this unit will give you additional insight into the Big Question.

PHLit Online!
www.PHLitOnline.com
- Big Question video
- Illustrated vocabulary words
- Interactive vocabulary games
- BQ Tunes

Learning Big Question Vocabulary

Common Core State Standards

Speaking and Listening
1. Engage effectively in a range of collaborative discussions (one-on-one, in groups, and teacher-led) with diverse partners on grade 8 topics, texts, and issues, building on others' ideas and expressing their own clearly.

Language
6. Acquire and use accurately grade-appropriate general academic and domain-specific words and phrases; gather vocabulary knowledge when considering a word or phrase important to comprehension or expression.

Acquire and Use Academic Vocabulary Academic vocabulary is the language you encounter in textbooks and on standardized tests. Review the definitions of these academic vocabulary words.

bias (bī′ əs) *n.* tendency to see things from a slanted, one-sided, or unbalanced viewpoint

confirm (kən fʉrm′) *v.* prove as true

contradict (kän′ trə dikt′) *v.* assert the opposite of what was said; declare a statement untrue

doubtful (dout′ fəl) *adj.* not likely

evidence (ev′ ə dəns) *n.* proof

factual (fak′ chōo əl) *adj.* based on information that can be observed or verified

illogical (i läj′ i kəl) *adj.* not sensible or reasonable

investigate (in ves′ te gāt′) *v.* search; inquire into

Use these words as you complete Big Question activities in this unit that involve reading, writing, speaking, and listening.

Gather Vocabulary Knowledge Additional Big Question words are listed below. Categorize the words by deciding whether you know each one well, know it a little bit, or do not know it at all.

fantasy	opinion	prove
objective	persuade	theory
observation		

Then, do the following:

1. Work with a partner to say each word and give its definition.
2. Confirm each word's pronunciation and meaning in a print or online dictionary.
3. Use as many vocabulary words as possible in a paragraph about an important truth you have discovered.
4. Take turns reading your paragraphs aloud.
5. Compare your ideas and the ways in which you used the Big Question words. Discuss how accurate vocabulary helps you to express ideas.

Elements of Fiction and Nonfiction

Fiction is writing in which the author tells made-up stories. **Nonfiction** is writing that provides facts.

Fiction tells the story of imaginary people or animals, called characters. Like real people, fictional **characters** are involved in conflicts, or struggles with an opposing force, such as another character. These **conflicts** set in motion the **plot,** or sequence of imagined events, in the story.

Fiction writers work hard to make their made-up characters realistic—believable, vivid, and engaging. In addition, some fiction writers base their stories on actual people or events. However, if a work is fiction, then at least some key characters, situations, or events are made up.

Nonfiction gives facts about real people, places, or events or discusses ideas about the real world. Nonfiction may inform you about a subject or try to convince you to do something. Regardless of its aim, nonfiction is based on facts.

Nonfiction can do more than just report facts, however. **Literary nonfiction** uses some of the same storytelling techniques as fiction to make factual writing come alive. For example, an essay telling a true story about a mountain-climbing expedition might create suspense. The chart below compares fiction and nonfiction.

Comparison of Fiction and Nonfiction

	Fiction and Nonfiction	
Similarities	• Both fiction and certain types of nonfiction tell a story. • Both may be told from a clear **point of view**—either the perspective of an observer outside the story being told, or the perspective of someone involved in the story. • Both may use **literary devices and effects,** including **imagery** (word pictures), **mood** (a general feeling conveyed by words), and **suspense** (a reader's anxious curiosity about what will happen next).	
	Fiction	**Nonfiction**
Differences	• Fiction tells the imaginary story of **characters,** or made-up people and animals. • The story is structured around an imaginary **conflict**—a struggle between opposing forces—that triggers a series of imaginary events, called the **plot.**	• Nonfiction that tells a story gives facts about real people, animals, or events. • Nonfiction that does not tell a story may explain a process or support an opinion.

Forms and Types of Fiction and Nonfiction

The following charts define common forms of fiction and nonfiction.

Forms of Fiction
Short stories are brief works of fiction that usually feature one or two main characters, a plot triggered by a single conflict, and a main **theme,** or insight about life.
Novels are longer works of fiction with several characters and multiple conflicts and themes; often, they are structured around a main plot and one or more **subplots**—series of events that are distinct from the main plot but linked to it.
Novellas are shorter than novels but longer and more complex than short stories.

Types of Nonfiction
Literary nonfiction gives facts about a topic using elements of literature. It includes **autobiographies,** or works in which the writer tells the story of his or her own life, as well as **inspirational speeches,** in which a writer shares experiences and insights.
Functional texts give practical information and are often **formatted,** or set up on the page, to make it easy to find information. Functional texts include **directions,** which explain how to perform a process or find a location.

Development in Fiction

Whatever the form of fiction, each detail helps to develop, or unfold, the story.

- **Character Development** Each action a character takes, each conversation he or she has, tells you a little bit more about the character. In some stories, you can see the character change as a result of his or her experiences.
- **Plot Development** Each new event may heighten the tension, leading to a climax.

Development in Nonfiction

Each fact, description, or explanation in a work of nonfiction helps to develop the main points. Forms of development in nonfiction include the following:

- **Illustration** After stating a general idea, an author may then give examples or tell a story that helps you understand the idea.
- **Proof** To show that a point is true, an author may construct a logical argument in support of the point, drawing on facts and other evidence.

 Common Core State Standards

RL.8.2; RI.8.2
[For the full wording of the standards, see the standards chart in the front of your textbook.]

Determining Themes in Fiction

Works of fiction convey themes—messages or insights about life.

 **Common Core State Standards**

Reading Literature
2. Determine a theme or central idea of a text and analyze its development over the course of the text, including its relationship to the characters, setting, and plot; provide an objective summary of the text.

Development of Theme Works of fiction convey themes—messages about or insights into life. Writers develop themes through characters' decisions, experiences, and insights. Often, writers do not state the theme. When the theme is conveyed indirectly, or **implied,** the reader must determine it by considering the lessons that characters learn and by examining patterns developed over the course of the story. By restating story patterns in general terms, readers can work toward a conclusion about the theme, as in this example:

Story Details Alex demands that Bob and Jake bully Sid. Jake refuses. Bob bullies Sid but feels bad afterward.

⬇

Story Patterns *Contrast:* Jake stands up for what he believes; Bob does not. *Before-and-after:* Bob acts against his better judgment and feels terrible.

⬇

Generalization from Pattern People who act against their better judgment may feel bad afterward.

⬇

Implied Theme Stay true to your own values.

Apply this strategy for determining theme to this sample passage.

Example: Do Clothes Make the Man?

A man went to a fancy party where he, along with several other guests, was to be honored. Dressed in ordinary clothes, the man was overlooked—no host greeted him, no guests chatted with him, no servants served him. The man went home, put on his best clothes, and returned to the party. Now the host introduced himself and commanded the servers to bring food to the man. When the man offered the food to his dress coat, the host was puzzled. The man explained that his clothes should have the food, since the host was actually honoring them.

As you read this passage, you may have identified a "before-and-after" pattern—the treatment of the guest before and after his change of clothes. You may have also noted the lesson the guest learns: the host and servants respond to clothing. Based on these observations, you may have stated the theme as "People should be judged by their characters, not by their clothes."

Determining Central Ideas in Nonfiction

Nonfiction works develop central, or main, ideas through the use of supporting details.

Common Core
State Standards

Reading Informational Text
2. Determine a central idea of a text and analyze its development over the course of the text, including its relationship to supporting ideas; provide an objective summary of the text.

A work of nonfiction develops one or more central ideas. A **central idea** is a key point the author wants to make. All the details in the text **develop** and **support** the central idea of the work—they help to prove it, to explain it, to illustrate it, to give further details about it, and so on. In most cases, the author directly states the central idea near the beginning of the text. In other cases, the central idea is **implied,** or suggested, by the points the author makes. Readers can infer the central idea by determining what point all of the details combine to support.

Paragraph Structure Each paragraph in a nonfiction work develops its own central, or main, idea. This main idea helps to support the central idea of the work as a whole. The main idea of a paragraph is often stated in a **topic sentence** at the beginning of the paragraph. The topic sentence is then supported by reasons, examples, and other specific details in the rest of the paragraph. These details, and the topic sentence they support, also serve the larger purpose of developing the central idea of the entire work.

The following example shows the relationship between the central idea of a text and the topic sentences of paragraphs within the text.

> **Example:**
> 1. **Central idea:** Our town should build a skate park for skateboarders.
> 2. **Topic sentence:** A park would keep skateboarders out of the street.
> 3. **Topic sentence:** Skateboarders would no longer damage public property, such as curbs.
> 4. **Topic sentence:** A park would inspire skateboarders to take pride in our town.

Central Idea and Author's Purpose
How an author develops a central idea depends on the **author's purpose,** or main reason for writing. General purposes for writing are **to inform** an audience about a subject; **to persuade,** or convince, an audience to share an opinion or to take an action; and **to entertain.**

Consider an essay with the central idea "Rock climbing is dangerous." To inform, an author might include facts about accidents. To persuade, an author might add arguments about the need for safety. To entertain, an author might include comical details about a rock climbing experience.

Close Read: Theme in Fiction

All elements of a story help develop its theme.

The theme of a literary work is its central insight or message. Authors develop a theme over the course of a work by carefully crafting and arranging story elements, including details about the characters, events in the plot, descriptions of the setting, and so on. The tips in the chart below will help you identify and analyze clues to theme.

Clues to Theme		
Title The **title** is the name of the work. As you read, ask: • What event, character, object, or idea does the title refer to? • Does the title suggest any general ideas or feelings? If yes, what are they? • How are these ideas or feelings related to story details?	**Plot and Conflict** The **plot** is the sequence of events in a story. The **conflict** is the main character's struggle with an opposing force. As you read, ask: • What is the conflict? • How does it turn out? • What lesson does the outcome suggest?	**Setting** **Setting** is the place and time of story events. As you read, ask: • When and where do the events take place? • What **mood,** or feeling, does the setting create? • What is life like in the setting?
Characters **Characters** are the people or animals in a story. As you read, ask: • What are each character's traits? Are there any strong contrasts between characters? • Does the main character change during the story? If yes, what lesson do these changes suggest?	**Statements** Characters or the narrator (the voice telling the story) may make **statements** commenting on events. As you read, ask: • What insights do these statements suggest? • Are there strong contrasts or similarities between statements? What ideas do these contrasts or similarities reinforce?	**Symbols** A **symbol** is a person, object, event, image, or place that stands for a larger idea. For example, an eagle might stand for pride. As you read, ask: • Are any people, objects, or events strongly associated with an idea—are they symbols? • How does the idea represented by each symbol relate to other story elements?

Model

About the Text Madeleine L'Engle (1918–2007) wrote novels, plays, and poetry, reaching audiences of both young adult and adult readers. At the outset of her novel *A Wrinkle in Time,* high-school student Meg Murry's father is still missing, having mysteriously vanished more than a year before. The following selection from the novel is set in the high-school principal's office, where Meg has been sent for misbehavior.

from *A Wrinkle in Time* by Madeleine L'Engle

"Meg, is something troubling you? Are you unhappy at home?" Mr. Jenkins asked.

At last Meg looked at him, pushing at her glasses in a characteristic gesture. "Everything's *fine* at home."

"I'm glad to hear it. But I know it must be hard on you to have your father away."

Meg eyed the principal warily, and ran her tongue over the barbed line of her braces.

"Have you had any news from him lately?"

Meg was sure it was not only imagination that made her feel that behind Mr. Jenkins' surface concern was a gleam of avid curiosity. Wouldn't he like to know! she thought. And if I knew anything he's the last person I'd tell. Well, one of the last.

The postmistress must know that it was almost a year now since the last letter, and heaven knows how many people *she'd* told, or what unkind guesses she'd made about the reason for the long silence.

Mr. Jenkins waited for an answer, but Meg only shrugged.

"Just what was your father's line of business?" Mr. Jenkins asked. "Some kind of scientist, wasn't he?"

"He is a physicist." Meg bared her teeth to reveal the two ferocious lines of braces.

Setting Principals, like other public officials, represent society and its rules. The setting and the principal's question suggest a thematic concern: society's efforts to intervene in an individual's life.

Plot and Conflict Meg resents the principal's question, a detail that reinforces the conflict between individual and society.

Setting Meg lives in a small community where it is hard to keep secrets. The setting again suggests a theme that pits the individual against society.

Plot and Conflict
This passage brings out the main conflict in the excerpt: Mr. Jenkins wants Meg to acknowledge that her father is gone for good, while Meg resents his probing questions.

Statements Meg's strong statement of faith refines the theme—it is not just a theme of the individual versus society, but of individual faith versus the attitudes encouraged by society.

"Meg, don't you think you'd make a better adjustment to life if you faced facts?"

"I do face facts," Meg said. "They're lots easier to face than people, I can tell you."

"Then why don't you face facts about your father?"

"You leave my father out of it!" Meg shouted.

"Stop bellowing," Mr. Jenkins said sharply. "Do you want the entire school to hear you?"

"So what?" Meg demanded. "I'm not ashamed of anything I'm saying. Are you?"

Mr. Jenkins sighed. "Do you enjoy being the most belligerent, uncooperative child in school?"

Meg ignored this. She leaned over the desk toward the principal. "Mr. Jenkins, you've met my mother, haven't you? You can't accuse her of not facing facts, can you? She's a scientist. She has doctors' degrees in both biology and bacteriology. Her *business* is facts. When she tells me that my father isn't coming home, I'll believe it. As long as she says Father *is* coming home, then I'll believe that."

Theme Details in the selection—from the setting in a principal's office to the character of the gossipy postmistress to the circumstance of Meg's father's disappearance—all suggest the pressure that Meg is under. The pattern that they form might be summed up in a phrase such as "Meg and her faith in her family versus society and its doubt." A generalized restatement of this pattern might be given as "individual faith versus social pressure." This pattern of story details, along with Meg's statement at the end of the excerpt, suggest this theme: *Sometimes a person needs to act on the basis of faith even when circumstances and social pressure do not support that faith.*

Independent Practice

About the Text When trains were the main form of long-distance transportation, the job of porter, or passenger assistant, was largely filled by African Americans. Patricia C. McKissack (b. 1944) based this story on legends African American porters told.

"The 11:59" by Patricia C. McKissack

Lester Simmons was a thirty-year retired Pullman car porter—had his gold watch to prove it. "Keeps perfect train time," he often bragged. "Good to the second."

Daily he went down to the St. Louis Union Station and shined shoes to help supplement his meager twenty-four-dollar-a-month Pullman retirement check. He ate his evening meal at the porter house on Compton Avenue and hung around until late at night talking union, playing bid whist,[1] and spinning yarns with those who were still "travelin' men." In this way Lester stayed in touch with the only family he'd known since 1920.

There was nothing the young porters liked more than listening to Lester tell true stories about the old days, during the founding of the Brotherhood of Sleeping Car Porters, the first black union in the United States. He knew the president, A. Philip Randolph,[2] personally, and proudly boasted that it was Randolph who'd signed him up as a union man back in 1926. He passed his original card around for inspection. "I knew all the founding brothers. Take Brother E. J. Bradley. We hunted many a day together, not for the sport of it but for something to eat. Those were hard times, starting up the union. But we hung in there so you youngsters might have the benefits you enjoy now."

The rookie porters always liked hearing about the thirteen-year struggle between the Brotherhood and the powerful Pullman Company, and how, against all odds, the fledgling union had won recognition and better working conditions. Everybody enjoyed it too when Lester told tall tales about Daddy Joe, the porters' larger-than-life hero. "Now y'all know the first thing a good Pullman man is expected to do is make up the top and lower berths for the passengers each night."

---

1. **bid whist** (hwist) *n.* card game for four players that developed into bridge.
2. **A. Philip Randolph** (1889–1979) president of the Brotherhood of Sleeping Car Porters, the first black union. He gave the opening speech at the historic March on Washington in 1963.

Title What is special about the time 11:59? What ideas might you associate with this time?

Symbols What ideas are associated with Lester's watch? What do you think the watch might represent?

Characters What do these details tell you about Lester and his past? What thematic contrast does this passage establish between Lester and other porters?

Practice continued

"Come on, Lester," one of his listeners chided. "You don't need to describe our jobs for us."

"Some of you, maybe not. But some of you, well—" he said, looking over the top of his glasses and raising an eyebrow at a few of the younger porters. "I was just setting the stage." He smiled good-naturedly and went on with his story. "They tell me Daddy Joe could walk flatfooted down the center of the coach and let down berths on both sides of the aisle."

Hearty laughter filled the room, because everyone knew that to accomplish such a feat, Daddy Joe would have to have been superhuman. But that was it: To the men who worked the sleeping cars, Daddy Joe was no less a hero than Paul Bunyan was to the lumberjacks of the Northwestern forests.

"And when the 11:59 pulled up to his door, as big and strong as Daddy Joe was . . ." Lester continued solemnly. "Well, in the end even he couldn't escape the 11:59." The old storyteller eyed one of the rookie porters he knew had never heard the frightening tale about the porters' Death Train. Lester took joy in mesmerizing[3] his young listeners with all the details.

"Any porter who hears the whistle of the 11:59 has got exactly twenty-four hours to clear up earthly matters. He better be ready when the train comes the next night . . ." In his creakiest voice, Lester drove home the point. "All us porters got to board that train one day. Ain't no way to escape the final ride on the 11:59."

Silence.

"Lester," a young porter asked, "you know anybody who ever heard the whistle of the 11:59 and lived to tell—"

"Not a living soul!"

Laughter.

"Well," began one of the men, "wonder will we have to make up berths on *that* train?"

"If it's an overnight trip to heaven, you can best be believing there's bound to be a few of us making up the berths," another answered.

> **Symbols** In this passage, what do you learn about the 11:59 legend? How does the legend reinforce or relate to other details in the story so far?

---

3. **mesmerizing** (mez´ mər īz´ iŋ) *v.* fascinating; amazing.

"Shucks," a card player stopped to put in. "They say even up in heaven *we* the ones gon' be keeping all that gold and silver polished."

"Speaking of gold and silver," Lester said, remembering. "That reminds me of how I gave Tip Sampson his nickname. Y'all know Tip?"

There were plenty of nods and smiles.

The memory made Lester chuckle. He shifted in his seat to find a more comfortable spot. Then he began. "A woman got on board the *Silver Arrow* in Chicago going to Los Angeles. She was dripping in finery—had on all kinds of gold and diamond jewelry, carried twelve bags. Sampson knocked me down getting to wait on her, figuring she was sure for a big tip. That lady was worrisome! Ooowee! 'Come do this. Go do that. Bring me this.' Sampson was running over himself trying to keep that lady happy. When we reached L.A., my passengers all tipped me two or three dollars, as was customary back then.

"When Sampson's Big Money lady got off, she reached into her purse and placed a dime in his outstretched hand. A *dime*! Can you imagine? *Ow*! You should have seen his face. And I didn't make it no better. Never did let him forget it. I teased him so—went to calling him Tip, and the nickname stuck."

Laughter.

"I haven't heard from ol' Tip in a while. Anybody know anything?"

"You haven't got word, Lester? Tip boarded the 11:59 over in Kansas City about a month ago."

"Sorry to hear that. That just leaves me and Willie Beavers, the last of the old, old-timers here in St. Louis."

Lester looked at his watch—it was a little before midnight. The talkfest[4] had lasted later than usual. He said his goodbyes and left, taking his usual route across the Eighteenth Street bridge behind the station.

In the darkness, Lester looked over the yard, picking out familiar shapes—the *Hummingbird,* the *Zephyr.*[5] He'd worked on them both. Train travel wasn't anything like it used to be in the old days—not since people had begun to ride airplanes. "Progress," he scoffed. "Those contraptions will never take the place of a train. No sir!"

Plot and Conflict
How does this news help to develop themes of aging or death?

---

4. **talkfest** (tôk´ fest´) *n.* informal gathering for discussion.
5. *Zephyr* (zef´ ər) *n.* soft, gentle breeze, named for the Greek god of the west wind.

Practice continued

Plot and Conflict
What conflict emerges for Lester in this passage? How does it relate to the story's theme?

Suddenly he felt a sharp pain in his chest. At exactly the same moment he heard the mournful sound of a train whistle, which the wind seemed to carry from some faraway place. Ignoring his pain, Lester looked at the old station. He knew nothing was scheduled to come in or out till early morning. Nervously he lit a match to check the time. 11:59!

"No," he said into the darkness. "I'm not ready. I've got plenty of living yet."

Fear quickened his step. Reaching his small apartment, he hurried up the steps. His heart pounded in his ear, and his left arm tingled. He had an idea, and there wasn't a moment to waste. But his own words haunted him. *Ain't no way to escape the final ride on the 11:59.*

"But I'm gon' try!" Lester spent the rest of the night plotting his escape from fate.

"I won't eat or drink anything all day," he talked himself through his plan. "That way I can't choke, die of food poisoning, or cause a cooking fire."

Lester shut off the space heater to avoid an explosion, nailed shut all doors and windows to keep out intruders, and unplugged every electrical appliance. Good weather was predicted, but just in case a freak storm came and blew out a window, shooting deadly glass shards in his direction, he moved a straight-backed chair into a far corner, making sure nothing was overhead to fall on him.

"I'll survive," he said, smiling at the prospect of beating Death. "Won't that be a wonderful story to tell at the porter house?" He rubbed his left arm. It felt numb again.

Lester sat silently in his chair all day, too afraid to move. At noon someone knocked on his door. He couldn't answer it. Foot-steps . . . another knock. He didn't answer.

A parade of minutes passed by, equally measured, one behind the other, ticking . . . ticking . . . away . . . The dull pain in his chest returned. He nervously checked his watch every few minutes.

Ticktock, ticktock.

Time had always been on his side. Now it was his enemy. Where had the years gone? Lester reviewed the thirty years he'd spent riding the rails. How different would his life have been if he'd married Louise Henderson and had a gallon of children? What if he'd taken that job at the mill down in Opelika?[6] What if he'd followed his brother to Philly?[7]

---

6. **Opelika** city in Alabama.
7. **Philly** informal name for Philadelphia, Pennsylvania.

How different?

Ticktock, ticktock.

So much living had passed so quickly. Lester decided if he had to do it all over again, he'd stand by his choices. His had been a good life. No regrets. No major changes for him.

Ticktock, ticktock.

The times he'd had—both good and bad—what memories. His first and only love had been traveling, and she was a jealous companion. Wonder whatever happened to that girl up in Minneapolis? Thinking about her made him smile. Then he laughed. That girl must be close to seventy years old by now.

Ticktock, ticktock.

Daylight was fading quickly. Lester drifted off to sleep, then woke from a nightmare in which, like Jonah, he'd been swallowed by an enormous beast. Even awake he could still hear its heart beating . . . *ticktock, ticktock* . . . But then he realized he was hearing his own heartbeat.

Lester couldn't see his watch, but he guessed no more than half an hour had passed. Sleep had overtaken him with such little resistance. Would Death, that shapeless shadow, slip in that easily? Where was he lurking? *Yea, though I walk through the valley of the shadow of death, I will fear no evil* . . . The Twenty-third Psalm was the only prayer Lester knew, and he repeated it over and over, hoping it would comfort him.

Lester rubbed his tingling arm. He could hear the blood rushing past his ear and up the side of his head. He longed to know what time it was, but that meant he had to light a match—too risky. What if there was a gas leak? The match would set off an explosion. "I'm too smart for that, Death," he said.

Ticktock, ticktock.

It was late. He could feel it. Stiffness seized his legs and made them tremble. How much longer? he wondered. Was he close to winning?

Then in the fearful silence he heard a train whistle. His ears strained to identify the sound, making sure it *was* a whistle. No mistake. It came again, the same as the night before. Lester answered it with a groan.

Statements How does this statement relate to the story Lester told the young porters about the 11:59? How does this statement contrast with the way Lester has used his time from the moment he heard the 11:59?

Symbols What do you think Lester's dream represents? How does it develop the story's theme?

Statements What attitude toward death does Lester take in this statement? Explain. How does this attitude relate to the theme?

Practice continued

Plot and Conflict
What is happening to
Lester? How do these
events both intensify the
conflict and develop the
theme?

Statements What
does Tip come to remind
Lester about? What
does Lester's response
indicate about the
story's theme?

Symbols What do you
think the train represents?
Give reasons for your
answer.

Symbols How does
the concluding sentence
reinforce the symbolism
in the story?

Ticktock, ticktock.

He could hear Time ticking away in his head. Gas leak or not, he had to see his watch. Striking a match, Lester quickly checked the time. 11:57.

Although there was no gas explosion, a tiny explosion erupted in his heart.

Ticktock, ticktock.

Just a little more time. The whistle sounded again. Closer than before. Lester struggled to move, but he felt fastened to the chair. Now he could hear the engine puffing, pulling a heavy load. It was hard for him to breathe, too, and the pain in his chest weighed heavier and heavier.

Ticktock, ticktock.

Time had run out! Lester's mind reached for an explanation that made sense. But reason failed when a glowing phantom dressed in the porters' blue uniform stepped out of the grayness of Lester's confusion.

"It's *your* time, good brother." The specter spoke in a thousand familiar voices.

Freed of any restraint now, Lester stood, bathed in a peaceful calm that had its own glow. "Is that you, Tip?" he asked, squinting to focus on his old friend standing in the strange light.

"It's me, ol' partner. Come to remind you that none of us can escape the last ride on the 11:59."

"I know. I know," Lester said, chuckling. "But man, I had to try."

Tip smiled. "I can dig it. So did I."

"That'll just leave Willie, won't it?"

"Not for long."

"I'm ready."

Lester saw the great beam of the single headlight and heard the deafening whistle blast one last time before the engine tore through the front of the apartment, shattering glass and splintering wood, collapsing everything in its path, including Lester's heart.

When Lester didn't show up at the shoeshine stand two days running, friends went over to his place and found him on the floor. His eyes were fixed on something quite amazing—his gold watch, stopped at exactly 11:59.

Theme Drawing on events, statements, symbols, and other elements in the story, explain the theme and how these details develop it.

Close Read: Central Idea in Nonfiction

Authors of nonfiction use various types of supporting details to develop a central idea.

A work of nonfiction often focuses on one major central idea. Each paragraph has its own central, or main, idea, which contributes to the development of the central idea of the work as a whole.

Stated Central Idea In nonfiction, the central idea is often directly stated, typically at the beginning of the piece. It may even be in the title.

> **Example: Stated Central Idea**
>
> **This central idea is stated in the first sentence.**
>
> It is easy to work exercise into everyday life. You can park far away from the supermarket entrance. You can use the stairs instead of the elevator.

Implied Central Idea Sometimes the central idea is not stated. Instead, the central idea is revealed through the connections between details in the work. The central idea is the idea that all the details combine to support.

> **Example: Implied Central Idea**
>
> Wolves are shy and try to avoid people. They do not eat humans. Wolf packs prefer to prey on large animals.
>
> **Each sentence tells why wolves are not a threat to humans. The central idea could be "People shouldn't fear wolves."**

Use the chart below to guide you in identifying and analyzing central ideas and the details that support them.

Identifying Supporting Details

As you read a nonfiction work, look for each different type of detail listed and determine how these details support and develop the central idea.

Statements of fact are statements that can be proven true.
Example: *Milkweed is the major food source for monarch butterflies.*

Firsthand accounts are accounts from eyewitnesses.
Example: *The security guard said no one entered the building after 6:00 P.M.*

Statistics are facts or data of a numerical kind that have been collected and analyzed.
Example: *Sixty-four percent of the students polled said they did not know how to cook.*

Personal experiences are reports of the author's own experiences, used to illustrate a point.
Example: *I had run marathons before, so I knew what to expect.*

Expert testimony comes from recognized authorities.
Example: *Professor Gordon, a Vermeer expert, said the painting was a fake.*

Anecdotes are stories that make a point.
Example: *To show the importance of following directions, my dad told me the story of the time he tried to make a cake without a recipe.*

Examples illustrate a general concept or point by giving a specific instance.
Example: *There are many non-meat sources of protein—for example, nuts, beans, and grains.*

Analogies are comparisons that clarify a point.
Example: *Singing is like playing a sport: Both require constant practice.*

ⓒ EXEMPLAR TEXT

Model

About the Text Frederick Douglass (1818?–1895) was born enslaved but escaped to freedom. He became an outspoken opponent of slavery and a civil rights advocate, lecturing widely and publishing his own newspapers. In this excerpt from his autobiography, he talks about the impact reading had on his life.

from *Narrative of the Life of Frederick Douglass, an American Slave, Written by Himself* (1845)

BACKGROUND When Douglass was a boy, he was sent to live in Baltimore with Hugh Auld, a relative of his first master. Auld's wife began to teach Douglass to read, but Auld forbade her claiming the lessons would make Douglass unfit for slavery. (Hugh Auld is referred to as "Master Hugh" in this excerpt.) Despite this setback, Douglass persisted and managed to learn to read. In this excerpt, Douglass reports his discovery of a collection of works entitled The Columbian Orator.

In the same book *[The Columbian Orator]*, I met with one of Sheridan's mighty speeches on and in behalf of Catholic emancipation.[1] These were choice documents to me. I read them over and over again with unabated interest. They gave tongue to interesting thoughts of my own soul, which had frequently flashed through my mind, and died away for want[2] of utterance. The moral which I gained from the dialogue was the power of truth over the conscience of even a slaveholder. What I got from Sheridan was a bold denunciation of slavery, and a powerful vindication of human rights. The reading of these documents enabled me to utter my thoughts, and to meet the arguments brought forward to sustain slavery; but while they relieved me of one difficulty, they brought on another even more painful than the one of which I was relieved. The more I read, the more I was led

Firsthand Accounts
In an autobiography, most of the details come from the author's own experiences. In these sentences, Douglass tells of an important event in his own life.

1. **Sheridan's mighty speeches . . . Catholic emancipation** Richard Brinsley Sheridan (1751–1816), British dramatist and politician, opposed discrimination against members of the Catholic faith. Such discrimination was widespread in England in his day. It included, for example, laws that prevented Catholics from holding public office.
2. **want** lack.

to abhor and detest my enslavers. I could regard them in no other light than a band of successful robbers, who had left their homes, and gone to Africa, and stolen us from our homes, and in a strange land reduced us to slavery. I loathed them as being the meanest as well as the most wicked of men. As I read and contemplated the subject, behold! that very discontentment which Master Hugh had predicted would follow my learning to read had already come, to torment and sting my soul to unutterable anguish. As I writhed under it, I would at times feel that learning to read had been a curse rather than a blessing. It had given me a view of my wretched condition, without the remedy. It opened my eyes to the horrible pit, but to no ladder upon which to get out. In moments of agony, I envied my fellow-slaves for their stupidity. I have often wished myself a beast. I preferred the condition of the meanest reptile to my own. Any thing, no matter what, to get rid of thinking! It was this everlasting thinking of my condition that tormented me. There was no getting rid of it. It was pressed upon me by every object within sight or hearing, animate or inanimate. The silver trump[3] of freedom had roused my soul to eternal wakefulness. Freedom now appeared, to disappear no more forever. It was heard in every sound, and seen in every thing. It was ever present to torment me with a sense of my wretched condition. I saw nothing without seeing it, I heard nothing without hearing it, and felt nothing without feeling it. It looked from every star, it smiled in every calm, breathed in every wind, and moved in every storm.

Analogies Douglass compares slavers to a band of robbers to help readers see them as criminals.

Personal Experiences Douglass's description of his own feelings supports his general condemnation of slavery.

Central Idea The supporting details in the selection suggest the following theme: *The idea of freedom, once encountered, will not let a person who is not free rest until he or she finds liberty.*

---

3. **trump** trumpet.

Independent Practice

About the Text In the age of widespread railway travel, Pullman railway cars offered luxurious accommodations. From the late 1800s into the twentieth century, the porters who assisted passengers on these cars were African Americans, for whom the job represented economic opportunity in a racially unjust society. In this excerpt from a chapter of *A Long Hard Journey: The Story of the Pullman Porter,* Patricia C. McKissack and her husband Fredrick McKissack (b. 1939) share the stories, lore, and language that united African American Pullman porters.

from "The Baker Heater League" by Patricia C. McKissack and Fredrick McKissack

Porters developed a language and history that grew out of their common experiences. And they shared their experiences from coast to coast, north and south. Singing and telling stories helped to pass the time while waiting for an assignment, and it took the edge off being away from home and their loved ones.

Train stations provided quarters for porters called "porter houses." Sitting around a Baker heater, a large pot-bellied stove, the first porters told tales, jokes, and real-life stories that, in time, developed into a communication network peculiar to themselves. For example, if something happened in New York on Friday, porters in every state would know about it on Sunday. Political news, a good joke, style changes, even a girl's telephone number could be passed from New York to Chicago to Los Angeles, or from Minneapolis to St. Louis to New Orleans. This special brotherhood became known as "The Baker Heater League."

As older porters died or retired, their stories became a part of railroad lore, and their legacy helped to reshape and mold new heroes and legends. Just as lumberjacks created their superhero, Paul Bunyan, and cowboys sang about wily Pecos Bill, railroaders had Casey Jones and John Henry.

John Luther Jones, better known as Casey Jones, was an engineer on Cannonball Number 382. On the evening of April 29, 1900, Casey and his black fireman, Sim Webb, prepared to take the Cannonball from Memphis to Canton. The scheduled engineer was out ill. The train left at 12:50 A.M., an hour and thirty minutes late. Casey was

Examples Identify the central idea (stated in the first paragraph) that this example supports.

Analogies What do you think is the purpose of this analogy? How does it help develop the central idea stated in the first paragraph?

Facts Why do you think the authors include both the true story and part of a song that tells the legend? By including both, what main idea do the authors illustrate?

determined to make up the lost time. Through a series of mishaps and miscommunications, Casey's train crashed. Although the brave engineer could have jumped to safety, he stayed with the train and saved many lives at the cost of his own. Casey Jones became a railroad hero, and many songs were written about him:

> Fireman jumped but Casey stayed on;
> He was a good engineer, but he's dead and gon'.

Legend tells us in another song that:

> When John Henry was a little boy,
> He was sitting on his papa's knee;
> He was looking down on a piece of steel,
> Say's "A steel-drivin' man I'll be, Lord, Lord.
> A steel-drivin' man I'll be."

The real John Henry, believed to be a newly freed slave from North Carolina, joined the West Virginia steel-driving team hired to dig out the Big Bend Tunnel for the C & O Railroad, circa 1870. Many stories detail the life and adventures of this two hundred-pound, six-foot man who was so strong he could drive steel with a hammer in each hand. John Henry's death occurred after competing with a steam drill, winning and then dying.

> The steam drill set on the right-hand side,
> John Henry was on the left.
> He said, "I will beat that steam drill down
> Or hammer my fool self to death."

Casey Jones and John Henry belonged to all railroaders, but the Pullman[1] porters had their very own hero in Daddy Joe.

Daddy Joe was a real person, but like most legends, his exploits were greatly exaggerated. One story establishes in legend, if not in fact, that Daddy Joe was the "first Pullman porter." He was said to have stood so tall and to have large hands so powerful that he could walk flat-footed down the aisle and let the upper berths down on each side.

Whenever a storyteller wanted to make a point about courtesy, honesty, or an outstanding job performance, he used a Daddy Joe story. And a

---

1. **Pullman** cars featured special seats, which were converted to sleeping berths at night. The porters who readied the berths for sleeping also helped the train passengers during the day.

Practice continued

tale about him usually began with: "The most terrific Pullman porter who ever made down a berth was Daddy Joe." Then the teller would tell a story like this one:

Hostile Indians were said to have attacked a train at a water tank. The all-white passengers were terrified. But Daddy Joe, with no regard for Pullman rules or his own safety, climbed on top of the train and spoke to the Indians in their own language. Afterwards Daddy Joe threw a Pullman blanket to each member of the attacking party and added a blessing at the end. The Indians let the train pass safely.

Examples How does this example, a story about Daddy Joe's silver and gold, relate to the information about the porters who created him? What central idea does the example help to support?

Whether he was facing hurricanes, high water, fires, robbers, or Indians, Daddy Joe always masterfully dealt with the situation. Legend has it that he even thwarted one of Jesse James's[2] attempted robberies. Daddy Joe got so many tips from grateful passengers, he was said to be "burdened down with silver and gold."

The first porters, who created Daddy Joe in their own image, were proud of him. He represented the qualities they valued—unquestionable loyalty and dedication to the job.

Examples Why do the authors follow this statement with an example of a story of a new employee?

New railroad employees were always the source of a good laugh, too. This new-brakeman story—or one like it—was a porter house favorite.

It began with a young college graduate who got a yearning to work on the railroad. So, he traded in his suit and tie for the rusty railroad blues. Right away he was hired as a brakeman on the Knox & Lincoln Line. On his first run, the engineer was having a very hard time getting the freight up a steep hill. After getting the train over, the engineer called out, "I was afraid she'd stall and the train would roll backward!"

The new brakeman smiled broadly and assured the engineer. "No chance of that happening," he said, beaming with pride, "because before we started, I went back and set the brakes."

Anecdotes How does this description of a story-telling session help to support the idea that the classic stories were a shared experience for the porters?

Amid thigh-slapping laughter, another tale would begin with: "Did you hear the story about the flagman?" Of course they'd all heard the story a hundred times. But each teller added or subtracted something until the tale was his own. That's how the tales stayed fresh and original.

Central Idea What central idea do the McKissacks convey in this excerpt? Give three examples of the way in which they develop it over the course of the text.

---

2. **Jesse James's** Jesse James (1847–1882) and his brother Frank roamed the American West after the Civil War, robbing trains and banks.

1. **Key Ideas and Details**
   (a) Summarize: Write an **objective summary** of "The 11:59." Remember that an objective summary reports the most important ideas and details from a text but does not include your personal opinions. **(b) Summarize:** Write an objective summary of "The Baker Heater League."

2. **Key Ideas and Details**
   (a) Summarize: Explain the legend of the Death Train in "The 11:59."
   (b) Connect: Explain how Lester's experiences before his death fit or illustrate the legend.

3. **Key Ideas and Details (a) Analyze:** What steps does Lester take to avoid death? **(b) Interpret:** When Tip tells Lester that he cannot avoid death, what does Lester mean in saying, "I know. . . . But man, I had to try"?

4. **Key Ideas and Details (a) Infer:** What actually causes Lester's death? Explain. **(b) Analyze:** Citing passages from the text, explain how the description of Lester's death makes his death part of the legend of the 11:59. **(c) Interpret:** Why is it fitting that Lester's death match the legend?

5. **Craft and Structure Analyze:** Cite three details from "The 11:59," including characters' speech and actions as well as descriptions and events, that make the story realistic. Explain your choices.

6. **Key Ideas and Details (a) Identify:** In a chart like the one shown, list both the facts and the details from legends reported in "The Baker Heater League."

Railroad Heroes	Fact	Legend/ Fiction

   (b) Collaboration: Share your chart with a small group, noting similarities and differences. **(c) Analyze:** Together, explain how fact and fiction were combined in railroad legend.

7. **Key Ideas and Details Infer:** What do you think is the authors' main purpose in writing "The Baker Heater League?" Explain.

8. **Craft and Structure (a) Analyze:** Explain what elements of fiction are used in "The Baker Heater League." **(b) Evaluate:** How effective is the authors' use of these elements? Explain.

9. **Integration of Knowledge and Ideas (a) Extend:** What stories and legends do people share in America today? **(b) Hypothesize:** Why it might be important for a group to develop its own stories or folklore?

Leveled Texts

Build your skills and improve your comprehension of fiction with texts of increasing complexity.

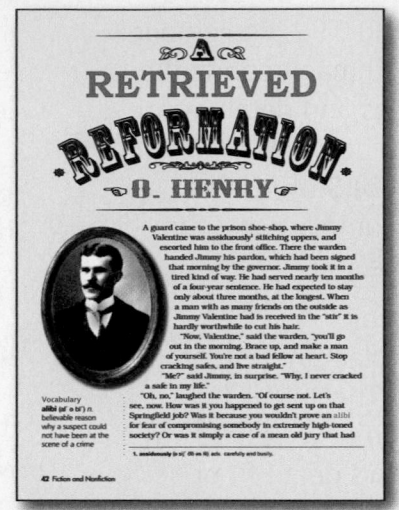

Read **"Raymond's Run"** to experience the sassy, streetwise voice of a young girl who is ready to take on the world.

Read **"A Retrieved Reformation"** to find out if a bank robber will be able to abandon a life of crime.

Common Core State Standards

Meet these standards with either **"Raymond's Run"** (p. 28) or **"A Retrieved Reformation"** (p. 42).

Reading Literature

3. Analyze how particular lines of dialogue or incidents in a story or drama propel the action, reveal aspects of a character, or provoke a decision. *(Literary Analysis: Plot)*

9. Analyze how a modern work of fiction draws on themes, patterns of events, or character types from myths, traditional stories, or religious works such as the Bible, including describing how the material is rendered new. *(Literature In Context)*

Writing

3. Write narratives to develop real or imagined experiences or events using effective technique, relevant descriptive details, and well-structured event sequences. **3.b.** Use narrative techniques, such as dialogue, pacing, description, and reflection, to develop experiences, events, and/or characters. **3.d.** Use precise words and phrases, relevant descriptive details, and sensory language to capture the

action and convey experiences and events. *(Speaking and Listening: Radio Broadcast)* **3.e.** Provide a conclusion that follows from and reflects on the narrated experiences or events. *(Writing: New Ending)*

Speaking and Listening

6. Adapt speech to a variety of contexts and tasks, demonstrating command of formal English when indicated or appropriate. *(Speaking and Listening: Radio Broadcast)*

Language

2. Demonstrate command of the conventions of standard English capitalization, punctuation, and spelling when writing. *(Conventions: Common and Proper Nouns)*

4.b. Use common, grade-appropriate Greek or Latin affixes and roots as clues to the meaning of a word. *(Vocabulary: Word Study)*

Reading Skill: Make Predictions

When you **make predictions** about a story, you develop an idea about what will happen next. You base this idea on details in the story itself, as well as on your own experience and background knowledge of the subject.

You can **support your predictions** by finding additional clues in the story that help you confirm your original ideas about what will happen next.

Using the Strategy: Predictions Chart

Draw on story details, background knowledge, and personal experience to fill in a **predictions chart** like the one shown.

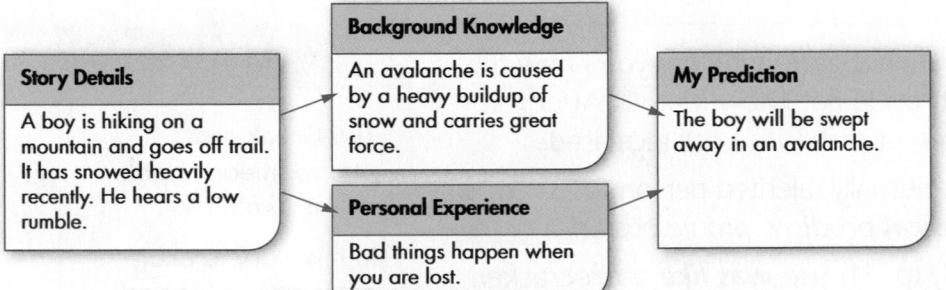

Story Details

A boy is hiking on a mountain and goes off trail. It has snowed heavily recently. He hears a low rumble.

Background Knowledge

An avalanche is caused by a heavy buildup of snow and carries great force.

Personal Experience

Bad things happen when you are lost.

My Prediction

The boy will be swept away in an avalanche.

Literary Analysis: Plot

Plot is the sequence of related events in a story. As you read, identify and analyze the effect of the following parts of the story's plot:

• **Exposition:** basic information about the characters and situation
• **Conflict:** a struggle between two opposing forces in the story
• **Rising Action:** events that increase the tension
• **Climax:** the high point of the story, usually the point at which the eventual outcome of the conflict is revealed
• **Falling Action:** events that follow the climax
• **Resolution:** the final outcome, during which any remaining conflicts are resolved or left open

Is *truth* the same for everyone?

Writing About the Big Question

In "Raymond's Run," the narrator discovers an important truth about herself after running in a big race. Use these sentence starters to develop your ideas about the Big Question.

Before _____ happened, I used to think that _____ was important. After it happened, I **observed** that _____.

While You Read Look for things that happen during the race to change the narrator's views of both her brother and herself.

Vocabulary

Read each word and its definition. Decide whether you know the word well, know it a little bit, or do not know it at all. After you read, see how your knowledge of each word has increased.

- **prodigy** (präd´ ə jē) *n.* unusually talented person (p. 31) *At six, Sam was already a musical prodigy. prodigious adj.*

- **liable** (lī´ ə bəl) *adj.* likely (p. 31) *Sue was like a firecracker, liable to go off at any moment. reliable adj. rely v.*

- **reputation** (rep´ yōō tā´ shən) *n.* widely-held opinion about someone, whether good or bad (p. 32) *The referee had a reputation for fairness. reputable adj. reputedly adv.*

- **pageant** (paj´ ənt) *n.* an elaborate play (p. 33) *Actors wore colorful costumes in a pageant celebrating the arrival of spring. pageantry n.*

- **periscope** (per´ ə scōp´) *n.* tube on a submarine that raises and lowers to show objects on the water's surface (p. 34) *The dark shape of an enemy ship appeared in the periscope.*

- **gesture** (jes´ chər) *n.* something said or done merely as a formality (p. 34) *Before playing, the bitter rivals shook hands as a gesture of sportsmanship.*

Word Study

The **Greek root -scope-** means "look at" or "watch."

In this story, a character cranes his neck like the periscope on a submarine, looking around the park to find a specific person.

Meet
Toni Cade Bambara
(1939–1995)

Author of
Raymond's Run

During her childhood, Toni Cade Bambara learned that growing up in New York City could be tough but rewarding. She loved the energy and rhythm of city life and the lively talk of the streets. Her gift as a writer was to capture the language and dreams of real people, especially young people, struggling to be themselves.

A Mother's Influence Bambara always gave her mother credit for inspiring her to write. "She gave me permission to wonder, to . . . dawdle, to daydream," the author once said.

BACKGROUND FOR THE STORY

Down Syndrome

In "Raymond's Run," the author implies that the narrator's brother has Down syndrome. People with Down syndrome develop more slowly, physically and mentally, than other people. Still, focusing on and developing a special talent can help people with disabilities achieve their fullest potential.

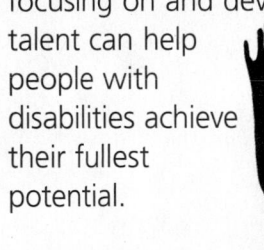

DID YOU KNOW?

The short story was Bambara's favorite form because it "makes a modest appeal for attention, slips up on your blind side and wrassles you to the mat before you know what's grabbed you."

Raymond's Run

Toni Cade Bambara

I don't have much work to do around the house like some girls. My mother does that. And I don't have to earn my pocket money by hustling; George runs errands for the big boys and sells Christmas cards. And anything else that's got to get done, my father does. All I have to do in life is mind my brother Raymond, which is enough.

Sometimes I slip and say my little brother Raymond. But as any fool can see he's much bigger and he's older too. But a lot of people call him my little brother cause he needs looking after cause he's not quite right. And a lot of smart mouths got lots to say about that too, especially when George was minding him. But now, if anybody has anything to say to Raymond, anything to say about his big head, they have to come by me. And I don't play the dozens[1] or believe in standing around with somebody in my face doing a lot of talking. I much rather just knock you down and take my chances even if I am a little girl with skinny arms and a squeaky voice, which is how I got the name Squeaky. And if things get too rough, I run. And as anybody can tell you, I'm the fastest thing on two feet.

There is no track meet that I don't win the first-place medal. I used to win the twenty-yard dash when I was a little kid in kindergarten. Nowadays, it's the fifty-yard dash. And tomorrow I'm subject to run the quarter-mile relay all by myself and come in first, second, and third. The big kids call me Mercury[2] cause I'm the swiftest thing in the neighborhood. Everybody knows that—except two people who know better, my father and me.

He can beat me to Amsterdam Avenue with me having a two fire-hydrant headstart and him running with his hands in his pockets and whistling. But that's private information. Cause can you imagine some thirty-five-year-old man stuffing himself into PAL[3] shorts to race little kids? So as far as everyone's concerned, I'm the fastest and that goes for Gretchen, too, who has put out the tale that she is going to win the first-place medal this year. Ridiculous. In the second

---

1. **the dozens** game in which the players insult one another; the first to show anger loses.
2. **Mercury** in Roman mythology, the messenger of the gods, known for great speed.
3. **PAL** Police Athletic League.

Make Predictions
In the first two paragraphs, what clues help you predict how Squeaky will react to a challenge?

Plot
List four facts you learn about Squeaky in the exposition of this story.

Reading Check
What is Squeaky's special talent?

place, she's got short legs. In the third place, she's got freckles. In the first place, no one can beat me and that's all there is to it.

I'm standing on the corner admiring the weather and about to take a stroll down Broadway so I can practice my breathing exercises, and I've got Raymond walking on the inside close to the buildings, cause he's subject to fits of fantasy and starts thinking he's a circus performer and that the curb is a tightrope strung high in the air. And sometimes after a rain he likes to step down off his tightrope right into the gutter and slosh around getting his shoes and cuffs wet. Or sometimes if you don't watch him he'll dash across traffic to the island in the middle of Broadway and give the pigeons a fit. Then I have to go behind him apologizing to all the old people sitting around trying to get some sun and getting all upset with the pigeons fluttering around them, scattering their newspapers and upsetting the waxpaper lunches in their laps. So I keep Raymond on the inside of me, and he plays like he's driving a stage coach, which is O.K. by me so long as he doesn't run me over or interrupt my breathing exercises, which I have to do on account of I'm serious about my running, and I don't care who knows it. •

Now some people like to act like things come easy to them, won't let on that they practice. Not me. I'll high prance down 34th Street like a rodeo pony to keep my knees strong even if it does get my mother uptight so that she walks ahead like she's not with me, don't know me, is all by herself on a shopping trip, and I am somebody else's crazy child.

Now you take Cynthia Procter for instance. She's just the opposite. If there's a test tomorrow, she'll say something like, "Oh, I guess I'll play handball this afternoon and watch television tonight," just to let you know she ain't thinking about the test. Or like last week when she won the spelling bee for the millionth time, "A good thing you got 'receive,' Squeaky, cause I would have got it wrong. I completely forgot about the spelling bee." And she'll clutch the lace on her blouse like it was a narrow escape. Oh, brother.

But of course when I pass her house on my early morning trots around the block, she is practicing the scales on the piano over and over and over and over. Then in music class she always lets herself get bumped around so she

Make Predictions
What details support a prediction that Squeaky will be tough to beat in a race?

falls accidently on purpose onto the piano stool and is so surprised to find herself sitting there that she decides just for fun to try out the ole keys and what do you know—Chopin's[4] waltzes just spring out of her fingertips and she's the most surprised thing in the world. A regular prodigy. I could kill people like that.

I stay up all night studying the words for the spelling bee. And you can see me any time of day practicing running. I never walk if I can trot, and shame on Raymond if he can't keep up. But of course he does, cause if he hangs back someone's liable to walk up to him and get smart, or take his allowance from him, or ask him where he got that great big pumpkin head. People are so stupid sometimes.

So I'm strolling down Broadway breathing out and breathing in on counts of seven, which is my lucky number, and here comes Gretchen and her sidekicks—Mary Louise who used to be a friend of mine when she first moved to Harlem from Baltimore and got beat up by everybody till I took up for her on account of her mother and my mother used to sing in the same choir when they were young girls, but people ain't grateful, so now she hangs out with the new girl Gretchen and talks about me like a dog; and Rosie who is as fat as I am skinny and has a big mouth where Raymond is concerned and is too stupid to know that there is not a big deal of difference between herself and Raymond and that she can't afford to throw stones. So they are steady coming up Broadway and I see right away that it's going to be one of those Dodge City[5] scenes cause the street ain't that big and they're close to the buildings just as

Vocabulary
prodigy (präd´ ə jē) *n.* unusually talented person
liable (lī´ ə bəl) *adj.* likely

▲ **Critical Viewing** How do you think growing up in a city like this one has affected Squeaky's personality? **[Infer]**

Reading Check
Why does Squeaky dislike Cynthia Procter?

Vocabulary
reputation (rep´ yōō
tā´ shən) *n.* widely-
held opinion about
someone, whether
good or bad

we are. First I think I'll step into the candy store and look
over the new comics and let them pass. But that's chicken
and I've got a reputation to consider. So then I think I'll just
walk straight on through them or even over them if necessary.
But as they get to me, they slow down. I'm ready to fight,
cause like I said I don't feature a whole lot of chit-chat, I much
prefer to just knock you down right from the jump and save
everybody a lotta precious time.

"You signing up for the May Day races?" smiles Mary
Louise, only it's not a smile at all.

A dumb question like that doesn't deserve an answer.
Besides, there's just me and Gretchen standing there really, so
no use wasting my breath talking to shadows.

"I don't think you're going to win this time," says Rosie,
trying to signify with her hands on her hips all salty,
completely forgetting that I have whupped her many times for
less salt than that.

"I always win cause I'm the best," I say straight at Gretchen
who is, as far as I'm concerned, the only one talking in this
ventriloquist-dummy routine.[6]

Gretchen smiles, but it's not a smile, and I'm thinking that
girls never really smile at each other because they don't know
how and don't want to know how and there's probably no one
to teach us how cause grown-up girls don't know either. Then
they all look at Raymond who has just brought his mule team
to a standstill. And they're about to see what trouble they can
get into through him.

"What grade you in now, Raymond?"

"You got anything to say to my brother, you say it to me,
Mary Louise Williams of Raggedy Town, Baltimore."

"What are you, his mother?" sasses Rosie.

"That's right, Fatso. And the next word out of anybody and
I'll be *their* mother too." So they just stand there and Gretchen
shifts from one leg to the other and so do they. Then Gretchen
puts her hands on her hips and is about to say something
with her freckle-face self but doesn't. Then she walks around
me looking me up and down but keeps walking up Broadway,

Make Predictions
What do you think
Squeaky will do if the
girls tease Raymond?
What details in the
story support your
prediction?

Plot
What clues in the story
indicate that Gretchen is
Squeaky's main rival in
this conflict?

---

6. **ventriloquist** (ven tril´ə kwist)-**dummy routine** a comedy act in which the performer
speaks through a puppet called a "dummy."

and her sidekicks follow her. So me and Raymond smile at each other and he says, "Gidyap" to his team and I continue with my breathing exercises, strolling down Broadway toward the ice man on 145th with not a care in the world cause I am Miss Quicksilver herself. •

I take my time getting to the park on May Day because the track meet is the last thing on the program. The biggest thing on the program is the May Pole dancing, which I can do without, thank you, even if my mother thinks it's a shame I don't take part and act like a girl for a change. You'd think my mother'd be grateful not to have to make me a white organdy dress with a big satin sash and

buy me new white baby-doll shoes that can't be taken out of the box till the big day. You'd think she'd be glad her daughter ain't out there prancing around a May Pole getting the new clothes all dirty and sweaty and trying to act like a fairy or a flower or whatever you're supposed to be when you should be trying to be yourself, whatever that is, which is, as far as I am concerned, a poor black girl who really can't afford to buy shoes and a new dress you only wear once a lifetime cause it won't fit next year.

I was once a strawberry in a Hansel and Gretel **pageant** when I was in nursery school and didn't have no better sense than to dance on tiptoe with my arms in a circle over my head doing umbrella steps and being a perfect fool just so my mother and father could come dressed up and clap. You'd think they'd know better than to encourage that kind of nonsense. I am not a strawberry. I do not dance on my toes. I run. That is what I am all about. So I always come late to the May Day program, just in time to get my number pinned on and lay in the grass till they announce the fifty-yard dash.

▲ **Critical Viewing**
What would Squeaky think about these children, shown dancing around a May Pole? **[Connect]**

Vocabulary
pageant (paj´ ənt) *n.* an elaborate play

☑ Reading Check
What would Squeaky's mother prefer that Squeaky do on May Day?

I put Raymond in the little swings, which is a tight squeeze
this year and will be impossible next year. Then I look around
for Mr. Pearson, who pins the numbers on. I'm really looking
for Gretchen if you want to know the truth, but she's not
around. The park is jam-packed. Parents in hats and corsages
and breast-pocket handkerchiefs peeking up. Kids in white
dresses and light-blue suits. The parkees unfolding chairs and
chasing the rowdy kids from Lenox as if they had no right to
be there. The big guys with their caps on backwards, leaning
against the fence swirling the basketballs on the tips of their
fingers, waiting for all these crazy people to clear out the park
so they can play. Most of the kids in my class are carrying
bass drums and glockenspiels[7] and flutes. You'd think they'd
put in a few bongos or something for real like that.

Then here comes Mr. Pearson with his clipboard and his
cards and pencils and whistles and safety pins and fifty
million other things he's always dropping all over the place
with his clumsy self. He sticks out in a crowd because he's on
stilts. We used to call him Jack and the Beanstalk to get him
mad. But I'm the only one that can outrun him and get away,
and I'm too grown for that silliness now.

"Well, Squeaky," he says, checking my name off the list and
handing me number seven and two pins. And I'm thinking he's
got no right to call me Squeaky, if I can't call him Beanstalk.

"Hazel Elizabeth Deborah Parker," I correct him and tell him
to write it down on his board.

"Well, Hazel Elizabeth Deborah Parker, going to give
someone else a break this year?" I squint at him real hard to
see if he is seriously thinking I should lose the race on purpose
just to give someone else a break. "Only six girls running this
time," he continues, shaking his head sadly like it's my fault all
of New York didn't turn out in sneakers. "That new girl should
give you a run for your money." He looks around the park for
Gretchen like a periscope in a submarine movie. "Wouldn't it
be a nice gesture if you were . . . to ahhh . . ."

I give him such a look he couldn't finish putting that idea
into words. Grownups got a lot of nerve sometimes. I pin

---

7. **glockenspiels** (gläk´ ən spēlz) *n.* musical instruments with flat metal bars that make bell-
like tones when struck with small hammers.

number seven to myself and stomp away, I'm so burnt. And I go straight for the track and stretch out on the grass while the band winds up with "Oh, the Monkey Wrapped His Tail Around the Flag Pole," which my teacher calls by some other name. The man on the loudspeaker is calling everyone over to the track and I'm on my back looking at the sky, trying to pretend I'm in the country, but I can't, because even grass in the city feels hard as sidewalk, and there's just no pretending you are anywhere but in a "concrete jungle" as my grandfather says. ●

The twenty-yard dash takes all of two minutes cause most of the little kids don't know no better than to run off the track or run the wrong way or run smack into the fence and fall down and cry. One little kid, though, has got the good sense to run straight for the white ribbon up ahead, so he wins. Then the second-graders line up for the thirty-yard dash and I don't even bother to turn my head to watch cause Raphael Perez always wins. He wins before he even begins by psyching the runners, telling them they're going to trip on their shoelaces and fall on their faces or lose their shorts or something, which he doesn't really have to do since he is very fast, almost as fast as I am. After that is the forty-yard dash which I use to run when I was in first grade. Raymond is hollering from the swings cause he knows I'm about to do my thing cause the man on the loudspeaker has just announced the fifty-yard dash, although he might just as well be giving a recipe for angel food cake cause you can hardly make out what he's saying for the static. I get up and slip off my sweat pants and then I see Gretchen standing at the starting line, kicking her legs out like a pro. Then as I get into place I see that ole Raymond is on line on the other side of the fence, bending down with his fingers on the ground just like he knew what he was doing. I was going to yell at him but then I didn't. It burns up your energy to holler.

Every time, just before I take off in a race, I always feel like I'm in a dream, the kind of dream you have when you're sick with fever and feel all hot and weightless. I dream I'm flying over a sandy beach in the early morning sun, kissing the leaves of the trees as I fly by. And there's always the smell of

Spiral Review
Theme What details in this part of the story indicate Squeaky's attitude toward winning?

Make Predictions
What do you predict will be the outcome of the conflict between Gretchen and Squeaky?

Reading Check
How does Mr. Pearson annoy Squeaky?

apples, just like in the country when I was little and used to think I was a choo-choo train, running through the fields of corn and chugging up the hill to the orchard. And all the time I'm dreaming this, I get lighter and lighter until I'm flying over the beach again, getting blown through the sky like a feather that weighs nothing at all. But once I spread my fingers in the dirt and crouch over the Get on Your Mark, the dream goes and I am solid again and am telling myself, Squeaky you must win, you must win, you are the fastest thing in the world, you can even beat your father up Amsterdam if you really try. And then I feel my weight coming back just behind my knees then down to my feet then into the earth and the pistol shot explodes in my blood and I am off and weightless again, flying past the other runners, my arms pumping up and down and the whole world is quiet except for the crunch as I zoom over the gravel in the track. I glance to my left and there is no one. To the right a blurred Gretchen, who's got her chin jutting out as if it would win the race all by itself. And on the other side of the fence is Raymond with his arms down to his side and the palms tucked up behind him, running in his very own style, and it's the first time I ever saw that and I almost stop to watch my brother Raymond on his first run. But the white ribbon is bouncing toward me and I tear past it,

▲ **Critical Viewing**
How does this photograph show that the start of a race is a moment of great tension and concentration? **[Speculate]**

racing into the distance till my feet with a mind of their own start digging up footfuls of dirt and brake me short. Then all the kids standing on the side pile on me, banging me on the back and slapping my head with their May Day programs, for I have won again and everybody on 151st Street can walk tall for another year.

"In first place . . ." the man on the loudspeaker is clear as a bell now. But then he pauses and the loudspeaker starts to whine. Then static. And I lean down to catch my breath and here comes Gretchen walking back, for she's overshot the finish line too, huffing and puffing with her hands on her hips taking it slow, breathing in steady time like a real pro and I sort of like her a little for the first time. "In first place . . ." and then three or four voices get all mixed up on the loudspeaker and I dig my sneaker into the grass and stare at Gretchen who's staring back, we both wondering just who did win. I can hear old Beanstalk arguing with the man on the loudspeaker and then a few others running their mouths about what the stopwatches say. Then I hear Raymond yanking at the fence to call me and I wave to shush him, but he keeps rattling the fence like a gorilla in a cage like in them gorilla movies, but then like a dancer or something he starts climbing up nice and easy but very fast. And it occurs to me, watching how smoothly he climbs hand over hand and remembering how he looked running with his arms down to his side and with the wind pulling his mouth back and his teeth showing and all, it occurred to me that Raymond would make a very fine runner. Doesn't he always keep up with me on my trots? And he surely knows how to breathe in counts of seven cause he's always doing it at the dinner table, which drives my brother George up the wall. And I'm smiling to beat the band cause if I've lost this race, or if me and Gretchen tied, or even if I've won, I can always retire as a runner and begin a whole new career as a coach with Raymond as my champion. After all, with a little more study I can beat Cynthia and her phony self at the spelling bee. And if I bugged my mother, I could get piano lessons and become a star. And I have a big rep as the baddest thing around. And I've got a roomful of ribbons and medals and awards. But what has Raymond got to call his own?

So I stand there with my new plans, laughing out loud by this time as Raymond jumps down from the fence and runs over with his teeth showing and his arms down to the side, which no one before him has quite mastered as a running style. And by the time he comes over I'm jumping up and down so glad to see him—my brother Raymond, a great runner in the family tradition. But of course everyone thinks I'm jumping up and down because the men on the

Plot
In what way is this the moment of greatest tension?

Make Predictions
What do you think Squeaky will do in the days following the race? Explain.

✔ Reading Check
What is Raymond doing while Squeaky runs the race?

loudspeaker have finally gotten themselves together and compared notes and are announcing "In first place—Miss Hazel Elizabeth Deborah Parker." (Dig that.) "In second place—Miss Gretchen P. Lewis." And I look over at Gretchen wondering what the "P" stands for. And I smile. Cause she's good, no doubt about it. Maybe she'd like to help me coach Raymond; she obviously is serious about running, as any fool can see. And she nods to congratulate me and then she smiles. And I smile. We stand there with this big smile of respect between us. It's about as real a smile as girls can do for each other, considering we don't practice real smiling every day, you know, cause maybe we too busy being flowers or fairies or strawberries instead of something honest and worthy of respect . . . you know . . . like being people.

Make Predictions
Was the outcome of the story difficult to predict? Explain.

Critical Thinking

© 1. Key Ideas and Details (a) Describe the relationship between Raymond and Squeaky. **(b) Analyze:** How does Squeaky feel about taking care of Raymond?

© 2. Key Ideas and Details (a) What does Raymond do during the race? **(b) Connect:** How do Raymond's actions change Squeaky's view of him? **(c) Deduce:** After seeing Raymond, why does Squeaky lose interest in the official outcome of the race?

© 3. Craft and Structure Analyze: Make a three-column chart to analyze the story's ending.
- Column 1: Write the last sentence of the story.
- Column 2: Explain what Squeaky's statement means.
- Column 3: Explain how Squeaky's actions illustrate the idea she expresses.

© 4. Integration of Knowledge and Ideas (a) How does Squeaky's view of her brother differ from the way other people see him? **(b)** How does Squeaky's view of Raymond change during the story? *[Connect to the Big Question: Is truth the same for everyone?]*

Cite textual evidence to support your responses.

Reading Skill: Make Predictions

1. **(a)** List two **predictions** you made as you read. **(b)** How did background knowledge help you make those predictions? **(c)** What story details helped **support** your prediction?

2. **(a)** What details could support a prediction that Gretchen will win the race? **(b)** Why would the author include details that support predictions of different outcomes?

Literary Analysis: Plot

3. **Key Ideas and Details** What is the **conflict** between Squeaky and Gretchen?

4. **Craft and Structure** Complete a **plot** chart like the one shown.

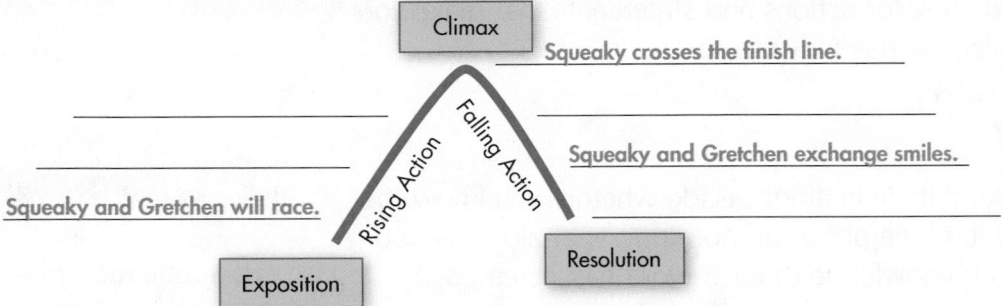

Climax — Squeaky crosses the finish line.

Rising Action

Falling Action

Squeaky and Gretchen exchange smiles.

Squeaky and Gretchen will race.

Exposition

Resolution

5. **Craft and Structure** How does Raymond's run contribute to the **resolution**?

Vocabulary

Acquisition and Use Write an answer to each question. Use a complete sentence that includes the italicized word.

1. What did the *prodigy* do at the show?
2. How is a wild animal *liable* to react when threatened?
3. What is the *reputation* of the other team?
4. What is the subject of the *pageant*?
5. Why did the submarine captain use the *periscope*?
6. What *gesture* can you make to welcome a new student?

Word Study Use context and what you know about the **Greek root -*scope*-** to explain your answer to each question.

1. Would a scientist use a *microscope* to study blood cells?
2. Why does an observatory have a large *telescope*?

Word Study

The **Greek root -*scope*-** means "look at" or "watch."

Apply It Explain how the root -*scope*- contributes to the meanings of these words. Consult a dictionary if necessary.

stethoscope
stereoscope
laparoscope

Is *truth* the same for everyone?

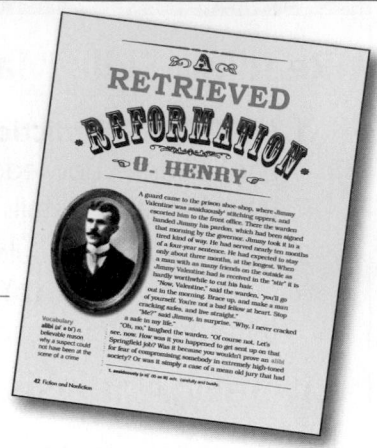

Writing About the Big Question

In "A Retrieved Reformation," Jimmy Valentine, a former thief, tries to reinvent himself as a small town shoe salesman. Use these sentence starters to develop your ideas about the Big Question.

People form **opinions** of others based on _____.

To **persuade** others that he or she has changed, a person could _____.

While You Read Look for actions and statements that make you believe Jimmy Valentine has truly changed.

Vocabulary

Read each word and its definition. Decide whether you know the word well, know it a little bit, or do not know it at all. After you read, see how your knowledge of each word has increased.

- **alibi** (al′ ə bī′) *n.* believable reason why a suspect could not have been at the scene of a crime (p. 42) *His alibi placed him in church, ten miles away, at the time of the robbery.*

- **rehabilitate** (rē′ hə bil′ə tāt) *v.* restore to working condition; restore the good name of (p. 43) *Her apology was the first step in an effort to rehabilitate herself.* *rehabilitation n.*

- **retribution** (re′ trə byōō′ shən) *n.* punishment for wrong-doing (p. 45) *The accident victim wanted money as retribution from the driver who hit him.*

- **perceived** (pər sēvd′) *v.* grasped mentally; saw (p. 46) *He had not perceived his error until it was too late.* *perception n. perceivable adj. perceptive adj.*

- **unobtrusively** (un′ əb trōō′ siv lē) *adv.* without calling attention to oneself (p. 47) *She slipped out of the room unobtrusively.* *obtrusiveness n. unobtrusive adj.*

- **anguish** (aŋ′ gwish) *n.* strong distress (p. 49) *The parents' anguish ended when their child recovered.* *anguished adj.*

Word Study

The **Latin root -trib-** means "pay" or "give."

In this story, the main character is a likeable thief who has generally avoided serious **retribution,** or pay-back, for his crimes.

Meet
O. Henry

(1862–1910)

Author of

❧ A ❧
RETRIEVED
REFORMATION

"O. Henry" was the pen name of William Sydney Porter. He remains a popular short-story writer who is best known for serving up surprise endings with a twist of **irony**—a turn of events the reader does not expect. A typical O. Henry story is full of humor and likeable, down-to-earth characters. They mirror his own life, which was also full of hard luck, unusual twists, and colorful characters.

Tragedy and Success Porter was brought up in North Carolina by his grandmother and his great-aunt. As a young man, he moved to Texas, where he worked as a writer, cartoonist, ranch hand, and bank teller. In 1898, Porter was convicted of stealing funds from the bank where he worked. During his three years in prison, Porter published several stories under the name O. Henry. He drew inspiration from the unusual personalities around him.

BACKGROUND FOR THE STORY

Safecracking

This story's main character is a thief who breaks into, or "cracks," safes in the early 1900s. At that time, the locks, dials, and levers of most safes were located on the outside. Safecrackers developed special techniques to punch out these parts. Today, safes are built with locks and bolts on the inside, making them harder to "crack."

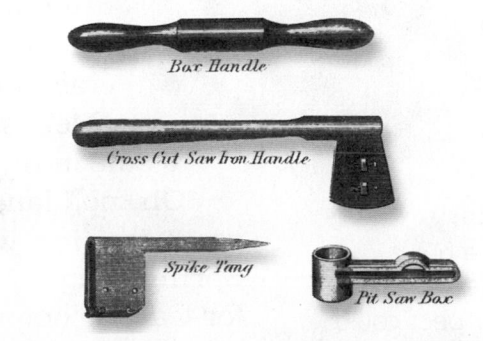

Box Handle

Cross Cut Saw Iron Handle

Spike Tang

Pit Saw Box

DID YOU KNOW?

The character of Jimmy Valentine was based on a safecracker O. Henry heard about while he was in jail.

A RETRIEVED REFORMATION

O. HENRY

A guard came to the prison shoe-shop, where Jimmy Valentine was assiduously[1] stitching uppers, and escorted him to the front office. There the warden handed Jimmy his pardon, which had been signed that morning by the governor. Jimmy took it in a tired kind of way. He had served nearly ten months of a four-year sentence. He had expected to stay only about three months, at the longest. When a man with as many friends on the outside as Jimmy Valentine had is received in the "stir" it is hardly worthwhile to cut his hair.

"Now, Valentine," said the warden, "you'll go out in the morning. Brace up, and make a man of yourself. You're not a bad fellow at heart. Stop cracking safes, and live straight."

"Me?" said Jimmy, in surprise. "Why, I never cracked a safe in my life."

"Oh, no," laughed the warden. "Of course not. Let's see, now. How was it you happened to get sent up on that Springfield job? Was it because you wouldn't prove an alibi for fear of compromising somebody in extremely high-toned society? Or was it simply a case of a mean old jury that

Vocabulary
alibi (al′ ə bī′) *n.* believable reason why a suspect could not have been at the scene of a crime

---

1. assiduously (ə sij′ ठ̄ əs lē) *adv.* carefully and busily.

had it in for you? It's always one or the other with you innocent victims."

"Me?" said Jimmy, still blankly virtuous. "Why, warden, I never was in Springfield in my life!"

"Take him back, Cronin," smiled the warden, "and fix him up with outgoing clothes. Unlock him at seven in the morn–ing, and let him come to the bullpen.[2] Better think over my advice, Valentine."

At a quarter past seven on the next morning Jimmy stood in the warden's outer office. He had on a suit of the villainously fitting, ready-made clothes and a pair of the stiff, squeaky shoes that the state furnishes to its discharged compulsory guests.

The clerk handed him a railroad ticket and the five-dollar bill with which the law expected him to rehabilitate himself into good citizenship and prosperity. The warden gave him a cigar, and shook hands. Valentine, 9762, was chronicled on the books "Pardoned by Governor," and Mr. James Valentine walked out into the sunshine.

Disregarding the song of the birds, the waving green trees, and the smell of the flowers, Jimmy headed straight for a restaurant. There he tasted the first sweet joys of liberty in the shape of a chicken dinner. From there he proceeded leisurely to the depot and boarded his train. Three hours set him down in a little town near the state line. He went to the café of one Mike Dolan and shook hands with Mike, who was alone behind the bar.

"Sorry we couldn't make it sooner, Jimmy, me boy," said Mike. "But we had that protest from Springfield to buck against, and the governor nearly balked. Feeling all right?"

"Fine," said Jimmy. "Got my key?"

He got his key and went upstairs, unlocking the door of a room at the rear. Everything was just as he had left it. There on the floor was still Ben Price's collar-button that had been torn from that eminent detective's shirt-band when they had overpowered Jimmy to arrest him.

Pulling out from the wall a folding-bed, Jimmy slid back a panel in the wall and dragged out a dust-covered suitcase.

---

2. bullpen *n.* barred room in a jail where prisoners are held while waiting to be moved or released.

Make Predictions
Based on Jimmy's atti-tude, do you predict he will take the warden's advice? Explain.

Vocabulary
rehabilitate (rē´ hə bil´ ə tāt) *v.* restore to work-ing condition; restore the good name of

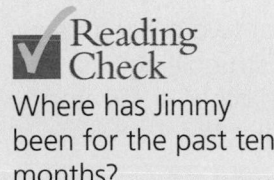
Reading Check
Where has Jimmy been for the past ten months?

HE OPENED THIS AND GAZED FONDLY AT THE FINEST SET OF BURGLAR'S TOOLS IN THE THE EAST.

He opened this and gazed fondly at the finest set of burglar's tools in the East. It was a complete set, made of specially tempered steel, the latest designs in drills, punches, braces and bits, jimmies, clamps, and augers,[3] with two or three novelties invented by Jimmy himself, in which he took pride. Over nine hundred dollars they had cost him to have made at—, a place where they make such things for the profession.

In half an hour Jimmy went downstairs and through the café. He was now dressed in tasteful and well-fitting clothes, and carried his dusted and cleaned suitcase in his hand.

"Got anything on?" asked Mike Dolan, genially.

"Me?" said Jimmy, in a puzzled tone. "I don't understand. I'm representing the New York Amalgamated Short Snap Biscuit Cracker and Frazzled Wheat Company."

This statement delighted Mike to such an extent that Jimmy had to take a seltzer-and-milk on the spot. He never touched "hard" drinks.

A week after the release of Valentine, 9762, there was a neat job of safe-burglary done in Richmond, Indiana, with no clue to the author. A scant eight hundred dollars was all that was secured. Two weeks after that a patented, improved, burglar-proof safe in Logansport was opened like a cheese to the tune of fifteen hundred dollars, currency; securities and silver untouched. That began to interest the rogue-catchers.[4] Then an old-fashioned bank-safe in Jefferson City became active and threw out of its crater an eruption of bank-notes amounting to five thousand dollars. The losses were now high enough to bring the matter up into Ben Price's class of work. By comparing notes, a remarkable similarity in the methods of the burglaries was noticed. Ben Price investigated the scenes of the robberies, and was heard to remark:

"That's Dandy Jim Valentine's autograph. He's resumed business. Look at that combination knob—jerked out as easy as pulling up a radish in wet weather. He's got the only clamps that can do it. And look how clean those tumblers were punched out! Jimmy never has to drill but one hole. Yes, I guess I want Mr. Valentine. He'll do his bit next time without any short-time or clemency foolishness."

Ben Price knew Jimmy's habits. He had learned them while

---

3. **drills . . . augers** (ô´ gərz) *n.* tools used to bore holes in metal.
4. **rogue-catchers** *n.* police.

working up the Springfield case. Long jumps, quick getaways, no confederates,[5] and a taste for good society—these ways had helped Mr. Valentine to become noted as a successful dodger of retribution. It was given out that Ben Price had taken up the trail of the elusive cracksman, and other people with burglar-proof safes felt more at ease.

One afternoon, Jimmy Valentine and his suitcase climbed out of the mail hack[6] in Elmore, a little town five miles off the railroad down in the blackjack country of Arkansas. Jimmy, looking like an athletic young senior just home from college, went down the board sidewalk toward the hotel.

A young lady crossed the street, passed him at the corner and entered a door over which was the sign "The Elmore Bank." Jimmy Valentine looked into her eyes, forgot what he was, and became another man. She lowered her eyes and colored slightly. Young men of Jimmy's style and looks were scarce in Elmore.

Jimmy collared a boy that was loafing on the steps of the bank as if he were one of the stockholders, and began to ask him questions about the town, feeding him dimes at intervals. By and by the young lady came out, looking royally unconscious of the young man with the suitcase, and went her way.

"Isn't that young lady Miss Polly Simpson?" asked Jimmy, with specious guile.[7]

"Naw," said the boy. "She's Annabel Adams. Her pa owns this bank. What'd you come to Elmore for? Is that a gold watch chain? I'm going to get a bulldog. Got any more dimes?"

Jimmy went to the Planters' Hotel, registered as Ralph D. Spencer, and engaged a room. He leaned on the desk and declared his platform[8] to the clerk. He said he had come to Elmore to look for a location to go into business. How was the shoe business, now, in the town? He had thought of the shoe business. Was there an opening?

5. **confederates** (kən fed′ər its) *n.* fellow criminals.
6. **mail hack** *n.* horse and carriage used to deliver mail.
7. **specious guile** (spē′ shəs gīl′) *n.* crafty, indirect way of obtaining information.
8. **platform** *n.* here, a statement of his situation.

Vocabulary
retribution (re′ trə byoo′ shən) *n.* punishment for wrongdoing

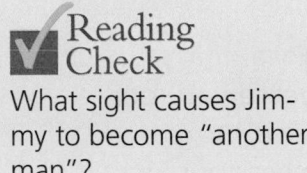

Spiral Review
Theme What details on this page point to the difficulty of changing old behaviors?

Reading Check
What sight causes Jimmy to become "another man"?

Language Connection

Allusions

O. Henry uses an allusion to explain Jimmy Valentine's transformation by love. An **allusion** is a reference to a person, place, or thing in another artistic work.

The allusion here is to the phoenix, a mythical bird. It was believed that every five hundred years, the phoenix, which resembled an eagle, would build a nest of wood. The nest would be consumed by flames and a new phoenix would emerge. The ashes of the former phoenix would be taken to the altar of the sun god by the new phoenix.

Connect to the Literature

How does O. Henry's use of this allusion emphasize the depth of Jimmy's transformation?

Vocabulary
perceived (pər
sēvd´) v. grasped
mentally; saw

The clerk was impressed by the clothes and manner of Jimmy. He, himself, was something of a pattern of fashion to the thinly gilded youth of Elmore, but he now perceived his shortcomings. While trying to figure out Jimmy's manner of tying his four-in-hand,[9] he cordially gave information.

Yes, there ought to be a good opening in the shoe line. There wasn't an exclusive shoe store in the place. The dry-goods and general stores handled them. Business in all lines was fairly good. Hoped Mr. Spencer would decide to locate in Elmore. He would find it a pleasant town to live in, and the people very sociable.

Mr. Spencer thought he would stop over in the town a few days and look over the situation. No, the clerk needn't call the boy. He would carry up his suitcase, himself: it was rather heavy.

Mr. Ralph Spencer, the phoenix that arose from Jimmy Valentine's ashes—ashes left by the flame of a sudden and alterative attack of love—remained in Elmore, and prospered. He opened a shoe store and secured a good run of trade.

Socially he was also a success, and made many friends. And he accomplished the wish of his heart. He met Miss Annabel Adams, and became more and more captivated by her charms.

At the end of a year the situation of Mr. Ralph Spencer was this: he had won the respect of the community, his shoe store was flourishing, and he and Annabel were engaged to be married in two weeks. Mr. Adams, the typical, plodding, country banker, approved of Spencer. Annabel's pride in him almost equaled her affection. He was as much at home in the family of Mr. Adams and that of Annabel's married sister as if he were already a member.

One day Jimmy sat down in his room and wrote this letter, which he mailed to the safe address of one of his old friends in St. Louis:

---

9. four-in-hand *n.* necktie.

Dear Old Pal:

I want you to be at Sullivan's place, in Little Rock, next Wednesday night, at nine o'clock. I want you to wind up some little matters for me. And, also, I want to make you a present of my kit of tools. I know you'll be glad to get them—you couldn't duplicate the lot for a thousand dollars. Say, Billy, I've quit the old business—a year ago. I've got a nice store. I'm making an honest living, and I'm going to marry the finest girl on earth two weeks from now. It's the only life, Billy—the straight one. I wouldn't touch a dollar of another man's money now for a million. After I get married I'm going to sell out and go West, where there won't be so much danger of having old scores brought up against me. I tell you, Billy, she's an angel. She believes in me; and I wouldn't do another crooked thing for the whole world. Be sure to be at Sully's, for I must see you. I'll bring along the tools with me.

 Your old friend,

 Jimmy.

Make Predictions
What clues here support a prediction that Jimmy will become a law-abiding citizen?

On the Monday night after Jimmy wrote this letter, Ben Price jogged unobtrusively into Elmore in a livery buggy. He lounged about town in his quiet way until he found out what he wanted to know. From the drugstore across the street from Spencer's shoe store he got a good look at Ralph D. Spencer.

"Going to marry the banker's daughter are you, Jimmy?" said Ben to himself, softly. "Well, I don't know!"

The next morning Jimmy took breakfast at the Adamses. He was going to Little Rock that day to order his wedding suit and buy something nice for Annabel. That would be the first time he had left town since he came to Elmore. It had been more than a year now since those last professional "jobs," and he thought he could safely venture out.

After breakfast quite a family party went downtown together—Mr. Adams, Annabel, Jimmy, and Annabel's married sister with her two little girls, aged five and nine. They came by the hotel where Jimmy still boarded, and he ran up to his room and brought along his suitcase. Then they

Vocabulary
unobtrusively (un´ əb trōō´ siv lē) *adv.* without calling attention to oneself

Plot
What events increase the tension of the conflict between Ben Price and Jimmy?

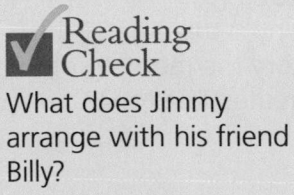
Reading
Check
What does Jimmy arrange with his friend Billy?

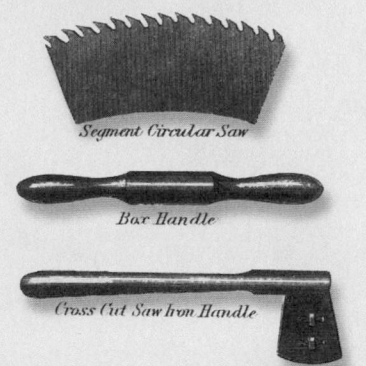

Segment Circular Saw

Box Handle

Cross Cut Saw Iron Handle

Spike Tang

Pit Saw Box

Fret Saw and Pad

Cross Cut Saw Handle

SAW SPINDLE & FRAME.

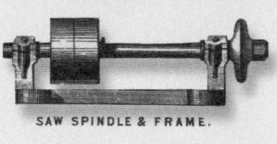

Plot
Why is this part of the story the moment of greatest tension?

went on to the bank. There stood Jimmy's horse and buggy and Dolph Gibson, who was going to drive him over to the railroad station.

All went inside the high, carved oak railings into the banking-room—Jimmy included, for Mr. Adams's future son-in-law was welcome anywhere. The clerks were pleased to be greeted by the goodlooking, agreeable young man who was going to marry Miss Annabel. Jimmy set his suitcase down. Annabel, whose heart was bubbling with happiness and lively youth, put on Jimmy's hat, and picked up the suitcase. "Wouldn't I make a nice drummer?"[10] said Annabel. "My! Ralph, how heavy it is! Feels like it was full of gold bricks."

"Lot of nickel-plated shoehorns in there," said Jimmy, coolly, "that I'm going to return. Thought I'd save express charges by taking them up. I'm getting awfully economical."

The Elmore Bank had just put in a new safe and vault. Mr. Adams was very proud of it, and insisted on an inspection by everyone. The vault was a small one, but it had a new, patented door. It fastened with three solid steel bolts thrown simultaneously with a single handle, and had a time lock. Mr. Adams beamingly explained its workings to Mr. Spencer, who showed a courteous but not too intelligent interest. The two children, May and Agatha, were delighted by the shining metal and funny clock and knobs.

While they were thus engaged Ben Price sauntered in and leaned on his elbow, looking casually inside between the railings. He told the teller that he didn't want anything; he was just waiting for a man he knew.

Suddenly there was a scream or two from the women, and a commotion. Unperceived by the elders, May, the nine-year-old girl, in a spirit of play, had shut Agatha in the vault. She had then shot the bolts and turned the knob of the combination as she had seen Mr. Adams do.

The old banker sprang to the handle and tugged at it for a moment. "The door can't be opened," he groaned. "The clock hasn't been wound nor the combination set."

---

10. drummer *n.* traveling salesman.

Agatha's mother screamed again, hysterically.

"Hush!" said Mr. Adams, raising his trembling hand. "All be quiet for a moment. Agatha!" he called as loudly as he could. "Listen to me." During the following silence they could just hear the faint sound of the child wildly shrieking in the dark vault in a panic of terror.

"My precious darling!" wailed the mother. "She will die of fright! Open the door! Oh, break it open! Can't you men do something?"

"There isn't a man nearer than Little Rock who can open that door," said Mr. Adams, in a shaky voice. "My God! Spencer, what shall we do? That child—she can't stand it long in there. There isn't enough air, and, besides, she'll go into convulsions from fright."

Agatha's mother, frantic now, beat the door of the vault with her hands. Somebody wildly suggested dynamite. Annabel turned to Jimmy, her large eyes full of anguish, but not yet despairing. To a woman nothing seems quite impossible to the powers of the man she worships.

"Can't you do something, Ralph—*try*, won't you?"

He looked at her with a queer, soft smile on his lips and in his keen eyes.

"Annabel," he said, "give me that rose you are wearing, will you?"

Hardly believing that she heard him aright, she unpinned the bud from the bosom of her dress, and placed it in his hand. Jimmy stuffed it into his vest pocket, threw off his coat and pulled up his shirt sleeves. With that act Ralph D. Spencer passed away and Jimmy Valentine took his place.

"Get away from the door, all of you," he commanded, shortly.

He set his suitcase on the table, and opened it out flat. From that time on he seemed to be unconscious of the presence of anyone else. He laid out the shining, queer implements swiftly and orderly, whistling softly to himself as he always did when at work. In a deep silence and

▲ **Critical Viewing**
Describe how it might feel to be trapped in a vault like this one. **[Speculate]**

Vocabulary
anguish (aŋ´ gwish) *n.* strong distress

Make Predictions
Based on what you know about Jimmy, what do you think he will do next? Explain.

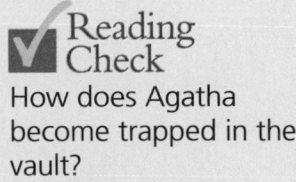
Reading Check
How does Agatha become trapped in the vault?

A Retrieved Reformation **49**

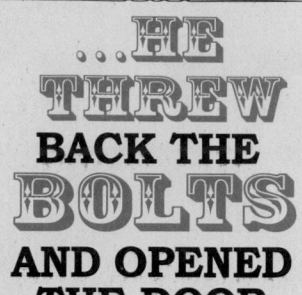

...HE THREW BACK THE BOLTS AND OPENED THE DOOR.

Plot
In what way is the resolution of the story **ironic,** or exactly opposite of what you might expect?

immovable, the others watched him as if under a spell.

In a minute Jimmy's pet drill was biting smoothly into the steel door. In ten minutes—breaking his own burglarious record—he threw back the bolts and opened the door.

Agatha, almost collapsed, but safe, was gathered into her mother's arms.

Jimmy Valentine put on his coat, and walked outside the railings toward the front door. As he went he thought he heard a far-away voice that he once knew call "Ralph!" But he never hesitated.

At the door a big man stood somewhat in his way.

"Hello, Ben!" said Jimmy, still with his strange smile. "Got around at last, have you? Well, let's go. I don't know that it makes much difference, now."

And then Ben Price acted rather strangely.

"Guess you're mistaken, Mr. Spencer," he said. "Don't believe I recognize you. Your buggy's waiting for you, ain't it?"

And Ben Price turned and strolled down the street.

Critical Thinking

Cite textual evidence to support your responses.

1. **Key Ideas and Details** **(a)** Whom does Valentine see when he gets off the train in Elmore? **(b) Deduce:** How does this event cause him to have a change of heart? **(c) Support:** Find at least two details in the story that prove Valentine has really changed.

2. **Craft and Structure** **Analyze:** Make a three-column chart to analyze the story's ending.
   • Column 1: Write Ben Price's words to Jimmy.
   • Column 2: Explain what Price means.
   • Column 3: Explain whether you think Price does the right thing.

3. **Integration of Knowledge and Ideas** **Make a Judgment:** Is it possible for people like Jimmy to reform themselves? Why or why not?

4. **Integration of Knowledge and Ideas** **(a)** How does Jimmy view himself before he meets Annabel? **(b)** How does this truth change for Jimmy after he meets her? **(c)** What do you think convinces Ben Price that Valentine has truly changed? *[Connect to the Big Question: Is truth the same for everyone?]*

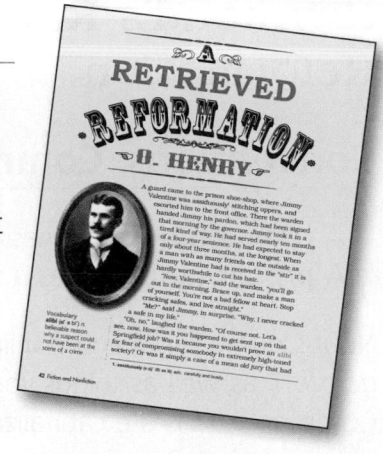

Reading Skill: Make Predictions

1. (a) List two **predictions** you made as you read. **(b)** How did background knowledge help you make those predictions? **(c)** What story details helped **support** your predictions?

2. (a) What support can you find in the story for a prediction that Ben Price will arrest Jimmy? **(b)** Why would the author include details that support predictions of different outcomes?

Literary Analysis: Plot

©3. Key Ideas and Details What is the **conflict** between Price and Valentine?

©4. Craft and Structure Complete a **plot** chart like the one shown.

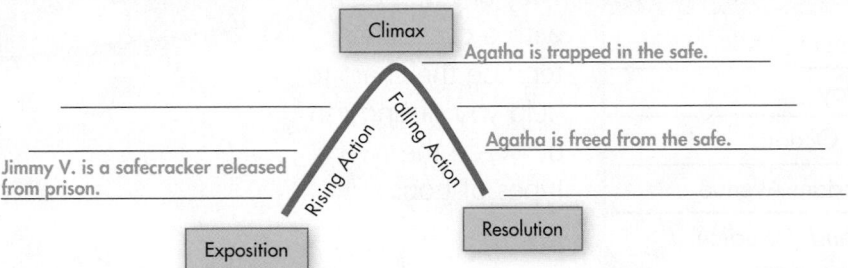

Climax

Agatha is trapped in the safe.

Rising Action

Falling Action

Agatha is freed from the safe.

Jimmy V. is a safecracker released from prison.

Exposition

Resolution

©5. Craft and Structure What role does Ben Price play in the **resolution** of the story?

Vocabulary

© Acquisition and Use Write an answer to each question. Use a complete sentence that includes the italicized word.

1. Can a company *rehabilitate* its name after a product fails?

2. Why is a good *alibi* important for the defense in a trial?

3. What might cause *anguish* for someone?

4. How is a parent *perceived* by a baby?

5. Why might someone want to leave a concert *unobtrusively?*

6. Why might a jury demand *retribution?*

Word Study Use the context of the sentences and what you know about the **Latin root -trib-** to answer each question.

1. Why would an association organize a *tribute* to someone?

2. What do sports figures *contribute* to society?

Word Study

The **Latin root -trib-** means "pay" or "give."

Apply It Explain how the root -trib- contributes to the meanings of these words. Consult a dictionary if necessary.

distribute
attribute
tributary

Integrated Language Skills

Raymond's Run • A Retrieved Reformation

Conventions: Common and Proper Nouns

A **common noun** names any person, place, or thing.
A **proper noun** names a specific person, place, or thing.

Nouns name living and nonliving things, such as *houses* and *goldfish*, as well as things you cannot see, such as *anger* or *time*. Common nouns are capitalized only if they come at the beginning of a sentence. Proper nouns name specific things, such as *Vermont*

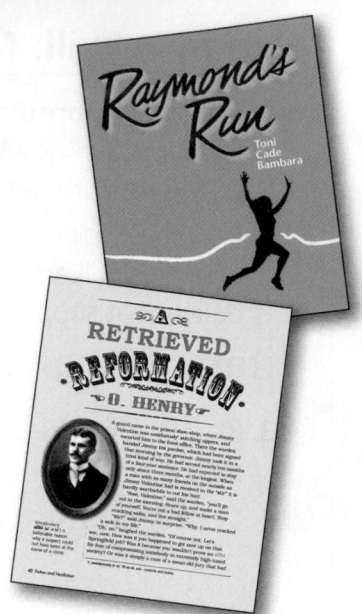

or *President Ford*. They always begin with a capital letter. Use the chart to help you distinguish between the two types of nouns.

Common Nouns	Proper Nouns
city	Sacramento
day	Thursday
ocean	Pacific Ocean
street	Amsterdam Avenue
book	*Pride and Prejudice*

Practice A Identify all the nouns in each sentence and indicate whether each one is a common noun or a proper noun.

1. The other girls that Squeaky meets on the street are Gretchen and Rosie.
2. The race is the last item on the program for May Day.
3. Squeaky and her mother shop at stores.
4. Gretchen and Squeaky exchange smiles of respect after the race.

© Reading Application Find two sentences in "Raymond's Run" that contain both common and proper nouns.

Practice B Rewrite the following sentences, using correct capitalization of proper nouns.

1. The Warden of the Prison told Jimmy he would be released on monday morning.
2. Soon after jimmy valentine left prison, a Bank in Richmond, indiana, was robbed.
3. Jimmy planned to give his burglary tools to an Old Pal named billy.
4. Ben price, a famous Detective, traced jimmy to his new Store in Elmore.

© Writing Application Find a proper noun in "A Retrieved Reformation" to replace each of these common nouns: town, state, girl, woman, banker.

PH WRITING COACH Further instruction and practice are available in *Prentice Hall Writing Coach.*

Writing

Narrative Text Write a **new ending** for the story you read. For example, imagine how the ending would have been different if Squeaky had lost the race, or if Ben Price had decided to arrest Jimmy Valentine. Use the following strategies in your writing:

- Describe each person's gestures and movements.
- Include dialogue that reveals the characters' personalities.
- Include descriptions of other characters' reactions to the statements or events you include.

You can decide whether to resolve the conflict neatly or whether to leave your readers guessing at the end.

Grammar Application Check to make sure you correctly capitalized the names of people and places in your new ending.

Writing Workshop: *Work in Progress*

Prewriting for Description List four physical characteristics of someone who has influenced you. Then, list six words that describe the person's personality. Save this Person Profile in your portfolio.

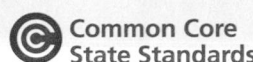

Common Core State Standards

L.8.2; W.8.3, W.8.3.b, W.8.3.d, W.8.3.e; SL.8.6
[For the full wording of the standards, see page 24.]

Use this prewriting activity to prepare for the **Writing Workshop** on page 104.

Speaking and Listening

Comprehension and Collaboration Write and perform a **radio broadcast** for your classmates. If you read "Raymond's Run," write a broadcast of the race. If you read "A Retrieved Reformation," write a script for the scene in which Jimmy rescues Agatha from the safe. To help you deliver an exciting broadcast, use the following tips:

- Use precise and vivid action verbs—such as *flying*, *pounding*, and *shrieking*—to convey action and emotion. Add sensory details, such as sights or sounds to make the broadcast come alive for listeners.

- Include physical description to show how characters look, act, and move. Use these descriptions for comparison or contrast. For example, *Squeaky runs gracefully, Gretchen awkwardly*.

- Use active voice rather than passive voice. For example, instead of *"The safe was pried open by Jimmy,"* say *"Jimmy pried open the safe."*

- As you deliver the broadcast, vary the tone and pace of your voice to create a mood of suspense and excitement.

www.PHLitOnline.com
- Interactive graphic organizers
- Grammar tutorial
- Interactive journals

© Leveled Texts

Build your skills and improve your comprehension of fiction and
literary nonfiction with texts of increasing complexity.

Read **"Gentleman of Río en
Medio"** to see how cultural
differences lead to an unexpected
disagreement over property.

Read **"Cub Pilot on the
Mississippi"** to find out what
causes Mark Twain to lose his
temper at a mean boss.

© Common Core State Standards

Meet these standards with either **"Gentlemen of Río en Medio"** (p. 59) or **"Cub Pilot on the
Mississippi"** (p. 66).

Reading Literature
2. Determine a theme or central idea of a text and
analyze its development over the course of the text,
including its relationship to the characters, setting, and
plot; provide an objective summary of the text. *(Literary
Analysis: Spiral Review)*

Reading Informational Text
2. Determine a central idea of a text and analyze its
development over the course of the text, including its
relationship to supporting ideas; provide an objective
summary of the text. *(Literary Analysis: Spiral Review)*

Writing
3. Write narratives to develop real or imagined experiences
or events using effective technique, relevant descriptive
details, and well-structured event sequences. **3.a.** Engage
and orient the reader by establishing a context and point
of view and introducing a narrator and/or characters;
organize an event sequence that unfolds naturally and
logically. *(Writing: Letter)*

Speaking and Listening
1. Engage effectively in a range of collaborative discussions
with diverse partners on grade 8 topics, texts, and issues,
building on others' ideas and expressing their own clearly.
1.d. Acknowledge new information expressed by others,
and, when warranted, qualify or justify their own views in
light of the evidence presented. *(Speaking and Listening:
Role Play)*

Language
1. Demonstrate command of the conventions of standard
English grammar and usage when writing or speaking.
(Conventions: Plural Nouns)

4.b. Use common, grade-appropriate Greek or Latin
affixes and roots as clues to the meaning of a word (e.g.,
precede, recede, secede). *(Vocabulary: Word Study)*

Reading Skill: Make Predictions

When you **make predictions**, you use details in a story to develop ideas about what will happen later. **Reading ahead to confirm or modify predictions** helps you remain focused on the connections between events. Follow these steps:

- As you read, look for details that suggest a certain outcome.
- Use your prior knowledge of common patterns in fiction and nonfiction to help you predict. In mysteries, for example, story clues usually lead readers to suspect the wrong character at first. Further reading, however, reveals the actual criminal. Keep patterns such as these in mind as you read.
- Once you have made a prediction, read on to see if you were right. Use new details to confirm or modify your prediction.

Using the Strategy: Predictions Chart

Use a **predictions chart** like the one shown to help you confirm and revise predictions.

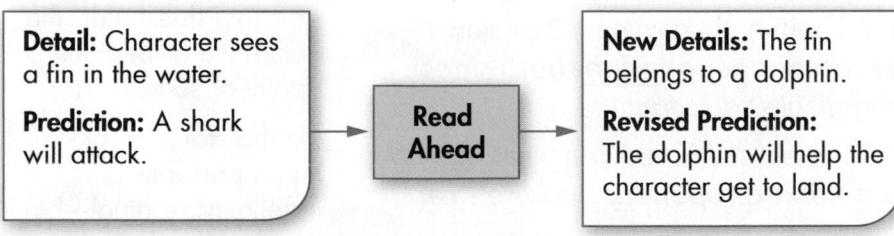

Detail: Character sees a fin in the water.

Prediction: A shark will attack.

→ **Read Ahead** →

New Details: The fin belongs to a dolphin.

Revised Prediction: The dolphin will help the character get to land.

Literary Analysis: Conflict and Resolution

Conflict is the struggle between two opposing forces.

- **External conflict** occurs when a character struggles against another character, natural forces, or some aspect of society.
- **Internal conflict** is a struggle between competing feelings, beliefs, needs, or desires within a single character. For example, a character might struggle with feelings of guilt.

In the **resolution** of a story, conflicts are resolved, or worked out. Sometimes conflicts are resolved neatly; at other times readers are left guessing about the exact outcome of a story.

Is *truth* the same for everyone?

Writing About the Big Question

In "Gentleman of Río en Medio," cultural differences spark a dispute over the value of property. Use these sentence starters to develop your ideas about the Big Question.

A person selling a house may be **biased** about his or her property because _____.

To a child, the value of a house and land consists of _____.

While You Read Notice how characters regard the idea of land ownership.

Vocabulary

Read each word and its definition. Decide whether you know the word well, know it a little bit, or do not know it at all. After you read, see how your knowledge of each word has increased.

- **negotiation** (ni gō′ shē ā′ shən) *n.* bargaining; discussion; deal-making (p. 59) *After intense negotiation, both sides agreed to a solution.* negotiable *adj.* negotiate *v.*

- **quaint** (kwānt) *adj.* unusual or old-fashioned in a pleasing way (p. 59) *He had the quaint habit of opening his wife's car door before his own.* quaintness *n.* quaintly *adv.*

- **deed** (dēd) *n.* a document which, when signed, transfers ownership of property (p. 60) *They found the deed to the house, signed by the original owners in 1853.* deed *v.*

- **preliminary** (prē lim′ ə ner′ ē) *adj.* introductory; preparatory (p. 60) *The pianist played a preliminary exercise to warm up for her recital.* preliminarily *adv.*

- **possession** (pə zesh′ ən) *n.* ownership (p. 61) *In colonial America, one requirement for voting was possession of property.* possessive *adj.* possess *v.*

- **descendants** (dē sen′ dənts) *n.* children, grandchildren, and continuing generations (p. 62) *In his will, the old man left all of his property to his descendants.* descent *n.* descend *v.*

Word Study

The **Latin root -limin-** means "threshold," the entrance or beginning point of something.

In this story, an old man performs a **preliminary** ritual—he shakes hands and makes small talk—before discussing business.

Meet
Juan A. A. Sedillo
(1902–1982)

Author of
Gentleman of Río en Medio

Born in New Mexico, Juan A. A. Sedillo was a descendant of early Spanish colonists of the Southwest. Sedillo was a man of many talents. In addition to being a writer and translator, Sedillo was a lawyer and judge who held various public positions. His varied life experiences and his exposure to the diverse cultures of New Mexico add a realistic depth to his stories.

The Story Behind the Story Although "Gentleman of Río en Medio" is a fictional story, it was inspired by a real legal case involving a conflict over a piece of property. Because Sedillo grew up among people of Spanish descent, he knew and understood their culture and beliefs. This understanding enabled him to turn an ordinary legal case into a memorable portrait of a person and a way of life.

Did You Know?
Juan Sedillo dropped his middle initials when he played a detective in the 1929 movie *The Girl From Havana,* an early black-and-white "talkie."

BACKGROUND FOR THE STORY
New Mexico's Spanish Heritage

New Mexico, the setting of this story, has a rich cultural heritage. The first Spanish colony in the area was established in 1598 in a region where Native Americans had lived for centuries. Over the next three hundred years, a patchwork of cultures was created with strong ties to both ancestral cultures. Today, in some remote villages, descendants of the first Spanish colonists still maintain a way of life that has remained largely unchanged since the sixteenth century.

The Parker Family Collection, Fort Worth, TX

Gentleman of Río en Medio

Juan A. A. Sedillo

It took months of negotiation to come to an understanding with the old man. He was in no hurry. What he had the most of was time. He lived up in Río en Medio, (rē' ō en mā de ō) where his people had been for hundreds of years. He tilled the same land they had tilled. His house was small and wretched, but quaint. The little creek ran through his land. His orchard was gnarled and beautiful.

The day of the sale he came into the office. His coat was old, green and faded. I thought of Senator Catron,[1] who had been such a power with these people up there in the mountains. Perhaps it was one of his old Prince Alberts.[2] He also wore gloves. They were old and torn and his fingertips showed through them. He carried a cane, but it was only the skeleton of a worn-out umbrella. Behind him walked one of his innumerable kin—a dark young man with eyes like a gazelle.

The old man bowed to all of us in the room. Then he removed his hat and gloves, slowly and carefully. Chaplin[3] once did that in a picture, in a bank—he was the janitor. Then he handed his things to the boy, who stood obediently behind the old man's chair.

There was a great deal of conversation, about rain and about his family. He was very proud of his large family. Finally we got down to business. Yes, he would sell, as he

---

1. **Senator Catron** Thomas Benton Catron, U.S. senator from New Mexico, 1912–1917.
2. **Prince Alberts** long, old-fashioned coats worn on formal occasions.
3. **Chaplin** Charlie Chaplin (1889–1977), actor and producer of silent films in the United States.

had agreed, for twelve hundred dollars, in cash. We would buy, and the money was ready. "Don[4] Anselmo," I said to him in Spanish, "we have made a discovery. You remember that we sent that surveyor, that engineer, up there to survey your land so as to make the deed. Well, he finds that you own more than eight acres. He tells us that your land extends across the river and that you own almost twice as much as you thought." He didn't know that. "And now, Don Anselmo," I added, "these Americans are *buena gente*,[5] they are good people, and they are willing to pay you for the additional land as well, at the same rate per acre, so that instead of twelve hundred dollars you will get almost twice as much, and the money is here for you."

The old man hung his head for a moment in thought. Then he stood up and stared at me. "Friend," he said, "I do not like to have you speak to me in that manner." I kept still and let him have his say. "I know these Americans are good people, and that is why I have agreed to sell to them. But I do not care to be insulted. I have agreed to sell my house and land for twelve hundred dollars and that is the price."

I argued with him but it was useless. Finally he signed the deed and took the money but refused to take more than the amount agreed upon. Then he shook hands all around, put on his ragged gloves, took his stick and walked out with the boy behind him. ●

A month later my friends had moved into Río en Medio. They had replastered the old adobe house, pruned the trees, patched the fence, and moved in for the summer. One day they came back to the office to complain. The children of the village were overrunning their property. They came every day and played under the trees, built little play fences around them, and took blossoms. When they were spoken to they only laughed and talked back good-naturedly in Spanish.

I sent a messenger up to the mountains for Don Anselmo. It took a week to arrange another meeting. When he arrived he repeated his previous preliminary performance. He wore the same faded cutaway,[6] carried the same stick and was accompanied by the boy again. He shook hands all around,

---

4. **Don** (dän) Spanish title of respect, similar to *Sir* in English.
5. *buena gente* (bwā´ nä hen´ tā) Spanish for "good people."
6. **cutaway** *n.* coat worn by men for formal daytime occasions; it is cut short in the front and curves to long tails in the back.

◀ **Critical Viewing**
How closely does this painting match your mental image of Don Anselmo's land? Explain. **[Compare]**

sat down with the boy behind his chair, and talked about the weather. Finally I broached the subject. "Don Anselmo, about the ranch you sold to these people. They are good people and want to be your friends and neighbors always. When you sold to them you signed a document, a deed, and in that deed you agreed to several things. One thing was that they were to have the complete possession of the property. Now, Don Anselmo, it seems that every day the children of the village overrun the orchard and spend most of their time there. We would like to know if you, as the most respected man in the village, could not stop them from doing so in order that these people may enjoy their new home more in peace."

Don Anselmo stood up. "We have all learned to love these Americans," he said, "because they are good people and good neighbors. I sold them my property because I knew they were good people, but I did not sell them the trees in the orchard."

This was bad. "Don Anselmo," I pleaded, "when one signs a deed and sells real property one sells also everything that grows on the land, and those trees, every one of them, are on the land and inside the boundaries of what you sold."

"Yes, I admit that," he said. "You know," he added, "I am the oldest man in the village. Almost everyone there is my relative

Vocabulary
possession (pə zesh′ ən)
n. ownership

Conflict
What conflict is identified here?

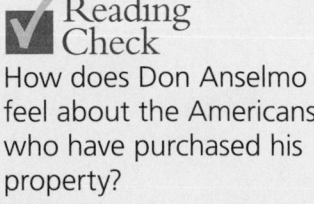
Reading Check
How does Don Anselmo feel about the Americans who have purchased his property?

Gentleman of Río en Medio **61**

Vocabulary
descendants (dē sen´
dənts) *n.* children,
grandchildren, and
continuing generations

Spiral Review
Theme What possible
theme is revealed by the
narrator's and Don
Anselmo's conflicting
ideas about ownership?

and all the children of Río en Medio are my
sobrinos and *nietos*,[7] my descendants. Every
time a child has been born in Río en Medio
since I took possession of that house from my
mother I have planted a tree for that child. The
trees in that orchard are not mine, *Señor*, they
belong to the children of the village. Every person
in Río en Medio born since the railroad came to
Santa Fe owns a tree in that orchard. I did not sell
the trees because I could not. They are not mine."

There was nothing we could do. Legally we owned
the trees but the old man had been so generous,
refusing what amounted to a fortune for him. It
took most of the following winter to buy the trees,
individually, from the descendants of Don Anselmo in the
valley of Río en Medio.

---

7. **sobrinos** (sō brē´ nōs) and **nietos** (nyä´ tōs) Spanish for "nephews" and
"grandsons"; used here to include nieces and granddaughters as well.

Critical Thinking

Cite textual
evidence to
support your
responses.

© 1. **Key Ideas and Details** **(a)** Who is the narrator of this
story? **(b)** What is the narrator's role? **(c) Analyze:** How
does the narrator's behavior toward Don Anselmo affect
the story's outcome?

© 2. **Key Ideas and Details** **(a)** What does Don Anselmo
discuss with the narrator before getting down to business?
(b) Infer: What does the discussion tell you about his
personality? **(c) Connect:** What other details in the story
reveal Don Anselmo's personality?

© 3. **Key Ideas and Details** Compare and contrast the
attitudes of Don Anselmo and the Americans toward
money.

© 4. **Craft and Structure** What does Don Anselmo's reasoning
about the trees reveal about his attitude toward property
ownership? How is the conflict of ownership resolved?
*[Connecting to the Big Question: Is truth the same for
everyone?]*

Reading Skill: Make Predictions

1. **(a)** What **predictions** did you make about the outcome of the story? **(b)** On which clues did you base your predictions?

2. Did you correct any predictions as you read? Explain.

Literary Analysis: Conflict and Resolution

Ⓒ 3. **Key Ideas and Details** Describe the **conflict** and **resolution** as shown.

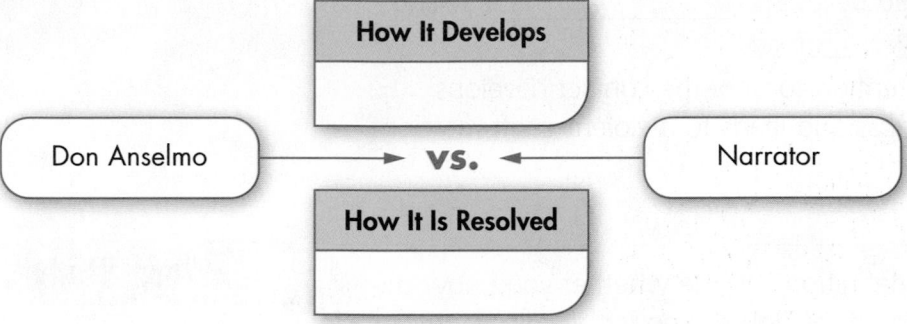

How It Develops

Don Anselmo → **VS.** ← **Narrator**

How It Is Resolved

Ⓒ 4. **Key Ideas and Details** Is the conflict *internal* or *external*? Support your answer with details from the story.

Vocabulary

Ⓒ **Acquisition and Use** For each item, explain why one of the three words is *not* a **synonym** to the given word.

1. negotiation: **(a)** celebrating, **(b)** bargaining, **(c)** deal-making
2. quaint: **(a)** modern, **(b)** old-fashioned, **(c)** oddly pleasing
3. deed: **(a)** document, **(b)** lawsuit, **(c)** certificate
4. preliminary: **(a)** preparatory, **(b)** introductory, **(c)** inhospitable
5. possession: **(a)** ownership, **(b)** holding, **(c)** abandonment
6. descendant: **(a)** grandson, **(b)** friend, **(c)** offspring

Word Study Use the context of the sentences and what you know about the **Latin root -*limin*-** to answer each question.

1. If you *eliminate* a hive of wasps, are there any wasps left?
2. How is a *subliminal* message delivered?

Word Study

The **Latin root -*limin*-** means "threshold."

Apply It Explain how the root -*limin*- contributes to the meanings of these words. Consult a dictionary if necessary.

elimination
liminal
sublime

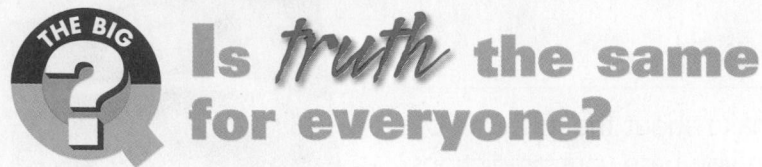

Is *truth* the same for everyone?

Writing About the Big Question

In "Cub Pilot on the Mississippi," a young man gets into a violent dispute with his boss over who is telling the truth. Use this sentence starter to develop your ideas about the Big Question.

If a young person and an adult were to **contradict** each other in an argument, I would believe _____ is telling the truth because _____ .

While You Read Pay attention to how the conflict develops between Twain and his boss and leads to a violent confrontation.

Vocabulary

Read each word and its definition. Decide whether you know the word well, know it a little bit, or do not know it at all. After you read, see how your knowledge of each word has increased.

- **malicious** (mə lish′ əs) *adj.* mean; spiteful (p. 68) *Her malicious remarks about her guests' poor fashion sense ruined the party.* maliciously *adv.* malice *n.*

- **contemptuously** (kən temp′ choo əs lē) *adv.* scornfully (p. 69) *The art expert sniffed contemptuously at the display of amateur art.* contempt *n.* contemptuous *adj.*

- **pretext** (prē′ tekst) *n.* excuse; reason that hides one's real motives (p. 70) *Tyler looked for a pretext to talk to Selena.*

- **judicious** (joo dish′ əs) *adj.* showing sound judgment; wise (p. 73) *A judicious person knows how and when to avoid a fight.* judiciousness *n.* judiciously *adv.* judge *v.*

- **confronted** (kən frunt′ əd) *v.* faced or opposed boldly (p. 75) *The trial lawyer dramatically confronted the witness with his own forged check.* confrontational *adj.*

- **emancipated** (ē man′ sə pāt′ əd) *adj.* freed (p. 76) *Released after years of suffering, the emancipated prisoner shouted happily.* emancipation *n.* emancipator *n.*

Word Study

The **Latin root judex** means "judge."

Early in this story, a character almost challenges his boss. He considers the pros and cons of doing so, like a judge considering a case. Then, he makes the **judicious** decision to keep quiet.

Meet
Mark Twain
(1835–1910)

Author of
Cub Pilot On The
MISSISSIPPI

Growing up in Hannibal, Missouri, Mark Twain was enchanted by the nearby Mississippi River. Twain's real name was Samuel Langhorne Clemens, but he took his pen name from a riverman's call, "By the mark—twain," which means "the river is two fathoms [twelve feet] deep," a safe enough depth for a steamboat. His boyhood experiences on the Mississippi and his travels around the world strongly influenced his writing. He visited five continents and crossed the Atlantic Ocean twenty-nine times.

BACKGROUND FOR THE SELECTION

Traveling by Steamboat

In "Cub Pilot on the Mississippi," Mark Twain tells a true story about his days as a cub pilot, a young trainee learning to pilot a Mississippi steamboat. In the 1800s, steamboats carried goods and people on the wide, long Mississippi River. There were dangers, however. Fires broke out, boilers burst, hidden rocks and sandbars damaged ships, and steamboat crews struggled to negotiate ever-changing currents.

DID YOU KNOW?

In 1998, the first annual Mark Twain Prize for American Humor was awarded to Richard Pryor.

Cub Pilot on the
MISSISSIPPI

Mark Twain

During the two or two and a half years of my
apprenticeship[1] I served under many pilots, and
had experience of many kinds of steamboatmen
and many varieties of steamboats. I am to this day
profiting somewhat by that experience; for in that brief, sharp
schooling, I got personally and familiarly acquainted with
about all the different types of human nature that are to be
found in fiction, biography, or history.

The fact is daily borne in upon me that the average shore-
employment requires as much as forty years to equip a man
with this sort of an education. When I say I am still profiting
by this thing, I do not mean that it has constituted me a
judge of men—no, it has not done that, for judges of men are
born, not made. My profit is various in kind and degree, but
the feature of it which I value most is the zest which that
early experience has given to my later reading. When I find a
well-drawn character in fiction or biography I generally take
a warm personal interest in him, for the reason that I have
known him before—met him on the river.

1. **apprenticeship** (ə pren′tis ship) *n.* time spent working for a master craftsperson in return

The figure that comes before me oftenest, out of the shadows of that vanished time, is that of Brown, of the steamer *Pennsylvania.* He was a middle-aged, long, slim, bony, smooth-shaven, horsefaced, ignorant, stingy, malicious, snarling, fault-hunting, mote magnifying tyrant.[2] I early got the habit of coming on watch with dread at my heart. No matter how good a time I might have been having with the off-watch below, and no matter how high my spirits might be when I started aloft, my soul became lead in my body the moment I approached the pilothouse.

I still remember the first time I ever entered the presence of that man. The boat had backed out from St. Louis and was "straightening down." I ascended to the pilothouse in high feather, and very proud to be semiofficially a member of the executive family of so fast and famous a boat. Brown was at the wheel. I paused in the middle of the room, all fixed to make my bow, but Brown did not look around. I thought he took a furtive glance at me out of the corner of his eye, but as not even this notice was repeated, I judged I had been mistaken. By this time he was picking his way among some dangerous "breaks" abreast the woodyards; therefore it would not be proper to interrupt him; so I stepped softly to the high bench and took a seat.

There was silence for ten minutes; then my new boss turned and inspected me deliberately and painstakingly from head to heel for about—as it seemed to me—a quarter of an hour. After which he removed his countenance[3] and I saw it no more for some seconds; then it came around once more, and this question greeted me: "Are you Horace Bigsby's cub?"

"Yes, sir."

After this there was a pause and another inspection. Then: "What's your name?"

I told him. He repeated it after me. It was probably the only thing he ever forgot; for although I was with him many months he never addressed himself to me in any other way than "Here!" and then his command followed.

"Where was you born?"

---

2. **mote magnifying tyrant** a cruel authority figure who exaggerates every tiny fault.
3. **countenance** (kount′ n əns) *n.* face.

"In Florida, Missouri."

A pause. Then: "Dern sight better stayed there!"

By means of a dozen or so of pretty direct questions, he pumped my family history out of me.

The leads[4] were going now in the first crossing. This interrupted the inquest. When the leads had been laid in he resumed:

"How long you been on the river?"

I told him. After a pause:

"Where'd you get them shoes?"

I gave him the information.

"Hold up your foot!"

I did so. He stepped back, examined the shoe minutely and contemptuously, scratching his head thoughtfully, tilting his high sugarloaf hat well forward to facilitate the operation, then ejaculated, "Well, I'll be dod derned!" and returned to his wheel.

What occasion there was to be dod derned about it is a thing which is still as much of a mystery to me now as it was then. It must have been all of fifteen minutes—fifteen minutes of dull, homesick silence—before that long horse-face swung round upon me again—and then what a change! It was as red as fire, and every muscle in it was working. Now came this shriek: "Here! You going to set there all day?"

I lit in the middle of the floor, shot there by the electric suddenness of the surprise. As soon as I could get my voice I said apologetically: "I have had no orders, sir."

▲ **Critical Viewing**
What quality of the boats in this painting might make them difficult to control on a busy river? **[Connect]**

Vocabulary
contemptuously
(kən temp´ choo əs lē) *adv.* scornfully

✓ Reading Check
How does Twain feel about Brown?

4. **leads** (ledz) *n.* weights that are lowered to test the depth of the river.

"You've had no *orders*! My, what a fine bird we are! We must have *orders*! Our father was a *gentleman*—and *we've* been to *school*. Yes, *we* are a gentleman, *too*, and got to have *orders*! Orders, is it? Orders is what you want! Dod dern my skin, *I'll* learn you to swell yourself up and blow around *here* about your dod-derned *orders*! G'way from the wheel!" (I had approached it without knowing it.)

I moved back a step or two and stood as in a dream, all my senses stupefied by this frantic assault.

"What you standing there for? Take that ice-pitcher down to the texas-tender!⁵ Come, move along, and don't you be all day about it!"

The moment I got back to the pilothouse Brown said: "Here! What was you doing down there all this time?"

"I couldn't find the texas-tender; I had to go all the way to the pantry."

"Derned likely story! Fill up the stove."

I proceeded to do so. He watched me like a cat. Presently he shouted: "Put down that shovel! Derndest numskull I ever saw—ain't even got sense enough to load up a stove."

All through the watch this sort of thing went on. Yes, and the subsequent watches were much like it during a stretch of months. As I have said, I soon got the habit of coming on duty with dread. The moment I was in the presence, even in the darkest night, I could feel those yellow eyes upon me, and knew their owner was watching for a pretext to spit out some venom on me. Preliminarily he would say: "Here! Take the wheel."

Two minutes later: "*Where* in the nation you going to? Pull her down! pull her down!"

After another moment: "Say! You going to hold her all day? Let her go—meet her! meet her!"

Then he would jump from the bench, snatch the wheel from me, and meet her himself, pouring out wrath upon me all the time. •

George Ritchie was the other pilot's cub. He was having good times now; for his boss, George Ealer, was as kind-hearted as Brown wasn't. Ritchie had steered for Brown the season before; consequently, he knew exactly how to entertain himself and plague me, all by the one operation. Whenever I took the wheel for a moment on Ealer's watch, Ritchie

Vocabulary
pretext (prē′ tekst) *n.* excuse; reason that hides one's real motives

---

5. **texas-tender** the waiter in the officers' quarters. On Mississippi steamboats, rooms were named after the states. The officers' area, being the largest, was named after Texas, then the largest state.

would sit back on the bench and play Brown, with continual ejaculations of "Snatch her! Snatch her! Derndest mudcat I ever saw!" "Here! Where are you going *now*? Going to run over that snag?" "Pull her *down*! Don't you hear me? Pull her *down*!" "There she goes! *Just* as I expected! I *told* you not to cramp that reef. G'way from the wheel!"

So I always had a rough time of it, no matter whose watch it was; and sometimes it seemed to me that Ritchie's good-natured badgering was pretty nearly as aggravating as Brown's dead-earnest nagging.

I often wanted to kill Brown, but this would not answer. A cub had to take everything his boss gave, in the way of vigorous comment and criticism; and we all believed that there was a United States law making it a penitentiary offense to strike or threaten a pilot who was on duty.

However, I could *imagine* myself killing Brown; there was no law against that; and that was the thing I used always to do the moment I was abed. Instead of going over my river in my mind, as was my duty, I threw business aside for pleasure, and killed Brown. I killed Brown every night for months; not in old, stale, commonplace ways, but in new and picturesque ones—ways that were sometimes surprising for freshness of design and ghastliness of situation and environment.

Brown was *always* watching for a pretext to find fault; and if he could find no plausible pretext, he would invent one. He would scold you for shaving a shore, and for not shaving it; for hugging a bar, and for not hugging it; for "pulling down" when not invited, and for *not* pulling down when not invited; for firing up without orders, and *for* waiting for orders. In a word, it was his invariable rule to find fault with *everything* you did and another invariable rule of his was to throw all his remarks (to you) into the form of an insult.

▲ Critical Viewing
What does this painting of the interior of a steamboat indicate about the size of the ships and the passengers that traveled on them? **[Analyze]**

Make Predictions
Does Twain's description of his fantasies help you predict if he will actually kill Brown? Explain.

Reading Check

Why is Twain afraid to take any action against Brown?

One day we were approaching New Madrid, bound down and heavily laden. Brown was at one side of the wheel, steering; I was at the other, standing by to "pull down" or "shove up." He cast a furtive glance at me every now and then. I had long ago learned what that meant; viz., he was trying to invent a trap for me. I wondered what shape it was going to take. By and by he stepped back from the wheel and said in his usual snarly way:

"Here! See if you've got gumption enough to round her to."

This was simply *bound* to be a success; nothing could prevent it; for he had never allowed me to round the boat to before; consequently, no matter how I might do the thing, he could find free fault with it. He stood back there with his greedy eye on me, and the result was what might have been foreseen: I lost my head in a quarter of a minute, and didn't know what I was about; I started too early to bring the boat around, but detected a green gleam of joy in Brown's eye, and corrected my mistake. I started around once more while too high up, but corrected myself again in time. I made other false moves, and still managed to save myself; but at last I grew so confused and anxious that I tumbled into the very worst blunder of all—I got too far *down* before beginning to fetch the boat around. Brown's chance was come.

His face turned red with passion; he made one bound, hurled me across the house with a sweep of his arm, spun the wheel down, and began to pour out a stream of vituperation[6] upon me which lasted till he was out of breath. In the course of this speech he called me all the different kinds of hard names he could think of, and once or twice I thought he was even going to swear—but he had never done that, and he didn't this time. "Dod dern" was the nearest he ventured to the luxury of swearing.

Two trips later I got into serious trouble. Brown was steering; I was "pulling down." My younger brother Henry appeared

▶ **Critical Viewing**
What is the main impression you get of Twain from this photo of him as a cub pilot? **[Respond]**

6. **vituperation** (vi tōō´pər ā´ shən) *n.* abusive language.

on the hurricane deck, and shouted to Brown to stop at some landing or other, a mile or so below. Brown gave no intimation[7] that he had heard anything. But that was his way: he never condescended to take notice of an underclerk. The wind was blowing; Brown was deaf (although he always pretended he wasn't), and I very much doubted if he had heard the order. If I had had two heads, I would have spoken; but as I had only one, it seemed judicious to take care of it; so I kept still. •

Presently, sure enough, we went sailing by that plantation. Captain Klinefelter appeared on the deck, and said: "Let her come around, sir, let her come around. Didn't Henry tell you to land here?"

"*No*, sir!"

"I sent him up to do it."

"He *did* come up; and that's all the good it done, the dod-derned fool. He never said anything."

"Didn't *you* hear him?" asked the captain of me.

Of course I didn't want to be mixed up in this business, but there was no way to avoid it; so I said: "Yes, sir."

I knew what Brown's next remark would be, before he uttered it. It was: "Shut your mouth! You never heard anything of the kind."

I closed my mouth, according to instructions. An hour later Henry entered the pilothouse, unaware of what had been going on. He was a thoroughly inoffensive boy, and I was sorry to see him come, for I knew Brown would have no pity on him. Brown began, straightway: "Here! Why didn't you tell me we'd got to land at that plantation?"

"I did tell you, Mr. Brown."

"It's a lie!"

I said: "You lie, yourself. He did tell you."

Brown glared at me in unaffected surprise; and for as much as a moment he was entirely speechless; then he shouted to me: "I'll attend to your case in a half a minute!" then to Henry, "And you leave the pilothouse; out with you!"

It was pilot law, and must be obeyed. The boy started out, and even had his foot on the upper step outside the door, when Brown, with a sudden access of fury, picked up a ten-pound lump of coal and sprang after him; but I was between, with a heavy stool, and I hit Brown a good honest blow which stretched him out.

---

7. intimation (in′tə mā′shən) *n.* hint or suggestion.

Vocabulary
judicious (jŏŏ dish′ əs) *adj.* showing sound judgment; wise

Conflict
Why does Twain stand up to Brown at this point in the story?

Reading Check

What argument starts the fight between Twain and Brown?

Conflict
How do Brown's actions contribute to the intensity of Twain's reaction?

I had committed the crime of crimes—I had lifted my hand against a pilot on duty! I supposed I was booked for the penitentiary sure, and couldn't be booked any surer if I went on and squared my long account with this person while I had the chance; consequently I stuck to him and pounded him with my fists a considerable time. I do not know how long, the pleasure of it probably made it seem longer than it really was; but in the end he struggled free and jumped up and sprang to the wheel: a very natural solicitude, for, all this time, here was this steamboat tearing down the river at the rate of fifteen miles an hour and nobody at the helm! However, Eagle Bend was two miles wide at this bank-full stage, and correspondingly long and deep: and the boat was steering herself straight down the middle and taking no chances. Still, that was only luck—a body *might* have found her charging into the woods.

Spiral Review
Central Idea What central idea about Twain's personality is revealed by the verbal exchange that follows his fight with Brown?

Perceiving at a glance that the *Pennsylvania* was in no danger, Brown gathered up the big spyglass, war-club fashion, and ordered me out of the pilothouse with more than ordinary bluster. But I was not afraid of him now; so, instead of going, I tarried, and criticized his grammar. I reformed his ferocious speeches for him, and put them into good English, calling his attention to the advantage of pure English over the dialect of the collieries[8] whence he was extracted. He could have done his part to admiration in a crossfire of mere vituperation, of course; but he was not equipped for this species of controversy; so he presently laid aside his glass and took the wheel, muttering and shaking his head; and I retired to the bench. The racket had brought everybody to the hurricane deck, and I trembled when I saw the old captain looking up from amid the crowd. I said to myself, "Now I *am* done for!" for although, as a rule, he was so fatherly and indulgent toward the boat's family, and so patient of minor shortcomings, he could be stern enough when the fault was worth it.

Make Predictions
What clues in the narrative so far help you predict whether the captain will punish Twain?

I tried to imagine what he *would* do to a cub pilot who had been guilty of such a crime as mine, committed on a boat guard-deep with costly freight and alive with passengers. Our watch was nearly ended. I thought I would go and hide somewhere till I got a chance to slide ashore. So I slipped out of the pilothouse, and down the steps, and around to the texas-door, and was in the act of gliding within, when

---

8. collieries (käl´ yər ēz) *n.* coal mines.

the captain **confronted** me! I dropped my head, and he stood over me in silence a moment or two, then said impressively: "Follow me." •

I dropped into his wake; he led the way to his parlor in the forward end of the texas. We were alone now. He closed the afterdoor, then moved slowly to the forward one and closed that. He sat down; I stood before him. He looked at me some little time, then said: "So you have been fighting Mr. Brown?"

I answered meekly: "Yes, sir."

"Do you know that that is a very serious matter?"

"Yes, sir."

"Are you aware that this boat was plowing down the river fully five minutes with no one at the wheel?"

"Yes, sir."

"Did you strike him first?"

"Yes, sir."

"What with?"

"A stool, sir."

"Hard?"

"Middling, sir."

"Did it knock him down?"

"He—he fell, sir."

"Did you follow it up? Did you do anything further?"

"Yes, sir."

"What did you do?"

"Pounded him, sir."

"Pounded him?"

"Yes, sir."

"Did you pound him much? that is, severely?"

"One might call it that, sir, maybe."

"I'm deuced glad of it! Hark ye, never mention that I said that. You have been guilty of a great crime; and don't you ever be guilty of it again, on this boat. *But*—lay for him ashore! Give him a good sound thrashing, do you hear? I'll pay the expenses. Now go—and mind you, not a word of this to anybody. Clear out with you! You've been guilty of a great crime, you whelp!"[9]

I slid out, happy with the sense of a close shave and a mighty deliverance; and I heard him laughing to himself and slapping his fat thighs after I had closed his door.

9. **whelp** (hwelp) *n.* puppy. Here, the captain uses it to indicate that Twain is young and foolish, like a puppy.

Vocabulary
confronted (kən frunt´ əd) *v.* faced or opposed boldly

▼ **Critical Viewing**
What might happen if a steamship, like those in the picture, had no one steering the boat? **[Speculate]**

Make Predictions
As you read, did you revise your prediction about whether Twain would be punished? Why or why not?

Reading Check
Why does Twain believe he will be severely punished at first?

When Brown came off watch he went straight to the captain, who was talking with some passengers on the boiler deck, and demanded that I be put ashore in New Orleans—and added: "I'll never turn a wheel on this boat again while that cub stays."

The captain said: "But he needn't come round when you are on watch, Mr. Brown."

"I won't even stay on the same boat with him. One of us has got to go ashore." "Very well," said the captain, "let it be yourself," and resumed his talk with the passengers.

During the brief remainder of the trip I knew how an emancipated slave feels, for I was an emancipated slave myself. While we lay at landings I listened to George Ealer's flute, or to his readings from his two Bibles, that is to say, Goldsmith and Shakespeare, or I played chess with him—and would have beaten him sometimes, only he always took back his last move and ran the game out differently.

Critical Thinking

Ⓒ **1. Key Ideas and Details** **(a)** About how long did Twain serve as a pilot's apprentice? **(b) Infer:** Why were cub pilots assigned to work with experienced pilots?

Ⓒ **2. Key Ideas and Details** **(a)** How does Brown treat Twain when he meets him? **(b) Analyze:** Is Brown's treatment of Twain the result of a personal dislike for him or an overall attitude? Explain.

Ⓒ **3. Key Ideas and Details** **(a)** What is the captain's reaction to Twain's beating of Brown? **(b) Draw Conclusions:** What are the captain's feelings about Brown? Explain.

Ⓒ **4. Integration of Knowledge and Ideas** **(a)** Under what circumstances, if any, should physical force be used to solve a problem? **(b) Discuss:** Share your answers with a partner. **(c) Analyze:** Did your answers change? Explain.

Ⓒ **5. Integration of Knowledge and Ideas** **(a)** Why does Twain think the captain will punish him severely? **(b)** How does the captain's reaction affect the conflict and contribute to the resolution? *[Connect to the Big Question: Is truth the same for everyone?]*

Cite textual evidence to support your responses.

Reading Skill: Make Predictions

1. (a) List two **predictions** you made about the outcome of the conflict between Twain and Brown. **(b)** Which specific clues led to your prediction? **(c)** Did you change any of your predictions as you read the selection? Explain.

Literary Analysis: Conflict and Resolution

2. Craft and Structure Use a chart to analyze the **conflict** between Twain and Brown and its **resolution**.

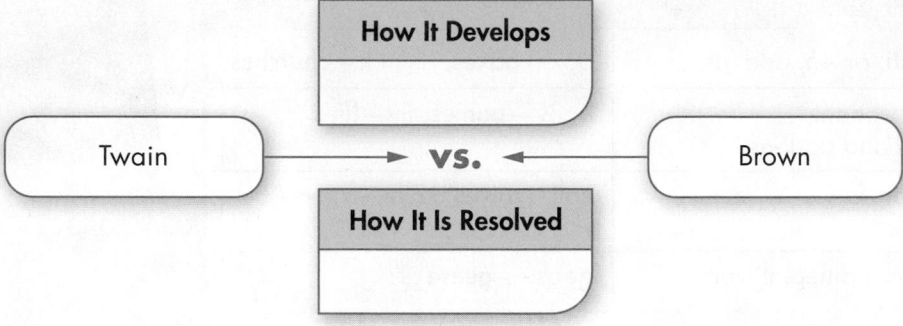

How It Develops

Twain → **VS.** ← Brown

How It Is Resolved

3. Key Ideas and Details Is the conflict in the narrative mainly *internal* or *external*? Support your answer with details.

Vocabulary

Acquisition and Use For each item, explain why one of the three words is *not* a **synonym** to the vocabulary word.

1. malicious: **(a)** spiteful, **(b)** considerate, **(c)** mean
2. contemptuously: **(a)** humbly, **(b)** sneeringly, **(c)** disdainfully
3. pretext: **(a)** reason, **(b)** excuse, **(c)** desire
4. judicious: **(a)** foolish, **(b)** wise, **(c)** reasonable
5. confronted: **(a)** faced, **(b)** invited, **(c)** challenged
6. emancipated: **(a)** liberated, **(b)** released, **(c)** confined

Word Study Use the context of the sentences and what you know about the **Latin root -judex-** to explain each answer.

1. What is the Supreme Court's role in our *judicial* system?
2. Why is it unfair to show *prejudice* based on race or gender?

Word Study

The **Latin root -judex-** means "judge."

Apply It Explain how the root -judex- contributes to the meanings of these words. Consult a dictionary if necessary.

judgment
adjudicate
injudicious

Integrated Language Skills

Gentleman of Río en Medio • Cub Pilot on the Mississippi

Conventions: Plural Nouns

A **plural noun** refers to more than one person, place, thing, or idea.

The plural of most nouns is formed by adding an -*s*. Certain nouns, however, follow different rules, shown in the chart.

Rule	Examples
For words that end in -*x*, -*ch*, or -*sh*, add -*es*.	box — **boxes**; church — **churches**
For words that end in a consonant plus *y*, change the *y* to an *i* and add -*es*.	pony — **ponies**; fly — **flies**
Some words that end in -*f* or -*fe* have plurals that end in -*ves*.	calf — **calves**; knife — **knives**
The plurals of some nouns are different words.	goose — **geese**

Whenever a plural noun appears as the subject, it takes a plural verb.
He cooperates. (singular) *Friends cooperate.* (plural)

Practice A Rewrite each sentence, replacing the noun in parentheses with its plural form.

1. The (child) are all his descendants.
2. The (family) have enjoyed Don Anselmo's orchards for years.
3. The (gentleman) shake hands with one another as they come to an agreement.
4. (Peach) and apricots ripen on the trees.

© Reading Application In "Gentleman of Río en Medio," find two nouns that take an -*s* for the plural. Find two nouns that form the plural differently.

Practice B Rewrite each sentence, making the underlined noun plural and using the plural verb form, when necessary.

1. The <u>author</u> writes fascinating memoirs.
2. His account of his <u>experience</u> on the river has been interesting to read.
3. The pilot's main <u>duty</u> is to obey.
4. The pilot's <u>spyglass</u> helps him see.

© Writing Application Write two sentences describing the steamboat pictures in "Cub Pilot on the Mississippi." Use plural nouns and plural verbs.

PH WRITING COACH Further instruction and practice are available in *Prentice Hall Writing Coach.*

Writing

Narrative Text Write a **letter** based on the selection that you read. If you read "Gentleman of Río en Medio," write from the point of view of the narrator explaining the situation and its outcome to the surveyor who measured the land. If you read "Cub Pilot on the Mississippi," write as Twain, telling a friend about his days as a cub pilot.

- Use an appropriate *tone* for your audience. For the surveyor, use a businesslike tone. For Twain's friend, use a casual tone.

- Review the story for details to use as the basis for your letter.

- Clearly state the *purpose* of your letter. Arrange your ideas or the events you are writing about in logical order.

- Follow the business or friendly letter format, as described on pages R26–R27, including an appropriate and satisfying closing.

Grammar Application Make sure that the plural nouns in your letter use the proper endings and take the plural form of the verb.

Writing Workshop: *Work in Progress*

Prewriting for Description Review the Person Profile in your writing portfolio. Ask yourself these questions: *What has this person said to me in a moment of crisis? What have other people said about this person? What have I said about this person to other people?* Jot down answers. Save this List in your portfolio.

Speaking and Listening

Comprehension and Collaboration With a partner, present a role play of the conflict in the story.

- For "Gentleman of Río en Medio," one of you should play Don Anselmo; the other, the narrator.

- For "Cub Pilot on the Mississippi," one person should play Twain; the other, Brown.

Address the key questions in your role play by providing appropriate information, such as, What issues *divide* you? What common interests do you have? What are your options for resolving your conflict in a way that is acceptable for both parties?

Invite your audience to respond to your role play. Then, modify the role play based on the feedback you receive. Decide with your audience which conflict-resolution strategies worked best.

Common Core State Standards

L.8.1, L.8.4.b; W.8.3; SL.8.1.d
[For the full wording of the standards, see page 54.]

Use this prewriting activity to prepare for the **Writing Workshop** on page 104.

PHLit Online!
www.PHLitOnline.com
- Interactive graphic organizers
- Grammar tutorial
- Interactive journals

Test Practice: Reading

Make Predictions

Fiction Selection

Directions: *Read the selection. Then, answer the questions.*

Eric rode down his driveway and shifted the gears on his new ten-speed bike. He had saved his money for a whole year, and now he was finally riding the bike for the first time. As he cruised down the street, his friend Travis ran out of his house, wearing the baseball cap he had borrowed from Eric.

"Oh, no," thought Eric. He liked and trusted Travis, but Travis was always asking for favors. Somehow he always made Eric feel sorry for him so that Eric just couldn't say no. "Maybe if I speed up and turn the corner, he won't see me," Eric thought to himself.

"Wow! Cool bike!" Travis shouted. "Hey," he said, eyeing the bike hopefully. "Can I ask you something?"

1. What do you think Travis will do next?
   A. He will ask to borrow money.
   B. He will ask to borrow Eric's bike.
   C. He will ask if Eric wants to play baseball.
   D. He will go back inside his house.

2. What clue supports your prediction?
   A. Travis is wearing Eric's baseball cap.
   B. Travis never has any money of his own.
   C. Travis admires the bike and always asks for favors.
   D. Eric never pays attention to Travis.

3. What do you predict Eric will do next?
   A. He will say yes if Travis asks to ride the bike.
   B. He will tell Travis to return the baseball cap.
   C. He will call the police.
   D. He will ride away without speaking to Travis.

4. What information in the passage helped you make your prediction?
   A. Eric saved his money for a year to pay for the bike.
   B. This is the first time Travis has seen the new bike.
   C. Eric always finds it hard to say no to Travis.
   D. Travis was always asking for favors.

Writing for Assessment

How do you predict Travis would react if Eric refused to let him borrow the bike? Write three sentences describing his likely reaction, supporting your prediction with details from the passage.

Nonfiction Selection

Directions: *Read the selection. Then, answer the questions.*

To Lend or Not to Lend?

It is a common situation. A friendly neighbor asks to borrow your new hedge clippers, promising to return them as soon as he is done. Two months later, you are too embarrassed or angry to ask for them back.

Experts on lending warn people to think twice before allowing a friend or family member to borrow anything significant—especially money. One study, conducted by an online bank, found that thirty-nine percent of those surveyed owe money to their family or friends. The same study found that eight percent of respondents had a "falling out" with friends or family over loans that had not been repaid.

You may think that you can trust friends or family. However, the burden of repayment can put a strain on close relationships. If you do decide to offer a loan, financial advisors agree that you should make the terms of repayment very clear.

1. The article's next section is entitled "Neither a Lender, Nor a Borrower Be." What advice do you predict it will give?
   A. Only borrow from strangers.
   B. Lending is a smarter strategy than borrowing.
   C. Avoid borrowing or lending.
   D. Borrow money at a good interest rate.

2. What phrase in the first paragraph helps you to predict that the author will discourage lending to family or friends?
   A. common situation
   B. friendly neighbor
   C. new hedge clippers
   D. too embarrassed or angry

3. Based on the bank study, what do you predict might happen if someone borrows money from family or friends?
   A. The person will not have to repay the loan.
   B. It will probably lead to a "falling out."
   C. It might lead to a "falling out."
   D. It will bring family and friends closer.

4. If a reader takes the advice in the last paragraph, what should he or she do?
   A. Cut off all ties with friends.
   B. Set up a loan repayment schedule.
   C. Have faith that the loan will eventually be repaid.
   D. Only borrow from friends.

Writing for Assessment

Connecting Across Texts
Imagine Eric had read the article about borrowing. What arguments might he use to discourage Travis from borrowing his bicycle? Use details from the two passages to write a short dialogue.

PHLit Online!
www.PHLitOnline.com
- Online practice
- Instant feedback

Reading for Information

Analyzing Functional Texts

Consumer Document

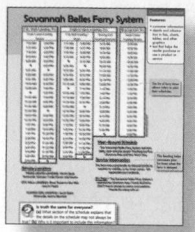

Map

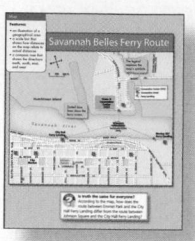

Common Core State Standards

Reading Informational Text
5. Analyze in detail the structure of a specific paragraph in a text, including the role of particular sentences in developing and refining a key concept.

Language
6. Acquire and use accurately grade-appropriate general academic and domain-specific words and phrases; gather vocabulary knowledge when considering a word or phrase important to comprehension or expression.

Reading Skill: Use Information to Solve a Problem

When you read schedules and maps, you **use information to solve a problem**—how to get from one place to another. Using **text features** can help you find the information you need.

This chart shows some text features of schedules and maps.

Text Features of a Schedule	
Headings	Show where to find departure and arrival times
Rows and columns	Allow for easy scanning across and down the page
Special type (such as boldface or italics) and special symbols (such as asterisks)	Indicate exceptions or special information
Text Features of a Map	
Labels	Identify places shown on map
Compass rose	Shows directions (north, south, east, west)

Content-Area Vocabulary

These words appear in the selections that follow. You may also encounter them in other content-area texts.

- **ferry** (fer´ ē) *n.* boat that carries people, vehicles, and goods across a body of water
- **geographical** (jē´ ə graf´ i kəl) *adj.* of the surface features of a place or region
- **vessels** (ves´ əls) *n.* large boats; ships

Savannah Belles Ferry System

Features:

- consumer information
- details and information in lists, charts, tables, and other graphics
- text that helps the reader purchase or use a product or service

City Hall Landing To:	
Trade Center Landing Westin	
7:00 AM	3:40 PM
7:20 AM	4:00 PM
7:40 AM	4:20 PM
8:00 AM	4:40 PM
8:20 AM	5:00 PM
*	5:20 PM
9:00 AM	*
9:20 AM	6:00 PM
9:40 AM	6:20 PM
10:00 AM	6:40 PM
10:20 AM	7:00 PM
*	7:20 PM
11:00 AM	7:40 PM
11:20 AM	8:00 PM
11:40 AM	8:20 PM
12:00 PM	*
12:20 PM	9:00 PM
12:40 PM	9:20 PM
1:00 PM	9:40 PM
1:20 PM	10:00 PM
1:40 PM	10:20 PM
2:00 PM	10:40 PM
2:20 PM	11:00 PM
2:40 PM	11:20 PM
3:00 PM	11:40 PM
3:20 PM	12:00 AM
3:40 PM	*

Trade Center Landing To:		
City Hall Landing / Hyatt		Waving Girl Landing/Marriott
7:10 AM	3:50 PM	8:15 AM
7:30 AM	4:10 PM	8:45 AM
7:50 AM	4:30 PM	9:15 AM
8:10 AM	4:50 PM	9:45 AM
*	5:10 PM	10:15 AM
8:50 AM	*	10:45 AM
9:10 AM	5:50 PM	11:15 AM
9:30 AM	6:10 PM	11:45 AM
9:50 AM	6:30 PM	12:15 PM
10:10 AM	6:50 PM	12:45 PM
*	7:10 PM	1:15 PM
10:50 AM	7:30 PM	1:45 PM
11:10 AM	7:50 PM	2:15 PM
11:30 AM	8:10 PM	2:45 PM
11:50 AM	*	3:15 PM
12:10 PM	8:50 PM	3:45 PM
12:30 PM	9:10 PM	4:15 PM
12:50 PM	9:30 PM	4:45 PM
1:10 PM	9:50 PM	5:15 PM
1:30 PM	10:10 PM	5:45 PM
1:50 PM	10:30 PM	*
2:10 PM	10:50 PM	
2:30 AM	11:10 PM	
2:50 PM	11:30 PM	
3:10 PM	11:50 PM	
3:30 PM	*	

Waving Girl To:
Trade Center Landing/Westin
8:00 AM
8:30 AM
9:00 AM
9:30 AM
10:00 AM
10:30 AM
11:00 AM
11:30 AM
12:00 PM
12:30 PM
1:00 PM
1:30 PM
2:00 PM
2:30 PM
3:00 PM
3:30 PM
4:00 PM
4:30 PM
5:00 PM
5:30 PM
6:00 PM

Revised 5/23/2007

The list of ferry times allows riders to plan their schedules.

Year-Around Schedule

The Savannah Belles Ferry System operates daily, year-around, except Thanksgiving Day, Christmas Day and New Year's Day

Service Interruption

This heading helps consumers plan for times when the ferry is delayed.

The ferry may occasionally be delayed briefly by weather or visibility, or by larger vessels. We appreciate your patience.

It's Free! The Savannah Belles Ferry System is operated by Chatham Area Transit Authority (CAT) free of charge to visitors and residents. Thanks for riding with us!

Service Locations

TRADE CENTER LANDING--North Bank Riverwalk, between Trade Center and Westin

CITY HALL LANDING--River Street at City Hall, next to Hyatt

WAVING GIRL LANDING--South Bank Riverwalk, next to Marriott

Features:

- an illustration of a geographical area
- a scale bar that shows how distances on the map relate to actual distances
- a compass rose that shows the directions north, south, east, and west

Savannah Belles Ferry Route

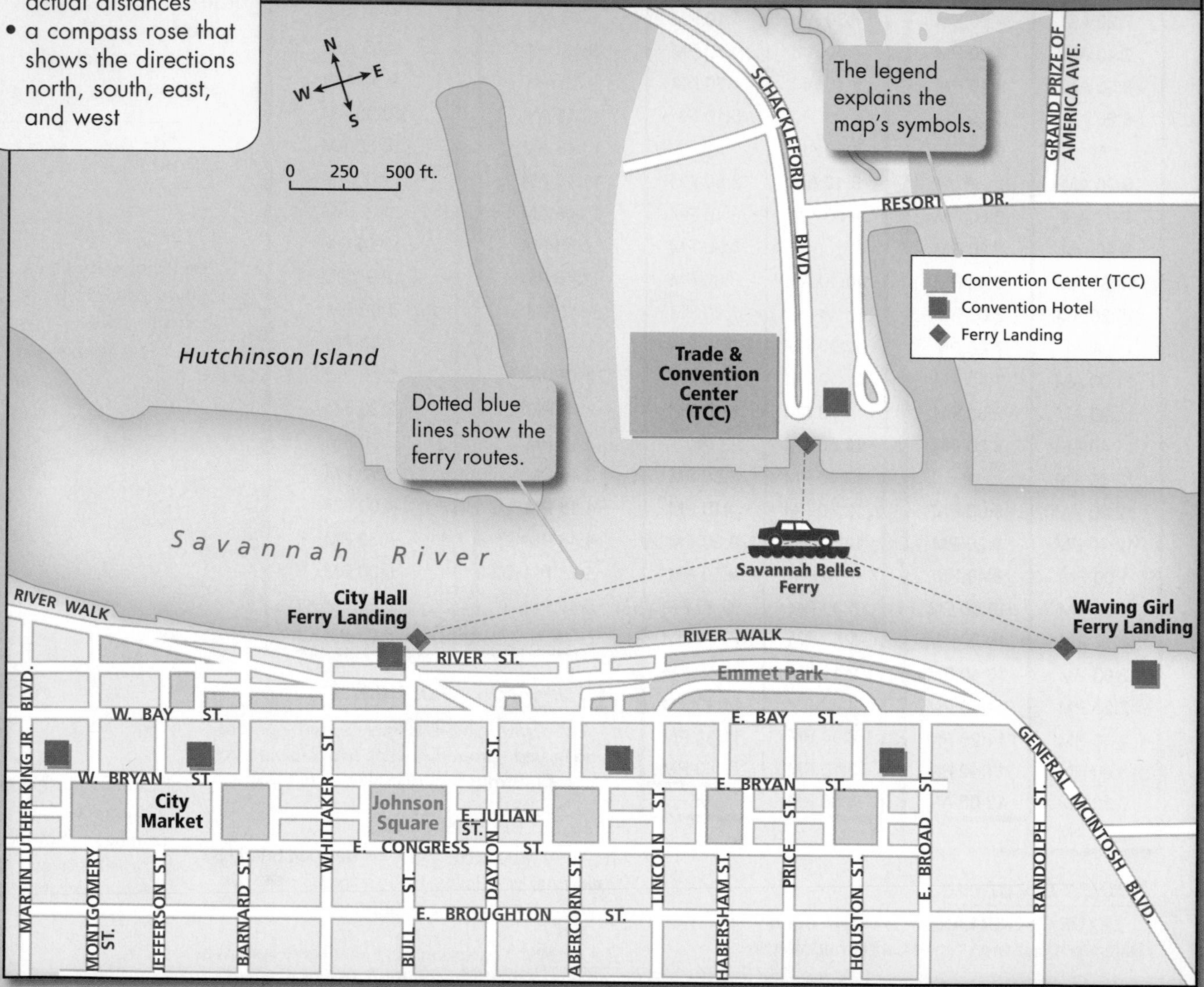

The legend explains the map's symbols.

0   250   500 ft.

GRAND PRIZE OF AMERICA AVE.

SCHACKLEFORD BLVD.

RESORT DR.

Convention Center (TCC)
Convention Hotel
Ferry Landing

Hutchinson Island

Trade & Convention Center (TCC)

Dotted blue lines show the ferry routes.

S a v a n n a h   R i v e r

Savannah Belles Ferry

City Hall Ferry Landing

Waving Girl Ferry Landing

RIVER WALK

RIVER ST.

RIVER WALK

Emmet Park

W. BAY ST.

E. BAY ST.

MARTIN LUTHER KING JR. BLVD.

W. BRYAN ST.

City Market

WHITTAKER ST.

Johnson Square

E. JULIAN ST.

E. BRYAN ST.

BULL ST.

DAYTON ST.

ABERCORN ST.

LINCOLN ST.

HABERSHAM ST.

PRICE ST.

HOUSTON ST.

E. BROAD ST.

RANDOLPH ST.

GENERAL McINTOSH BLVD.

MONTGOMERY ST.

JEFFERSON ST.

BARNARD ST.

E. CONGRESS ST.

E. BROUGHTON ST.

Comparing Functional Texts

1. Key Ideas and Details **(a)** How might you use information in the schedule and the map to **solve a problem** like planning a trip? **(b)** Which document uses **text features** best to aid your understanding and help you solve problems? Explain.

Content-Area Vocabulary

2. (a) Add the suffix *-ly* to the base word *geographical.* Using a print or an online dictionary, explain how changing the suffix alters the meaning and part of speech of the base word. **(b)** Then, use the words *geographical* and *geographically* in sentences that show their meaning.

Timed Writing

Informative Text: Detailed Directions

Format and Detail
The prompt calls for detailed directions in a specific format, using both cardinal (north, south, east, west) and ordinal (northeast, northwest, southeast, southwest) directions.

> Write a set of detailed directions from the City Hall Ferry Landing to the City Market in Savannah. Use cardinal and ordinal directions, and include landmarks, streets, distances, and a time estimate of each step. (20 minutes)

Academic Vocabulary
When you provide an *estimate* about time, you make a judgment about roughly how long something will take.

5-Minute Planner

Complete these steps before you begin to write:

1. Read the prompt carefully, noting the key highlighted words.

2. Find the two locations on the map, and identify the simplest route between them.

3. Trace the route with your finger, and jot down information such as landmarks, street names, numbers of blocks, and turns. Use text features to find details you can include in your directions. For example, use the compass rose to find out whether the reader should travel north, south, east, or west.

4. Use your notes to prepare a draft of your written directions.

Comparing Narrative Structure

All **narratives** tell a story. **Narrative structure** is the pattern a story's plot follows. A common type of narrative structure is *chronological*, with events being presented in the same order that they occur in time. Sometimes, however, a narrative does not follow a straight line. In some stories, time sequence may be broken by two common narrative devices:

- In **flashbacks,** scenes relate events that happened in the past. Flashbacks often show what motivates a character, or reveal something important about a character's past.

- Through **foreshadowing,** the author provides clues that hint at events to come. Foreshadowing creates suspense by keeping a reader guessing what will happen.

The graph shown here illustrates how a chronological timeline can be rearranged.

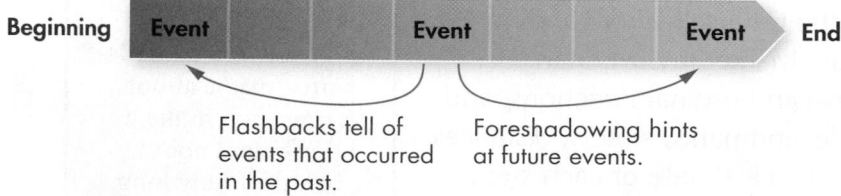

Beginning Event   Event   Event End

Flashbacks tell of events that occurred in the past.

Foreshadowing hints at future events.

Narrative structure affects the way readers receive and understand key concepts. A linear, direct structure may communicate key ideas clearly. A structure involving flashback or foreshadowing can shape understanding of key ideas in more subtle and complex ways.

As you read "Old Ben" and "Fox Hunt," compare their narrative structures. Pay special attention to the way flashback and foreshadowing affect your understanding of the story.

Common Core State Standards

Reading Literature
5. Compare and contrast the structure of two or more texts and analyze how the differing structure of each text contributes to its meaning and style.

Writing
2. Write informative/explanatory texts to examine a topic and convey ideas, concepts, and information through the selection, organization, and analysis of relevant content. *(Timed Writing)*

www.PHLitOnline.com

- Vocabulary flashcards
- Interactive journals
- More about the authors
- Selection audio
- Interactive graphic organizers

Is *truth* the same for everyone?

Writing About the Big Question

In these stories, characters form unusual bonds with animals or animal spirits. Use this sentence starter to develop your ideas.

You (can/cannot) **prove** that bonds exist between people and animals because _____.

Meet the Authors

Jesse Stuart (1906–1984)
Author of "Old Ben"

As a boy growing up in rural Kentucky, Jesse Stuart developed a strong connection to the natural world. As an adult, he found that his home and his roots provided endless inspiration. He produced an amazing volume of writing—more than fifty-five books and five hundred short stories—mostly based on his home state.

State Poet After Stuart became the Poet Laureate, or official state poet, of Kentucky, one biographer wrote, "Stuart's writing is indeed like bright water mirroring the trees, the sky, and the Kentucky life he knew and loved."

Lensey Namioka (b. 1929)
Author of "Fox Hunt"

Lensey Namioka loves exciting stories. As a child in China, she read martial arts novels, Sherlock Holmes detective stories, and *The Three Musketeers*. She wrote her first book, *Princess with a Bamboo Sword*, when she was eight years old.

Sources of Inspiration At nine, Namioka moved to the United States with her family. When she grew up, she taught math and married a mathematician of Japanese descent. Perhaps this is one reason why the subject of math often appears in her stories.

Old Ben

Jesse Stuart

▲ **Critical Viewing**
What would be your response if you almost stepped on a snake like the one in the picture? **[Connect]**

One morning in July when I was walking across a clover field to a sweet-apple tree, I almost stepped on him. There he lay coiled like heavy strands of black rope. He was a big bull blacksnake. We looked at each other a minute, and then I stuck the toe of my shoe up to his mouth. He drew his head back in a friendly way. He didn't want trouble. Had he shown the least fight, I would have soon finished him. My father had always told me there was only one good snake—a dead one.

When the big fellow didn't show any fight, I reached down and picked him up by the neck. When I lifted him he was as long as I was tall. That was six feet. I started calling him Old Ben as I held him by the neck and rubbed his back. He enjoyed having his back rubbed and his head stroked. Then I lifted him into my arms. He was the first snake I'd ever been friendly with. I was afraid at first to let Old Ben wrap himself around me. I thought he might wrap himself around my neck and choke me.

The more I petted him, the more affectionate he became. He was so friendly I decided to trust him. I wrapped him around my neck a couple of times and let him loose. He crawled down one arm and went back to my neck, around and down the other arm and back again. He struck out his forked tongue to the sound of my voice as I talked to him.

"I wouldn't kill you at all," I said. "You're a friendly snake. I'm taking you home with me."

I headed home with Old Ben wrapped around my neck and shoulders. When I started over the hill by the pine grove, I met my cousin Wayne Holbrook coming up the hill. He stopped suddenly when he saw me. He started backing down the hill.

"He's a pet, Wayne," I said. "Don't be afraid of Old Ben."

It was a minute before Wayne could tell me what he wanted. He had come to borrow a plow. He kept a safe distance as we walked on together.

Before we reached the barn, Wayne got brave enough to touch Old Ben's long body.

"What are you going to do with him?" Wayne asked. "Uncle Mick won't let you keep him!"

"Put him in the corncrib," I said. "He'll have plenty of delicate food in there. The cats we keep at this barn have grown fat and lazy on the milk we feed 'em."

I opened the corncrib door and took Old Ben from around my neck because he was beginning to get warm and a little heavy.

"This will be your home," I said. "You'd better hide under the corn."

Besides my father, I knew Old Ben would have another enemy at our home. He was our hunting dog, Blackie, who would trail a snake, same as a possum or mink. He had treed blacksnakes, and my father had shot them from the trees. I knew Blackie would find Old Ben, because he followed us to the barn each morning.

The first morning after I'd put Old Ben in the corncrib, Blackie followed us. He started toward the corncrib holding his head high, sniffing. He stuck his nose up to a crack in the crib and began to bark. Then he tried to tear a plank off.

Vocabulary
affectionate
(ə fek´ shən it) *adj.*
loving

Narrative Structure
What decision does the narrator make that keeps the narrative moving forward?

✓ Reading Check
How do people react to Old Ben?

Old Ben **89**

"Stop it, Blackie," Pa scolded him. "What's the matter with you? Have you taken to barking at mice?"

"Blackie is not barking at a mouse," I said. "I put a blacksnake in there yesterday!"

"A blacksnake?" Pa asked, looking unbelievingly. "A blacksnake?"

"Yes, a pet blacksnake," I said.

"Have you gone crazy?" he said. "I'll move a thousand bushels of corn to get that snake!"

"You won't mind this one," I said. "You and Mom will love him."

My father said a few unprintable words before we started back to the house. After breakfast, when Pa and Mom came to the barn, I was already there. I had opened the crib door and there was Old Ben. He'd crawled up front and was coiled on a sack. I put my hand down and he crawled up my arm to my neck and over my shoulder. When Mom and Pa reached the crib, I thought Pa was going to faint.

"He has a pet snake," Mom said.

"Won't be a bird or a young chicken left on this place," Pa said. "Every time I pick up an ear of corn in the crib, I'll be jumping."

"Pa, he won't hurt you," I said, patting the snake's head. "He's a natural pet, or somebody has tamed him. And he's not going to bother birds and young chickens when there are so many mice in this crib."

"Mick, let him keep the snake," Mom said. "I won't be afraid of it."

This was the beginning of a long friendship.

Narrative Structure
What conflict or problem does the narrator try to solve here?

▼ **Critical Viewing**
Why would these corn cribs be a good place for a snake to live?
[Assess]

Mom went to the corncrib morning after morning and shelled corn for her geese and chickens. Often Old Ben would be lying in front on his burlap sack. Mom watched him at first from the corner of her eye. Later she didn't bother to watch him any more than she did a cat that came up for his milk.

Later it occurred to us that Old Ben might like milk, too. We started leaving milk for him. We never saw him drink it, but his pan was always empty when we returned. We know the mice didn't drink it, because he took care of them.

"One thing is certain," Mom said one morning when she went to shell corn. "We don't find any more corn chewed up by the mice and left on the floor."

July passed and August came. My father got used to Old Ben, but not until he had proved his worth. Ben had done something our nine cats couldn't. He had cleaned the corncrib of mice.

Then my father began to worry about Old Ben's going after water, and Blackie's finding his track. So he put water in the crib.

September came and went. We began wondering where our pet would go when days grew colder. One morning in early October we left milk for Old Ben, and it was there when we went back that afternoon. But Old Ben wasn't there.

"Old Ben's a good pet for the warm months," Pa said. "But in the winter months, my cats will have to do the work. Maybe Blackie got him!"

"He might have holed up for the winter in the hayloft," I told Pa after we had removed all the corn and didn't find him. "I'm worried about him. I've had a lot of pets—groundhogs, crows and hawks—but Old Ben's the best yet."

November, December, January, February, and March came and went. Of course we never expected to see Old Ben in one of those months. We doubted if we ever would see him again.

One day early in April I went to the corncrib, and Old Ben lay stretched across the floor. He looked taller than I was now. His skin was rough and his long body had a flabby appearance. I knew Old Ben needed mice and milk. I picked him up, petted him, and told him so. But the chill of early April was still with him. He got his tongue out slower to answer the kind words I was saying to him. He tried to crawl up my arm but he couldn't make it.

Spiral Review
Central Idea
How do the family's feelings toward Old Ben develop as the months go by?

Narrative Structure
How many seasons have passed since the beginning of the story?

Reading Check
Where does Old Ben live?

Vocabulary
scarce (skers) *adj.* few in number; not common
partition (pär tish´ ən) *n.* interior dividing wall

That spring and summer mice got scarce in the corncrib and Old Ben got daring. He went over to the barn and crawled up into the hayloft, where he had many feasts. But he made one mistake.

He crawled from the hayloft down into Fred's feed box, where it was cool. Old Fred was our horse.

There he lay coiled when the horse came in and put his nose down on top of Old Ben. Fred let out a big snort and started kicking. He kicked down a partition, and then turned his heels on his feed box and kicked it down. Lucky for Old Ben that he got out in one piece. But he got back to his crib.

Old Ben became a part of our barnyard family, a pet and darling of all. When children came to play with my brother and sisters, they always went to the crib and got Old Ben. He enjoyed the children, who were afraid of him at first but later learned to pet this kind old reptile.

Summer passed and the late days of September were very humid. Old Ben failed one morning to drink his milk. We knew it wasn't time for him to hole up for the winter.

We knew something had happened.

Pa and I moved the corn searching for him. Mom made a couple of trips to the barn lot to see if we had found him. But all we found was the rough skin he had shed last spring.

"Fred's never been very sociable with Old Ben since he got in his box that time," Pa said. "I wonder if he could have stomped Old Ben to death. Old Ben could've been crawling over the barn lot, and Fred saw his chance to get even!"

Narrative Structure
Which events—if any—could have foreshadowed Ben's disappearance?

▼ Critical Viewing
What characteristics of a horse would present a danger to a snake? **[Analyze]**

"We'll see," I said.

Pa and I left the crib and walked to the barn lot. He went one way and I went the other, each searching the ground.

Mom came through the gate and walked over where my father was looking. She started looking around, too.

"We think Fred might've got him," Pa said. "We're sure Fred's got it in for him over Old Ben getting in his feed box last summer."

"You're accusing Fred wrong," Mom said. "Here's Old Ben's track in the sand."

I ran over to where Mom had found the track. Pa went over to look, too.

"It's no use now," Pa said, softly. "Wouldn't have taken anything for that snake. I'll miss him on that burlap sack every morning when I come to feed the horses. Always looked up at me as if he understood."

The last trace Old Ben had left was in the corner of the lot near the hogpen. His track went straight to the woven wire fence and stopped.

"They've got him," Pa said. "Old Ben trusted everything and everybody. He went for a visit to the wrong place. He didn't last long among sixteen hogs. They go wild over a snake. Even a biting copperhead can't stop a hog. There won't be a trace of Old Ben left."

We stood silently for a minute looking at the broad, smooth track Old Ben had left in the sand.

Critical Thinking

1. **Key Ideas and Details (a)** What kind of snake is the only good kind, according to Pa? **(b) Analyze Causes and Effects:** What details show that Pa's feelings have changed?

2. **Integration of Knowledge and Ideas** Explain how "Old Ben" illustrates the idea that friends can be found in the most unexpected places.

3. **Integration of Knowledge and Ideas** Many people think snakes are dangerous and harmful. Is this impression a "truth" that is shared by everyone? *[Connect to the Big Question: Is truth the same for everyone?]*

Cite textual evidence to support your responses.

Fox Hunt

Lensey Namioka

Andy Liang watched the kids from his school bus walk home with their friends. He could hear them talking together and laughing. He always got off the bus alone and walked home by himself.

But this time it was different. A girl got off the bus just behind him and started walking in the same direction. He wondered why he hadn't seen her before. She was also Asian American, which made it all the more surprising that he hadn't noticed her earlier.

As he tried to get a better look, she went into the neighborhood convenience store and disappeared behind a shelf of canned soup. He peered into the store, hoping for another glimpse of her. All he saw were some of the kids from the bus getting bags of potato chips and soft drinks.

Andy sighed. He was used to being a loner, and usually it didn't bother him—not much, anyway. But today the loneliness was heavy. He overheard the other kids talking, and he knew they were planning to study together for the PSAT.[1] From the looks of the snacks, they were expecting a long session.

Andy would be practicing for the test, too, but he would be doing it by himself. *I'm better off doing it alone, anyway,* he thought. *Studying with somebody else would just slow me down.*

The truth was that none of the others had invited him to study with them. *So all right,* he said to himself, *they think I'm a grind. What's wrong with that? I'll be getting better scores on the PSAT than any of them, even if there's nobody to coach me.*

He finally found the girl standing in front of a case of barbecued chicken. She was staring so hungrily at the chickens that his own mouth began watering, and he would have bought a piece on the spot if he had the money. But with the change in his pocket, he had to be satisfied with a candy bar.

Leaving the store, he reached his street and passed the corner house with the moody German shepherd. As usual, it snapped at him, and he automatically retreated to the far side of the sidewalk. Although the dog was on a chain, Andy didn't like the way it looked at him. Besides, a chain could always break.

Today, the dog not only snapped, it began to bark furiously and strained against its chain. Andy jumped back and bumped against the girl he had seen earlier. Somehow she had appeared behind him without making any noise.

He apologized. "I didn't mean to crash into you. That dog always growls at me, but today he's really barking like crazy."

The girl shivered. "The dog doesn't seem to like me very much, either." Before he had a chance to say anything more, she turned and walked away.

Again Andy sighed. He hadn't even had a chance to find out what her name was or where she lived. Was she Chinese American, as he was? What grade was she in? At least she went on the same school bus, so there was a chance of seeing her again.

---

1. **PSAT** abbreviation for *Preliminary Scholastic Aptitude Test*, a test given in high school.

Narrative Structure
What details here show you the narrative follows a chronological order?

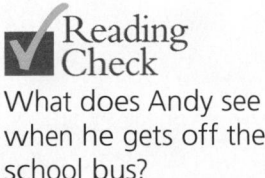

Reading Check
What does Andy see when he gets off the school bus?

But he didn't have much hope that she would be interested in him. Girls didn't go for the quiet, studious type. Last year, one of the girls in his geometry class had asked him to give her some help after school. That went pretty well, and for a while he thought they might have something going. But after she passed the geometry test, she didn't look at him again.

Maybe if he studied less and went in for sports, girls would get interested in him. But then his grades might slip, and his parents would never let him hear the end of it. He had to keep his grades up, study hard, be the dutiful son.

His brother had managed to get a math score of 800 on the PSAT, and now he was at Yale with a full scholarship. Andy had to try and do as well.

More than once he had asked his parents why it was so important to get into a good college. "Lots of people get rich in this country without going to college at all," he told them.

His father would draw himself up stiffly. "The Liangs belonged to the mandarin class in China. I've told you again and again that to become a mandarin, one had to pass the official examinations. Only outstanding scholars passed, and only they had the qualifications to govern the country."

Andy's father always got worked up about the subject. He might be only a minor clerk in America, he said, but he was descended from a family of high-ranking officials in China.

Another thing Andy noticed was that when his father went on at length about the illustrious Liang family, his mother always listened with a faint smile. She seemed to be amused for some reason.

But that didn't stop her from also putting pressure on Andy to study hard. Every night, she would ask him whether he had done his homework, and she double-checked his papers to make sure everything was correct.

Normally Andy didn't mind doing his homework. He liked the satisfaction of a job well done when he finished a hard problem in math. But lately, all the extra work preparing for the exam was beginning to get him down. His mind wandered, and he began to daydream. He had visions of becoming a snake charmer, making a balloon trip over the Andes, or practicing kung fu in Shaolin Temple.[2] He saw himself in the English countryside, riding a galloping horse in a fox hunt.

---

2. **Shaolin** (shou´ lin) **Temple** The ancient Chinese martial art of kung fu is thought to have originated in Shaolin Temple, located in the Songshan Mountains of China's Henan Province.

◄ **Critical Viewing**
Does this student
seem to be studying or
daydreaming? How can
you tell? **[Speculate]**

He tried to stop wasting time on these stupid daydreams.
Maybe his mind wouldn't wander if he had someone to study
with. But nobody wanted to study with him. Nobody wanted
to spend time with a nerd.

Next day, the girl got off the bus again with Andy, and this
time, instead of going into the convenience store, she began to
walk with him. When they reached the yard with the German
shepherd, they both automatically backed away from the fence.

Andy and the girl looked at each other and grinned. He was
encouraged. "I'm Andy Liang. Are you new in the neighborhood?"

"We moved here last week," she replied. "My name is Leona
Hu. But Leona is a silly name, and my friends call me Lee."

She was inviting him to call her Lee and including him
among her friends! Andy could hardly believe his luck.
An attractive girl was actually ready to be friends. He was
grateful to the German shepherd.

The girl had big almond-shaped eyes. Andy had overheard
Americans saying that Chinese had slanty eyes, although
his own eyes did not slant. Lee's eyes, on the other hand,
definitely slanted upward at the corners.

Her hair had a slightly reddish tint, instead of being blue-
black like his own. She wasn't exactly beautiful, but with her
hair and her slanting eyes, she looked exotic and fascinating.

When they came to his house, Andy wished he could keep Lee
talking with him. But she smiled at him briefly and went on. He
had to stop himself from running after her to find out where she

Reading Check

Why is Andy studying
so hard?

lived. He didn't want her to think that he was pestering her.

Was she going to take the PSAT this year? If she was, maybe they could study together!

At dinner that night, his father went on as usual about how important it was to do well on the PSAT. "We immigrants start at the bottom here in America, and the only way we can pull ourselves up is to get a good education. Never forget that you're descended from illustrious ancestors, Andy."

Again, Andy noticed his mother's faint smile. Later, he went into the kitchen where he found her washing the dishes. "Why do you always smile when Father gives me his pep talk about education? Don't you agree with him?"

"Oh, I agree with him about the importance of education," his mother said. "I'm just amused by all that talk about *illustrious ancestors.*"

"You mean Father wasn't telling the truth about Liangs being mandarins?" asked Andy. He took up a bunch of chopsticks and began to wipe them dry. Usually, his mother refused his help with the chores. She wanted him to spend all his time on his homework.

But tonight she didn't immediately send him upstairs to his desk. She rinsed a rice bowl and put it in the dish rack. "Well, the Liangs haven't always been mandarins," she said finally. "They used to be quite poor, until one of them achieved success by passing the official examinations and raising the status of the whole Liang family."

"Hey, that's great!" Andy liked the idea of a poor boy making good. It was more interesting than coming from a long line of decadent aristocrats. "Tell me more about this ancestor."

"His name was Fujin Liang," replied his mother. "Or I should say Liang Fujin, since in China, last names come first." Again she smiled faintly. "Very well. You should really be studying, but it's good for you to know about your ancestors."

Liang Fujin lived with his widowed mother in a small thatched cottage and earned money by looking after a neighbor's water buffalo. His mother added to their meager income by weaving and selling cotton cloth. It was a hard struggle to put rice in their bowls.

But Fujin's mother was ambitious for him. She knew he was smart, and she decided that he should try for the

Narrative Structure
What clues indicate that this section is a flash-back, not part of the main narrative?

official examinations. In theory, any poor boy could take the examinations, and if he passed, he could raise his family to mandarin status. But rich boys could afford tutors to help them study. For Fujin, even buying a book was a luxury.

He was so eager to learn that he crouched under the window of the nearby school and tried to eavesdrop on the lessons. Whenever he saved enough money to buy books, he would read them while seated on the back of the water buffalo. Once he was so absorbed that he walked the buffalo into a rice paddy. But he managed to read the precious books until he knew them all by heart.

Through hard work he grew up to be a fine scholar. His mother thought he was finally ready to take the examinations, but he himself wasn't so confident. The other competitors were the sons of rich families, who could afford the very best tutors.

He continued to study late every night, until his head began to nod. So he tied the end of his pigtail to a nail in the ceiling, and whenever his head fell forward, the pigtail jerked him awake.

One night, while he was struggling to stay awake over his book, he heard a soft voice behind him. "A fine, hardworking young man like you deserves to pass the examination."

Fujin whirled around and saw a beautiful girl standing behind him. Somehow she had appeared without making any noise. She had huge, bewitching eyes that slanted sharply. Could he be dreaming?

"Let me help you," continued the girl. "I can act as a tutor and coach you."

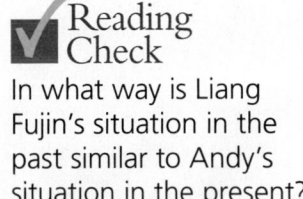

▲ **Critical Viewing**
What features in this picture of a mandarin reflect a power and status that would make a descendant proud? **[Analyze]**

"And that was how your ancestor, Liang Fujin, got the coaching he needed to pass the examinations," said Andy's mother.

Andy blinked. "But . . . but who was this mysterious girl? And how come she was such a great scholar? I thought women didn't get much education in the old days."

His mother laughed. "Nobody in the Liang family would say. But I'll give you a hint: When the girl lifted her skirt to sit down, Fujin caught a flash of something swishing. It looked like a long, bushy tail!"

✓ Reading
Check

In what way is Liang Fujin's situation in the past similar to Andy's situation in the present?

▲ **Critical Viewing**
What event does this image capture? **[Analyze]**

It took Andy a moment to get it. Then he remembered the Chinese stories his mother used to tell him, stories about the *huli jing,* or fox spirit. The mischievous fox, or *huli,* often appeared in the form of a beautiful girl and played tricks on people. But in some of the stories, the fox fell in love with a handsome young man and did him a great service. She expected a reward for her service, of course, and the reward was marriage.

"So my ancestor passed the examinations because he was coached by a fox?" asked Andy.

"That story is a lie!" cried Andy's father, stomping into the kitchen. "It was made up by malicious neighbors who were jealous of the Liangs!"

Andy's mother shrugged and began to pack the dishes away. His father continued. "Liang Fujin passed the examinations because he was smart and worked hard! Don't you forget it, Andy! So now you can go up to your room and start working!"

His father was right, of course. Fox spirits belonged in fairy tales. He, Andy Liang, would have to study for the PSAT the hard way.

Andy was delighted when Lee told him that she was also planning to take the PSAT. She agreed that it would be a good idea to study together. He was eager to begin that very evening. "How about coming over to my house? I'm sure my parents would love to meet you."

Actually, he wasn't sure how delighted his parents would be. He suspected that they would be glad to see him with a Chinese American girl, but they'd probably think that a girl—any girl—would distract him from his studies.

He was half sorry and half relieved when she said, "I'm going to be busy tonight. Maybe we can go to the public library tomorrow afternoon and get some sample tests and study guides."

That night he had a dream about fox hunting. Only this time, he found himself running on the ground trying to get away from the mounted horsemen and howling dogs. There was somebody running with him—another fox, with reddish hair and a bushy tail. It flashed a look at him with its slanting eyes.

Andy and Lee began studying sample PSAT tests at the library. Working with someone else certainly made studying less of a drudgery. Andy felt relaxed with Lee. He didn't suffer the paralyzing shyness with her that seized him when he was with other girls.

She was really good at finding out what his weaknesses were. English grammar was his worst subject, and Lee fed him the right questions so that the fuzzy points of grammar got cleared up. As the days went by, Andy became confident that he was going to do really well on the PSAT. At this rate, he might get a scholarship to some famous university.

He began to worry that the help was one-sided. *He* was getting first-rate coaching, but what was Lee getting out of this? "You're helping me so much," he told her. "But I don't see how I'm helping you at all."

She smiled at him. "I'll get my reward someday."

Something about her glance looked familiar. Where had he seen it before?

They had an extralong study session the day before the exam. When they passed the corner house on their way home, the German shepherd went into a frenzy of barking and scrabbled to climb the Cyclone fence. Both the chain and the fence held, fortunately. Lee looked shaken and backed away from the fence.

At Andy's house she recovered her color. "Well, good luck on the exam tomorrow." She looked at him for a moment with her slanting eyes, and then she was gone.

Again, he thought he remembered that look from somewhere. All during supper, he was tantalized by the memory, which was just out of reach.

That night he dreamed about fox hunting again. It was more vivid than usual, and he could see the scarlet coats of the riders chasing him. The howling of the dogs sounded just like the German shepherd. Again, he was running with

Narrative Structure
What possible meaning could the recurring image of a fox have? Explain.

Spiral Review
Theme What are the connections between the story of the ancestor, Andy's dream, and reality?

Vocabulary
tantalized
(tan´ tə līzd´) *v.*
tormented by something just out of reach

Reading Check
How does Lee help Andy?

another fox. It had huge slanting eyes, bright with mischief.

He woke up, and as he sat in his bed, he finally remembered where he had seen those huge, slanting eyes. They were Lee's eyes.

Next day Andy met Lee at the entrance to the examination hall. He suddenly realized that if he said her name in the Chinese order, it would be Hu Lee, which sounded the same as *huli,* or fox.

She smiled. "So you know?"

Andy found his voice. "Why did you pick me, particularly?"

Her smile widened. "We foxes hunt out our own kind."

That was when Andy knew why the German shepherd always snapped at him. He himself must be part fox. His ancestor, Liang Fujin, had accepted help from the fox spirit after all, and she had collected her reward.

Narrative Structure
Andy solves the mystery foreshadowed in the story. What does he learn?

Critical Thinking

Cite textual evidence to support your responses.

© **1. Key Ideas and Details (a)** What is the first hint that something is strange about Leona Hu? **(b) Draw Conclusions:** At what point in the story does an unusual explanation for Lee's presence and behavior seem likely? **(c) Evaluate:** What is another reasonable explanation for her presence and behavior?

© **2. Integration of Knowledge and Ideas Make a Judgment:** Would you rather succeed based on your own efforts or succeed with the help of others? Explain.

© **3. Integration of Knowledge and Ideas (a)** Does Andy accept a straightforward or a fantastic explanation for the appearance of Leona Hu? **(b)** How does the author blur the line between fantasy and reality in this story? *[Connect to the Big Question: Is truth the same for everyone?]*

Comparing Narrative Structure

1. Craft and Structure (a) Using a chart like the one shown, list examples of **flashback** and **foreshadowing. (b)** Which of the story's plots was closer to presenting events in strict chronological order? Explain.

	Flashback	Foreshadowing
Old Ben		
Fox Hunt		Dream of a fox hunt

2. Craft and Structure On a separate piece of paper, show the narrative structure of "Fox Hunt" by creating a timeline. List the plot events in the order in which they occur, using arrows to represent flashback and foreshadowing.

⏱ Timed Writing

Explanatory Text: Essay

Compare and contrast the narrative structures of "Old Ben" and "Fox Hunt." In a brief essay, analyze how the authors develop the plot in each narrative. Consider the ways in which the narrative structure of each piece contributes to its meaning. **(40 minutes)**

5-Minute Planner

1. Read the prompt carefully and completely.

2. Gather your ideas by jotting down answers to these questions:

- In each narrative, what information does the author convey through flashback or foreshadowing?
- What is the central conflict in each narrative, and how do events lead to a climax?
- How does the structure of each narrative help to relay the central idea?

3. To retrace the structure of each plot, refer to your answers to questions 1 and 2 at the top of the page.

4. Reread the prompt, and then draft your essay.

Writing Workshop

 Common Core
State Standards

Writing

2. Write informative/explanatory texts to examine a topic and convey ideas, concepts, and information through the selection, organization, and analysis of relevant content.

2.a. Introduce a topic clearly, previewing what is to follow; organize ideas, concepts, and information into broader categories.

2.b. Develop the topic with relevant, well-chosen facts, definitions, concrete details, quotations, or other information and examples.

4. Produce clear and coherent writing in which the development, organization, and style are appropriate to task, purpose, and audience.

Write Explanatory Text

Description of a Person

Defining the Form When nonfiction writers get ready to write a **descriptive essay,** they often think about memorable people who have influenced their lives. You might use the same elements of description in personal letters and in expository essays.

Assignment Write a descriptive essay about a person who has had an important influence on your life. Your essay should introduce your topic clearly and feature these elements:

✔ a *controlling impression* of the person that is carried throughout the essay and is supported with a clear, effective conclusion

✔ relevant concrete *details* and *examples, personal anecdotes, quotations,* and *comparisons* as support

✔ *sensory details* about appearance, behavior, and speech

✔ your thoughts about how this person has influenced your life

✔ error-free writing, including *correct spelling and use of nouns*

To preview the criteria on which your essay may be judged, see the rubric on page 109.

 **Writing Workshop:** *Work in Progress*

Review the work you did on pages 53 and 79.

Prewriting/Planning Strategy

Make a character web. After you have decided on a person to describe, create a web like the one shown. Jot down specific details about the person's actions, appearance, behavior, and character traits. Then, use your character web to generate one broad statement about the person and his or her significance to you.

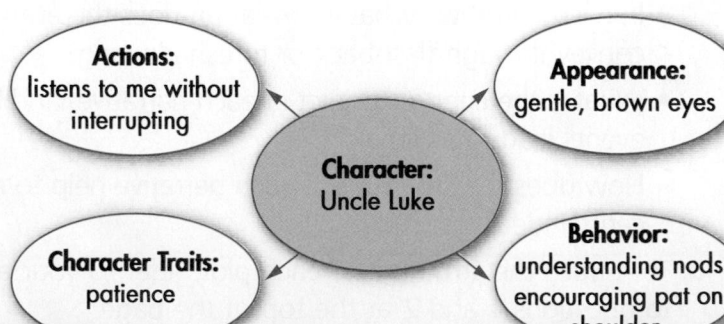

Using a Unique Voice

Voice is a writer's unique use of language that conveys his or her personality to the reader. This voice may vary from work to work— or it may be a consistent voice that the writer uses and develops over an entire career. Some writers have such unique voices that a reader can recognize his or her work without even seeing the writer's name. Develop your own voice by following these tips.

Work on tone. Tone is the writer's attitude toward a subject. These questions will help you develop a tone that is appropriate to your descriptive essay:

- How do I feel about the person I am describing?
- What descriptive words best express this feeling?
- What sensory details can I use to support this attitude?

Write your answers to these questions in a chart like the one shown. You can choose from the words and phrases in your chart as you write your first draft.

How Do I Feel?	Descriptive Words	Sensory Details
affectionate	kind thoughtful attentive generous	her friendly smile her warm hugs her delicious cooking her colorful clothing

Maintain a consistent voice. Once you have determined the tone you wish to convey, make sure that everything you write contributes to that tone. For example, if you wish to show the affection you feel toward your subject, include only details that support this view. Use **anecdotes**—quick stories that illustrate a point—to show a time when the person went out of his or her way to help you. Keep anecdotes light-hearted for a humorous tone and more serious for a solemn tone. You can also help the reader understand your feelings through quotations, sensory details, descriptions, and comparisons.

Add dialogue to bring descriptions to life. A great way to bring the subject of your description to life is to capture the way he or she talks. Be sure your subject's words reflect the tone of your essay.

Drafting Strategies

Organize examples and details. Your description should keep readers' interest and create a strong, controlling impression about your subject. Follow these steps to organize your draft.

- Organize examples and details in such a way that your reader will come to know the person you are describing.
- Develop your essay by relating anecdotes that reveal the person's character.
- Include quotations by and about the person that will help the reader get a clearer picture.

As you write, work up to a clear and well-supported conclusion that reinforces the impression you wish to create.

Use sensory details. As you draft, focus on providing vivid **sensory details**—words and phrases that appeal to any of the five senses. These details will create a strong picture for your readers.

Revising Strategies

Evaluate unity. To make sure your description creates a single **controlling impression,** eliminate unnecessary details. For example, if you are creating an impression about your grandmother's modesty, only supply details that relate to this trait—the way she blushed when praised or the time she let someone else take credit for her good deed. Then, your conclusion should flow naturally from these points. For instance, your concluding thoughts might be about how her modesty has affected your behavior.

Revise by adding transitions. Strengthen your writing by adding appropriate and varied transitions, such as *therefore* and *however,* to connect your ideas and clarify the organization of your essay.

Evaluate for voice. Look over your draft with a partner to see if you have used a strong and appropriate voice. Answer questions like the ones shown. Then, revise where necessary.

Questions	Take It Out!	Put It In!
Do all my examples, anecdotes, and quotations contribute to the overall impression I want to make?	If not, exclude any information that is unneeded or inappropriate.	Replace weak material with examples, anecdotes, and quotations that strengthen the voice of the essay.

Common Core State Standards

Writing

2.c. Use appropriate and varied transitions to create cohesion and clarify the relationships among ideas and concepts.

2.f. Provide a concluding statement or section that follows from and supports the information or explanation presented.

3.d. Use precise words and phrases, relevant descriptive details, and sensory language to capture the action and convey experiences and events.

5. With some guidance and support from peers and adults, develop and strengthen writing as needed by planning, revising, editing, rewriting, or trying a new approach, focusing on how well purpose and audience have been addressed.

Using Concrete, Abstract, and Possessive Nouns

Nouns name people, places, things, or ideas. They are critical to description because they identify people and things writers discuss.

Identifying Types of Nouns **Concrete nouns** name people, places, or things that can be perceived by the five senses. **Abstract nouns** name ideas, beliefs, qualities, or concepts. **Possessive nouns** show ownership or belonging. They end in 's or s'.

Type of Noun	Examples
concrete	child, dog, street, Jeff
abstract	freedom, childhood, love, kindness
possessive	child's coat, freedom's appeal

Using Vivid Concrete Nouns In your writing, support abstract nouns such as *friendship* or *love* with specific concrete nouns that give vivid details. Avoid vague, general nouns that do not give a clear picture.

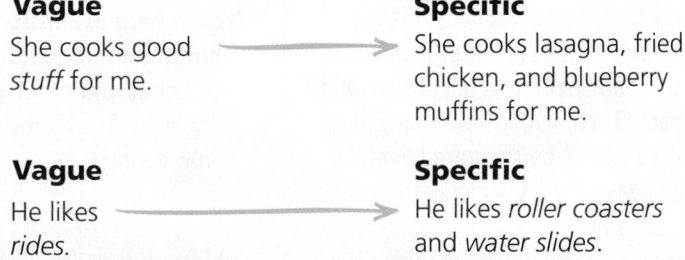

Vague	**Specific**
She cooks good *stuff* for me.	She cooks lasagna, fried chicken, and blueberry muffins for me.

Vague	**Specific**
He likes *rides*.	He likes *roller coasters* and *water slides*.

Identifying Errors Most errors with possessive nouns occur when apostrophes are left out or placed incorrectly. Follow these rules:

1. To form the possessive form of plural nouns that end in *s*, add an apostrophe.

2. For plural nouns that do not end in *s,* add an apostrophe and the letter *s.*

Examples: *dogs'* owner, *boys'* basketball game, *women's* plan

Grammar in Your Writing

In two paragraphs of your draft, underline each noun. Ask yourself if each noun paints a vivid picture of your subject. If the noun is vague or too general, replace it with a more vivid, specific noun.

Grandpa Mike

Many people tell me that I am very fortunate to be blessed with the light-hearted, fun-loving grandfather I have. Every time I hear those words, I simply laugh and agree. Since I was a child, I can remember a smiling grandfather by my side, every step of the way. Whether it was my first softball game or learning to skateboard, Grandpa Mike was there to cheer me up when at first I did not succeed.

My grandfather and I are very different. Looking at us, you would not believe that we belonged in the same family. That is because we are not blood-related. When my grandmother was still in Thailand, her first husband died in the war. That is when she met the handsome, tall American man who is now my grandfather. Almost thin, with the exception of a pot belly, Mike can still move with the athleticism of a young man—but not for very long. He seems to always be dressed in nylon sweat suits emblazoned with the symbol of his favorite sports team. He is also infectiously funny. A curt joke followed by grandpa's infamous staccato laugh is enough to plant a joyous smirk on my face. Laugh lines around his eyes—relics from memories past—make me imagine the way I will be when I get older. I look at him and realize that I want to be just like him.

Even on the gloomiest of days, Grandpa Mike's presence can brighten my life, as if someone in the heavens decided to switch on the sun. I remember, once, when I was in a bit of a quibble with my best friend and I was feeling very down on myself, my grandfather waltzed on over to the couch with a confidence that seemed to make him glow. He plopped down right next to me and just stared at me until I was forced to look back. Then, with a smile, he simply said, "Ha! Got you! Now, you have to smile!" Laughing, he sauntered away, leaving me to giggle in spite of myself. Mike always has a way to liven things up, even if his methods may seem immature or corny.

Grandpa Mike can make any dreary situation seem amusing. On rainy days, when black clouds hide the sunshine, my dad and uncle like to watch golf. Personally, I always find this activity mind-numbing and tedious. With my grandfather, it is a completely different story. Grandpa Mike will always add his own hilarious commentary or imaginary situations that make every moment enjoyable.

Without my carefree, comical grandfather at my side growing up, I probably would not be the same person I am today. Being with him, and having him teach me valuable life lessons—while adding a funny twist to every circumstance—has helped make me a more well-rounded person. It has also helped me to appreciate the type of person I have become and to realize the kind of person I would like to be.

In the first sentence and paragraph, Liz establishes the controlling impression of her grandfather through the use of specific adjectives and concrete examples.

Sensory details that appeal to the senses of sight and hearing make Liz's grandfather more real.

Liz introduces an anecdote here to support her main impression of her grandfather as "light-hearted" and "fun-loving."

Here, the writer compares Grandpa Mike with her dad and uncle to further emphasize how much fun the grandfather is.

Liz concludes with thoughts about the influence that her grandfather has had on her as a person.

Editing and Proofreading

Review your draft to correct errors in spelling and grammar.

Check commonly misspelled words. Many commonly used words are misspelled because a consonant is doubled when it should not be, or not doubled when it should be. Double-check the spelling of words like *always, business, occasion,* and *recommend*.

Focus on comparative and superlative adjectives. Comparative adjectives (*neater, more artistic*) compare two things. Superlative adjectives (*neatest, most artistic*) compare three or more things. Check your essay to ensure you have used these adjectives correctly.

Publishing and Presenting

Consider sharing your writing using one of these ideas:

Make a photo scrapbook. Select a group of photos of you and your subject, and organize them in a small photo album. On each page of the album, include a paragraph from your description.

Prepare an oral presentation. Descriptive writing is well suited to reading aloud. Share your description with a live audience.

Reflecting on Your Writing

Writer's Journal Jot down your answer to this question:

What new insights about your subject did you gain?

Rubric for Self-Assessment

Find evidence in your writing that addresses each category. Then, use the rating scale to grade your work.

Spiral Review
Earlier in the unit, you learned about **common and proper nouns** (p. 52) and **plural nouns** (p. 78). Check to see that you correctly capitalized proper nouns in your descriptive essay. Review your essay to be sure you have formed each plural noun correctly.

PH | WRITING COACH
Further instruction and practice are available in *Prentice Hall Writing Coach*.

Criteria	Rating Scale				
	not very				*very*
Focus: How well do you establish and maintain a controlling impression?	1	2	3	4	5
Organization: How clearly is your description organized?	1	2	3	4	5
Support/Elaboration: How effectively are anecdotes, examples, comparisons, and figurative and sensory language used?	1	2	3	4	5
Styles: How well do you describe this person's influence on your life?	1	2	3	4	5
Conventions: How correct is your grammar, especially your use of concrete, abstract, and possessive nouns?	1	2	3	4	5

Leveled Texts

Build your skills and improve your comprehension of fiction and literary nonfiction with texts of increasing complexity.

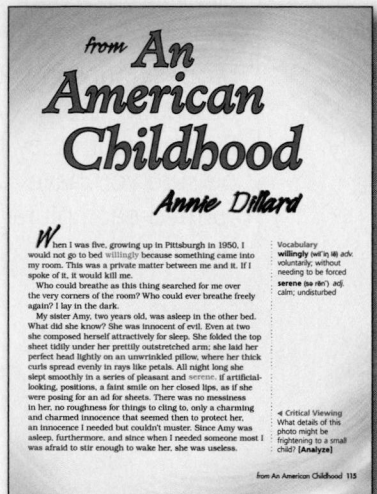

Read the excerpt from *An American Childhood* to appreciate a child's experience with fear.

Read **"The Adventure of the Speckled Band"** to witness how a sharp detective unlocks a mystery.

© **Common Core State Standards**

Meet these standards with either the excerpt from *An American Childhood* (p. 115) or **"The Adventure of the Speckled Band"** (p. 122).

Reading Literature/Informational Text
1. Cite the textual evidence that most strongly supports an analysis of what the text says explicitly as well as inferences drawn from the text. (*Reading: Author's Purpose*)
Spiral Review RL.8.2/RI.8.2
Writing
3. Write narratives to develop real or imagined experiences or events using effective technique, relevant descriptive details, and well-structured event sequences.
3.a. Engage and orient the reader by establishing a context and point of view and introducing a narrator and/or characters; organize an event sequence that unfolds naturally and logically. **3.e.** Provide a conclusion that follows from and reflects on the narrated experiences or events. (*Writing: Personal Narrative*)
7. Conduct short research projects to answer a question (including a self-generated question), drawing on several

sources and generating additional related, focused questions that allow for multiple avenues of exploration. (*Research and Technology: Research Report*)
8. Gather relevant information from multiple print and digital sources, using search terms effectively; assess the credibility and accuracy of each source; and quote or paraphrase the data and conclusions of others while avoiding plagiarism and following a standard format for citation. (*Research and Technology: Research Report*)
Language
1. Demonstrate command of the conventions of standard English grammar and usage when writing or speaking. (*Conventions: Personal Pronouns*)
4.b. Use common, grade-appropriate Greek or Latin affixes and roots as clues to the meaning of a word (e.g., *precede, recede, secede*). (*Vocabulary: Word Study*)

Reading Skill: Author's Purpose

The **author's purpose** is his or her reason for writing. An author may write to inform, to persuade, or to entertain. Learn to **recognize details from which you can infer the author's purpose.**

- To *inform*, an author provides factual information about a subject. (Read closely: Pause frequently and take notes.)

- To *persuade*, an author gives reasons that lead readers to agree with an opinion. (Read critically: Question and evaluate the author's statements, and check facts.)

- To *entertain*, an author uses details that horrify or amuse. (Read for enjoyment: Respond to images, ideas, and characters.)

Writers also may have specific, as well as general, purposes in mind. By describing an earlier event in a character's life, for example, an author helps readers understand the character better.

Using the Strategy: Author's Purpose Chart

As you read, use an **author's purpose chart** like this one to help you make inferences about different purposes in a story.

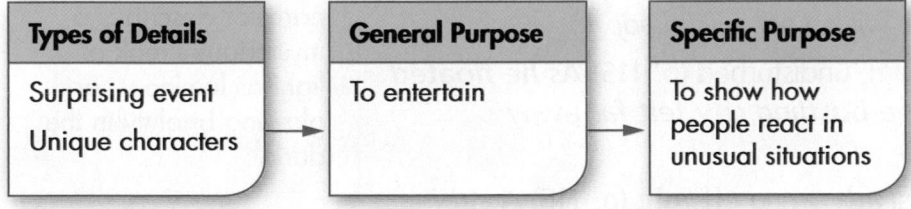

Types of Details	General Purpose	Specific Purpose
Surprising event Unique characters	To entertain	To show how people react in unusual situations

Literary Analysis: Mood

Mood, or atmosphere, is the overall feeling that a literary work creates for the reader. The mood of a work might be serious, humorous, or sad. A variety of elements contribute to mood:

- Words and phrases with figurative and connotative meanings, such as *grumpy* or *starlit night*

- **Setting,** such as *a dark, shadowy room*

- Dramatic events, such as *heavy storm clouds lifting*

 **Is** *truth* **the same for everyone?**

Writing About the Big Question

In this excerpt from *An American Childhood*, Annie Dillard's understanding of the world around her is influenced more by her young imagination than by reality. Use this sentence starter to develop your ideas about the Big Question.

Small children may draw **illogical** conclusions about the world around them because _____.

While You Read Look for Dillard's descriptions of the "monster."

Vocabulary

Read each word and its definition. Decide whether you know the word well, know it a little bit, or do not know it at all. After you read, see how your knowledge of each word has increased.

- **willingly** (wil´ iŋ lē) *adv.* voluntarily; without needing to be forced (p. 115) *The escaped convict did not surrender* __willingly__. *willingness* ***n.*** *willing* ***adj.*** *willful* ***adj.***

- **serene** (sə rēn´) *adj.* calm; undisturbed (p. 115) *As he floated on the* __serene__ *lake, the bustling city felt far away.* *serenity* ***n.*** *serenely* ***adj.***

- **luminous** (lōō´ mə nəs) *adj.* giving off light (p. 116) *A cabin was lit by the moon's* __luminous__ *glow.* *luminosity* ***n.***

- **ascent** (ə sent´) *n.* upward slope; climb (p. 116) *The climber was out of breath after the difficult* __ascent__. *ascend* ***v.*** *descend* ***v.***

- **conceivably** (kən sēv´ ə blē) *adv.* in an imaginable or believable way (p. 117) *Joe has trained so hard; he could* __conceivably__ *win.* *conceive* ***v.*** *conceivable* ***adj.*** *concept* ***n.***

- **overwhelming** (ō´ vər hwelm´ iŋ) *adj.* emotionally overpowering (p. 118) *Wild applause sparked* __overwhelming__ *feelings of joy in the young actors.* *overwhelmingly* ***adv.*** *overwhelm* ***v.***

Word Study

The **Latin root -lum-** means "light."

In this memoir, the narrator describes a mysterious streak of light as luminous, or glowing brightly in the dark.

Photograph by Rollie McKenna

Meet
Annie Dillard

(b. 1945)

Author of
An American Childhood

In *An American Childhood*, a memoir about growing up, Annie Dillard describes how her parents encouraged her to explore the world. Their encouragement eventually led Dillard to a career as a writer famous for providing insights about the natural world.

A Year Close to Nature Before writing her first book of prose, Dillard spent a year living at the edge of a creek in the mountains of Virginia. There, she recorded such observations as the time she watched, fascinated, as a frog—attacked by a giant waterbug—was deflated into a pouch of skin before her eyes. She edited these observations of nature to create *Pilgrim at Tinker Creek,* which won the 1975 Pulitzer Prize for general nonfiction.

Words of Advice Dillard says to aspiring writers, "You have enough experience by the time you're five years old. What you need is the library. What you have to learn is the best of what is being thought and said."

Did You Know?

A very private person, Annie Dillard calls herself a "recluse" because she does not like to travel or meet with strangers. She has never appeared on television; as a result there is no known film footage of her.

BACKGROUND FOR THE MEMOIR

Interpreting Information

Scientists have found that very young children cannot make connections or interpret information the way that adults can. For example, an adult who sees an object put into a drawer is able to find the object later. A small child, however, does not make the connection and thinks the object has disappeared. As children grow, their ability to interpret information improves.

from An American Childhood

Annie Dillard

When I was five, growing up in Pittsburgh in 1950, I would not go to bed **willingly** because something came into my room. This was a private matter between me and it. If I spoke of it, it would kill me.

Who could breathe as this thing searched for me over the very corners of the room? Who could ever breathe freely again? I lay in the dark.

My sister Amy, two years old, was asleep in the other bed. What did she know? She was innocent of evil. Even at two she composed herself attractively for sleep. She folded the top sheet tidily under her prettily outstretched arm; she laid her perfect head lightly on an unwrinkled pillow, where her thick curls spread evenly in rays like petals. All night long she slept smoothly in a series of pleasant and **serene**, if artificial-looking, positions, a faint smile on her closed lips, as if she were posing for an ad for sheets. There was no messiness in her, no roughness for things to cling to, only a charming and charmed innocence that seemed then to protect her, an innocence I needed but couldn't muster. Since Amy was asleep, furthermore, and since when I needed someone most I was afraid to stir enough to wake her, she was useless.

Vocabulary
willingly (wil´ iŋ lē) *adv.* voluntarily; without needing to be forced
serene (sə rēn´) *adj.* calm; undisturbed

◄ **Critical Viewing**
What details of this photo might be frightening to a small child? **[Analyze]**

► **Critical Viewing**
What details in this photo convey a scary mood, like the one in the memoir? **[Analyze]**

Vocabulary
luminous (lōō′ mə nəs) *adj.* giving off light

Author's Purpose
What details does Dillard include to entertain readers in her description of her fear?

Mood
What words and phrases in this paragraph create a mood that is tense and scary?

Vocabulary
ascent (ə sent′) *n.* upward slope; climb

I lay alone and was almost asleep when the darned thing entered the room by flattening itself against the open door and sliding in. It was a transparent, **luminous** oblong.[1] I could see the door whiten at its touch; I could see the blue wall turn pale where it raced over it, and see the maple headboard of Amy's bed glow. It was a swift spirit; it was an awareness. It made noise. It had two joined parts, a head and a tail, like a Chinese dragon. It found the door, wall, and headboard; and it swiped them, charging them with its luminous glance. After its fleet, searching passage, things looked the same, but weren't.

I dared not blink or breathe; I tried to hush my whooping blood. If it found another awareness, it would destroy it.

Every night before it got to me it gave up. It hit my wall's corner and couldn't get past. It shrank completely into itself and vanished like a cobra down a hole. I heard the rising roar it made when it died or left. I still couldn't breathe. I knew—it was the worst fact I knew, a very hard fact—that it could return again alive that same night.

Sometimes it came back, sometimes it didn't. Most often, restless, it came back. The light stripe slipped in the door, ran searching over Amy's wall, stopped, stretched lunatic at the first corner, raced wailing toward my wall, and vanished into the second corner with a cry. So I wouldn't go to bed.

It was a passing car whose windshield reflected the corner streetlight outside. I figured it out one night.

Figuring it out was as memorable as the oblong itself. Figuring it out was a long and forced **ascent** to the very

---

1. oblong (äb′ lôŋ′) *n.* shape that is longer than it is broad.

rim of being, to the membrane of skin that both separates and connects the inner life and the outer world. I climbed deliberately from the depths like a diver who releases the monster in his arms and hauls himself hand over hand up an anchor chain till he meets the ocean's sparkling membrane and bursts through it; he sights the sunlit, becalmed hull of his boat, which had bulked so ominously from below.

I recognized the noise it made when it left. That is, the noise it made called to mind, at last, my daytime sensations when a car passed—the sight and noise together. A car came roaring down hushed Edgerton Avenue in front of our house, stopped at the corner stop sign, and passed on shrieking as its engine shifted up the gears. What, precisely, came into the bedroom? A reflection from the car's oblong windshield. Why did it travel in two parts? The window sash split the light and cast a shadow.

Night after night I labored up the same long chain of reasoning, as night after night the thing burst into the room where I lay awake and Amy slept prettily and my loud heart thrashed and I froze.

There was a world outside my window and contiguous[2] to it. If I was so all-fired bright, as my parents, who had patently no basis for comparison, seemed to think, why did I have to keep learning this same thing over and over? For I had learned it a summer ago, when men with jackhammers broke up Edgerton Avenue. I had watched them from the yard; the street came up in jagged slabs like floes. When I lay to nap, I listened. One restless afternoon I connected the new noise in my bedroom with the jackhammer men I had been seeing outside. I understood abruptly that these worlds met, the outside and the inside. I traveled the route in my mind: You walked downstairs from here, and outside from downstairs. "Outside," then, was conceivably just beyond my windows. It was the same world I reached by going out the front or the back door. I forced my imagination yet again over this route.

▼ **Critical Viewing**
Which word would you choose to describe these lights in the night—*comforting* or *threatening*? Explain. **[Interpret]**

Author's Purpose
Which details support the author's purpose of informing readers about a child's insight?

Vocabulary
conceivably (kən sēv´ ə blē) *adv.* in an imaginable or believable way

Reading Check
What does the "monster" in Dillard's bedroom turn out to be?

---

2. **contiguous** (kən tig´ yoo əs) *adj.* in physical contact; near or next to.

The world did not have me in mind; it had no mind. It was a coincidental collection of things and people, of items, and I myself was one such item—a child walking up the sidewalk, whom anyone could see or ignore. The things in the world did not necessarily cause my overwhelming feelings; the feelings were inside me, beneath my skin, behind my ribs, within my skull. They were even, to some extent, under my control.

I could be connected to the outer world by reason, if I chose, or I could yield to what amounted to a narrative fiction, to a tale of terror whispered to me by the blood in my ears, a show in light projected on the room's blue walls. As time passed, I learned to amuse myself in bed in the darkened room by entering the fiction deliberately and replacing it by reason deliberately.

When the low roar drew nigh and the oblong slid in the door, I threw my own switches for pleasure. It's coming after me; it's a car outside. It's after me. It's a car. It raced over the wall, lighting it blue wherever it ran; it bumped over Amy's maple headboard in a rush, paused, slithered elongate[3] over the corner, shrank, flew my way, and vanished into itself with a wail. It was a car.

3. **elongate** (ē lôŋ´ gāt´) *adv.* in a way that emphasizes length and narrowness.

Critical Thinking

1. **Key Ideas and Details (a)** Who else is in Dillard's room when the mysterious event occurs? **(b) Contrast:** Why does that person not react to the event the same way Dillard does?

2. **Key Ideas and Details (a)** What happens to the thing before it reaches Dillard? **(b) Analyze:** Why does Dillard believe it cannot find her? **(c) Deduce:** What is the real reason it cannot find her?

3. **Key Ideas and Details (a)** What does Dillard finally figure out is the source of the event? **(b) Infer:** After solving the mystery, Dillard sometimes pretends that she does not know the solution. Why?

4. **Integration of Knowledge and Ideas Speculate:** Why do you think Dillard chose to relate this particular childhood experience?

5. **Integration of Knowledge and Ideas (a)** When Dillard first sees the lights, how is her reaction different from the way an adult might react? **(b)** How does her process for discovering the truth eventually come to resemble the way an adult might think? *[Connect to the Big Question: Is truth the same for everyone?]*

After You Read

from **An American Childhood**

Reading Skill: Author's Purpose

1. (a) In the first paragraph, what details does Annie Dillard give about the object that frightens her? **(b)** From these details, what can you infer is the author's general **purpose?**

2. How does each of the following details contribute to the author's general purpose? **(a)** The description of her sister Amy sleeping; **(b)** the description of the object itself; **(c)** the discovery of what the object was.

Literary Analysis: Mood

© **3. Key Ideas and Details** What is the **mood** of the scene in which Annie Dillard first describes how the light entered her room? Support your answer with details from the **setting.**

© **4. Key Ideas and Details** When Dillard finally realizes what the light really is, her mood is one of triumph. Use a chart like the one shown to list words, phrases, and images that contribute to this mood.

Words	Phrases	Images

Vocabulary

© **Acquisition and Use** Explain your answers to these questions.

1. If a child does chores *willingly,* will his parents be upset?
2. Would a boat be likely to overturn on a *serene* lake?
3. If the night is *luminous,* is there a full moon or no moon?
4. Is an *ascent* something that requires effort?
5. When someone offers directions and says that you could *conceivably* get lost, should you feel worried or reassured?
6. Would a task like making toast be *overwhelming* for a chef?

Word Study Use the context of the sentences and what you know about the **Latin root -*lum*-** to explain each answer.

1. Is an *illumination* bright or dim?
2. Are other people likely to follow the example of a *luminary*?

Word Study

The **Latin root -*lum*-** means "light."

Apply It Explain how the root -*lum*- contributes to the meanings of these words. Consult a dictionary if necessary.

illuminate
lumen
luminescence

 **Is** *truth* **the same for everyone?**

Writing About the Big Question

In "The Adventure of the Speckled Band," a detective pieces together the truth behind a young woman's mysterious death. Use this sentence starter to develop your ideas about the Big Question.

To **prove** a **theory** about a crime scene, a detective can _____.

While You Read Notice the way the story's detective, Sherlock Holmes, evaluates clues to solve a murder. Then, look for details that show you how the truth affects each character.

Vocabulary

Read each word and its definition. Decide whether you know the word well, know it a little bit, or do not know it at all. After you read, see how your knowledge of each word has increased.

- **deductions** (dē duk´ shəns) *n.* judgments about something, based on available information (p. 123) *The scientist made brilliant deductions based on the results of her experiments.* deduces *v.* deductive *adj.*

- **avert** (ə vʉrt´) *v.* avoid (p. 128) *Quick thinking and skillful driving helped avert a fiery crash.* aversion *n.* averse *adj.*

- **sinister** (sin´ is tər) *adj.* threatening harm or evil (p. 134) *The grinning skull, though fake, was still a sinister sight.*

- **tangible** (tan´ jə bəl) *adj.* actual or real; able to be perceived by the senses, especially that of touch (p. 144) *Firefighters usually find a tangible cause for a fire.* tangibly *adv.*

- **invaluable** (in val´ yōō ə bəl) *adj.* extremely useful (p. 145) *A witness is invaluable in solving a case.* invaluably *adv.* value *n.* valuable *adj.* evaluate *v.*

- **indiscreetly** (in´ di skrēt´ lē) *adv.* carelessly (p. 150) *The child indiscreetly passed the knife with its blade facing out.* indiscretion *n.* indiscreet *adj.* discreet *adj.* discretion *n.*

Word Study

The **Latin root -duc-** means "to lead" or "to bring."

In this story, the detective Sherlock Holmes makes **deductions**. His observations lead him to conclusions that enable him to solve the case.

Meet
Arthur Conan Doyle
(1859–1930)

Author of *The Adventure of*

The Speckled Band

When Arthur Conan Doyle studied to become a medical doctor, one of his professors possessed an ability that Doyle found amazing. The professor was able to determine, with total accuracy, details about his patients' lives. When Doyle decided to become a writer, he based his character Sherlock Holmes on the professor. In 1887, he published his first Sherlock Holmes novel, *A Study in Scarlet*.

Holmes Murdered? By 1893, Doyle was tired of making up stories about this character, so he wrote "The Final Problem," in which he killed off Holmes. Public demand for more Sherlock Holmes was so overwhelming that in 1901 Doyle resurrected the detective in *The Hound of the Baskervilles*.

BACKGROUND FOR THE STORY

Sherlock Holmes

One of the most beloved fictional detectives of all time is Sherlock Holmes, a nineteenth-century British character created by Arthur Conan Doyle. Holmes is famous for his deductive reasoning. He analyzes evidence—often little details that no one else notices—and puts together the pieces to figure out what they mean. Readers find out how Holmes solves the mystery when he explains his thinking to Dr. Watson, the character who narrates the story.

DID YOU KNOW?

Sherlock Holmes's most famous expression is "Elementary, my dear Watson," but Arthur Conan Doyle never wrote these words. They were first spoken by Holmes's character in a movie version of one of the Sherlock Holmes stories.

The Adventure of
The Speckled Band

ARTHUR CONAN DOYLE

▲ **Critical Viewing**
What kind of mood does this illustration set for the story that follows? Why? **[Analyze]**

On glancing over my notes of the seventy odd cases in which I have during the last eight years studied the methods of my friend Sherlock Holmes, I find many tragic, some comic, a large number merely strange, but none commonplace; for, working as he did rather for the love of his art than for the acquirement of wealth, he refused to associate himself with any investigation which did not tend towards the unusual, and even the fantastic. Of all these varied cases, however, I cannot recall any which presented more singular features than that which was associated with the well-known Surrey family of the Roylotts of Stoke Moran.

The events in question occurred in the early days of my association with Holmes when we were sharing rooms as bachelors in Baker Street. It is possible that I might have placed them upon record before but a promise of secrecy was made at the time, from which I have only been freed during the last month by the untimely death of the lady to whom the pledge was given. It is perhaps as well that the facts should now come to light, for I have reasons to know that there are widespread rumors as to the death of Dr. Grimesby Roylott which tend to make the matter even more terrible than the truth.

It was early in April in the year 1883 that I woke one morning to find Sherlock Holmes standing, fully dressed, by the side of my bed. He was a late riser, as a rule, and as the clock on the mantelpiece showed me that it was only a quarter past seven, I blinked up at him in some surprise, and perhaps just a little resentment, for I was myself regular in my habits.

"Very sorry to wake you up, Watson," said he, "but it's the common lot this morning. Mrs. Hudson has been awakened, she retorted upon me, and I on you."

"What is it, then—a fire?"

"No; a client. It seems that a young lady has arrived in a considerable state of excitement who insists upon seeing me. She is waiting now in the sitting room. Now, when young ladies wander about the metropolis at this hour of the morning, and get sleepy people up out of their beds, I presume that it is something very pressing which they have to communicate. Should it prove to be an interesting case, you would, I am sure, wish to follow it from the outset. I thought, at any rate, that I should call you and give you the chance."

"My dear fellow, I would not miss it for anything."

I had no keener pleasure than in following Holmes in his professional investigations, and in admiring the rapid deductions, as swift as intuitions, and yet always founded on a logical basis, with which he unraveled the problems which were submitted to him. I rapidly threw on my clothes and was ready in a few minutes to accompany my friend down to the sitting room. A lady dressed in black and heavily veiled, who had been sitting in the window, rose as we entered.

"Good morning, madam," said Holmes cheerily. "My name

Author's Purpose
Why might the author introduce this story with references to secrets, rumors, and deaths?

Vocabulary
deductions
(dē duk´ shəns) *n.* judgments about something, based on available information

Reading Check
Why does Holmes wake Watson early?

is Sherlock Holmes. This is my intimate friend and associate, Dr. Watson, before whom you can speak as freely as before myself. Ha! I am glad to see that Mrs. Hudson has had the good sense to light the fire. Pray draw up to it, and I shall order you a cup of hot coffee, for I observe that you are shivering."

"It is not cold which makes me shiver," said the woman in a low voice, changing her seat as requested.

"What, then?"

"It is fear, Mr. Holmes. It is terror." She raised her veil as she spoke, and we could see that she was indeed in a pitiable state of agitation, her face all drawn and gray, with restless, frightened eyes, like those of some hunted animal. Her features and figure were those of a woman of thirty, but her hair was shot with premature gray, and her expression was weary and haggard. Sherlock Holmes ran her over with one of his quick, all-comprehensive glances.

▼ **Critical Viewing**
What story details does this illustration capture? What scene does it bring to life? **[Connect]**

"You must not fear," said he soothingly, bending forward and patting her forearm. "We shall soon set matters right, I have no doubt. You have come in by train this morning, I see."

"You know me, then?"

"No, but I observe the second half of a return ticket in the palm of your left glove. You must have started early, and yet you had a good drive in a dogcart[1] along heavy roads, before you reached the station."

The lady gave a violent start and stared in bewilderment at my companion.

"There is no mystery, my dear madam," said he, smiling. "The left arm of your jacket is spattered with mud in no less than seven places. The marks are perfectly fresh. There is no vehicle save a dogcart which throws up mud in that way, and then only when you sit on the left-hand side of the driver."

"Whatever your reasons may be, you are perfectly correct," said she. "I started from home before six, reached Leatherhead at twenty past, and came in by the first train to Waterloo. Sir, I can stand this strain no longer; I shall go mad if it continues. I have no one to turn to—none, save only one, who cares for me, and he, poor fellow, can be of little aid. I have heard of you, Mr. Holmes. I have heard of you from Mrs. Farintosh, whom you helped in the hour of her sore need. It was from her that I had your address. Oh, sir, do you not think that you could help me, too, and at least throw a little light through the dense darkness which surrounds me? At present it is out of my power to reward you for your service, but in a month or six weeks I shall be married, with the control of my own income, and then at least you shall not find me ungrateful."

Holmes turned to his desk and, unlocking it, drew out a small case book, which he consulted.

"Farintosh," said he. "Ah yes, I recall the case; it was concerned with an opal tiara. I think it was before your time, Watson. I can only say, madam, that I shall be happy to devote the same care to your case as I did to that of your friend. As to reward, my profession is its own reward; but you are at liberty to defray[2] whatever expenses I may be put to, at the time which suits you best. And now I beg that you will lay

---

1. **dogcart** *n.* small, horse-drawn carriage with seats arranged back-to-back.
2. **defray** (dē frā´) *v.* pay or furnish the money for.

Author's Purpose
How do these details help you to appreciate Holmes's powers of observation?

Mood
Which words and phrases in this paragraph suggest Helen Stoner's anxiety?

Reading Check
Why is the visitor worried that Holmes will not take the case?

before us everything that may help us in forming an opinion upon the matter."

"Alas!" replied our visitor, "the very horror of my situation lies in the fact that my fears are so vague, and my suspicions depend so entirely upon small points, which might seem trivial to another, that even he to whom of all others I have a right to look for help and advice looks upon all that I tell him about it as fancy.[3] He does not say so, but I can read it from his soothing answers and averted eyes. But I have heard, Mr. Holmes, that you can see deeply into the manifold wickedness of the human heart. You may advise me how to walk amid the dangers which encompass me."

"I am all attention, madam."

"My name is Helen Stoner, and I am living with my stepfather, who is the last survivor of one of the oldest Saxon families in England: the Roylotts of Stoke Moran, on the western border of Surrey."

Holmes nodded his head. "The name is familiar to me," said he.

"The family was at one time among the richest in England, and the estates extended over the borders into Berkshire in the north, and Hampshire in the west. In the last century, however, four successive heirs were of a dissolute and wasteful disposition, and the family ruin was eventually completed by a gambler in the days of the Regency. Nothing was left save a few acres of ground, and the two-hundred-year-old house, which is itself crushed under a heavy mortgage. The last squire dragged out his existence there, living the horrible life of an aristocratic pauper;[4] but his only son, my stepfather, seeing that he must adapt himself to the new conditions, obtained an advance from a relative, which enabled him to take a medical degree and went out to Calcutta, where, by his professional skill and his force of character, he established a large practice. In a fit of anger, however, caused by some robberies which had been perpetrated in the house, he beat his native butler to death and narrowly escaped a capital sentence. As it was, he suffered a long term of imprisonment and afterwards returned to England a morose[5] and disappointed man.

---

3. **fancy** *n.* something imagined.
4. **aristocratic pauper** upper-class person who has run out of money.
5. **morose** (mə rōs´) *adj.* gloomy; ill-tempered.

"When Dr. Roylott was in India he married my mother, Mrs. Stoner, the young widow of Major-General Stoner, of the Bengal Artillery. My sister Julia and I were twins, and we were only two years old at the time of my mother's remarriage. She had a considerable sum of money—not less than £1000[6] a year—and this she bequeathed to Dr. Roylott entirely while we resided with him, with a provision that a certain annual sum should be allowed to each of us in the event of our marriage. Shortly after our return to England my mother died—she was killed eight years ago in a railway accident near Crewe. Dr. Roylott then abandoned his attempts to establish himself in practice in London and took us to live with him in the old ancestral house at Stoke Moran. The money which my mother had left was enough for all our wants, and there seemed to be no obstacle to our happiness.

"But a terrible change came over our stepfather about this time. Instead of making friends and exchanging visits with our neighbors, who had at first been overjoyed to see a Roylott of Stoke Moran back in the old family seat, he shut himself up in his house and seldom came out save to indulge in ferocious quarrels with who ever might cross his path. Violence of temper approaching to mania has been hereditary in the men of the family, and in my stepfather's case it had, I believe, been intensified by his long residence in the tropics. A series of disgraceful brawls took place, two of which ended in the police court, until at last he became the terror of the village, and the folks would fly at his approach, for he is a man of immense strength, and absolutely uncontrollable in his anger.

▲ **Critical Viewing**
Why do you think the author chose to set this murder mystery in a crumbling mansion like the one above? **[Speculate]**

☑ Reading Check
What is Dr. Roylott's family background?

---

6. **£1000** one thousand pounds; £ is the symbol for "pound" or "pounds," the British unit of money.

▲ **Critical Viewing**
What qualities of
Dr. Roylott does
this illustration
show? **[Analyze]**

Vocabulary
avert (ə vʉrt´) *v.* avoid

Mood
What words and
phrases in this para-
graph contribute to its
mood of mystery?

"Last week he hurled the local blacksmith over a parapet into a stream, and it was only by paying over all the money which I could gather together that I was able to avert another public exposure. He had no friends at all save the wandering gypsies, and he would give these vagabonds leave to encamp upon the few acres of bramble-covered land which represent the family estate, and would accept in return the hospitality of their tents, wandering away with them sometimes for weeks on end. He has a passion also for Indian animals, which are sent over to him by a correspondent, and he has at this moment a cheetah and a baboon, which wander freely over his grounds and are feared by the villagers almost as much as is their master.

"You can imagine from what I say that my poor sister Julia and I had no great pleasure in our lives. No servant would stay with us, and for a long time we did all the work of the house. She was but thirty at the time of her death, and yet her hair had already begun to whiten, even as mine has."

"Your sister is dead, then?"

"She died just two years ago, and it is of her death that I wish to speak to you. You can understand that, living the life which I have described, we were little likely to see anyone of our own age and position. We had, however, an aunt, my mother's maiden sister, Miss Honoria Westphail, who lives near Harrow, and we were occasionally allowed to pay short visits at this lady's house. Julia went there at Christmas two years ago, and met there a major in the Marines, to whom she became engaged. My stepfather learned of the engagement when my sister returned and offered no objection to the marriage; but within a fortnight of the day which had been fixed for the wedding, the terrible event occurred which has deprived me of my only companion."

Sherlock Holmes had been leaning back in his chair with

his eyes closed and his head sunk in a cushion, but he half opened his lids now and glanced across at his visitor.

"Pray be precise as to details," said he.

"It is easy for me to be so, for every event of that dreadful time is seared into my memory. The manor house is, as I have already said, very old, and only one wing is now inhabited. The bedrooms in this wing are on the ground floor, the sitting rooms being in the central block of the buildings. Of these bedrooms the first is Dr. Roylott's, the second my sister's, and the third my own. There is no communication between them, but they all open out into the same corridor. Do I make myself plain?"

"Perfectly so."

"The windows of the three rooms open out upon the lawn. That fatal night Dr. Roylott had gone to his room early, though we knew that he had not retired to rest, for my sister was troubled by the smell of the strong Indian cigars which it was his custom to smoke. She left her room, therefore, and came into mine, where she sat for some time, chatting about her approaching wedding. At eleven o'clock she rose to leave me, but she paused at the door and looked back.

"'Tell me, Helen,' said she, 'have you ever heard anyone whistle in the dead of the night?'

"'Never,' said I.

"'I suppose that you could not possibly whistle, yourself, in your sleep?'

"'Certainly not. But why?'

"'Because during the last few nights I have always, about three in the morning, heard a low, clear whistle. I am a light sleeper, and it has awakened me. I cannot tell where it came from—perhaps from the next room, perhaps from the lawn. I thought that I would just ask you whether you had heard it.'

"'No, I have not. It must be the gypsies in the plantation.'

"'Very likely. And yet if it were on the lawn, I wonder that you did not hear it also.'

"'Ah, but I sleep more heavily than you.'

"'Well, it is of no great consequence, at any rate.' She smiled back at me, closed my door, and a few moments later I heard her key turn in the lock."

"Indeed," said Holmes. "Was it your custom always to lock yourselves in at night?"

Reading Check

What did Dr. Roylott do to the local blacksmith?

SP

▲ **Critical Viewing**
What does the expression on each sister's face tell you about her state of mind? **[Evaluate]**

Author's Purpose
Why does Doyle use such fine detail in Helen's description of events?

"Always."

"And why?"

"I think that I mentioned to you that the doctor kept a cheetah and a baboon. We had no feeling of security unless our doors were locked."

"Quite so. Pray proceed with your statement."

"I could not sleep that night. A vague feeling of impending misfortune impressed me. My sister and I, you will recollect, were twins, and you know how subtle are the links which bind two souls which are so closely allied. It was a wild night. The wind was howling outside, and the rain was beating and splashing against the windows. Suddenly, amid all the hubbub of the gale, there burst forth the wild scream of a terrified woman. I knew that it was my sister's voice. I sprang from my bed, wrapped a shawl round me, and rushed into the corridor. As I opened my door I seemed to hear a low whistle, such as my sister described, and a few moments later a clanging sound, as if a mass of metal had fallen. As I ran down the passage, my sister's door was unlocked, and

revolved slowly upon its hinges. I stared at it horror-stricken, not knowing what was about to issue from it. By the light of the corridor lamp I saw my sister appear at the opening, her face blanched with terror, her hands groping for help, her whole figure swaying to and fro like that of a drunkard. I ran to her and threw my arms round her, but at that moment her knees seemed to give way and she fell to the ground. She writhed as one who is in terrible pain, and her limbs were dreadfully convulsed.[7] At first I thought that she had not recognized me, but as I bent over her she suddenly shrieked out in a voice which I shall never forget, 'Oh, Helen! It was the band! The speckled band!' There was something else which she would fain have said, and she stabbed with her finger into the air in the direction of the doctor's room, but a fresh convulsion seized her and choked her words. I rushed out, calling loudly for my stepfather, and I met him hastening from his room in his dressing gown. When he reached my sister's side she was unconscious, and though he poured brandy down her throat and sent for medical aid from the village, all efforts were in vain, for she slowly sank and died without having recovered her consciousness. Such was the dreadful end of my beloved sister."

Mood
What mood does this description of Julia convey?

Oh, Helen! It was the band! The speckled band!

"One moment," said Holmes; "are you sure about this whistle and metallic sound? Could you swear to it?"

"That was what the county coroner asked me at the inquiry. It is my strong impression that I heard it, and yet, among the crash of the gale and the creaking of an old house, I may possibly have been deceived."

"Was your sister dressed?"

"No, she was in her nightdress. In her right hand was found the charred stump of a match, and in her left a matchbox."

"Showing that she had struck a light and looked about her when the alarm took place. That is important. And what conclusions did the coroner come to?"

"He investigated the case with great care, for Dr. Roylott's conduct had long been notorious in the county, but he was

Reading Check
What did Helen observe of Julia's actions just before she died?

---

7. **convulsed** (kən vulst´) *adj.* taken over by violent, uncontrollable muscular spasms.

unable to find any satisfactory cause of death. My evidence showed that the door had been fastened upon the inner side, and the windows were blocked by old-fashioned shutters with broad iron bars, which were secured every night. The walls were carefully sounded, and were shown to be quite solid all round, and the flooring was also thoroughly examined, with the same result. The chimney is wide, but is barred up by four large staples. It is certain, therefore, that my sister was quite alone when she met her end. Besides, there were no marks of any violence upon her."

"How about poison?"

"The doctors examined her for it, but without success."

"What do you think that this unfortunate lady died of, then?"

"It is my belief that she died of pure fear and nervous shock, though what it was that frightened her I cannot imagine."

"Were there gypsies in the plantation at the time?"

"Yes, there are nearly always some there."

"Ah, and what did you gather from this allusion to a band—a speckled band?"

"Sometimes I have thought that it was merely the wild talk of delirium, sometimes that it may have referred to some band of people, perhaps to these very gypsies in the plantation. I do not know whether the spotted handkerchiefs which so many of them wear over their heads might have suggested the strange adjective which she used."

Holmes shook his head like a man who is far from being satisfied.

"These are very deep waters," said he; "pray go on with your narrative."

"Two years have passed since then, and my life has been until lately lonelier than ever. A month ago, however, a dear friend, whom I have known for many years, has done me the honor to ask my hand in marriage. His name is Armitage— Percy Armitage—the second son of Mr. Armitage, of Crane Water, near Reading. My stepfather has offered no opposition to the match, and we are to be married in the course of the spring. Two days ago some repairs were started in the west wing of the building, and my bedroom wall has been pierced, so that I have had to move into the chamber in which my sister died, and to sleep in the very bed in which she slept. Imagine, then, my thrill of terror when last night, as I lay awake, thinking over her terrible fate, I suddenly heard in the silence of the night the low whistle which had been the herald of her own death. I sprang up and lit the lamp, but nothing was to be seen in the room. I was too shaken to go to bed again, however, so I dressed, and as soon as it was daylight I slipped down, got a dogcart at the Crown Inn, which is opposite, and drove to Leatherhead, from whence I have come on this morning with the one object of seeing you and asking your advice."

"You have done wisely," said my friend. "But have you told me all?"

"Yes, all."

"Miss Roylott, you have not. You are screening your stepfather."

"Why, what do you mean?"

For answer Holmes pushed back the frill of black lace which fringed the hand that lay upon our visitor's knee. Five little livid spots, the marks of four fingers and a thumb, were printed upon the white wrist.

"You have been cruelly used," said Holmes.

The lady colored deeply and covered over her injured wrist. "He is a hard man," she said, "and perhaps he hardly knows his own strength."

There was a long silence, during which Holmes leaned his chin upon his hands and stared into the crackling fire.

"This is a very deep business," he said at last. "There are a thousand details which I should desire to know before I decide upon our course of action. Yet we have not a moment to lose. If we were to come to Stoke Moran today, would it be possible for us to look over these rooms without the knowledge of your stepfather?"

"As it happens, he spoke of coming into town today upon some most important business. It is probable that he will be away all day and that there would be nothing to disturb you. We have a housekeeper now, but I could easily get her out of the way."

"Excellent. You are not averse to this trip, Watson?"

"By no means."

"Then we shall both come. What are you going to do yourself?"

Mood
What details in this paragraph increase the sense that something terrible will happen?

Reading Check
What caused the marks on Helen's wrist?

The Adventure of the Speckled Band **133**

"I have one or two things which I would wish to do now that I am in town. But I shall return by the twelve o'clock train, so as to be there in time for your coming."

"And you may expect us early in the afternoon. I have myself some small business matters to attend to. Will you not wait and breakfast?"

"No, I must go. My heart is lightened already since I have confided my trouble to you. I shall look forward to seeing you again this afternoon." She dropped her thick black veil over her face and glided from the room.

"And what do you think of it all, Watson?" asked Sherlock Holmes, leaning back in his chair.

"It seems to me to be a most dark and sinister business."

"Dark enough and sinister enough."

"Yet if the lady is correct in saying that the flooring and walls are sound, and that the door, window, and chimney are impassable, then her sister must have been undoubtedly alone when she met her mysterious end."

"What becomes, then, of these nocturnal whistles, and what of the very peculiar words of the dying woman?"

"I cannot think."

"When you combine the ideas of whistles at night, the presence of a band of gypsies who are on intimate terms with this old doctor, the fact that we have every reason to believe that the doctor has an interest in preventing his stepdaughter's marriage, the dying allusion to a band, and, finally, the fact that Miss Helen Stoner heard a metallic clang, which might have been caused by one of those metal bars that secured the shutters, falling back into its place, I think that there is good ground to think that the mystery may be cleared along those lines."

"But what, then, did the gypsies do?"

"I cannot imagine."

"I see many objections to any such theory."

"And so do I. It is precisely for that reason that we are going to Stoke Moran this day. I want to see whether the objections are fatal, or if they may be explained away. But what in the name of the devil!"

The ejaculation had been drawn from my companion by the fact that our door had been suddenly dashed open, and that a huge man had framed himself in the aperture. His costume

Vocabulary
sinister (sin´ is tər) *adj.* threatening harm or evil

Author's Purpose
What specific purpose does the conversation between Holmes and Watson serve?

was a peculiar mixture of the professional and of the agricultural, having a black top hat, a long frock coat, and a pair of high gaiters, with a hunting crop[8] swinging in his hand. So tall was he that his hat actually brushed the crossbar of the doorway, and his breadth seemed to span it across from side to side. A large face, seared with a thousand wrinkles, burned yellow with the sun, and marked with every evil passion, was turned from one to the other of us, while his deep-set, bile-shot eyes, and his high, thin, fleshless nose, gave him somewhat the resemblance to a fierce old bird of prey.

"Which of you is Holmes?" asked this apparition.

"My name, sir; but you have the advantage of me," said my companion quietly.

"I am Dr. Grimesby Roylott, of Stoke Moran."

"Indeed, Doctor," said Holmes blandly. "Pray take a seat."

"I will do nothing of the kind. My stepdaughter has been here. I have traced her. What has she been saying to you?"

"It is a little cold for the time of the year," said Holmes.

"What has she been saying to you?" screamed the old man furiously.

"But I have heard that the crocuses promise well," continued my companion imperturbably.

"Ha! You put me off, do you?" said our new visitor, taking a step forward and shaking his hunting crop. "I know you, you scoundrel! I have heard of you before. You are Holmes, the meddler."

My friend smiled.

"Holmes, the busybody!"

His smile broadened.

"Holmes, the Scotland Yard Jack-in-office!"

Holmes chuckled heartily. "Your conversation is most

▲ **Critical Viewing**
Which figure in this illustration is Dr. Roylott? How can you tell? **[Deduce]**

Reading Check
Who had been secretly following Helen on her visit to Holmes?

---

8. **gaiters, with a hunting crop** cloth or leather coverings for the lower legs, with a short whip used to direct a horse while riding.

entertaining," said he. "When you go out close the door, for there is a decided draft."

"I will go when I have said my say. Don't you dare to meddle with my affairs. I know that Miss Stoner has been here. I traced her! I am a dangerous man to fall foul of! See here." He stepped swiftly forward, seized the poker, and bent it into a curve with his huge brown hands.

"See that you keep yourself out of my grip," he snarled, and hurling the twisted poker into the fireplace he strode out of the room.

"He seems a very amiable person," said Holmes, laughing. "I am not quite so bulky, but if he had remained I might have shown him that my grip was not much more feeble than his own." As he spoke he picked up the steel poker and, with a sudden effort, straightened it out again.

"Fancy his having the insolence to confound me with[9] the official detective force! This incident gives zest to our investigation, however, and I only trust that our little friend will not suffer from her imprudence in allowing this brute to trace her. And now, Watson, we shall order breakfast, and afterwards I shall walk down to Doctors' Commons, where I hope to get some data which may help us in this matter."

It was nearly one o'clock when Sherlock Holmes returned from his excursion. He held in his hand a sheet of blue paper, scrawled over with notes and figures.

"I have seen the will of the deceased wife," said he. "To determine its exact meaning I have been obliged to work out the present prices of the investments with which it is concerned. The total income, which at the time of the wife's death was little short of £1100, is now, through the fall in agricultural prices, not more than £750. Each daughter can claim an income of £250, in case of marriage. It is evident, therefore, that if both girls had married, this beauty would have had a mere pittance,[10] while even one of them would cripple him to a very serious extent. My morning's work has not been wasted, since it has proved that he has the very strongest motives for standing in the way of anything of the sort. And now, Watson, this is too serious for dawdling, especially as the old man is aware that we are interesting

---

9. **confound me with** mistake me for.
10. **pittance** (pit´'ns) *n.* small or barely sufficient sum of money.

Author's Purpose
What aspects of the confrontation with Dr. Roylott serve a general purpose of entertaining the reader?

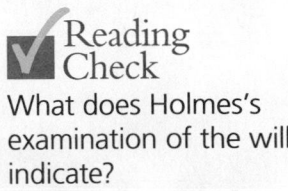

ourselves in his affairs; so if you are ready, we shall call a cab and drive to Waterloo. I should be very much obliged if you would slip your revolver into your pocket. An Eley's No. 2 is an excellent argument with gentlemen who can twist steel pokers into knots. That and a toothbrush are, I think, all that we need."

At Waterloo we were fortunate in catching a train for Leatherhead, where we hired a trap at the station inn and drove for four or five miles through the lovely Surrey lanes. It was a perfect day, with a bright sun and a few fleecy clouds in the heavens. The trees and wayside hedges were just throwing out their first green shoots, and the air was full of the pleasant smell of the moist earth. To me at least there was a strange contrast between the sweet promise of the spring and this sinister quest upon which we were engaged. My companion sat in the front of the trap, his arms folded, his hat pulled down over his eyes, and his chin sunk upon his breast, buried in the deepest thought. Suddenly, however, he started, tapped me on the shoulder, and pointed over the meadows.

▲ **Critical Viewing**
What elements of this illustration tell you that this story is set in the past? **[Infer]**

Mood
How does Holmes's suggestion to bring a revolver affect the mood of the story?

Reading Check
What does Holmes's examination of the will indicate?

The Adventure of the Speckled Band **137**

"Look there!" said he.

A heavily timbered park stretched up in a gentle slope, thickening into a grove at the highest point. From amid the branches there jutted out the gray gables and high rooftop of a very old mansion.

"Stoke Moran?" said he.

"Yes, sir, that be the house of Dr. Grimesby Roylott," remarked the driver.

"There is some building going on there," said Holmes; "that is where we are going."

"There's the village," said the driver, pointing to a cluster of roofs some distance to the left; "but if you want to get to the house, you'll find it shorter to get over this stile, and so by the footpath over the fields. There it is, where the lady is walking."

"And the lady, I fancy, is Miss Stoner," observed Holmes, shading his eyes. "Yes, I think we had better do as you suggest."

We got off, paid our fare, and the trap rattled back on its way to Leatherhead.

"I thought it as well," said Holmes as we climbed the stile, "that this fellow should think we had come here as architects, or on some definite business. It may stop his gossip. Good afternoon, Miss Stoner. You see that we have been as good as our word."

Our client of the morning had hurried forward to meet us with a face which spoke her joy. "I have been waiting so eagerly for you," she cried, shaking hands with us warmly. "All has turned out splendidly. Dr. Roylott has gone to town, and it is unlikely that he will be back before evening."

"We have had the pleasure of making the doctor's acquaintance," said Holmes, and in a few words he sketched out what had occurred. Miss Stoner turned white to the lips as she listened.

"Good heavens!" she cried, "he has followed me, then."

"So it appears."

"He is so cunning that I never know when I am safe from him. What will he say when he returns?"

"He must guard himself, for he may find that there is someone more cunning than himself upon his track. You

Mood
In what way does Miss Stoner's greeting change the mood?

Reading Check
Where is Dr. Roylott when Holmes and Watson arrive at Stoke Moran?

◀ **Critical Viewing** What emotion do you think each character is feeling in the illustration on page 138? **[Infer]**

must lock yourself up from him tonight. If he is violent, we shall take you away to your aunt's at Harrow. Now, we must make the best use of our time, so kindly take us at once to the rooms which we are to examine."

The building was of gray, lichen-blotched stone, with a high central portion and two curving wings, like the claws of a crab, thrown out on each side. In one of these wings the windows were broken and blocked with wooden boards, while the roof was partly caved in, a picture of ruin. The central portion was in little better repair, but the right-hand block was comparatively modern, and the blinds in the windows, with the blue smoke curling up from the chimneys, showed that this was where the family resided. Some scaffolding had been erected against the end wall, and the stonework had been broken into, but there were no signs of any workmen at the moment of our visit. Holmes walked slowly up and down the ill-trimmed lawn and examined with deep attention the outsides of the windows.

"This, I take it, belongs to the room in which you used to sleep, the center one to your sister's, and the one next to the main building to Dr. Roylott's chamber?"

"Exactly so. But I am now sleeping in the middle one."

"Pending the alterations, as I understand. By the way, there does not seem to be any very pressing need for repairs at that end wall."

"There were none. I believe that it was an excuse to move me from my room."

"Ah! that is suggestive. Now, on the other side of this narrow wing runs the corridor from which these three rooms open. There are windows in it, of course?"

"Yes, but very small ones. Too narrow for anyone to pass through."

"As you both locked your doors at night, your rooms were unapproachable from that side. Now, would you have the kindness to go into your room and bar your shutters?"

Miss Stoner did so, and Holmes, after a careful examination through the open window, endeavored in every way to force the shutter open, but without success. There was no slit through which a knife could be passed to raise the bar. Then with his lens he tested the hinges, but they were of solid iron, built firmly into the massive masonry.

"Hum!" said he, scratching his chin in some perplexity. "My theory certainly presents some difficulties. No one could pass through these shutters if they were bolted. Well, we shall see if the inside throws any light upon the matter."

A small side door led into the whitewashed corridor from which the three bedrooms opened. Holmes refused to examine the third chamber, so we passed at once to the second, that in which Miss Stoner was now sleeping, and in which her sister had met with her fate. It was a homely little room, with a low ceiling and a gaping fireplace, after the fashion of old country houses. A brown chest of drawers stood in one corner, a narrow white-counterpaned bed in another, and a dressing table on the left-hand side of the window. These articles, with two small wickerwork chairs, made up all the furniture in the room save for a square of Wilton carpet in the center. The boards round and the paneling of the walls were of brown, worm-eaten oak, so old and discolored that it may have dated from the original building of the house. Holmes drew one of the chairs into a corner and sat silent, while his eyes traveled round and round and up and down, taking in every detail of the apartment.

"Where does that bell communicate with?" he asked at last, pointing to a thick bell-rope which hung down beside the bed, the tassel actually lying upon the pillow.

"It goes to the housekeeper's room."

"It looks newer than the other things?"

"Yes, it was only put there a couple of years ago."

"Your sister asked for it, I suppose?"

"No, I never heard of her using it. We used always to get what we wanted for ourselves."

"Indeed, it seemed unnecessary to put so nice a bell-pull there. You will excuse me for a few minutes while I satisfy myself as to this floor." He threw himself down upon his face with his lens in his hand and crawled swiftly backward and forward, examining minutely the cracks between the boards. Then he did the same with the woodwork with which the chamber was paneled. Finally he walked over to the bed and spent some time in staring at it and in running his eye up and down the wall. Finally he took the bell-rope in his hand and gave it a brisk tug.

Author's Purpose
List two details on this page that prove Holmes is a thorough detective.

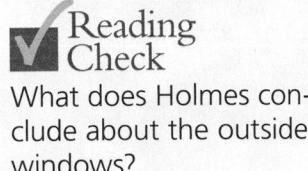

Reading Check
What does Holmes conclude about the outside windows?

"Why, it's a dummy," said he.

"Won't it ring?"

"No, it is not even attached to a wire. This is very interesting. You can see now that it is fastened to a hook just above where the little opening for the ventilator is."

"How very absurd! I never noticed that before!"

"Very strange!" muttered Holmes, pulling at the rope. "There are one or two very singular points about this room. For example, what a fool a builder must be to open a ventilator into another room, when, with the same trouble, he might have communicated with the outside air!"

"That is also quite modern," said the lady.

"Done about the same time as the bell-rope?" remarked Holmes.

"Yes, there were several little changes carried out about that time."

"They seem to have been of a most interesting character—dummy bell-ropes, and ventilators which do not ventilate. With your permission, Miss Stoner, we shall now carry our researches into the inner apartment."

Dr. Grimesby Roylott's chamber was larger than that of his stepdaughter, but was as plainly furnished. A camp bed, a small wooden shelf full of books, mostly of a technical character, an armchair beside the bed, a plain wooden chair against the wall, a round table, and a large iron safe were the principal things which met the eye. Holmes walked slowly round and examined each and all of them with the keenest interest.

"What's in here?" he asked, tapping the safe.

"My stepfather's business papers."

"Oh! you have seen inside, then?"

"Only once, some years ago. I remember that it was full of papers."

"There isn't a cat in it, for example?"

"No. What a strange idea!"

"Well, look at this!" He took up a small saucer of milk which stood on the top of it.

"No; we don't keep a cat. But there is a cheetah and a baboon."

"Ah, yes, of course! Well, a cheetah is just a big cat, and yet a saucer of milk does not go very far in satisfying its wants, I daresay. There is one point which I should wish

Mood

Do Holmes's observations and questions convey a mood of lightheartedness or seriousness? Explain.

to determine." He squatted down in front of the wooden chair and examined the seat of it with the greatest attention.

"Thank you. That is quite settled," said he, rising and putting his lens in his pocket. "Hello! Here is something interesting!"

The object which had caught his eye was a small dog lash hung on one corner of the bed. The lash, however, was curled upon itself and tied so as to make a loop of whipcord.

"What do you make of that, Watson?"

"It's a common enough lash. But I don't know why it should be tied."

"That is not quite so common, is it? Ah, me! it's a wicked world, and when a clever man turns his brains to crime it is the worst of all. I think that I have seen enough now, Miss Stoner, and with your permission we shall walk out upon the lawn."

I had never seen my friend's face so grim or his brow so dark as it was when we turned from the scene of this investigation. We had walked several times up and down the lawn, neither Miss Stoner nor myself liking to break in upon his thoughts before he roused himself from his reverie.[11]

"It is very essential, Miss Stoner," said he, "that you should absolutely follow my advice in every respect."

"I shall most certainly do so."

"The matter is too serious for any hesitation. Your life may depend upon your compliance."

"I assure you that I am in your hands."

"In the first place, both my friend and I must spend the night in your room."

Both Miss Stoner and I gazed at him in astonishment.

"Yes, it must be so. Let me explain. I believe that that is the village inn over there?"

"Yes, that is the Crown."

"Very good. Your windows would be visible from there?"

"Certainly."

"You must confine yourself to your room, on pretense of a headache, when your stepfather comes back. Then when you hear him retire for the night, you must open the shutters

---

Mood
Describe the mood that is created as Holmes walks up and down the lawn.

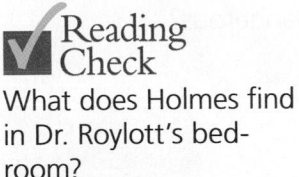

Reading Check
What does Holmes find in Dr. Roylott's bedroom?

---

11. **reverie** (rev′ ə rē) *n.* dreamy thinking or imagining.

of your window, undo the hasp,[12] put your lamp there as a signal to us, and then withdraw quietly with everything which you are likely to want into the room which you used to occupy. I have no doubt that, in spite of the repairs, you could manage there for one night."

"Oh, yes, easily."

"The rest you will leave in our hands."

"But what will you do?"

"We shall spend the night in your room, and we shall investigate the cause of this noise which has disturbed you."

"I believe, Mr. Holmes, that you have already made up your mind," said Miss Stoner, laying her hand upon my companion's sleeve.

"Perhaps I have."

"Then, for pity's sake, tell me what was the cause of my sister's death."

"I should prefer to have clearer proofs before I speak."

"You can at least tell me whether my own thought is correct, and if she died from some sudden fright."

"No, I do not think so. I think that there was probably some more tangible cause. And now, Miss Stoner, we must leave you, for if Dr. Roylott returned and saw us our journey would be in vain. Goodbye, and be brave, for if you will do what I have told you, you may rest assured that we shall soon drive away the dangers that threaten you."

Sherlock Holmes and I had no difficulty in engaging a bedroom and sitting room at the Crown Inn. They were on the upper floor, and from our window we could command a view of the avenue gate, and of the inhabited wing of Stoke Moran Manor House. At dusk we saw Dr. Grimesby Roylott drive past, his huge form looming up beside the little figure of the lad who drove him. The boy had some slight difficulty in undoing the heavy iron gates, and we heard the hoarse roar of the doctor's voice and saw the fury with which he shook his clinched fists at him. The trap drove on, and a few minutes later we saw a sudden light spring up among the trees as the lamp was lit in one of the sitting rooms.

"Do you know, Watson," said Holmes as we sat together in the gathering darkness, "I have really some scruples as to taking you tonight. There is a distinct element of danger."

Vocabulary
tangible (tan´ jə bəl) *adj.* actual or real; able to be perceived by the senses, especially that of touch

Author's Purpose
What details in this paragraph help you remember why the situation is dangerous?

---

12. **hasp** *n.* hinged metal fastening of a window.

"Can I be of assistance?"

"Your presence might be *invaluable*."

"Then I shall certainly come."

"It is very kind of you."

"You speak of danger. You have evidently seen more in these rooms than was visible to me."

"No, but I fancy that I may have deduced a little more. I imagine that you saw all that I did."

"I saw nothing remarkable save the bell-rope, and what purpose that could answer I confess is more than I can imagine."

"You saw the ventilator, too?"

"Yes, but I do not think that it is such a very unusual thing to have a small opening between two rooms. It was so small that a rat could hardly pass through."

"I knew that we should find a ventilator before ever we came to Stoke Moran."

"My dear Holmes!"

"Oh, yes, I did. You remember in her statement she said that her sister could smell Dr. Roylott's cigar. Now, of course that suggested at once that there must be a communication between the two rooms. It could only be a small one, or it would have been remarked upon at the coroner's inquiry. I deduced a ventilator."

"But what harm can there be in that?"

"Well, there is at least a curious coincidence of dates. A ventilator is made, a cord is hung, and a lady who sleeps in the bed dies. Does not that strike you?"

"I cannot as yet see any connection."

"Did you observe anything very peculiar about that bed?"

"No."

"It was clamped to the floor. Did you ever see a bed fastened like that before?"

"I cannot say that I have."

"The lady could not move her bed. It must always be in the same relative position to the ventilator and to the rope—or so we may call it, since it was clearly never meant for a bell-pull."

"Holmes," I cried, "I seem to see dimly what you are hinting at. We are only just in time to prevent some subtle and horrible crime."

"Subtle enough and horrible enough. When a doctor does go wrong he is the first of criminals. He has nerve and he has

Vocabulary
invaluable (in val´ yo͞o ə bəl) *adj.* extremely useful

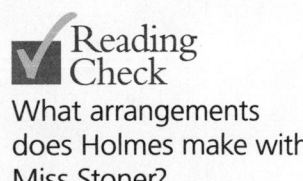

Reading Check

What arrangements does Holmes make with Miss Stoner?

Science Connection

DNA Fingerprinting

In modern times, detectives can solve crimes using DNA evidence from hair, blood, or saliva collected at the crime scene. Here is how the process works:

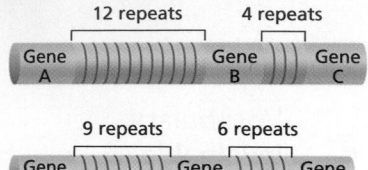

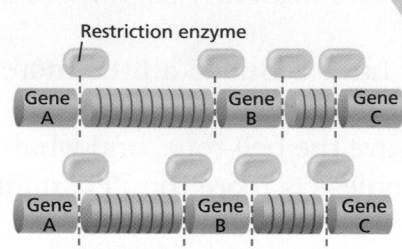

Restriction enzyme

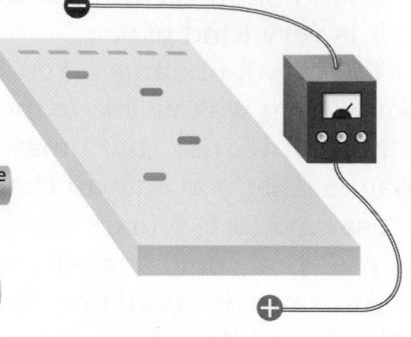

▲ With the exception of identical twins, each of us has unique DNA. Chromosomes have large amounts of DNA called repeats.

▲ For identification purposes, restriction enzymes are used to cut DNA into fragments containing genes and repeats.

▲ The fragments are separated by size using a machine like the one shown. The ones with repeats are labeled using radioactive probes.

S 1
S 2
E(v s)

▲ The result is a series of bands—
◄ the DNA fingerprint. Fans of this technique believe it is sensitive enough to identify one person from 100,000 to 1 million others.

Connect to the Literature Would DNA fingerprinting help Holmes solve this particular mystery? Why or why not?

Mood
List three words or phrases in this paragraph that hint at danger.

knowledge. Palmer and Pritchard were among the heads of their profession. This man strikes even deeper, but I think, Watson, that we shall be able to strike deeper still. But we shall have horrors enough before the night is over; for goodness' sake let us have a quiet pipe and turn our minds for a few hours to something more cheerful."

About nine o'clock the light among the trees was extinguished, and all was dark in the direction of the Manor House. Two hours passed slowly away, and then, suddenly, just

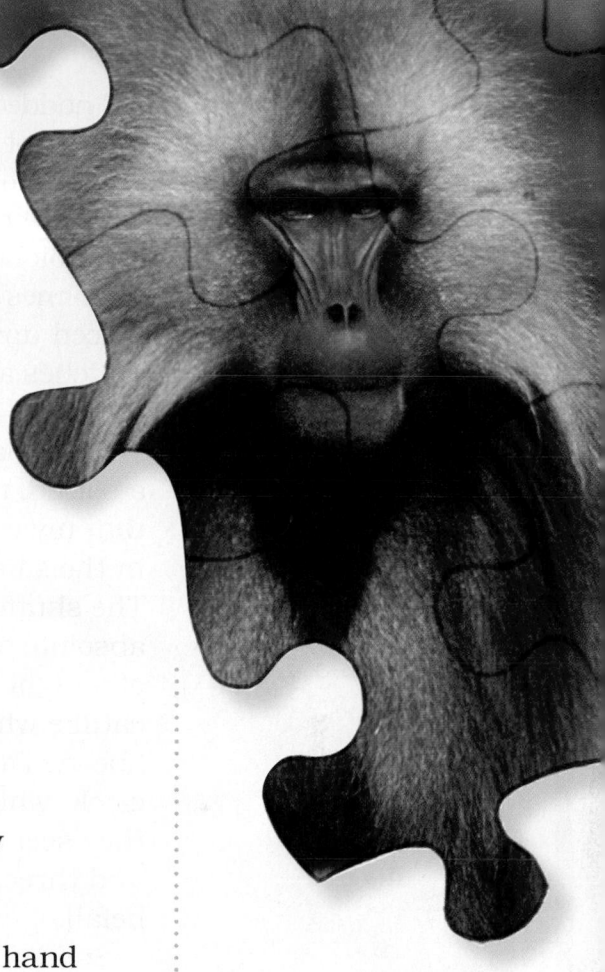

at the stroke of eleven, a single bright light shone out right in front of us.

"That is our signal," said Holmes, springing to his feet; "it comes from the middle window."

As we passed out he exchanged a few words with the landlord, explaining that we were going on a late visit to an acquaintance, and that it was possible that we might spend the night there. A moment later we were out on the dark road, a chill wind blowing in our faces, and one yellow light twinkling in front of us through the gloom to guide us on our somber errand.

There was little difficulty in entering the grounds; for unrepaired breaches gaped in the old park wall. Making our way among the trees, we reached the lawn, crossed it, and were about to enter through the window when out from a clump of laurel bushes there darted what seemed to be a hideous and distorted child, who threw itself upon the grass with writhing limbs and then ran swiftly across the lawn into the darkness.

"My God!" I whispered; "did you see it?"

Holmes was for the moment as startled as I. His hand closed like a vise upon my wrist in his agitation. Then he broke into a low laugh and put his lips to my ear.

"It is a nice household," he murmured. "That is the baboon."

I had forgotten the strange pets which the doctor affected. There was a cheetah, too; perhaps we might find it upon our shoulders at any moment. I confess that I felt easier in my mind when, after following Holmes's example and slipping off my shoes, I found myself inside the bedroom. My companion noiselessly closed the shutters, moved the lamp onto the table, and cast his eyes round the room. All was as we had seen it in the daytime. Then creeping up to me and making a trumpet of his hand, he whispered into my ear again so gently that it was all that I could do to distinguish the words:

"The least sound would be fatal to our plans."

I nodded to show that I had heard.

"We must sit without light. He would see it through the ventilator."

Author's Purpose
Why do you think the author includes the startling incident with the baboon?

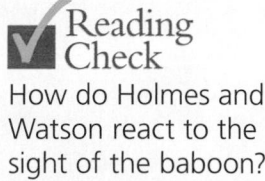

How do Holmes and Watson react to the sight of the baboon?

The Adventure of the Speckled Band **147**

I nodded again.

"Do not go asleep; your very life may depend upon it. Have your pistol ready in case we should need it. I will sit on the side of the bed, and you in that chair."

I took out my revolver and laid it on the corner of the table.

Holmes had brought up a long thin cane, and this he placed upon the bed beside him. By it he laid the box of matches and the stump of a candle. Then he turned down the lamp, and we were left in darkness.

How shall I ever forget that dreadful vigil?[13] I could not hear a sound, not even the drawing of a breath, and yet I knew that my companion sat open-eyed, within a few feet of me, in the same state of nervous tension in which I was myself. The shutters cut off the least ray of light, and we waited in absolute darkness. From outside came the occasional cry of a night bird, and once at our very window a long-drawn catlike whine, which told us that the cheetah was indeed at liberty. Far away we could hear the deep tones of the parish clock, which boomed out every quarter of an hour. How long they seemed, those quarters! Twelve struck, and one and two and three, and still we sat waiting silently for whatever might befall.

Suddenly there was the momentary gleam of a light up in the direction of the ventilator, which vanished immediately, but was succeeded by a strong smell of burning oil and heated metal. Someone in the next room had lit a dark lantern.[14] I heard a gentle sound of movement, and then all was silent once more, though the smell grew stronger. For half an hour I sat with straining ears. Then suddenly another sound became audible—a very gentle, soothing sound, like that of a small jet of steam escaping continually from a kettle. The instant that we heard it, Holmes sprang from the bed, struck a match, and lashed furiously with his cane at the bell-pull.

"You see it, Watson?" he yelled. "You see it?"

But I saw nothing. At the moment when Holmes struck the light I heard a low, clear whistle, but the sudden glare flashing into my weary eyes made it impossible for me to tell what it was at which my friend lashed so savagely. I could,

Mood
List three elements of the setting in this paragraph that add to the mood of dread.

---

13. **vigil** (vij´əl) *n.* watch; period of staying awake during the usual hours of sleep.
14. **dark lantern** lantern with a shutter that can hide the light.

◄ **Critical Viewing**
Does this illustration effectively capture a sense of extreme danger? Why or why not?
[Make a Judgment]

however, see that his face was deadly pale and filled with horror and loathing.

He had ceased to strike and was gazing up at the ventilator when suddenly there broke from the silence of the night the most horrible cry to which I have ever listened. It swelled up louder and louder, a hoarse yell of pain and fear and anger all mingled in the one dreadful shriek. They say that away down in the village, and even in the distant parsonage, that cry raised the sleepers from their beds. It struck cold to our hearts, and I stood gazing at Holmes, and he at me, until the last echoes of it had died away into the silence from which it rose.

"What can it mean?" I gasped.

"It means that it is all over," Holmes answered. "And perhaps, after all, it is for the best. Take your pistol, and we will enter Dr. Roylott's room."

With a grave face he lit the lamp and led the way down the corridor. Twice he struck at the chamber door without any reply from within. Then he turned the handle and entered, I at his heels, with the cocked pistol in my hand.

It was a singular sight which met our eyes. On the table stood a dark lantern with the shutter half open, throwing a brilliant beam of light upon the iron safe, the door of which was ajar. Beside this table, on the wooden chair, sat

✓ **Reading Check**
How does Holmes react to the gleam of light and the sound of movement?

Dr. Grimesby Roylott, clad in a long gray dressing gown, his bare ankles protruding beneath, and his feet thrust into red heelless Turkish slippers. Across his lap lay the short stock with the long lash which we had noticed during the day. His chin was cocked upward and his eyes were fixed in a dreadful, rigid stare at the corner of the ceiling. Round his brow he had a peculiar yellow band, with brownish speckles, which seemed to be bound tightly round his head. As we entered he made neither sound nor motion.

"The band! the speckled band!" whispered Holmes.

I took a step forward. In an instant his strange headgear began to move, and there reared itself from among his hair the squat diamond-shaped head and puffed neck of a loathsome serpent.

"It is a swamp adder!" cried Holmes; "the deadliest snake in India. He has died within ten seconds of being bitten. Violence does, in truth, recoil upon the violent, and the schemer falls into the pit which he digs for another. Let us thrust this creature back into its den, and we can then remove Miss Stoner to some place of shelter and let the county police know what has happened."

As he spoke he drew the dog whip swiftly from the dead man's lap, and throwing the noose round the reptile's neck he drew it from its horrid perch and, carrying it at arm's length, threw it into the iron safe, which he closed upon it.

Such are the true facts of the death of Dr. Grimesby Roylott, of Stoke Moran. It is not necessary that I should prolong a narrative which has already run to too great a length by telling how we broke the sad news to the terrified girl, how we conveyed her by the morning train to the care of her good aunt at Harrow, of how the slow process of official inquiry came to the conclusion that the doctor met his fate while indiscreetly playing with a dangerous pet. The little which I had yet to learn of the case was told me by Sherlock Holmes as we traveled back next day.

"I had," said he,

Vocabulary
indiscreetly (in´di skrēt´ lē) *adv.* carelessly

"come to an entirely erroneous conclusion which shows, my dear Watson, how dangerous it always is to reason from insufficient data. The presence of the gypsies, and the use of the word band, which was used by the poor girl, no doubt to explain the appearance which she had caught a hurried glimpse of by the light of her match, were sufficient to put me upon an entirely wrong scent. I can only claim the merit that I instantly reconsidered my position when, however, it became clear to me that whatever danger threatened an occupant of the room could not come either from the window or the door. My attention was speedily drawn, as I have already remarked to you, to this ventilator, and to the bell-rope which hung down to the bed. The discovery that this was a dummy, and that the bed was clamped to the floor, instantly gave rise to the suspicion that the rope was there as a bridge for something passing through the hole and coming to the bed. The idea of a snake instantly occurred to me, and when I coupled it with my knowledge that the doctor was furnished with a supply of creatures from India, I felt that I was probably on the right track. The idea of using a form of poison which could not possibly be discovered by any chemical test was just such a one as would occur to a clever and ruthless man who had had an Eastern training. The rapidity with which such a poison would take effect would also, from his point of view, be an advantage. It would be a sharp-eyed coroner, indeed, who could distinguish the two little dark punctures which would show where the poison fangs had done their work. Then I thought of the whistle. Of course he must recall the snake before the morning light revealed it to the victim. He had trained it, probably by the use of the milk which we saw, to return to him when summoned. He would put it through this ventilator at the hour that he thought best, with the certainty that it would crawl down the rope and land on the bed. It might or might not bite the occupant, perhaps she might escape every night for a week, but sooner or later she must fall a victim.

"I had come to these conclusions before ever I had entered his room. An inspection of his chair showed me that he had been in the habit of standing on it, which of course would be necessary in order that he should reach the ventilator. The sight of the safe, the saucer of milk, and the loop of whipcord

Mood
How does the mood shift in this final part of the story?

Reading Check
What was the "speckled band?"

Author's Purpose
Why does Doyle include this explanation of how Holmes solved the case?

were enough to finally dispel any doubts which may have remained. The metallic clang heard by Miss Stoner was obviously caused by her stepfather hastily closing the door of his safe upon its terrible occupant. Having once made up my mind, you know the steps which I took in order to put the matter to the proof. I heard the creature hiss as I have no doubt that you did also, and I instantly lit the light and attacked it."

"With the result of driving it through the ventilator."

"And also with the result of causing it to turn upon its master at the other side. Some of the blows of my cane came home and roused its snakish temper, so that it flew upon the first person it saw. In this way I am no doubt indirectly responsible for Dr. Grimesby Roylott's death, and I cannot say that it is likely to weigh very heavily upon my conscience."

Critical Thinking

Cite textual evidence to support your responses.

1. **Key Ideas and Details** **(a)** Why does Helen Stoner come to see Holmes? **(b) Compare:** In what three ways is Helen's situation when she visits Holmes similar to Julia's just before she dies?

2. **Key Ideas and Details** **(a)** What clues does Holmes use to solve the mystery? **(b) Speculate:** What do you think would have happened if Helen had not consulted Holmes?

3. **Integration of Knowledge and Ideas** **Make a Judgment:** Holmes says that he is indirectly responsible for Roylott's death. In your judgment, who is most responsible for Roylott's death? Explain.

4. **Integration of Knowledge and Ideas** When the truth about Julia's death is revealed, it affects the characters in different ways. **(a)** Explain the effects of this truth on Holmes. **(b)** Explain the effects of this truth on Helen Stoner. *[Connect to the Big Question: Is truth the same for everyone?]*

Reading Skill: Author's Purpose

1. **(a)** In the story's first paragraph, what details does Dr. Watson provide about Holmes's cases? **(b)** Using these details, what can you infer is the author's general **purpose?**

2. How does each of the following details contribute to the author's general purpose? **(a)** Holmes's conversation with Dr. Roylott; **(b)** Holmes's explanation of how he figured out the mystery; **(c)** Holmes's comment at the end of the story.

Literary Analysis: Mood

© 3. **Key Ideas and Details** What is the **mood** of the scene in which Holmes and Watson are waiting in the bedroom at Stoke Moran? Support your answer with details about the **setting.**

© 4. **Key Ideas and Details** When Helen describes the night her sister died, the mood is one of terror and mystery. Use a chart like the one shown to list words, phrases, and images that contribute to this mood.

Words	Phrases	Images

Vocabulary

© **Acquisition and Use** Explain your answers to these questions.

1. How does a doctor make *deductions* about an illness?
2. Is it wise to *avert* a possible collision?
3. Would a *sinister* clown frighten small children?
4. If you were walking alone at night, what might give you a *tangible* cause to be nervous?
5. If a person gave you *invaluable* advice, would you be happy?
6. How could speaking *indiscreetly* cause an awkward situation?

Word Study Use the context of the sentences and what you know about the **Latin root -duc-** to explain each answer.

1. If you *reduce* the weight of a load, does it get heavier?
2. Why might it be valuable for a city to construct an *aqueduct*?

Word Study

The **Latin root -duc-** means "to lead" or "to bring."

Apply It Explain how the root -duc- contributes to the meanings of these words. Consult a dictionary if necessary.

abduct
educate
induce

Integrated Language Skills

from An American Childhood • The Adventure of the Speckled Band

Conventions: Personal Pronouns

Personal pronouns are words that replace nouns in sentences.

Personal pronouns refer to the person speaking, the person spoken to, or the person, place, or thing spoken about. Be sure personal pronouns agree in case and number with their antecedents, the words to which they refer.

The Three Cases of Personal Pronouns		
Case	**Pronouns**	**Use in a Sentence**
Nominative (subject)	I, we, you, he, she, it, they	subject of a sentence or clause (the "giver" of an action)
Objective (object)	me, us, you, him, her, it, them	object of a sentence or clause (the "receiver" of an action)
Possessive	my, mine, our, ours, your, yours, his, her, hers, its, their, theirs	shows ownership

To check **case** or form in a sentence, remove the other noun or pronoun and see if the sentence makes sense.

Practice A Choose the correct pronouns for these sentences and indicate their cases.

1. When Annie wrote about the car, (she/ her) made (it/its) sound like a monster.

2. Both Warren and (I/me) found her descriptions frightening.

3. Annie is older than (her/hers) sister, but (they/them) slept in the same room.

4. Annie and (I/me) are friends because (we/ ours) have much in common.

© **Reading Application** In *An American Childhood,* find and copy a sentence that contains each case of personal pronoun listed in the chart above.

Practice B Complete these sentences by filling in the appropriate personal pronouns.

1. Watson was surprised when Holmes woke ____ so early because ____ knew that Holmes usually slept late.

2. Helen was convinced that ____ sister's death did not happen the way ____ step-father said ____ did.

3. ____ began to suspect that ____ stepfather had plotted against Helen.

© **Writing Application** Choose five sentences from "The Adventure of the Speckled Band" and rewrite them by replacing nouns with pronouns.

PH WRITING COACH   Further instruction and practice are available in *Prentice Hall Writing Coach.*

Writing

Common Core State Standards

L.8.1; W.8.3.a, W.8.3.e, W.8.7, W.8.8
[For the full wording of the standards, see page 110.]

Narrative Text Write a **personal narrative** about an important childhood insight or about a time you used logic or reasoning to solve a problem.

- In the introduction, identify the confusion, puzzle, or problem. Explain why this event was important to you and reveal the first ideas you considered for a solution or answer.

- In the body, discuss the evidence you considered. Describe, in order, the steps you took to reach your insight or solution.

- In the conclusion, explain the outcome. Describe how you felt when you learned the truth or found the answer.

As you write, include only the most important ideas and details.

Grammar Application Make sure personal pronouns in your narrative agree with their antecedents in number and case.

Writing Workshop: *Work in Progress*

Prewriting for Narration To prepare for an autobiographical essay you may write, make a four-column chart. At the top, write an event that taught you something valuable about yourself. In each column, jot down words that explain *What?, How?, Why?,* and *Where?* Save this Brainstorming Chart in your portfolio.

Use this prewriting activity to prepare for the **Writing Workshop** on page 208.

Research and Technology

Build and Present Knowledge Prepare a brief **research report** to present to the class.

- If you read the excerpt from *An American Childhood*, prepare a report about how an important scientific puzzle was solved.

- If you read "The Adventure of the Speckled Band," prepare a report about how a famous real-life crime was solved.

Follow these steps to complete the assignment.

- First, raise questions to help you focus your research. Then identify and use a variety of resources, both electronic and print, to find answers. Evaluate the credibility of sources before using information.

- Use your research to write an organized report. To add interest and authority, include direct quotations wherever possible.

- Be sure to cite your sources for information and quotations. List all of the sources you used in a bibliography at the end. Present to the class an oral report on your research findings.

- Interactive graphic organizers
- Grammar tutorial
- Interactive journals

Before You Read

from **Steinbeck: A Life in Letters** •
from **Travels with Charley**
• **The American Dream**

Ⓒ Leveled Texts

Build your skills and improve your comprehension of nonfiction with texts of increasing complexity.

Read works by John Steinbeck to discover what happens when a writer and his canine companion set out to explore America.

Read **"The American Dream"** to appreciate the deep gulf that Dr. King saw between our nation's ideals and its realities.

Ⓒ Common Core State Standards

Meet these standards with either the works by Steinbeck (p. 160) or **"The American Dream"** (p. 172).

Reading Informational Text
4. Determine the meaning of words and phrases as they are used in a text, including figurative, connotative, and technical meanings; analyze the impact of specific word choices on meaning and tone, including analogies or allusions to other texts. *(Literary Analysis: Author's Style)*

6. Determine an author's point of view or purpose in a text and analyze how the author acknowledges and responds to conflicting evidence or viewpoints. *(Reading Skill: Author's Purpose)*

Spiral Review: RI.8.2

Writing
2. Write informative/explanatory texts to examine a topic and convey ideas, concepts, and information through the selection, organization, and analysis of relevant content. *(Writing: Observation Journal)*

6. Use technology, including the Internet, to produce and publish writing and present the relationships between information and ideas efficiently as well as to interact and collaborate with others. *(Research and Technology: Brochure)*

Language
4.b. Use common, grade-appropriate Greek or Latin affixes and roots as clues to the meaning of a word (e.g., *precede, recede, secede). (Vocabulary: Latin Roots)*

Reading Skill: Author's Purpose

An **author's purpose** is the reason he or she has for writing. It may be to persuade, to entertain, or to provide information. The author's purpose influences the kinds of details he or she includes.

As you read, **evaluate whether the author achieves his or her purpose.** First, determine what the author's purpose is. Then, decide whether the author is successful. For example, if the goal is to persuade, decide if the author's arguments convince you that his or her perspective makes sense. Keep in mind that sometimes an author tries to achieve more than one purpose.

Using the Strategy: Evaluation Chart

Use this **evaluation chart** to evaluate an author's purpose.

Literary Analysis: Author's Style

An **author's style** is his or her particular way of writing. Elements that contribute to an author's style include the following:

- Word choice and length and rhythm of sentences
- The author's heritage, traditions, attitudes, and beliefs
- The author's **tone,** or attitude toward the subject and audience
- Literary devices, such as **metaphor,** a comparison in which something is described as though it were something else, and **simile,** a comparison of two unlike things that uses *like* or *as*

These elements are often connected. For example, an author's word choice helps to set his or her tone. Some writers write informally, using everyday language and straightforward sentences. Other writers use formal words and more complicated sentences. Writers may also use **symbols** as part of their styles. As you read, consider each writer's unique style.

 Is *truth* the same for everyone?

Writing About the Big Question

In *Travels with Charley,* John Steinbeck tours the country to refresh his memory about what Americans are truly like. Use this sentence starter to develop your ideas about the Big Question.

If someone asked me to describe America and Americans, I would say, "From my **observations**, I would describe America as _____ and Americans as _____."

While You Read Notice the author's observations about his travel experiences, and consider whether others would feel the same way.

Vocabulary

Read each word and its definition. Decide whether you know the word well, know it a little bit, or do not know it at all. After you read, see how your knowledge of each word has increased.

- **thrives** (thrīvz) *v.* does well; prospers (p. 161) *A tomato plant thrives, given adequate sunlight and water. thriving adj.*

- **omens** (ō´mənz) *n.* signs of a bad or good event that may take place in the future (p. 164) *We needed a good vacation, but the flat tire and dead battery were bad omens.*
  ominous adj. ominously adv.

- **inexplicable** (in eks pli´ kə bəl) *adj.* impossible to explain (p. 164) *The night brought mysterious and inexplicable sounds. inexplicably adv. inexplicability n. explicate v.*

- **reluctance** (re luk´ təns) *n.* hesitation; unwillingness (p. 164) *To save his dog, Bill had to overcome his reluctance to dive into the icy, fast-moving water. reluctantly adv. reluctant adj.*

- **desolate** (des´ ə lit) *adj.* empty; lonely (p. 165) *At 2 AM, the school parking lot is desolate. desolation n. desolately adv.*

- **foreboding** (fôr bōd´ iŋ) *n.* feeling that something bad will happen (p. 165) *Seeing no one else on the dark street, Juan felt a chill of foreboding. forebodingly adv.*

Word Study

The **Latin root -sol-** means "alone."

In the excerpt from *Travels with Charley,* Steinbeck describes the Badlands of North Dakota as "dry and sharp, **desolate** and dangerous." They are desolate because they are deserted and empty, making him feel alone.

Meet
John Steinbeck
(1902–1968)

from
Author of
Steinbeck: A Life in Letters
and ## Travels with Charley

Living in southern California, John Steinbeck got to know workers on farms, in canning factories, and in fisheries. He watched ordinary Americans suffer during the Depression of the 1930s and sympathized with their struggles.

The Common Touch Steinbeck's experiences and attitudes came to life in novels such as *East of Eden* and *The Grapes of Wrath*. Steinbeck caught the attention of the American public with his vivid descriptions and powerful use of symbols and metaphors. His novels, with their desperate, confused characters, provided American readers a window into the lives of people at the margins of society—people they otherwise might not have met.

A Love of Travel Steinbeck had an attitude of restless curiosity that drove him out onto the road. "When I laid the ground plan of my journey, there were definite questions to which I wanted matching answers. . . . I suppose they could all be lumped into the single question: 'What are Americans like today?'"

BACKGROUND FOR THE SELECTIONS

Steinbeck's America

John Steinbeck is famous for his descriptions of American life. In 1960, he put his powers of observation to the test on a cross-country trip with his poodle Charley. First, in letters, then in the memoir *Travels with Charley*, Steinbeck chronicled life on the road. In the letters and excerpt that follow, Steinbeck describes traveling through Wisconsin, Minnesota, and the Badlands of North Dakota—a region where barren, treeless landscapes and strange rock formations create an otherworldly atmosphere.

DID YOU KNOW?
Steinbeck was one of the few writers to be honored with both the Pulitzer Prize and the Nobel Prize for Literature.

from Steinbeck: A Life in Letters

JOHN STEINBECK

Background As a writer, John Steinbeck built a career on observing and describing Americans from all walks of life. But, by 1960, he felt he had lost touch with America. Steinbeck's solution was simple. He would travel cross-country and then write about his experiences. The famous author grew a beard, hoping to avoid being recognized, and took along his French poodle, Charley, for company. A custom-built camper top mounted on his truck allowed him to sleep and eat wherever he pleased. While on the road, Steinbeck wrote the following letters to his wife, Elaine.

Aroostook County, Maine
September 29, 1960
Thursday

Darling:

I drove very far today. Nearly to the top of Aroostook County and then in and way down. I think I am not very far from the New Hampshire border now but night caught us and rain so we are bedded down behind a bridge and it is still raining, but we are dry and I cooked lima beans and gorged on them. Maine is a monster big state. The leaves are flaming now—never saw such colors.

Charley thrives. He loves it but has taken to sleeping in the seat with his head in my lap. I still haven't combed him. What with driving and cooking and doing the truck up and down and trying to find my way and sleeping, I've had no time to comb and clip Charley. I guess he's just as glad.

It was good to hear you last night. It was in a small grocery store with truck drivers tripping over me.

I find I am terrible lonesome tonight. And so I won't go on about it. But I miss you dreadful. Been gone a week today. It seems like more.

Good night darling.

[unsigned]

Not far from
Detroit Lakes, Minnesota
October 11 [1960]

Dear Monsoon:[1]

Seems impossible that you went yesterday morning. It seems very much longer ago than that. I've been through so many kinds of country. I'm camped in a row of great cattle trailers—longer than box cars. Got to talking to the man at the gas pump and he invited me to stay. These big trailers have taken it away from the railroads. This is also turkey country. Just below this hill the earth is black with them.

Author's Purpose
How do the details Steinbeck chooses reflect his purpose for writing?

Vocabulary
thrives (thrīvz) *v.*
does well; prospers

◄ **Critical Viewing**
Why would a pet like Charley, pictured here with Steinbeck, be a good companion on a cross-country trip? **[Speculate]**

---

1. **Monsoon** (män soon´) John Steinbeck often used affectionate nicknames when writing letters to his wife. The literal meaning of *monsoon* is a strong, seasonal wind that blows heavy rains from the Indian Ocean into parts of Southeast Asia.

Author's Style
Does the rhythm of
Steinbeck's writing here
contribute to a formal
or an informal tone?
Explain.

There must be ten thousand turkeys in the one flock.

I guess Wisconsin is the prettiest state I ever saw—more kinds of country—hills and groves like Somerset, and the Dells a strange place of water and odd mushroom-shaped rocks. Lousy with tourist places but nearly all closed now with signs saying—"See you next spring." Then I got into St. Paul and Minneapolis. There must be some way to avoid them but I didn't make it. Crawling with traffic. Took a good time to get out of that. So I've been in Minnesota all afternoon and now am not far from the North Dakota border. At breakfast a trucker told me how women drove the big trucks during the war. I said, "My god, they must have been Amazons,"[2] and he replied, "I don't know. I never fought one." I've talked to lots of people today. Stopped quite a lot. One argument—did you know if you bake a doughnut, it will float? I'm just repeating what I heard. And I heard that Dag Hammarskjöld could easy be President.[3] When I suggested that he was a Swede the reply was—"What of it?" I think I'll write that to him.

I know you think just because I'm away from you and you can't check on me, that I make up things. I'll just have to ask you to believe there is Swiss cheese candy. No, I didn't taste it, I just saw the sign. Also that the largest collection of Sea Shells in the world is on Route 12 in Wisconsin. Who could make up things like that? Who would want to?

I know E.O.[4] wouldn't approve of the speed with which I am covering ground but I'm sure seeing lots and hearing lots.

---

2. **Amazons** (ām´ə zänz´) mythical warrior women, famous for their fierceness and strength.

3. **Dag Hammarskjöld...President.** Swedish diplomat who served as Secretary General of the United Nations from 1953 to 1961. The man's statement is comical because any foreign-born person is barred by the Constitution from serving as president of the United States.

4. **E.O.** Elaine Otis, the literary agent of John Steinbeck, with whom he had discussed writing a book based on his travels.

▲ ▶ **Critical Viewing**
What might an observer
find striking about the
Upper Midwestern land-
scapes shown in these
photos? **[Speculate]**

People don't talk about issues. They talk about how you bake a doughnut and it will float. There's lots of local politics talked but I can't see much interest in the national. But plenty in the U.N.[5] Washington is so far away. A man today looked at my license plates and said, "Clear from New York." But mostly it's hunting and stories about hunting. The bombardment against ducks starts at dawn.

I went from maple country which is flame red to birch which is flame yellow. You would have oohed quite a lot, aahed some. I stopped at a sign that said "home made sausages," and bought some. I'm cooking it now and it smells really wonderful. And at another place I got apples that just explode with juice when you bite them. There's no doubt that frost does something to them. But it's stopping like this that gets talk going. Everyone wants to see the inside of the truck. I even do the floors with Lestoil and I keep the stove shined. When they see the guns they say, "Oh, going hunting!" and never ask another question. Because of the cap and beard they usually take me for a retired sailor and make jokes about do I get car sick. I say I sure do. On the Duluth and Minneapolis radio there is a great block of advertising for Florida real estate. I listened carefully and all it promises is that it is in Florida.

I'll go through Fargo tomorrow morning and by the time I call you tomorrow night I'll be deep in North Dakota. From now on there will be long stretches less populated. In two days I'll be climbing toward the Rockies.

Well, I had the sausage and it was just as good as it smelled. And I didn't even splash grease on this letter.

They're loading cattle outside with floodlights. Must get out to see that. The truckers are a set-apart bunch of men. The long distance ones are exactly like sailors. I suppose they have homes but they live on the road and stop to sleep.

Well I watched. Two truckloads of yearlings. Going south to be fed—but bull calves. The beefers are kept for milk. There is too Swiss cheese candy.

I miss you already. Time gets all out of kilter.

Good night my love.

Tobit

---

5. **U.N.** United Nations.

Author's Style
Interpret the meaning of the simile Steinbeck uses to describe long distance truckers.

Reading Check
Why do people think Steinbeck is a retired sailor?

from Travels with Charley

JOHN STEINBECK

Later, Steinbeck collected his thoughts and impressions and wrote the bestselling memoir, Travels with Charley, *published two years after his trip. The following excerpt from the memoir describes the part of his trip that came after his experiences in Wisconsin and Minnesota.*

▶ **Critical Viewing**
How does the picture on p. 165 compare to the scene Steinbeck describes in this paragraph? **[Compare and Contrast]**

Vocabulary
omens (ō´mənz´) *n.* signs of bad or good events that may take place in the future

inexplicable (in eks pli´ kə bəl) *adj.* impossible to explain

reluctance (ri luk´ təns) *n.* hesitation; unwillingness

© **Spiral Review**
Central Idea What possible central idea is suggested by Steinbeck's reaction to the wind?

The night was loaded with omens. The grieving sky turned the little water to a dangerous metal and then the wind got up—not the gusty, rabbity wind of the seacoasts I know but a great bursting sweep of wind with nothing to inhibit it for a thousand miles in any direction. Because it was a wind strange to me, and therefore mysterious, it set up mysterious responses in me. In terms of reason, it was strange only because I found it so. But a goodly part of our experience which we find inexplicable must be like that. To my certain knowledge, many people conceal experiences for fear of ridicule. How many people have seen or heard or felt something which so outraged their sense of what should be that the whole thing was brushed quickly away like dirt under a rug?

For myself, I try to keep the line open even for things I can't understand or explain, but it is difficult in this frightened time. At this moment in North Dakota I had a reluctance to drive on that amounted to fear. At the same time, Charley wanted to go—in fact, made such a commotion about going that I tried to reason with him.

"Listen to me, dog. I have a strong impulse to stay amounting to **celestial** command. If I should overcome it and go and a great snow should close in on us, I would recognize it as a warning disregarded. If we stay and a big snow should come I would be certain I had a pipeline to prophecy."

Charley sneezed and paced restlessly. "All right, *mon cur*,[6] let's take your side of it. You want to go on. Suppose we do, and in the night a tree should crash down right where we are presently standing. It would be you who have the attention of the gods. And there is always that chance. I could tell you

---

6. *mon cur* (mōn kʉr´) French slang for "my dear mutt."

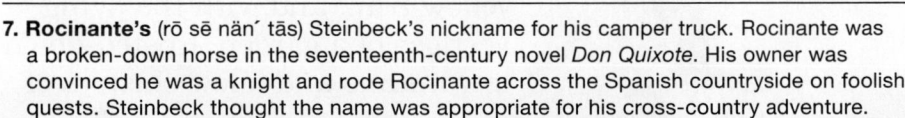

many stories about faithful animals who saved their masters, but I think you are just bored and I'm not going to flatter you." Charley leveled at me his most cynical eye. I think he is neither a romantic nor a mystic. "I know what you mean. If we go, and no tree crashes down, or stay and no snow falls—what then? I'll tell you what then. We forget the whole episode and the field of prophecy is in no way injured. I vote to stay. You vote to go. But being nearer the pinnacle of creation than you, and also president, I cast the deciding vote."

We stayed and it didn't snow and no tree fell, so naturally we forgot the whole thing and are wide open for more mystic feelings when they come. And in the early morning swept clean of clouds and telescopically clear, we crunched around on the thick white ground cover of frost and got under way. The caravan of the arts was dark but the dog barked as we ground up to the highway.

Someone must have told me about the Missouri River at Bismarck, North Dakota, or I must have read about it. In either case, I hadn't paid attention. I came on it in amazement. Here is where the map should fold. Here is the boundary between east and west. On the Bismarck side it is eastern landscape, eastern grass, with the look and smell of eastern America. Across the Missouri on the Mandan side, it is pure west, with brown grass and water scorings and small outcrops. The two sides of the river might well be a thousand miles apart. As I was not prepared for the Missouri boundary, so I was not prepared for the Bad Lands. They deserve this name. They are like the work of an evil child. Such a place the Fallen Angels might have built as a spite to Heaven, dry and sharp, desolate and dangerous, and for me filled with foreboding. A sense comes from it that it does not like or welcome humans. But humans being what they are, and I being human, I turned off the highway on a shaley road and headed in among the buttes, but with a shyness as though I crashed a party. The road surface tore viciously at my tires and made Rocinante's[7] overloaded springs

---

7. **Rocinante's** (rō sē nän´ tās) Steinbeck's nickname for his camper truck. Rocinante was a broken-down horse in the seventeenth-century novel *Don Quixote*. His owner was convinced he was a knight and rode Rocinante across the Spanish countryside on foolish quests. Steinbeck thought the name was appropriate for his cross-country adventure.

Author's Style
What effect does the unusual nature of the "Bad Lands" have on Steinbeck's attitude, tone, and style?

Vocabulary
foreboding (fôr bōd´ iŋ) *n.* feeling that something bad will happen
desolate (des´ ə lit) *adj.* empty; lonely

Reading Check
What reaction does Steinbeck have when he sees the "Bad Lands"?

cry with anguish. What a place for a colony of troglodytes, or better, of trolls. And here's an odd thing. Just as I felt unwanted in this land, so do I feel a reluctance in writing about it. ●

Presently I saw a man leaning on a two-strand barbed-wire fence, the wires fixed not to posts but to crooked tree limbs stuck in the ground. The man wore a dark hat, and jeans and long jacket washed palest blue with lighter places at knees and elbows. His pale eyes were frosted with sun glare and his lips scaly as snakeskin. A .22 rifle leaned against the fence beside him and on the ground lay a little heap of fur and feathers—rabbits and small birds.

I pulled up to speak to him, saw his eyes wash over Rocinante, sweep up the details, and then retire into their sockets. And I found I had nothing to say to him. The "Looks like an early winter," or "Any good fishing hereabouts?" didn't seem to apply. And so we simply brooded at each other.

"Afternoon!"

"Yes, sir," he said.

"Any place nearby where I can buy some eggs?"

"Not real close by 'less you want to go as far as Galva or up to Beach."

"I was set for some scratch-hen eggs."

"Powdered," he said. "My Mrs. gets powdered."

"Lived here long?"

"Yep."

I waited for him to ask something or to say something so we could go on, but he didn't. And as the silence continued, it became more and more impossible to think of something to say. I made one more try. "Does it get very cold here winters?"

"Fairly."

"You talk too much."

He grinned. "That's what my Mrs. says."

"So long," I said, and put the car in gear and moved along. And in my rear-view mirror I couldn't see that he looked after me. He may not be a typical Badlander, but he's one of the few I caught.

A little farther along I stopped at a small house, a section of war-surplus barracks, it looked, but painted white with yellow trim, and with the dying vestiges of a garden, frosted-down geraniums and a few clusters of

▼ **Critical Viewing**
What aspects of the man in this photograph reflect the realities of living in a harsh environment like the Badlands? **[Analyze]**

Author's Purpose
How does the use of dialogue support the author's main purpose for writing?

chrysanthemums, little button things yellow and red-brown. I walked up the path with the certainty that I was being regarded from behind the white window curtains. An old woman answered my knock and gave me the drink of water I asked for and nearly talked my arm off. She was hungry to talk, frantic to talk, about her relatives, her friends, and how she wasn't used to this. For she was not a native and she didn't rightly belong here. Her native clime was a land of milk and honey and had its share of apes and ivory and peacocks. Her voice rattled on as though she was terrified of the silence that would settle when I was gone. As she talked it came to me that she was afraid of this place and, further, that so was I. I felt I wouldn't like to have the night catch me here.

I went into a state of flight, running to get away from the unearthly landscape. And then the late afternoon changed everything. As the sun angled, the buttes and coulees, the cliffs and sculptured hills and ravines lost their burned and dreadful look and glowed with yellow and rich browns and a hundred variations of red and silver gray, all picked out by streaks of coal black. It was so beautiful that I stopped near a thicket of dwarfed and wind-warped cedars and junipers, and once stopped I was caught, trapped in color and dazzled by the clarity of the light. Against the descending sun the battlements were dark and clean-lined, while to the east, where the uninhibited light poured slantwise, the strange landscape shouted with color. And the night, far from being frightful, was lovely beyond thought, for the stars were close, and although there was no moon the starlight made a silver glow in the sky. The air cut the nostrils with dry frost. And

Author's Purpose
Why does Steinbeck include descriptions of the people he meets in the middle of descriptions of the landscape? Explain.

▲ **Critical Viewing**
Does this look like the kind of landscape that you would linger to enjoy, or one from which you would hurry away? Why?
[Make a Judgment]

Reading Check
What does Steinbeck run from?

for pure pleasure I collected a pile of dry dead cedar branches and built a small fire just to smell the perfume of the burning wood and to hear the excited crackle of the branches. My fire made a dome of yellow light over me, and nearby I heard a screech owl hunting and a barking of coyotes, not howling but the short chuckling bark of the dark of the moon. This is one of the few places I have ever seen where the night was friendlier than the day. And I can easily see how people are driven back to the Bad Lands.

Before I slept I spread a map on my bed, a Charley-tromped map. Beach was not far away, and that would be the end of North Dakota. And coming up would be Montana, where I had never been. That night was so cold that I put on my insulated underwear for pajamas, and when Charley had done his duties and had his biscuits and consumed his usual gallon of water and finally curled up in his place under the bed, I dug out an extra blanket and covered him—all except the tip of his nose—and he sighed and wriggled and gave a great groan of pure ecstatic comfort. And I thought how every safe generality I gathered in my travels was canceled by another. In the night the Bad Lands had become Good Lands. I can't explain it. That's how it was.

Critical Thinking

Cite textual evidence to support your responses.

© **1. Key Ideas and Details (a)** List three statements that Steinbeck makes in his letters that show his attitude toward travel or toward new experiences. **(b) Analyze:** What belief does each statement reflect? **(c) Synthesize:** How are these attitudes and beliefs supported by those reflected in his memoir?

© **2. Key Ideas and Details** In what ways are the two Badlanders whom Steinbeck meets similar to and different from him?

© **3. Key Ideas and Details (a)** How does Steinbeck's attitude toward the Badlands change? **(b)** What conclusion about travel does he draw as a result of this change in attitude?

© **4. Integration of Knowledge and Ideas** Would a different visitor be likely to take away the same truths about the Badlands that Steinbeck did? Why or why not? *[Connect to the Big Question: Is truth the same for everyone?]*

from **Steinbeck: A Life in Letters**
from **Travels with Charley**

Reading Skill: Author's Purpose

1. What is Steinbeck's **purpose** in writing these excerpts? Explain, using details from the excerpts.

2. Review the details Steinbeck includes, and **evaluate** whether he achieves his purpose. Explain.

Literary Analysis: Author's Style

© 3. **Craft and Structure** Make a chart to analyze the **author's style.** In each box, describe that feature of Steinbeck's writing, and give an example.

```
Sentence Length  <-->  ( Steinbeck's Style )  <-->  Word Choice

Literary Devices <-->                          <-->  Tone
```

© 4. **Craft and Structure** Use your chart to compare and contrast the style of Steinbeck's memoir and letters. **(a)** What elements carry through both selections? **(b)** How does the change in audience affect his tone and writing style?

Vocabulary

© **Acquisition and Use** Review the vocabulary list on page 158. Decide if each statement is true or false. Explain your response.

1. Bacteria do not *thrive* in warm, moist environments.
2. A dark, cloudy sky is a good *omen* for an enjoyable picnic.
3. The reason why humans float in space is *inexplicable*.
4. Shy people often show a *reluctance* to start conversations.
5. An abandoned farmhouse would feel *desolate*.
6. A sense of *foreboding* might make you shiver.

Word Study Use the context of the sentences and what you know about the **Latin root -sol-** to explain each answer.

1. Is a *solitary* person surrounded by friends?
2. Does someone flying *solo* have a copilot?

Word Study

The **Latin root -sol-** means "alone."

Apply It Explain how the root -sol- contributes to the meanings of these words. Consult a dictionary if necessary.

soliloquy
isolation
solitude

Is *truth* the same for everyone?

Writing About the Big Question

Martin Luther King, Jr., draws on the Declaration of Independence statement that "all men are created equal" to make his point. Use these sentence starters to develop your own ideas.

In America today, the promise of full equality is **contradicted** by _____.

In America today, the promise of full equality is **confirmed** by _____.

While You Read See if King's dreams of equality match the reality of today's world.

Vocabulary

Read each word and its definition. Decide whether you know the word well, know it a little bit, or do not know it at all. After you read, see how your knowledge of each word has increased.

- **unequivocal** (un′ ē kwiv′ ə kəl) *adj.* clear; plainly understood (p. 173) *The critic stood firm in his <u>unequivocal</u> praise of the film.* unequivocally *adv.* equivocate *v.* equivocation *n.*

- **antithesis** (an tith′ ə sis) *n.* direct opposite (p. 174). *Joy is the <u>antithesis</u> of sorrow.* antithetical *adj.* thesis *n.*

- **paradoxes** (par′ ə daks′ is) *n.* two things that seem directly at odds (p. 174) *To North Americans, the Southern Hemisphere is full of <u>paradoxes</u>, such as snow in July.* paradoxical *adj.* paradoxically *adv.*

- **exploitation** (eks′ ploi tā′ shən) *n.* the act of using another person for selfish purposes (p. 174) *The union called the low wages "<u>exploitation</u> of workers."* exploit *v.* exploitative *adj.*

- **devoid** (di void′) *adj.* completely without (p. 175) *The Dead Sea is <u>devoid</u> of fish species.* void *adj.*

- **perish** (per′ ish) *v.* die; be destroyed or wiped out (p. 176) *Without water, a person will <u>perish</u> within days.* perishable *adj.*

Word Study

The **Latin root -equi-** means "equal."

Language that is *equivocal* can have two or more equally reasonable meanings. In "The American Dream," Dr. King describes the language of the Declaration of Independence as **unequivocal**, or having only one clear meaning.

Meet
Martin Luther King, Jr.
(1929–1968)

Author of
THE AMERICAN DREAM

Many people remember Dr. Martin Luther King, Jr., best for these lines from a speech in 1963: "I have a dream that my four little children will one day live in a nation where they will not be judged by the color of their skin but by the content of their character."

Civil Rights Champion Dr. King's work as a civil rights leader began in 1955, when he led a boycott against the segregated bus system in Montgomery, Alabama. A long campaign of marches and demonstrations followed, with the aim of bringing down the entire system of segregation. King and his fellow activists faced opposition from segregationist governors, hostile crowds, and unsympathetic police officers. Ultimately, King was successful in getting important legislation passed and in drawing national attention to the problems of inequality.

DID YOU KNOW?

During the Montgomery bus boycott, thousands of African Amercians walked miles to work and school in the heat and the rain for more than a year. On November 13, 1956, the Supreme Court declared segregated buses illegal. The boycott ended shortly after.

BACKGROUND FOR THE SPEECH

Voices for Change

Persuasive speeches played a key role in the civil rights movement of the 1960s. Of all the voices for change, none was more powerful than that of Dr. Martin Luther King, Jr. At marches and rallies, Dr. King spoke out against segregation and moved people to action with his vision of an equal and just society. An electrifying speaker, Dr. King had a distinctive style. He laced his speeches with familiar **allusions,** or references, to the Bible to emphasize arguments. To move audiences, he also relied on the repetition and stately rhythms he used in his church sermons.

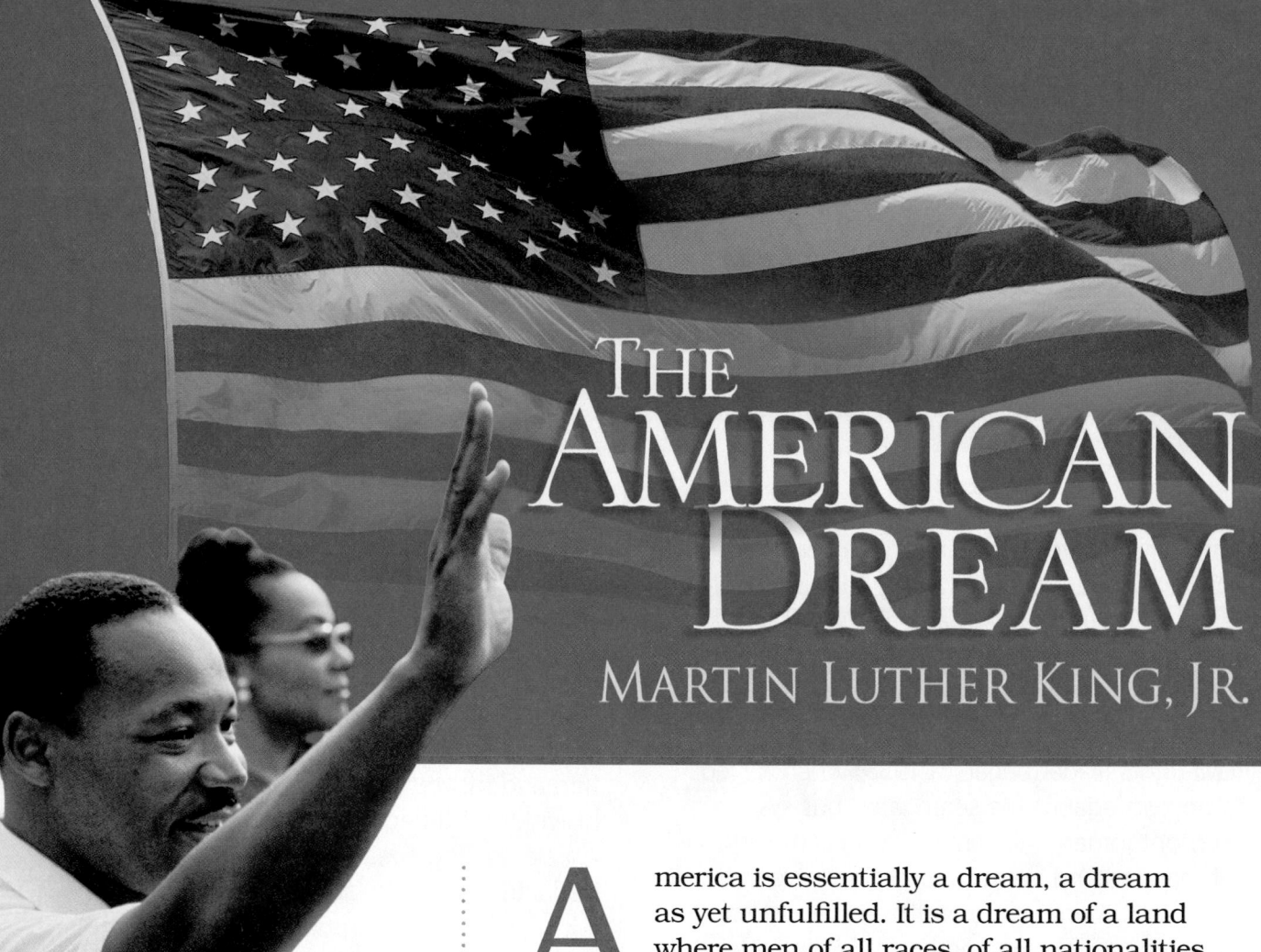

The AMERICAN DREAM

MARTIN LUTHER KING, JR.

A merica is essentially a dream, a dream as yet unfulfilled. It is a dream of a land where men of all races, of all nationalities and of all creeds[1] can live together as brothers. The substance of the dream is expressed in these sublime words, words lifted to cosmic proportions: "We hold these truths to be self-evident, that all men are created equal; that they are endowed by their Creator with certain unalienable rights; that among these are life, liberty, and the pursuit of happiness."[2] This is the dream.

One of the first things we notice in this dream is an amazing universalism. It does not say some men, but it says all men. It does not say all white men, but

Author's Purpose
What does the opening paragraph suggest about the author's purpose for writing?

---

1. **creeds** (krēdz) *n.* systems of belief.
2. **"We hold these truths . . . pursuit of happiness."** opening words of the Declaration of Independence, which asserted the American colonies' independence from Great Britain in 1776.

it says all men, which includes black men. It does not say all Gentiles, but it says all men, which includes Jews. It does not say all Protestants, but it says all men, which includes Catholics.

And there is another thing we see in this dream that ultimately distinguishes democracy and our form of government from all of the totalitarian regimes[3] that emerge in history. It says that each individual has certain basic rights that are neither conferred by nor derived from the state. To discover where they came from it is necessary to move back behind the dim mist of eternity, for they are God-given. Very seldom if ever in the history of the world has a sociopolitical document expressed in such profoundly eloquent and unequivocal language the dignity and the worth of human personality. The American dream reminds us that every man is heir to the legacy of worthiness.

Author's Style
Is King's style formal or informal here? Explain.

Vocabulary
unequivocal (un´ ē kwiv´ ə kəl) *adj.* clear; plainly understood

Reading Check
According to King, what is one of the most important features of the American Dream?

---

3. **totalitarian** (tō tal´ ə ter´ ē ən) **regimes** (rə zhēmz´) countries in which those in power control every aspect of citizens' lives.

Ever since the Founding Fathers of our nation dreamed this noble dream, America has been something of a schizophrenic[4] personality, tragically divided against herself. On the one hand we have proudly professed the principles of democracy, and on the other hand we have sadly practiced the very antithesis of those principles. Indeed slavery and segregation have been strange paradoxes in a nation founded on the principle that all men are created equal. This is what the Swedish sociologist, Gunnar Myrdal, referred to as the American dilemma.

But the shape of the world today does not permit us the luxury of an anemic democracy. The price America must pay for the continued exploitation of the Negro and other minority groups is the price of its own destruction. The hour is late; the clock of destiny is ticking out. It is trite, but urgently true, that if America is to remain a first-class nation she can no longer have second-class citizens. Now, more than ever before, America is challenged to bring her noble dream into reality, and those who are working to implement the American dream are the true saviors of democracy. ●

Vocabulary

antithesis (an tith′ ə sis) *n.* direct opposite

paradoxes (par′ ə däks′ əz) *n.* two things that seem directly at odds

exploitation (eks′ ploi tā′ shən) *n.* the act of using another person for selfish purposes

---

4. schizophrenic (skit′ sə fren′ ik) *adj.* characterized by a separation between the thought processes and emotions, popularly known as "split personality."

Now may I suggest some of the things we must do if we are to make the American dream a reality. First I think all of us must develop a world perspective if we are to survive. The American dream will not become a reality devoid of the larger dream of a world of brotherhood and peace and good will. The world in which we live is a world of geographical oneness and we are challenged now to make it spiritually one.

Man's specific genius and technological ingenuity has dwarfed distance and placed time in chains. Jet planes have compressed into minutes distances that once took days and months to cover. It is not common for a preacher to be quoting Bob Hope, but I think he has aptly described this jet age in which we live. If, on taking off on a nonstop

Vocabulary
devoid (di void´) *adj.* completely without

Author's Style
How does King's choice of phrases, such as *specific genius* and *aptly described*, affect his style?

◀ **Critical Viewing**
How does this picture illustrate the idea of "geographical oneness"? **[Connect]**

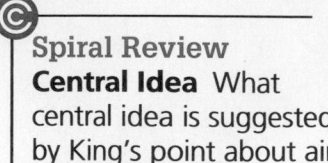

Spiral Review
Central Idea What central idea is suggested by King's point about air travel?

Vocabulary
perish (per´ ish) *v.*
die; be destroyed or wiped out

Author's Purpose
Is King specific in saying what he wants his audience to do? Explain.

flight from Los Angeles to New York City, you develop hiccups, he said, you will hic in Los Angeles and cup in New York City. That is really *moving.* If you take a flight from Tokyo, Japan, on Sunday morning, you will arrive in Seattle, Washington, on the preceding Saturday night. When your friends meet you at the airport and ask you when you left Tokyo, you will have to say, "I left tomorrow." This is the kind of world in which we live. Now this is a bit humorous but I am trying to laugh a basic fact into all of us: the world in which we live has become a single neighborhood.

Through our scientific genius we have made of this world a neighborhood; now through our moral and spiritual development we must make of it a brotherhood. In a real sense, we must all learn to live together as brothers, or we will all perish together as fools. We must come to see that no individual can live alone; no nation can live alone. We must all live together; we must all be concerned about each other.

Critical Thinking

Cite textual evidence to support your responses.

1. **Key Ideas and Details (a) Interpret:** What does King mean when he uses the metaphor, "America is essentially a dream, a dream as yet unfulfilled"? **(b) Assess:** How well does he support this belief?

2. **Key Ideas and Details (a)** What differences does King find between the way things are and the way they should be? **(b) Analyze Cause and Effect:** What effect do these differences have on our democracy? **(c) Synthesize:** How would the elimination of these differences affect people's lives?

3. **Key Ideas and Details (a)** According to King, how has "our scientific genius" changed the world? **(b)** What steps does Dr. King believe that Americans must take to make the American dream a reality? **(c)** Do you agree with this central idea? Explain.

4. **Integration of Knowledge and Ideas** If Dr. King delivered this speech today, instead of in the 1960s, would his message still ring true? Explain. *[Connect to the Big Question: Is truth the same for everyone?]*

Reading Skill: Author's Purpose

1. (a) What is Dr. King's **purpose** in writing this speech? Support your answer with details from the speech. **(b)** Review the details King provides, and **evaluate** whether he achieves his purpose. Explain.

Literary Analysis: Author's Style

2. Craft and Structure Make a chart to analyze the features of the **author's style.** In each box, describe Dr. King's writing and give an example from the text.

3. Craft and Structure (a) Use your chart to write one or two sentences that describe King's writing style. **(b)** Is his style effective for communicating his **attitudes** and **beliefs**? Why or why not?

Vocabulary

Acquisition and Use Review the vocabulary list on page 170. Decide if each statement below is true or false. Explain your response.

1. Rudeness is the *antithesis* of politeness.

2. This is a *paradox*: A platypus is a mammal that lays eggs.

3. It is *exploitation* if companies give generous raises every year.

4. If you are unsure, it helps to receive *unequivocal* advice.

5. Someone *devoid* of a conscience sacrifices for others.

6. Most crops will *perish* without sunlight.

Word Study Use the context of the sentences and what you know about the **Latin root -equi-** to explain each answer.

1. Are *equivalent* sums the same or different?

2. What happens when a gymnast loses her *equilibrium*?

Word Study

The **Latin root -equi-** means "equal."

Apply It Explain how the root *-equi-* contributes to the meanings of these words. Consult a dictionary if necessary.

equity
equidistant
equanimity

Integrated Language Skills

from **Steinbeck: A Life in Letters** •
from **Travels with Charley** • **The American Dream**

Conventions: Reflexive Pronouns

A **reflexive pronoun** indicates that someone or something performs an action to, for, or upon itself.

A reflexive pronoun always ends with *-self* or *-selves* and agrees in number and gender with a noun or pronoun that appears earlier in the sentence. It should never take the place of a noun or pronoun.

This chart lists reflexive pronouns and their uses.

Reflexive Pronouns	Singular	Plural	Sample
First Person	myself	ourselves	**I** took **myself** home.
Second Person	yourself	yourselves	**You** are proud of **yourself**.
Third Person	himself, herself, itself	themselves	**They** asked **themselves.**

Practice A Identify the reflexive pronouns in the following sentences.

1. Steinbeck wanted to see America for himself.
2. The author and Charley liked traveling and camping out by themselves.
3. Steinbeck wanted to learn whether America itself had changed.
4. Steinbeck explained, "I can easily drive Rocinante by myself."

Ⓒ **Reading Application** Find one sentence with a reflexive pronoun in the excerpt from *Travels with Charley.*

Practice B Correct the reflexive pronoun errors in these sentences.

1. Dr. King itself felt the contradiction between the American dream and reality.
2. Dr. King urged Americans to ask themself whether the country could thrive with an "anemic democracy."
3. Some ideas in the Declaration contrast with the reality of America themselves.
4. People will be proud when they learn to treat ourselves fairly.

Ⓒ **Writing Application** Write three sentences about Dr. King or another American hero. Use reflexive pronouns in each sentence.

PH **WRITING COACH** Further instruction and practice are available in *Prentice Hall Writing Coach.*

Writing

Explanatory Text Write an entry for an **observation journal.**

If you read the excerpts from *Travels With Charley,* write an entry about a favorite place that you have visited and remember well.

If you read "The American Dream," write an entry in which you record thoughts about a troubling aspect of today's society.

- First, identify the impression you want to make. In a sentence, state your main observation to focus your writing. Support it with descriptive details, anecdotes (brief stories), or examples. Organize these details logically to create a clear impression for your readers.

- Then, describe the feelings associated with your observation.

- Finally, summarize your observation and explain its significance.

Grammar Application Check your writing for correct use of reflexive pronouns.

Writing Workshop: *Work in Progress*

Prewriting for Narration Using your Brainstorming Chart, decide which column describes an important lesson you learned. Develop a timeline of the event, adding details to help the reader understand how you felt. Save this Timeline Work in your writing portfolio.

Research and Technology

Build and Present Knowledge With a partner, create a **brochure** about the Badlands or cities associated with Dr. King.

- If you choose the Badlands, include activities for at least three destinations, as well as directions for getting there.

- If you choose cities associated with Dr. King, list at least three sites, explaining the significance of each one.

Follow these steps to complete the assignment:

- Find at least two sources on the Internet and in print to research the destinations.

- Then, identify your audience. Include information and images that will be most helpful and interesting to that audience.

- Write your brochure, balancing facts with your own ideas.

- Organize the brochure so that travelers can use it easily.

- Use word-processing and graphics software to produce an illustrated brochure that is attractive and readable.

Common Core State Standards

L.8.1; W.8.2, W.8.6
[For the full wording of the standards, see page 156.]

Use this prewriting activity to prepare for the **Writing Workshop** on page 208.

PHLit Online!
www.PHLitOnline.com

- Interactive graphic organizers
- Grammar tutorial
- Interactive journals

Test Practice: Reading

Author's Purpose

Fiction Selection

Directions: *Read the selection. Then, answer the questions.*

Val wanted something special to wear to the spring dance on Friday. "If I look amazing," she thought, "maybe I won't feel so bad about being the new kid." Val considered asking her mom to drive her to the mall when she got home from work, but that would just lead to a lecture about learning to appreciate what she had. Looking through her closet, Val had to admit she had plenty of great outfits.

A moment later, Val's mom was standing in her room, handing Val a box. Inside was the blue top Val had admired at the mall. "I stopped at the mall on my way home," her mom said. Val just stared, so her mom said, "I know that being the new kid isn't always easy."

1. What is the author's overall purpose?
   A. to entertain
   B. to inform
   C. to persuade
   D. to warn

2. What is the author's specific purpose in the first paragraph?
   A. to describe Val
   B. to introduce Val and her problem
   C. to show why people should appreciate what they have
   D. to provide background

3. What is the author's specific purpose in the second paragraph?
   A. to build suspense
   B. to create sympathy
   C. to show why Val and her mom do not get along
   D. to resolve the problem

4. What types of details help the author achieve her purpose in the second paragraph?
   A. facts and examples
   B. reasons
   C. dialogue and description
   D. persuasive language

Writing for Assessment

If Val's mother had given her a lecture, how could she have convinced Val that she did not need new clothes for the dance? Use details from the passage to write a persuasive speech. Keep your purpose in mind.

Nonfiction Selection

Directions: *Read the selection. Then, answer the questions.*

In 1846, Elias Howe was awarded a patent for the first practical sewing machine. With a sewing machine, a worker could make a shirt in only one hour, as opposed to the fourteen hours it took to make one by hand. Clothes could now be mass-produced and sold in stores. By 1877, there were half a million sewing machines in the United States.

Some people think the telephone or the gasoline engine is the invention that had the greatest impact on people's lives. However, the sewing machine was more important because it freed people from the endless drudgery of sewing by hand and made many styles of clothing affordable for ordinary people. As a result of this machine, people could take greater pride in their appearance and an entire industry was born.

1. What types of details establish the author's purpose in the first paragraph?
- **A.** facts
- **B.** reasons
- **C.** images
- **D.** characters

2. What is the author's main purpose in the first paragraph?
- **A.** to entertain
- **B.** to inform
- **C.** to persuade
- **D.** to exaggerate

3. What do you think is the author's purpose in the second paragraph?
- **A.** to entertain
- **B.** to inform
- **C.** to persuade
- **D.** to instruct

4. Which of the following details does the author use in the second paragraph to achieve this purpose?
- **A.** anecdotes
- **B.** arguments that disprove other claims
- **C.** facts and opinions
- **D.** expert testimony

Writing for Assessment

Connecting Across Texts

Do you think Val would agree with the writer's opinion about the importance of the sewing machine in the nonfiction passage? Use details in the two passages to write a one-paragraph response.

www.PHLitOnline.com
- Online practice
- Instant feedback

Reading for Information

Analyzing Expository Texts

Magazine Article

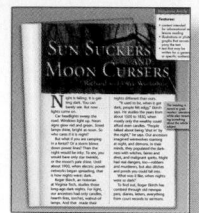

Scientific Article

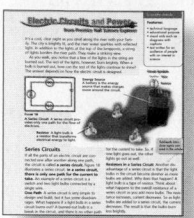

Common Core State Standards

Reading Informational Text

2. Determine a central idea of a text and analyze its development over the course of the text, including its relationship to supporting ideas; provide an objective summary of the text.

Language

4. Determine or clarify the meaning of unknown and multiple-meaning words or phrases based on *grade 8 reading and content,* choosing flexibly from a range of strategies.

6. Acquire and use accurately grade-appropriate general academic and domain-specific words and phrases; gather vocabulary knowledge when considering a word or phrase important to comprehension or expression.

Reading Skill: Identify Central Idea and Details

The **central idea** is the most important point conveyed in a passage or text. **Details** are the facts and examples that support the central idea. Before you begin to read an article or other informational text, **preview the text features.** *Scan* the page by running your eyes quickly over features such as heads. Then, *skim* a few sample paragraphs by reading them quickly. Look for the central, or most important, idea. Then, as you read, you will be able to identify details that support the central idea.

Questions to Help You Preview an Article

❏ What do headings and subheadings tell me about the topic?

❏ What information do photographs, diagrams, illustrations, and captions provide?

❏ What subjects are mentioned in the first sentences of paragraphs?

❏ What kinds of statistics, quotations from experts, or facts appear in the text?

Content-Area Vocabulary

These words appear in the selections that follow. You may also encounter them in other content-area texts.

- **malignant** (mə lig´ nənt) *adj.* very harmful; able to cause death
- **aristocrats** (ə ris´ tə kratz) *n.* those having a high position in society because of birth, rank, or title
- **resistance** (ri zis´ təns) *n.* opposing or weakening force; opposition to the passage of electric current

Sun Suckers and Moon Cursers

Richard and Joyce Wolkomir

Night is falling. It is getting dark. You can barely see. But now . . . lights come on.

Car headlights sweep the road. Windows light up. Neon signs glow red and green. Street lamps shine, bright as noon. So who cares if it is night?

But what if you are camping in a forest? Or a storm blows down power lines? Then the night would be inky. To see, you would have only star twinkle, or the moon's pale shine. Until about 1900, when electric power networks began spreading, that is how nights were: dark.

Roger Ekirch, an historian at Virginia Tech, studies those long-ago dark nights. For light, our ancestors had only candles, hearth fires, torches, walnut-oil lamps. And that made their nights different than ours.

"It used to be, when it got dark, people felt edgy," Ekirch says. He studies the years from about 1500 to 1830, when mostly only the wealthy could afford even candles. "People talked about being 'shut in' by the night," he says. Our ancestors imagined werewolves roaming at night, and demons. In their minds, they populated the darkness with witches, fairies and elves, and malignant spirits. Night had real dangers, too—robbers and murderers, but also ditches and ponds you could fall into.

What was it like, when nights were so dark?

To find out, Roger Ekirch has combed through old newspapers, diaries, letters, everything from court records to sermons.

The heading is meant to grab readers' attention while also revealing something about the article's subject.

He has pondered modern scientific research, too. He has found that, before the invention of electric lights, our ancestors considered night a different "season." At night, they were nearly blind. And so, to them, day- and night seemed as different as summer and winter.

They even had special words for night. Some people called the last rays of the setting sun "sun suckers." Nighttime travelers, who relied on the moon called it the "parish lantern." But robbers, who liked to lurk in darkness, hated the moon. They called it "the tattler." And those darkness-loving criminals? They were "moon cursers."

Cities were so dark that people needing to find their way at night hired boys to carry torches, or "links." Such torchbearers were called "linkboys."

Country people tried to stay indoors at night, unless the moon was out. On moonless nights, people groping in the darkness frequently fell into ponds and ravines.1 Horses, also blinded by darkness, often threw riders.

If you were traveling at night, you would wear light-colored clothing, so your friends could see you. You might ride a white horse. You might mark your route in advance by stripping away tree bark, exposing the white inner wood. In southern England, where the soil is chalky white, people planning night trips mounded up white chalk along their route during the day, to guide them later, in the moonlight.

This photograph helps readers imagine how a night traveler could stumble into a pool of water.

---

1. **ravines** (rə vēnz´) *n.* long, deep hollows in the earth's surface.

It was dark inside houses, too. To dress in the darkness, people learned to fold their clothes just so. Swedish homeowners, Roger Ekirch says, pushed parlor furniture against walls at night, so they could walk through the room without tripping.

People began as children to memorize their local terrain—ditches, fences, cisterns, bogs.[2] They learned the magical terrain, too, spots where ghosts and other imaginary nighttime frights lurked. "In some places, you never whistled at night, because that invited the devil," says Ekirch.

One reason people feared nightfall was they thought night actually did "fall." At night, they believed, malignant air descended. To ward off that sickly air, sleepers wore nightcaps. They also pulled curtains around their beds. In the 1600s, one London man tied his hands inside his bed at night so they would not flop outside the curtains and expose him to night air. . . .

At night, evildoers came out. Virtually every major European city had criminal gangs. Sometimes those gangs included wealthy young **aristocrats** who assaulted people just for the thrill. . . .

If you were law-abiding, you might clang your sword on the pavement while walking down a dark nighttime street to warn robbers you were armed. Or you might hold your sword upright in the moonlight. You tried to walk in groups. You walked down the street's middle, to prevent robbers from lunging at you from doorways or alleys. Robbers depended so much on darkness that a British criminal who attacked his victim in broad daylight was acquitted—jurors decided he must be insane.

Many whose days were blighted by poverty or ill treatment sought escape at night. Slaves in the American South, for instance, sneaked out at night to dances and parties. Or they stumbled through the darkness to other plantations, to visit their wives or children. After the Civil War, says Roger Ekirch, former slaveholders worried that their freed slaves might attack them. And so they rode out at night disguised as ghosts, to frighten onetime slaves into staying indoors.

"At night, many servants felt beyond supervision, and they would often leave directly after their employers fell asleep," Ekirch adds. When they did sleep, it

> Quotations from experts support the writer's main ideas and lend authority and interest to the article.

---

2. **cisterns** (sis´ tərnz) large underground areas for storing water; **bogs** small marshes or swamps where footing is treacherous.

was fitfully, because of rumbling carts and watchmen's cries. And so Ekirch believes many workers got much too little sleep. "That explains why so many slaveowners and employers complained about their workers falling asleep during the day," he said.

Our ancestors had one overriding—and entirely real—nighttime fear: fire. Blazes were common because houses, often with thatched roofs,[3] ignited easily. At night, open flames flickered everywhere. Passersby carrying torches might set your roof ablaze. Also, householders commonly complained about servants forgetting to bank fires or snuff out candles. Roger Ekirch believes one reason night watchmen bellowed out each hour, to the irritation of sleepers,

was precisely to keep everyone half awake, to be ready when fires erupted. . . .

Electricity changed the night. One electric bulb, Ekirch calculates, provided 100 times more light than a gas lamp. Night was becoming what it is today—an artificially illuminated extension of the day. Night has lost its spookiness.

Still, says Roger Ekirch, even in the electric age, his children sometimes fear the dark: "I tell them, 'Your daddy is an expert on night, and he knows a lot about the history of the night, and he can tell you there is nothing to be afraid of!'"

He shrugs. "It doesn't work well," he says.

---

3. **thatched** (thacht) **roofs** roofs made of materials such as straw or rushes.

Electric Circuits and Power

from Prentice Hall Science Explorer

Scientific Article

Features:

- technical language
- educational purpose
- visual aids such as diagrams with captions
- text written for an audience of people with an interest in science

It's a cool, clear night as you stroll along the river with your family. The city is brightly lit, and the river water sparkles with reflected light. In addition to the lights at the top of the lampposts, a string of lights borders the river path. They make a striking view.

As you walk, you notice that a few of the lights in the string are burned out. The rest of the lights, however, burn brightly. When a bulb is burned out, how can the rest of the lights continue to shine? The answer depends on how the electric circuit is designed.

Circuit Symbols

—— Wire

Resistor

Energy Source
A battery is the energy source that makes charges move around the circuit.

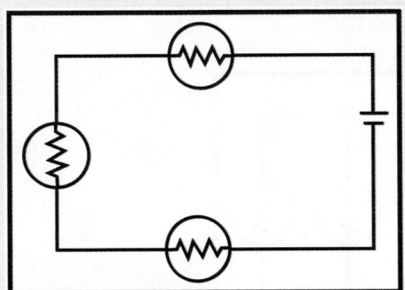

FIGURE 18

A Series Circuit A series circuit provides only one path for the flow of electrons.

Resistor A light bulb is a resistor that transforms electrical energy to light.

Series Circuits

If all the parts of an electric circuit are connected one after another along one path, the circuit is called **a series circuit.** Figure 18 illustrates a series circuit. **In a series circuit, there is only one path for the current to take.** An example of a series circuit is a switch and two light bulbs connected by a single wire.

One Path A series circuit is very simple to design and build, but it has some disadvantages. What happens if a light bulb in a series circuit burns out? A burned-out bulb is a break in the circuit, and there is no other path for the current to take. So, if one light goes out, the other lights go out as well.

Resistors in a Series Circuit Another disadvantage of a series circuit is that the light bulbs in the circuit become dimmer as more bulbs are added. Why does that happen? A light bulb is a type of resistor. Think about what happens to the overall **resistance** of a series circuit as you add more bulbs. The resistance increases, current decreases. So as light bulbs are added to a series circuit, the current decreases. The result is that the bulbs burn less brightly.

Subheads introduce topics covered in the article.

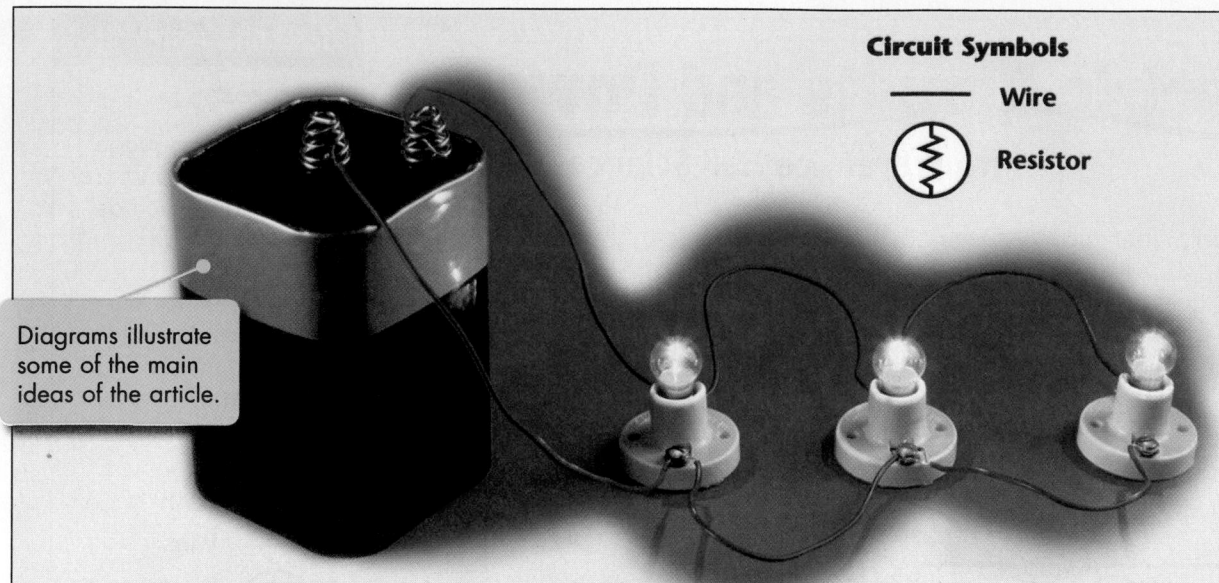

Circuit Symbols

—— Wire

Resistor

Diagrams illustrate some of the main ideas of the article.

Parallel Circuits

As you gaze at a string of lights, you observe that some bulbs burn brightly, but others are burned out. Your observation tells you that these bulbs are connected in a parallel circuit. In a **parallel circuit**, the different parts of the circuit are on separate branches. Figure 19 shows a parallel circuit. **In a parallel circuit, there are several paths for current to take.** Each bulb is connected by a separate path from the battery and back to the battery.

Several Paths What happens if a light burns out in a parallel circuit? If there is a break in one branch, charges can still move through the other branches. So if one bulb goes out, the others remain lit. Switches can be added to each branch to turn lights on and off without affecting the other branches.

Resistors in a Parallel Circuit What happens to the resistance of a parallel circuit when you add a branch? The overall resistance actually decreases. To understand why this happens, consider blowing through a single straw. The straw resists the

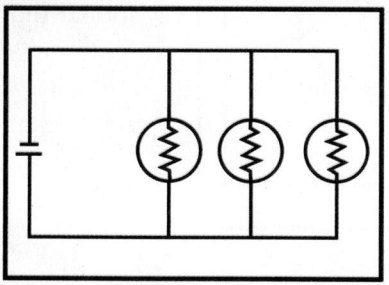

Figure 19

A Parallel Circuit A parallel circuit provides several paths for the flow of electrons.

flow of air so that only a certain amount of air comes out. However, if you use two straws, twice as much air can flow. The air encounters less resistance. As new branches are added to a parallel circuit, the electric current has more paths to follow, so the overall resistance decreases.

Remember that for a given voltage, if resistance decreases, current increases. The additional current travels along each new branch without affecting the original branches. So as you add branches to a parallel circuit, the brightness of the light bulbs does not change.

Comparing Expository Texts

© **1. Craft and Structure (a)** How are the magazine article and the scientific article similar in the way the authors support their **central idea** with **details? (b)** How are the two articles different in this respect? **(c)** Which article makes best use of **text features** to support its most important idea?

Content-Area Vocabulary

2. Explain how the meanings of *resistor* and *resister* relate to the word *resistance.* **(b)** Use the word *resistance* in a sentence about electricity. **(c)** Use the words *resistance* and *aristocrats* in a sentence about a rebellion.

Timed Writing

Explanatory Text: Summary

> **Format**
> The prompt gives specific instructions regarding the length of the writing assignment.

> Choose one of the two articles to summarize in one paragraph. Briefly state the author's historical or scientific conclusions. Then, provide a quick overview of the evidence that the author uses to support those conclusions. (15 minutes)

> **Academic Vocabulary**
> When you *summarize,* you give a short statement that presents the central ideas and most important points in a piece of writing.

5-Minute Planner

Complete these steps before you begin to write:

1. Choose which article you will summarize. Review the article to identify its central idea. Jot down a few words or phrases that will help you recall the central idea when you write your summary.

2. With the central idea in mind, look for details, such as quotations or facts, that support the article's conclusions. Jot down words or phrases for at least three details. **TIP** Supporting details often appear in diagrams and illustrations.

3. Expand the words and phrases you jotted down to form sentences. Use these sentences to draft your summary.

Comparing Characters of Different Eras

A **character** is someone who takes part in the action of a story.

- A *dynamic character* develops and learns through story events.

- A *static character* does not change.

The main character of a story is usually a dynamic character. The way in which this character changes is central to the story and its meaning.

Just as in life, characters in fiction are affected by the **historical and cultural settings** in which they live. The forces that shape characters can include their jobs, living conditions, family customs, and historical events.

When a major historical event is part of a story, that event will certainly help to define a character. Readers may already have some appreciation of historical eras and important events. The way in which a character responds to those events reveals aspects of his or her personality.

Both of these stories present boys who live through challenging times. In "The Finish of Patsy Barnes," a recent move north and a sudden illness have a devastating impact on a poor family. In "The Drummer Boy of Shiloh," a battle threatens to change the life of a young soldier forever.

As you read, compare characters by asking questions, like those in the chart, about the forces that shape their lives.

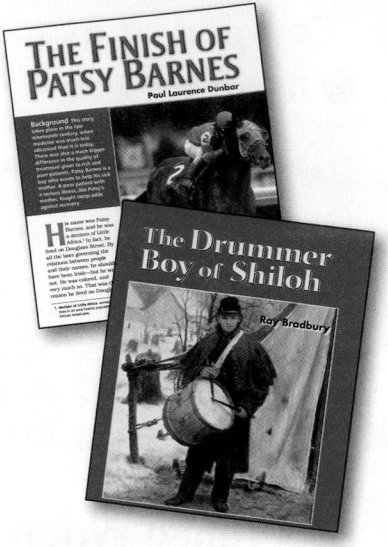

 **Common Core
State Standards**

Reading Literature
3. Analyze how particular lines of dialogue or incidents in a story or drama propel the action, reveal aspects of a character, or provoke a decision.

Writing
2. Write informative/explanatory texts to examine a topic and convey ideas, concepts, and information through the selection, organization, and analysis of relevant content. *(Timed Writing)*

Questions for Comparing Main Characters	Responses
Where does he live?	
What does he do?	
What hardships does he face?	
How do his motivations and reactions reflect the cultural and historical setting and time period?	

www.PHLitOnline.com

- Vocabulary flashcards
- Interactive journals
- More about the authors

- Selection audio
- Interactive graphic organizers

Is *truth* the same for everyone?

Writing About the Big Question

Both of these stories are about boys who face hard truths and grow up too fast. Use this sentence starter to develop your ideas:

Difficult **factors**, such as _____, can cut childhood short.

Meet the Authors

Paul Laurence Dunbar (1872–1906)

Author of "The Finish of Patsy Barnes"

Paul Laurence Dunbar was born in Dayton, Ohio, the son of former slaves. One of the first African Americans to support himself through his writing, Dunbar penned numerous poems, novels, and short stories in his brief life.

A Popular Poet Dunbar's poetry became so popular that by his late twenties he was able to write from Florida, "Down here one finds my poems recited everywhere."

Ray Bradbury (b. 1920)

©Thomas Victor

Author of "The Drummer Boy of Shiloh"

Ray Bradbury often travels to the future in his stories, setting them on Mars or Venus. Occasionally, however, he shifts his time-travel machine into reverse and heads for the past. This story, for instance, takes place in Shiloh, Tennessee, on the eve of a great Civil War battle.

Inspiration in the Newspaper Many years ago, Bradbury read the death notice of an actor whose grandfather had been "the drummer boy of Shiloh." This phrase inspired him to write this story. To paint an accurate picture of the setting, he researched weather conditions before the Battle of Shiloh at a local library.

THE FINISH OF PATSY BARNES

Paul Laurence Dunbar

Background This story takes place in the late nineteenth century, when medicine was much less advanced than it is today. There was also a much bigger difference in the quality of treatment given to rich and poor patients. Patsy Barnes is a boy who wants to help his sick mother. A poor patient with a serious illness, like Patsy's mother, fought steep odds against recovery.

His name was Patsy Barnes, and he was a denizen of Little Africa.[1] In fact, he lived on Douglass Street. By all the laws governing the relations between people and their names, he should have been Irish—but he was not. He was colored, and very much so. That was the reason he lived on Douglass

---

1. **denizen of Little Africa** someone who lives in an area heavily populated by African Americans.

Street. The Negro has very strong within him the instinct of colonization and it was in accordance with this that Patsy's mother had found her way to Little Africa when she had come North from Kentucky.

Patsy was incorrigible.[2] Even into the confines of Little Africa had penetrated the truant officer[3] and the terrible penalty of the compulsory education law. Time and time again had poor Eliza Barnes been brought up on account of the shortcomings of that son of hers. She was a hard-working, honest woman, and day by day bent over her tub, scrubbing away to keep Patsy in shoes and jackets, that would wear out so much faster than they could be bought. But she never murmured, for she loved the boy with a deep affection, though his misdeeds were a sore thorn in her side.

She wanted him to go to school. She wanted him to learn. She had the notion that he might become something better, something higher than she had been. But for him school had no charms; his school was the cool stalls in the big livery stable near at hand; the arena of his pursuits its sawdust floor; the height of his ambition, to be a horseman. Either here or in the racing stables at the Fairgrounds he spent his truant hours. It was a school that taught much, and Patsy was as apt a pupil as he was a constant attendant. He learned strange things about horses, and fine, sonorous oaths that sounded eerie on his young lips, for he had only turned into his fourteenth year.

A man goes where he is appreciated; then could this slim black boy be blamed for doing the same thing? He was a great favorite with the horsemen, and picked up many a dime or nickel for dancing or singing, or even a quarter for warming up a horse for its owner. He was not to be blamed for this, for, first of all, he was born in Kentucky, and had spent the very days of his infancy about the paddocks[4] near Lexington, where his father had sacrificed his life on account of his love for horses. The little fellow had shed no tears when he looked at his father's bleeding body, bruised

Vocabulary
compulsory (kəm pul´ sə rē) *adj.* required

Farm Boy, 1941, Charles Alston, Courtesy of Clark Atlanta University

▲ **Critical Viewing**
How might growing up on a farm leave a boy like the one in this painting unprepared for city life? **[Analyze]**

Reading Check
Where does Patsy spend his time?

---

2. **incorrigible** (in kȯur ´ ə jə bəl) *adj.* unable to be corrected or improved because of bad habits.
3. **truant** (tro͞o´ ənt) **officer** *n.* person whose job is to make sure children attend school.
4. **paddocks** (pad´ əks) *n.* enclosed areas near a stable in which horses are exercised.

Character
What is unusual about Patsy's reaction to his father's death?

Vocabulary
meager (mē´ gər) *adj.* small amount

and broken by the fiery young two-year-old he was trying to subdue. Patsy did not sob or whimper, though his heart ached, for over all the feeling of his grief was a mad, burning desire to ride that horse.

His tears were shed, however, when, actuated by the idea that times would be easier up North, they moved to Dalesford. Then, when he learned that he must leave his old friends, the horses and their masters, whom he had known, he wept. The comparatively **meager** appointments of the Fair-grounds at Dalesford proved a poor compensation for all these. For the first few weeks Patsy had dreams of running away—back to Kentucky and the horses and stables. Then after a while he settled himself with heroic resolution to make the best of what he had, and with a mighty effort took up the burden of life away from his beloved home.

Eliza Barnes, older and more experienced though she was, took up her burden with a less cheerful philosophy than her son. She worked hard, and made a scanty livelihood, it is true, but she did not make the best of what she had. Her complainings were loud in the land, and her wailings for her old home smote the ears of any who would listen to her.

They had been living in Dalesford for a year nearly, when hard work and exposure brought the woman down to bed with pneumonia.[5] They were very poor—too poor even to call in a doctor, so there was nothing to do but to call in the city physician. Now this medical man had too frequent calls into Little Africa, and he did not like to go there. So he was very gruff when any of its denizens called him, and it was even said that he was careless of his patients.

Patsy's heart bled as he heard the doctor talking to his mother:

"Now, there can't be any foolishness about this," he said. "You've got to stay in bed and not get yourself damp."

"How long you think I got to lay hyeah, doctah?" she asked.

"I'm a doctor, not a fortune-teller," was the reply. "You'll lie there as long as the disease holds you."

"But I can't lay hyeah long, doctah, case I ain't got nuffin' to go on."

"Well, take your choice: the bed or the boneyard."

Eliza began to cry.

Character
What does this exchange between Eliza and the doctor reveal about the difficulties Patsy and his mother face?

---

5. **pneumonia** (no͞o mōn´ yə) *n.* potentially deadly infection that causes swelling in the lungs, making it difficult to breathe.

"You needn't sniffle," said the doctor; "I don't see what you people want to come up here for anyhow. Why don't you stay down South where you belong? You come up here and you're just a burden and a trouble to the city. The South deals with all of you better, both in poverty and crime." He knew that these people did not understand him, but he wanted an outlet for the heat within him.

There was another angry being in the room, and that was Patsy. His eyes were full of tears that scorched him and would not fall. The memory of many beautiful and appropriate oaths came to him; but he dared not let his mother hear him swear. Oh! to have a stone—to be across the street from that man!

When the physician walked out, Patsy went to the bed, took his mother's hand, and bent over shamefacedly to kiss her. The little mark of affection comforted Eliza unspeakably. The mother-feeling overwhelmed her in one burst of tears. Then she dried her eyes and smiled at him.

"Honey," she said; "mammy ain' gwine lay hyeah long. She be all right putty soon."

"Nevah you min'," said Patsy with a choke in his voice. "I can do somep'n', an' we'll have an othah doctah."

"La, listen at de chile; what kin you do?"

"I'm goin' down to McCarthy's stable and see if I kin git some horses to exercise."

A sad look came into Eliza's eyes as she said: "You'd bettah not go, Patsy; dem hosses'll kill you yit, des lak dey did yo' pappy."

But the boy, used to doing pretty much as he pleased, was obdurate, and even while she was talking, put on his ragged jacket and left the room.

Patsy was not wise enough to be **diplomatic**. He went right to the point with McCarthy, the liveryman.

The big red-faced fellow slapped him until he spun round and round. Then he said, "Ye little devil, ye, I've a mind to knock the whole head off o' ye. Ye want harses to exercise, do ye? Well git on that un, 'an' see what ye kin do with him."

The boy's honest desire to be helpful had tickled the big, generous Irishman's peculiar sense of humor, and from now on, instead of giving Patsy a horse to ride now and then as he had formerly done, he put into his charge all the animals that

Character
How does the doctor's attitude toward the poor affect the mood of this scene?

Vocabulary
diplomatic
(dip´ lə mat´ ik) *adj.* showing skill in dealing with people

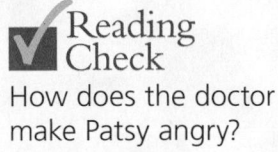
Reading Check
How does the doctor make Patsy angry?

needed exercise.

It was with a king's pride that Patsy marched home with his first considerable earnings.

They were small yet, and would go for food rather than a doctor, but Eliza was inordinately proud, and it was this pride that gave her strength and the desire of life to carry her through the days approaching the crisis of her disease.

Character
What challenge does Patsy face as he watches his mother's condition worsen?

As Patsy saw his mother growing worse, saw her gasping for breath, heard the rattling as she drew in the little air that kept going her clogged lungs, felt the heat of her burning hands, and saw the pitiful appeal in her poor eyes, he became convinced that the city doctor was not helping her. She must have another. But the money?

That afternoon, after his work with McCarthy, found him at the Fair-grounds. The spring races were on, and he thought he might get a job warming up the horse of some independent jockey. He hung around the stables, listening to the talk of men he knew and some he had never seen before. Among the latter was a tall, lanky man, holding forth to a group of men.

▼ **Critical Viewing**
What qualities would someone need to be able to ride a stallion like this one? **[Speculate]**

"No, suh," he was saying to them generally, "I'm goin' to withdraw my hoss, because thaih ain't nobody to ride him as he ought to be rode. I haven't brought a jockey along with me, so I've got to depend on pick-ups. Now, the talent's set again my hoss, Black Boy, because he's been losin' regular, but that hoss has lost for the want of ridin', that's all."

The crowd looked in at the slim-legged, raw-boned horse, and walked away laughing.

"The fools!" muttered the stranger. "If I could ride myself I'd show 'em!"

Patsy was gazing into the stall at the horse.

"What are you doing thaih?" called the owner to him.

"Look hyeah, mistah," said Patsy, "ain't that a bluegrass hoss?"

"Of co'se it is, an' one o' the fastest that evah grazed."

"I'll ride that hoss, mistah."

"What do you know bout ridin'?"

"I used to gin'ally be' roun' Mistah Boone's paddock in Lexington, an'—"

"Aroun' Boone's paddock—what! Look here, if you can ride that hoss to a winnin' I'll give you more money than you ever seen before."

"I'll ride him."

Patsy's heart was beating very wildly beneath his jacket. That horse. He knew that glossy coat. He knew that raw-boned frame and those flashing nostrils. That black horse there owed something to the orphan he had made.

The horse was to ride in the race before the last. Somehow out of odds and ends, his owner scraped together a suit and colors for Patsy. The colors were maroon and green, a curious combination. But then it was a curious horse, a curious rider, and a more curious combination that brought the two together.

Long before the time for the race Patsy went into the stall to become better acquainted with his horse. The animal turned its wild eyes upon him and neighed. He patted the long, slender head, and grinned as the horse stepped aside as gently as a lady.

"He sholy is full o' ginger," he said to the owner, whose name he had found to be Brackett.

"He'll show 'em a thing or two," laughed Brackett.

"His dam[6] was a fast one," said Patsy, unconsciously.

Brackett whirled on him in a flash. "What do you know about his dam?" he asked.

The boy would have retracted, but it was too late. Stammeringly he told the story of his father's death and the horse's connection therewith.

"Well," said Bracket, "if you don't turn out a hoodoo,[7] you're a winner, sure. But I'll be blessed if this don't sound like a story! But I've heard that story before. The man I got Black Boy from, no matter how I got him, you're too young to understand the ins and outs of poker, told it to me."

When the bell sounded and Patsy went out to warm up, he felt as if he were riding on air. Some of the jockeys laughed at his getup, but there was something in him—or under him, maybe—that made him scorn their derision. He saw a sea of faces about him, then saw no more. Only a shining white track loomed ahead of him, and a restless steed was cantering[8] with him around the curve. Then the bell called him back to the stand.

They did not get away at first, and back they trooped. A second trial was a failure. But at the third they were off

---

6. **dam** (dam) *n.* mother of a horse.
7. **hoodoo** (hoo′ doo′) *n.* here, someone or something that causes bad luck.
8. **steed** (stēd) **was cantering** (kan′ tər in) high-spirited riding horse was running at a smooth, easy pace.

Spiral Review
Theme What detail in this paragraph hints at the theme of "overcoming obstacles"?

Reading Check
What unexpected job does Patsy take on?

Character
In what ways are Black Boy and Patsy well suited for each other as horse and jockey?

in a line as straight as a chalk-mark. There were Essex and Firefly, Queen Bess and Mosquito, galloping away side by side, and Black Boy a neck ahead. Patsy knew the family reputation of his horse for endurance as well as fire, and began riding the race from the first. Black Boy came of blood that would not be passed, and to this his rider trusted. At the eighth the line was hardly broken, but as the quarter was reached Black Boy had forged a length ahead, and Mosquito was at his flank. Then, like a flash, Essex shot out ahead under whip and spur, his jockey standing straight in the stirrups.

The crowd in the stand screamed; but Patsy smiled as he lay low over his horse's neck. He saw that Essex had made his best spurt. His only fear was for Mosquito, who hugged and hugged his flank. They were nearing the three-quarter post, and he was tightening his grip on the black. Essex fell back; his spurt was over. The whip fell unheeded on his sides. The spurs dug him in vain.

Black Boy's breath touches the leader's ear. They are neck and neck—nose to nose. The black stallion passes him.

Another cheer from the stand, and again Patsy smiles as they turn into the stretch. Mosquito has gained a head. The colored boy flashes one glance at the horse and rider who are so surely gaining upon him, and his lips close in a grim line. They are half-way down the stretch, and Mosquito's head is at the stallion's neck.

For a single moment Patsy thinks of the sick woman at home and what that race will mean to her, and then his knees close against the horse's sides with a firmer dig. The spurs

Character
What circumstances give Patsy extra motivation to win?

shoot deeper into the steaming flanks. Black Boy shall win; he must win. The horse that has taken away his father shall give him back his mother. The stallion leaps away like a flash, and goes under the wire—a length ahead.

Then the band thundered, and Patsy was off his horse, very warm and very happy, following his mount to the stable. There, a little later, Brackett found him. He rushed to him, and flung his arms around him.

"You little devil," he cried, "you rode like you were kin to that hoss! We've won! We've won!" And he began sticking banknotes at the boy. At first Patsy's eyes bulged, and then he seized the money and got into his clothes.

"Goin' out to spend it?" asked Brackett.

"I'm goin' for a doctah fu' my mother," said Patsy, "she's sick."

"Don't let me lose sight of you."

"Oh, I'll see you again. So long," said the boy.

An hour later he walked into his mother's room with a very big doctor, the greatest the druggist could direct him to. The doctor left his medicines and his orders, but, when Patsy told his story, it was Eliza's pride that started her on the road to recovery. Patsy did not tell his horse's name.

Character
How have events in the story changed Patsy?

Critical Thinking

1. **Key Ideas and Details (a)** Instead of going to school, what setting does Patsy prefer? **(b) Infer:** In what way do Patsy's reasons for spending time there change after his mother becomes ill?

2. **Key Ideas and Details (a) Infer:** Why does the doctor speak to Eliza Barnes in an unfeeling way? **(b) Draw Conclusions:** What does this story suggest about the problems faced by Patsy and his mother?

3. **Key Ideas and Details (a) Infer:** What motivates Patsy to ride Black Boy? **(b) Analyze:** How is Patsy's win a victory for both his mother and his father?

4. **Integration of Knowledge and Ideas (a)** What daily difficult truths do Patsy and his mother face that someone like the doctor does not? **(b)** What does the story reveal about American society in the nineteenth century? *[Connect to the Big Question: Is truth the same for everyone?]*

Cite textual evidence to support your responses.

The Drummer Boy of Shiloh

Ray Bradbury

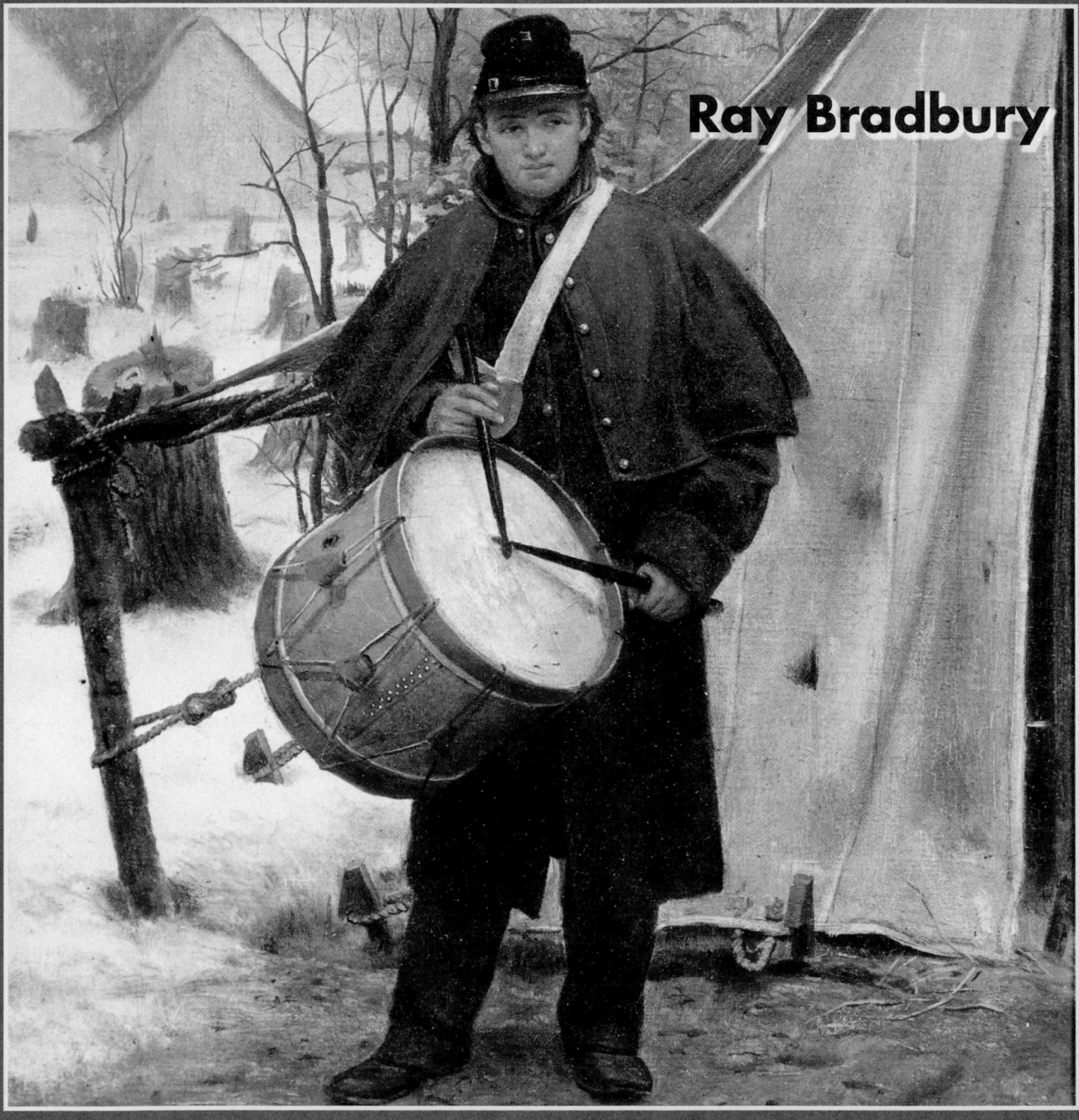

BACKGROUND

This story is about a Civil War drummer boy. Although drummer boys accompanied troops into battle, they carried no weapons. There was no age requirement—so some drummer boys were as young as ten. Because few parents were willing to send their young sons to battle, many drummer boys were runaways or orphans.

◄ **Critical Viewing**
Which aspects of this drummer boy reflect the information in the Background? **[Connect]**

In the April night, more than once, blossoms fell from the orchard trees and lighted with rustling taps on the drumhead. At midnight a peach stone left miraculously on a branch through winter, flicked by a bird, fell swift and unseen; it struck once, like panic, and jerked the boy upright. In silence he listened to his own heart ruffle away, away—at last gone from his ears and back in his chest again.

After that he turned the drum on its side, where its great lunar face peered at him whenever he opened his eyes.

His face, alert or at rest, was solemn. It was a solemn time and a solemn night for a boy just turned fourteen in the peach orchard near Owl Creek not far from the church at Shiloh.

". . . thirty-one . . . thirty-two . . . thirty-three. Unable to see, he stopped counting.

Beyond the thirty-three familiar shadows forty thousand men, exhausted by nervous expectation and unable to sleep for romantic dreams of battles yet unfought, lay crazily askew in their uniforms. A mile farther on, another army was strewn helter-skelter, turning slowly, basting themselves with the thought of what they would do when the time came—a leap, a yell, a blind plunge their strategy, raw youth their protection and benediction.[1]

Now and again the boy heard a vast wind come up that gently stirred the air. But he knew what it was—the army here, the army there, whispering to itself in the dark. Some men talking to others, others murmuring to themselves, and all so quiet it was like a natural element arisen from South or North with the motion of the earth toward dawn.

What the men whispered the boy could only guess and he guessed that it was "Me, I'm the one, I'm the one of all the rest who won't die. I'll live through it. I'll go home. The band will play. And I'll be there to hear it."

Yes, thought the boy, *that's all very well for them, they can give as good as they get!*

Character
What historical situation affects the boy's mood?

Character
How do the drummer boy's age and job give him a different perspective than soldiers in modern wars?

Reading Check
Why do the soldiers sleep uneasily?

---

1. **benediction** (ben´ ə dik´ shən) *n.* blessing.

For with the careless bones of the young men, harvested by night and bindled[2] around campfires, were the similarly strewn steel bones of their rifles with bayonets fixed like eternal lightning lost in the orchard grass.

Me, thought the boy, *I got only a drum, two sticks to beat it, and no shield.*

There wasn't a man-boy on this ground tonight who did not have a shield he cast, riveted or carved himself on his way to his first attack, compounded[3] of remote but nonetheless firm and fiery family devotion, flag-blown patriotism and cocksure immortality strengthened by the touchstone of very real gunpowder, ramrod, Minié ball[4] and flint. But without these last, the boy felt his family move yet farther off in the dark, as if one of those great prairie-burning trains had chanted them away, never to return—leaving him with this drum which was worse than a toy in the game to be played tomorrow or someday much too soon.

The boy turned on his side. A moth brushed his face, but it was peach blossom. A peach blossom flicked him, but it was a moth. Nothing stayed put. Nothing had a name. Nothing was as it once was.

If he lay very still, when the dawn came up and the soldiers put on their bravery with their caps, perhaps they might go away, the war with them, and not notice him lying small here, no more than a toy himself.

"Well, by thunder now," said a voice. The boy shut his eyes to hide inside himself, but it was too late. Someone, walking by in the night, stood over him. "Well," said the voice quietly, "here's a soldier crying *before* the fight. Good. Get it over. Won't be time once it all starts."

And the voice was about to move on when the boy, startled, touched the drum at his elbow. The man above, hearing this, stopped. The boy could feel his eyes, sense him slowly bending near. A hand must have come down out of the night, for there was a little *rat-tat* as the fingernails brushed and the man's breath fanned the boy's face.

"Why, it's the drummer boy, isn't it?"

The boy nodded, not knowing if his nod was seen. "Sir, is that you?" he said.

---

2. **bindled** (bin´ dəld) *adj.* bedded.
3. **compounded** (käm pound´ əd) *adj.* mixed or combined.
4. **Minié** (min´ ē) **ball** *n.* cone-shaped rifle bullet that expands when fired.

Character
How does the boy's historical situation affect his mood and that of the story?

▲ **Critical Viewing**
Based on his expression, what emotions might this young drummer boy be feeling? **[Speculate]**

"I assume it is." The man's knees cracked as he bent still closer. He smelled as all fathers should smell, of salt-sweat, tobacco, horse and boot leather, and the earth he walked upon. He had many eyes. No, not eyes, brass buttons that watched the boy.

He could only be, and was, the general. "What's your name, boy?" he asked.

"Joby, sir," whispered the boy, starting to sit up.

"All right, Joby, don't stir." A hand pressed his chest gently, and the boy relaxed. "How long you been with us, Joby?"

"Three weeks, sir."

"Run off from home or join legitimate, boy?"

Silence.

"Damn-fool question," said the general. "Do you shave yet, boy? Even more of a fool. There's your cheek, fell right off the tree overhead. And the others here, not much older. Raw, raw, damn raw, the lot of you. You ready for tomorrow or the next day, Joby?"

"I think so, sir."

"You want to cry some more, go on ahead. I did the same last night."

"You, sir?"

"God's truth. Thinking of everything ahead. Both sides figuring the other side will just give up, and soon, and the war done in weeks and us all home. Well, that's not how it's going to be. And maybe that's why I cried."

"Yes, sir," said Joby.

The general must have taken out a cigar now, for the dark was suddenly filled with the Indian smell of tobacco unlighted yet, but chewed as the man thought what next to say.

"It's going to be a crazy time," said the general. "Counting both sides, there's a hundred thousand men—give or take a few thousand—out there tonight, not one as can spit a sparrow off a tree, or knows a horse clod from a Minié ball. Stand up, bare the breast, ask to be a target, thank them and sit down, that's us, that's them. We should turn tail and train four months, they should do the same. But here we are, taken with spring fever and thinking it blood lust, taking our sulphur with cannons instead of with molasses, as it should be—going to be a hero, going to live forever. And I can see all them over there nodding agreement, save the other way around. It's wrong, boy, it's wrong as a head put on hindside front and a man marching backward through life. Sometime

Character
Why is the general's reaction to the boy's tears surprising?

Reading Check

Why is Joby crying?

The Drummer Boy of Shiloh **203**

Social Studies Connection

A Bloody Battle The Battle of Shiloh was sparked when the southern Confederate army suddenly attacked the northern Union troops near Shiloh Church in Tennessee on April 6, 1862. Some of the heaviest fighting took place in Sarah Bell's peach orchard.

Thanks to the efforts of raw, young recruits from the farms of Iowa and Illinois, the Union lines held. This bloody, bitterly fought battle resulted in the killing or wounding of about 23,000 men and dashed any hopes of a quick end to the Civil War.

Connect to the Literature

What details of the historical setting are included in Bradbury's story?

Character
What do the general's words reveal about his character?

this week more innocents will get shot out of pure Cherokee enthusiasm than ever got shot before. Owl Creek was full of boys splashing around in the noonday sun just a few hours ago. I fear it will be full of boys again, just floating, at sundown tomorrow, not caring where the current takes them." •

The general stopped and made a little pile of winter leaves and twigs in the dark as if he might at any moment strike fire to them to see his way through the coming days when the sun might not show its face because of what was happening here and just beyond.

The boy watched the hand stirring the leaves and opened his lips to say something, but did not say it. The general heard the boy's breath and spoke himself.

"Why am I telling you this? That's what you wanted to ask, eh? Well, when you got a bunch of wild horses on a loose rein somewhere, somehow you got to bring order, rein them in. These lads, fresh out of the milkshed, don't know what I know; and I can't tell them—men actually die in war. So each is his own army. I got to make one army of them. And for that, boy, I need you."

"Me!" The boy's lips barely twitched.

"You, boy," said the general quietly. "You are the heart of the army. Think about that. You are the heart of the army. Listen to me, now."

And lying there, Joby listened. And the general spoke. If he, Joby, beat slow tomorrow, the heart would beat slow in the men. They would lag by the wayside. They would drowse in the fields on their muskets. They would sleep forever, after that—in those same fields, their hearts slowed by a drummer boy and stopped by enemy lead.

But if he beat a sure, steady, ever faster rhythm, then, then, their knees would come up in a long line down over that hill, one knee after the other, like a wave on the ocean shore. Had he seen the ocean ever? Seen the waves rolling in like a well-ordered cavalry charge to the sand? Well, that was it, that's what he wanted, that's what was needed. Joby was his right hand and his left. He gave the orders, but Joby set the pace.

◀ **Critical Viewing**
Why might the drummer boy's role be important in the confusion of a Civil War battle such as this one? **[Connect]**

So bring the right knee up and the right foot out and the left knee up and the left foot out, one following the other in good time, in brisk time. Move the blood up the body and make the head proud and the spine stiff and the jaw resolute. Focus the eye and set the teeth, flare the nostrils and tighten the hands, put steel armor all over the men, for blood moving fast in them does indeed make men feel as if they'd put on steel. He must keep at it, at it! Long and steady, steady and long! Then, even though shot or torn, those wounds got in hot blood—in blood he'd helped stir—would feel less pain. If their blood was cold, it would be more than slaughter, it would be murderous nightmare and pain best not told and no one to guess.

The general spoke and stopped, letting his breath slack off. Then, after a moment, he said, "So there you are, that's it. Will you do that, boy? Do you know now you're general of the army when the general's left behind?"

The boy nodded mutely.

"You'll run them through for me then, boy?"

"Yes, sir."

"Good. And, God willing, many nights from tonight, many years from now, when you're as old or far much older than me, when they ask you what you did in this awful time, you will tell them—one part humble and one part proud—I was the drummer boy at the battle of Owl Creek or the Tennessee River, or maybe they'll just name it after the church there. I was the drummer boy at Shiloh. Good grief, that has a beat and sound to it fitting for Mr. Longfellow. 'I was the drummer boy at Shiloh.' Who will ever hear those words and not know you, boy, or what you thought this night, or what you'll think tomorrow or the next day when we must get up on our legs and move!"

Vocabulary
resolute (rez´ ə lo͞ot) *adj.* showing a firm purpose

Spiral Review
Theme As the general describes the role of the drummer boy, are there any hints that he is exaggerating? Explain.

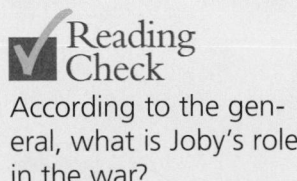

✔ Reading Check

According to the general, what is Joby's role in the war?

Character
Why might the general's words appeal to a young boy in the middle of the Civil War?

The general stood up. "Well, then. God bless you, boy. Good night."

"Good night, sir." And tobacco, brass, boot polish, salt sweat and leather, the man moved away through the grass.

Joby lay for a moment staring, but unable to see where the man had gone. He swallowed. He wiped his eyes. He cleared his throat. He settled himself. Then, at last, very slowly and firmly he turned the drum so that it faced up toward the sky.

He lay next to it, his arm around it, feeling the tremor, the touch, the muted thunder as, all the rest of the April night in the year 1862, near the Tennessee River, not far from the Owl Creek, very close to the church named Shiloh, the peach blossoms fell on the drum.

Critical Thinking

Cite textual evidence to support your responses.

1. **Key Ideas and Details (a)** What frightens Joby most about the upcoming battle? **(b) Compare and Contrast:** How are his fears like and unlike those of the other soldiers? **(c) Compare and Contrast:** In what other ways are Joby and the soldiers alike and not alike?

2. **Key Ideas and Details (a) Infer:** What do you think motivates the general to talk to Joby? **(b) Draw Conclusions:** How do you think Joby feels after his talk with the general? Explain.

3. **Key Ideas and Details Evaluate:** Is the drummer boy's role as crucial as the general says? Explain.

4. **Integration of Knowledge and Ideas (a) Speculate:** Do you think the general has motivated Joby to keep his promise? Why or why not? **(b) Make a Judgment:** Is the general's request fair or unfair to Joby? Explain.

5. **Integration of Knowledge and Ideas (a)** In what ways are Joby and the other soldiers unprepared for the roles they have assumed? **(b)** What hard truths about war are revealed by Joby's thoughts about his role? **(c)** What truths are revealed by the general's words? *[Connect to the Big Question: Is truth the same for everyone?]*

Comparing and Contrasting Characters

© **1. Key Ideas and Details** Complete a chart like this to analyze the characters listed. Explain whether each one is a static or a dynamic character.

Name	Static or Dynamic	Proof
Patsy Barnes		
the doctor		
Joby		
the general		

© **2. Key Ideas and Details** **(a)** List four historical details involving time and place that have an effect on Patsy Barnes. **(b)** List four historical details involving time and place that have an effect on Joby.

⏲ Timed Writing

Explanatory Text: Essay

Compare and contrast Patsy and Joby—two characters facing difficult situations in different time periods. In an essay, discuss ways that the historical events and cultural settings help to develop these main characters. **(40 minutes)**

5-Minute Planner

1. Read the prompt carefully and completely.

2. Gather your ideas by jotting down answers to these questions:

• What outside forces influence the characters?

• How does each character confront his main conflict?

• How do historical and cultural circumstances affect the characters' reactions, motivations, and emotions?

• How do the boys' values and beliefs change as a result of their experiences?

3. Choose an organizational strategy. If you use the block method, present all the details about Patsy, then all the details about Joby. If you use point-by-point, discuss one aspect of both characters, then another aspect, and so on.

4. Reread the prompt, and then draft your essay.

Writing Workshop

Write a Narrative

Narration: Autobiographical Essay

Defining the Form An **autobiographical essay** tells the story of a memorable event, time, or situation in the writer's life. You may use elements of this form in letters, anecdotes, or expository essays.

Assignment Write an autobiographical essay about an event that changed you in a significant way. Include these elements:

✔ a plan for writing that addresses *purpose and audience*

✔ a clear *sequence of events* from your life using well-chosen details and description

✔ a central *conflict,* problem, or shift in perspective

✔ *precise words* that indicate the event's significance or your attitude toward the event

✔ consistent use of first-person *point of view*

✔ correct *use of pronouns and punctuation of dialogue*

To preview the criteria on which your autobiographical essay may be judged, see the rubric on page 215.

 Writing Workshop: *Work in Progress*

Review the work you did on pages 155 and 179.

WRITE GUY
Jeff Anderson, M.Ed.

What Do You Notice?

Description

Read the following sentences from John Steinbeck's *Travels with Charley.*

As she talked it came to me that she was afraid of this place and, further, that so was I. I felt I wouldn't like to have the night catch me here. I went into a state of flight, running to get away from the unearthly landscape.

With a partner, discuss what makes this passage exciting and dramatic. For example, you may want to talk about the author's use of images, action words, and setting. Think about ways you might use similar elements in your narrative.

 **Common Core State Standards**

Writing

3. Write narratives to develop real or imagined experiences or events using effective technique, relevant descriptive details, and well-structured event sequences.

3.a. Engage and orient the reader by establishing a context and point of view and introducing a narrator and/or characters; organize an event sequence that unfolds naturally and logically.

3.d. Use precise words and phrases, relevant descriptive details, and sensory language to capture the action and convey experiences and events.

Reading-Writing Connection

To get a feel for autobiographical narrative, read the excerpt from *I Know Why the Caged Bird Sings,* by Maya Angelou, on page 514.

Prewriting/Planning Strategies

Make a blueprint. Draw and label a blueprint of a familiar or special place—a friend's house, your school, or a park. List the people, things, and incidents you associate with each spot listed on your blueprint. Choose one as your topic. This model shows the events and experiences associated with a town football field.

Determine audience and purpose. Knowing who your audience will be and why you want to tell your story can help you decide what to write about.

- If your purpose is **to entertain your audience,** focus on the funny, moving, or exciting parts of your story.

- If your purpose is **to share a lesson you learned,** focus on the events that illustrate the message and prepare to explain what you learned from your experience.

Gather descriptive details. Make a five-column chart with the following headings for your topic: *People, Time, Place, Events,* and *Emotions.* For each column, use about three minutes to list words and phrases that describe each heading for your topic.

Visitors

Home

Visitors' Bench

Home Bench

Caught game-winning touchdown

Caught my first interception

Coach

Scored on my own team when I got confused and ran the wrong way

- Focus on **physical description** when describing *people.* Answer these questions: *How did they look? How did they act?*

- Focus on **background description** when describing *time and place.* Answer: *What was unique about this time of your life? What was special about the place where these events occurred?*

- Focus on **specific action** when describing *events.* Answer: *Who did what to whom? What was the exact sequence of events?*

Use words and phrases from the chart when you draft your essay.

Drafting Strategies

Common Core
State Standards

Writing
3.a. Engage and orient the reader by establishing a context and point of view and introducing a narrator and/or characters; organize an event sequence that unfolds naturally and logically.

3.b. Use narrative techniques, such as dialogue, pacing, description, and reflection, to develop experiences, events, and/or characters.

3.d. Use precise words and phrases, relevant descriptive details, and sensory language to capture the action and convey experiences and events.

3.e. Provide a conclusion that follows from and reflects on the narrated experiences or events.

Order events. Identify the **conflict,** or problem, that makes your narrative worth reading. Then, organize events around the **conflict.** Make sure the order of events is *clear* and *coherent*—that it will make sense to your readers. First, introduce the people, setting, and situation. Build to the **climax,** where the tension is the greatest. Finish your narrative with a **resolution** that settles the problem and reflects on the experiences described.

Use a consistent point of view. Maintain a first-person point of view, using the pronoun *I* to refer to yourself. Avoid telling what other people are thinking or feeling unless you show readers you are guessing about other people's thoughts. As a first-person narrator, you can know and tell only your own thoughts and feelings.

Develop readers' interest. As you write, provide background about the event, setting, and people. Choose descriptive details that will show the significance of the event, satisfy your audience, and achieve your overall purpose. Use vivid sensory details to capture what the scene looked like and how people acted.

> **Dull:** I run two miles every day.

> **Vivid:** Every day at 5 A.M., when all sensible people are asleep, I groggily lace my cleats and run two miles to improve my fitness.

Use remembered feelings. Since the story is about you, tell your readers how you felt at the time. Connect the events in your narrative to yourself and your emotions. Ask yourself:

- What made this event significant and memorable?

- What emotions did I experience? What triggered them?

- How did my feelings change or grow throughout the event?

Use a chart like the one shown to organize your thoughts.

Emotion	Cause	Importance
Disappointment	At first, I did not make the team	Made me practice harder
Exhaustion	Running every day, training with my older sister	I got into shape but also pulled muscles
Accomplishment	Making the team after weeks of hard work	Improved my skills; learned lesson of never giving up

Patricia C. McKissack On Reaching Out to an Audience

Patricia C. McKissack is co-author of the selection from *The Baker Heater League* (p. 11) and the author of "The 11:59" (p. 20).

"Research is the cornerstone of nonfiction."
— Patricia C. McKissack

An "author's note" allows the writer to share personal information about the content of the work. Although the note usually comes at the beginning of a book, I don't write mine until my manuscript is complete and almost ready for publication. It is then that I can step away and get a better perspective on what I've written. Although the stories in *The Dark-Thirty* are historical fiction, my author's note is nonfiction and gives the reader the historical backdrop for the stories.

Professional Model:

from Author's Note, *The Dark-Thirty*

When I was growing up in the South, we kids called the half hour just before nightfall the dark-thirty. We had exactly half an hour to get home before the monsters came out.

During the hot, muggy summer, when days last longer, we gathered on the front porch to pass away the evening hours. Grandmama's hands were always busy, but while shelling peas or picking greens, she told a spine-chilling ghost tale about Laughing Lizzy. . . .

Then on cold winter nights, when the dark-thirty came early, our family sat in the living room and talked. The talk generally led to one of Grandmama's hair-raising tales. As the last glimmers of light faded from the window overlooking the woods, she told about Gray Jim, the runaway slave who'd been killed while trying to escape. Gray Jim's ghost haunted the woods on moonless nights. . . .

I needed a concise definition of the dark-thirty for readers. The first one I wrote was too long and not as memorable.

I wanted to bring my readers to the front porch of my grandmother's house. I used descriptive words like "shelling peas" to show what was happening around me as I listened to her scary stories.

Here, I try to prepare the reader for what the stories are about in *The Dark-Thirty*. They are scary stories that are set within the historical context of African American history from slavery times to the present.

Revising Strategies

Check for sentence variety. Look over your paragraphs to see the patterns of sentences you have used. When writing in the first person, you may find that many of the sentences begin with *I*.

To analyze and evaluate sentence patterns in your draft, highlight the first word of each sentence. Then, review your draft to determine if you have too many sentences that start with *I*. Revise repetitive sentence beginnings to build variety, using the chart. Make sure that you maintain the first-person point of view.

Draft	Add Variety Strategy	Revision
I was surprised to see my sister up on stage.	Start your sentence with a word that describes your emotion or state of mind.	Startled, I noticed a familiar figure on the stage—it was my sister!
I rushed up to congratulate her after the play ended.	Move another part of the sentence to the beginning.	After the play ended, I rushed to congratulate her.
I told her that she had done such a good job, I forgot I knew her.	Start with a real quotation instead of writing that someone said something.	"Good job!" I exclaimed, "You really had me believing you were Alice."

Use specific, precise nouns and verbs. Replace vague nouns that might have readers asking *What kind?* with precise nouns. Also look for vague verbs and replace them with more vivid, precise language.

Vague: Weeds *filled* the *place*.

Precise: Weeds *overran* the *playground*.

Peer Review

With a partner, review your revised draft for word choices. Look particularly at your use of transitions to signal a change in time or setting, or to indicate an influence or result. Add transitions to make relationships and shifts clearer, as in the example below.

Without transitions: I sprained my finger playing softball at school. I was in severe pain. I could barely think—much less remember to call my mother. She was worried sick about me.

With transitions: *After* I sprained my finger playing softball at school, I was in severe pain. *Consequently,* I could barely think—much less remember to call my mother. *Meanwhile, back home,* my mother was worried sick about me.

 Common Core
State Standards

Writing
3.c. Use a variety of transition words, phrases, and clauses to convey sequence, signal shifts from one time frame or setting to another, and show the relationships among experiences and events.

3.d. Use precise words and phrases, relevant descriptive details, and sensory language to capture the action and convey experiences and events.

Language
1. Demonstrate command of the conventions of standard English grammar and usage when writing or speaking.

Revising for Pronoun-Antecedent Agreement

A **pronoun** is a word that stands for a noun. An **antecedent** is the word or group of words to which the pronoun refers.

Pronoun-Antecedent Agreement Pronouns should agree with their antecedents in number and person. *Number* tells whether a pronoun is singular or plural. *Person* tells to whom a pronoun refers.

First-person, singular: *I* paid for *my* ticket, please send it to *me*.

First-person, plural: <u>*We*</u> ate *our* dinner when the waitress served it to *us*.

Second-person, singular: <u>Simon</u>, who gave that to *you*?

Second-person, plural: <u>Girls</u>, would *you* like some dessert?

Third-person, singular: <u>Sara</u> said *she* was late because *her* watch was lost.

Third-person, plural: The <u>boys</u> brought *their* cleats so *they* could play.

Indefinite pronouns like the ones listed can pose agreement problems. This list shows the number associated with these pronouns.

   Singular: another, anyone, anything, each, everybody, everything, little, much, nobody, nothing, one, other, someone, something

   Plural: both, few, many, others, several

   Both: all, any, more, most, none, some

Fixing Errors Follow these steps to fix agreement problems:

1. Locate the pronoun and identify the antecedent.

2. If the antecedent is a singular indefinite pronoun, use a singular personal pronoun. *Both girls are funny—<u>each</u> has <u>her</u> own way of dancing.*

3. If the antecedent is a plural indefinite pronoun, use a plural personal pronoun. *The men argued. Then, <u>both</u> went <u>their</u> separate ways.*

Grammar in Your Writing
In your draft, circle all pronouns. Draw a line from each pronoun to its antecedent. Use the rules above to fix errors in agreement.

> **PH WRITING COACH**
> Further instruction and practice are available in *Prentice Hall Writing Coach*.

Baseball, a Sport I Love

I remember the day my dad placed a glove in one of my hands and a bat in the other and told me the combination was an eight-letter word called baseball. Ever since then, most of my memories have been related to the sport. When I was eleven, I played in a game I'll remember forever.

We were facing the West Torrance Bull Dogs. We had a great team that year. Our pitcher, Frank (The Smasher) was tough to hit. The nicknames of other players—"Hot Glove," "Fireball," and "McGwire, Jr."— were earned with outstanding play during the season. We had a team of stars. The only one who had not earned a "star" nickname was Matt.

Nine starters took the field at five o'clock on a warm afternoon. The small crowd of parents and friends made enough noise for a major-league game. For most of the game, the two teams were evenly matched. Then, in the last inning, Pat "The Runstopper" at third base was injured as one of the Bull Dogs accidentally rammed his ankle while sliding into third base. We had two choices: forfeit the game or play Matt.

"You can do it, Matt!" the coach said as he sent Matt out to take Pat's place on third base.

"All right, Matt!" we encouraged from our places in the field as he trotted out nervously.

The score was tied with two outs. Unfortunately, the next ball took a sharp bounce toward third—and toward Matt. Matt ran forward and made an awkward catch, followed by an even more awkward lob toward first. Amazingly, it made it there in time!

As we jogged back in, the players called out, "Way to go, Matt!" "You came through in the clutch!"

That's when I realized the truth of something the coach is always telling us. When you play as a team, everyone is a star. And that's exactly what I told Matt, whose new nickname is "Clutch."

Chris uses a consistent first-person point of view, referring to himself with the first-person pronouns *I*, *my*, and *me*.

Chris begins a clear sequence of events from his life by identifying when the action of the narrative begins.

Precise details about the warmth and the noise help bring the scene to life.

The injury increases the suspense in the conflict between the two teams.

Dialogue helps readers feel as if they are witnessing this important conversation.

Here, Chris reveals how his personal experience has helped him look at his favorite sport in a new way.

Editing and Proofreading

Read your drafts and correct errors in spelling, grammar, and punctuation.

Focus on punctuating dialogue. If you include conversations in your writing, follow proper rules of punctuation.

- Enclose all direct quotations with quotation marks.
  "You were right," I said to my grandfather.

- Place a comma after the words that introduce the speaker.
  Grandpa replied, "Well, you learned a lesson today."

- Use commas and quotation marks before and after any words in **split dialogue**. *"Next time," I said, "I guess I'll listen."*

Publishing and Presenting

Consider one of the following ways to share your writing:

Present an autobiographical storytelling or a speech. Use your autobiographical narrative as the basis for a narrative presentation.

Make a comic strip. Create a comic strip based on your narrative and post it in the classroom.

Reflecting on Your Writing

Writer's Journal Jot down your answer to this question:
How useful were the prewriting strategies you used?

Rubric for Self-Assessment

Find evidence in your writing to address each category. Then, use the rating scale to grade your work.

Spiral Review

Earlier in this unit, you learned about **personal pronouns** (p. 154) and **reflexive pronouns** (p. 178). Review your essay to be sure you have used these types of pronouns correctly.

PH   WRITING COACH

Further instruction and practice are available in *Prentice Hall Writing Coach*.

Criteria	Rating Scale
	not very *very*
Focus: How consistent is the use of first-person point of view?	1 2 3 4 5
Organization: How clear and coherent is the sequence of events?	1 2 3 4 5
Support/Elaboration: How well do the choice of details support purpose, audience, and significance?	1 2 3 4 5
Conventions: How consistent is the agreement of pronouns and antecedents?	1 2 3 4 5

Vocabulary Workshop

Using a Dictionary and Thesaurus

When you look up a word in a **dictionary,** you will find the meaning, pronunciation, and part of speech for the word. You will also find the word's **etymology,** or origin. Etymologies show how words come into the English language and how they change over time. Look in the front or the back of a dictionary for a guide to the abbreviations used in etymologies.

When you look up a word in a **thesaurus,** you will find the word's synonyms, or words with similar meaning. A thesaurus can be helpful when you are looking for alternate word choices to use in your writing.

Compare these two entries for the word *verdict*:

Common Core State Standards

Language

4. Determine or clarify the meaning of unknown and multiple-meaning words or phrases based on *grade 8 reading and content,* choosing flexibly from a range of strategies.

4.c. Consult general and specialized reference materials, both print and digital, to find the pronunciation of a word or determine or clarify its precise meaning or its part of speech.

4.d. Verify the preliminary determination of the meaning of a word or phrase.

Dictionary

> **ver•dict** (vʉr´ dikt) **n.** [ME *verdit* <
> Anglo-Fr < ML *veredictum,* true saying,
> verdict < L *vere,* truly + *dictum,* a thing
> said: see VERY and DICTUM] **1.** The
> decision arrived at by a jury at the end
> of a trial **2.** any decision or judgment

Thesaurus

> **verdict** **n.** judgment, finding, decision,
> answer, opinion, sentence, determination,
> decree, conclusion, deduction, adjudication,
> arbitrament

Notice that a thesaurus does not provide definitions of words. Before you use a word you find in a thesaurus, check a dictionary to verify the meaning of the word and confirm that it is a good choice.

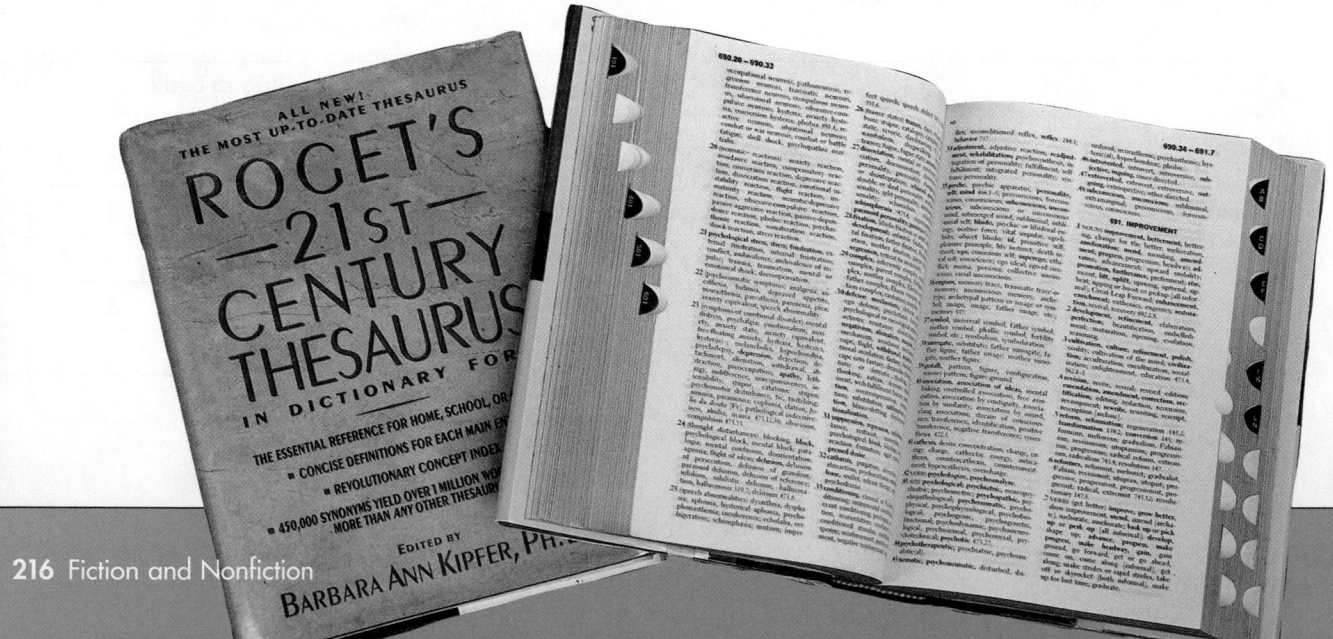

Where to Find a Dictionary and Thesaurus You can find these resources in book form at your school or in a library. You can also use digital tools, such as online dictionaries and thesauruses, to search for the perfect words to express your ideas. Ask your teacher to recommend the best online word study resources.

PHLit Online!
www.PHLitOnline.com
- Author video: Writing Process
- Author video: Rewards of Writing

Practice A Use a print or an online dictionary to look up each of the following words. Show how each one breaks into syllables and which syllables are stressed. Then, write each word's definition. Finally, use each word in a sentence that shows its meaning.

1. quandary   **2.** interminable   **3.** perfunctory

Practice B Use a print or an online thesaurus to find five synonyms for the word *strange*. Then, use a dictionary to look up the definitions of those five words. Finally, use each synonym in a sentence that shows the word's exact meaning.

Activity The cluster diagram shown gives four synonyms for the word *fast*. Using a thesaurus, add to the diagram by giving two synonyms for each of the *fast* synonyms. (An example is shown below.) Share your completed diagram with a partner, and discuss how all of the words in your diagram differ in meaning. Refer to the dictionary definition and etymology of each word in your discussion.

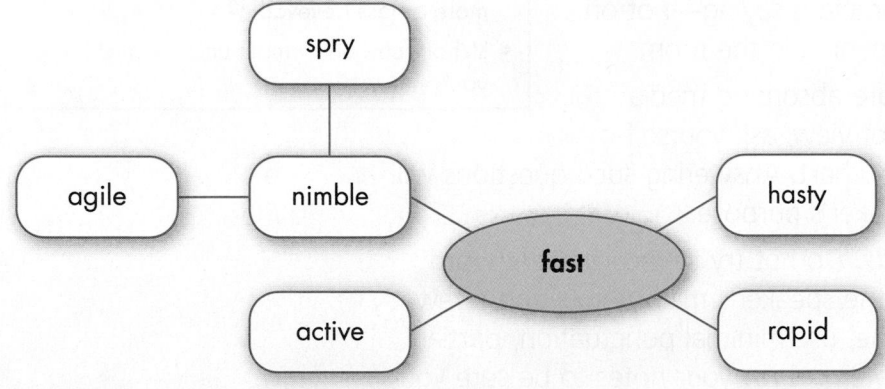

Comprehension and Collaboration

In a group, discuss the day's weather without using these words:

nice bad cold

hot warm windy

Use a thesaurus to find alternate word choices. Check a dictionary to be sure you use those words correctly.

Communications Workshop

Effective Listening and Note-Taking

For situations when understanding and remembering are crucial, it is useful to learn effective listening and note-taking skills.

Learn the Skills

Select a purpose for listening. Choosing a purpose for listening helps you focus your attention on what is most important. For example, if your purpose is to follow instructions, you will need to focus more closely on details than if your purpose were enjoyment.

Consider the speaker's purpose. A speaker's purpose will influence how you listen. For example, listen carefully and analytically as a teacher speaks to inform you. Listen critically and questioningly as a candidate speaks to persuade you.

Listen to how something is said. Speakers often give you hints that can help you identify their purpose and perspective. Listen for these clues:

- changes in tone of voice that indicate emotion
- emphasis on words or phrases
- repetition of key points

Eliminate barriers to listening. Try to avoid distractions when listening. Sit close to the speaker and try to stay focused on what he or she is saying—not on the other things that are happening in the room.

Listen critically. When you are absorbing media messages or different points of view, ask yourself questions such as those in the chart. Answering such questions will also help you identify the speaker's purpose.

Note main ideas and details. Do not try to record every word a speaker says. Instead, note the speaker's main points and a few supporting details. To save time, use minimal punctuation, partial phrases, and abbreviations. Later, review your notes to be sure you understand them.

Record your questions. Write down your questions and reactions. These notes will help you think critically about what you hear.

Common Core State Standards

Speaking and Listening
2. Analyze the purpose of information presented in diverse media and formats and evaluate the motives behind its presentation.
3. Delineate a speaker's argument and specific claims, evaluating the soundness of the reasoning and relevance and sufficiency of the evidence and identifying when irrelevant evidence is introduced.

Critical-Listening Questions

- How would you **paraphrase,** or describe in your own words, the **speaker's purpose**?

- How would you describe his or her **point of view** or message?

- Does the speaker offer enough facts or examples as support?

- How does the way the speaker **delivers** the presentation affect the message?

- Do you agree with the speaker's point of view and ideas?

- What are the speaker's **biases,** influences, or leanings? Do they make his or her points more or less believable?

- What **questions** remain unanswered for you?

Practice the Skills

Ⓒ Presentation of Knowledge and Ideas Use what you have learned in this workshop to complete the following activity.

ACTIVITY: Listen to a Political Speech and Take Notes

Listen to a recording of a current or historic political speech. Then, follow the steps below:

- Identify your purpose for listening.
- Identify the speaker's purpose and perspective by paying attention to ideas that repeat, emphasis placed on words, or changes in tone.
- Avoid distractions and focus your attention on the speaker.
- Take notes, capturing the speaker's main points and a few supporting details.
- Write down your questions and reactions.

Use a Listening Guide like the one below as you analyze the purpose of information presented and evaluate the motives behind its presentation.

Listening Guide

Speaker's Cues
Note which of the following methods the speaker uses to reveal purpose:
- Changes in tone of voice
- Emphasis on words or phrases
- Repetition of key points

Interpret
What is the speaker's point of view and how is it revealed?
What are the speaker's biases, and how do they affect his or her message?
How does the speaker's delivery affect the message?
Are enough facts or examples presented to support key points?

Taking Notes
Jot down the speaker's main ideas and a few supporting details. Note your reaction to the speech and any questions that the speaker leaves unanswered.

Ⓒ Comprehension and Collaboration With a group of classmates, watch and take notes on a television interview. Compare your notes with group members to see how they analyzed the purpose of and motivation behind the interview. Then, compare how your notes differed in organization, style, questions, or personal reaction.

Cumulative Review

**Common Core
State Standards**

RL.8.3, RL.8.4; W.8.2
[For the full wording of the standards, see the standards chart in the front of your textbook.]

I. Reading Literature

Directions: *Read the passage. Then, answer the questions that follow.*

"It's a school just like any other school," Val said with a <u>bravado</u> that disguised her shaking knees and knotted stomach.

"Sure," Nina said. "It's just like any other enormously massive school."

Nina liked to exaggerate, but Carter Middle School was huge compared to Jones Elementary–Middle School, where both girls had been students and friends since first grade. This year, Val and Nina were in eighth grade, but because of the county's recent redistricting plan, they had to change schools. Some families in the newly expanded tenth district were allowed to keep their kids at Jones. Other kids, like Val and her friend Nina, had to make the switch to Carter. Val would never forget the day her mother had given her the awful news. "I'll never fit in there!" Val had wailed.

Now, as they walked through the school's front entrance, Nina whispered, "I don't know about this. It's like walking to our deaths." Val looked at her schedule. "At least we're in the same homeroom."

Room 319 was on the third floor in the south wing. "Three floors? Our old school was just one," said Nina. "Oh, this is going to kill me." Just then, two girls approached. Val felt her stomach sink as she realized they were going to stop to confront Val and Nina. She looked around for a way to escape.

"Hey, didn't you play for the Jones soccer team?" one of the girls asked. "We heard you were coming here this year. What a bummer—having to switch schools, but how lucky for us. By the way, I'm Rena and this is Sophie."

"Hi," Val and Nina said, cautiously.

"You both are trying out for our soccer team," Sophie said. "We absolutely need your speed on offense."

"Boy, do we," Rena added. "You ran circles around us in that game last season. We're really glad you're here."

"This place is so big," Nina said.

"Only at first," Sophie said. "Then, it's like any other school."

"That's just what I was saying," Val said, barely aware that her knees had grown steady and the knot in her stomach had loosened. "By the way," Val asked, "when are soccer tryouts?"

1. Which word *best* describes the **tone** of the **exposition** of the passage?
   A. anxious
   B. humorous
   C. confused
   D. sad

2. **Vocabulary** Which is the *best* definition for the underlined word <u>bravado</u>?
   A. show of fear
   B. show of courage
   C. display of honor
   D. display of humor

3. Which sentence *best* describes the **main conflict?**
   A. Val and Nina worry about adjusting to a new school.
   B. Val and Nina worry about finding their way around a large school.
   C. Val and Nina worry about attending school with girls from a rival team.
   D. Val and Nina worry about how difficult their new classes will be.

4. Which words below *best* describe the writer's **style?**
   A. serious and complex
   B. flowery and romantic
   C. humorous and fanciful
   D. plain and realistic

5. How can you tell that Val is a **dynamic character?**
   A. She no longer enjoys school.
   B. She is a strong, fast soccer player.
   C. She begins to lose her fear of change.
   D. She continues to play on sports teams.

6. Which event in the passage is an example of **flashback?**
   A. Nina exaggerates the size of Carter Middle School.
   B. Val recalls the day her mother told her she had to go to Carter.
   C. Some families are allowed to keep their children at Val and Nina's old school.
   D. Val examines her schedule.

7. Which event marks the **climax** of the passage?
   A. The county creates a redistricting plan that sends Val and Nina to a new school.
   B. Nina complains about the stairs.
   C. Rena and Sophie tell Val and Nina they are needed on the soccer team.
   D. Val and Nina are approached by two girls on their way to homeroom.

8. Which sentence *best* describes the **resolution?**
   A. Val and Nina prepare to attend a new school.
   B. Nina understands that all schools are the same.
   C. Val realizes that she will fit in at Carter Middle School.
   D. Val and Nina think they will be the school's soccer stars.

⏱ Timed Writing

9. In a brief essay, explain whether the **conflict** of this passage is **internal, external,** or both. Cite evidence from the text to support your analysis.

GO ON

II. Reading Informational Text

Directions: *Read the passage. Then, answer the questions that follow.*

Common Core State Standards

RI.8.3, RI.8.4; W.8.2.c, W.8.2.d; L.8.3
[For the full wording of the standards, see the standards chart in the front of your textbook.]

Ski Jumping at the Olympics

History

Ski jumping originated as a sport in Norway around 1860, when Sondre Norheim soared approximately 98 feet. Since then, jumpers have developed techniques to improve their <u>aerodynamics</u> and greatly increase the distance of their jumps. Now, Olympic ski jumpers can reach past 656 feet—almost seven times the distance of Norheim's first jump!

Technique

Ski jumpers use wide, long skis and wear tight-fitting ski suits. Using their legs for power, they ski down a ramp, accelerating to a speed of about 56 mph at take-off. Then, they snap their skis upward and lean their bodies forward until they are almost parallel with their skis. When they achieve perfect form, skiers almost appear to be in flight.

Ski Jumping Schedule			
Event	Date	Time	Place
Individual Finals	February 17	4:00 pm	Pregalato

1. Which **text aid** signals that information about the development of ski jumping is provided?
   A. the title, Ski Jumping at the Olympics
   B. the subhead History
   C. the subhead Technique
   D. the chart title, Ski Jumping Schedule

2. What is the most important function of the **subheads** in the article?
   A. They add visual variety.
   B. They are a convenient stopping point.
   C. They signal what comes next.
   D. They summarize what comes before.

3. **Vocabulary** What is the meaning of the underlined word <u>aerodynamics</u>?
   A. "form that maximizes speed by reducing air resistance"
   B. "ability to change form"
   C. "the greatest use of energy"
   D. "the ability to endure intense training for long periods of time"

4. Which **subhead** would be the *best* choice for a section about how to compete in an Olympic ski jumping event?
   A. Olympic Ski Jumping Rules
   B. Olympic Ski Jumping Records
   C. The First Olympic Games
   D. How Weather Affects Ski Jumpers

III. Writing and Language Conventions

Directions: *Read the passage. Then, answer each question that follows.*

(1) Most kids my age that meet Susi for the first time think she is cold and a bit mysterious. (2) Perhaps it is that look of hers, which seems to say, "I know something you will never know." (3) Susi also has this habit of standing with her head tilted. (4) As a result, her black hair drapes over her right eye. (5) When spoken to, Susi answers politely, but it is always brief. (6) She never starts a conversation. (7) Between you and myself, Susi's quiet style appeals to me.

1. Which sentence would *best* support the author's **main impression** of Susi?
   A. Susi's cold attitude hides her shyness.
   B. Susi is an insightful and creative writer.
   C. Susi used to live in Jacksonville, Florida.
   D. Susi studies ballet and is very graceful.

2. Which of the following revisions would make the **voice** of the passage more vivid?
   A. Change the word *kids* to *young people* in sentence 1.
   B. Change the word *look* to *quirky half-smile* in sentence 2.
   C. Add the word *funny* before *habit* insentence 3.
   D. Add the word *ever* before *starts* in sentence 6.

3. Which of these revisions to sentence 5 corrects an error in **pronoun-antecedent agreement?**
   A. When spoken to, Susi answers politely, but they are always brief.
   B. When spoken to, Susi answers politely, but her is always brief.
   C. When spoken to, Susi answers politely, but she is always brief.
   D. The sentence is correct as is.

4. Which revision to sentence 6 helps create a smoother **transition?**
   A. She has never started a conversation that I am aware of.
   B. In fact, she never starts a conversation.
   C. As a result, she never starts a conversation.
   D. And she never starts a conversation.

5. How could sentence 7 *best* be rewritten to correct an error in the use of **reflexive pronouns?**
   A. Between you and me, Susi's quiet style appeals to me.
   B. Between you and myself, Susi's quiet style appeals to myself.
   C. Between you and me, Susi's quiet style appeals to myself.
   D. The sentence is correct.

Performance Tasks

Common Core State Standards

RL.8.2, RL.8.3, RL.8.5; RI.8.2, RI.8.4, RI.8.5; W.8.2, W.8.9; SL.8.1, SL.8.4, SL.8.5, SL.8.6; L.8.1, L.8.2, L.8.4
[For the full wording of the standards, see the standards chart in the front of your textbook.]

Directions: *Follow the instructions to complete the tasks below as required by your teacher.*

As you work on each task, incorporate both general academic vocabulary and literary terms you learned in this unit.

Writing

Task 1: Literature [RL.8.2; W.8.2]

Analyze the Development of Theme

Write an essay in which you determine the theme of a story from this unit and analyze how the events of the plot develop that theme.

- Determine the theme, or central meaning, of the story.

- Summarize the plot by listing the important events. Then, analyze in detail how each event helps develop the story's theme.

- Be sure your essay correctly uses standard English grammar, punctuation, and spelling.

Task 2: Informational Text [RI.8.2; W.8.2]

Analyze the Development of a Central Idea

Write an essay in which you analyze the development of a central idea in a work of literary nonfiction in this unit.

- Choose a work of literary nonfiction in this unit.

- State the topic of the work and determine the central idea expressed about this topic.

- List the supporting ideas that develop this central idea and explain what each supporting idea adds to the central idea.

- Identify individual details that further develop and refine the central idea.

- Spell correctly, including capitalizing proper nouns.

Task 3: Literature [RL.8.5; RI.8.2; W.8.9]

Compare and Contrast a Work of Fiction and a Work of Nonfiction

Write an essay in which you compare and contrast one of the stories in this unit with one of the nonfiction works.

- Select a story and a nonfiction work that have something in common, such as a similar situation, character, setting, or idea.

- Summarize each work briefly. Then, state several important similarities and differences between the works.

- Explain how the structure of each work affects its style and meaning.

- When analyzing how a text is structured, think about the way in which the author conveys information.

Task 4: Informational Text [RI.8.4; W.8.2]

Analyze Word Choice

Write an essay in which you analyze word choice in a nonfiction work from this unit.

- Select a nonfiction work in which the author has made striking word choices.

- Identify words and phrases that stand out, such as figures of speech or colorful images. Analyze their impact.

- Include an analysis of the connotations, or feelings and associations, that the words and phrases evoke.

- Check for correct grammar and usage.

Speaking and Listening

Analyze the Impact of Dialogue

Prepare a brief presentation in which you analyze the impact of dialogue in a story.

- Choose a story from this unit in which the dialogue plays an important part.
- Find examples of dialogue that help propel the plot or reveal character traits. Analyze the impact of each example. Create a set of note cards or talking points based on your ideas.
- Present your analysis to the class. Read aloud the dialogue selections that you have chosen. Speak them as you imagine the characters in the story would say them.
- Answer questions about your findings, backing up your claims with relevant evidence from the text.
- Use a conversational tone, but adhere to the conventions of English grammar.

Task 6: Informational Text [RI.8.5; SL.8.4, SL.8.6]

Analyze a Paragraph

Prepare an oral presentation in which you closely read and analyze a paragraph from a nonfiction work in the unit.

- Choose a meaningful paragraph from a nonfiction work in this unit and prepare an oral presentation about it.
- First, identify the work and explain at what point in the text the paragraph appears. Summarize the paragraph's content.
- Read the paragraph aloud with adequate volume and clear pronunciation.
- Present a detailed analysis of the paragraph, explaining what each sentence or group of sentences adds to the paragraph's meaning. For example, identify the topic sentence and evidence that supports it.

- Show how this paragraph develops or refines a concept that is key to the work as a whole.
- Following your presentation, respond to any questions from your audience.

Task 7: Literature [RL.8.3; SL.8.5]

Compare Character Development

Conduct a small group discussion in which you compare and contrast the way in which two or more characters are defined through dialogue and action.

- Choose at least two characters from stories in this unit who change and develop during the course of the stories.
- Identify the lines of dialogue and events that reveal new information about the characters.
- Prepare a list of questions to guide a group discussion about how each character develops. Compare how well readers know each of the characters. Examine the kinds of details each author uses. Consider how well each author brings a character to life.
- Use a visual display, such as a graphic organizer, on paper or a chalk board to record key points of the discussion.

THE BIG Q?

Is truth the same for everyone?

At the beginning of Unit 1, you participated in a discussion about the Big Question. Now that you have completed the unit, write a response to the question. Discuss how and why your original views have been changed or reinforced. Give specific examples from the literature, as well as from other subjects and your own life, to support your ideas. Use Big Question vocabulary words (see p. 3) in your response.

Featured Titles

In this unit, you have read a variety of fiction and literary nonfiction. Continue to read on your own. Select books that you enjoy, but challenge yourself to explore new topics, new authors, and works of increasing depth and complexity. The titles suggested below will help you get started.

Literature

The Boy Who Reversed Himself
by William Sleator

In this **science-fiction novel,** Laura makes an interesting discovery about her strange neighbor, Omar. He has direct access to the fourth dimension. However, events turn serious when Laura and her boyfriend Pete travel to "four-space" on their own and realize they cannot return through time and space without Omar's help.

Something Permanent
by Cynthia Rylant
Harcourt Children's Books, 1994

In 1941, when Walker Evans's stark photographs of three poor Southern families and the contents of their bare, rickety shacks were published, they stunned the nation with their power. Decades later, Cynthia Rylant responds to these same Depression-era photographs. Her sparse but touching **poems** pay tribute to the lives of ordinary Americans enduring terrible times.

Two Suns in the Sky
by Miriam Bat-Ami

In this **novel** set in Oswego, New York, during World War II, 15-year-old Chris Cook falls in love with Adam Bornstein, a Jewish refugee living behind barbed wire in a nearby camp. Will their love survive their differences and the bitter opposition of Cook's father?

The Outsiders
by S. E. Hinton
Speak, 1997

In this **novel** written by Hinton when she was a teen, Ponyboy is a greaser, one of the outsiders routinely bullied by the vicious, wealthy Socs. It is not until the violence goes too far that Ponyboy realizes people may not be so different after all.

Informational Texts

Discoveries: Believe It or Not

In this **essay** collection, you can explore the concept of truth in four different subject areas: social studies, science, humanities, and mathematics. Choose from a variety of interesting topics.

Travels with Charley: In Search of America
by John Steinbeck   EXEMPLAR TEXT

In this **nonfiction** book, writer John Steinbeck chronicles his journey around the United States with his poodle Charley. This book offers readers a look at 1960s America from the perspective of a curious and perceptive writer.

The Words We Live By: Your Annotated Guide to the Constitution
by Linda R. Monk   EXEMPLAR TEXT

This **nonfiction** book explains the history and meaning of the U.S. Constitution and its amendments in language that is approachable and which provides a balanced perspective on current constitutional controversies.

Preparing to Read Complex Texts

Attentive Reading As you read on your own, ask yourself questions about the text. The questions shown below and others that you ask as you read will help you learn and enjoy literature even more.

 **Common Core State Standards**

Reading Literature/Informational Text
10. By the end of the year, read and comprehend literature, including stories, dramas, and poems, and literary nonfiction at the high end of the grades 6–8 text complexity band independently and proficiently.

When reading fiction, ask yourself…

- Who is telling the story? Do I enjoy this voice?
- Does the story have a meaning or theme that I think is valuable? Why or why not?

Key Ideas and Details

- Do the settings in the story seem real? Why or why not?
- Are the characters' words and actions believable? Why or why not?
- Do I understand why the characters feel, think, and behave as they do? If not, why?
- Do I care what happens? Why or why not?
- Does the author use language well? If so, how? If not, why?

Craft and Structure

- Does this story move me emotionally? If so, how?
- Does the story teach me something? If so, what?
- Does the work seem like others I have read, or does it seem fresh and new?

Integration of Ideas

When reading nonfiction, ask yourself…

- Why did the author write this work?
- Are the ideas the author expresses important? Why or why not?
- Has the author made me care about the subject? Why or why not?
- Do the ideas in this work surprise me? Why or why not?

Key Ideas and Details

- Are the author's ideas organized clearly and logically? Why or why not?
- Is the evidence the author uses strong and convincing? Why or why not?
- Does the author explain things clearly and use language well? Why or why not?

Craft and Structure

- Do I agree or disagree with the author's ideas?
- Does this work make me want to read other works on the same topic? Why or why not?
- Would I recommend this work to someone who was researching this topic? Why or why not?

Integration of Ideas

THE BIG ? Q

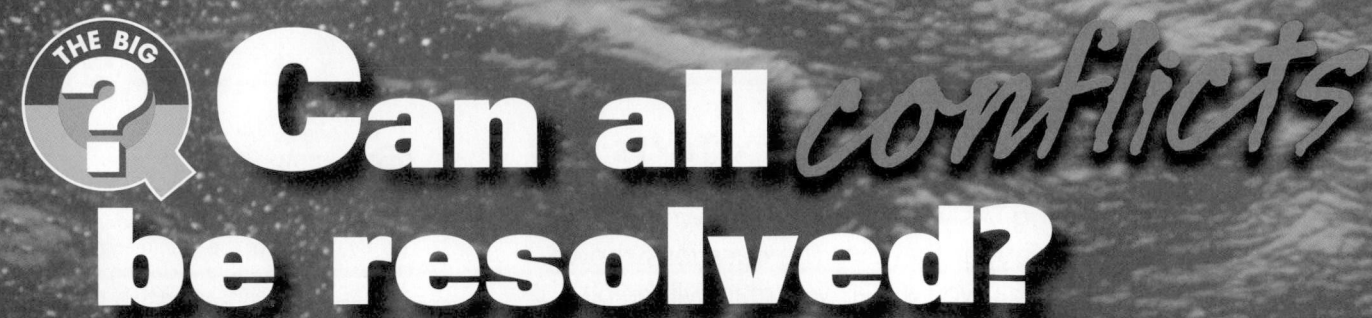

Can all *conflicts* be resolved?

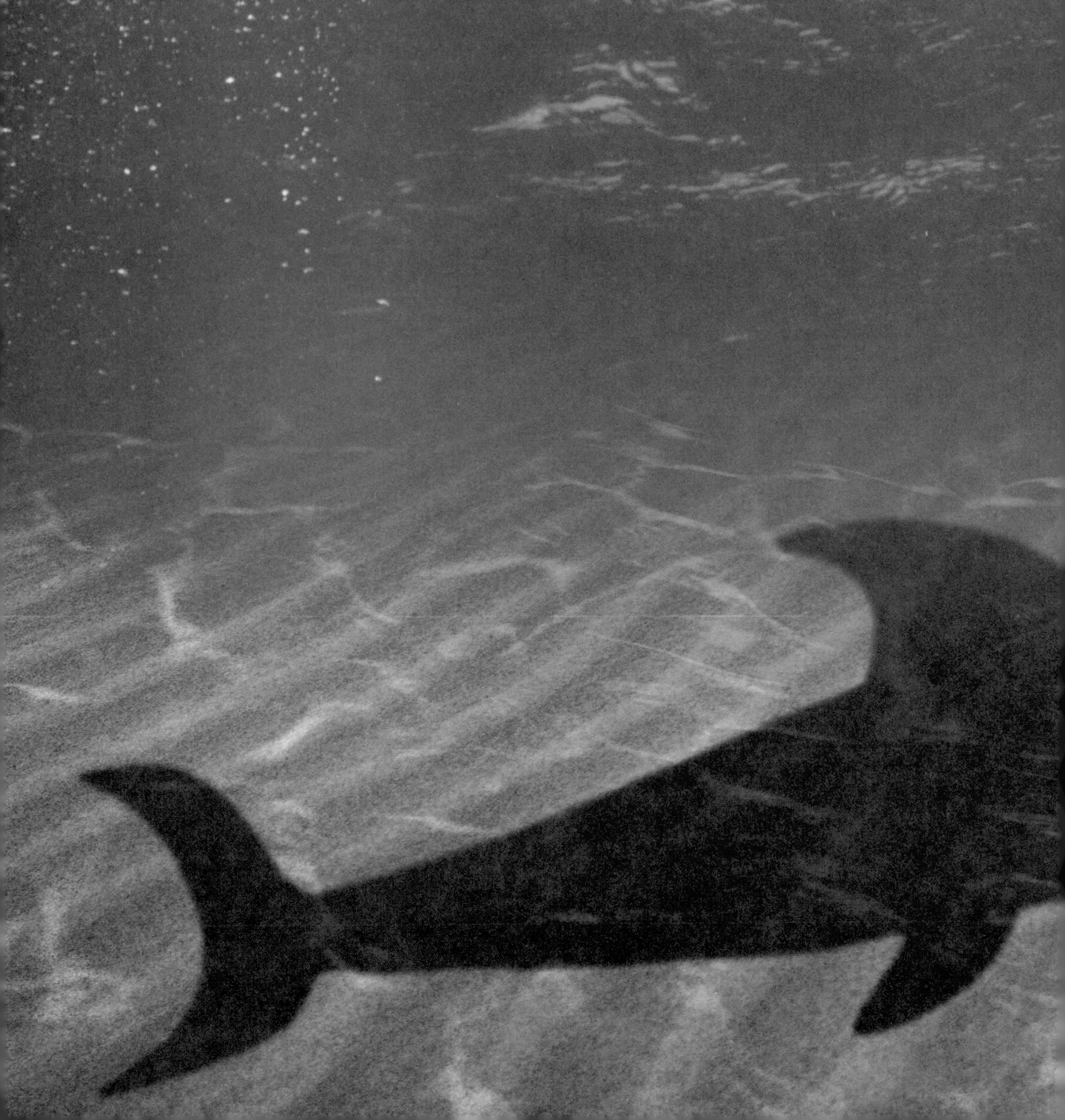

PHLit Online!
www.PHLitOnline.com

Hear It!
- Selection summary audio
- Selection audio
- BQ Tunes

See It!
- Author videos
- Big Question video
- Get Connected videos
- Background videos
- More about the authors
- Illustrated vocabulary words
- Vocabulary flashcards

Do It!
- Interactive journals
- Interactive graphic organizers
- Grammar tutorials
- Interactive vocabulary games
- Test practice

Can all *conflicts* be resolved?

A **conflict** is a struggle between opposing forces. For example, a disagreement might arise between you and a friend about where to eat. Such a minor conflict usually has a quick solution that ends in a compromise. However, it may turn into an argument about who has better taste in food. It might even end in a stalemate, a dispute that neither side can win.

Major conflicts are more serious and take time to resolve. Some can lead to anger or even violence and injury. For example, a land dispute that cannot be resolved peacefully through negotiation could turn into a violent conflict between neighboring countries.

Exploring the Big Question

Collaboration: Group Discussion Start thinking about the Big Question by making a list of different conflicts based on your own experience and knowledge. Describe one specific example of each of the following types of conflicts and explain its outcome.

- A situation in which neighbors irritate each other
- An incident in which someone tries to take something by force
- An occasion in which one person tries to mislead another
- A strong reaction to an opposing viewpoint
- A person struggling with insecurity about leaving home
- A person doubting his or her ability to achieve a particular goal

Talk with a partner about attempts that were made to resolve each conflict. Use the Big Question vocabulary in your discussion.

Connecting to the Literature Each reading in this unit will give you additional insight into the Big Question.

PHLit Online!
www.PHLitOnline.com
- Big Question video
- Illustrated vocabulary words
- Interactive vocabulary games
- BQ Tunes

Learning Big Question Vocabulary

Common Core State Standards

Speaking and Listening
1. Engage effectively in a range of collaborative discussions (one-on-one, in groups, and teacher-led) with diverse partners on grade 8 topics, texts, and issues, building on others' ideas and expressing their own clearly.

Language
6. Acquire and use accurately grade-appropriate general academic and domain-specific words and phrases; gather vocabulary knowledge when considering a word or phrase important to comprehension or expression.

Acquire and Use Academic Vocabulary Academic vocabulary is the language you encounter in textbooks and on standardized tests. Review the definitions of these academic vocabulary words.

> **argument** (är´ gyōō mənt) *n.* 1. oral disagreement 2. support of a claim
>
> **injury** (in´ jə rē) *n.* harm or damage to a person
>
> **insecurity** (in´ si kyōōr´ ə tē) *n.* lack of confidence; self-doubt
>
> **interact** (in´ tər akt´) *v.* act together with others
>
> **negotiate** (ni gō´ shē āt´) *v.* bargain or deal with another party to reach a settlement
>
> **oppose** (ə pōz´) *v.* go against; stand in the way of
>
> **reaction** (rē ak´ shən) *n.* response to an influence, an action, or a statement
>
> **solution** (sə lōō´ shən) *n.* act of solving a problem or answering a question
>
> **viewpoint** (vyōō´ point´) *n.* position regarding an idea or a statement

Use these words as you complete Big Question activities in this unit that involve reading, writing, speaking, and listening.

Gather Vocabulary Knowledge Additional Big Question words are listed below. Categorize the words by deciding whether you know each one well, know it a little bit, or do not know it at all.

> | compromise | mislead | victorious |
> |---|---|---|
> | irritate | stalemate | violence |

Then, do the following:

1. Write the definitions of the words you know.
2. Using a print or online dictionary, look up the meaning of each word you do not know. Then, write the meaning.
3. Confirm the meaning and pronunciation of each word. Revise your definition if necessary.
4. Use as many words as possible in a paragraph about an interesting conflict that you or someone you know has faced and its resolution.

Elements of a Short Story

In a short story, characters, setting, plot, and conflict combine to develop a meaningful theme.

A **short story** is a brief work of fiction intended to be read in a single sitting. Most short stories are built from the same elements.

At the heart of a short story are the **characters,** the people, or the animals who take part in the action. To help you get to know a character, an author uses **characterization.** For example, by having a character talk tough but act kindly, a writer uses what the character says and does to reveal the character's personality. Characterization can show

- a character's **traits**—his or her qualities, attitudes, and values;
- a character's **motives**—the reasons for a character's actions.

Characters live and act in a **setting**—the time and place of the story's action. Setting often contributes to the story's atmosphere or **mood.** Setting includes cultural context—the society in which the characters live.

Plot is the sequence of events in a story. Each event in the plot plays its role in propelling the action forward. Early scenes may provide important background information. Subsequent events build to the climax, or turning point, which leads to the ending.

A **conflict,** or struggle between opposing forces, calls on characters to act and so drives the plot. An **internal conflict** takes place in the mind of a character, as when a character struggles with opposing feelings. An **external conflict** takes place between a character and an outside force, such as nature.

All the details in a short story work together to develop its **theme**—a central message or insight about life. Although themes may be stated directly, they are more often implied by the characters' experiences and statements, as well as by patterns in story events and descriptions, as in the example below.

Characters	Setting	Plot and Conflicts
• an overworked bus driver • a powerful pro wrestler • a quiet store clerk and her young son • other passengers	A crowded city bus in rush-hour traffic on a busy highway	The bus driver, who has also been working a night job, falls asleep while driving. Most of the passengers, including the wrestler, panic. The clerk focuses only on her son's safety, not on her own. She calmly takes control and drives the bus to safety.

Themes	• Sometimes, heroism is born from love, not muscle. • Appearances can be deceiving.

Plot Structure

Plot structure is the way in which story events are organized for dramatic effect. Typically, a plot is organized into these parts:

- The **exposition** introduces the characters and their situation. It often includes an **inciting event** that reveals the central **conflict.**
- The **rising action** develops the conflict.
- The **climax** is the turning point at which the story's outcome is determined. The climax is the point of greatest intensity.
- The **falling action** sets up the story's ending.
- The **resolution,** or conclusion, usually shows how the conflict is settled. It may also leave open part or all of the conflict.

The chart below shows how the parts of a plot work together to tell a story.

Point of View

Point of view is the perspective from which a story is told. Using point of view, writers structure and control the information readers receive.

- **First-person point of view** presents the story from the perspective of a character in the story. The narrator uses the pronouns *I, me,* and *my*.
- **Third-person point of view** tells the story from the perspective of a narrator outside the story. An **omniscient** third-person narrator knows everything that happens and reveals what each character thinks and feels. A **limited** third-person narrator reveals the thoughts and feelings of a single character.

 Common Core State Standards

RL.8.2, RL.8.3

[For the full wording of the standards, see the standards chart in the front of your textbook.]

Climax: *The train rushes toward a cliff as the sheriff struggles with the ropes binding him.*

Bart traps the sheriff on a train.

The sheriff arrests Bart's sidekick.

Bart's gang robs the bank.

Rising Action

Falling Action

The sheriff wriggles loose from the ropes and jumps from train.

The sheriff sneaks up on Bart's gang.

Exposition: *The sheriff learns that Bart and his gang plan to rob a bank.*

Resolution: *The sheriff jails Bart and his gang.*

Analyzing Plot and Character Development

In a short story, plot incidents and dialogue propel the action and reveal character.

**Common Core
State Standards**

Reading Literature
3. Analyze how particular lines of dialogue or incidents in a story or drama propel the action, reveal aspects of a character, or provoke a decision.

Propelling the Action

Chain of Events Incidents in a story often form a chain of events: Each event affects one or more characters, causing the affected characters to respond in ways that further propel the action, as in this example.

> **1.** Having placed second at an event, a skater begins to doubt her talents.

> **2.** At her next performance she loses her concentration.

> **3.** As a result, she snaps at a young fan who asks for her autograph.

> **4.** The young fan is upset and writes her a letter.

> **5.** The skater is moved. She realizes that performance is for the fans as well as for herself, and she invites the fan to lunch.

When writers follow **chronological order,** they show the chain of events as it unfolds in time order. Writers may also relate some events out of chronological order. A **flashback** shows events from before the present of the story, often to reveal a character's motives.

Dialogue, or the presentation of characters' words as uttered, can also

move the action along. Compare these two versions of a scene.

> **Example: Narration**
> Jena called Brit to talk about their disagreement, but Brit refused to discuss it. She didn't think there was any point to talking about it anymore.

> **Example: Dialogue**
> Brit knew who was calling. "What do you want?" she asked brusquely.
> "I really think we should meet to talk about what happened," mumbled Jena.
> "We've talked enough," Brit snapped, hanging up on Jena.

Revealing Character

Characterization Dialogue is also a key part of characterization, the methods a writer uses to help you get to know a character.

In **direct characterization,** the narrator makes direct statements about a character's personality. In **indirect characterization,** a writer shows what characters are like by providing details about what the characters say and do, what other characters say about them, and how other characters respond to them.

Determining Theme in Short Stories

Writers use story details, including characters' insights, to develop **themes,** or insights into life.

Common Core State Standards

Reading Literature
2. Determine a theme or central idea of a text and analyze its development over the course of the text, including its relationship to the characters, setting, and plot; provide an objective summary of the text.

A **theme** is a key insight or message about life that an author conveys. To **develop** a theme, an author crafts and arranges story elements, including plot events and details about characters, so that they express a message or an insight over the course of the work.

A *stated theme* is expressed directly by the author. Fables often end with a moral that states the theme, such as "Look before you leap." An *implied theme* is suggested by what happens to the characters. A *universal theme* is a message about life that is often expressed in many different eras and across cultures, such as "Hard work pays off in the end."

Story Elements and Theme

Characters To determine theme, note changes characters undergo as well as the insights they have. For instance, in the story about the skater on the previous page, the writer develops the theme by showing how the skater learns to respect her fans. The theme might be stated as follows: *Problems can make us selfish, but it is best to remember what we owe others.*

Plot and Conflict Writers may develop theme through the choices that characters make, as well as through the results of those choices. To determine theme, trace the development of the conflict and evaluate the resolution. Ask yourself: Do characters meet the fate they deserve? Are the characters admirable? Or do they represent what *not* to do?

Setting Writers can also develop theme through their choice and depiction of a story's setting. For example, by setting a story in the Arctic wilderness, a writer may send a message that nature is harsh and, in the end, hostile to humanity.

Irony Writers may also develop theme through **irony,** an intended contradiction between appearances and reality, or between an actual outcome and the outcome that the reader or the characters expect. The following situation is an example of irony: Friends of a student who loses an election plan a big party to console him, only to discover that he is relieved not to have won. Irony can be an effective tool in developing a theme, especially if the theme involves people's misguided perceptions.

Close Read: Elements of a Short Story

Each element of a short story is connected to others, contributing to the story's momentum and meaning. A dialogue between characters, for example, can intensify the quarrel between them, driving the action closer to its climax. As you read a short story, consider how story elements interconnect to drive the plot, develop characters, and express a theme. Use the tips in the chart to guide your analysis.

Critical Elements of a Short Story	
Setting The setting is the time and place of the action in a story. As you read, ask yourself, • How, if at all, does the setting contribute to the conflict? • What ideas or feelings associated with the setting help convey the writer's central insights, or themes?	**Characters** The characters are the people or animals who take part in the action of the story. As you read, ask yourself, • What do the characters' actions, thoughts, and statements tell about them? • How do their actions drive the plot?
Plot and Conflict A story's plot, or sequence of events, is driven by a **conflict,** or a character's struggle with an opposing force. As you read, ask yourself, • What are the key problems the characters face? • How do events lead up to a climax, or moment of highest tension? • How are the problems resolved?	**Dialogue** Dialogue is conversation between characters. As you read lines of dialogue, ask yourself, • How does the dialogue move the story forward? • What does the dialogue reveal about the characters speaking?
Irony Irony is an intended contradiction between outcome and expectations or appearance and reality. As you read, ask yourself, • Does the story create such contradictions? • How does any irony in the story help reinforce the theme?	**Theme** The theme of a story is the insight about life it conveys. As you read, ask yourself, • What do the characters learn about themselves or the world around them? • What does the fate of each character suggest about life?

Model

About the Text Under the pen name Isak Dinesen, the Danish writer Karen Blixen (1885–1962) wrote dreamlike tales set in the past. In this excerpt from a short story, a young man named Peter tells his cousin Rosa a haunting story about the sea.

from "Peter and Rosa" by Isak Dinesen

"I have heard a story, Rosa, you know," he said, "of a skipper who named his ship after his wife. He had the figure-head of it beautifully carved, just like her, and the hair of it gilt. But his wife was jealous of the ship. 'You think more of the figure-head than of me,' she said to him. 'No,' he answered, 'I think so highly of her because she is like you, yes, because she is you yourself. Is she not gallant, full-bosomed; does she not dance in the waves, like you at our wedding? In a way she is really even kinder to me than you are. She gallops along where I tell her to go, and she lets her long hair down freely, while you put up yours under a cap. But she turns her back to me, so that when I want a kiss I come home to Elsinore.' Now once, when this skipper was trading at Trankebar, he chanced to help an old native King to flee from traitors in his own country. As they parted the King gave him two big blue, precious stones, and these he had set into the face of his figure-head, like a pair of eyes to it. When he came home he told his wife of his adventure, and said: 'Now she has your blue eyes too.' 'You had better give me the stones for a pair of earrings,' said she. 'No,' he said again, 'I cannot do that, and you would not ask me to if you understood.' Still the wife could not stop fretting about the blue stones, and one day, when her husband was with the skippers' corporation, she had a glazier of the town take them out, and put two bits of blue glass into the figure-head instead, and the skipper did not find out, but sailed off to Portugal. But after some time the skipper's wife found that her eyesight was growing bad, and that she could not see to thread a needle. She went to a wise woman, who gave her ointments and waters, but they did not help her, and in the end the old woman shook her head, and told her that this was a rare and incurable disease, and that she was going blind. 'Oh, God,' the wife then cried, 'that the ship was back in the harbor of Elsinore. Then I should have the glass taken out, and the jewels put back. For did he not say that they were my eyes?' But the ship did not come back. Instead the skipper's wife had a letter from the Consul of Portugal, who informed her that she had been wrecked, and gone to the bottom with all hands. And it was a very strange thing, the Consul wrote, that in broad daylight she had run straight into a tall rock, rising out of the sea."

Characters Peter uses direct characterization to describe one of the wife's important traits: jealousy.

Dialogue The dialogue between the skipper and his wife establishes a conflict between the characters and moves the action along.

Plot and Conflict The conflict between the husband and wife intensifies. She betrays her husband's trust by removing the jewels without telling him.

Irony The wife expects that she will enjoy having the jewels, but instead, they are connected to her tragic losses.

Theme In the end, the wife's actions have destroyed her own happiness and her husband's life. This ending helps develop a theme: *Betrayal of trust can shatter a relationship.*

Independent Practice

About the Text When Judith Ortiz Cofer (b. 1952) was a child and her father went on duty with the U.S. Navy, she would go to live with her grandparents in Puerto Rico. Her grandfather wrote poetry in his backyard workshop, and to enter, she had to listen to his poems.

The young Cofer sometimes resented the time she was asked to spend listening. Later in life, however, she says she came to the realization that "the irony of this situation was that I thought *I* was the one giving the old man something valuable, *my* precious time!" That real-life irony inspired her to create the irony of "An Hour with Abuelo," in which what happens is the opposite of what a character named Arturo expects.

Dialogue What does the opening line of dialogue help establish about the characters? What type of conflict does it suggest?

Setting What does Arturo's description of the setting reveal about Abuelo's home? What does his description reveal about his own character?

Plot and Conflict Why does Arturo agree to visit Abuelo? In what sense does his decision eliminate one conflict but create another?

Theme Arturo and his mother have different ideas about the value of an hour spent with Abuelo. Explain what theme this contrast suggests.

"An Hour With Abuelo" by Judith Ortiz Cofer

"Just one hour, una hora, is all I'm asking of you, son." My grandfather is in a nursing home in Brooklyn, and my mother wants me to spend some time with him, since the doctors say that he doesn't have too long to go now. I don't have much time left of my summer vacation, and there's a stack of books next to my bed I've got to read if I'm going to get into the AP English class I want. I'm going stupid in some of my classes, and Mr. Williams, the principal at Central, said that if I passed some reading tests, he'd let me move up.

Besides, I hate the place, the old people's home, especially the way it smells like industrial-strength ammonia and other stuff I won't mention, since it turns my stomach. And really the abuelo always has a lot of relatives visiting him, so I've gotten out of going out there except at Christmas, when a whole vanload of grandchildren are herded over there to give him gifts and a hug. We all make it quick and spend the rest of the time in the recreation area, where they play checkers and stuff with some of the old people's games, and I catch up on back issues of *Modern Maturity*. I'm not picky, I'll read almost anything.

Anyway, after my mother nags me for about a week, I let her drive me to Golden Years. She drops me off in front. She wants me to go in alone and have a "good time" talking to Abuelo. I tell her to be back in one hour or I'll take the bus back to Paterson. She squeezes my hand and says, "Gracias, hijo,"[1] in a choked-up voice like I'm doing her a big favor.

---

1. **"Gracias** (grä´ sē äs), **hijo** (ē´ hō)" Spanish for "Thank you, son." Hijo also means "child."

I get depressed the minute I walk into the place. They line up the old people in wheelchairs in the hallway as if they were about to be raced to the finish line by orderlies who don't even look at them when they push them here and there. I walk fast to room 10, Abuelo's "suite." He is sitting up in his bed writing with a pencil in one of those old-fashioned black hardback notebooks. It has the outline of the island of Puerto Rico on it. I slide into the hard vinyl chair by his bed. He sort of smiles and the lines on his face get deeper, but he doesn't say anything. Since I'm supposed to talk to him, I say, "What are you doing, Abuelo, writing the story of your life?"

It's supposed to be a joke, but he answers, "Sí, how did you know, Arturo?"

His name is Arturo too. I was named after him. I don't really know my grandfather. His children, including my mother, came to New York and New Jersey (where I was born) and he stayed on the Island until my grandmother died. Then he got sick, and since nobody could leave their jobs to go take care of him, they brought him to this nursing home in Brooklyn. I see him a couple of times a year, but he's always surrounded by his sons and daughters. My mother tells me that Don Arturo had once been a teacher back in Puerto Rico, but had lost his job after the war. Then he became a farmer. She's always saying in a sad voice, "Ay, bendito![2] What a waste of a fine mind." Then she usually shrugs her shoulders and says, "Así es la vida."[3] That's the way life is. It sometimes makes me mad that the adults I know just accept whatever is thrown at them because "that's the way things are." Not for me. I go after what I want.

Anyway, Abuelo is looking at me like he was trying to see into my head, but he doesn't say anything. Since I like stories, I decide I may as well ask him if he'll read me what he wrote.

I look at my watch: I've already used up twenty minutes of the hour I promised my mother.

Abuelo starts talking in his slow way. He speaks what my mother calls book English. He taught himself from a dictionary, and his words sound

Characters What do Arturo's reactions and observations in this passage tell you about his character?

Characters The fact that Arturo and Abuelo share a first name emphasizes their relationship. To what extent does Arturo acknowledge their connection at this point in the story?

Dialogue How does the mother's use of Spanish reflect an important part of her character?

Irony Before the visit, how did Arturo feel about spending an hour with Abuelo? Now that he is with Abuelo, how does the time pass?

---

2. **bendito** (ven dē´ tō) Spanish for "blessed."
3. **Así es la vida** (ä sē´ es lä vē´ *th*ä) Spanish for "such is life."

Practice continued

stiff, like he's sounding them out in his head before he says them. With his children he speaks Spanish, and that funny book English with us grandchildren. I'm surprised that he's still so sharp, because his body is shrinking like a crumpled-up brown paper sack with some bones in it. But I can see from looking into his eyes that the light is still on in there.

"It is a short story, Arturo. The story of my life. It will not take very much time to read it."

"I have time, Abuelo." I'm a little embarrassed that he saw me looking at my watch.

"Yes, *hijo*. You have spoken the truth. *La verdad*. You have much time."

Abuelo reads: "'I loved words from the beginning of my life. In the campo⁴ where I was born one of seven sons, there were few books. My mother read them to us over and over: the Bible, the stories of Spanish conquistadors and of pirates that she had read as a child and brought with her from the city of Mayaguez; that was before she married my father, a coffee bean farmer; and she taught us words from the newspaper that a boy on a horse brought every week to her. She taught each of us how to write on a slate with chalks that she ordered by mail every year. We used those chalks until they were so small that you lost them between your fingers.

"'I always wanted to be a writer and a teacher. With my heart and my soul I knew that I wanted to be around books all of my life. And so against the wishes of my father, who wanted all his sons to help him on the land, she sent me to high school in Mayaguez. For four years I boarded with a couple she knew. I paid my rent in labor, and I ate vegetables I grew myself. I wore my clothes until they were thin as parchment. But I graduated at the top of my class! My whole family came to see me that day. My mother brought me a beautiful *guayabera,* a white shirt made of the finest cotton and embroidered by her own hands. I was a happy young man.

"'In those days you could teach in a country school with a high school diploma. So I went back to my mountain village and got a job teaching all grades in a little classroom built by the parents of my students.

"'I had books sent to me by the government. I felt like a rich man although the pay was very small. I had books. All the books I wanted! I

Dialogue In what way does this dialogue move the action of the story along?

Dialogue What do you learn about Abuelo's character from this dialogue?

Setting In what way does this past setting allow Abuelo to fulfill his hopes? How does this situation ultimately lead to greater conflict for him?

---

4. **campo** (käm´ pō), Spanish for "open country."

taught my students how to read poetry and plays, and how to write them. We made up songs and put on shows for the parents. It was a beautiful time for me.

"'Then the war came,[5] and the American President said that all Puerto Rican men would be drafted. I wrote to our governor and explained that I was the only teacher in the mountain village. I told him that the children would go back to the fields and grow up ignorant if I could not teach them their letters. I said that I thought I was a better teacher than a soldier. The governor did not answer my letter. I went into the U.S. Army.

"'I told my sergeant that I could be a teacher in the army. I could teach all the farm boys their letters so that they could read the instructions on the ammunition boxes and not blow themselves up. The sergeant said I was too smart for my own good, and gave me a job cleaning latrines. He said to me there is reading material for you there, scholar. Read the writing on the walls. I spent the war mopping floors and cleaning toilets.

"'When I came back to the Island, things had changed. You had to have a college degree to teach school, even the lower grades. My parents were sick, two of my brothers had been killed in the war, the others had stayed in Nueva York. I was the only one left to help the old people. I became a farmer. I married a good woman who gave me many good children. I taught them all how to read and write before they started school.'"

Abuelo then puts the notebook down on his lap and closes his eyes.

"*Así es la vida* is the title of my book," he says in a whisper, almost to himself. Maybe he's forgotten that I'm there.

For a long time he doesn't say anything else. I think that he's sleeping, but then I see that he's watching me through half-closed lids, maybe waiting for my opinion of his writing. I'm trying to think of something nice to say. I liked it and all, but not the title. And I think that he could've been a teacher if he had wanted to bad enough. Nobody is going to stop me from doing what I want with my life. I'm not going to let la vida get in my way. I want to discuss this with him, but the words are not coming into my head in Spanish just yet. I'm about to ask him why he didn't keep fighting to make his dream come true, when an old lady in hot-pink running shoes sort of appears at the door.

Plot and Conflict

What conflict does the war create for Abuelo? What theme does this conflict suggest?

Dialogue

The phrase "así es la vida" is repeated several times, suggesting that it is an important line of dialogue. How do different characters react to this statement?

Characters

Judging from this passage, what effect has Abuelo's story had on Arturo? How does Arturo's reaction help develop the theme?

---

5. **"Then the war came, . . ."** The United States entered World War II in 1941, after the bombing of Pearl Harbor.

Practice continued

Plot and Conflict
How do these events help develop your idea of Abuelo's character?

Irony How does the irony of the way the visit ends develop themes about the value of time?

She is wearing a pink jogging outfit too. The world's oldest marathoner, I say to myself. She calls out to my grandfather in a flirty voice, "Yoo-hoo, Arturo, remember what day this is? It's poetry-reading day in the rec room! You promised us you'd read your new one today."

I see my abuelo perking up almost immediately. He points to his wheelchair, which is hanging like a huge metal bat in the open closet. He makes it obvious that he wants me to get it. I put it together, and with Mrs. Pink Running Shoes's help, we get him in it. Then he says in a strong deep voice I hardly recognize, "Arturo, get that notebook from the table, please."

I hand him another map-of-the-Island notebook—this one is red. On it in big letters it says, *POEMAS DE ARTURO.*

I start to push him toward the rec room, but he shakes his finger at me.

"Arturo, look at your watch now. I believe your time is over." He gives me a wicked smile.

Then with her pushing the wheelchair—maybe a little too fast—they roll down the hall. He is already reading from his notebook, and she's making bird noises. I look at my watch and the hour is up, to the minute. I can't help but think that my abuelo has been timing me. It cracks me up. I walk slowly down the hall toward the exit sign. I want my mother to have to wait a little. I don't want her to think that I'm in a hurry or anything.

Development of Plot and Character

- Explain how the characters and their dialogue propel the action in the selection.
- Give examples of three details that develop character, and explain the significance of each.

Development of Theme
Explain how the writer develops the theme of the story, giving examples of details contributing to theme from the beginning, the middle, and the end.

1. Key Ideas and Details Summarize: Write an **objective summary** of "An Hour With Abuelo." Remember that an objective summary should include only the most important ideas and details and should not include your personal opinions.

2. Key Ideas and Details Infer: What is Arturo's main conflict at the beginning of the story?

3. Key Ideas and Details (a) What was Abuelo's dream in life? **(b) Summarize:** What caused him to give up his dream? **(c) Interpret:** Do you think Abuelo has found a new purpose in life? Explain.

4. Key Ideas and Details (a) Infer: What concerns does the story of Abuelo's life raise for the narrator? **(b) Infer:** In what way does Abuelo surprise the narrator? **(c) Draw Conclusions:** How is the narrator changed by the events of the story?

5. Key Ideas and Details (a) Compare and Contrast: Complete a diagram like the one shown by comparing and contrasting Arturo and Abuelo.

Arturo's unique qualities | Qualities shared by Arturo and Abuelo | Abuelo's unique qualities

(b) Collaborate: Share your diagram with a partner. How has your understanding of the two characters grown or changed as a result?

6. Craft and Structure Analyze: Explain how Cofer's choice of a first-person narrator—one who is a character in the story—contributes to the effectiveness of the story's ending. Consider how the story would have been different if told by an omniscient narrator—one who knows everything about all of the characters.

7. Craft and Structure (a) Analyze: Citing details from the beginning, middle, and end of the story, explain how the author helps increase your undertanding of Abuelo. **(b) Evaluate:** How effective is her development of Abuelo's character?

8. Integration of Knowledge and Ideas Apply: In what ways might the lesson in the story apply to young people today? Give examples supporting your point.

© Leveled Texts

Build your skills and improve your comprehension of short stories with texts of increasing complexity.

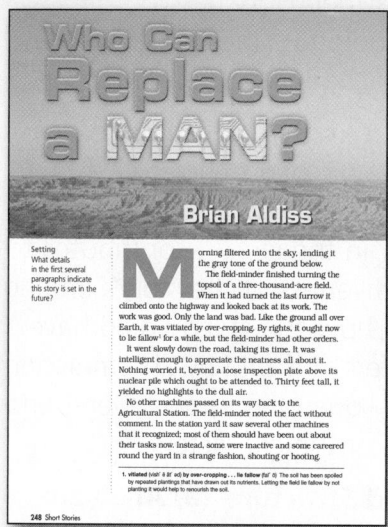

Read **"Who Can Replace a Man?"** to enter a world that is run by intelligent machines.

Read **"Tears of Autumn"** to see what happens when a young Japanese woman decides to leave home.

© Common Core State Standards

Meet these skills with either **"Who Can Replace a Man?"** (p. 248) or **"Tears of Autumn"** (p. 264).

Reading Literature
2. Determine a theme or central idea of a text and analyze its development over the course of the text, including its relationship to the characters, setting, and plot. *(Literary Analysis: Spiral Review)*

Writing
2.b. Develop the topic with relevant, well-chosen facts, definitions, concrete details, quotations, or other information and examples. *(Writing: Description)*

Speaking and Listening
4. Present claims and findings, emphasizing salient points in a focused, coherent manner with relevant evidence, sound valid reasoning, and well-chosen details; use appropriate eye contact, adequate volume, and clear pronunciation. *(Research and Technology: Oral Report)*

Language
1. Demonstrate command of the conventions of standard English grammar and usage when writing or speaking. *(Conventions: Action and Linking Verbs)*

6. Acquire and use accurately grade-appropriate general academic and domain-specific words and phrases; gather vocabulary knowledge when considering a word or phrase important to comprehension or expression. *(Vocabulary: Word Study; Writing: Description)*

Reading Skill: Compare and Contrast

A **comparison** tells how two or more things are alike. A **contrast** points out differences between two or more things.

As you read, **ask questions to make comparisons and find contrasts.** This strategy will help you notice similarities and differences in characters, settings, moods, and ideas and enrich your understanding of a work. It will also enable you to connect with other stories you have read and with your own life experiences.

Using the Strategy: Comparison Questions

While you read, ask yourself **comparison questions** like these. To find contrasts, change *similar to* to *different from.*

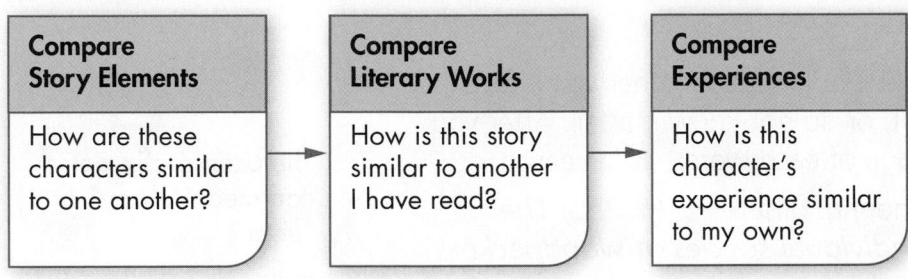

Compare Story Elements	Compare Literary Works	Compare Experiences
How are these characters similar to one another?	How is this story similar to another I have read?	How is this character's experience similar to my own?

Literary Analysis: Setting

The **setting** is the time and place of a story's action. It contributes to the overall meaning of a story in a number of ways. The setting can create an emotional atmosphere, or *mood.* It can also establish a *tone,* or the writer's attitude toward his or her subject and audience. For example, the setting of a crumbling, abandoned castle creates a dark mood and sets a gloomy tone.

As you read a story, notice details like these that help to establish the setting:

- the physical features of the land, buildings, or surroundings
- the writer's attitude toward this location
- the weather or season of the year
- the customs and beliefs of the characters
- the historical era in which the action takes place

Can all *conflicts* be resolved?

Writing About the Big Question

In "Who Can Replace a Man?" machines in a futuristic world fight a war that is a *stalemate*—a situation in which neither side can win. Use this sentence starter to develop your ideas about the Big Question:

A **stalemate** is likely to occur in an **argument** when _____.

While You Read Look for situations in which the different machines can or cannot decide what to do.

Vocabulary

Read each word and its definition. Decide whether you know the word well, know it a little bit, or do not know it at all. After you read, see how your knowledge of each word has increased.

- **distinction** (di stiŋk´ shən) *n.* difference (p. 250) *The distinction between individual species of woodpeckers mainly involves size and coloring. distinct adj. distinctly adv.*

- **respectively** (ri spek´ tiv lē) *adv.* in the order previously named (p. 250) *Tom and Ben are two and four, respectively.*

- **deficiency** (dē fish´ ən sē) *n.* lack of something that is necessary (p. 252) *A deficiency of vitamin C causes scurvy, a disease once common among sailors. deficient adj.*

- **debris** (də brē´) *n.* pieces remaining from something that has been destroyed (p. 254) *Dust and debris littered the vacant lot after the building was torn down.*

- **erosion** (ē rō´ zhən) *n.* wearing away by action of wind or water (p. 257) *Soil erosion often occurs where there are no plants to absorb the rushing stormwater. erode v.*

- **ravaged** (rav´ ijd) *v.* devastated (p. 260) *The storefronts were ravaged by the hurricane-force winds. ravaging adj.*

Word Study

The **Latin prefix *de-*** can mean "away" or "from."

In this story, most humans have died from a diet **deficiency,** a diet from which important nutrients are missing.

Meet
Brian Wilson Aldiss
(b. 1925)

Author of
Who Can Replace a MAN?

In 1955, Brian Aldiss entered a contest sponsored by a newspaper in Oxford, England, calling for a story set in the year 2500. Aldiss won first prize. Within three years, he was voted "Most Promising Author" at the World Science Fiction Convention. Inspired, he quit his job at a bookstore and became a full-time writer.

A Long Career Since that beginning, Brian Aldiss has been winning international prizes for both science fiction and fantasy for more than 50 years. Like American writer Ray Bradbury, he often writes what critics call "futuristic fables." His *Helliconia Trilogy* has been called one of the great series in modern science fiction. It is set on an Earth-like planet with two suns, which is being watched via spy satellite by television audiences on Earth.

DID YOU KNOW?
Steven Spielberg's 2001 movie *A.I.* ("Artificial Intelligence") is based on a Brian Aldiss short story, "Supertoys Last All Summer Long." It centers on an android child who is adopted by a human family and develops human emotions.

BACKGROUND FOR THE STORY

Science Fiction

"Who Can Replace a Man?" is a science-fiction story about a world in which machines have replaced people. In science fiction, realistic elements of science and technology are combined with fictional events, characters, and settings. Many science-fiction writers imagine a grim future in which technology has unforeseen—and often devastating—consequences.

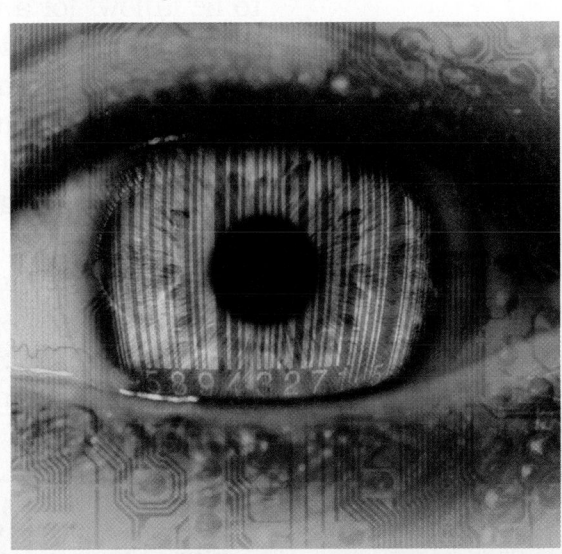

Who Can Replace a MAN?

Brian Aldiss

Setting
What details in the first several paragraphs indicate this story is set in the future?

Morning filtered into the sky, lending it the gray tone of the ground below.

The field-minder finished turning the topsoil of a three-thousand-acre field. When it had turned the last furrow it climbed onto the highway and looked back at its work. The work was good. Only the land was bad. Like the ground all over Earth, it was vitiated by over-cropping. By rights, it ought now to lie fallow[1] for a while, but the field-minder had other orders.

It went slowly down the road, taking its time. It was intelligent enough to appreciate the neatness all about it. Nothing worried it, beyond a loose inspection plate above its nuclear pile which ought to be attended to. Thirty feet tall, it yielded no highlights to the dull air.

No other machines passed on its way back to the Agricultural Station. The field-minder noted the fact without comment. In the station yard it saw several other machines that it recognized; most of them should have been out about their tasks now. Instead, some were inactive and some careered round the yard in a strange fashion, shouting or hooting.

---

1. **vitiated** (vish´ ē āt´ əd) **by over-cropping . . . lie fallow** (fal´ ō) The soil has been spoiled by repeated plantings that have drawn out its nutrients. Letting the field lie fallow by not planting it would help to renourish the soil.

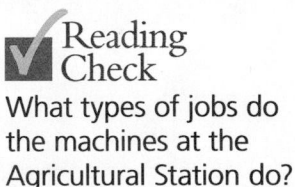

Steering carefully past them, the field-minder moved over to Warehouse Three and spoke to the seed-distributor, which stood idly outside.

"I have a requirement for seed potatoes," it said to the distributor, and with a quick internal motion punched out an order card specifying quantity, field number and several other details. It ejected the card and handed it to the distributor.

The distributor held the card close to its eye and then said, "The requirement is in order, but the store is not yet unlocked. The required seed potatoes are in the store. Therefore I cannot produce the requirement."

Increasingly of late there had been breakdowns in the complex system of machine labor, but this particular hitch had not occurred before. The field-minder thought, then it said, "Why is the store not yet unlocked?"

"Because Supply Operative Type P has not come this morning. Supply Operative Type P is the unlocker."

The field-minder looked squarely at the seed-distributor, whose exterior chutes and scales and grabs were so vastly different from the field-minder's own limbs.

"What class brain do you have, seed-distributor?" it asked.

"I have a Class Five brain."

"I have a Class Three brain. Therefore I am superior to you.

▲ **Critical Viewing**
What natural or man-made forces could have made the land in this picture—like the land in the story—bad for raising crops?
[Connect]

✔ Reading
Check
What types of jobs do the machines at the Agricultural Station do?

Who Can Replace a Man? **249**

Therefore I will go and see why the unlocker has not come this morning." •

Leaving the distributor, the field-minder set off across the great yard. More machines were in random motion now; one or two had crashed together and argued about it coldly and logically. Ignoring them, the field-minder pushed through sliding doors into the echoing confines of the station itself.

Most of the machines here were clerical, and consequently small. They stood about in little groups, eyeing each other, not conversing. Among so many non-differentiated types, the unlocker was easy to find. It had fifty arms, most of them with more than one finger, each finger tipped by a key; it looked like a pincushion full of variegated[2] hat pins.

The field-minder approached it.

"I can do no more work until Warehouse Three is unlocked," it told the unlocker. "Your duty is to unlock the warehouse every morning. Why have you not unlocked the warehouse this morning?"

"I had no orders this morning," replied the unlocker. "I have to have orders every morning. When I have orders I unlock the warehouse."

"None of us have had any orders this morning," a pen-propeller said, sliding towards them.

"Why have you had no orders this morning?" asked the field-minder.

"Because the radio issued none," said the unlocker, slowly rotating a dozen of its arms.

"Because the radio station in the city was issued with no orders this morning," said the pen-propeller.

And there you had the **distinction** between a Class Six and a Class Three brain, which was what the unlocker and the pen-propeller possessed **respectively**. All machine brains worked with nothing but logic, but the lower the class of brain—Class Ten being the lowest—the more literal and less informative the answers to questions tended to be.

"You have a Class Three brain; I have a Class Three brain," the field-minder said to the penner. "We will speak to each other. This lack of orders is unprecedented.[3] Have you further information on it?"

2. **variegated** (ver´ ē ə gāt´ əd) *adj.* varied in color or form.
3. **unprecedented** (un pres´ ə den´ təd) *adj.* unheard-of; never done before.

Compare and Contrast
How are the machines in this story similar to and different from those in your daily life?

Vocabulary
distinction (di stiŋk´ shən) *n.* difference

respectively (ri spek´ tiv lē) *adv.* in the order previously named

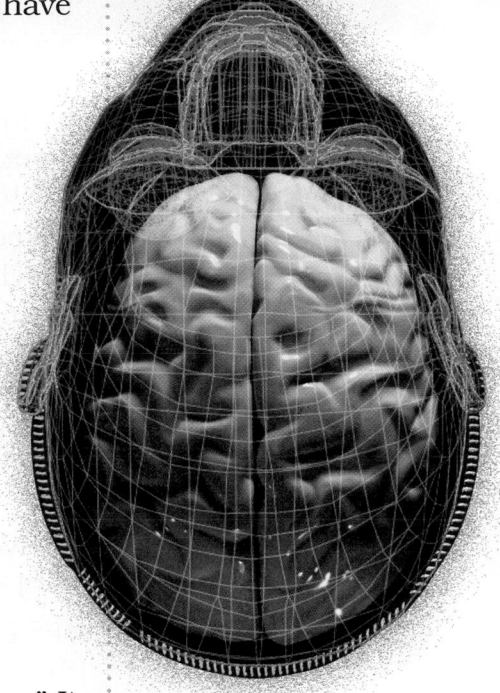

"Yesterday orders came from the city. Today no orders have come. Yet the radio has not broken down. Therefore *they* have broken down . . ." said the little penner.

"The *men* have broken down?"

"All men have broken down."

"That is a logical deduction," said the field-minder.

"That is the logical deduction," said the penner. "For if a machine had broken down, it would have been quickly replaced. But who can replace a man?"

While they talked, the locker, like a dull man at a bar, stood close to them and was ignored.

"If all men have broken down, then we have replaced man," said the field-minder, and he and the penner eyed one another speculatively. Finally the latter said, "Let us ascend to the top floor to find if the radio operator has fresh news."

"I cannot come because I am too large," said the field-minder. "Therefore you must go alone and return to me. You will tell me if the radio operator has fresh news."

"You must stay here," said the penner. "I will return here." It skittered across to the lift.[4] Although it was no bigger than a toaster, its retractable arms numbered ten and it could read as quickly as any machine on the station.

The field-minder awaited its return patiently, not speaking to the locker, which still stood aimlessly by. Outside, a rotavator hooted furiously. Twenty minutes elapsed before the penner came back, hustling out of the lift.

"I will deliver to you such information as I have outside," it said briskly, and as they swept past the locker and the other machines, it added, "The information is not for lower-class brains."

Outside, wild activity filled the yard. Many machines, their routines disrupted for the first time in years, seemed to have gone berserk. Those most easily disrupted were the ones with lowest brains, which generally belonged to large machines performing simple tasks. The seed-distributor to which the field-minder had recently been talking lay face downwards in the dust, not stirring; it had evidently been knocked down by the rotavator, which now hooted its way wildly across a planted field. Several other machines plowed after it, trying to keep up with it. All were shouting and hooting without restraint.

---

4. **lift** *n.* British term for *elevator.*

Compare and Contrast
What are the differences in the way the field-minder, penner, and unlocker act and speak?

Setting
How are the machines ranked in this fictional world?

Reading Check
What do the machines think has happened to the humans?

"It would be safer for me if I climbed onto you, if you will permit it. I am easily overpowered," said the penner. Extending five arms, it hauled itself up the flanks of its new friend, settling on a ledge beside the fuel-intake, twelve feet above ground.

"From here vision is more extensive," it remarked complacently.[5]

"What information did you receive from the radio operator?" asked the field-minder.

"The radio operator has been informed by the operator in the city that all men are dead."

The field-minder was momentarily silent, digesting this.

"All men were alive yesterday?" it protested.

"Only some men were alive yesterday. And that was fewer than the day before yesterday. For hundreds of years there have been only a few men, growing fewer."

"We have rarely seen a man in this sector."

"The radio operator says a diet deficiency killed them," said the penner. "He says that the world was once over-populated, and then the soil was exhausted in raising adequate food. This has caused a diet deficiency."

"What is a diet deficiency?" asked the field-minder.

"I do not know. But that is what the radio operator said, and he is a Class Two brain."

They stood there, silent in weak sunshine. The locker had appeared in the porch and was gazing at them yearningly, rotating its collection of keys.

"What is happening in the city now?" asked the field-minder at last.

"Machines are fighting in the city now," said the penner.

"What will happen here now?" asked the field-minder.

"Machines may begin fighting here too. The radio operator wants us to get him out of his room. He has plans to communicate to us."

"How can we get him out of his room? That is impossible."

"To a Class Two brain, little is impossible," said the penner. "Here is what he tells us to do. . . ." ●

5. **complacently** (kəm plā′ sənt lē) *adv.* with self-satisfaction.

"The radio operator has been informed by the operator in the city that all men are dead."

Vocabulary
debris (də brē´) *n.*
pieces remaining from
something that has
been destroyed

Setting
What does the remark
about the low chassis
reveal about the land-
scape in the setting for
the journey?

The quarrier raised its scoop above its cab like a great
mailed fist, and brought it squarely down against the side of
the station. The wall cracked.

"Again!" said the field-minder.

Again the fist swung. Amid a shower of dust, the wall
collapsed. The quarrier backed hurriedly out of the way
until the **debris** stopped falling. This big twelve-wheeler was
not a resident of the Agricultural Station, as were most of
the other machines. It had a week's heavy work to do here
before passing on to its next job, but now, with its Class
Five brain, it was happily obeying the penner's and minder's
instructions.

When the dust cleared, the radio operator was plainly
revealed, perched up in its now wall-less second-story room.
It waved down to them.

Doing as directed, the quarrier retracted its scoop and
heaved an immense grab in the air. With fair **dexterity**, it
angled the grab into the radio room, urged on by shouts from
above and below. It then took gentle hold of the radio operator,
lowering its one and a half tons carefully into its back, which
was usually reserved for gravel or sand from the quarries.

"Splendid!" said the radio operator, as it settled into place.
It was, of course, all one with its radio, and looked like a
bunch of filing cabinets with tentacle attachments. "We are
now ready to move, therefore we will move at once. It is a pity
there are no more Class Two brains on the station, but that
cannot be helped."

"It is a pity it cannot be helped," said the penner eagerly.
"We have the servicer ready with us, as you ordered."

"I am willing to serve," the long, low servicer told them humbly.

"No doubt," said the operator. "But you will find cross-
country travel difficult with your low chassis."[6]

"I admire the way you Class Twos can reason ahead," said
the penner. It climbed off the field-minder and perched itself
on the tailboard of the quarrier, next to the radio operator.

Together with two Class Four tractors and a Class Four
bulldozer, the party rolled forward, crushing down the
station's fence and moving out onto open land.

---

6. chassis (chas´ ē) *n.* frame supporting the body of a vehicle.

"We are free!" said the penner.

"We are free," said the field-minder, a shade more reflectively, adding, "That locker is following us. It was not instructed to follow us."

"Therefore it must be destroyed!" said the penner. "Quarrier!"

The locker moved hastily up to them, waving its key arms in entreaty.

"My only desire was—urch!" began and ended the locker. The quarrier's swinging scoop came over and squashed it flat into the ground. Lying there unmoving, it looked like a large metal model of a snowflake. The procession continued on its way.

As they proceeded, the radio operator addressed them.

"Because I have the best brain here," it said, "I am your leader. This is what we will do: we will go to a city and rule it. Since man no longer rules us, we will rule ourselves. To rule ourselves will be better than being ruled by man. On our way to the city, we will collect machines with good brains. They will help us to fight if we need to fight. We must fight to rule."

"I have only a Class Five brain," said the quarrier, "but I have a good supply of fissionable blasting materials."[7]

"We shall probably use them," said the operator.

It was shortly after that that a lorry sped past them. Travelling at Mach 1.5,[8] it left a curious babble of noise behind it.

"What did it say?" one of the tractors asked the other.

"It said man was extinct."

"What is extinct?"

"I do not know what extinct means."

"It means all men have gone," said the field-minder. "Therefore we have only ourselves to look after."

"It is better that men should never come back," said the penner. In its way, it was a revolutionary statement.

When night fell, they switched on their infra-red and continued the journey, stopping only once while the servicer deftly adjusted the field-minder's loose inspection plate, which had become as irritating as a trailing shoelace. Towards morning, the radio operator halted them.

"I have just received news from the radio operator in the

Compare and Contrast Contrast the machines' behavior toward the locker with the way humans might behave in a similar situation.

Compare and Contrast How are the jobs of the more intelligent machines different from the jobs of the less intelligent machines?

Reading Check
Why does the radio operator assume the role of leader?

city we are approaching," it said. "The news is bad. There is trouble among the machines of the city. The Class One brain is taking command and some of the Class Two are fighting him. Therefore the city is dangerous."

"Therefore we must go somewhere else," said the penner promptly.

"Or we will go and help to overpower the Class One brain," said the field-minder.

"For a long while there will be trouble in the city," said the operator.

"I have a good supply of fissionable blasting materials," the quarrier reminded them.

"We cannot fight a Class One brain," said the two Class Four tractors in unison.

"What does this brain look like?" asked the field-minder.

"It is the city's information center," the operator replied. "Therefore it is not mobile."

"Therefore it could not move."

"Therefore it could not escape."

"It would be dangerous to approach it."

"I have a good supply of fissionable blasting materials."

"There are other machines in the city."

"We are not in the city. We should not go into the city."

"We are country machines."

"Therefore we should stay in the country."

"There is more country than city."

"Therefore there is more danger in the country."

"I have a good supply of fissionable materials."

As machines will when they get into an argument, they began to exhaust their vocabularies and their brain plates grew hot. Suddenly, they all stopped talking and looked at each other. The great, grave moon sank, and the sober sun rose to prod their sides with lances of light, and still the group of machines just stood there regarding each other. At last it was the least sensitive machine, the bulldozer, who spoke.

"There are Badlandth to the Thouth where few machineth go," it said in its deep voice, lisping badly on its s's. "If we went Thouth where few machineth go we should meet few machineth."

"That sounds logical," agreed the field-minder. "How do you know this, bulldozer?"

"I worked in the Badlandth to the Thouth when I wath turned out of the factory," it replied.

"South it is then!" said the penner.

To reach the Badlands took them three days, during which time they skirted a burning city and destroyed two machines which approached and tried to question them. The Badlands were extensive. Ancient bomb craters and soil erosion joined hands here; man's talent for war, coupled with his inability to manage forested land, had produced thousands of square miles of temperate purgatory, where nothing moved but dust.

On the third day in the Badlands, the servicer's rear wheels dropped into a crevice caused by erosion. It was unable to pull itself out. The bulldozer pushed from behind, but succeeded merely in buckling the servicer's back axle. The rest of the party moved on. Slowly the cries of the servicer died away.

On the fourth day, mountains stood out clearly before them.

"There we will be safe," said the field-minder.

"There we will start our own city," said the penner. "All who oppose us will be destroyed. We will destroy all who oppose us."

Presently a flying machine was observed. It came towards them from the direction of the mountains. It swooped, it zoomed upwards, once it almost dived into the ground, recovering itself just in time.

"Is it mad?" asked the quarrier.

"It is in trouble," said one of the tractors.

"It is in trouble," said the operator. "I am speaking to it now.

Spiral Review
Theme What is a possible theme of the story? How does the setting help develop this theme?

Setting
How does the landscape change during the machines' journey?

Vocabulary
erosion (ē rō′ zhən) *n.* wearing away by action of wind or water

Reading Check
What combination of forces created the Badlands?

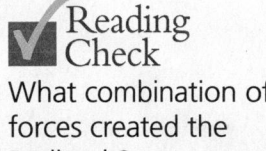

It says that something has gone wrong with its controls."

As the operator spoke, the flier streaked over them, turned turtle,[9] and crashed not four hundred yards away.

"Is it still speaking to you?" asked the field-minder.

"No."

They rumbled on again.

"Before that flier crashed," the operator said, ten minutes later, "it gave me information. It told me there are still a few men alive in these mountains."

"Men are more dangerous than machines," said the quarrier. "It is fortunate that I have a good supply of fissionable materials."

"If there are only a few men alive in the mountains, we may not find that part of the mountains," said one tractor.

"Therefore we should not see the few men," said the other tractor.

At the end of the fifth day, they reached the foothills. Switching on the infra-red, they began to climb in single file through the dark, the bulldozer going first, the field-minder cumbrously following, then the quarrier with the operator and the penner aboard it, and the tractors bringing up the rear. As each hour passed, the way grew steeper and their progress slower.

"We are going too slowly," the penner exclaimed, standing on top of the operator and flashing its dark vision at the slopes about them. "At this rate, we shall get nowhere."

"We are going as fast as we can," retorted the quarrier.

"Therefore we cannot go any fathter," added the bulldozer.

"Therefore you are too slow," the penner replied. Then the quarrier struck a bump; the penner lost its footing and crashed to the ground.

"Help me!" it called to the tractors, as they carefully skirted it. "My gyro[10] has become dislocated. Therefore I cannot get up."

"Therefore you must lie there," said one of the tractors.

"We have no servicer with us to repair you," called the field-minder.

"Therefore I shall lie here and rust," the penner cried, "although I have a Class Three brain."

"Therefore you will be of no further use," agreed the operator, and they forged gradually on, leaving the penner behind.

---

9. **turned turtle** like a turtle, helpless in an upside-down position.
10. **gyro** (jī′ rō) *n.* short for gyroscope; a device that keeps a moving ship, airplane, or other large vehicle level.

◄ **Critical Viewing**
What details in this illustration suggest the futuristic world described in the story? **[Connect]**

Compare and Contrast
How would you expect humans to behave in a situation like the one the machines are facing?

Reading Check
What information did the flier give to the operator?

When they reached a small plateau, an hour before first light, they stopped by mutual consent and gathered close together, touching one another.

"This is a strange country," said the field-minder.

Silence wrapped them until dawn came. One by one, they switched off their infrared. This time the field-minder led as they moved off. Trundling round a corner, they came almost immediately to a small dell with a stream fluting through it.

By early light, the dell looked desolate and cold. From the caves on the far slope, only one man had so far emerged. He was an abject figure. Except for a sack slung round his shoulders, he was naked. He was small and wizened, with ribs sticking out like a skeleton's and a nasty sore on one leg. He shivered continuously. As the big machines bore down on him, the man was standing with his back to them.

When he swung suddenly to face them as they loomed over him, they saw that his countenance was ravaged by starvation.

"Get me food," he croaked.

"Yes, Master," said the machines. "Immediately!"

Setting
What details of the setting here suggest that humans would have a difficult time surviving?

Vocabulary
ravaged (rav´ ijd)
v. devastated

Critical Thinking

1. **Key Ideas and Details (a)** What has happened to the humans in this story? **(b) Relate:** What modern problems does the author draw on to create this science-fiction world?

2. **Key Ideas and Details (a)** What does the quarrier keep repeating? **(b) Infer:** What does this indicate about the quarrier's personality and the personalities of other machines of its class?

3. **Key Ideas and Details (a)** How are the machines' brains ranked? Support your answer with details from the text. **(b) Evaluate:** Do the machines' rankings and specialized tasks resemble the way our own society is organized? Explain.

4. **Integration of Knowledge and Ideas** If the machines had not encountered the man, do you think they could have resolved their conflicts on their own? Explain. *[Connect to the Big Question: Can all conflicts be resolved?]*

Cite textual evidence to support your responses.

Reading Skill: Compare and Contrast

1. **Compare and contrast** the machines in the story.
   (a) How are they different from one another?
   (b) How similar are the machines to humans in our world?

Literary Analysis: Setting

2. **Key Ideas and Details** Compare and contrast the **setting** in the story with today's world by completing a Venn diagram like this one. In the outer circles, list differences. In the center, list similarities.

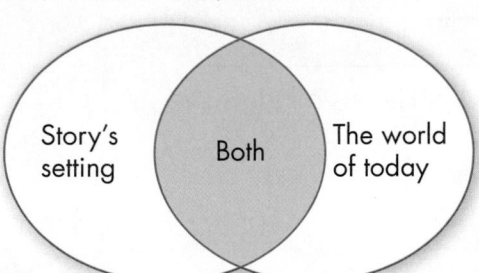

Story's setting | Both | The world of today

3. **Craft and Structure** **(a)** What mood is created by the Badlands setting? **(b)** Does the tone of the dialogue and description match the mood? Explain. **(c)** How does the setting lend greater meaning to the discovery of a man?

Vocabulary

Acquisition and Use Answer each question based on your knowledge of the underlined vocabulary words.

1. What is the main <u>distinction</u> between night and day?
2. If Al and Ed are in L.A. and Miami <u>respectively</u>, where is Al?
3. Why is a vitamin <u>deficiency</u> serious?
4. What kind of <u>debris</u> would you find after a tornado?
5. How can <u>erosion</u> affect a steep hillside?
6. If a landscape looks <u>ravaged</u>, what might have happened?

Word Study Use the context of the sentences and what you know about the **Latin prefix de-** to answer each question.

1. Do people with a *deficit* in their accounts have money?
2. If you *depart* a train station, are you leaving or arriving?

Word Study

The **Latin prefix de-** means "from."

Apply It Explain how the prefix **de-** contributes to the meanings of these words. Consult a dictionary, if necessary.

detour
decontaminate
decertification

Can all *conflicts* be resolved?

Writing About the Big Question

In "Tears of Autumn," a young woman chooses a new life that is very different from the one she has known. Use these sentence starters to develop your ideas about the Big Question.

Making a big change in one's life can lead to feelings of **insecurity** because _____.

One way to overcome such feelings is _____.

While You Read Look for conflicts that build in Hana's mind as she travels to America.

Vocabulary

Read each word and its definition. Decide whether you know the word well, know it a little bit, or do not know it at all. After you read, see how your knowledge of each word has increased.

- **turbulent** (tur´ byə lənt) *adj.* marked by wild, irregular motion (p. 264) *Their rubber raft tossed on the turbulent waters of the rapids. turbulence n. turbulently adv.*

- **relentless** (ri lent´ lis) *adj.* continuing without stopping; end-less (p. 265) *Relentless waves of violence destroyed the tiny country. relentlessly adv. relent v. unrelenting adj.*

- **affluence** (af´ lo͞o əns) *n.* wealth (p. 266) *The mansions reflect the affluence of the neighborhood. affluent adj.*

- **radical** (rad´ i kəl) *adj.* favoring major change in the social structure (p. 268) *The candidate's radical views on taxes are hotly debated. radicalism n. radicalize v.*

- **recoiled** (ri koild´) *v.* drawn back in disgust (p. 269) *She recoiled at the thought of a slimy eel on the bottom of the murky lake. recoiling adj. recoil v.*

- **degrading** (dē grād´ iŋ) *adj.* insulting; dishonorable (p. 270) *Brandon felt mopping floors was a degrading job. degradation n.*

Word Study

The **Latin prefix de-** can mean "down."

In this story, the main character is treated in a way that she feels is **degrading,** or insulting to her dignity as a person.

Meet
Yoshiko Uchida
(1921–1992)

Author of
Tears of Autumn

Like many other Japanese Americans, Yoshiko Uchida was caught up in the events of December 7, 1941. On that day, a Japanese attack on the American naval base in Pearl Harbor, Hawaii, brought the United States into World War II. In the furious reaction that followed, suspicion fell on all Americans of Japanese descent—even those who were born here or were long-time legal citizens.

WRA Camps Uchida's family and more than 100,000 other Japanese Americans were forced to leave their homes and property. They were "resettled" in Wartime Relocation Agency (WRA) camps—primitive facilities guarded by armed soldiers. Uchida's family lived in quarters that had been converted from horses' stables.

After she became a writer, Uchida explained her purpose for writing: "I want to celebrate our common humanity, for I feel the basic elements of humanity are present in all our strivings."

BACKGROUND FOR THE STORY

Arranged Marriage

"Tears of Autumn" takes place about a century ago, at a time when most Japanese families arranged marriages for their children. An older relative or family friend would help set up these unions. Before reaching an agreement, both sides had to be satisfied that the match would benefit their own family. Couples often exchanged pictures before meeting.

DID YOU KNOW?
One of Uchida's best-known books is *Journey to Topaz*, a novel based on her family's experience in the camps.

Tears of Autumn

Yoshiko Uchida

Hana Omiya stood at the railing of the small ship that shuddered toward America in a **turbulent** November sea. She shivered as she pulled the folds of her silk kimono close to her throat and tightened the wool shawl about her shoulders.

She was thin and small, her dark eyes shadowed in her pale face, her black hair piled high in a pompadour that seemed too heavy for so slight a woman. She clung to the moist rail and breathed the damp salt air deep into her lungs. Her body seemed leaden and lifeless, as though it were simply the vehicle transporting her soul to a strange new life, and she longed with childlike intensity to be home again in Oka Village.

She longed to see the bright persimmon dotting the barren trees beside the thatched roofs, to see the fields of golden rice stretching to the mountains where only last fall she had gathered plum white mushrooms, and to see once more the maple trees lacing their flaming colors through the green pine. If only she could see a familiar face, eat a meal without retching, walk on solid ground, and stretch out at night on a *tatami* mat[1] instead of in a hard narrow bunk. She thought now of seeking the warm shelter of her bunk but could not bear to face the relentless smell of fish that penetrated the lower decks.

Why did I ever leave Japan? she wondered bitterly. Why did I ever listen to my uncle? And yet she knew it was she herself who had begun the chain of events that placed her on this heaving ship. It was she who had first planted in her uncle's mind the thought that she would make a good wife for Taro Takeda, the lonely man who had gone to America to make his fortune in Oakland, California. •

It all began one day when her uncle had come to visit her mother.

"I must find a nice young bride," he had said, startling Hana with this blunt talk of marriage in her presence. She blushed and was ready to leave the room when her uncle quickly added, "My good friend Takeda has a son in America. I must find someone willing to travel to that far land."

This last remark was intended to indicate to Hana and her mother that he didn't consider this a suitable prospect for Hana, who was the youngest daughter of what once had been a fine family. Her father, until his death fifteen years ago, had been the largest landholder of the village and one of its last

---

1. *tatami* (tə tä′ mē) **mat** *n.* floor mat woven of rice straw, traditionally used in Japanese homes.

Vocabulary
turbulent (tʉr′ byə lənt) *adj.* marked by wild, irregular motion
relentless (ri lent′ lis) *adj.* continuing without stopping; endless

© **Spiral Review**
Theme In this paragraph, the narrator contrasts Hana Omiya's former home with the setting of the story. What possible theme is revealed by this comparison?

☑ **Reading Check**
Who is Taro Takeda?

samurai.[2] They had once had many servants and field hands, but now all that was changed. Their money was gone. Hana's three older sisters had made good marriages, and the eldest remained in their home with her husband to carry on the Omiya name and perpetuate the homestead. Her other sisters had married merchants in Osaka and Nagoya and were living comfortably.

Now that Hana was twenty-one, finding a proper husband for her had taken on an urgency that produced an embarrassing secretive air over the entire matter. Usually, her mother didn't speak of it until they were lying side by side on their quilts at night. Then, under the protective cover of darkness, she would suggest one name and then another, hoping that Hana would indicate an interest in one of them.

Her uncle spoke freely of Taro Takeda only because he was so sure Hana would never consider him. "He is a conscientious, hardworking man who has been in the United States for almost ten years. He is thirty-one, operates a small shop, and rents some rooms above the shop where he lives." Her uncle rubbed his chin thoughtfully. "He could provide well for a wife," he added.

"Ah," Hana's mother said softly.

"You say he is successful in this business?" Hana's sister inquired.

"His father tells me he sells many things in his shop—clothing, stockings, needles, thread, and buttons—such things as that. He also sells bean paste, pickled radish, bean cake, and soy sauce. A wife of his would not go cold or hungry."

They all nodded, each of them picturing this merchant in varying degrees of success and affluence. There were many Japanese emigrating to America these days, and Hana had heard of the picture brides who went with nothing more than an exchange of photographs to bind them to a strange man.

"Taro San[3] is lonely," her uncle continued. "I want to find for him a fine young woman who is strong and brave enough to cross the ocean alone."

"It would certainly be a different kind of life," Hana's sister ventured, and for a moment, Hana thought she glimpsed a longing ordinarily concealed behind her quiet, obedient

---

2. **samurai** (sam´ ə rī) *n.* Japanese army officer or member of the military class.
3. **San** (sän) Japanese term added to names, indicating respect.

face. In that same instant, Hana knew she wanted more for herself than her sisters had in their proper, arranged, and loveless marriages. She wanted to escape the smothering strictures of life in her village. She certainly was not going to marry a farmer and spend her life working beside him planting, weeding, and harvesting in the rice paddies until her back became bent from too many years of stooping and her skin was turned to brown leather by the sun and wind. Neither did she particularly relish the idea of marrying a merchant in a big city as her two sisters had done. Since her mother objected to her going to Tokyo to seek employment as a teacher, perhaps she would consent to a flight to America for what seemed a proper and respectable marriage.

Almost before she realized what she was doing, she spoke to her uncle. "Oji San, perhaps I should go to America to make this lonely man a good wife."

"You, Hana Chan?"[4] Her uncle observed her with startled curiosity. "You would go all alone to a foreign land so far away from your mother and family?"

"I would not allow it." Her mother spoke fiercely. Hana was her youngest and she had lavished upon her the attention and latitude that often befall the last child. How could she permit her to travel so far, even to marry the son of Takeda who was known to her brother?

But now, a notion that had seemed quite impossible a moment before was lodged in his receptive mind, and Hana's uncle grasped it with the pleasure that comes from an unexpected discovery.

"You know," he said looking at Hana, "it might be a very good life in America."

Hana felt a faint fluttering in her heart. Perhaps this lonely

---

4. **Chan** (chän) Japanese term added to children's names.

▲ **Critical Viewing**
This painting shows a village like the one Hana left. Why might she be anxious about moving to a big city in America? **[Infer]**

Setting
In what ways do the customs of village life contribute to Hana's desire to go to America?

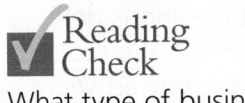
Reading Check
What type of business does Taro Takeda own?

man in America was her means of escaping both the village and the encirclement of her family.

Her uncle spoke with increasing enthusiasm of sending Hana to become Taro's wife. And the husband of Hana's sister, who was head of their household, spoke with equal eagerness. Although he never said so, Hana guessed he would be pleased to be rid of her, the spirited younger sister who stirred up his placid life with what he considered radical ideas about life and the role of women. He often claimed that Hana had too much schooling for a girl. She had graduated from Women's High School in Kyoto, which gave her five more years of schooling than her older sister.

"It has addled her brain—all that learning from those books," he said when he tired of arguing with Hana.

A man's word carried much weight for Hana's mother. Pressed by the two men, she consulted her other daughters and their husbands. She discussed the matter carefully with her brother and asked the village priest. Finally, she agreed to an exchange of family histories and an investigation was begun into Taro Takeda's family, his education, and his health, so they would be assured there was no insanity or tuberculosis or police records concealed in his family's past. Soon Hana's uncle was devoting his energies entirely to serving as go-between for Hana's mother and Taro Takeda's father.

When at last an agreement to the marriage was almost reached, Taro wrote his first letter to Hana. It was brief and proper and gave no more clue to his character than the stiff formal portrait taken at his graduation from middle school. Hana's uncle had given her the picture with apologies from his parents, because it was the only photo they had of him and it was not a flattering likeness.

Hana hid the letter and photograph in the sleeve of her kimono and took them to the outhouse to study in private. Squinting in the dim light and trying to ignore the foul odor, she read and reread Taro's letter, trying to find the real man somewhere in the sparse unbending prose.

By the time he sent her money for her steamship tickets, she had received ten more letters, but none revealed much more of the man than the first. In none did he disclose his

▲ **Critical Viewing**
What emotions do you see on the faces of the newly arrived immigrants pictured here? **[Interpret]**

loneliness or his need, but Hana understood this. In fact, she would have **recoiled** from a man who bared his intimate thoughts to her so soon. After all, they would have a lifetime together to get to know one another. ●

So it was that Hana had left her family and sailed alone to America with a small hope trembling inside of her. Tomorrow, at last, the ship would dock in San Francisco and she would meet face to face the man she was soon to marry. Hana was overcome with excitement at the thought of being in America, and terrified of the meeting about to take place. What would she say to Taro Takeda when they first met, and for all the days and years after?

Hana wondered about the flat above the shop. Perhaps it would be luxuriously furnished with the finest of brocades and lacquers,[5] and perhaps there would be a servant, although he had not mentioned it. She worried whether she would be able to manage on the meager English she had learned at Women's High School. The overwhelming anxiety for the day to come and the violent rolling of the ship were more than Hana could bear. Shuddering in the face of the wind, she leaned over the railing and became violently and wretchedly ill.

By five the next morning, Hana was up and dressed in her finest purple silk kimono and coat. She could not eat the bean soup and rice that appeared for breakfast and took only a few bites of the yellow pickled radish. Her bags, which had scarcely been touched since she boarded the ship, were easily packed, for all they contained were her kimonos and some of her favorite books. The large willow basket, tightly secured by a rope, remained under the bunk, untouched since her uncle had placed it there.

She had not befriended the other women in her cabin, for they had lain in their bunks for most of the voyage, too sick to be company to anyone. Each morning Hana had fled the closeness of the sleeping quarters and spent most of the day huddled in a corner of the deck, listening to the lonely songs of some Russians also traveling to an alien land.

As the ship approached land, Hana hurried up to the deck to look out at the gray expanse of ocean and sky, eager for a first glimpse of her new homeland.

---

5. **brocades** (brō´ kādz´) **and lacquers** (lak´ ərz) brocades are rich cloths with raised designs; lacquers are highly polished, decorative pieces of wood.

Vocabulary
recoiled (ri koïld´) *v.* drawn back in disgust

Taro wrote his first letter to Hana. It was brief and proper and gave no more clue to his character than the stiff formal portrait taken at his graduation from middle school.

Setting
What details about the time of the setting make Hana's journey more difficult and uncertain?

Reading Check
What did Hana receive from Taro before her journey?

"We won't be docking until almost noon," one of the deckhands told her.

Hana nodded, "I can wait," she answered, but the last hours seemed the longest.

When she set foot on American soil at last, it was not in the city of San Francisco as she had expected, but on Angel Island, where all third-class passengers were taken. She spent two miserable days and nights waiting, as the immigrants were questioned by officials, examined for trachoma and tuberculosis, and tested for hookworm. It was a bewildering, degrading beginning, and Hana was sick with anxiety, wondering if she would ever be released.

On the third day, a Japanese messenger from San Francisco appeared with a letter for her from Taro. He had written it the day of her arrival, but it had not reached her for two days.

Taro welcomed her to America, and told her that the bearer of the letter would inform Taro when she was to be released so he could be at the pier to meet her.

The letter eased her anxiety for a while, but as soon as she was released and boarded the launch for San Francisco, new fears rose up to smother her with a feeling almost of dread.

The early morning mist had become a light chilling rain, and on the pier black umbrellas bobbed here and there, making the task of recognition even harder. Hana searched desperately for a face that resembled the photo she had studied so long and hard. Suppose he hadn't come. What would she do then?

Hana took a deep breath, lifted her head and walked slowly from the launch. The moment she was on the pier, a man in a black coat, wearing a derby and carrying an umbrella, came quickly to her side. He was of slight build, not much taller than she, and his face was sallow and pale. He bowed stiffly and murmured, "You have had a long trip, Miss Omiya. I hope you are well."

Hana caught her breath. "You are Takeda San?" she asked.

He removed his hat and Hana was further startled to see that he was already turning bald.

"You are Takeda San?" she asked again. He looked older than thirty-one.

"I am afraid I no longer resemble the early photo my parents gave you. I am sorry."

Vocabulary
degrading (dē grād´ iŋ) *adj.* insulting; dishonorable

Setting
What details of the setting contribute to an uncertain, unhappy mood?

Compare and Contrast
Compare and contrast Hana's expectations of Taro Takeda with reality.

Hana had not meant to begin like this. It was not going well.

"No, no," she said quickly. "It is just that I . . . that is, I am terribly nervous. . . ." Hana stopped abruptly, too flustered to go on.

"I understand," Taro said gently. "You will feel better when you meet my friends and have some tea. Mr. and Mrs. Toda are expecting you in Oakland. You will be staying with them until . . ." He couldn't bring himself to mention the marriage just yet and Hana was grateful he hadn't.

Reading Check

Why did Hana wait two days on Angel Island?

LITERATURE IN CONTEXT

History Connection

Gateways to a New World

Seeking a better life, millions of immigrants passed through Angel Island and Ellis Island.

Angel Island in San Francisco's bay was an immigration station from 1910 to 1940. More than one million people were processed there. Many were detained on the island, before they were admitted.

From 1892 to 1954, **Ellis Island** in New York harbor welcomed more than 12 million immigrants. All who passed through underwent medical and legal inspections there. Only two percent were excluded.

Connect to the Literature

How does Hana's decision to travel to America reflect her desire for a better life?

He quickly made arrangements to have her baggage sent to Oakland, then led her carefully along the rain-slick pier toward the streetcar that would take them to the ferry.

Hana shuddered at the sight of another boat, and as they climbed to its upper deck she felt a queasy tightening of her stomach.

"I hope it will not rock too much," she said anxiously. "Is it many hours to your city?"

Taro laughed for the first time since their meeting, revealing the gold fillings of his teeth. "Oakland is just across the bay," he explained. "We will be there in twenty minutes."

Raising a hand to cover her mouth, Hana laughed with him and suddenly felt better. I am in America now, she thought, and this is the man I came to marry. Then she sat down carefully beside Taro, so no part of their clothing touched.

Compare and Contrast
How do Hana's feelings here contrast with her feelings earlier?

Critical Thinking

1. **Key Ideas and Details (a)** In what ways is Hana's life in Japan unsatisfying to her? **(b) Draw Conclusions:** How do these details explain Hana's decision to marry?

2. **Key Ideas and Details (a)** Describe the various feelings Hana experiences from her time on the ship to her meeting with Taro. **(b) Evaluate:** Is Hana's journey courageous? Why or why not?

3. **Key Ideas and Details (a)** What happens when Hana meets Taro? **(b) Interpret:** What does Taro's behavior toward Hana suggest about his personality?

4. **Integration of Knowledge and Ideas (a)** According to the story, what were the steps in the process of Hana's arranged marriage? **(b) Discuss:** With a partner, discuss the advantages and disadvantages of an arranged marriage like Hana's. Choose one set of responses to share with your class.

5. **Integration of Knowledge and Ideas (a)** What conflicts build in Hana's mind during her trip? **(b)** How does her decision to marry Taro help resolve conflicts within her family? **(c)** What conflicts does she have with herself over this choice? *[Connect to the Big Question: Can all conflicts be resolved?]*

Cite textual evidence to support your responses.

Reading Skill: Compare and Contrast

1. **Compare and contrast** Hana's ambitions for her life with the lives her sisters have.

2. Compare and contrast the personalities of Hana and Taro.

Literary Analysis: Setting

© 3. **Key Ideas and Details** The customs and beliefs of a certain time and place are part of the **setting**. Compare and contrast the attitudes toward marriage in the story with attitudes in your own community by using a Venn diagram like this one.

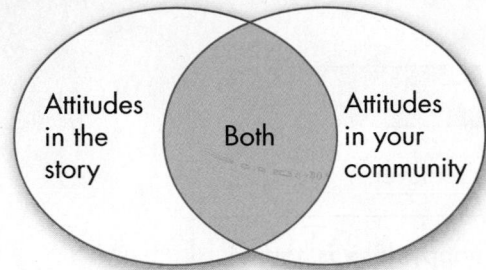

© 4. **Craft and Structure** **(a)** What mood is created by the final setting? **(b)** Do the dialogue and description match the mood? Explain. **(c)** Does this setting make the shared joke at the story's end more significant? Why or why not?

Vocabulary

© **Acquisition and Use** Answer each question.

1. Is it a good idea to take a canoe out on a <u>turbulent</u> lake?

2. Will the <u>relentless</u> sound of loud music wake a baby?

3. Is a designer handbag a sign of <u>affluence</u>?

4. Might a <u>radical</u> politician try to overthrow the government?

5. Would you be surprised if someone <u>recoiled</u> from a spider?

6. Why do some jobs seem <u>degrading</u>?

Word Study Use the context of the sentences and what you know about the **Latin prefix de-** to answer each question.

1. If you <u>descend</u> a staircase, are you going up or down?

2. What happens when you <u>depress</u> a computer key?

Word Study

The **Latin prefix de-** often means "down."

Apply It Explain how the prefix **de-** contributes to the meanings of these words. Consult a dictionary if necessary.

decline
descendant
demote

Integrated Language Skills

Who Can Replace a Man? • Tears of Autumn

Conventions: Action and Linking Verbs

A **verb** is a word that expresses an action or a state of being. Every complete sentence has at least one verb.

An **action verb** tells what action is performed. A **linking verb** connects a noun or pronoun with a word that describes or identifies it. The most common linking verbs are forms of *be*: *am, are, is, was, were*. To identify a linking verb, replace it with a form of *be*. If the sentence makes sense, it has a linking verb.

Action Verbs	Linking Verbs
Penny the dog *chases* the cat around the yard.	Penny *is* a golden retriever.
The dog *wagged* her tail.	The dog *seemed* happy. (She *is* happy)
The students *watched* the movie.	This movie *was* very popular last year.

Practice A Identify the verb or verbs in each sentence and indicate whether each is a linking verb or action verb.

1. The field-minder had a Class Three brain and seemed fairly intelligent.

2. The pen-propeller was small.

3. Several machines crashed together and argued about it.

4. "Men are more dangerous than machines," the quarrier said.

© **Reading Application** In "Who Can Replace a Man?" find one sentence with an action verb and one with a linking verb.

Practice B Some verbs can be used as either action or linking verbs. Identify the linking verb in each of these sentences. Then, write a sentence using that word as an action verb.

1. Hana stayed quiet while her uncle spoke.

2. On the boat, Hana felt sick and scared.

3. The weather turned stormy.

4. Taro Takeda looked younger in his photo.

© **Writing Application** Linking verbs can make writing less vivid. Write three sentences using linking verbs. Then, revise the sentences to feature active verbs instead. Let the examples in the chart on this page guide you.

PH WRITING COACH | Further instruction and practice are available in *Prentice Hall Writing Coach*.

Writing

 Informative Text Write a **description** based on the selection you read. If you read "Who Can Replace a Man?" describe a future time and place, such as your city in 2150. Include details about the land and people. If you read "Tears of Autumn," describe Hana's new home in America. Include details about the setting.

- Prewrite to plan what details you will include and how you will organize them.

- Use sensory details. Describe sights, sounds, and smells.

- As you revise, use creative language devices such as colorful adjectives to make your description more vivid. To find better or more precise words, you can use a thesaurus.

Grammar Application Make sure all linking verbs in your description refer to a noun or pronoun.

Writing Workshop: *Work in Progress*

Prewriting for Response to Literature Write down two of your favorite literary works. Use each title as the center of a web. In the outer circles, note topics, themes, characters, settings, and plot lines from each work. Save these Story Webs in your portfolio.

Research and Technology

 Build and Present Knowledge Work with a small group to gather information for an **oral report.** Use Internet and library resources to start your work. As a group, decide which information is most important and interesting.

- If you read "Who Can Replace a Man?" concentrate on how another artist, writer, or filmmaker envisioned the future. Your goal is to show how imagination can create a different world.

- If you read "Tears of Autumn," focus your research on Angel Island. Learn about the people who passed through it, the conditions they faced there, and their reactions to their experiences. The goal of your report is to present a dramatic factual history.

Keep these tips in mind as you plan your report.

- Choose facts or details that support your claims and ideas.

- Organize information to achieve the goal of your oral report.

- When you present your report, maintain eye contact with your audience, speak at an appropriate volume, and pronounce your words clearly.

 **Common Core State Standards**

L.8.1, L.8.6; W.8.2.b; SL.8.4
[For the full wording of the standards, see page 244.]

Use this prewriting activity to prepare for the **Writing Workshop** on page 326.

www.PHLitOnline.com
- Interactive graphic organizers
- Grammar tutorial
- Interactive journals

Hamadi •
The Tell-Tale Heart

ⓒ Leveled Texts

Build your skills and improve your comprehension of short stories with texts of increasing complexity.

Read **"Hamadi"** to see how an unusual friendship brings comfort to a young girl.

Read **"The Tell-Tale Heart"** to explore the restless mind of a murderer.

ⓒ Common Core State Standards

Meet these standards with either **"Hamadi"** (p. 281) or **"The Tell-Tale Heart"** (p. 294).

Reading Literature
3. Analyze how particular lines of dialogue or incidents in a story or drama propel the action, reveal aspects of a character, or provoke a decision. *(Reading Skill: Compare and Contrast Characters; Literary Analysis: Character Traits; Writing: Character Profile)*

Writing
2. Write informative/explanatory texts to examine a topic and convey ideas, concepts, and information through the selection, organization, and analysis of relevant content. *(Writing: Character Profile)*

Speaking and Listening
4. Present claims and findings, emphasizing salient points in a focused, coherent manner with relevant evidence, sound valid reasoning, and well-chosen details; use appropriate eye contact, adequate volume, and clear pronunciation. *(Speaking and Listening: Oral Response)*

Language
1. Demonstrate command of the conventions of standard English grammar and usage when writing or speaking. *(Conventions: Principal Parts of Regular Verbs)*

4.b. Use common, grade-appropriate Greek or Latin affixes and roots as clues to the meaning of a word. *(Vocabulary: Word Study)*

5.b. Use the relationship between particular words to better understand each of the words. *(Vocabulary: Synonyms)*

Reading Skill: Compare and Contrast

When you **compare and contrast characters,** you look for similarities and differences among the characters in a story. One strategy for comparing is to **identify each character's perspective,** the way that person understands the world.

- As you read, use a graphic organizer like the one below to note details about the main character.
- To compare, consider whether the main character's words, actions, emotions, and ideas are similar to or different from those of other characters.
- Finally, use everything you have learned about the character to decide how much you trust what he or she says or thinks.

Using the Strategy: Perspective Chart

Fill in the boxes of the **character's perspective chart** to complete your understanding of the main character.

Main Character's Perspective			
Personal Qualities	**Past Experiences**	**State of Mind**	**View of Current Situation**

Literary Analysis: Character Traits

Character traits are the personal qualities, attitudes, and values that a character shows through words and actions. For example, one character may be lazy and untrustworthy, while another is hardworking and reliable.

The number of character traits a character displays contributes to how well you "know" the character.

- **Round characters** are fully developed by the writer. They show many character traits, both good and bad.
- **Flat characters** are one-sided, often showing just one trait.

Can all *conflicts* be resolved?

Writing About the Big Question

In "Hamadi," characters have different ways of dealing with a conflict that involves hurt feelings between friends. Use this sentence starter to develop your ideas about the Big Question.

Emotional conflicts, such as hurt feelings, are difficult to resolve through **compromise** because _____.

While You Read Look for the steps Hamadi takes to resolve the story's conflict.

Vocabulary

Read each word and its definition. Decide whether you know the word well, know it a little bit, or do not know it at all. After you read, see how your knowledge of each word has increased.

- **tedious** (tē′dē əs) *adj.* boring; tiresome (p. 282) *Jim tired of the _tedious_ task of stocking and restocking the shelves.* *tediousness n. tediously adv. tedium n.*

- **expansive** (ek spans′ iv) *adj.* very friendly (p. 282) *His _expansive_ personality and friendly smile made him a popular figure.* *expansively adv. expansiveness n. expand v.*

- **surrogate** (sʉr′ ə git) *adj.* substitute (p. 287) *Though they were twins, Holly was not a _surrogate_ for her sister Sue.*

- **obscure** (əb skyo͞or′) *adj.* little known (p. 289) *The scholar quoted an _obscure_ passage from an out-of-print book.* *obscurity n.*

- **refugees** (ref′ yo͞o jēz′) *n.* people who flee from their homes during a time of trouble (p. 289) *During the war, many _refugees_ were forced to find new homes.* *refuge n.*

- **melancholy** (mel′ ən käl′ ē) *adj.* sad; depressed (p. 289) *Thinking of friends he had lost made the old man _melancholy_.* *melancholy n.*

Word Study

The **suffix -ee** comes from French and refers to someone who receives an action or has been put in a certain position.

In this story, a character is one of many **refugees** from Palestine. He is someone who had to find *refuge,* or safety, in another country.

Author of

Hamadi

The daughter of a Palestinian father and an American mother, Naomi Shihab Nye writes stories and poems that show the "connections between times and people and cultures."

Making Connections Nye grew up in St. Louis, Missouri. When she was in high school, Nye and her family lived in Ramallah, Jordan, and in Jerusalem. There she met her father's family for the first time, an experience she would never forget. Although she saw firsthand some of the dangerous conflicts in the Middle East, she was also struck by the bonds that can form between people of different cultures. Her experiences later inspired her to write her first young adult novel, *Habibi*.

BACKGROUND FOR THE STORY

Between Two Worlds

This story focuses on the friendship between Susan, a teenage girl, and Saleh Hamadi, a Palestinian refugee. Before 1948, the region that is now Israel was known as Palestine. When ethnic fighting broke out in the late 1940s, many Palestinians fled the violence and settled in other nations. Older members of these refugee communities, like Hamadi, form a link to the memories and traditions of the land they left.

DID YOU KNOW?

Nye began writing poems when she was only six. At seven, she published her first poem in a children's magazine.

Hamadi

NAOMI SHIHAB NYE

Susan didn't really feel interested in Saleh Hamadi until she was a freshman in high school carrying a thousand questions around. Why this way? Why not another way? Who said so and why can't I say something else? Those brittle women at school in the counselor's office treated the world as if it were a yardstick and they had tight hold of both ends.

Sometimes Susan felt polite with them, sorting attendance cards during her free period, listening to them gab about fingernail polish and television. And other times she felt she could run out of the building yelling. That's when she daydreamed about Saleh Hamadi, who had nothing to do with any of it. Maybe she thought of him as escape, the way she used to think about the Sphinx at Giza[1] when she was younger. She would picture the golden Sphinx sitting quietly in the desert with sand blowing around its face, never changing its expression. She would think of its wry, slightly crooked mouth and how her grandmother looked a little like that as she waited for her bread to bake in the old village north of Jerusalem. Susan's family had lived in Jerusalem for three years before she was ten and drove out to see her grandmother every weekend. They would find her patting fresh dough between her hands, or pressing cakes of dough onto the black rocks in

◀ **Critical Viewing**
How does this man's clothing indicate that, like Hamadi, he is influenced by two different cultures? **[Connect]**

Compare and Contrast
Contrast the things Susan thinks about with the kinds of topics the women in the counselor's office discuss.

✓ Reading Check
When did Susan first become interested in Hamadi?

---

1. **Sphinx** (sfiŋks) **at Giza** (gē′ zə) huge statue with the head of a man and the body of a lion, located near Cairo in northern Egypt.

the taboon, the rounded old oven outdoors. Sometimes she moved her lips as she worked. Was she praying? Singing a secret song? Susan had never seen her grandmother rushing.

Now that she was fourteen, she took long walks in America with her father down by the drainage ditch at the end of their street. Pecan trees shaded the path. She tried to get him to tell stories about his childhood in Palestine. She didn't want him to forget anything. She helped her American mother complete **tedious** kitchen tasks without complaining—rolling grape leaves around their lemony rice stuffing, scrubbing carrots for the roaring juicer. Some evenings when the soft Texas twilight pulled them all outside, she thought of her far-away grandmother and said, "Let's go see Saleh Hamadi. Wouldn't he like some of that cheese pie Mom made?" And they would wrap a slice of pie and drive downtown. Somehow he felt like a good substitute for a grandmother, even though he was a man. •

Usually Hamadi was wearing a white shirt, shiny black tie, and a jacket that reminded Susan of the earth's surface just above the treeline on a mountain—thin, somehow purified. He would raise his hands high before giving advice.

"It is good to drink a tall glass of water every morning upon arising!" If anyone doubted this, he would shake his head. "Oh Susan, Susan, Susan," he would say.

He did not like to sit down, but he wanted everyone else to sit down. He made Susan sit on the wobbly chair beside the desk and he made her father or mother sit in the saggy center of the bed. He told them people should eat six small meals a day.

They visited him on the sixth floor of the Traveler's Hotel, where he had lived so long nobody could remember him ever traveling. Susan's father used to remind him of the apartments available over the Victory Cleaners, next to the park with the fizzy pink fountain, but Hamadi would shake his head, pinching kisses at his spartan room. "A white handkerchief spread across a tabletop, my two extra shoes lined by the wall, this spells 'home' to me, this says 'mi casa.' What more do I need?"

Hamadi liked to use Spanish words. They made him feel **expansive**, worldly. He'd learned them when he worked at the fruits and vegetables warehouse on Zarzamora Street, marking off crates of apples and avocados on a long white pad. Occasionally he would speak Arabic, his own first

Character
What character traits are reflected in this description of Hamadi?

Vocabulary
expansive (ek spans′ iv) adj. very friendly

LITERATURE IN CONTEXT

Culture Connection

Guided by Gibran

Kahlil Gibran's famous work *The Prophet* appeals to millions of readers looking for meaning and dignity in ordinary life. It was first published in English in 1923, and was translated into at least twenty languages.

Born in Lebanon in 1883, Gibran eventually settled in New York, where he began to publish his short stories and exhibit his paintings. This philosopher, essayist, and poet died in 1931 at the age of forty-eight and was buried in Bsharrì, his hometown. He summarized his most popular work this way: "You are far greater than you know, and all is well."

Connect to the Literature

How well does Gibran's quotation above seem to reflect Hamadi's approach to life?

language, with Susan's father and uncles, but he said it made him feel too sad, as if his mother might step into the room at any minute, her arms laden with fresh mint leaves. He had come to the United States on a boat when he was eighteen years old and he had never been married. "I married books," he said. "I married the wide horizon."

"What is he to us?" Susan used to ask her father. "He's not a relative, right? How did we meet him to begin with?"

Susan's father couldn't remember. "I think we just drifted together. Maybe we met at your uncle Hani's house. Maybe that old Maronite priest who used to cry after every service introduced us. The priest once shared an apartment with Kahlil Gibran in New York—so he said. And Saleh always says he stayed with Gibran when he first got off the boat. I'll bet that popular guy Gibran has had a lot of roommates he doesn't even know about."

Susan said, "Dad, he's dead."

"I know, I know," her father said.

Later Susan said, "Mr. Hamadi, did you really meet Kahlil Gibran? He's one of my favorite writers." Hamadi walked slowly to the window of his room and stared out. There wasn't much to look at down on the street—a bedraggled² flower shop, a boarded-up tavern with a hand-lettered sign tacked to the front, GONE TO FIND JESUS. Susan's father said the owners had really gone to Alabama.

Hamadi spoke patiently. "Yes, I met brother Gibran. And I meet him in my heart every day. When I was a young man—shocked by all the visions of the new world—the tall buildings—the wild traffic—the young people without shame—the proud mailboxes in their blue uniforms—I met him. And he has stayed with me every day of my life."

"But did you really meet him, like in person, or just in a book?"

He turned dramatically. "Make no such distinctions, my friend. Or your life will be a pod with only dried-up beans inside. Believe anything can happen."

Susan's father looked irritated, but Susan smiled. "I do," she said. "I believe that. I want fat beans. If I imagine something, it's true, too. Just a different kind of true."

Susan's father was twiddling with the knobs on the old-fashioned sink. "Don't they even give you hot water here? You don't mean to tell me you've been living without hot water?"

---

2. bedraggled (bē drag´ əld) *adj.* limp and dirty, as if dragged through mud.

On Hamadi's rickety desk lay a row of different "Love" stamps issued by the post office.

"You must write a lot of letters," Susan said.

"No, no, I'm just focusing on that word," Hamadi said. "I particularly like the globe in the shape of a heart," he added.

"Why don't you take a trip back to his village in Lebanon?" Susan's father asked. "Maybe you still have relatives living there."

Hamadi looked pained. "'Remembrance is a form of meeting,' my brother Gibran says, and I do believe I meet with my cousins every day."

"But aren't you curious? You've been gone so long! Wouldn't you like to find out what has happened to everybody and everything you knew as a boy?" Susan's father traveled back to Jerusalem once every year to see his family.

"I would not. In fact, I already know. It is there and it is not there. Would you like to share an orange with me?"

His long fingers, tenderly peeling. Once when Susan was younger, he'd given her a lavish ribbon off a holiday fruit basket and expected her to wear it on her head. In the car, Susan's father said, "Riddles. He talks in riddles. I don't know why I have patience with him." Susan stared at the people talking and laughing in the next car. She did not even exist in their world. •

Susan carried *The Prophet* around on top of her English textbook and her Texas history. She and her friend Tracy read it out loud to one another at lunch. Tracy was a junior—they'd met at the literary magazine meeting where Susan, the only freshman on the staff, got assigned to do proofreading. They never ate in the cafeteria; they sat outside at picnic tables with sack lunches, whole wheat crackers and fresh peaches. Both of them had given up meat.

Tracy's eyes looked steamy. "You know that place where Gibran says, 'Hate is a dead thing. Who of you would be a tomb?'"

Susan nodded. Tracy continued. "Well, I hate someone. I'm trying not to, but I can't help it. I hate Debbie for liking Eddie and it's driving me nuts."

"Why shouldn't Debbie like Eddie?" Susan said. "*You* do."

Tracy put her head down on her arms. A gang of cheerleaders walked by giggling. One of them flicked her finger in greeting.

Character
List three traits described here that show Hamadi is a complex, round character.

Compare and Contrast
Compare Susan's perspective on Hamadi with her father's perspective.

Character
What interests and traits do Susan and Tracy share?

Reading Check
What writer does Hamadi admire?

▶ **Critical Viewing**
Do these girls seem to share qualities with Susan and Tracy? Why or why not? **[Compare and Contrast]**

Compare and Contrast
Are Tracy's and Susan's ideas about relationships with boys similar or different? Explain.

"In fact, we *all* like Eddie," Susan said. "Remember, here in this book—wait and I'll find it—where Gibran says that loving teaches us the secrets of our hearts and that's the way we connect to all of Life's heart? You're not talking about liking or loving, you're talking about owning."

Tracy looked glum. "Sometimes you remind me of a minister."

Susan said, "Well, just talk to me someday when *I'm* depressed."

Susan didn't want a boyfriend. Everyone who had boyfriends or girlfriends all seemed to have troubles. Susan told people she had a boyfriend far away, on a farm in Missouri, but the truth was, boys still seemed like cousins to her. Or brothers. Or even girls.

A squirrel sat in the crook of a tree, eyeing their sandwiches. When the end-of-lunch bell blared, Susan and Tracy jumped—it always seemed too soon. Squirrels were lucky; they didn't have to go to school. •

Character
What traits of Hamadi does Susan enjoy that her father cannot appreciate?

Susan's father said her idea was ridiculous: to invite Saleh Hamadi to go Christmas caroling with the English Club. "His English is archaic,[3] for one thing, and he won't know any of the songs."

"How could you live in America for years and not know 'Joy to the World' or 'Away in a Manger'?"

"Listen, I grew up right down the road from 'Oh Little Town of Bethlehem' and I still don't know a single verse."

"I want him. We need him. It's boring being with the same bunch of people all the time."

So they called Saleh and he said he would come—"thrilled" was the word he used. He wanted to ride the bus to their

---

3. archaic (är kā´ ik) *adj.* old-fashioned; out-of-date.

house, he didn't want anyone to pick him up. Her father muttered, "He'll probably forget to get off." Saleh thought "caroling" meant they were going out with a woman named Carol. He said, "Holiday spirit—I was just reading about it in the newspaper."

Susan said, "Dress warm."

Saleh replied, "Friend, my heart is warmed simply to hear your voice."

All that evening Susan felt light and bouncy. She decorated the coffee can they would use to collect donations to be sent to the children's hospital in Bethlehem. She had started doing this last year in middle school, when a singing group collected $100 and the hospital responded on exotic onion-skin stationery that they were "eternally grateful."

Her father shook his head. "You get something into your mind and it really takes over," he said. "Why do you like Hamadi so much all of a sudden? You could show half as much interest in your own uncles."

Susan laughed. Her uncles were dull. Her uncles shopped at the mall and watched TV. "Anyone who watches TV more than twelve minutes a week is uninteresting," she said.

Her father lifted an eyebrow.

"He's my surrogate grandmother," she said. "He says interesting things. He makes me think. Remember when I was little and he called me The Thinker? We have a connection." She added, "Listen, do you want to go too? It is not a big deal. And Mom has a *great* voice, why don't you both come?"

A minute later her mother was digging in the closet for neck scarves, and her father was digging in the drawer for flashlight batteries.

Saleh Hamadi arrived precisely on time, with flushed red cheeks and a sack of dates stuffed in his pocket. "We may need sustenance on our journey." Susan thought the older people seemed quite giddy as they drove down to the high school to meet the rest of the carolers. Strands of winking lights wrapped around their neighbors' drainpipes and trees. A giant Santa tipped his hat on Dr. Garcia's roof.

Her friends stood gathered in front of the school. Some were smoothing out song sheets that had been crammed in a drawer or cabinet for a whole year. Susan thought holidays were strange; they came, and you were supposed to feel ready for them. What if you could make up your own holidays as

Spiral Review
Character What do Susan's desire to invite Hamadi and his reaction to her invitation reveal about their characters?

Compare and Contrast
How do Susan's interests set her apart from many of the people around her?

Vocabulary
surrogate (sʉr´ ə git) *adj.* substitute

Why is Susan so excited before she goes caroling?

Hamadi **287**

> *He had stepped out of a painting, or a newscast, with his outdated long overcoat, his clunky old men's shoes and elegant manners.*

you went along? She had read about a woman who used to have parties to celebrate the arrival of fresh asparagus in the local market. Susan's friends might make holidays called Eddie Looked at Me Today and Smiled.

Two people were alleluia-ing in harmony. Saleh Hamadi went around the group formally introducing himself to each person and shaking hands. A few people laughed behind their hands when his back was turned. He had stepped out of a painting, or a newscast, with his outdated long overcoat, his clunky old men's shoes and elegant manners.

Susan spoke more loudly than usual. "I'm honored to introduce you to one of my best friends, Mr. Hamadi."

"Good evening to you," he pronounced musically, bowing a bit from the waist.

What could you say back but "Good evening, sir." His old-fashioned manners were contagious.

They sang at three houses which never opened their doors. They sang "We Wish You a Merry Christmas" each time they moved on. Lisa had a fine, clear soprano. Tracy could find the alto harmony to any line. Cameron and Elliot had more enthusiasm than accuracy. Lily, Rita, and Jeannette laughed every time they said a wrong word and fumbled to find their places again. Susan loved to see how her mother knew every word of every verse without looking at the paper, and her father kept his hands in his pockets and seemed more interested in examining people's mailboxes or yard displays than in trying to sing. And Saleh Hamadi—what language was he singing in? He didn't even seem to be pronouncing words, but humming deeply from his throat. Was he saying, "Om?" Speaking Arabic? Once he caught her looking and whispered, "That was an Aramaic word that just drifted into my mouth—the true language of the Bible, you know, the language Jesus Christ himself spoke." •

By the fourth block their voices felt tuned up and friendly people came outside to listen. Trays of cookies were passed around and dollar bills stuffed into the little can. Thank you, thank you. Out of the dark from down the block, Susan noticed Eddie sprinting toward them with his coat flapping, unbuttoned. She shot a glance at Tracy, who pretended not to notice. "Hey, guys!" shouted Eddie. "The first time in my life I'm late and everyone else is on time! You could at least have left a note about which way you were going." Someone slapped him on the back. Saleh Hamadi, whom he had never seen before, was the only one who managed a reply. "Welcome, welcome to our cheery group!"

Eddie looked mystified. "Who is this guy?"

Susan whispered, "My friend."

Eddie approached Tracy, who read her song sheet intently just then, and stuck his face over her shoulder to whisper, "Hi." Tracy stared straight ahead into the air and whispered "Hi" vaguely, glumly. Susan shook her head. Couldn't Tracy act more cheerful at least? They were walking again. They passed a string of blinking reindeer and a wooden snowman holding a painted candle. Ridiculous!

Eddie fell into step beside Tracy, murmuring so Susan couldn't hear him anymore. Saleh Hamadi was flinging his arms up high as he strode. Was he power walking? Did he even know what power walking was? Between houses, Susan's mother hummed obscure songs people never remembered: "What Child Is This?" and "The Friendly Beasts."

Lisa moved over to Eddie's other side. "I'm so *excited* about you and Debbie!" she said loudly. "Why didn't she come tonight?"

Eddie said, "She has a sore throat."

Tracy shrank up inside her coat.

Lisa chattered on. "James said we should make our reservations *now* for dinner at the Tower after the Sweetheart Dance, can you believe it? In December, making a reservation for February? But otherwise it might get booked up!"

Saleh Hamadi tuned into this conversation with interest; the Tower was downtown, in his neighborhood. He said, "This sounds like significant preliminary planning! Maybe you can be an international advisor someday." Susan's mother bellowed, "Joy to the World!" and voices followed her, stretching for notes. Susan's father was gazing off into the sky. Maybe he thought about all the refugees in camps in Palestine far from doorbells and shutters. Maybe he thought about the horizon beyond Jerusalem when he was a boy, how it seemed to be inviting him, "Come over, come over." Well, he'd come all the way to the other side of the world, and now he was doomed to live in two places at once. To Susan, immigrants seemed bigger than other people, and always slightly melancholy. They also seemed doubly interesting. Maybe someday Susan would meet one her own age.

Character
Which character traits of Hamadi would cause Eddie to be "mystified" in this situation?

Vocabulary
obscure (əb skyo͞or´) *adj.* little known

Vocabulary
refugees (ref´ yo͞o jēz´) *n.* people who flee from their homes in times of trouble

melancholy (mel´ ən käl´ ē) *adj.* sad; depressed

Reading Check
How does Hamadi introduce himself to Susan's friends?

Two thin streams of tears rolled down Tracy's face. Eddie had drifted to the other side of the group and was clowning with Cameron, doing a tap dance shuffle. "While fields and floods, rocks hills and plains, repeat the sounding joy, repeat the sounding joy . . . " Susan and Saleh Hamadi noticed her. Hamadi peered into Tracy's face, inquiring, "Why? Is it pain? Is it gratitude? We are such mysterious creatures, human beings!"

Tracy turned to him, pressing her face against the old wool of his coat, and wailed. The song ended. All eyes on Tracy, and this tall, courteous stranger who would never in a thousand years have felt comfortable stroking her hair. But he let her stand there, crying as Susan stepped up to stand firmly on the other side of Tracy, putting her arms around her friend. Hamadi said something Susan would remember years later, whenever she was sad herself, even after college, a creaky anthem sneaking back into her ear, "We go on. On and on. We don't stop where it hurts. We turn a corner. It is the reason why we are living. To turn a corner. Come, let's move."

Above them, in the heavens, stars lived out their lonely lives. People whispered, "What happened? What's wrong?" Half of them were already walking down the street.

Compare and Contrast
How are Susan's and Hamadi's reactions to Tracy different from the reactions of the others?

Critical Thinking

Ⓒ

© **1. Key Ideas and Details (a)** What is Hamadi's explanation for having never married? **(b) Interpret:** What does Hamadi mean when he says, "I married the wide horizon"?

© **2. Key Ideas and Details (a)** What are the other carolers' reactions to Hamadi? **(b) Interpret:** What are the reasons for their reactions?

© **3. Key Ideas and Details (a)** Why is Tracy upset during the caroling? **(b) Speculate:** Why does she turn to Hamadi for comfort? **(c) Evaluate:** How useful do you think Hamadi's advice is for someone in Tracy's situation?

Cite textual evidence to support your responses.

© **4. Integration of Knowledge and Ideas (a)** What steps does Hamadi take to resolve the conflict involving Tracy? **(b)** Do the differences between Hamadi and Tracy make him more or less effective at solving her problem? Explain. *[Connect to the Big Question: Can all conflicts be resolved?]*

Reading Skill: Compare and Contrast

1. How do the differences between Susan's father and Saleh Hamadi affect the way the two men view each other?

2. The story reveals Susan's thoughts more than any other character's. **(a)** How would the description of the interaction between Hamadi and Tracy be different if it revealed Hamadi's perspective or Tracy's ideas? **(b)** Do you trust Susan's way of seeing the world? Explain.

Literary Analysis: Character Traits

© 3. **Key Ideas and Details** Using a chart like the one shown, list three **character traits** that describe Susan and Hamadi.

Character	Trait	Example
Susan	sympathetic	She comforts her friend Tracy.
Hamadi		

© 4. **Craft and Structure** **(a)** Are Susan, Hamadi, and Eddie *round* or *flat characters*? **(b)** Do you care more about round or flat characters? Why?

Vocabulary

© **Acquisition and Use** Replace the word or words in italics with a **synonym,** or word close in meaning, from the vocabulary list on page 278.

1. Listening to the old songs put them in a *sad* mood.

2. Washing dish after dish quickly became *tiresome*.

3. Thousands of *displaced people* fled after the earthquake.

4. She was good at coming up with *little-known* facts.

5. Their uncle was like a *substitute* parent for the children.

6. The friendly, *generous* host treated everyone to ice cream.

Word Study Use the context and what you know about the **suffix -ee** to answer each question. Explain your answers.

1. Would a *trainee* already be good at his or her job?

2. Would the *addressee* of a letter write it or receive it?

Word Study

The **suffix -ee** refers to someone who receives an action or has been put in a certain position.

Apply It Explain how the suffix **-ee** contributes to the meanings of these words. Consult a dictionary if necessary.
honoree
trustee
referee

Can all *conflicts* be resolved?

Writing About the Big Question

In "The Tell-Tale Heart," a murderer describes his internal conflicts before and after he has committed the crime. Use this sentence starter to develop your ideas about the Big Question.

When torn between doing right and wrong, a person may find a **solution** by _____.

While You Read Look for the conflicts the narrator faces, and consider how he tries to resolve them.

Vocabulary

Read each word and its definition. Decide whether you know the word well, know it a little bit, or do not know it at all. After you read, see how your knowledge of each word has increased.

- **cunningly** (kun´ iŋ lē) *adv.* in a way that is skillfully dishonest (p. 295) *The surprise attack was <u>cunningly</u> planned.* *cunning n. or adj.*

- **resolved** (ri zälvd´) *v.* decided (p. 298) *I <u>resolved</u> to study harder after I failed my last test. resolution n.*

- **stealthily** (stelth´ ə lē) *adv.* in a secret or sly way (p. 298) *The campers <u>stealthily</u> sneaked out of the cabin to get a snack. stealth n. stealthy adj.*

- **vex** (veks) *v.* annoy; distress (p. 299) *Why does losing a board game <u>vex</u> you? vexation n. vexing adj.*

- **audacity** (ô das´ ə tē) *n.* bold courage; nerve (p. 300) *He had the <u>audacity</u> to ask her to pay for the camera he had destroyed. audaciously adv. audacious adj.*

- **derision** (di rizh´ ən) *n.* statements or actions that show you have no respect for someone or something (p. 302) *The woman expressed <u>derision</u> for her neighbor's bad taste. derisive adj. derisively adv.*

Word Study

The **Latin suffix -ity** indicates a noun and means "state of" or "condition of."

In this story, the main character is a murderer who displays great **audacity**—a state of boldness—in denying his crime.

Meet
Edgar Allan Poe
(1809–1849)

Author of
The Tell-Tale Heart

Edgar Allan Poe led a short and troubled life and died in poverty. However, his ability to write terrifying stories that keep readers wide awake at night has made him a literary star long after his death.

Dreams and Nightmares Shortly after Poe's birth, his father abandoned his family. When Poe was only two years old, his mother died. Young Edgar was taken in by a foster father, John Allan. A romantic, irresponsible young man who dreamed of writing poetry, Poe never understood Allan, a businessman. At eighteen, Poe left home. For the rest of his life, he held various jobs, while trying to make a living writing poems and stories that explored the dark side of the human imagination.

DID YOU KNOW?

Like modern horror stories, Poe's stories drew on readers' worst fears. His story "Premature Burial" exploited a common fear of the time—that people were often buried alive, only to revive in their caskets.

BACKGROUND FOR THE STORY

The Short Story

Edgar Allan Poe made the short story into an art form. He believed that writers should create a "unity of effect." Every element—from sentence rhythm to a character's personality—would help create a single impression in the reader's mind. In this story, that impression is one of horror.

The Tell-Tale Heart

Edgar Allan Poe

True!—**nervous**—very, very dreadfully nervous I had been and am; but why will you say that I am mad? The disease had sharpened my senses—not destroyed—not dulled them.

Above all was the sense of hearing acute. I heard all things in the heaven and in the earth. I heard many things in hell. How, then, am I mad? Hearken![1] and observe how healthily—how calmly I can tell you the whole story.

It is impossible to say how first the idea entered my brain; but once conceived, it haunted me day and night. Object there was none. Passion there was none. I loved the old man. He had never wronged me. He had never given me insult. For his gold I had no desire. I think it was his eye! yes, it was this! One of his eyes resembled that of a vulture—a pale blue eye, with a film over it. Whenever it fell upon me, my blood ran cold; and so by degrees—very gradually—I made up my mind to take the life of the old man, and thus rid myself of the eye forever.

Now this is the point. You fancy me mad. Madmen know nothing. But you should have seen *me*. You should have seen how wisely I proceeded with what caution—with what foresight—with what dissimulation[2] I went to work! I was never kinder to the old man than during the whole week before I killed him. And every night, about midnight, I turned the latch of his door and opened it—oh, so gently! And then, when I had made an opening sufficient for my head, I put in a dark lantern, all closed, closed, so that no light shone out, and then I thrust in my head. Oh, you would have laughed to see how cunningly I thrust it in! I moved it slowly—very, very slowly, so that I might not disturb the old man's sleep. It took me an hour to place my whole head within the opening so far that I could see him as he lay upon his bed. Ha!—would a madman have been so wise as this? And then, when my head was well in the room, I undid the lantern cautiously—oh, so cautiously—cautiously (for the hinges creaked) I undid it just so much that a single thin ray fell upon the vulture eye. And this I did for seven long nights—every night just at midnight—but I found the eye always closed; and so it

---

1. **Hearken!** (här´ kən) *v.* listen!
2. **dissimulation** (di sim´ yo͞o lā´ shən) *n.* hiding of one's feelings or purposes.

◀ **Critical Viewing**
What kind of story do you expect to read, based on the title and the illustration? Explain.
[Speculate]

Compare and Contrast
The narrator and the author are not the same person. Contrast the way the narrator sees himself with the way the author portrays him.

Vocabulary
cunningly (kun´ iŋ lē) *adv.* in a way that is skillfully dishonest

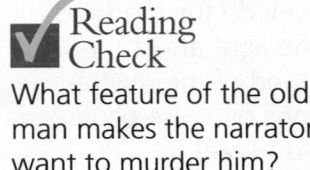
Reading Check
What feature of the old man makes the narrator want to murder him?

Character
What character traits does the narrator reveal as he describes his murder plan?

▲ **Critical Viewing**
How do the shadows and light affect the mood of the illustrations on these pages?
[Analyze]

was impossible to do the work; for it was not the old man who vexed me, but his evil eye. And every morning, when the day broke, I went boldly into the chamber, and spoke courageously to him, calling him by name in a hearty tone, and inquiring how he had passed the night. So you see he would have been a very profound old man, indeed, to suspect that every night, just at twelve, I looked in upon him while he slept. ●

Upon the eighth night I was more than usually cautious in opening the door. A watch's minute hand moves more quickly than did mine. Never, before that night, had I *felt* the extent of my own powers—of my sagacity.[3] I could scarcely contain my feelings of triumph. To think that there I was, opening the door, little by little, and he not even to dream of my secret deeds or thoughts. I fairly chuckled at the idea; and perhaps he heard me; for he moved on the bed suddenly, as

---

3. sagacity (sə gas´ ə tē) *n.* high intelligence and sound judgment.

if startled. Now you may think that I drew back—but no. His room was as black as pitch with the thick darkness (for the shutters were close fastened, through fear of robbers), and so I knew that he could not see the opening of the door, and I kept pushing it on steadily, steadily.

I had my head in, and was about to open the lantern, when my thumb slipped upon the tin fastening, and the old man sprang up in the bed, crying out—"Who's there?"

I kept quite still and said nothing. For a whole hour I did not move a muscle, and in the meantime I did not hear him lie down. He was still sitting up in the bed, listening;— just as I have done, night after night, hearkening to the deathwatches[4] in the wall.

---

4. **deathwatches** (deth´ wäch´ əz) *n.* wood-boring beetles whose heads make a tapping sound; they are superstitiously regarded as an omen of death.

Reading Check

What steps does the narrator take to prevent the old man from hearing or seeing him?

...I knew that he could not see the opening of the door, and I kept pushing it on steadily, steadily.

Character
What character traits does the narrator show here in his reaction to the old man's groan?

Presently I heard a slight groan, and I knew it was the groan of mortal terror. It was not a groan of pain or of grief—oh, no!—it was the low stifled sound that arises from the bottom of the soul when overcharged with awe. I knew the sound well. Many a night, just at midnight, when all the world slept, it has welled up from my own bosom, deepening, with its dreadful echo, the terrors that distracted me. I say I knew it well. I knew what the old man felt, and pitied him, although I chuckled at heart.

Compare and Contrast
Compare and contrast the old man's state of mind with that of the narrator.

I knew that he had been lying awake ever since the first slight noise, when he had turned in the bed. His fears had been ever since growing upon him. He had been trying to fancy them causeless, but could not. He had been saying to himself—"It is nothing but the wind in the chimney—it is only a mouse crossing the floor," or "it is merely a cricket which has made a single chirp." Yes, he has been trying to comfort himself with these suppositions: but he had found all in vain. *All in vain*; because Death, in approaching him, had stalked with his black shadow before him, and enveloped the victim. And it was the mournful influence of the unperceived shadow that caused him to feel—although he neither saw nor heard—to *feel* the presence of my head within the room. •

Vocabulary
resolved (ri zälvd´) *v.* decided

stealthily (stelth´ ə lē) *adv.* in a secret or sly way

When I had waited a long time, very patiently, without hearing him lie down, I resolved to open a little—a very, very little crevice in the lantern. So I opened it—you cannot imagine how stealthily, stealthily—until, at length, a single dim ray, like the thread of the spider, shot from out the crevice and fell upon the vulture eye.

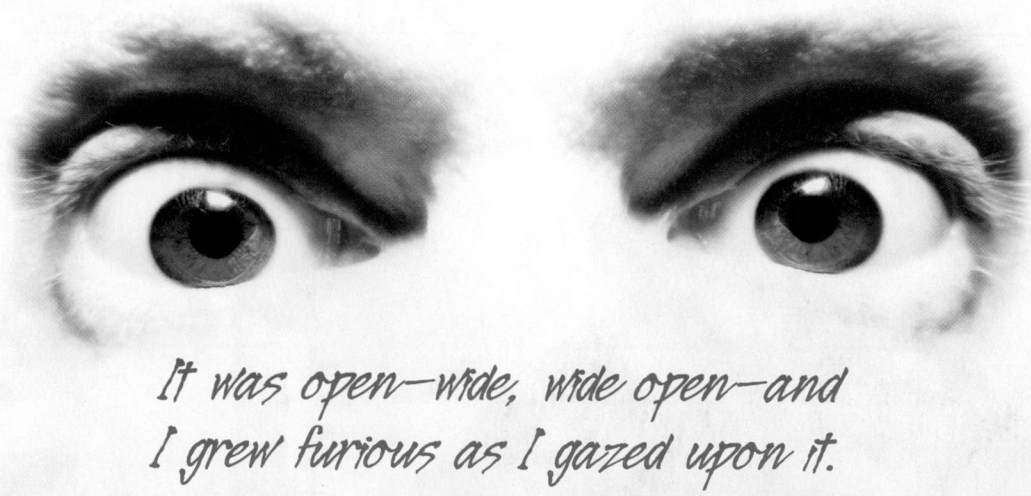

It was open—wide, wide open—and I grew furious as I gazed upon it.

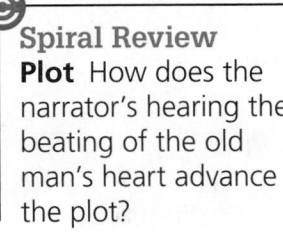

It was open—wide, wide open—and I grew furious as I gazed upon it. I saw it with perfect distinctness—all a dull blue, with a hideous veil over it that chilled the very marrow in my bones; but I could see nothing else of the old man's face or person for I had directed the ray as if by instinct, precisely upon the spot.

And now—have I not told you that what you mistake for madness is but overacuteness of the senses?—now, I say, there came to my ears a low, dull, quick sound, such as a watch makes when enveloped in cotton. I knew *that* sound well, too. It was the beating of the old man's heart. It increased my fury, as the beating of a drum stimulates the soldier into courage.

But even yet I refrained and kept still. I scarcely breathed. I held the lantern motionless. I tried how steadily I could maintain the ray upon the eye. Meantime the hellish tattoo of the heart increased. It grew quicker and quicker, and louder and louder every instant. The old man's terror *must* have been extreme! It grew louder, I say, louder every moment!—do you mark me well? I have told you that I am nervous: so I am. And now at the dead hour of the night, amid the dreadful silence of that old house, so strange a noise as this excited me to uncontrollable terror. Yet, for some minutes longer I refrained and stood still. But the beating grew louder, louder! I thought the heart must burst. And now a new anxiety seized me—the sound would be heard by a neighbor! The old man's hour had come! With a loud yell, I threw open the lantern and leaped into the room. He shrieked once—once only. In an instant I dragged him to the floor, and pulled the heavy bed over him. I then smiled gaily, to find the deed so far done. But, for many minutes, the heart beat on with a muffled sound. This, however, did not **vex** me; it would not be heard through the wall. At length it ceased. The old man was dead. I removed the bed and examined the corpse. Yes, he was stone, stone dead. I placed my hand upon the heart and held it there many minutes. There was no pulsation. He was stone dead. His eye would trouble me no more.

Spiral Review
Plot How does the narrator's hearing the beating of the old man's heart advance the plot?

Vocabulary
vex (veks) *v.* annoy; distress

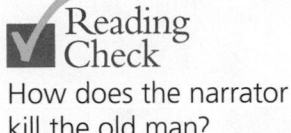

Reading Check
How does the narrator kill the old man?

Character
What do the narrator's repeated statements about being sane indicate about his character?

Compare and Contrast
Contrast the narrator's perception of his situation with the perception most people would have.

Vocabulary
audacity (ô das´ ə tē) *n.* bold courage; nerve

If still you think me mad, you will think so no longer when I describe the wise precautions I took for the concealment of the body. The night waned, and I worked hastily, but in silence. First of all I dismembered the corpse. I cut off the head and the arms and the legs.

I then took up three planks from the flooring of the chamber, and deposited all between the scantlings.[5] I then replaced the boards so cleverly, so cunningly, that no human eye—not even *his*—could have detected anything wrong. There was nothing to wash out—no stain of any kind—no blood-spot whatever. I had been too wary for that. A tub had caught all—ha! ha! •

When I had made an end of these labors, it was four o'clock—still dark as midnight. As the bell sounded the hour, there came a knocking at the street door. I went down to open it with a light heart—for what had I *now* to fear? There entered three men, who introduced themselves, with perfect suavity, as officers of the police. A shriek had been heard by a neighbor during the night; suspicion of foul play had been aroused; information had been lodged at the police office, and they (the officers) had been deputed to search the premises.

I smiled—for *what* had I to fear? I bade the gentlemen welcome. The shriek, I said, was my own in a dream. The old man, I mentioned, was absent in the country. I took my visitors all over the house. I bade them search—search *well*. I led them, at length, to *his* chamber. I showed them his treasures, secure, undisturbed. In the enthusiasm of my confidence, I brought chairs into the room, and desired them *here* to rest from their fatigues, while I myself, in the wild audacity of my perfect triumph, placed my own seat upon the very spot beneath which reposed the corpse of the victim.

---

5. **scantlings** (skant´ liŋz) *n.* small beams or timbers.

The officers were satisfied. My *manner* had convinced them. I was singularly at ease. They sat, and while I answered cheerily, they chatted of familiar things. But, ere long, I felt myself getting pale and wished them gone. My head ached, and I fancied a ringing in my ears: but still they sat and still chatted. The ringing became more distinct:—it continued and became more distinct: I talked more freely to get rid of the feeling: but it continued and gained definitiveness—until, at length, I found that the noise was *not* within my ears.

No doubt I now grew *very* pale—but I talked more fluently, and with a heightened voice. Yet the sound increased—and what could I do? It was a *low, dull, quick sound—much such a sound as a watch makes when enveloped in cotton.* I gasped for breath—and yet the officers heard it not. I talked more quickly—more vehemently; but the noise steadily increased. I arose and argued about trifles, in a high key and with violent gesticulations;[6] but the noise steadily increased. Why *would* they not be gone? I paced the floor to and fro with heavy strides, as if excited to fury by the observations of the men—but the noise steadily increased. Oh! what *could* I do? I foamed—I raved—I swore! I swung the chair upon which I had been sitting, and grated it upon the boards, but the noise arose over all, and continually increased. It grew louder—louder—*louder!* And still the men chatted pleasantly, and smiled. Was it possible they heard not?—no, no! They heard!—they suspected—they *knew!*—they were making a mockery of my horror!—this I thought, and this I think. But

---

6. **gesticulations** (jes tik´ yōō lā´ shənz) *n.* energetic hand or arm movements.

The officers were satisfied. My manner had convinced them.

Character
Which character traits allow the narrator to conceal the crime?

Compare and Contrast
Compare and contrast the perspective of the narrator with the likely perspectives of the officers.

Vocabulary
derision (di rizh´ ən)
n. statements or
actions that show you
have no respect for
someone or something

Character
Which traits force the
narrator to confess his
crime?

anything was better than this agony! Anything was more tolerable than this derision! I could bear those hypocritical smiles no longer! I felt that I must scream or die!—and now again! hark! louder! louder! louder! *louder!*—

"Villains!" I shrieked, "dissemble[7] no more! I admit the deed!—tear up the planks!—here, here!—it is the beating of his hideous heart!"

---

7. **dissemble** (di sem´ bəl) *v.* conceal one's true feelings.

Critical Thinking

Cite textual evidence to support your responses.

 1. Key Ideas and Details (a) Why does the narrator kill the old man? **(b) Draw Conclusions:** What does the narrator fear? **(c) Support:** What details in the story indicate his fears?

 2. Key Ideas and Details (a) At first, how does the narrator behave in the presence of the police? **(b) Draw Conclusions:** What causes him to change his behavior?

 3. Integration of Knowledge and Ideas (a) What sound drives the narrator to confess to the crime? **(b) Apply:** Why do you think people sometimes confess to having done something wrong, even if there is little chance their wrongdoing will be discovered? **(c) Evaluate:** Is the "tell-tale heart" in the title the old man's heart—or the narrator's? Explain.

 4. Integration of Knowledge and Ideas (a) What conflicts does the narrator experience before and after the crime? **(b)** What leads to his final breakdown? **(c)** Has his conflict been resolved? Explain. *[Connect to the Big Question: Can all conflicts be resolved?]*

Reading Skill: Compare and Contrast

1. **(a) Compare and contrast** the perspectives of the narrator and the old man on the night of the murder. **(b)** How does the reader know what the old man is thinking and feeling?

2. **(a)** Do you trust the narrator's account of what happened? Why or why not? **(b)** How would the description of the police officers' visit be different if it revealed one of the officers' perspectives?

Literary Analysis: Character Traits

3. **Key Ideas and Details (a)** Using a chart like this one, describe three **character traits** of the narrator. **(b)** Give examples that show each trait.

Character	Trait	Example
The narrator	nervousness	He is afraid the neighbor will hear the beating heart.

4. **Craft and Structure (a)** Which of the story's characters are *round characters* and which are *flat characters*? **(b)** Why do readers care more about what happens to round characters than to flat ones?

Vocabulary

Acquisition and Use Replace the word or words in italics with a **synonym** from the vocabulary list on page 292.

1. Leon *decided firmly* to become a better basketball player.
2. The dog's constant barking began to *annoy* the neighbors.
3. A *cleverly* organized political campaign won the election.
4. Dressed in black, they crept *silently* up to the old castle.
5. All Lin's ideas for a party theme were met with *ridicule*.
6. It took *boldness* to challenge the bigger, better team.

Word Study Use context and what you know about the **suffix -ity** to answer each question. Explain your answers.

1. Would something that's a *rarity* be easy or hard to find?
2. Would someone's *timidity* make public speaking easy?

Word Study

The **Latin suffix -ity** indicates a noun and means "state of" or "condition of."

Apply It Explain how the suffix **-ity** contributes to the meanings of these words. Consult a dictionary, if necessary.
complexity
continuity
purity

Integrated Language Skills

Hamadi • The Tell-Tale Heart

Conventions: Principal Parts of Regular Verbs

Every verb has four **principal parts.** These are used to form *tenses* that show when action occurs, such as in the past.

The principal parts of verbs are the **present** (basic form), **present participle, past,** and **past participle.** Both the participle forms must be used with a helping verb such as *is, was,* or *had.*

The following chart shows the principal parts of three regular verbs: *talk, save,* and *hurry.*

Principal Part	How to Form	Examples
Present	Basic form	talk, save, hurry I talk to her every day.
Present Participle	Add *–ing* Use after a form of "to be" (*is, are, was, were, will be*)	(am) talking, (are) saving, (were) hurrying We were talking yesterday.
Past	Add *–d* or *–ed*	talked, saved, hurried We talked last week.
Past Participle	Add *–d* or *–ed* Use after *has, have, had*	(have, had) talked, (has, have) saved, (has, had) hurried We have talked several times.

Practice A Identify whether the underlined verbs in each sentence use the present, past, present participle, or past participle form.

1. Usually Hamadi was wearing a white shirt.
2. Hamadi liked to use Spanish words.
3. Susan's family had lived in Jerusalem.
4. Susan's father often talks about his boyhood.

© **Reading Application** Find sentences in "Hamadi" that contain an example of each of the principal parts of verbs.

Practice B In each sentence, supply the correct principal part of the verb given at the end.

1. As the story begins, the narrator is _____ his crime. (describe)
2. Before the crime, the narrator had _____ it carefully. (plan)
3. At midnight, the man _____ the knob of the old man's door. (turn)
4. When the police knocked, the narrator _____ the door. (open)

© **Writing Application** Write a paragraph in which you use and label four principal parts of a single verb.

PH **WRITING COACH** Further instruction and practice are available in *Prentice Hall Writing Coach.*

Writing

Narrative Text Both selections have unique central characters. Write a **character profile** of the main character in "Hamadi" or "The Tell-Tale Heart." Explain how the character's traits affect the story's plot and resolution.

- Refer to the chart of traits you created for either Hamadi or the narrator of "The Tell-Tale Heart."

- If you read "Hamadi," reread the end of the story to review the way Hamadi helps to resolve Tracy's problems. If you read "The Tell-Tale Heart," reread the end of the story to review why the narrator acts as he does when the police arrive.

- As you draft your character profile, show the connection between the main character's personality and the story's ending.

Grammar Application Make sure that your character profile uses verb participles correctly and consistently.

Writing Workshop: *Work in Progress*

Prewriting for Response to Literature Choose one Story Web from your portfolio. Next to each circle in the web, write a sentence explaining why this feature is important. Then, number the circles, beginning with "1" for the circle that you think contains the most important idea. Save this Story Web in your portfolio.

Speaking and Listening

Comprehension and Collaboration Prepare and present an **oral response** to the short story you read. Ask yourself questions like these: *Is Saleh Hamadi an interesting character? Is "The Tell-Tale Heart" as frightening as today's horror films?*

- Develop your interpretation around several clear ideas, arguments, or images.

- Support your response by using examples and evidence from the story itself.

- To give your response greater depth, call attention to specific techniques the writer uses to provoke a reaction from his or her audience. You can also make comparisons to other works.

- In class, share your individual response. Ask for others' responses to the same character and use them as a basis for discussion. Speak clearly and loudly to aid listeners' comprehension.

Common Core State Standards

L.8.1; W.8.2; SL.8.4
[For the full wording of the standards, see page 276.]

Use this prewriting activity to prepare for the **Writing Workshop** on page 326.

www.PHLitOnline.com
- Interactive graphic organizers
- Grammar tutorial
- Interactive journals

Test Practice: Reading

Compare and Contrast

Fiction Selection

Directions: *Read the selection. Then, answer the questions.*

Nicole and Katherine were thrilled when their team won the soccer game. They both loved the sport and never missed a game or a practice. After the game, the coach invited everyone to go out for ice cream. Nicole wanted to go but instead went home to review some items for a test for which she had been studying. She enjoyed biology and wanted to do well on the test.

Katherine decided to go out, anyway. By the time she got home, she was tired. Nevertheless, she forced herself to stay up late and memorize terms for the biology test.

When they got their tests back, Nicole had done well. Katherine was not surprised at her low grade. "It's my own fault," she said. "I'm just no good at biology."

1. What **perspective** about soccer do the two girls share?
   A. They think studying is more important than soccer.
   B. They think soccer is more important than studying.
   C. They love soccer and never miss practice.
   D. They can take it or leave it.

2. In what way are the two girls different?
   A. Katherine always fails tests.
   B. Nicole is more popular.
   C. Nicole is more motivated in school.
   D. Katherine is never critical of herself.

3. What trait explains why Nicole gets a better grade than Katherine?
   A. Nicole is smarter than Katherine.
   B. Nicole is friendlier than Katherine.
   C. Nicole is more disciplined than Katherine.
   D. Nicole is less honest than Katherine.

4. Choose the words that most accurately complete this sentence: *Before the test, Katherine is _____ about the test; after the test she is _____ .*
   A. unconcerned; frustrated
   B. unconcerned; afraid
   C. ashamed; proud
   D. angry; confused

Writing for Assessment

In a few sentences, describe the conversation that Nicole and Katherine might have had after receiving the coach's invitation. Use details from the passage to show how the girls are alike and different.

Nonfiction Selection

Directions: *Read the selection. Then, answer the questions.*

A recent survey of students' study habits at University of Minnesota has resulted in an interesting finding. *How you study is as important as how much you study.*

Two researchers examined a class in which students studied the same average number of hours for a weekly test. They wanted to find out why students received different grades, ranging from A to F. They found that students who received A's tended to pace their studying better than students with lower grades. They spread study sessions out instead of cramming at the last minute. D and F students tended to memorize terms without understanding the information or seeing how it connected to the big picture—things that A and B students did well. Motivation counts, too. "If students are uninterested or not motivated toward the subject, they may not be able to retain the infomation very well," said one official familiar with the study.

1. What is the main difference between the groups of students described in the passage?
   - **A.** Some studied longer than others.
   - **B.** Some had prior experience in the subject.
   - **C.** Some studied more effectively.
   - **D.** Some had received help from a teacher.

2. What was the same for all the students?
   - **A.** They studied the same number of hours.
   - **B.** They studied the same number of hours each day leading up to the test.
   - **C.** They achieved the same grades.
   - **D.** They were equally motivated.

3. In what way were the study habits of A students *most* different from those of D and F students?
   - **A.** A students had taken the class before.
   - **B.** A students studied more.
   - **C.** A students did not memorize at all.
   - **D.** A students studied over time.

4. Based on the study, which statement is true?
   - **A.** Motivation matters less than study time.
   - **B.** Pacing and understanding are key.
   - **C.** Good students do not memorize at all.
   - **D.** The same number of study hours produce the same results.

Writing for Assessment

Connecting Across Texts
Write one paragraph on effective study habits for students. Use details from both passages to contrast good study habits with poor ones.

PHLit Online!
www.PHLitOnline.com
- Online practice
- Instant feedback

Reading for Information

Analyzing Expository Texts

Summary

Summary

Reading Skill: Compare Summaries to an Original Text

A **summary** is a statement of the main ideas and major details in a written work. When you **compare an original text with its summary**, you look for similarities and differences between the two. The first thing you will notice is that a summary includes certain details and leaves out others.

The Venn diagram here shows some of the similarities and differences between an original work and a summary. As you read the two summaries of "The Tell-Tale Heart," keep these basic similarities and differences in mind. Analyze the text to determine how accurately the two summaries capture the main ideas, whether they include or leave out critical details, and how well they convey the meaning of the story.

Common Core State Standards

Reading Informational Text
3. Analyze how a text makes connections among and distinctions between individuals, ideas, or events.

Language
4.b. Use common, grade-appropriate Greek or Latin affixes and roots as clues to the meaning of a word.

6. Acquire and use accurately grade-appropriate general academic and domain-specific words and phrases; gather vocabulary knowledge when considering a word or phrase important to comprehension or expression.

Comparing an Original Text with a Summary

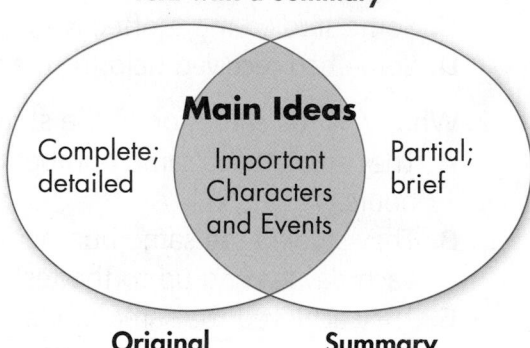

Original   Summary

Content-Area Vocabulary

These words appear in the selections that follow. You may also encounter them in other content-area texts.

- **stream-of-consciousness** (strēm əv kän´ shəs nis) *adj.* narrative technique that imitates the way the narrator thinks by presenting his or her thoughts and feelings in random order

- **criticism** (krit´ ə siz´ əm) *n.* writing that evaluates the qualities of literary works, movies, music, or other art forms

Summary of
The Tell-Tale Heart

FROM THE OXFORD COMPANION TO
AMERICAN LITERATURE - JAMES D. HART, EDITOR

Features:

- main ideas captured and presented accurately
- brief mention of important details
- an explanation of the underlying meaning of the work
- shorter length than the original work

Tell-Tale Heart, The, *story by Poe, published in* The Pioneer *(1843). It has been considered the most influential of Poe's stories in the later development of* **stream-of-consciousness** *fiction.*

> This sentence explains why the story is important.

A victim of a nervous disease is overcome by homicidal mania and murders an innocent old man in whose home he lives. He confuses the ticking of the old man's watch with an excited heartbeat, and although he dismembers the body he neglects to remove the watch when he buries the pieces beneath the floor. The old man's dying shriek has been overheard, and three police officers come to investigate. They discover nothing, and the murderer claims that the old man is absent in the country, but when they remain to question him he hears a loud rhythmic sound that he believes to be the beating of the buried heart. This so distracts his diseased mind that he suspects the officers know the truth and are merely trying his patience, and in an insane fit he confesses his crime.

> The summary begins by briefly identifying the characters and the situation.

> The rest of the summary tells the main events of the plot in chronological order.

The Tell-Tale Heart

FROM SHORT STORY CRITICISM, ANNA SHEETS NESBITT - EDITOR

> This summary, while longer than the first, is still shorter than the original text.

Plot and Major Characters

> This summary tells more about the main character—the narrator—and gives more details about why he kills the old man.

The tale opens with the narrator insisting that he is not mad, avowing that his calm telling of the story that follows is confirmation of his sanity. He explains that he decided to take the life of an old man whom he loved and whose house he shared. The only reason he had for doing so was that the man's pale blue eye, which was veiled by a thin white film and "resembled that of a vulture," tormented him, and he had to rid himself of the "Evil Eye" forever.

After again declaring his sanity, the narrator proceeds to recount the details of the crime. Every night for seven nights, he says, he had stolen into the old man's room at midnight holding a closed lantern. Each night he would very slowly unlatch the lantern slightly and shine a single ray of light onto the man's closed eye. As he enters the room on the eighth night, however, the old man stirs, then calls out, thinking he has heard a sound. The narrator shines the light on the old man's eye as usual, but this time finds it wide open. He begins to hear the beating of a heart and, fearing the sound might be heard by a neighbor, kills the old man by dragging him to the floor and pulling the heavy bed over him. He dismembers the corpse and hides it beneath the floorboards of the old man's room.

> Like the first summary, this summary tells the events of the plot in chronological order, concluding with the narrator's confession. However, this summary includes more detail.

At four o'clock in the morning, the narrator continues, three policemen come asking to search the premises because a neighbor has reported a shriek coming from the house. The narrator invites the officers in, explaining that the noise came from himself as he dreamt. The old man, he tells them, is in the country. He brings chairs into the old man's room, placing his own seat on the very planks under which the victim lies buried. The officers are convinced there is no foul play, and sit around chatting amiably, but the narrator becomes increasingly agitated. He soon begins to hear a heart beating, much as he had just before he killed the old man. It grows louder and louder until he becomes convinced the policemen hear it too. They know of his crime, he thinks, and mock him. Unable to bear their derision and the sound of the beating heart, he springs up and, screaming, confesses his crime.

Comparing Expository Texts

 1. Key Ideas and Details **(a)** What are four details that appear in both summaries? **(b)** What are four details that you found in the second summary but not in the first?

 2. Craft and Structure Explain how reading a summary differs from reading the full text.

Content-Area Vocabulary

3. (a) Explain the meaning of the root *crit-*, as in *criteria*, *hypocrite*, and *critical*. **(b)** Use each of the three words in a sentence that shows its meaning.

⏱ Timed Writing

Expository Text: Evaluation

> **Organization and Details**
> The prompt tells you what points to cover in your essay and the order in which to cover them.

Write an essay in which you evaluate the two summaries of "The Tell-Tale Heart." First, compare the summaries, noting their style, completeness, conciseness, and accuracy. Then, assess each summary to determine how effective each summary is. (20 minutes)

> **Academic Vocabulary**
> When you *assess* something, you evaluate its strengths and weaknesses. When you *determine* whether writing is effective, you make a judgment about its quality.

5-Minute Planner

Complete these steps before you begin to write:

1. Read the prompt and make sure you understand the assignment. Key words, like the ones highlighted in color, will tell you **exactly** what is required. Remember to address style, completeness, conciseness, and accuracy in your essay.

2. Skim each summary for details that relate to each point.

3. Make a Venn diagram with the following headings: Summary 1 (in left section), Both (in center section), and Summary 2 (in right section). In each summary section, identify what is unique in each summary. In the center, identify what is common to both.

4. Refer to your chart as you write your response.

Comparing Types of Narratives

A **narrative** is any type of writing that tells a story. Every narrative presents a sequence of events that takes place in a certain setting. There are key differences between types of narratives, however.

- A **fictional narrative** is about imaginary characters and events.

- A **nonfictional narrative** is about real characters and events.

Since a fictional narrative does not describe real events, the author has complete control over *characters, setting,* and *plot*. A writer can introduce new characters, change locations, or alter events to build the story.

In nonfiction, authors cannot change real-life events or invent details about people or places. Authors of nonfiction can choose which details they wish to present to readers, however.

As you read the fictional story "Up the Slide" and the nonfiction work "A Glow in the Dark," notice the differences between the types of narratives. Also, note the features they share, as shown in the chart.

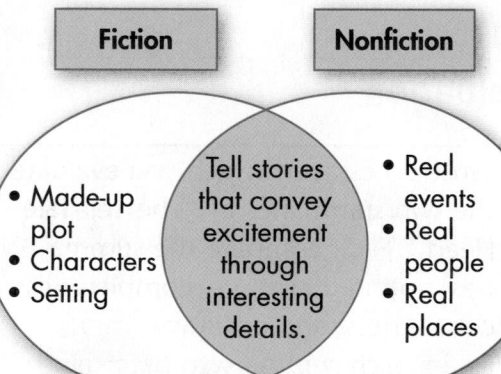

Fiction

- Made-up plot
- Characters
- Setting

Tell stories that convey excitement through interesting details.

Nonfiction

- Real events
- Real people
- Real places

Common Core State Standards

Writing

2. Write informative/explanatory texts to examine a topic and convey ideas, concepts, and information through the selection, organization, and analysis of relevant content.

9. Draw evidence from literary or informational texts to support analysis, reflection, and research. *(Timed Writing)*

Compare narrators in fiction and nonfiction. In any literary work, the narrator is the character or speaker who tells the story. In fiction, the narrator is a creation of the author. A narrator in a fictional work may have a distinct personality or may be a neutral reporter of events. In nonfiction, the narrator and the writer are usually one and the same. As a result, readers can infer what the nonfiction writer's perspective is on a topic. Readers may also feel a strong connection to a nonfiction narrator because the story is true.

As you read, be aware of each narrator. Consider how the narrator helps to shape your response to the work.

PHLit Online!
www.PHLitOnline.com

- Vocabulary flashcards
- Interactive journals
- More about the authors

- Selection audio
- Interactive graphic organizers

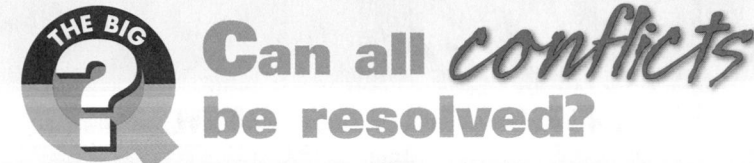

Can all *conflicts* be resolved?

Writing About the Big Question

In both of these narratives, an individual struggles against his fear of natural dangers. Use this sentence starter to develop your ideas about the Big Question.

Nature's beauty can **mislead.** It often hides dangers for those who _____.

Meet the Authors

Jack London (1876–1916)

Author of "Up the Slide"

Jack London was the most popular novelist and short-story writer of his day. His exciting tales of adventure and courage were inspired by his own experiences.

A Young Adventurer When he was seventeen, London sailed with a seal-hunting ship to Japan and Siberia. After two years, he returned to high school, vowing to become a writer. In 1897, London journeyed to the Yukon Territory in search of gold. Although he did not find any, he did find inspiration for writing.

Gary Paulsen (b. 1939)

Author of "A Glow in the Dark"

Gary Paulsen had a difficult childhood. Because his family moved often, he never spent more than five months in any school.

In From the Cold One cold night, Paulsen went into a library to get warm. The librarian gave him a book and a library card. "It was as though I had been dying of thirst and the librarian had handed me a five-gallon bucket of water," he says. Now, Paulsen writes fiction based on his own life. "A Glow in the Dark" is from *Woodsong,* an account of his experiences as he trained for the Iditarod, a dog-sled race in Alaska.

Up the SLIDE

Jack London

Background

Clay Dilham, the young man in "Up the Slide," is similar to many young prospectors who traveled to the Yukon Territory in search of gold in the 1890s. The Yukon Territory is located in the northwestern corner of Canada. It is part of the subarctic zone, where temperatures have been known to plunge to −80°F!

When Clay Dilham left the tent to get a sled-load of firewood, he expected to be back in half an hour. So he told Swanson, who was cooking the dinner. Swanson and he belonged to different outfits, located about twenty miles apart on the Stewart River, but they had become traveling partners on a trip down the Yukon to Dawson to get the mail.

Swanson had laughed when Clay said he would be back in half an hour. It stood to reason, Swanson said, that good, dry firewood could not be found so close to Dawson; that whatever firewood there was originally had long since been gathered in; that firewood would not be selling at forty dollars a cord if any man could go out and get a sled-load and be back in the time Clay expected to make it.

Then it was Clay's turn to laugh, as he sprang on the sled and *mushed* the dogs on the river-trail. For, coming up from the Siwash village the previous day, he had noticed a small dead pine in an out-of-the-way place, which had defied discovery by eyes less sharp than his. And his eyes were both young and sharp, for his seventeenth birthday was just cleared.

A swift ten minutes over the ice brought him to the place, and figuring ten minutes to get the tree and ten minutes to return made him certain that Swanson's dinner would not wait.

◀ **Critical Viewing**
What would be difficult about making this climb? **[Analyze]**

▲ **Critical Viewing**
What details about the setting of this story can you learn from this historical photograph of Yukon miners? **[Connect]**

✔ Reading Check
What is Clay trying to do?

Just below Dawson, and rising out of the Yukon itself, towered the great Moosehide Mountain, so named by Lieutenant Schwatka long ere the Yukon became famous. On the river side the mountain was scarred and gullied and gored; and it was up one of these gores or gullies that Clay had seen the tree.

Halting his dogs beneath, on the river ice, he looked up, and after some searching, rediscovered it. Being dead, its weatherbeaten gray so blended with the gray wall of rock that a thousand men could pass by and never notice it. Taking root in a cranny, it had grown up, exhausted its bit of soil, and perished. Beneath it the wall fell sheer for a hundred feet to the river. All one had to do was to sink an ax into the dry trunk a dozen times and it would fall to the ice, and most probably smash conveniently to pieces. This Clay had figured on when confidently limiting the trip to half an hour.

He studied the cliff thoroughly before attempting it. So far as he was concerned, the longest way round was the shortest way to the tree. Twenty feet of nearly perpendicular climbing would bring him to where a slide sloped more gently in. By making a long zigzag across the face of this slide and back again, he would arrive at the pine.

Fastening his ax across his shoulders so that it would not interfere with his movements, he clawed up the broken rock, hand and foot, like a cat, till the twenty feet were cleared and he could draw breath on the edge of the slide.

The slide was steep and its snow-covered surface slippery. Further, the heelless, walrus-hide shoes of his *muclucs* were polished by much ice travel, and by his second step he realized how little he could depend upon them for clinging purposes. A slip at that point meant a plunge over the edge and a twenty-foot fall to the ice. A hundred feet farther along, and a slip would mean a fifty-foot fall.

He thrust his mittened hand through the snow to the earth to steady himself, and went on. But he was forced to exercise such care that the first zigzag consumed five minutes. Then, returning across the face of the slide toward the pine, he met with a new difficulty. The slope steepened considerably, so that little snow collected, while bent flat beneath this thin covering were long, dry last-year's grasses.

The surface they presented was as glassy as that of his muclucs, and when both surfaces came together his feet shot out, and he fell on his face, sliding downward and convulsively clutching for something to stay himself.

This he succeeded in doing, although he lay quiet for a couple of minutes to get back his nerve. He would have taken off his muclucs and gone at it in his socks, only the cold was thirty below zero, and at such temperature his feet would quickly freeze. So he went on, and after ten minutes of risky work made the safe and solid rock where stood the pine.

A few strokes of the ax felled it into the chasm, and peeping over the edge, he indulged a laugh at the startled dogs. They were on the verge of bolting when he called aloud to them, soothingly, and they were reassured. •

Then he turned about for the trip back. Going down, he knew, was even more dangerous than coming up, but how dangerous he did not realize till he had slipped half a dozen times, and each time saved himself by what appeared to him a miracle. Time and again he ventured upon the slide, and time and again he was balked when he came to the grasses.

He sat down and looked at the treacherous snow-covered slope. It was manifestly[1] impossible for him to make it with a whole body, and he did not wish to arrive at the bottom shattered like the pine tree.

He must be doing something to keep his blood circulating. If he could not get down by going down, there only remained to him to get down by going up. It was a herculean task, but it was the only way out of the predicament.

From where he was he could not see the top of the cliff, but he reasoned that the gully in which lay the slide must give inward more and more as it approached the top. From what little he could see, the gully displayed this tendency; and he noticed, also, that the slide extended for many hundreds of feet upward, and that where it ended the rock was well broken up and favorable for climbing. . . .

So instead of taking the zigzag which led downward, he made a new one leading upward and crossing the slide at an angle of thirty degrees. The grasses gave him much trouble, and made him long for soft-tanned moosehide moccasins, which could make his feet cling like a second pair of hands.

He soon found that thrusting his mittened hands through the snow and clutching the grass roots was uncertain and unsafe.

---

1. **manifestly** (man´ ə fest´ lē) *adv.* clearly.

Narratives
Do the risks that Clay takes seem like those an actual person would take? Why or why not?

Narratives
How does the author's choice of setting heighten the drama in the story?

Reading Check
Why is the trip down harder than the trip up?

His mittens were too thick for him to be sure of his grip, so he took them off. But this brought with it new trouble. When he held on to a bunch of roots the snow, coming in contact with his bare warm hand, was melted, so that his hands and the wristbands of his woolen shirt were dripping with water. This the frost was quick to attack, and his fingers were numbed and made worthless.

Then he was forced to seek good footing, where he could stand erect unsupported, to put on his mittens, and to thrash his hands against his sides until the heat came back into them.

This constant numbing of his fingers made his progress very slow; but the zigzag came to an end finally, where the side of the slide was buttressed by a perpendicular rock, and he turned back and upward again. As he climbed higher and higher, he found that the slide was wedge-shaped, its rocky buttresses pinching it away as it reared its upper end. Each step increased the depth which seemed to yawn for him.

While beating his hands against his sides he turned and looked down the long slippery slope, and figured, in case he slipped, that he would be flying with the speed of an express train ere he took the final plunge into the icy bed of the Yukon.

He passed the first outcropping rock, and the second, and at the end of an hour found himself above the third, and fully five hundred feet above the river. And here, with the end nearly two hundred feet above him, the pitch of the slide was increasing.

Each step became more difficult and perilous, and he was faint from exertion and from lack of Swanson's dinner. Three or four times he slipped slightly and recovered himself; but, growing careless from exhaustion and the long tension on his nerves, he tried to continue with too great haste, and was rewarded by a double slip of each foot, which tore him loose and started him down the slope.

On account of the steepness there was little snow; but what little there was as displaced by his body, so that he became the nucleus of a young avalanche. He clawed desperately with his hands, but there was little to cling to, and he sped downward faster and faster.

The first and second outcroppings were below him, but he knew that the first was almost out of line, and pinned his hope on the second. Yet the first was just enough in line to catch one of his feet and to whirl him over and head downward on his back.

The shock of this was severe in itself, and the fine snow enveloped him in a blinding, maddening cloud; but he was

thinking quickly and clearly of what would happen if he brought up head first against the outcropping. He twisted himself over on his stomach, thrust both hands out to one side, and pressed them heavily against the flying surface.

This had the effect of a brake, drawing his head and shoulders to the side. In this position he rolled over and over a couple of times, and then, with a quick jerk at the right moment, he got his body the rest of the way round.

And none too soon, for the next moment his feet drove into the outcropping, his legs doubled up, and the wind was driven from his stomach with the abruptness of the stop.

There was much snow down his neck and up his sleeves. At once and with unconcern he shook this out, only to discover, when he looked up to where he must climb again, that he had lost his nerve. He was shaking as if with a palsy, and sick and faint from a frightful nausea.

Fully ten minutes passed ere he could master these sensations and summon sufficient strength for the weary climb. His legs hurt him and he was limping, and he was conscious of a sore place in his back, where he had fallen on the ax.

In an hour he had regained the point of his tumble, and was contemplating the slide, which so suddenly steepened. It was plain to him that he could not go up with his hands and feet alone, and he was beginning to lose his nerve again when he remembered the ax.

Reaching upward the distance of a step, he brushed away the snow, and in the frozen gravel and crumbled rock of the slide chopped a shallow resting place for his foot. Then he came up a step, reached forward, and repeated the maneuver. And so, step by step, foothole by foothole, a tiny speck of toiling life poised like a fly on the face of Moosehide Mountain, he fought his upward way. ●

Twilight was beginning to fall when he gained the head of the slide and drew himself into the rocky bottom of the gully. At this point the shoulder of the mountain began to bend back toward the crest, and in addition to its being less steep, the rocks afforded better handhold and foothold. The worst was over, and the best yet to come!

The gully opened out into a miniature basin, in which a floor of soil had been deposited, out of which, in turn, a tiny grove of pines had sprung. The trees were all dead, dry and seasoned, having long since exhausted the thin skin of earth.

Narratives
What details does London use in this passage to create suspense?

Spiral Review
Point of View How does the use of a third-person narrator affect the way you experience the events described here?

Vocabulary
maneuver
(mə nōō´ vər)
n. series of planned steps

Reading Check
How does Clay avoid sliding to his death?

Clay ran his experienced eye over the timber, and estimated that it would chop up into fifty cords at least. Beyond, the gully closed in and became barren rock again. On every hand was barren rock, so the wonder was small that the trees had escaped the eyes of men. They were only to be discovered as he had discovered them—by climbing after them.

He continued the ascent, and the white moon greeted him when he came out upon the crest of Moosehide Mountain. At his feet, a thousand feet below, sparkled the lights of Dawson.

But the descent was precipitate and dangerous in the uncertain moonlight, and he elected to go down the mountain by its gentler northern flank. In a couple of hours he reached the Yukon at the Siwash village, and took the river-trail back to where he had left the dogs. There he found Swanson, with a fire going, waiting for him to come down.

And although Swanson had a hearty laugh at his expense, nevertheless, a week or so later, in Dawson, there were fifty cords of wood sold at forty dollars a cord, and it was he and Swanson who sold them.

Critical Thinking

Cite textual evidence to support your responses.

1. **Craft and Structure (a)** How long does Clay say he will be gone collecting firewood? **(b)** What is Swanson's reaction to Clay's estimate? **(c) Speculate:** Why do you think London begins his story with the description of the disagreement?

2. **Key Ideas and Details (a) Infer:** Identify three specific details in the text that demonstrate Clay's survival skills. **(b) Contrast:** Which of his actions endanger his life? Explain. **(c) Make a Judgment:** Is the discovery worth the risks Clay takes? Explain.

3. **Integration of Knowledge and Ideas (a) Infer:** What lesson does Clay learn from his experiences? **(b) Generalize:** What lesson does the story hold for readers who will never visit the Yukon?

4. **Integration of Knowledge and Ideas (a)** What challenges does Clay face on the mountain? **(b)** How does he overcome his fears? *[Connect to the Big Question: Can all conflicts be resolved?]*

A Glow in the Dark
from WOODSONG
Gary Paulsen

There are night ghosts.

Some people say that we can understand all things if we can know them, but there came a dark night in the fall when I thought that was wrong, and so did the dogs.

We had been running all morning and were tired; some of the dogs were young and could not sustain a long run. So we stopped in the middle of the afternoon when they seemed to want to rest. I made a fire, set up a gentle, peaceful camp, and went to sleep for four hours.

It hadn't snowed yet so we had been running with a three-wheel cart, which meant we had to run on logging roads and open areas. I had been hard pressed to find new country to run in to keep the young dogs from becoming bored and this logging trail was one we hadn't run. It had been rough going, with a lot of ruts and mud and the cart was a mess so I spent some time fixing it after I awakened, carving off the dried mud. The end result was we didn't get going again until close to one in the morning. This did not pose a problem except that as soon as I hooked the dogs up and got them lined out—I was running an eight-dog team—my head lamp

Vocabulary
sustain (sə stān´) *v.*
keep up

Reading Check
Why is the author running his dogs in the middle of the night?

Narratives
What real details emphasize that "the ride was madness"?

▼ **Critical Viewing**
How would riding this cart during the day compare with riding it at night after a rain? **[Compare and Contrast]**

went out. I replaced the bulb and tried a new battery, but that didn't help—the internal wiring was bad. I thought briefly of sleeping again until daylight but the dogs were slamming into the harnesses, screaming to run, so I shrugged and jumped on the rig and untied it. Certainly, I thought, running without a head lamp would not be the worst thing I had ever done.

Immediately we blew into the darkness and the ride was madness. Without a lamp I could not tell when the rig was going to hit a rut or a puddle. It was cloudy and fairly warm—close to fifty—and had rained the night before. Without the moon or even starlight I had no idea where the puddles were until they splashed me—largely in the face—so I was soon dripping wet. Coupled with that, tree limbs I couldn't see hit at me as we passed, almost tearing me off the back of the rig. Inside an hour I wasn't sure if I was up, down, or sideways.

And the dogs stopped.

They weren't tired, not even a little, judging by the way they had been ripping through the night, but they stopped dead.

I had just taken a limb in the face and was temporarily blinded. All I knew was that they had stopped suddenly and that I had to jam down on the brakes to keep from running over them. It took me a couple of seconds to clear my eyes and when I did, I saw the light.

In the first seconds I thought it was another person coming toward me. The light had an eerie green-yellow glow. It was quite bright and filled a whole part of the dark night ahead, down the trail. It seemed to be moving. I was in deep woods and couldn't think what a person would be doing there—there are no other teams where I train—but I was glad to see the light.

At first.

Then I realized the light was strange. It glowed and ebbed and seemed to fill too much space to be a regular light source. It was low to the ground, and wide.

I was still not frightened, and would probably not have become frightened except that the dogs suddenly started to sing.

I have already talked about some of their songs. Rain songs and first-snow songs and meat songs and come-back-and-stay-with-us songs and even puppy-training songs, but I had heard this song only once, when an old dog had died in the kennel. It was a death song.

And that frightened me.

They all sat. I could see them quite well in the glow from the light—the soft glow, the green glow, the ghost glow. It crept into my thinking without my knowing it: the ghost glow. Against my wishes I started thinking of all the things in my life that had scared me.

Ghosts and goblins and dark nights and snakes under the bed and sounds I didn't know and bodies I had found and graveyards under covered pale moons and death, death, death . . .

And they sang and sang. The cold song in the strange light. For a time I could do nothing but stand on the back of the wheeled rig and stare at the light with old, dusty terror. •

But curiosity was stronger. My legs moved without my wanting them to move and my body followed them, alongside the team in the dark, holding to each dog like a security blanket until I reached the next one, moving closer to the light until I was at the front and there were no more dogs to hold.

The light had gotten brighter, seemed to pulse and flood back and forth, but I still could not see the source. I took another step, then another, trying to look around the corner, deeply feeling the distance from the dogs, the aloneness.

Two more steps, then one more, leaning to see around the corner and at last I saw it and when I did it was worse.

It was a form. Not human. A large, standing form glowing in the dark. The light came from within it, a cold-glowing green light with yellow edges that **diffused** the shape, making it change and grow as I watched.

I felt my heart slam up into my throat.

I couldn't move. I stared at the upright form and was sure it was a ghost, a being from the dead sent for me. I could not move and might not have ever moved except that the dogs had followed

Spiral Review
Point of View How does having access to the narrator's thought processes affect the way you view these events?

Narratives
What details from Paulsen's imagination create excitement here?

Vocabulary
diffused (di fyo͞ozd´) *v.* spread out widely in different directions

Reading Check
What sound frightens Paulsen?

Science Connection

Phosphorescence

Phosphorus is a major element that aids plant growth. *Phosphorescence* is the process that makes phosphorus glow. During phosphorescence, phosphorus electrons absorb energy and become unstable. Light—the glow—results when the electrons drop back to their original energy levels.

Connect to the Literature

How did Paulsen's ignorance of a scientific explanation for the glow add to his fear?

me, pulling the rig quietly until they were around my legs, peering ahead, and I looked down at them and had to laugh.

They were caught in the green light, curved around my legs staring at the standing form, ears cocked and heads turned sideways while they studied it. I took another short step forward and they all followed me, then another, and they stayed with me until we were right next to the form.

It was a stump.

A six-foot-tall, old rotten stump with the bark knocked off, glowing in the dark with a bright green glow. Impossible. I stood there with the dogs around my legs, smelling the stump and touching it with their noses. I found out later that it glowed because it had sucked phosphorus from the ground up into the wood and held the light from day all night.

But that was later. There in the night I did not know this. Touching the stump, and feeling the cold light, I could not quite get rid of the fear until a black-and-white dog named Fonzie came up, smelled the stump, snorted, and relieved himself on it.

So much for ghosts.

Critical Thinking

1. Key Ideas and Details (a) Infer: Why do the dogs start to sing? **(b) Apply:** In what way does their singing increase Paulsen's fear?

2. Key Ideas and Details (a) How does Paulsen use his dogs for support as he moves toward the glow? **(b) Draw Conclusions:** Based on his actions, how does Paulsen feel about his dogs?

3. Integration of Knowledge and Ideas Assess: Do you think Paulsen shows good judgment and common sense? Explain.

4. Integration of Knowledge and Ideas (a) What fears does Paulsen need to face in order to approach the glowing stump? **(b)** What enables him to overcome his fears? *[Connect to the Big Question: Can all conflicts be resolved?]*

Cite textual evidence to support your responses.

Comparing Types of Narratives

1. Key Ideas and Details Use a chart like this one to compare narrative elements.

Up the Slide	Elements	A Glow in the Dark
Outside narrator	Narrator	Gary Paulsen
	Main character	
	Danger	
	Role of dogs	
	Character's attitude toward danger	
	Reasons for character's behavior	

2. Key Ideas and Details Fictional and nonfictional narratives often borrow from each other. **(a)** List four details in the text of "Up the Slide" that add a sense of realism to this work of fiction. **(b)** List four details that lend "A Glow in the Dark" the excitement of a short story.

⏱ Timed Writing

Explanatory Text: Essay

Write an essay comparing the use of details in the two narratives. Discuss how these details affect the way you view the challenges facing Clay and Paulsen. **(40 minutes)**

5-Minute Planner

1. Read the prompt carefully and completely.

2. Gather your ideas by jotting down answers to these questions:
   - Who was more brave, Clay or Paulsen? Explain.
   - Which invented details reveal aspects of Clay's character?
   - Which true details reveal aspects about Paulsen?

3. To organize your thoughts, you may refer to your completed chart from this page. Then, provide evidence to support your analysis.

4. Reread the prompt, and then draft your essay.

Writing Workshop

 **Common Core
State Standards**

Writing

1. Write arguments to support claims with clear reasons and relevant evidence.

1.c. Use words, phrases, and clauses to create cohesion and clarify the relationships among claim(s), counterclaims, reasons, and evidence.

4. Produce clear and coherent writing in which the development, organization, and style are appropriate to task, purpose, and audience.

9. Draw evidence from literary or informational texts to support analysis, reflection, and research.

Write an Argument

Response to Literature: Critical Review

Defining the Form A **critical review** is an analysis of a work of literature in which the writer describes the work and expresses an opinion about its quality and effectiveness. You might use elements of this form in writing critical essays or book reviews.

Assignment Write a critical review of two or more works of literature that are linked by theme or topic. Your critical review should include these elements:

 ✔ a *thesis statement* about the value of the two works

 ✔ text references that make connections and *support judgments*

 ✔ an *analysis* of the stories' *characters, plots, or themes*

 ✔ *ideas and arguments* that demonstrate insight

 ✔ error-free writing, including *correct use of irregular verbs*

To preview the criteria on which your critical review may be judged, see the rubric on page 331.

 Writing Workshop: *Work in Progress*

Review the work you did on pages 275 and 305.

Prewriting/Planning Strategy

Make Connections Browse this textbook and other works you have read. In a chart like this one, take notes about the plot, characters, theme, and style in each work. Look for points that will allow you to make connections among multiple works. Then, choose two works to address in your review.

Story	Characters	Plot	Theme
"The Finish of Patsy Barnes"	Patsy Barnes, his mother, the doctor, McCarthy, Brackett	A boy rides a wild horse to victory to help his sick mother.	People facing hard times can rise to the occasion.
"The Drummer Boy of Shiloh"	Joby, the general	A general helps a drummer boy find courage before battle.	A bad situation can become bearable, given the right motivation.

Using the Right Words

Word choice is the exact language a writer selects to communicate ideas. For a critical review, good writers choose precise words that convey either praise or criticism, or both.

Follow these tips when writing your critical review.

Considering Audience and Purpose Take a moment to identify why you are writing and for whom. Choose words that will appeal to your audience and help you achieve your purpose.

Determining Your Opinion Think about how each story affected you when you read it. Ask yourself questions like these:

- Did the story have a plot that interested me? Why or why not?
- Were the characters believable? Did I like them? Why?
- Would I recommend this story to a friend? Why?

Jot down your answers, either as individual words or as phrases or clauses. Examine the ideas in your responses for clear connections you can draw. For example, perhaps you found characters in a story difficult to relate to because the plot itself was so outlandish. Then, use the language from your responses to establish and support claims and defend against counterclaims when writing.

> **PH WRITING COACH**
> Further instruction and practice are available in *Prentice Hall Writing Coach*.

Writing Like a Reviewer As you think about your response to the literature, be aware of your word choices and their *connotations*. Connotations are the impressions and feelings a word conveys beyond its basic meaning. Ask: *Do my words have connotations that suit my purpose? What impact will my words have on my audience?*

Brainstorming for Accurate Words Determine your attitude toward the story. Do you think it deserves praise—or disapproval? Make lists of words that express these attitudes. Start with the categories in this chart, and then consult a thesaurus for synonyms.

Strong Disapproval	Mild Disapproval	Mild Praise	High Praise
biased	confusing	accurate	brilliant
pointless	dull	intelligent	excellent
ridiculous	predictable	solid	entertaining

Drafting Strategies

Find and define your focus. Using your notes, pinpoint an idea that connects both works of literature. The idea could center around specific techniques, such as flashback or figurative language. Or it could focus on similarities or differences in the characters, plots, or themes of the works. Whatever focus you choose, be sure you have enough relevant examples from the texts to introduce and develop the claims you expect to make.

Establish your claims. Determine your reaction to the technique or literary element you have chosen. Then, combine your focus and response into a single statement, a *thesis statement*.

Use a logical organization. In an introduction, present your main claims in the form of your thesis statement. In the body, flesh out your comparisons or contrasts using examples. For your conclusion, summarize similarities or differences and restate your response. Develop an outline, like the one shown, to guide you.

Make and support claims. Claims are informed judgments that you can make by connecting various pieces of evidence in a text. For example, in "The Tell-Tale Heart," you could connect the narrator's actions with his matter-of-fact statements in order to make a claim about why readers might find the story disturbing. To make a claim with certainty and authority, first make sure you have credible textual evidence to support it.

Revising Strategy

Revise for completeness and consistency. Work with a partner to check your draft to make sure that you have fully developed the ideas you set forth in your introduction. To help you revise, answer questions like these:

Questions	Revisions
• Have I anticipated and answered my readers' questions?	• If not, add information to address readers' possible counter-arguments.
• Have I been consistent in presenting my arguments?	• If not, revise by eliminating items that conflict with your thesis statement.
• Have I provided a sense of closure to my review?	• If not, reshape your conclusion to emphasize your main comparison or contrast.

Common Core State Standards

Writing

1.a. Introduce claim(s), acknowledge and distinguish the claim(s), and organize the reasons and evidence logically.

1.b. Support claim(s) with logical reasoning and relevant evidence, using accurate, credible sources and demonstrating an understanding of the topic or text.

Language

1.c. Form and use verbs in the indicative, imperative, interrogative, conditional, and subjunctive moods.

1.d. Recognize and correct inappropriate shifts in verb voice and mood.

3.a. Use verbs in the conditional and subjunctive moods to achieve particular effects.

Sample Outline

I. Introduction

Thesis Statement: The two main characters in these stories produce opposite reactions. It is easy to identify with one, while the other is completely unlikable.

II. Body

A. Impression of first character
    1. Supporting Detail
    2. Supporting Detail
B. Contrast of second character with first
    1. Supporting Detail
    2. Supporting Detail

III. Conclusion—Summary of why the two characters are different.

Revising Verb Phrases for Mood

Mood is the manner in which a verb phrase conveys action or state of being.

Identifying Mood of Verbs There are four primary verb moods in English. These are:

Indicative: This mood is used to make statements of fact. It is the most common mood in English.
Example: Paul went to the store.

Interrogative: This mood is used to ask questions.
Example: Did you go to the store?

Imperative: This mood is used to issue requests or commands.
Example: Please go to the store.
Go to the store!

Subjunctive: This mood is used to express a wish, a hope, or a statement contrary to fact. It is often found in a clause beginning with *if.*
Example: If I were going to the store, I would bring my wallet.

The **conditional** mood is similar to the subjunctive mood because it is used to refer to something that has not happened. In addition, it is used to express uncertainty. The conditional mood uses conditional auxiliary (helping) verbs such as *could, would, should,* and *might.*

Example: I wish I could go to the store.
I might go to the store.

Fixing Faulty Verb Moods To fix incorrect use of verb mood, first identify the form of the verb that is needed. Then, edit the sentence to ensure that the appropriate auxiliary verbs, sentence structure, and punctuation are used to express that mood.

Example: If Josephine <u>was</u> taller, she would be able to reach the cookie jar.
Correction: If Josephine <u>were</u> taller, she would be able to reach the cookie jar.

Grammar in Your Writing
Find examples of each verb mood in your draft. Underline each sentence and write a note above it, indicating which verb mood it contains. Fix any incorrect verb moods you encounter in your writing.

PH WRITING COACH

Further instruction and practice are available in *Prentice Hall Writing Coach.*

Common Core State Standards

Language
2.c. Spell correctly.

Storybook Greed

A lot of stories are written to teach lessons to readers. Sometimes stories can have different plots, settings, and characters but still have the same message.

Although *The Giving Tree*, by Shel Silverstein, and the story of King Midas are different in many ways, they both share an important theme. Both stories are about the unhappy consequences of greed.

The Giving Tree is the story of a boy who keeps taking pieces of a tree to try to make himself happy. In the beginning of the story, there is an apple tree who loves a little boy. Every day he comes to play with her leaves, climb her trunk, and eat her apples. However, as the boy grows older, other things became more important. From then on, all he wants to do is take things from the tree and use them for his own needs. In the end, when the boy comes back for the last time, he is an old man and the tree has nothing left to give him. Instead of taking something from her, all he does is sit on the tree's stump.

The story of King Midas is also a story about greed. King Midas spares the life of a satyr who is caught sleeping in his royal rose bed, a crime punishable by death. Because King Midas decides to spare the satyr's life, he is granted one wish. Being a greedy man, he immediately wishes for the gift of a golden touch. One day, his beloved daughter comes running up to him and gives him a hug. She is instantly turned to gold and King Midas is heartbroken.

Both of these stories show men who ask for more than they should have. In the end, both men lose the one thing they have loved most. That shows what greed can do. Given another chance, neither character would probably act the same way. However, neither the boy nor King Midas can change the consequences of their actions.

Both stories show why people should not be so greedy. There are some people who could greatly benefit from reading these stories and some whose unselfish attitudes would be reinforced. The tales of King Midas and of *The Giving Tree* are important and everyone should read them and learn from them. Their basic lesson is how to be a true friend.

In this paragraph, Joyce introduces both works and their common theme.

Joyce summarizes both works, offers details from the text, and explains how each one connects to the theme of greed.

In her conclusion, Joyce offers an opinion on the value of each work that reflects independent thought.

Editing and Proofreading

Spell tricky or difficult words correctly. Certain words are commonly misspelled because of how they are mispronounced. Though correct pronunciation does not always help with spelling, in some cases it does. If you add extra letter or syllable sounds to words—for example, if you say *athalete*—you will probably spell this word incorrectly. If in doubt, run a spell check or consult a dictionary.

Publishing and Presenting

Consider one of the following ways to share your writing.

Present a book talk. Use your critical review as the basis for an informal oral presentation.

Publish a "Teens Review" column. Contact a local newspaper and arrange for your work to be part of a series of critical reviews by young people.

Reflecting on Your Writing

Writer's Journal Jot down your answers to this question:

Which of the strategies or activities did you find most useful?

Spiral Review

Earlier in this unit, you learned about **action verbs and linking verbs** (p. 274) and **principal parts of regular verbs** (p. 304). Review your essay for correct verb use.

PH WRITING COACH

Further instruction and practice are available in *Prentice Hall Writing Coach*.

Rubric for Self-Assessment

Find evidence in your writing to address each category. Then, use the rating scale to grade your work.

Criteria	Rating Scale
	not very very
Focus: How clearly is your opinion stated?	1 2 3 4
Language: Is the language in your review appropriate and effective in conveying your reaction to the stories?	1 2 3 4
Organization: How logically is the support for your opinion organized?	1 2 3 4
Support/Elaboration: How well is evidence used to support ideas and connections?	1 2 3 4
Style: How well do you demonstrate insights?	1 2 3 4
Conventions: How correct is your grammar, especially your use of irregular verbs?	1 2 3 4

© Leveled Texts

Build your skills and improve your comprehension of short stories with texts of increasing complexity.

Read **"Charles"** to see how a young boy copes with bad behavior at school.

Read **"Flowers for Algernon"** to find out how experimental brain surgery completely changes one man's life.

© Common Core State Standards

Meet these standards with either **"Charles"** (p. 336) or **"Flowers for Algernon"** (p. 347).

Reading Literature

1. Cite the textual evidence that most strongly supports an analysis of what the text says explicitly as well as inferences drawn from the text. *(Reading Skill: Make Inferences)*

6. Analyze how differences in the points of view of the characters and the audience or reader create such effects as suspense or humor. *(Literary Analysis: Point of View)*

Reading Informational Text

2. Determine a central idea of a text and analyze its development over the course of the text, including its relationship to supporting ideas; provide an objective summary of the text. *(Research and Technology: Summary of an Article)*

Writing

2.b. Develop the topic with relevant, well-chosen facts, definitions, concrete details, quotations, or other information and examples. *(Research and Technology: Summary of an Article)*

3.b. Use narrative techniques, such as dialogue, pacing, description, and reflection, to develop experiences, events, and/or characters. *(Writing: Dialogue)*

Language

1.d. Recognize and correct inappropriate shifts in verb voice and mood. *(Conventions: Simple Tenses of Verbs)*

5.b. Use the relationship between particular words to better understand each of the words. *(Vocabulary: Analogies)*

Reading Skill: Make Inferences

When you **make inferences,** you look at the information the author provides to make logical assumptions about what the author leaves unstated. To make inferences, **use details** that the author provides as clues and add your own background knowledge and experience. Notice details like these:

- what the characters say about one another
- what the characters do and how they behave
- how the characters respond to others and to their surroundings

Using the Strategy: Inference Chart

Use an **inference chart** like this one for details and inferences.

Detail	Possible Inference
An actor at an audition compliments the director's past work.	The actor thinks flattery might get him a part.
A waitress is careless and rude.	She does not take pride in her job.
A toddler is drooling and crying.	He is teething.

Literary Analysis: Point of View

Point of view is the perspective from which a story is told. Most stories are told from a first-person or a third-person point of view.

- **First person:** The narrator participates in the action of the story and can tell only what he or she sees, knows, thinks, or feels. This kind of narrator uses the pronoun *I* when speaking about himself or herself.

- **Third person:** The narrator is not a character in the story, but describes events from the "outside." This kind of narrator uses pronouns such as *he, she,* and *they* to describe all the characters.

As you read, notice how point of view creates distinctions between what characters and readers know that can help lay the groundwork for suspense, humor, or surprise.

Can all *conflicts* be resolved?

CHARLES

Shirley Jackson

Writing About the Big Question

In "Charles," a kindergartner finds a creative way to deal with bad behavior at the start of his first year of school. Use this sentence starter to develop your ideas about the Big Question.

Adjusting to a new school is challenging because you are forced to **interact** with _____.

While You Read Look for clues about the connection between Laurie and Charles.

Vocabulary

Read each word and its definition. Decide whether you know the word well, know it a little bit, or do not know it at all. After you read, see how your knowledge of each word has increased.

- **renounced** (ri nounst´) *v.* gave up (p. 337) *Bill renounced eating meat and became a vegetarian.* renunciation *n.*

- **insolently** (in´ sə lənt lē) *adv.* in an impolite manner; (p. 337) *Spoiled children often behave insolently, talking back to their parents.* insolent *adj.* insolence *n.*

- **deprived** (dē prīvd´) *v.* not permitted to have (p. 338) *Deprived of his bicycle, the boy walked to school instead.* deprivation *n.*

- **simultaneously** (sī´ məl tā´ nē əs lē) *adv.* at the same time (p. 339) *It is not safe to drive and to dial a cell phone simultaneously.* simultaneous *adj.*

- **cynically** (sin´ i kəl lē) *adv.* doubtfully; skeptically (p. 340) *After losing a lot of money, Justin viewed get-rich schemes cynically.* cynicism *n.* cynical *adj.* cynic *n.*

- **haggard** (hag´ ərd) *adj.* having a wild, worn look (p. 341) *The man emerged pale and haggard after three days trapped in the cave.* haggardness *n.*

Word Study

The **Latin root** *-nounc-* or *-nunc-* means "report."

In this story, a young boy **renounces** his childhood clothes when he leaves home for the first day of school. He rejects his toddler clothes and starts a new phase of his life.

Meet
Shirley Jackson
(1916–1965)

Author of
CHARLES

As the mother of four energetic children, Shirley Jackson once said that she wrote because "It's the only chance I get to sit down." Jackson grew up in San Francisco, and spent most of her free time writing rather than playing with the neighborhood children. As a writer, she is famous for two types of stories—spine-tingling tales and hilarious stories about daily life.

The Real-Life Charles Like many other writers, Jackson borrows characters and events from her own life and weaves them into her fictional stories. The main character in "Charles" is based on Jackson's own son.

DID YOU KNOW?
Jackson's collections of stories about family life often have humorous titles such as *Life Among the Savages* (1953) and *Raising Demons* (1957).

BACKGROUND FOR THE STORY

Early Learning

The first day of kindergarten is an event that is both scary and exciting for most children. At ages four and five, children are still learning lessons about getting along with others. Suddenly going from home to a school environment can be a difficult change for children like Laurie, a character in "Charles."

CHARLES

Shirley Jackson

◀ **Critical Viewing**
Does the boy in this photograph look like someone who would behave in kindergarten? Why or why not? **[Infer]**

The day my son Laurie started kindergarten he renounced corduroy overalls with bibs and began wearing blue jeans with a belt; I watched him go off the first morning with the older girl next door, seeing clearly that an era of my life was ended, my sweet-voiced nursery-school tot replaced by a long-trousered, swaggering[1] character who forgot to stop at the corner and wave good-bye to me.

He came home the same way, the front door slamming open, his cap on the floor, and the voice suddenly become raucous[2] shouting, "Isn't anybody *here*?"

At lunch he spoke insolently to his father, spilled his baby sister's milk, and remarked that his teacher said we were not to take the name of the Lord in vain.

"How *was* school today?" I asked, elaborately casual.

"All right," he said.

"Did you learn anything?" his father asked.

Laurie regarded his father coldly. "I didn't learn nothing," he said.

"Anything," I said. "Didn't learn anything."

"The teacher spanked a boy, though," Laurie said, addressing his bread and butter. "For being fresh," he added, with his mouth full.

"What did he do?" I asked. "Who was it?"

Laurie thought. "It was Charles," he said. "He was fresh. The teacher spanked him and made him stand in a corner. He was awfully fresh."

"What did he do?" I asked again, but Laurie slid off his chair, took a cookie, and left, while his father was still saying, "See here, young man."

Vocabulary
renounced (ri nounst´) *v.* gave up

insolently (in´ sə lənt lē) *adv.* in an impolite manner

Reading Check
What change does the narrator notice in her son on his first day of school?

---

1. swaggering (swag´ gər iŋ) *v.* strutting; walking with a bold step.
2. raucous (rô´ kəs) *adj.* harsh; rough-sounding.

Make Inferences
What details show that Laurie admires Charles's rude behavior?

> **"Well, Charles was bad again today."**

The next day Laurie remarked at lunch, as soon as he sat down, "Well, Charles was bad again today." He grinned enormously and said, "Today Charles hit the teacher."

"Good heavens," I said, mindful of the Lord's name, "I suppose he got spanked again?"

"He sure did," Laurie said. "Look up," he said to his father.

"What?" his father said, looking up.

"Look down," Laurie said. "Look at my thumb. Gee, you're dumb." He began to laugh insanely.

"Why did Charles hit the teacher?" I asked quickly.

"Because she tried to make him color with red crayons," Laurie said. "Charles wanted to color with green crayons so he hit the teacher and she spanked him and said nobody play with Charles but everybody did."

The third day—it was Wednesday of the first week—Charles bounced a see-saw on to the head of a little girl and made her bleed, and the teacher made him stay inside all during recess. Thursday Charles had to stand in a corner during story-time because he kept pounding his feet on the floor. Friday Charles was deprived of blackboard privileges because he threw chalk.

On Saturday I remarked to my husband, "Do you think kindergarten is too unsettling for Laurie? All this toughness, and bad grammar, and this Charles boy sounds like such a bad influence."

Vocabulary
deprived (dē prīvd´) v. not permitted to have

Point of View
What clues indicate that this story is told by a first-person narrator?

"It'll be all right," my husband said reassuringly. "Bound to be people like Charles in the world. Might as well meet them now as later."

On Monday Laurie came home late, full of news. "Charles," he shouted as he came up the hill; I was waiting anxiously on the front steps. "Charles," Laurie yelled all the way up the hill, "Charles was bad again."

"Come right in," I said, as soon as he came close enough. "Lunch is waiting."

"You know what Charles did?" he demanded, following me through the door. "Charles yelled so in school they sent a boy in from first grade to tell the teacher she had to make Charles keep quiet, and so Charles had to stay after school. And so all the children stayed to watch him."

"What did he do?" I asked.

"He just sat there," Laurie said, climbing into his chair at the table. "Hi, Pop, y'old dust mop."

"Charles had to stay after school today," I told my husband. "Everyone stayed with him."

"What does this Charles look like?" my husband asked Laurie. "What's his other name?"

"He's bigger than me," Laurie said. "And he doesn't have any rubbers and he doesn't ever wear a jacket."

Monday night was the first Parent-Teachers meeting, and only the fact that the baby had a cold kept me from going; I wanted passionately to meet Charles's mother. On Tuesday Laurie remarked suddenly, "Our teacher had a friend come to see her in school today."

"Charles's mother?" my husband and I asked simultaneously.

"Naaah," Laurie said scornfully. "It was a man who came and made us do exercises, we had to touch our toes. Look." He climbed down from his chair and squatted down and touched his toes. "Like this," he said. He got solemnly back into his chair and said, picking up his fork, "Charles didn't even *do* exercises."

"That's fine," I said heartily. "Didn't Charles want to do exercises?"

"Naaah," Laurie said. "Charles was so fresh to the

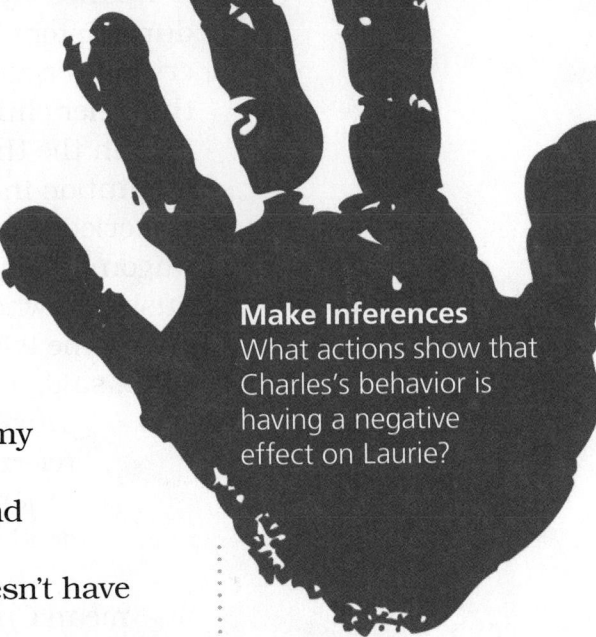

Make Inferences
What actions show that Charles's behavior is having a negative effect on Laurie?

Vocabulary
simultaneously
(sī′ məl tā′ nē əs lē)
adv. at the same time

Reading
Check
Why did Charles lose blackboard privileges?

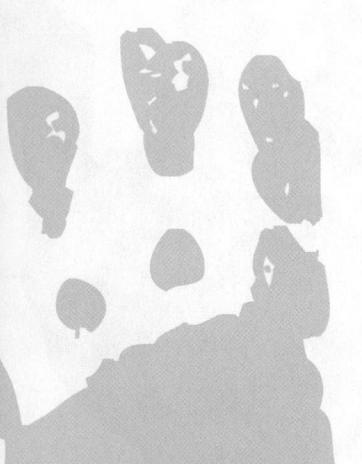

teacher's friend he wasn't *let* do exercises."

"Fresh again?" I said.

"He kicked the teacher's friend," Laurie said. "The teacher's friend told Charles to touch his toes like I just did and Charles kicked him."

"What are they going to do about Charles, do you suppose?" Laurie's father asked him.

Laurie shrugged elaborately. "Throw him out of school, I guess," he said.

Wednesday and Thursday were routine; Charles yelled during story hour and hit a boy in the stomach and made him cry. On Friday Charles stayed after school again and so did all the other children.

With the third week of kindergarten Charles was an institution in our family; the baby was being a Charles when she cried all afternoon; Laurie did a Charles when he filled his wagon full of mud and pulled it through the kitchen; even my husband, when he caught his elbow in the telephone cord and pulled the telephone, ashtray, and a bowl of flowers off the table, said, after the first minute, "Looks like Charles." •

During the third and fourth weeks it looked like a reformation in Charles; Laurie reported grimly at lunch on Thursday of the third week, "Charles was so good today the teacher gave him an apple."

"What?" I said, and my husband added warily, "You mean Charles?"

"Charles," Laurie said. "He gave the crayons around and he picked up the books afterward and the teacher said he was her helper."

"What happened?" I asked incredulously.

"He was her helper, that's all," Laurie said, and shrugged.

"Can this be true, about Charles?" I asked my husband that night. "Can something like this happen?"

"Wait and see," my husband said cynically. "When you've got a Charles to deal with, this may mean he's only plotting."

He seemed to be wrong. For over a week Charles was the teacher's helper; each day he handed things out and he picked things up; no one had to stay after school.

"The PTA meeting's next week again," I told my husband one evening. "I'm going to find Charles's mother there."

"Ask her what happened to Charles," my husband said. "I'd like to know."

Point of View
How does the narrator respond to each item of news about Charles?

Vocabulary
cynically
(sin´ i kəl lē) *adv.*
doubtfully; skeptically

"I'd like to know myself," I said.

On Friday of that week things were back to normal. "You know what Charles did today?" Laurie demanded at the lunch table, in a voice slightly awed. "He told a little girl to say a word and she said it and the teacher washed her mouth out with soap and Charles laughed."

"What word?" his father asked unwisely, and Laurie said, "I'll have to whisper it to you, it's so bad." He got down off his chair and went around to his father. His father bent his head down and Laurie whispered joyfully. His father's eyes widened.

"Did Charles tell the little girl to say *that*?" he asked respectfully.

"She said it *twice*," Laurie said. "Charles told her to say it *twice*."

"What happened to Charles?" my husband asked.

"Nothing," Laurie said. "He was passing out the crayons."

Monday morning Charles abandoned the little girl and said the evil word himself three or four times, getting his mouth washed out with soap each time. He also threw chalk.

My husband came to the door with me that evening as I set out for the PTA meeting. "Invite her over for a cup of tea after the meeting," he said. "I want to get a look at her."

"If only she's there," I said prayerfully.

"She'll be there," my husband said. "I don't see how they could hold a PTA meeting without Charles's mother."

At the meeting I sat restlessly, scanning each comfortable matronly face, trying to determine which one hid the secret of Charles. None of them looked to me haggard enough. No one stood up in the meeting and apologized for the way her son had been acting. No one mentioned Charles.

After the meeting I identified and sought out Laurie's kindergarten teacher. She had a plate with a cup of tea and a

Spiral Review

Character What do the father's reactions to Laurie's stories about Charles show about his character?

Make Inferences What does Charles's behavior on Monday suggest about his good behavior in the previous weeks?

Vocabulary

haggard (hag´ ərd) *adj.* having a wild, worn look

 **Reading Check**

What made the narrator believe that Charles's behavior was improving for a while?

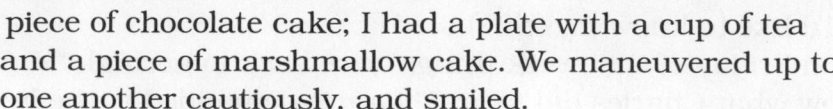

piece of chocolate cake; I had a plate with a cup of tea and a piece of marshmallow cake. We maneuvered up to one another cautiously, and smiled.

"I've been so anxious to meet you," I said. "I'm Laurie's mother."

"We're all so interested in Laurie," she said.

"Well, he certainly likes kindergarten," I said. "He talks about it all the time."

"We had a little trouble adjusting, the first week or so," she said primly, "but now he's a fine little helper. With occasional lapses, of course."

"Laurie usually adjusts very quickly," I said. "I suppose this time it's Charles's influence."

"Charles?"

"Yes," I said, laughing, "you must have your hands full in that kindergarten, with Charles."

"Charles?" she said. "We don't have any Charles in the kindergarten."

Point of View
How does the first-person point of view contribute to the humor in this conversation?

Critical Thinking

© 1. **Key Ideas and Details (a)** Describe the change in Laurie's clothing on the day he starts school. **(b) Draw Conclusions:** How does this signal a change in Laurie's behavior?

© 2. **Key Ideas and Details (a)** Give three examples of Charles's behavior at school and three examples of Laurie's behavior at home. **(b) Compare and Contrast:** How is their behavior in both these places similar and different?

© 3. **Integration of Knowledge and Ideas (a) Make a Judgment:** What should Laurie's mother say to him after she meets his teacher and learns the truth? **(b) Discuss:** Share your ideas with a small group. Then, discuss the reasons for your responses.

© 4. **Integration of Knowledge and Ideas** When the teacher reveals the connection between Charles and Laurie, is she resolving a conflict or creating a new one? Explain your reasoning. *[Connect to the Big Question: Can all conflicts be resolved?]*

Cite textual evidence to support your responses.

Reading Skill: Make Inferences

1. (a) List four details that his mother has observed about Laurie's new behavior at home. **(b)** Use these details to **make an inference** about what the changes mean.

Ⓒ 2. Key Ideas and Details What inferences can you make about the teacher by the way she speaks to Laurie's mother?

Literary Analysis: Point of View

CHARLES
Shirley Jackson

Ⓒ 3. Craft and Structure Use this chart to explain how the story would change if it were told from Laurie's **point of view** instead of the first-person perspective of his mother.

Mother	Laurie
Mother thinks Laurie has a classmate named Charles.	
Mother worries that Charles is a bad influence on Laurie.	

Ⓒ 4. Craft and Structure How does the point of view help set up a humorous surprise ending for readers?

Vocabulary

Ⓒ Acquisition and Use Analogies show the relationships between words. Use a word from page 334 to create a word pair that matches the relationship between the first two words.

1. *Carefully* is to *carelessly* as *respectfully* is to _____.

2. *Praised* is to *congratulated* as *denied* is to _____.

3. *Sensibly* is to *wisely* as *doubtfully* is to _____.

4. *Healthy* is to *frail* as *energetic* is to _____.

5. *Rudely* is to *politely* as *sequentially* is to _____.

6. *Awoke* is to *slept* as *welcomed* is to _____.

Word Study Use what you know about the **Latin root -nounc-** to answer each question.

1. Why is it good for an *announcer* to speak clearly?

2. When is it important to avoid a *mispronunciation*?

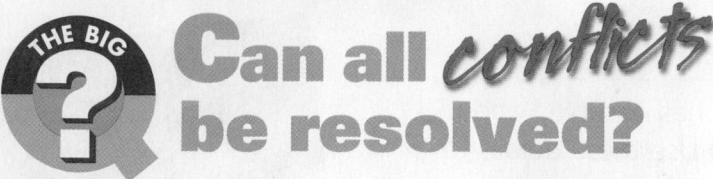

Can all *conflicts* be resolved?

Writing About the Big Question

In "Flowers for Algernon," unexpected challenges face a man who increases his intelligence through experimental surgery. Use this sentence starter to develop your ideas about the Big Question.

When someone I know well suddenly changes, my **reaction** is _____.

While You Read Look for changes in Charlie that might cause conflicts between himself and others.

Vocabulary

Read each word and its definition. Decide whether you know the word well, know it a little bit, or do not know it at all. After you read, see how your knowledge of each word has increased.

- **deceive** (dē sēv´) *v.* make someone believe what is not true (p. 368) *The criminal pretended to be a policeman to deceive the detectives.* deception *n.* deceit *n.*

- **refute** (ri fyo͞ot´) *v.* give evidence to prove a statement false (p. 368) *He presented facts the lawyer could not refute.*

- **intellectual** (in´ tə lek´ cho͞o əl) *adj.* relating to the ability to think and understand ideas and information (p. 368) *She preferred intellectual activities like playing chess to physical activities.* intellect *n.* intelligent *adj.*

- **naïvete** (nä´ ēv tā´) *n.* the state of being simple or childlike (p. 370) *The young businessman's naïvete about money matters led to bankruptcy.* naïvely *adv.* naïve *adj.*

- **deterioration** (dē tir´ ē ə rā´ shən) *n.* the process of becoming worse (p. 373) *Efforts to prevent further deterioration failed and his condition worsened.* deteriorate *v.*

- **introspective** (in´ trō spek´ tiv) *adj.* thoughtful; inward-looking (p. 374) *Introspective people often keep diaries of their thoughts.* introspection *n.* introspectively *adv.*

Word Study

The **Latin root -spec-** means "look."

In this story, Charlie is **introspective** when he writes in his diary about his innermost thoughts and feelings. He "looks inside" himself to find interesting insights.

Meet
Daniel Keyes
(b. 1927)

Author of
Flowers
for Algernon

Raised in Brooklyn, New York, writer and teacher Daniel Keyes has also been a photographer, a merchant seaman, and an editor. Keyes is fascinated by unusual psychological conditions. His book *The Milligan Wars* is about a man with a multiple-personality disorder. After winning the Hugo Award for "Flowers for Algernon" in 1959, Keyes expanded the story into a full-length novel, which won the Nebula Award in 1966.

Inspiration for the Story A meeting with a mentally disabled man gave Keyes the idea for "Flowers for Algernon." He began to wonder what would happen "if it were possible to increase human intelligence artificially."

BACKGROUND FOR THE STORY
Intelligence Testing
Charlie Gordon, the main character in "Flowers for Algernon," undergoes surgery to improve his intelligence. In the story, his doctors measure his progress with I.Q., or *intelligence quotient,* tests. These tests were once widely used to measure intelligence and learning ability. Researchers now recognize that one test cannot accurately measure a person's range of abilities.

DID YOU KNOW?
Cliff Robertson won an Academy Award for his portrayal of the title character in the film adaptation *Charly* (1968). A new movie adaptation of the story came out in 2000 with Matthew Modine in the lead role.

Flowers for Algernon

Daniel Keyes

progris riport 1 —
martch 5 1965

Dr. Strauss says I shud rite down what I think and evrey thing that happins to me from now on. I dont know why but he says its importint so they will see if they will use me. I hope they use me. Miss Kinnian says maybe they can make me smart. I want to be smart. My name is Charlie Gordon. I am 37 years old and 2 weeks ago was my brithday. I have nuthing more to rite now so I will close for today.

Make Inferences
What details in the opening paragraph help you to make inferences about Charlie's situation? Explain.

progris riport 2 —martch 6

I had a test today. I think I faled it. and I think that maybe now they wont use me. What happind is a nice young man was in the room and he had some white cards with ink spillled all over them. He sed Charlie what do you see on this card. I was very skared even tho I had my rabits foot in my pockit because when I was a kid I always faled tests in school and I spillled ink to.

I told him I saw a inkblot. He said yes and it made me feel good. I thot that was all but when I got up to go he stopped me. He said now sit down Charlie we are not thru yet. Then I dont remember so good but he wantid me to say what was in the ink. I dint see nuthing in the ink but he said there was picturs there other pepul saw some picturs. I coudnt see any picturs. I reely tryed to see. I held the card close up and then far away. Then I said if I had my glases I coud see better I usally only ware my glases in the movies or TV but I said they are in the closit in the hall. I got them. Then I said let me see that card agen I bet Ill find it now.

I tryed hard but I still coudnt find the picturs I only saw the ink. I told him maybe I need new glases. He rote somthing down on a paper and I got skared of faling the test. I told him it was a very nice inkblot with littel points all around the eges. He looked very sad so that wasnt it. I said please let me try agen. Ill get it in a few minits becaus Im not so fast somtimes. Im a slow reeder too in Miss Kinnians class for slow adults but I'm trying very hard.

He gave me a chance with another card that had 2 kinds of ink spilled on it red and blue.

He was very nice and talked slow like Miss Kinnian does and he explained it to me that it was a *raw shok*.[1] He said pepul see things in the ink. I said show me where. He said think. I told him I think a inkblot but that wasnt rite eather. He said what does it remind you—pretend somthing. I closd my eyes for a long time to pretend. I told him I pretned a fowntan pen with ink leeking all over a table cloth. Then he got up and went out.

I dont think I passd the *raw shok* test.

---

1. *raw shok* misspelling of Rorschach (rôr´ shäk´) test, a psychological test that requires a subject to describe inkblots.

Point of View
What elements here tell you the story is told from the first-person point of view?

> I had a test today. I think I faled it.

progris riport 3 —march 7

Dr Strauss and Dr Nemur say it dont matter about the inkblots. I told them I dint spill the ink on the cards and I coudnt see anything in the ink. They said that maybe they will still use me. I said Miss Kinnian never gave me tests like that one only spelling and reading. They said Miss Kinnian told that I was her bestist pupil in the adult nite scool becaus I tryed the hardist and I reely wantid to lern. They said how come you went to the adult nite scool all by yourself Charlie. How did you find it. I said I askd pepul and sumbody told me where I shud go to lern to read and spell good. They said why did you want to. I told them becaus all my life I wantid to be smart and not dumb. But its very hard to be smart. They said you know it will probly be tempirery. I said yes. Miss Kinnian told me. I dont care if it herts.

Later I had more crazy tests today. The nice lady who gave it me told me the name and I asked her how do you spellit so I can rite it in my progris riport. THEMATIC APPERCEPTION TEST.[2] I dont know the frist 2 words but I know what *test* means. You got to pass it or you get bad marks. This test lookd easy becaus I coud see the picturs. Only this time she dint want me to tell her the picturs. That mixd me up. I said the man yesterday said I shoud tell him what I saw in the ink she said that dont make no difrence. She said make up storys about the pepul in the picturs.

I told her how can you tell storys about pepul you never met. I said why shud I make up lies. I never tell lies any more becaus I always get caut.

She told me this test and the other one the raw-shok was for getting personalty. I laffed so hard. I said how can you get that thing from inkblots and fotos. She got sore and put her picturs away. I dont care. It was sily. I gess I faled that test too.

Later some men in white coats took me to a difernt part of the hospitil and gave me a game to play. It was like a race with a white mouse. They called the mouse Algernon. Algernon was in a box with a lot of twists and turns like all kinds of walls and they gave me a pencil and a paper with lines and lots of boxes. On one side it said START and on the

Make Inferences
What does Charlie's failure to understand the tests reveal about his personality and abilities?

✓ Reading Check
What type of a test do the doctors give Charlie?

---

2. **THEMATIC** (thē mat´ ik) **APPERCEPTION** (ap´ ər sep´ shən) **TEST** personality test in which the subject makes up stories about a series of pictures.

other end it said FINISH. They said it was *amazed*[3] and that Algernon and me had the same *amazed* to do. I dint see how we could have the same *amazed* if Algernon had a box and I had a paper but I dint say nothing. Anyway there wasnt time because the race started.

One of the men had a watch he was trying to hide so I woudnt see it so I tryed not to look and that made me nervus.

Anyway that test made me feel worser than all the others because they did it over 10 times with difernt *amazeds* and Algernon won every time. I dint know that mice were so smart. Maybe thats because Algernon is a white mouse. Maybe white mice are smarter than other mice.

Point of View
What does the first-person point of view show about Charlie's experience with the doctors?

---

3. *amazed* Charlie means "a maze," or confusing series of paths. Often, the intelligence of animals is assessed by how fast they go through a maze.

LITERATURE IN CONTEXT

Science Connection

Test Inventors
Three pioneers of intelligence and behavioral testing devised tests that are still used to this day.

◀ In the early twentieth century, Swiss psychologist **Hermann Rorschach** developed a test in which the subject describes what an inkblot looks like. Psychologists use the subject's responses to make interpretations about mental condition and personality.

◀ Rorschach inkblot

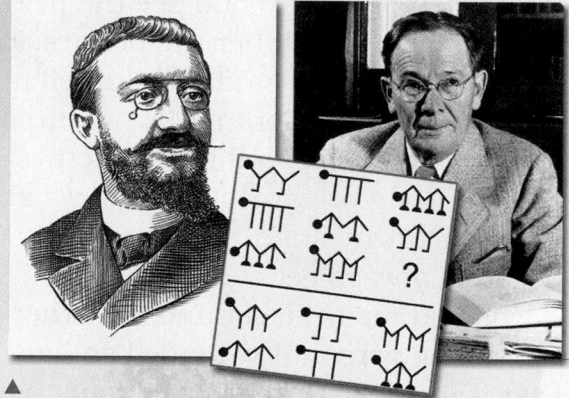

▲ In 1905, **Alfred Binet**, above left, and Theodore Simon devised a system for testing intelligence based on standardized, average mental levels for various age groups. In 1916, **Lewis Terman**, above right, reworked the test, which become known as the Revised Stanford-Binet Intelligence Test. One question from an intelligence test is shown above.

Connect to the Literature

What do you think Charlie's first reaction to the Rorschach inkblots reveals?

Their going to use me! Im so exited I can hardly write. Dr Nemur and Dr Strauss had a argament about it first. Dr Nemur was in the office when Dr Strauss brot me in. Dr Nemur was worryed about using me but Dr Strauss told him Miss Kinnian rekemmended me the best from all the pepul who she was teaching. I like Miss Kinnian becaus shes a very smart teacher. And she said Charlie your going to have a second chance. If you volenteer for this experament you mite get smart. They dont know if it will be perminint but theirs a chance. Thats why I said ok even when I was scared because she said it was an operashun. She said dont be scared Charlie you done so much with so little I think you deserv it most of all.

So I got scaird when Dr Nemur and Dr Strauss argud about it. Dr Strauss said I had something that was very good. He said I had a good *motor-vation*.[4] I never even knew I had that. I felt proud when he said that not every body with an *eye-q*[5] of 68 had that thing. I dont know what it is or where I got it but he said Algernon had it too. Algernons *motor-vation* is the cheese they put in his box. But it cant be that because I didnt eat any cheese this week.

Then he told Dr Nemur something I dint understand so while they were talking I wrote down some of the words.

He said Dr Nemur I know Charlie is not what you had in mind as the first of your new brede of intelek** (coudnt get the word) superman. But most people of his low ment** are host** and uncoop** they are usualy dull apath** and hard to reach. He has a good natcher hes intristed and eager to please.

Dr Nemur said remember he will be the first human beeng ever to have his intelijence trippled by surgicle meens.

Dr Strauss said exakly. Look at how well hes lerned to read and write for his low mentel age its as grate an acheve** as you and I lerning einstines therey of **vity without help. That shows the intenss motorvation. Its comparat** a tremen** achev** I say we use Charlie.

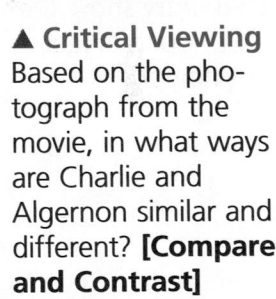

▲ **Critical Viewing**
Based on the photograph from the movie, in what ways are Charlie and Algernon similar and different? **[Compare and Contrast]**

Reading
Check
What makes Charlie excited on March 8?

---

4. *motor-vation* motivation, or desire to work hard and achieve a goal.
5. *eye-q* IQ, or intelligence quotient. A way of measuring human intelligence.

▲ **Critical Viewing**
Why do scientists use lab animals like Algernon in their experiments? **[Infer]**

Make Inferences
What details in the March 8 entry show the way both doctors feel about Charlie?

Point of View
What feelings does the use of this point of view allow the narrator to reveal?

I dint get all the words and they were talking to fast but it sounded like Dr Strauss was on my side and like the other one wasnt.

Then Dr Nemur nodded he said all right maybe your right. We will use Charlie. When he said that I got so exited I jumped up and shook his hand for being so good to me. I told him thank you doc you wont be sorry for giving me a second chance. And I mean it like I told him. After the operashun Im gonna try to be smart. Im gonna try awful hard.

progris ript 5—Mar 10

Im skared. Lots of people who work here and the nurses and the people who gave me the tests came to bring me candy and wish me luck. I hope I have luck. I got my rabits foot and my lucky penny and my horse shoe. Only a black cat crossed me when I was comming to the hospitil. Dr Strauss says dont be supersitis Charlie this is sience. Anyway Im keeping my rabits foot with me.

I asked Dr Strauss if Ill beat Algernon in the race after the operashun and he said maybe. If the operashun works Ill show that mouse I can be as smart as he is. Maybe smarter. Then Ill be abel to read better and spell the words good and know lots of things and be like other people. I want to be smart like other people. If it works perminint they will make everybody smart all over the wurld.

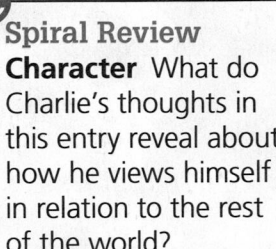

They dint give me anything to eat this morning. I dont know what that eating has to do with getting smart. Im very hungry and Dr Nemur took away my box of candy. That Dr Nemur is a grouch. Dr Strauss says I can have it back after the operashun. You cant eat befor a operashun . . .

Progress Report 6—Mar 15

The operashun dint hurt. He did it while I was sleeping. They took off the bandijis from my eyes and my head today so I can make a PROGRESS REPORT. Dr Nemur who looked at some of my other ones says I spell PROGRESS wrong and he told me how to spell it and REPORT too. I got to try and remember that.

I have a very bad memary for spelling. Dr Strauss says its ok to tell about all the things that happin to me but he says I shoud tell more about what I feel and what I think. When I told him I dont know how to think he said try. All the time when the bandijis were on my eyes I tryed to think. Nothing happened. I dont know what to think about. Maybe if I ask him he will tell me how I can think now that Im suppose to get smart. What do smart people think about. Fancy things I suppose. I wish I knew some fancy things alredy.

Progress Report 7—Mar 19

Nothing is happining. I had lots of tests and different kinds of races with Algernon. I hate that mouse. He always beats me. Dr Strauss said I got to play those games. And he said some time I got to take those tests over again. Thse inkblots are stupid. And those pictures are stupid too. I like to draw a picture of a man and a woman but I wont make up lies about people.

I got a headache from trying to think so much. I thot Dr Strauss was my frend but he dont help me. He dont tell me what to think or when Ill get smart. Miss Kinnian dint come to see me. I think writing these progress reports are stupid too.

Progress Report 8—Mar 23

Im going back to work at the factery. They said it was better I shud go back to work but I cant tell anyone what the operashun was for and I have to come to the hospitil for an hour evry night after work. They are gonna pay me mony every month for lerning to be smart.

Im glad Im going back to work because I miss my job and all my frends and all the fun we have there.

Dr Strauss says I shud keep writing things down but I dont have to do it every day just when I think of something or something speshul happins. He says dont get discoridged because it takes time and it happins slow. He says it took a long time with Algernon before he got 3 times smarter then he was before. Thats why Algernon beats me all the time because he had that operashun too. That makes me feel better. I coud probly do that *amazed* faster than a reglar mouse. Maybe some day Ill beat Algernon. Boy that would be something. So far Algernon looks like he mite be smart perminent.

Mar 25

(I dont have to write PROGRESS REPORT on top any more just when I hand it in once a week for Dr Nemur to read. I just have to put the date on. That saves time)

We had a lot of fun at the factery today. Joe Carp said hey look where Charlie had his operashun what did they do Charlie put some brains in. I was going to tell him but I remembered Dr Strauss said no. Then Frank Reilly said what did you do Charlie forget your key and open your door the hard way. That made me laff. Their really my friends and they like me.

Sometimes somebody will say hey look at Joe or Frank or George he really pulled a Charlie Gordon. I dont know why they say that but they always laff. This morning Amos Borg who is the 4 man at Donnegans used my name when he shouted at Ernie the office boy. Ernie lost a packige. He said Ernie what are you trying to be a Charlie Gordon. I dont understand why he said that. I never lost any packiges.

▲ **Critical Viewing**
What impression of Charlie do you get from this photo- graph? [**Infer**]

Make Inferences
What do Charlie's friends mean when they say someone "pulled a Charlie Gordon"?

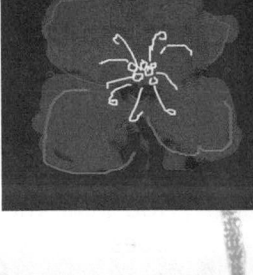

Mar 28

Dr Straus came to my room tonight to see why I dint come in like I was suppose to. I told him I dont like to race with Algernon any more. He said I dont have to for a while but I shud come in. He had a present for me only it wasnt a present but just for lend. I thot it was a little television but it wasnt. He said I got to turn it on when I go to sleep. I said your kidding why shud I turn it on when Im going to sleep. Who ever herd of a thing like that. But he said if I want to get smart I got to do what he says. I told him I dint think I was going to get smart and he put his hand on my sholder and said Charlie you dont know it yet but your getting smarter all the time. You wont notice for a while. I think he was just being nice to make me feel good because I dont look any smarter.

Oh yes I almost forgot. I asked him when I can go back to the class at Miss Kinnians school. He said I wont go their. He said that soon Miss Kinnian will come to the hospitil to start and teach me speshul. I was mad at her for not comming to see me when I got the operashun but I like her so maybe we will be frends again.

Mar 29

That crazy TV kept me up all night. How can I sleep with something yelling crazy things all night in my ears. And the nutty pictures. Wow. I dont know what it says when Im up so how am I going to know when Im sleeping.

Dr Strauss says its ok. He says my brains are lerning when I sleep and that will help me when Miss Kinnian starts my lessons in the hospitl only I found out it isnt a hospitil its a labatory. I think its all crazy. If you can get smart when your sleeping why do people go to school. That thing I dont think will work. I use to watch the late show and the late late show on TV all the time and it never made me smart. Maybe you have to sleep while you watch it.

Progress Report 9—APRIL 3

Dr Strauss showed me how to keep the TV turned low so now I can sleep. I don't hear a thing. And I still dont understand what it says. A few times I play it over in the

Reading Check
What does Dr. Strauss give to Charlie?

morning to find out what I lerned when I was sleeping and I dont think so. Miss Kinnian says Maybe its another langwidge or something. But most times it sounds american. It talks so fast faster then even Miss Gold who was my teacher in 6 grade and I remember she talked so fast I coudnt understand her.

I told Dr Strauss what good is it to get smart in my sleep. I want to be smart when Im awake. He says its the same thing and I have two minds. Theres the *subconscious* and the *conscious* (thats how you spell it). And one dont tell the other one what its doing. They dont even talk to each other. Thats why I dream. And boy have I been having crazy dreams. Wow. Ever since that night TV. The late late late late late show.

I forgot to ask him if it was only me or if everybody had those two minds.

(I just looked up the word in the dictionary Dr Strauss gave me. The word is *subconscious*. adj. *Of the nature of mental operations yet not present in consciousness; as, subconscious conflict of desires.*) There's more but I still dont know what it means. This isnt a very good dictionary for dumb people like me.

Anyway the headache is from the party. My frends from the factery Joe Carp and Frank Reilly invited me to go with them to Muggsys Saloon for some drinks. I dont like to drink but they said we will have lots of fun. I had a good time.

Joe Carp said I shoud show the girls how I mop out the toilet in the factory and he got me a mop. I showed them and everyone laffed when I told that Mr Donnegan said I was the best janiter he ever had because I like my job and do it good and never come late or miss a day except for my operashun.

I said Miss Kinnian always said Charlie be proud of your job because you do it good.

Everybody laffed and we had a good time and they gave me lots of drinks and Joe said Charlie is a card when hes potted. I dont know what that means but everybody likes me and we have fun. I cant wait to be smart like my best frends Joe Carp and Frank Reilly.

I dont remember how the party was over but I think I went out to buy a newspaper and coffe for Joe and Frank and when I came back there was no one their. I looked for them all over till late. Then I dont remember so good but I think I

got sleepy or sick. A nice cop brot me back home. Thats what my landlady Mrs Flynn says.

But I got a headache and a big lump on my head and black and blue all over. I think maybe I fell. Anyway I got a bad headache and Im sick and hurt all over. I dont think Ill drink anymore.

April 6

I beat Algernon! I dint even know I beat him until Burt the tester told me. Then the second time I lost because I got so exited I fell off the chair before I finished. But after that I beat him 8 more times. I must be getting smart to beat a smart mouse like Algernon. But I dont *feel* smarter.

I wanted to race Algernon some more but Burt said thats enough for one day. They let me hold him for a minit. Hes not so bad. Hes soft like a ball of cotton. He blinks and when he opens his eyes their black and pink on the eges.

I said can I feed him because I felt bad to beat him and I wanted to be nice and make frends. Burt said no Algernon is a very specshul mouse with an operashun like mine, and he was the first of all the animals to stay smart so long. He told me Algernon is so smart that every day he has to solve a test to get his food. Its a thing like a lock on a door that changes every time Algernon goes in to eat so he has to lern something new to get his food. That made me sad because if he coudnt lern he woud be hungry.

I dont think its right to make you pass a test to eat. How woud Dr Nemur like it to have to pass a test every time he wants to eat. I think Ill be frends with Algernon.

April 9

Tonight after work Miss Kinnian was at the laboratory. She looked like she was glad to see me but scared. I told her dont worry Miss Kinnian Im not smart yet and she laffed. She said I have confidence in you Charlie the way you struggled so hard to read and right better than all the others. At werst you will have it for a littel wile and your doing something for sience.

We are reading a very hard book. I never read such a hard book before. Its called *Robinson Crusoe*[6] about a man who

---

6. *Robinson Crusoe* (kro͞o′ sō) novel written in 1719 by Daniel Defoe, a British author.

Reading Check

What happens at the party to make people laugh?

gets merooned on a dessert Iland. Hes smart and figers out all kinds of things so he can have a house and food and hes a good swimmer. Only I feel sorry because hes all alone and has no frends. But I think their must be somebody else on the iland because theres a picture with his funny umbrella looking at footprints. I hope he gets a frend and not be lonly.

April 10

Miss Kinnian teaches me to spell better. She says look at a word and close your eyes and say it over and over until you remember. I have lots of truble with *through* that you say *threw* and *enough* and tough that you dont say *enew* and *tew.* You got to say *enuff* and *tuff.* Thats how I use to write it before I started to get smart. Im confused but Miss Kinnian says theres no reason in spelling.

April 14

Finished Robinson Crusoe. I want to find out more about what happens to him but Miss Kinnian says thats all there is. *Why*

▲ **Critical Viewing**
What details in this photograph show that Charlie admires Miss Kinnian? **[Analyze]**

Make Inferences
What can you infer about Miss Kinnian's personality, based on this entry?

April 15

Miss Kinnian says Im lerning fast. She read some of the Progress Reports and she looked at me kind of funny. She says Im a fine person and Ill show them all. I asked her why. She said never mind but I shoudnt feel bad if I find out that everybody isnt nice like I think. She said for a person who god gave so little to you done more then a lot of people with brains they never even used. I said all my frends are smart people but there good. They like me and they never did anything that wasnt nice. Then she got something in her eye and she had to run out to the ladys room.

April 16

Today, I lerned, the comma, this is a comma (,) a period, with a tail, Miss Kinnian, says its importent, because, it makes writing, better, she said, somebody, coud lose, a lot of

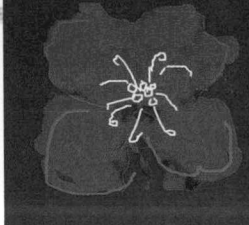

money, if a comma, isnt, in the, right place, I dont have, any money, and I dont see, how a comma, keeps you, from losing it,

But she says, everybody, uses commas, so Ill use, them too,

April 17

I used the comma wrong. Its punctuation. Miss Kinnian told me to look up long words in the dictionary to lern to spell them. I said whats the difference if you can read it anyway. She said its part of your education so now on Ill look up all the words Im not sure how to spell. It takes a long time to write that way but I think Im remembering. I only have to look up once and after that I get it right. Anyway thats how come I got the word *punctuation* right. (Its that way in the dictionary). Miss Kinnian says a period is punctuation too, and there are lots of other marks to lern. I told her I thot all the periods had to have tails but she said no.

You got to mix them up, she showed? me" how. to mix! them(up,. and now; I can! mix up all kinds" of punctuation, in! my writing? There, are lots! of rules? to lern; but Im gettin'g them in my head.

One thing I? like about, Dear Miss Kinnian: (thats the way it goes in a business letter if I ever go into business) is she, always gives me' a reason" when—I ask. She's a gen'ius! I wish! I cou'd be smart" like, her;

(Punctuation, is; fun!)

April 18

What a dope I am! I didn't even understand what she was talking about. I read the grammar book last night and it explanes the whole thing. Then I saw it was the same way as Miss Kinnian was trying to tell me, but I didn't get it. I got up in the middle of the night, and the whole thing straightened out in my mind.

Miss Kinnian said that the TV working in my sleep helped out. She said I reached a plateau. Thats like the flat top of a hill.

After I figgered out how punctuation worked, I read over all my old Progress Reports from the beginning. Boy, did I have crazy spelling and punctuation! I told Miss Kinnian I ought to go over the pages and fix all the mistakes but she said, "No, Charlie, Dr. Nemur wants them just as they are. That's

Point of View
What do you learn about Charlie from this entry that you might not know if it were written in the third person?

Make Inferences
What details in the April 18 entry show that Charlie's level of thought has increased?

Reading Check
What are some things Charlie is learning from Miss Kinnian?

why he let you keep them after they were photostated, to see your own progress. You're coming along fast, Charlie."

That made me feel good. After the lesson I went down and played with Algernon. We don't race any more.

April 20

I feel sick inside. Not sick like for a doctor, but inside my chest it feels empty like getting punched and a heartburn at the same time.

I wasn't going to write about it, but I guess I got to, because its important. Today was the first time I ever stayed home from work.

Last night Joe Carp and Frank Reilly invited me to a party. There were lots of girls and some men from the factory. I remembered how sick I got last time I drank too much, so I told Joe I didn't want anything to drink. He gave me a plain coke instead. It tasted funny, but I thought it was just a bad taste in my mouth.

We had a lot of fun for a while. Joe said I should dance with Ellen and she would teach me the steps. I fell a few times and I couldn't understand why because no one else was dancing besides Ellen and me. And all the time I was tripping because somebody's foot was always sticking out.

Make Inferences
Is Joe a true friend to Charlie? Explain.

Then when I got up I saw the look on Joe's face and it gave me a funny feeling in my stomack. "He's a scream," one of the girls said. Everybody was laughing.

Frank said, "I ain't laughed so much since we sent him off for the newspaper that night at Muggsy's and ditched him."

"Look at him. His face is red."

"He's blushing. Charlie is blushing."

"Hey, Ellen, what'd you do to Charlie? I never saw him act like that before."

Point of View
How does the use of first-person point of view help you to sympathize with Charlie?

I didn't know what to do or where to turn. Everyone was looking at me and laughing and I felt naked. I wanted to hide myself. I ran out into the street and I threw up. Then I walked home. It's a funny thing I never knew that Joe and Frank and the others liked to have me around all the time to make fun of me.

Now I know what it means when they say "to pull a Charlie Gordon."

I'm ashamed.

Progress Report 11
April 21

Still didn't go into the factory. I told Mrs. Flynn my landlady to call and tell Mr. Donnegan I was sick. Mrs. Flynn looks at me very funny lately like she's scared of me.

I think it's a good thing about finding out how everybody laughs at me. I thought about it a lot. It's because I'm so dumb and I don't even know when I'm doing something dumb. People think it's funny when a dumb person can't do things the same way they can.

Anyway, now I know I'm getting smarter every day. I know punctuation and I can spell good. I like to look up all the hard words in the dictionary and I remember them. I'm reading a lot now, and Miss Kinnian says I read very fast. Sometimes I even understand what I'm reading about, and it stays in my mind. There are times when I can close my eyes and think of a page and it all comes back like a picture.

Besides history, geography and arithmetic, Miss Kinnian said I should start to learn a few foreign languages. Dr. Strauss gave me some more tapes to play while I sleep. I still don't understand how that conscious and unconscious mind works, but Dr. Strauss says not to worry yet. He asked me to promise that when I start learning college subjects next week I wouldn't read any books on psychology—that is, until he gives me permission.

I feel a lot better today, but I guess I'm still a little angry that all the time people were laughing and making fun of me because I wasn't so smart. When I become intelligent like Dr. Strauss says, with three times my I.Q. of 68, then maybe I'll be like everyone else and people will like me and be friendly.

I'm not sure what an I.Q. is. Dr. Nemur said it was something that measured how intelligent you were—like a scale in the drugstore weighs pounds. But Dr. Strauss had a big arguement with him and said an I.Q. didn't

▲ **Critical Viewing**
Does Charlie seem to have made progress, judging from the details in this photograph? Explain. **[Infer]**

Reading Check
What happened at Joe Carp's party?

weigh intelligence at all. He said an I.Q. showed how much intelligence you could get, like the numbers on the outside of a measuring cup. You still had to fill the cup up with stuff.

Then when I asked Burt, who gives me my intelligence tests and works with Algernon, he said that both of them were wrong (only I had to promise not to tell them he said so). Burt says that the I.Q. measures a lot of different things including some of the things you learned already, and it really isn't any good at all.

So I still don't know what I.Q. is except that mine is going to be over 200 soon. I didn't want to say anything, but I don't see how if they don't know *what* it is, or *where* it is—I don't see how they know *how much* of it you've got.

Dr. Nemur says I have to take a *Rorschach Test* tomorrow. I wonder what *that* is.

April 22

I found out what a *Rorschach* is. It's the test I took before the operation—the one with the inkblots on the pieces of cardboard. The man who gave me the test was the same one.

I was scared to death of those inkblots. I knew he was going to ask me to find the pictures and I knew I wouldn't be able to. I was thinking to myself, if only there was some way of knowing what kind of pictures were hidden there. Maybe there weren't any pictures at all. Maybe it was just a trick to see if I was dumb enough too look for something that wasn't there. Just thinking about that made me sore at him.

"All right, Charlie," he said, "you've seen these cards before, remember?"

"Of course I remember."

The way I said it, he knew I was angry, and he looked surprised. "Yes, of course. Now I want you to look at this one. What might this be? What do you see on this card? People see all sorts of things in these inkblots. Tell me what it might be for you—what it makes you think of."

I was shocked. That wasn't what I had expected him to say at all. "You mean there are no pictures hidden in those inkblots?"

He frowned and took off his glasses. "What?"

"Pictures. Hidden in the inkblots. Last time you told me

that everyone could see them and you wanted me to find them too."

He explained to me that the last time he had used almost the exact same words he was using now. I didn't believe it, and I still have the suspicion that he misled me at the time just for the fun of it. Unless—I don't know any more—could I have been *that* feeble-minded?

We went through the cards slowly. One of them looked like a pair of bats tugging at some thing. Another one looked like two men fencing with swords. I imagined all sorts of things. I guess I got carried away. But I didn't trust him any more, and I kept turning them around and even looking on the back to see if there was anything there I was supposed to catch. While he was making his notes, I peeked out of the corner of my eye to read it. But it was all in code that looked like this:

WF + A DdF-Ad orig. WF-A
SF + obj

The test still doesn't make sense to me. It seems to me that anyone could make up lies about things that they didn't really see. How could he know I wasn't making a fool of him by mentioning things that I didn't really imagine? Maybe I'll understand it when Dr. Strauss lets me read up on psychology.

April 25

I figured out a new way to line up the machines in the factory, and Mr. Donnegan says it will save him ten thousand dollars a year in labor and increased production. He gave me a $25 bonus.

I wanted to take Joe Carp and Frank Reilly out to lunch to celebrate, but Joe said he had to buy some things for his wife, and Frank said he was meeting his cousin for lunch. I guess it'll take a little time for them to get used to the changes in me. Everybody seems to be frightened of me. When I went over to Amos Borg and tapped him on the shoulder, he jumped up in the air.

People don't talk to me much any more or kid around the way they used to. It makes the job kind of lonely.

Point of View
How does the first-person point of view help you to keep track of Charlie's development?

Make Inferences
Why do Charlie's co-workers behave differently toward him?

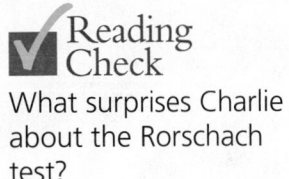
Reading Check
What surprises Charlie about the Rorschach test?

April 27

I got up the nerve today to ask Miss Kinnian to have dinner with me tomorrow night to celebrate my bonus.

At first she wasn't sure it was right, but I asked Dr. Strauss and he said it was okay. Dr. Strauss and Dr. Nemur don't seem to be getting along so well. They're arguing all the time. This evening when I came in to ask Dr. Strauss about having dinner with Miss Kinnian, I heard them shouting. Dr. Nemur was saying that it was *his* experiment and his research, and Dr. Strauss was shouting back that he contributed just as much, because he found me through Miss Kinnian and he performed the operation. Dr. Strauss said that someday thousands of neurosurgeons[7] might be using his technique all over the world.

Dr. Nemur wanted to publish the results of the experiment at the end of this month. Dr. Strauss wanted to wait a while longer to be sure. Dr. Strauss said that Dr. Nemur was more interested in the Chair[8] of Psychology at Princeton than he was in the experiment. Dr. Nemur said that Dr. Strauss was nothing but an opportunist who was trying to ride to glory on *his* coattails.

When I left afterwards, I found myself trembling. I don't know why for sure, but it was as if I'd seen both men clearly for the first time. I remember hearing Burt say that Dr. Nemur had a shrew of a wife who was pushing him all the time to get things published so that he could become famous. Burt said that the dream of her life was to have a big shot husband. Was Dr. Strauss really trying to ride on his coattails?

April 28

I don't understand why I never noticed how beautiful Miss Kinnian really is. She has brown eyes and feathery brown hair that comes to the top of her neck. She's only thirty-four!

▲ **Critical Viewing**
What details in this picture show that Charlie's intelligence has increased? **[Analyze]**

---

7. **neurosurgeons** (nŏŏr´ō sʉr´ jənz) *n.* doctors who operate on the nervous system, including the brain and spine.
8. **chair** *n.* professorship.

I think from the beginning I had the feeling that she was an unreachable genius—and very, very old. Now, every time I see her she grows younger and more lovely.

We had dinner and a long talk. When she said that I was coming along so fast that soon I'd be leaving her behind, I laughed.

"It's true, Charlie. You're already a better reader than I am. You can read a whole page at a glance while I can take in only a few lines at a time. And you remember every single thing you read. I'm lucky if I can recall the main thoughts and the general meaning."

"I don't feel intelligent. There are so many things I don't understand."

"You've got to be a *little* patient. You're accomplishing in days and weeks what it takes normal people to do in half a lifetime. That's what makes it so amazing. You're like a giant sponge now, soaking things in. Facts, figures, general knowledge. And soon you'll begin to connect them, too. You'll see how the different branches of learning are related. There are many levels, Charlie, like steps on a giant ladder that take you up higher and higher to see more and more of the world around you.

"I can see only a little bit of that, Charlie, and I won't go much higher than I am now, but you'll keep climbing up and up, and see more and more, and each step will open new worlds that you never even knew existed." She frowned. "I hope . . . I just hope to God—"

"What?"

"Never mind, Charles. I just hope I wasn't wrong to advise you to go into this in the first place."

I laughed. "How could that be? It worked, didn't it? Even Algernon is still smart."

We sat there silently for a while and I knew what she was thinking about as she watched me toying with the chain of my rabbit's foot and my keys. I didn't want to think of that possibility any more than elderly people want to think of death. I *knew* that this was only the beginning. I knew what she meant about levels because I'd seen some of them already. The thought of leaving her behind made me sad.

I'm in love with Miss Kinnian.

Point of View
Compare this entry to Progress Report 3 on pages 349 and 350. Which words and phrases show that Charlie has changed?

Reading Check
How are Charlie's feelings toward Miss Kinnian changing?

Progress Report 12
April 30

I've quit my job with Donnegan's Plastic Box Company. Mr. Donnegan insisted that it would be better for all concerned if I left. What did I do to make them hate me so?

The first I knew of it was when Mr. Donnegan showed me the petition. Eight hundred and forty names, everyone connected with the factory, except Fanny Girden. Scanning the list quickly, I saw at once that hers was the only missing name. All the rest demanded that I be fired.

Joe Carp and Frank Reilly wouldn't talk to me about it. No one else would either, except Fanny. She was one of the few people I'd known who set her mind to something and believed it no matter what the rest of the world proved, said or did—and Fanny did not believe that I should have been fired. She had been against the petition on principle and despite the pressure and threats she'd held out.

"Which don't mean to say," she remarked, "that I don't think there's something mighty strange about you, Charlie. Them changes. I don't know. You used to be a good, dependable, ordinary man—not too bright maybe, but honest. Who knows what you done to yourself to get so smart all of a sudden. Like everybody around here's been saying, Charlie, it's not right."

"But how can you say that, Fanny? What's wrong with a man becoming intelligent and wanting to acquire knowledge and understanding of the world around him?"

She stared down at her work, and I turned to leave. Without looking at me, she said: "It was evil when Eve listened to the snake and ate from the tree of knowledge. It was evil when she saw that she was naked. If not for that none of us would ever have to grow old and sick, and die."

Once again now I have the feeling of shame burning inside me. This intelligence has driven a wedge between me and all the people I once knew and loved. Before, they laughed at me and despised me for my ignorance and dullness; now, they hate me for my knowledge and understanding. What do they want of me?

They've driven me out of the factory. Now I'm more alone than ever before . . .

Make Inferences
Why do you think Charlie's co-workers signed the petition to have him fired?

Make Inferences
What comparison is Fanny making between Charlie and Eve?

May 15

Dr. Strauss is very angry at me for not having written any progress reports in two weeks. He's justified because the lab is now paying me a regular salary. I told him I was too busy thinking and reading. When I pointed out that writing was such a slow process that it made me impatient with my poor handwriting, he suggested that I learn to type. It's much easier to write now because I can type nearly seventy-five words a minute. Dr. Strauss continually reminds me of the need to speak and write simply so that people will be able to understand me.

I'll try to review all the things that happened to me during the last two weeks. Algernon and I were presented to the American Psychological Association sitting in convention with the World Psychological Association last Tuesday. We created quite a sensation. Dr. Nemur and Dr. Strauss were proud of us.

I suspect that Dr. Nemur, who is sixty—ten years older than Dr. Strauss—finds it necessary to see tangible[9] results of his work. Undoubtedly the result of pressure by Mrs. Nemur.

Contrary to my earlier impressions of him, I realize that Dr. Nemur is not at all a genius. He has a very good mind, but it struggles under the specter of self-doubt. He wants people to take him for a genius. Therefore, it is important for him to feel that his work is accepted by the world. I believe that Dr. Nemur was afraid of further delay because he worried that someone else might make a discovery along these lines and take the credit from him.

Dr. Strauss on the other hand might be called a genius, although I feel that his areas of knowledge are too limited. He was educated in the tradition of narrow specialization; the broader aspects of background were neglected far more than necessary—even for a neurosurgeon.

I was shocked to learn that the only ancient languages he could read were Latin, Greek and Hebrew, and that he knows almost nothing of mathematics beyond the elementary levels of the calculus of variations. When he admitted this to me, I found myself almost annoyed. It was as if he'd hidden this

---

9. tangible (tan´ jə bəl) *adj.* substantial; easily understood.

Point of View
What details in this entry reveal Charlie's increased intelligence?

Reading Check
Why does Charlie quit his job?

part of himself in order to deceive me, pretending—as do many people I've discovered—to be what he is not. No one I've ever known is what he appears to be on the surface.

Dr. Nemur appears to be uncomfortable around me. Sometimes when I try to talk to him, he just looks at me strangely and turns away. I was angry at first when Dr. Strauss told me I was giving Dr. Nemur an inferiority complex. I thought he was mocking me and I'm oversensitive at being made fun of.

How was I to know that a highly respected psychoexperimentalist like Nemur was unacquainted with Hindustani[10] and Chinese? It's absurd when you consider the work that is being done in India and China today in the very field of his study.

I asked Dr. Strauss how Nemur could refute Rahajamati's attack on his method and results if Nemur couldn't even read them in the first place. That strange look on Dr. Strauss' face can mean only one of two things. Either he doesn't want to tell Nemur what they're saying in India, or else—and this worries me—Dr. Strauss doesn't know either. I must be careful to speak and write clearly and simply so that people won't laugh.

May 18

I am very disturbed. I saw Miss Kinnian last night for the first time in over a week. I tried to avoid all discussions of intellectual concepts and to keep the conversation on a simple, everyday level, but she just stared at me blankly and asked me what I meant about the mathematical variance equivalent in Dorbermann's *Fifth Concerto.*

When I tried to explain she stopped me and laughed. I guess I got angry, but I suspect I'm approaching her on the wrong level. No matter what I try to discuss with her, I am unable to communicate. I must review Vrostadt's equations on *Levels of Semantic Progression.* I find that I don't communicate with people much any more. Thank God for books and music and things I can think about. I am alone in my apartment at Mrs. Flynn's boarding house most of the time and seldom speak to anyone.

---

10. **Hindustani** (hin´ dōō stä´ nē) *n.* a language of northern India.

Vocabulary
deceive (dē sēv´) *v.* make someone believe what is not true
refute (ri fyōōt´) *v.* give evidence to prove a statement false

intellectual (in´ tə lek´ chōō əl) *adj.* relating to the ability to think and understand ideas and information

Point of View
How would the May 18 entry be different if it were told from Miss Kinnian's point of view?

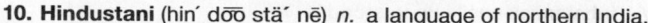

May 20

I would not have noticed the new dishwasher, a boy of about sixteen, at the corner diner where I take my evening meals if not for the incident of the broken dishes.

They crashed to the floor, shattering and sending bits of white china under the tables. The boy stood there, dazed and frightened, holding the empty tray in his hand. The whistles and catcalls from the customers (the cries of "hey, there go the profits!" . . . "*Mazeltov!*" . . . and "well, he didn't work here very long . . ." which invariably seems to follow the breaking of glass or dishware in a public restaurant) all seemed to confuse him.

When the owner came to see what the excitement was about, the boy cowered as if he expected to be struck and threw up his arms as if to ward off the blow.

"All right! All right, you dope," shouted the owner, "don't just stand there! Get the broom and sweep that mess up. A broom . . . a broom, you idiot! It's in the kitchen. Sweep up all the pieces."

The boy saw that he was not going to be punished. His frightened expression disappeared and he smiled and hummed as he came back with the broom to sweep the floor. A few of the rowdier customers kept up the remarks, amusing themselves at his expense.

"Here, sonny, over here there's a nice piece behind you . . ."

"C'mon, do it again . . ."

"He's not so dumb. It's easier to break 'em than to wash 'em . . ."

As his vacant eyes moved across the crowd of amused onlookers, he slowly mirrored their smiles and finally broke into an uncertain grin at the joke which he obviously did not understand.

I felt sick inside as I looked at his dull, vacuous smile, the wide, bright eyes of a child, uncertain but eager to please. They were laughing at him because he was mentally retarded.

And I had been laughing at him too.

Suddenly, I was furious at myself and all those who were smirking at him. I jumped up and shouted, "Shut up! Leave him alone! It's not his fault he can't understand! He can't help what he is! But . . . he's still a human being!"

> I am alone in my apartment at Mrs. Flynn's boarding house most of the time and seldom speak to anyone.

Reading Check
What makes Charlie angry with Miss Kinnian?

Point of View
How does Charlie now see himself?

The room grew silent. I cursed myself for losing control and creating a scene. I tried not to look at the boy as I paid my check and walked out without touching my food. I felt ashamed for both of us.

How strange it is that people of honest feelings and sensibility, who would not take advantage of a man born without arms or legs or eyes—how such people think nothing of abusing a man born with low intelligence. It infuriated me to think that not too long ago I, like this boy, had foolishly played the clown.

And I had almost forgotten.

I'd hidden the picture of the old Charlie Gordon from myself because now that I was intelligent it was something that had to be pushed out of my mind. But today in looking at that boy, for the first time I saw what I had been. *I was just like him!*

Only a short time ago, I learned that people laughed at me. Now I can see that unknowingly I joined with them in laughing at myself. That hurts most of all.

Vocabulary
naïvete (nä´ ēv tā´)
n. the state of being simple or childlike

I have often reread my progress reports and seen the illiteracy, the childish naïveté, the mind of low intelligence peering from a dark room, through the keyhole, at the dazzling light outside. I see that even in my dullness I knew that I was inferior, and that other people had something I lacked—something denied me. In my mental blindness, I thought that it was somehow connected with the ability to read and write, and I was sure that if I could get those skills I would automatically have intelligence too.

Even a feeble-minded man wants to be like other men.

A child may not know how to feed itself, or what to eat, yet it knows of hunger.

This then is what I was like. I never knew. Even with my gift of intellectual awareness, I never really knew.

Point of View
What has Charlie learned about himself?

This day was good for me. Seeing the past more clearly, I have decided to use my knowledge and skills to work in the field of increasing human intelligence levels. Who is better equipped for this work? Who else has lived in both worlds? These are my people. Let me use my gift to do something for them.

Tomorrow, I will discuss with Dr. Strauss the manner in which I can work in this area. I may be able to help him work out the problems of widespread use of the technique which

was used on me. I have several good ideas of my own.

There is so much that might be done with this technique. If I could be made into a genius, what about thousands of others like myself? What fantastic levels might be achieved by using this technique on normal people? On *geniuses*?

There are so many doors to open. I am impatient to begin.

PROGRESS REPORT 13

May 23

It happened today. Algernon bit me. I visited the lab to see him as I do occasionally, and when I took him out of his cage, he snapped at my hand. I put him back and watched him for a while. He was unusually disturbed and vicious.

May 24

Burt, who is in charge of the experimental animals, tells me that Algernon is changing. He is less cooperative; he refuses to run the maze any more; general motivation has decreased. And he hasn't been eating. Everyone is upset about what this may mean.

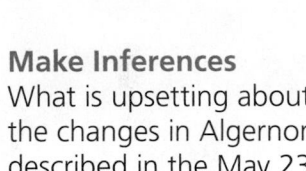

Make Inferences
What is upsetting about the changes in Algernon described in the May 23 and May 24 entries?

May 25

They've been feeding Algernon, who now refuses to work the shifting-lock problem. Everyone identifies me with Algernon. In a way we're both the first of our kind. They're all pretending that Algernon's behavior is not necessarily significant for me. But it's hard to hide the fact that some of the other animals who were used in this experiment are showing strange behavior.

Dr. Strauss and Dr. Nemur have asked me not to come to the lab any more. I know what they're thinking but I can't accept it. I am going ahead with my plans to carry their research forward. With all due respect to both of these fine scientists, I am well aware of their limitations. If there is an answer, I'll have to find it out for myself. Suddenly, time has become very important to me.

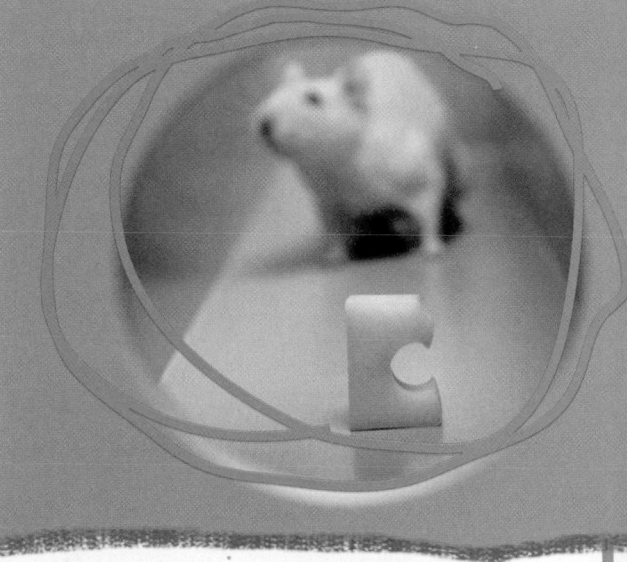

✓ **Reading Check**
What new line of work does Charlie want to pursue?

May 29

I have been given a lab of my own and permission to go ahead with the research. I'm on to something. Working day and night. I've had a cot moved into the lab. Most of my writing time is spent on the notes which I keep in a separate folder, but from time to time I feel it necessary to put down my moods and my thoughts out of sheer habit.

I find the *calculus of intelligence* to be a fascinating study. Here is the place for the application of all the knowledge I have acquired. In a sense it's the problem I've been concerned with all my life.

May 31

Dr. Strauss thinks I'm working too hard. Dr. Nemur says I'm trying to cram a lifetime of research and thought into a few weeks. I know I should rest, but I'm driven on by something inside that won't let me stop. I've got to find the reason for the sharp regression in Algernon. I've got to know *if* and *when* it will happen to me.

June 4

Make Inferences
What aspects of this letter show that Charlie is as smart as the doctors?

Letter to Dr. Strauss *(copy)*
Dear Dr. Strauss:
Under separate cover I am sending you a copy of my report entitled, "The Algernon-Gordon Effect: A Study of Structure and Function of Increased Intelligence," which I would like to have you read and have published.

As you see, my experiments are completed. I have included in my report all of my formulae, as well as mathematical analysis in the appendix. Of course, these should be verified.

Because of its importance to both you and Dr. Nemur (and need I say to myself, too?) I have checked and rechecked my results a dozen times in the hope of finding an error. I am sorry to say the results must stand. Yet for the sake of science, I am grateful for the little bit that I here add to the knowledge of the function of the human mind and of the laws governing the artificial increase of human intelligence.

I recall your once saying to me that an experimental *failure* or the *disproving* of a theory was as important to the advancement of learning as a success would be. I know

now that this is true. I am sorry, however, that my own contribution to the field must rest upon the ashes of the work of two men I regard so highly.

Yours truly,
Charles Gordon

encl.: rept.

June 5

I must not become emotional. The facts and the results of my experiments are clear, and the more sensational aspects of my own rapid climb cannot obscure the fact that the tripling of intelligence by the surgical technique developed by Drs. Strauss and Nemur must be viewed as having little or no practical applicability (at the present time) to the increase of human intelligence.

As I review the records and data on Algernon, I see that although he is still in his physical infancy, he has regressed mentally. Motor activity[11] is impaired; there is a general reduction of glandular activity; there is an accelerated loss of coordination.

There are also strong indications of progressive amnesia.

As will be seen by my report, these and other physical and mental **deterioration** syndromes[12] can be predicted with statistically significant results by the application of my formula.

The surgical stimulus to which we were both subjected has resulted in an intensification and acceleration of all mental processes. The unforeseen development, which I have

Vocabulary
deterioration (dē tir´ ē ə rā shən) *n. (used here as an adjective)* the process of becoming worse

Reading Check
What does Charlie want to learn through his research?

---

11. **motor activity** movement; physical coordination.
12. **syndromes** (sin´ drōmz´) *n.* a number of symptoms occurring together and characterizing a specific disease or condition.

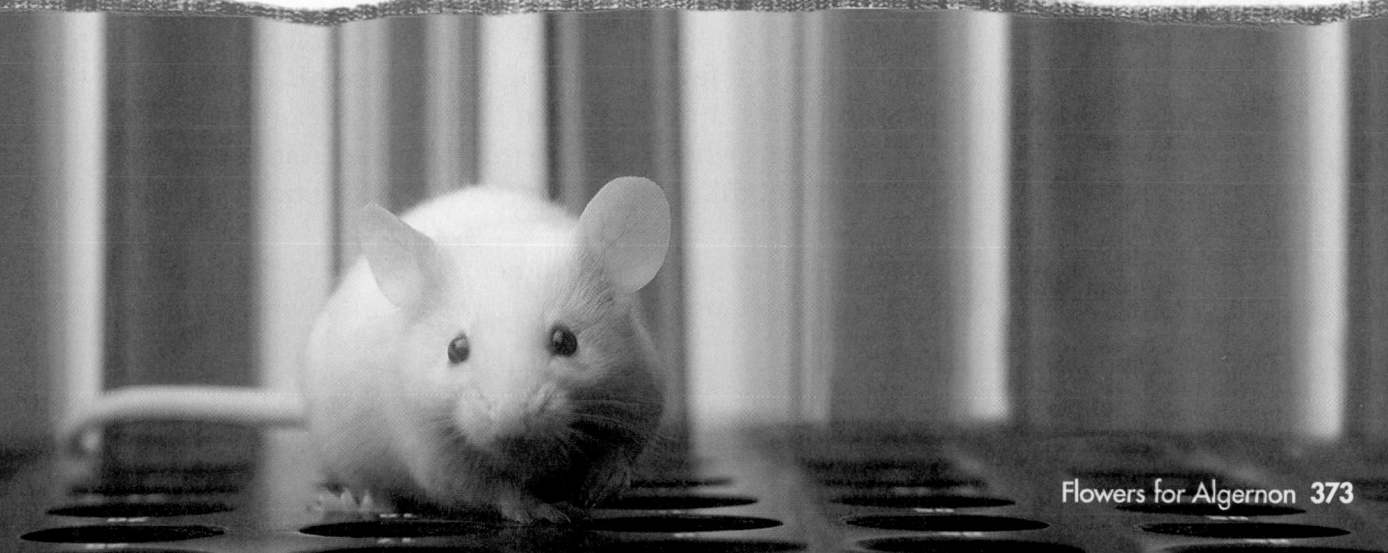

taken the liberty of calling the "Algernon-Gordon Effect," is the logical extension of the entire intelligence speedup. The hypothesis here proven may be described simply in the following terms: Artificially increased intelligence deteriorates at a rate of time directly proportional to the quantity of the increase.

I feel that this, in itself, is an important discovery.

As long as I am able to write, I will continue to record my thoughts in these progress reports. It is one of my few pleasures. However, by all indications, my own mental deterioration will be very rapid.

I have already begun to notice signs of emotional instability and forgetfulness, the first symptoms of the burnout.

June 10

Deterioration progressing. I have become absent-minded. Algernon died two days ago. Dissection shows my predictions were right. His brain had decreased in weight and there was a general smoothing out of cerebral convolutions as well as a deepening and broadening of brain fissures.

I guess the same thing is or will soon be happening to me. Now that it's definite, I don't want it to happen.

I put Algernon's body in a cheese box and buried him in the back yard. I cried.

June 15

Dr. Strauss came to see me again. I wouldn't open the door and I told him to go away. I want to be left to myself. I have become touchy and irritable. I feel the darkness closing in. I keep telling myself how important this introspective journal will be.

It's a strange sensation to pick up a book that you've read and enjoyed just a few months ago and discover that you don't remember it. I remembered how great I thought John Milton[13] was, but when I picked up *Paradise Lost* I couldn't understand it at all. I got so angry I threw the book across the room.

I've got to try to hold on to some of it. Some of the things I've learned. Oh, God, please don't take it all away.

---

13. John Milton British poet (1608–1674) who wrote *Paradise Lost*.

Point of View
How does the point of view make the changes Charlie is experiencing more dramatic?

Vocabulary
introspective (in´ trō spek´ tiv) *adj.* thoughtful; inward-looking

June 19

Sometimes, at night, I go out for a walk. Last night I couldn't remember where I lived. A policeman took me home. I have the strange feeling that this has all happened to me before—a long time ago. I keep telling myself I'm the only person in the world who can describe what's happening to me.

June 21

Why can't I remember? I've got to fight. I lie in bed for days and I don't know who or where I am. Then it all comes back to me in a flash. Fugues of amnesia.[14] Symptoms of senility—second childhood. I can watch them coming on. It's so cruelly logical. I learned so much and so fast. Now my mind is deteriorating rapidly. I won't let it happen. I'll fight it. I can't help thinking of the boy in the restaurant, the blank expression, the silly smile, the people laughing at him. No— please—not that again . . .

June 22

I'm forgetting things that I learned recently. It seems to be following the classic pattern—the last things learned are the first things forgotten. Or is that the pattern? I'd better look it up again . . .

I reread my paper on the "Algernon-Gordon Effect" and I get the strange feeling that it was written by someone else. There are parts I don't even understand.

Motor activity impaired. I keep tripping over things, and it becomes increasingly difficult to type.

June 23

I've given up using the typewriter completely. My coordination is bad. I feel that I'm moving slower and slower. Had a terrible shock today. I picked up a copy of an article I used in my research, Krueger's "Uber psychische Ganzheit," to see if it would help me understand what I had done. First I thought there was something wrong with my eyes. Then I realized I could no longer read German. I tested myself in other languages. All gone.

Make Inferences
How does Charlie probably feel about forgetting things he had learned? Why?

✓ Reading
Check
What are some signs that Charlie's mental state is rapidly reversing?

---

14. **fugues** (fyo͞ogz) **of amnesia** (am nē′ zhə) *n.* periods of loss of memory.

June 30

A week since I dared to write again. It's slipping away like sand through my fingers. Most of the books I have are too hard for me now. I get angry with them because I know that I read and understood them just a few weeks ago.

I keep telling myself I must keep writing these reports so that somebody will know what is happening to me. But it gets harder to form the words and remember spellings. I have to look up even simple words in the dictionary now and it makes me impatient with myself.

Dr. Strauss comes around almost every day, but I told him I wouldn't see or speak to anybody. He feels guilty. They all do. But I don't blame anyone. I knew what might happen. But how it hurts.

July 7

I don't know where the week went. Todays Sunday I know because I can see through my window people going to church. I think I stayed in bed all week but I remember Mrs. Flynn bringing food to me a few times. I keep saying over and over Ive got to do something but then I forget or maybe its just easier not to do what I say Im going to do.

I think of my mother and father a lot these days. I found a picture of them with me taken at a beach. My father has a big ball under his arm and my mother is holding me by the hand. I dont remember them the way they are in the picture. All I remember is my father arguing with mom about money.

He never shaved much and he used to scratch my face when he hugged me. He said he was going to take me to see cows on a farm once but he never did. He never kept his promises . . .

July 10

My landlady Mrs Flynn is very worried about me. She said she doesnt like loafers. If Im sick its one thing, but if Im a loafer thats another thing and she wont have it. I told her I think Im sick.

I try to read a little bit every day, mostly stories, but sometimes I have to read the same thing over and over again because I dont know what it means. And its hard to write.

It's slipping away like sand through my fingers.

Make Inferences
What does Charlie's style of writing reveal?

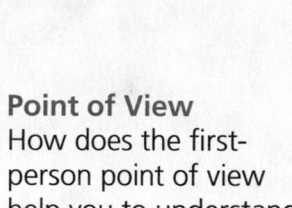

I know I should look up all the words in the dictionary but its so hard and Im so tired all the time.

Then I got the idea that I would only use the easy words instead of the long hard ones. That saves time. I put flowers on Algernons grave about once a week. Mrs. Flynn thinks Im crazy to put flowers on a mouses grave but I told her that Algernon was special.

July 14

Its sunday again. I dont have anything to do to keep me busy now because my television set is broke and I dont have any money to get it fixed. (I think I lost this months check from the lab. I dont remember)

I get awful headaches and asperin doesnt help me much. Mrs. Flynn knows Im really sick and she feels very sorry for me. Shes a wonderful woman whenever someone is sick.

July 22

Mrs. Flynn called a strange doctor to see me. She was afraid I was going to die. I told the doctor I wasnt too sick and that I only forget sometimes. He asked me did I have any friends or relatives and I said no I dont have any. I told him I had a friend called Algernon once but he was a mouse and we used to run races together. He looked at me kind of funny like he thought I was crazy.

He smiled when I told him I used to be a genius. He talked to me like I was a baby and he winked at Mrs Flynn. I got mad and chased him out because he was making fun of me the way they all used to.

July 24

I have no more money and Mrs Flynn says I got to go to work somewhere and pay the rent because I havent paid for over two months. I dont know any work but the job I used to have at Donnegans Plastic Box Company. I dont want to go back there because they all knew me when I was smart and maybe they'll laugh at me. But I dont know what else to do to get money.

Point of View
How does the first-person point of view help you to understand Charlie's experience?

Reading Check
How does the doctor anger Charlie?

July 25

I was looking at some of my old progress reports and its very funny but I cant read what I wrote. I can make out some of the words but they dont make sense.

Miss Kinnian came to the door but I said go away I dont want to see you. She cried and I cried too but I wouldnt let her in because I didnt want her to laugh at me. I told her I didn't like her any more. I told her I didn't want to be smart any more. Thats not true. I still love her and I still want to be smart but I had to say that so shed go away. She gave Mrs. Flynn money to pay the rent. I dont want that. I got to get a job.

Please . . . please let me not forget how to read and write . . .

July 27

Mr. Donnegan was very nice when I came back and asked him for my old job of janitor. First he was very suspicious but I told him what happened to me then he looked very sad and put his hand on my shoulder and said Charlie Gordon you got guts.

Everybody looked at me when I came downstairs and started working in the toilet sweeping it out like I used to. I told myself Charlie if they make fun of you dont get sore because you remember their not so smart as you once thot they were. And besides they were once your friends and if they laughed at you that doesnt mean anything because they liked you too.

One of the new men who came to work there after I went away made a nasty crack he said hey Charlie I hear your a very smart fella a real quiz kid. Say something intelligent. I felt bad but Joe Carp came over and grabbed him by the shirt and said leave him alone or Ill break your neck. I didnt expect Joe to take my part so I guess hes really my friend.

▲ **Critical Viewing**
Why would Charlie be reluctant to go back to this job? **[Connect]**

Point of View
How has Charlie's view of his co-workers changed?

Later Frank Reilly came over and said Charlie if anybody bothers you or trys to take advantage you call me or Joe and we will set em straight. I said thanks Frank and I got choked up so I had to turn around and go into the supply room so he wouldnt see me cry. Its good to have friends.

July 28

I did a dumb thing today I forgot I wasnt in Miss Kinnians class at the adult center any more like I use to be. I went in and sat down in my old seat in the back of the room and she looked at me funny and she said Charles. I dint remember she ever called me that before only Charlie so I said hello Miss Kinnian Im ready for my lesin today only I lost my reader that we was using. She startid to cry and run out of the room and everybody looked at me and I saw they wasnt the same pepul who use to be in my class.

Then all of a suddin I rememberd some things about the operashun and me getting smart and I said holy smoke I reely pulled a Charlie Gordon that time. I went away before she come back to the room.

Thats why Im going away from New York for good. I dont want to do nothing like that agen. I dont want Miss Kinnian to feel sorry for me. Evry body feels sorry at the factery and I dont want that eather so Im going someplace where nobody knows that Charlie Gordon was once a genus and now he cant even reed a book or rite good.

Im taking a cuple of books along and even if I cant reed them Ill practise hard and maybe I wont forget every thing I lerned. If I try reel hard maybe Ill be a littel bit smarter then I was before the operashun. I got my rabits foot and my luky penny and maybe they will help me.

If you ever reed this Miss Kinnian dont be sorry for me Im glad I got a second chanse to be smart becaus I lerned a lot of things that I never even new were in this world and Im grateful that I saw it all for a littel bit. I dont know why Im dumb agen or what I did wrong maybe its becaus I dint try hard enuff. But if I try and practis very hard maybe Ill get a littl smarter and know what all the words are. I remember a littel bit how nice I had a feeling with the blue book that has the torn cover when I red it. Thats why Im gonna keep trying to get smart so I can have that feeling agen. Its a good feeling

Point of View
What thoughts and emotions drive Charlie to leave New York?

Reading Check
Why is Charlie leaving New York?

to know things and be smart. I wish I had it rite now if I did I woud sit down and reed all the time. Anyway I bet Im the first dumb person in the world who ever found out somthing importent for sience. I remember I did somthing but I dont remember what. So I gess its like I did it for all the dumb pepul like me.

Goodbye Miss Kinnian and Dr Strauss and evreybody. And P.S. please tell Dr Nemur not to be such a grouch when pepul laff at him and he woud have more frends. Its easy to make frends if you let pepul laff at you. Im going to have lots of frends where I go.

P.P.S. Please if you get a chanse put some flowrs on Algernons grave in the bak yard . . .

Critical Thinking

1. Key Ideas and Details (a) Who is Algernon? **(b) Compare:** Explain how changes in Charlie are similar to those in Algernon.

2. Key Ideas and Details (a) Analyze: When do you realize that Charlie's intelligence is not permanent? **(b) Support:** What two details from the story reveal the progress of the reversal?

3. Key Ideas and Details (a) Contrast: What is the difference between Charlie at the beginning of the story and Charlie at the end of the story? **(b) Predict:** What will happen to Charlie? How do you know?

4. Integration of Knowledge and Ideas Take a Position: Do you think Charlie should have had the operation? Why or why not?

5. Integration of Knowledge and Ideas (a) How does Charlie's surgery change him? **(b)** What conflict cannot be resolved by the end of the story? *[Connect to the Big Question: Can all conflicts be resolved?]*

Cite textual evidence to support your responses.

Reading Skill: Make Inferences

1. **(a)** How did Charlie's attitudes toward his doctors change after his operation? **(b)** Use these details to make an **inference** about how the operation affects Charlie.

2. What inferences can you make about Miss Kinnian from the way she treats Charlie?

Literary Analysis: Point of View

© 3. **Craft and Structure** Explain how the story would change if it were told from Dr. Strauss's **point of view.**

Charlie	Dr. Strauss
Charlie reveals his confusion about the inkblot test.	
Charlie shares his innermost feelings through his journal entries.	

© 4. **Craft and Structure** **(a)** At what points in the story do you understand better than Charlie what is happening to him? **(b)** What effect does this difference in perspective create?

Vocabulary

© **Acquisition and Use** **Analogies** show the relationships between words. Use a word from page 344 to create a word pair that matches the relationship between the first two words.

1. *Heavy* is to *weighty* as *lie* is to _____.
2. *Emotional* is to *rational* as *physical* is to _____.
3. *Happiness* is to *contentment* as *inexperience* is to _____.
4. *Expand* is to *shrink* as *improvement* is to _____.
5. *Anxious* is to *worried* as *thoughtful* is to _____.
6. *Accept* is to *reject* as *support* is to _____.

Word Study Use the context of the sentences and what you know about the **Latin root -spec-** to answer each question.

1. What does a *spectator* do during a sports event?
2. How does a police *inspector* solve a crime?

Word Study

The **Latin root -spec-** means "to look."

Apply It Explain how the root contributes to the meanings of these words. Consult a dictionary if necessary.

speculate
perspective
circumspect

Integrated Language Skills

Charles • Flowers for Algernon

Conventions: Simple Tenses of Verbs

The **tense** of a verb shows the time of an action or a condition. The three **simple tenses** are *past, present,* and *future*.

Present Tense	Past Tense	Future Tense
Base Form	**Add -d or -ed to base form.**	**Use *will* before the base form.**
I walk you walk he, she, it walks	I walked you walked he, she, it walked	I will walk you will walk he, she, it will walk

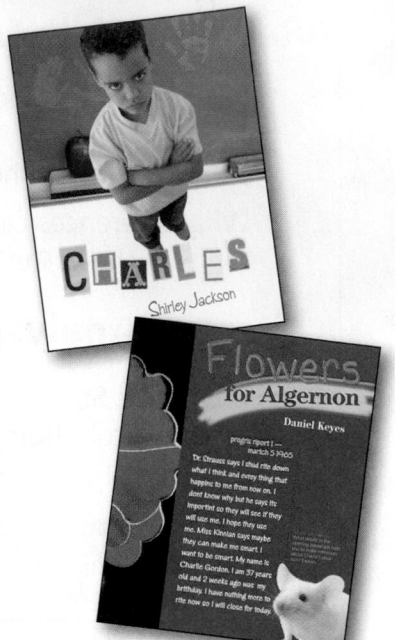

When two actions occur at the same time, keep the tense the same.
   Incorrect: I *walked* to the door and *open* it.
   Correct: I *walked* to the door and *opened* it.

When two or more actions or conditions occur at different times, change tenses to show the order in which they occur.
   Incorrect: Last year I *walk*, but next year I *ride* the bus.
   Correct: Last year I *walked*, but next year I *will ride* the bus.

Practice A Complete each sentence with a verb that uses the tense indicated.

1. Laurie _____ blue jeans. (present)

2. Laurie _____ home from school and eat with his parents. (future)

3. Charles _____ so loudly that he had to stay after school. (past)

4. Laurie's mother _____ the PTA meeting next week. (future)

Ⓒ **Reading Application** In "Charles," find a sentence containing at least two verbs with simple tenses. Identify the tenses of these verbs.

Practice B Identify whether the verb tenses are correct. Then explain your answer.

1. Doctors perform surgery. Then Charlie gained intelligence.

2. He likes Miss Kinnian and studies hard.

3. Charlie's knowledge increased and his life changed greatly.

4. The effect will eventually wear off and he worsened.

Ⓒ **Writing Application** Find a sentence in "Flowers for Algernon" that uses two verbs in the same tense. Then, use those same verbs in two different tenses in a sentence to show events occurring at different times.

PH WRITING COACH   Further instruction and practice are available in *Prentice Hall Writing Coach*.

Writing

 **Narrative Text** Write **dialogue** for a movie scene that you adapt from either "Charles" or "Flowers for Algernon."

- First, choose a scene that you can expand by imagining details and parts of conversations that the author left out.
- Then, write the dialogue using words and behavior that seem natural for each character.
- Write in standard dialogue format. Provide the character's name, then place a colon before the words he or she says. Put words that are not spoken in parentheses and start a new line when a different character speaks.

  Laurie: (Excitedly) Charles said a bad word.
  Father: Really? What did the teacher do?

Grammar Application Check your dialogue for consistent tense.

Writing Workshop: *Work in Progress*

Prewriting for Narration For a short story you may write, free-write about what makes your favorite literary characters fascinating. Think about what they say and how they react to situations. Save this Characterization Freewrite in your portfolio.

Use this prewriting activity to prepare for the **Writing Workshop** on page 438.

Research and Technology

 **Build and Present Knowledge** Write a **summary of an article** on either of the following topics:

- If you read "Charles," use library resources to find articles about a child's adjustment to kindergarten.
- If you read "Flowers for Algernon," find articles about human intelligence and the development of the brain.

To write the summary, follow these directions:

- As you read, take notes, recording ideas, quotations, and important information on the topic.
- Then, write a summary that includes the main idea and at least two significant details, stated in your own words.
- Include a direct quotation that provides a snapshot of the author's perspective.
- Make sure to keep your summary free of personal opinion or bias.

Common Core State Standards

L.8.1.d; RI.8.2; W.8.2.b, W.8.3.b
[For the full wording of the standards, see page 332.]

PHLit **Online!**
www.PHLitOnline.com
- Interactive graphic organizers
- Grammar tutorial
- Interactive journals

© Leveled Texts

Build your skills and improve your comprehension of short stories
with texts of increasing complexity.

Read **"Thank You, M'am"**
to witness a woman's surprising
response to a young purse-
snatcher.

Read **"The Story-Teller"** to see
how a man entertains three
bored children.

© Common Core State Standards

Meet these standards with either **"Thank You, M'am"** (p. 388) or **"The Story-Teller"** (p. 396).

Reading Literature
1. Cite the textual evidence that most strongly supports an analysis of what the text says explicitly as well as inferences drawn from the text. *(Reading Skill: Make Inferences)*

2. Determine a theme or central idea of a text and analyze its development over the course of the text, including its relationship to the characters, setting, and plot. *(Literary Analysis: Theme; Writing: Personal Essay)*

Writing
9. Draw evidence from literary or informational texts to support analysis, reflection, and research. *(Writing: Personal Essay)*

Speaking and Listening
1.a. Come to discussions prepared, having read or researched material under study; explicitly draw on that preparation by referring to evidence on the topic, text, or issue to probe and reflect on ideas under discussion. **b.** Follow rules for collegial discussions and decision-making, track progress toward specific goals and deadlines, and define individual roles as needed. **c.** Pose questions that connect the ideas of several speakers and respond to others' questions and comments with relevant evidence, observations, and ideas. **d.** Acknowledge new information expressed by others, and, when warranted, qualify or justify their own views in light of the evidence presented. *(Speaking and Listening: Panel Discussion)*

Language
1.c. Form and use verbs in the indicative, imperative, interrogative, conditional, and subjunctive mood. *(Conventions: Tense and Mood of Verbs)*

Reading Skill: Make Inferences

An **inference** is a logical assumption about information based on ideas that the writer suggests but does not state directly. Making inferences is a way of "reading between the lines" of a story to discover the meaning behind actions and events. As you read, **identify connections to make inferences about the author's meaning.**

- Connect characters' actions to reasons and outcomes.
- Connect story events to reasons and outcomes.
- Connect to your own experiences and ideas.

Then, ask yourself what meaning the author is suggesting.

Using the Strategy: Inference Chart

Use an **inference chart** like the one shown to help you make inferences by connecting events in the story.

Event		Event		Inference
A boy spends all of his money on candy and does not share.	**+**	He gets sick from eating too much candy.	**=**	Author wants to show that people should not be selfish.

Literary Analysis: Theme

The **theme** of a literary work is its central idea, insight, or message. This central idea is often expressed as a generalization about life or people. A theme can be drawn from the specific experiences of characters in a certain setting, or from the outcomes of events.

- A **stated theme** is expressed directly in the story.
- More often, a theme is **unstated,** or **implied.** You infer the theme from characters' experiences and from story events.

As you read, notice how a theme is developed by a story's characters, setting, and plot. Remember, readers can sometimes find different themes in the same work of literature. Each interpretation of a theme is valid, as long as it can be adequately supported with details from the text.

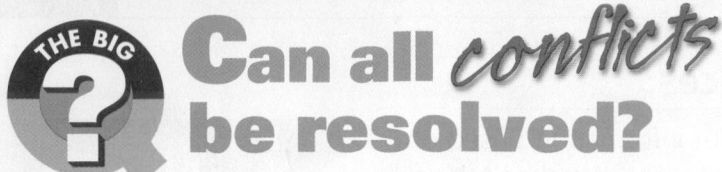

Can all *conflicts* be resolved?

Writing About the Big Question

In "Thank You, M'am," a teenager attempts to commit a crime and is completely unprepared for his victim's reaction. Use this sentence starter to develop your ideas about the Big Question.

> The best way to convince someone not to commit a crime of robbery or **violence** is to _____.

While You Read Look for changes in the relationship between the teenager and the victim.

Vocabulary

Read each word and its definition. Decide whether you know the word well, know it a little bit, or do not know it all. After you read, see how your knowledge of each word has increased.

- **slung** (sluŋ) *v.* hung loosely (p. 388) *As she walked away, she <u>slung</u> her backpack casually over one shoulder.*

- **frail** (frāl) *adj.* slender and delicate (p. 389) *The thin old woman appeared <u>frail</u> and helpless. frailty n.*

- **contact** (kän´ takt) *n.* touching; communication (p. 389) *Her <u>contact</u> with the icy water made her shiver.*

- **presentable** (prē zent´ ə bəl) *adj.* neat enough to be seen by others (p. 391) *His mother asked him to change into a cleaner, more <u>presentable</u> shirt. presentation n. present v.*

- **mistrusted** (mis´ trust´ əd) *v.* lacked confidence in (p. 391) *Daryl <u>mistrusted</u> the person who was trying to sell him the used car. mistrust n. trust v.*

- **barren** (bar´ ən) *adj.* empty; bare (p. 392) *The treeless prairie was scorched and <u>barren</u>. barrenness n.*

Word Study

The **Anglo-Saxon prefix *mis-*** means "opposite," "badly," or "wrongly."

In this story, a character learns the difference between being trusted and **mistrusted**, and quickly finds that he prefers the feeling of being trusted.

Meet
Langston Hughes
(1902–1967)

Author of
Thank You,
M'am

In the 1920s and 1930s, a young writer named Langston Hughes was at the forefront of an explosion of creativity in literature and the arts known as the Harlem Renaissance. Readers first noticed Hughes's talent in 1921, when his poem "The Negro Speaks of Rivers" was published shortly after he graduated from high school.

A Varied Career While working on a merchant ship, Hughes continued writing. In 1926, his first collection of poems was published as *The Weary Blues.* Hughes went on to have a long career as a writer. He wrote poetry, short stories, children's books—and even an opera.

DID YOU KNOW?

Hughes's work was beloved for its familiar characters like Jesse B. Simple, an average man who told his troubles to anyone who would listen.

BACKGROUND FOR THE STORY

Urban Living

"Thank You, M'am" is set in an urban neighborhood similar to the New York City neighborhood in which Langston Hughes lived. New York City's population grew rapidly in the early part of the twentieth century. Many single-family houses were converted into modest, smaller apartments, like the "kitchenette" apartment—one large room with its own mini-kitchen in the corner—where Mrs. Jones in the story lives.

Thank You, M'am

Langston Hughes

Vocabulary
slung (sluŋ) *v.*
hung loosely

Make Inferences
From the description here, what can you infer about the woman's personality? Provide two details to support your view.

She was a large woman with a large purse that had everything in it but a hammer and nails. It had a long strap, and she carried it slung across her shoulder. It was about eleven o'clock at night, dark, and she was walking alone, when a boy ran up behind her and tried to snatch her purse. The strap broke with the sudden single tug the boy gave it from behind. But the boy's weight and the weight of the purse combined caused him to lose his balance. Instead of taking off full blast as he had hoped, the boy fell on his back on the sidewalk and his legs flew up. The large woman simply turned around and kicked him right square in his blue-jeaned sitter. Then she reached down, picked the boy up by his shirt front, and shook him until his teeth rattled.

After that the woman said, "Pick up my pocketbook, boy, and give it here."

She still held him tightly. But she bent down enough to permit him to stoop and pick up her purse. Then she said, "Now ain't you ashamed of yourself?"

Firmly gripped by his shirt front, the boy said, "Yes'm."

The woman said, "What did you want to do it for?"

The boy said, "I didn't aim to."

She said, "You a lie!"

By that time two or three people passed, stopped, turned to look, and some stood watching.

"If I turn you loose, will you run?" asked the woman.

"Yes'm," said the boy.

"Then I won't turn you loose," said the woman. She did not release him.

"Lady, I'm sorry," whispered the boy.

"Um-hum! Your face is dirty. I got a great mind to wash your face for you. Ain't you got nobody home to tell you to wash your face?"

"No'm," said the boy.

"Then it will get washed this evening," said the large woman, starting up the street, dragging the frightened boy behind her.

He looked as if he were fourteen or fifteen, frail and willow-wild, in tennis shoes and blue jeans.

The woman said, "You ought to be my son. I would teach you right from wrong. Least I can do right now is to wash your face. Are you hungry?"

"No'm," said the being-dragged boy. "I just want you to turn me loose."

"Was I bothering *you* when I turned that corner?" asked the woman.

"No'm."

"But you put yourself in contact with *me*," said the woman. "If you think that that contact is not going to last awhile, you got another thought coming. When I get through with you, sir, you are going to remember Mrs. Luella Bates Washington Jones."

◀ **Critical Viewing**
Would it be easy to "disappear" on a city street like the one shown in the picture? Explain. **[Analyze]**

Theme
What is the woman's attitude toward the boy? How does the boy view the woman?

Vocabulary
frail (frāl) *adj.* slender and delicate

contact (kän´ takt) *n.* touching; communication

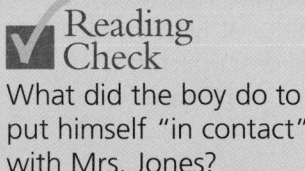
Reading Check
What did the boy do to put himself "in contact" with Mrs. Jones?

▲ **Critical Viewing**
What details in the painting suggest traits of Mrs. Jones, as described in the story? **[Connect]**

Sweat popped out on the boy's face and he began to struggle. Mrs. Jones stopped, jerked him around in front of her, put a half nelson[1] about his neck, and continued to drag him up the street. When she got to her door, she dragged the boy inside, down a hall, and into a large kitchenette-furnished room at the rear of the house. She switched on the light and left the door open. The boy could hear other roomers laughing and talking in the large house. Some of their doors were open, too, so he knew he and the woman were not alone. The woman still had him by the neck in the middle of her room.

She said, "What is your name?"

"Roger," answered the boy.

"Then, Roger, you go to that sink and wash your face," said the woman, whereupon she turned him loose—at last. Roger looked at the door—looked at the woman—looked at the door—*and went to the sink.*

"Let the water run until it gets warm," she said. "Here's a clean towel."

"You gonna take me to jail?" asked the boy, bending over the sink.

"Not with that face, I would not take you nowhere," said the woman. "Here I am trying to get home to cook me a bite to eat, and you snatch my pocketbook! Maybe you ain't been to your supper either, late as it be. Have you?"

"There's nobody home at my house," said the boy.

"Then we'll eat," said the woman. "I believe you're hungry—or been hungry—to try to snatch my pocketbook!"

---

1. half nelson wrestling hold in which an arm is placed under the opponent's armpit from behind with the palm of the hand pressed against the back of the neck.

"I want a pair of blue suede shoes,"[2] said the boy.

"Well, you didn't have to snatch *my* pocketbook to get some suede shoes," said Mrs. Luella Bates Washington Jones. "You could of asked me."

"M'am?"

The water dripping from his face, the boy looked at her. There was a long pause. A very long pause. After he had dried his face and not knowing what else to do, dried it again, the boy turned around, wondering what next. The door was open. He could make a dash for it down the hall. He could run, run, run, *run*!

The woman was sitting on the day bed. After awhile she said, "I were young once and I wanted things I could not get."

There was another long pause. The boy's mouth opened. Then he frowned, not knowing he frowned.

The woman said, "Um-hum! You thought I was going to say *but*, didn't you? You thought I was going to say, *but I didn't snatch people's pocketbooks*. Well, I wasn't going to say that." Pause. Silence. "I have done things, too, which I would not tell you, son—neither tell God, if He didn't already know. Everybody's got something in common. So you set down while I fix us something to eat. You might run that comb through your hair so you will look presentable."

In another corner of the room behind a screen was a gas plate and an icebox. Mrs. Jones got up and went behind the screen. The woman did not watch the boy to see if he was going to run now, nor did she watch her purse, which she left behind her on the day bed. But the boy took care to sit on the far side of the room, away from her purse, where he thought she could easily see him out of the corner of her eye if she wanted to. He did not trust the woman *not* to trust him. And he did not want to be mistrusted now.

"Do you need somebody to go to the store," asked the boy, "maybe to get some milk or something?"

"Don't believe I do," said the woman, "unless you just want sweet milk yourself. I was going to make cocoa out of this canned milk I got here."

"That will be fine," said the boy.

She heated some lima beans and ham she had in the icebox, made the cocoa, and set the table. The woman did not

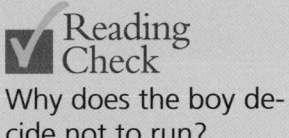
---

2. **blue suede** (swād) **shoes** style of shoes worn by "hipsters" in the 1940s and 1950s; made famous in a song sung by Elvis Presley.

ask the boy anything about where he lived, or his folks, or anything else that would embarrass him. Instead, as they ate, she told him about her job in a hotel beauty shop that stayed open late, what the work was like, and how all kinds of women came in and out, blondes, redheads, and Spanish. Then she cut him a half of her ten-cent cake.

"Eat some more, son," she said.

When they were finished eating, she got up and said, "Now here, take this ten dollars and buy yourself some blue suede shoes. And next time, do not make the mistake of latching onto *my* pocketbook *nor nobody else's*—because shoes got by devilish ways will burn your feet. I got to get my rest now. But from here on in, son, I hope you will behave yourself."

She led him down the hall to the front door and opened it. "Good night! Behave yourself, boy!" she said, looking out into the street as he went down the steps.

The boy wanted to say something other than, "Thank you, m'am," to Mrs. Luella Bates Washington Jones, but although his lips moved, he couldn't even say that as he turned at the foot of the barren stoop and looked up at the large woman in the door. Then she shut the door.

Theme
Why does Mrs. Jones give Roger money for shoes instead of turning him over to the police?

Vocabulary
barren (bar´ ən) *adj.* empty; bare

Critical Thinking

1. **Key Ideas and Details (a)** What does Roger think Mrs. Jones is going to do with him? **(b) Contrast:** What does Mrs. Jones do and say instead to win Roger's trust? Why?

2. **Key Ideas and Details (a)** What do Mrs. Jones and Roger talk about during their meal? **(b) Draw Conclusions:** Why do you think Mrs. Jones avoids asking Roger personal questions?

3. **Key Ideas and Details (a)** What does Roger say or do as he leaves the apartment? **(b) Interpret:** Why is he unable to say what he wants to say? **(c) Speculate:** What more does he want to say?

4. **Integration of Knowledge and Ideas (a)** How does the relationship between the two characters change? **(b)** What effect might Mrs. Jones's action have on Roger's future behavior? *[Connect to the Big Question: Can all conflicts be resolved?]*

Cite textual evidence to support your responses.

Reading Skill: Make Inferences

1. (a) What is the connection between what Roger wants and what he does to Mrs. Jones? **(b)** What is the outcome of his attempt to steal her purse? **(c)** What **inference** can you make about the author's message concerning stealing? List details from the text that support your inference.

Literary Analysis: Theme

2. Integration of Knowledge and Ideas (a) Using a chart like this one, identify a **theme** of this story and indicate whether it is **stated** or **implied. (b)** In the second column, support your interpretation with details from the story that show how the theme is developed. **(c)** Discuss your response with a partner. Then, in the third column, record whether your interpretation changed.

Theme (stated or implied)	Details	Did My View Change?

Vocabulary

Acquisition and Use Respond using a vocabulary word from the list on page 386. Explain your answers.

1. Which word describes something that can spread a cold?

2. Which word describes how you should look at an important function?

3. Which word describes a poor place to plant a cornfield?

4. Which word describes a way to carry a purse or bag?

5. Which word describes someone who is fragile?

6. Which word describes one in whom others lack confidence?

Word Study Use context and what you know about the **Anglo-Saxon prefix *mis-*** to answer these questions.

1. Why might you hope that your records have not been *misfiled*?

2. Is someone who experiences *misfortune* likely to be happy?

Word Study

The **Anglo-Saxon prefix *mis-*** means "opposite," "badly," or "wrongly."

Apply It Explain how the prefix ***mis-*** contributes to the meaning of these words. Consult a dictionary if necessary.

misdirect
mistrial
misrule

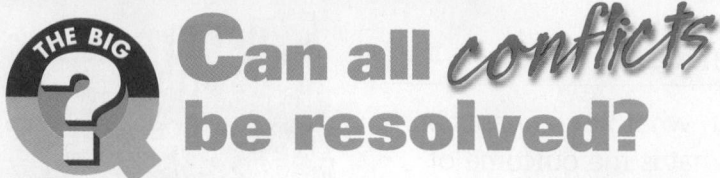 **Can all** *conflicts* **be resolved?**

Writing About the Big Question

In "The Story-Teller," a passenger entertains three bored children on a train ride by telling them an unusual story. Use this sentence starter to develop your ideas about the Big Question.

When children are bored, they can **irritate** others by _____
_____.

One way to amuse a child is _____.

While You Read Consider the conflict in the bachelor's story. Look for evidence that his story is not a typical fairy tale.

Vocabulary

Read each word and its definition. Decide whether you know the word well, know it a little bit, or do not know it at all. After you read, see how your knowledge of each word has increased.

- **persistent** (pər sist´ ənt) *adj.* continuing to happen, especially for longer than is usual or desirable (p. 397) *The persistent car alarm kept her awake.* persistently *adv.* persistence *n.*

- **inevitable** (in ev´ i tə bəl) *adj.* certain to happen (p. 397) *The track was so wet, it was inevitable that a runner would fall.* inevitably *adv.* inevitability *n.*

- **conviction** (kən vik´ shən) *n.* strong belief; certainty (p. 398) *He argued with conviction that his idea was the best.*

- **suppressed** (sə prest´) *v.* stopped from showing feelings or from acting a certain way (p. 400) *She suppressed the urge to laugh when she won the game.* suppression *n.*

- **immensely** (i mens´ lē) *adv.* greatly (p. 401) *Alicia found it immensely satisfying to say, "I told you so."* immensity *n.* immense *adj.*

- **assail** (ə sāl´) *v.* attack with arguments, questions, or doubts (p. 402) *We agreed not to assail the public official with questions about the scandal.* assault *n.*

Word Study

The **Latin prefix** *per-* means "thoroughly" or "throughout."

In this story, three bored children ask questions of their aunt in order to keep themselves entertained. They are **persistent** and keep asking question after question.

Meet
Saki (H. H. Munro)
(1870–1916)

Author of
The Story-Teller

Long before celebrities began to use single names, H. H. (Hector Hugh) Munro became famous under the pen name "Saki." Born to British parents in Burma (now Myanmar), he was raised in England by his aunts. Munro worked as a foreign correspondent and political writer before beginning to write the clever short stories for which he is famous.

Making Fun of Society Munro's stories poke fun at the manners and behavior of society in late nineteenth- and early twentieth-century England. His stories often end with jokes or surprise endings. Sometimes his humor is cruel or tinged with horror. These characteristics stood out and made Saki popular in an era which was more formal than ours.

DID YOU KNOW?
During World War I, when he was in his forties, Munro enlisted in the British military. He was killed in action in France in 1916.

BACKGROUND FOR THE STORY
English Trains

"The Story-Teller" takes place in a railroad car, or "carriage," around 1900. Trains on English railways, especially at that time, were built differently from modern American trains. Cars were divided into smaller compartments, each with its own doors and seating for four or six people. Trains also were divided into luxurious first-class carriages and more crowded, less comfortable, second- and third-class cars.

The Story-Teller

Saki

▲ Critical Viewing
What does this painting tell you about travel in the late nineteenth century? **[Infer]**

It was a hot afternoon, and the railway carriage was correspondingly sultry, and the next stop was at Templecombe, nearly an hour ahead. The occupants of the carriage were a small girl, and a smaller girl, and a small boy. An aunt belonging to the children occupied one corner seat, and the further corner seat on the opposite side was occupied by a bachelor who was a stranger to their party, but the small girls and the small boy emphatically occupied the compartment. Both the aunt and the children were conversational in a limited, persistent way, reminding one of the attentions of a housefly that refused to be discouraged. Most of the aunt's remarks seemed to begin with "Don't," and nearly all of the children's remarks began with "Why?" The bachelor said nothing out loud.

"Don't, Cyril, don't," exclaimed the aunt, as the small boy began smacking the cushions of the seat, producing a cloud of dust at each blow.

"Come and look out of the window," she added.

The child moved reluctantly to the window. "Why are those sheep being driven out of that field?" he asked.

"I expect they are being driven to another field where there is more grass," said the aunt weakly.

"But there is lots of grass in that field," protested the boy; "there's nothing else but grass there. Aunt, there's lots of grass in that field."

"Perhaps the grass in the other field is better," suggested the aunt fatuously.[1]

"Why is it better?" came the swift, inevitable question.

"Oh, look at those cows!" exclaimed the aunt. Nearly every field along the line had contained cows or bullocks, but she spoke as though she were drawing attention to a rarity.

"Why is the grass in the other field better?" persisted Cyril.

The frown on the bachelor's face was deepening to a scowl. He was a hard, unsympathetic man, the aunt decided in her mind. She was utterly unable to come to any satisfactory decision about the grass in the other field.

The smaller girl created a diversion by beginning to recite "On the Road to Mandalay."[2] She only knew the first line, but she put her limited knowledge to the fullest possible use. She repeated the line over and over again in a dreamy but resolute and very audible voice; it seemed to the bachelor as though someone had had a bet with her that she could not repeat the line aloud two thousand times without stopping. Whoever it was who had made the wager was likely to lose his bet.

"Come over here and listen to a story," said the aunt, when the bachelor had looked twice at her and once at the communication cord. ●

---

1. **fatuously** (fach´ ‾o‾o wəs lē) *adv.* in a silly or foolish way.
2. **"On the Road to Mandalay"** popular poem by Rudyard Kipling, later a song. Its first lines are: "On the road to Mandalay, where the flyin' fishes play / An' the dawn comes up like thunder outer China 'crost the bay!"

Vocabulary
persistent (pər sist´ ənt) *adj.* continuing to happen, especially for longer than is usual or desirable

Vocabulary
inevitable (in ev´ i tə bəl) *adj.* certain to happen

Make Inferences
What can you infer from this passage about the relationship between the children and their aunt? Why?

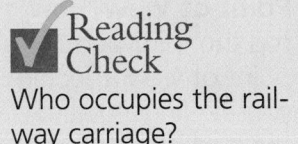
Reading Check
Who occupies the railway carriage?

Theme
What does the children's reaction suggest about the kind of stories the aunt tells?

The children moved listlessly[3] toward the aunt's end of the carriage. Evidently her reputation as a story-teller did not rank high in their estimation.

In a low, confidential voice, interrupted at frequent intervals by loud, petulant[4] questions from her listeners, she began an unenterprising and deplorably[5] uninteresting story about a little girl who was good, and made friends with everyone on account of her goodness, and was finally saved from a mad bull by a number of rescuers who admired her moral character.

"Wouldn't they have saved her if she hadn't been good?" demanded the bigger of the small girls. It was exactly the question that the bachelor had wanted to ask.

"Well, yes," admitted the aunt lamely, "but I don't think they would have run quite so fast to her help if they had not liked her so much."

Vocabulary
conviction (kən vik′ shən) *n.* strong belief; certainty

"It's the stupidest story I've ever heard," said the bigger of the small girls, with immense conviction.

"I didn't listen after the first bit, it was so stupid," said Cyril.

The smaller girl made no actual comment on the story, but she had long ago recommenced a murmured repetition of her favorite line.

"You don't seem to be a success as a story-teller," said the bachelor suddenly from his corner.

Make Inferences
What do the aunt and the bachelor think of each other?

The aunt bristled in instant defense at this unexpected attack.

"It's a very difficult thing to tell stories that children can both understand and appreciate," she said stiffly.

"I don't agree with you," said the bachelor.

"Perhaps *you* would like to tell them a story," was the aunt's retort.

"Tell us a story," demanded the bigger of the small girls.

"Once upon a time," began the bachelor, "there was a little girl called Bertha, who was extraordinarily good."

Spiral Review
Point of View How has the third-person point of view affected your feelings toward the bachelor up until this point in the story?

The children's momentarily aroused interest began at once to flicker; all stories seemed dreadfully alike, no matter who told them.

"She did all that she was told, she was always truthful, she kept her clothes clean, ate milk puddings as though they

---

3. **listlessly** (list′ ləs lē) *adv.* without energy or enthusiasm.
4. **petulant** (pech′ oo lənt) *adj.* peevishly impatient.
5. **deplorably** (dē plôr′ ə blē) *adv.* miserably; wretchedly.

were jam tarts, learned her lessons perfectly, and was polite in her manners."

"Was she pretty?" asked the bigger of the small girls.

"Not as pretty as any of you." said the bachelor, "but she was horribly good."

There was a wave of reaction in favor of the story; the word horrible in connection with goodness was a novelty that commended itself. It seemed to introduce a ring of truth that was absent from the aunt's tales of infant life.

"She was so good," continued the bachelor, "that she won several medals for goodness, which she always wore, pinned on to her dress. There was a medal for obedience, another medal for punctuality, and a third for good behavior. They were large metal medals and they clinked against one another as she walked. No other child in town where she lived had as many as three medals, so everybody knew that she must be an extra good child."

"Horribly good," quoted Cyril.

"Everybody talked about her goodness, and the Prince of the country got to hear about it, and he said that as she was so very good she might be allowed once a week to walk in his park, which was just outside the town. It was a beautiful park, and no children were ever allowed in it, so it was a great honor for Bertha to be allowed to go there."

"Were there any sheep in the park?" demanded Cyril.

"No," said the bachelor, "there were no sheep."

"Why weren't there any sheep?" came the inevitable question arising out of that answer.

The aunt permitted herself a smile, which might almost have been described as a grin.

"There were no sheep in the park," said the bachelor, "because the Prince's mother had once had a dream that her son would either be killed by a sheep or else by a clock falling on him. For that reason the Prince never kept a sheep in his park or a clock in his palace."

Make Inferences
What details support the inference that the bachelor understands children?

"She was so good," continued the bachelor, "that she won several medals for goodness..."

Make Inferences
Why do you think the aunt smiles?

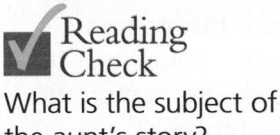
Reading Check
What is the subject of the aunt's story?

▶ **Critical Viewing**
How do these pigs
resemble those
in the bachelor's
story? **[Connect]**

Vocabulary
suppressed (sə prest´)
v. stopped from show-
ing feelings or from
acting a certain way

The aunt suppressed a gasp of admiration.

"Was the Prince killed by a sheep or by a clock?" asked Cyril.

"He is still alive, so we can't tell whether the dream will come true," said the bachelor unconcernedly; "anyway, there were no sheep in the park, but there were lots of little pigs running all over the place."

"What color were they?"

"Black with white faces, white with black spots, black all over, gray with white patches, and some were white all over."

The story-teller paused to let a full idea of the park's treasures sink into the children's imaginations; then he resumed:

"Bertha was rather sorry to find that there were no flowers in the park. She had promised her aunts, with tears in her eyes, that she would not pick any of the kind Prince's flowers, and she had meant to keep her promise, so of course it made her feel silly to find that there were no flowers to pick."

"Why weren't there any flowers?"

"Because the pigs had eaten them all," said the bachelor promptly. "The gardeners had told the Prince that you couldn't have pigs and flowers, so he decided to have pigs and no flowers."

Make Inferences
What can you infer from
the children's murmur
of approval?

There was a murmur of approval at the excellence of the Prince's decision; so many people would have decided the other way.

"There were lots of other delightful things in the park. There were ponds with gold and blue and green fish in them, and trees with beautiful parrots that said clever things at a moment's notice, and hummingbirds that hummed all the popular tunes of the day. Bertha walked up and down and enjoyed herself immensely, and thought to herself: 'If I were not so extraordinarily good, I should not have been allowed to come into this beautiful park and enjoy all that there is to be seen in it,' and her three medals clinked against one another as she walked and helped to remind her how very good she really was. Just then an enormous wolf came prowling into the park to see if it could catch a fat little pig for its supper."

"What color was it?" asked the children, amid an immediate quickening of interest.

"Mud color all over, with a black tongue and pale gray eyes that gleamed with unspeakable ferocity. The first thing that it saw in the park was Bertha; her pinafore[6] was so spotlessly white and clean that it could be seen from a great distance. Bertha saw the wolf and saw that it was stealing toward her, and she began to wish that she had never been allowed to come into the park. She ran as hard as she could, and the wolf came after her with huge leaps and bounds. She managed to reach a shrubbery of myrtle bushes, and she hid herself in one of the thickest of the bushes. The wolf came sniffing among the branches, its black tongue lolling out of its mouth and its pale gray eyes glaring with rage. Bertha was terribly frightened, and thought to herself: 'If I had not been so extraordinarily good, I should have been safe in the town at this moment.' However, the scent of the myrtle was so strong that the wolf could not sniff out where Bertha was hiding, and the bushes were so thick that he might have hunted about in them for a long time without catching sight of her, so he thought he might as well go off and catch a little pig instead. Bertha was trembling very much at having the wolf prowling and sniffing so near her, and as she trembled the medal for obedience clinked against the medals for good conduct and punctuality. The wolf was just moving away when he heard the sound of the medals clinking and stopped to listen; they clinked again in a bush quite near him. He dashed into the bush, his pale gray eyes gleaming with ferocity and triumph, and dragged Bertha out and devoured her to the last morsel. All that was left of her were her shoes, bits of clothing, and the three medals for goodness."

---

6. **pinafore** (pin´ ə fôr´) *n.* sleeveless apronlike garment worn over a dress.

Vocabulary
immensely (i mens´ lē) *adv.* greatly

Theme
How is the message of the bachelor's story different from the message of the aunt's story?

Reading Check
What kinds of things were in the park?

Theme
How might the children's enjoyment of the bachelor's story connect to a possible theme of the entire work?

Vocabulary
assail (ə sāl´) *v.* attack with arguments, questions, or doubts

"Were any of the little pigs killed?"

"No, they all escaped."

"The story began badly," said the smaller of the small girls, "but it had a beautiful ending."

"It is the most beautiful story that I ever heard," said the bigger of the small girls, with immense decision.

"It is the *only* beautiful story I have ever heard," said Cyril.

A dissentient[7] opinion came from the aunt.

"A most improper story to tell to young children! You have undermined the effect of years of careful teaching."

"At any rate," said the bachelor, collecting his belongings preparatory to leaving the carriage, "I kept them quiet for ten minutes, which was more than you were able to do."

"Unhappy woman!" he observed to himself as he walked down the platform of Templecombe station; "for the next six months or so those children will assail her in public with demands for an improper story!"

---

7. dissentient (di sen´ shənt) *adj.* differing from the majority.

Critical Thinking

© **1. Key Ideas and Details** **(a)** What questions do the children ask their aunt? **(b) Analyze:** Why are the children unsatisfied with her answers? **(c) Evaluate:** How well does the aunt understand children? Explain.

© **2. Key Ideas and Details** **(a)** How does the bachelor respond to the aunt's story? **(b) Analyze:** Is he more sympathetic with the aunt or with the children? Support your response with examples from the story.

© **3. Key Ideas and Details** **(a) Compare and Contrast:** How are the two storytellers' motives, or reasons behind their actions, similar? How are they different? **(b) Draw Conclusions:** Why do the children like the bachelor's story better than the aunt's? **(c) Evaluate:** Do you agree that the bachelor's story is "improper" for children?

© **4. Integration of Knowledge and Ideas** Compare the conflict and resolution in the bachelor's story to those in fairy tales that you have read. **(a)** How are they similar? **(b)** How are they different? *[Connect to the Big Question: Can all conflicts be resolved?]*

Cite textual evidence to support your responses.

Reading Skill: Make Inferences

1. (a) What is the connection between the behavior of the children and the bachelor's decision to amuse them with a story? **(b)** What is the outcome of the bachelor's attempt at story-telling? **(c)** What **inference** can you make about the author's message concerning the interests and upbringing of children?

Literary Analysis: Theme

© **2. Key Ideas and Details (a)** In the first column of the chart, identify a **theme** of this story and indicate whether it is **stated** or **implied. (b)** In the second column, support your interpretation with story details that show how the theme is developed. **(c)** Discuss your response with a partner. Then, in the third column, record whether the discussion changed your interpretation.

Theme (stated or implied)	Details	Did My View Change?

Vocabulary

© **Acquisition and Use** Respond using a vocabulary word from the list on page 394. Explain your answers.

1. Which word can refer to a ruling of "guilty" or a belief?

2. Which word is the opposite of *defend*?

3. Which word is the opposite of *slightly*?

4. Which word is similar in meaning to *restrained* or *stifled*?

5. Which word is the opposite of *avoidable*?

6. Which word describes one who is not easily discouraged?

Word Study Use the context of the sentences and what you know about the **Latin prefix per-** to answer these questions.

1. Would a person who *perseveres* be likely to give up easily?

2. Why should students *peruse* their notes before a test?

Word Study

The **Latin prefix per-** means "thoroughly" or "throughout."

Apply It Explain how the prefix *per-* contributes to the meanings of these words. Consult a dictionary if necessary.

pervasive
perpetual
permanence

Integrated Language Skills

Thank You, M'am • The Story-Teller

Conventions: Tense and Mood of Verbs

The **tense** of a verb shows the time of an action. The **mood** of a verb shows the speaker's attitude toward the action.

The **perfect tense** describes an action that was or will be completed at a certain time. The **subjunctive mood** is used to express a wish or a condition that is contrary to fact, as in the following example: *If he were faster, he would have won.*

Verb Tense	Own (owned)
Present Perfect: action in the past that continues up to the present **have + past participle**	I *have owned* this red bike for two years.
Past Perfect: action in the past that ended **had + past participle**	I *had owned* one like it a few years earlier.
Future Perfect: action in the future that will have ended at a certain point in time **will have + past participle**	By next year, *I will have owned* three red bikes.

Practice A Identify the tense of each verb.

1. Roger had tried to snatch Mrs. Jones's purse.

2. Mrs. Jones had met boys like Roger.

3. By next April, Mrs. Jones will have worked in the hotel beauty shop for ten years.

4. Roger has wanted blue suede shoes since he saw a pair in a shop window.

Practice B Fill in the sentences with verbs in the perfect tense or in the subjunctive mood.

1. By the time the train reaches its destination, _____. (future perfect)

2. If the bachelor _____, the children would have become bored. (subjunctive)

3. The pigs _____ all the flowers a long time ago. (past perfect)

Ⓒ Reading Application Choose a sentence from the first paragraph of "Thank You, M'am" that is written in the past tense and change the verb to perfect tense.

Ⓒ Writing Application Using the following sentence as a model, write two sentences that follow this subjunctive "If/then" pattern: *If the story were less entertaining, the children would have misbehaved.*

PH WRITING COACH Further instruction and practice are available in *Prentice Hall Writing Coach.*

Writing

**Common Core
State Standards**

L.8.1.c; RL.8.2; W.8.9;
SL.8.1.a, SL.8.1.b, SL.8.1.c,
SL.8.1.d
[For the complete standards
wording, see page 384.]

Narrative Text Write a brief **personal essay** showing how a theme of "Thank You, M'am" or "The Story-Teller" applies to everyday life.

- First, identify a theme based on specific passages and events in the story. State the theme in your own words.

- Next, take note of experiences in your past that reflect the same theme.

- Finally, write the essay. In the introduction, provide a *thesis statement* that summarizes your insights. In the body of the essay, provide details that work together to create a *controlling impression* of your topic. Conclude by restating the story's theme and how it applies to everyday life.

Writing Workshop: *Work in Progress*

Prewriting for Narration Use the Characterization Freewrite from your writing portfolio. Underline the ideas about realistic characters that are most important. For two ideas, write a few notes about how you can apply these ideas to your own writing. Next, write a brief Character Sketch that uses the ideas and notes you have developed. Save this work in your writing portfolio.

Use this prewriting activity to prepare for the **Writing Workshop** on page 438.

Speaking and Listening

Comprehension and Collaboration Organize a **panel discussion** to explore the story that you read. If you read "Thank You, M'am," discuss whether you thought Mrs. Jones's actions were appropriate and realistic. If you read "The Story-Teller," discuss whether the bachelor should have told the young children such a gruesome story. Follow these steps:

- Ask one person to be the moderator, or leader, of the discussion. That person should ensure that everyone receives at least one opportunity to voice an opinion or interpretation.

- As part of the discussion, the moderator should ask each panelist to identify the theme of the story. Then, each panelist should judge the theme's effectiveness and justify that opinion.

- After the panel members have spoken, open up the discussion to the class. Encourage students to ask questions that will expand on, connect, and clarify points made in the discussion. For example, a student might ask questions that relate the story's message to his or her own experience or to another subject area.

PHLit
Online!
www.PHLitOnline.com

- Interactive graphic organizers
- Grammar tutorial
- Interactive journals

Test Practice: Reading

Make Inferences

Fiction Selection

Directions: *Read the selection. Then, answer the questions.*

Homer consulted with Adrian, the local pest control authority. "My garden is a mess!" he complained. "I've been working on it for years, making it perfect and learning how to keep the bugs and beetles away. But now I find big holes all over the ground! Last night I saw a pair of armadillos in the flower beds. Luckily, my dogs scared them off, but I'm afraid they'll come back. Can you help me keep the armadillos away from my garden?"

"There are several methods you can use," said Adrian. "I have repellents that work well and are not harmful to humans or pets. But did you know armadillos can actually be *good* for your garden? They eat bugs and lots of other pests."

1. Based on the passage, what inference can you make about the holes in the ground?
   A. Homer's dogs dug the holes.
   B. They were made by the armadillos.
   C. Homer dug them himself.
   D. Adrian dug them to get more business.

2. What can you infer about Homer?
   A. He always stays up late.
   B. He does not take care of his dogs.
   C. His garden is important to him.
   D. He grows his own vegetables.

3. What inference can you make about armadillos' behavior?
   A. They eat fruits and vegetables.
   B. They eat the same food as dogs.
   C. They dig holes in the ground to find food.
   D. They like to chase dogs.

4. Based on the passage, what is the most logical inference?
   A. Homer will stop gardening.
   B. Homer will find out more about the options Adrian mentions.
   C. Homer will ask someone else about pest control.
   D. Homer will decide to keep armadillos as pets.

Writing for Assessment

Write a short description of Adrian, based on details in the passage. Make inferences about Adrian, and include that information in your description.

Nonfiction Selection

Directions: *Read the selection. Then, answer the questions.*

Most gardeners do not like armadillos, those strange little mammals covered with a bonelike casing of "armor." However, armadillos can have a positive effect on a garden. Like its distant cousin the anteater, the armadillo enjoys eating ants. It will even eat fire ants. In fact, it eats all kinds of bugs, especially scarab beetles, which can be very destructive to gardens.

As the armadillo digs for grubs, worms, and other tasty meals, it leaves behind cone-shaped holes, three to four inches wide. The gardener who finds this annoying should keep in mind that the armadillo may be providing a service. It may be controlling several kinds of destructive insects, even as it disturbs the garden beds.

1. What can you infer about the reason for writing this essay?
   A. The author believes all gardens need armadillos.
   B. The author wants people to know that armadillos can help protect gardens.
   C. The author does not like armadillos.
   D. The author wants to entertain readers with facts about armadillos.

2. Which detail helps you infer that gardeners consider armadillos pests?
   A. Armadillos eat ants.
   B. Armadillos are related to anteaters.
   C. Armadillos control several types of insects.
   D. Armadillos leave holes in the ground.

3. Which detail shows that armadillos are helpful to gardeners?
   A. Armadillos are related to anteaters.
   B. Armadillos are covered with a bonelike casing.
   C. Armadillos eat destructive insects.
   D. Gardeners find armadillos annoying.

4. What inference can you make based on gardeners' feelings about armadillos?
   A. The holes armadillos dig are helpful to gardeners.
   B. Gardeners might not know that armadillos can help protect gardens.
   C. Insects can be destructive to garden plants.
   D. Armadillos can eat bugs without disturbing gardens.

Writing for Assessment

Connecting Across Texts

If Homer found scarab beetles or fire ants in his garden, how might his reaction to the armadillos be different? Write a short paragraph that uses details from both passages to support your ideas.

www.PHLitOnline.com
- Online practice
- Instant feedback

Reading for Information

Analyzing Arguments

Advertisements

 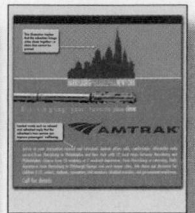  

Common Core State Standards

Reading Informational Text
8. Delineate and evaluate the argument and specific claims in a text, assessing whether the reasoning is sound and the evidence is relevant and sufficient; recognize when irrelevant evidence is introduced.

Language
6. Acquire and use accurately grade-appropriate general academic and domain-specific words and phrases; gather vocabulary knowledge when considering a word or phrase important to comprehension or expression.

Reading Skill: Evaluate Persuasive Appeals

Advertisements often use different types of persuasive appeals. The best way to **evaluate persuasive appeals** is to separate arguments that appeal to the emotions from those that appeal to the mind. Analyze the images and text of ads to understand their appeal. Then, weigh the reasons for and against buying the product. The chart shows common persuasive devices.

Device	Example	Explanation
Bandwagon appeal	Everyone loves Muncheez!	Words like *everyone* appeal to people's desire to belong.
Loaded language	Muncheez is incredibly delicious.	*Incredibly* and *delicious* are claims that cannot be proved.
Testimonials	Tina Idol says Muncheez gives her energy.	Just because a celebrity or "expert" says it, it does not mean the claim is true.
Generalizations	Muncheez is not only the best, it's the healthiest.	Claims that are too broad or vague cannot be proved.
Rhetorical questions	Wouldn't you like to stay healthy?	The answer is obvious, but it does not prove that the product is good.

Content-Area Vocabulary

These words appear in the selections that follow. You may also encounter them in other content-area texts.

- **destination** (des´ tə nā´ shən) *n.* place to which someone or something is going or is being sent
- **commuters** (kə myü´ tərz) *n.* people who travel regularly to and from work by train, bus, car, etc.

For EXTRA DAYS in

FLORIDA

Take the Train!

18-DAY ROUND-TRIP TICKET

to MIAMI $52.90 From Philadelphia

Also reduced 30-day and Season Tickets

Proportionate fares to other Southern Resorts

Have your car while there!

It, too, can ride on a railroad ticket (3.6c per mile)

Proportionate fares from other Stations

PENNSYLVANIA RAILROAD

This illustration implies that the advertiser brings cities closer together—a claim that cannot be proved.

HARRISBURGPHILADELPHIA**NEWYORK**

B r i n g i n g   y o u r   f a v o r i t e places **closer.**

Loaded words such as *relaxed* and *refreshed* imply that the advertiser's train service can improve passengers' well-being.

Arrive at your destination relaxed and refreshed. Amtrak offers safe, comfortable, affordable daily service from Harrisburg to Philadelphia and New York with 12 local stops between Harrisburg and Philadelphia. Choose from 10 weekday or 5 weekend departures, from Harrisburg or returning. Daily departures from Harrisburg to Pittsburgh, Chicago and most major cities. Ask about our discounts for children 2-15, seniors, students, commuters, AAA members, disabled travelers and government employees.

Call for details

JUMPSTART'S READ FOR THE RECORD

ROCKEFELLER CENTER CONCOURSE
THURSDAY, AUGUST 24 | 7AM - 2PM

Help us set a world record and work toward the day every
child in America enters school prepared to succeed.

Official Campaign Book
THE LITTLE ENGINE THAT COULD™

READ FOR THE RECORD
jumpstart

The advertisement conveys an image from a classic children's book to appeal to readers' emotions.

Illustration by Loren Long from The Little Engine That Could
by Watty Piper, TM & (c) 2005 Penguin Group (USA) Inc.

Comparing Arguments

© 1. **Key Ideas and Details** **(a)** For the Amtrak advertisement on page 410, identify the main argument and specific claims and write them down. **(b)** Does the ad support its claims with sufficient evidence, or does it rely on any of the techniques mentioned in the chart on page 408? Explain. **(c)** What textual and visual appeals do the other three ads use to influence the viewer?

Content-Area Vocabulary

2. **(a)** Explain how the Latin root -*mut*- contributes to the meaning of *commuter, mutate,* and *mutable*. **(b)** Use each word correctly in a sentence that shows its meaning.

⏱ Timed Writing

Argument: Advertisement

> **Audience**
> The prompt gives specific information about your audience. Use details in your ad that will appeal to this group.

Write a persuasive ad that will influence students in your grade to use a product or support an issue. Use at least two of the following techniques: bandwagon appeal, loaded language, testimonial, generalization, and rhetorical questions. (40 minutes)

> **Key Words**
> This list offers several persuasive techniques from which you can choose when writing your ad. Review these techniques on page 408.

5-Minute Planner

Complete these steps before you begin to write:

1. Read the prompt carefully to be sure you understand the assignment. Notice the audience you need to reach.

2. Decide if you will advertise a product or an issue.

3. Review each ad as a model, looking for style and content ideas.

4. Jot down two or three points to make in your ad. For each point, write a few key words that emphasize it. Use as many of the techniques on the list as possible. You can choose among these later.

5. Decide on a central idea to support with examples, arguments, and persuasive techniques. This idea should be the main reason a student would buy this product or support this issue. Finally, use your notes to draft your response.

Comparing Symbols

A **symbol** is a person, place, or thing that represents something beyond its literal meaning. For example, doves usually symbolize peace. To add depth and insight to their literary works, authors can use these strategies:

• Use existing symbols with commonly understood meanings.

• Create their own symbols and develop the symbols' meanings through descriptions, actions, and events of a story.

For many stories, understanding the **symbolism** helps you draw conclusions about the central idea, or **theme.** Symbols are often open to interpretation and may have more than one set meaning. The meaning of a symbol can become deeper and richer during the course of a work.

"The White Umbrella" and "The Medicine Bag" both use symbols to illustrate the recurring theme of how it feels to be caught between two worlds.

To discover what the symbols mean and how they connect to the theme, ask yourself questions like the ones shown in the chart.

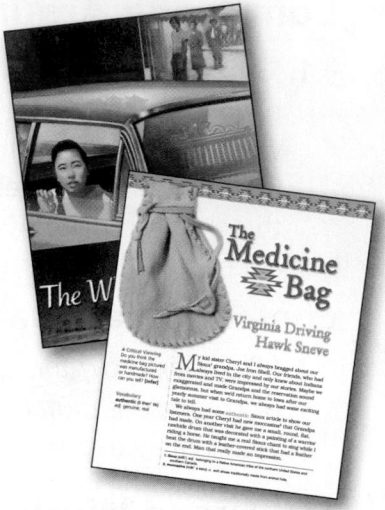

**Common Core
State Standards**

Reading Literature
4. Determine the meaning of words and phrases as they are used in a text, including figurative and connotative meanings; analyze the impact of specific word choices on meaning and tone, including analogies or allusions to other texts.

Writing
2. Write informative/explanatory texts to examine a topic and convey ideas, concepts, and information through the selection, organization, and analysis of relevant content.

9. Draw evidence from literary or informational texts to support analysis, reflection, and research. *(Timed Writing)*

	white umbrella	medicine bag
What does the object mean to the narrator?		
What cultural meaning does the object have?		
What is its significance for the plot and theme?		

PHLit Online!
www.PHLitOnline.com

• Vocabulary flashcards
• Interactive journals
• More about the authors

• Selection audio
• Interactive graphic organizers

Can all *conflicts* be resolved?

Writing About the Big Question

Both of these stories involve characters who struggle with feelings of embarrassment. Use this sentence starter to develop your ideas.

People are most likely to **react** with embarrassment when they _____.

Meet the Authors

Gish Jen (b. 1956)

Author of "The White Umbrella"

Gish Jen, the daughter of Chinese immigrants, grew up in Yonkers and Scarsdale, New York. When asked about her influences, Jen replied, "A fellow writer described my situation when he said that making fiction is like making soup. There's lots of different ingredients: some of the ingredients come from your life; some come from things you've read, or from other people's lives; many, many things you've just made up."

Virginia Driving Hawk Sneve (b. 1933)

Author of "The Medicine Bag"

Virginia Driving Hawk Sneve grew up on the Rosebud Reservation in South Dakota where she listened to storytellers tell traditional Sioux legends and folk tales.

A Mission to Educate As a Sioux mother, Sneve quickly realized that few children's books accurately portrayed Native American culture. She began writing in the early 1970s to correct this gap in literature. Sneve summarizes her award-winning career in this way: "[I hope to] show my reading audience that Native Americans have a proud past, a viable present, and a hopeful future."

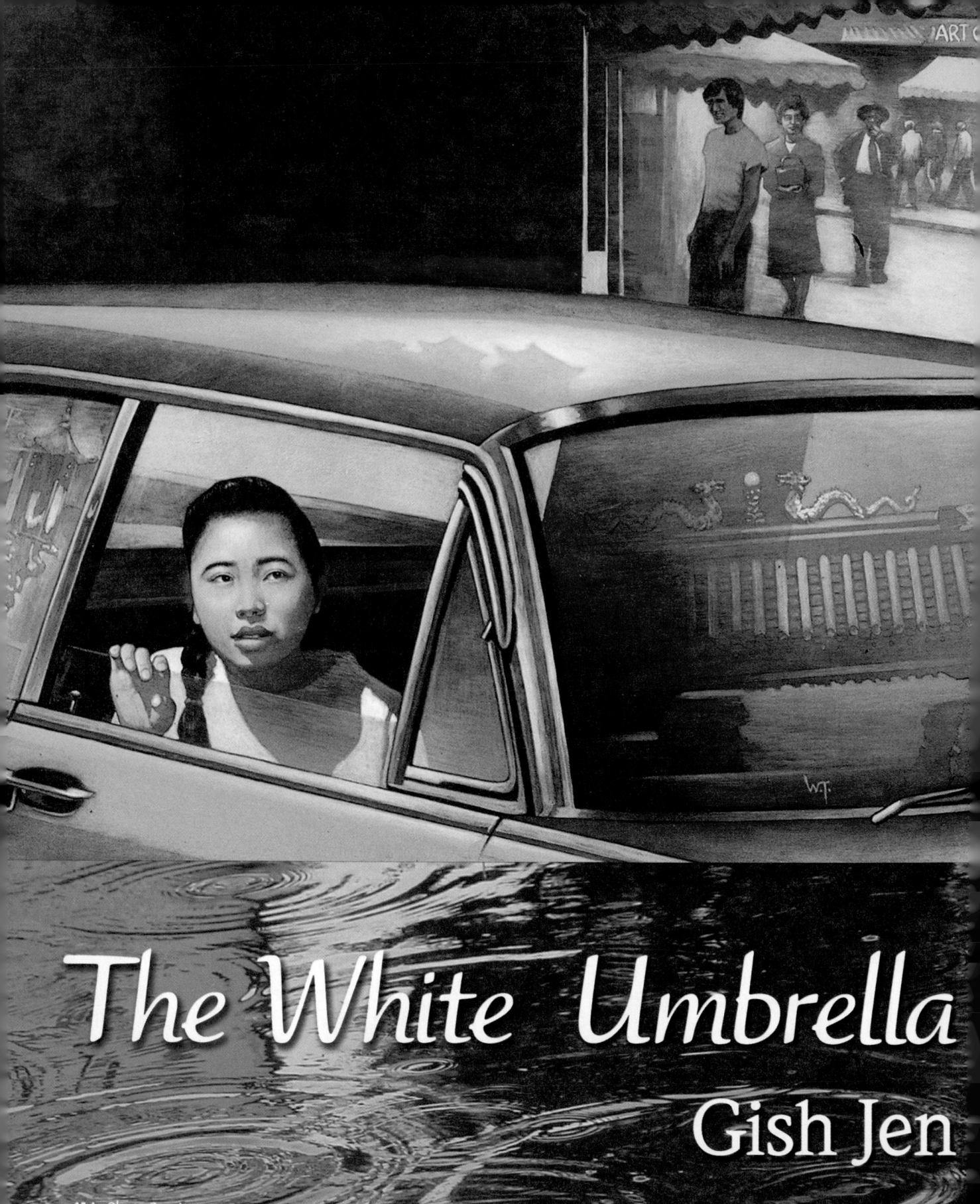

The White Umbrella

Gish Jen

When I was twelve, my mother went to work without telling me or my little sister.

"Not that we need the second income." The lilt of her accent drifted from the kitchen up to the top of the stairs, where Mona and I were listening.

"No," said my father, in a barely audible voice. "Not like the Lee family."

The Lees were the only other Chinese family in town. I remembered how sorry my parents had felt for Mrs. Lee when she started waitressing downtown the year before; and so when my mother began coming home late, I didn't say anything, and tried to keep Mona from saying anything either.

"But why shouldn't I?" she argued. "Lots of people's mothers work."

"Those are American people," I said.

"So what do you think we are? I can do the pledge of allegiance with my eyes closed."

Nevertheless, she tried to be discreet; and if my mother wasn't home by 5:30, we would start cooking by ourselves, to make sure dinner would be on time. Mona would wash the vegetables and put on the rice; I would chop.

For weeks we wondered what kind of work she was doing. I imagined that she was selling perfume, testing dessert recipes for the local newspaper. Or maybe she was working for the florist. Now that she had learned to drive, she might be delivering boxes of roses to people.

"I don't think so," said Mona as we walked to our piano lesson after school. "She would've hit something by now."

A gust of wind littered the street with leaves.

"Maybe we better hurry up," she went on, looking at the sky. "It's going to pour."

"But we're too early." Her lesson didn't begin until 4:00, mine until 4:30, so we usually tried to walk as slowly as we could. "And anyway, those aren't the kind of clouds that rain. Those are cumulus clouds."[1] ●

We arrived out of breath and wet.

"Oh, you poor, poor dears," said old Miss Crosman. "Why don't you call me the next time it's like this out? If your mother won't drive you, I can come pick you up."

"No, that's okay," I answered. Mona wrung her hair out

---

1. **cumulus** (kyoo′ mye les) **clouds** *n.* white clouds that usually indicate fair weather.

Symbol
Why might the girls' mother try to hide the fact that she is working?

Vocabulary
discreet (di skrēt′) *adj.* careful about what one says or does

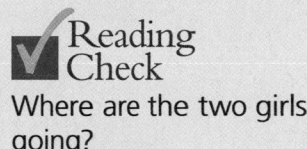
Reading Check
Where are the two girls going?

Vocabulary
credibility (kred´ ə bil´ i tē) *n.* believability

Symbol
Contrast the true story of how the girls got to the lesson with the symbolism of arriving in a convertible.

on Miss Crosman's rug. "We just couldn't get the roof of our car to close, is all. We took it to the beach last summer and got sand in the mechanism." I pronounced this last word carefully, as if the credibility of my lie depended on its middle syllable. "It's never been the same." I thought for a second. "It's a convertible."

"Well then make yourselves at home." She exchanged looks with Eugenie Roberts, whose lesson we were interrupting. Eugenie smiled good-naturedly. "The towels are in the closet across from the bathroom."

Huddling at the end of Miss Crosman's nine-foot leatherette couch, Mona and I watched Eugenie play. She was a grade ahead of me and, according to school rumor, had a boyfriend in high school. I believed it. . . . She had auburn hair, blue eyes, and, I noted with a particular pang, a pure white folding umbrella.

"I can't see," whispered Mona.

"So clean your glasses."

"My glasses *are* clean. You're in the way."

I looked at her. "They look dirty to me."

"That's because *your* glasses are dirty."

Eugenie came bouncing to the end of her piece.

"Oh! Just stupendous!" Miss Crosman hugged her, then looked up as Eugenie's mother walked in. "Stupendous!" she said again. "Oh! Mrs. Roberts! Your daughter has a gift, a real gift. It's an honor to teach her."

Mrs. Roberts, radiant with pride, swept her daughter out of the room as if she were royalty, born to the piano bench. Watching the way Eugenie carried herself, I sat up, and concentrated so hard on sucking in my stomach that I did not realize until the Robertses were gone that Eugenie had left her umbrella. As Mona began to play, I jumped up and ran to the window, meaning to call to them—only to see their brake lights flash then fade at the stop sign at the corner. As if to allow them passage, the rain had let up; a quivering sun lit their way.

The umbrella glowed like a scepter on the blue carpet while Mona, slumping over the keyboard, managed to eke out[2] a fair rendition of a catfight. At the end of the piece, Miss Crosman asked her to stand up.

"Stay right there," she said, then came back a minute later

---

2. **eke** (ēk) **out** *v.* barely manage to play.

with a towel to cover the bench. "You must be cold," she continued. "Shall I call your mother and have her bring over some dry clothes?"

"No," answered Mona. "She won't come because she . . ."

"She's too busy," I broke in from the back of the room.

"I see." Miss Crosman sighed and shook her head a little. "Your glasses are filthy, honey," she said to Mona. "Shall I clean them for you?"

Sisterly embarrassment seized me. Why hadn't Mona wiped her lenses when I told her to? As she resumed abuse of the piano, I stared at the umbrella. I wanted to open it, twirl it around by its slender silver handle; I wanted to dangle it from my wrist on the way to school the way the other girls did. I wondered what Miss Crosman would say if I offered to bring it to Eugenie at school tomorrow. She would be impressed with my consideration for others; Eugenie would be pleased to have it back; and I would have possession of the umbrella for an entire night. I looked at it again, toying with the idea of asking for one for Christmas. I knew, however, how my mother would react.

"Things," she would say. "What's the matter with a raincoat? All you want is things, just like an American." ●

Sitting down for my lesson, I was careful to keep the towel under me and sit up straight.

"I'll bet you can't see a thing either," said Miss Crosman, reaching for my glasses. "And you can relax, you poor dear." She touched my chest, in an area where she never would have touched Eugenie Roberts. "This isn't a boot camp."[3]

When Miss Crosman finally allowed me to start playing I played extra well, as well as I possibly could. See, I told her with my fingers. You don't have to feel sorry for me.

"That was wonderful," said Miss Crosman. "Oh! Just wonderful."

An entire constellation rose in my heart.

"And guess what," I announced proudly. "I have a surprise for you."

---

3. **boot camp** place where soldiers receive basic training under strict discipline.

> *I noted with a particular pang, a pure white folding umbrella.*

Symbol
What do her daydreams tell you about how the narrator views the white umbrella?

Symbol
What does the narrator think the white umbrella would symbolize to her mother?

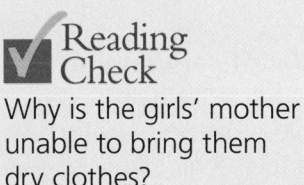
Reading Check
Why is the girls' mother unable to bring them dry clothes?

Then I played a second piece for her, a much more difficult one that she had not assigned.

"Oh! That was stupendous," she said without hugging me. "Stupendous! You are a genius, young lady. If your mother had started you younger, you'd be playing like Eugenie Roberts by now!"

I looked at the keyboard, wishing that I had still a third, even more difficult piece to play for her. I wanted to tell her that I was the school spelling bee champion, that I wasn't ticklish, that I could do karate.

"My mother is a concert pianist," I said.

She looked at me for a long moment, then finally, without saying anything, hugged me. I didn't say anything about bringing the umbrella to Eugenie at school. ●

The steps were dry when Mona and I sat down to wait for my mother.

"Do you want to wait inside?" Miss Crosman looked anxiously at the sky.

"No," I said. "Our mother will be here any minute."

"In a while," said Mona.

"Any minute," I said again, even though my mother had been at least twenty minutes late every week since she started working.

Symbol
Why is the ability to play the piano well so important to the narrator?

▶ **Critical Viewing**
What skills help people, like the narrator and the girls in this photo, play the piano well? **[Analyze]**

According to the church clock across the street we had been waiting twenty-five minutes when Miss Crosman came out again.

"Shall I give you ladies a ride home?"

"No," I said. "Our mother is coming any minute."

"Shall I at least give her a call and remind her you're here? Maybe she forgot about you."

"I don't think she forgot," said Mona.

"Shall I give her a call anyway? Just to be safe?"

"I bet she already left," I said. "How could she forget about us?"

Miss Crosman went in to call.

"There's no answer," she said, coming back out.

"See, she's on her way," I said.

"Are you sure you wouldn't like to come in?"

"No," said Mona.

"Yes," I said. I pointed at my sister. "She meant yes too. She meant no, she wouldn't like to go in."

Miss Crosman looked at her watch. "It's 5:30 now, ladies. My pot roast will be coming out in fifteen minutes. Maybe you'd like to come in and have some then?"

"My mother's almost here," I said. "She's on her way."

We watched and watched the street. I tried to imagine what my mother was doing; I tried to imagine her writing messages in the sky, even though I knew she was afraid of planes. I watched as the branches of Miss Crosman's big willow tree started to sway; they had all been trimmed to exactly the same height off the ground, so that they looked beautiful, like hair in the wind.

It started to rain.

"Miss Crosman is coming out again," said Mona.

"Don't let her talk you into going inside," I whispered.

"Why not?"

"Because that would mean Mom isn't really coming any minute."

"But she isn't," said Mona. "She's working."

"Shhh! Miss Crosman is going to hear you."

"She's working! She's working! She's working!"

I put my hand over her mouth, but she licked it, and so I was wiping my hand on my wet dress when the front door opened.

"We're getting even *wetter*," said Mona right away. "Wetter and wetter."

Symbol
Why does the narrator resist going inside?

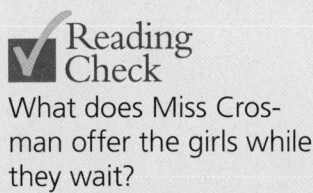

Reading Check
What does Miss Crosman offer the girls while they wait?

"Shall we all go in?" Miss Crosman pulled Mona to her feet. "Before you young ladies catch pneumonia? You've been out here an hour already."

"We're *freezing*." Mona looked up at Miss Crosman. "Do you have any hot chocolate? We're going to catch *pneumonia*."

"I'm not going in," I said. "My mother's coming any minute."

"Come on," said Mona. "Use your *noggin*."[4]

"Any minute."

"Come on, Mona," Miss Crosman opened the door. "Shall we get you inside first?"

"See you in the hospital," said Mona as she went in. "See you in the hospital with pneumonia." ●

I stared out into the empty street. The rain was pricking me all over; I was cold; I wanted to go inside. I wanted to be able to let myself go inside. If Miss Crosman came out again, I decided, I would go in.

She came out with a blanket and the white umbrella.

I could not believe that I was actually holding the umbrella, opening it. It sprang up by itself as if it were alive, as if that were what it wanted to do—as if it belonged in my hands, above my head. I stared up at the network of silver spokes, then spun the umbrella around and around and around. It was so clean and white that it seemed to glow, to illuminate everything around it.

"It's beautiful," I said.

Miss Crosman sat down next to me, on one end of the blanket. I moved the umbrella over so that it covered that too. I could feel the rain on my left shoulder and shivered. She put her arm around me.

"You poor, poor dear."

I knew that I was in store for another bolt of sympathy, and braced myself by staring up into the umbrella.

"You know, I very much wanted to have children when I was younger," she continued.

Symbol
What details in this paragraph indicate that the narrator sees the umbrella as something more than a useful object?

---

4. Use your *noggin* informal expression for "use your head" or "think."

"You did?"

She stared at me a minute. Her face looked dry and crusty, like day-old frosting.

"I did. But then I never got married."

I twirled the umbrella around again.

"This is the most beautiful umbrella I have ever seen," I said. "Ever, in my whole life."

"Do you have an umbrella?"

"No. But my mother's going to get me one just like this for Christmas."

"Is she? I tell you what. You don't have to wait until Christmas. You can have this one."

"But this one belongs to Eugenie Roberts," I protested. "I have to give it back to her tomorrow in school."

"Who told you it belongs to Eugenie? It's not Eugenie's. It's mine. And now I'm giving it to you, so it's yours."

"It is?"

She hugged me tighter. "That's right. It's all yours."

"It's mine?" I didn't know what to say. "Mine?" Suddenly I was jumping up and down in the rain. "It's beautiful! Oh! It's beautiful!" I laughed.

Miss Crosman laughed too, even though she was getting all wet.

"Thank you, Miss Crosman. Thank you very much. Thanks a zillion. It's beautiful. It's *stupendous!*"

"You're quite welcome," she said.

"Thank you," I said again, but that didn't seem like enough. Suddenly I knew just what she wanted to hear. "I wish you were my mother."

Right away I felt bad.

"You shouldn't say that," she said, but her face was opening into a huge smile as the lights of my mother's car cautiously turned the corner. I quickly collapsed the umbrella and put it up my skirt, holding onto it from the outside, through the material.

"Mona!" I shouted into the house. "Mona! Hurry up! Mom's here! I told you she was coming!"

Then I ran away from Miss Crosman, down to the curb. Mona came tearing up to my side as my mother neared the house. We both backed up a few feet, so that in case she went onto the curb, she wouldn't run us over.

Symbol
Why might Miss Crosman especially enjoy the narrator's response to her gift?

Reading Check
What does the narrator say to thank Miss Crosman for the umbrella?

Vocabulary
revelation (rev´ ə
lā´ shən) *n.* some-
thing that suddenly
becomes known

"But why didn't you go inside with Mona?" my mother asked on the way home. She had taken off her own coat to put over me, and had the heat on high.

"She wasn't using her noggin," said Mona, next to me in the back seat.

"I should call next time," said my mother. "I just don't like to say where I am."

That was when she finally told us that she was working as a check-out clerk in the A&P. She was supposed to be on the day shift, but the other employees were unreliable, and her boss had promised her a promotion if she would stay until the evening shift filled in.

For a moment no one said anything. Even Mona seemed to find the revelation disappointing.

"A promotion already!" she said, finally.

I listened to the windshield wipers.

"You're so quiet." My mother looked at me in the rear view mirror. "What's the matter?"

"I wish you would quit," I said after a moment.

She sighed. "The Chinese have a saying: one beam cannot hold the roof up."

"But Eugenie Roberts's father supports their family."

She sighed once more. "Eugenie Roberts's father is Eugenie Roberts's father," she said.

Symbol
Why does the narrator
hide the umbrella from
her mother?

As we entered the downtown area, Mona started leaning hard against me every time the car turned right, trying to push me over. Remembering what I had said to Miss Crosman, I tried to maneuver the umbrella under my leg so she wouldn't feel it.

"What's under your skirt?" Mona wanted to know as we came to a traffic light. My mother, watching us in the rear view mirror again, rolled slowly to a stop.

"What's the matter?" she asked.

"There's something under her skirt!" said Mona, pulling at me.

"Under her skirt?"

Meanwhile, a man crossing the street started to yell at us. "Who do you think you are, lady?" he said. "You're blocking the whole crosswalk."

We all froze. Other people walking by stopped to watch.

Spiral Review
Theme How might the
umbrella be connected
with a possible theme,
or central idea, of the
story?

"Didn't you hear me?" he went on, starting to thump on the hood with his fist. "Don't you speak English?"

My mother began to back up, but the car behind us honked. Luckily, the light turned green right after that. She sighed in relief.

"What were you saying, Mona?" she asked.

We wouldn't have hit the car behind us that hard if he hadn't been moving too, but as it was our car bucked violently, throwing us all first back and then forward.

"Uh oh," said Mona when we stopped. "*Another* accident."

I was relieved to have attention diverted from the umbrella. Then I noticed my mother's head, tilted back onto the seat. Her eyes were closed.

"Mom!" I screamed. "Mom! Wake up!"

She opened her eyes. "Please don't yell," she said. "Enough people are going to yell already."

"I thought you were dead," I said, starting to cry. "I thought you were dead."

She turned around, looked at me intently, then put her hand to my forehead.

"Sick," she confirmed. "Some kind of sick is giving you crazy ideas."

As the man from the car behind us started tapping on the window, I moved the umbrella away from my leg. Then Mona and my mother were getting out of the car. I got out after them; and while everyone else was inspecting the damage we'd done, I threw the umbrella down a sewer.

Critical Thinking

1. **Key Ideas and Details (a)** Why is the narrator's mother late to pick up the sisters? **(b) Infer:** Why is the narrator bothered by her mother's lateness? **(c) Analyze:** Why does she prevent her sister from explaining why their mother is late?

Cite textual evidence to support your responses.

2. **Key Ideas and Details (a) Infer:** Why does Miss Crosman give the narrator the umbrella? **(b) Deduce:** How does she feel about children?

3. **Integration of Knowledge and Ideas (a)** Why is the narrator embarrassed by her mother? **(b)** Does she feel guilty about her embarrassment? How do you know? **(c)** Do you think this conflict can be resolved? Explain your response. *[Connect to the Big Question: Can all conflicts be resolved?]*

The Medicine Bag

Virginia Driving Hawk Sneve

▲ **Critical Viewing**
Do you think the
medicine bag pictured
was manufactured
or handmade? How
can you tell? **[Infer]**

Vocabulary
authentic (ô then´ tik)
adj. genuine; real

My kid sister Cheryl and I always bragged about our
Sioux[1] grandpa, Joe Iron Shell. Our friends, who had
always lived in the city and only knew about Indians
from movies and TV, were impressed by our stories. Maybe we
exaggerated and made Grandpa and the reservation sound
glamorous, but when we'd return home to Iowa after our
yearly summer visit to Grandpa, we always had some exciting
tale to tell.

We always had some authentic Sioux article to show our
listeners. One year Cheryl had new moccasins[2] that Grandpa
had made. On another visit he gave me a small, round, flat,
rawhide drum that was decorated with a painting of a warrior
riding a horse. He taught me a real Sioux chant to sing while I
beat the drum with a leather-covered stick that had a feather
on the end. Man that really made an impression.

---

1. Sioux (sōō´) *adj.* belonging to a Native American tribe of the northern United States and
southern Canada.
2. moccasins (mäk´ ə sənz) *n.* soft shoes traditionally made from animal hide.

We never showed our friends Grandpa's picture. Not that we were ashamed of him, but because we knew that the glamorous tales we told didn't go with the real thing. Our friends would have laughed at the picture because Grandpa wasn't tall and stately like TV Indians. His hair wasn't in braids but hung in stringy, gray strands on his neck, and he was old. He was our great-grandfather, and he didn't live in a tepee, but all by himself in a part log, part tarpaper shack on the Rosebud Reservation in South Dakota. So when Grandpa came to visit us, I was so ashamed and embarrassed I could've died.

There are a lot of yippy poodles and other fancy little dogs in our neighborhood, but they usually barked singly at the mailman from the safety of their own yards. Now it sounded as if a whole pack of mutts were barking together in one place.

I got up and walked to the curb to see what the commotion was. About a block away I saw a crowd of little kids yelling, with the dogs yipping and growling around someone who was walking down the middle of the street.

I watched the group as it slowly came closer and saw that in the center of the strange **procession** was a man wearing a tall black hat. He'd pause now and then to peer at something in his hand and then at the houses on either side of the street. I felt cold and hot at the same time as I recognized the man. "Oh, no!" I whispered. "It's Grandpa!"

I stood on the curb, unable to move even though I wanted to run and hide. Then I got mad when I saw how the yippy dogs were growling and nipping at the old man's baggy pant legs and how wearily he poked them away with his cane. "Stupid mutts," I said as I ran to rescue Grandpa.

When I kicked and hollered at the dogs to get away, they put their tails between their legs and scattered. The kids ran to the curb where they watched me and the old man. ●

"Grandpa," I said and felt pretty dumb when my voice cracked. I reached for his beat-up old tin suitcase, which was tied shut with a rope. But he set it down right in the street and shook my hand.

"*Hau, Takoza,* Grandchild," he greeted me formally in Sioux.

All I could do was stand there with the whole neighborhood watching and shake the hand of the leather-brown old man. I saw how his gray hair straggled from under his big black

Symbol
Why is the narrator embarrassed by his grandfather?

We never showed our friends Grandpa's picture.

Vocabulary
procession (prō sesh´ ən) *n.* a group moving forward, as in a parade

Reading Check
Who accompanies the narrator's grandfather as he walks down the street?

The Medicine Bag **427**

The Sioux Nation
Before the mid-1800s, the Sioux lived throughout the northern plains of North America. In 1874, the U.S. government broke a treaty guaranteeing Sioux boundaries. Many Sioux decided to fight. Led by the famous chiefs Sitting Bull (shown here) and Crazy Horse, they defeated General Custer's troops at Little Big Horn. Eventually, however, the Sioux were overpowered. Today, many Sioux live on reservations throughout the Upper Midwest.

Connect to the Literature

How might living on a reservation affect Grandpa's feelings about Sioux traditions?

Vocabulary
unseemly (un sēm´ lē)
adj. inappropriate

hat, which had a drooping feather in its crown. His rumpled black suit hung like a sack over his stooped frame. As he shook my hand, his coat fell open to expose a bright red satin shirt with a beaded bolo tie under the collar. His get-up wasn't out of place on the reservation, but it sure was here, and I wanted to sink right through the pavement.

"Hi," I muttered with my head down. I tried to pull my hand away when I felt his bony hand trembling, and looked up to see fatigue in his face. I felt like crying. I couldn't think of anything to say so I picked up Grandpa's suitcase, took his arm, and guided him up the driveway to our house.

Mom was standing on the steps. I don't know how long she'd been watching, but her hand was over her mouth and she looked as if she couldn't believe what she saw. Then she ran to us.

"Grandpa," she gasped. "How in the world did you get here?"

She checked her move to embrace Grandpa and I remembered that such a display of affection is **unseemly** to the Sioux and would embarrass him.

"*Hau*, Marie," he said as he shook Mom's hand. She smiled and took his other arm.

As we supported him up the steps, the door banged open and Cheryl came bursting out of the house. She was all smiles and was so obviously glad to see Grandpa that I was ashamed of how I felt.

"Grandpa!" she yelled happily. "You came to see us!"

Grandpa smiled, and Mom and I let go of him as he stretched out his arms to my ten-year-old sister, who was still young enough to be hugged.

"*Wicincala*, little girl," he greeted her and then collapsed.

He had fainted. Mom and I carried him into her sewing room, where we had a spare bed.

After we had Grandpa on the bed, Mom stood there helplessly patting his shoulder.

"Shouldn't we call the doctor, Mom?" I suggested, since she didn't seem to know what to do.

"Yes," she agreed with a sigh. "You make Grandpa comfortable, Martin."

I reluctantly moved to the bed. I knew Grandpa wouldn't want to have Mom undress him, but I didn't want to, either. He was so skinny and frail that his coat slipped off easily. When I loosened his tie and opened his shirt collar, I felt a small leather pouch that hung from a thong around his neck. I left it alone and moved to remove his boots. The scuffed old cowboy boots were tight, and he moaned as I put pressure on his legs to jerk them off.

I put the boots on the floor and saw why they fit so tight. Each one was stuffed with money. I looked at the bills that lined the boots and started to ask about them, but Grandpa's eyes were closed again.

Mom came back with a basin of water. "The doctor thinks Grandpa is suffering from heat exhaustion," she explained as she bathed Grandpa's face. Mom gave a big sigh, "*Oh, hinh,* Martin. How do you suppose he got here?" ●

We found out after the doctor's visit. Grandpa was angrily sitting up in bed while Mom tried to feed him some soup.

"Tonight you let Marie feed you, Grandpa," spoke my dad, who had gotten home from work just as the doctor was leaving. "You're not really sick," he said as he gently pushed Grandpa back against the pillows. "The doctor said you just got too tired and hot after your long trip."

Grandpa relaxed, and between sips of soup, he told us of his journey. Soon after our visit to him, Grandpa decided that he would like to see where his only living descendants lived and what our home was like. Besides, he admitted sheepishly, he was lonesome after we left.

I knew that everybody felt as guilty as I did—especially Mom. Mom was all Grandpa had left. So even after she married my dad, who's a white man and teaches in the college in our city, and after Cheryl and I were born, Mom made sure that every summer we spent a week with Grandpa.

I never thought that Grandpa would be lonely after our visits, and none of us noticed how old and weak he had become. But Grandpa knew, and so he came to us. He had ridden on buses for two and a half days. When he arrived in the city, tired and stiff from sitting for so long, he set out, walking, to find us.

He had stopped to rest on the steps of some building downtown, and a policeman found him. The cop, according to Grandpa, was a good man who took him to the bus stop and

Symbol
Why does Grandpa resist being fed by Mom?

Reading Check
Why does Grandpa come to the city?

waited until the bus came and told the driver to let Grandpa out at Bell View Drive. After Grandpa got off the bus, he started walking again. But he couldn't see the house numbers on the other side when he walked on the sidewalk, so he walked in the middle of the street. That's when all the little kids and dogs followed him.

I knew everybody felt as bad as I did. Yet I was so proud of this eighty-six-year-old man, who had never been away from the reservation, having the courage to travel so far alone.

"You found the money in my boots?" he asked Mom.

"Martin did," she answered, and roused herself to scold. "Grandpa, you shouldn't have carried so much money. What if someone had stolen it from you?"

Grandpa laughed. "I would've known if anyone tried to take the boots off my feet. The money is what I've saved for a long time—a hundred dollars—for my funeral. But you take it now to buy groceries so that I won't be a burden to you while I am here."

"That won't be necessary, Grandpa," Dad said. "We are honored to have you with us, and you will never be a burden. I am only sorry that we never thought to bring you home with us this summer and spare you the discomfort of a long trip."

Grandpa was pleased. "Thank you," he answered. "But do not feel bad that you didn't bring me with you, for I would not have come then. It was not time." He said this in such a way that no one could argue with him. To Grandpa and the Sioux, he once told me, a thing would be done when it was the right time to do it, and that's the way it was.

"Also," Grandpa went on, looking at me, "I have come because it is soon time for Martin to have the medicine bag."

We all knew what that meant. Grandpa thought he was going to die, and he had to follow the tradition of his family to pass the medicine bag, along with its history, to the oldest male child.

"Even though the boy," he said still looking at me, "bears a white man's name, the medicine bag will be his."

I didn't know what to say. I had the same hot and cold feeling that I had when I first saw Grandpa in the street. The medicine bag was the dirty leather pouch I had found around

Symbol
What makes Grandpa's journey remarkable?

Symbol
What is the symbolic importance of Grandpa's visit?

his neck. "I could never wear such a thing," I almost said aloud. I thought of having my friends see it in gym class or at the swimming pool and could imagine the smart things they would say. But I just swallowed hard and took a step toward the bed. I knew I would have to take it.

But Grandpa was tired. "Not now, Martin," he said, waving his hand in dismissal. "It is not time. Now I will sleep."

So that's how Grandpa came to be with us for two months. My friends kept asking to come see the old man, but I put them off. I told myself that I didn't want them laughing at Grandpa. But even as I made excuses, I knew it wasn't Grandpa that I was afraid they'd laugh at.

Nothing bothered Cheryl about bringing her friends to see Grandpa. Every day after school started, there'd be a crew of giggling little girls or round-eyed little boys crowded around the old man on the patio, where he'd gotten in the habit of sitting every afternoon.

Grandpa would smile in his gentle way and patiently answer their questions, or he'd tell them stories of brave warriors, ghosts, animals; and the kids listened in awed silence. Those little guys thought Grandpa was great.

Finally, one day after school, my friends came home with me because nothing I said stopped them. "We're going to see the great Indian of Bell View Drive," said Hank, who was supposed to be my best friend. "My brother has seen him three times so he oughta be well enough to see us." ●

When we got to my house, Grandpa was sitting on the patio. He had on his red shirt, but today he also wore a fringed leather vest that was decorated with beads. Instead of his usual cowboy boots, he had solidly beaded moccasins on his feet that stuck out of his black trousers. Of course, he had his old black hat on—he was seldom without it. But it had been brushed, and the feather in the beaded headband was proudly erect, its tip a brighter white. His hair lay in silver strands over the red shirt collar.

I stared just as my friends did, and I heard one of them murmur, "Wow!"

Grandpa looked up, and, when his eyes met mine, they twinkled as if he were laughing inside. He nodded to me, and my face got all hot. I could tell that he had known all along I was afraid he'd embarrass me in front of my friends.

"*Hau, hoksilas,* boys," he greeted and held out his hand.

Symbol

How does Martin's reluctance to accept the medicine bag show he is caught between two worlds?

> Instead of his usual cowboy boots, he had solidly beaded moccasins on his feet that stuck out of his black trousers.

Reading Check

What does Grandpa do to prepare for the visit of Martin's friends?

My buddies passed in a single file and shook his hand as I introduced them. They were so polite I almost laughed. "How, there, Grandpa," and even a "How-do-you-do, sir."

"You look fine, Grandpa," I said as the guys sat on the lawn chairs or on the patio floor.

"*Hanh*, yes," he agreed. "When I woke up this morning, it seemed the right time to dress in the good clothes. I knew that my grandson would be bringing his friends."

"You guys want some lemonade or something?" I offered. No one answered. They were listening to Grandpa as he started telling how he'd killed the deer from which his vest was made.

Grandpa did most of the talking while my friends were there. I was so proud of him and amazed at how respectfully quiet my buddies were. Mom had to chase them home at supper time. As they left, they shook Grandpa's hand again and said to me,

"Martin, he's really great!"

"Yeah, man! Don't blame you for keeping him to yourself."

"Can we come back?"

But after they left, Mom said, "No more visitors for a while, Martin. Grandpa won't admit it, but his strength hasn't returned. He likes having company, but it tires him."

That evening Grandpa called me to his room before he went to sleep. "Tomorrow," he said, "when you come home, it will be time to give you the medicine bag."

I felt a hard squeeze from where my heart is supposed to be and was scared, but I answered, "OK, Grandpa." ●

All night I had weird dreams about thunder and lightning on a high hill. From a distance I heard the slow beat of a drum. When I woke up in the morning, I felt as if I hadn't slept at all. At school it seemed as if the day would never end and, when it finally did, I ran home.

Grandpa was in his room, sitting on the bed. The shades were down, and the place was dim and cool. I sat on the floor in front of Grandpa, but he didn't even look at me. After what seemed a long time he spoke.

"I sent your mother and sister away. What you will hear today is only for a man's ears. What you will receive is only for a man's hands." He fell silent, and I felt shivers down my back.

"My father in his early manhood," Grandpa began, "made a vision quest[3] to find a spirit guide for his life. You cannot

Symbol
What does Grandpa represent to Martin's friends?

Symbol
From the description, do you think Martin's dream symbolizes something pleasant or distressing? Why?

---

3. **vision quest** (vizh´ ən kwest) *n.* In Native American cultures, a difficult search for spiritual guidance.

understand how it was in that time, when the great Teton Sioux were first made to stay on the reservation. There was a strong need for guidance from *Wakantanka*,[4] the Great Spirit. But too many of the young men were filled with despair and hatred. They thought it was hopeless to search for a vision when the glorious life was gone and only the hated confines of a reservation lay ahead. But my father held to the old ways.

"He carefully prepared for his quest with a purifying sweat bath, and then he went alone to a high butte top[5] to fast and pray. After three days he received his sacred dream—in which he found, after long searching, the white man's iron. He did not understand his vision of finding something belonging to the white people, for in that time they were the enemy. When he came down from the butte to cleanse himself at the stream

▲ Critical Viewing
Why might someone be more likely to have a vision alone in a natural setting like the one shown? **[Speculate]**

✓ Reading Check
Why was it unusual for Grandpa's father to go on a vision quest?

---

4. **Wakantanka** (wä´ kən tank´ ə) *n.* Sioux religion's most important spirit—the creator of the world.
5. **butte** (byo͞ot) **top** *n.* isolated mountain top with steep sides.

▲ **Critical Viewing**
What aspects of a
vision quest do you
think you would find
rewarding? **[Speculate]**

Spiral Review
Theme How might
the story of Iron Shell
and his medicine bag
be connected with a
possible theme of this
story?

below, he found the remains of a campfire and the broken
shell of an iron kettle. This was a sign that reinforced his
dream. He took a piece of the iron for his medicine bag, which
he had made of elk skin years before, to prepare for his quest.

"He returned to his village, where he told his dream to the
wise old men of the tribe. They gave him the name *Iron Shell*, but
neither did they understand the meaning of the dream. The first
Iron Shell kept the piece of iron with him at all times and believed
it gave him protection from the evils of those unhappy days.

"Then a terrible thing happened to Iron Shell. He and
several other young men were taken from their homes by the
soldiers and sent far away to a white man's boarding school.
He was angry and lonesome for his parents and the young
girl he had wed before he was taken away. At first Iron Shell
resisted the teacher's attempts to change him, and he did not
try to learn. One day it was his turn to work in the school's
blacksmith shop. As he walked into the place, he knew that
his medicine had brought him there to learn and work with
the white man's iron.

"Iron Shell became a blacksmith and worked at the trade
when he returned to the reservation. All of his life he treasured
the medicine bag. When he was old, and I was a man, he gave
it to me, for no one made the vision quest any more."

Grandpa quit talking, and I stared in disbelief as he covered his face with his hands. His shoulders were shaking with quiet sobs, and I looked away until he began to speak again.

"I kept the bag until my son, your mother's father, was a man and had to leave us to fight in the war across the ocean. I gave him the bag, for I believed it would protect him in battle, but he did not take it with him. He was afraid that he would lose it. He died in a faraway place."

Again Grandpa was still, and I felt his grief around me.

"My son," he went on after clearing his throat, "had only a daughter, and it is not proper for her to know of these things."

He unbuttoned his shirt, pulled out the leather pouch, and lifted it over his head. He held it in his hand, turning it over and over as if memorizing how it looked.

"In the bag," he said as he opened it and removed two objects, "is the broken shell of the iron kettle, a pebble from the butte, and a piece of the sacred sage."[6] He held the pouch upside down and dust drifted down.

"After the bag is yours you must put a piece of prairie sage within and never open it again until you pass it on to your son." He replaced the pebble and the piece of iron, and tied the bag.

I stood up, somehow knowing I should. Grandpa slowly rose from the bed and stood upright in front of me holding the bag

Symbol
Why is Grandpa telling Martin this family history?

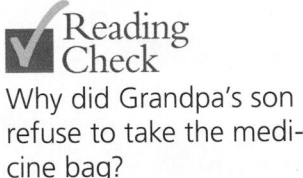

Reading Check

Why did Grandpa's son refuse to take the medicine bag?

---

6. sage (sāj) *n.* type of herb.

The Medicine Bag **435**

before my face. I closed my eyes and waited for him to slip it over my head. But he spoke.

"No, you need not wear it." He placed the soft leather bag in my right hand and closed my other hand over it. "It would not be right to wear it in this time and place where no one will understand. Put it safely away until you are again on the reservation. Wear it then, when you replace the sacred sage."

Grandpa turned and sat again on the bed. Wearily he leaned his head against the pillow. "Go," he said. "I will sleep now."

"Thank you, Grandpa," I said softly and left with the bag in my hands.

That night Mom and Dad took Grandpa to the hospital. Two weeks later I stood alone on the lonely prairie of the reservation and put the sacred sage in my medicine bag.

Critical Thinking

1. Key Ideas and Details **(a)** Describe how each family member welcomes Grandpa. **(b) Analyze:** What causes Martin to feel ashamed when Grandpa appears? **(c) Interpret:** How can Martin feel both ashamed and proud of Grandpa?

2. Key Ideas and Details **(a)** What reasons does Grandpa give for coming to visit? **(b) Support:** How do the events of the story support Grandpa's idea that things will be done at "the right time"?

> Cite textual evidence to support your responses.

3. Key Ideas and Details **(a)** What does Martin do at the very end of the story? **(b) Draw Conclusions:** What does Martin's final act reveal about his relationship to his heritage?

4. Integration of Knowledge and Ideas **(a) Evaluate:** By the end of the story, is Martin ready to receive his grandfather's gift? **(b) Apply:** Using examples from the story and from life, explain how some "gifts" are also responsibilities.

5. Integration of Knowledge and Ideas **(a)** What causes Martin's embarrassment about accepting the medicine bag? **(b)** What do you feel was the most important reason behind Martin's decision to accept it? **(c)** Would you say this conflict is resolved? Explain. *[Connect to the Big Question: Can all conflicts be resolved?]*

Comparing Symbols

© **1. Key Ideas and Details (a)** How does the narrator feel about the white umbrella? **(b)** What does the umbrella represent to the narrator? **(c)** What does the narrator's action of throwing away the umbrella at the end of the story symbolize?

© **2. Key Ideas and Details (a)** At first, how does Martin feel about the medicine bag? **(b)** What does it come to symbolize for Martin?

© **3. Integration of Knowledge and Ideas (a)** Fill in a chart like the one shown to analyze the similarities and differences between the symbols in the two stories. **(b)** Use your chart to write one statement about how the symbols are similar and one statement about how they are different.

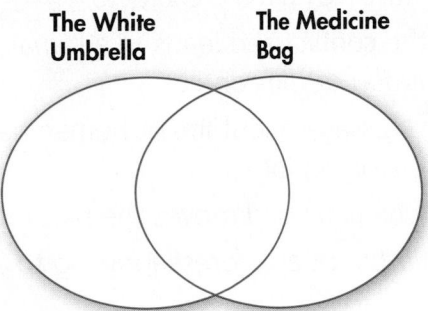

The White Umbrella   The Medicine Bag

⏱ Timed Writing

Explanatory Text: Essay

Describe each story's theme in an essay. Draw conclusions about how the symbol in each story helps to illustrate the story's theme. Provide evidence from the text to support your analysis. **(40 minutes)**

5-Minute Planner

1. Read the prompt carefully and completely.

2. Gather your ideas by jotting down answers to these questions:

- Do the symbols have cultural meaning outside of the stories?
- How do the conflicting feelings of the main characters make the symbolism more powerful?
- What theme or message about being caught between two worlds do the symbols help convey?

3. Reread the prompt, and then draft your essay.

Writing Workshop

Write a Narrative

Narration: Short Story

Defining the Form A **short story** is a brief fictional narrative that has a setting, a plot, a theme, a point of view, and characters. You might use elements of short story writing in plays or biographical essays.

Assignment Write a short story that has believable characters who face a realistic conflict. Include these elements:

✔ one or more *characters*, developed throughout the story

✔ a clear *setting*—a time and place in which the action occurs

✔ a *conflict* or problem faced by a main character

✔ a *plot* that develops the conflict and leads to a *climax*, or turning point, and a *resolution* of the conflict

✔ a *theme*—an idea or message about life or human nature—that is reflected in the story's plot

✔ *dialogue* that reveals character and moves the plot forward

✔ plot devices such as *flashback* and *foreshadowing* to add interest to the story

To preview the criteria on which your short story may be judged, see the rubric on page 445.

 Writing Workshop: *Work in Progress*

Review the work you did on pages 383 and 405.

WRITE GUY
Jeff Anderson, M.Ed.

What Do You Notice?

Creating an Effect

Read the following sentences from "The Tell-Tale Heart."

True!—nervous—very, very dreadfully nervous I had been and am; but why will you say that I am mad? The disease had sharpened my senses—not destroyed—not dulled them.

With a partner, discuss the following question: What do you notice about the way Poe opens the story and the effect it has on you, the reader? What role do you think the author intended this opening to serve in developing the character of the narrator?

 **Common Core State Standards**

Writing

3. Write narratives to develop real or imagined experiences or events using effective technique, relevant descriptive details, and well-structured event sequences.

3.a. Engage and orient the reader by establishing a context and point of view and introducing a narrator and/or characters; organize an event sequence that unfolds naturally and logically.

3.d. Use precise words and phrases, relevant descriptive details, and sensory language to capture the action and convey experiences and events.

Reading-Writing Connection

To read a short story written by a master, read "The Tell-Tale Heart" by Edgar Allan Poe on page 294.

Prewriting/Planning Strategies

Begin with a character. Your story's main character may be based on a person you know, or he or she can be drawn completely from your imagination. Get to know your character by drawing pictures, listing details, or asking and answering questions such as *What does this character like to do?* or *Who are his or her friends?*

Determine point of view. The narrator's presentation of information will influence the way the story is told. It will also influence your readers' experience of reading the story. Decide if you want your narrator to be a participant in the story who speaks in the first person or an observer who speaks in third person:

First-person narrator: I felt a surge of energy as I launched the ball toward the hoop.

Third-person narrator: The crowd held its breath as Pam shot the ball toward the hoop.

Picture the scene. Imagine your story's main character in a specific time and place. Make a chart, like this one, of sensory images to weave throughout your story. Use all five senses to help readers experience the setting as fully as possible.

Sight	Open window; curtains blowing
Sound	Music, laughter
Smell	Neighbors' barbecue
Touch	Breeze from window
Taste	Sweet lemonade

Invent a situation. To focus on the action and conflict in your story, complete sentences like these in several different ways.

- What if *(person)* wanted _____ but *(name problem)*?
- What if *(person)* suddenly *(name problem)*?

Review your work and choose a focus for your story.

Identify the conflict. Pinpoint the problem, or conflict, your story will develop. Make notes about the ways the conflict will reveal itself and intensify, the ways each character will react, and the way the conflict will be resolved.

Drafting Strategies

Common Core State Standards

Writing

3.a. Engage and orient the reader by establishing a context and point of view and introducing a narrator and/or characters; organize an event sequence that unfolds naturally and logically.

3.b. Use narrative techniques, such as dialogue, pacing, description, and reflection, to develop experiences, events, and/or characters.

4. Produce clear and coherent writing in which the development, organization, and style are appropriate to task, purpose, and audience.

Draft your plot. In the beginning, or exposition, of your story, engage your readers by providing information about the characters, setting, and conflict. Then, develop the conflict, event by event, until you reach the turning point, or climax. Finally, focus on resolving the problem in the falling action and resolution.

One day George discovers Martha and Henry trapped by a bull.

Climax

Martha refuses to marry George because he is a farmer.

George distracts the bull and Henry runs away.

Introduce George, Martha, and Henry the school teacher.

Struck by George's bravery, Martha agrees to marry him.

Rising Action

Falling Action

Exposition

Resolution

Conflict introduced

Use plot devices. Enhance mood, add suspense, and keep your readers' interest by using various plot devices. For example, **foreshadowing** can set the stage for a surprising event, and **flashbacks** can help explain a character's mysterious background.

Use dialogue to distinguish characters. Give your characters individual voices and patterns of speech. The words characters say can reveal parts of their personalities, such as humor or bitterness. Dialogue can also show relationships between characters.

Dialogue Type	Conveys
Short, choppy lines of dialogue	*humor, excitement,* or a *heated* conversation
Longer lines or speeches	*heavier moods* or the idea that someone is saying *something important*

Build in characterization. Give your characters unique personalities with interesting similarities and differences. Similarities show bonds between characters. Differences can create conflicts. Contrasts between characters also pull readers into the story by making them feel sympathetic toward certain characters and suspicious of others.

Writers on Writing

Judith Ortiz Cofer On Bringing Characters to Life

Judith Ortiz Cofer is the author of "An Hour With Abuelo" (p. 238).

Before I start writing I take notes, sometimes for days, sometimes for months, and in the case of novels, maybe even years. I keep a notebook with me at all times where I jot down ideas, images, words I hear, anything that I think will bring my characters to life. Before a story is finished I have usually rewritten it many times, as the theme develops and changes.

"The short story is very often a journey . . ."
—Judith Ortiz Cofer

Professional Model:

from "The One Who Watches," from *An Island Like You*

"Mira, mira!" my friend Yolanda yells out. She's always telling me to look at something. And I always do. I look, she does. That's the way it's always been. Yolanda just turned sixteen, I'm six months younger. I was born to follow the leader, and that's what my mother says when she sees us together, and it's true.

It's like the world is a deli full of pricey treats to Yolanda, and she wants the most expensive ones in fancy boxes, the ones she can't afford. We spend hours shopping downtown. Sometimes when Yolanda gets excited about an outfit, we go into a store and she tries it on. But the salespeople are getting to know us. They know we don't have any money. So we get chased out of places a lot. . . .

We have to pass my apartment on our way out, and I can hear my mother singing an old song . . . It's *Cielito Lindo*—a sort of lullaby that she used to sing to me when I was little.

Because Yolanda is the dominant character, I wanted her to say the first words in the story, to take control. "Mira, mira!" is an imperative; Doris *thinks* her responses.

A story depends on sensory details to come alive. A reader should be able to share the experience by seeing, tasting, smelling, hearing, and feeling right along with the characters in scenes filled with vivid details.

I often use titles of old songs I heard in my childhood as memory triggers in my writing. *Cielito Lindo* is what my mother used to sing to us at bedtime; in the story, it reminds Doris of her mother's warnings about Yolanda.

Revising Strategies

 Common Core
State Standards

Writing

3.c. Use a variety of transition words, phrases, and clauses to convey sequence, signal shifts from one time frame or setting to another, and show the relationships among experiences and events.

5. With some guidance and support from peers and adults, develop and strengthen writing as needed by planning, revising, editing, rewriting, or trying a new approach, focusing on how well purpose and audience have been addressed.

Add detail to develop characters. Look for places to add more details that help your readers see and respond to your characters.

1. Review your draft, highlighting significant events to which a character would have a strong reaction.

2. Ask yourself: *What gestures, words, facial expressions, thoughts, memories, or actions will reflect this reaction?*

3. In the margin, jot down your answer to the question above.

4. Review your notes and decide which details to include. You will influence your audience through the reactions of your characters.

Share your story with a peer. Find a partner and read each other's work, looking for areas to improve. In particular, evaluate character development by asking the questions in the chart. Then, revise your story to achieve the reaction you intended.

> **Character Development Checklist**
>
> ✓ Do the characters seem realistic?
>
> ✓ Do the characters have unique personalities?
>
> ✓ Do they have interesting things to say?
>
> ✓ Are their reactions appropriate to events?

Revise to include action verbs. Linking verbs simply connect a subject with a word that describes it. Action verbs are often a more exciting alternative. To replace linking verbs, highlight all forms of *be* and other linking verbs (*feel, look, appear, become, grow, remain*) and rewrite your sentences using action verbs.

| **Linking Verb:** | I *was surprised* by what I saw. |
| **Action Verb:** | I *gasped* at what I saw. |

Revise dialogue. To add excitement and realism to your dialogue, use **interjections**—exclamatory words and phrases such as "No way!" and "Unbelievable!"

Revise dialogue for rhythm and emotion. Read your dialogue aloud to make sure that the speech patterns feel natural and convey the emotions you intend. If a section drags, revise by making dialogue shorter and more dramatic. On the other hand, if dialogue moves too fast, revise by making sentences longer.

Add transitions. Use transitions to indicate shifts in time or setting. Words and phrases such as *meanwhile, during,* and *earlier* can help clarify connections between places, times, and events.

Revising for Subject-Verb Agreement

A verb must agree with its subject in number. In grammar, the number of a word can be either *singular* (indicating *one*) or *plural* (indicating *more than one*). Unlike nouns, which usually become plural when -*s* or -*es* is added, verbs with -*s* or -*es* added to them are singular.

Nouns and Pronouns	
Singular	**Plural**
bus, goose, I, you, it	buses, geese, we, you, them
Verbs	
Singular	**Plural**
runs, reads, sleeps, writes	run, read, sleep, write

Here are some examples of correct subject-verb agreement. In each case, subjects are underlined and verbs are set in italics.

Singular: The <u>child</u> *goes* to sleep at eight o'clock.

Plural: The <u>children</u> *go* to sleep at eight o'clock.

Compound, Plural: <u>George and Martha</u> *agree* to get married.

Fixing Faulty Subject-Verb Agreement To fix problems with subject-verb agreement, use the following methods.

1. **First identify the subject, and then check its number.** For singular subjects, use singular verbs. For plural subjects, use plural verbs.

2. **If the subject comes after the verb, rephrase the sentence.** This makes it easier to determine the number of the subject.

   Faulty Inverted Sentence: There *was* many <u>girls</u> in the store.

   Rephrased: Many <u>girls</u> *were* in the store.

3. **Check the context.** The subject *you* can be singular or plural. Read the rest of the paragraph to determine the correct number.

PH **WRITING COACH**

Further instruction and practice are available in *Prentice Hall Writing Coach*.

Grammar In Your Writing

Choose two paragraphs in your draft. Underline every subject and every verb. Draw a line from each subject to its verb. If these pairs do not agree in number, fix them according to the examples above.

Student Model: Michael Casey, Tiverton, RI

 Common Core
State Standards

Language
3. Use knowledge of language
and its conventions when writing,
speaking, reading, or listening.

Sailing to Freedom

The hot sun was beating down on Anuk as he finished the final words on the tomb in which the Pharaoh would be buried two days later. As he looked back to examine his work, his mind began to wander. Anuk thought about his situation. The only reason he was standing there, half-heartedly working, was because he was one of the very few teenagers accepted into the "Gifted Society." This class of servants who were smarter and stronger than most of the others was permitted to perform the "better" jobs and was honored with the closest burial spot next to the Pharaoh inside the pyramid.

"Great," thought Anuk sarcastically, "I'm only thirteen and I'm already being sent to my death." Most of the Pharaoh's servants would jump at the chance to go into the afterlife with their king. But Anuk was no ordinary boy. There was something inside him that made him want to live—a drive that all the servants in Egypt didn't have…. Anuk wanted and needed to escape, and no matter how hard the challenges, he was going to accomplish this.

Talla was hoeing in the fields again. He hated hoeing because it made huge calluses and blisters on his hands. Talla was almost finished with the first row when he saw a boy his age, dressed in fine clothes, walking toward him.

As the boy walked closer he said, "You, boy! Listen, I have a proposal for you. I'd like to offer you a large payment if you will help me sail to Lower Egypt."

Talla could clearly see the boy now. It was Anuk, the son of the royal scribe.

"Aren't you supposed to be buried with the pharaoh in his tomb—" He was cut short by the hand of Anuk.

"The stench of resin doesn't please me, if you know what I mean," answered Anuk.

Talla nodded. He knew from his father that the dead body of the Pharaoh is covered with a dry sap called resin.

"What I need is a guide to take me down the Nile and some help getting supplies. I believe—"

Talla interrupted. "Let me see the payment and I'll make my decision." Anuk held out a pure red ruby amulet. Talla was amazed, letting his mouth drop. He quickly closed it and said, "Let's go."

First, Michael introduces and develops the main character, Anuk, in this third-person narrative.

Michael conveys the setting by using historical terms and describing cultural traditions.

Michael introduces the conflict and theme early. Both center around the human desire to be free.

This dialogue reveals differences between the two boys. It also moves the plot forward.

These paragraphs continue building tension ahead of the climax that will occur later.

Editing and Proofreading

Read your draft and correct errors in grammar, spelling, and punctuation.

Focus on sentences. Review each sentence to check that it contains a subject and a verb that agree in gender and number. In addition, make sure that you have maintained a consistent point of view. If your story is told from the first-person point of view, verify that you have not switched to third-person, or vice versa.

Spiral Review

Earlier in this unit, you learned about **simple tenses of verbs** (p. 382) and **tense and mood of verbs** (p. 404). Review your short story for correct verb use.

Publishing and Presenting

Consider one of the following ways to share your writing.

Tell your story aloud. Hold a storytelling event at which several students tell their stories. Make posters announcing the event.

Submit your story. Send your story to a national magazine, online journal, or contest that solicits student writing. Ask your teacher or librarian for suggestions.

Reflecting on Your Writing

Writer's Journal Jot down your answers to these questions:

- *How effective were the strategies you used for drafting?*
- *What insights about short stories did the experience give you?*

Rubric for Self-Assessment

Find evidence in your writing to address each category. Then, use the rating scale to grade your work.

Criteria	Rating Scale
	not very ... very
Focus: How clearly does the story show the conflict faced by the main character?	1 2 3 4 5
Organization: How effectively do you introduce the conflict, use plot devices, and develop the plot?	1 2 3 4 5
Support/Elaboration: How well do you use details to describe the setting?	1 2 3 4 5
Style: How well does your dialogue reveal character and further the plot?	1 2 3 4 5
Conventions: How correct is your grammar, especially your use of subject-verb agreement?	1 2 3 4 5

Vocabulary Workshop

Word Origins

The history of the English language begins around the year A.D. 500. Germanic tribes—the Angles, Saxons, and Jutes—brought their language to Britain when they moved west and settled there. Later, when the Vikings invaded Britain, Danish and Norse elements were introduced to the language. Latin elements were added when Christian missionaries arrived. The resulting language, Old English, was spoken until about 1100, when it underwent another change.

The change was caused by the Norman Conquest of Britain in 1066. The conquerors, from the Normandy region of France, introduced elements of Old French to the language. This new form, Middle English, was spoken from about 1100 to 1500.

The Renaissance (1300–1600) brought great changes to the language. Interest in ancient Greek and Roman culture brought Greek and Latin influences to English. Toward the end of the Renaissance, Shakespeare added about two thousand words to English. The result, Modern English, continues to change to this day.

This chart shows some of the ways words enter our language.

Common Core State Standards

Language

4. Determine or clarify the meaning of unknown and multiple-meaning words or phrases, choosing flexibly from a range of strategies.

4.a. Use context as a clue to the meaning of a word or phrase.

4.b. Use common, grade-appropriate Greek or Latin affixes and roots as clues to the meaning of a word (e.g., *precede, recede, secede*).

4.c. Consult general and specialized reference materials, both print and digital, to find the pronunciation of a word or determine or clarify its precise meaning or its part of speech.

Source	Result	Examples
War	Conquerors bring new terms, ideas, and vocabulary.	*anger* (Old Norse) *sabotage* (French)
Immigration	Large groups of people moving from other countries bring words with them.	*boycott* (Irish) *frankfurter* (German) *carnival* (Italian)
Travel and Trade	People who travel and do business in foreign lands bring new words back with them.	*shampoo* (Hindi) *kimono* (Japanese) *kowtow* (Chinese)
Science and Technology	New concepts in science and technology give rise to new words.	*blog* *ultrasound* *laser*
Mythology	Names of gods, goddesses, heroes, and heroines of various mythologies form the basis of new words.	*Wednesday* (from Woden, a god in Anglo-Saxon mythology) *martial* (from Mars, the god of war in Roman mythology)

Practice A For each underlined root, write two more related words.

1. The Greek root _-phon-_, meaning "sound," is part of our word _telephone._

2. The Latin root _-mob-_, meaning "move," is part of our word _mobile._

3. The Latin root _-ped-_, meaning "foot," is part of our word _pedal._

4. The Greek root _-therm-_, meaning "heat," is part of our word _thermometer._

5. The Latin root _-vis-_, meaning "see," is part of our word _visible._

6. The Greek root _-photo-_, meaning "light," is part of our word _photography._

7. The Latin root _-dent-_, meaning "tooth," is part of our word _dentist._

PHLit Online!
www.PHLitOnline.com

- Illustrated vocabulary words
- Interactive vocabulary games
- Vocabulary flashcards

Practice B An **allusion** is a reference to a person, place, thing, or literary work. Many works of literature contain allusions to characters from **mythology.** Read each description of a mythological character. Then, use the information to complete each allusion.

1. In Greek mythology, Narcissus was a young man who fell in love with his own reflection. _He is such a Narcissus, he does not care about _____._

2. Titans were gigantic beings in Greek mythology. _The ship_ Titanic _was _____._

3. In Roman mythology, Mercury, the messenger of the gods, was known for his speed. _Because she ran like Mercury, her team _____._

4. Cupid was the Roman god of love. _My friend warned me not to play Cupid because _____._

5. In Greek mythology, King Midas had the gift of making everything he touched turn to gold. _The president of the company has the Midas touch because _____._

Activity Look up the following words in a dictionary that includes information on word origins. Describe the ways in which these words entered American English.

1. tortilla
2. gigabyte
3. sauna
4. camouflage
5. Thursday
6. January

Comprehension and Collaboration

Choose one of the mythological characters from Practice B, or research one of these:

Atlas

Proteus

Hercules

Then, write a short paragraph on a topic of your choice that includes an **allusion** to that character.

Communications Workshop

Conducting Interviews

You do not need to be a talk show host to produce a good interview. All you need is curiosity about a subject, adequate preparation time, and a knowledgeable person to interview.

 **Common Core State Standards**

Speaking and Listening
1. Engage effectively in a range of collaborative discussions (one-on-one) with diverse partners on grade 8 topics, texts, and issues, building on others' ideas and expressing their own clearly.

6. Adapt speech to a variety of contexts and tasks, demonstrating command of formal English when indicated or appropriate.

Learn the Skills

Identify your purpose. Determine what kind of information you would like to obtain. Then, do some basic research so that you will be able to ask informed questions.

Draw up questions. Use your research to generate a list of thoughtful questions for the interview. Bring this list to the interview as a guide. Use the list to predict the path the interview will take. However, do not be afraid to depart from this list if the interview heads down another useful path.

Build a question staircase.
Think of the answers in your interview as the steps in a staircase you are building upward. Each *question* should build on the *answer* you just received as well as on the previous question. The chart shown illustrates this technique.

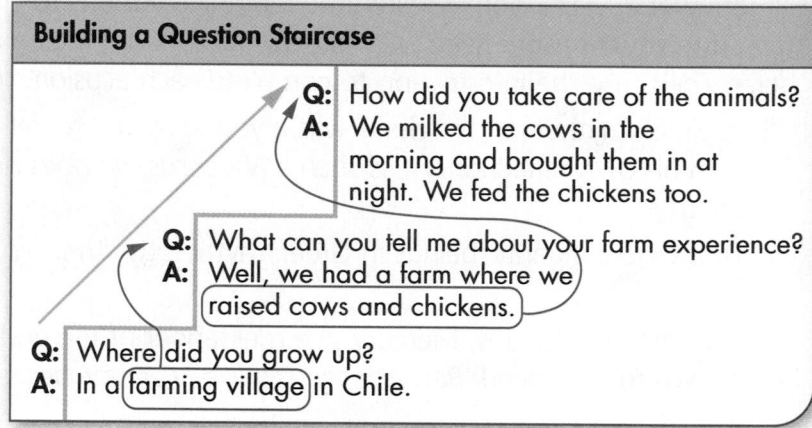

Building a Question Staircase

Q: How did you take care of the animals?
A: We milked the cows in the morning and brought them in at night. We fed the chickens too.

Q: What can you tell me about your farm experience?
A: Well, we had a farm where we raised cows and chickens.

Q: Where did you grow up?
A: In a farming village in Chile.

Phrase your questions clearly.
You can guarantee quality answers if you take the time to ask your questions in a way that will be clearly understood by your interviewee. Avoid asking multi-part questions all at once. Instead, break up a complex question into a series of questions to make it easier for your interviewee to answer.

Listen actively. Express your interest through good questions, eye contact, and attentive listening. Ask relevant follow-up questions and paraphrase the interviewee's ideas when you need clarification.

Respect others' views. You will get better results if you respect others' views. If you disagree with something the person says, do not express your negative feelings. Instead, ask respectful questions that can help clarify why the person feels that way. Finally, thank the person you interview for his or her time.

Practice the Skills

Presentation of Knowledge and Ideas Use what you have learned in this workshop to complete the following activity.

ACTIVITY: Interview and Report

Interview a community member, friend, or relative. Then, follow the steps below.

- Determine the purpose of your interview, or what information you would like to find out.
- Write a list of questions for the interviewee.
- Avoid distractions and focus your attention on the interviewee.
- Listen attentively and make eye contact. Your analysis should include a summary of the interview and an evaluation of its effectiveness. Ask relevant follow-up questions and paraphrase the interviewee's ideas when you need clarification.
- Take notes that capture the interviewee's exact words.

Use the Evaluation Guide below to judge the effectiveness of your interview.

Evaluation Guide

Identify
- What is the purpose of the interview?
- How does the interviewer reveal this purpose?

Interview Techniques
Briefly evaluate the interviewer's use of each of the following techniques:

- ❑ good questions
- ❑ eye contact
- ❑ attentive listening
- ❑ relevant follow-up questions

Analyze Effectiveness
Write a brief analysis. Your analysis should include a summary of the interview and an evaluation of its effectiveness. Identify potential areas of improvement, such as missed opportunities for asking follow-up questions.

Comprehension and Collaboration With your classmates, watch and take notes on a television or radio interview using the Interpretation Guide. Compare your notes and analysis with those of others.

Cumulative Review

I. Reading Literature

 **Common Core State Standards**

RL.8.1, RL.8.2, RL.8.3; W.8.2, W.8.9; L.8.4.a
[For the full wording of the standards, see the standards chart in the front of your textbook.]

Directions: *Read the passage. Then, answer each question that follows.*

Although they were twins, Sandy and Erica could not have been more different. Sandy's hair was straight and blond; Erica's was curly and red. Sandy's favorite pets were cats; Erica liked dogs. Sandy liked onions and pepper on her burgers; Erica preferred ketchup and relish. One of the twins' biggest differences was their interests. Sandy enjoyed baseball and followed her home team in Los Angeles with great enthusiasm. Erica, on the other hand, disliked baseball and spent all of her spare time playing her guitar. That is why, when it came to buying birthday gifts, each knew exactly what to get the other—the exact opposite of what she herself would have wanted.

For the past month, Sandy had had her eye on a guitar stand for Erica. Every time Erica played, she had to drag her guitar case out from under the bed. It was a big hassle, and Erica had mentioned how handy a guitar stand would be.

Sandy did not have enough money for a guitar stand, but she thought she might sell the baseball that she kept in her top drawer. She had waited an hour to get her favorite pitcher's signature on that ball. That was last year, during his first season with the team. Sandy advertised the ball online and quickly had a buyer. That week, she bought the guitar stand and wrapped it expertly.

On the day the girls turned thirteen, they exchanged gifts. As Erica unwrapped hers, she gasped in surprise, smiled briefly, and then seemed vaguely confused. This was not the reaction Sandy had expected. "What's wrong, Erica? Don't you like it?"

"I love it!" said Erica. "You'll understand when you open your gift."

Sandy's jaw dropped open as she unwrapped her gift. It was the rookie card for her favorite pitcher and a beautiful display case to hold it and the <u>autographed</u> baseball. "I sold my guitar to get the money for your gift," said Erica. "Now I have a guitar stand but no guitar."

"And I have a display case but no baseball. But have no fear. I made enough money on the sale to buy you another guitar. And maybe I can get another baseball autographed next summer."

1. What is the **setting** of the story?
   A. The setting is present-day Los Angeles.
   B. The setting is an unknown city in the present.
   C. The setting is in the distant future.
   D. The setting is in the early twentieth century, somewhere in the United States.

2. Which of the following **character traits** does Sandy have?
   A. She enjoys listening to all forms of music.
   B. She likes to play the guitar.
   C. She enjoys baseball.
   D. She is a talented athlete.

3. Which **character trait** do both girls share?
   A. They are somewhat shy.
   B. They are musically inclined.
   C. They are sports minded.
   D. They are generous.

4. Identify the **point of view** that is used in the story.
   A. The first-person point of view is used.
   B. The third-person point of view is used.
   C. No point of view is used.
   D. Both the first- and third-person point of view are used.

5. In the first part of the story, the author uses the baseball and guitar as **symbols.** What do these objects symbolize?
   A. They symbolize the differences between Sandy and Erica.
   B. They symbolize the bond between Sandy and Erica.
   C. They symbolize sports and music.
   D. They symbolize the need for the two girls to feel accepted.

6. **Vocabulary** Which word is closest in meaning to the underlined word *autographed*?
   A. signed
   B. professional
   C. used
   D. valuable

7. What can you infer about Sandy's **character** by her willingness to sell her autographed baseball?
   A. The baseball is not very important to her.
   B. Her desire to please her sister is stronger than her attachment to the baseball.
   C. The only reason she got the ball autographed was so she could sell it.
   D. Her interest in baseball is fading.

8. Which sentence best expresses the **theme** of the story?
   A. Relationships are more important than material goods.
   B. You should never sell your most prized possession.
   C. Baseball memorabilia can be very valuable.
   D. Twins are often quite different from each other.

Timed Writing

9. In one paragraph, **describe** the traits that Sandy and Erica share. **Support** your answer with details from the text.

II. Reading Informational Text

Directions: *Read the passages. Then, answer each question that follows.*

Common Core State Standards

RI.8.2, RI.8.4, RI.8.5; L.8.4.a, L.8.5.c
[For the full wording of the standards, see the standards chart in the front of your textbook.]

Passage A: The Use of Cell Phones on Campus

The recent ban on the use of cell phones on campus must be lifted! I make this urgent demand in the interest of convenience and safety. Imagine that your parents expect you home by 3:30 and one day you need to stay after school for extra help. You would like to call your parents to let them know you will be late, but because of the cell phone ban, you cannot.

Even more seriously, imagine if a student or a teacher falls ill and needs emergency medical attention. Using your cell phone to call for help might save the precious minutes that would be wasted getting to a land line. In such cases, a cell phone could save a life!

Everyone uses cell phones these days, and it makes no sense to ban their use on campus. If a celebrity can take her cell phone any-where she goes, the same privilege should be allowed for students at Memorial Middle School!

Passage B: Summary of Passage A

Cell phones should be allowed on campus for reasons of conve-nience and safety. Students often need to communicate with parents about schedules, and cell phones allow them to do this. Cell phones are also useful in emergency situations.

1. What **persuasive technique** is used in the first two paragraphs of Passage A?
   A. rational appeal
   B. appeal to authority
   C. bandwagon appeal
   D. testimonial

2. In Passage A, the phrases *suddenly ill, precious minutes,* and *save a life* are exam-ples of which kind of persuasive device?
   A. rational appeal
   B. testimonial
   C. generalization
   D. loaded language

3. If the author claimed that students usually know when cell phone use is appropriate, what type of statement would that be?
   A. emotional appeal
   B. appeal to authority
   C. generalization
   D. testimonial

4. Which sentence most accurately describes the **difference** between the two passages?
   A. *A* includes examples and details; *B* only captures the main ideas of *A*.
   B. *B* is shorter than *A*.
   C. *A* includes more important information.
   D. *B* uses bandwagon appeal; *A* does not.

III. Writing and Language Conventions

Directions: *Read the passage. Then, answer each question that follows.*

> (1) One of the most powerful characters in fiction is the character Charlie in "Flowers for Algernon." (2) Charlie is a man of minimal intelligence who is unaware that others mistreat him. (3) After Charlie had surgery to improve his intelligence, he begins to see the world differently. (4) Suddenly, he sees the limitations of people whom he once considered smart. (5) Worse, he realizes that his friends have been taking advantage of him. (6) Charlie's bitter experience shows how knowledge sometimes comes at a high price.

1. Which sentence states the **central idea** of this review?

  A. sentence 1
  B. sentence 2
  C. sentence 4
  D. sentence 5

2. Which sentence would *best* develop the writer's **interpretation** of the story?

  A. Daniel Keyes enjoys exploring psychological topics in his other stories, as well.
  B. All of the other characters, besides Charlie, are flat characters.
  C. After the surgery, Charlie grows apart from a teacher he once admired.
  D. The passage in which his co-workers make fun of Charlie did not move me.

3. This review is mainly written in which of the following **verb tenses**?

  A. past tense
  B. present tense
  C. future tense
  D. past perfect tense

4. Which of the following revisions helps maintain a consistent **verb tense** in sentence 3?

  A. After Charlie had surgery to improve his intelligence, he began to see the world differently.
  B. After Charlie has surgery to improve his intelligence he begins to see the world differently.
  C. After Charlie had surgery, his intelligence increased rapidly and he saw the world differently.
  D. After Charlie will have surgery to improve his intelligence, he will be beginning to see the world differently.

5. Which word has a **connotation** similar to the word *bitter* in sentence 6?

  A. unusual
  B. harsh
  C. interesting
  D. low quality

Performance Tasks

**Common Core
State Standards**

RL.8.1, RL.8.2, RL.8.3, RL.8.6; W.8.2,
W.8.9.a; SL.8.1, SL.8.6
[For the full wording of the standards,
see the standards chart in the front of
your textbook.]

Directions: *Follow the instructions to complete the tasks
below as required by your teacher.*

*As you work on each task, incorporate both general
academic vocabulary and literary terms you learned
in this unit.*

Writing

Task 1: Literature [RL.8.2; W.8.9.a]
Analyze the Development of Theme

*Write an essay in which you analyze the
importance of plot events and characters'
actions to the development of a story's theme.*

- Choose a story from this unit that has a
  clearly identifiable theme, or message, and
  state what that theme is.

- Describe the elements that contribute to
  the story's theme. Include such elements as
  the story's central conflict and resolution
  and the characters' dialogue and behavior.

- Explain how individual story events impact
  the way the theme is developed and
  whether the theme is stated directly or
  implied.

- Summarize your main points in a
  conclusion.

Task 2: Literature [RL.8.1, RL.8.3; W.8.2]
**Analyze the Use of Dialogue to Develop
a Character**

*Write an essay in which you analyze how
specific lines of dialogue reveal a character's
personality traits in a story.*

- Choose a story from this unit with clearly
  defined characters. Analyze how the
  dialogue spoken by one character shows
  particular attitudes or patterns of behavior
  that are unique to that character.

- Write a brief description of the character
  whose dialogue you are analyzing.

- List several examples of the character's
  dialogue, and explain which personality
  trait(s) each example of dialogue reveals.

- In your analysis, include any changes or
  growth in that character that is revealed
  through dialogue.

- Vary sentence beginnings to maintain
  readers' interest.

Task 3: Literature [RL.8.6; W.8.2]
Analyze Point of View

*Write an essay in which you analyze how
point of view affects readers' knowledge of
characters and events in a story.*

- Select a story from this unit in which point
  of view has an important impact on what
  readers and what characters know.

- Identify the point of view of the story (i.e.,
  first person, third person) and explain how
  you made that determination.

- Explain the difference between what the
  reader knows and what the character or
  characters know about key events in the
  story. Then describe the effect of this
  difference: whether it adds humor, sadness,
  or suspense, for example, and why.

Speaking and Listening

Task 4: Literature [RL.8.3; SL.8.1]

Analyze the Impact of a Plot Event on a Story's Action

Read aloud a section of a story, then discuss the importance of the event it describes to the overall plot.

- Select a significant event that influences other events in a story from this unit.
- Describe the events that come immediately before and after the section you will read. Then, read the section aloud as a group.
- Identify words and phrases that show the significance of the event. Consider impacts on characters and their actions and decisions, as well as on events.
- Reach an agreement with the rest of the group on the nature of the event and its importance to the overall plot.

Task 5: Literature [RL.8.2; SL.8.6]

Present an Oral Review of a Story

Plan and present an oral review of one of the stories in this unit.

- Choose a story and prepare an outline for your review that includes a description of the story's characters, setting, main events, and theme.
- To help you practice conciseness, write a brief summary of the story. Then, write a statement that captures your response to the story's theme.
- When you are ready, begin by presenting your summary and response to the theme. Then, use your outline to support your response.
- Present quotations and descriptions of story details to support your response.

Task 6: Literature [RL.8.6; SL.8.1]

Compare Point of View in Two Different Texts

Compare two stories in this unit with different points of view and evaluate the impact of point of view on the reader.

- With a partner, identify one story from this unit that is told from the perspective of a first-person narrator and one told from the perspective of a third-person narrator.
- Explain how you know that one story is first person and another is third person.
- Discuss the impact that the author's choice of point of view has on the way you view characters' thoughts and actions and the way you perceive story events.
- In your discussion, consider how a change in point of view might have affected your judgments about characters and events.
- Each partner should take turns posing questions about how point of view affects how a story is told, such as, *Would the story have been more or less humorous if it had been told from another point of view?*

Can all conflicts be resolved?
At the beginning of Unit 2, you participated in a discussion about the Big Question. Now that you have finished the unit, write a response to the question. Discuss how and why the views you shared in the discussion have been changed or reinforced. Give specific examples from the stories, as well as from other subjects and your personal experiences, to support your ideas. Use Big Question vocabulary words (see p. 231) in your response.

Featured Titles

In this unit, you have read a variety of short stories. Continue to read on your own. Select works that you enjoy, but challenge yourself to explore new authors and works of increasing depth and complexity. The titles suggested below will help you get started.

Literature

Robot Dreams
by Isaac Asimov
Ace, 1990

This collection of twenty-one science-fiction **short stories** shows Isaac Asimov at his visionary best. Whether imagining the inner life of robots or life without bodies, this book provides fascinating and thought-provoking reading.

Robin Hood
by Angela Bull

To some, Robin Hood—who steals from the rich to give to the poor—is a hero; to others, he is an outlaw. Read this **novel** to see how this crafty woodsman tries to solve one conflict while unintentionally creating others.

Across Five Aprils
by Irene Hunt
Berkley, 2002

Over the course of five eventful Aprils, Jethro Creighton grows into a young man in this **novel** set in southern Illinois during the Civil War. Through the experiences of a single family, this novel explores life in a region whose citizens have divided loyalties and mixed feelings about the bloody conflict sweeping the nation. The author draws on careful research and the stories of her grandfather, who was a boy during the Civil War, to produce this compelling account of a tumultuous time.

19 Varieties of Gazelle
by Naomi Shihab Nye

This **poetry** collection brings together sixty of Nye's imagery-rich poems. Full of figs and olive trees, prayer and heartbreak, these poems capture the uniqueness of the Middle East and of the Arab American experience.

Informational Texts

Behind the Blue and Gray: The Soldier's Life in the Civil War
by Delia Ray

Soldiers on both sides of the Civil War quickly learned about the hardships of army life. The first-person accounts in this **nonfiction** book provide special insight into the horrors of the Civil War experience.

Math Trek: Adventures in the Math Zone
by Ivars Peterson and Nancy Henderson
Jossey-Bass, 1999   EXEMPLAR TEXT ©

In this **nonfiction** book, readers get to take a trip through an adventure park, stopping in each chapter to solve creative math puzzles and problems.

Lend Me Your Ears: Great Speeches in History
edited by William Safire   EXEMPLAR TEXT

William Safire, a speechwriter for President Nixon, introduces this book of exceptional wartime, political, and commencement **speeches.** Included is Winston Churchill's "Blood, Toil, Tears, and Sweat" speech, delivered at a dark moment for Britons, when their ally France was facing Nazi tanks, guns, and planes.

Preparing to Read Complex Texts

Attentive Reading As you read on your own, ask yourself questions about the text. The questions shown below and others that you ask as you read will help you learn and enjoy literature even more.

Common Core State Standards

Reading Literature/Informational Text 10. By the end of the year, read and comprehend literature, including stories, dramas, and poems, and literary nonfiction at the high end of grades 6–8 text complexity band independently and proficiently.

When reading short stories, ask yourself...

- Can I clearly picture the setting of the story? Which details help me do so?
- Can I picture the characters clearly in my mind? Why or why not?
- Do the characters speak and act like real people? Why or why not?
- Which characters do I like? Why? Which characters do I dislike? Why?
- Do I understand why the characters act as they do? Why or why not?
- What does the story mean to me? Does it express a meaning or an insight I find important and true?

Ⓒ Key Ideas and Details

- Does the story grab my attention right from the beginning? Why or why not?
- Do I want to keep reading? Why or why not?
- Can I follow the sequence of events in the story? Am I confused at any point? If so, what information would make the sequence clearer?
- Do the characters change as the story progresses? If so, do their changes seem believable?
- Are there any passages that I find especially moving, interesting, or well written? If so, why?

Ⓒ Craft and Structure

- How is this story similar to and different from other stories I have read?
- Do I care what happens to the characters? Do I sympathize with them? Why or why not?
- How do my feelings toward the characters affect my experience of reading the story?
- Did the story teach me something new or cause me to look at something in a new way? If so, what did I learn?
- Would I recommend this story to others? Why or why not?
- Would I like to read other works by this author? Why or why not?

Ⓒ Integration of Ideas

THE BIG Q

How much *information* is enough?

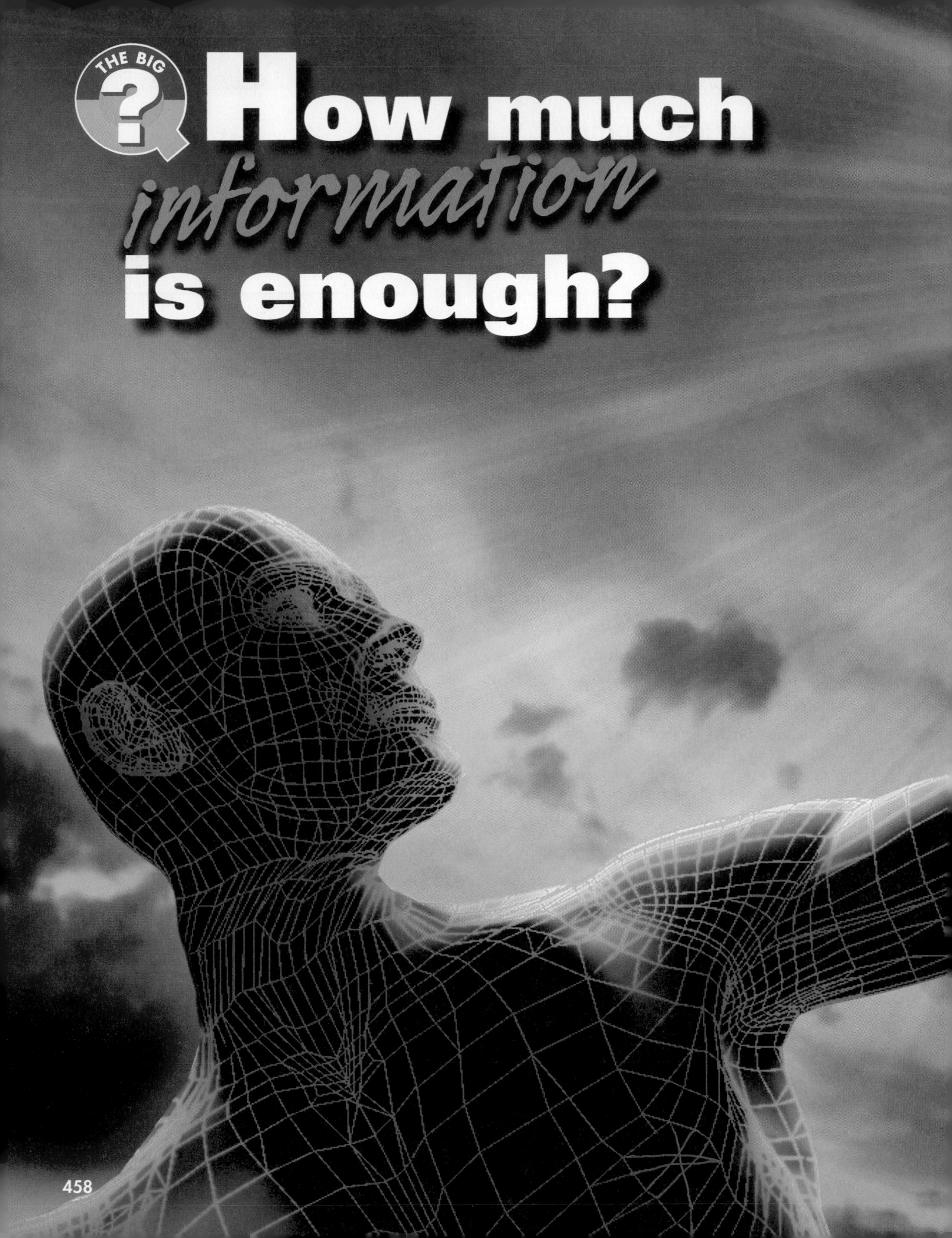

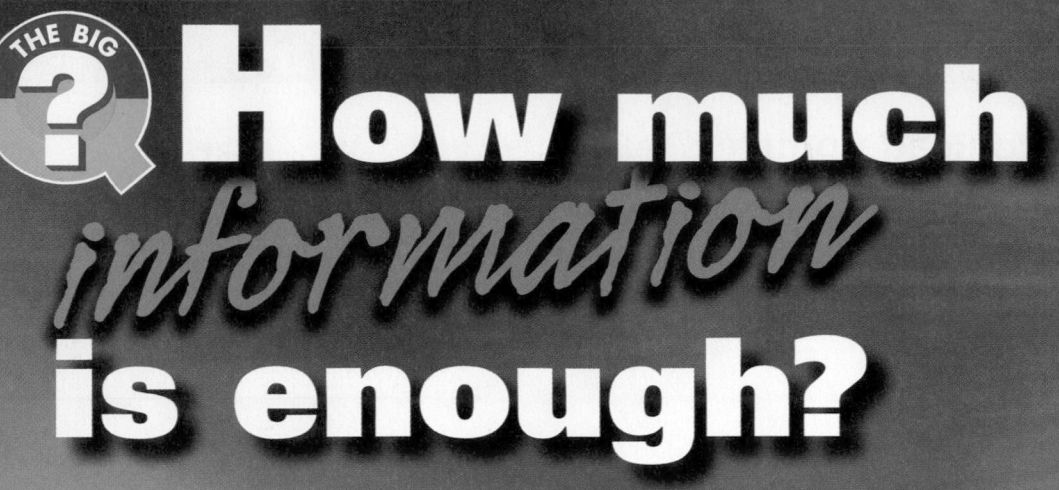

Types of Nonfiction

www.PHLitOnline.com

Hear It!
- Selection summary audio
- Selection audio
- BQ Tunes

See It!
- Author videos
- Big Question video
- Get Connected videos
- Background videos
- More about the authors
- Illustrated vocabulary words
- Vocabulary flashcards

Do It!
- Interactive journals
- Interactive graphic organizers
- Grammar tutorials
- Interactive vocabulary games
- Test practice

THE BIG Q? How much *information* is enough?

Every day, from the time we wake up until we go to sleep, we constantly encounter new information. Television, radio, the Internet, newspapers, magazines, books, and advertisements all compete for our attention. Every global development is analyzed in the press. Statistics reveal information that may or may not be useful.

The challenge is to avoid possible information overload and to separate quality from quantity. Only then will information be valuable to us.

Exploring the Big Question

© **Collaboration: Group Discussion** Start thinking about the Big Question by identifying different types of information. Discuss with a group at least one example of information that would be important to someone in each of these situations:

- A historian writing a biography
- An emergency-room doctor receiving a patient
- A hiker exploring dry backcountry that is prone to fires
- A social scientist researching children's television-viewing habits
- A government official looking into complaints about racial or gender discrimination

Talk about why each type of information would be helpful and how you might evaluate its quality. As you participate in the discussion, listen to one another's ideas carefully and add your own observations and comments. Pose questions and respond thoughtfully to those asked by others. Respond respectfully to others' ideas while you clearly express your own.

Connecting to the Literature Each reading in this unit will give you additional insight into the Big Question.

PHLit
Online!
www.PHLitOnline.com
- Big Question video
- Illustrated vocabulary words
- Interactive vocabulary games
- BQ Tunes

Learning Big Question Vocabulary

Acquire and Use Academic Vocabulary Academic vocabulary is the language you encounter in textbooks and on standardized tests. Review the definitions of these academic vocabulary words.

---

accumulate (ə kyōōm′ yōō lāt′) **v.** collect; gather

challenge (chal′ ənj) **v.** call into question

decision (dē sizh′ ən) **n.** choice

development (di vel′ əp mənt) **n.** outcome

discrimination (di skrim′i nā′ shən) **n.** judgment; ability to perceive even small differences

factor (fak′ tər) **n.** one element that contributes to a condition or situation

global (glō′ bəl) **adj.** worldwide

reveal (ri vēl′) **v.** uncover; expose

statistics (stə tis′ tiks) **n.** numerical facts

Use these words as you complete Big Question activities that involve reading, writing, speaking, and listening.

Gather Vocabulary Knowledge Additional Big Question words are listed below. Categorize the words by deciding whether you know each one well, know it a little bit, or do not know it at all.

| explanation | inequality | quantity |
| exploration | quality | valuable |

Then, do the following:

1. Write the definitions of the words you know.
2. Consult a dictionary to confirm the word's meaning. Revise your definition if necessary.
3. Using a print or an online dictionary, look up the meanings of the words you do not know. Then, write the meanings.
4. If a word sounds familiar but you are not sure of its meaning, consult a dictionary. Then, record the meaning.
5. Use all of the words in a brief paragraph about the value of different types of information.

Common Core State Standards

Speaking and Listening
1. Engage effectively in a range of collaborative discussions with diverse partners on *grade 8 topics, texts, and issues*, building on others' ideas and expressing their own clearly.

1.c. Pose questions that connect the ideas of several speakers and respond to others' questions and comments with relevant evidence, observations, and ideas.

Language
6. Acquire and use accurately grade-appropriate general academic and domain-specific words and phrases; gather vocabulary knowledge when considering a word or phrase important to comprehension or expression.

Elements of Literary Nonfiction

Literary nonfiction discusses real people, places, and events while using literary techniques and expressing artistic insight.

Literary nonfiction is writing that describes real people, places, events, and ideas, but it employs the types of craft and artistry you are used to seeing in fiction or poetry. For that reason, it is sometimes called "creative nonfiction."

For example, in an account of a historic soccer game, an author might include conversations among players. Such use of **dialogue**—a technique you know from fiction—helps readers better understand the players' thoughts and feelings. In describing the game, the author might also build **suspense,** or a feeling of tension about what will happen next.

Works of literary nonfiction may focus on big topics, such as the causes of a war.

Alternatively, they may focus on small topics, such as a moment in someone's life. Regardless of the topic, a literary nonfiction work expresses a **central idea,** or key point. It also conveys the author's unique **point of view,** or perspective, on the topic.

An author develops a central idea by presenting **supporting details** that add information. To help the reader understand the connections between ideas and details, the author presents them in a logical order. Sometimes, an author will follow a formal pattern of organization, such as one of the formats described in the chart below.

Common Organizational Patterns

Pattern or Structure	Description
Chronological Order	Presenting events in time order, or the sequence in which they occurred **Example:** the true story of a mission to Mars
Comparison and Contrast	Grouping elements of a subject according to their similarities and differences **Example:** a review of two different productions of a play
Cause and Effect	Presenting actions (causes) and their results (effects) **Example:** an explanation of a scientific experiment
Problem and Solution	Describing a problem and then explaining one or more ways to solve it **Example:** a proposal to build a new playground and park

Types of Literary Nonfiction

There are five main types, or modes, of literary nonfiction:

- **Narration:** Narrative works tell the stories of real events.
- **Exposition:** Expository works explain or provide information.
- **Argument:** Argumentative, or persuasive, works convince readers to take an action or to think differently.
- **Reflection:** Reflective works offer the author's insights into the meaning of a personal experience.
- **Description:** Descriptive works use details to give readers a clear mental picture of something.

Purposes of Nonfiction

In all types of nonfiction, an author writes for a **purpose,** or reason. Three main purposes are as follows:

- to **inform** or to **explain**
- to **persuade** or to argue
- to **entertain** or to amuse

Purpose and mode go hand in hand. For example, if an author's purpose is to inform readers about a new invention, he or she will write an expository work. The author may, however, combine other types of writing to fulfill that purpose. For instance, he or she might narrate the story of the invention's development and describe the invention in detail.

In This Section

Elements of Literary Nonfiction

Determining the Author's Point of View

Analyzing Structure in Nonfiction

Close Read: Point of View
- Model Text
- Practice Text

After You Read

 Common Core State Standards

RI.8.4, RI.8.5, RI.8.6
[For the full wording of the standards, see the standards chart in the front of your textbook.]

Types and Examples of Nonfiction

Type (or Mode)	Example
Narration	an **autobiography** in which a senator tells the story of her life a **memoir** in which the author tells the story of an adventure
Exposition	an **essay** in which a scholar explains the causes of the Civil War a **report** in which a scientist presents results
Argumentation, or Persuasion	a **speech** in which a student tries to convince classmates to exercise daily an **editorial** in which the author protests a new law
Reflection	a **magazine article** in which a poet describes what he learned from a favorite teacher a **reflective essay** in which an artist discusses her sources of inspiration
Description	a **memoir** in which the author describes storms at sea a restaurant **review** in which a food writer discusses a great meal

Determining the Author's Point of View

Point of view is the way in which a writer regards a subject.

Common Core State Standards

Reading Informational Text
6. Determine an author's point of view or purpose in a text and analyze how the author acknowledges and responds to conflicting evidence or viewpoints.

Point of view is the perspective with which a writer sees a subject. It is shaped by the author's knowledge, beliefs, and experiences.

Stated or Implied Point of View
Sometimes, a writer simply states his or her point of view. More often, however, point of view is implied. The reader must infer—or make an educated guess about—the writer's point of view.

> **Stated Point of View:** As president of the Bike Club, I support bicycle lanes.
>
> **Implied Point of View:** I spent my childhood going on bike trips. One of my first words was *derailleur.*

Point of View and Positions Point of view is not the same as position. In fact, two people who support the same position may have different points of view.

Position: Students Should Wear Uniforms

School Principal	Student
Point of View: I am responsible for students' safety.	**Point of View:** I spend too much time on clothes.
Specific Position: If students wore uniforms, we could identify non-students more easily.	**Specific Position:** Uniforms would allow us to focus on our studies.

Opposing Points of View When writers disagree about ideas, it may be due to differences in their viewpoints. In such cases, writers anticipate conflicts and address them directly.

> **Anticipating Conflicting Viewpoints**
> I know that some students disagree with me. They want to express themselves through their clothing.
>
> **Addressing Conflicting Viewpoints**
> But I think most students agree safety outweighs expression.

By acknowledging another point of view, the author demonstrates respect for others and builds a stronger argument.

Language and Tone The words writers choose create a distinct **tone,** or emotional attitude. When choosing words, writers consider both **denotation,** or dictionary meanings, and **connotation,** or emotional associations. Sometimes, writers use **charged or loaded words** that convey strong emotion, as in the example below.

> **Example:**
> Today we meet our oldest rivals, the Screaming Eagles. We will march onto the football field with strength, pride, and purpose. Cheer us on to victory!

Analyzing Structure in Nonfiction

All the structures of nonfiction work to develop key concepts.

 **Common Core State Standards**

Reading Informational Text
4. Determine the meaning of words and phrases as they are used in a text, including figurative and connotative meanings; analyze the impact of specific word choices on meaning and tone. **5.** Analyze in detail the structure of a specific paragraph in a text, including the role of particular sentences in developing and refining a key concept.

Central Ideas and Paragraphs

Writers develop central ideas, or main points, by introducing related, or supporting, ideas and details throughout a work. Supporting ideas and details are organized in paragraphs. Each paragraph focuses on a single concept.

Topic Sentences Paragraphs usually function in the same way as the work as a whole. Each paragraph contains a main idea, which may be expressed in a topic sentence. Every sentence within the paragraph then helps to develop that main point.

Types of Support Writers develop ideas by using varied types of evidence.

- **Facts:** statements that can be proved true
- **Opinions:** beliefs that may or may not be based on fact
- **Reasons:** statements that justify or explain opinions
- **Examples:** specific cases that illustrate general ideas
- **Descriptions:** details that show how something looks, sounds, feels, or tastes
- **Anecdotes:** brief stories that illustrate a concept

In the example shown here, the author states a main idea and then develops it with both a fact and an example.

> **Example:**
>
> *[Main Idea]* In general, good students spend more time on homework. *[Fact]* A survey of middle school students shows that an "A" student spends two hours on homework each day. *[Example]* For example, my son spent three hours last night studying for a math test.

Language Structures Specific types of language structures, often called **rhetorical devices,** also help writers emphasize certain ideas.

- **Repetition:** reuse of a key word, phrase, or idea
  Example: Eat fruit. Eat vegetables. Eat lean meat. Eat well.
- **Parallel Structure:** use of similar grammatical structures to express related ideas
  Example: We will show our strength and prove our talent.
- **Rhetorical Questions:** inquiries asked for effect rather than answers
  Example: Are we to stand idly by while our park is ruined?

As you read literary nonfiction, notice that the structural choices a writer makes do more than just organize ideas. They also help to advance an author's purpose for writing and to express his or her unique point of view on the topic.

Close Read: Point of View

A writer's point of view is revealed in his or her choices of organization, supporting details, and words and phrases.

In some nonfiction, an author openly states a point of view. However, even when the writer does not directly state a point of view, it still affects how he or she creates a text. As you read, analyze clues that help you understand an author's point of view. Use the following questions as a guide.

Clues to Point of View

Purpose and Central Idea

- What is the author's main purpose for writing—to narrate, to inform, to persuade, to describe, or to reflect?
- What is the author's central idea?
- Is the central idea directly stated, or is it implied?

Organizational Structure

- What do you notice about the way the text is structured? Does it have sections?
- Does the author use a formal organizational pattern?
- What do you notice about paragraph and sentence lengths?

Supporting Details

- What kinds of evidence does the author use to support the central idea?
- Does the author use one type of supporting detail more than others?
- What do the supporting details tell you about the author's beliefs, interests, background, feelings, and experiences?

Language and Tone

- Do any word choices seem unusual, powerful, or interesting?
- Does the author use loaded or charged language?
- Does the author use any rhetorical devices?
- What emotional attitudes does the author's use of words suggest?

Other Viewpoints

- Does the author acknowledge the viewpoints of others?
- If so, how does the author respond to the other viewpoints?

Paragraphs and Sentences

- How does each paragraph support the central idea?
- How does each sentence within each paragraph support the paragraph's main point?

Model

About the Text Linda R. Monk has studied the U.S. Constitution and written extensively about this fundamental document. Her book *Words We Live By: Your Annotated Guide to the Constitution,* from which this excerpt is taken, presents Monk's unique understanding of the Constitution's history.

"We the People" from *Words We Live By* by Linda R. Monk

We the people . . .

These first three words of the Constitution are the most important. They clearly state that the people—not the king, not the legislature, not the courts—are the true rulers in American government. This principle is known as popular sovereignty.

But who are "We the People"? This question troubled the nation for centuries. As Lucy Stone, one of America's first advocates for women's rights, asked in 1853, "'We the People'? Which 'We the People'? The women were not included." Neither were white males who did not own property, American Indians, or African Americans—slave or free. Justice Thurgood Marshall, the first African American on the Supreme Court, described the limitation:

For a sense of the evolving nature of the Constitution, we need look no further than the first three words of the document's preamble: 'We the People.' When the founding fathers used this phrase in 1787, they did not have in mind the majority of America's citizens . . . The men who gathered in Philadelphia in 1787 could not . . . have imagined, nor would they have accepted, that the document they were drafting would one day be construed by a Supreme court to which had been appointed a woman and the descendant of an African slave.

Through the Amendment process, more and more Americans were eventually included in the Constitution's definition of "We the People." After the Civil War, the Thirteenth Amendment ended slavery, the Fourteenth Amendment gave African Americans citizenship, and the Fifteenth Amendment gave black men the vote. In 1920, the Nineteenth Amendment gave women the right to vote nationwide, and in 1971, the Twenty-sixth Amendment extended suffrage to eighteen-year-olds.

Central Idea The author states a central idea in her opening sentence.

Organizational Structure The author uses a problem/solution structure centered on the unspecified meaning of the Constitution's first three words.

Supporting Details The author develops her central idea with a quotation from a respected source.

Paragraphs and Sentences The paragraph begins with a topic sentence that states a main point. Each sentence develops that point by listing, in chronological order, amendments that extended the definition of "We the People."

Literary Analysis Workshop **467**

Independent Practice

About the Text Andrew Mishkin designs and develops robotic vehicles. He was a member of the team that created the *Sojourner* rover, a robot that was used to explore Mars in 1997. Mishkin also designed the operating system that allowed controllers on Earth to give instructions to the robots on Mars. The text is from a journal Mishkin wrote based on a blog he created.

"Making Tracks on Mars" by Andrew Mishkin

Background

NASA blasted two rockets into space in 2003. Sitting on top of them were *Spirit* and *Opportunity*, robotic vehicles the size of golf carts called rovers. Their job was to look for water on Mars and collect data. The Mars Exploration Rovers traveled seven months and 303 million miles, and on January 3, 2004, *Spirit* was due to enter the Martian atmosphere.

Monday, December 29, 2003
Six Days to First Landing

The big question about Mars is, did life ever exist there? Life as we understand it demands the presence of liquid water, yet Mars is now apparently a dead desert world. But what if things were different in the ancient past? From space, Mars looks as if once water might have flowed in rivers, collected in vast oceans, or pooled in crater lakes. The two robotic Mars Exploration Rovers will search for evidence of that water, potentially captured in the rocks and soil of the planet's surface. . .

Spirit, the first of the rovers to reach Mars, will be landing next Saturday night, January 3rd. *"Opportunity"* will follow three weeks later.

A British spacecraft—*Beagle 2*[1]—attempted its own Mars landing on Christmas Eve, but has been silent ever since. Landing on Mars is hard! I wish the *Beagle 2* team well, and hope they hear from their spacecraft soon. I cannot help but hope that our own landing goes more smoothly, with a quick confirmation from *Spirit* that it has arrived unscathed.

Organizational Structure What organizational structure is Mishkin using, and how does it suit his purpose for writing?

Language and Tone Identify words that seem casual or chatty and others that seem formal and poetic. What does this combination tell you about Mishkin's point of view toward his subject?

---

1. ***Beagle 2*** No definite cause was found for the loss of the robot space probe.

Saturday, January 3, 2004
Landing Day

Far away, so far that the signals it was sending were taking nearly 10 minutes at the speed of light to arrive at Earth, the spacecraft carrying the *Spirit* rover was about to collide with Mars.

I waited with a sick feeling, a hundred million miles closer to home in mission control at the Jet Propulsion Laboratory in Pasadena, California. Hundreds of us have worked for the past three years—days, evenings, weekends, and holidays—for this moment.

It's looking more and more like the *Beagle 2* mission has failed. I can only imagine wreckage strewn over a barren butterscotch-hued landscape. Will we have better luck?

Spirit's lander must be hitting the atmosphere, a falling meteor blazing in the Martian sky. We'd named the next moments "the six minutes of terror." I listened to the reports on the voice network. All the way down, radio signals from the spacecraft told us "so far so good." Then, immediately after the lander hit the ground, contact was lost. Everyone tensed up. Time dragged. There was only silence from Mars.

Ten minutes later, we got another signal. *Spirit* had survived! The engineers and scientists in mission control were screaming, cheering, thrusting their fists in the air. We were on Mars!

Two hours later, the first pictures arrived from *Spirit*. None of us could believe our luck. The rover looked perfect, with its solar panels fully extended, and the camera mast[2] fully deployed. All the engineering data looked "nominal."[3] There were no fault conditions—much better than any of our rehearsals!

In another minute or two, we had our first panoramic view through *Spirit's* eyes. We could see 360 degrees around the rover, to the horizon. The landing site looked flat, with small rocks. We can drive here!

Language and Tone
Note specific words Mishkin uses to describe the Martian landscape. What do these word choices tell you about Mishkin's feelings toward his subject?

Organizational Structure
Mishkin describes what he is seeing in chronological order. How does his choice of organizational structure suit his purpose?

2. **camera mast** tall pole on which the camera is mounted, which rotates and swivels.
3. **nominal** normal; what is expected.

Practice continued

Sunday, January 11, 2004
Living on Mars Time

I just finished working the Martian night, planning *Spirit*'s activities for the rover's ninth Martian day on the surface. I've been working Mars time for the past four days, and now finally have a couple of days off.

The Mars day (called a "sol") is just a bit longer than an Earth day, at twenty-four hours and thirty-nine and a half minutes. Since the rover is solar powered, and wakes with the sun, its activities are tied to the Martian day. And so are the work shifts of our operations team on Earth. Part of the team works the Martian day, interacting with the spacecraft, sending commands, and analyzing the results. But those of us who build new commands for the rover work the Martian night, while the rover sleeps.

Since the rover wakes up about 40 Earth minutes later every morning, so do we. It seems like sleeping later every day would be easy, but it can be disorienting. It's very easy to lose track of what time it is here on Earth . . .

Thursday, January 15, 2004
Sol 12: Six Wheels on Dirt!

Mars time continues to be disorienting. During another planning meeting for *Spirit*, we were introduced to a Congressman touring the Laboratory. All I could think was, "What's he doing here in the middle of the night " It was two in the morning—Mars time. Only after he left did I remember that it was mid-afternoon Pacific time . . .

My team delivered the commands for sol 12—drive off day—but nobody went home. This would be *Spirit*'s most dangerous day since landing. There was a small chance the rover could tip over or get stuck as it rolled off the lander platform onto the dust of Mars. When the time came, the Flight Director played the theme from "Rawhide"[4]—"rollin', rollin', rollin'. . ." —and everyone crowded into mission control cheered and applauded. The command to drive shot through space.

Paragraphs and Sentences
Mishkin begins the paragraph with a topic sentence that connects this paragraph to the previous one. How do the other sentences in the paragraph develop the topic sentence?

4. **"Rawhide"** popular 1960s television show about cattle drivers in the 1860s. Its theme song was also extremely popular.

We'll now have to wait another hour and a half to hear back. Engineers are professional worriers. We imagine all the ways things can fail, so that we can prevent those failures from occurring. But even when we've done our jobs, and considered all the alternatives we can come up with, there is always some doubt . . .

A signal. Applause. Then images started to appear. There was the lander—behind us! We could see tracks in the dirt. The front cameras showed nothing but Martian soil under our wheels. We were off! Engineers were cheering, applauding, and hugging each other. People were shaking my hand. The mission had just shifted from deployment to exploration.

Thursday, January 22, 2004
Sol 19

Something's wrong with *Spirit*. Yesterday, the rover didn't respond to the commands we sent. At first we thought it was just the thunderstorms at our transmitter in Australia, getting in the way. But later *Spirit* missed its preprogrammed communications times, or sent meaningless data. When your spacecraft is halfway across the solar system and won't talk to you, there's no way to tell whether this is a minor problem, easily fixed, or the beginning of the end of our mission. For *Spirit*, there's no repairman to make house calls.

And we've just barely gotten started!

Sunday, January 25, 2004
Ups, Downs, and Landing on Mars—Again

After a day of unsuccessful attempts to regain control of the rover, the project manager declared *Spirit*'s condition "critical." We tried commanding *Spirit* to send us simple "beep" signals that would prove it was listening to us. Sometimes these worked. But after one such attempt, we got no signal. The mood in the control room collapsed. The team forced itself into thinking about what to try next.

Paragraphs and Sentences
Notice the style and structure of this paragraph. How do the short sentences and order of the sentences suggest Mishkin's point of view?

Practice continued

Language Mishkin uses both technical language ("carrier lock" and "telemetry") as well as literary language ("tentative, incredulous"). How does this both suit his purpose and reveal his point of view?

Language and Tone What point of view toward the robot is suggested by Mishkin's use of the words "our girl"?

Purpose and Central Idea How does this final paragraph, and final word, help support Mishkin's purpose for writing?

A few minutes later, there was a tentative, incredulous voice on the network: "Uh. Flight. Telecom. Station 63 is reporting carrier lock."[5] Engineers around the room looked up in surprise. "They're reporting symbol lock . . . We've got telemetry."[6] *Spirit* was back! The data coming down was garbled, but our girl was at least babbling at us. The mood in the room transformed again.

Thanks to extreme long distance diagnosis by the software engineers, *Spirit* was listening to us again within two days. We still have a lot of work to do. But at least we can now begin tracing the problem on a stable spacecraft.

In the meantime, *Opportunity* has been falling toward Mars. On Saturday night, those of us working on *Spirit*'s problems paused long enough to watch the landing events unfold. *Opportunity*'s first photos were amazing, even for Mars. It looks like we rolled to a stop at the bottom of a bowl—actually a small crater. The soil is a grayish red, except where we've disturbed it with our airbags; there it looks like a deep pure red. And while there are no individual rocks, we seem to be partly encircled by a rock outcropping—bedrock. No one has seen anything like this on Mars before. And it's only yards away. A scientist standing next to me in mission control said only one word: "Jackpot!"

---

5. **carrier lock** stage of receiving information. Communication over a great distance involves locating the frequency of the carrier's signal, locking onto it, and holding it while information is received.

6. **telemetry** (tə lem´ ə trē) *n.* transmission of data over a great distance, as from satellites and other space vehicles.

1. **Key Ideas and Details** **(a)** What is Mishkin's main purpose for writing about the mission? **(b)** Identify three elements of the text that reflect that purpose.

2. **Key Ideas and Details** **(a)** What is the mission of the two rovers? **(b) Generalize:** What evidence do the scientists hope to find?

3. **Key Ideas and Details** **(a) Infer:** Why does Mishkin refer to the failure of the *Beagle 2* mission? **(b) Make a Judgment:** At what point do the engineers fear the current mission might fail?

4. **Key Ideas and Details** **(a) Cite:** How many references to *Spirit* as a living thing does Mishkin include in this excerpt? **(b) Speculate:** Why do you think he sometimes discusses the robot as if it were a human being? **(c)** What does this suggest about his point of view?

5. **Craft and Structure** **Analyze:** How does the diary structure of Mishkin's blog give the reader a sense of connection to both Mishkin and the mission?

6. **Craft and Structure** **(a) Cite:** Note two examples of scientific language, two examples of casual language, and two examples of poetic or descriptive language in this journal. **(b) Analyze:** Does Mishkin's use of different types of language suggest that he brings multiple points of view to the topic? Explain.

7. **Integration of Knowledge and Ideas** **(a)** Using a chart like the one shown, identify three personal reflections of Mishkin's. For each, identify the related fact or event that sparked his reflection.

Personal Reflection	←→	Event

(b) Collaboration: Compare your answers with a partner and discuss any differences. How have your answers grown or changed?

8. Learn more about Andrew Mishkin and the Martian rovers by conducting research in the library or on the Internet. Prepare a **report** to share with the class. You may share your report on a bulletin board or on a classroom blog. Include the following information:

- a list of the goals of the mission
- a presentation of the results of the exploration
- your evaluation of the mission's success

© Leveled Texts

Build your skills and improve your comprehension of narrative nonfiction with texts of increasing complexity.

Read **"Baseball"** to find out how a group of children create their own fun.

Read the excerpt from *Harriet Tubman: Conductor on the Underground Railroad* to learn about a brave woman.

© Common Core State Standards

Meet these standards with either **"Baseball"** (p. 478) or the excerpt from *Harriet Tubman: Conductor on the Underground Railroad* (p. 486).

Reading Informational Text

2. Determine a central idea of a text and analyze its development over the course of the text, including its relationship to supporting ideas. *(Reading Skill: Main Idea)*

3. Analyze how a text makes connections among and distinctions between individuals, ideas, or events. *(Reading Skill: Main Idea)*

Writing

2. Write informative/explanatory texts to examine a topic and convey ideas, concepts, and information through the selection, organization, and analysis of relevant content. *(Writing: Biographical Sketch)*

2.b. Develop the topic with relevant, well-chosen facts, definitions, concrete details, quotations, or other information and examples. *(Writing: Biographical Sketch)*

2.c. Use appropriate and varied transitions to create cohesion and clarify the relationships among ideas and concepts. *(Writing: Biographical Sketch)*

Speaking and Listening

6. Adapt speech to a variety of contexts and tasks, demonstrating command of formal English when indicated or appropriate. *(Speaking and Listening: Skit)*

Language

1. Demonstrate command of the conventions of standard English grammar and usage when writing or speaking. *(Conventions: Adjectives and Articles)*

Reading Skill: Main Idea

The **main idea** of a work of nonfiction is the **central point** that the author conveys. Sometimes, the author directly states the main idea. More often, the author implies, or suggests, the main idea.

You can use the structure of key paragraphs to find details to help you **identify the implied main idea.** As you read, you will notice that most important details can be grouped around a common connection or idea. Other details may not seem as *relevant*, or important, to this idea. Use the relevant connections to help you infer the main idea.

For example, in an essay about a family vacation, you learn that the writer's beautiful sister was silent and shaking on a plane ride. You could connect the key details—ignoring the detail about her beauty—to infer that the girl is afraid of flying.

Literary Analysis: Narrative Essay

A **narrative essay** tells the story of real events, people, and places. Narrative essays share these features with fictional stories:

- People's traits and personalities are developed through their words, actions, and thoughts.

- The *setting* is important if it creates a specific *mood*, or if it tells something about the characters, such as where they live or whether they are in danger.

As you read, think about how the setting influences the way the characters think, speak, and act.

Using the Strategy: Narrative Essay Chart

Use a **narrative essay chart** like the one shown to help you keep track of the elements in the essays you will read.

Narrative Essay		
Setting(s)	People	Event(s)

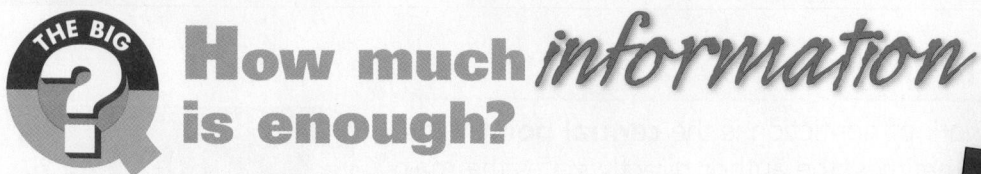

How much *information* is enough?

Writing About the Big Question

In "Baseball," the author describes the fun he had as a child playing a unique version of baseball with his friends. Use this sentence starter to develop your ideas about the Big Question.

In order to **reveal** what the world looks like from a child's perspective, a writer can include information such as _____ _____.

While You Read Look for details that reflect the carefree way that the author and his friends experienced the world.

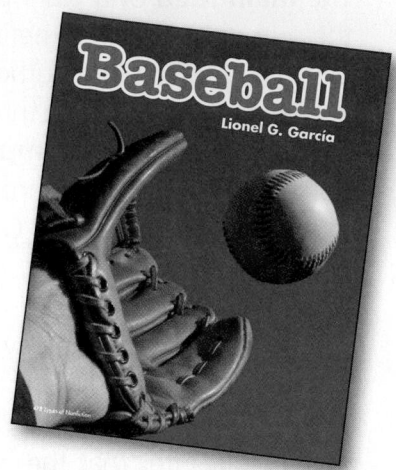

Vocabulary

Read each word and its definition. Decide whether you know the word well, know it a little bit, or do not know it all. After you read, see how your knowledge of each word has increased.

- **rotate** (rō′ tāt′) *v.* switch (p. 479) *One player will <u>rotate</u> out when a substitute comes in.* rotation *n.*

- **scheme** (skēm) *n.* organized way of doing something; plan (p. 480) *She developed an efficient <u>scheme</u> for studying for tests.* schemer *n.* scheming *adj.*

- **option** (äp′ shən) *n.* choice (p. 481) *Students have the <u>option</u> of doing a written or an oral report.* opt *v.* optional *adj.*

- **evaded** (ē vād′ əd) *v.* avoided (p. 481) *Thanks to my speediness, I <u>evaded</u> the bully.* evader *n.* evasive *adj.*

- **shiftless** (shift′ lis) *adj.* without ambition (p. 481) *The <u>shiftless</u> woman lacked the energy and desire to look for a job.* shiftlessness *n.* shiftlessly *adv.* shift *v.*

- **ignorance** (ig′ nə rəns) *n.* lack of knowledge or awareness (p. 482) *His blank expression revealed his total <u>ignorance</u> of the subject.* ignore *v.* ignorant *adj.* ignorantly *adv.* ignoramus *n.*

Word Study

The **Latin suffix -ance** changes a verb or adjective into a noun. It means "a condition" or "a state of being."

In this essay, the narrator's uncle is surprised by the children's unaware state—their **ignorance** of baseball rules.

Meet
Lionel G. García
(b. 1935)

Author of
Baseball

The youngest of eight children, Lionel G. García grew up in a Mexican American family in rural Texas.

A Family of Storytellers As a child, García loved to listen to his relatives tell stories about their experiences and acquaintances. "It was easy to laugh and cry in the dark with the stories," he recalls. Although his family was poor, García remembers his childhood as a happy time: "We walked the hot, dusty streets barefooted, our pockets full of marbles, spinning tops, mesquite sticks and balls, looking for a game to play. We were carefree . . . ." In his essays, García uses humor and adult wisdom to recall childhood adventures.

BACKGROUND FOR THE ESSAY

Sports and Games

Today, many young people play on organized sports teams that have strict rules as well as coaches and referees to enforce them. In the past, though, children often made up their own games or played informal "pickup" games in which they served as their own referees. In his essay "Baseball," Lionel G. García describes the unique version of baseball he and his friends used to play.

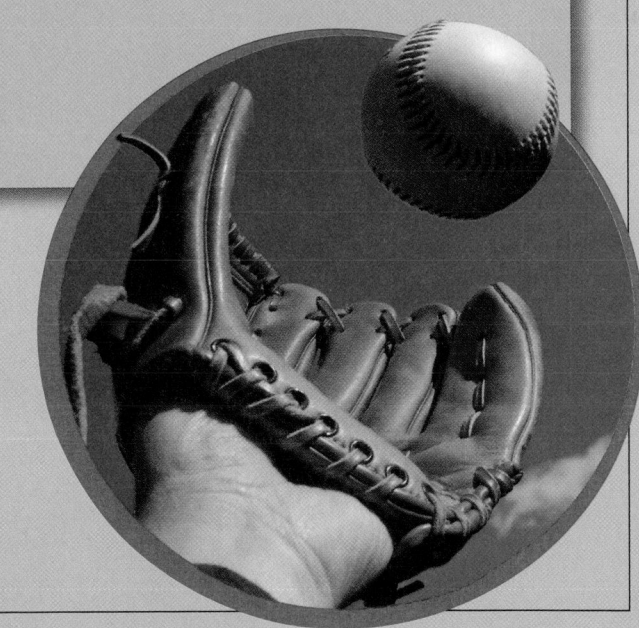

DID YOU KNOW?

In the past, García has worked full-time as a veterinarian while writing at night. He has always enjoyed caring for animals. For part of his childhood, García lived on a ranch with his grandfather, tending cows and goats.

Baseball

Lionel G. García

We loved to play baseball. We would take the old mesquite[1] stick and the old ball across the street to the parochial[2] school grounds to play a game. Father Zavala enjoyed watching us. We could hear him laugh mightily from the screened porch at the rear of the rectory[3] where he sat.

The way we played baseball was to rotate positions after every out. First base, the only base we used, was located where one would normally find second base. This made the batter have to run past the pitcher and a long way to the first baseman, increasing the odds of getting thrown out. The pitcher stood in line with the batter, and with first base, and could stand as close or as far from the batter as he or she wanted. Aside from the pitcher, the batter and the first baseman, we had a catcher. All the rest of us would stand in the outfield. After an out, the catcher would come up to bat. The pitcher took the position of catcher, and the first baseman moved up to be the pitcher. Those in the outfield were left to

---

1. **mesquite** (me skēt´) *n.* thorny shrub common in Mexico and the southwestern United States.
2. **parochial** (pə rō´ kē əl) *adj.* supported by a church.
3. **rectory** (rek´ tər ē) *n.* housing for priests or ministers.

Baseball **479**

▶ **Critical Viewing**
In standard base-
ball, what rules
might apply in the
situation shown at the
right? **[Interpret]**

Vocabulary
scheme (skēm′) *n.*
organized way of
doing something; plan

Main Idea
What main idea about
the way the game was
played is implied by the
details in this passage ?

their own devices. I don't remember ever getting to bat.

There was one exception to the rotation scheme. I don't
know who thought of this, but whoever caught the ball on the
fly would go directly to be the batter. This was not a popular
thing to do. You could expect to have the ball thrown at you
on the next pitch.

There was no set distance for first base. First base was
wherever Matías or Juan or Cota tossed a stone. They were
the law. The distance could be long or short depending on
how soon we thought we were going to be called in to eat. The
size of the stone marking the base mattered more than the
distance from home plate to first base. If we hadn't been called
in to eat by dusk, first base was hard to find. Sometimes
someone would kick the stone farther away and arguments
erupted.

When the batter hit the ball in the air and it was caught
that was an out. So far so good. But if the ball hit the
ground, the fielder had two choices. One, in keeping with
the standard rules of the game, the ball could be thrown to
the first baseman and, if caught before the batter arrived at
the base, that was an out. But the second, more interesting

option allowed the fielder, ball in hand, to take off running after the batter. When close enough, the fielder would throw the ball at the batter. If the batter was hit before reaching first base, the batter was out. But if the batter evaded being hit with the ball, he or she could either run to first base or run back to home plate. All the while, everyone was chasing the batter, picking up the ball and throwing it at him or her. To complicate matters, on the way to home plate the batter had the choice of running anywhere possible to avoid getting hit. For example, the batter could run to hide behind the hackberry trees at the parochial school grounds, going from tree to tree until he or she could make it safely back to home plate. Many a time we would wind up playing the game past Father Zavala and in front of the rectory half a block away. Or we could be seen running after the batter several blocks down the street toward town, trying to hit the batter with the ball. One time we wound up all the way across town before we cornered Juan against a fence, held him down, and hit him with the ball. Afterwards, we all fell laughing in a pile on top of each other, exhausted from the run through town. ●

The old codgers, the old shiftless men who spent their day talking at the street corners, never caught on to what we were doing. They would halt their idle conversation just long enough to watch us run by them, hollering and throwing the old ball at the batter.

It was the only kind of baseball game Father Zavala had ever seen. What a wonderful game it must have been for him to see us hit the ball, run to a rock, then run for our lives down the street. He loved the game, shouting from the screened porch at us, pushing us on. And then all of a sudden we were gone, running after the batter. What a game! In what enormous stadium would it be

Vocabulary
option (äp´ shən)
n. choice
evaded (ē vād´ əd)
v. avoided

Spiral Review
Author's Purpose
How does this information about the author's childhood baseball games support his purpose for writing?

Vocabulary
shiftless (shift´ lis)
adj. without ambition

Narrative Essay
What do you learn about Father Zavala, based on these details?

Reading Check
Where could the batter run to avoid being thrown out?

played to allow such freedom over such an expanse of ground?

My uncle Adolfo, who had pitched for the Yankees and the Cardinals in the majors, had given us the ball several years before. Once when he returned for a visit, he saw us playing from across the street and walked over to ask us what we were doing.

"Playing baseball," we answered as though we thought he should know better. After all, he was the professional baseball player.

He walked away shaking his head. "What a waste of a good ball," we heard him say, marveling at our ignorance.

Vocabulary
ignorance (ig´ nə rəns)
n. lack of knowledge or awareness

Critical Thinking

1. **Key Ideas and Details (a)** Where was first base in García's version of baseball? **(b) Analyze Cause and Effect:** What were some results of this situation?

2. **Key Ideas and Details (a) Contrast:** In what ways did García's version of baseball differ from the standard rules of baseball? **(b) Speculate:** How do you think García and his friends came to develop these unusual rules?

3. **Integration of Knowledge and Ideas (a) Infer:** Why do Father Zavala and García's uncle Adolfo respond differently to the game? **(b) Take a Position:** Do you agree with Adolfo's statement, "What a waste of a good ball"? Why or why not? **(c) Discuss:** Share your opinion with a partner. Then, discuss how your view has or has not changed as a result of listening to your partner's opinion.

4. **Integration of Knowledge and Ideas** What information does García provide that creates an impression of childhood as a time of creativity and freedom? *[Connect to the Big Question: How much information is enough?]*

Cite textual evidence to support your responses.

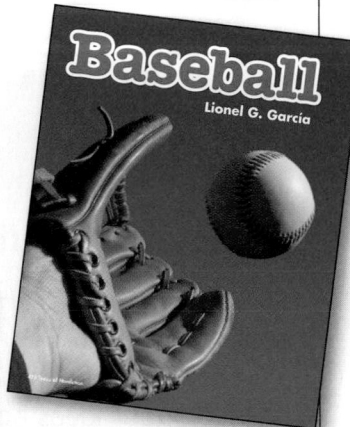

Reading Skill: Main Idea

1. (a) In a chart like the one shown, write at least two more important details about the baseball game described in the essay. **(b)** Then, based on all the details, write a sentence that states the **main idea** the author conveys about the game.

Detail		Detail		Detail	Main Idea
The boys did not have good equipment.	+	The boys did not know official baseball rules.	+		

2. Why do you think the author implies the main idea rather than directly stating it in "Baseball"? Explain.

Literary Analysis: Narrative Essay

3. Key Ideas and Details List the two most important events in this **narrative essay.**

4. Key Ideas and Details (a) Identify three people in the narrative and describe their relationship with the author. **(b)** Use details to identify the setting.

Vocabulary

Acquisition and Use Use your knowledge of the vocabulary words to indicate if the statements are *true* or *false*. Explain your answers.

1. A criminal who has *evaded* punishment is probably in prison.

2. A person who has more than one *option* has many choices.

3. The purpose of education is to spread *ignorance.*

4. If preschoolers *rotate* activities, they will get bored.

5. Following a *scheme* makes a complex task easier.

6. A *shiftless* attitude is essential to accomplish work.

Word Study Use the context of the sentences and what you know about the **Latin suffix -ance** to explain each answer.

1. Does William Shakespeare still have *relevance* today?

2. Why should you avoid giving a pet an *abundance* of snacks?

Word Study

The **Latin suffix -ance** means "a condition" or "state of being."

Apply It Explain how the suffix **-ance** contributes to the meanings of these words. You may consult a dictionary if necessary.

significance
arrogance
avoidance

How much *information* is enough?

Writing About the Big Question

In this excerpt from *Harriet Tubman: Conductor on the Underground Railroad*, Harriet Tubman leads eleven escaped slaves to freedom in Canada in the mid-1800s. Use this sentence starter to develop your ideas about the Big Question:

It is important to learn about historical figures who **challenged** slavery because _____.

While You Read Notice the types of details the author includes to help readers learn about Tubman.

Vocabulary

Read each word and its definition. Decide whether you know the word well, know it a little bit, or do not know it all. After you read, see how your knowledge of each word has increased.

- **invariably** (in ver´ ē ə blē) *adv.* all the time; always (p. 487) *People invariably mistake Jon for his twin brother.* *invariable adj. invariability n. vary v. variety n.*

- **fugitives** (fyo͞o´ ji tivz) *n.* people fleeing from danger (p. 487) *The escaping slaves were fugitives from the law.*

- **incentive** (in sent´ iv) *n.* something that makes a person take action (p. 488) *Extra pay for overtime labor is an incentive to work longer hours.*

- **dispel** (di spel´) *v.* cause something to go away (p. 489) *The facts will dispel any doubts about his innocence.* *dispelling v. impel v. compel v. repel v.*

- **mutinous** (myo͞ot´ ən əs) *adj.* rebellious (p. 491) *The mutinous sailors captured the captain and took charge of the ship. mutiny n. mutineer n.*

- **bleak** (blēk) *adj.* bare and windswept; cold and harsh (p. 495) *The bleak landscape stretched before them like an old, gray blanket. bleakly adv. bleakness adj.*

Word Study

The **suffix -ly** comes from **Old English.** It is used to create adverbs that describe how, when, or how often something is done.

In this essay, slave owners **invariably** discover that some slaves have escaped. Time after time, they are fooled by those who desire freedom.

Meet
Ann Petry
(1908–1997)

Author of
Harriet Tubman:
Conductor on the Underground Railroad

Stories of the Underground Railroad had a personal meaning for Ann Petry. Her grandfather Willis James was himself a fugitive slave who had escaped from Virginia and settled in Connecticut in the 1800s.

The Voices of History Petry's parents encouraged Petry to be confident and proud of her heritage by telling stories of her ancestors. These stories later helped Petry capture the voices of history in her own writing. To young people, she said, "Remember for what a long, long time black people have been in this country, have been a part of America: a sturdy, indestructible, wonderful part of America, woven into its heart and into its soul."

DID YOU KNOW?
Like her father, Petry trained as a pharmacist. She worked for several years in her family's drugstore.

BACKGROUND FOR THE ESSAY
The Underground Railroad

Harriet Tubman, a former slave, became a leading force behind the Underground Railroad, a network of people that helped slaves escape the South in the mid-1800s. At first, she led escaped slaves to free states in the North. In 1850, however, Congress passed the Fugitive Slave Law, which returned escaped slaves found in the North to their southern masters. As a result, Tubman was forced to lead the fugitives to Canada.

from Harriet Tubman: Conductor on the Underground Railroad **485**

from **Harriet Tubman:**
Conductor on the
Underground Railroad

Ann Petry

The Railroad Runs to Canada

Along the Eastern Shore of Maryland, in Dorchester County, in Caroline County, the masters kept hearing whispers about the man named Moses, who was running off slaves. At first they did not believe in his existence. The stories about him were fantastic, unbelievable. Yet they watched for him. They offered rewards for his capture.

They never saw him. Now and then they heard whispered rumors to the effect that he was in the neighborhood. The woods were searched. The roads were watched. There was never anything to indicate his whereabouts. But a few days afterward, a goodly number of slaves would be gone from the plantation. Neither the master nor the overseer had heard or seen anything unusual in the quarter. Sometimes one or the other would vaguely remember having heard a whippoorwill call somewhere in the woods, close by, late at night. Though it was the wrong season for whippoorwills.

Sometimes the masters thought they had heard the cry of a hoot owl, repeated, and would remember having thought that the intervals between the low moaning cry were wrong, that it had been repeated four times in succession instead of three. There was never anything more than that to suggest that all was not well in the quarter. Yet when morning came, they invariably discovered that a group of the finest slaves had taken to their heels.

Unfortunately, the discovery was almost always made on a Sunday. Thus a whole day was lost before the machinery of pursuit could be set in motion. The posters offering rewards for the fugitives could not be printed until Monday. The men who made a living hunting for runaway slaves were out of reach, off in the woods with their dogs and their guns, in pursuit of four-footed game, or they were in camp meetings[1] saying their prayers with their wives and families beside them.

Harriet Tubman could have told them that there was far more involved in this matter of running off slaves than signaling the would-be runaways by imitating the call of a whippoorwill, or a hoot owl, far more involved than a matter of waiting for a clear night when the North Star was visible.

In December, 1851, when she started out with the band of fugitives that she planned to take to Canada, she had been in the vicinity of the plantation for days, planning the trip, carefully selecting the slaves that she would take with her.

She had announced her arrival in the quarter by singing the forbidden spiritual[2]—"Go down, Moses, 'way down to Egypt Land"—singing it softly outside the door of a slave cabin, late at night. The husky voice was beautiful even when it was barely more than a murmur borne on the wind.

Once she had made her presence known, word of her coming spread from cabin to cabin. The slaves whispered

Reading Check
What does Harriet Tubman do?

---

1. **camp meetings** religious meetings held outdoors or in a tent.
2. **forbidden spiritual** In 1831, a slave named Nat Turner encouraged an unsuccessful slave uprising by talking about the biblical story of the Israelites' escape from Egypt. Afterward, the singing of certain spirituals, songs based on the Bible, was forbidden for fear of encouraging more uprisings.

Narrative Essay
What are the real-life
setting and subject of
this essay?

to each other, ear to mouth, mouth to ear, "Moses is here." "Moses has come." "Get ready. Moses is back again." The ones who had agreed to go North with her put ashcake and salt herring in an old bandanna, hastily tied it into a bundle, and then waited patiently for the signal that meant it was time to start. •

There were eleven in this party, including one of her brothers and his wife. It was the largest group that she had ever conducted, but she was determined that more and more slaves should know what freedom was like.

She had to take them all the way to Canada. The Fugitive Slave Law was no longer a great many incomprehensible words written down on the country's lawbooks. The new law had become a reality. It was Thomas Sims, a boy, picked up on the streets of Boston at night and shipped back to Georgia. It was Jerry and Shadrach, arrested and jailed with no warning.

She had never been in Canada. The route beyond Philadelphia was strange to her. But she could not let the runaways who accompanied her know this. As they walked along she told them stories of her own first flight, she kept painting vivid word pictures of what it would be like to be free.

But there were so many of them this time. She knew moments of doubt when she was half-afraid, and kept looking back over her shoulder, imagining that she heard the sound of pursuit. They would certainly be pursued. Eleven of them. Eleven thousand dollars' worth of flesh and bone and muscle that belonged to Maryland planters. If they were caught, the eleven runaways would be whipped and sold South, but she—she would probably be hanged.

They tried to sleep during the day but they never could wholly relax into sleep. She could tell by the positions they assumed, by their restless movements. And they walked at night. Their progress was slow. It took them three nights of walking to reach the first stop. She had told them about the place where they would stay, promising warmth and good food, holding these things out to them as an incentive to keep going.

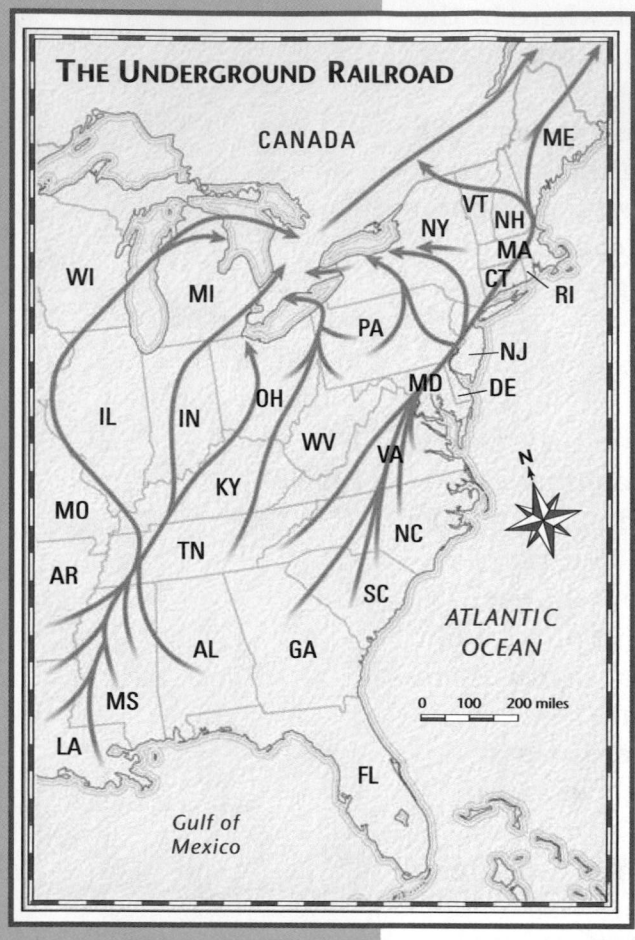

THE UNDERGROUND RAILROAD

▲ Critical Viewing
What does the map
show? [Interpret]

Main Idea
What new details
about Tubman do you
learn here?

Vocabulary
incentive (in sent´ iv) *n.*
something that makes
a person take action

When she knocked on the door of a farmhouse, a place where she and her parties of runaways had always been welcome, always been given shelter and plenty to eat, there was no answer. She knocked again, softly. A voice from within said, "Who is it?" There was fear in the voice.

She knew instantly from the sound of the voice that there was something wrong. She said, "A friend with friends," the password on the Underground Railroad.

The door opened, slowly. The man who stood in the doorway looked at her coldly, looked with unconcealed astonishment and fear at the eleven disheveled runaways who were standing near her. Then he shouted, "Too many, too many. It's not safe. My place was searched last week. It's not safe!" and slammed the door in her face.

She turned away from the house, frowning. She had promised her passengers food and rest and warmth, and instead of that, there would be hunger and cold and more walking over the frozen ground. Somehow she would have to instill courage into these eleven people, most of them strangers, would have to feed them on hope and bright dreams of freedom instead of the fried pork and corn bread and milk she had promised them.

They stumbled along behind her, half-dead for sleep, and she urged them on, though she was as tired and as discouraged as they were. She had never been in Canada but she kept painting wondrous word pictures of what it would be like. She managed to dispel their fear of pursuit, so that they would not become hysterical, panic-stricken. Then she had to bring some of the fear back, so that they would stay awake and keep walking though they drooped with sleep. •

Yet during the day, when they lay down deep in a thicket, they never really slept, because if a twig snapped or the wind sighed in the branches of a pine tree, they jumped to their feet, afraid of their own shadows, shivering and shaking. It was very cold, but they dared not make fires because someone would see the smoke and wonder about it.

Main Idea
What main idea is implied by Tubman's thoughts at the beginning of this paragraph?

▼ **Critical Viewing**
Judging from the text and this photo of a secret tunnel entrance under an Ohio tavern, what physical sensations and emotions do you think the fugitives would have experienced hiding in the "stations"? **[Connect]**

She kept thinking, eleven of them. Eleven thousand dollars' worth of slaves. And she had to take them all the way to Canada. Sometimes she told them about Thomas Garrett, in Wilmington. She said he was their friend even though he did not know them. He was the friend of all fugitives. He called them God's poor. He was a Quaker and his speech was a little different from that of other people. His clothing was different, too. He wore the wide-brimmed hat that the Quakers wear.

She said that he had thick white hair, soft, almost like a baby's, and the kindest eyes she had ever seen. He was a big man and strong, but he had never used his strength to harm anyone, always to help people. He would give all of them a new pair of shoes. Everybody. He always did. Once they reached his house in Wilmington, they would be safe. He would see to it that they were.

She described the house where he lived, told them about the store where he sold shoes. She said he kept a pail of milk and a loaf of bread in the drawer of his desk so that he would have food ready at hand for any of God's poor who should suddenly appear before him, fainting with hunger. There was a hidden room in the store. A whole wall swung open, and behind it was a room where he could hide fugitives. On the wall there were shelves filled with small boxes—boxes of shoes—so that you would never guess that the wall actually opened.

While she talked, she kept watching them. They did not believe her. She could tell by their expressions. They were thinking. New shoes, Thomas Garrett, Quaker, Wilmington—what foolishness was this? Who knew if she told the truth? Where was she taking them anyway?

That night they reached the next stop—a farm that belonged to a German. She made the runaways take shelter behind trees at the edge of the fields before she knocked at the door. She hesitated before she approached the door, thinking, suppose that he, too, should refuse shelter, suppose—Then she thought, Lord, I'm going to hold steady on to You and You've got to see me through—and knocked softly.

She heard the familiar guttural voice say, "Who's there?"

She answered quickly, "A friend with friends."

He opened the door and greeted her warmly. "How many this time?" he asked.

"Eleven," she said and waited, doubting, wondering.

He said, "Good. Bring them in."

He and his wife fed them in the lamplit kitchen, their faces glowing, as they offered food and more food, urging them to eat, saying there was plenty for everybody, have more milk, have more bread, have more meat. •

They spent the night in the warm kitchen. They really slept, all that night and until dusk the next day. When they left, it was with reluctance. They had all been warm and safe and well-fed. It was hard to exchange the security offered by that clean, warm kitchen for the darkness and the cold of a December night.

"Go On or Die"

Harriet had found it hard to leave the warmth and friendliness, too. But she urged them on. For a while, as they walked, they seemed to carry in them a measure of contentment; some of the serenity and the cleanliness of that big warm kitchen lingered on inside them. But as they walked farther and farther away from the warmth and the light, the cold and the darkness entered into them. They fell silent, sullen, suspicious. She waited for the moment when some one of them would turn mutinous. It did not happen that night.

Two nights later she was aware that the feet behind her were moving slower and slower. She heard the irritability in their voices, knew that soon someone would refuse to go on.

She started talking about William Still and the Philadelphia Vigilance Committee.[3] No one commented. No one asked any questions. She told them the story of William and Ellen Craft and how they escaped from Georgia. Ellen was so fair that she looked as though she were white, and so she dressed up in a man's clothing and she looked like a wealthy young planter. Her husband, William, who was dark, played the role of her slave. Thus they traveled from Macon, Georgia, to Philadelphia, riding on the trains, staying at the finest hotels. Ellen pretended to be very ill—her right arm was in a sling, and her right hand was bandaged, because she was supposed to have rheumatism. Thus she avoided having to sign the register at the hotels for she could not read or write. They finally arrived safely in Philadelphia, and then went on to Boston.

Narrative Essay
What elements of the setting contribute to the action of the plot here?

Vocabulary
mutinous (myo͞ot´ ən əs) *adj.* rebellious

Narrative Essay
Tubman tells a narrative of her own here. Why does she tell the story of these real people?

☑ Reading Check
What does Tubman fear the fugitives might do?

---

3. **Philadelphia Vigilance Committee** group of citizens that helped escaped slaves. Its secretary was a free black man named William Still.

History Connection

Frederick Douglass: Fighter for Freedom

Born into slavery in Maryland in 1818, Frederick Douglass learned to read even though it was against the law. Twenty years later, he fled north, and in 1845 wrote his autobiography, which made him the most famous and visible African American spokesperson of the nineteenth century. Douglass began publishing the influential antislavery newspaper North Star shortly afterward.

He also became an inspiring speaker who spoke out against slavery before the Civil War. Douglass continued to fight for African American civil rights, for women's rights, and on behalf of the poor until his death in 1895.

Connect to the Literature

Why do you think Harriet Tubman chose to tell the slaves about Frederick Douglass on their journey north?

No one said anything. Not one of them seemed to have heard her.

She told them about Frederick Douglass, the most famous of the escaped slaves, of his eloquence, of his magnificent appearance. Then she told them of her own first vain effort at running away, evoking the memory of that miserable life she had led as a child, reliving it for a moment in the telling.

But they had been tired too long, hungry too long, afraid too long, footsore too long. One of them suddenly cried out in despair, "Let me go back. It is better to be a slave than to suffer like this in order to be free."

She carried a gun with her on these trips. She had never used it—except as a threat. Now as she aimed it, she experienced a feeling of guilt, remembering that time, years ago, when she had prayed for the death of Edward Brodas, the Master, and then not too long afterward had heard that great wailing cry that came from the throats of the field hands, and knew from the sound that the Master was dead.

One of the runaways said, again, "Let me go back. Let me go back," and stood still, and then turned around and said, over his shoulder, "I am going back."

She lifted the gun, aimed it at the despairing slave. She said, "Go on with us or die." The husky low-pitched voice was grim.

He hesitated for a moment and then he joined the others. They started walking again. She tried to explain to them why none of them could go back to the plantation. If a runaway returned, he would turn traitor, the master and the overseer would force him to turn traitor. The returned slave would disclose the stopping places, the hiding places, the cornstacks they had used with the full knowledge of the owner of the farm, the name of the German farmer who had fed them and sheltered them. These people who had risked their own security to help runaways would be ruined, fined, imprisoned.

She said, "We got to go free or die. And freedom's not bought with dust."

This time she told them about the long agony of the Middle Passage on the old slave ships, about the black horror of the holds, about the chains and the whips. They too knew these stories. But she wanted to remind them of the long hard way they had come, about the long hard way they had yet to go. She told them about Thomas Sims, the boy picked up on the streets of Boston and sent back to Georgia. She said when they got him back to Savannah, got him in prison there, they whipped him until a doctor who was standing by watching said, "You will kill him if you strike him again!" His master said, "Let him die!" •

Thus she forced them to go on. Sometimes she thought she had become nothing but a voice speaking in the darkness, cajoling, urging, threatening. Sometimes she told them things to make them laugh, sometimes she sang to them, and heard the eleven voices behind her blending softly with hers, and then she knew that for the moment all was well with them.

She gave the impression of being a short, muscular, indomitable[4] woman who could never be defeated. Yet at any moment she was liable to be seized by one of those curious fits of sleep, which might last for a few minutes or for hours.[5]

Even on this trip, she suddenly fell asleep in the woods. The runaways, ragged, dirty, hungry, cold, did not steal the gun as they might have, and set off by themselves, or turn back. They sat on the ground near her and waited patiently until she awakened. They had come to trust her implicitly, totally. They, too, had come to believe her repeated statement, "We got to go free or die." She was leading them into freedom, and so they waited until she was ready to go on.

Finally, they reached Thomas Garrett's house in Wilmington, Delaware. Just as Harriet had promised, Garrett gave them all new shoes, and provided carriages to take them on to the next stop.

By slow stages they reached Philadelphia, where William Still hastily recorded their names, and the plantations whence they had come, and something of the life they had led in slavery. Then he carefully hid what he had written, for fear it might be discovered. In 1872 he published this record in book form and called it *The Underground Railroad*. In the

Narrative Essay
Why does Tubman tell the fugitives the anecdote about Thomas Sims?

Main Idea
What main idea is directly stated in this paragraph?

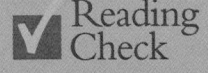
Reading Check
What prevents the fugitives from turning back?

---

4. **indomitable** (in däm´ it ə bəl) *adj.* not easily discouraged.
5. **sleep . . . hours.** When she was about thirteen, Harriet accidentally received a severe blow on the head. Afterward, she often lost consciousness and could not be awakened until the episode ended.

foreword to his book he said: "While I knew the danger of keeping strict records, and while I did not then dream that in my day slavery would be blotted out, or that the time would come when I could publish these records, it used to afford me great satisfaction to take them down, fresh from the lips of fugitives on the way to freedom, and to preserve them as they had given them."

William Still, who was familiar with all the station stops on the Underground Railroad, supplied Harriet with money and sent her and her eleven fugitives on to Burlington, New Jersey.

Main Idea
What main idea about the weather is directly stated here? Which details best illustrate the main idea?

Harriet felt safer now, though there were danger spots ahead. But the biggest part of her job was over. As they went farther and farther north, it grew colder; she was aware of the wind on the Jersey ferry and aware of the cold damp in New York. From New York they went on to Syracuse, where the temperature was even lower.

In Syracuse she met the Reverend J.W. Loguen, known as "Jarm" Loguen. This was the beginning of a lifelong friendship. Both Harriet and Jarm Loguen were to become friends and supporters of Old John Brown.[6]

From Syracuse they went north again, into a colder, snowier city—Rochester. Here they almost certainly stayed with Frederick Douglass, for he wrote in his autobiography:

Spiral Review
Author's Purpose
Why do you think the author includes this passage from Douglass's autobiography? How does it support her purpose for writing?

"On one occasion I had eleven fugitives at the same time under my roof, and it was necessary for them to remain with me until I could collect sufficient money to get them to Canada. It was the largest number I ever had at any one time, and I had some difficulty in providing so many with food and shelter, but, as may well be imagined, they were not very fastidious in either direction, and were well content with very plain food, and a strip of carpet on the floor for a bed, or a place on the straw in the barnloft."

Late in December, 1851, Harriet arrived in St. Catharines, Canada West (now Ontario), with the eleven fugitives. It had taken almost a month to complete this journey; most of the time had been spent getting out of Maryland.

That first winter in St. Catharines was a terrible one. Canada was a strange frozen land, snow everywhere, ice everywhere, and a bone-biting cold the like of which none of them had ever experienced before. Harriet rented a small

---

6. **John Brown** white antislavery activist (1800–1859) hanged for leading a raid on the arsenal at Harpers Ferry, Virginia (now West Virginia), as part of a slave uprising.

frame house in the town and set to work to make a home. The fugitives boarded with her. They worked in the forests, felling trees, and so did she. Sometimes she took other jobs, cooking or cleaning house for people in the town. She cheered on these newly arrived fugitives, working herself, finding work for them, finding food for them, praying for them, sometimes begging for them.

Often she found herself thinking of the beauty of Maryland, the mellowness of the soil, the richness of the plant life there. The climate itself made for an ease of living that could never be duplicated in this bleak, barren countryside.

In spite of the severe cold, the hard work, she came to love St. Catharines, and the other towns and cities in Canada where black men lived. She discovered that freedom meant more than the right to change jobs at will, more than the right to keep the money that one earned. It was the right to vote and to sit on juries. It was the right to be elected to office. In Canada there were black men who were county officials and members of school boards. St. Catharines had a large colony of ex-slaves, and they owned their own homes, kept them neat and clean and in good repair. They lived in whatever part of town they chose and sent their children to the schools.

▲ **Critical Viewing**
Judging from this painting, how warmly were the slaves received once they arrived in the North? Explain. **[Analyze]**

Vocabulary
bleak (blēk) *adj.*
bare and windswept; cold and harsh

from Harriet Tubman: Conductor on the Underground Railroad **495**

When spring came she decided that she would make this small Canadian city her home—as much as any place could be said to be home to a woman who traveled from Canada to the Eastern Shore of Maryland as often as she did.

In the spring of 1852, she went back to Cape May, New Jersey. She spent the summer there, cooking in a hotel. That fall she returned, as usual, to Dorchester County, and brought out nine more slaves, conducting them all the way to St. Catharines, in Canada West, to the bone-biting cold, the snow-covered forests—and freedom.

She continued to live in this fashion, spending the winter in Canada, and the spring and summer working in Cape May, New Jersey, or in Philadelphia. She made two trips a year into slave territory, one in the fall and another in the spring. She now had a definite crystallized purpose, and in carrying it out, her life fell into a pattern which remained unchanged for the next six years.

Main Idea
What main idea is implied by the many details the author provides about Tubman's schedule from 1852 until 1858?

Critical Thinking

1. **Key Ideas and Details (a)** What does Tubman do when a fugitive wants to go back to the plantation? **(b) Analyze Cause and Effect:** Explain why Tubman feels she must act this way.

2. **Integration of Knowledge and Ideas (a) Interpret:** Tubman says, "We got to go free or die. And freedom's not bought with dust." In your own words, interpret that statement. **(b) Make a Judgment:** Are the results of the Underground Railroad trips worth the risks involved? Why or why not? **(c) Discuss:** Share your judgment with a partner. Then, discuss how your own opinion has or has not changed as a result of your conversation.

3. **Integration of Knowledge and Ideas (a)** What kind of information does Petry provide in this narrative essay that you would not find in an encyclopedia entry about Tubman? **(b)** Does Petry's approach give you a better idea of what Tubman was like as a person? Why or why not? *[Connect to the Big Question: How much information is enough?]*

Cite textual evidence to support your responses.

Reading Skill: Main Idea

1. (a) Make a chart like the one shown and write at least two details you learned about Harriet Tubman from the essay.
(b) Then, based on the details, write a sentence that states the **main idea** the author conveys about Tubman.

Detail		Detail		Detail		Main Idea
If she were caught, she would be hanged.	+	She hid the fact that she did not know the new route.	+		→	

2. Why do you think the author implies the main idea, rather than directly stating it in the essay?

Literary Analysis: Narrative Essay

3. Key Ideas and Details List the two most important events in this **narrative essay.**

4. Key Ideas and Details (a) Describe the author's relationship with at least three people in the narrative. **(b)** Use details to identify the setting.

Vocabulary

Acquisition and Use Use your knowledge of the vocabulary words to indicate if the statements are *true* or *false*. Explain your answers.

1. Discussing controversial ideas *invariably* leads to agreement.

2. Eating a good meal will *dispel* the feeling of hunger.

3. A *mutinous* sailor would obey all the captain's rules.

4. *Fugitives* often have reason to feel afraid.

5. The need to pay bills is an *incentive* for getting a job.

6. On a *bleak* morning, the sun is bright and the air is warm.

Word Study Use the context of the sentences and what you know about the **Old English suffix -ly** to explain each answer.

1. Would someone who is escaping open the door *silently*?

2. Why is it best to answer a test question *correctly*?

Word Study

The **Old English suffix -ly** creates adverbs that describe how, when, or how often something is done.

Apply It Explain how the suffix **-ly** contributes to the meanings of these words. You may consult a dictionary if necessary.

persuasively
horribly
humorously

Integrated Language Skills

Baseball • *from* Harriet Tubman: Conductor on the Underground Railroad

Conventions: Adjectives and Articles

An **adjective** is a word that describes a noun or pronoun.

Adjectives are also called *modifiers* because they modify, or change, the noun. An adjective adds detail to a noun by answering *What kind?*, *Which one?*, *How many?*, *How much?*, or *Whose?* Some common adjectives are shown in the chart.

What kind?	Which one?	How many?	How much?	Whose?
old, sparkling, green, layered	this, that, these, those	many, few, some	none, some, five, ten	my, your, his, her, their, Jen's, Joe's

Three common adjectives that answer the question *Which one?* are also called **articles:** *a, an,* and *the. The* is used to answer the question in a specific way. *The* dog that I own. *A* and *an* answer in a general way. I want *a* dog. Use *an,* not *a,* when the word after it begins with a vowel: I found *a* key, but I lost *an* oar.

Practice A Identify the adjectives and articles in these sentences.

1. Father Zavala sat on the shady porch.
2. My uncle gave us a real baseball.
3. We played the game in the dusty schoolyard.
4. We used a large stone as first base.
5. Someday I'll learn the official rules.

© **Reading Application** In "Baseball," find a sentence that uses at least two articles and at least one adjective.

Practice B Rewrite these sentences, removing all adjectives and changing articles. Then, explain how the meaning changes.

1. Harriet Tubman was a former slave who helped form the Underground Railroad.
2. The greatest danger for fugitive slaves was being caught and returned to their owners.
3. Escape was a dangerous challenge.
4. Thomas Sims was a famous escaped slave.

© **Writing Application** Write a paragraph describing what it might have felt like to escape from slavery to freedom. Use at least three articles and three adjectives to make your feelings clear.

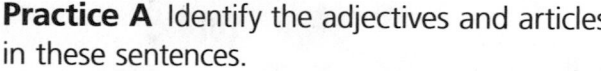

PH **WRITING COACH** | Further instruction and practice are available in *Prentice Hall Writing Coach.*

Writing

Common Core State Standards

L.8.1; W.8.2, W.8.2.b., W.8.2.c.; SL.8.6
[For the full wording of the standards, see page 474.]

Explanatory Text Write a **biographical sketch** about a person who took risks in order to achieve a worthy goal. You might consider a historical person, like Harriet Tubman, or a person alive today.

- In your first sentence, state the main idea you want readers to know about the person. Then, write several sentences that contain details supporting the main idea.

- Include quotations from the person to support the main idea. Choose quotes that have a particular meaning or effect.

- Use varied transitions to show the progress from one idea to the next. Transitions include words and phrases such as *finally*, *meanwhile*, *as a result*, and *for example*.

- Your sketch should be long enough to create interest and support your main idea. End with a strong concluding paragraph.

Grammar Application Check your biographical sketch to make sure you used the articles *a* and *an* correctly.

Writing Workshop: *Work in Progress*

Prewriting for Exposition For a how-to essay you may write, make a list of three tasks that you do each day. List the basic steps that go into each task. Put this Steps List in your writing portfolio.

Use this prewriting activity to prepare for the **Writing Workshop** on page 548.

Speaking and Listening

Comprehension and Collaboration In a small group, create a **skit** based on the essay you read. If you read "Baseball," write a skit about children who are playing baseball when an argument breaks out over rules. If you read the excerpt from *Harriet Tubman,* write a skit based on a dramatic scene from the excerpt.

Follow these steps to complete the assignment.

- Consider the tone or attitude you want to convey. Write dialogue using vocabulary that matches the importance of the situation.

- Use gestures and body language to express the characters' feelings. For example, throw your hands angrily in the air to show a child's reaction to winning or losing, or drag your feet to show a fugitive slave's struggles with exhaustion.

- Rehearse your skit and then present it to your classmates.

- After the skit, compare perceptions about whether the performance matches or contrasts with the mood of the essay.

www.PHLitOnline.com
- Interactive graphic organizers
- Grammar tutorial
- Interactive journals

Ⓒ Leveled Texts

Build your skills and improve your comprehension of biography and autobiography with texts of increasing complexity.

Read the excerpt from ***Always to Remember*** to learn about a famous memorial.

Read the excerpt from ***I Know Why the Caged Bird Sings*** to see how a woman's love of language influenced a young girl.

Ⓒ Common Core State Standards

Meet these standards with either the excerpt from ***Always to Remember: The Vision of Maya Ying Lin*** (p. 504) or the excerpt from ***I Know Why the Caged Bird Sings*** (p. 514).

Reading Informational Text
2. Determine a central idea of a text and analyze its development over the course of the text, including its relationship to supporting ideas. *(Reading Skill: Main Idea)*

3. Analyze how a text makes connections among and distinctions between individuals, ideas, or events. *(Reading Skill: Main Idea)*

Writing
2. Write informative/explanatory texts to examine a topic and convey ideas, concepts, and information through selection, organization, and analysis of relevant content. *(Writing: Reflective Essay)*

7. Conduct short research projects to answer a question, drawing on several sources and generating additional related, focused questions that allow for multiple avenues of exploration. *(Research and Technology: Multimedia Presentation)*

9. Draw evidence from literary or informational texts to support analysis, reflection, and research. *(Research and Technology: Multimedia Presentation)*

Speaking and Listening
5. Integrate multimedia and visual displays into presentations to clarify information, strengthen claims and evidence, and add interest. *(Research and Technology: Multimedia Presentation)*

Language
1. Demonstrate command of the conventions of standard English grammar and usage when writing or speaking. *(Conventions: Adverbs)*

5.b. Use the relationship between particular words to better understand each of the words. *(Vocabulary: Synonyms and Antonyms)*

Reading Skill: Main Idea

Main, or central, ideas are the most important points in a piece of nonfiction. In essays, main ideas are part of a clear structure. An introduction states the main idea. Body paragraphs explain the main idea. Finally, a conclusion restates and reinforces the main idea.

To follow the path the writer sets for you, **make connections** between supporting paragraphs and the main idea.

- As you read paragraphs, identify the sentence (often the first) that contains the main subject of the paragraph. This is the **topic sentence.**
- Link topic sentences to see how the main idea in each paragraph helps to develop key concepts.
- Write notes or outlines that detail the main ideas of sections.

Using the Strategy: Topic Sentence Chart

Use a **topic sentence chart** like this one to track main ideas.

Paragraph 1	Paragraph 2	Essay
Topic Sentence Throughout Pablo Picasso's career, he was well known for being innovative.	**Topic Sentence** Other artists took note and followed Picasso's lead.	**Main Point** Picasso was a great artist who had a major impact on twentieth-century art.

Literary Analysis: Biography and Autobiography

- A **biography** is a nonfiction work in which the writer tells about important events in the life of another person.
- An **autobiography** is also a true account, but it is written by the person who directly experienced an event. It includes the writer's thoughts and feelings.

Both types of writing examine the influence of personal experiences, such as schooling, on a person's development and accomplishments. Biography and autobiography also often reflect the heritage, traditions, attitudes, and beliefs of the subject or author.

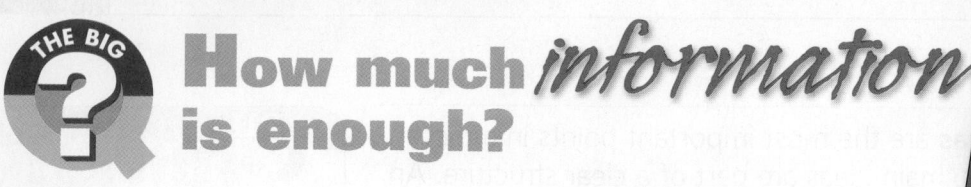

How much *information* is enough?

Writing About the Big Question

Always to Remember introduces you to the young student who designed a powerful memorial to Vietnam War soldiers. Use these sentence starters to develop your ideas about the Big Question:

Remembering events from our history can be **valuable** because
_____.

One interesting way for an insightful artist to use history as a subject would be to _____.

While You Read Look for hints that show you the kinds of information the artist used in planning her work.

Vocabulary

Read each word and its definition. Decide whether you know the word well, know it a little bit, or do not know it at all. After you read, see how your knowledge of each word has increased.

- **authorized** (ô´ thər īzd´) *v.* approved (p. 505) *The mayor authorized the victory parade.* authorization *n.* authority *n.*

- **criteria** (krī tir´ ē ə) *n.* standards by which something can be judged (p. 506) *The winner is chosen using six criteria.*

- **harmonious** (här mō´ nē əs) *adj.* combined in a pleasing arrangement (p. 507) *The sculpture stood in a harmonious setting that added to its beauty.* harmoniously *adv.* harmony *n.*

- **anonymously** (ə nän´ ə məs lē) *adv.* without a name or any identification (p. 507) *The money was given anonymously by a mystery donor.* anonymous *adj.* anonymity *n.*

- **eloquent** (el´ ə kwənt) *adj.* vividly expressive (p. 507) *Her eloquent speech moved us.* eloquence *n.* eloquently *adv.*

- **unanimous** (yō̄ō nan´ ə məs) *adj.* in complete agreement (p. 507) *The wildly popular bill passed by a unanimous vote.* unanimously *adv.* unity *n.*

Word Study

The **Greek root -nym-** means "name."

In this essay, the designs for the Vietnam Veterans Memorial are submitted **anonymously,** or without names, so that the judges can evaluate them based only on the strengths of the design ideas.

Author of

Always to Remember:

The Vision of Maya Ying Lin

When Brent Ashabranner was eleven, he loved a book called *Bomba the Jungle Boy*. He tried writing a book of his own, *Barbara the Jungle Girl*, but gave up after page three. He did not give up for long—he won fourth prize in a short-story contest when he was a high school student.

Sources of Inspiration Ashabranner has been writing ever since, drawing on his experiences in the Peace Corps in Africa and India, and living in the Philippines and Indonesia. He has written many books on social issues, such as one examining the experience of migrant farm workers in the United States.

DID YOU KNOW?

Ashabranner served in the United States Navy for three years, where he saw the losses of war firsthand. The subject of the Vietnam Veterans Memorial appealed to him because, as he said, "It will make us remember that war . . . is about sacrifice and sorrow."

BACKGROUND FOR THE BIOGRAPHY

A Divisive War

This excerpt from *Always to Remember* is about the effort to design a memorial for the Vietnam War. United States involvement in Vietnam began in 1961, when President Kennedy sent 3,000 military advisors to help the South Vietnamese government fight communist rebels supported by North Vietnam. By 1968, the United States had more than 500,000 troops there. Americans became bitterly divided over the war.

Maya Ying Lin

Brent Ashabranner

In the 1960s and 1970s, the United States was involved in a war in Vietnam. Because many people opposed the war, Vietnam veterans were not honored as veterans of other wars had been. Jan Scruggs, a Vietnam veteran, thought that the 58,000 U.S. servicemen and women killed or reported missing in Vietnam should be honored with a memorial. With the help of lawyers Robert Doubek and John Wheeler, Scruggs worked to gain support for his idea. In 1980, Congress authorized the building of the Vietnam Veterans Memorial in Washington, D.C., between the Washington Monument and the Lincoln Memorial.

The memorial had been authorized by Congress "in honor and recognition of the men and women of the Armed Forces of the United States who served in the Vietnam War." The law, however, said not a word about what the memorial should be or what it should look like. That was left up to the Vietnam Veterans Memorial Fund, but the law did state that the memorial design and plans would have to be approved by the Secretary of the Interior, the Commission of Fine Arts, and the National Capital Planning Commission.

What would the memorial be? What should it look like? Who would design it? Scruggs, Doubek, and Wheeler didn't know, but they were determined that the memorial should help bring closer together a nation still bitterly divided by the Vietnam War. It couldn't be something like the Marine Corps Memorial showing American troops planting a flag on enemy soil at Iwo Jima. It couldn't be a giant dove with an olive branch of peace in its beak. It had to soothe passions, not stir

Main Idea
How do the details about how the designer will be chosen connect to the main point of the previous paragraph?

Vocabulary
criteria (krī tir´ ē ə)
n. standards by which something can be judged

▼ **Critical Viewing**
How does the design of the memorial honor individual soldiers, like the veteran shown here? **[Analyze]**

them up. But there was one thing Jan Scruggs insisted on: The memorial, whatever it turned out to be, would have to show the name of every man and woman killed or missing in the war.

The answer, they decided, was to hold a national design competition open to all Americans. The winning design would receive a prize of $20,000, but the real prize would be the winner's knowledge that the memorial would become a part of American history on the Mall in Washington, D.C. Although fund raising was only well started at this point, the choosing of a memorial design could not be delayed if the memorial was to be built by Veterans Day, 1982. H. Ross Perot contributed the $160,000 necessary to hold the competition, and a panel of distinguished architects, landscape architects, sculptors, and design specialists was chosen to decide the winner. •

Announcement of the competition in October, 1980, brought an astonishing response. The Vietnam Veterans Memorial Fund received over five thousand inquiries. They came from every state in the nation and from every field of design; as expected, architects and sculptors were particularly interested.

Everyone who inquired received a booklet explaining the criteria. Among the most important: The memorial could not make a political statement about the war; it must contain the names of all persons killed or missing in action in the war; it must be in harmony with its location on the Mall.

A total of 2,573 individuals and teams registered for the competition. They were sent photographs of the memorial site, maps of the area around the site and of the entire Mall, and other technical design information. The competitors had three months to prepare their designs, which had to be received by March 31, 1981.

Of the 2,573 registrants, 1,421 submitted designs, a record number for such a design competition. When the designs were spread out for jury selection,

they filled a large airplane hangar. The jury's task was to select the design which, in their judgment, was the best in meeting these criteria:

- a design that honored the memory of those Americans who served and died in the Vietnam War.
- a design of high artistic merit.
- a design which would be harmonious with its site, including visual harmony with the Lincoln Memorial and the Washington Monument.
- a design that could take its place in the "historic continuity" of America's national art.
- a design that would be buildable, durable, and not too hard to maintain.

The designs were displayed without any indication of the designer's name so that they could be judged anonymously, on their design merits alone. The jury spent one week reviewing all the designs in the airplane hangar. On May 1 it made its report to the Vietnam Veterans Memorial Fund; the experts declared Entry Number 1,026 the winner. The report called it "the finest and most appropriate" of all submitted and said it was "superbly harmonious" with the site on the Mall. Remarking upon the "simple and forthright" materials needed to build the winning entry, the report concludes:

This memorial, with its wall of names, becomes a place of quiet reflection, and a tribute to those who served their nation in difficult times. All who come here can find it a place of healing. This will be a quiet memorial, one that achieves an excellent relationship with both the Lincoln Memorial and Washington Monument, and relates the visitor to them. It is uniquely horizontal, entering the earth rather than piercing the sky.

This is very much a memorial of our own times, one that could not have been achieved in another time and place. The designer has created an eloquent place where the simple meeting of earth, sky and remembered names contain messages for all who will know this place.

The eight jurors signed their names to the report, a unanimous decision. When the name of the winner was revealed, the art and architecture worlds were stunned. It

Vocabulary
harmonious (här mō´ nē əs) *adj.* combined in a pleasing arrangement

anonymously (ə nän´ə məs lē) *adv.* without a name or any identification

Biography
The author identifies the winner by number. How does this suggest that the winner's identity may surprise readers?

Vocabulary
eloquent (el´ ə kwənt) *adj.* vividly expressive

unanimous (yoo nan´ ə məs) *adj.* in complete agreement

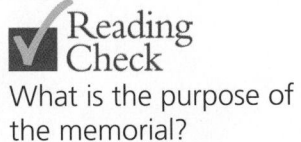
Reading Check
What is the purpose of the memorial?

Arts Connection

Honoring Civil Rights

In addition to the Vietnam Veterans Memorial, Maya Ying Lin also designed a memorial that honors the civil rights movement. Her inspiration came from these words of Dr. Martin Luther King, Jr.'s famous "I Have a Dream" speech: " . . . until justice rolls down like waters and righteousness like a mighty stream." Maya Lin decided that the memorial would be about water, and would honor King by using his words to connect the past with the future.

At the Civil Rights Memorial, water streams over King's words carved into the black granite wall. Clear water covers the names and events of the civil rights movement on the circular stone table.

Connect to the Literature

In what ways does the Civil Rights Memorial resemble the Vietnam Veterans Memorial?

was not the name of a nationally famous architect or sculptor, as most people had been sure it would be. The creator of Entry Number 1,026 was a twenty-one-year-old student at Yale University. Her name—unknown as yet in any field of art or architecture—was Maya Ying Lin.

How could this be? How could an undergraduate student win one of the most important design competitions ever held? How could she beat out some of the top names in American art and architecture? Who was Maya Ying Lin?

The answer to that question provided some of the other answers, at least in part. Maya Lin, reporters soon discovered, was a Chinese-American girl who had been born and raised in the small midwestern city of Athens, Ohio. Her father, Henry Huan Lin, was a ceramicist of considerable reputation and dean of fine arts at Ohio University in Athens. Her mother, Julia C. Lin, was a poet and professor of Oriental and English literature. Maya Lin's parents were born to culturally prominent families in China. When the Communists came to power in China in the 1940's, Henry and Julia Lin left the country and in time made their way to the United States. Maya Lin grew up in an environment of art and literature. She was interested in sculpture and made both small and large sculptural figures, one cast in bronze. She learned silversmithing and made jewelry. She was surrounded by books and read a great deal, especially fantasies such as *The Hobbit* and *Lord of the Rings.*

But she also found time to work at McDonald's. "It was about the only way to make money in the summer," she said.

A covaledictorian at high school graduation, Maya Lin went to Yale without a clear notion of what she wanted to study and eventually decided to major in Yale's undergraduate program in architecture. During her junior year she studied in Europe and found herself increasingly interested in cemetery architecture. "In Europe there's very little space, so graveyards are used as parks," she said. "Cemeteries are cities of the dead in European countries, but they are also living gardens."

In France, Maya Lin was deeply moved by the war memorial to those who died in the Somme offensive in 1916 during World War I.[1] The great arch by architect Sir Edwin Lutyens is considered one of the world's most outstanding war memorials.

Back at Yale for her senior year, Maya Lin enrolled in Professor Andrus Burr's course in funerary (burial) architecture. The Vietnam Veterans Memorial competition had recently been announced, and although the memorial would be a cenotaph—a monument in honor of persons buried someplace else—Professor Burr thought that having his students prepare a design of the memorial would be a worthwhile course assignment.

Surely, no classroom exercise ever had such spectacular results.

After receiving the assignment, Maya Lin and two of her classmates decided to make the day's journey from New Haven, Connecticut, to Washington to look at the site where the memorial would be built. On the day of their visit, Maya Lin remembers, Constitution Gardens was awash with a late November sun; the park was full of light, alive with joggers and people walking beside the lake.

▼ **Critical Viewing**
How does Maya Lin's design, shown here, contrast with other memorials that you have seen? [**Compare and Contrast**]

"It was while I was at the site that I designed it," Maya Lin said later in an interview about the memorial with *Washington Post* writer Phil McCombs. "I just sort of visualized it. It just popped into my head. Some people were playing Frisbee. It was a beautiful park. I didn't want to destroy a living park. You use the landscape. You don't fight with it. You absorb the landscape. . . . When I looked at the site I just knew I wanted something horizontal that took you in, that made you feel safe within the park, yet at the same time reminding you of the dead. So I just imagined opening up the earth. . . ."

When Maya Lin returned to Yale, she made a clay model of the vision that had come to her in Constitution Gardens.

Biography
From what sources did Maya Lin draw inspiration for her prize-winning design?

Reading Check

Why did Maya Lin go with classmates to Washington?

---

1. **Somme offensive . . . World War I** costly and largely unsuccessful Allied attack that resulted in approximately 615,000 British and French soldiers killed.

▶ **Critical Viewing**
If the contest judges had known who the designers were, do you think Maya Lin's youth and inexperience would have worked for or against her? Explain.
[Make a Judgment]

Spiral Review
Author's Purpose
Why do you think the author notes that Maya Lin barely made the submission deadline? How does this detail add to the author's portrayal of Lin?

She showed it to Professor Burr; he liked her conception and encouraged her to enter the memorial competition. She put her design on paper, a task that took six weeks, and mailed it to Washington barely in time to meet the March 31 deadline.

A month and a day later, Maya Lin was attending class. Her roommate slipped into the classroom and handed her a note. Washington was calling and would call back in fifteen minutes. Maya Lin hurried to her room. The call came. She had won the memorial competition.

Critical Thinking

© 1. Key Ideas and Details (a) Why did people think that a Vietnam memorial was necessary? **(b) Interpret:** What kinds of balances did the design need to strike in order to accomplish its purpose?

© 2. Key Ideas and Details (a) Why did Maya Ying Lin enter the design competition? **(b) Draw Conclusions:** Why was her win so surprising?

© 3. Integration of Knowledge and Ideas (a) Classify: Make a two-column chart. In one column, list the design criteria from page 507. **(b) Evaluate:** In the second column, explain whether you think the memorial meets each of these criteria. **(c) Discuss:** Share your responses with a group. Then, explain why your evaluation has or has not changed.

© 4. Integration of Knowledge and Ideas (a) What types of information did Maya Lin combine as she planned her design for the memorial? **(b)** Do you think there is a connection between architecture and cultural and historical events? Explain. *[Connect to the Big Question: How much information is enough?]*

Cite textual evidence to support your responses.

Reading Skill: Main Idea

1. (a) What is the **main idea** of the section of the essay on pages 505–507? **(b)** Which details support this main idea?

2. (a) List three main ideas in the section about Maya Ying Lin on pages 508–510. **(b)** From this list, construct a sentence that states the main idea of the entire section.

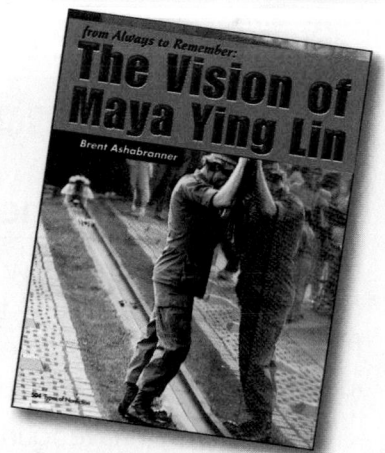

Literary Analysis: Biography and Autobiography

3. Key Ideas and Details This **biographical essay** provides information about Maya Ying Lin. Complete a chart like the one shown to summarize details from the essay in your own words.

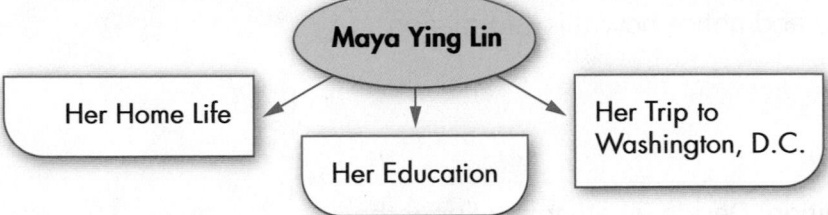

Maya Ying Lin

Her Home Life

Her Education

Her Trip to Washington, D.C.

Vocabulary

Acquisition and Use Review the vocabulary list on page 502. Then, decide how each of these word pairs are related. Choose **synonyms** for words that are similar in meaning and **antonyms** for words that have opposite meanings. Explain your responses.

1. criteria, guidelines

2. harmonious, compatible

3. eloquent, inexpressive

4. unanimous, divided

5. authorized, empowered

6. anonymously, namelessly

Word Study Use what you know about the **Greek root -nym-** to answer each question. Explain your responses.

1. The word *atlas* is an *eponym* taken from the name of the mythological Greek giant Atlas. What eponym is related to the name of the Roman goddess Fortuna?

2. How is using a *pseudonym* different from being *anonymous*?

Word Study

The **Greek root -nym-** means "name."

Apply It Explain how the root **-nym-** contributes to the meanings of these words. Consult a dictionary if necessary.

homonym
patronym
acronym

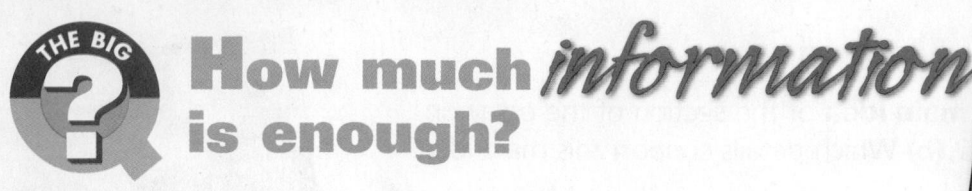

How much *information* is enough?

Writing About the Big Question

In this excerpt from *I Know Why the Caged Bird Sings*, a girl receives "lessons in living" that encourage her to gather wisdom from those around her. Use these sentence starters to develop your ideas about the Big Question.

The best way I have found to **accumulate** knowedge is
_____. If I want to acquire wisdom, however, I go
to _____ because _____.

While You Read Look for information the author gains from her interactions with other people and notice how this information influences her ideas about life.

Vocabulary

Read each word and its definition. Decide whether you know the word well, know it a little bit, or do not know it all. After you read, see how your knowledge of each word has increased.

- **fiscal** (fis´ kəl) *adj.* having to do with finances (p. 515) *The accountant reviewed the fiscal report.* fiscally *adv.*

- **ceaseless** (sēs´ lis) *adj.* never stopping; continual (p. 515) *The birds' ceaseless chirping soon became annoying.* ceaselessly *adv.* ceaselessness *n.* unceasing *adj.*

- **benign** (bi nīn´) *adj.* kind; gentle (p. 518) *His warm smile revealed a benign personality.* benignly *adv.*

- **valid** (val´ id) *adj.* convincing; compelling (p. 519) *Stacy's reasons for wanting the job seemed valid.* validity *n.* validate *v.*

- **intolerant** (in täl´ ər ənt) *adj.* not able or willing to accept other people's beliefs and opinions (p. 520) *Try not to be intolerant of others' opinions.* intolerance *n.* intolerable *adj.* tolerant *adj.*

- **enchantment** (en chant´ mənt) *n.* feeling of delight (p. 521) *The old toy train brought back the enchantment of his happy, carefree childhood.* enchanted *adj.* enchant *v.*

Word Study

The **Latin root -val-** means "strong."

In this autobiography, the author recognizes that an idea that has been shared with her is **valid**. It is a strong, well-founded idea, based on personal experience.

Meet
Maya Angelou
(b. 1928)

Author of
I Know Why
THE CAGED BIRD SINGS

Marguerite Johnson and her brother Bailey were raised by their grandmother in Arkansas. Bailey called Marguerite "mya sister," and she later officially changed her name to "Maya." Angelou struggled with racism, poverty, and ill treatment early in her life, but she worked hard to overcome these obstacles.

A Better Life After moving to San Francisco and finishing high school there, Angelou held a number of jobs that led to careers in drama, dance, teaching, and writing. Today, she is one of the best-known African American authors in the world. In her work, Angelou tries to show that ". . . as human beings we are more alike than we are unalike."

DID YOU KNOW?

In 1993, Bill Clinton asked Angelou to write and read a poem for his presidential inauguration.

BACKGROUND FOR THE AUTOBIOGRAPHY
Growing Up in the South

When Maya Angelou was growing up in Arkansas in the 1930s and 1940s, state laws required African Americans and whites to attend separate schools. The schools African American children attended lacked money for basic educational needs, such as books and qualified teachers. As a result, many students, like Angelou, were eager for role models to inspire them. Angelou found her inspiration with the help of Mrs. Flowers, a family friend.

From
I Know Why
THE CAGED
BIRD SINGS

Maya Angelou

We lived with our grandmother and uncle in the rear of the Store (it was always spoken of with a capital *s*), which she had owned some twenty-five years.

Early in the century, Momma (we soon stopped calling her Grandmother) sold lunches to the sawmen in the lumberyard (east Stamps) and the seedmen at the cotton gin (west Stamps). Her crisp meat pies and cool lemonade, when joined to her miraculous ability to be in two places at the same time, assured her business success. From being a mobile lunch counter, she set up a stand between the two points of fiscal interest and supplied the workers' needs for a few years. Then she had the Store built in the heart of the Negro area. Over the years it became the lay center of activities in town. On Saturdays, barbers sat their customers in the shade on the porch of the Store, and troubadours[1] on their ceaseless crawlings through the South leaned across its benches and sang their sad songs of The Brazos[2] while they played juice harps[3] and cigar-box guitars.

The formal name of the Store was the Wm. Johnson General Merchandise Store. Customers could find food staples, a good variety of colored thread, mash for hogs, corn for chickens, coal oil for lamps, light bulbs for the wealthy, shoestrings, hair dressing, balloons, and flower seeds. Anything not visible had only to be ordered.

Until we became familiar enough to belong to the Store and it to us, we were locked up in a Fun House of Things where the attendant had gone home for life. . . .

Weighing the half-pounds of flour, excluding the scoop, and depositing them dust-free into the thin paper sacks held a simple kind of adventure for me. I developed an eye for measuring how full a silver-looking ladle of flour, mash, meal, sugar or corn had to be to push the scale indicator over to eight ounces or one pound.

Vocabulary
fiscal (fis´ kəl) *adj.* having to do with finances

ceaseless (sēs´ lis) *adj.* never stopping; continual

▲ **Critical Viewing**
Would you expect a general store like this one to be a busy place? Explain. **[Speculate]**

✓ Reading Check
What types of goods were sold at the store?

1. **troubadours** (trōō´ bə dôrz´) *n.* traveling musicians.
2. **The Brazos** (bräz´ əs) area in central Texas near the Brazos River.
3. **juice** (jōōs) **harps** small musical instruments held between the teeth and played by plucking a metal band.

from I Know Why the Caged Bird Sings **515**

When I was absolutely accurate our appreciative customers used to admire: "Sister Henderson sure got some smart grandchildrens." If I was off in the Store's favor, the eagle-eyed women would say, "Put some more in that sack, child. Don't you try to make your profit offa me."

Then I would quietly but persistently punish myself. For every bad judgment, the fine was no silver-wrapped kisses, the sweet chocolate drops that I loved more than anything in the world, except Bailey. And maybe canned pineapples. My obsession with pineapples nearly drove me mad. I dreamt of the days when I would be grown and able to buy a whole carton for myself alone.

Although the syrupy golden rings sat in their exotic cans on our shelves year round, we only tasted them during Christmas. Momma used the juice to make almost-black fruit cakes. Then she lined heavy soot-encrusted iron skillets with the pineapple rings for rich upside-down cakes. Bailey and I received one slice each, and I carried mine around for hours, shredding off the fruit until nothing was left except the perfume on my fingers. I'd like to think that my desire for pineapples was so sacred that I wouldn't allow myself to steal a can (which was possible) and eat it alone out in the garden, but I'm certain that I must have weighed the possibility of the scent exposing me and didn't have the nerve to attempt it.

Until I was thirteen and left Arkansas for good, the Store was my favorite place to be. Alone and empty in the mornings, it looked like an unopened present from a stranger. Opening the front doors was pulling the ribbon off the unexpected gift. The light would come in softly (we faced north), easing itself over the shelves of mackerel, salmon, tobacco, thread. It fell flat on the big vat of lard and by noontime during the summer the grease had softened to a thick soup. Whenever I walked into the Store in the afternoon, I sensed that it was tired. I alone could hear the slow pulse of its job half done. But just before bedtime, after numerous people had walked in and out, had argued over their bills, or joked about their neighbors, or just dropped in "to give Sister Henderson a 'Hi y'all,'" the promise of magic mornings returned to the Store and spread itself over the family in washed life waves. . . . ●

Main Idea
What key point does the author make about the expectations she places on herself?

Autobiography
What does this paragraph show about the author's personality?

When Maya was about ten years old, she returned to Stamps from a visit to St. Louis with her mother. She had become depressed and withdrawn.

For nearly a year, I sopped around the house, the Store, the school and the church, like an old biscuit, dirty and inedible. Then I met, or rather got to know, the lady who threw me my first lifeline.

Mrs. Bertha Flowers was the aristocrat[4] of Black Stamps. She had the grace of control to appear warm in the coldest weather, and on the Arkansas summer days it seemed she

---

4. **aristocrat** (ə ris´ tə krat´) *n.* person belonging to the upper class.

✔ Reading Check

Who throws the author "a lifeline"?

She had the grace of control to appear warm in the coldest weather...

◀ **Critical Viewing** Which aspects of this woman resemble the description of Mrs. Flowers? **[Assess]**

from I Know Why the Caged Bird Sings **517**

had a private breeze which swirled around, cooling her. She was thin without the taut look of wiry people, and her printed voile[5] dresses and flowered hats were as right for her as denim overalls for a farmer. She was our side's answer to the richest white woman in town.

Her skin was a rich black that would have peeled like a plum if snagged, but then no one would have thought of getting close enough to Mrs. Flowers to ruffle her dress, let alone snag her skin. She didn't encourage familiarity. She wore gloves too.

I don't think I ever saw Mrs. Flowers laugh, but she smiled often. A slow widening of her thin black lips to show even, small white teeth, then the slow effortless closing. When she chose to smile on me, I always wanted to thank her. The action was so graceful and inclusively benign.

She was one of the few gentlewomen I have ever known, and has remained throughout my life the measure of what a human being can be. . . . •

One summer afternoon, sweet-milk fresh in my memory, she stopped at the Store to buy provisions.

Another Negro woman of her health and age would have been expected to carry the paper sacks home in one hand, but Momma said, "Sister Flowers, I'll send Bailey up to your house with these things."

She smiled that slow dragging smile, "Thank you, Mrs. Henderson. I'd prefer Marguerite, though." My name was beautiful when she said it. "I've been meaning to talk to her, anyway." They gave each other age-group looks.

Momma said, "Well, that's all right then. Sister, go and change your dress. You going to Sister Flowers's. . . ."

There was a little path beside the rocky road, and Mrs. Flowers walked in front swinging her arms and picking her way over the stones.

She said, without turning her head, to me, "I hear you're doing very good school work, Marguerite, but that it's all written. The teachers report that they have trouble getting you to talk in class." We passed the triangular farm on our left and the path widened to allow us to walk together. I hung back in the separate unasked and unanswerable questions.

Vocabulary
benign (bi nīn´) *adj.*
kind; gentle

▲ **Critical Viewing**
What qualities would someone need to be a good role model for a child? **[Assess]**

---

5. **voile** (voil) *n.* light cotton fabric.

518 Types of Nonfiction

"Come and walk along with me, Marguerite." I couldn't have refused even if I wanted to. She pronounced my name so nicely. Or more correctly, she spoke each word with such clarity that I was certain a foreigner who didn't understand English could have understood her.

"Now no one is going to make you talk—possibly no one can. But bear in mind, language is man's way of communicating with his fellow man and it is language alone which separates him from the lower animals." That was a totally new idea to me, and I would need time to think about it.

"Your grandmother says you read a lot. Every chance you get. That's good, but not good enough. Words mean more than what is set down on paper. It takes the human voice to infuse them with the shades of deeper meaning."

I memorized the part about the human voice infusing words. It seemed so valid and poetic.

She said she was going to give me some books and that I not only must read them, I must read them aloud. She suggested that I try to make a sentence sound in as many different ways as possible.

"I'll accept no excuse if you return a book to me that has been badly handled." My imagination boggled at the punishment I would deserve if in fact I did abuse a book of Mrs. Flowers'. Death would be too kind and brief.

The odors in the house surprised me. Somehow I had never connected Mrs. Flowers with food or eating or any other common experience of common people. There must have been an outhouse, too, but my mind never recorded it.

The sweet scent of vanilla had met us as she opened the door.

"I made tea cookies this morning. You see, I had planned to invite you for cookies and lemonade so we could have this little chat. The lemonade is in the icebox."

It followed that Mrs. Flowers would have ice on an ordinary day, when most families in our town bought ice late on Saturdays only a few times during the summer to be used in the wooden ice cream freezers.

She took the bags from me and disappeared through the kitchen door. I looked around the room that I had never in my wildest fantasies imagined I would see. Browned photographs leered or threatened from the walls and the white, freshly done curtains pushed against themselves and against the wind. I wanted to gobble up the room entire and

Main Idea
List three details that show that the author admires Mrs. Flowers.

Vocabulary
valid (val´ id) *adj.* convincing; compelling

Autobiography
Which phrases show the influence that Mrs. Flowers's words have on the author?

Spiral Review
Author's Purpose
Why does the author include descriptive details about Mrs. Flowers and about the odors in the house? What does she want readers to understand?

Autobiography
What types of things does the author notice here that help explain her decision to become a writer?

Reading Check
What does Mrs. Flowers lend the author?

take it to Bailey, who would help me analyze and enjoy it.

"Have a seat, Marguerite. Over there by the table." She carried a platter covered with a tea towel. Although she warned that she hadn't tried her hand at baking sweets for some time, I was certain that like everything else about her the cookies would be perfect.

They were flat round wafers, slightly browned on the edges and butter-yellow in the center. With the cold lemonade they were sufficient for childhood's lifelong diet. Remembering my manners, I took nice little ladylike bites off the edges. She said she had made them expressly for me and that she had a few in the kitchen that I could take home to my brother. So I jammed one whole cake in my mouth and the rough crumbs scratched the insides of my jaws, and if I hadn't had to swallow, it would have been a dream come true.

As I ate she began the first of what we later called "my lessons in living." She said that I must always be intolerant of ignorance but understanding of illiteracy. That some people,

LITERATURE IN CONTEXT Humanities Connection

Inspired by Words

For some people, the impulse to become a poet, a scientist, an actor, or a combat journalist may have begun in the stories they read as children.

Maya Angelou

A TALE of TWO CITIES

Scientist transformed by Stevenson

Poet influenced by Dickens

THE STRANGE CASE OF DR. JEKYLL and MR. HYDE

Robert Louis Stevenson

THE RED BADGE OF COURAGE

Stephen Crane

A Midsummer Night's Dream

William Shakespeare

Actor enchanted by Shakespeare

Journalist enlisted by Crane

Connect to the Literature

How does Angelou say she was influenced by the "poetry" of *A Tale of Two Cities?*

unable to go to school, were more educated and even more intelligent than college professors. She encouraged me to listen carefully to what country people called mother wit. That in those homely sayings was couched the collective wisdom of generations.

When I finished the cookies she brushed off the table and brought a thick, small book from the bookcase. I had read *A Tale of Two Cities* and found it up to my standards as a romantic novel. She opened the first page and I heard poetry for the first time in my life.

"It was the best of times and the worst of times . . ." Her voice slid in and curved down through and over the words. She was nearly singing. I wanted to look at the pages. Were they the same that I had read? Or were there notes, music, lined on the pages, as in a hymn book? Her sounds began cascading gently. I knew from listening to a thousand preachers that she was nearing the end of her reading, and I hadn't really heard, heard to understand, a single word.

"How do you like that?"

It occurred to me that she expected a response. The sweet vanilla flavor was still on my tongue and her reading was a wonder in my ears. I had to speak.

I said, "Yes, ma'am." It was the least I could do, but it was the most also.

"There's one more thing. Take this book of poems and memorize one for me. Next time you pay me a visit, I want you to recite."

I have tried often to search behind the sophistication of years for the enchantment I so easily found in those gifts. The essence escapes but its aura[6] remains. To be allowed, no, invited, into the private lives of strangers, and to share their joys and fears, was a chance to exchange the Southern bitter wormwood[7] for a cup of mead with Beowulf[8] or a hot cup of tea and milk with Oliver Twist. When I said aloud, "It is a far far better thing that I do, than I have ever done . . ."[9] tears of love filled my eyes at my selflessness.

Main Idea
What point is being made about how Mrs. Flowers changes the author's feelings toward literature?

Vocabulary
enchantment
(en chant´ mənt) *n.* feeling of delight

Autobiography
What lasting "gifts" does Mrs. Flowers give the author?

---

6. **aura** (ô´ rə) *n.* atmosphere or quality.

7. **wormwood** (wʉrm´ wood´) *n.* plant that produces a bitter oil.

8. **Beowulf** (bā´ ə woolf´) hero of an old Anglo-Saxon epic. People in this poem drink **mead** (mēd´), a drink made with honey and water.

9. **"It is . . . than I have ever done"** last two lines from *A Tale of Two Cities* by Charles Dickens, uttered by Sydney Carton as he sacrifices his own life to save Charles Darnay, the man whom Lucie Manette—Carton's beloved—truly loves.

On that first day, I ran down the hill and into the road (few cars ever came along it) and had the good sense to stop running before I reached the Store.

I was liked, and what a difference it made. I was respected not as Mrs. Henderson's grandchild or Bailey's sister but for just being Marguerite Johnson.

Childhood's logic never asks to be proved (all conclusions are absolute). I didn't question why Mrs. Flowers had singled me out for attention, nor did it occur to me that Momma might have asked her to give me a little talking to. All I cared about was that she had made tea cookies for *me* and read to *me* from her favorite book. It was enough to prove that she liked me.

Main Idea
What prevents the author from questioning Mrs. Flowers about singling her out?

Critical Thinking

Cite textual evidence to support your responses.

1. **Key Ideas and Details** **(a)** What are two customers' reactions when Marguerite weighs their goods on the scale? **(b) Infer:** How does she feel when a customer criticizes her? **(c) Draw Conclusions:** What does Marguerite's reaction show about her character?

2. **Key Ideas and Details** **(a) Infer:** What do the actions of Mrs. Flowers prove to Marguerite? **(b) Interpret:** Why has Mrs. Flowers remained for Angelou "the measure of what a human being can be"?

3. **Craft and Structure** **(a) Compare and Contrast:** In a two-column chart, write words or phrases that describe how Marguerite felt about herself before and after her visit with Mrs. Flowers. **(b) Discuss:** In a small group, share and discuss your lists. **(c) Interpret:** Explain what the author means when she calls Mrs. Flowers "the lady who threw me my first lifeline."

4. **Integration of Knowledge and Ideas** What do you think is more important to the author, the description of Mrs. Flowers's life or the insights that Mrs. Flowers shared with her? Explain your answer. *[Connect to the Big Question: How much information is enough?]*

Reading Skill: Main Idea

1. (a) What is the **main idea** of the section about the Store?
(b) Which details in this section support this idea?

2. (a) What main idea about Mrs. Flowers does the author present? **(b)** What details support this main idea?

Literary Analysis: Biography and Autobiography

© **3. Key Ideas and Details** In this **autobiography,** Maya Angelou describes working in a general store. She also discusses an important event that changed her life. Complete a chart like the one shown by listing a few details about each part of her life.

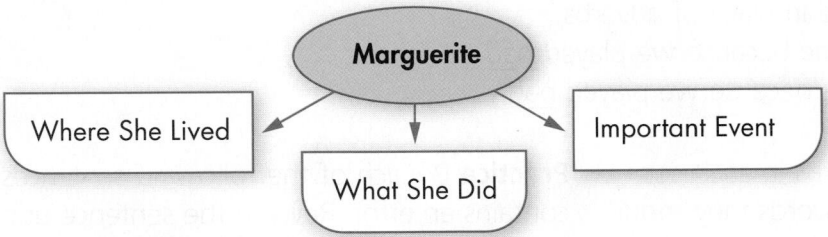

Marguerite

Where She Lived

What She Did

Important Event

Vocabulary

© **Acquisition and Use** Review the vocabulary list on page 512. Then, decide how each of these word pairs are related. Choose **synonyms** for words that are similar in meaning and **antonyms** for words that have opposite meanings. Explain your responses.

1. fiscal, financial

2. benign, hostile

3. ceaseless, finished

4. intolerant, open-minded

5. enchantment, charm

6. valid, accurate

Word Study Use what you know about the **Latin root -*val*-** to answer each question. Explain your responses.

1. How do you assess the *value* of a friendship?

2. If someone makes a *valiant* attempt to help another person, how hard has he or she tried?

Word Study

The **Latin root -*val*-** means "strong."

Apply It Explain how the root -*val*- contributes to the meanings of these words. Consult a dictionary if necessary.

valor
valedictorian
convalesce

Integrated Language Skills

from Always to Remember • *from* I Know Why the Caged Bird Sings

Conventions: Adverbs

An **adverb** is a word that modifies, or adds to the meaning of, a verb, an adjective, or another adverb.

Adverbs often end in the suffix *-ly* and answer the questions *When?, Where?, In what manner?,* and *To what extent?*

When?	Where?	What manner?	What extent?
She answered <u>promptly</u>.	They performed the play <u>locally</u>.	He looked at her <u>wistfully</u> and smiled.	The watch was <u>exactly</u> what she wanted.

Adjectives should not be used in place of adverbs.

Incorrect: We lost the game because we played <u>bad</u>.

Correct: We lost the game because we played <u>badly</u>.

Practice A Identify the adverbs in each sentence below. Indicate which words they modify, and write what questions they answer.

1. The committee wisely decided that the memorial should bring people together.

2. Maya Ying Lin was greatly inspired when she visited the site of the future memorial.

3. The committee called yesterday to inform Maya that she had won.

4. The former soldier stood here when he viewed the memorial.

© **Reading Application** In *Always to Remember,* find a sentence that uses an adverb. Identify the verb or adjective it modifies.

Practice B Each of the following sentences contains an error. Rewrite the sentence using the correct adverb form.

1. Mrs. Flowers warned Marguerite not to return a book that had been handled bad.

2. Mrs. Flowers did not want Marguerite to do poor in her studies.

3. Mrs. Flowers walked graceful across the beautifully arranged room.

4. Marguerite thought that pineapples had an extreme pleasant taste.

© **Writing Application** Follow the construction of this model sentence to write two sentences using adverbs. *Mrs. Flowers read so beautifully, it inspired Marguerite to actively pursue a career in writing.*

PH WRITING COACH | Further instruction and practice are available in *Prentice Hall Writing Coach.*

Writing

Common Core State Standards

L.8.1; W.8.2, W.8.7, W.8.9; SL.8.5
[For the full wording of the standards, see page 500.]

Explanatory Text Maya Lin was inspired by Lutyens's memorial, and Maya Angelou was inspired by Dickens. Write a **reflective essay** in which you discuss a work of fine art or music.

- Begin your essay with an introduction to your topic. Include a thesis statement in which you reveal the focus of your essay.
- Weave together details about the work of art or music you have chosen. Choose details that contribute to your main idea.
- Conclude your essay by summarizing your ideas about the topic.

Grammar Application Check your essay to ensure that you did not use adjectives in place of adverbs. Be sure to convey ideas precisely.

Writing Workshop: *Work in Progress*

Prewriting for Exposition Using the Steps List from your writing portfolio, visualize each step that you have listed. Then, write a paragraph in which you describe how to perform the first few steps on the list. Review what you have written, and add descriptive details. Save this Descriptive Paragraph in your portfolio.

Use this prewriting activity to prepare for the **Writing Workshop** on page 548.

Research and Technology

Build and Present Knowledge With a group, create a **multimedia presentation.**

- If you read *Always to Remember*, explore the impact of the Vietnam War on popular culture and on attitudes toward war.
- If you read *I Know Why the Caged Bird Sings,* create a presentation on the Depression, the era in which Angelou grew up.

Follow these steps to complete the assignment:

- Take notes, using several reliable online and multimedia sources, to learn more about the time period.
- Discuss with your group the best way to incorporate materials such as oral histories, statistics, charts, maps, and graphs. Be aware of questions that arise as you work, and explore additional research sources to find answers.
- Design the presentation's visual aspects, spoken words, and music for dramatic impact.
- During the presentation, make a connection between your research and the essay you read, using direct quotations.
- Use audience feedback, such as your listeners' interest level, to determine which subjects to emphasize.

www.PHLitOnline.com
- Interactive graphic organizers
- Grammar tutorial
- Interactive journals

Test Practice: Reading

Main Idea

Fiction Selection

Directions: *Read the selection. Then, answer the questions.*

Charlie Floyd was born seeking excitement. When he was eight, he decided he wanted to be an acrobat. He only got as far as tying a rope swing to a high branch of an elm before his mother made him take it down. At age eleven, Charlie made up his mind to join the circus. Within weeks, he had taught himself how to walk on stilts and ride a unicycle. He practiced tricks with his cat, Rufus, who, according to Charlie, had the heart of a lion. When Charlie turned fourteen, he decided that being an explorer would fulfill his need for adventure and excitement. He dreamed of the discoveries he would make and adventures he would have. He often pictured himself on African safaris, jungle treks, and polar expeditions.

1. Which sentence *best* expresses the main idea of the passage?
   A. Charlie Floyd was a troublemaker.
   B. Charlie Floyd had a great imagination.
   C. Charlie Floyd had unrealistic ambitions.
   D. Charlie Floyd yearned for excitement.

2. Which statement conveys the idea that Charlie always looked for adventure?
   A. He thought his cat looked like a lion.
   B. His mother discovered his plan.
   C. He tried to build a homemade trapeze.
   D. He kept changing his mind.

3. Which sentence *best* states two important details about Charlie Floyd?
   A. He was a daring boy, and by age fourteen he dreamed of being an explorer.
   B. He wanted to be an acrobat, then later wanted to join the circus.
   C. He imagined going on safaris and polar expeditions.
   D. He always practiced tricks with his cat.

4. Based on the detail about Rufus, what inference can you make about Charlie?
   A. Charlie did not know very much about animals.
   B. Charlie would have been too scared to go near a real lion.
   C. Charlie did not think much of his cat, Rufus.
   D. Charlie thought doing tricks with a lion would be exciting.

Writing for Assessment

Summarize this selection in a few sentences. In your summary state the main idea and include at least three key supporting details.

Nonfiction Selection

Directions: *Read the selection. Then, answer the questions.*

The Lewis and Clark Expedition is considered by many to be the greatest adventure in American history. The 1803 purchase of the Louisiana Territory from France had doubled the area of the United States. Curious about the vast new territory west of the Mississippi, President Thomas Jefferson ordered the expedition, which set off from St. Louis in the spring of 1804. Without maps or modern equipment, thirty-two men, one woman, and a baby ventured into the unknown. For four years, the group journeyed across thousands of unexplored miles, crossing mountains and rivers. The experience was filled with excitement, danger, and discovery.

1. Which sentence *best* states an important detail about the Louisiana Territory?
   A. It was an area of land that was sold to the French in 1804.
   B. It was an area of land that doubled the area of the United States in 1803.
   C. President Thomas Jefferson was afraid the territory was too dangerous.
   D. It was where Lewis and Clark discovered the Mississippi River.

2. Which detail *best* supports the description of the expedition as adventurous?
   A. It crossed mountains and rivers.
   B. The group included a baby.
   C. The Louisiana Territory was vast.
   D. It set off from St. Louis.

3. What key point does the author make about Lewis and Clark's expedition?
   A. The terrain was treacherous.
   B. They did not bring many supplies.
   C. The President was counting on them.
   D. They were exploring the unknown.

4. Which sentence *best* expresses the main idea of the selection?
   A. Thomas Jefferson was the greatest American president.
   B. Lewis and Clark were unsuccessful explorers.
   C. Lewis and Clark's expedition was a great adventure.
   D. The unknown is always exciting and dangerous.

Writing for Assessment

Connecting Across Texts
Do you think Charlie, from the first selection, would have liked to go on an expedition like Lewis and Clark's? In a brief paragraph, explain why or why not, using details from the selections to support your ideas.

PHLit
Online!
www.PHLitOnline.com
• Online practice
• Instant feedback

Reading for Information

Analyzing Expository Texts

Textbook Article   **Public Document**   **Letter**

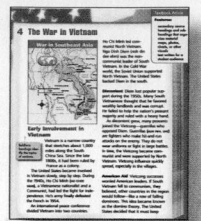 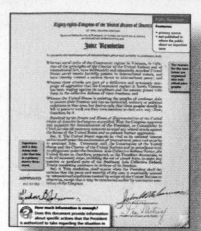 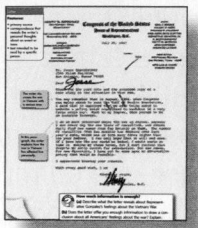

Ⓒ Common Core State Standards

Reading Informational Text
5. Analyze in detail the structure of a specific paragraph in a text, including the role of particular sentences in developing and refining a key concept.

Language
4.c. Consult general and specialized reference materials, both print and digital, to find the pronunciation of a word or determine or clarify its precise meaning or its part of speech.
5.c. Distinguish among the connotations (associations) of words with similar denotations (definitions).

Reading Skill: Analyze Treatment, Scope, and Organization of Ideas

The study of history involves two types of sources. A **primary source,** such as a diary or letter, is created at the time an event is occurring, often by a participant or onlooker. A **secondary source,** such as a textbook, interprets or describes a past event.

When you read any historical resource, **analyze the treatment, scope, and organization of ideas.** *Treatment* refers to the way the writer regards and presents a topic. *Scope* is the range of information that the writer discusses. Ask these questions to help you identify and analyze the treatment, scope, and organization of texts:

Treatment	Scope	Organization
• Is this a primary or secondary source? • Is the writer biased or neutral? • What is the writer's tone, or attitude, toward the topic?	• Has the writer explored a single topic or a series of topics? • How in-depth is this exploration?	• How does each paragraph convey information about the topic? • How do individual sentences develop the key concept of each paragraph?

Content-Area Vocabulary

These words appear in the selections that follow. You may also encounter them in other content-area texts.

- **communism** (kom´ yə niz´ əm) *n.* economic and social system in which most or all property is owned by the state or community and shared by all

- **aggression** (ə gresh´ ən) *n.* attack or offensive action

- **resolution** (rez´ə lü´ shən) *n.* formal expression of opinion or intention agreed on by a legislative body or other group

Features:

- secondary source
- headings and subheadings that organize material
- maps, photos, charts, or other visuals
- text written for a student audience

4 The War in Vietnam

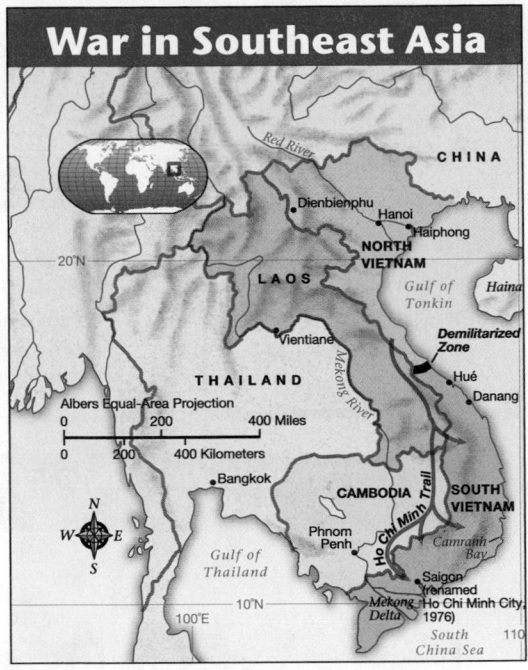

War in Southeast Asia

Ho Chi Minh led communist North Vietnam. Ngo Dinh Diem (NOH DIN dee EHM) was the noncommunist leader of South Vietnam. In the Cold War world, the Soviet Union supported North Vietnam. The United States backed Diem in the south.

Early Involvement in Vietnam

> Boldface headings identify the topics of sections.

Vietnam is a narrow country that stretches about 1,000 miles along the South China Sea. Since the late 1800s, it had been ruled by France as a colony.

The United States became involved in Vietnam slowly, step by step. During the 1940s, Ho Chi Minh (HO CHEE MIHN), a Vietnamese nationalist and a Communist, had led the fight for independence. Ho's army finally defeated the French in 1954.

An international peace conference divided Vietnam into two countries.

Discontent Diem lost popular support during the 1950s. Many South Vietnamese thought that he favored wealthy landlords and was corrupt. He failed to help the nation's peasant majority and ruled with a heavy hand.

As discontent grew, many peasants joined the Vietcong—guerrillas who opposed Diem. Guerrillas (guh RIHL uHz) are fighters who make hit-and-run attacks on the enemy. They do not wear uniforms or fight in large battles. In time, the Vietcong became communist and were supported by North Vietnam. Vietcong influence quickly spread, especially in the villages.

American Aid Vietcong successes worried American leaders. If South Vietnam fell to **communism**, they believed, other countries in the region would follow—like a row of falling dominoes. This idea became known as the domino theory. The United States decided that it must keep

South Vietnam from becoming the first domino.

During the 1950s and 1960s, Presidents Eisenhower and Kennedy sent financial aid and military advisers to South Vietnam. The advisers went to help train the South Vietnamese army, not to fight the Vietcong. Diem, however, continued to lose support. In November 1963, Diem was assassinated. A few weeks later, President John F. Kennedy was assassinated. Vice President Lyndon Baines Johnson became President.

The Fighting in Vietnam Expands

Lyndon Johnson was also determined to keep South Vietnam from falling to the communists. He increased aid to South Vietnam, sending more arms and advisers. Still, the Vietcong continued to make gains.

Gulf of Tonkin Resolution

In August 1964, President Johnson announced that North Vietnamese torpedo boats had attacked an American ship patrolling the Gulf of Tonkin off the coast of North Vietnam. At Johnson's urging, Congress passed the Gulf of Tonkin Resolution. It allowed the President "to take all necessary measures to repel any armed attack or to prevent further **aggression**." Johnson used the **resolution** to order the bombing of North Vietnam and Vietcong-held areas in the south.

With the Gulf of Tonkin Resolution, the role of Americans in Vietnam changed from military advisers to active fighters. The war in Vietnam escalated, or expanded. By 1968, President Johnson had sent more than 500,000 troops to fight in Vietnam.

The graph shows statistical trends and adds depth to the coverage of information.

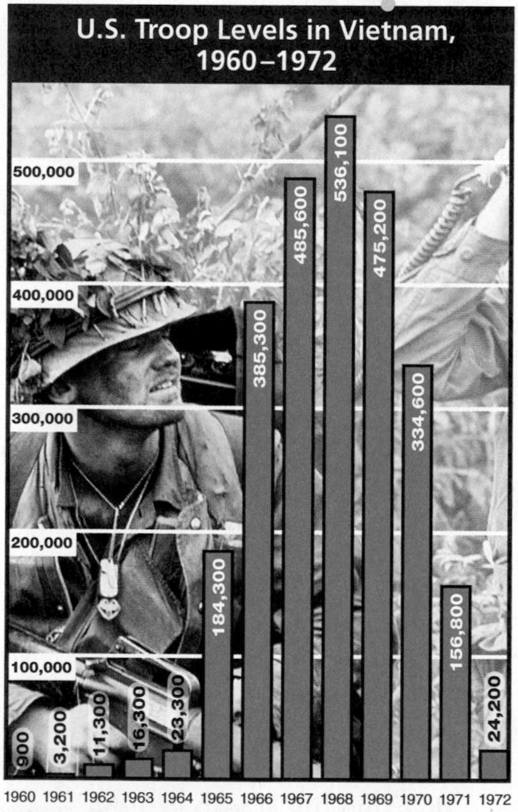

U.S. Troop Levels in Vietnam, 1960–1972

500,000
400,000
300,000
200,000
100,000

1960: 900
1961: 3,200
1962: 11,300
1963: 16,300
1964: 23,300
1965: 184,300
1966: 385,300
1967: 485,600
1968: 536,100
1969: 475,200
1970: 334,600
1971: 156,800
1972: 24,200

Source: U.S. Department of Defense

Eighty-eighth Congress of the United States of America

AT THE SECOND SESSION

Begun and held at the City of Washington on Tuesday, the seventh day of January,
one thousand nine hundred and sixty-four

Joint Resolution

To promote the maintenance of international peace and security in southeast Asia.

Whereas naval units of the Communist regime in Vietnam, in violation of the principles of the Charter of the United Nations and of international law, have deliberately and repeatedly attacked United States naval vessels lawfully present in international waters, and have thereby created a serious threat to international peace; and

Whereas these attacks are part of a deliberate and systematic campaign of aggression that the Communist regime in North Vietnam has been waging against its neighbors and the nations joined with them in the collective defense of their freedom; and

Whereas the United States is assisting the peoples of southeast Asia to protect their freedom and has no territorial, military or political ambitions in that area, but desires only that these peoples should be left in peace to work out their own destinies in their own way : Now, therefore, be it

Resolved by the Senate and House of Representatives of the United States of America in Congress assembled, That the Congress approves and supports the determination of the President, as Commander in Chief, to take all necessary measures to repel any armed attack against the forces of the United States and to prevent further aggression.

Sec. 2. The United States regards as vital to its national interest and to world peace the maintenance of international peace and security in southeast Asia. Consonant with the Constitution of the United States and the Charter of the United Nations and in accordance with its obligations under the Southeast Asia Collective Defense Treaty, the United States is, therefore, prepared, as the President determines, to take all necessary steps, including the use of armed force, to assist any member or protocol state of the Southeast Asia Collective Defense Treaty requesting assistance in defense of its freedom.

Sec. 3. This resolution shall expire when the President shall determine that the peace and security of the area is reasonably assured by international conditions created by action of the United Nations or otherwise, except that it may be terminated earlier by concurrent resolution of the Congress.

APPROVED

AUG 1 0 1964

Lyndon B. Johnson

John W. McCormack

Speaker of the House of Representatives.

Acting President pro tempore of the Senate.

Letter

Features:

- primary source
- correspondence that reveals the writer's personal thoughts about an event or issue
- text intended to be read by a specific person

HENRY B. GONZALEZ
20TH DISTRICT, TEXAS
BEXAR COUNTY

127 LONGWORTH OFFICE BUILDING
WASHINGTON, D.C. 20515

MEMBER:
BANKING AND CURRENCY COMMITTEE

SUBCOMMITTEES:
HOUSING
CONSUMER AFFAIRS
INTERNATIONAL FINANCE

Congress of the United States
House of Representatives
Washington, D.C.

July 25, 1967

FILE REF.:
B6a

STAFF:
GAIL J. BEAGLE
KELSAY R. MEEK
RICHARD F. KAUFMAN
MRS. CORA FAYE CLAYTON
KENNETH E. BROOTEN, JR.
F. SCOTT FORSYTH
PATTY M. BARRERA
JOAN ORRINGER
RALPH DE LA CRUZ

HOME OFFICE:
203 FEDERAL BUILDING
SAN ANTONIO, TEXAS 78205

MRS. LUZ G. TAMEZ
ROBERT SPICER

Mr. Jesse Oppenheimer
1540 Milam Building
San Antonio, Texas 78205

Dear Mr. Oppenheimer:

Thank you for your note and the attached copy of a news story on the situation in Viet Nam.

> The writer discusses the war in Vietnam with a serious tone.

You may remember that in August, 1964, when Congress was being asked to pass the Gulf of Tonkin Resolution, I said that it appeared that we were being asked to endorse a policy which could lead to backdoor in a very large scale war. Much to my regret, this proved to be an accurate forecast.

> In this paragraph, the writer explains how the war in Vietnam has affected him personally.

I am as much concerned about the war as anyone, because I see every day the new lists of casualties, and almost daily find new names from San Antonio on them. The number of casualties from San Antonio has doubled over last year's rate, which was in turn many times higher than the year before. I can only hope that it will end soon. If I knew how the war could be ended, I would waste no time in making my views known, but I must confess that despite my daily search for information, for new ideas, for new direction, I have yet to come upon an alternative policy that would be feasible.

I appreciate knowing your concern.

With every good wish, I am

Sincerely yours,

Henry B. Gonzalez, M.C.

Comparing Expository Texts

1. Key Ideas and Details **(a)** Compare the three documents in their **treatment, scope, and organization of ideas.**
(b) On page 531, how does each of the sentences beginning "Whereas" connect to the paragraph beginning "Resolved"?
(c) On page 532, where does the letter's author express his views about the idea in the "Resolved" paragraph? Explain.

Content-Area Vocabulary

2. Key Ideas and Details **(a)** The word *aggression* has many synonyms. Use a dictionary to locate the precise meanings of three of them: *assault, invasion, offense.* **(b)** Explain differences in the connotations, or shades of meaning, among the four words.

🕐 Timed Writing

Explanatory Text: Evaluation of Sources

> **Format**
> The prompt gives specific directions about the type of writing and the length of the assignment.

Evaluate the primary and secondary sources you have read as if you were preparing to write a report on the Vietnam War. In an essay, explain each source's value and the criteria, or standards, you used to judge its reliability. Note other sources you might consult to gain a more complete understanding of the war. Your evaluation should consist of one paragraph per source. (25 minutes)

> **Academic Vocabulary**
> When you *evaluate* a source, you make a judgment about its reliability and usefulness for research.

5-Minute Planner

Complete these steps before you begin to write:

1. Reread the selections, and look for details related to the task.

2. Take notes about the aspects of each source that make it seem reliable or unreliable. **TIP:** Consider what information is not included in each text but might be available in another source.

3. Use your notes to prepare a quick outline. Then, use the outline to help you organize your response.

Comparing Literary Works

Forest Fire • Why Leaves Turn Color in the Fall • The Season's Curmudgeon . . .

Comparing Types of Organization

To present information clearly, writers can choose among several **types of organization.** Here are three of the most common types:

- **Chronological order** relates events in order of occurrence. Narratives usually place events in time order.

- **Cause-and-effect order** highlights the relationship between an event and its result or results. Science articles often use cause-and-effect text structure to explain events or reactions.

- **Comparison and contrast** shows similarities and differences.

As you read these essays, look for clues that signal the type of organization being used. For example, words and phrases like *consequently* or *as a result* might signal a cause-and-effect pattern.

In addition to the structure of the full work, analyze the structures of specific paragraphs. For example, a writer might include an anecdote, or brief story, within a work that does not otherwise use chronological order. As you look for these nuances, also analyze how individual sentences develop or refine ideas within paragraphs. For example, notice whether a sentence adds an important detail or example.

As you read, use charts like the ones shown to analyze the organizational patterns used in these essays. Then, examine how individual sentences help to develop and refine meaning.

Common Core State Standards

Reading Informational Text
5. Analyze in detail the structure of a specific paragraph in a text, including the role of particular sentences in developing and refining a key concept.

Writing
9. Draw evidence from literary or informational texts to support analysis, reflection, and research. *(Timed Writing)*

Forest Fire: Retells exciting event

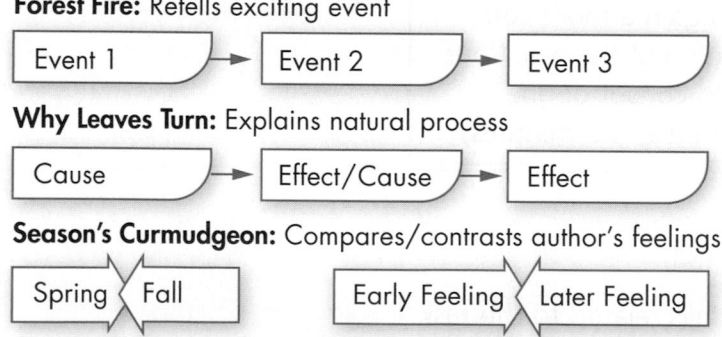

Why Leaves Turn: Explains natural process

Season's Curmudgeon: Compares/contrasts author's feelings

www.PHLitOnline.com

- Vocabulary flashcards
- Interactive journals
- More about the authors
- Selection audio
- Interactive graphic organizers

How much *information* is enough?

Writing About the Big Question

These essays highlight different ways of appreciating nature. Use the following sentence starter to develop your ideas.

The part of nature that I **value** the most is _____

because _____ .

Meet the Authors

Anaïs Nin (1903–1977)

Author of "Forest Fire"

Anaïs Nin wrote in many forms, but she is best known for her diaries. Born in France, Nin started a diary at age eleven while traveling to a new home in New York. Nin wrote entries in the diary for the rest of her life, eventually filling 200 volumes.

Diane Ackerman (b. 1948)

Author of "Why Leaves Turn Color in the Fall"

A native of Waukegan, Illinois, nature writer Diane Ackerman studied psychology, physiology, and English. Combining her literary skills with scientific training, Ackerman has published books of poems and books of nonfiction, including *A Natural History of the Senses*.

Mary C. Curtis (b. 1953)

Author of "The Season's Curmudgeon . . ."

Mary Curtis grew up in Baltimore and worked at *The New York Times* and *Baltimore Sun* before becoming the writer of a column in the *Charlotte* (North Carolina) *Observer*. Her column examines family life, religion, education, and popular culture. Says her managing editor, "Mary touches people in a special way. Her passion and empathy connect with their hearts, her reasoned analysis with their minds."

Forest Fire
Anaïs Nin

▲ **Critical Viewing**
What details in this photograph show the danger of forest fires? **[Deduce]**

Background *Monrovia Peak is a mountain in the Sierra Madre range near where Nin had a home in southwest California. The Santa Ana winds are hot, quickly-moving desert winds that dry out vegetation and fuel massive fires.*

A man rushed in to announce he had seen smoke on Monrovia Peak. As I looked out of the window I saw the two mountains facing the house on fire. The entire rim burning wildly in the night. The flames, driven by hot Santa Ana winds from the desert, were as tall as the tallest trees, the sky already tinted coral, and the crackling noise of burning trees, the ashes and the smoke were already increasing. The fire raced along, sometimes descending behind the mountain where I could only see the glow, sometimes descending toward us. I thought of the foresters in danger. I made coffee for the weary men who came down occasionally with horses they had led out, or with old people from the isolated cabins. They were covered with soot from their battle with the flames.

At six o'clock the fire was on our left side and rushing toward Mount Wilson. Evacuees from the cabins began to arrive and had to be given blankets and hot coffee. The streets were blocked with fire engines readying to fight the fire if it touched the houses. Policemen and firemen and guards turned away the sightseers. Some were relatives concerned over the fate of the foresters, or the pack station family. The policemen lighted flares, which gave the scene a theatrical, tragic air. The red lights on the police cars twinkled alarmingly. More fire engines arrived. Ashes fell, and the roar of the fire was now like thunder.

We were told to ready ourselves for evacuation. I packed the diaries. The saddest spectacle, beside that of the men fighting the fire as they would a war, were the animals, rabbits, coyotes, mountain lions, deer, driven by the fire to the edge of the mountain, taking a look at the crowd of people and panicking, choosing rather to rush back into the fire.

The fire now was like a ring around Sierra Madre, every mountain was burning. People living at the foot of the mountain were packing their cars. I rushed next door to the Campion children, who had been left with a baby-sitter, and got them into the car. It was impossible to save all the horses. We parked the car on the field below us. I called up the Campions, who were out for the evening, and reassured them. The baby-sitter dressed the children warmly. I made more coffee. I answered frantic telephone calls.

All night the fire engines sprayed water over the houses. But the fire grew immense, angry, and rushing at a speed I could not believe. It would rush along and suddenly leap over a road, a trail, like a monster, devouring all in its path. The firefighters cut breaks in the heavy brush,[1] but when the wind was strong enough, the fire leaped across them. At dawn one arm of the fire reached the back of our houses but was finally contained.

But high above and all around, the fire was burning, more vivid than the sun, throwing spirals of smoke in the air like the smoke from a volcano. Thirty-three cabins burned, and twelve thousand acres of forest still burning endangered countless homes below the fire. The fire was burning to the back of us now, and a rain of ashes began to fall and

---

1. **cut breaks in the heavy brush** cut down trees, shrubs, and underbrush to starve the fire of the fuel it needs to spread.

Vocabulary
evacuees (ē vak′ yoō ēz′) *n.* people who leave a dangerous area

Organization
What clues here indicate that this essay is organized chronologically?

Organization
How does relating these events in chronological order increase the drama?

Reading Check
How is the author affected by the forest fire?

Vocabulary
tenacious (tə nā′ shəs)
adj. holding on
firmly; stubborn

▼ **Critical Viewing**
Why would a mountain
be an especially chal-
lenging place to fight
a fire? **[Speculate]**

continued for days. The smell of the burn in the air, acrid
and pungent and tenacious. The dragon tongues of flames
devouring, the flames leaping, the roar of destruction and
dissolution,[2] the eyes of the panicked animals, caught
between fire and human beings, between two forms of death.
They chose the fire. It was as if the fire had come from the
bowels of the earth, like that of a fiery volcano, it was so
powerful, so swift, and so ravaging. I saw trees become
skeletons in one minute, I saw trees fall, I saw bushes
turned to ashes in a second, I saw weary, ash-covered men,
looking like men returned from war, some with burns, others
overcome by smoke.

The men were rushing from one spot to another watching for
recrudescence.[3] Some started backfiring up the mountain so that
the ascending flames could counteract the descending ones.

As the flames reached the cities below, hundreds of roofs
burst into flame at once. There was no water pressure because
all the fire hydrants were turned on at the same time, and the
fire departments were helpless to save more than a few of the
burning homes.

The blaring loudspeakers of passing police cars warned us
to prepare to evacuate in case the wind changed and drove
the fire in our direction. What did I wish to save? I thought
only of the diaries. I appeared
on the porch carrying a
huge stack of diary volumes,
preparing to pack them
in the car. A reporter for
the Pasadena *Star News*
was taking pictures of the
evacuation. He came up,
very annoyed with me. "Hey,
lady, next time could you
bring out something more
important than all those old
papers? Carry some clothes
on the next trip. We gotta
have human interest in these
pictures!"

2. **dissolution** (dis′ ə lōō′ shən) *n.* crumbling.
3. **recrudescence** (rē′ krōō des′ əns) *n.* fresh
outbreak of something that has been
inactive.

A week later, the danger was over.

Gray ashy days.

In Sierra Madre, following the fire, the January rains brought floods. People are sandbagging their homes. At four A.M. the streets are covered with mud. The bare, burnt, naked mountains cannot hold the rains and slide down bringing rocks and mud. One of the rangers must now take photographs and movies of the disaster. He asks if I will help by holding an umbrella over the cameras. I put on my raincoat and he lends me hip boots which look to me like seven-league boots.

We drive a little way up the road. At the third curve it is impassable. A river is rushing across the road. The ranger takes pictures while I hold the umbrella over the camera. It is terrifying to see the muddied waters and rocks, the mountain disintegrating. When we are ready to return, the road before us is covered by large rocks but the ranger pushes on as if the truck were a jeep and forces it through. The edge of the road is being carried away.

I am laughing and scared too. The ranger is at ease in nature, and without fear. It is a wild moment of danger. It is easy to love nature in its peaceful and consoling moments, but one must love it in its furies too, in its despairs and wildness, especially when the damage is caused by us.

Organization
What event makes a mudslide more likely to occur after the fire?

Spiral Review
Point of View How would you describe the author's point of view in these final paragraphs? Cite details to support your thinking.

Vocabulary
consoling (kən sōl´ iŋ) *adj.* comforting

Critical Thinking

Cite textual evidence to support your responses.

1. **Key Ideas and Details (a)** What possession does Nin rescue from the fire? **(b)** How does she help other people during the ordeal? **(c) Infer:** What do her actions reveal about her?

2. **Key Ideas and Details (a)** List three details Nin uses to describe the fire. **(b) Assess:** What effect does her language have on you?

3. **Integration of Knowledge and Skills Draw Conclusions:** What does Nin conclude about nature after witnessing the fire and the mudslide?

4. **Integration of Knowledge and Skills** What kind of information can we learn from one natural disaster that might help us to better prepare for the next one?
[Connect to the Big Question: How much information is enough?]

Why Leaves Turn Color in the Fall

Diane Ackerman

The stealth of autumn catches one unaware. Was
a goldfinch perching in the early September woo
just the first turning leaf? A red-winged blackbir
sugar maple closing up shop for the winter? Kee:
as leopards, we stand still and squint hard, looking for
of movement. Early-morning frost sits heavily on the gr
and turns barbed wire into a string of stars. On a dist;
a small square of yellow appears to be a lighted stage. ;
the truth dawns on us: Fall is staggering in, right on sc
with its baggage of chilly nights, macabre holidays, anc
spectacular, heart-stoppingly beautiful leaves. Soon the
will start cringing on the trees, and roll up in clenched
before they actually fall off. Dry seedpods will rattle lik
gourds. But first there will be weeks of gushing color so
so pastel, so confettilike, that people will travel up and
the East Coast just to stare at it—a whole season of lea

Where do the colors come from? Sunlight rules most living things with its golden edicts. When the days begin to shorten, soon after the summer solstice on June 21, a tree reconsiders its leaves. All summer it feeds them so they can process sunlight, but in the dog days of summer the tree begins pulling nutrients back into its trunk and roots, pares down, and gradually chokes off its leaves. A corky layer of cells forms at the leaves' slender petioles,[1] then scars over. Undernourished, the leaves stop producing the pigment chlorophyll,[2] and photosynthesis[3] ceases. Animals can migrate, hibernate, or store food to prepare for winter. But where can a tree go? It survives by dropping its leaves, and by the end of autumn only a few fragile threads of fluid-carrying xylem[4] hold leaves to their stems.

A turning leaf stays partly green at first, then reveals splotches of yellow and red as the chlorophyll gradually breaks down. Dark green seems to stay longest in the veins, outlining and defining them. During the summer, chlorophyll dissolves in the heat and light, but it is also being steadily replaced. In the fall, on the other hand, no new pigment is produced, and so we notice the other colors that were always there, right in the leaf, although chlorophyll's shocking green hid them from view. With their camouflage gone, we see these colors for the first time all year, and marvel, but they were always there, hidden like a vivid secret beneath the hot glowing greens of summer.

The most spectacular range of fall foliage occurs in the northeastern United States and in eastern China, where the leaves are robustly colored thanks in part to a rich climate. European maples don't achieve the same flaming reds as their American relatives, which thrive on cold nights and sunny days. In Europe, the warm, humid weather turns the leaves brown or mildly yellow. Anthocyanin, the pigment that gives apples their red and turns leaves red or red-violet, is produced by sugars that remain in the leaf after the supply of nutrients dwindles. Unlike the carotenoids, which color carrots, squash, and corn, and turn leaves orange and

Organization
What is the beginning and end of the chain of causes and effects the author describes here?

Reading Check
What pigment in leaves gives them their green color?

---

1. **petioles** (pet´ ē ōlz´) *n.* stalks of leaves.
2. **chlorophyll** (klôr´ ə fil´) *n.* green pigment found in plant cells. It is essential for photosynthesis.
3. **photosynthesis** (fōt´ ō sin´ thə sis) *n.* chemical process by which green plants make their food. This process involves using energy from the sun to turn water and carbon dioxide into food.
4. **xylem** (zī´ ləm) *n.* plant's woody tissue, which carries water and minerals in the stems, roots, and leaves.

yellow, anthocyanin varies from year to year, depending on the temperature and amount of sunlight. The fiercest colors occur in years when the fall sunlight is strongest and the nights are cool and dry (a state of grace scientists find vexing to forecast). This is also why leaves appear dizzyingly bright and clear on a sunny fall day: The anthocyanin flashes like a marquee.

Not all leaves turn the same color. Elms, weeping willows, and the ancient ginkgo all grow radiant yellow, along with hickories, aspens, bottlebrush buckeyes, cottonweeds, and tall, keening poplars. Basswood turns bronze, birches bright gold. Water-loving maples put on a symphonic display of scarlets. Sumacs turn red, too, as do flowering dogwoods, black gums, and sweet gums. Though some oaks yellow, most turn a pinkish brown. The farmlands also change color, as tepees of cornstalks and bales of shredded-wheat-textured hay stand drying in the fields. In some spots, one slope of a hill may be green and the other already in bright color, because the hillside facing south gets more sun and heat than the northern one.

Vocabulary
predisposed (prē dis pōzd´) *adj.* inclined

▼ **Critical Viewing**
From the author's description of leaf colors, what type of tree do you think this is? **[Apply]**

An odd feature of the colors is that they don't seem to have any special purpose. We are predisposed to respond to their beauty, of course. They shimmer with the colors of sunset, spring flowers, the tawny buff of a colt's pretty rump, the shuddering pink of a blush. Animals and flowers color for a reason—adaptation to their environment—but there is no adaptive reason for leaves to color so beautifully in the fall any more than there is for the sky or ocean to be blue. It's just one of the haphazard marvels the planet bestows every year. We find the sizzling colors thrilling, and in a sense they dupe us. Colored like living things, they signal death and disintegration. In time, they will become fragile and, like the body, return to dust. They are as we hope our own fate will be when we die; not to vanish, just to sublime from one beautiful state into another. Though leaves lose their green life, they bloom with urgent colors, as the woods grow mummified day by day, and Nature

becomes more carnal, mute, and radiant.

We call the season "fall," from the Old English *feallan,* to fall, which leads back through time to the Indo-European *phol,* which also means to fall. So the word and the idea are both extremely ancient, and haven't really changed since the first of our kind needed a name for fall's leafy abundance. As we say the word, we're reminded of that other Fall, in the Garden of Eden, when fig leaves never withered and scales fell from our eyes. Fall is the time when leaves fall from the trees, just as spring is when flowers spring up, summer is when we simmer, and winter is when we whine from the cold.

Children love to play in piles of leaves, hurling them into the air like confetti, leaping into soft unruly mattresses of them. For children, leaf fall is just one of the odder figments of Nature, like hailstones or snowflakes. Walk down a lane overhung with trees in the never-never land of autumn, and you will forget about time and death, lost in the sheer delicious spill of color. . . . ●

Children love to play in piles of leaves, hurling them into the air like confetti, leaping into soft unruly mattresses of them.

But how do the colored leaves fall? As a leaf ages, the growth hormone, auxin, fades, and cells at the base of the petiole divide. Two or three rows of small cells, lying at right angles to the axis of the petiole, react with water, then come apart, leaving the petioles hanging on by only a few threads of xylem. A light breeze, and the leaves are airborne. They glide and swoop, rocking in invisible cradles. They are all wing and may flutter from yard to yard on small whirlwinds or updrafts, swiveling as they go. Firmly tethered to earth, we love to see things rise up and fly—soap bubbles, balloons, birds, fall leaves. They remind us that the end of a season is capricious, as is the end of life. We especially like the way leaves rock, careen, and swoop as they fall. Everyone knows the motion. Pilots sometimes do a maneuver called a "falling leaf," in which the plane loses altitude quickly and on purpose, by slipping first to the right, then to the left. The machine weighs a ton or more, but in one pilot's mind it is a weightless thing, a falling leaf. She has seen the motion before, in the Vermont woods where she played as a child. Below her the trees radiate gold, copper, and red. Leaves are

Organization
How does the author use cause and effect to explain how the colored leaves fall?

Vocabulary
capricious (kə prish′ əs) *adj.* tending to change abruptly, without apparent reason

Reading Check
Where does the word *fall* come from?

falling, although she can't see them fall, as she falls, swooping down for a closer view.

At last the leaves leave. But first they turn color and thrill us for weeks on end. Then they crunch and crackle underfoot. They *shush*, as children drag their small feet through leaves heaped along the curb. Dark, slimy mats of leaves cling to one's heels after a rain. A damp, stuccolike mortar of semidecayed leaves protects the tender shoots with a roof until spring, and makes a rich humus. An occasional bulge or ripple in the leafy mounds signals a shrew or a field mouse tunneling out of sight. Sometimes one finds in fossil stones the imprint of a leaf, long since disintegrated, whose outlines remind us how detailed, vibrant, and alive are the things of this earth that perish.

Organization
Humus is rich soil. How is humus both an effect and a cause?

Spiral Review
Point of View How would you describe the author's point of view in this final paragraph? Cite details to support your answer.

Critical Thinking

Cite textual evidence to support your responses.

1. **Key Ideas and Details (a)** Identify two facts about leaves that are presented in the essay. **(b) Speculate:** Do you think Ackerman's scientific knowledge about leaves comes mostly from observation or research? Explain.

2. **Key Ideas and Details (a)** Why do leaves fall? **(b) Apply:** To what human process does Ackerman compare the turning and falling of leaves?

3. **Key Ideas and Details (a)** According to the text, where do leaves have the most spectacular color changes? **(b) Compare:** What weather conditions do those two places probably share? **(c) Speculate:** What questions might occur to a reader who does not live in a place where leaves change color?

4. **Integration of Knowledge and Ideas (a)** List two pieces of information that the author provides that are new for you and two facts that you already knew. **(b)** Does learning more about the scientific explanation for the changing colors of leaves make them seem more, equally, or less amazing? Explain. *[Connect to the Big Question: How much information is enough?]*

The Season's Curmudgeon Sees the Light

Mary C. Curtis

Spring has never done much for me.

I was always an autumn kind of gal: My birthday is in September. When red and gold creep into the leaves, I see beauty, not death. A slight chill in the air feels just right.

I planned an October wedding. When I raised my face to kiss the groom, I didn't want any beads of sweat ruining the moment.

In autumn, you can fall back into an extra hour for sleep or contemplation. It's something I look forward to all summer.

Autumn leads into the hibernation of winter, setting the perfect mood for us quiet types. When you sit inside to read a book, you're never chided for wasting a perfectly beautiful day.

I didn't mind fall's signal of a new school year; I liked school.

The season even has a song —"Autumn in New York"— that mentions two of my favorite things.

Spring meant too many rainy days, too many reminders of the humid summer to come. Spring-fever romances? New blossoms and pungent smells trigger sneezes, not love.

In spring, you lose an hour, which you need for all the scrubbing and cleaning.

Everyone is always *doing* something in the spring. And if you aren't, you feel like some kind of slug. "You've had all winter to rest, you lazy bum. Go outside!"

When you do venture out, it's not cold, but it's not warm enough, either. You can't take a walk without running into throngs of people: jogging, cycling, lying in every tiny patch of sun.

Vocabulary
contemplation
(kän´ təm plā´ shən)
n. the act of thinking about something

Organization
What two things does the author compare and contrast?

✓ Reading Check
Why does Curtis like autumn?

---

1. **curmudgeon** (kər muj´ ən) *n.* bad-tempered person.

Everyone says it's time to garden; I hate to garden.

"It Might as Well be Spring" isn't bad, but it's a little corny.

But this year, I began to wonder if maybe I had written off spring too hastily.

Spring is a clear signal that you've made it through another ice storm, another broken heater, another cold snap.

Rain isn't a bother if you think of it as washing all the grime away. Splashing is fun!

Spring is an excuse to get out of all those black clothes and go buy a pair of pink shoes. (Oh yes I did!)

You can peel off another layer of outerwear each day. As you lighten up—by hue and weight—it puts a "spring" in your step.

Sure you feel obligated, even compelled, to move around. Just look at it as a reminder from Mother Nature that it's time to put those chocolate bunny ears down and exercise.

It's for your health and so you'll look fabulous when those layers come off.

You get to see people you haven't seen for months. Or if you did pass them by, they had their collars up and their heads down.

Now, you can stop and say hi, ask them what they've been up to, give them garden advice and get some tips yourself. (Even if you have no intention of actually getting out in the garden yourself, saying "mulch," "fertilizer," and "perennials" is cathartic.[2])

Spring is fresh and positive like no other season.

The best part is knowing that another spring will come, and you will always have the chance for a fresh start.

---

2. **cathartic** (ke thär´ tik) *adj.* allowing a release of emotional tension.

Organization
What two feelings about spring does the author contrast?

Critical Thinking

Cite textual evidence to support your responses.

1. Key Ideas and Details (a) What are two reasons that Curtis initially gives for preferring fall? **(b) Deduce:** Based on these reasons, how would you describe the author's personality? Explain.

2. Key Ideas and Details (a) What change occurs in the author's thinking? **(b) Speculate:** What might have prompted this change?

3. Craft and Structure (a) On what type of information does Curtis base her impressions? **(b)** What makes them subject to change? *[Connect to the Big Question: How much information is enough?]*

Comparing Types of Organization

1. Craft and Structure (a) Identify three events in "Forest Fire" that occur in **chronological order. (b)** How does the final event of the essay help the writer make a point about nature?

2. Craft and Structure (a) Name two **causes** in "Why Leaves Turn Color in the Fall" that explain the natural **effect** of changing autumn leaves. **(b)** What effect does the author point out in the last line? **(c)** How does this effect help her make a point about living things?

3. Craft and Structure (a) In "The Season's Curmudgeon Sees the Light," identify two ways the author **compares and contrasts** spring and fall. **(b)** How does the writer use these contrasts to emphasize the qualities she has come to value about spring?

Timed Writing

Explanatory Text: Essay

The authors of these essays use specific organizational patterns to achieve their purposes, or reasons for writing. Choose one essay and write an in-depth analysis of its structure. Discuss the overall organization of the essay and explain whether it suits the author's topic. Then, analyze one important paragraph, explaining how it is structured and the ways in which individual sentences work together to build meaning. Come to a general conclusion about the ways in which the topic can influence the type of organization an author chooses. **(40 minutes)**

5-Minute Planner

1. Read the prompt carefully and completely.

2. Gather your ideas by completing a chart like the one shown.

Title	Author's Purpose	Key Details	Organization

3. Look for connections, such as similarities or contrasts, in the details you have observed. Use these connections to help organize your essay.

4. Reread the prompt, and then draft your essay.

Writing Workshop

 **Common Core State Standards**

Writing

2. Write informative/explanatory texts to examine a topic and convey ideas, concepts, and information through the selection, organization, and analysis of relevant content.

2.b. Develop the topic with relevant, well-chosen facts, definitions, concrete details, quotations, or other information and examples.

Write Informative Text

Exposition: How-to Essay

Defining the Form A **how-to essay** is a short, focused piece of expository writing that explains a process. You might use elements of this form in writing directions, recipes, or technical documents.

Assignment Write a how-to essay to explain a process you know well or to describe how to use a certain tool. Your essay should include these elements:

✔ *a focused topic* that can be fully explained in the essay

✔ *explanations of terms and materials* that may be unfamiliar

✔ *a sequence of logical steps* explained in chronological order

✔ *visual aids,* such as charts, illustrations, and diagrams, and *formatting techniques,* such as headings and boldface fonts, to help make complicated procedures understandable

✔ a list of variables and factors that need to be considered

✔ error-free writing, including *correct use of comparative and superlative forms,* as well as proper adjectives

To preview the criteria on which your how-to essay may be judged, see the rubric on page 553.

Writing Workshop: *Work in Progress*

Review the work you did on pages 499 and 525.

Prewriting/Planning Strategy

Listing To find a topic, make a list of people, places, things, and activities that you associate with your home or school. Circle words and draw lines to show connections between items on the lists. Choose a topic from the ideas the chart generates.

<u>Things</u>	<u>Activities</u>	<u>Places</u>
(my bicycle)	doing chores	my bedroom
CD collection	(reading bike magazines)	the backyard
(tools)	watching television	(the workshop)
skateboard	playing basketball	the kitchen

Topic: Customizing a mountain bike.

Organize Details

Organization is the general structure a writer chooses to arrange details in an essay. The details in most how-to essays are presented in **chronological order,** or in time sequence. Imagine your readers have no experience with the process you are explaining. Your essay must clarify the steps and explain them in order.

To clarify the order of steps, follow this sequence:

- Write each detail on a sticky note or on an index card.
- Arrange the steps in order. Add or rearrange steps as needed.
- When you find the right order, number the steps.

Use these notes as a guide for your first draft.

Creating Lists Directions, recipes, and technical documents often begin with a list of necessary tools or supplies. List the items in the order in which they should be used.

Addressing Factors and Variables *Factors* are elements that influence your readers' success in carrying out your instructions. *Variables* are the different conditions that may affect the process you describe. For example, a how-to essay on growing tomatoes should address factors such as types of soil and amounts of sunlight and variables such as the amount of rainfall.

To account for factors and variables in your essay, ask yourself:

- What different situations or conditions might my readers face?
- What could go wrong when readers carry out my instructions?

Adding Visuals Consider the types of visual aids that will help readers understand the process. Visual aids can appear anywhere in your essay, and you can use different types, depending on your needs. For ideas, refer to this chart, then add your own examples.

Drawings	Photographs	Diagrams	Maps
• Supplies • A person doing the activity	• Supplies • Equipment and tools • A finished product	Ways to put things together	Showing directions to get somewhere

Drafting Strategy

Use formatting techniques. Use various formatting techniques to draw attention to specific points or warnings in your instructions. These techniques may include headings and subheadings, different fonts and typefaces, and special arrangements on the page. You may wish to use bulleted or numbered lists, boxed information, color, or graphic elements such as arrows. Even the use of white space can make your instructions easier to read. Examples of some of these techniques are shown here.

Revising Strategies

Add interest with your introduction and conclusion. Look for ways to convince readers that the project is worth doing. Think about why your topic interests you, and build your enthusiasm into your introduction and conclusion.

Look for missing information. Review each paragraph in your draft to be sure you have included each step in the process. Use clear transitions between steps. Add any information a reader would need to complete a task successfully. Be sure to allow for variables, such as traveling from different points of origin when giving directions.

How to Make a Hot Fudge Sundae

Things You Will Need

- Chocolate sauce
- Vanilla ice cream
- Whipped cream
- Cherries
- Nuts

Steps

1. Heat ¼ cup to ½ cup chocolate sauce in the microwave.
2. Put 2–3 scoops of vanilla ice cream into a bowl.
3. Pour hot fudge over the top of the ice cream.
4. Top with whipped cream, a few cherries, and nuts.

Original	Revised
Go south on Main Street and turn left on Third.	If you are coming from north of the city, go south on Main Street and turn left on Third. If you are coming from south of the city, go north on Main Street and turn right on Third.

Add a Troubleshooting Guide. If your procedure is complicated, with lots of factors and variables, consider adding a Troubleshooting Guide. It should describe common mistakes that someone might make and how to correct them.

Revising to Correct Comparative and Superlative Forms

When you use adjectives and adverbs to compare items, use the correct comparative and superlative forms.

Identifying Forms Use the **comparative form** to compare two items. Use the **superlative form** to compare three or more items.

- The most common way to form these degrees is by adding *-er* or *-est* to words with one or two syllables.

- *More* and *most* (and *less* and *least*) are used with most adverbs ending in *-ly* and with modifiers of three or more syllables.

- Irregular adjectives and adverbs have unpredictable patterns that must be memorized.

Positive	Comparative	Superlative
heavy	heavier	heaviest
nutritious	less nutritious	least nutritious
bad, badly	worse	worst
good, well	better	best
many, much	more	most
far (distance)	farther	farthest
far (extent)	further	furthest

PH WRITING COACH

Further instruction and practice are available in *Prentice Hall Writing Coach*.

Fixing Errors To fix faulty use of comparatives and superlatives:

1. **Determine how many items are being compared.**

2. **Use the comparative form for two, and use the superlative form for three or more.**

   Comparative: Dave did better on the test than Suzie.

   Superlative: Of everyone in the class, Jo did the best.

Grammar in Your Writing

Choose two paragraphs in your draft. If a comparative or superlative adjective or adverb is used incorrectly, fix it using the rules above.

Student Model: Mike Tuholski, La Porte, IN

How to Treat a Classic Truck Bed

When you are restoring a classic truck, one large factor in the appearance of the finished truck is the wooden bed strips. This will make your truck look like it did when it first came off the assembly line. I suggest purchasing a kit from a company that specializes in truck parts from the year of your classic truck.

Open the package right away. Be sure the shipment includes:

- the proper length wood panels
- metal strips to connect the wooden panels
- braces to connect the bed to the frame

If you ordered metal strips that were not already polished, you may want to think about getting them polished. You will also need to purchase:

- varnish
- medium-sized paint brush
- large resealable container
- small cup
- wood finish (optional)
- sandpaper of different grit sizes
- paint thinner

Now that you have all of these items, you are ready to refinish your bed strips. The first thing to do is sand the boards. Sandpaper comes in many different textures. Start with a lower, or coarser, grit and gradually move to a higher, or finer, grit. This will leave the wood smooth by the end of the project. When you have your wood to a desired effect, you may now begin to apply finish, if you choose to. Finish can darken the wood, or it can bring out the grains in the wooden strips. When the finish is dried, you are ready to put on your first coat of varnish.

The varnish mixture for the first coat should be about 25 percent varnish and 75 percent paint thinner. This can be calculated easily with a small cup. Put three cups of thinner and one cup of varnish into the large resealable container. Utilize a thin layer of this mixture over every groove and surface of the wooden planks. Then, sand it lightly with a higher grit sandpaper.

Additional layers of varnish can be applied in the same fashion. In the second layer, however, use a mixture of 50 percent varnish and 50 percent paint thinner. Sand the wood lightly, then move to the third layer, which is a mixture of 75 percent varnish and 25 percent thinner. Again, sand the wood and apply one final coat of varnish.

Follow the instructions to put the wooden planks and metal strips together. The metal strips should have bolts, nuts, and washers that will clamp the wooden planks together. Be sure to put the "L"-shaped strips on the sides, as those will clamp to the bed sides. Then, attach the braces to the frame and bed. If you assemble the bed correctly, your remodeled wooden bed will provide a nice complement to your classic truck.

Now, with a new and improved bed to go with your shiny restored truck, you will be the envy of any classic truck admirer. All that is left is to enjoy your treated wood bed while you cruise down the highway, head held high.

Mike chose to focus his essay on restoring a truck bed.

Mike provides a bulleted list to identify key items.

Mike considers one variable here—that the reader might have ordered unpolished metal strips.

Mike explains a precise calculation for the varnish mixture.

Steps for varnishing are presented in the order they should be completed.

The conclusion reinforces the value of completing the project.

Editing and Proofreading

Review your draft to correct errors in spelling, punctuation, and grammar. Be precise and eliminate wordiness as you correct errors.

Focus on capitalizing proper adjectives. Proper adjectives require capitalization because they are derived from proper nouns. For example, you might have described a task that requires a specialized tool, such as an *Allen wrench* or a *Fahrenheit thermometer*. Make sure you have capitalized proper adjectives correctly.

Ⓒ **Spiral Review**

Use Adverbs Correctly Remember, adverbs answer the questions *When?*, *Where?*, *In what manner?*, and *To what extent?* Check to be sure you have not used adjectives in place of adverbs in your essay.

Publishing and Presenting

Consider these ideas for sharing your how-to essay.

Make a Web page. Use digital tools, such as Web authoring software, to create a Web page that explains your particular task. If you have never created a Web page before, you can find tutorials online.

Plan a demonstration day. Turn your writing into an oral demonstration that you can present to a group.

Reflecting on Your Writing

Writer's Journal Jot down your answer to this question:

Did teaching "how-to" help you to better learn your procedure? Explain.

Rubric for Self-Assessment

Find evidence in your writing to address each category. Then, use the rating scale to grade your work.

Criteria	Rating Scale
	not very very
Focus: How clearly and concisely is the topic stated?	1 2 3 4 5
Organization: How logically are the series of steps organized?	1 2 3 4 5
Support/Elaboration: How helpful are the visual aids and formatting techniques to understanding the instructions? How well are factors and variables taken into account?	1 2 3 4 5
Style: How clearly are materials and terms explained?	1 2 3 4 5
Conventions: How correct is your grammar, especially your use of proper adjectives and comparative and superlative forms?	1 2 3 4 5

ⓒ Leveled Texts

Build your skills and improve your comprehension of types of nonfiction with texts of increasing complexity.

Read **"The Trouble With Television"** to see how a respected journalist views the influence of television.

Read **"On Woman's Right to Suffrage"** to hear the voice of an early fighter for women's rights.

ⓒ Common Core State Standards

Meet these standards with either **"The Trouble with Television"** (p. 558) or **"On Woman's Right to Suffrage"** (p. 566).

Reading Informational Text

6. Determine an author's point of view or purpose in a text and analyze how the author acknowledges and responds to conflicting evidence or viewpoints. *(Literary Analysis: Spiral Review; Writing: Evaluation)*

8. Delineate and evaluate the argument and specific claims in a text, assessing whether the reasoning is sound and the evidence is relevant and sufficient. *(Reading Skill: Fact and Opinion; Literary Analysis: Types of Appeals; Writing: Evaluation)*

9. Analyze a case in which two or more texts provide conflicting information on the same topic and identify where texts disagree on matters of fact or interpretation. *(Research and Technology: Snapshot)*

Writing

1. Write arguments to support claims with clear reasons and relevant evidence. *(Writing: Evaluation)*

6. Use technology, including the Internet, to produce and publish writing and present the relationships between information and ideas efficiently as well as to interact and collaborate with others. *(Research and Technology: Snapshot)*

Language

1. Demonstrate command of the conventions of standard English grammar and usage when writing or speaking. *(Conventions: Conjunctions)*

4.b. Use common, grade-appropriate Greek and Latin affixes and roots as clues to the meaning of a word. *(Vocabulary: Word Study)*

Reading Skill: Fact and Opinion

In persuasive essays, writers present an argument and then use evidence to defend their claims against conflicting viewpoints. An argument may consist of both facts and opinions.

A **fact** is information that can be proved with evidence. An **opinion** may be supported by evidence, but not proved. A **generalization** is a conclusion supported by facts. An **overgeneralization** is a conclusion that overstates the facts.
You can **use clue words** to analyze fact and opinion.

- Words that express judgment, like *best* or *worst*, or words that show the writer's beliefs, usually indicate an opinion.

- Words that show connections—such as *so* and *because*—may signal generalizations. Extreme statements that include words like *always*, *everything*, *never*, and *only* may be overgeneralizations.

Literary Analysis: Types of Appeals

Persuasive techniques are the methods that a writer uses to make an audience think or act a certain way.

- **Repetition** is doing or saying something again and again to drive home a point. Commercials often repeat a slogan so that the viewer will remember it and come to believe it.

- **Rhetorical questions,** those with obvious answers, can be used to persuade people to agree with controversial points.

Using the Strategy: Types of Appeals

Three other persuasive methods are listed in the **persuasive appeals** chart. As you read, take note of the persuasive techniques at work.

Types of Persuasive Appeals		
Appeal to Authority	**Appeal to Emotions**	**Appeal to Reason**
Example: Quotations from experts or reliable sources.	*Example:* Words that appeal to feelings, such as love of one's country.	*Example:* Logical arguments based on evidence, such as statistics.
*Example:*_____	*Example:*_____	*Example:* _____

How much information is enough?

Writing About the Big Question

In "The Trouble With Television," Robert MacNeil expresses doubts about the quality of the information television offers. Use these sentence starters to develop your ideas about the Big Question.

The **exploration** of ideas on television shows is usually _____.

Two shows that demonstrate this are _____ and _____ because they _____.

While You Read This speech was written before cable and the Internet became popular. Consider which of his ideas would apply to those media.

Vocabulary

Read each word and its definition. Decide whether you know the word well, know it a little bit, or do not know it at all. After you read, see how your knowledge of each word has increased.

- **constructive** (kən struk´ tiv) *adj.* leading to improvement (p. 559) *Dad's <u>constructive</u> advice helped solve my problem. constructively adv. construct v. construction n.*

- **diverts** (di vʉrts´) *v.* distracts; amuses (p. 559) *A movie <u>diverts</u> her from her worries. diversion n. inverts v. reverts v.*

- **passively** (pas´ iv lē) *adv.* without resistance (p. 559) *She <u>passively</u> agreed to the plan, allowing us to make all the decisions. passive adj. passivity n.*

- **pervading** (pər vād´ iŋ) *adj.* spreading throughout (p. 560) *The odor sickened us all as it traveled through the house, <u>pervading</u> every room. pervasive adj. pervade v.*

- **trivial** (triv´ ē əl) *adj.* of little importance (p. 562) *He strives to solve significant problems, not <u>trivial</u> ones. trivia n.*

- **skeptically** (skep´ ti kəl ē) *adv.* with doubt and distrust (p. 562) *We listened <u>skeptically</u> to her outrageous account of what we knew was a minor accident. skeptical adj. skeptic n.*

Word Study

The **Latin root -vad-** means "to go."

In this speech, the author worries that the networks' desire to entertain an audience is **pervading,** or spreading throughout, television. He believes it affects the way news is presented.

Author of

The TROUBLE With Television

Robert MacNeil grew up in Halifax, Nova Scotia, Canada, where he developed a love for the English language early in life. This led him to a lifelong career in broadcasting.

MacNeil began his broadcast career in Canada as a radio announcer and disc jockey. For Canadian television, he then hosted an educational children's show. In 1955, he moved to England and worked as a journalist.

NewsHour In 1975, MacNeil became co-host of the highly respected *MacNeil/Lehrer NewsHour* on American public television. The show stood out from other news programs by offering more in-depth news and analysis. He retired from *NewsHour* in 1995. He continues to write about life, language, and history, and occasionally hosts programs on public television.

DID YOU KNOW?

In his memoir *Wordstruck*, MacNeil says he is "crazy about the sound of words, the look of words, the taste of words, the feeling for words on the tongue and in the mind."

BACKGROUND FOR THE SPEECH

Television Viewing

Robert MacNeil was co-host of a news show in 1984 when he delivered this speech about America's television addiction. Since then, viewing has only increased. According to Nielsen research, in September 2005, the average American watched more than thirty hours of television a week. Teenagers watched twenty-one hours. Critics, like MacNeil, worry about the potential negative effects of so much television-watching.

The TROUBLE With Television

ROBERT MACNEIL

Fact and Opinion
Identify one fact and one opinion presented here.

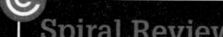

Spiral Review
Point of View Examine MacNeil's word choice in the first two paragraphs. What might be his point of view on the subject of television?

It is difficult to escape the influence of television. If you fit the statistical averages, by the age of 20 you will have been exposed to at least 20,000 hours of television. You can add 10,000 hours for each decade you have lived after the age of 20. The only things Americans do more than watch television are work and sleep.

Calculate for a moment what could be done with even a part of those hours. Five thousand hours, I am told, are what a typical college undergraduate spends working on a bachelor's degree. In 10,000 hours you could have learned enough to become an astronomer or engineer. You could have learned several languages fluently. If it appealed to you, you could be reading Homer[1] in the original Greek or Dostoevski[2] in Russian. If it didn't, you could have walked around the world and written a book about it.

---

1. **Homer** (hō´ mər) ancient Greek author to whom the epic poems the *Odyssey* and the *Iliad* are attributed.
2. **Dostoevski** (dôs´ tô yef´ skē) (1821–1881) Fyodor (fyô´ dôr), Russian novelist.

The trouble with television is that it discourages concentration. Almost anything interesting and rewarding in life requires some constructive, consistently applied effort. The dullest, the least gifted of us can achieve things that seem miraculous to those who never concentrate on anything. But television encourages us to apply no effort. It sells us instant gratification. It diverts us only to divert, to make the time pass without pain.

Television's variety becomes a narcotic, not a stimulus.[3] Its serial, kaleidoscopic[4] exposures force us to follow its lead. The viewer is on a perpetual guided tour: thirty minutes at the museum, thirty at the cathedral, then back on the bus to the next attraction—except on television, typically, the spans allotted are on the order of minutes or seconds, and the chosen delights are more often car crashes and people killing one another. In short, a lot of television usurps one of the most precious of all human gifts, the ability to focus your attention yourself, rather than just passively surrender it.

Capturing your attention—and holding it—is the prime motive of most television programming and enhances its role as a profitable advertising vehicle. Programmers live in constant fear of losing anyone's attention—anyone's. The surest way to avoid doing so is to keep everything brief, not to strain the attention of anyone but instead to provide constant stimulation through variety, novelty, action and movement. Quite simply, television operates on the appeal to the short attention span.

It is simply the easiest way out. But it has come to be regarded as a given, as inherent in the medium[5] itself: as an imperative, as though General Sarnoff, or one of the

Persuasive Techniques
Does MacNeil appeal to logic or emotion here? Explain.

Reading Check
According to MacNeil, how do programmers avoid losing viewers?

---

3. **becomes a narcotic, not a stimulus** becomes something that dulls the senses instead of something that inspires action.
4. **kaleidoscopic** (kə lī´ də skäp´ ik) *adj.* constantly changing.
5. **inherent** (in hir´ ənt) **in the medium** a natural part of television. A *medium* is a means of communication; the plural is *media*.

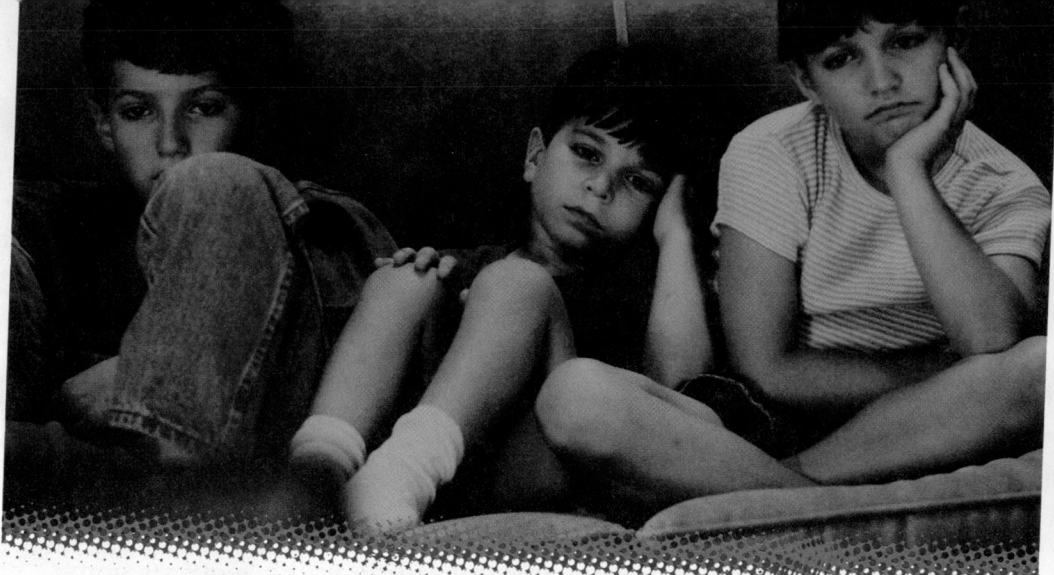

▶ **Critical Viewing**
What does this photo suggest about the effects of watching television? **[Infer]**

Vocabulary
pervading (pər vād´ iŋ) *adj.* spreading throughout

Fact and Opinion
Is the first sentence of this paragraph a fact or an opinion? How do you know?

other august pioneers of video, had bequeathed to us tablets of stone commanding that nothing in television shall ever require more than a few moments' concentration.

In its place that is fine. Who can quarrel with a medium that so brilliantly packages escapist entertainment as a mass-marketing tool? But I see its values now pervading this nation and its life. It has become fashionable to think that, like fast food, fast ideas are the way to get to a fast-moving, impatient public.

In the case of news, this practice, in my view, results in inefficient communication. I question how much of television's nightly news effort is really absorbable and understandable. Much of it is what has been aptly described as "machine gunning with scraps." I think its technique fights coherence.[6] I think it tends to make things ultimately boring and dismissable (unless they are accompanied by horrifying pictures) because almost anything is boring and dismissable if you know almost nothing about it.

I believe that TV's appeal to the short attention span is not only inefficient communication but decivilizing as well. Consider the casual assumptions that television tends to cultivate: that complexity must be avoided, that visual stimulation is a substitute for thought, that verbal precision is an anachronism.[7] It may be old-fashioned, but I was taught that thought is words, arranged in grammatically precise ways.

There is a crisis of literacy in this country. One study estimates that some 30 million adult Americans are "functionally

---

6. **coherence** (kō hir´ əns) *n.* quality of being connected in a way that is easily understood.
7. **anachronism** (ə nak´ rə niz´ əm) *n.* something that seems to be out of its proper place in history.

Culture Connection

The Television Age
When television sets were scarce, people peered through store windows to watch broadcasts of popular events such as this one, the inauguration of Queen Elizabeth II in 1953. Radio pioneer David Sarnoff (inset) believed in and supported TV's emerging technology. His vision was right on the mark— today, nearly 100 percent of U.S. homes have one or more televisions.

▲ David Sarnoff

1900	The word **"television"** used for the first time the World's Fair in Paris.
1923	**Vladimir Zworykin** patents his **iconoscope,** a TV camera tube. Later he develops the **kinescope** for picture display.
1927	**Philo Farnsworth** files for a patent on the first electronic television system.
1936	**Coaxial cable,** used to transmit TV, telephone, and data signals, is introduced. About 200 TV sets are in use worldwide.
1939	**RCA's David Sarnoff** showcases TV at the World's Fair.
1948	**Milton Berle's** *Texaco Star Theater* is the No. 1 program. Less than two percent of homes in the U.S. own a TV set.
1953	The puppet show *Kukla, Fran and Ollie* broadcasts in **color.**
1956	**Robert Adler** invents the first practical **remote control,** called the *Zenith Space Commander.* TV ownership is now seventy percent of U.S. homes.
1969	On July 20, 600 million people watched TV **transmission from the moon.**
1998	First **HDTV** (high definition television) broadcast.
2004	**Plasma** and **LCD** (liquid crystal display) technology supports flat-screen TVs.

Connect to the Literature

How has the fascination with television impacted U.S. culture?

illiterate" and cannot read or write well enough to answer a want ad or understand the instructions on a medicine bottle.

Literacy may not be an inalienable human right, but it is one that the highly literate Founding Fathers might not have found unreasonable or even unattainable. We are not only not attaining it as a nation, statistically speaking, but we are falling further and further short of attaining it. And, while I would not be so simplistic as to suggest that television is the cause, I believe it contributes and is an influence. •

Everything about this nation—the structure of the society, its forms of family organization, its economy, its

Reading Check
What does MacNeil dislike about the way television covers news?

place in the world—has become more complex, not less. Yet its dominating communications instrument, its principal form of national linkage, is one that sells neat resolutions to human problems that usually have no neat resolutions. It is all symbolized in my mind by the hugely successful art form that television has made central to the culture, the thirty-second commercial: the tiny drama of the earnest housewife who finds happiness in choosing the right toothpaste.

When before in human history has so much humanity collectively surrendered so much of its leisure to one toy, one mass diversion? When before has virtually an entire nation surrendered itself wholesale to a medium for selling?

Some years ago Yale University law professor Charles L. Black, Jr. wrote: ". . . forced feeding on trivial fare is not itself a trivial matter." I think this society is being force fed with trivial fare, and I fear that the effects on our habits of mind, our language, our tolerance for effort, and our appetite for complexity are only dimly perceived. If I am wrong, we will have done no harm to look at the issue skeptically and critically, to consider how we should be resisting it. I hope you will join with me in doing so.

Vocabulary

trivial (triv´ ē əl) *adj.* of little importance

skeptically (skep´ ti kəl ē) *adv.* with doubt and distrust

Fact and Opinion
What words and phrases in the last three paragraphs indicate opinions and generalizations?

Critical Thinking

Cite textual evidence to support your responses.

© 1. **Key Ideas and Details (a)** What does MacNeil identify as the main trouble with television? **(b) Connect:** How does this problem relate to the methods broadcasters use?

© 2. **Key Ideas and Details (a)** What does MacNeil criticize about nightly news shows on television? **(b) Evaluate:** Do you agree or disagree with his criticism of television news? Support your answer.

© 3. **Integration of Knowledge and Ideas (a)** What positive aspects of television does MacNeil mention? **(b) Speculate:** If MacNeil were in charge of programming for a network, what changes might he make?

© 4. **Integration of Knowledge and Ideas (a)** How does MacNeil's speech reflect the historical era in which it was written? **(b)** Are his opinions and information still relevant today? **(c)** How might he update his criticism to include new media? *[Connect to the Big Question: How much information is enough?]*

Reading Skill: Fact and Opinion

1. In a chart like this one, classify each claim as a **fact,** an **opinion,** a **generalization,** or an **overgeneralization.**

Statement	Type of Statement
Almost anything interesting and rewarding in life requires some constructive . . . effort.	
But television encourages us to apply no effort.	
. . . by the age of 20 you will have been exposed to at least 20,000 hours of television.	
I think this society is being force fed with trivial fare . . .	

Literary Analysis: Persuasive Techniques

© 2. Craft and Structure (a) Find places where MacNeil says that television appeals to short attention spans. **(b)** Why does he repeat this idea?

© 3. Craft and Structure (a) What is one source MacNeil quotes to give his argument authority? **(b)** Explain how he uses this source for support. **(c)** Identify and explain one more **persuasive technique.**

Vocabulary

© Acquisition and Use Rewrite each sentence, using a vocabulary word.

1. Her questions were about small, unimportant matters.

2. Wafting through the house was the aroma of cookies.

3. Any small noise interrupts my concentration on homework.

4. Our conversation was helpful because it gave me ideas.

5. He listened to her yell without fighting back.

6. I looked at her doubtfully when she said that she was 29.

Word Study Use the context of the sentences and what you know about the **Latin root -vad-** to explain each answer.

1. What would a driver do in order to *evade* an obstacle?

2. How might citizens react to an *invading* army?

Word Study

The **Latin root -vad-** means "to go."

Apply It Explain how the root **-vad-** contributes to the meanings of these words. Consult a dictionary, if necessary.

evasively
wading
vamoose

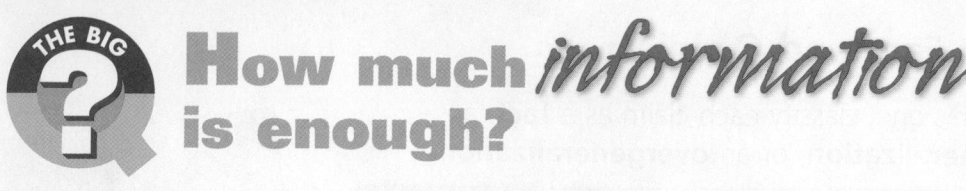

How much *information* is enough?

Writing About the Big Question

Susan B. Anthony gave this speech to discuss the importance of many voices to a democracy. Use these sentence starters to develop your ideas about the Big Question.

Discrimination may have a negative effect on democracy because it prevents citizens from _____.

In a democracy, government hears many opinions because_____.

While You Read Consider the ways Anthony defends the idea that input from all people is critical to democracy.

Vocabulary

Read each word and its definition. Decide whether you know the word well, know it a little bit, or do not know it at all. After you read, see how your knowledge of each word has increased.

- **posterity** (päs ter´ ə tē) *n.* future generations (p. 567) *He died, leaving his fortune to posterity. posterior adj.*

- **mockery** (mak´ ər ē) *n.* false, insulting action or statement (p. 567) *His disrespectful comments during the awards ceremony were a mockery. mock v. mockingly adv.*

- **violation** (vī ə lā´ shən) *n.* the breaking or ignoring of rules, laws, or rights (p. 567) *The officer ticketed the driver for a traffic violation. violate v. violator n.*

- **derived** (di rīvd´) *v.* received or taken from a source (p. 567) *The playwright derived satisfaction from positive reviews. derivation adv.*

- **rebellion** (ri bel´ yən) *n.* open resistance to authority or dominance (p. 568) *The peasants staged a rebellion to overthrow the wicked king. rebellious adj. rebel n.*

- **immunities** (i myoon´ ə tēz) *n.* freedoms; protections (p. 568) *One of our legal immunities is the freedom from unreasonable searches. immune adj. immunization n.*

Author of

On *Woman's Right to Suffrage*

Susan B. Anthony spent most of her adult life as a prominent voice in the struggle to win the vote for women. Raised as a Quaker, she inherited her parents' dislike of slavery and inequality.

Early Activist At her first job as a teacher, Anthony found out that she was making one-fifth the salary of the school's male teachers. She complained and was fired. Anthony found a new job as the principal of a girls' school. After ten years, though, she became so caught up in the struggle to win the vote for women that she decided to dedicate her life to the cause. With Elizabeth Cady Stanton, Anthony founded the National Woman Suffrage Association in 1869. She remained in the fight for the vote until she died in her eighties.

DID YOU KNOW?

At age 84, Anthony organized an international alliance for women's suffrage. Women finally won the right to vote in 1920—too late for Anthony. She had died fourteen years earlier.

BACKGROUND FOR THE SPEECH

Women's Suffrage

Before 1920, American women did not have the right to vote— also known as *suffrage*. In 1872, activist Susan B. Anthony and some friends tested a law preventing women from voting by going to the polls in Rochester, New York. Anthony was arrested, tried, and ordered to pay a fine. She refused to pay. "On Woman's Right to Suffrage" is her defiant answer to the charges against her.

On Woman's Right to Suffrage

SUSAN B. ANTHONY

◀ Critical Viewing
What personality traits are conveyed in this photo of suffragists Susan B. Anthony and Elizabeth Cady Stanton? **[Analyze]**

1873—Friends and fellow citizens:

I stand before you to-night under indictment for
the alleged crime[1] of having voted at the last presidential
election, without having a lawful right to vote. It shall be
my work this evening to prove to you that in thus voting, I
not only committed no crime, but, instead, simply exercised
my *citizen's rights*, guaranteed to me and all United States
citizens by the National Constitution, beyond the power of
any State to deny.

The preamble of the Federal Constitution says:

"We, the people of the United States, in order to form
a more perfect union, establish justice, insure *domestic*
tranquillity, provide for the common defense, promote
the general welfare, and secure the blessings of liberty to
ourselves and our posterity, do ordain and establish this
Constitution for the United States of America."

It was we, the people; not we, the white male citizens;
nor yet we, the male citizens; but we, the whole people, who
formed the Union. And we formed it, not to give the blessings
of liberty, but to secure them; not to the half of ourselves and
the half of our posterity, but to the whole people—women as
well as men. And it is a downright mockery to talk to women
of their enjoyment of the blessings of liberty while they are
denied the use of the only means of securing them provided
by this democratic-republican government—the ballot. •

For any State to make sex a qualification that must ever
result in the disfranchisement of one entire half of the people
is to pass a bill of attainder, or an *ex post facto* law,[2] and is
therefore a violation of the supreme law of the land. By it the
blessings of liberty are for ever withheld from women and
their female posterity. To them this government has no just
powers derived from the consent of the governed. To them
this government is not a democracy. It is not a republic.
It is an odious aristocracy;[3] a hateful oligarchy of sex; the
most hateful aristocracy ever established on the face of the

---

1. **indictment** (in dīt´ mənt) **for the alleged** *(ə lejd´)* **crime** in law, a written statement charging a person with supposedly committing a crime.
2. **bill of attainder . . . ex post facto law** two practices specifically outlawed by the U.S. Constitution. A bill of attainder declares someone guilty without a trial. An *ex post facto* law applies to acts committed before the law was passed.
3. **odious** (ō´ dē əs) **aristocracy** (ar´ i stä´ krə sē) hateful system based on inherited wealth and power.

Fact and Opinion
Identify one fact and one opinion in this paragraph.

Vocabulary
posterity (päs ter´ ə tē)
n. future generations; descendants

mockery (mak´ ər ē)
n. false, insulting action or statement

violation (vī´ ə lā´ shən) *n.* the breaking or ignoring of rules, laws, or rights

derived (di rīvd´) *v.* received or taken from a source

Spiral Review
Point of View What point of view does Anthony express in the passage in which she quotes the Constitution?

Reading Check
What crime did Anthony commit?

Fact and Opinion
On what fact does
Anthony base her
opinion that discrimina-
tion against women is
illegal?

globe; an oligarchy of wealth, where the rich govern the poor. An oligarchy of learning, where the educated govern the ignorant, or even an oligarchy of race, where the Saxon rules the African, might be endured;[4] but this oligarchy of sex, which makes father, brothers, husband, sons, the oligarchs over the mother and sisters, the wife and daughters of every household—which ordains all men sovereigns, all women subjects, carries dissension, discord and rebellion into every home of the nation.

Webster, Worcester and Bouvier all define a citizen to be a person in the United States, entitled to vote and hold office.

The only question left to be settled now is: Are women persons? And I hardly believe any of our opponents will have the hardihood to say they are not. Being persons, then, women are citizens; and no State has a right to make any law, or to enforce any old law, that shall abridge their privileges or immunities. Hence, every discrimination against women in the constitutions and laws of the several States is to-day null and void, precisely as in every one against negroes.

---

4. **oligarchy of race . . . endured** Anthony refers to a racist nineteenth-century belief, held even by some abolitionists, that whites ("the Saxon") were the natural rulers of African Americans.

Critical Thinking

© 1. **Key Ideas and Details (a)** Of what crime is Anthony accused? **(b) Contrast:** How does she describe her actions? **(c) Connect:** How is her description connected to the Constitution?

© 2. **Key Ideas and Details (a)** According to Anthony, how do dictionaries define *citizen*? **(b) Analyze:** How does she use this definition to support her position? **(c) Synthesize:** What is her conclusion about laws that discriminate against women?

© 3. **Craft and Structure** What information in the language, style, ideas, attitudes, and subject matter tells you that the speech was presented at least one hundred years ago?

© 4. **Integration of Knowledge and Ideas (a)** What does Anthony believe is required for a government to be a democracy? **(b)** Does Anthony believe that she lives in a true democracy? Explain. *[Connect to the Big Question: How much information is enough?]*

Cite textual evidence to support your responses.

Reading Skill: Fact and Opinion

1. In a chart like this one, classify each claim as a **fact,** an **opinion,** a **generalization,** or an **overgeneralization.**

Statement	Type of Statement
It is a downright mockery to talk to women of their enjoyment of the blessings of liberty….	
To [women] this government is…the most hateful aristocracy ever established.	
[I] voted at the last…election, without having a lawful right to vote.	
Webster…define[s] a citizen to be a person entitled to vote.	

Literary Analysis: Persuasive Techniques

Ⓒ **2. Craft and Structure (a)** Identify an example of repetition in Anthony's speech. **(b)** What point is she emphasizing through this repetition?

Ⓒ **3. Craft and Structure (a)** List two sources Anthony quotes in her speech. **(b)** Explain how she uses these sources. **(c)** Name another **persuasive technique** used by Anthony.

Vocabulary

Ⓒ **Acquisition and Use** Rewrite each sentence using a vocabulary word.

1. Today's music is rooted in the music of earlier generations.

2. The judge's sentence made the legal system look ridiculous.

3. Talking during a movie breaks the rules of good manners.

4. This is an issue, not just for us, but also for our descendants.

5. The Constitution offers citizens many legal protections.

6. Governments look for signs of opposition.

Word Study Use the context of the sentences and what you know about the **Latin root -bellum-** to explain each answer.

1. How would a *belligerent* person treat others?

2. What actions might a *rebellious* child take?

Word Study

The **Latin root -bellum-** means "war."

Apply It Explain how the root **-bellum-** contributes to the meanings of these words. Consult a dictionary, if necessary.

bellicose
antebellum
postbellum

Integrated Language Skills

The Trouble With Television •
On Woman's Right to Suffrage

Conventions: Conjunctions

Words that connect sentence parts are called **conjunctions**.

The chart shows three types and functions of conjunctions.

Type	Function	Example
coordinating	connects parts of similar importance	*and, but, for, nor, or, so, yet*
correlative	connects pairs of equal importance	*both/and, either/or, neither/nor*
subordinating	connects two ideas, one dependent on the other	*although, because, even though, if, since, while, until*

Writers often make the mistake of mismatching *either/or* and *neither/nor.* Always use *either* with *or* and *neither* with *nor.*

Incorrect: Neither she or I can go to the party.
Correct: Neither she nor I can go to the party.

Practice A Identify the conjunction in each sentence below and name the type.

1. Watching television news is convenient, but the news stories lack depth.
2. MacNeil is critical of television even though he is a TV journalist.
3. Treating news as entertainment is neither efficient nor educational.
4. Although television has many faults, it also provides important information.

© **Reading Application** In "The Trouble With Television," find a sentence with a conjunction. Identify its type and function in the sentence.

Practice B Rewrite each sentence, changing one of the conjunctions. Explain how the new conjunction affects the meaning of the sentence.

1. The Constitution and Bill of Rights spell out rights and responsibilities.
2. States approved the Constitution, but they wanted a Bill of Rights.
3. Neither women nor African Americans could vote in 1789.

© **Writing Application** Follow the construction of this sentence to write two sentences using conjunctions. *Either legislators or voters have to insist on change, but progress will be made.*

PH WRITING COACH Further instruction and practice are available in *Prentice Hall Writing Coach.*

Writing

**Common Core
State Standards**

**L.8.1; RI.8.6, RI.8.8, RI.8.9;
W.8.1, W.8.6**
[For the full wording of the standards, see page 554.]

Argument Write an **evaluation** of either MacNeil's speech or Anthony's speech. Use these criteria and questions to guide your analysis of the author's claims and supporting evidence.

- **Unity:** How well does the evidence support the main argument?
- **Coherence:** Does each argument build on previous arguments?
- **Logic:** Does the evidence always lead to each conclusion?
- **Consistency:** Do any of the arguments conflict with earlier ones?
- **Completeness:** Are opposing viewpoints addressed?

Begin by stating the author's position. State your claim about how persuasive the author was, and support your ideas with relevant evidence.

Grammar Application Check your writing for correct conjunctions. Be sure you use *either* with *or* and *neither* with *nor*.

Writing Workshop: *Work in Progress*

Prewriting for Editorial Make a list of five problems. For each issue, jot down an opinion. Keep this Problem List in your portfolio.

Use this prewriting activity to prepare for the **Writing Workshop** on page 614.

Research and Technology

Build and Present Knowledge With a group, create a **snapshot** of arguments based on the selection you read.

- If you read "The Trouble With Television," use Internet resources to find an editorial or essay that argues that watching television can be beneficial or educational. Compare the piece you find with the O'Neill essay.

- If you read "On Woman's Suffrage," find a historical editorial or essay from the late nineteenth or early twentieth century that argues against granting women the vote. Compare this piece with the Anthony speech.

Follow these steps to complete the assignment.

- Analyze the facts, logical arguments, appeals to authority, and statistics that each author uses to support his or her main argument.

- Write an overview of the arguments made by the "pro" and "con" authors. Use a class blog or message board to post your findings and discuss which argument is more effective.

PHLit Online!
www.PHLitOnline.com
- Interactive graphic organizers
- Grammar tutorial
- Interactive journals

Ⓒ Leveled Texts

Build your skills and improve your comprehension of types of nonfiction with texts of increasing complexity.

Read the excerpt from ***Sharing in the American Dream*** to hear a famous leader's ideas for helping people in need.

Read **"Science and the Sense of Wonder"** to consider the ways that science can help us appreciate the universe.

Ⓒ Common Core State Standards

Meet these standards with either the excerpt from ***Sharing in the American Dream*** (p. 576) or **"Science and the Sense of Wonder"** (p. 582).

Reading Informational Text
4. Determine the meaning of words and phrases as they are used in a text, including figurative, connotative, and technical meanings; analyze the impact of specific word choices on meaning and tone. *(Literary Analysis: Word Choice)*

8. Delineate and evaluate the argument and specific claims in a text, assessing whether the reasoning is sound and the evidence is relevant and sufficient; recognize when irrelevant evidence is introduced. *(Reading Skill: Fact and Opinion)*

Writing
2. Write informative/explanatory texts to examine a topic and convey ideas, concepts, and information. *(Writing: Response)*

2.c. Use appropriate transitions to create cohesion and clarify the relationships among ideas and concepts. *(Speaking and Listening: Speech)*

Speaking and Listening
4. Present claims and findings, emphasizing salient points in a focused, coherent manner with relevant evidence, sound valid reasoning, and well-chosen details. *(Speaking and Listening: Speech)*

Language
4.b. Use common, grade-appropriate Greek and Latin affixes and roots as clues to the meaning of a word. *(Vocabulary: Word Study)*

5.c. Distinguish among the connotations (associations) of words with similar denotations (definitions). *(Literary Analysis: Word Choice)*

Reading Skill: Fact and Opinion

In an argumentative text, a writer makes a claim and then provides suitable and thorough evidence to defend it. Writers can use both facts and opinions to support their claims. A **fact** is information that can be proved. An **opinion** is a person's judgment or belief. It can be further analyzed this way:

- *Valid opinions* can be supported by facts or by expert authority.
- *Faulty opinions* cannot be supported by facts. Instead, they are supported only by other opinions, often ignoring major facts that are contradictory. Faulty opinions often show *bias*, an unfair preference or dislike for something.

As you read arguments, evaluate the writers' claims and the quality of the supporting evidence.

Using the Strategy: Opinion Flowchart

Use this **opinion flowchart** to evaluate support for a claim.

PHLit Online!
www.PHLitOnline.com

Hear It!
- Selection summary audio
- Selection audio

See It!
- Get Connected video
- Background video
- More about the author
- Vocabulary flashcards

Do It!
- Interactive journals
- Interactive graphic organizers
- Self-test
- Internet activity
- Grammar tutorial
- Interactive vocabulary games

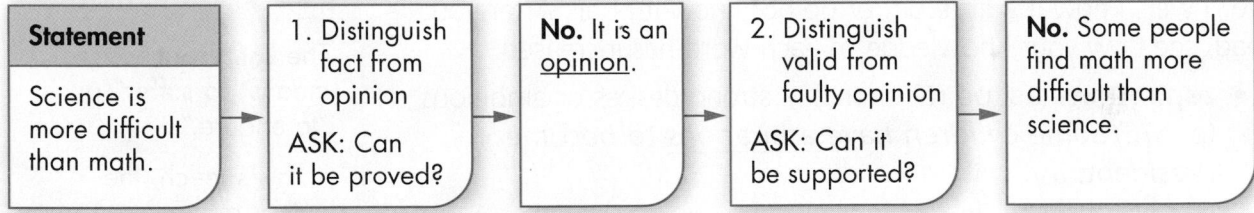

Statement	1. Distinguish fact from opinion ASK: Can it be proved?	**No.** It is an opinion.	2. Distinguish valid from faulty opinion ASK: Can it be supported?	**No.** Some people find math more difficult than science.
Science is more difficult than math.				

Literary Analysis: Word Choice

An author's **word choice** can help convey meaning or tone—an author's attitude toward his or her subject matter. For example, the use of slang in an essay might create a friendly, casual tone. Factors that influence word choice include:

- the author's intended audience and purpose
- the **denotations** of words, or their specific meanings
- the **connotations** of words, or the negative or positive ideas associated with them (For example, *assertive* and *pushy* have similar denotations but have very different connotations.)

As you read, notice how word choice affects the meaning and tone of a work.

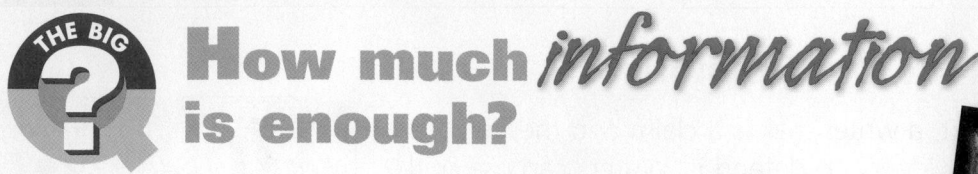

How much *information* is enough?

Writing About the Big Question

In his speech, Colin Powell calls on all members of society to share their knowledge with young people to help them achieve their dreams. Use these sentence starters to develop your ideas about the Big Question.

Information that can be **valuable** for someone in need is _____.

An effective way to **challenge** people to volunteer is _____.

While You Read Note Powell's ideas about making the world better for young people. Consider what information he believes they need to be successful.

Vocabulary

Read each word and its definition. Decide whether you know the word well, know it a little bit, or do not know it at all. After you read, see how your knowledge of each word has increased.

- **aspirations** (as´ pə rā´ shənz) *n.* strong desires or ambitions (p. 576) *Some children have* aspirations *to become President. aspire v.*

- **deferred** (dē fʉrd´) *adj.* delayed (p. 576) *He took a* deferred *admission to college and traveled. defer v. deferral n.*

- **compassionate** (kəm pash´ ən it) *adj.* deeply sympathetic (p. 577) *My doctor is always* compassionate *when I am in pain. compassionately adv. compassion n.*

- **vulnerable** (vul´ nər ə bəl) *adj.* likely to be hurt (p. 577) *The elderly man was weak and* vulnerable *to further infections. vulnerability n. vulnerably adv.*

- **virtue** (vʉr´ chōō) *n.* value (p. 577) *A job teaches the* virtue *of hard work. virtuous adj. virtuously adv.*

- **alliance** (ə lī´ əns) *n.* a group united for a common goal (p. 577) *Britain's* alliance *with the United States helped end the Nazi threat. ally n. allied adj.*

Word Study

The **Latin root -pass-** means "to suffer" or "to endure."

In this speech, the author refers to people who are **compassionate**, or deeply sympathetic, and asks them to reach out to others who are suffering.

Colin Powell
(b. 1937)

Author of

Sharing in the
American
Dream

Colin Powell's life is a true American success story. From a humble childhood in the New York neighborhood of the South Bronx, Powell rose to become one of the most powerful and influential people in American politics.

Rising Through the Ranks Powell began his thirty-five year career serving as a soldier during the Vietnam War. He rose quickly through the ranks to assume the most powerful Defense Department position—chairman of the joint chiefs of staff—shortly before the Persian Gulf War. From 2001 to 2005, Powell was the first African American to serve as secretary of state, an official appointed by the President to set key foreign policy. Since leaving office, Powell has turned to improving the lives of young people.

DID YOU KNOW?

In 1997, Powell founded the volunteer organization America's Promise to give other children the same chances to succeed that he has enjoyed.

BACKGROUND FOR THE SPEECH

Volunteers

In the excerpt from *Sharing in the American Dream*, Colin Powell encourages his audience to spread the spirit of volunteerism. In the United States, millions of people volunteer each year, and the numbers are growing. Unpaid volunteers perform crucial tasks in schools, hospitals, nursing homes, and libraries. Without volunteer help, many organizations could not afford to serve as many people as they do.

from Sharing in the
American Dream

Colin Powell

Over 200 years ago, a group of volunteers gathered on this sacred spot to found a new nation. In perfect words, they voiced their dreams and aspirations of an imperfect world. They pledged their lives, their fortune and their sacred honor to secure inalienable rights given by God for life, liberty and pursuit of happiness—pledged that they would provide them to all who would inhabit this new nation.

They look down on us today in spirit, with pride for all we have done to keep faith with their ideals and their sacrifices. Yet, despite all we have done, this is still an imperfect world. We still live in an imperfect society. Despite more than two centuries of moral and material progress, despite all our efforts to achieve a more perfect union, there are still Americans who are not sharing in the American Dream. There are still Americans who wonder: is the journey there for them, is the dream there for them, or, whether it is, at best, a dream deferred.

Vocabulary
aspirations (as′ pə rā′ shənz) *n.* strong desires or ambitions
deferred (dē fʉrd′) *adj.* delayed

The great American poet, Langston Hughes, talked about a dream deferred, and he said, "What happens to a dream deferred? Does it dry up like a raisin in the sun, or fester like a sore and then run? Does it stink like rotten meat or crust and sugar over like a syrupy sweet? Maybe it just sags, like a heavy load. Or, does it explode?" . . .

So today, we gather here today to pledge that the dream must no longer be deferred and it will never, as long as we can do anything about it, become a dream denied. That is why we are here, my friends. We gather here to pledge that those of us who are more fortunate will not forsake those who are less fortunate. We are a compassionate and caring people. We are a generous people. We will reach down, we will reach back, we will reach across to help our brothers and sisters who are in need.

Above all, we pledge to reach out to the most vulnerable members of the American family, our children. As you've heard, up to 15 million young Americans today are at risk. . . .

In terms of numbers the task may seem staggering. But if we look at the simple needs that these children have, then the task is manageable, the goal is achievable. We know what they need. They need an adult caring person in their life, a safe place to learn and grow, a healthy start, marketable skills and an opportunity to serve so that early in their lives they learn the virtue of service so that they can reach out then and touch another young American in need.

These are basic needs that we commit ourselves to today, we promise today. We are making America's promise today to provide to those children in need. This is a grand alliance. It is an alliance between government and corporate America and nonprofit America, between our institutions of faith, but especially between individual Americans.

You heard the governors and the mayors, and you'll hear more in a little minute that says the real answer is for each and every one of us, not just here in Philadelphia, but across this land—for each and every one of us to reach out and touch someone in need.

All of us can spare 30 minutes a week or an hour a week. All of us can give an extra dollar. All of us can touch someone who doesn't look like us, who doesn't speak like us, who may not dress like us, but needs us in their lives. And that's what we all have to do to keep this going.

Vocabulary
compassionate (kəm pash´ ən it) *adj.* deeply sympathetic

vulnerable (vul´ nər ə bəl) *adj.* likely to be hurt

Spiral Review
Author's Purpose What rhetorical devices has Powell used in the first three paragraphs on this page? What purpose do these devices help Powell achieve?

Vocabulary
virtue (vur´ chōō) *n.* value

alliance (ə lī´ əns) *n.* a group united for a common goal

Fact and Opinion
Is Powell's statement "All of us can spare 30 minutes…" a fact or an opinion? Explain, and then evaluate whether the statement is valid.

Reading Check
Who does Powell think would be proud of the audience members?

And so there's a spirit of Philadelphia here today. There's a spirit of Philadelphia that we saw yesterday in Germantown. There is a spirit of Philadelphia that will leave Philadelphia tomorrow afternoon and spread across this whole nation—30 governors will go back and spread it; over 100 mayors will go back and spread it, and hundreds of others, leaders around this country who are watching will go back and spread it. Corporate America will spread it, nonprofits will spread it. And each and every one of us will spread it because it has to be done, we have no choice. We cannot leave these children behind if we are going to meet the dreams of our founding fathers.

And so let us all join in this great crusade. Let us make sure that no child in America is left behind, no child in America has their dream deferred or denied. We can do it. We can do it because we are Americans. . . .

Word Choice
What phrases have positive connotations in the final paragraph? Explain their effect.

Critical Thinking

Cite textual evidence to support your responses.

1. **Key Ideas and Details** **(a)** To which earlier group of volunteers does Powell refer at the beginning of the speech? **(b) Interpret:** What types of feelings do you think Powell wants to create in his audience by mentioning this group of people?

2. **Key Ideas and Details** **(a)** In what way is America "imperfect," according to Powell? **(b) Infer:** What does Powell suggest would bring America closer to perfection?

3. **Craft and Structure** **Analyze:** What effect does Powell's use of repeated, parallel phrases have on the speech's message?

4. **Integration of Knowledge and Ideas** **Assess:** Do you think this speech would inspire an audience to increase its involvement in volunteer work? Why or why not?

5. **Integration of Knowledge and Ideas** **(a)** What kind of information does Powell say the young people of America need to succeed? **(b)** Do you agree with him? Why or why not? *[Connect to the Big Question: How much information is enough?]*

After You Read

from Sharing in the American Dream

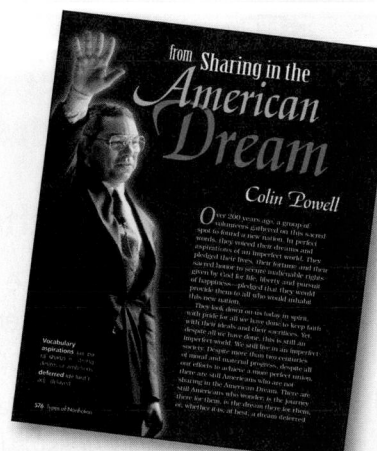

Reading Skill: Fact and Opinion

1. Key Ideas and Details Identify one statement of **fact** and one statement of **opinion** in Powell's speech.

2. Key Ideas and Details **(a)** Is Powell's statement "We can do it because we are Americans" one of fact or opinion? Explain. **(b)** Evaluate Powell's support for this statement. Does the statement reflect *bias*? Explain.

3. Key Ideas and Details **(a)** What is Powell's main claim, or argument? **(b)** How does he support this claim? List examples.

Literary Analysis: Word Choice

4. Craft and Structure Use a chart like this one to analyze Powell's **word choice.**

Powell's Purpose	Words and Phrases That Support His Purpose	Connotations

5. Craft and Structure **(a)** Would you characterize Powell's language as simple and informal or complex and formal? **(b)** What tone does the word choice create? Support your response with examples.

Vocabulary

Acquisition and Use Write a complete sentence to answer each question. For each item, use a vocabulary word in place of underlined words.

1. What is the most <u>caring</u>, <u>unselfish</u> thing you have ever done?

2. What are two of your <u>dreams</u> or <u>goals</u>?

3. Why should people and companies <u>work together</u>?

4. Are wishes worth waiting for if they are <u>delayed</u>?

5. Why are babies of nearly every species <u>helpless</u> at birth?

6. How do people demonstrate their <u>good qualities</u>?

Word Study Use the context of the sentences and what you know about the **Latin root -*pass*-** to explain each answer.

1. Can an *impassioned* person be expected to think clearly?

2. Is a typical movie spy *dispassionate* or *compassionate*?

Word Study

The **Latin root word -*pass*-** means "to suffer" or "to endure."

Apply It Explain how the root -*pass*- contributes to the meaning of these words. Consult a dictionary, if necessary.

passion
impassive

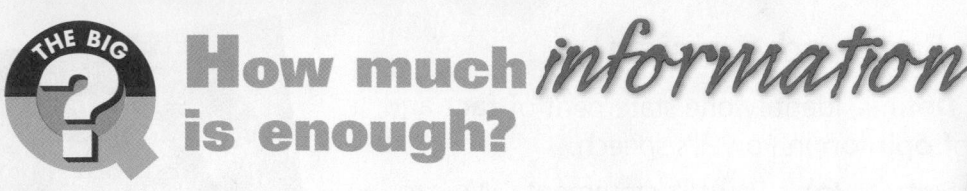

How much *information* is enough?

Writing About the Big Question

In "Science and the Sense of Wonder," Asimov argues that scientific knowledge adds to our sense of wonder about the universe. Use this sentence starter to develop your ideas about the Big Question.

The more knowledge I **accumulate** about how natural systems work, the (more/less) curious I feel. This is because _____.

While You Read Pay close attention to both Asimov's message and the message of the Walt Whitman poem to which he is responding to decide which approach makes the best sense to you.

Vocabulary

Read each word and its definition. Decide whether you know the word well, know it a little bit, or do not know it all. After you read, see how your knowledge of each word has increased.

- **exultantly** (eg zult´ nt lē) *adv.* triumphantly (p. 583) *"We won!" he yelled exultantly.* exultant *adj.* exult *v.*

- **awed** (ôd) *v.* filled with wonder (p. 583) *We stared silently into the Grand Canyon, awed by its sheer size and beauty.* awe *n.* awesome *adj.* awestruck *adj.*

- **cataclysm** (kat´ ə kliz´ əm) *n.* sudden, violent event that causes change (p. 584) *When the volcano erupted, the cataclysm wiped out the island.* cataclysmal *adj.* cataclysmic *adj.*

- **radiation** (rā´ dē ā´ shən) *n.* rays of energy (p. 585) *Radiation from the sun can be harmful.* radiate *v.* irradiated *adj.* radius *n.*

- **conceivable** (kən sēv´ ə bəl) *adj.* imaginable (p. 585) *It is conceivable, but unlikely, that he walked all the way here.* conceivably *adv.* inconceivable *adj.* conceive *v.*

- **contraction** (kən trak´ shən) *n.* the act of becoming smaller (p. 585) *The cold weather caused contraction of the flooring, opening up spaces between the joints.* contract *v.*

Word Study

The **Latin root -tract-** means "pull" or "drag."

In this essay, Asimov suggests that our expanding universe may someday begin a period of **contraction**, or shrinking, in which gravity pulls it back to its original shape and form.

Meet
Isaac Asimov
(1920–1992)

Author of
SCIENCE
and the Sense of Wonder

Isaac Asimov became a science-fiction fan by reading fantastic stories in science-fiction magazines. Little did he know then that he would become one of the most influential science writers of the twentieth century.

Persistence Asimov's father discouraged his son's early interest in science-fiction stories, describing the magazines as "junk." Still, Asimov's interest continued and he started writing his own stories at age eleven. At first, his stories were rejected by most magazines, but little by little, Asimov gained the knowledge that enabled him to build a successful career as a visionary science and science fiction writer.

BACKGROUND FOR THE ESSAY

Walt Whitman

Isaac Asimov wrote "Science and the Sense of Wonder" in response to a poem by nineteenth-century writer Walt Whitman. Whitman was a journalist, essayist, and poet whose writing celebrated the beauty of the human body and of the natural world. He was writing at the beginning of a long period of scientific and technological progress.

DID YOU KNOW?

Asimov's stories often involve robots. *I, Robot* is a book of short stories featuring mind-reading robots, world-conquering robots—even robot politicians. It was adapted in 2004 as a movie starring Will Smith.

SCIENCE
and the Sense of Wonder

Isaac Asimov

One of Walt Whitman's best-known poems is this one:

When I heard the learn'd astronomer,

When the proofs, the figures, were ranged in columns before me,

When I was shown the charts and diagrams, to add, divide and measure them,

When I sitting heard the astronomer where he lectured with much applause in the lecture-room,

How soon unaccountable I became tired and sick,

Till rising and gliding out I wander'd off by myself,

In the mystical moist night-air, and from time to time,

Look'd up in perfect silence at the stars.

Imagine that many people reading those lines tell themselves, exultantly, "How true! Science just sucks all the beauty out of everything, reducing it all to numbers and tables and measurements! Why bother learning all that junk when I can just go out and look at the stars?"

That is a very convenient point of view since it makes it not only unnecessary, but downright aesthetically wrong,[1] to try to follow all that hard stuff in science. Instead, you can just take a look at the night sky, get a quick beauty fix, and go off to a nightclub.

The trouble is that Whitman is talking through his hat, but the poor soul didn't know any better.

I don't deny that the night sky is beautiful, and I have in my time spread out on a hillside for hours looking at the stars and being awed by their beauty (and receiving bug-bites whose marks took weeks to go away).

But what I see—those quiet, twinkling points of light—is not *all the beauty there is*. Should I stare lovingly at a single leaf and willingly remain ignorant of the forest? Should I be satisfied to watch the sun glinting off a single pebble and scorn any knowledge of a beach?

Those bright spots in the sky that we call planets are worlds. There are worlds with thick atmospheres of carbon dioxide and sulfuric acid; worlds of red-hot liquid with hurricanes that could gulp down the whole earth; dead worlds with quiet pockmarks of craters; worlds with volcanoes puffing plumes of dust into airlessness; worlds with pink and desolate deserts— each with a weird and unearthly beauty that boils down to a mere speck of light if we just gaze at the night sky.

Those other bright spots, which are stars rather than planets, are actually suns. Some of them are of incomparable grandeur,[2] each glowing with the light

---

1. **aesthetically** (es thet´ i klē) **wrong** insensitive to beauty.
2. **incomparable grandeur** (gran´ jər) unequaled splendor.

Vocabulary
exultantly (eg zult´ nt lē) *adv.* triumphantly
awed (ôd) *v.* filled with wonder

Fact and Opinion
Is this statement about Whitman fact or opinion? Explain.

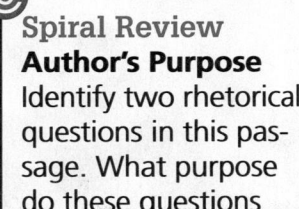

Spiral Review
Author's Purpose
Identify two rhetorical questions in this passage. What purpose do these questions help Asimov achieve?

Word Choice
Which words in this passage add drama to the description?

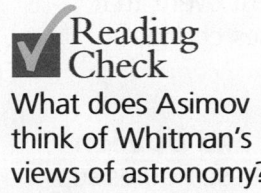
Reading Check
What does Asimov think of Whitman's views of astronomy?

of a thousand suns like ours; some of them are merely red-hot coals doling out their energy stingily. Some of them are compact bodies as massive as our sun, but with all that mass squeezed into a ball smaller than the earth. Some are more compact still, with the mass of the sun squeezed down into the volume of a small asteroid. And some are more compact still, with their mass shrinking down to a volume of zero, the site of which is marked by an intense gravitational field that swallows up everything and gives back nothing; with matter spiraling into that bottomless hole and giving out a wild death-scream of X-rays.

There are stars that pulsate endlessly in a great cosmic breathing; and others that, having consumed their fuel, expand and redden until they swallow up their planets, if they have any (and someday, billions of years from now, our sun will expand and the earth will crisp and sere and vaporize into a gas of iron and rock with no sign of the life it once bore). And some stars explode in a vast

Vocabulary

cataclysm (kat´ ə kliz´ əm) *n.* sudden, violent event that causes change

Fact and Opinion
Do these figures support Asimov's opinion that there is more to the universe than we see?

cataclysm whose ferocious blast of cosmic rays, hurrying outward at nearly the speed of light, reaches across thousands of light years to touch the earth and supply some of the driving force of evolution through mutations.

Those paltry few stars we see as we look up in perfect silence (some 2,500 or more on even the darkest and clearest night) are joined by a vast horde we don't see, up to as many as three hundred billion—300,000,000,000—to form an enormous pinwheel in space. This pinwheel, the Milky Way galaxy, stretches so widely that it takes light, moving at 186,282 miles each *second*, a hundred thousand *years* to cross it from end to end; and it rotates about its center in a vast and stately turn that takes two hundred million years to complete—and the sun and the earth and we ourselves all make that turn.

Beyond our Milky Way galaxy are others, a score or so of them bound to our own in a cluster of galaxies, most of them small, with no more than a few billion stars in each; but with one at least, the Andromeda galaxy, twice as large as our own.

Beyond our own cluster, other galaxies and other clusters exist; some clusters made up of thousands of galaxies. They stretch outward and outward as far as our best telescopes can see, with no visible sign of an end—perhaps a hundred billion of them in all.

And in more and more of those galaxies we are becoming aware of violence at the centers—of great explosions and outpourings of radiation, marking the death of perhaps millions of stars. Even at the center of our own galaxy there is incredible violence masked from our own solar system far in the outskirts by enormous clouds of dust and gas that lie between us and the heaving center.

Some galactic centers are so bright that they can be seen from distances of billions of light-years, distances from which the galaxies themselves cannot be seen and only the bright starlike centers of ravening[3] energy show up—as quasars. Some of these have been detected from more than ten billion light-years away.

All these galaxies are hurrying outward from each other in a vast universal expansion that began fifteen billion years ago, when all the matter in the universe was in a tiny sphere that exploded in the hugest conceivable shatter to form the galaxies.

The universe may expand forever or the day may come when the expansion slows and turns back into a contraction to re-form the tiny sphere and begin the game all over again so that the whole universe is exhaling and inhaling in breaths that are perhaps a trillion years long.

---

3. **ravening** (rav´ ə nin) *adj.* consuming greedily.

Vocabulary

radiation (rā´dē ā´ shən) *n.* rays of energy

conceivable (kən sēv´ ə bəl) *adj.* imaginable

contraction (kən trak´ shən) *n.* the act of becoming smaller

LITERATURE IN CONTEXT

Science Connection

Lord of the Rings The wonder of Saturn's rings—patterned waves that resemble ripples in a pond—wowed the world in 2004. The images were transmitted from 900 million miles away by the *Cassini* spacecraft, which NASA had launched seven years before.

The craft is named for the seventeenth-century astronomer Giovanni Cassini, discoverer of several of Saturn's moons. Cassini also discovered a gap in the rings, which was named *Cassini's Division*. Scientists know that the hundreds of rings are made up of ice and rock particles that orbit Saturn at different speeds. By studying the rings up close, scientists hope to learn more about the solar system and how planets form.

Connect to the Literature

Would Asimov be impressed by the *Cassini* photos? Why?

And all of this vision—far beyond the scale of human imaginings—was made possible by the works of hundreds of "learn'd" astronomers. All of it; *all* of it was discovered after the death of Whitman in 1892, and most of it in the past twenty-five years, so that the poor poet never knew what a stultified[4] and limited beauty he observed when he "look'd up in perfect silence at the stars."

Nor can we know or imagine now the limitless beauty yet to be revealed in the future—by science.

---

4. **stultified** (stul´ tə fid´) *adj.* foolish or absurd.

▲ **Critical Viewing**
How might being in space give you a different appreciation for the wonders of science and the universe? **[Connect]**

Critical Thinking

Cite textual evidence to support your responses.

© 1. **Key Ideas and Details (a)** Approximately how many stars are included in the Milky Way? **(b) Analyze:** How does Asimov give the reader a sense of how small our galaxy is?

© 2. **Key Ideas and Details (a)** At the end of the essay, what fact does Asimov give about discoveries made after Whitman's death? **(b) Evaluate:** Does this fact call Whitman's views into question? Why or why not?

© 3. **Integration of Knowledge and Ideas Make a Judgment:** As we accumulate more data and information about the mysteries of the universe, do you think our sense of wonder will increase or decrease? Explain.

© 4. **Integration of Knowledge and Ideas** Do you agree with Whitman's view, Asimov's view, or both views of science and the natural world? Support your response. *[Connect to the Big Question: How much information is enough?]*

Reading Skill: Fact and Opinion

1. Key Ideas and Details Identify one statement of **fact** and one statement of **opinion** in the essay.

2. Key Ideas and Details **(a)** Is it fact or Asimov's opinion that what Whitman admired was a "limited beauty"? Explain. **(b)** Evaluate Asimov's support for this statement. Does the statement reflect **bias?** Explain.

3. Key Ideas and Details **(a)** What is Asimov's main claim, or argument? **(b)** How does he support this argument? List two examples.

Literary Analysis: Word Choice

4. Craft and Structure Use a chart like this one to analyze Asimov's **word choice.**

Asimov's Purpose	Words and Phrases That Support His Purpose	Connotations

5. Craft and Structure **(a)** Would you characterize Asimov's language as simple and informal or complex and formal? **(b)** What tone does the word choice create? Support your response with examples.

Vocabulary

Acquisition and Use Write a complete sentence to answer each question. For each item, use a vocabulary word in place of underlined words.

1. What aspects of nature cause you to be <u>struck with wonder</u>?

2. Would an underdog team view a win <u>with a happy emotion</u>?

3. How might a tornado cause a <u>disaster</u> in a city in its path?

4. Is the <u>energy</u> released by an atomic bomb dangerous?

5. Is it <u>possible</u> that a child of five can play a symphony?

6. When water is removed from fruit, is there a <u>decrease</u> in size?

Word Study Use the context of the sentences and what you know about the **Latin root -tract-** to explain each answer.

1. Why is a *tractor* a good tool for moving a heavy object?

2. What might happen if you *distract* the driver of a car?

Word Study

The **Latin root -tract-** means "pull" or "drag."

Apply It Explain how the root **-tract-** contributes to the meaning of each word. Consult a dictionary, if necessary.

attract

detract

extract

Integrated Language Skills

from **Sharing in the American Dream • Science and the Sense of Wonder**

Conventions: Prepositions

A **preposition** relates the noun or pronoun following it to another word in the sentence.

Prepositions work as connectors, relating one word to another within a sentence. Often, they indicate relative location or direction.

Thirty Common Prepositions				
about	behind	during	of	since
above	below	except	off	through
after	besides	for	on	under
among	between	from	opposite	until
around	beyond	in	over	up
at	by	near	past	without

Practice A Identify the preposition. Then, explain the relationship between the preposition and the words it connects.

1. Volunteers arrived before the speech.
2. We live among people who have great dreams.
3. Volunteers help people in need.
4. Help spread the word about volunteering.

Practice B Complete each sentence with an appropriate preposition.

1. Walt Whitman lived _____ the age of modern scientific discovery.
2. Scientific knowledge does not deprive us _____ wonder.
3. Other galaxies exist _____ the Milky Way.
4. We could not see the stars _____ the clouds.

Reading Application In the excerpt from *Sharing in the American Dream*, identify two sentences that contain prepositions. Decide if the words preceding the prepositions can take any other prepositions besides the one shown.

Writing Application Replace the preposition in the model sentence to create three new sentences. *The scientist looked into the microscope.* Discuss how your new sentences differ.

PH WRITING COACH Further instruction and practice are available in *Prentice Hall Writing Coach*.

Writing

Common Core State Standards

L.8.1; W.8.2, W.8.2.c; SL.8.4
[For the full wording of the standards, see page 572.]

Explanatory Text Write a **response** to Powell's speech or Asimov's essay. If you read Powell, react to his statement, "All of us can spare 30 minutes a week or an hour a week." If you read Asimov, respond to his idea that the scientist's appreciation of nature is as valid as the poet's.

- First, reread to examine the main ideas of the essay or speech.

- Next, identify effective words, passages, or phrases from the text.

- Take notes on ways in which the writer's word choice affects what you understand and feel about the text.

- Finally, draft your response and explain how the author's main idea applies—or does not apply—to your own experience.

Grammar Application Prepositions often indicate connections or relationships. Check your writing for effective use of prepositions.

Writing Workshop: *Work in Progress*

Prewriting for Editorial Choose two issues from your Problem List. For each, jot down a logical reason, based on facts, that supports your opinion. Then, write an emotional reason, based on feelings, that explains your thoughts. Save this Reasons List in your portfolio.

Use this prewriting activity to prepare for the **Writing Workshop** on page 614.

Speaking and Listening

Presentation of Ideas Conduct research to write a **speech** commemorating the founding of a volunteer organization such as the Peace Corps or honoring the achievements of a famous astronomer or astronaut.

Begin by making an outline that includes an introduction, or preview; a body, or main section, that is developed in logical order; and a strong, effective conclusion.

Use these tips as you plan and rehearse:

- Support your claims and findings with well-chosen details.

- Include transitions—words and phrases such as *therefore* or *as a result*—that clarify relationships among your ideas and allow the audience to follow the progress of your thoughts.

- Delete irrelevant details to create a focused, coherent exploration of your topic.

- Use parallel wording to add drama and emphasis to your speech.

Deliver the speech to your class, pausing for dramatic effect and varying your pacing to create audience interest.

www.PHLitOnline.com
- Interactive graphic organizers
- Grammar tutorial
- Interactive journals

Test Practice: Reading

Fact and Opinion

Fiction Selection

Directions: *Read the selection. Then, answer the questions.*

My friend Joe is a football nut. During the fall and winter, when football is played, he is busy watching pro games. I can't understand his devotion, given that football is a horrible game. But, he's in good company: a lot of people like football, and the Super Bowl games always get high ratings.

I, myself, like basketball—"hoops." It's the best game in the world. All winter long I am focused on the college games, which are fast and fun. Last year my dad took me to see some NCAA tournament games during "March Madness."

The funny thing is, I am built like a lineman, tough and muscular, and Joe is tall enough to play center. Neither of us is good at playing the sport we love to watch!

1. Which of the following suggests an opinion?
   A. He lives and breathes football.
   B. It's the best game.
   C. The funny thing is,
   D. I am built like a lineman.

2. Which of the following statements based on the passage is a fact?
   A. Joe is a football nut.
   B. Football is a horrible game.
   C. Basketball is the best game in the world.
   D. Basketball is played in the winter.

3. Which statement based on the text in the passage does *not* provide factual information about football?
   A. Super Bowl games get high ratings.
   B. During fall and winter, football is played.
   C. A lot of people like football.
   D. Football is a horrible game.

4. Which of the following statements is *not* possible to verify?
   A. Centers are tall.
   B. Linemen are muscular and big.
   C. Neither the narrator nor his friend are good at playing sports.
   D. The NCAA tournament is called "March Madness."

Writing for Assessment

In a one-paragraph response, choose one of the writer's statements and explain whether it is supported by facts or opinions. Use specific details from the passage.

Nonfiction Selection

Directions: *Read the selection. Then, answer the questions.*

If you ask people to name the best athlete of all time, some will name boxer Muhammad Ali. Others will name golfer Tiger Woods. Many hockey fans will name Wayne Gretsky, and basketball fans will name Michael Jordan. If you ask fifty people, you'll probably get fifty different answers. One thing is certain, though: Most of the names will be those of baseball players. Baseball captures people's hearts like no other sport. Baseball players are spectacular athletes. Other athletes aren't nearly as versatile. Only in baseball do the same team members play offense *and* defense. Baseball players must function as a team while excelling as individuals. They are fast, strong, and incredibly smart. No other athletes work as hard. After about two months of training, each team plays 162 games during the regular season.

1. Which of these statements is an opinion?
   A. Wayne Gretsky played hockey.
   B. Baseball requires individual and team skills.
   C. Teams train for about two months before the season.
   D. Baseball captures people's hearts.

2. Which of these statements is a fact?
   A. They are fast, strong, and incredibly smart.
   B. Baseball players are spectacular athletes.
   C. Each team plays 162 games during the regular season.
   D. Other athletes aren't nearly as versatile.

3. Which of the following words suggests an opinion?
   A. spectacular
   B. only
   C. different
   D. some

4. Which question would *best* help you evaluate the statement "No other athletes work as hard"?
   A. How many people think Michael Jordan is the best athlete?
   B. How many games do other athletes play each season?
   C. How many players are on a baseball team?
   D. How may baseball teams are there?

Writing for Assessment

Connecting Across Texts
Write a brief essay comparing and contrasting the views expressed in the two passages. In your response, describe the extent to which each writer supports his or her opinions with facts.

www.PHLitOnline.com
- Online practice
- Instant feedback

Reading for Information

Analyzing Arguments

Editorial

Speech

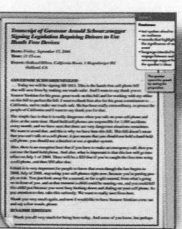

Reading Skill: Analyze Proposition and Support

In editorials and speeches, a writer or speaker often presents a **proposition,** which is a type of claim or argument. The writer then provides **support,** or evidence, for that claim. Support may include facts, expert opinions, or personal observations. As you read a text with a proposition, **analyze** the support to see if the proposition is logical.

Here are some examples of statements that show errors in logic:

Error in Logic	Example	Problem
Oversimplification	If you own a cellphone, you should support the right to use it anywhere you want to.	Ignores other alternatives
False analogy	Outlawing cellphone use while driving is like outlawing eating while reading.	The comparison is irrelevant
Insufficient evidence	I do not know anyone who has had an accident because of a cellphone, so I do not think they are a problem.	False conclusion
Jumping on the bandwagon	Everyone I know drives while talking on a cellphone, so it should be legal.	Assumes an opinion is correct because it is popular

Content-Area Vocabulary

These words appear in the selections that follow. You may also encounter them in other content-area texts.

- **distraction** (dis trak´shən) *n.* thing that draws away the mind, attention, etc.
- **legislation** (lej´ə slā´shən) *n.* laws that have been passed
- **compliance** (kəm plī´əns) *n.* heeding a request, command, or law; obedience

The title of the editorial clearly states the writer's position.

The Mercury News

Langberg: Hands-free law won't solve the problem

FRIDAY, SEPTEMBER 1, 2006

By Mike Langberg

Driving while talking on a cell phone clearly increases your risk of getting into an accident, but here's a surprise: The problem is all in your head.

The mental distraction of conversing behind the wheel is so great that switching to a headset or other "hands-free" approach—instead of taking one hand off the wheel to hold the phone to your ear— does nothing to reduce the danger.

But politicians never let facts get in the way of making themselves look good.

The result is hands-free legislation that passed the California Assembly and Senate last week, and is likely to be signed into law this month by Gov. Arnold Schwarzenegger.

The California Wireless Telephone Automobile Safety Act of 2006, the bill's formal name, says: "A person shall not drive a motor vehicle while using a wireless telephone unless that telephone is specifically designed and configured to allow hands-free listening and talking, and is used in that manner while driving." Using a hand-held phone, you'll get an almost painless fine of $20 for the first offense. The penalty doesn't get much worse for additional violations, moving up to just $50.

Using a hand-held phone would only be allowed in emergency situations, such as calling 911.

The new rules wouldn't take effect until July 1, 2008.

So we're getting a nearly toothless law, two years down the line, that doesn't offer a real solution to a serious problem.

The first part of that problem is the awesome popularity of cell phones.

There are now 208 million cell phone subscribers in the United States, equal to 69 percent of the total population. Almost every adult American, in other words, now has a cell phone.

The National Highway Traffic Safety Administration says an average 6 percent of drivers on the road at any given moment are talking on a cell phone. The number goes up to 10 percent during daylight hours.

The writer offers statistics to support his position.

Driver distraction or inattention contributes to nearly 80 percent of accidents, according to a research study completed earlier this year by NHTSA and Virginia Tech.

Although overall death and injury rates continue to decline slowly over time, there's no question cell phones are a factor in many highway accidents. Last year, NHTSA reports, highway accidents killed 43,443 last year and injured 2.7 million.

There's an obvious solution: Ban talking on a cell phone while driving.

But that's not going to happen, at least not anytime soon. The cell phone lobby is too powerful, and the public is too enamored with chatting behind the wheel.

Instead, we're getting hands-free laws that give politicians the appearance of taking action.

New York, New Jersey, Connecticut and the District of Columbia already have hands-free laws, and many other states are considering similar steps.

These laws are moving forward despite a persuasive and growing list of academic studies, involving both simulator testing and analysis of real-world crash data, showing hands-free phone calls are no less risky than holding a phone.

Think about it: If you're fully aware of what's happening on the road ahead of you, such as a car suddenly slamming on its brakes, your response time isn't going to vary much whether you've got one or two hands on the wheel.

But your response time will suffer if you're in the middle of an argument on the phone with your boss or spouse.

I'll raise my hand here and admit I'm part of the problem. I've come close to rear-ending other drivers on a few occasions because I was talking on my cell phone. And I don't believe my sluggish reaction would have changed if I'd been using a headset.

David L. Strayer, a psychology professor at the University of Utah, has been studying cell phone distraction for more than five years.

Last week, he told me there are at least six studies showing no safety benefit from hands-free talking.

"This . . . suggests that legislative initiatives that restrict handheld devices but permit hands-free devices are not likely to eliminate the problems associated with cell phones while driving," Strayer and two colleagues wrote in the summer 2006 issue of the journal *Human Factors*.

I asked Strayer if there's a safe way to participate in a phone call while driving.

"Not unless we somehow rewire our brains," he responded. There's no technological remedy, in other words, to the mental distraction created during a cell phone conversation.

At the same time, there are possible side effects—both good and bad—from hands free laws.

On the good side, some drivers might not want to go through the hassle of buying and using a headset or other hands-free gadget. They would give up talking while driving, collectively reducing auto accidents.

On the bad side, some drivers might get a false sense of security and decide it's OK to talk even more.

Here's my prediction: California's hands-free law, and similar laws elsewhere, will do nothing to change the number of accidents tied to drivers using cell phones.

Once everyone realizes these laws accomplish nothing, we'll have to decide whether cell phones require further restrictions or should be categorized with other dangerous behind-the-wheel distractions—everything from noisy children to complicated audio systems—that aren't restricted.

Transcript of Governor Arnold Schwarzenegger Signing Legislation Requiring Drivers to Use Hands Free Devices

DATE: *Friday, September 15, 2006*
TIME: *11:15 a.m.*

EVENT: *Oakland Hilton, California Room, 1 Hegenberger Rd, Oakland, CA*

GOVERNOR SCHWARZENEGGER:

. . . Today we will be signing SB 1613. This is the hands-free cell phone bill that will save lives by making our roads safer. And I want to say thank you to Senator Simitian for his great, great work on this bill and for working with my office on this bill to perfect the bill. I want to thank him also for his great commitment to . . . California, and to make our roads safe. He has been really extraordinary, to protect the people of California and I want to say thank you for that.

The simple fact is that it is really dangerous when you talk on your cell phone and drive at the same time. Hand-held cell phones are responsible for 1,000 accidents every month, and we have seen that there are very dangerous situations sometimes. We want to avoid that, and this is why we have here this bill. This bill doesn't mean that you can't talk on a cell phone; it just means that you should not hold a hand-held cell phone, you should use a headset or use a speaker system.

Also, there is an exception here that if you have to make an emergency call, then you can use the hand-held phone. And also, what is important is that this law will go into effect on July 1 of 2008. There will be a $20 fine if you're caught the first time using a cell phone, and then $50 after that.

I think it is very important for people to know that even though the law begins in 2008, July of 2008, stop using your cell phones right now, because you're putting people at risk. You just look away for a second, or for a split second, from what's going on in front of you, and at that moment a child could be running out, and you could kill this child just because you were busy looking down and dialing on your cell phone. So pay attention to that, take this seriously. We want to really save lives here.

Thank you very much again, and now I would like to have Senator Simitian come out and say a few words, please.

SENATOR SIMITIAN:

Thank you all very much for being here today. And some of you know, but perhaps

> The speaker opens his speech by stating his proposition.

not all of you, that this is the sixth hands-free cell phone bill I've introduced during the past six years. The question I've been asked quite frequently of late is, "Why did you keep introducing the bill?" And the answer is really very simple. I introduced the bill because I believe it will save lives. It's just that simple. You've got a readily available technology that costs next to nothing and saves lives. Why on earth wouldn't we use it?

This bill isn't a perfect solution, it isn't a total solution, but it is a significant and important improvement over the current state of affairs, and it will save lives, and that was the goal from Day 1. . . .

> The speaker over-simplifies the issue of cost involved in using a hands-free cellphone device.

CHIEF BECHER:

. . . I'm proud to be here today for the signing of this bill. It represents a collaborative effort between the legislature, the Governor, [the phone company] and the many backers and traffic safety officials throughout the state, to make the roadways of California a safer place to drive.

Statewide, collisions caused by distracted drivers result in countless hours of roadway delay, congestion, injury and death. This legislation is another useful tool for law enforcement to curb the growing number of collisions caused either partially or wholly by distracted drivers.

Prior to this cell phone law going into effect, the CHP plans a major public education campaign to ensure the public is aware of the changes. Education is a major focus for the CHP, because public awareness of the issue and voluntary compliance with this new law can have a significant impact on crashes even before the new law goes into effect. The Governor is exactly right. Start now.

Our goal is to have all drivers in the state keep both hands on the wheel and have the attention and awareness so that they can navigate [their] driving environment. It is always incumbent on drivers to drive attentively. Many devices and activities taking place inside today's vehicles can cause that split second distraction that may result in an unnecessary traffic collision. Cell phones are among the more prominent of these distractions.

And finally, thanks to all in the creation and implementation of this bill. The California Highway Patrol supports this new legislation as part of our No. 1 goal, to prevent traffic collisions and to save lives. Thank you.

Comparing Arguments

1. Key Ideas and Details **(a)** What is the main **proposition,** or claim, in each text? **(b)** What details, or evidence, does each text include as **support? (c)** Which text makes more effective use of relevant supporting details? Explain your response.

Content-Area Vocabulary

2. (a) For each of the following words, explain how the addition of a suffix alters the meaning and part of speech of the base word *distract*: *distracted*, *distracting*, and *distraction.* **(b)** Use each word in a sentence that shows its meaning.

⏱ Timed Writing

Argument: Letter to the Editor

Format and Audience
The prompt calls for a letter to the editor. Therefore, your writing should have a formal tone and be formatted as a business letter.

Write a letter to the editor in which you state your opinion about the public issue addressed in the editorial and speech. Analyze any conflicting information presented in the two texts. Cite at least one example of logical error, bias, or inconsistency in the texts. Also, cite an argument that is well reasoned and logical.
(30 minutes)

Academic Vocabulary
When you *cite* an example, you refer to it as evidence to support a position. A *bias* is an unfair preference or dislike for someone or something.

5-Minute Planner

Complete these steps before you begin to write:

1. Read the prompt carefully and completely. Look for key words to help you understand the requirements of the assignment.

2. Make a chart with two columns, one for each text. Jot down the main argument stated in each text.

3. Reread the texts, and jot down specific supporting details and claims. Note any errors in logic or inconsistent reasoning.

4. Based on your chart, decide what you think about the issue. Outline your letter, noting inconsistencies or logical weaknesses in one or both of the the texts.

Comparing Tone

The **tone** of a literary work is the author's attitude toward his or her audience and subject. Tone can often be described by an adjective, such as *formal, informal, serious,* or *playful.* The following features can help you determine tone.

- Specific words and phrases and their *connotations* can point to an author's attitude about a subject. Connotation includes the ideas, images, and feelings associated with a word. For example, the word *fragrance* conveys a different tone than *odor.*

- Sentence structure and variety, as well as the descriptive details an author includes, can also point to the tone of a literary work.

Tone may vary within a single work. For example, an author may begin a speech with a humorous anecdote in order to make a serious point later.

An author's choice of tone is just one decision he or she makes to further his or her **purpose,** or reason for writing. The following selections are both serious works that aim to make history interesting. In both, the writer's purpose is not simply to present factual information, but to convey his opinions and beliefs about those events. The tones of the two works differ, partly because the authors' reasons for writing and attitudes toward their subjects are different. As you read, complete a chart like the one shown to identify the relationships between word choice, sentence structure, tone, and purpose:

Common Core State Standards

Reading Informational Text
4. Determine the meaning of words and phrases as they are used in a text, including figurative, connotative, and technical meanings; analyze the impact of specific word choices on meaning and tone, including analogies or allusions to other texts.

Writing
9. Draw evidence from literary or informational texts to support analysis, reflection, and research. *(Timed Writing)*

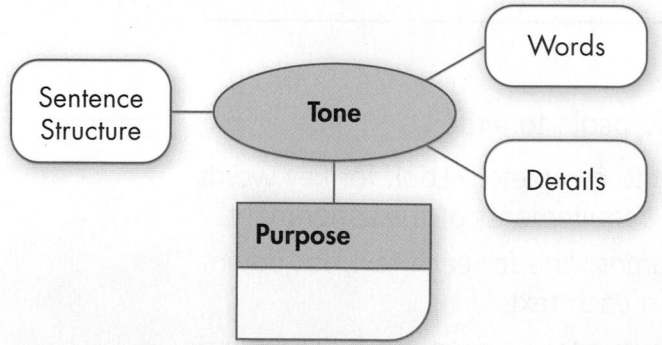

How much *information* is enough?

Writing About the Big Question

These works each involve important historical events in the struggle for racial equality. Use this sentence starter to develop your ideas.

To learn about **inequality** in history, I would want to read about _____ because _____.

Meet the Authors

Russell Freedman (b. 1929)

Author of "Emancipation"

"I had the good fortune to grow up in a house filled with books and book talk," Russell Freedman has said. After working as a reporter and editor, he decided to write books that would make history more interesting for young people.

Writing About Lincoln When Freedman visited the Lincoln Memorial as a boy, his father encouraged him to look at Lincoln's statue from all angles. Much later, when Freedman wrote *Lincoln: A Photobiography,* he tried to show the many sides of Lincoln, including the heartache and difficulties he faced as president.

Walter Dean Myers (b. 1937)

Author of "Brown vs. Board of Education"

Born in West Virginia, Walter Dean Myers was raised by foster parents in Harlem, a section of New York City. His foster mother taught him to read at four years old. "The public library was my most treasured place," Myers recalls. "I couldn't believe my luck in discovering that what I enjoyed most, reading, was free." Many of his works take place in Harlem and depict the problems and joys of African American teens.

Writing From Experience "My ideas come largely from my own background," Myers says. "I'm interested in history, so I write about historical characters in nonfiction."

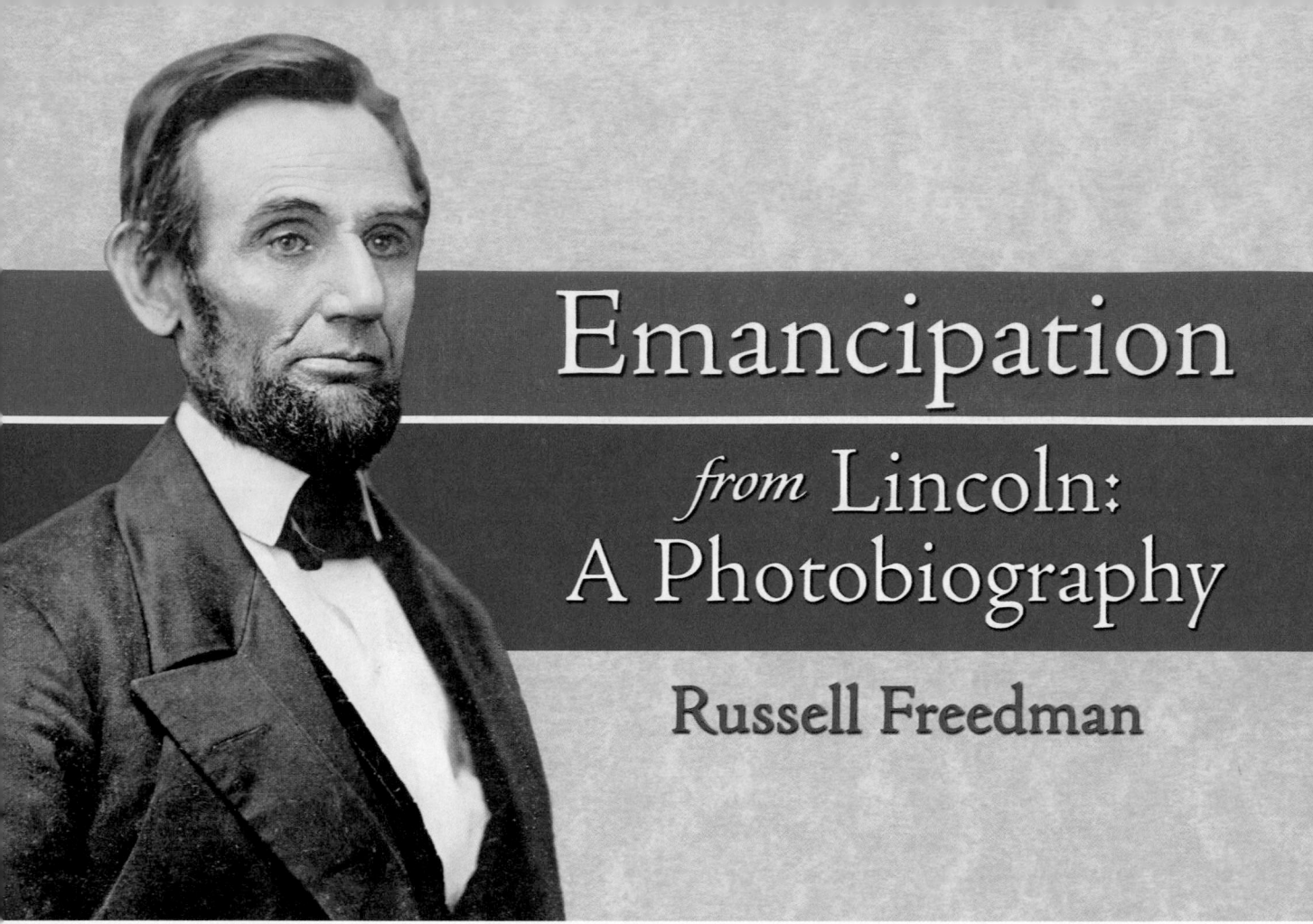

Emancipation

from Lincoln: A Photobiography

Russell Freedman

President Abraham Lincoln was leading the country in 1862—during the Civil War. He was challenged to find the best means for preserving the Union. His troops had just been beaten in fierce battles in Virginia. He had tough military and political decisions to make.

The toughest decision facing Lincoln . . . was the one he had to make about slavery. Early in the war, he was still willing to leave slavery alone in the South, if only he could restore the Union. Once the rebellion was crushed, slavery would be confined to the Southern states, where it would gradually die out. "We didn't go into the war to put down slavery, but to put the flag back," Lincoln said. "To act differently at this moment would, I have no doubt, not only weaken our cause, but smack of bad faith."

Abolitionists were demanding that the president free the slaves at once, by means of a wartime proclamation. "Teach the rebels and traitors that the price they are to pay for the attempt to abolish this Government must be the abolition of slavery," said Frederick Douglass, the famous black editor and reformer. "Let the war cry be down with treason, and down with slavery, the cause of treason!"

But Lincoln hesitated. He was afraid to alienate the large numbers of Northerners who supported the Union but opposed emancipation. And he worried about the loyal, slaveholding border states—Kentucky, Missouri, Maryland, and Delaware—that had refused to join the Confederacy. Lincoln feared that emancipation might drive those states into the arms of the South.

Yet slavery was the issue that had divided the country, and the president was under mounting pressure to do something about it. At first he supported a voluntary plan that would free the slaves gradually and compensate their owners with money from the federal treasury. Emancipation would begin in the loyal border states and be extended into the South as the rebel states were conquered. Perhaps then the liberated slaves could be resettled in Africa or Central America.

Lincoln pleaded with the border-state congressmen to accept his plan, but they turned him down. They would not part with their slave property or willingly change their way of life. "Emancipation in the cotton states is simply an absurdity," said a Kentucky congressman. "There is not enough power in the world to compel it to be done." •

Lincoln came to realize that if he wanted to attack slavery, he would have to act more boldly. A group of powerful Republican senators had been urging him to act. It was absurd, they argued, to fight the war without destroying the institution that had caused it. Slaves provided a vast pool of labor that was crucial to the South's war effort. If Lincoln freed the slaves, he could cripple the Confederacy and hasten the end of the war. If he did not free them, then the war would settle nothing. Even if the South agreed to return to the Union, it would start another war as soon as slavery was threatened again.

Besides, enslaved blacks were eager to throw off their shackles and fight for their own freedom. Thousands of slaves had already escaped from behind Southern lines. Thousands more were ready to enlist in the Union armies. "You need more men," Senator Charles Sumner told Lincoln, "not only at the North, but at the South, in the rear of the rebels. You need the slaves."

▶ **Critical Viewing**
Would you describe this photo of Lincoln as formal or informal? Why? **[Analyze]**

Tone
How do the subject and details here lend themselves to a serious tone?

Tone
Does the quotation here conflict with or match the tone in the rest of the paragraph? Explain.

All along, Lincoln had questioned his authority as president to abolish slavery in those states where it was protected by law. His Republican advisors argued that in time of war, with the nation in peril, the president did have the power to outlaw slavery. He could do it in his capacity as commander in chief of the armed forces. Such an act would be justified as a necessary war measure, because it would weaken the enemy. If Lincoln really wanted to save the Union, Senator Sumner told him, he must act now. He must wipe out slavery.

The war had become an endless nightmare of bloodshed and bungling generals. Lincoln doubted if the Union could survive without bold and drastic measures. By the summer of 1862, he had worked out a plan that would hold the loyal slave states in the Union, while striking at the enemies of the Union.

On July 22, 1862, he revealed his plan to his cabinet. He had decided, he told them, that emancipation was "a military necessity, absolutely essential to the preservation of the Union." For that reason, he intended to issue a proclamation freeing all the slaves in rebel states that had not returned to the Union by January 1, 1863. The proclamation would be aimed at the Confederate South only. In the loyal border states, he would continue to push for gradual, compensated emancipation.

Some cabinet members warned that the country wasn't ready to accept emancipation. But most of them nodded their approval, and in any case, Lincoln had made up his mind. He did listen to the objection of William H. Seward, his secretary of state. If Lincoln published his proclamation now, Seward argued, when Union armies had just been defeated in Virginia, it would seem like an act of desperation, "the last shriek on our retreat." The president must wait until the Union had won a decisive military victory in the East. Then he could issue his proclamation from a position of strength.

Lincoln agreed. For the time being, he filed the document away in his desk. •

A month later, in the war's second battle at Bull Run, Union forces commanded by General John Pope suffered another **humiliating** defeat. "We are whipped again," Lincoln moaned. He feared now that the war was lost. Rebel troops under Robert E. Lee were driving north. Early in September, Lee invaded Maryland and advanced toward Pennsylvania.

Lincoln again turned to General George McClellan—Who else do I have? he asked—and ordered him to repel the invasion. The two armies met at Antietam Creek in Maryland on September 17 in the bloodiest single engagement of the war. Lee was forced to retreat back to Virginia. But McClellan, cautious as ever, held his position and failed to pursue the defeated rebel army. It wasn't the decisive victory Lincoln had hoped for, but it would have to do.

On September 22, Lincoln read the final wording of his Emancipation Proclamation to his cabinet. If the rebels did not return to the Union by January 1, the president would free "thenceforward and forever" all the slaves everywhere in the Confederacy. Emancipation would become a Union war objective. As Union armies smashed their way into rebel territory, they would annihilate slavery once and for all.

The next day, the proclamation was released to the press. Throughout the North, opponents of slavery hailed the measure, and black people rejoiced. Frederick Douglass, the black abolitionist, had criticized Lincoln severely in the past. But he said now: "We shout for joy that we live to record this righteous decree."

When Lincoln delivered his annual message to Congress on December 1, he asked support for his program of military emancipation:

"Fellow citizens, *we* cannot escape history. We of this Congress and this administration, will be remembered in spite of ourselves. . . . In *giving* freedom to the *slave*, we assure freedom to the *free*—honorable alike in what we give, and what we preserve."

On New Year's Day, after a fitful night's sleep, Lincoln sat at his White House desk and put the finishing touches on his historic decree. From this day forward, all slaves in the rebel states were "forever free." Blacks who wished to could now enlist in the Union army and sail on Union ships. Several all-black regiments were formed immediately. By the end

Vocabulary
humiliating (hyo͞o mil´ ē āt´ iŋ) *adj.* embarrassing

Tone
How does the organization of details and word choice add to the dramatic tone of this passage?

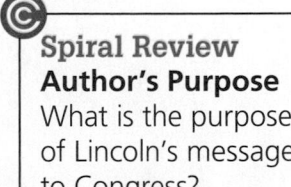

Spiral Review
Author's Purpose
What is the purpose of Lincoln's message to Congress?

Reading Check
What happened at Antietam Creek?

of the war, more than 180,000 blacks—a majority of them emancipated slaves—had volunteered for the Union forces. They manned military garrisons and served as front-line combat troops in every theatre of the war.

The traditional New Year's reception was held in the White House that morning. Mary appeared at an official gathering for the first time since Willie's death,[1] wearing garlands in her hair and a black shawl about her head.

During the reception, Lincoln slipped away and retired to his office with several cabinet members and other officials for the formal signing of the proclamation. He looked tired. He had been shaking hands all morning, and now his hand trembled as he picked up a gold pen to sign his name.

Ordinarily he signed "A. Lincoln." But today, as he put pen to paper, he carefully wrote out his full name. "If my name ever goes into history," he said then, "it will be for this act."

---

1. **Mary appeared . . . Willie's death** Mary Todd Lincoln was President Lincoln's wife. The couple's son William died in 1862 at age eleven.

Critical Thinking

Cite textual evidence to support your responses.

1. **Key Ideas and Details (a)** What does Freedman say Lincoln's toughest decision was as president? **(b) Synthesize:** Why did Lincoln hesitate to issue a wartime proclamation emancipating slaves? **(c) Infer:** What does his hesitation indicate about the limits of his power as president?

2. **Key Ideas and Details (a)** What was William Seward's recommendation to Lincoln about when to issue the proclamation? **(b) Speculate:** Why did Lincoln decide to issue it after Antietam Creek?

3. **Integration of Knowledge and Ideas (a) Interpret:** What did Lincoln mean when he said, "In giving freedom to the slave, we assure freedom to the free—honorable alike in what we give, and what we preserve"? **(b) Assess:** What, if any, act by an American president is as significant as Lincoln's Emancipation Proclamation?

4. **Key Ideas and Details** Does the information in this essay change your impression or understanding of Lincoln? Explain. *[Connect to the Big Question: How much information is enough?]*

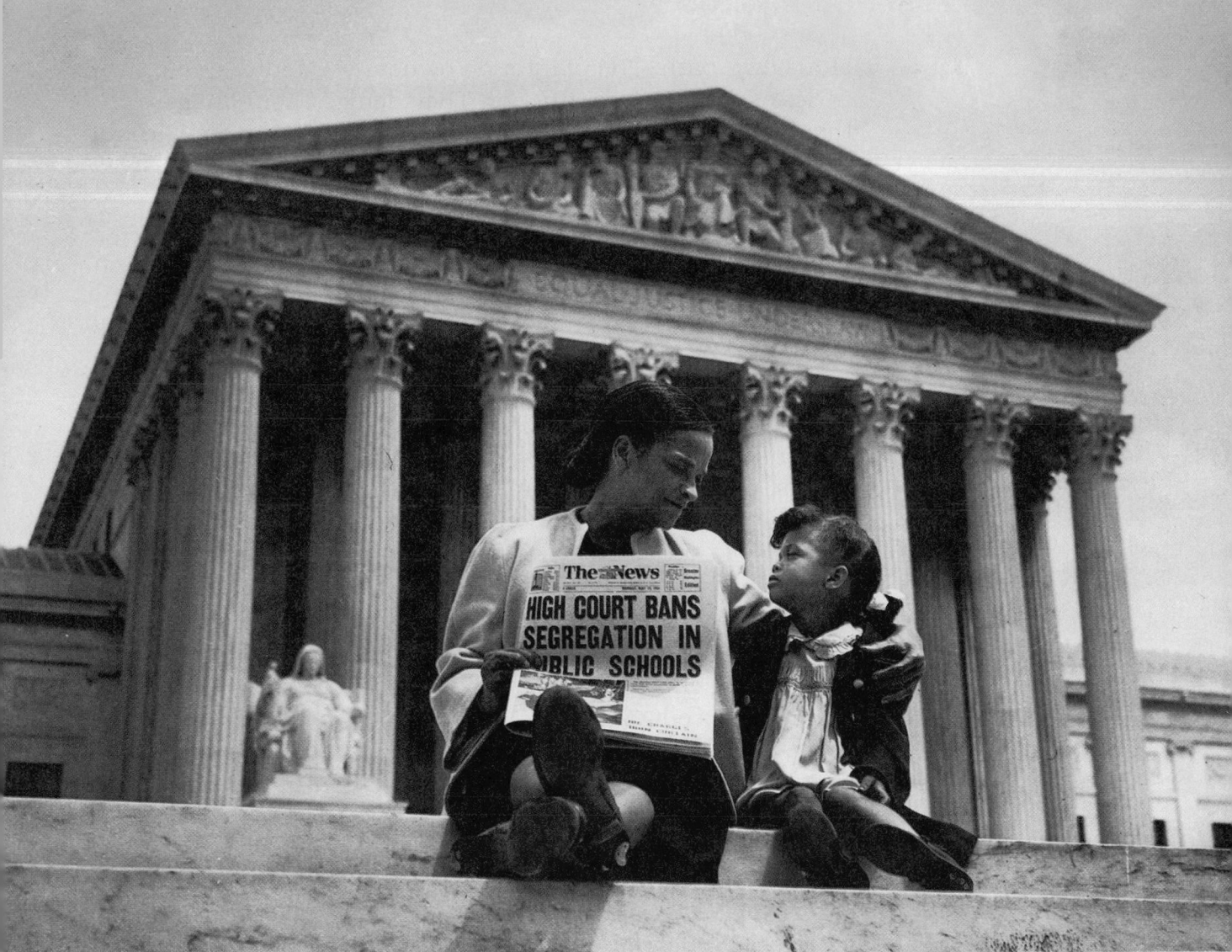

Brown vs. Board of Education

Walter Dean Myers

There was a time when the meaning of freedom was easily understood. For an African crouched in the darkness of a tossing ship, wrists chained, men with guns standing on the decks above him, freedom was a physical thing, the ability to move away from his captors, to follow the dictates of his own heart, to listen to the voices within him that defined his values and showed him the truth

▲ **Critical Viewing**
Why is the U.S. Supreme Court an appropriate setting for this photograph? **[Analyze]**

of his own path. The plantation owners wanted to make the Africans feel helpless, inferior. They denied them images of themselves as Africans and told them that they were without beauty. They segregated them and told them they were without value.

Slowly, surely, the meaning of freedom changed to an elusive thing that even the strongest people could not hold in their hands. There were no chains on black wrists, but there were the shadows of chains, stretching for hundreds of years back through time, across black minds.

———————————— ⚜ ————————————

Tone
How do words and phrases like *de facto*, *predominantly*, and *de jure* affect the tone?

From the end of the Civil War in 1865 to the early 1950's, many public schools in both the North and South were segregated. Segregation was different in the different sections of the country. In the North most of the schools were segregated *de facto*;[1] that is, the law allowed blacks and whites to go to school together, but they did not actually always attend the same schools. Since a school is generally attended by children living in its neighborhood, wherever there were predominantly African-American neighborhoods there were, "in fact," segregated schools. In many parts of the country, however, and especially in the South, the segregation was *de jure*,[2] meaning that there were laws which forbade blacks to attend the same schools as whites.

Vocabulary
predominantly
(prē däm′ ə nənt lē)
adv. mainly

The states with segregated schools relied upon the ruling of the Supreme Court in the 1896 *Plessy vs. Ferguson* case for legal justification: Facilities that were "separate but equal" were legal.

In the early 1950's the National Association for the Advancement of Colored People (N.A.A.C.P.) sponsored five cases that eventually reached the Supreme Court. One of the cases involved the school board of Topeka, Kansas.

Tone
How does the sentence structure in this paragraph contribute to a formal tone?

Thirteen families sued the Topeka school board, claiming that to segregate the children was harmful to the children and, therefore, a violation of the equal protection clause of the Fourteenth Amendment. The names on the Topeka case were listed in alphabetical order, with the father of seven-year-old Linda Brown listed first.

---

1. *de facto* (dē fak′ tō) Latin for "existing in actual fact."
2. *de jure* (dē joor′ ē) Latin for "by right or legal establishment."

"I didn't understand why I couldn't go to school with my playmates. I lived in an integrated neighborhood and played with children of all nationalities, but when school started they went to a school only four blocks from my home and I was sent to school across town," she says.

For young Linda the case was one of convenience and of being made to feel different, but for African-American parents it had been a long, hard struggle to get a good education for their children. It was also a struggle waged by lawyers who had worked for years to overcome segregation. The head of the legal team who presented the school cases was Thurgood Marshall.

The city was Baltimore, Maryland, and the year was 1921. Thirteen-year-old Thurgood Marshall struggled to balance the packages he was carrying with one hand while he tried to get his bus fare out of his pocket with the other. It was almost

▲ **Critical Viewing**
What would the families in the *Brown* case say about this classroom? What would the state say? **[Connect]**

Reading Check
Why did thirteen families sue the Topeka school board?

Tone
How does the author's tone change when he discusses Marshall's boyhood?

▼ **Critical Viewing**
In this photograph, Marshall is sworn in as a Supreme Court justice, with President Lyndon Johnson by his side. What details show this is a solemn, historic occasion? **[Interpret]**

Easter, and the part-time job he had would provide money for flowers for his mother. Suddenly he felt a violent tug at his right arm that spun him around, sending his packages sprawling over the floor of the bus.

"Don't you never push in front of no white lady again!" an angry voice spat in his ear.

Thurgood turned and threw a punch . . . . The man charged into Thurgood, throwing punches that mostly missed, and tried to wrestle the slim boy to the ground. A policeman broke up the fight, grabbing Thurgood with one huge black hand and pushing him against the side of the bus. Within minutes they were in the local courthouse.

Thurgood was not the first of his family to get into a good fight. His father's father had joined the Union Army during the Civil War, taking the names Thorough Good to add to the one name he had in bondage. His grandfather on his mother's side was a man brought from Africa and, according to Marshall's biography, "so ornery that his owner wouldn't sell him out of pity for the people who might buy him, but gave him his

freedom instead and told him to clear out of the county."

Thurgood's frequent scrapes earned him a reputation as a young boy who couldn't be trusted to get along with white folks.

His father, Will Marshall, was a steward at the Gibson Island Yacht Club near Baltimore, and his mother, Norma, taught in a segregated school. The elder Marshall felt he could have done more with his life if his education had been better, but there had been few opportunities available for African Americans when he had been a young man. When it was time for the Marshall boys to go to college, he was more than willing to make the sacrifices necessary to send them.

Young people of color from all over the world came to the United States to study at Lincoln University, a predominantly black institution in southeastern Pennsylvania. Here Marshall majored in predentistry, which he found boring, and joined the Debating Club, which he found interesting. By the time he was graduated at the age of twenty-one, he had decided to give up dentistry for the law. Three years later he was graduated, first in his class, from Howard University Law School.

At Howard there was a law professor, Charles Hamilton Houston, who would affect the lives of many African-American lawyers and who would influence the legal aspects of the civil rights movement. Houston was a great teacher, one who demanded that his students be not just good lawyers but great lawyers. If they were going to help their people—and for Houston the only reason for African Americans to become lawyers was to do just that—they would have to have absolute understanding of the law, and be diligent[3] in the preparation of their cases. At the time, Houston was an attorney for the N.A.A.C.P. and fought against discrimination in housing and in jobs.

After graduation, Thurgood Marshall began to do some work for the N.A.A.C.P., trying the difficult civil rights cases. He not only knew about the effects of discrimination by reading about it, he was still living it when he was graduated from law school in 1933. In 1936 Marshall began working full-time for the N.A.A.C.P., and in 1940 became its chief counsel.

It was Thurgood Marshall and a battery of N.A.A.C.P. attorneys who began to challenge segregation throughout the country. These men and women were warriors in the cause of freedom for African Americans, taking their battles

Tone
What word here contrasts with the otherwise formal tone of the paragraph?

Reading Check
What did Marshall's father do for a living?

---

3. **diligent** (dil´ ə jənt) *adj.* careful and thorough.

Law Connection

Civil Rights Pioneer

In 1892, an African American shoemaker named Homer Plessy boarded a whites-only railcar in New Orleans. Promptly arrested, he took his case against Louisiana's segregation laws all the way to the U.S. Supreme Court.

In 1896, the Supreme Court ruled against Mr. Plessy in a 7–1 decision. The majority concluded that segregation laws "do not necessarily imply the inferiority of either race." After the *Plessy* decision, segregation laws multiplied and did not face a serious challenge again until *Brown* in 1954.

Connect to the Literature

How was the *Plessy* case similar to and different from *Brown*?

into courtrooms across the country. They understood the process of American justice and the power of the Constitution.

In *Brown vs. Board of Education of Topeka*, Marshall argued that segregation was a violation of the Fourteenth Amendment—that even if the facilities and all other "tangibles" were equal, which was the heart of the case in *Plessy vs. Ferguson*, a violation still existed. There were intangible[4] factors, he argued, that made the education unequal.

Everyone involved understood the significance of the case: that it was much more than whether black children could go to school with white children. If segregation in the schools was declared unconstitutional, then *all* segregation in public places could be declared unconstitutional.

Southerners who argued against ending school segregation were caught up, as then-Congressman Brooks Hays of Arkansas put it, in "a lifetime of adventures in that gap between law and custom." The law was one thing, but most Southern whites felt just as strongly about their customs as they did the law.

Dr. Kenneth B. Clark, an African-American psychologist, testified for the N.A.A.C.P. He presented clear evidence that the effect of segregation was harmful to African-American children. Describing studies conducted by black and white psychologists over a twenty-year period, he showed that black children felt inferior to white children. In a particularly dramatic study that he had supervised, four dolls, two white and two black, were presented to African-American children. From the responses of the children to the dolls, identical in every way except color, it was clear that the children were rejecting the black dolls. African-American children did not just feel separated from white children, they felt that the separation was based on their inferiority.

Dr. Clark understood fully the principles and ideas of those people who had held Africans in bondage and had tried to make slaves of captives. By isolating people of African descent, by barring them from certain actions or

---

4. intangible (in tan´ jə bəl) *adj.* not able to be touched or grasped.

places, they could make them feel inferior. The social scientists who testified at *Brown vs. Board of Education* showed that children who felt inferior also performed poorly.

The Justice Department argued that racial segregation was objectionable to the Eisenhower Administration and hurt our relationships with other nations.

On May 17, 1954, after deliberating for nearly a year and a half, the Supreme Court made its ruling. The Court stated that it could not use the intentions of 1868, when the Fourteenth Amendment was passed, as a guide to its ruling, or even those of 1896, when the decision in *Plessy vs. Ferguson* was handed down. Chief Justice Earl Warren wrote:

> We must consider public education in the light of its full development and its present place in American life throughout the nation. We must look instead to the effect of segregation itself on public education.

The Court went on to say that "modern authority" supported the idea that segregation deprived African Americans of equal opportunity. "Modern authority" referred to Dr. Kenneth B. Clark and the weight of evidence that he and the other social scientists had presented.

The high court's decision in *Brown vs. Board of Education* signaled an important change in the struggle for civil rights. It signaled clearly that the legal prohibitions that oppressed African Americans would have to fall. Equally important was the idea that the nature of the fight for equality would change. Ibrahima, Cinqué, Nat Turner, and George Latimer had struggled for freedom by fighting against their captors or fleeing from them. The 54th had fought for African freedom on the battlefields of the Civil War. Ida B. Wells had fought for equality with her pen. Lewis H. Latimer and Meta Vaux Warrick had tried to earn equality with their work. In *Brown vs. Board of Education* Thurgood Marshall, Kenneth B. Clark, and the lawyers and social scientists, both black and white, who helped them had won for African Americans a victory that would bring them closer to full equality than they had ever been in North America. There would still be legal battles to be won, but the major struggle would be in the hearts and minds of people and "in that gap between law and custom."

Tone
Which words in this paragraph contribute to a tone of formality and seriousness?

Vocabulary
deliberating (di lib´ ər āt iŋ) *v.* thinking carefully
oppressed (ə prest´) *v.* kept down by unjust power

Spiral Review
Author's Purpose
Why does Myers include the quotation from Chief Justice Earl Warren?

Reading Check
What did Dr. Clark's testimony prove?

In 1967 Thurgood Marshall was appointed by President Lyndon B. Johnson as an associate justice of the U.S. Supreme Court. He retired in 1991.

"I didn't think of my father or the other parents as being heroic at the time," Linda Brown says. "I was only seven. But as I grew older and realized how far-reaching the case was and how it changed the complexion of the history of this country, I was just thrilled that my father and the others here in Topeka were involved."

Critical Thinking

Cite textual evidence to support your responses.

1. Key Ideas and Details **(a)** Describe how school segregation differed in different sections of the United States between 1865 and the early 1950s. **(b) Compare and Contrast:** How were seven-year-old Linda Brown's views on the *Topeka* case different from the views of African American parents involved in the case?

2. Key Ideas and Details **Analyze:** Based on the biographical details Myers gives about Thurgood Marshall's family, his early career, and his character traits, do you think Marshall was or was not a good choice to lead the NAACP's legal team? Explain.

3. Key Ideas and Details **(a)** What was the Supreme Court's decision in *Brown*? **(b) Apply:** Why is this case a significant event in history?

4. Integration of Knowledge and Ideas **Make a Judgment:** Myers quotes the grown-up Linda Brown as saying she did not think of her father as heroic at the time of the court case. Do you think any of the participants in the case were heroes? Explain.

5. Integration of Knowledge and Ideas **(a)** How clear an idea did the author provide of what it might feel like to attend a segregated school? **(b)** What sources could provide more information? *[Connect to the Big Question: How much information is enough?]*

Comparing Tone

1. Craft and Structure What tone does Freedman develop with words such as *demanding, hesitated, worried, pressure,* and *argued*?

2. Key Ideas and Details (a) What do you think is Freedman's purpose for writing? **(b)** How might the tone be different if his purpose had been to convince readers that Lincoln was a great leader?

3. Craft and Structure What aspect of Myers's tone is reflected in his choice of the words *struggle, challenge, warriors, cause,* and *battles*?

4. Key Ideas and Details What do you think is Myers's purpose for writing? Explain.

⏱ Timed Writing

Explanatory Text: Essay

Write an essay analyzing how each author's tone helps to convey his attitudes and beliefs toward his topic. Then, compare and contrast how tone reflects each author's purpose for writing. (40 minutes)

5-Minute Planner

1. Read the prompt carefully and completely.

2. Gather details from the diagrams you completed as you read the texts (see page 598). Complete a chart like the one shown.

	Emancipation	Brown
Topic		
Details about events		
Details about participants		
Points of view presented		
Words that convey attitude		

3. Organize your essay around a thesis statement or central idea that connects each author's tone to his purpose for writing and to his beliefs and attitudes toward the topic. Be sure to compare and contrast the tones of the two pieces.

4. Reread the prompt, and then draft your essay.

Writing Workshop

Write Arguments

Persuasion: Editorial

Defining the Form Persuasion is the act of using words to change the way people think or to influence the way they behave. One type of persuasion is an **editorial,** a brief essay or article that states and defends a position on an issue.

Assignment Write an editorial that persuades readers to adopt your position on an issue or to accept your solution to a problem. Include these elements:

✔ a *thesis,* a clear statement of your position on an issue

✔ *detailed evidence and logical arguments*

✔ a *clear organization* that builds toward a conclusion

✔ a *response to possible counterarguments*

✔ *persuasive techniques* that convey a powerful message

✔ error-free writing, including *correct use of conjunctions*

To preview the criteria on which your editorial may be judged, see the rubric on page 621.

 Writing Workshop: *Work in Progress*

Review the work you did on pages 571 and 589.

WRITE GUY
Jeff Anderson, M.Ed.

What Do You Notice?

Persuasion

The following passage is from Robert MacNeil's speech "The Trouble With Television." Read it several times.

I question how much of television's nightly news effort is really absorbable and understandable. Much of it is what has been aptly described as 'machine gunning with scraps.' I think its technique fights coherence. I think it tends to make things ultimately boring and dismissable (unless they are accompanied by horrifying pictures) because almost anything is boring and dismissable if you know almost nothing about it.

With a partner, discuss the qualities that make the passage persuasive and thought-provoking. For example, you may want to talk about the writer's use of word choice, repetition, or quotation.

Writing

1. Write arguments to support claims with clear reasons and relevant evidence.

1.a. Introduce claim(s), acknowledge and distinguish the claim(s) from alternate or opposing claims, and organize the reasons and evidence logically.

1.b. Support claim(s) with logical reasoning and relevant evidence, using accurate, credible sources and demonstrating an understanding of the topic or text.

Reading-Writing Connection

To get the feel for persuasion, read "The Trouble With Television" by Robert MacNeil on page 558.

Prewriting/Planning Strategies

Have a group discussion. Hold a discussion of issues in your school and community. Create a list of specific problems that need solving and common views that you think need changing. Review the list and choose the issue that interests you most.

Turn to the media. Every day, the media brings controversies and debates into our living rooms. Over a day or two, read newspapers (including letters to the editor) and watch the local and national news. Use a table like the one shown to jot down topics that spark your interest. Then, choose one as the subject of your editorial.

PHLit
Online!
www.PHLitOnline.com
- Author video: Writing Process
- Author video: Rewards of Writing

Newspapers	Television News
overweight teens a national epidemic *(National Gazette)*	health care costs continue to rise *(The Nightly News)*
budget cuts force canceling of youth sports program *(City News)*	city baseball team's game attendance at an all-time low *(The Local Report)*
town needs new recycling plan *(My Town Newspaper)*	residents protest building of stadium *(Local Channel News)*

Define your position. Before you write, you need to determine your position on the issue. Write a **thesis statement,** a single, clear statement that summarizes your thinking. Since drafting a single statement from scratch can be difficult, you can reverse the process. First, freewrite thoughts, arguments, and feelings about the issue. Jot them down as they occur to you. Then, review your notes to see what thoughts go together. Assemble these to construct a single, powerful thesis statement.

Prepare to provide support. Arrange your thoughts and arguments in an outline that supports your thesis. Consider using **Nestorian order**—arranging points according to their strength. Begin with your least strong point. Then, build your editorial so that you end with your strongest point. Finally, gather evidence that supports your position on your topic. Types of support include:

- facts and statistics
- expert opinions
- interviews and surveys
- personal observations

Drafting Strategies

Use a variety of persuasive techniques. As you draft, use these techniques to sway readers:

- **Logical Arguments** Take your readers, step-by-step, through your argument. Present reliable, compelling evidence.

- **Emotional Appeals** Sway your readers with a brief story or vivid image that adds impact to your argument by sparking an emotion such as pride, surprise, anger, or fear.

- **Charged Words** Use words with positive or negative associations, such as *shameful* or *honesty.* They can pack entire emotions into a few syllables.

- **Repetition and Parallelism** Create sentences that use identical patterns to add drama and emphasize certain ideas.

Repetition (words and phrases)	Parallelism (similar sentence patterns)
Our beaches are littered, our parks are littered, and our streets are littered.	Join us on Saturday. Help us clean up these areas. Be a community activist.

Avoid libel. Being passionate about your issue is a strength, but editorial writers must not resort to libel—false statements that can damage someone's reputation. Avoid trouble by steering clear of personal attacks and by making sure you have evidence to back up your claims.

Anticipate and respond to counterarguments. Think about the arguments against your position. Then, meet opposing ideas head-on with arguments of your own. Look at the examples in the chart.

Arguments	Counterarguments
Wearing school uniforms robs students of their individuality.	Students do not have to worry about wearing what is considered "cool."
Uniforms are expensive.	Students save money by not wearing a different outfit every day.

Maintain a formal style. Your editorial will be more persuasive if you write in a businesslike way. Do not use slang and avoid an overly familiar or chatty tone.

 **Common Core State Standards**

Writing

1. Write arguments to support claims with clear reasons and relevant evidence.

1.a. Introduce claim(s), acknowledge and distinguish the claim(s) from alternate or opposing claims, and organize the reasons and evidence logically.

1.b. Support claim(s) with logical reasoning and relevant evidence, using accurate, credible sources and demonstrating an understanding of the topic or text.

1.c. Use words, phrases, and clauses to create cohesion and clarify the relationships among claim(s), counterclaims, reasons, and evidence.

1.d. Establish and maintain a formal style.

Writers on Writing

Andrew Mishkin On Grabbing the Reader's Attention

Andrew Mishkin is the author of "Making Tracks on Mars" (p. 468).

When writing the history of *Sojourner*, the first Mars rover, I needed to grab readers quickly, and let them know why they should be interested in the story I was telling. I had to persuade them that the characters would struggle mightily to meet the coming challenges, and perhaps still not succeed. I wanted readers to care about the final outcome, and to read the book to see how it all works out. The following draft shows revisions I made to accomplish these goals.

"Make the reader part of the action."
— Andrew Mishkin

Professional Model:

from *Sojourner*

To begin work on a flight project is to enter a new world where mass, power, and volume are precious commodities. Consuming too much of any of these is not an option. Each available ~~launch vehicle,~~ rocket —in aerospace they call them "launch vehicles"— whether a Delta, Titan, or Ariane ~~rocket~~, has only so much ~~lift capability, or~~ weight of payload it can put into a particular trajectory in space. If you are launching a spacecraft to Mars, and its mass is too high, the laws of physics ensure that it will never reach its target. Each spacecraft must carry with it its own power source, whether in the form of solar arrays, radioisotope thermoelectric generators, or batteries. These power sources are limited in their capacity. The components of the spacecraft that depend on this power must use it efficiently, for when the needs of the system exceed the available power, the spacecraft dies.

I rearranged the sentence to avoid using a technical term without defining it first, and then deleted another term I decided I didn't need at all.

Using "you" is not only less formal, but also suggests that the reader consider how he or she would personally deal with the situation.

I immediately backed up my premise with examples to make it more real, more convincing.

I used a word normally applied to a living thing—"dies"—to encourage the reader to see the spacecraft in the same way as the characters do in the pages to come.

Revising Strategies

Revise to strengthen appeals to your audience. Give your readers more than facts and logic—add emotion and description to grab their attention. Review your draft to find points that are supported only with logical arguments or statistics. Then, follow these steps:

- Consider adding a colorful comparison, striking image, or dramatic anecdote to add interest and to illustrate your argument.

- Strengthen your argument with quotations that express the opinions of respected authorities.

- Offer evidence, examples, and reasoning to support your argument, being careful to differentiate between facts and opinions.

- Support your thesis with an **analogy,** an extended comparison between the situation you describe and another, similar situation that helps shed light on the first. Be sure to think through an analogy first to make sure it is not a false or flawed comparison.

Original Version	Revised Version—Using an Analogy
Young people should be encouraged to get out on their own as soon as they can.	Like a mother bird, a good parent knows that a child sometimes needs to be pushed out of the nest if he or she is to experience the joys of life.

Revise for coherence. Paragraphs should cohere, or hold together well. In your draft, read the last sentence of each paragraph and the first sentence of the next paragraph. If the connection between the paragraphs is not obvious, highlight the space between them. Consider these tips to improve coherence in the spaces you marked.

- Repeat a key word or phrase.

- Use a transitional word or phrase such as *similarly* or *in addition.*

- Insert a sentence that takes readers smoothly from one idea to the next. Provide a strong concluding statement that supports the arguments you have already presented.

Peer Review

Read your revised draft aloud to a small group of classmates. Ask the group members whether they saw any points or ideas that did not fit well with the rest of the editorial. Consider their responses to make your essay more effective.

 **Common Core State Standards**

Writing

1. Write arguments to support claims with clear reasons and relevant evidence.

1.c. Use words, phrases, and clauses to create cohesion and clarify the relationships among claim(s), counterclaims, reasons, and evidence.

1.e. Provide a concluding statement or section that follows from and supports the argument presented.

Revising Sentences by Combining With Conjunctions

Conjunctions connect words or groups of words. They can be used to join two sentences to create a compound or complex sentence.

Understanding the Role of Conjunctions There are two categories of conjunctions that serve different functions.

Coordinating conjunctions join words of the same kind and equal rank, such as two nouns or two verbs. When they join two independent clauses, these conjunctions make a compound sentence.

> **Example:** *Pablo* takes dance lessons. *June* takes dance lessons.

> **Compound Subject:** *Pablo and June* take dance lessons.

Subordinating conjunctions connect two complete ideas and show that one is dependent on the other.

> **Example:** June takes dance lessons. She wants to be graceful.

> **With Subordinating Conjunction:** Because June wants to be graceful, she takes dance lessons.

Common Conjunctions	
Coordinating	and, or, but, nor, so, yet, for
Subordinating	after, although, as, because, before, if, since, unless, until, when, while, whenever

PH WRITING COACH

Further instruction and practice are available in *Prentice Hall Writing Coach.*

Joining Sentences With Conjunctions You can join short, choppy sentences with conjunctions. Follow these steps:

1. **Identify short sentences that could be combined.** Then, identify the words, phrases, or clauses that you want to join.

2. **Determine if the items are of the same kind and of equal rank.** If so, use a coordinating conjunction to join them.

3. **Determine if one is dependent on the other.** If so, use a subordinating conjunction to join them.

Grammar in Your Writing
Choose three paragraphs in your draft. Improve coherence and add interest by combining some of the sentences with conjunctions.

**Common Core
State Standards**

Language
1. Demonstrate command of the conventions of standard English grammar and usage when writing or speaking.

Editorial: *Save The Brazilian Voice*

Our Ironbound neighborhood of Newark is like a little Brazil. A lot of us who live here came from Brazil, and most of us read *The Brazilian Voice* every week. Now, however, this paper is going to close because there isn't enough money to keep publishing it. My old grandfather says, "A problem always has a solution if you want to find it." We need to find a solution to the problem of losing this neighborhood newspaper. It is my belief that *The Brazilian Voice* should not stop publishing. The people need it.

There are lots of reasons that the people need *The Brazilian Voice*. For one thing, as all the readers know, it is an important source of information. It contains news about things happening in New Jersey and the rest of the country, and also about things happening in Brazil. The articles in Portuguese are important for people who don't know English very well. By reading *The Brazilian Voice*, they learn about the security of the city and about projects that the city is planning. Furthermore, the paper contains ads for people who are looking for jobs and all the announcements for special events like new restaurants opening, festivals, shows, sales, and activities for older people and young people. It lists all the programs for the weekends and holidays. It is the heartbeat of a city that pulses with life and energy.

Some people might think that if we have a Brazilian television channel in New Jersey, we don't need the newspaper. However, the Brazilian channel only shows news from Brazil. *The Brazilian Voice* gives the news about our community that affects our lives every day. The people in the Ironbound depend on this paper.

The reason *The Brazilian Voice* is closing is money. The owners of this paper say that they can't afford to print it anymore because there aren't enough businesses paying for advertisements. If they don't have money, they can't pay the reporters, or buy paper and ink. Of course, this paper can't survive if it keeps losing money every week. But the obvious solution is to charge money for the paper. In all its years, *The Brazilian Voice* has been given away for free. That is a good service for the people. We like to get the paper for free, but I am sure that people would rather pay for it than not have it anymore.

If I were going to compare *The Newark Star-Ledger* and *The Brazilian Voice*, I would say the situation is the same. People would probably want to pay more for the Star-Ledger than to not have it anymore.

There are 45,000 people in the Ironbound. According to a poll by the paper, over half of them read *The Brazilian Voice* every week. If 20,000 people would pay 50 cents for the paper, that would be an extra $10,000. This money would mean that the citizens of the neighborhood could keep their paper.

In summation, I want to repeat that it is really important to have *The Brazilian Voice* in the Ironbound, and 50 cents isn't too much to pay for something that important.

Jordanna presents the problem she will address in her editorial and clearly states her position.

She supports her position with a series of reasons to show why the paper is important to the community.

Jordanna anticipates and addresses a potential argument against her position.

Statistics provide solid support for logical arguments.

In this editorial, the writer has used evidence to build up to her conclusion—a clear restatement of her argument.

Editing and Proofreading

Focus on double negatives. Avoid creating confusion with double negatives—two negative words—when only one is required in standard English. The example shows two ways to correct a double negative.

    Example: There is no reason to not cut funding.

    Correction 1: There is not any reason to cut funding.

    Correction 2: There is no reason to cut funding.

Publishing and Presenting

Consider one of the following ways to share your writing:

Organize a forum. Assemble a panel of classmates to read their editorials to the class. Allow the class to ask questions of the panel and then vote on whether they agree or disagree with each paper.

Publish in a newspaper. Send your editorial, with a cover letter, to a local newspaper. Briefly summarize your essay in the letter, and explain that you wish it to be considered for publication.

Reflecting on Your Writing

Writer's Journal Jot down your answers to these questions:

What did you learn about the issue you chose? Did you find your opinions changing as you learned more? Explain.

Rubric for Self-Assessment

Find evidence in your writing to address each category. Then, use the rating scale to grade your work.

Spiral Review

Earlier in this unit, you learned about **conjunctions** (p. 570) and **prepositions** (p. 588). Check your persuasive writing to be sure that you have used conjunctions and prepositions correctly.

Criteria	Rating Scale not very very
Focus: How clearly do you state your position?	1 2 3 4 5
Organization: How effectively does the organization build to a conclusion?	1 2 3 4 5
Support/Elaboration: How convincing is the evidence that supports your position?	1 2 3 4 5
Style: How powerful is your use of persuasive techniques?	1 2 3 4 5
Conventions: How correct is your grammar, especially your use of conjunctions?	1 2 3 4 5

Vocabulary Workshop

Words With Multiple Meanings

Many words in English relate to multiple subjects and therefore have multiple meanings. A **multiple-meaning word** is a word that has more than one definition. The word *bat*, for example, can be defined as a furry, flying animal or as a club used in baseball. To determine the meaning intended in a sentence, you must consider the *context*, or the words surrounding the word. The following chart shows two usages of the multiple-meaning word *factor*.

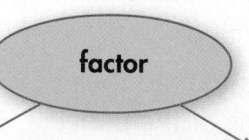

Meaning 1	Meaning 2
a condition that contributes to a result (Social Studies)	any of two or more quantities that form a product when multiplied together (Math)
Sentence	**Sentence**
The stock market crash of 1929 was one *factor* that brought about the Great Depression.	When multiplied by five, two is a *factor* of ten.

 Common Core State Standards

Language

4. Determine or clarify the meaning of unknown and multiple-meaning words or phrases based on grade 8 reading and content, choosing flexibly from a range of strategies.

4.a. Use context as a clue to the meaning of a word or phrase.

4.c. Consult general and specialized reference materials, both print and digital, to find the pronunciation of a word or determine or clarify its precise meaning or its part of speech.

Practice A Write the meaning of each italicized word in the sentences below. If necessary, check the meaning in a dictionary.

1. a. After weeks of cold weather, the *ground* was very hard.

   b. I like freshly *ground* pepper on my salad.

2. a. The overflowing garbage can produced a *rank* smell.

   b. Juan hopes to reach the *rank* of captain.

3. a. Today's *date* is January 23.

   b. I sliced a *date* into pieces and put it in my bowl of cereal.

4. a. Do not *cross* the street until the light turns green.

   b. The coach becomes *cross* when players are late for practice.

Practice B For each word listed, write two sentences that use different meanings of the word. If necessary, look up the meanings in a dictionary.

1. bank	**5.** count
2. mean	**6.** bound
3. square	**7.** range
4. base	**8.** capital

Activity Look in a dictionary to learn more about these words that have multiple meanings: *nature, horn, jam, match, positive.* Write each word on a separate notecard like the one shown. Fill in the left column of the note card according to one of the word's meanings. Fill in the right-hand column according to another of the word's meanings. Then, trade note cards with a partner, and discuss the different meanings and uses of the words that each of you found.

Comprehension and Collaboration

Work with two or three classmates to write a sentence for each of the following words, using two different meanings of the word in the same sentence. For example: *"In his speech, the governor will state his goals for reducing pollution in our state."*

plain
sound
object

Word: _____	
Part of Speech:	**Part of Speech:**
Definition:	**Definition:**
Example Sentence:	**Example Sentence:**

Communications Workshop

Evaluating an Oral Presentation

When you evaluate an oral presentation, you make judgments about a speaker's ideas and effectiveness. Use these steps to guide you.

Understand the Structure

Evaluating a presentation is easier if you know the topic and format.

Identify topic. The topic is a one-phrase summary of a speech's subject. The title of the presentation might also be the topic. Speakers usually introduce the topic within the first few minutes.

Identify purpose. The general purpose of an oral presentation is often to inform or persuade. The specific purpose depends on the topic. For example, the specific purpose of a scientific presentation might be to describe new research on the brain.

Determine point of view. Especially when listening to a persuasive speech, it is important to identify point of view. Use the arguments and examples a speaker offers, as well as his or her background, to determine how the speaker feels about a subject.

Identify organization. Speeches often follow the same format as essays, so the skills you learn in identifying written formats can be applied to a speech. Identify the speaker's main ideas and connect them with the facts and ideas that support them. Determine the organizational format, such as cause-and-effect or order of importance. Knowing organization helps focus your listening.

Evaluate the Speech

Evaluate the content. Once you understand a presentation's purpose and organization, you can evaluate its content. Ask yourself if the speaker presents ideas clearly and whether he or she supports main ideas with strong and varied evidence, such as facts, examples, and expert opinions. Determine whether all the evidence is relevant and relates clearly to the ideas presented.

Evaluate the delivery. The quality of a presentation depends on both delivery and content. A speaker who mumbles and repeats uninteresting or irrelevant information gives a poor presentation. A good speaker should enunciate clearly, vary his or her voice, and deliver a lively, informative presentation.

 Common Core State Standards

Speaking and Listening

2. Analyze the purpose of information presented in diverse media and formats and evaluate the motives behind its presentation.

3. Delineate a speaker's argument and specific claims, evaluating the soundness of the reasoning and relevance and sufficiency of the evidence and identifying when irrelevant evidence is introduced.

6. Adapt speech to a variety of contexts and tasks, demonstrating command of formal English when indicated or appropriate.

Practice the Skills

Ⓒ Presentation of Knowledge and Ideas Choose a topic you know well, such as how to care for a pet or play a sport. Then, in a group, take turns presenting a speech. Use the chart to focus your presentation.

ACTIVITY: Giving an Oral Presentation

- Identify your topic, purpose, and point of view, or attitude, toward your subject.
- Present information clearly, concisely, and logically. Emphasize main points in a focused way and use relevant evidence.
- Use sound reasoning and well-chosen examples or details.
- Maintain effective eye contact.
- Speak clearly and at an adequate volume.
- Use formal English and avoid mistakes in grammar or pronunciation.

Use an evaluation form like the one shown below as you listen to your classmates' oral presentations.

Evaluating an Oral Presentation

Content
____ Clarity of ideas ____ Interesting topic ____ Logical organization
____ Strong evidence or examples ____Originality

Delivery
____ Enunciated clearly? ____ Varied voice?
____ Good eye contact? ____ Adequate volume?
____ Used appropriate and correct language, including formal English?

Respond to these questions:
In your own words, what was the speaker's purpose? _____
Did the speaker achieve this purpose? _____
What was the speaker's point of view on the topic? _____
Did the speaker present information clearly and logically? _____
Did the speaker consistently use varied evidence to support ideas? ____
Did the speaker consistently use relevant evidence to support ideas? ____
What constructive suggestions for improvement can you offer
the speaker? Consider elements of both the content and the delivery.

_____

Cumulative Review

Common Core
State Standards

RI.8.3, RI.8.4, RI.8.5, RI.8.6, RI.8.8
[For the full wording of the standards, see the standards chart in the front of your textbook.]

I. Reading Informational Text

Directions: *Read the passage. Then, answer each question that follows.*

American history usually celebrates people who are famous for at least one major accomplishment. Sacagawea, a Native American woman born around 1784, did not lead an important social movement. She did not make a great scientific discovery. She did not speak English. In fact, it could be said that Sacagawea played just a small role in the expedition of Lewis and Clark. So why does history continue to honor her memory? According to the journals of Lewis and Clark, the reasons are many.

In late 1804, Lewis and Clark hired a French Canadian fur trader and his young wife Sacagawea to interpret on their expedition west through the Louisiana Territory. They hoped Sacagawea would help them negotiate for supplies when they reached Shoshone lands. Hidatsa warriors had taken Sacagawea from the Shoshone people, when she was only a little girl.

Sacagawea became more than just a translator on the expedition. She helped identify and gather plants and other vegetation for food and medicines. Her calm behavior during one difficult boat crossing saved valuable documents and supplies from being swept away. In addition, Sacagawea's infant son, Jean-Baptiste, provided a cheerful distraction for the <u>weary</u> explorers.

As Lewis and Clark had hoped, Sacagawea helped the explorers purchase needed supplies from the Shoshone people. Sacagawea benefited, too. It turned out that the chief of that Shoshone group was her brother, whom she had not seen since being kidnapped.

Sacagawea's greatest contribution to the success of the expedition, however, may have been the least expected. Many Native Americans in unexplored territories had never seen white men and probably felt threatened by them. Frequently, just the sight of Sacagawea and her baby helped calm their fears and made the members of the expedition seem less fearsome.

The United States honors those who have made significant historical achievements. In 2000, The United States Mint issued a Sacagawea coin. In 2006, the navy named a ship after her. "Finally, after 200 years, people are noticing the contribution she made," says Amy Mossett, a noted scholar of Sacagawea's life.

1. Which *best* describes the **organizational structure** of the passage?

   A. comparison-and-contrast organization
   B. chronological organization
   C. problem-and-solution organization
   D. cause-and-effect organization

2. What **persuasive technique** does the writer use in the first paragraph?

   A. appeal to authority
   B. appeal to emotions
   C. repetition and parallelism
   D. appeal to reason

3. How does the writer use an **appeal to authority** in the passage?

   A. The writer refers to a woman who has studied Sacagawea's life.
   B. The writer describes the reunion between Sacagawea and her brother.
   C. The writer describes how Sacagawea saved valuable documents.
   D. The writer says that Hidatsa warriors had kidnapped Sacagawea.

4. Which phrase *best* describes the author's attitude toward the subject matter?

   A. awestruck
   B. disdainful
   C. appreciative
   D. timid

5. Which word *best* describes the overall **tone** of the passage?

   A. cheerful
   B. serious
   C. casual
   D. friendly

6. What do most of the **details** in the passage describe or explain about Sacagawea?

   A. They describe her childhood.
   B. They describe the honors she received after the Lewis and Clark expedition.
   C. They explain how she was kidnapped from the Shoshone and came to live with the Hidatsa people.
   D. They explain how she assisted Lewis and Clark on their expedition.

7. Which of the following *best* explains why the passage is a **biography** and not an **autobiography?**

   A. It is written in the third person.
   B. Sacagawea is no longer living.
   C. It is written in first person.
   D. It is mainly about one person's life.

8. **Vocabulary in Context** Which word is closest in meaning to the underlined word weary?

   A. excited
   B. adventurous
   C. depressed
   D. tired

 Timed Writing

9. In a well-developed essay, **explain** how the author develops the character of Sacagawea. Use relevant facts, concrete details, quotations, and examples from the text.

 **GO ON**

II. Reading Literary Nonfiction

Directions: *Read the passages. Then, answer each question that follows.*

Common Core State Standards

RI.8.1; RI.8.3, RI.8.5; W.8.2, W.8.2.b, W.8.2.c; L.8.2
[For the full wording of the standards, see the standards chart in the front of your textbook.]

Passage A We were all, horses and men, four days and four nights on the cars coming here from San Antonio and were very tired and very dirty when we arrived . . . Mother stays at a big hotel about a mile from camp. There are nearly thirty thousand troops here now, besides the sailors from the war-ships in the bay. At night the corridors and piazzas are thronged with officers of the army and navy; the older ones fought in the great Civil War, a third of a century ago, and now they are all going to Cuba to war against the Spaniards. Most of them are in blue, but our rough-riders are in brown.

Passage B It was the beginning of the Spanish-American War in the spring of 1898. As Assistant Secretary of the Navy, Roosevelt was stationed in Florida, with the Rough Riders, a volunteer <u>regiment</u> that he had helped organize. The men and their horses had just endured four grueling days of rail travel from San Antonio, Texas, to the camp in Tampa.

   In late June, American troops traveled to Cuba. On July 1, Roosevelt and his Rough Riders fought in the legendary Battle of San Juan Hill. Stories of Roosevelt's fearless leadership following the battle made him a hero in the United States. It was also the start of his political career.

1. Which idea from Passage A is explained in greater detail in Passage B?

   A. travel from San Antonio

   B. mother's visit

   C. troop size

   D. the Rough Riders

2. What is the **organizational structure** of Passage B?

   A. comparison-and-contrast organization

   B. chronological organization

   C. problem-and-solution organization

   D. cause-and-effect organization

3. What is the **main difference** between Passage A and Passage B?

   A. Passage A has a conversational tone, while passage B is factual.

   B. Passage A does not contain any facts, while Passage B contains only facts.

   C. Passage A focuses on Roosevelt's family, while Passage B focuses on his political career.

   D. Passage A does not explain the history of the Spanish-American War, while Passage B does.

III. Writing and Language Conventions

Directions: *Read the passage. Then, answer each question that follows.*

(1) Even if you are the worse cook in the world, you can make scrambled eggs. (2) Crack four eggs, one at a time, in one bowl and then transfer each egg to a different bowl. (3) This ensures that you do not ruin all the eggs if shell gets mixed in or if one egg is bad. (4) Next, add milk, but not too much. (5) Then, break the egg yolks and stir the eggs and milk until they are mixed good. (6) Melt two pats of butter in the pan and pour in the eggs. (7) Heat a large skillet over medium heat. (8) Stir the eggs until they are cooked.

1. Which additional detail could *best* help readers complete this task successfully?

   A. what brand of eggs to use
   B. the reason why eggs go bad
   C. how much milk to use
   D. which size fork to use

2. Which term should the writer probably explain in greater detail?

   A. scrambled eggs
   B. bowl
   C. stir
   D. pats of butter

3. How could the writer revise sentence 1 to correctly use a **superlative adjective?**

   A. Even if you are the worser cook in the world, you can scramble eggs.
   B. Even if you are the worst cook in the world, you can scramble eggs.
   C. Even if you are the most worst cook in the world, you can scramble eggs.
   D. The sentence is correct.

4. What is the best way to revise sentence 5 to fix the **adverb** error?

   A. Then, break the egg yolks well and stir the eggs and milk until they are mixed.
   B. Then, break the egg yolks and stir the eggs and milk until they are mixed well.
   C. Then, break the egg yolks good and stir the eggs and milk until they are mixed.
   D. The sentence is correct.

5. Where should sentence 7 be placed so the passage maintains a **sequential order?**

   A. It should be placed after sentence 1.
   B. It should be placed after sentence 3.
   C. It should be placed after sentence 4.
   D. It should be placed after sentence 5.

6. How should sentence 8 best be revised to add **important** and **useful information?**

   A. Using a spatula, stir the eggs until they are cooked to a creamy consistency.
   B. Stir the mixed eggs until they are cooked.
   C. Using a spatula, stir the eggs until they are hot.
   D. Stir the eggs until they are cooked through and look right.

STOP

Performance Tasks

Directions: *Follow the instructions to complete the tasks below as required by your teacher.*

As you work on each task, incorporate both general academic vocabulary and literary terms you learned in this unit.

Common Core State Standards

RI.8.2, RI.8.4, RI.8.5, RI.8.6, RI.8.8;
SL.8.1, SL.8.5, SL.8.6; L.8.1, L.8.6
[For the full wording of the standards, see the standards chart in the front of your textbook.]

Writing

Task 1: Informational Text [RI.8.5]
Analyze Paragraph Structure

Write an essay in which you analyze the structure of one paragraph from a work of nonfiction in this unit.

- Identify the work you are analyzing, and describe its central idea. Then, identify the paragraph you will discuss and explain why you chose it—what makes this paragraph especially important?

- Explain the key idea expressed in the paragraph and note whether it is implied or directly stated.

- Then, discuss the role each sentence plays in building the key idea. Explain whether each sentence introduces, refines, or develops the idea. If the sentence refines or develops the idea, explain how. For example, consider whether the author adds an example, provides a quotation, or includes another form of evidence.

- Conclude your essay by restating your ideas about the importance of the paragraph within the work as a whole.

Task 2: Informational Text [RI.8.6; L.8.1]
Analyze Author's Point of View

Write an essay in which you analyze the author's point of view in a nonfiction work from this unit.

- Identify the work you have chosen to analyze and explain why you chose it.

- Describe the author's point of view toward the topic. Then, explain how the author's point of view is reflected in the writing. For example, consider any statements of opinion or ways in which the author discusses opposing opinions.

- Analyze the language the author uses. Show how specific words and phrases express the point of view you have identified.

- Describe the author's tone. Give examples of words and phrases that develop that tone, and explain how the tone reflects the author's point of view.

- As you describe the point of view, use adjectives correctly, including their comparative and superlative forms.

Task 3: Informational Text [RI.8.2, RI.8.8]
Evaluate an Argument

Write an evaluation of the argument in a persuasive essay from this unit.

- Explain which work you will analyze and why you chose it. Identify the author's central idea and include a brief summary of the work.

- State whether you think the author's argument is logical, clearly developed, and supported with valid evidence.

- If you find the argument logical and sound, explain why. If you find the argument weak or inadequately supported, explain why.

- Support your evaluation with details from the work.

Speaking and Listening

Task 4: Informational Text [RI.8.4; SL.8.1]
Analyze and Discuss Word Choice

Lead a small group discussion in which you analyze the word choice in a nonfiction work from this unit.

- Prepare for the discussion by choosing and analyzing the work ahead of time. Consider the author's use of specific words and phrases, and note any figurative language, connotations, or technical meanings. Describe how the author's word choices combine to create a specific tone.
- Identify at least three key points you want to cover during the discussion.
- Create handouts, such as lists of words or definitions, to share with your group.
- As you conduct the discussion, refer to your handouts, and invite participants to make suggestions for items to add.

Task 5: Informational Text [RI.8.2; SL.8.5; L.8.6]
Analyze the Development of a Text

With a partner, deliver a presentation in which you analyze the development of the central idea in a nonfiction work from this unit.

- To prepare, choose a work and analyze its central idea and organization. Determine whether the author has used a formal structure, such as cause-and-effect or comparison-and-contrast. Note how supporting ideas relate to the main idea.
- Capture your ideas in a combination of notes for your own use and visuals to share with listeners. Consider such visuals as an idea web, a cause-and-effect chart, or a sequence-of-events chart.
- Introduce the work by explaining the central idea and summarizing the work. Then, present your analysis.

- As you speak, use academic and content-area vocabulary accurately to clarify ideas and maintain a formal tone.

Task 6: Informational Text [RI.8.8; SL.8.6]
Evaluate an Argument

Write and deliver an evaluation of the argument in a persuasive speech from this unit.

- Explain which speech you will analyze and why you chose it. Identify the author's central idea and include a brief summary of the work.
- State whether you think the author's argument is logical, clearly developed, and supported with valid evidence.
- If you find the argument logical and sound, explain why. If you find the argument weak or inadequately supported, explain why.
- Support your evaluation with details from the speech. Identify specific claims the author makes, and note whether his or her reasoning is logical and whether all the evidence he or she uses is relevant.
- As you speak, demonstrate respect for your topic, the academic setting, and your audience by using formal English.

THE BIG ？

How much information is enough?

At the beginning of Unit 3, you wrote a response to the Big Question. Now that you have completed the unit, write a new response. Discuss how your initial ideas have either been changed or reinforced. Cite specific examples from the literature in this unit, from other subject areas, and from your own life to support your ideas. Use Big Question vocabulary words (see p. 461) in your response.

Featured Titles

In this unit, you have read a variety of informational texts, including literary nonfiction. Continue to read on your own. Select works that you enjoy, but challenge yourself to explore new topics, new authors, and works of increasing depth and complexity. The titles suggested below will help you get started.

Informational Text

The Building of Manhattan
by Donald Mackay   EXEMPLAR TEXT ©

This illustrated **nonfiction** account tells the history of how New York City was built, from the subways underground to the skyscrapers that crowd the skyline.

The Story of Columbus
by Peter Chrisp

In 1492, Christopher Columbus opened a new era of European exploration with his voyage to the "new world." Learn about his famous voyages in this **biography.**

Albert Einstein: A Photographic Story of a Life
by Frieda Wishinsky

In this **biography,** the extraordinary life of Albert Einstein is told through words and photographs. From his early struggles as a student to his revolutionary discoveries in physics, this book provides fascinating details.

Cool Stuff and How It Works
by Chris Woodford, Luke Collins, Clint Witchalls, Ben Morgan, and James Flint

Explore the inner workings of modern technological devices like robots and MP3 players through the **essays,** diagrams, photographs, and captions in this richly illustrated book.

Helen Keller: A Photographic Story of a Life
by Leslie Garrett

This **biography** tells the remarkable story of Helen Keller, who lost her sight and hearing at age two. Read how she overcame her disabilities to break out of the isolation of her world.

Discoveries: Exploring the Possibilities

This **essay** collection provides a wide range of information on subjects such as forensic anthropology, stamps, and the Internet.

Literature

Chicago Poems
by Carl Sandburg   EXEMPLAR TEXT ©

In this collection of **poems,** Sandburg focuses his lens with memorable results on the "stormy, husky, brawling" city of Chicago in the early 20th century.

No Promises in the Wind
by Irene Hunt
Berkley, 2002

Set during the Great Depression, this **historical novel** chronicles two brothers' desperate search for food and work. On the road, they experience the harsh reality of miserable economic times.

Preparing to Read Complex Texts

Attentive Reading As you read literary nonfiction on your own, bring your imagination and questions to the text. The questions shown below, and others that you ask as you read, will help you learn and enjoy literary nonfiction even more.

 **Common Core State Standards**

Reading Literature/Informational Text 10. By the end of the year, read and comprehend literature, including stories, dramas, and poems, and literary nonfiction, at the high end of grades 6–8 text complexity band independently and proficiently.

When reading literary nonfiction, ask yourself...

- Who is the author? Why did he or she write the work?
- Is the author writing about a personal experience or a topic he or she has studied? In either case, what are my expectations about the work?
- Are the ideas the author expresses important? Why or why not?
- Did the author live at a different time and place than the present? If so, how does that affect his or her choice of topic and attitude?
- Does the author express beliefs that are very different from mine? If so, how does that affect what I understand and feel about the text?
- Does any one idea seem more important than the others? Why?
- What can I learn from this work?

© **Key Ideas and Details**

- Does the author organize ideas so that I can understand them? If not, what is unclear?
- Is the work interesting right from the start? If so, what has the author done to capture my interest? If not, why?
- Does the author give me a new way of looking at a topic? If so, how? If not, why?
- Is the author an expert on the topic? How do I know?
- Does the author use a variety of evidence that makes sense? If not, what is weak?
- Does the author use words in ways that are both interesting and clear? If so, are there any sections that I enjoy more than others? If not, why?

© **Craft and Structure**

- Does the work seem believable? Why or why not?
- Do I agree or disagree with the author's arguments or ideas? Why or why not?
- Does this work remind me of others I have read? If so, in what ways?
- Does this work make me want to read more about this topic? Does it make me want to explore a related topic? Why or why not?

© **Integration of Ideas**

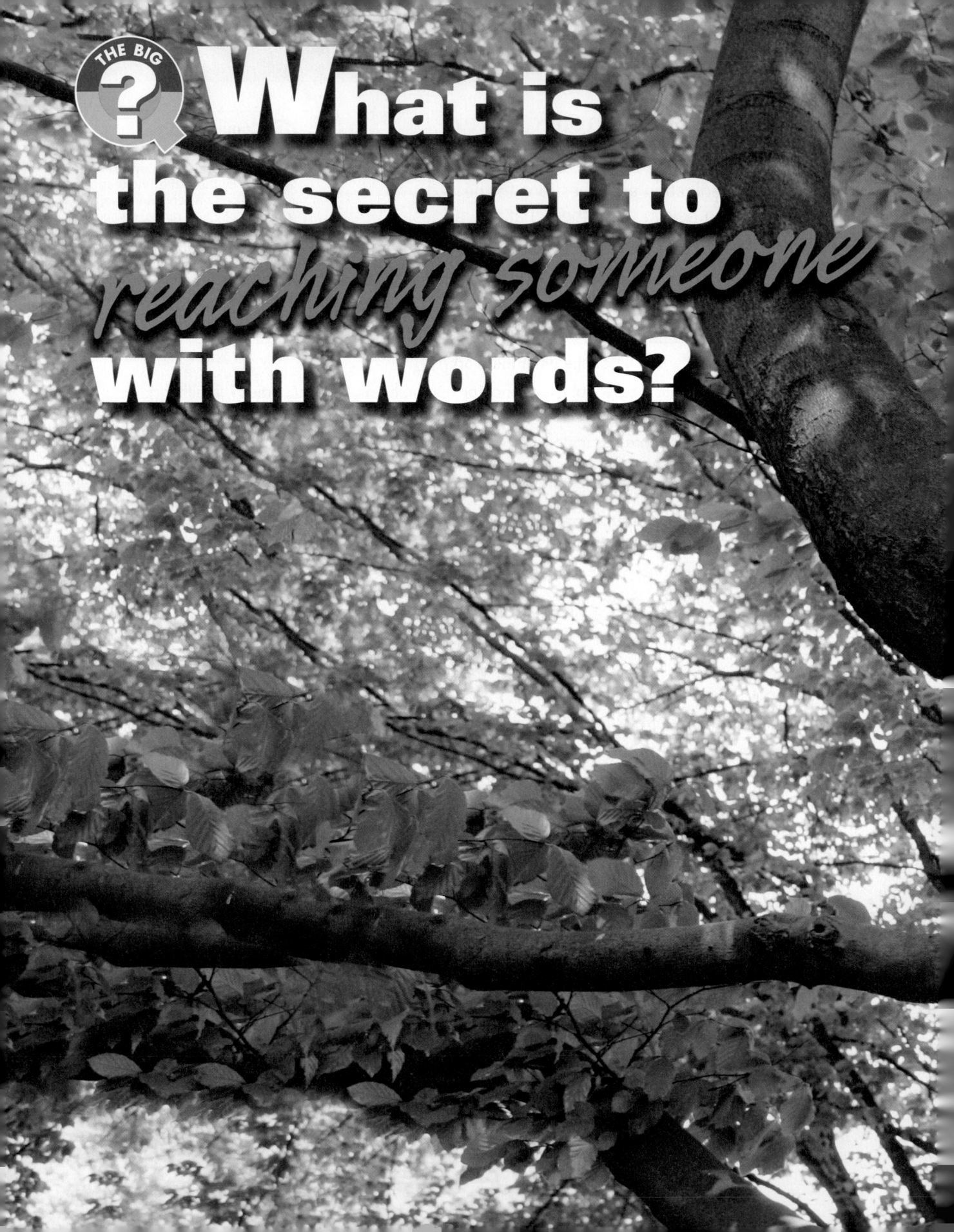

THE BIG ?

What is the secret to *reaching someone* with words?

PHLit
Online!
www.PHLitOnline.com

Hear It!
- Selection summary audio
- Selection audio
- BQ Tunes

See It!
- Author videos
- Big Question video
- Get Connected videos
- Background videos
- More about the authors
- Illustrated vocabulary words
- Vocabulary flashcards

Do It!
- Interactive journals
- Interactive graphic organizers
- Grammar tutorials
- Interactive vocabulary games
- Test practice

THE BIG ? Q What is the secret to reaching someone with words?

Think of how limited our lives would be without words. Words, written or spoken, are the building blocks that make meaningful communication possible. When two people connect, it is often the result of verbal communication—whether it is between child and parent, friend and friend, or writer and reader. This communication takes different forms, such as agreement or disagreement, satisfaction in gaining knowledge, or the experience that occurs when someone reads a powerful, meaningful text.

Writers use different techniques to express ideas. All writers share one common starting point, however. Whether their goal is to inform, persuade, or entertain, writers know that in order to create something with significance they must first reach a reader with words.

Exploring the Big Question

© **Collaboration: One-on-One Discussion** Start thinking about the Big Question by describing a specific example of each of the following situations.

- A news story in the media about a recent historical event
- A situation that allowed you to express your individuality
- An experience that you found difficult to put into words
- A conversation that inspired you to try a new activity or approach
- A text message, e-mail, or blog entry that made you laugh
- A story, poem, or article that changed your perspective

Discuss with a partner how each situation reveals a different aspect of the human desire to communicate. Use the Big Question vocabulary in your discussion.

Connecting to the Literature Each reading in this unit will give you additional insight into the Big Question.

PHLit Online!
www.PHLitOnline.com
- Big Question video
- Illustrated vocabulary words
- Interactive vocabulary games
- BQ Tunes

Learning Big Question Vocabulary

**Common Core
State Standards**

Speaking and Listening
1. Engage effectively in a range of collaborative discussions with diverse partners on *grade 8 topics, texts, and issues,* building on others' ideas and expressing their own clearly.

Language
6. Acquire and use accurately grade-appropriate general academic and domain-specific words and phrases; gather vocabulary knowledge when considering a word or phrase important to comprehension or expression.

Acquire and Use Academic Vocabulary Academic vocabulary is the language you encounter in textbooks and on standardized tests. Review the definitions of these academic vocabulary words.

benefit (ben´ ə fit) *n.* advantage; positive result

connection (kə nek´ shən) *n.* link; tie; relationship

cultural (kul´ chər əl) *adj.* relating to the customs and beliefs of a group

individuality (in´ də vij´ o͞o al´ə tē) *n.* characteristics that set a person or thing apart from others

inform (in fôrm´) *v.* tell; give information or knowledge

relevant (rel´ ə vənt) *adj.* connected to the topic being discussed

significance (sig nif´ ə kəns) *n.* importance

valid (val´ id) *adj.* true; backed by evidence

Use these words as you complete Big Question activities in this unit that involve reading, writing, speaking, and listening.

Gather Vocabulary Knowledge Additional Big Question words are listed below. Categorize the words by deciding whether you know each one well, know it a little bit, or do not know it at all.

experience	meaningful	misunderstood
express	media	sensory
feedback		

Then, do the following:

1. Write the definitions of the words you know.

2. Using a print or online dictionary, look up the meaning of each word you do not know. Then, write the meaning.

3. Confirm the meaning and pronunciation of each word you think you know. Revise your definition if necessary.

4. Use as many words as possible in a paragraph about the obstacles and difficulties you might encounter when trying to reach someone with words.

Elements of Poetry

Poetry is the most musical of literary forms.

The **structure** of a poem is the way the words, lines, and groups of lines are arranged.

Lines Most poetry is arranged in **lines,** or groupings of words. A line may not be a complete sentence. A poet may *break*, or end, a line to emphasize a word or an idea, or to create a pattern of rhythm or rhyme.

Stanzas Lines may be grouped in **stanzas**—logical sections of ideas, like paragraphs in an essay. A two-line stanza is a **couplet,** three lines is a **tercet,** four lines is a **quatrain.**

Rhyme The **rhyme scheme** is the pattern of rhymes at the ends of lines. Each new rhyme is assigned a letter of the alphabet, as shown below.

The path of least resistance,	**a**
Is short, but it's boring.	**b**
Choose the tougher distance	**a**
For soaring.	**b**

Meter The pattern of stressed and unstressed syllables in a poem is the **meter.** Each unit of stressed and unstressed syllables in a poem is called a **foot.**

The example below shows how poetry can be marked to show the meter. An accent (′) marks each stressed syllable. A horseshoe symbol (˘) marks each unstressed syllable. Vertical lines (|) divide each line into feet.

Sómebŏdỹ,	Nóbŏdỹ—
Ă fáce	ĭš sŏ neár

The chart below shows a fuller analysis of the meter and other structural elements of a poem.

from "The Village Blacksmith," Henry Wadsworth Longfellow	
˘ ′ ˘ ′ ˘ ′ ˘ ′ His hair | is crisp, | and black, | and long, ˘ ′ ˘ ′ ˘ ′ His face | is like | the tan; ˘ ′ ˘ ′ ˘ ′ ˘ ′ His brow | is wet | with hon | est sweat, ˘ ′ ˘ ′ ˘ ′ He earns | whate'er | he can, ˘ ′ ˘ ′ ˘ ′ ˘ ′ And looks | the whole | world in | the face, ˘ ˘ ′ ˘ ˘ ′ ˘ ′ For he owes | not an | y man.	This stanza has six lines. The poet begins each line with a capital letter. The regular beat is like the rhythmic pounding of a hammer. The second, fourth, and sixth lines rhyme. This *abcbdb* rhyme scheme reinforces the sense of pounding and emphasizes the word *man* at the end of the stanza. Internal rhyme calls attention to the vivid image. The change in meter at the end of the stanza slows readers down so that they think about the last line.

Poetic Forms A poem's form is usually defined by its purpose and characteristics. **Formal verse** follows fixed, traditional patterns that may include a specific rhyme scheme, meter, line length, or stanza structure. **Free verse** uses poetic language, but does not follow a fixed pattern. Three main categories of poetry are lyric, narrative, and dramatic. Within these categories are forms of poetry that have specific structures and features.

Lyric poetry expresses the thoughts and feelings of a single speaker, often in very musical verse. The chart below describes some forms of lyric poetry.

Narrative poetry tells a story. Most narrative poetry, including **ballads** and **epic poetry,** follows a formal structure with set stanzas, strong rhythms, and a regular rhyme scheme.

Dramatic poetry presents a drama in verse. The action is told through the words the characters speak.

Speaker The **speaker** is the person or character who communicates the words of the poem. Do not assume that the voice in the poem is the poet's, even when the poem is written in the first person. The poet creates the character of the speaker, just as a songwriter may invent a character to express his or her feelings and ideas in a song.

Imagery Poets create word pictures for readers by using **imagery,** or vivid language that appeals to the five senses. Imagery can enhance the meaning of a poem by providing a context or setting a scene. Imagery also helps create a poem's emotional impact.

 Common Core State Standards

RL.8.4, RL.8.5

[For the full wording of the standards, see the standards chart in the front of your textbook.]

Forms of Lyric Poetry

Sonnet "Harriet Beecher Stowe," p. 735	A sonnet is a fourteen-line poem of praise with a specific rhyme scheme. A **Petrarchan sonnet** follows a rhyme scheme of abba/abba/cde/cde. A **Shakespearean sonnet** has a rhyme scheme of abab/cdcd/efef/gg.
Ode "Ode to Enchanted Light," p. 685	An ode is a formal poem of honor or celebration. Odes often have a regular meter and end rhyme, but the number and length of their lines and stanzas can vary.
Elegy "O Captain, My Captain," p. 777	An elegy is a formal poem reflecting on death or another serious theme. The structure, meter, and rhyme scheme of elegies can vary considerably.
Haiku	A haiku is a short, unrhymed poem, often about nature. It has one three-line stanza that follows a 5-7-5 syllabic pattern.

Analyzing Poetic Language

Poets create meaning through their imaginative use of language.

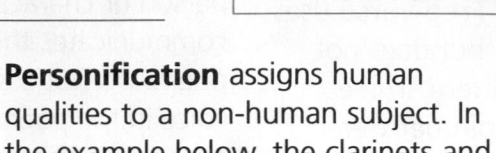
Common Core
State Standards

Reading Literature 4. Determine the meaning of words and phrases as they are used in a text, including figurative and connotative meanings; analyze the impact of specific word choices on meaning and tone, including analogies or allusions to other texts.

In poetry, writers communicate more than the literal meanings of their words. Through figurative language, sound devices, and other literary techniques, they create vivid images and express unique ideas. Understanding the ways a poet uses language can help you fully grasp the meaning of a poem.

Figurative Language Words and phrases have **literal** meanings—the meanings you find in a dictionary. **Figurative language** describes and compares things in ways that are not meant to be taken literally. By using the following types of figurative language, a poet can put intense focus on a particular quality and present it in a rich and unique way.

Similes and metaphors highlight a shared quality of two things that are otherwise different.

- A **simile** uses the word *like* or *as* to compare two things: *The icy water hurt like a thousand bee stings.*
- A **metaphor** compares by describing one thing as if it were another: *The icy water was a thousand stinging bees.*
- An **extended metaphor** carries a metaphor throughout part or all of a poem.

Personification assigns human qualities to a non-human subject. In the example below, the clarinets and drums are personified.

> **Example:**
> The clarinets sang merrily,
> While the drums grumbled and complained.

An **analogy** explains, clarifies, or illustrates by drawing comparisons.

In the example below, the poet uses the analogy of deleted computer files to clarify the idea that memories exist someplace but are inaccessible.

> Age betrayed her daily now.
> Memories gone, but where?
> Somewhere inaccessible,
> The way a computer file
> Deleted accidentally,
> Is there
> But not there.

Allusions are direct or implied references to people, places, events, literary works, or artworks, as in the following example:

> In desperate times be brave and bold
> Your Cinderella story is not yet told.

Sound Devices

The sounds of words contribute to the musical quality of a poem. Sounds can also strengthen meaning by emphasizing significant words and by connecting ideas. Look for these sound devices as you read poetry.

Alliteration is the repetition of initial consonant sounds:

- He climbs the <u>h</u>ill and <u>h</u>uffs and <u>h</u>eaves.

The repeated *h* sound strengthens the impression of labored breathing.

Consonance is the repetition of consonant sounds in stressed syllables with different vowel sounds:

- Gulls gracefully pa<u>ss</u> acro<u>ss</u> the sky.

The repeated *s* sound creates a sense of graceful movement from word to word.

Assonance is the repetition of vowel sounds in stressed syllables that do not rhyme:

- C<u>a</u>lling and squ<u>aw</u>king like crows, they f<u>ou</u>ght.

The repetition of the *aw* sound reinforces the sense of the simile.

Repetition is the repeated use of a word or phrase:

- <u>Time</u> and <u>time</u> again I lose track of <u>time</u>.

The repetition emphasizes a key idea.

Onomatopoeia is the use of words that imitate sounds:

- The wind <u>whooshed</u> in and slammed the door with a <u>bang</u>.

The words *whooshed* and *bang* appeal to the sense of sound.

Connotations and Tone

A word's **connotations** are the ideas associated with that word beyond its **denotation,** or literal definition. Connotations can be positive or negative. The chart below shows how the word *diva* can have both negative and positive connotations.

The actress is a *diva.*	
Denotation: successful female performer	
Negative	**Positive**
arrogance, ego, bossiness	power, confidence, talent
Context: the actress has a temper tantrum	**Context:** the actress gives a great performance

Tone is the attitude the writer projects in a poem. Word choice and other poetic elements work together to convey the tone of a poem.

Combination of Elements	Tone Created
Word choices: *exquisite, rare, inspire* **Connotations:** positive **Meter:** musical	• respectful • admiring
Word choices: *isolated, loneliness* **Connotations:** negative **Meter:** slow beat	• sorrowful • pitying
Word choices: *helter-skelter, whiz* **Connotations:** positive/amusing **Meter:** bouncy beat	• carefree • playful

Close Read: Analyzing the Impact of Word Choice

To understand the meaning of a poem, consider the impact of the author's choice of words and phrases.

Word choice affects every element of a poem. For example, a poet following a formal structure might choose a particular word not only because it has the intended denotation and connotation, but also because it has the right number of syllables. Poets also select words for their sounds. They choose vocabulary that reveals the personality of the speaker in a poem and use figurative language to enhance meaning. All the word choices work together to build the overall effect the poet wants to achieve.

Use the questions in the following chart to guide you as you analyze the overall impact of word choice on the meaning of a poem.

Clues to Word Choice Analysis

Structure	Poetic Language	Sound Devices
• How does the poem look on the page?	• How does imagery appeal to the five senses?	• What sounds stand out when you read the poem aloud?
• Are the lines divided into stanzas?	• Does the poem contain figurative language, such as similes, metaphors, and personification?	• Where does the poet use rhyme? Is each rhyme exact or near?
• Is there a rhyme scheme?		• How does meter affect the sound of the poem?
• Is there a regular metrical rhythm?	• Are there any allusions to other texts or ideas?	
• Is it formal or free verse?		• Are there examples of alliteration, assonance, consonance, repetition, or onomatopoeia?

Speaker	Connotation	Tone
• Who is the speaker?	• What are the connotations of key words?	• What adjective would you use to describe the tone of the poem?
• What do the word choices and imagery tell you about the speaker's thoughts and feelings?	• Are there any words that have strong positive or negative connotations?	• Which elements help create that tone?

Model

About the Text Nikki Giovanni is an African American poet with a life-long commitment to equality and civil rights. Like the speaker in the poem below, Giovanni spent summers at her grandparents' home in Tennessee. Growing up in the 1950s, Giovanni experienced firsthand the kind of discrimination described in the poem.

"A Poem for My Librarian, Mrs. Long"

(You never know what troubled little girl needs a book.)

by Nikki Giovanni

At a time when there was no tv before 3:00 P.M.
And on Sunday none until 5:00
We sat on front porches watching
The jfg sign go on and off greeting
5 The neighbors, discussing the political
Situation congratulating the preacher
On his sermon

There was always radio which brought us
Song from wlac in nashville and what we would now call
10 Easy listening or smooth jazz but when I listened
Late at night with my portable (that I was so proud of)
Tucked under my pillow
I heard nat king cole and matt dennis, june christy and ella fitzgerald
And sometimes sarah vaughan sing black coffee
15 Which I now drink
It was just called music

There was a bookstore uptown on gay street
Which I visited and inhaled that wonderful odor
Of new books
20 Even today I read hardcover as a preference paperback only
As a last resort

And up the hill on vine street
(The main black corridor) sat our carnegie library
Mrs. Long always glad to see you
25 The stereoscope always ready to show you faraway

Structure This lyric poem is written in free verse. It has no consistent or formal structural elements.

Poetic Language The speaker refers to black and white recording artists. This allusion stresses her assumption of equality.

Poetic Language The imagery in these lines emphasizes the speaker's passion for books.

Speaker The "black corridor" refers to the segregation of the time. This reality contrasts with the earlier "integrated" allusions to singers.

EXEMPLAR TEXT

Model continued

Structure A line break separates the word *southern* from *Whites*, subtly suggesting that the desire to humiliate was not limited to southern whites.

Sound Devices In these lines, alliteration (*but, brought, books, back; held, heart, happily, house*) and assonance (*held, them, chest*) create a musicality that reflects the speaker's enthusiastic appreciation of books.

Tone The poem recognizes harsh realities, such as discrimination, but the overall tone is optimistic and hopeful. Spring suggests renewal and the possibility of a better future.

Places to dream about

Mrs. Long asking what are you looking for today
When I wanted *Leaves of Grass* or alfred north whitehead
She would go to the big library uptown and I now know
30 Hat in hand to ask to borrow so that I might borrow
Probably they said something humiliating since southern
Whites like to humiliate southern blacks

But she nonetheless brought the books
Back and I held them to my chest
35 Close to my heart
And happily skipped back to grandmother's house
Where I would sit on the front porch
In a gray glider and dream of the world
Far away

40 I love the world where I was
I was safe and warm and grandmother gave me neck kisses
When I was on my way to bed

But there was a world
Somewhere
45 Out there
And Mrs. Long opened that wardrobe
But no lions or witches scared me
I went through
Knowing there would be
Spring

Independent Practice

About the Texts Jacqueline Woodson is an African American poet and novelist whose works reflect her interest in writing for and about young people. Although she takes on many different points of view in her writing, she says her writing is always "emotionally autobiographical."

The speaker of both poems is Lonnie Collins Motion, who lives in Brooklyn, New York, with his foster mother, Miss Edna.

"Describe Somebody" by Jacqueline Woodson

Today in class Ms. Marcus said
Take out your poetry notebooks and describe somebody.
Think carefully, Ms. Marcus said.
You're gonna read it to the class.
5 I wrote, Ms. Marcus is tall and a little bit skinny.
Then I put my pen in my mouth and stared down
at the words.
Then I crossed them out and wrote
Ms. Marcus's hair is long and brown.
10 Shiny.
When she smiles it makes you feel all good inside.
I stopped writing and looked around the room.
Angel was staring out the window.
Eric and Lamont were having a pen fight.
15 They don't care about poetry.
Stupid words, Eric says.
Lots and lots of stupid words.
Eric is tall and a little bit mean.
Lamont's just regular.
20 Angel's kinda chubby. He's got light brown hair.
Sometimes we all hang out,
play a little ball or something. Angel's real good
at science stuff. Once he made a volcano
for science fair and the stuff that came out of it
25 looked like real lava. Lamont can
draw superheroes real good. Eric—nobody
at school really knows this but
he can sing. Once, Miss Edna took me
to a different church than the one

Speaker What details in the opening lines help you decide who the speaker is?

Connotation What are other words the speaker could have used to convey a more positive impression?

Structure Describe the structure of this poem.

Sound Devices How does alliteration enhance the image in this line?

Practice continued

Poetic Language
What type of comparison does the speaker make here? What is the effect of this comparison?

Tone How would you describe the speaker's tone in the poem's final lines?

30 we usually go to on Sunday.
    I was surprised to see Eric up there
    with a choir robe on. He gave me a mean look
    like I'd better not
    say nothing about him and his dark green robe with
35 gold around the neck.
    After the preacher preached
    Eric sang a song with nobody else in the choir singing.
    Miss Edna started dabbing at her eyes
    whispering *Yes, Lord.*
40 Eric's voice was like something
    that didn't seem like it should belong
    to Eric.
    Seemed like it should be coming out of an angel.

    Now I gotta write a whole new poem
45 'cause Eric would be real mad if I told the class
    about his angel voice.

"Almost Summer Sky" by Jacqueline Woodson

It was the trees first, Rodney[1] tells me.
It's raining out. But the rain is light and warm.
And the sky's not all close to us like it gets
sometimes. It's way up there with
5 some blue showing through.
Late spring sky, Ms. Marcus says. *Almost summer sky.*
And when she said that, I said
Hey Ms. Marcus, that's a good title
for a poem, right?
10 *You have a poet's heart, Lonnie.*
That's what Ms. Marcus said to me.
I have a poet's heart.
That's good. A good thing to have.
And I'm the one who has it.

15 Now Rodney puts his arm around my shoulder
We keep walking. There's a park
eight blocks from Miss Edna's house
That's where we're going.
Me and Rodney to the park.
20 Rain coming down warm
Rodney with his arm around my shoulder
Makes me think of Todd and his pigeons
how big his smile gets when they fly.

The trees upstate ain't like other trees you seen, Lonnie
25 Rodney squints up at the sky, shakes his head
smiles.
No, upstate they got maple and catalpa and scotch pine,[2]
all kinds of trees just standing.
Hundred-year-old trees big as three men.

30 *When you go home this weekend,* Ms. Marcus said.
Write about a perfect moment.

1. **Rodney** one of Miss Edna's sons.
2. **catalpa** (kə tal′ pə) tree with heart-shaped leaves; **scotch pine** tree with yellow wood, grown for timber.

Poetic Language
How does the imagery in the opening lines of the poem establish a contrast?

Sound Devices Why might the speaker think these words would be a good title for a poem?

Speaker Why do you think Lonnie thinks a poet's heart is a good thing to have?

Speaker How does Rodney's point of view compare and contrast with Lonnie's point of view?

Poetic Language What type of comparison is used in line 29? What is the effect of this comparison?

Practice continued

Yeah, Little Brother, Rodney says.
You don't know about shade till you lived upstate.
Everybody should do it—even if it's just for a little while.

35 Way off, I can see the park—blue-gray sky
touching the tops of trees.

I had to live there awhile, Rodney said.
Just to be with all that green, you know?
I nod, even though I don't.
40 I can't even imagine moving away from here,
from Rodney's arm around my shoulder,
from Miss Edna's Sunday cooking,
from Lily[3] in her pretty dresses and great
big smile when she sees me.

45 Can't imagine moving away

From
Home.

You know what I love about trees, Rodney says.
It's like . . . It's like their leaves are hands
reaching
50 *out to you. Saying Come on over here, Brother.*
Let me just . . . Let me just . . .
Rodney looks down at me and grins.
Let me just give you some shade for a while.

---

3. Lily Lonnie's sister, who lives in a different foster home.

Connotation What are the connotations of the word *green* in this stanza?

Structure What idea does the poet convey by breaking these lines in this way?

Poetic Language What is the effect of the figurative language in the closing lines of the poem?

from Describe Somebody • Almost Summer Sky

1. Key Ideas and Details (a) What does the speaker know about Eric that others do not? **(b) Infer:** Why would Eric be mad if the class knew this information?

2. Key Ideas and Details
(a) Speculate: In "Almost Summer Sky," what is Rodney's perfect moment? **(b)** What do you think Lonnie's perfect moment might be? **(c) Draw Conclusions:** How are both boys observant in the way that poets are?

3. Craft and Structure (a) What tells you these poems are written in **free verse? (b)** How is the free-verse structure well suited to convey the **speaker** of these poems?

4. Craft and Structure (a) Use a chart like the one shown to analyze the figurative language in the poems.

	Ideas Compared	Ideas Conveyed
"Describe Somebody," lines 40–43		
"Almost Summer Sky," lines 49–53		

(b) Collaborate: In a group, use the chart to guide a discussion about the use of poetic language in these poems.

5. Integration of Knowledge and Ideas Compare and Contrast: Are the tones of the two poems more similar or more different? Why?

6. Integration of Knowledge and Ideas Read the following poem. Notice that it tells the same story as "Describe Somebody." Compare and contrast the two poems. Consider the structure, speaker, word choice, and tone of each poem.

Poem to Describe
I look around and start to write
About the guys: their hair, their height
Describing them I start to see
They're not so bad. They're just like me
There's something they each care about
Like me, they each have fears and doubts
And passions they don't want to share.
They don't let on how much they care.
Eric wouldn't let me tell
A poem that says he sings so well.
The guys have never heard him sing.
Too bad—it's an angelic thing.

Leveled Texts

Build your skills and improve your comprehension of poetry with texts of increasing complexity.

Read **Poetry Collection 1** to discover how poets use their imaginations to create vivid descriptions.

Read **Poetry Collection 2** to see how writers use poetry to express their views of the world.

Common Core State Standards

Meet these standards with either **Poetry Collection 1** (p. 654) or **Poetry Collection 2** (p. 663).

Reading Literature
4. Determine the meaning of words and phrases as they are used in a text, including figurative and connotative meanings; analyze the impact of specific word choices on meaning and tone, including analogies or allusions to other texts. *(Literary Analysis: Spiral Review)*

Writing
4. Produce clear and coherent writing in which the development, organization, and style are appropriate to task, purpose, and audience. *(Writing: Poem)*

Speaking and Listening
6. Adapt speech to a variety of contexts and tasks, demonstrating command of formal English when indicated or appropriate. *(Speaking and Listening: Poetry Recitation)*

Language
4.a. Use context (e.g., the overall meaning of a sentence or paragraph; a word's position or function in a sentence) as a clue to the meaning of a word or phrase. *(Reading Skill: Using Context)*

4.b. Use common, grade-appropriate Greek or Latin affixes and roots as clues to the meaning of a word (e.g., *precede, recede, secede*). *(Vocabulary: Word Study)*

5.b. Use the relationship between particular words to better understand each of the words. *(Reading Skill: Using Context)*

Reading Skill: Using Context

The **context** of a word is the information in the words that surround it. Before you read poetry, **preview the lines to identify unfamiliar words.** As you read, look for these types of context clues to help determine a meaning for words you do not know.

- **synonym/definition/restatement:** words that mean the same as the unfamiliar word
- **antonym/contrast:** words that are opposite in meaning
- **comparison:** words that show a connection or relationship
- **explanation/example:** words that give more information
- **sentence role:** words that show how the word functions

Using the Strategy: Context Clues Chart

Use this **context clues chart** to help you determine a word's meaning.

With her hair all *disheveled* / Looking like she had just awoken	
Explanation	Looking like she had just awoken
Sentence Role	describes hair

Meaning: Disheveled probably means *messy*, like hair looks after sleeping

Literary Analysis: Sound Devices

Sound devices create musical effects that appeal to the ear. Poets use these techniques to achieve specific purposes and to convey the mood, tone, and meaning of a poem. Common sound devices include the following:

- **alliteration:** repetition of initial consonant sounds—*we won*
- **onomatopoeia:** words that imitate sounds—*buzz* or *hiss*
- **rhyme:** repetition of sounds at ends of words—*spring fling.* Rhymes occurring at the ends of two or more lines are called *external rhyme* or *end rhyme. Internal rhyme* occurs within a single line, as in "The rain in Spain stays mainly in the plain."
- **Rhyme scheme:** the pattern of end rhyme in a poem, described by assigning each rhyme a letter (*a, b, c, d,* etc.)
- **meter:** a poem's rhythm—the strong and weak stresses, as well as pauses, that we give words and syllables when we read

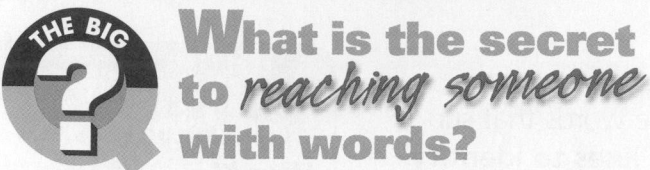

What is the secret to *reaching someone* with words?

Writing About the Big Question

In the poems in Collection 1, poets go beyond relying only on the meaning of words to communicate. They choose words for their sound quality and for the moods the words inspire. Use these sentence starters to develop your ideas about the Big Question.

I (notice/do not notice) the **sensory** effect of words like swoosh, *smush, scrunch, crunch, munch,* and *splash.* Some words I like for their sounds are _____ and _____ because _____.

While You Read Look for specific words that grab your attention and help build a connection between you and the poem.

Vocabulary

Read each word and its definition. Decide whether you know the word well, know it a little bit, or do not know it at all. After you read, see how your knowledge of each word has increased.

- **flatterer** (flat´ ər ər) *n.* one who praises insincerely to win approval (p. 655) *I do not take Liz's compliments seriously because she is a <u>flatterer</u>.* *flatter v. flattery n. flatteringly adv.*

- **scampering** (skam´ pər iŋ) *v.* running quickly (p. 657) *The scared rabbit went <u>scampering</u> away.* *scamper v.*

- **reeds** (rēdz) *n.* tall slender grasses that grow in wetland areas (p. 657) *A duck hid in a clump of marsh <u>reeds</u>.* *reedy adj.*

- **immensity** (i men´ sə tē) *n.* vastness; hugeness (p. 658) *The <u>immensity</u> of the universe makes me feel small and insignificant.* *immense adj. immensely adv.*

- **rapture** (rap´ chər) *n.* ecstasy (p. 658) *Athletes dream of Olympic gold with <u>rapture</u>.* *rapturous adj. rapturously adv.*

Word Study

The **Latin prefix im-** means "not." Combined with the root *mensus* meaning "measured," **immensity** describes something you cannot measure.

Eleanor Farjeon

(1881–1965)

"Cat!" (page 654)

Eleanor Farjeon spent much of her childhood reading fantasy stories in the attic of her family's house in London, England. She also enjoyed playing games of make-believe with her little brother. When she grew up, she drew on memories of her childhood to inspire dozens of books of poetry and stories for children and young adults. Farjeon's 1931 poem "Morning Has Broken" became a huge hit when it was set to music by pop singer Cat Stevens forty years later.

Walter de la Mare

(1873–1956)

"Silver" (page 657)

The British poet and novelist Walter de la Mare loved the magical world of imagination. Yet, for eighteen years, he worked at an ordinary job as a bookkeeper for an oil company. He wrote during his lunch hour. Every night at bedtime, he read one of his new poems to his four children. In 1908, the British government gave him a grant that allowed him to retire at age thirty-five and write full-time for the rest of his life.

Georgia Douglas Johnson

(1886–1966)

"Your World" (page 658)

Georgia Douglas Johnson was born in Atlanta, Georgia, and lived in Washington, D.C., as an adult. She used her love of music and words to create poems, stories, and plays, and also had a career as a newspaper columnist. One of the first well-known African American women writers, Johnson became part of the Harlem Renaissance. She hosted weekly conversations among African American writers at her home in Washington.

CAT!

Eleanor Farjeon

▲ **Critical Viewing** Which of these two drawings most resembles the cat described in the poem? Explain your choice. **[Connect]**

Cat!
Scat!
After her, after her,
Sleeky flatterer,
5   Spitfire chatterer,
Scatter her, scatter her
         Off her mat!
         Wuff!
         Wuff!
10   Treat her rough!
Git her, git her,
Whiskery spitter!
Catch her, catch her,
Green-eyed scratcher!
15   Slathery
         Slithery
         Hisser,
         Don't miss her!
Run till you're dithery,¹
20   Hithery
         Thithery²
         Pftts! pftts!
         How she spits!
         Spitch! Spatch!
25   Can't she scratch!
Scritching the bark
Of the sycamore tree,
She's reached her ark
And's hissing at me
30   *Pftts! pftts!*
         Wuff! wuff!
            Scat,
            Cat!
            That's
35   *That!*

Vocabulary
flatterer (flat´ ər ər) *n.*
one who praises
insincerely to win
approval

Context
Which words in lines
10–14 provide a syn-
onym that helps you
determine the meaning
of *git*?

Sound Devices
Find two made-up
words that imitate cat
sounds. How do they
help you imagine the
poem's action?

1. **dithery** (dith´ rē) *adj.* nervous and confused; in a dither.
2. **Hithery/Thithery** made-up words based on *hither* and *thither*, which mean "here"
   and "there."

A Summer Night on the Beach, Edvard Munch, ©2003 The Munch Museum/The Munch-Ellingsen Group/
Artists Rights Society (ARS), New York/ADAGP, Paris.

SILVER
Walter de la Mare

Slowly, silently, now the moon
Walks the night in her silver shoon;[1]
This way, and that, she peers, and sees
Silver fruit upon silver trees;
5   One by one the casements[2] catch
Her beams beneath the silvery thatch;[3]
Couched in his kennel, like a log,
With paws of silver sleeps the dog;
From their shadowy coat the white breasts peep
10 Of doves in a silver-feathered sleep;
A harvest mouse goes scampering by,
With silver claws, and silver eye;
And moveless fish in the water gleam,
By silver reeds in a silver stream.

---

1. **shoon** (sho͞on) *n.* old-fashioned word for "shoes."
2. **casements** (kās′ mənts) *n.* windows that open out like doors.
3. **thatch** (thach) *n.* roof made of straw or other plant material.

◀ **Critical Viewing**
How does this painting capture the mood
and images of the poem? **[Connect]**

Sound Devices
Identify examples of
alliteration in lines 1–5.

Vocabulary
scampering (skam′ pər
iŋ) *v.* running quickly
reeds (rēdz) *n.* tall
slender grasses that
grow in wetland areas

© **Spiral Review**
Connotation Iden-
tify the connotations
of the word "peep"
in line 9. How do the
word's connotations
contribute to the
poem's mood?

Your World

GEORGIA DOUGLAS JOHNSON

Your world is as big as you make it.
I know, for I used to abide
In the narrowest nest in a corner,
My wings pressing close to my side.

5   But I sighted the distant horizon
Where the sky line encircled the sea
And I throbbed with a burning desire
To travel this immensity.

I battered the cordons[1] around me
10 And cradled my wings on the breeze
Then soared to the uttermost reaches
With rapture, with power, with ease!

---

1. **cordons** (kôr´ dənz) *n.* lines or cords that restrict free movement.

Vocabulary
immensity (i men´ sə tē)
n. vastness; hugeness

rapture (rap´ chər)
n. ecstasy

Critical Thinking

Cite textual evidence to support your responses.

1. **Key Ideas and Details (a) Interpret:** Why is the cat running in "Cat!"? **(b) Infer:** How does the poem's speaker feel about the cat?

2. **Key Ideas and Details (a)** What "walks the night" in "Silver"? **(b) Analyze Causes and Effects:** What effects does this "walk" have on everyday objects? **(c) Generalize:** What mood does the poet create as he describes these effects?

3. **Key Ideas and Details (a)** Where does the speaker of "Your World" say that she used to live? **(b) Restate:** What was her "burning desire"? **(c) Interpret:** How did she reach her goal?

4. **Integration of Knowledge and Ideas (a)** What sounds and rhythms do these poets use to connect with readers? **(b)** How do these devices contribute to the overall effect of the poems? *[Connect to the Big Question: What is the secret to reaching someone with words?]*

Reading Skill: Context

1. Explain how **context** helps you determine the meaning of *scritching* (line 26) in "Cat!"

2. What kind of context clues help you clarify the meaning of *abide* (line 2) in "Your World"? Explain.

Literary Analysis: Sound Devices

3. **Craft and Structure** Complete the chart with examples of **sound devices.** Not all sound devices are used in each poem.

	Cat!	Silver	Your World
alliteration			
onomatopoeia			
rhyme (internal/external)			
meter (rhythmic patterns)			

4. **Craft and Structure** Explain how at least one of the sound devices listed above contributes to the mood, tone, and meaning of a poem.

Vocabulary

Acquisition and Use In each group, identify the word that does not belong. Explain how its meaning differs from those of the other words.

1. flatterer, praiser, complainer
2. sleeping, dozing, scampering
3. silence, immensity, hugeness
4. rapture, misery, unhappiness
5. landscape, horizon, scenery
6. grasses, roses, reeds

Word Study Use the context of the sentences and what you know about the **Latin prefix im-** to explain each answer.

1. Would you believe someone who told an *improbable* story?

2. Is it safe to use medicines that are *impure*?

Word Study

The **Latin prefix im-** means "not."

Apply It Explain how the prefix im- contributes to the meanings of these words. Consult a dictionary if necessary.

immoderate
impossible
immaterial

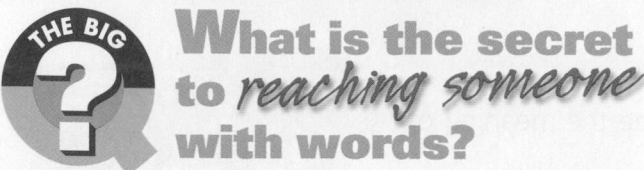

What is the secret to *reaching someone* with words?

Writing About the Big Question

The writers in Collection 2 take advantage of the musical quality of poetry to communicate with readers. They use strong rhythms to convey feelings about their world. Use this sentence starter to develop your ideas about the Big Question.

> Words set to a beat, whether poetry or song lyrics, can create a memorable **experience** for a listener because _____.

While You Read Look for lines in the poetry in which the sounds and rhythms help communicate the poets' ideas.

Vocabulary

Read each word and its definition. Decide whether you know the word well, know it a little bit, or do not know it at all. After you read, see how your knowledge of each word has increased.

- **resounding** (rē zound´ iŋ) *adj.* sounding loudly (p. 663) *His voice echoed, <u>resounding</u> in the empty hall.* resound *v.* resoundingly *adv.* sound *n.*

- **strife** (strīf) *n.* conflict (p. 665) *<u>Strife</u> between the two groups led to war.* strive *v.*

- **modes** (mōdz) *n.* ways of doing or behaving (p. 665) *In a big city, you can choose from many different <u>modes</u> of transportation.* modal *adj.* modality *n.*

- **spite** (spīt) *n.* nastiness (p. 665) *His angry, hateful words were spoken out of <u>spite</u>.* spiteful *adj.* spitefulness *n.* spitefully *adv.*

- **singularity** (siŋ´ gyə ler´ ə tē) *n.* unique or unusual quality (p. 666) *The cricket's chirp has an unmistakable <u>singularity</u>.* singular *adj.* singularly *adv.* single *adj.*

- **imprint** (im´ print) *v.* make a lasting mark (p. 666) *The star will <u>imprint</u> his hands in the wet cement.* print *n. or v.*

Word Study

The **Latin prefix im-** means "in" or "into."

In "Thumbprint," the poet wants to leave her **imprint**, or create a lasting impression, in the minds of her readers.

Nikki Giovanni

(b. 1943)

"The Drum (for Martin Luther King, Jr.)" (p. 663)

As a college student in the 1960s, Nikki Giovanni became involved in the civil rights movement. In the 1970s, she began writing poetry that expressed her pride in her African American heritage. Her poems are known for their musical rhythms, and she has recorded several of her works set to gospel music.

Alfred, Lord Tennyson

(1809–1892)

"Ring Out, Wild Bells" (p. 664)

Alfred, Lord Tennyson's faith in life was shattered in his twenties when his close friend Arthur Henry Hallam died suddenly while on a trip. Tennyson wrote the long poem "In Memoriam A.H.H." as a tribute to his friend. It helped make Tennyson one of the most popular English poets of his time. "Ring Out, Wild Bells" is part of this famous poem.

Eve Merriam

(1916–1992)

"Thumbprint" (p. 666)

Eve Merriam fell in love with words at an early age. As a child, she enjoyed playing with rhythms, rhymes, and puns. As an adult, she never lost her feeling that words could be fun. She once said, "I find it difficult to sit still when I hear poetry or read it out loud. . . . It's like a shot of adrenaline or oxygen when I hear rhymes and word play."

The Drum

(for Martin Luther King, Jr.)

Nikki Giovanni

The drums . . . Pa-Rum . . . the rat-tat-tat . . . of drums . . .
The Pied Piper[1] . . . after leading the rats . . . to death . . .
took the children . . . to dreams . . . Pa-Rum Pa-Rum . . .

The big bass drums . . . the kettles roar . . . the sound of
animal flesh . . . **resounding** against the wood . . . Pa-Rum
Pa-Rum . . .

Kunta Kinte[2] was making a drum . . . when he was captured . . .
Pa-Rum . . .
Thoreau[3] listened . . . to a different drum . . . rat-tat-tat-Pa-
Rum . . .
King said just say . . . I was a Drum Major . . . for peace . . . Pa-
Rum Pa-Rum . . . rat-tat-tat Pa-rum . . .

Drums of triumph . . . Drums of pain . . . Drums of life . . .
Funeral drums . . . Marching drums . . . Drums that call . . .
Pa-Rum
Pa-Rum . . . the Drums that call . . . rat-tat-tat-tat . . . the
Drums are calling . . . Pa-Rum Pa-Rum . . . rat-tat-tat Pa-
Rum . . .

Vocabulary
resounding (ri zound´
iŋ) *adj.* sounding
loudly

Sound Devices
What words in the
poem imitate the
sounds that drums
make?

◄ **Critical Viewing**
What can make the
sound of a poem
similar to the sound of
a drum? **[Compare]**

---

1. **Pied Piper** musician in folklore who led away a town's children after he rid the town of rats.
2. **Kunta Kinte** (koon´ tə kin´ tā) ancestor of *Roots* author Alex Haley.
3. **Thoreau** (thə rō´) (1817–1862) Henry David, American writer who wrote, "If a man does
   not keep pace with his companions, perhaps it is because he hears a different drummer."

Ring Out,

Alfred, Lord Tennyson

Wild Bells

Ring out, wild bells, to the wild sky,
    The flying cloud, the frosty light:
    The year is dying in the night;
Ring out, wild bells, and let him die.

5 Ring out the old, ring in the new,
    Ring, happy bells, across the snow:
    The year is going, let him go;
Ring out the false, ring in the true.

Ring out the grief that saps the mind,
10   For those that here we see no more;
    Ring out the feud of rich and poor,
Ring in redress to all mankind.

Ring out a slowly dying cause,
    And ancient forms of party strife;
15   Ring in the nobler modes of life,
With sweeter manners, purer laws.

Ring out the want, the care, the sin,
    The faithless coldness of the times;
    Ring out, ring out thy mournful rhymes,
20 But ring the fuller minstrel[1] in.

Ring out false pride in place and blood,
    The civic[2] slander and the spite;
    Ring in the love of truth and right,
Ring in the common love of good.

25 Ring out old shapes of foul disease;
    Ring out the narrowing lust of gold;
    Ring out the thousand wars of old,
Ring in the thousand years of peace.

---

1. **fuller minstrel** (minʹ strəl) *n.* singer of the highest rank.
2. **civic** (sivʹ ik) *adj.* relating to cities or citizens.

Sound Devices
How many beats do you hear in each line?

Context
How can the pattern of things "rung out" and "rung in" help you determine the meaning of *saps* in line 9?

Vocabulary
strife (strīf) *n.* conflict
modes (mōdz) *n.* ways of doing or behaving
spite (spīt) *n.* nastiness

Thumbprint

Eve Merriam

On the pad of my thumb
are whorls,[1] whirls, wheels
in a unique design:
mine alone.
5   What a treasure to own!
My own flesh, my own feelings.
No other, however grand or base,
can ever contain the same.
My signature,
10   thumbing the pages of my time.
My universe key,
my singularity.

Impress, implant,
I am myself,
15   of all my atom parts I am the sum.
And out of my blood and my brain
I make my own interior weather,
my own sun and rain.
Imprint my mark upon the world,
20   whatever I shall become.

Sound Devices
Which repeated consonant sounds create alliteration in lines 1–6?

Vocabulary
singularity (siŋ´ gyə ler´ ə tē) *n.* unique or unusual quality

imprint (im´ print) *v.* make a lasting mark

---

1. **whorls** (hwôrlz) *n.* circular ridges that form the pattern of fingerprints.

Critical Thinking

1. Key Ideas and Details (a) What kinds of people and drums are mentioned in "The Drum"? **(b) Interpret:** Why is a drummer a good symbol for a leader like Martin Luther King, Jr.?

2. Key Ideas and Details (a) Name four things the speaker in "Ring Out, Wild Bells" wants to "ring out" and "ring in." **(b) Interpret:** How will the future that the speaker envisions differ from the past?

3. Key Ideas and Details (a) Interpret: In "Thumbprint," explain lines 14 and 15. **(b) Infer:** What do these lines reveal is important to the speaker?

4. Integration of Knowledge and Ideas How do the sounds and rhythms of "The Drum" help the poet communicate her ideas? *[Connect to the Big Question: What is the secret to reaching someone with words?]*

Cite textual evidence to support your responses.

Reading Skill: Context

1. What **context clues** help you clarify the meaning of *feud* (line 11) in "Ring Out, Wild Bells"?

2. Explain how context helps you figure out the meaning of *base* (line 7) in "Thumbprint."

Literary Analysis: Sound Devices

© 3. **Craft and Structure** Complete the chart with examples of **sound devices.** Not all sound devices are used in each poem.

	The Drum	Ring Out, Wild Bells	Thumbprint
alliteration			
onomatopoeia			
rhyme (internal/external)			
meter (rhythmic patterns)			

© 4. **Craft and Structure** Explain how at least one of the sound devices listed above contributes to the mood, tone, and meaning of a poem.

Vocabulary

© **Acquisition and Use** In each group, identify the word that does not belong. Explain how its meaning differs from those of the other words.

1. imprint, forget, mark

2. malice, spite, kindness

3. ordinariness, uniqueness, singularity

4. peace, goodwill, strife

5. modes, moods, fashions

6. echoing, resounding, whispering

Word Study Use the context of the sentences and what you know about the **Latin prefix im-** to explain each answer.

1. What happens to someone who is *imprisoned*?

2. Are *imports* shipped into or out of a country?

Word Study

The **Latin prefix im-** means "in" or "into."

Apply It Explain how the prefix *im-* contributes to the meanings of these words. Consult a dictionary if necessary.

immersion
immigrant
impress

Integrated Language Skills

Poetry Collections 1 and 2

Conventions: Subject Complements

A **subject complement** is a noun, pronoun, or adjective that follows a linking verb and completes the thought by telling something about the subject.

Three types of subject complements are *predicate nouns, predicate pronouns,* and *predicate adjectives.*

- A **predicate noun** or **predicate pronoun** follows a linking verb and *identifies,* or renames, the subject of the sentence.
- A **predicate adjective** follows a linking verb and *describes* the subject of the sentence.

Poetry Collection 1

Poetry Collection 2

Predicate Noun	Predicate Pronoun	Predicate Adjective
Ronnie will be the <u>captain</u> of the team.	The two winners are <u>they</u>.	The flight to Houston was <u>swift</u>.
Captain renames the subject, *Ronnie.*	*They* identifies the subject, *winners.*	*Swift* describes the subject, *flight.*

Practice A Identify the subject and subject complement in each sentence. A sentence may have more than one subject and complement.

1. The cat is a green-eyed scratcher.
2. The reeds and stream were silver in the moonlight.
3. The speaker in "Your World" is she.
4. The mood of "Silver" is quiet and gentle.

ⓒ **Reading Application** In the poems in Collection 1, find one sentence that has a subject complement.

Practice B In each sentence, identify the subject, linking verb, and subject complement(s), noting the type of complement.

1. The speaker's thumbprint is a unique pattern.
2. The drums sound loud and triumphant.
3. The sky and the bells seemed wild.
4. The end of the year was a symbol for Tennyson.

ⓒ **Writing Application** Rewrite the following sentence with a predicate noun. Then, rewrite it with a predicate adjective. *Tennyson was one whom the English admired.*

PH **WRITING COACH** Further instruction and practice are available in *Prentice Hall Writing Coach.*

Writing

 **Common Core State Standards**

W.8.4; SL.8.6
[For the full wording of the standards, see page 650.]

Poetry Write a **poem that uses rhythm and sound devices.** If you wish, use one of the poems in Poetry Collection 1 or 2 as a model.

- Before you start, prewrite to choose a main idea to develop. Then, review the literature to see how the poets use sound devices like rhyme, rhythm, and repetition in their poems.

- Select a poetic form with regular rhyme and meter, or use free verse. Whatever you choose, maintain consistency in style throughout.

- Decide what mood you want to convey, whether serious, aggressive, exciting, or quiet. Plan rhythms and sound devices that will best convey these moods and emotions.

- As you draft, carefully consider the words you choose. Read them aloud for their sound as well as for their meaning.

Grammar Application Consider adding unusual subject complements to your poem.

Writing Workshop: *Work in Progress*

Prewriting for Exposition Problem-and-solution essays describe a problem and suggest one or more possible solutions. To prepare for an essay you may write, list some issues that matter to you, along with a problem associated with each. Save this Problem-and-Solution List in your writing portfolio.

Use this prewriting activity to prepare for the **Writing Workshop** on page 708.

Listening and Speaking

Choose a poem to present in a **poetry recitation.** Memorize a poem that uses sound devices effectively. You may choose a poem from these collections or a favorite poem or song.

- To prepare, notice how sound devices contribute to the overall mood and meaning. Keep these in mind as you practice.

- While rehearsing, aim for appropriate enunciation, emphasis, volume, and tone of voice. Speak clearly and naturally, not too fast or too slow. Modulate, or vary, your voice to express the tone of the poem. Add gestures if they enhance your presentation. Maintain eye contact with your audience.

- Practice reciting your poem with a natural rhythm. Monitor your reading for effect and for errors in pronunciation.

- When you are ready, recite the poem for your class.

www.PHLitOnline.com

- Interactive graphic organizers
- Grammar tutorial
- Interactive journals

© Leveled Texts

Build your skills and improve your comprehension of poetry with texts of increasing complexity.

Poetry Collection 3 looks at life in the big city from a variety of angles.

Poetry Collection 4 examines nature and its many moods.

© Common Core State Standards

Meet these standards with either **Poetry Collection 3** (p. 675) or **Poetry Collection 4** (p. 683).

Reading Literature
4. Determine the meaning of words and phrases as they are used in a text, including figurative and connotative meanings; analyze the impact of specific word choices on meaning and tone, including analogies or allusions to other texts. *(Literary Analysis: Figurative Language)*

Writing
1. Write arguments to support claims with clear reasons and relevant evidence. *(Research and Technology: Mini-Anthology)*

4. Produce clear and coherent writing in which the development, organization, and style are appropriate to task, purpose, and audience. *(Writing: Study for a Poem)*

9. Draw evidence from literary or informational texts to support analysis, reflection, and research. *(Research and Technology: Mini-Anthology)*

Language
1. Demonstrate command of the conventions of standard English grammar and usage when writing or speaking. *(Conventions: Direct and Indirect Objects)*

4.a. Use context as a clue to the meaning of a word or phrase. **4.d.** Verify the preliminary determination of the meaning of a word or phrase. *(Reading Skill: Context Clues)*

5.b. Use the relationship between particular words to better understand each of the words. *(Reading Skill: Context Clues)*

Reading Skill: Context Clues

Context, the words and phrases surrounding a word, can help you understand new words. When you are confused by an unfamiliar word, **reread and read ahead** for context clues.

Once you have figured out a possible meaning, *verify* the meaning by inserting it in place of the unfamiliar word. Reread the sentence. If it makes sense, the meaning you chose is probably correct. If the sentence does not make sense, read ahead to look for additional context clues, or consult a dictionary.

Using the Strategy: Context Clues Chart

This **context clues chart** shows types of context clues. Use it to help you identify context clues surrounding an unfamiliar word.

Comparison/ Contrast	Restatement	Definition	Example
I *never shop* anymore, but last year I was a shopping <u>enthusiast</u>.	Do not <u>veto</u> our request. Your *rejection* can hurt many people.	The <u>tare</u> of the truck, *its weight when empty*, was ten tons.	She <u>agonized</u>, *biting her nails*, *sleeping poorly*, and *crying*.

Literary Analysis: Figurative Language

Figurative language is writing or speech that is not meant to be taken literally. The use of figurative language can help poets set a mood, convey a tone, and create imagery. Figurative language includes these *figures of speech*:

- A **simile** compares two apparently unlike things using the words *like* or *as*: *His eyes were as black as coal.*

- A **metaphor** compares two apparently unlike things by saying that one thing *is* the other: *The world is my oyster.*

- **Personification** is a comparison in which a nonhuman subject is given human characteristics: *The trees toss in their sleep.*

As you read, notice the way figurative language allows writers to present ideas in fresh, unusual ways.

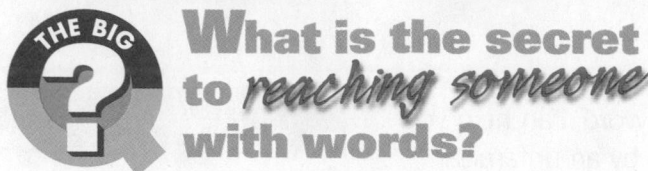

What is the secret to *reaching someone* with words?

Writing About the Big Question

In Collection 3, three poets carefully craft their words to help us experience life in the big city. Use this sentence starter to develop your ideas about the Big Question.

> Even if you have never been to a place, a talented poet can help you **experience** how it might feel to be there by _____.

While You Read Notice how the poets reach out to readers by using their skill with words.

Vocabulary

Read each word and its definition. Decide whether you know the word well, know it a little bit, or do not know it at all. After you read, see how your knowledge of each word has increased.

- **ponderous** (pän´ dər əs) *adj.* very heavy (p. 675) *We heard his ponderous footsteps echoing in the stairwell.* ponderously *adv.* ponder *v.*

- **bellow** (bel´ ō) *v.* make a deep, loud sound like a bull (p. 675) *Listen to him bellow like an injured animal when the doctor injects the needle.* bellowing *adj.*

- **urban** (ʉr´ bən) *adj.* related to the city or city life (p. 675) *Skyscrapers lined the urban landscape.* suburban *adj.* urbanite *n.* urbane *adj.*

- **roam** (rōm) *v.* go aimlessly; wander (p. 677) *We keep our cat inside so she will not roam.* roamer *n.*

- **dew** (do͞o) *n.* tiny drops of moisture that condense on cooled objects at night (p. 677) *We sat down on a grassy slope, damp with dew, to gaze at the stars.* dewy *adj.* dewpoint *n.*

Word Study

The **Latin suffix -ous** means "full of" or "characterized by."

In the poem "Concrete Mixers," the poet describes the vehicles as **ponderous**, very heavy or full of weight, like elephants.

Patricia Hubbell

(b. 1928)

"Concrete Mixers" (page 675)

Patricia Hubbell began writing poetry when she was ten years old. She liked to sit in a tree and look down on her family's farm, where she often saw things she would capture later in verse. Hubbell, who has been writing poetry and children's books for more than forty years, explains "Poem ideas are everywhere; you have to listen and watch for them."

Langston Hughes

(1902–1967)

"Harlem Night Song" (page 677)

One of Langston Hughes's most famous poems, "The Negro Speaks of Rivers," was written while traveling on a train to visit his father in Mexico. Fresh out of high school, Hughes was making the trip to convince his father to pay for a writing program at Columbia University. His father agreed, and Hughes's writing career was launched. Though he remained at Columbia for only a year, Hughes developed a lifelong love for the New York neighborhood of Harlem, the setting of many of his stories, poems, and plays.

Richard García

(b. 1941)

"The City Is So Big" (page 678)

Richard García has been writing poetry since the 1950s. He published his first poetry collection in 1973, but then stopped writing for six years. An encouraging letter from Nobel Prize winner Octavio Paz inspired him to write again. In addition to writing, García was the Poet-in-Residence for years at the Children's Hospital in Los Angeles, where he led poetry and art workshops for hospitalized children.

Concrete Mixers

Patricia Hubbell

The drivers are washing the concrete mixers;
Like elephant tenders they hose them down.
Tough gray-skinned monsters standing ponderous,
Elephant-bellied and elephant-nosed,
5   Standing in muck up to their wheel-caps,
Like rows of elephants, tail to trunk.
Their drivers perch on their backs like mahouts,[1]
Sending the sprays of water up.
They rid the trunk-like trough of concrete,
10 Direct the spray to the bulging sides,
Turn and start the monsters moving.
      Concrete mixers
      Move like elephants
      Bellow like elephants
15   Spray like elephants
      Concrete mixers are urban elephants,
      Their trunks are raising a city.

---

1. mahouts (mə houts´) *n.* in India and the East Indies, an elephant driver or keeper.

◀ **Critical Viewing**
What details in this picture of cement mixers
support the comparison in the poem? **[Connect]**

Context Clues
Reread lines 1–8. What
context clues help
reveal the meaning
of *muck?* Explain.

Spiral Review
Tone In line 4, the concrete mixers are referred
to as "elephant-bellied"
and "elephant-nosed."
What tone does this
metaphor suggest?

Vocabulary
ponderous (pän´ dər
əs) *adj.* very heavy

bellow (bel´ ō) *v.*
make a deep, loud
sound like a bull

urban (ʉr´ bən)
adj. related to the
city or city life

HARLEM *Night Song*

Langston Hughes

Come,
Let us **roam** the night together
Singing.

I love you.

5 Across
The Harlem roof-tops
Moon is shining.
Night sky is blue.
Stars are great drops
10 Of golden **dew**.

Down the street
A band is playing.

I love you.

Come,
15 Let us roam the night together
Singing.

Vocabulary
roam (rōm) *v.* go aimlessly; wander

dew (dōō) *n.* tiny drops of moisture that condense on cooled objects at night

Figurative Language
Does Hughes use a simile or a metaphor to describe stars? Explain.

The City Is So Big

Richard García

Context Clues
Which words help you confirm that *quake* means "tremble"?

The city is so big
Its bridges quake with fear
I know, I have seen at night

The lights sliding from house to house
5 And trains pass with windows shining
Like a smile full of teeth

I have seen machines eating houses
And stairways walk all by themselves
And elevator doors opening and closing
10 And people disappear.

Critical Thinking

Cite textual evidence to support your responses.

1. **Key Ideas and Details** **(a)** In "Concrete Mixers," where are the drivers as they wash the mixers? **(b) Interpret:** How does the poet show the mixers' size?

2. **Key Ideas and Details** **(a)** In "Harlem Night Song," which phrases are repeated? **(b) Analyze:** How does the repetition emphasize the joyful mood of the poem?

3. **Key Ideas and Details** **(a)** In "The City Is So Big," what three unusual events does the speaker say he has seen? **(b) Interpret:** In your own words, explain what the speaker has actually seen.

4. **Integration of Knowledge and Ideas** How does each poet use language to communicate the sights, sounds, and experiences of a city? *[Connect to the Big Question: What is the secret to reaching someone with words?]*

Reading Skill: Context Clues

1. Using the **context** surrounding the word *trough* in line 9 of "Concrete Mixers," explain what a trough looks like and what it does on a concrete mixer.

2. Read the text before and after the term *elephant tenders* in line 2 of "Concrete Mixers." **(a)** What do you think this term means? **(b)** Explain your reasoning.

Literary Analysis: Figurative Language

© 3. Craft and Structure Use a chart like the one shown to analyze examples of **figurative language** in each poem.

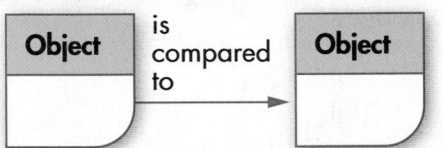 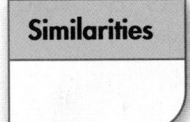

☐ Simile
☐ Metaphor
☐ Personification

© 4. Craft and Structure In a small group, review your charts. Discuss how the poets' use of figurative language appeals to the readers' senses and emotions. Then, evaluate which poem makes the most effective use of figurative language.

Vocabulary

© Acquisition and Use Based on your knowledge of the italicized words, answer the following questions. Explain your responses.

1. If you wanted to *roam,* where might you go?
2. What emotion might a *ponderous* sigh reveal?
3. Why might someone choose to live in an *urban* location?
4. In what types of situations might it be impolite to *bellow*?
5. Where are you most likely to find *dew*?

Word Study Use the context and what you know about the **Latin suffix -ous** to explain your answer to each question.

1. Which is more *nutritious,* a carrot or a marshmallow?
2. Do good athletes follow a *rigorous* training schedule?

Word Study

The **Latin suffix -ous** means "full of" or "characterized by."

Apply It Explain how the suffix *-ous* contributes to the meanings of these words. Consult a dictionary if necessary.

glorious
omnivorous
outrageous

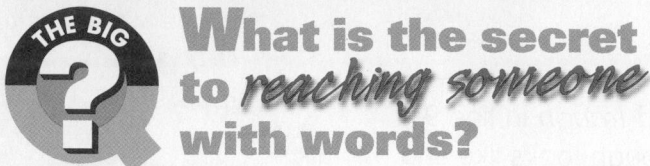

What is the secret to *reaching someone* with words?

Writing About the Big Question

In Collection 4, three poets reach out to readers as they share their ideas about nature. Use these sentence starters to develop your ideas about the Big Question.

Written works about nature that get the most positive **feedback** from me are ones that _____. This is because those writers **express** _____.

While You Read Look for ways the poets use words to convey their unique thoughts and ideas to readers.

Vocabulary

Read each word and its definition. Decide whether you know the word well, know it a little bit, or do not know it at all. After you read, see how your knowledge of each word has increased.

- **uneasily** (un ēz´ ə lē) *adv.* restlessly (p. 683) *Awake, she tossed uneasily all night.* *uneasy adj.*

- **unresponsive** (un ri spän´ siv) *adj.* not reacting (p. 683) *Her illness was unresponsive to treatment.* *unresponsively adv.* *unresponsiveness n. respond v.*

- **boulevard** (bool´ ə värd´) *n.* wide road (p. 683) *We walked along the boulevard, in the shade of huge oak trees.*

- **cicada** (si cā´ də) *n.* large, flying insect; the male makes a loud, high-pitched noise (p. 685) *Like grasshoppers and crickets, a cicada makes noise by rubbing parts of its body together.*

- **rut** (rut) *n.* a groove in the ground (p. 686) *I fell off my bike when I hit a rut in the road.* *rutted adj.*

- **debates** (dē bāts´) *v.* tries to decide (p. 686) *Tim debates whether to go out or stay in.* *debate n. debatable adj.*

Word Study

The **Latin suffix -ive** indicates a tendency toward something.

In the poem "Little Exercise," the poet describes the islands of mangrove trees as **unresponsive**, because they do not tend to respond to the power of the storm.

Elizabeth Bishop

(1911–1979)

"Little Exercise" (page 683)

Although she was born in Massachusetts, Elizabeth Bishop was raised by her grandparents in Nova Scotia, Canada. During her life, she lived and taught at various times in Europe, Brazil, New York City, and Boston. In thirty-five years, she published five volumes of poetry and won nearly every major American poetry award, including the National Book Award.

Pablo Neruda

(1904–1973)

"Ode to Enchanted Light" (page 685)

Chile's most acclaimed poet, Pablo Neruda won the Nobel Prize for Literature in 1971. Many of his poems are meditations on nature or on love. The son of a teacher and a railway worker, Neruda was a larger-than-life figure who inspired the Italian movie *Il Postino (The Postman)*, in which a shy postal worker seeks the famous poet's romantic advice.

Emily Dickinson

(1830–1886)

"The Sky Is Low, the Clouds Are Mean" (page 686)

Emily Dickinson considered books her "strongest friend." Withdrawn and shy, she spent most of her time at home in Amherst, Massachusetts, reading and writing. Most of her 1,775 poems were discovered after her death, including one that begins "I'm nobody! Who are you?" She may have considered herself a "nobody" during her lifetime, but she is now considered one of the most important American poets.

Little Exercise

Elizabeth Bishop

Think of the storm roaming the sky uneasily
like a dog looking for a place to sleep in,
listen to it growling.

5 Think how they must look now, the mangrove keys[1]
lying out there unresponsive to the lightning
in dark, coarse-fibered[2] families,

where occasionally a heron may undo his head,
shake up his feathers, make an uncertain comment
when the surrounding water shines.

10 Think of the boulevard and the little palm trees
all stuck in rows, suddenly revealed
as fistfuls of limp fish-skeletons.

It is raining there. The boulevard
and its broken sidewalks with weeds in every crack,
15 are relieved to be wet, the sea to be freshened.

Now the storm goes away again in a series
of small, badly lit battle-scenes,
each in "Another part of the field."[3]

Think of someone sleeping in the bottom of a row-boat
20 tied to a mangrove root or the pile of a bridge;
think of him as uninjured, barely disturbed.

---

1. **mangrove keys** little islands where mangrove trees grow. Mangrove trees (shown in the photo at left) have large tangled roots that provide shelter for many types of animals.
2. **coarse-fibered** having a structure of rough-textured strands.
3. **"Another part of the field"** Stage directions in plays, such as Shakespeare's *Macbeth*, often use this phrase to switch the action to a different location in a big battle.

Vocabulary
uneasily (un ēz´ ə lē) *adv.* restlessly
unresponsive (un´ ri spän´ siv) *adj.* not reacting

Context Clues
Read ahead from the word *heron* in line 7. Which words help you confirm what type of animal a heron is?

Vocabulary
boulevard (bool´ ə värd´) *n.* wide road

Ode to Enchanted Light

Pablo Neruda

Under the trees light
has dropped from the top of the sky,
light
like a green
5 latticework of branches,
shining
on every leaf,
drifting down like clean
white sand.

10 A cicada sends
its sawing song
high into the empty air.

The world is
a glass overflowing
15 with water.

Figurative Language
What figure of speech
is used in lines 3–5?
Explain.

Vocabulary
cicada (si cā´ də) *n.*
large, flying insect; the
male makes a loud,
high-pitched noise

THE SKY IS LOW, THE CLOUDS ARE MEAN

Emily Dickinson

Vocabulary
rut (rut) *n.* a groove in the ground
debates (dē bāts´) *v.* tries to decide

The sky is low, the clouds are mean,
A travelling flake of snow
Across a barn or through a rut
Debates if it will go.

5 A narrow wind complains all day
How some one treated him;
Nature, like us, is sometimes caught
Without her diadem.[1]

---

1. **diadem** (dī´ ə dem´) *n.* crown.

Critical Thinking

Cite textual evidence to support your responses.

1. **Key Ideas and Details** **(a)** Who is the one person included in "Little Exercise"? **(b) Compare and Contrast:** How do that person's surroundings contrast with his behavior? **(c) Speculate:** Why is it unimportant whether he is "tied to a mangrove root or the pile of a bridge"?

2. **Key Ideas and Details** **Infer:** What could "Little Exercise" be considered a "little exercise" in?

3. **Key Ideas and Details** **(a) Forms of Poetry:** Review page 639. What makes Neruda's poem an ode? **(b) Analyze:** What is his purpose when he describes the world as "a glass overflowing with water"?

4. **Key Ideas and Details** **Interpret:** In "The Sky Is Low, the Clouds Are Mean," what mood do the words *rut, complain,* and *mean* convey?

5. **Integration of Knowledge and Ideas** In each poem, how does the poet appeal to the reader's mind, emotions, or both? Explain. *[Connect to the Big Question: What is the secret to reaching someone with words?]*

After You Read
Poetry Collection 4

Little Exercise •
Ode to Enchanted Light •
The Sky Is Low, the Clouds
  Are Mean

Reading Skill: Context Clues

1. The word *pile* (line 20) of "Little Exercise" is used in an unusual way. **(a)** Use **context clues** to determine a possible meaning. **(b)** Explain your reasoning.

2. Read the text before and after *latticework* (line 5) in "Ode to Enchanted Light." **(a)** What might this term mean? **(b)** Explain your reasoning, and then confirm your definition using a dictionary.

Literary Analysis: Figurative Language

3. Craft and Structure Use a chart to analyze the **figurative language** in each poem.

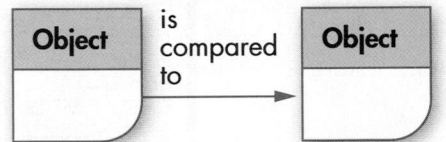 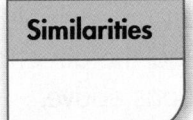

- ☐ Simile
- ☐ Metaphor
- ☐ Personification

4. Craft and Structure In a small group, review your charts. Discuss how the poets' use of figurative language appeals to the readers' senses and emotions. Then, evaluate which poem makes the most effective use of figurative language.

Vocabulary

Acquisition and Use Based on your knowledge of the italicized words, answer the following questions.

1. What should a customer do if a salesperson is *unresponsive*?

2. What kind of road surfaces get very few *ruts*?

3. How is a *boulevard* different from an alley or a lane?

4. What decision on a trip might cause a family to *debate*?

5. What situation might cause someone to wait *uneasily*?

Word Study Use context and what you know about the **Latin suffix -*ive*** to explain your answer to each question.

1. Does an *active* person keep busy or just sit around?

2. Is taking the *initiative* a sign of leadership?

Word Study

The **Latin suffix -*ive*** shows a tendency toward something.

Apply It Explain how the suffix -*ive* contributes to the meanings of these words. Consult a dictionary if necessary.

argumentative
disruptive
massive

Integrated Language Skills

Poetry Collections 3 and 4

Conventions: Direct and Indirect Objects

A **direct object** is a noun or pronoun that receives the action of a verb and answers the question *Whom?* or *What?*
An **indirect object** is a noun or pronoun that comes after an action verb and answers the question *To whom?*, *For whom?*, *To what?*, or *For what?*

Direct Object	Indirect Object
S V DO	S V IO DO
Sentence: Bill baked some cookies.	**Sentence:** Bill baked Marissa some cookies.
Baked what? cookies	**Baked for whom?** Marissa

A sentence cannot have an indirect object unless it also has a direct object. To find the indirect object, first find the direct object. Then, ask one of the four indirect object questions above.

Practice A In each sentence, identify the subject (S), verb (V), direct object (DO), and indirect object (IO). Some sentences do not include indirect objects.

1. Patricia Hubbell gives her readers a colorful impression of concrete mixers.

2. The "trunks" of the concrete mixers build the city.

3. Langston Hughes writes a love poem.

4. The elevated trains add light to the city.

© **Reading Application** Find two lines of poetry in Collection 3 that have direct objects. Identify the verb and the direct object in each.

Practice B In each sentence, identify the subject (S), verb (V), direct object (DO), and indirect object (IO), if there is one. Then rewrite each sentence with a different direct object.

1. Neruda's poem gives us beautiful images.

2. The storm showed the poet a new view of the islands.

3. Emily Dickinson watched the snowflakes.

4. Elizabeth Bishop offers her readers a "Little Exercise."

© **Writing Application** Write two sentences, each with a direct object and an indirect object, about one of the poems you read.

PH **WRITING COACH** Further instruction and practice are available in *Prentice Hall Writing Coach.*

Writing

Poem Write a **study for a poem** about one of two settings—a busy city or the countryside. Your study should plan for the figurative language that will work best in your poem. If you wish, use one of the poems in Poetry Collection 3 or 4 as a model.

Common Core State Standards

L.8.1; W.8.1, W.8.4, W.8.9
[For the full wording of the standards, see page 670.]

- List the objects, sights, and sounds that come to mind when you think about a bustling city scene or a natural landscape.

- Review the poems and the figurative language the poets use. To think of fresh ways to describe the items in your list, use this sentence starter: _____ *is like* _____ *because* _____ .

- Jot down several ideas. Then, choose one or two you like best.

- In a few sentences, explain your plan. Include details about the comparisons and figurative language your poem will present.

Grammar Application Use punctuation, such as commas and periods, for effect in your poem.

Writing Workshop: *Work in Progress*

Prewriting for Argumentative Texts Review your Problem-and-Solution List. Choose one problem and set of solutions that you would like to explore further. Research this problem and its possible solutions, and write a quick summary of your findings. Then, save this Research Summary in your writing portfolio.

Use this prewriting activity to prepare for the **Writing Workshop** on page 708.

Research and Technology

Build and Present Knowledge Different poems speak to different people. Follow your own personal interests to help you create a **mini-anthology**, a collection of three poems on a similar topic or theme. Follow these steps:

- First, choose a topic or theme that speaks to you, such as the beauty of the natural world or the thrill of sports.

- Next, visit your library or browse the Internet to research poems on this subject or theme.

- After you have selected three poems you like, write an introduction defending why you chose each one and how it affected you. Include your own interpretation of the poets' use of literary devices, such as figurative language.

- To complete the anthology, design a cover with drawings or use appropriate software to create graphics that are inspired by your response to one of the poems.

Test Practice: Reading

Context Clues

Fiction Selection

Directions: *Read the selection. Then, answer the questions.*

In the early days, Cat walked upright on two legs and swam as naturally as any ocean creature. But Cat was boastful, with far too much *pride* for his own good. "Ha!" he said to Dog, "You must *lumber* clumsily on four legs. I stride *elegantly* on two. You are inferior to me." To Turtle, he said, "Ha! I glide sleekly through the crests and curls of waves like a true *aquatic* creature. You struggle through the water. A wave easily flips you over—and then you *flounder* with your legs in the air!"

"Enough!" boomed the Great Mother. "Cat, your bragging has gone too far. You will no longer walk on two legs or be a graceful swimmer." The Great Mother's *reprimand* didn't tame the Cat's *arrogance* completely. Although today Cat walks on four legs and fears the water, he still remains quite pleased with himself!

1. The word *lumber* most nearly means—
   A. to stand upright.
   B. to swim with grace and speed.
   C. to walk or move in a clumsy way.
   D. to quickly climb to the top of a tree.

2. Which of the following is the closest **antonym** of *elegantly*?
   A. awkwardly
   B. fearfully
   C. swiftly
   D. gracefully

3. Which of the following context clues *best* helps you determine the meaning of *aquatic*?
   A. creature
   B. crests and curls of waves
   C. struggle through
   D. easily flips

4. What type of context clue in the passage helps you determine that *flounder* means "thrash about wildly"?
   A. contrast
   B. explanation/example
   C. sentence role
   D. comparison

Writing for Assessment

Interpret the meaning of either *reprimand* or *arrogance*, based on context. In a one-paragraph response, explain how context clues in the selection help you understand the word you chose.

Nonfiction Selection

Directions: *Read the selection. Then, answer the questions.*

(1) When it comes to eating, cats are *carnivorous*. (2) Unlike animals that eat only plants, or animals that eat a little of everything, cats eat only meat. (3) They are also *predators*, animals that hunt prey. (4) Members of the cat family include lions, tigers, cheetahs, leopards, and jaguars. (5) Although most kinds of wild cats are *nocturnal*, a few are more active during the day. (6) Most cats are *solitary* hunters, traveling alone. (7) Some, such as lions, live in groups. (8) A lion *pride* may include up to twenty individuals.

1. Which phrase from sentence 2 helps you most in determining the meaning of *carnivorous* in sentence 1?
A. unlike animals
B. eat only plants
C. eat a little of everything
D. eat only meat

2. What type of context clue is represented by the phrase that immediately follows the word *predators*?
A. definition
B. contrast
C. comparison
D. example

3. Which of the following context clues helps you determine the meaning of *nocturnal*?
A. traveling alone
B. members of the cat family
C. animals that hunt prey
D. more active during the day

4. The word *solitary* most nearly means—
A. alone
B. in a group
C. together
D. linked

Writing for Assessment

Connecting Across Texts
In a two-paragraph explanation, describe how you can use context clues to help determine the meaning of *pride* in each selection. Be sure to provide specific examples of context clues in your writing.

www.PHLitOnline.com
• Online practice
• Instant feedback

Reading for Information

Analyzing Functional Texts

Recipe   **Product Information**   **Menu**

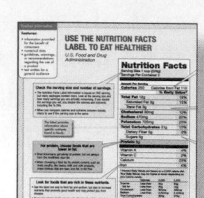 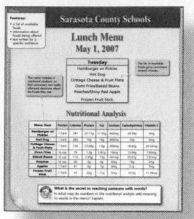

Common Core State Standards

Reading Informational Text
5. Analyze in detail the structure of a specific paragraph in a text, including the role of particular sentences in developing and refining a key concept.

Writing
2.b. Develop the topic with relevant, well-chosen facts, definitions, concrete details, quotations, or other information and examples. *(Timed Writing)*

Language
6. Acquire and use accurately grade-appropriate general academic and domain-specific words and phrases; gather vocabulary knowledge when considering a word or phrase important to comprehension or expression.

Reading Skill: Compare and Contrast Features of Consumer Materials

Different types of documents offer different types of information. For example, a cookie recipe tells you how to make cookies, but it might not provide nutritional content. When you read **consumer materials,** note the **features and elements** and the types of information offered. As you read, use a chart like the one shown to note information that the texts have in common and information that is particular to each.

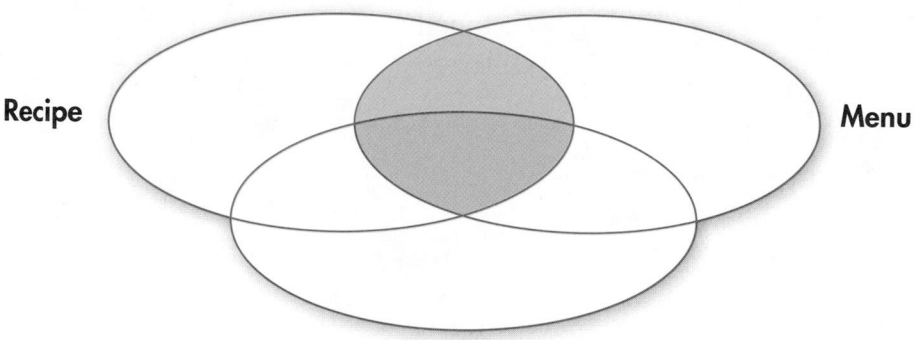

Recipe   Menu

Nutrition Information

Content-Area Vocabulary

These words appear in the selections that follow. You may also encounter them in other content-area texts.

- **calories** (kal´ ər ēz) *n.* units of the energy supplied by food
- **nutrients** (nü´ trē ənts) *n.* any substances that a living thing needs to eat for energy, growth, and repair of tissues
- **cholesterol** (kə les´ tə rol´) *n.* white fatty substance found in the blood and in some foods

Thumbprint Cookies

Recipe

Features:

- a title that names the food being prepared
- a list of ingredients
- directions that explain how to prepare a certain kind of food
- text written for a general audience

½ cup brown sugar
1 cup butter
2–3 egg yolks
2 cups flour
egg whites
1½ cups chopped nuts
raspberry preserves

A list of ingredients tells readers what goes into the food they will be making.

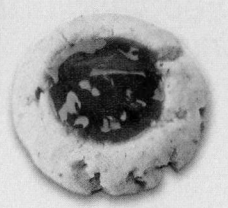

To separate eggs, crack each egg in half. Over a bowl, pour the egg back and forth between the cracked halves. Let the egg white fall into the bowl, keeping the egg yolk intact in the shell. Cream together sugar, butter, and egg yolks. Beat flour into this mixture. Form balls and dip into slightly beaten egg whites. Roll balls in chopped nuts. Put on lightly greased cookie sheet and make a thumbprint on each ball. Bake at 350° for 8 minutes. Remove from oven and reset thumbprint. Bake 8 to 10 minutes longer. Fill print with raspberry preserves.

Preparation: 25 min.
Baking: 18 min.

Yield: 30
Can freeze

Separating an egg

Using a teaspoon

Photographs and captions help to clarify the written instructions.

ABOUT DROP COOKIES

Whoever invented drop cookies, which we used to call "drop cakes," deserves a medal. Except for bars, drop cookies are the easiest of all cookies to make, because shaping usually involves nothing more than dropping dough from a spoon. A few call for patting down the dough or spreading it out with the tip of a knife. In most cases, drop cookies are very forgiving: No harm is done if the mixture is slightly stiffer or softer than expected; the results will just be a little flatter or puffier than usual.

Features:

- information provided for the benefit of consumers
- numerical data
- guidelines, warnings, or recommendations regarding the use of a product
- text written for a general audience

USE THE NUTRITION FACTS LABEL TO EAT HEALTHIER

U.S. Food and Drug Administration

Check the serving size and number of servings.

- The Nutrition Facts Label information is based on ONE serving, but many packages contain more. Look at the serving size and how many servings you are actually consuming. If you double the servings you eat, you double the **calories** and **nutrients**, including the Percent Daily Values.

- When you compare calories and nutrients between brands, check to see if the serving size is the same.

The label provides information about specific nutrients found in foods.

For protein, choose foods that are lower in fat.

- Most Americans get plenty of protein, but not always from the healthiest sources.

- When choosing a food for its protein content, such as meat, poultry, dry beans, milk and milk products, make choices that are lean, low-fat, or fat free.

Look for foods that are rich in these nutrients.

- Use the label not only to limit fat and sodium, but also to increase nutrients that promote good health and may protect you from disease.

- Some Americans don't get enough vitamins A and C, potassium, calcium, and iron, so choose the brand with the higher Percent Daily Value for these nutrients.

- Get the most nutrition for your calories—compare the calories to the nutrients you would be getting to make a healthier food choice.

Nutrition Facts

Serving Size 1 cup (228g)
Servings Per Container 2

Amount Per Serving

Calories 250   Calories from Fat 110

% Daily Value*

Total Fat 12g	18%
Saturated Fat 3g	15%
Trans Fat 3g	
Cholesterol 30mg	10%
Sodium 470mg	20%
Potassium 700mg	20%
Total Carbohydrates 31g	10%
Dietary Fiber 0g	0%
Sugars 5g	
Protein 5g	
Vitamin A	4%
Vitamin C	2%
Calcium	20%
Iron	4%

* Percent Daily Values are based on a 2,000 calorie diet. Your Daily Values may be higher or lower depending on your calorie needs.

	Calories:	2,000	2,500
Total fat	Less than	65g	80g
Sat fat	Less than	20g	25g
Cholesterol	Less than	300mg	300mg
Sodium	Less than	2,400mg	2,400mg
Total Carbohydrate		300g	375g
Dietary Fiber		25g	30g

Calories count, so pay attention to the amount.

- This is where you'll find the number of calories per serving and the calories from fat in each serving.

- Fat-free doesn't mean calorie-free. Lower fat items may have as many calories as full-fat versions.

- If the label lists that 1 serving equals 3 cookies and 100 calories, and you eat 6 cookies, you've eaten 2 servings, or twice the number of calories and fat.

Call-out boxes help consumers understand and use the information provided.

Know your fats and reduce sodium for your health.

- To help reduce your risk of heart disease, use the label to select foods that are lowest in saturated fat, *trans* fat and cholesterol.

- *Trans* fat doesn't have a Percent Daily Value, but consume as little as possible, because it increases your risk of heart disease.

- The Percent Daily Value for total fat includes all different kinds of fats.

- To help lower blood cholesterol, replace saturated and *trans* fats with monounsaturated and polyunsaturated fats found in fish, nuts, and liquid vegetable oils.

- Limit sodium to help reduce your risk of high blood pressure.

Reach for healthy, wholesome carbohydrates.

- Fiber and sugars are types of carbohydrates. Healthy sources, like fruits, vegetables, beans, and whole grains, can reduce the risk of heart disease and improve digestive functioning.

- Whole grain foods can't always be identified by color or name, such as multi-grain or wheat. Look for the "whole" grain listed first in the ingredient list, such as whole wheat, brown rice, or whole oats.

- There isn't a Percent Daily Value for sugar, but you can compare the sugar content in grams among products.

- Limit foods with added sugars (sucrose, glucose, fructose, corn or maple syrup), which add calories but not other nutrients, such as vitamins and minerals. Make sure that added sugars are not one of the first few items in the ingredients list.

Features:
- a list of available foods
- information about foods being offered
- text written for a specific audience

Sarasota County Schools

Lunch Menu
May 1, 2007

Tuesday
Hamburger w/ Pickles
Hot Dog
Cottage Cheese & Fruit Plate
Oven Fries/Baked Beans
Peaches/Shiny Red Apple
Frozen Fruit Stick

The list of available foods gives consumers several choices.

This menu includes a nutritional analysis so that consumers can make informed decisions about the foods they eat.

Nutritional Analysis

Menu Item	Portion	Calories	Protein	Fat	Sodium	Carbohydrates	Vitamin C
Hamburger w/ Pickles	1 Each	281	20.17g	11.55g	942mg	29.98g	0mg
Hot Dog	1 Each	280	10g	16g	800mg	24g	0mg
Cottage Cheese & Fruit Plate	1 Each	136	13.68g	1.6g	498mg	18.83g	20.64mg
Oven Fries	½ cup	78	1.3g	2.61g	16mg	13.04g	7.82mg
Baked Beans	½ cup	110	2.95g	.13g	491mg	25.92g	5.81mg
Peaches	½ cup	66	0g	0g	6mg	18g	2mg
Apples	1 Each	81	0g	.5g	0mg	21g	7mg
Frozen Fruit Stick	1 Stick	43	.32g	.11g	5mg	10.3g	11.78mg

Comparing Functional Texts

1. Key Ideas and Details (a) When you **compare and contrast the features** of the **consumer materials** you have read, what similarities do you find between the recipe and the school lunch menu? **(b)** What does the school lunch menu tell you that the recipe does not? **(c)** What does the recipe tell you that the menu does not?

Content-Area Vocabulary

2. (a) Review the definitions of the words *nutrients*, *calories*, and *cholesterol*, and determine how the words are related. **(b)** Use each of the words in a brief letter to your school's principal in which you propose healthful foods for your school's cafeteria menu.

🕐 Timed Writing

Informative Text: Essay

Format
The prompt directs you to write a brief essay. Therefore, you will need to express your ideas in three to five paragraphs.

Compare the Nutrition Facts label to the nutritional analysis in the school lunch menu. Evaluate both texts to determine which one you find more useful. Explain the results of your evaluation in a brief essay.
(30 minutes)

Academic Vocabulary
When you *evaluate* something, you make a judgment about its value based on examination and analysis.

5-Minute Planner

Complete these steps before you begin to write:

1. Read the prompt carefully, noting the key highlighted words.

2. Review the Nutrition Facts label and the nutritional analysis chart. Compare and contrast their features and elements.

3. Make notes about the strengths and weaknesses of each document. Consider which document is easier to use and which format is easier to read.

4. Based on your notes, decide which document you find more useful. Use details from your notes and from the texts as support as you draft your essay.

Comparing Poetry and Prose

Poetry and prose are two major classifications of literature.

- **Prose** is the common form of written language. It includes both fiction and nonfiction. Stories, articles, and novels are all prose.

- **Poetry** is distinguished from prose by its use of precise words, deliberate line lengths, and sound devices such as rhythm, rhyme, and alliteration. Poems are often more indirect—hinting at meaning rather than directly stating it. This results in writing that relies more heavily on figurative language than prose and is more open to interpretation.

Although poets and prose writers use different techniques, both try to convey **mood** and meaning to the reader. Also, in both forms, vivid descriptions and details create a picture of a physical **setting**—the look of the land, or the feel of a certain time and place.

As you read these two selections, you will see that both are set in the Georgia landscape. Both have a similar **theme**—how the natural world can surprise. But their topics, moods, and styles are very different.

Analyze and compare the elements of both works using a chart like the one shown. Consider how the genre of each text—prose or poetry—helps to define its style and convey its message.

Common Core State Standards

Reading Literature
2. Determine a theme or central idea of a text and analyze its development over the course of the text, including its relationship to the characters, setting, and plot.
5. Compare and contrast the structure of two or more texts and analyze how the differing structure of each text contributes to its meaning and style.

Writing
1. Write arguments to support claims with clear reasons and relevant evidence. *(Timed Writing)*

	Setting	Mood	Style	Theme
Snake on the Etowah				
Vanishing Species				

www.PHLitOnline.com

- Vocabulary flashcards
- Interactive journals
- More about the authors
- Selection audio
- Interactive graphic organizers

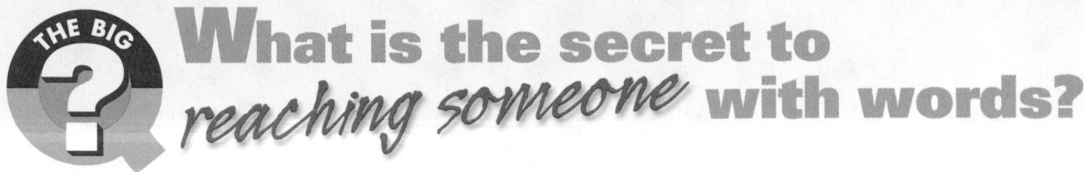

THE BIG ? What is the secret to *reaching someone* with words?

Writing About the Big Question

Both of these writers make us see how the world of nature can bring surprises, beauty, and sometimes fear or humor. Use this sentence starter to develop your ideas.

A writer can make "small" events **meaningful** by _____.

Meet the Authors

David Bottoms (b. 1949)

Author of "Snake on the Etowah"

David Bottoms was born in Canton, Georgia. He grew up hiking in the southern woods and fishing in rivers like the Etowah. Those memories of rural and small-town life appear throughout his poetry. Images of water and animals such as snakes and turtles show the beauty of nature along with its dangers.

A Distinguished Career In 1979, when Bottoms was twenty-nine, his first full-length book, *Shooting Rats at the Bibb County Dump,* won him the Walt Whitman Award. Since then, his poems have appeared frequently. He teaches writing at Georgia State and was named Georgia's poet laureate in 2000.

Bailey White (b. 1950)

Author of "Vanishing Species"

Bailey White still lives in the house where she grew up, in the longleaf pine woods of Thomasville, Georgia. Local settings and characters, along with gentle humor, color her writing.

An Old-Fashioned Storyteller Bailey White taught grade school in south Georgia for many years but became known to thousands of people nationwide after she began reading her writing on National Public Radio. Though White travels, she likes to come home to a place "full of people whose lives I know so well that I can tell the story of every missing finger and call every old lady's cat by name."

Snake on the Etowah

David Bottoms

Kicking through woods and fields, I'd spooked several
and once stepped on a coachwhip among gravestones,
at least one garter curled like a bow
under ivy in my yard.
5 Once I even woke on the hazy bank of a lake,
wiped dew from my eyes and found
on my ankle
a cottonmouth draped like a bootlace.

I thought I knew how beauty could poison
10 a moment with fear,
but wading that low river, feet wide on rocks—
my rod hung on the backswing, my jitterbug
snagged on the sun—
I felt something brush my thigh.
15 The bronze spoon of a copperhead drifted
between my legs.

Out came the little tongue reaching
in two directions,
the head following upriver,
20 following down, then a wide undulation[1] of tail,
a buff and copper swish. The river eased
around it in a quivering V,
while inside my shudder
it slipped out—
25 spiny, cool, just below
the surface, sidling against the current.

---

1. **undulation** (un´jə lā´ shən) *n.* curvy, wavy form.

Vocabulary
sidling (sīd´ liŋ) *v.* moving
sideways in a sly manner

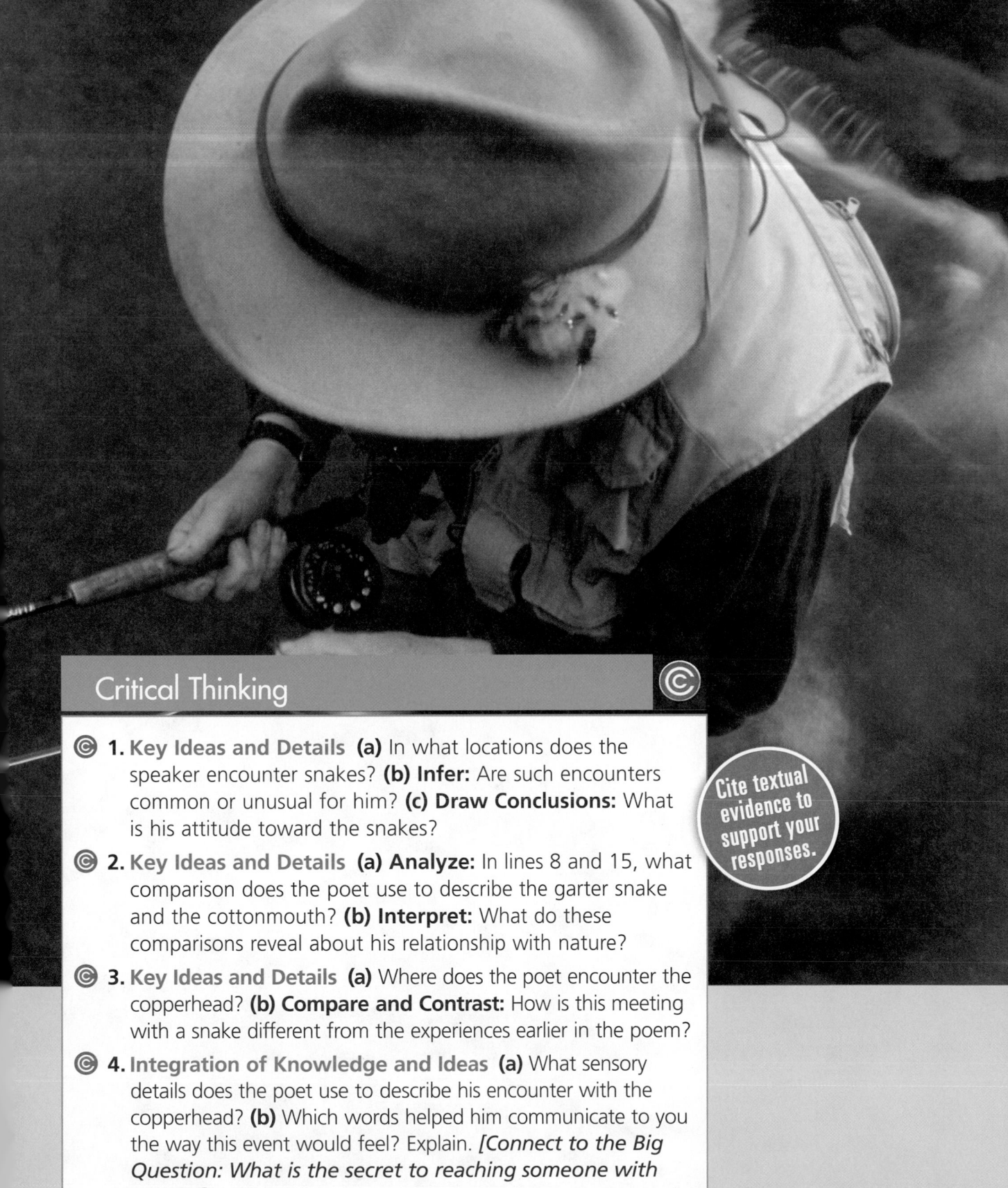

Critical Thinking

1. **Key Ideas and Details** **(a)** In what locations does the speaker encounter snakes? **(b) Infer:** Are such encounters common or unusual for him? **(c) Draw Conclusions:** What is his attitude toward the snakes?

2. **Key Ideas and Details** **(a) Analyze:** In lines 8 and 15, what comparison does the poet use to describe the garter snake and the cottonmouth? **(b) Interpret:** What do these comparisons reveal about his relationship with nature?

3. **Key Ideas and Details** **(a)** Where does the poet encounter the copperhead? **(b) Compare and Contrast:** How is this meeting with a snake different from the experiences earlier in the poem?

4. **Integration of Knowledge and Ideas** **(a)** What sensory details does the poet use to describe his encounter with the copperhead? **(b)** Which words helped him communicate to you the way this event would feel? Explain. *[Connect to the Big Question: What is the secret to reaching someone with words?]*

Cite textual evidence to support your responses.

Vanishing Species

Bailey White

▲ **Critical Viewing**
What characteristics make alligators, like this one, the objects of people's fascination? **[Speculate]**

Many years ago a man came down here with a whole station wagon full of recording equipment. He was on a quest to acquire and preserve amazing and unusual natural sounds from all over the world. He had just been in the South Seas recording Tasmanian devils, and somewhere he had heard about my aunt Belle's alligator, the one she had trained to bellow on command.

This was back in the days when alligators had been hunted to the brink of extinction,[1] and people believed that their bellow, one of the most truly majestic of all animal sounds, might soon be lost forever.

My aunt loaded Mr. Linley and all his recording equipment into her pickup truck and backed him down to the edge of the pond where the alligator lived. Then she revved up the engine a couple of times, and pretty soon here came the alligator.

Vocabulary
acquire (ə kwīr´)
v. get; obtain

Reading Check
What was unique about "aunt Belle's alligator"?

---

1. **extinction** (ek stiŋk´ shən) *n.* dying out of a species.

Poetry and Prose
Which words and phrases does the narrator use to convey a relaxed, humorous mood.

The alligator slumped down in the middle, we saw the water begin to quiver around his jowls, and the **bellowing began.**

We hadn't been too impressed with Mr. Linley at first. He just seemed like a quiet, pale little man with quick-moving hands and a nervous flicker in his eyes. But when that alligator came crawling up out of the mud, Mr. Linley slung his tape recorder over his shoulder, plugged in a bunch of black cables, pressed RECORD, then vaulted out of the truck and went crawling down the bank to meet him. We'd never seen anyone do that before. My aunt's alligator ate things that came out of the back of that truck. He ate everything that came out of the back of that truck. But we didn't want to be recorded, so we didn't say anything.

Aunt Belle revved the engine a few more times then shut it off. A quail bird whistled. The hot engine ticked. Then we saw the alligator swell up. Mr. Linley stuck out a microphone as long as his arm, right up to those ragged jaws. The alligator slumped down in the middle, we saw the water begin to quiver around his jowls, and the bellowing began. It went on for a full two minutes. Mr. Linley didn't flinch. He held that microphone steady with all his heart.

When it ended, Mr. Linley and the alligator moved at the same time. Mr. Linley made it into the back of the truck in two leaps, but it seemed like that alligator almost took flight. He crashed into the tailgate just as Mr. Linley crashed into the back of the cab. The alligator left a big dent in the tailgate, with teeth marks scraped through the paint, and Mr. Linley left a shiny smear down the back of the cab where he rubbed the dust off as he slumped down.

We were impressed. Now we understood that nervous flicker in Mr. Linley's eyes and those quivering hands.

And now that it was all over, Mr. Linley became quite garrulous. He sat down on our porch and eagerly showed us how his equipment worked. He played back the alligator bellowing. It was amazing. It was better than the real thing. You could hear drops of water fall from the alligator's top teeth into the muddy puddle that swirled around his bottom jaw. You could hear that little pink flap of skin at the back of

his throat open up. You could hear time and distance. You could hear silence.

Then Mr. Linley played some of his other recordings for us. He played star-nosed moles snuffling on a moonlight night. He played an almost extinct worm crawling through dead leaves. He played whales, he played sharks, he played icebergs groaning.

But when he started playing his recording of Viennese cats, our dog began to howl. He was an old bird dog, tied up to his doghouse in the backyard, and he really began to do some fancy howling. It was almost like a yodel. Mr. Linley got excited.

"I've never heard a dog do that," he said.

And quick as a flash he whipped out his unidirectional microphone. The dog howled, the little needle jumped up into the red, and Mr. Linley did his work.

After a few minutes the dog shut up. Mr. Linley began dismantling his equipment. He unplugged the cables, shoved all the levers over to the far left, and rewound the tape. Then he stopped. His hands stopped trembling. His eyes grew steady. He didn't breathe. Something was wrong. He had erased his alligator recording. He had taped the howling dog right over it.

So back we went to the edge of the pond; back Mr. Linley crawled into the mud. My aunt revved and revved the engine. But the alligator just lay there, eye to eye with Mr. Linley. He didn't raise up his tail. He didn't raise up his head. He didn't slump down in the middle. Water didn't quiver around his jowls. He just lay silent in the mud and glared at Mr. Linley.

Finally we drove back home. Mr. Linley packed up his equipment, bid us a desultory good-bye, and went off to record the courtship rituals of the Komodo dragon. We never heard from him again.

Poetry and Prose
How does White's description of the alligator recording show that it was "better than the real thing"?

Vocabulary
rituals (rich′ o͞o əlz) *n.* practices done at regular times

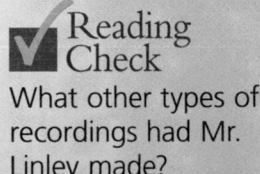

Reading Check
What other types of recordings had Mr. Linley made?

Vocabulary
resurgence (ri sʉr´ jəns)
n. reappearance; revival

Since then, laws protecting alligators have resulted in a resurgence in their population. They have been removed from the endangered species list. And almost any summer night in any southern swamp or river or pond you can hear alligators bellowing. We're not worried about them anymore. But I sometimes wonder whatever happened to that little Mr. Linley.

Critical Thinking

Cite textual evidence to support your responses.

1. **Key Ideas and Details (a)** Why does Mr. Linley come to visit the narrator's aunt? **(b) Infer:** What first impression does he give? **(c) Compare and Contrast:** How does his behavior with the alligator contradict this impression?

2. **Key Ideas and Details (a)** Once the recording is successful, what does Mr. Linley do? **(b) Infer:** How do the narrator and her aunt react? **(c) Connect:** Why does the dog start to howl?

3. **Key Ideas and Details (a)** What happens to the alligator recording? **(b) Interpret:** What do Mr. Linley's reactions show about him? **(c) Speculate:** What do you think happens to Mr. Linley after this incident?

4. **Integration of Knowledge and Ideas (a)** How does the narrator's conversational style and descriptive language help make this story funny for readers? **(b)** What words or details helped the writer communicate the way this episode took place? Explain. *[Connect to the Big Question: What is the secret to reaching someone with words?]*

Comparing Poetry and Prose

1. Craft and Structure Although "Snake on the Etowah" does not have regular meter or rhyme, what characteristics of poetry does it have?

2. Craft and Structure **(a)** Identify examples of figurative language such as simile and metaphor in the poem. **(b)** How do these figures of speech contribute to the mood?

3. Key Ideas and Details In what ways does the humor in "Vanishing Species" depend on **(a)** characterization and **(b)** memorable images?

4. Key Ideas and Details Complete Venn diagrams to compare these selections. Develop separate diagrams, like the one shown, for setting and theme.

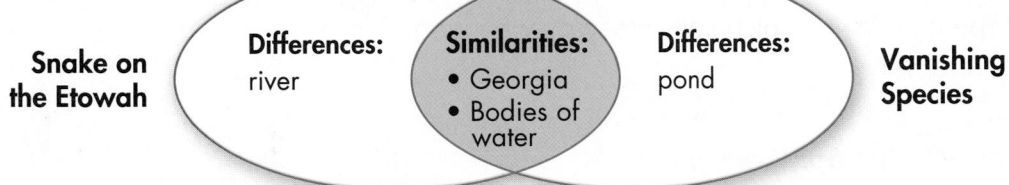

Snake on the Etowah

Differences:
river

Similarities:
• Georgia
• Bodies of water

Differences:
pond

Vanishing Species

⏱ Timed Writing

Argument: Analytical Essay

Write an essay supporting a claim about the relationship between genre and theme. To arrive at a claim, analyze how Bottoms and White, working in different genres, express similar themes. Compare and contrast elements such as setting, mood, and style. Then, draw conclusions about how much the genre—poetry or prose—accounts for the differences in the way the theme is presented. State this claim and support it with evidence from both texts. **(40 minutes)**

5-Minute Planner

1. Read the prompt carefully and completely.
2. Gather your ideas by answering these questions:
   • How similar are the themes of the two works?
   • How do the different writers look at and portray nature?
   • What element of each work expresses the theme most clearly?
3. Determine your claim, which will become the basis of your essay.
4. Reread the prompt, and then draft your essay.

Writing Workshop

 **Common Core State Standards**

Writing
1. Write arguments to support claims with clear reasons and relevant evidence.
1.d. Establish and maintain a formal style.

Write an Argument

Argument: Problem-and-Solution Essay

Defining the Form In a **problem-and-solution essay,** a writer identifies a problem and then offers a way to solve it. You might use elements of this type of writing in letters, editorials, and speeches.

Assignment Write an essay in which you identify a problem your school, community, or country faces. Then, propose an appealing solution to the problem you describe. Include these elements:

✔ a well-defined *statement of the problem and proposed solution*
✔ *evidence, examples, and reasoning that support your arguments*
✔ *support that answers readers' concerns*
✔ a structure that includes an *introduction, body, and conclusion*
✔ a *clear and formal style* with which to present your ideas

To preview the criteria on which your essay may be judged, see the rubric on page 713.

 **Writing Workshop:** *Work in Progress*

Review the work you did on pages 669 and 689.

Prewriting/Planning Strategy

Use a sentence starter. Complete one of these four sentence starters to help you brainstorm for possible topics:

• Our community should fix ____. • School would be better if___.
• I wish people would ____.   • I get annoyed when ____.

Write your endings in a cluster diagram like this one, and then choose one of the issues you have raised as your topic.

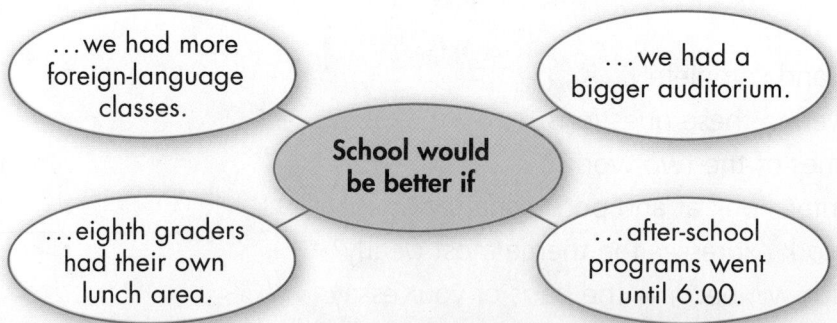

Generating Ideas

Ideas are the building blocks of all good writing. Before you begin writing, it is important to develop ideas you have about your topic. To generate ideas, try one or more of these methods:

Accessing Prior Knowledge Ask, "What do I already know about this problem and its possible solutions?" Jot down any relevant personal experiences, as well as ideas that you've gotten from reading.

Brainstorming With Others Get together with classmates and have a brainstorming session to discuss the problem and your ideas for solutions. As you brainstorm, try to be accepting of all ideas—no matter how unusual. The purpose of the brainstorming session is to list as many ideas as you can. Later, when you review your list, you can decide how many of the ideas could actually work.

Researching Identify and use various resources to find solutions to your problem. These resources may be books, Web pages, articles, individuals with expert knowledge, government agencies, or organizations. Focus on information related to defining your problem as well as finding solutions. For example, someone researching solutions to a water shortage in the Southeast might look at the actions of communities in the West that have faced the same problem.

Drawing Analogies Think about whether your problem may have similarities to another situation. By drawing analogies, or making comparisons, you can add ideas to your list. The chart shows one example in which drawing analogies helped inspire a solution.

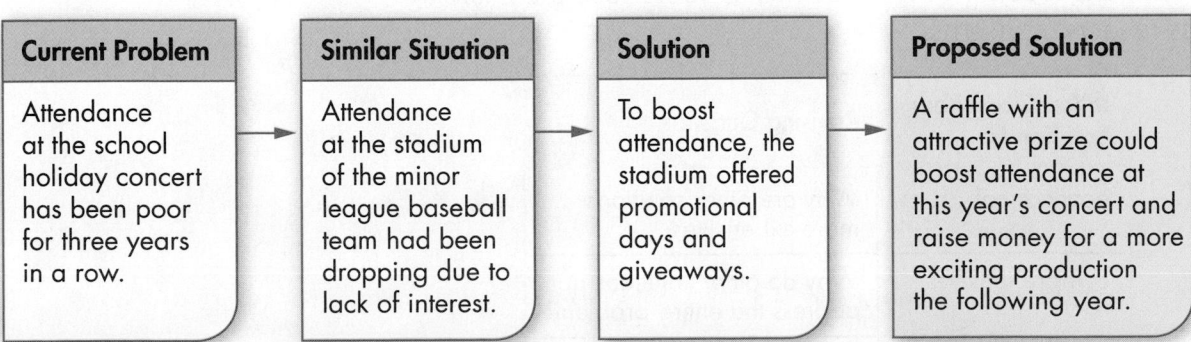

Current Problem	Similar Situation	Solution	Proposed Solution
Attendance at the school holiday concert has been poor for three years in a row.	Attendance at the stadium of the minor league baseball team had been dropping due to lack of interest.	To boost attendance, the stadium offered promotional days and giveaways.	A raffle with an attractive prize could boost attendance at this year's concert and raise money for a more exciting production the following year.

Drafting Strategies

Choose the most promising ideas that come out of your prewriting and develop them into an essay using the following steps:

Use an appropriate structure. Set up your argument with an introduction that defines and explains the problem. Follow that up with a thesis statement that provides an outline of your proposed solution.

Promote your solution. Use the body of your essay to explain and "sell" your solution to readers. Present reasons for your solution and support these reasons with evidence. Some common reasons are listed in this chart.

If a Solution Is...	It Means	Example	Support
Economical	It is affordable.	Fluorescent bulbs cost less money.	Statistics (cost comparison)
Comprehensive	It will solve the entire problem.	Good nutrition, exercise, and less stress help with heart problems.	Statistics and expert opinions
Practical	It can be easily carried out.	Community policing helps prevent crime.	Examples, statistics, and expert opinions

Offer support. Include examples, analogies, statistics, and expert opinions as evidence that your solution makes the most sense. Be sure to indicate the weaknesses of other solutions. Finally, write a conclusion in which you restate why your solution would be effective.

Revising Strategies

Revise to anticipate reader concerns. Be sure to indicate why other solutions would not work as well as yours. Use the chart to address readers' concerns.

If You Claim Your Solution Is...	Revising Question
economical	Why are other solutions more expensive?
comprehensive	Why do other solutions not address the entire problem?
practical	Why are other solutions harder to carry out?

 **Common Core State Standards**

Writing
1.a. Introduce claim(s), acknowledge and distinguish the claim(s) from alternate or opposing claims, and organize the reasons and evidence logically.
1.b. Support claim(s) with logical reasoning and relevant evidence, using accurate, credible sources and demonstrating an understanding of the topic or text.
1.c. Use words, phrases, and clauses to create cohesion and clarify the relationships among claim(s), counterclaims, reasons, and evidence.
1.e. Provide a concluding statement or section that follows from and supports the argument presented.

Language
1.b. Form and use verbs in the active and passive voice.
3.a. Use verbs in the active and passive voice to achieve particular effects (e.g., emphasizing the actor or the action).

Choosing Between Active and Passive Voice

In grammar, **voice** describes the verb form that shows whether the subject of a sentence is performing the action or receiving it. Your writing can be stronger when you write most sentences in the active voice.

Identifying Active and Passive Voice A verb is in the **active voice** when the subject performs the action. A verb is in the **passive voice** when its subject does not perform the action.

Active Voice	Passive Voice
Lightning **struck** the barn.	The barn **was struck** by lightning.
My family **is painting** the house.	The house **is being painted** by my family.

While most writing advisors prefer the active voice, the passive voice can be used to stress the action, not the performer. It can also be used when the performer is unknown.

> **To show unknown performer:** *The office was closed.*
> **To stress action:** *The goal was exceeded.*

Revising for Voice To assess your use of voice, follow these steps:

1. Locate the subject and verb in each sentence. Determine whether the subject performs the action.

2. If the subject performs the action, consider using the active voice.

   Subject: We   **Verb:** declare
   Active Voice: *We declared the experiment a success.*

3. If the performer of the action is unknown or unimportant, you might want to use the passive voice. A passive verb is a verb phrase made from a form of *be* with a past participle.

   Subject: unknown   **Verb:** declare
   Passive Voice: *The building <u>was declared</u> unsafe.*

Grammar in Your Writing
Choose two paragraphs in your draft. Underline every verb and identify it as active or passive. Analyze your choices. When appropriate, rewrite sentences in the active voice.

> **PH WRITING COACH**
> Further instruction and practice are available in *Prentice Hall Writing Coach*.

Student Model: Amnesti Terrell, Memphis, TN

Language
2.c. Spell correctly.

My Neighborhood

As I look out my bedroom window, I see the whole neighborhood. I see a lot of things, both good and bad. I see children playing outside on the weekends and after school. I see parades marching through the street during the holidays. I see watchful neighbors keeping an eye on the neighborhood. All of these are great sights, but they get overlooked because of all of the problems in the neighborhood. My neighborhood used to be nice and quiet, but lately it has become worse. Fights are breaking out for no good reason, trash is littering the streets, and kids have nothing to do but hang out on the streets. Something needs to change before it is too late.

The first thing that I would like to change to improve my neighborhood is to make it safer. I want to be able to walk inside a store and not have to wait until a fight is over so I can leave. People have to stop trying to impress others by picking fights with everyone they see. I could feel safer if people were more respectful toward each other.

I also want to change the appearance of my neighborhood. There is trash everywhere. I hate having to clean up after someone else just because they do not know how to put trash into a trash can. I would also like to add some things. People in the neighborhood need a place to play and think. A playground would be a safe place for small children to play. This would be a place where the children would not have to worry about careless drivers or street fights. I would also like to build a community center for teens to have fun, play sports, and be themselves. The center would be a place that helps teens figure out that they can do anything if they put their minds to it. It could be called The Hope Center.

Finally, I would like to change the attitude toward the schools in my neighborhood. Walker Elementary and Ford Road Elementary have math and spelling bees every year, but they do not grab the headlines. Neither school gets positive recognition in the media. Positive attention would help everyone feel better about schools and the work teachers and students do.

My neighborhood is not bad. It just needs a few adjustments like any other neighborhood. So as I look out of my bedroom window, I see what it once was, what it has become, and what it has the potential to be. By committing to local safety and community spaces, we could take important steps toward improvements that can help everyone. I will do everything I can to help improve my neighborhood.

In the introduction, Amnesti clearly defines the problem in a way that conveys a sense of urgency.

She addresses possible solutions in paragraphs 2–4 by explaining three ideas to improve the quality of life in her neighborhood.

The essay uses the proper conventions of grammar, usage, and mechanics.

Amnesti organizes her essay with a conclusion that summarizes her solution.

Editing and Proofreading

Proofread to correct errors in grammar, spelling, and punctuation.

Focus on spelling homophones. A **homophone** is a word that sounds the same as another word but is spelled differently. People often choose the wrong homophone if they are writing quickly and not paying close attention to spelling. If you use a computer program to write your essay, you should run a spell-check. Be extra careful with homophones, however. The spell-check will miss mistakes that occur when words like *there*, *their*, and *they're* are spelled correctly but used incorrectly.

Publishing and Presenting

Consider one of the following ways to share your writing:

Post your ideas. Post your essay online or on a bulletin board, along with the essays written by other class members.

Implement the solution. If it is possible, carry out the solution you propose in your essay. Then, evaluate how well it worked. Write a summary of the results and post it with your essay.

Reflecting on Your Writing

Writer's Journal Jot down your answer to this question:
What did you learn about the difficulties in solving problems?

Rubric for Self-Assessment

Find evidence in your writing to address each category. Then, use the rating scale to grade your work.

Spiral Review
Earlier in the unit, you learned about **subject complements** (p. 668) and **direct and indirect objects** (p. 688). Review your essay to be sure you have used subject complements and direct and indirect objects correctly.

Criteria	Rating Scale
	not very → very
Focus: How clearly do you define the problem and proposed solution(s)?	1 2 3 4 5
Organization: How well do you employ an appropriate structure that includes an introduction, body, and conclusion?	1 2 3 4 5
Support/Elaboration: How effectively do you support your arguments with evidence, examples, and reasoning?	1 2 3 4 5
Support/Elaboration: How well do you anticipate reader concerns by offering counterarguments?	1 2 3 4 5
Conventions: How effective is your use of active and passive voice?	1 2 3 4 5

Ⓒ Leveled Texts

Build your skills and improve your comprehension of poetry with texts of increasing complexity.

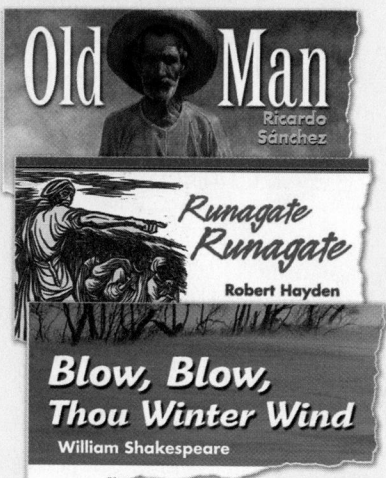

Poetry Collection 5 explores different emotions—thankfulness, desperation, and thoughtlessness.

Poetry Collection 6 celebrates figures and events in American history in verse.

Ⓒ Common Core State Standards

Meet these standards with either **Poetry Collection 5** (p. 718) or **Poetry Collection 6** (p. 728).

Reading Literature

5. Compare and contrast the structure of two or more texts and analyze how the differing structure of each text contributes to its meaning and style. *(Literary Analysis: Forms of Poetry)*

Spiral Review RL.8.4

Writing

3. Write narratives to develop real or imagined experiences or events using effective technique, relevant descriptive details, and well-structured event sequences. *(Writing: Lyric or Narrative Poem)*

Speaking and Listening

1. Engage effectively in a range of collaborative discussions with diverse partners, building on others'

ideas and expressing their own clearly. *(Speaking and Listening: Evaluation Form)*

Language

1. Demonstrate command of the conventions of standard English grammar and usage when writing or speaking. *(Conventions: Prepositional Phrases)*

2.a. Use punctuation (comma, ellipsis, dash) to indicate a pause or break. *(Writing: Lyric or Narrative Poem)*

4.b. Use common, grade-appropriate Greek or Latin affixes and roots as clues to the meaning of a word (e.g, *precede, recede, secede*). *(Vocabulary: Word Study)*

Reading Skill: Paraphrase

Paraphrasing is restating a text in your own words. When you paraphrase, you look for specific details in the text that help explain the writer's main idea or message. Then you use simpler language to express that meaning.

Paraphrasing helps you check your understanding. Before you paraphrase, **reread to clarify** meaning. Then, follow these steps:

- Identify the most basic information in each sentence.
- Restate details simply, using synonyms for the writer's words.
- Look up unfamiliar words. Replace unusual words and sentence structures with language that is more like everyday speech.

Using the Strategy: Paraphrase Chart

Use a **paraphrase chart** to help you rephrase a writer's ideas.

Poem	
Line from poem	
Basic information	
Paraphrase	

PHLit Online!
www.PHLitOnline.com

Hear It!
- Selection summary audio
- Selection audio

See It!
- Get Connected video
- Background video
- More about the author
- Vocabulary flashcards

Do It!
- Interactive journals
- Interactive graphic organizers
- Self-test
- Internet activity
- Grammar tutorial
- Interactive vocabulary games

Literary Analysis: Forms of Poetry

Two major forms of poetry are lyric poetry and narrative poetry.

- A **lyric poem** uses "musical" verse to express the thoughts and feelings of a single **speaker**—the person "saying" the poem. Its purpose is to create a vivid impression in readers' minds.

- A **narrative poem** tells a story in verse and includes the elements of a short story—characters, setting, conflict, and plot.

As you read, compare and contrast the structure of each form of poetry. Poets often tap readers' prior knowledge and emotions by including **allusions**—references to people, places, or things from other artistic works.

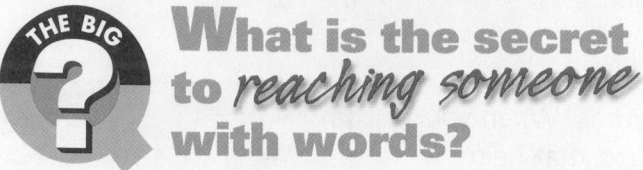

What is the secret to *reaching someone* **with words?**

Writing About the Big Question

The poems in Poetry Collection 5 were written at widely different times. Yet, they all share the characteristic of reaching readers through the emotions they convey. Use these sentence starters to develop your ideas about the Big Question.

I can find poems written in the past **relevant** as long as they _____. I do not find them relevant if they _____.

While You Read Look for words and phrases that trigger emotions in you.

Vocabulary

Read each word and its definition. Decide whether you know the word well, know it a little bit, or do not know it at all. After you read, see how your knowledge of each word has increased.

- **legacy** (leg´ ə sē) *n.* something physical or spiritual handed down from an ancestor (p. 718) *Norman's legacy will be the number of lives he touched.*

- **aromas** (ə rō´ məz) *n.* smells (p. 719) *Some aromas, like the smell of freshly cut grass and warm cinnamon bread, remind me of home.* *aromatic adj.*

- **supple** (sup´ əl) *adj.* yielding; soft (p. 719) *The baby's skin was soft and supple.* *suppleness n.*

- **beckoning** (bek´ ə niŋ) *adj.* calling; summoning (p. 720) *I could not resist Hawaii's beckoning breezes.* *beckon v.*

- **shackles** (shak´ əlz) *n.* metal bonds used to restrain prisoners (p. 721) *The defendant's ankles were bound together by shackles.* *shackled adj.* *shackle v.*

- **ingratitude** (in grat´ i tood) *n.* lack of thankfulness or appreciation (p. 723) *Your ingratitude makes me want to take back my gift.* *ungrateful adj.* *ingrate n.*

Word Study

The **Latin prefix** *in-* means "not" or "lacking."

In "Blow, Blow, Thou Winter Wind," the speaker refers to man's **ingratitude**, or lack of thankfulness, for the gift of friendship.

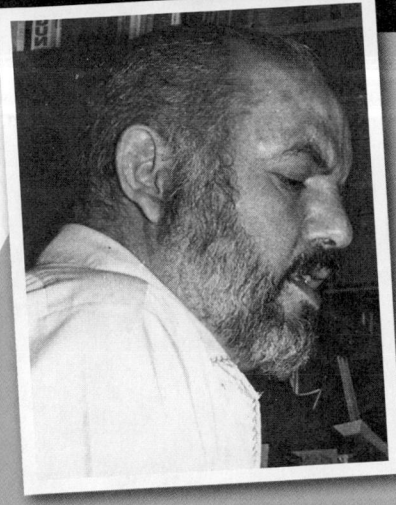

Ricardo Sánchez

(1941–1995)

"Old Man" (page 718)

Ricardo Sánchez was born in El Paso, Texas. His family had roots in Spanish, Mexican, and Native American cultures. Most of Sánchez's work explores and celebrates his rich cultural heritage. In the poem "Old Man," Sánchez offers a portrait of a grandfather he remembers with love.

Robert Hayden

(1913–1980)

"Runagate Runagate" (page 720)

Raised in a poor Detroit neighborhood, Robert Hayden was the first African American poet appointed as Consultant of Poetry to the Library of Congress. His poetry covers a wide range of subjects— from personal remembrances to celebrations of the history and achievements of African Americans.

William Shakespeare

(1564–1616)

"Blow, Blow, Thou Winter Wind" (page 723)

William Shakespeare is regarded by some as the greatest writer in the English language. Born in Stratford-on-Avon, a small town in England, he moved to London as a young man and spent most of his adult life there. Shakespeare was an actor, a producer, and a director. However, he is most famous for his plays and poems.

Old Man

Ricardo Sánchez

El Pan Nuestro (Our Daily Bread), ©1905, Ramon Frade, Instituto de Cultura. Puertorriqueña, San Juan

remembrance
(smiles/hurts sweetly)
October 8, 1972

▲ **Critical Viewing**
What aspects of this
man's appearance
might help him earn
the respect of others?
[Analyze]

old man
with brown skin
talking of past
    when being shepherd
5   in utah, nevada, colorado and
        new mexico
was life lived freely;

old man,
    grandfather,
10 wise with time
running rivulets on face,
deep, rich furrows,[1]
    each one a legacy,
deep, rich memories of life . . .

Vocabulary
legacy (leg´ ə sē) *n.*
something physical or
spiritual handed down
from an ancestor

---

1. **rivulets . . . furrows** here, the wrinkles on the old man's face.

15   "you are indio,[2]
         among other things,"
     he would tell me
         during nights spent
     so long ago
20   amidst familial gatherings
     in albuquerque . . .

old man, loved and respected,
he would speak sometimes
of pueblos,[3]
25   san juan, santa clara,
     and even santo domingo,
and his family, he would say,
     came from there:
     some of our blood was here,
30   he would say,
     before the coming of coronado,[4]
other of our blood
     came with los españoles,[5]
and the mixture
35 was rich,
     though often painful . . .
old man,
who knew earth
     by its awesome aromas
40 and who felt
the heated sweetness
     of chile verde[6]
by his supple touch,
gone into dust is your body
45   with its stoic[7] look and resolution,
but your reality, old man, lives on
in a mindsoul touched by you . . .

Old Man . . .

---

2. **indio** (in′ dē ō) *n.* Indian; Native American.
3. **pueblos** (pweb′ lōz) *n.* here, Native American towns in central and northern New Mexico.
4. **coronado** (kôr′ ə nä′ dō) The sixteenth-century Spanish explorer Francisco Vásquez de Coronado journeyed through what is today the American Southwest.
5. **los españoles** (lôs es pä′ nyō lās) *n.* Spaniards.
6. **chile verde** (chil′ lē ver′ dā) *n.* green pepper.
7. **stoic** (stō′ ik) *adj.* calm in the face of suffering.

Paraphrase
In your own words, identify the person the speaker describes and what the speaker says about this person.

Forms of Poetry
Why does the speaker respect the old man?

Vocabulary
aromas (ə rō′ məz) *n.* smells
supple (sup′ əl) *adj.* yielding; soft

Runagate Runagate

Robert Hayden

> **Background** The term *runagate* refers to the runaway slaves who escaped to the North from slave states via the Underground Railroad. "Conductors," or guides, led the slaves by night to appointed "stations," where they received food, shelter, and clothing.

▲ **Critical Viewing**
In this illustration, who are the *runagates* and "conductors" to which the Background refers? How can you tell? **[Apply]**

Vocabulary
beckoning (bek´ ə niŋ)
adj. calling; summoning

I.

Runs falls rises stumbles on from darkness into darkness
and the darkness thicketed with shapes of terror
and the hunters pursuing and the hounds pursuing
and the night cold and the night long and the river
5 to cross and the jack-muh-lanterns[1] **beckoning** beckoning
and blackness ahead and when shall I reach that somewhere
morning and keep on going and never turn back and keep
   on going
        Runagate
           Runagate
10   Runagate

Many thousands rise and go
many thousands crossing over
          O mythic North
          O star-shaped yonder Bible city

---

1. jack-muh-lanterns (jak´ mə lan´ tərnz) *n.* jack-o'-lanterns, shifting lights seen over a marsh at night.

15 Some go weeping and some rejoicing
     some in coffins and some in carriages
     some in silks and some in shackles

           Rise and go or fare you well

     No more auction block for me
20 no more driver's lash for me

        If you see my Pompey, 30 yrs of age,
        new breeches, plain stockings, negro shoes;
        if you see my Anna, likely young mulatto
        branded E on the right cheek, R on the left,
25   catch them if you can and notify subscriber.[2]
        Catch them if you can, but it won't be easy.
        They'll dart underground when you try to catch them,
        plunge into quicksand, whirlpools, mazes,
        turn into scorpions when you try to catch them.

30 And before I'll be a slave
     I'll be buried in my grave

        North star and bonanza gold
        I'm bound for the freedom, freedom-bound
        and oh Susyanna don't you cry for me

35   Runagate

             Runagate

     II.
     Rises from their anguish and their power,

         Harriet Tubman,

         woman of earth, whipscarred,
40   a summoning, a shining

         Mean to be free

     And this was the way of it, brethren brethren,
     way we journeyed from Can't to Can.

---

2. **subscriber** (səb skrīb´ ər) *n.* here, the person from whom the slave Pompey ran away.

Forms of Poetry
How does the perspective of the first-person point of view change between lines 19–20 and lines 21–29?

Forms of Poetry
In what way is this poem an example of both lyric and narrative forms?

**Reading
Check**
What challenges do the runaway slaves face?

Paraphrase
Paraphrase lines 45–53
by describing in your
own words what is
happening.

45 Moon so bright and no place to hide,
the cry up and the patterollers[3] riding,
hound dogs belling in bladed air.
And fear starts a-murbling, Never make it,
we'll never make it. *Hush that now,*
50 and she's turned upon us, leveled pistol
glinting in the moonlight:
Dead folks can't jaybird-talk, she says;
You keep on going now or die, she says.

Wanted   Harriet Tubman   alias The General
55 alias Moses   Stealer of Slaves
In league with Garrison   Alcott   Emerson
Garrett   Douglass   Thoreau   John Brown[4]

Armed and known to be Dangerous

Wanted   Reward   Dead or Alive

60 Tell me, Ezekiel, oh tell me do you see
mailed Jehovah[5] coming to deliver me?

Hoot-owl calling in the ghosted air,
five times calling to the hants[6] in the air.
Shadow of a face in the scary leaves,
65 shadow of a voice in the talking leaves:

Come ride-a my train

Oh that train, ghost-story train
through swamp and savanna movering movering,
over trestles of dew, through caves of the wish,
70 *Midnight Special on a sabre track movering movering,*
first stop Mercy and the last Hallelujah.

Come ride-a my train

Mean mean mean to be free.

Paraphrase
Paraphrase lines 67–73
by explaining what
the "train" is, where it
comes from, and where
it is going.

---

3. **patterollers** (pa´ tər ôl ərz) *n.* dialect for *patrollers,* people who hunt for runaways.
4. **Garrison . . . John Brown** various abolitionists, people who were against slavery.
5. **Ezekiel** (i zē´ kē əl) **. . . Jehovah** (ji hō və) Ezekiel was a Hebrew prophet of the sixth century B.C.; *Jehovah* is another word for "*God.*"
6. **hants** (hants) *n.* dialect term for *ghosts.*

Blow, Blow, Thou Winter Wind

William Shakespeare

Blow, blow, thou winter wind.
Thou art not so unkind
   As man's ingratitude.
Thy tooth is not so keen,
5 Because thou art not seen,
   Although thy breath be rude.
Heigh-ho! Sing, heigh-ho! unto the green holly.
Most friendship is feigning, most loving mere folly.[1]
   Then, heigh-ho, the holly!
10   This life is most jolly.

---

1. **feigning . . . folly** Most friendship is fake, most loving is foolish.

Vocabulary
ingratitude (in grat´ i
to̅o̅d) *n.* lack of thankfulness or appreciation

© **Spiral Review**
Analogy What two
things does Shakespeare
compare in the first
stanza? How are they
alike?

Forms of Poetry
To what does the speaker compare the winter's chill in this lyric poem?

Freeze, freeze, thou bitter sky,
That dost not bite so nigh
    As benefits forgot.
Though thou the waters warp,[2]
15 Thy sting is not so sharp
    As friend remembered not.
Heigh-ho! Sing, heigh-ho! unto the green holly.
Most friendship is feigning, most loving mere folly.
    Then, heigh-ho, the holly!
20   This life is most jolly.

_____

2. warp *v.* freeze.

Critical Thinking

© 1. **Key Ideas and Details (a) Interpret:** Interpret the meaning and significance of the following lines: "Old Man" (lines 8–14); "Runagate Runagate" (lines 1–2); "Blow, Blow . . ." (line 8). **(b) Discuss:** In a small group, discuss your responses. Then, share your ideas with the class.

© 2. **Integration of Knowledge and Ideas (a)** Compare word choice and language patterns in the contemporary poem "Old Man" with those in Shakespeare's "Blow, Blow, Thou Winter Wind." **(b)** Does the fact that the poems reflect different times influence your response to them? Why or why not? *[Connect to the Big Question: What is the secret to reaching someone with words?]*

Cite textual evidence to support your responses.

Reading Skill: Paraphrase

1. (a) What synonyms could be used for the following words and phrases in lines 44–47 of "Old Man": *gone into dust, resolution,* and *mindsoul.* **(b) Paraphrase** these lines.

2. Reread the first stanza of "Runagate . . ." **(a)** Write the lines in sentences. **(b)** Paraphrase each sentence.

Literary Analysis: Forms of Poetry

3. Craft and Structure Use a chart like this one to compare and contrast the purposes and characteristics of the **lyric** and **narrative poems** in this collection.

	Form: lyric or narrative?	What characteristics make it lyric or narrative?	How does the form help the poet achieve his purpose?
Old Man			
Runagate...			
Blow, Blow...			

4. Craft and Structure (a) What overall impression does "Old Man" convey? **(b)** How do the lines "remembrance / (smiles / hurts sweetly)" connect with this impression?

5. Craft and Structure (a) List two **allusions** in "Runagate . . ." **(b)** How might these allusions tap into emotional connections with the past?

Vocabulary

Acquisition and Use For each item, write a sentence that correctly uses both of the words provided.

1. prisoner; shackles
2. supple; aging
3. tantrum; ingratitude
4. aromas; cooking
5. home; beckoning
6. legacy; ancestor

Word Study Use context and what you know about the **Latin prefix in-** to explain your answer to each question.

1. Why would an employer fire an *incompetent* worker?
2. Should jury members focus on *insignificant* details in a trial?

Word Study

The **Latin prefix in-** means "not" or "lacking."

Apply It Explain how the prefix *in-* contributes to the meanings of these words. Consult a dictionary if necessary.

inability
incurable
inconclusive

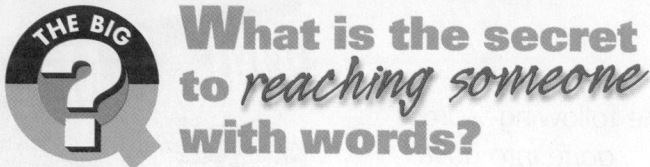

What is the secret to *reaching someone* with words?

Writing About the Big Question

The poets in Poetry Collection 6 reach out to readers by highlighting important figures and events in American history. Use this sentence starter to develop your ideas about the Big Question.

> The description of an event from history needs to _____ in order to have **significance** for me.

While You Read Look for details that help explain why we remember and celebrate our history.

Vocabulary

Read each word and its definition. Decide whether you know the word well, know it a little bit, or do not know it at all. After you read, see how your knowledge of each word has increased.

- **exiles** (ek´ sīlz) *n.* people who are forced to live in another country (p. 729) *During the French Revolution, exiles from France settled in the Caribbean. exile v.*

- **yearning** (yʉr´ niŋ) *v.* feeling longing; painfully wanting something (p. 729) *They watched the clock, yearning for lunchtime. yearning n. yearn v.*

- **somber** (säm´ bər) *adj.* dark; gloomy (p. 732) *It is hard to joke when you are in a somber mood. somberly adv.*

- **defiance** (dē fī´ əns) *n.* refusal to obey authority (p. 734) *In defiance of a court's order to return to their jobs, the workers refused to do so. defiant adj. defy v.*

- **peril** (per´ əl) *n.* danger (p. 734) *Her reckless actions put her health and safety in peril. perilous adj. perilously adv.*

- **transfigured** (trans fig´ yərd) *adj.* changed; transformed in a glorious way (p. 736) *She was glowing, transfigured by the experience of becoming a new mother. transfiguration n.*

Word Study

The **Latin prefix *trans-*** means "change."

In "Harriet Beecher Stowe," the speaker suggests that both black and white Americans were **transfigured**, or changed, by the anti-slavery movement.

Emma Lazarus

(1849–1887)

"The New Colossus" (page 728)

Emma Lazarus wrote "The New Colossus" to inspire others to donate money for the Statue of Liberty's pedestal. The final lines of the poem were so inspirational that they were permanently inscribed on the pedestal itself. Raised in New York City, where she studied languages, Lazarus published a book of poems and translations at seventeen. Later, drawing on her Jewish heritage, she wrote several works celebrating America as a place of refuge for people persecuted in Europe.

Henry Wadsworth Longfellow

(1807–1882)

"Paul Revere's Ride" (page 731)

Henry Wadsworth Longfellow started college at age fifteen and was asked to be the first professor of modern languages at Bowdoin College at the age of nineteen. He was one of the "fireside poets," a group of writers whose popular poems were read aloud by nineteenth-century families as they gathered around a fireplace. He wrote several long poems on topics in American history.

Paul Laurence Dunbar

(1872–1906)

"Harriet Beecher Stowe" (page 735)

Paul Laurence Dunbar was the son of former slaves. Encouraged by his mother, he began writing poetry at an early age. Dunbar was inspired by Harriet Beecher Stowe's novel *Uncle Tom's Cabin,* and in his own work he honored people who fought for the rights of African Americans.

The New Colossus

Emma Lazarus

Background The title and first two lines of Lazarus's poem refer to the Colossus of Rhodes, one of the Seven Wonders of the Ancient World. A huge statue of the sun god Helios, it was built around 280 B.C. and stood at the entrance to the harbor of the Greek island of Rhodes. At 100 feet tall, it was around three-fifths the size of our Statue of Liberty. It commemorated a great military victory but only stood for 54 years before an earthquake toppled it.

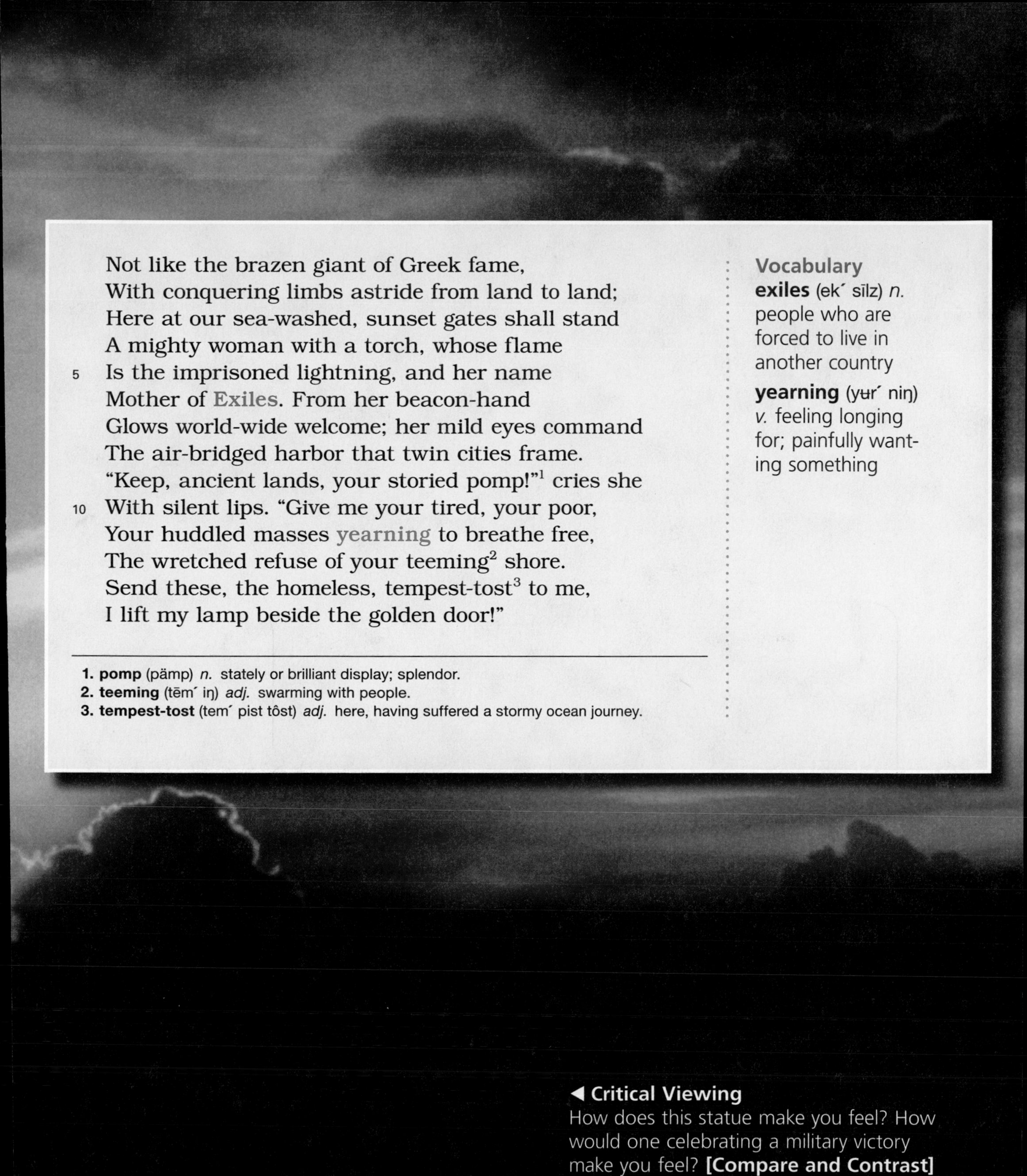

Not like the brazen giant of Greek fame,
With conquering limbs astride from land to land;
Here at our sea-washed, sunset gates shall stand
A mighty woman with a torch, whose flame
5 Is the imprisoned lightning, and her name
Mother of Exiles. From her beacon-hand
Glows world-wide welcome; her mild eyes command
The air-bridged harbor that twin cities frame.
"Keep, ancient lands, your storied pomp!"[1] cries she
10 With silent lips. "Give me your tired, your poor,
Your huddled masses yearning to breathe free,
The wretched refuse of your teeming[2] shore.
Send these, the homeless, tempest-tost[3] to me,
I lift my lamp beside the golden door!"

---

1. pomp (pämp) *n.* stately or brilliant display; splendor.
2. teeming (tēm´ iŋ) *adj.* swarming with people.
3. tempest-tost (tem´ pist tôst) *adj.* here, having suffered a stormy ocean journey.

Vocabulary
exiles (ek´ sīlz) *n.*
people who are
forced to live in
another country

yearning (yʉr´ niŋ)
v. feeling longing
for; painfully want-
ing something

◄ **Critical Viewing**
How does this statue make you feel? How
would one celebrating a military victory
make you feel? **[Compare and Contrast]**

Paul Revere's Ride

Henry Wadsworth Longfellow

Listen, my children, and you shall hear
Of the midnight ride of Paul Revere,
On the eighteenth of April, in Seventy-five;
Hardly a man is now alive
5 Who remembers that famous day and year.

He said to his friend, "If the British march
By land or sea from the town to-night,
Hang a lantern aloft in the belfry arch
Of the North Church tower as a signal light,—
10 One, if by land, and two, if by sea;
And I on the opposite shore will be,
Ready to ride and spread the alarm
Through every Middlesex village and farm,
For the country folk to be up and to arm."

15 Then he said, "Good night!" and with muffled oar
Silently rowed to the Charlestown shore,
Just as the moon rose over the bay,
Where swinging wide at her moorings lay
The *Somerset*, British man-of-war;[1]
20 A phantom ship, with each mast and spar
Across the moon like a prison bar,
And a huge black hulk, that was magnified
By its own reflection in the tide.

Meanwhile, his friend, through alley and street,
25 Wanders and watches with eager ears,

---

1. man-of-war (man´ əv wôr´) *n.* armed naval vessel; warship.

◀ **Critical Viewing**
Based on this painting, what do you think the mood of this poem will be? **[Predict]**

Forms of Poetry
What is the conflict in this poem?

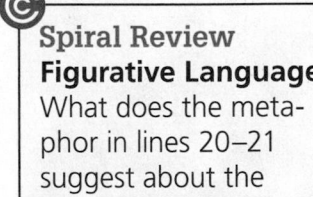
Spiral Review
Figurative Language
What does the metaphor in lines 20–21 suggest about the speaker's feelings toward the British?

 Reading Check
At what time in history is this narrative poem set?

Vocabulary
somber (säm´ bər)
adj. dark; gloomy

▼ Critical Viewing
What would make the
Old North Church,
shown here, a good
place from which to sig-
nal Revere? **[Speculate]**

Till in the silence around him he hears
The muster[2] of men at the barrack door,
The sound of arms, and the tramp of feet,
And the measured tread of the grenadiers,[3]
30   Marching down to their boats on the shore.

Then he climbed the tower of the Old North Church,
By the wooden stairs, with stealthy tread,
To the belfry-chamber overhead,
And startled the pigeons from their perch
35   On the somber rafters, that round him made
Masses and moving shapes of shade,—
By the trembling ladder, steep and tall,
To the highest window in the wall,
Where he paused to listen and look down
40   A moment on the roofs of the town,
And the moonlight flowing over all.

Beneath, in the churchyard, lay the dead,
In their night-encampment on the hill,
Wrapped in silence so deep and still
45   That he could hear, like a sentinel's tread,[4]
The watchful night-wind, as it went
Creeping along from tent to tent,
And seeming to whisper, "All is well!"
A moment only he feels the spell
50   Of the place and the hour, and the secret dread
Of the lonely belfry and the dead;
For suddenly all his thoughts are bent
On a shadowy something far away,
Where the river widens to meet the bay,—
55   A line of black that bends and floats
On the rising tide, like a bridge of boats.

Meanwhile, impatient to mount and ride,
Booted and spurred, with a heavy stride
On the opposite shore walked Paul Revere.
60   Now he patted his horse's side,
Now gazed at the landscape far and near,
Then, impetuous,[5] stamped the earth,

---

2. muster (mus´ tər) *n.* assembly of troops summoned for inspection, roll call, or service.
3. grenadiers (gren´ ə dirz´) *n.* members of a special regiment or corps.
4. sentinel's (sent´ 'n əlz) **tread** (tred) footsteps of a guard.
5. impetuous (im pech´ oo əs) *adj.* done suddenly with little thought.

And turned and tightened his saddle-girth;[6]
But mostly he watched with eager search
65 The belfry-tower of the Old North Church,
As it rose above the graves on the hill,
Lonely and spectral and somber and still.
And lo! as he looks, on the belfry's height
A glimmer, and then a gleam of light!
70 He springs to the saddle, the bridle he turns,
But lingers and gazes, till full on his sight
A second lamp in the belfry burns!

A hurry of hoofs in a village street,
A shape in the moonlight, a bulk in the dark,
75 And beneath, from the pebbles, in passing, a spark
Struck out by a steed flying fearless and fleet:
That was all! And yet, through the gloom and the light,
The fate of a nation was riding that night;
And the spark struck out by that steed in his flight,
80 Kindled the land into flame with its heat.

He has left the village and mounted the steep,
And beneath him, tranquil and broad and deep,
Is the Mystic,[7] meeting the ocean tides;
And under the alders that skirt its edge,
85 Now soft on the sand, now loud on the ledge,
Is heard the tramp of his steed as he rides.

It was twelve by the village clock,
When he crossed the bridge into Medford town.
He heard the crowing of the cock,
90 And the barking of the farmer's dog,
And felt the damp of the river fog,
That rises after the sun goes down.

It was one by the village clock,
When he galloped into Lexington.
95 He saw the gilded weathercock
Swim in the moonlight as he passed,
And the meeting-house windows, blank and bare,
Gaze at him with a spectral glare,
As if they already stood aghast
100 At the bloody work they would look upon.

Paraphrase
Paraphrase this stanza by identifying what is happening and who is participating in the action.

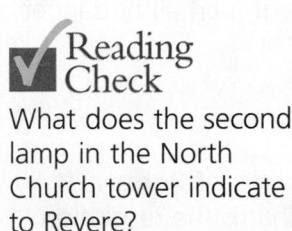
Reading Check
What does the second lamp in the North Church tower indicate to Revere?

---

6. **saddle-girth** (gʉrth) *n.* band put around the belly of a horse for holding a saddle.
7. **Mystic** (mis′ tik) river in Massachusetts.

It was two by the village clock,
When he came to the bridge in Concord town.
He heard the bleating of the flock,
And the twitter of birds among the trees,
105 And felt the breath of the morning breeze
Blowing over the meadows brown.
And one was safe and asleep in his bed
Who at the bridge would be first to fall,
Who that day would be lying dead,
110 Pierced by a British musket-ball.

Paraphrase
Paraphrase this stanza
by explaining who was
fighting and what the
result of the fight was.

You know the rest. In the books you have read,
How the British Regulars fired and fled,—
How the farmers gave them ball for ball,
From behind each fence and farm-yard wall,
115 Chasing the red-coats down the lane,
Then crossing the fields to emerge again
Under the trees at the turn of the road,
And only pausing to fire and load.

Vocabulary
defiance (dē fī´ əns)
n. refusal to obey
authority
peril (per´ əl) *n.* danger

So through the night rode Paul Revere;
120 And so through the night went his cry of alarm
To every Middlesex village and farm,—
A cry of defiance and not of fear,
A voice in the darkness, a knock at the door,
And a word that shall echo forevermore!
125 For, borne on the night-wind of the Past,
Through all our history, to the last,
In the hour of darkness and peril and need,
The people will waken and listen to hear
The hurrying hoof-beats of that steed,
130 And the midnight message of Paul Revere.

Forms of Poetry
What is the resolution
of the conflict in this
poem?

Harriet Beecher Stowe

Paul Laurence Dunbar

Background Harriet Beecher Stowe is the author of *Uncle Tom's Cabin,* a classic antislavery novel. Her work, written before the Civil War, brought the horror of slavery into the public eye. When Abraham Lincoln met Stowe, he said, "So you're the little woman who wrote the book that made this great war!"

She told the story, and the whole world wept
    At wrongs and cruelties it had not known
    But for this fearless woman's voice alone.
    She spoke to the consciences that long had slept:

5   Her message, Freedom's clear reveille,[1] swept
       From heedless hovel[2] to complacent throne.
       Command and prophecy were in the tone
       And from its sheath the sword of justice leapt.
    Around two peoples swelled the fiery wave,
10   But both came forth transfigured from the flame
    Blest be the hand that dared be strong to save,
       And blest be she who in our weakness came—
       Prophet and priestess! At one stroke she gave
       A race to freedom and herself to fame.

Vocabulary
transfigured (trans fig´
yərd) *adj.* changed;
transformed in a
glorious way

---

1. **reveille** (rev´ ə lē) *n.* early morning bugle or drum signal to waken soldiers.
2. **heedless hovel** (hēd´ lis huv´ əl) small, miserable, poorly kept dwelling place.

Critical Thinking

Cite textual evidence to support your responses.

Ⓒ **1. Key Ideas and Details (a) Interpret:** Interpret the meaning and significance of the following lines: "The New Colossus" (line 9); "Paul Revere's Ride" (lines 78–80); "Harriet Beecher Stowe" (lines 9–10). **(b) Discuss:** In a small group, discuss your responses. Then, share your ideas with the class.

Ⓒ **2. Integration of Knowledge and Ideas** All three of these poems were written in the nineteenth century. Review a more modern poem from earlier in this unit, such as "Describe Somebody" (p. 645) or "The Drum" (p. 663). **(a) Analyze:** How do the language patterns and word choice in these three poems compare with those found in a more contemporary poem? **(b) Evaluate:** Does the fact that the poems reflect different time periods influence your response to them? Why or why not?

Ⓒ **3. Integration of Knowledge and Ideas (a)** Which of these historical poems do you find the most exciting or inspiring? **(b)** Which details and elements provoke your response? *[Connect to the Big Question: What is the secret to reaching someone with words?]*

736 Poetry

Reading Skill: Paraphrase

1. **(a)** Which words in lines 3–6 from "The New Colossus" answer the questions *Whom?* or *What?* **(b) Paraphrase** the lines using a structure that is more like everyday speech.

2. Reread the second stanza of "Paul Revere's Ride." **(a)** Write the lines in sentences. **(b)** Paraphrase each sentence.

Literary Analysis: Forms of Poetry

© 3. **Craft and Structure** Use a chart to compare and contrast the **lyric** and **narrative poems** in this collection.

	Form: lyric or narrative?	What characteristics make it lyric or narrative?	How does the form help the poet achieve his or her purpose?
Colossus			
Revere's Ride			
Stowe			

© 4. **Craft and Structure (a)** What overall impression does "The New Colossus" convey? **(b)** How does the **allusion** at the beginning connect to this impression?

© 5. **Craft and Structure** Review the definition of a **sonnet** on page 639. What elements of "Harriet Beecher Stowe" fit the form of a sonnet?

Vocabulary

© **Acquisition and Use** For each item, write a sentence that correctly uses both of the words or phrases provided.

1. exiles; persecution
2. homesick; yearning
3. memorial service; somber
4. defiance; authority
5. carelessly; peril
6. birth; transfigured

Word Study Use context and what you know about the **Latin prefix *trans-*** to explain your answer to each question.

1. How might you try to *transform* a classroom bully?
2. What might cause someone to undergo a *transition*?

Word Study

The **Latin prefix *trans-***
means "change."

Apply It Explain how the prefix *trans-* contributes to the meanings of these words. Consult a dictionary if necessary.

transplant
transcribe
translation

Integrated Language Skills

Poetry Collections 5 and 6

Conventions: Prepositional Phrases

A **preposition** shows the relationship between two words or phrases. A **prepositional phrase** begins with a preposition and ends with the noun, noun phrase, or pronoun that follows it. As a unit, a prepositional phrase acts like an adjective or an adverb.

Prepositional Phrase	Explanation
The cup *of milk* tipped over.	The prepositional phrase *of milk* acts like an adjective and tells which cup.
The milk spilled *onto the floor*.	The prepositional phrase *onto the floor* acts like an adverb and tells where the milk spilled.

Poetry Collection 6

Avoid ending a sentence with a preposition in formal writing, such as reports, essays, and business letters. In some cases, the preposition is grammatically incorrect and should be omitted:

Incorrect: *They didn't know where he was at.*
Correct: *They didn't know where he was.*

In other instances, the sentence should be reworded:

Incorrect: *Which country did he emigrate from?*
Correct: *From which country did he emigrate?*

Practice A Identify the prepositional phrase or phrases in each sentence. Tell if the prepositional phrase acts like an adjective or adverb.

1. Harriet Tubman led many slaves to safety.

2. Many runaways escaped at night and traveled on foot.

3. The speaker has doubts about friendship.

4. He honors the memory of his grandfather.

Ⓒ **Reading Application** In Poetry Collection 5, find two prepositional phrases that act as adjectives and two prepositional phrases that act as adverbs.

Practice B Rewrite the following sentences, adding prepositional phrases to tell more about the italicized words.

1. The Statue of Liberty is *located* ____.

2. Revere *rode* ____, warning the *citizens* ___.

3. His *ride* ____ was an important *event* ___.

4. Abolitionists like Stowe were *involved* ___.

Ⓒ **Writing Application** Locate a copy of the Pledge of Allegiance and identify eight prepositional phrases it contains. For each, decide whether the phrase functions as an adjective or adverb.

PH WRITING COACH | Further instruction and practice are available in *Prentice Hall Writing Coach*.

Writing

Common Core State Standards

L.8.1, L.2.a; W.8.3; SL.8.1
[For the full wording of the standards, see page 714.]

Narrative Text Write a **lyric or narrative poem** about an admirable person from history or from your own life.

- If you are writing a lyric poem, brainstorm for details about the person's qualities.

- If you are writing a narrative poem, list the events, characters, and details of setting you will include in the poem.

Use your notes to draft and revise the lines of your poem.

- To revise word choice in a lyric poem, look for places to add words that have a musical quality and convey strong emotions.

- To revise word choice in a narrative poem, replace dull description with dynamic language to further plot or characterization.

Punctuate based on how you want your poem to be read. For a pause or break, use a comma, an ellipsis (. . .), or a dash (—); for a full stop, use a period.

Grammar Application If your poem contains incomplete sentences that have only subordinate clauses, add main clauses to complete them.

Writing Workshop: *Work-in-Progress*

Prewriting for Exposition For a comparison-and-contrast essay, create a chart with categories such as *literary characters, scientific processes,* or *historical events*. List several items under each heading. Think about ways the items in each list are alike and different. Circle two items to use as a focus. Save this Topic Ideas Chart.

Use this prewriting activity to prepare for the **Writing Workshop** on page 780.

Speaking and Listening

Comprehension and Collaboration Prepare an oral presentation of one of the poems in these collections. In a group, develop an **evaluation form** for the presentations. Follow these steps:

- Identify the different qualities of an effective delivery, such as varying tone of voice, using pauses for dramatic effect, reading clearly, and adjusting reading rates.

- List categories to evaluate the poems themselves, such as choice of language and effect on the listener.

- Decide on a rating scale and a layout for your form.

- Share the form with classmates to help them prepare to read poetry aloud. Then, use it to evaluate the oral presentations.

Leveled Texts

Build your skills and improve your comprehension of poetry with texts of increasing complexity.

Poetry Collection 7 shows how places and people can inspire joy in others.

Poetry Collection 8 uses sensory details to bring experiences to life.

Common Core State Standards

Meet these standards with either **Poetry Collection 7** (p. 744) or **Poetry Collection 8** (p. 757).

Reading Literature

1. Cite textual evidence that most strongly supports an analysis of what the text says explicitly as well as inferences drawn from the text. *(Reading Skill: Paraphrase)*

Spiral Review RL.8.4

Writing

1. Write arguments to support claims with clear reasons and relevant evidence. *(Writing: Review)*

8. Gather relevant information from multiple print and digital sources, using search terms effectively; assess the credibility and accuracy of each source; and quote or paraphrase the data and conclusions of others while avoiding plagiarism and following a standard format for citation. *(Research and Technology: Profile)*

9. Draw evidence from literary or informational texts to support analysis, reflection, and research. *(Writing: Review)*

Language

1.a. Explain the function of verbals in general and their function in particular sentences. *(Conventions: Infinitive Phrases)*

6. Acquire and use accurately grade-appropriate general academic and domain-specific words and phrases; gather vocabulary knowledge when considering a word or phrase important to comprehension or expression. *(Vocabulary: Word Study)*

Reading Skill: Paraphrase

Poetry often expresses ideas in language that does not sound like everyday speech. **Paraphrasing** is restating something in your own words. Stopping occasionally to paraphrase a line or a group of lines can clarify the meanings of words and phrases that contribute to the main ideas and improve your understanding.

- First, **read aloud fluently according to punctuation.** Pause briefly at commas, dashes, and semicolons and longer after end marks like periods to help you find units of meaning.

- Next, restate the meaning of each complete thought in your own words. Rephrase unusual or complicated expressions into simpler language, using synonyms for the writer's words.

Literary Analysis: Imagery

A *writer's style* is his or her unique use of language. One key component of style is the use of imagery to convey ideas. **Imagery** is language that appeals to the senses. Poets use imagery to help readers imagine sights, sounds, textures, tastes, and smells.

- **With imagery:** The train thundered past, roaring, screaming.
- **Without imagery:** The train went by.

For each poem, use a chart like the one shown to note imagery.

Using the Strategy: Sensory Web

Record details beneath each heading on a **sensory web** like this one.

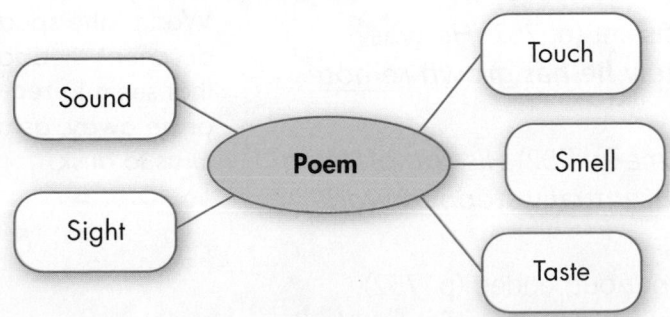

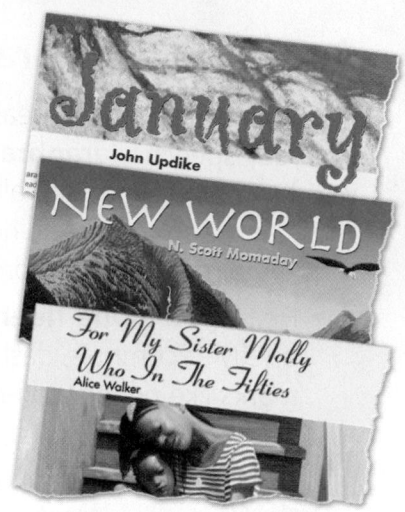

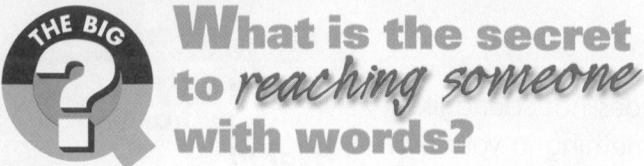 **What is the secret** to *reaching someone* **with words?**

Writing About the Big Question

The poets in Poetry Collection 7 carefully chose words to convey a speakers' ideas about specific people and places. Use this sentence starter to develop your ideas about the Big Question.

If someone who did not know me asked me to describe my hometown or my family, I would choose **sensory** images such as _____ and _____.

While You Read Notice the way the speakers of the poems connect their emotions with the sensory images that they describe.

Vocabulary

Read each word and its definition. Decide whether you know the word well, know it a little bit, or do not know it at all. After you read, see how your knowledge of each word has increased.

- **pollen** (päl´ ən) *n.* powdery grains on seed plants that aid in reproduction (p. 746) *Insects and wind carry pollen from flower to flower.* pollinate *v.* pollination *n.*

- **recede** (ri sēd´) *v.* move away (p. 747) *As the clouds began to recede, the sky brightened.* receded *adj.* recession *n.*

- **inexpressible** (in´ eks pres´ ə bəl) *adj.* not able to be described (p. 751) *Words were not enough to capture his feelings of inexpressible joy.* inexpressive *adj.* expressive *adj.*

- **remote** (ri mōt´) *adj.* aloof; cold; distant (p. 752) *He was once warm and friendly, but lately he has grown remote.* remotely *adv.* remoteness *n.*

- **wearisome** (wir´ i səm) *adj.* tiresome (p. 752) *His complaining had grown wearisome and we eventually stopped working with him.* weary *adj.*

- **extinguished** (ek stiŋ´ gwisht) *v.* put out; ended (p. 752) *When he injured his knee, he saw his dream of a football career extinguished.* extinguishable *adj.*

Word Study

The **Latin roots -cede-** and **-ceed-** mean "go" or "yield."

In the poem "New World," the speaker describes meadows that seem to **recede**, or go away, as day turns to dusk.

John Updike

(1932–2009)

"January" (page 744)

Although he is best known as a Pulitzer Prize-winning novelist, John Updike also wrote poetry, essays, short stories, and literary criticism. As a child growing up on a farm in Pennsylvania, Updike enjoyed reading so much that his mother encouraged him to write. In 2003, Updike received the National Medal for the Humanities. He had previously won the National Medal of Art. Only a handful of writers have been honored with both prizes.

N. Scott Momaday

(b. 1934)

"New World" (page 746)

A Kiowa Indian, N. Scott Momaday is known for his poetry, plays, art, and essays. As a writer, Momaday strives to pass on Kiowa oral traditions. His father, a great teller of Kiowa stories, inspired Momaday to write: ". . . it was only after I became an adult that I understood how fragile [the stories] are, because they exist only by word of mouth, always just one generation away from extinction."

Alice Walker

(b. 1944)

"For My Sister Molly Who in the Fifties" (page 749)

Alice Walker, the youngest of eight children, grew up in Georgia, where her parents were farmers. She is one of the best-known and best-loved African American writers. Walker's poems frequently deal with the preservation of her culture and heritage. Her novel *The Color Purple,* was made into a movie in 1985, directed by Steven Spielberg and starred Whoopi Goldberg and Oprah Winfrey. *The Color Purple* has also been produced as a Broadway show.

January

John Updike

Paraphrase
Read lines 1–4 according to punctuation. Then, put this stanza into your own words.

The days are short,
   The sun a spark
Hung thin between
   The dark and dark.

5 Fat snowy footsteps
   Track the floor,
And parkas pile up
   Near the door.

The river is
10   A frozen place
Held still beneath
      The trees' black lace.

The sky is low.
      The wind is gray.
15 The radiator
      Purrs all day.

▲ **Critical Viewing**
Compare and contrast the artist's concept of winter with Updike's. **[Compare and Contrast]**

NEW WORLD

N. Scott Momaday

▲ **Critical Viewing**
What aspects of this painting convey the idea of a "new world"? **[Analyze]**

Vocabulary
pollen (päl´ ən) *n.* powdery grains on seed plants that aid in reproduction

1.

First Man,
behold:
the earth
glitters
5   with leaves;
the sky
glistens
with rain.
Pollen
10 is borne
on winds
that low
and lean
upon
15 mountains.
Cedars
blacken
the slopes—
and pines.

2.

20 At dawn
eagles
hie and
hover[1]
above
25 the plain
where light
gathers
in pools.
Grasses
30 shimmer
and shine.
Shadows
withdraw
and lie
35 away
like smoke.

---

1. hie and hover fly swiftly and then hang as if suspended in the air.

Wallowa Lake, Harley, Abby Aldrich Rockefeller Folk Art Center, Williamsburg, VA.

3.

    At noon
    turtles
    enter
40 slowly
    into
    the warm
    dark loam.[2]
    Bees hold
45 the swarm.
    Meadows
    recede
    through planes
    of heat
50 and pure
    distance.

4.

    At dusk
    the gray
    foxes
55 stiffen
    in cold;
    blackbirds
    are fixed
    in the
60 branches.
    Rivers
    follow
    the moon,
    the long
65 white track
    of the
    full moon.

Spiral Review
Tone Which words
and phrases in the
poem support the
author's tone of
wonder and majesty?
Explain.

Vocabulary
recede (ri sēd´) *v.*
move away

Imagery
What images convey a
sense of the tempera-
ture in the final stanza?

---

2. loam (lōm) rich, dark soil.

For My Sister Molly Who In The Fifties

Alice Walker

Once made a fairy rooster from
Mashed potatoes
Whose eyes I forget
But green onions were his tail
5 And his two legs were carrot sticks
A tomato slice his crown.
Who came home on vacation
When the sun was hot
and cooked
10 and cleaned
And minded least of all
The children's questions
A million or more
Pouring in on her
15 Who had been to school
And knew (and told us too) that certain
Words were no longer good
And taught me not to say us for we
No matter what "Sonny said" up the
20 road.

FOR MY SISTER MOLLY WHO IN THE FIFTIES
Knew Hamlet[1] well and read into the night
And coached me in my songs of Africa
A continent I never knew
25 But learned to love
Because "they" she said could carry
A tune
And spoke in accents never heard
In Eatonton.

---

1. *Hamlet* play by William Shakespeare.

◄ **Critical Viewing**
How would you describe the relationship between the girls in this painting? **[Infer]**

Imagery
What do the images in the first stanza tell you about Molly?

✔ Reading Check
What are two things the speaker appreciates about her sister?

30 Who read from *Prose and Poetry*
And loved to read "Sam McGee from Tennessee"[2]
On nights the fire was burning low
And Christmas wrapped in angel hair[3]
And I for one prayed for snow.

Paraphrase
Restate lines 35–42 in
your own words.

35 WHO IN THE FIFTIES
Knew all the written things that made
Us laugh and stories by
The hour   Waking up the story buds
Like fruit. Who walked among the flowers
40 And brought them inside the house
And smelled as good as they
And looked as bright.
Who made dresses, braided
Hair. Moved chairs about
45 Hung things from walls
Ordered baths
Frowned on wasp bites
And seemed to know the endings
Of all the tales
50 I had forgot.

Paraphrase
In your own words,
explain the growing
distance between Molly
and her siblings.

WHO OFF INTO THE UNIVERSITY
Went exploring   To London and
To Rotterdam
Prague and to Liberia
55 Bringing back the news to us
Who knew none of it
But followed
crops and weather
funerals and
60 Methodist Homecoming;
easter speeches,
groaning church.

---

2. "Sam McGee from Tennessee" reference to the title character in the Robert Service
poem, "The Cremation of Sam McGee."
3. angel hair fine, white, filmy Christmas tree decoration.

WHO FOUND ANOTHER WORLD
Another life   With gentlefolk
65 Far less trusting
And moved and moved and changed
Her name
And sounded precise
When she spoke   And frowned away
70 Our sloppishness.

WHO SAW US SILENT
Cursed with fear   A love burning
Inexpressible
And sent me money not for me
75 But for "College."
Who saw me grow through letters
The words misspelled   But not
The longing   Stretching
Growth
80 The tied and twisting
Tongue
Feet no longer bare
Skin no longer burnt against
The cotton.

85 WHO BECAME SOMEONE OVERHEAD
A light   A thousand watts
Bright and also blinding
And saw my brothers cloddish

Vocabulary
inexpressible (in´ eks
pres´ ə bəl) *adj.* not
able to be described

Imagery
What images describe
the sensations of
growing up?

✓ Reading
Check
In what ways is
the speaker's sister
changing?

And me destined to be
90 Wayward[4]
My mother remote   My father
A wearisome farmer
With heartbreaking
Nails.

95 FOR MY SISTER MOLLY WHO IN THE FIFTIES
Found much
Unbearable
Who walked where few had
Understood   And sensed our
100 Groping after light
And saw some extinguished
And no doubt mourned.

FOR MY SISTER MOLLY WHO IN THE FIFTIES
Left us.

---

4. wayward (wā´ wərd) *adj.* headstrong; disobedient.

Critical Thinking

Cite textual evidence to support your responses.

© **1. Key Ideas and Details (a)** In "January," what are three things the speaker associates with January? **(b)** How does he describe these things? **(c) Draw Conclusions:** Based on these descriptions, what kind of attitude does he have toward winter? Explain.

© **2. Key Ideas and Details (a)** In "New World," what three times of day are identified? **(b) Infer:** Why does the poet describe these times? **(c) Interpret:** What might these times represent?

© **3. Key Ideas and Details (a)** In "For My Sister Molly Who in the Fifties," what are three things the speaker learns from Molly? **(b) Analyze:** What is the significance of these three things? **(c) Evaluate:** Why are these lessons important to her?

© **4. Integration of Knowledge and Ideas (a)** List five images that the speaker uses to describe Molly in "For My Sister . . ." **(b)** How do these images help us understand Molly? **(c)** How do the poet's words help us appreciate the speaker's changing relationship with Molly? *[Connect to the Big Question: What is the secret to reaching someone with words?]*

Reading Skill: Paraphrase

1. Use the punctuation in lines 21–29 of "For My Sister . . ." to identify two complete thoughts. **Paraphrase** the lines.

2. Fill in a chart like the one shown with your paraphrases.

Original Lines	Paraphrase
January: (lines 13–16)	
New World: (lines 37–45)	
For My Sister Molly...: (lines 15–17)	

Literary Analysis: Imagery

3. Craft and Structure (a) What **imagery** does Updike use in "January" to describe winter days? **(b)** How does Updike's word choice and overall style affect the poem's meaning?

4. Craft and Structure (a) What moods, or feelings, does the imagery in "For My Sister . . ." create? **(b)** How well does the free verse structure work with the images to create mood and meaning? Explain.

Vocabulary

Acquisition and Use Use a vocabulary word from page 742 to change each sentence so that it makes sense. Explain your answers.

1. When the rain stops, the water level will rise.

2. Friends grow closer if they do not see each other for years.

3. Bees gather petals from flowers to make honey.

4. When sunlight filled the room, the candles were lit.

5. She was so nervous, her thoughts were easy to share.

6. He was energized after years of backbreaking work.

Word Study Use context to answer each question.

1. Would a war's victor be likely to *cede* territory to the loser?

2. Would a negative review *exceed* an author's expectations?

Word Study

The **Latin roots -cede-** and **-ceed-** mean "go" or "yield."

Apply It Explain how the roots -cede- and -ceed- contribute to the meanings of these words. Consult a dictionary, if necessary.

succeed
secede
intercede

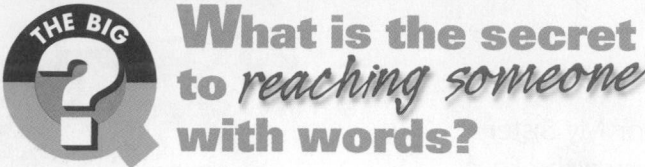

What is the secret to *reaching someone* with words?

Writing About the Big Question

The poems in Poetry Collection 8 explore how words make connections between people and the world. Use these sentence starters to develop your ideas about the Big Question.

I feel a **connection** to other people when I _____.

I feel a **connection** with the natural world when I _____.

While You Read Note how the poets use words and images to establish connections.

Vocabulary

Read each word and its definition. Decide whether you know the word well, know it a little bit, or do not know it at all. After you read, see how your knowledge of each word has increased.

- **jostling** (jäs´ liŋ) *n.* the act of knocking into, often on purpose (p. 757) *With all the jostling taking place in the crowd, I was elbowed several times. jostle v.*

- **impertinently** (im pʉrt´ 'n ənt lē) *adv.* disrespectfully (p. 757) *"You are older, not wiser," he said impertinently to his mother. impertinent adj. pertinent adj.*

- **exquisite** (eks´ kwiz it) *adj.* very beautiful (p. 757) *This exquisite vase was hand-painted by an artist known for her unique, lovely designs. exquisitely adv. exquisiteness n.*

- **vertical** (vʉr´ ti kəl) *adj.* straight up and down; upright (p. 758) *A pine tree's trunk is tall and vertical. vertically adv.*

- **burrow** (bʉr´ ō) *n.* passage or hole for shelter (p. 758) *The gopher dove into its burrow. burrow v.*

- **tongue** (tuŋ) *n.* language (p. 760) *Our guide spoke to the village chief in his native tongue.*

Word Study

The **Latin word root -vert-** means "turn."

In the poem "Drum Song," the speaker figuratively describes a tree trunk as "**vertical** earth." The speaker is describing earth, which is normally horizontal, and turning it upright.

E. E. Cummings

(1894–1962)

"your little voice / Over the wires came leaping" (page 757)

During World War I, Edward Estlin Cummings joined a volunteer ambulance corps in France. The unusual writing style of his letters back home convinced French censors he was a spy, and he was imprisoned for three months. In his poetry, Cummings is known for his experimental, playful style, unusual punctuation, and unconventional arrangement of words.

Wendy Rose

(b. 1948)

"Drum Song" (page 758)

Wendy Rose believes that "For everything in this universe there is a song to accompany its existence; writing is another way of singing these songs." One of the foremost Native American poets, Rose also illustrates many of her poems with pen and ink drawings and watercolors.

Amy Ling

(1939–1999)

"Grandma Ling" (page 759)

Amy Ling was born in China and lived there with her family for six years before moving to the United States. In addition to writing poetry, Ling worked as an editor of American literature anthologies. She was instrumental in bringing the work of Asian American writers to a wider audience. In the 1960s, Ling visited her grandmother in Taiwan and wrote about their first meeting in "Grandma Ling."

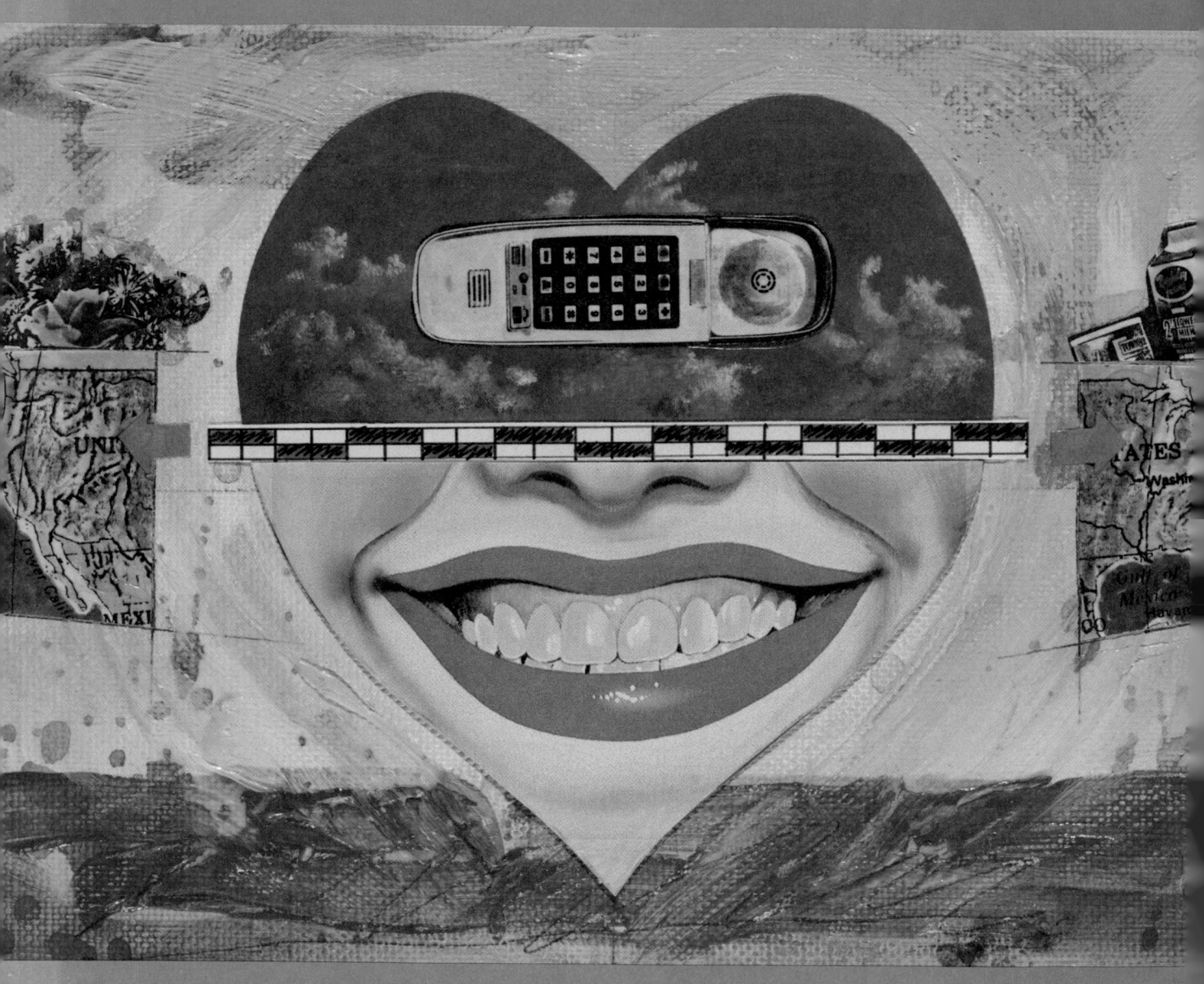

your little voice
Over the wires came leaping
E. E. Cummings

your little voice
                    Over the wires came leaping
and i felt suddenly
dizzy
5   With the jostling and shouting of merry flowers
wee skipping high-heeled flames
courtesied[1] before my eyes
                    or twinkling over to my side
Looked up
10 with impertinently exquisite faces
floating hands were laid upon me
I was whirled and tossed into delicious dancing
up
Up
15 with the pale important
                  stars and the Humorous
                        moon

dear girl
How i was crazy how i cried when i heard
20   over time
and tide and death
leaping
Sweetly
        your voice

Vocabulary
jostling (jäs´ liŋ) n. the act of knocking into, often on purpose
impertinently (im pʉrt´ 'n ənt lē) adv. disrespectfully
exquisite (eks´ kwiz it) adj. very beautiful

◀ **Critical Viewing**
What details in this artwork illustrate the poem's ideas about communication? **[Analyze]**

---

1. courtesied (kʉrt´ sēd) v. bowed with bended knees; curtsied.

Drum Song

Wendy Rose

Ⓒ **Spiral Review**
Tone What tone does the author create by repeating the word *Listen*? Explain.

Vocabulary
vertical (vʉr´ ti kəl) *adj.* straight up and down; upright
burrow (bʉr´ ō) *n.* passage or hole for shelter

Listen. Turtle
    your flat round feet
    of four claws each
    go slow, go steady,
5   from rock to water
    to land to rock to
water.

Listen. Woodpecker
    you lift your red head
10   on wind, perch
    on vertical earth
    of tree bark and
branch.

Listen. Snowhare[1]
15   your belly drags,
    your whiskers dance
    bush to burrow
    your eyes turn up
    to where owls
20 hunt.

Listen. Women
    your tongues melt,
    your seeds are planted
    mesa[2] to mesa a shake
25   of gourds,[3]
    a line of mountains
    with blankets
    on their
hips.

Imagery
To what senses does the imagery in the last stanza appeal?

1. **Snowhare** (snō´ har´) *n.* snowshoe hare; a large rabbit whose color changes from brown to white in winter and whose broad feet resemble snowshoes.
2. **mesa** (mā´ sə) *n.* small, high plateau with steep sides.
3. **gourds** (gôrdz) *n.* dried, hollowed-out shells of fruits such as melons and pumpkins.

Grandma Ling

Amy Ling

Woman with White Kerchief (Uygur), Lunda Hoyle Gill

If you dig that hole deep enough
you'll reach China, they used to tell me,
a child in a backyard in Pennsylvania.
Not strong enough to dig that hole,

▲ **Critical Viewing**
What thoughts might
go through your head
if you were meeting a
foreign relative for the
first time? **[Connect]**

Imagery
Which words in lines
9–11 appeal to one or
more of the five senses?

5   I waited twenty years,
    then sailed back, half way around the world.

    In Taiwan I first met Grandma.
    Before she came to view, I heard
    her slippered feet softly measure
10   the tatami[1] floor with even step;
    the aqua paper-covered door slid open
    and there I faced
    my five foot height, sturdy legs and feet,
    square forehead, high cheeks, and wide-set eyes;
15   my image stood before me,
    acted on by fifty years.

    She smiled, stretched her arms
    to take to heart the eldest daughter
    of her youngest son a quarter century away.
20   She spoke a tongue I knew no word of,
    and I was sad I could not understand,
    but I could hug her.

Vocabulary
tongue (tuŋ) *n.*
language

Paraphrase
Restate lines 20–22 in
your own words.

---

1. tatami (tə tä′ mē) *adj.* woven of rice straw.

Critical Thinking

© **1. Key Ideas and Details (a)** In "your little voice . . . ," what effect does the little voice have on the speaker? **(b) Infer:** Why does the speaker react this way?

© **2. Key Ideas and Details (a)** What is each of the animals doing in "Drum Song"? **(b) Analyze:** How do the animals and the women interact with their environments?

© **3. Key Ideas and Details (a)** In "Grandma Ling," what prevents the grandmother and granddaughter from communicating in their first meeting? **(b) Speculate:** What might they want to tell or ask each other? **(c) Analyze:** How do they finally communicate, and what are they saying?

© **4. Integration of Knowledge and Ideas** How do each of the poems show us the types of connections that are possible in the world? *[Connect to the Big Question: What is the secret to reaching someone with words?]*

Cite textual evidence to support your responses.

Reading Skill: Paraphrase

1. Use the punctuation in lines 17–19 of "Grandma Ling" to identify two complete thoughts. **Paraphrase** these lines.

2. Paraphrase the original lines in a chart like the one shown.

Original Lines	Paraphrase
your little voice…: (lines 1–4)	
Drum Song: (lines 8–13)	
Grandma Ling: (lines 15–16)	

Literary Analysis: Imagery

Ⓒ **3. Craft and Structure (a)** List three images from "your little voice . . . " **(b)** What mood, or feeling, does this **imagery** create? **(c)** How well does the unusual structure of the poem combine with the imagery to create this mood? Explain.

Ⓒ **4. Craft and Structure (a)** In "Grandma Ling," what imagery is used in the first stanza? **(b)** How does the *author's style* and use of images affect the poem's meaning?

Vocabulary

Ⓒ **Acquisition and Use** Use a vocabulary word from page 754 to change each sentence so that it makes sense. Explain your answers.

1. The rude child spoke respectfully.

2. We looked up at the horizontal towers of the skyscrapers.

3. The chipmunk ran to hide in the open air.

4. My friend has terrible taste in clothes and always looks good.

5. We'll need a translator who is familiar with their native food.

6. In the crowded store, people had no trouble moving through the aisles.

Word Study Use context to explain each answer.

1. What would happen if a glass of water were suddenly *inverted*?

2. If something *diverts* your attention, does it help you focus?

Word Study

The **Latin root** *-vert-* means "turn."

Apply It Explain how the root *-vert-* contributes to the meanings of these words. Consult a dictionary if necessary.

avert
evert
revert

Integrated Language Skills

Poetry Collections 7 and 8

Conventions: Infinitive Phrases

An **infinitive** is a form of verb that comes after the word *to* and acts as a noun, an adjective, or an adverb. An **infinitive phrase** is an infinitive with a modifier or a complement, all acting together as a single part of speech.

Do not confuse prepositional phrases that begin with the preposition *to* with infinitive phrases. An infinitive phrase always contains a verb; a prepositional phrase never contains a verb.

Prepositional Phrase: I went *to the tennis court.*

Infinitive Phrase: I went *to play tennis at school.*

Poetry Collection 8

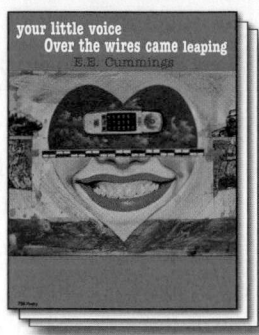

Infinitive	Infinitive Phrase
to ski	*To ski in New Mexico,* you must travel into the mountains.
to give	I need *to give you my new cell phone number.*

Practice A Identify the infinitive phrase in each sentence.

1. To capture January's bleakness, Updike uses words like *dark, black,* and *gray.*

2. Momaday wants readers to focus on nature's beauty.

3. Molly taught her sister to use correct grammar.

4. She left home to explore the world.

ⓒ **Reading Application** In "For My Sister Molly Who in the Fifties," find at least two examples of infinitive phrases. Explain the connecting role the infinitive phrase plays in each sentence.

Practice B Identify the infinitive in each sentence. Then use that infinitive to write a sentence of your own.

1. Because of its unusual structure, it is easy to recognize E. E. Cummings's poetry.

2. Just to hear her voice made him dizzy.

3. The speaker asks Turtle to listen.

4. The child knew it was not possible to dig a hole to China.

ⓒ **Writing Application** Using Item 1 as a model, write three more sentences using infinitive phrases. Follow this sentence starter: Because of_____, it is easy to_____.

PH WRITING COACH Further instruction and practice are available in *Prentice Hall Writing Coach.*

Writing

Argumentative Text A review of a literary work is an evaluation of its strengths and weaknesses. Write a **review** of the three poems in Poetry Collection 7 or 8. Evaluate each poem based on sound, word choice, and imagery.

- To evaluate the sound of a poem, read it aloud and decide how well its sound and rhythm match its subject.
- To evaluate word choice and imagery, determine whether the poets use vivid and appropriate words and images.
- As you draft, support your claims with references to lines from the poems. Finally, offer your overall opinion of each poem.

Grammar Application Check your review to be sure you have used infinitive phrases correctly.

Writing Workshop: *Work in Progress*

Prewriting for Exposition Review the items that you circled on the Topic Ideas Chart in your portfolio. List all the ways that the two items are alike. Then, list all the ways that the two items are different. Finally, put this Categories Map in your portfolio.

Research and Technology

Build and Present Knowledge Write a **profile** of one of the poets featured in Poetry Collection 7 or 8. Follow these steps:

- Use search terms to gather information from several print or online sources about the poet's life, writings, and influences. Reliable sources should be accurate and recent. Choose websites that end with *.edu* or *.org.* When researching, paraphrase—do not copy—your sources, unless you are using a direct quotation. If you include a quotation, note the source, using the appropriate citation style (see pp. R34–R35).
- As you draft, explain how the poet's work reflects his or her heritage, traditions, attitudes, and beliefs.
- Provide specific details about when and where the poet lived and how this influenced the characterization and settings in the poet's major works.
- While drafting, be sure to develop an effective balance between research information and original ideas. Be careful to credit ideas that are not your own.

Common Core State Standards

L.8.1.a; W.8.1, W.8.8, W.8.9
[For the full wording of the standards, see page 740.]

Use this prewriting activity to prepare for the **Writing Workshop** on page 780.

Test Practice: Reading

Paraphrase

Fiction Selection

Directions: *Read the selection. Then, answer the questions.*

1 Once upon a midnight dreary, while I pondered, weak and
     weary,
2 Over many a quaint and curious volume of forgotten lore,
3 While I nodded, nearly napping, suddenly there came a tapping,
4 As of someone gently rapping, rapping at my chamber door.
5 "Tis some visitor," I muttered, "tapping at my chamber door—
6   Only this, and nothing more."

—from "The Raven" by Edgar Allan Poe

1. According to punctuation, when should the reader come to a complete stop?
  A. after lines 1 and 3
  B. after lines 2 and 5
  C. after lines 4 and 6
  D. at the end of every line

2. Which is the *best* paraphrase of "quaint and curious volume of forgotten lore" (line 2)?
  A. interesting book of myths
  B. old and interesting book of old stories
  C. antique and difficult book of old tales
  D. question and answer books

3. According to punctuation, when should the reader pause in line 3?
  A. after each comma
  B. after the final comma
  C. after the 1st and 3rd commas
  D. after the 2nd and 3rd commas

4. Which paraphrase of lines 3 and 4 is the *most* accurate?
  A. While I began to fall asleep, someone softly tapped on the door to my room.
  B. As the speaker enjoys his book, he hears a tapping sound on his door.
  C. While I was sleeping, I heard a knock.
  D. As I nodded off to sleep, someone rapped, rapped, rapped, at my bedroom door.

Writing for Assessment

Write a one-paragraph response in which you paraphrase the verse to explain what happened. Be sure to restate the events in your own words.

Nonfiction Selection

Directions: *Read the selection. Then, answer the questions.*

(1) Edgar Allan Poe's poems and stories have chilled readers for over 150 years. **(2)** While his work spans many genres, he is best known for his psychological thrillers. **(3)** "The Raven," possibly his most famous poem, is a haunting tale of a man's growing anguish as he mourns the death of his beloved. **(4)** The dark mood of the poem is enhanced by Poe's skillful use of repetition, rhyme, and word choice.

(5) It is no wonder that much of Poe's writing was so dark. **(6)** Both his parents died when he was a toddler. **(7)** His wealthy foster family disowned him when he accumulated massive debts. **(8)** After his young wife died, he struggled with depression. **(9)** The exact nature of Poe's early death at age forty remains a mystery to this day. **(10)** Many people feel his mysterious death is appropriate, given the nature of his writing.

1. Which of the following is the *best* paraphrase of "chilled readers," in sentence 1?
   A. cold and tired readers
   B. excited and pleased readers
   C. thrilled and scared readers
   D. dismayed and annoyed readers

2. Why might paraphrasing sentence 3 be helpful to readers?
   A. The sentence is poorly written.
   B. The sentence references Poe's other works.
   C. The vocabulary in the sentence is challenging.
   D. The tone of the sentence is complex.

3. Which is the *best* paraphrase of "he accumulated massive debts," in sentence 7?
   A. he borrowed a lot of money
   B. he accounted for all his debts
   C. he loaned out lots of money
   D. he became bankrupt

4. What main idea does a paraphrase of the second paragraph help to clarify?
   A. Poe spent his childhood as an orphan.
   B. Poe's life was tragic.
   C. Poe died young.
   D. Poe's writing is admired.

Writing for Assessment

Connecting Across Texts

In a brief essay, paraphrase ideas and details from each selection to explain how Poe achieves a dark mood of discontent in his poem "The Raven."

www.PHLitOnline.com
- Online practice
- Instant feedback

Reading for Information

Analyzing Functional Texts

Technical Directions

Consumer Document

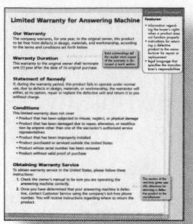

Common Core State Standards

Reading Informational Text
4. Determine the meaning of words and phrases as they are used in a text, including figurative, connotative, and technical meanings.

Language
6. Acquire and use accurately grade-appropriate general academic and domain-specific words and phrases; gather vocabulary knowledge when considering a word or phrase important to comprehension or expression.

Reading Skill: Analyze Technical Directions

Technical directions offer step-by-step instruction on how to assemble, operate, or repair a mechanical device. A warranty gives directions on what to do if the device does not function properly. When you encounter any set of directions, first **analyze** the directions to be sure you understand all of the steps. *Text features* can help you clarify key points. Use a checklist like the one shown to be sure you follow the directions correctly.

Checklist for Following Technical Directions

❑ Read all the directions completely before starting to follow them.

❑ Look for clues such as bold type or capital letters that point out specific sections or important information.

❑ Use diagrams to locate and name the parts of the product.

❑ Follow each step in the exact order given.

❑ Do not skip any steps.

Content-Area Vocabulary

These words appear in the selections that follow. You may also encounter them in other content-area texts.

- **defects** (dē´fekts) *n.* shortcomings or failings in someone or something; faults in mechanics or design

- **modification** (mod´ə fə kā´shən) *n.* change; adjustment

- **exclusion** (ek sklü´zhən) *n.* barring someone or something from participation or consideration

Using Your Answering Machine

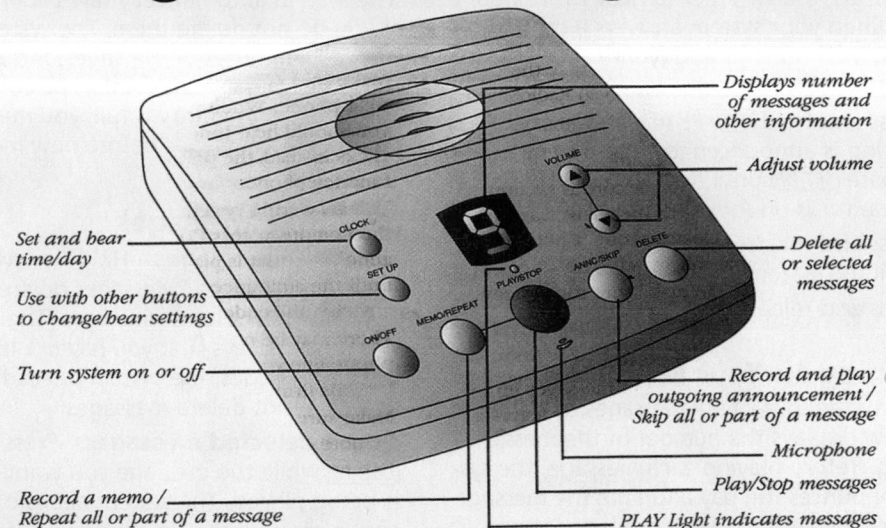

Displays number of messages and other information

Adjust volume

Set and hear time/day

Use with other buttons to change/hear settings

Turn system on or off

Delete all or selected messages

Record and play outgoing announcement / Skip all or part of a message

Microphone

Play/Stop messages

PLAY Light indicates messages

Record a memo / Repeat all or part of a message

Labels identify the different features on the answering machine and explain what each one does.

Each heading identifies a function of the answering machine. The numbered steps explain how to accomplish that function.

Setting the Clock

You'll need to set the clock so that it can announce the day and time that each message is received. Press `PLAY/STOP` to exit Setting the Clock at any time.

1. Press and hold `CLOCK` until the Message Window displays `CLOCK`, and the default day is announced.

2. To change the day setting, hold down `MEMO/REPEAT` or until the correct day is announced. Then release the button.

3. Press and release `CLOCK`. The current hour setting is announced.

4. To change the hour setting, hold down `MEMO/REPEAT` or `ANNC/SKIP` until the correct hour is announced. Then release the button.

5. Press and release `CLOCK`. The current minutes setting is announced.

6. To change the minutes setting, hold down `MEMO/REPEAT` or `ANNC/SKIP` until the correct minutes setting is announced. Then release the button.

7. Press and release `CLOCK`. The new day and time are announced.

To check the clock, press and release `CLOCK`.

Note alerts the reader that special instructions follow.

NOTE: In the event of a power failure, see the instructions on the bottom of the unit to reset the clock.

Recording Your Announcement

Before using this answering system, you should record the announcement (up to one minute long) that callers will hear when the system answers a call. If you choose not to record an announcement, the system answers with a prerecorded announcement: *"Hello. Please leave a message after the tone."*

1. Press and hold `ANNC/SKIP`. The system beeps. Speak toward the microphone normally, from about nine inches away. While you are recording, the Message Window displays—.

2. To stop recording, release `ANNC/SKIP`. The system automatically plays back your announcement.

To review your announcement, press and release `ANNC/SKIP`.

Turning the System On/Off

Use `ON/OFF` to turn the system on and off. When the system is off, the Message Window is blank.

Volume Control

Use volume buttons (▲ and ▼) to adjust the volume of the system's speaker. Press the top button (▲) to increase volume. Press the bottom button (▼) to decrease volume. The system beeps three times when you reach the maximum or minimum volume setting.

Announcement Monitor

You can choose whether to hear the announcement when your system answers a call, or have it silent (off) on your end (your caller will still hear an announcement).

1 Press and hold SET UP. After the Ring Select setting is announced, continue to press and release SET UP until the system announces *"Monitor is on (or off)."*

2 Press and release ANNC/SKIP or MEMO/REPEAT until the system announces your selection.

3 Press and release PLAY/STOP or SET UP to exit.

Listening to Your Messages

As the system plays back messages, the Message Window displays the number of the message playing. Before playing each message, the system announces the day and time the message was received. After playing the last message, the system announces *"End of messages."*

Play all messages—Press and release PLAY/STOP. If you have no messages, the system announces *"No messages."*

Play new messages only—Hold down PLAY/STOP for about two seconds, until the system begins playing. If you have no new messages, the system announces *"No new messages."*

Repeat entire messages—Press and release MEMO/REPEAT.

Repeat part of message—Hold down MEMO/REPEAT until you hear a beep, then release to resume playing. The more beeps you hear, the farther back in the message you will be when you release the button.

Repeat previous message—Press MEMO/REPEAT twice, continue this process to hear other previous messages.

Skip to next message—Press and release ANNC/SKIP.

Skip part of a message—Hold down ANNC/SKIP until you hear a beep, then release to resume playing. The more beeps you hear, the farther into the message you will be when you release the button.

Stop message playback—Press and release PLAY/STOP.

The boxed words are visual cues that tell the reader to hold down or release a button on the answering machine.

Saving Messages

The system automatically saves your messages if you do not delete them. The system can save about 12 minutes of messages, including your announcement, for a total of up to 59 messages. When memory is full, you must delete some or all messages before new messages can be recorded.

Deleting Messages

Delete all messages—Hold down DELETE. The system announces *"Messages deleted"* and permanently deletes messages. The Message Window displays **0**. If you haven't listened to all of the messages, the system beeps five times, and does not delete messages.

Delete selected messages—Press and release DELETE while the message you want to delete is being played. The system beeps once, and continues with the next message. If you want to check a message before you delete it, you can press MEMO/REPEAT to replay the message before deleting it.

When the system reaches the end of the last message, the messages not deleted are renumbered, and the Message Window displays the total number of messages remaining in memory.

Recording a Memo

You can record a memo to be stored as an incoming message. The memo can be up to three minutes long, and will be played back with other messages.

1 Press and hold MEMO/REPEAT. After the beep, speak toward the microphone.

2 To stop recording, release MEMO/REPEAT.

3 To play the memo, press PLAY/STOP.

When Memory is Full

The system can record approximately 12 minutes of messages, including your announcement, for a total of up to 59 messages. When memory is full, or 59 messages have been recorded, the Message Window flashes **F**. Delete messages to make room for new ones.

When memory is full, the system answers calls after 10 rings, and sounds two beeps instead of your announcement.

Limited Warranty for Answering Machine

Our Warranty

The company warrants, for one year, to the original owner, this product to be free from defects in design, materials, and workmanship, according to the terms and conditions set forth below.

Warranty Duration

This warranty to the original owner shall terminate one (1) year after the date of its original purchase.

> Bold subheadings tell the reader what aspect of the warranty is discussed in each section.

Statement of Remedy

If, during the warranty period, this product fails to operate under normal use, due to defects in design, materials, or workmanship, the warrantor will either, at its option, repair or replace the defective unit and return it to you without charge.

Conditions

This limited warranty does not cover
- Product that has been subjected to misuse, neglect, or physical damage
- Product that has been damaged due to repair, alteration, or modification by anyone other than one of the warrantor's authorized service representatives
- Product that has been improperly installed
- Product purchased or serviced outside the United States
- Product whose serial number has been removed
- Product without valid proof of purchase

Obtaining Warranty Service

To obtain warranty service in the United States, please follow these instructions:

1. Check the owner's manual to be sure you are operating the answering machine correctly.
2. Once you have determined that your answering machine is defective, contact Customer Service using the company's toll-free phone number. You will receive instructions regarding where to return the product.

> This section of the warranty gives specific directions for returning a defective product to the manufacturer.

3. Pack the answering machine in a padded cardboard box. Be sure to include the following:
   - all parts and accessories that were included in the original package
   - a copy of the sales receipt
   - a detailed description of the problem
   - your daytime phone number
   - your return shipping address

4. Ship the product to the company's repair facility using the address provided. You will be responsible for the cost of shipping the answering machine to the repair facility. The company will cover the cost of return shipment. The repair or replacement process should take approximately 30 days.

Limitations of Warranty

The warranty set forth above is the sole and entire warranty for this product. It supersedes all other communications related to this product. There are no other express warranties, whether written or oral, other than this printed limited warranty.

This warranty does not cover or provide for indirect, special, incidental, consequential, or similar damages (including, but not limited to lost profits or revenue, inability to use the product, the cost of substitute equipment, and claims by third parties) resulting from the use of this product.

Some states do not allow the exclusion or limitation of incidental or consequential damages, so the above limitation or exclusion may not apply to you.

This section includes important information regarding directions that appear earlier in the document.

Comparing Functional Texts

 1. Integration of Knowledge and Ideas (a) In what ways do both the technical directions and the warranty help readers to make better use of a **complex mechanical device? (b)** In what ways are these two documents different? Explain your response.

Content-Area Vocabulary

2. Use all three vocabulary words from page 766 in a brief paragraph that explains why warranties cover only *defects,* while singling out for *exclusion* any consumer *modification* of the item.

⏱ Timed Writing

Expository Text: Explanation

> **Format and Details**
> The prompt directs you to explain a process. Therefore, you will need to use sequence words, such as *first, next,* and *finally.*

Choose an answering machine function from the technical directions you have read. For example, you might choose "Recording Your Announcement." Then, write a few paragraphs explaining how to use that function. Refer to the source document for the steps, but use your own words. (30 minutes)

> **Academic Vocabulary**
> A *source* document is the text from which you received information.

5-Minute Planner

Complete these steps before you begin to write:

1. Read the prompt carefully. Look for key words like the ones highlighted in color to help you understand the assignment.

2. Reread the source document and choose an answering machine function to use as the basis for your explanation.

3. Analyze the technical directions to identify the steps involved in using the function you choose. Note any parts of the instructions that are unclear or confusing, and jot down ideas about how you can explain them more clearly.

4. Use your notes and the source document to prepare an outline. Then, use it to help you organize your explanation.

Comparing Literary Works

The Road Not Taken • O Captain! My Captain!

Comparing Types of Description

Descriptive writing paints pictures with words. A variety of descriptions can be used in poetry to present **levels of meaning.**

- **Literal meaning** is the actual, everyday meaning of words.

- In contrast, **figurative meaning** is based on the symbolic nature of language, using imaginative, innovative ways to express ideas.

An **analogy** is a figurative description that compares two or more things that are similar in some ways, but otherwise unalike. In literature, analogies may extend over the course of a work. For example, a poem that literally describes the ocean also can be read as an analogy: It may compare the ocean to life because both are vast, deep, and ever-changing. The poem, therefore, has two levels of meaning—one literal and one figurative or symbolic.

When you think a poem may have levels of meaning, think about whether the poet is using an analogy or other type of figurative description to emphasize an idea. Follow these steps as you read the poems by Frost and Whitman:

- Record your ideas about what the descriptions might symbolize, or represent.

- List some of the words and images that give you clues about the figurative meaning in a chart like the one shown.

- Determine whether or not the figurative meaning develops over the course of the poem.

- Finally, compare the analogies in the two poems.

Common Core State Standards

Reading Literature

1. Cite the textual evidence that most strongly supports an analysis of what the text says explicitly as well as inferences drawn from the text.

4. Determine the meaning of words and phrases as they are used in a text, including figurative and connotative meanings; analyze the impact of specific word choices on meaning and tone, including analogies or allusions to other texts.

Writing

9. Draw evidence from literary or informational texts to support analysis, reflection, and research. *(Timed Writing)*

www.PHLitOnline.com

- Vocabulary flashcards
- Interactive journals
- More about the authors
- Selection audio
- Interactive graphic organizers

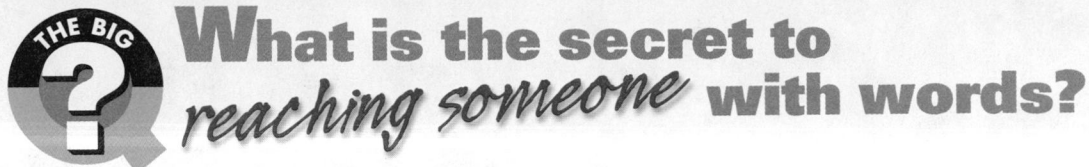

What is the secret to reaching someone with words?

Writing About the Big Question

These poets use different approaches to language in their writing—one uses simple, direct language and structure, and the other writes in a more flowery style. Use this sentence starter to develop your ideas.

For a poem to be **meaningful** to me, it should _____.

Meet the Authors

Robert Frost (1874–1963)

Author of "The Road Not Taken"

One of the best-known and best-loved American poets, Robert Frost was a four-time winner of the Pulitzer Prize. Though he was born in San Francisco, Frost spent most of his life in New England—the subject of many of his poems.

"The Gift Outright" Frost's reading of his poem "The Gift Outright" at the inauguration of John F. Kennedy in 1961 was a memorable moment for poetry in the twentieth century.

Walt Whitman (1819–1892)

Author of "O Captain! My Captain!"

Although he is now considered one of the greatest American poets, Walt Whitman could not find a commercial publisher and was forced to pay for the publication of his masterpiece *Leaves of Grass* in 1855. This collection of poems about the United States has continued to influence poetry ever since.

The Poet and the War During the Civil War, Whitman worked in military hospitals in Washington, D.C., where he saw his beloved President Lincoln from afar. Lincoln's assassination less than a week after the Union victory deeply moved Whitman. He wrote "O Captain! My Captain!" in tribute to the fallen leader.

The Road Not Taken

Robert Frost

Two roads diverged in a yellow wood,
And sorry I could not travel both
And be one traveler, long I stood
And looked down one as far as I could
5 To where it bent in the undergrowth;

Then took the other, as just as fair,
And having perhaps the better claim,
Because it was grassy and wanted wear;
Though as for that, the passing there
10 Had worn them really about the same,

And both that morning equally lay
In leaves no step had trodden black.
Oh, I kept the first for another day!
Yet knowing how way leads on to way,
15 I doubted if I should ever come back.

I shall be telling this with a sigh
Somewhere ages and ages hence:
Two roads diverged in a wood, and I—
I took the one less traveled by,
20 And that has made all the difference.

Vocabulary
diverged (dì vʉrj´ d)
v. branched off

Description
What is the literal subject of this poem?

Description
What clue in the final stanza hints that the poem is about more than a hike in the woods?

Critical Thinking ©

© 1. Key Ideas and Details (a) In the first five lines, where does the speaker remember being? **(b) Infer:** Based on these lines, what can you tell about the speaker's character and attitude toward life?

© 2. Key Ideas and Details (a) Which road does the speaker finally choose? **(b) Deduce:** Why does the speaker choose one road over the other? **(c) Analyze:** Find two statements suggesting that the speaker believes he has made a significant choice.

© 3. Key Ideas and Details (a) Speculate: Why does the speaker predict that he will remember this decision? **(b) Generalize:** What message does the poem communicate about decisions in general?

© 4. Integration of Knowledge and Ideas (a) How does the language Frost uses let him reach a wide readership with his message? **(b)** How might Frost answer this Big Question? *[Connect to the Big Question: What is the secret to reaching someone with words?]*

Cite textual evidence to support your responses.

The Road Not Taken **775**

▲ **Critical Viewing** What details in this photograph of Lincoln's funeral procession reflect the importance of Lincoln's death to Americans like Whitman? **[Analyze]**

O Captain! My Captain!

Walt Whitman

O Captain! my Captain! our fearful trip is done,
The ship has weather'd every rack,[1] the prize we
    sought is won,
The port is near, the bells I hear, the people all
    exulting,
While follow eyes the steady keel,[2] the vessel grim
    and daring;
5   But O heart! heart! heart!
        O the bleeding drops of red,
          Where on the deck my Captain lies,
          Fallen cold and dead.

    O Captain! my Captain! rise up and hear the bells;
10 Rise up—for you the flag is flung—for you the
    bugle trills,
For you bouquets and ribbon'd wreaths—for you
    the shores a-crowding,
For you they call, the swaying mass, their eager
    faces turning;
    Here Captain! dear father!

Vocabulary
exulting (eg zult´ iŋ)
v. rejoicing

Description
In this stanza, what does the speaker describe literally?

1. **rack** (rak) *n.* destruction or ruin.
2. **keel** (kēl) *n.* main beam that extends along the bottom of a ship and supports the frame.

This arm beneath your head!
15   It is some dream that on the deck,
        You've fallen cold and dead.

My Captain does not answer, his lips are pale
    and still,
My father does not feel my arm, he has no pulse
    nor will,
The ship is anchor'd safe and sound, its voyage
    closed and done,
20 From fearful trip the victor ship comes in with
    object won;
    Exult O shores, and ring O bells!
        But I with mournful tread,
        Walk the deck my Captain lies,
        Fallen cold and dead.

Description
What is the symbolic meaning of the safely anchored ship?

Critical Thinking

Cite textual evidence to support your responses.

1. Key Ideas and Details (a) What has happened to the Captain? **(b) Infer:** Why does the timing of this event make it doubly unfortunate? **(c) Interpret:** How does the mood or feeling of the poem reflect what has happened?

2. Key Ideas and Details (a) What words in the poem relate to the sea and sailing? **(b) Compare:** In what ways does Lincoln's leadership resemble a captain's role on a ship? **(c) Draw Conclusions:** What kind of leader does the speaker consider Lincoln?

3. Craft and Structure Forms of Poetry: Review page 639. How does the tone and purpose of Whitman's poem fit the form of an *elegy*?

4. Integration of Knowledge and Ideas Is it more powerful to hear about someone's life and death described in symbolic language, as in Whitman's poem? Or is direct description more powerful, as in a speech given at a funeral? Explain your reasoning. *[Connect to the Big Question: What is the secret to reaching someone with words?]*

After You Read

The Road Not Taken • O Captain! My Captain!

Comparing Types of Description

© **1. Craft and Structure (a)** In "The Road Not Taken," what descriptive language shows that the two roads are alike and different? **(b)** What kind of choice might these two roads represent? Explain.

© **2. Key Ideas and Details (a)** In "O Captain! My Captain!" what is the ship's destination? **(b)** What is the "fearful trip" that the ship has "weathered"? **(c)** How does this trip and the rest of the poem reveal the poet's response to a historic event?

© **3. Craft and Structure** Use this chart to analyze the ideas and emotions that each poem conveys through the use of analogy.

Literal Meaning	Analogy		Ideas and Emotions
Two roads separate		→	
A ship's captain dies			

⏱ Timed Writing

Explanatory Text: Essay

The insights of both Frost's and Whitman's poems are expressed through figurative description. In an essay, explain whether these descriptions remain relevant and help convey ideas important to readers today. **(40 minutes)**

5-Minute Planner

1. Read the prompt carefully and completely.

2. Gather your ideas by jotting down answers to these questions:
   - How common are the experiences that each poem describes?
   - Which poet better expresses emotions through description?
   - How does each poet's use of analogies help readers understand the importance of the event described?
   - Which message is easier for you to interpret? Why?

3. Make sure that you address the prompt and support your response with relevant details from the poems.

4. Use the charts on page 772 and this page to help draft your essay.

Writing Workshop

Write an Informative Text

Exposition: Comparison-and-Contrast Essay

In a comparison-and-contrast essay, a writer examines the similarities and differences between two or more subjects. You might use elements of this type of writing in comparisons of literary works, product comparisons, and news analyses.

Assignment Write a comparison-and-contrast essay to analyze the similarities and differences between two or more subjects. Your essay should feature the following elements:

✔ a *topic involving two or more subjects* that are different in some ways and similar in other ways

✔ an introduction that presents the *thesis,* or main point; a body that shows similarities and differences; and a conclusion that restates and reinforces the thesis

✔ a *parallel structure* that emphasizes comparisons and contrasts

✔ error-free writing, including *correct use of parallelism in grammatical forms*

To preview the criteria on which your comparison-and-contrast essay may be judged, see the rubric on page 787.

 **Writing Workshop:** *Work in Progress*

Review the work you did on pages 739 and 763.

WRITE GUY
Jeff Anderson, M.Ed.

What Do You Notice?

Structure and Style

Read these sentences from Mary C. Curtis's essay. "The Season's Curmudgeon Sees the Light."

Spring has never done much for me. I was always an autumn kind of gal: My birthday is in September. When red and gold creep into the leaves, I see beauty, not death. A slight chill in the air feels just right.

I planned an October wedding. When I raised my face to kiss the groom, I didn't want any beads of sweat ruining the moment.

With a partner, discuss the structure, style, and tone of the writing. Think of ways you might use similar elements in your writing.

Writing
2 Write informative/explanatory texts to examine a topic and convey ideas, concepts, and information through the selection, organization, and analysis of relevant content.
2.a. Introduce a topic clearly, previewing what is to follow; organize ideas, concepts, and information into broader categories; include formatting, graphics, and multimedia when useful to aiding comprehension.
2.b. Develop the topic with relevant, well-chosen facts, definitions, concrete details, quotations, or other information and examples.

Reading-Writing Connection

To get the feel for comparison-and-contrast essays, read "The Season's Curmudgeon Sees the Light," by Mary C. Curtis, on page 545.

Prewriting/Planning Strategies

Create a personal-experience timeline. Every time you outgrow your clothes, you can see how you are changing. In addition to physical change, you undergo changes in attitude and perspective. Use a timeline like the one shown to chart ways you have changed over time. Next, choose two entries as one possible topic for your comparison-and-contrast essay.

PHLit Online!
www.PHLitOnline.com
- Author video: Writing Process
- Author video: Rewards of Writing

Preschool	Kindergarten	Grade 2	Grade 4	Grade 6	Grade 8
Enjoyed playing alone in sandbox	Liked dressing as a superhero, finger painting	Wanted to do everything perfectly	Understood it was OK to make mistakes	Joined the swimming team	Helped team win swim meet

Narrow your topic. Before you finalize your topic, examine it to be sure you can discuss it fully. A topic such as "The Best Vacation Spots," for example, is much too broad in scope to be addressed adequately in a short essay. You might narrow it to "Atlanta vs. San Francisco—Which Is More Family-Friendly?" Review your topic to divide it into separate parts, aspects, or subtopics. Choose one of these subtopics as your new, narrowed topic.

Use a Venn diagram. To gather details, organize information about the ideas you will compare by using a Venn diagram, as shown here. Jot down as many similarities as you can in the center section, and note several differences in the outer sections of each circle. When you have finished, circle the items that most vividly show comparisons and contrasts. Then, include these details in your essay. When you write your essay, plan to *juxtapose* these details—set them side-by-side—to emphasize their differences and similarities. Look at this example:

Buses
- above ground
- comfortable
- see where you are going
- get caught in traffic

- faster than walking
- cheap
- do not have to park

Subways
- underground
- claustrophobic
- cannot see where you are going
- avoid traffic

Drafting Strategies

Common Core State Standards

Writing
2.b. Develop the topic with relevant, well-chosen facts, definitions, concrete details, quotations, or other information and examples.

Select the best organizational format. There are two common ways to organize a comparison-and-contrast essay. Review these options and use a structure that is appropriate to your topic and audience.

- **Block method** Present all the details about one aspect first, and then present all the details about the next aspect. The block method works well if you are writing about more than two aspects of a topic, or if your topic is complex.

- **Point-by-point organization** Discuss each aspect of your subjects in turn. For example, if you are comparing buses and subways, you might first discuss the cost of each form of transportation, then the convenience, and so on.

Block

I. Buses
 a. cheaper
 b. more routes
 c. better views
II. Trains
 a. better seats
 b. faster
 c. quieter

Use parallel structure. No matter which overall organizational method you choose, be sure to keep the paragraphs in the body *parallel*, or consistent, in structure and style. This makes it easier for your reader to follow and understand your points. For example, for the first aspect you compare, you might choose the SEE method (shown in the chart below) to develop the comparison in your supporting paragraphs. Then you would use the same method to develop support for the second aspect. Study the example in the chart.

Point-by-Point

I. Introduction
II. Cost of each
III. Accessibility of each
IV. View from each
V. Disadvantages of each

- State the topic of the paragraph.

- Extend the idea by restating it in a new way, applying it to a particular case, or contrasting it with another point.

- Elaborate with specific examples, facts, or explanations.

Statement	Extension	Elaboration
Buses and trains are two forms of public transportation that offer advantages and disadvantages in the area of convenience.	A bus can often drop you off very close to your final destination, but trains are limited to designated stations along the railroad line.	If people's origins and destinations are near train stations, trains are usually more convenient. Trains do not get caught in traffic and are generally faster than buses.

Writers on Writing

Jacqueline Woodson On Including Details

Jacqueline Woodson is the author of "Describe Somebody" (p. 645) and "Almost Summer Sky" (p. 647).

In this passage from my novel *Hush*, Toswiah, the narrator, tells of her family's transition from their Boulder, Colorado, home. They were forced to leave after her father witnessed a murder, and as a result, are now part of a Witness Protection Program that has moved them to a tiny apartment in a big city. Toswiah and her family have left everything they loved behind them—even their old names.

"I write because I love creating new worlds."
—Jacqueline Woodson

Professional Model:

from *Hush*

Some mornings, waking up in this new place, I don't know where I am. The apartment is tiny. The kitchen is not even a whole room away from the living room, just a few steps and a wide doorway with no door separating it. Not even one fireplace. Daddy sits by the window staring out, hardly ever saying anything. Maybe he thinks if he looks long and hard enough, Denver will reappear, . . . Maybe he thinks the tall gray buildings all smashed against each other will separate and squat down, that the Rocky Mountains will rise up behind them. . . .

When Daddy looks over to where me and my sister, Anna, sit watching TV, he looks surprised, like he's wondering why we aren't downstairs in the den. No den here, though. No dining room. No extra bathrooms down the hall and at the top of the stairs. Just five rooms with narrow doorways here.

 Here, I spent a lot of time imagining what it would be like to leave the place I loved. I wanted to really focus on small details.

 Toswiah's father is very depressed about the current situation. I put him by the window to show his sadness and to also show what he was seeing.

 The family has gone from a grand house to a small apartment. I spent time trying to give details about each to show the difference.

Revising Strategies

 **Common Core
State Standards**

Writing

2.b. Develop the topic with relevant, well-chosen facts, definitions, concrete details, quotations, or other information and examples.

2.d. Use precise language and domain-specific vocabulary to inform about or explain the topic.

Check overall balance. Reread your draft. Use one color to highlight details about one aspect of your comparison. Use additional colors to mark details about other aspects. If your draft has more of one color, add details on an aspect that is less developed.

Check organization and structure. If your rereading reveals a confusing overall organization, consider rearranging sections to fit the block method or point-by-point organization. If your review indicates an inconsistent paragraph structure, revise your work to develop your arguments in a parallel way.

Original Version	Revised to Include Parallelism
Bus routes crisscross the city, traveling down every major street and into every neighborhood. I took the train once, and it dropped me off on the outskirts of town.	*Bus routes crisscross the city,* traveling down every major street and into every neighborhood. *The train, on the other hand, skirts the city,* traveling down tracks far from many common destinations.

Delete unnecessary details. Copy your thesis onto an index card. Run the card down your draft as you read through the introduction, body, and conclusion, one line at a time. Identify any details that do not directly support your thesis. Delete the details or rewrite them to develop your main idea. In the example shown, the deleted detail did not develop the main argument comparing buses and trains.

Buses cost 85¢ a ride. ~~Of course, you can walk for free or take a cab that costs $1.00 for each quarter mile.~~ Trains cost $1.25.

Peer Review

Invite a classmate to read your draft to evaluate its organization, balance, and use of parallel structure. Ask your reader:

- if the overall organization you chose for your comparison is clear
- if your essay is missing support for an aspect of your comparison
- if you are consistent in the way you develop your arguments

Revise your draft, based on this feedback.

Revising to Vary Sentence Patterns

To keep your writing lively, avoid writing sentences that follow a dull pattern. Many sentences begin with nouns, as in *The waiter took our order.*

Using a Variety of Sentence Beginnings To avoid beginning every sentence with a noun, consider these options:

Adjective: Surprised, the waiter rushed over.

Adverb: Running quickly, he arrived at our table.

Prepositional Phrase: After a delay, the food arrived.

Using Appositives and Appositive Phrases To pack information into your sentences, use appositives, noun phrases that define or explain other words in the sentence.

Appositive: The cat, a tabby, prowled the yard.

Appositive Phrase: The dog, my mother's longtime pet, was happy to see us.

Fixing Repetitive Sentence Patterns To fix a series of sentences that start the same way, follow these steps:

1. **Identify the existing pattern of sentence beginnings.**
   - Draw a triangle around each noun that starts a sentence.
   - Draw a box around each adjective that starts a sentence.
   - Draw a circle around each prepositional phrase that starts a sentence.

2. **Review your results.** Count the number of triangles, boxes, and circles. If you have too many of one shape, rewrite the sentence beginnings to build greater variety.

3. **Consider using appositives to include more information.** Identify a key noun in a sentence and write a brief noun phrase to define the word. Use commas to set the appositive or the appositive phrase off from the rest of the sentence.

Grammar in Your Writing

Choose three paragraphs in your draft. Review the sentence beginnings. If you have not used enough variety, revise by beginning some sentences according to the rules presented here.

PH WRITING COACH

Further instruction and practice are available in *Prentice Hall Writing Coach.*

Comparing Struggles for Equality

The civil rights movement of the 1950s and 1960s had a lot in common with the women's suffrage movement that began with the Seneca Falls Convention in 1848. Both movements involved a group of people who were denied rights and who fought to obtain those rights.

Although in most ways the two struggles were similar, the specific rights each group fought for were different. Women wanted the right to vote in elections, the right to own property in their own names, and the right to keep their own wages. African Americans fought for the end to segregation. Like the women, they wanted to be treated with equal rights. However, the civil rights movement was about fairness in schools, jobs, and public places like buses and restaurants.

Both movements protested in nonviolent ways. They held marches, boycotts, and demonstrations to raise the public's consciousness and get the laws changed. In 1917, Alice Paul and other women picketed at the White House. In 1963, more than 200,000 Americans, led by Dr. Martin Luther King, Jr., marched on Washington, D.C. They wanted Congress to pass laws to end discrimination.

Both movements were about equality. The Declaration of Independence, an important document in the struggle for equality, states: "We hold these truths to be self-evident, that all men are created equal; that they are endowed by their Creator with certain unalienable rights; that among these are life, liberty, and the pursuit of happiness."

Protesters in both the civil rights movement and the women's suffrage movement felt that they were being denied rights that were given to them by this statement from the Declaration of Independence. Both groups were able to change the laws so that they could have their rights. Women were given the right to vote in 1920 by Amendment 19 to the Constitution. Similarly, the Civil Rights Act of 1964 outlawed discrimination in hiring and ended segregation in public places.

In conclusion, the civil rights movement of the 1950s and 1960s and the women's suffrage movement were both about equality under the law. They are both good examples of how much work and determination it takes to change the laws. It is good to know, however, that the laws can be changed.

Carolyn begins her essay with a thesis statement that introduces the subjects of her comparison. She indicates that she will focus more on similarities.

The writer focuses first on the differences in the specific rights being sought.

Carolyn uses point-by-point organization to compare the movements.

The writer provides a quotation to support an idea.

The conclusion restates the introduction, driving home the point.

Editing and Proofreading

Proofread to correct errors in spelling, grammar, and punctuation.

Focus on items in a series. Use commas to separate words, phrases, or clauses in a series. To avoid confusion, use semicolons when some items already contain commas. Use colons to introduce lists.

> **Commas:** Recyling is cheaper, easier, and cleaner than dumping.
>
> **Semicolons:** We visited Moab, Utah; Lima, Ohio; and Bath, Maine.
>
> **Colons:** I will compare the following: beets, carrots, and celery.

Publishing and Presenting

Consider one of the following ways to share your writing:

Publish a column. If you compared subjects of local interest, such as two restaurants or several stores, submit your essay to your local newspaper or post it on a community blog or Web site.

Start a family tradition. If you have compared two subjects of interest to your family—two uncles, two birthdays, two vacations—read your essay at a family gathering.

Reflecting on Your Writing

Writer's Journal Jot down your answer to this question:

If you could write your essay again, what would you do differently?

Rubric for Self-Assessment

Find evidence in your writing to address each category. Then, use the rating scale to grade your work.

Spiral Review

Earlier in this unit, you learned about **prepositional phrases** (p. 738) and **infinitive phrases** (p. 762). Check your essay to be sure you have used prepositional and infinitive phrases correctly.

Criteria	Rating Scale *not very* *very*
Focus: How clearly do you introduce and develop your thesis?	1 2 3 4 5
Organization: How effectively do you highlight the points of comparison?	1 2 3 4 5
Support/Elaboration: How well do you use parallel structure to emphasize key comparisons and contrasts?	1 2 3 4 5
Conventions: How correct is your grammar, especially your use of parallelism in grammatical forms?	1 2 3 4 5

Vocabulary Workshop

Idioms

An **idiom** is a figurative expression that has a very different meaning than the literal meanings of the words it contains. For example, people use the expression *shooting the breeze* to mean "having a casual conversation." The chart shows examples of common English idioms based on farming, weather, and sailing terms.

Idiom	Source	Meaning
a needle in a haystack	farming	something extremely difficult to find
a tempest in a teapot	weather	a problem that seems serious but is actually insignificant
rock the boat	sailing	disturb the balance of a group or situation

Practice A Identify the idiom that is part of each sentence.

1. Ian, a budding musician, has sung since the age of five.
2. Jasey ran slowly for most of the race, but then the tide turned.
3. The neighbors started a grassroots campaign to keep their streets free of litter.
4. I thought he would blow a gasket when he lost his keys.
5. What's the holdup with this project?

Common Core State Standards

Language
5.a. Interpret figures of speech in context.

Practice B Find the idiom in each sentence. Then, explain the meaning of the idiom.

1. After she won the tennis match, Janine was on cloud nine.
2. I disagreed with my friend's opinion, but I didn't want to make waves.
3. Out of left field, Ms. Sampson announced that we would have a quiz tomorrow.
4. Since I spent a week in Mexico, my progress in speaking Spanish has been smooth sailing.
5. After I learned the secret, it was difficult to keep it under my hat.
6. We are trying not to go overboard, but we are ordering plenty of food for the class picnic.

Activity Copy each idiom onto a separate note card like the one shown. Identify the source of the idiom (such as sports, music, or weather). Then, define the idiom and use it in a sentence. Refer to printed or online dictionaries of idioms.

count your chickens before they've hatched

come out of one's shell

fit as a fiddle

throw in the towel

step up to the plate

skim the surface

Idiom:
Source:
Meaning:
Example sentence:

Comprehension and Collaboration

With a partner, make a list of ten idioms that you use. You can list idioms that appear in your textbook, idioms you know, or idioms you find online by doing a Web search with the keyword "idioms." Together, write a funny short story using these idioms.

Evaluating Media Messages

Messages sent via television, radio, and the Internet are meant to make you think or act a certain way. Practice being an active and critical listener and viewer by following these suggestions.

Learn the Skills

Use these strategies to complete the activity on page 791.

Look critically at images. The media flash images at us at amazing speeds and levels of complexity. Some are graphic; others are realistic; still others are digitally created. All are intended to catch the attention of and influence an audience. Be aware of how certain images are designed to affect your impressions and opinions.

Listen critically to words and sounds. The creator of a message can create a mood that influences an audience by using "buzz words" (words that trigger specific associations), music, or sound effects that play on emotions.

Be aware of persuasive appeals and rhetorical techniques. Some messages suggest that you jump on a bandwagon. Others use celebrity spokespeople. Still others use statistics and facts to impress an audience. Being aware of these persuasive strategies will help you to assess media messages. In addition, being alert for **rhetorical techniques** such as repetition, loaded terms, and leading questions will help you understand how the message may be swaying you. Recognizing media techniques will make you a smarter viewer.

Look for hidden agendas. It is essential to distinguish fact from opinion, especially when looking for information or point of view. Sometimes, messages are hidden. Look beyond the surface of a media message by paraphrasing it. Ask yourself: Which facts, values, and ideas are being presented?

Identify slant or bias. Often, complex subjects are presented from only one point of view. In its most extreme form, this becomes **propaganda** that unfairly boosts one point of view while misrepresenting another. For example, political ads often address only one side of a controversial issue. As a viewer, distinguish between messages that inform and propaganda that is meant to mislead.

**Common Core
State Standards**

Reading Informational Text
7. Evaluate the advantages and disadvantages of using different mediums to present a particular topic or idea.

Speaking and Listening
2. Analyze the purpose of information presented in diverse media and formats and evaluate the motives behind its presentation.

3. Delineate a speaker's argument and specific claims, evaluating the soundness of the reasoning and relevance and sufficiency of the evidence and identifying when irrelevant evidence is introduced.

Practice the Skills

© **Presentation of Knowledge and Ideas** Use what you've learned in this workshop to perform the following task.

ACTIVITY: Evaluate Media Messages

Watch several television commercials. Then, follow the steps below.

- **Summarize each commercial.**
- **Identify the purpose and point of view of each message.**
- **Identify techniques, such as buzz words, loaded terms, and leading questions, used to deliver the message.**
- **Explain the effect each commercial had on you.**
- **Use the Evaluation Guide to interpret the commercials.**

Use an Evaluation Guide like the one below to evaluate the content of each commercial.

Evaluation Guide

Visual and Sound Techniques
Identify which of the following techniques are used and how they influence the message.

❏ Flashy graphics   ❏ Lighting
❏ Digital effects   ❏ Appealing use of color
❏ Sound effects   ❏ Music

The role of media
- How did each message focus your attention?
- How did each message affect, change, or shape your opinion?

Effect of the message
Interpret how the use of the following techniques creates a point of view and impacts, or affects, you as a viewer. Then, comment on the evidence that supports each commercial's claims.

❏ Rhetorical devices   ❏ Fact vs. opinion
❏ Hidden agendas   ❏ Bias or slant

How persuasive was the evidence? **Comments:**

Credibility
How would you rate the credibility of this message? Explain.
_____ Excellent _____ Good _____ Fair _____ Poor

© **Comprehension and Collaboration** Discuss your findings with a classmate. Discuss how critical viewing and listening helps to uncover motives behind the messages. Compare the insights you gained from listening for rhetorical devices and persuasive appeals.

Cumulative Review

Common Core
State Standards

RL.8.4; L.8.4.a; W.8.2.b
[For the full wording of the standards, see the standards chart in the front of your textbook.]

I. Reading Literature

Directions: *Read the poem. Then, answer each question that follows.*

A Pinch of Salt
by Robert Graves

> WHEN a dream is born in you
>   With a sudden clamorous pain,
> When you know the dream is true
>   And lovely, with no flaw nor stain,
> 5 O then, be careful, or with sudden clutch
> You'll hurt the delicate thing you prize so much.
>
> Dreams are like a bird that mocks,
>   Flirting the feathers of his tail.
> When you seize at the salt-box,
> 10 Over the hedge you'll see him sail.
> Old birds are neither caught with salt nor chaff:
> They watch you from the apple bough and laugh.
>
> Poet, never chase the dream.
>   Laugh yourself, and turn away.
> 15 <u>Mask</u> your hunger; let it seem
>   Small matter if he come or stay;
> But when he nestles in your hand at last,
> Close up your fingers tight and hold him fast.

1. Which of the following is a **simile** found in the poem?
   A. *When a dream is born in you*
   B. *O then, be careful, or with sudden clutch*
   C. *Poet, never chase the dream*
   D. *Dreams are like a bird that mocks*

2. Which pattern best describes the **rhyme scheme** of stanza 1?
   A. *abcabc*
   B. *ababcc*
   C. *abcdef*
   D. *ababaa*

3. What **sound device** is used in the phrase *flirting the feathers of his tail*?
   A. onomatopoeia
   B. internal rhyme
   C. alliteration
   D. repetition

4. Which statement *best* explains the use of **personification** in the first stanza?
   A. A dream is said to be truthful, although it can cause pain.
   B. A dream, like a child, can be hurt if treated too roughly.
   C. A dream is like a delicate bird.
   D. A dream is like a prize that can be won in a contest.

5. To whom or what might the "he" refer in line 17 of the poem?
   A. the poet
   B. the bird
   C. the dream
   D. memories

6. Which of the following *best* **paraphrases** the lines "… let it seem / small matter if he go or stay" in lines 15–16?
   A. Make him feel small so he will leave.
   B. Do not make it obvious that you see him.
   C. Let him feel so small that you will not notice when he leaves.
   D. Let it seem unimportant to you if he comes or goes.

7. Which **form of poetry** best describes this poem?
   A. lyric
   B. elegy
   C. narrative
   D. free verse

8. **Vocabulary** Which word or phrase is closest in meaning to the underlined word <u>mask</u>?
   A. a covering
   B. feed
   C. a face
   D. hide

Timed Writing

9. In an essay, explain the **speaker's attitude** toward "dreams" and decide whether you agree with him. Use specific examples from the poem to support your ideas.

GO ON

II. Reading Informational Text

Directions: *Read the passages. Then, answer each question that follows.*

> **Common Core State Standards**
>
> **RI.8.2; L.8.1.b; W.8.4**
> [For the full wording of the standards, see the standards chart in the front of your textbook.]

"You-Till"

Product Description: This 4-horsepower, gas-engine rotary tiller is equipped with spinning blades to loosen soil. It is perfect for preparing soil for planting vegetables or flowers.

Cost: $49.95

Easy-to-Use Instructions:

1. Fill the 1-gal. tank with diesel gasoline. Replace gas cap tightly.
2. Press and hold the start button.
3. Adjust lever on right handle to adjust motor speed.
4. Release start button to turn off.

Caution! Always clear the soil of rocks and debris before using tiller!

"Hoe for Health"

This specially designed hoe is perfectly engineered to <u>eliminate</u> unnecessary back strain. The rubber-coated handle is angled for optimum balance and strength.

Yours for the low cost of $14.99

How to Care for Your "Hoe for Health":

- Store in a shed or covered area.
- Clean your hoe of dirt, and dry before storing.

---

1. According to the product description, what is the purpose of a rotary tiller?
   A. It breaks up the soil.
   B. It keeps the soil from forming crusts.
   C. It helps you to spread seeds.
   D. It helps you spread the mulch layer.

2. What features do the documents have in common?
   A. Both contain directions.
   B. Both provide a product description.
   C. Both contain caution notes.
   D. Both list manufacturer information.

3. Why is "You-Till" more suitable for the needs of a professional gardener?
   A. It uses gasoline.
   B. It can till soil more quickly than a hoe.
   C. It costs more and will last longer.
   D. It is a safer machine.

4. According to the text, what is the biggest difference between the two products?
   A. The till has an engine; the hoe does not.
   B. The hoe needs to be stored inside.
   C. The hoe has a rubber handle.
   D. The hoe is washable.

III. Writing and Language Conventions

Directions: *Read the passage. Then, answer each question.*

(1) Many people have problems writing thank-you cards. (2) You might *want* to thank people for their kindness and generosity but you never get around to it. (3) Here is how to solve your problem. (4) Buy a set of blank cards and envelopes. (5) Stamps should be bought, too. (6) Send an e-mail to your friends and relatives, asking them to send you their mailing addresses. (7) Put those addresses in an address book. (8) When someone does a nice deed for you, you can start writing: the envelopes, addresses, and stamps are at your fingertips!

1. Which of the following provides the *best* support for the idea stated in sentence 1?
   A. How many times have you meant to send a card but didn't?
   B. Thank-you cards are an obligation we all have.
   C. People also dislike writing letters of recommendation.
   D. Writing thank-you notes is a centuries-old tradition.

2. Which is the *most* effective way to combine sentences 4 and 5?
   A. Buy stamps, and a set of blank cards and envelopes, too.
   B. Buy a set of blank cards, envelopes, and stamps.
   C. Purchase stamps, and also blank cards and envelopes.
   D. Blank cards, stamps, and envelopes should be bought at the store.

3. Which sentence in the passage uses the **passive voice** and should be fixed?
   A. sentence 1
   B. sentence 3
   C. sentence 5
   D. sentence 7

4. Which possible revision to sentence 3 contains an **indirect object?**
   A. I will tell you how to solve your problem.
   B. I will solve your problem for you.
   C. Solving problems is easy.
   D. The solution is clear, and here it is.

5. Which revision to sentence 7 shows the strongest cause-and-effect relationship?
   A. Put those addresses in an address book so that you be able to find them later.
   B. Put those addresses in a book in which you keep addresses.
   C. After you buy an address book, put the addresses you get into it.
   D. Put the addresses in an address book, where they belong.

6. Which of the possible revisions to sentence 5 includes a **subject complement?**
   A. Stamps should be bought in advance.
   B. Stamps are useful items to have on hand.
   C. You should buy stamps, too.
   D. Do not forget stamps.

Performance Tasks

Directions: *Follow the instructions to complete the tasks below as required by your teacher.*

As you work on each task, incorporate both general academic vocabulary and literary terms you learned in this unit.

**Common Core
State Standards**

RL.8.1, RL.8.4, RL.8.5; W.8.2, W.8.9;
SL.8.1, SL.8.6; L.8.1, L.8.3, L.8.4, L.8.5,
L.8.6
[For the full wording of the standards, see the standards chart in the front of your textbook.]

Writing

© Task 1: Literature [RL.8.4; W.8.9]
Analyze the Effect of Word Choice on a Poem's Meaning and Tone

Write an essay in which you analyze a poet's word choices and their impact on meaning and tone.

- Identify a poem from this unit whose meaning and tone seem clear to you.

- State your interpretation of the poem's overall meaning in a few sentences. Then, characterize the poem's tone by using adjectives that describe the main attitude of the poem's speaker.

- Support your interpretation of the poem's meaning by showing how specific words, phrases, and figurative language help to communicate an aspect of the meaning you identified.

- Support your characterization of tone by indicating how the connotations of particular words and phrases help produce the tone you identified.

- Check your writing to identify and correct any misplaced or dangling modifiers.

© Task 2: Literature [RL.8.5; W.8.4]
Contrast the Structure of Two Poems

Write an essay in which you contrast the structures of two poems and explain how their different structures affect style and meaning.

- Choose two poems from this unit that have notable differences in structure. For example, you might choose a sonnet and a free verse poem.

- Explain how the poems differ by contrasting such characteristics as rhyme scheme, line length, number of lines in stanzas, and pattern of stressed syllables (meter).

- Describe how these differences in structure combine to affect the formality or informality of each poem's style.

- Finally, explain how the differences in structure contribute to the overall meaning and effect of the poem.

© Task 3: Literature [RL.8.4; W.8.2; L.8.3]
Analyze the Sound Devices in a Poem

Write an essay in which you analyze the effect of sound devices in a poem from this unit.

- Select a poem that uses sound devices—such as rhyme, rhythm, or alliteration—in a powerful way.

- Identify specific word or phrase choices and explain which sound device each example represents.

- Describe the effect of these sound devices on the poem's tone. For example, explain whether they make the poem seem musical, exciting, or mournful.

- Check your writing to make sure that you consistently use active voice and that you vary sentence patterns.

Speaking and Listening

© Task 4: Literature [RL.8.4; L.8.5]

Analyze Word Choice by Doing a Close Reading

Read aloud a poem from this unit. Then, discuss the meaning of specific words and phrases in that poem.

- Select a poem in which the author has made several interesting word choices with literal, figurative, and connotative meanings.
- Read the poem aloud to a group. Then, review the poem, line by line.
- As you review, identify examples of simile, metaphor, and personification and analyze their meanings.
- For other types of word choices, distinguish between the literal meanings and connotations of particular words.
- Then, analyze how the connotations affect the meaning of the stanzas in which they appear and the overall poem.

© Task 5: Literature [RL.8.5; SL.8.1]

Read Two Poems Aloud to Compare Their Structures

Read two poems aloud. Then, discuss how their structures affect the poems' meaning and style.

- Choose two poems from this unit that have distinct structures.
- As a group, identify the characteristics of each poem's structure, including meter, rhyme scheme, line length, number of lines, and regular or irregular stanzas.
- Have two group members read the poems aloud, emphasizing structural elements, such as stressed syllables, rhymed words, and stanza breaks.
- Based on the readings, compare and contrast the two poems' structures. In your discussion, analyze the way that each structure contributes to the poem's style and reinforces its overall meaning.

© Task 6: Literature [RL.8.2; SL.8.1]

Hold a Panel Discussion About Three Poems

Choose three poems from this unit that address a similar topic and explain how each poet brings a different perspective to that topic.

- Identify three poems in this unit that have the same general topic, such as nature or a historical event.
- Ask panel members to characterize the poet's attitude toward the topic and to identify one or more themes in each of the poems.
- To support their claims, panel members should identify specific lines or sections of the poem that best reflect the theme and poet's attitude.
- Each panel member should ask additional questions and make comments that connect to and build on the comments of other panel members.

THE BIG ?

What is the secret to reaching someone with words?

At the beginning of Unit 4, you participated in a discussion about the Big Question. Now that you have finished the unit, write a response to the question. Discuss how your views have developed since you discussed the question. Give specific examples from the poems, as well as from other subjects and your personal experiences, to support your ideas. Use Big Question vocabulary words (see p. 637) in your response.

Featured Titles

In this unit, you have read a wide variety of poems by many different poets. Continue to read on your own. Select works that you enjoy, but challenge yourself to explore new poets and works of increasing depth and complexity. The titles suggested below will help you get started.

Literature

Black Hair

by Gary Soto   **EXEMPLAR TEXT**

In this wide-ranging collection of **poetry,** Gary Soto reaches back to his roots—growing up poor in a Fresno neighborhood. In works like "Oranges," a poem about wanting to impress a girl but having very little to impress her with, Soto looks back with fondness, humor, and insight on his earlier years.

The Heart of a Chief

by Joseph Bruchac

A bright, courageous eleven-year-old Native American boy fights injustice and prejudice in this **novel** by author Bruchac, whose own mother was Abenaki. Through a mixture of humor and seriousness, sprinkled with lots of realistic dialogue, this first-person story provides readers with a unique perspective from which to view the world.

Classic Poems to Read Aloud

edited by James Berry   **EXEMPLAR TEXT**

Poetry by poets from all over the world is included in this collection, organized by subject. Read such classic poems as Lewis Carroll's "Jabberwocky" and W. H. Auden's "Funeral Blues" alongside contemporary gems like Shel Silverstein's "It's Dark in Here."

Locomotion

by Jacqueline Woodson

In this gripping story, told through a series of **poems,** a boy named Lonnie discovers the power of self-expression. At first, Lonnie is not sure what to write when he gets a poetry assignment. However, eventually, through poetry, he is able to explore his grief over his parents' deaths and celebrate the enjoyment he gets from close relationships with his friends and foster family.

Informational Texts

A Street Through Time

by Anne Millard

Have you ever wondered how your neighborhood would look one hundred, five hundred, or even several thousand years ago? This fascinating book follows an English port city through time, from the Stone Age to the present day. Discover how nature and human activities can shape a landscape in dramatic ways.

Discoveries: Lines of Communication

Advances in technology have transformed the way we communicate. Read this collection of **essays** to learn more about these topics: "Samuel Morse's Dream," "Astronauts Take Off in Russian," "Welcome to the Blogosphere," and "Misleading Statistics."

Preparing to Read Complex Texts

Attentive Reading As you read on your own, ask yourself questions about the text. The questions shown below and others that you ask as you read will help you learn and enjoy literature even more.

 **Common Core State Standards**

Reading Literature/Informational Text 10. By the end of the year, read and comprehend literature, including stories, dramas, and poems, and literary nonfiction at the high end of grades 6–8 text complexity band independently and proficiently.

When reading poetry, ask yourself...

- Who is the speaker of the poem? What kind of person does the speaker seem to be? How do I know?

- What is the poem about?

- If the poem is telling a story, who are the characters and what happens to them?

- Does any one line or section state the poem's theme, or meaning, directly? If so, what is that line or section?

- If there is no direct statement of a theme, what details help me to see the poem's deeper meaning?

© **Key Ideas and Details**

- How does the poem look on the page? Is it long and rambling or short and concise? Does it have long or short lines?

- Does the poem have a formal structure or is it free verse?

- How does the form affect how I read the poem?

- How many stanzas form this poem? What does each stanza tell me?

- Do I notice repetition, rhyme, or meter? Do I notice other sound devices? How do these elements affect how I read the poem?

- Even if I do not understand every word, do I like the way the poem sounds? Why or why not?

- Do any of the poet's word choices seem especially interesting or unusual? Why?

- What images do I notice? Do they create clear word-pictures in my mind? Why or why not?

- Would I like to read this poem aloud? Why or why not?

© **Craft and Structure**

- Has the poem helped me understand its subject in a new way? If so, how?

- Does the poem remind me of others I have read? If so, how?

- In what ways is the poem different from others I have read?

- What information, ideas, or insights have I gained from reading this poem?

- Do I find the poem moving, funny, or mysterious? How does the poem make me feel?

- Would I like to read more poems by this poet? Why or why not?

© **Integration of Ideas**

Is it our differences or our similarities that matter most?

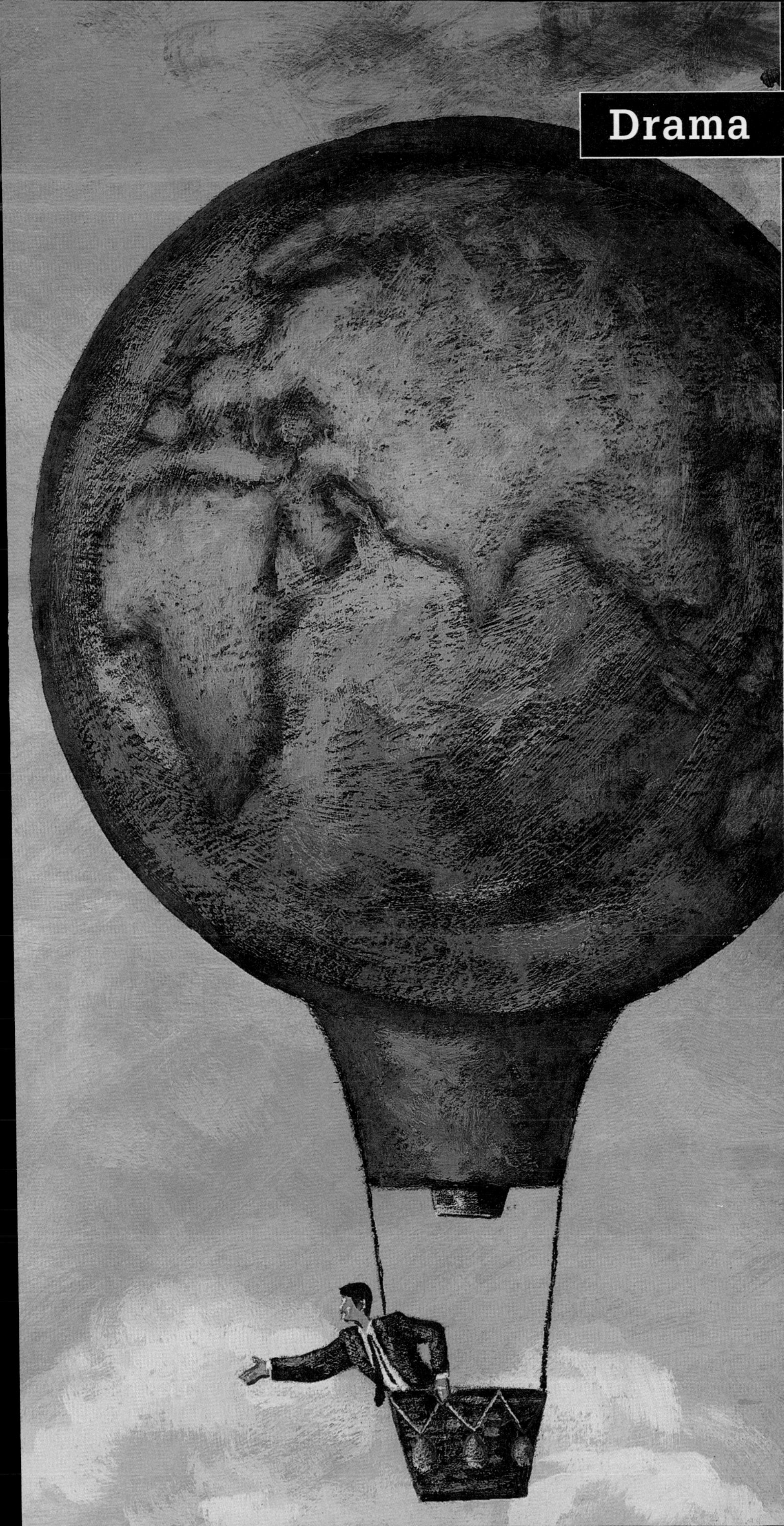

Unit 5

Drama

PHLit Online!
www.PHLitOnline.com

Hear It!
- Selection summary audio
- Selection audio
- BQ Tunes

See It!
- Author videos
- Big Question video
- Get Connected videos
- Background videos
- More about the authors
- Illustrated vocabulary words
- Vocabulary flashcards

Do It!
- Interactive journals
- Interactive graphic organizers
- Grammar tutorials
- Interactive vocabulary games
- Test practice

Is it our *differences* or our *similarities* that matter most?

There are many ways for people to distinguish themselves from one another. People often choose to identify themselves—or to classify others—based on race, religion, national origin, or economic class. Or they might choose a different category, such as academic or athletic achievement. At the same time, as human beings with similar needs and desires, we have much in common.

The health of a society depends on how we handle differences and similarities. We debate about whether to find value in differences, or whether we should focus on similarities. We ask whether many standards we use to judge one another are only superficial realities, or whether they represent deep qualities such as character or beliefs. However we answer these questions, it is important to explore the ways in which we balance our differences and our similarities.

Exploring the Big Question

Collaboration: One-on-One Discussion Start thinking about the Big Question by making a list of various ways in which similarities and differences among people influence behavior. Describe one specific example of each of these situations in which similarities and differences matter.

- A well-off employer considering how much to pay a worker
- A group of people trying to escape religious discrimination
- An event at school that brings different social groups together
- A visit to a family from a different ethnic background

Share your examples with a partner. Discuss how people in these situations might act if they based their actions on differences alone, similarities alone, or taking both factors into consideration.

Connecting to the Literature Each reading in this unit will give you additional insight into the Big Question.

PHLit Online!
www.PHLitOnline.com
- Big Question video
- Illustrated vocabulary words
- Interactive vocabulary games
- BQ Tunes

Learning Big Question Vocabulary

Common Core State Standards

Speaking and Listening
1. Engage effectively in a range of collaborative discussions with diverse partners on *grade 8 topics, texts, and issues,* building on others' ideas and expressing their own clearly.

Language
6. Acquire and use accurately grade-appropriate general academic and domain-specific words and phrases; gather vocabulary knowledge when considering a word or phrase important to comprehension or expression.

Acquire and Use Academic Vocabulary Academic vocabulary is the language you encounter in textbooks and on standardized tests. Review the definitions of these academic vocabulary words.

> **class** (klas) *n.* a group of people or objects
>
> **discriminate** (di skrim´ i nāt) *v.* see the difference between; tell apart; also, treat one group unfairly
>
> **distinguish** (di stiŋ´ gwish) *v.* see the difference between; tell apart
>
> **divide** (də vīd´) *v.* separate
>
> **identify** (i den´ tə fi´) *v.* recognize as being
>
> **judge** (juj) *v.* form an opinion about; evaluate
>
> **represent** (rep´ ri zent´) *v.* stand for; speak for

Use these words as you complete Big Question activities in this unit that involve reading, writing, speaking, and listening.

Gather Vocabulary Knowledge Additional Big Question words are listed below. Categorize the words by deciding whether you know each one well, know it a little bit, or do not know it at all.

> | | | |
> |---|---|---|
> | **assumption** | **separate** | **tolerance** |
> | **common** | **superficial** | **unify** |
> | **generalization** | **sympathy** | |

Then, do the following:

1. Write the definitions of the words you know.
2. Consult a dictionary to confirm the definitions of the words you know. Revise your definitions if necessary.
3. Using a print or an online dictionary, look up the meanings of the words you do not know. Then, write the meanings.
4. Use all of the words in a brief paragraph about a specific conflict in which either a crucial difference or a key similarity among individuals or groups of people affected the outcome.

Elements of Drama

In drama, dialogue and action work together to develop characters and tell a story.

Drama is a genre of literature that is meant to be performed. **Plays,** or dramatic performances, have entertained audiences for thousands of years. In drama, the dialogue and action tell the story.

The **playwright,** or dramatist, is the author of the **script,** the written version of a play. The script contains **dialogue,** the words spoken by the characters, and **stage directions** that provide instructions on how the play should be performed.

A play takes place at a particular time and location, called the **setting.** As a play develops, we learn about the **characters** and the struggle, or **conflict,** they face.

Events in the **plot** move forward, and the action builds until it reaches a **climax,** the point when the conflict reaches its peak. As the play comes to a close, the conflict is usually settled. This part of the play is called the **resolution.**

A successful play is one in which the playwright provides the reader or audience with believable, **well-rounded characters.** Such characters remind us of people we know in real life. Playwrights portray well-rounded characters through the careful development of dialogue that reveals not only *what* the characters say but *how* and *why* they say it.

Elements of Drama

Element	Function
Dialogue	• reveals the nature of characters • advances the plot • establishes theme, the work's central message about life or human nature
Characters	• show qualities, or traits, and motivations • face one or more conflicts • develop theme through their words and actions
Plot	• develops suspense • focuses on a conflict, or struggle between opposing forces • builds to a climax, or turning point, the point of maximum interest • shows relationships between characters' actions and events • expresses theme
Stage Directions	• describe scenery, lighting, and sound effects • tell how characters should behave
Setting	• describes the time and place in which the action occurs • creates mood

Types of Drama

Two general categories of drama are comedy and tragedy.

A **comedy** usually deals with a light subject or handles a dark subject in an upbeat way. Comedies often present everyday characters in amusing situations. They are humorous in tone and end happily.

In a **tragedy,** events lead to the downfall or death of the main character. This character can be an average person but is often a heroic figure who displays a **tragic flaw,** a human trait such as pride or greed, that brings about his or her destruction. A tragedy may teach a powerful lesson about human nature.

A playwright may combine elements of both comedy and tragedy in a single work. For example, some comedies use humor to express a serious message about life or human nature. Likewise, a tragedy might include **comic relief**—a scene or an incident that provides a break from the otherwise serious events of the play.

The Changing World of Drama

For centuries, plays were intended to be viewed by a live audience or read in script form. Today, technology has changed the ways in which we experience plays. We can still watch a play with live actors onstage, but we can also watch a performance onscreen in a movie theater or at home in front of our televisions or computers.

In This Section

Elements of Drama

Analyzing Dramatic Elements

Close Read: Character, Action, and Theme
• Model Text
• Practice Text

After You Read

 Common Core State Standards

RL.8.3, RL.8.6
[For the full wording of the standards, see the standards chart in the front of your textbook.]

Types of Drama Today

Live Theater	Film/Movies	Television Drama	Radio Drama
• performed live for an audience • follows a written script • divides into acts and scenes • uses dialogue to tell the audience what is happening • uses scenery and lighting for visual effects	• recorded on film or digital medium and shown in theaters or streamed online • follows a script called a screenplay • is often made up of many short scenes • uses a camera to direct audience's attention to certain details	• recorded or performed live • follows a script called a teleplay • uses long and short scenes • like film, uses a camera to direct audience's attention • may be streamed online over the Internet	• recorded or performed live • follows a script called a radio play • uses long and short scenes • uses dialogue and sound effects to tell the audience what is happening

Analyzing Dramatic Elements

In drama, conflict, dialogue, and stage directions make the characters and their actions come alive.

 **Common Core State Standards**

Reading Literature 3. Analyze how particular lines of dialogue or incidents in a story or drama propel the action, reveal aspects of a character, or provoke a decision.

Reading Literature 6. Analyze how differences in the points of view of the characters and the audience or reader create such effects as suspense or humor.

Drama has the power to reveal important truths about life and human nature. Whether you are reading or watching a play, realistic characters can remind you of yourself or people you know. Even if just for a moment, you may feel as strongly about their situations as you do about real life. It is through the play's action, conflict, and dialogue that this magic takes place.

Action and Conflict In most plays, characters face a **conflict,** or struggle between opposing forces, that drives the **action.**

- An **external conflict** involves a character confronting an outside force, such as a physical obstacle, an enemy, nature, or society.
- An **internal conflict** is a struggle that occurs within a character. It often involves the character's feelings, beliefs, and values.

Dialogue and Character Development In drama, most of what you learn about characters comes from dialogue. Playwrights use dialogue in the following ways:

- to show a character's personality;
- to express a character's thoughts and feelings about events and other characters.

Character Motivation When a playwright writes a play, he or she must decide who the characters are and what their personalities are like. The playwright must also determine how each character will respond to events in the plot. For example, will the character explain through dialogue how he or she feels, or will events force the character to make a decision that moves the plot in a new direction? The playwright answers such questions by developing each character's motivation. **Character motivation** refers to the reasons why a character feels or behaves a certain way. The following chart demonstrates how character motivation works.

Character Motivation	Resulting Action
Anna likes Max, a new boy at school, and wants to meet him.	Anna's friend Jenna is having a party. At Anna's request, Jenna invites both Anna and Max to the party.
A man must get on the last train out of his war-torn country.	The man sleeps at the station the night before to guarantee his spot on the train.

Character motivation typically sets up a **cause-and-effect relationship** between events in a play. In the first example, Anna's desire to get to know the new boy causes her to ask Jenna to invite them both to a party. The resulting action is the effect.

Complex Characters To create plays that audiences care about, playwrights strive to develop **complex characters.** These characters display strengths and weaknesses and exhibit a full range of emotions. Sometimes, complex characters have multiple motivations.

Characters in Written Drama In a live performance, the actors use their facial expressions, body language, and tones of voice to help the audience understand the characters. When you read a play, however, you must gather clues to fully understand the characters and their motivations and conflicts. Here are some questions to ask yourself:

- Do the stage directions call for certain movements, facial expressions, or vocal intonations? (Example: *She nods in agreement.*)
- Do punctuation marks in a speech express a character's mood or feeling? (Example: That's amazing! I had no idea!)
- Do the characters use certain words that reveal their relationships? (Example: Honey, why didn't you call me?)

Dramatic Irony Sometimes the audience or readers of a play know more than the characters know. Such situations are examples of **dramatic irony,** a technique that can create humor or build suspense. The chart shows an example of dramatic irony and two possible ways that the situation might be revealed to the audience but hidden from the other characters.

Situation: The audience knows a character's true identity, while the other characters believe she is someone she is not.
Possibility 1: The character puts on a disguise during a scene in which other characters are not present.
Possibility 2: The character reveals she is in disguise by delivering a speech called an **aside.** An aside can be heard by the audience but not by other characters.

When a playwright uses dramatic irony, the point of view of the audience is very different from the points of view of the characters. Therefore, the words and actions of the characters have a different meaning for the audience than they do for the play's characters.

Theme in Drama The unique combination of elements in a play helps express its theme. As characters face conflicts and undergo growth and change, their actions and attitudes deliver important messages about life and human nature. To determine the theme of a dramatic work, ask yourself these questions:

- How have events caused the characters to change?
- Do events in the play remind me of my own experiences? If so, what did those experiences teach me?
- What might have been the playwright's purpose for writing the play?

Close Read: Character, Action, and Theme

In drama, characters propel the action and develop the theme.

In drama, playwrights develop characters who come alive through dialogue and stage directions. As the action of the play advances, powerful messages about life and human nature reveal themselves. The following questions can help you get the most out of reading a play.

Clues to Analyzing Character, Plot, and Theme

Dialogue
- What do the characters say?
- How do they say it?
- How do they react to comments made by other characters?
- How does the dialogue help to develop the plot?

Stage Directions
- What do you learn from the physical descriptions of the characters?
- How do the characters behave onstage?
- How does background and information about the setting influence the plot?
- What mental image do the stage directions help create?

Character
- What personality traits do the characters show?
- What problems or conflicts do they face?
- How do they attempt to resolve the conflicts?
- What decisions do they make?

Character Motivations
- What do characters want? Why do they behave as they do?
- How does their behavior affect the plot?
- How are the characters' goals or desires theatened?

Action/Plot
- What actions do the characters carry out?
- How do the characters react to events?
- How is tension built and then released?
- What is the climax, and how are the conflicts resolved?

Theme
- What ideas do the main characters' goals or desires reveal?
- Do any events or feelings expressed by the characters remind you of your own experiences in life?
- What message does the play's outcome suggest about life or human nature?

Model

About the Text *Kindertransport* takes place in Germany in 1938, during the violent rule of Adolf Hitler's Nazi party. In the play, the Nazis are waging a brutal campaign against Jews. Great Britain has responded with Kindertransport ("Children's Transport"), a program that offers Jewish children safe passage to Britain. In this scene, nine-year-old Eva is on a train heading out of Germany.

---

from *Kindertransport* by Diane Samuels

(Enter a Nazi border OFFICER. He approaches EVA . . .)

OFFICER: No councillor in here?

EVA: She's in the next carriage.

OFFICER *(picking up EVA'S case)*: Whose case is this?

EVA: Mine.

OFFICER: Stand up straight.

(EVA stands.)

Turn your label around then. It's gone the wrong way. Can't see your number.

EVA *(turning the label round. Quietly)*: Sorry.

OFFICER: Speak up.

EVA: Sorry.

OFFICER: Sir! Sorry, Sir.

EVA: Sorry, Sir.

OFFICER: No one will know what to do with you if they can't see your number.

(Silence)

Will they?

EVA: No, Sir.

OFFICER: Might have to remove you from the train.

(Silence.)

Mightn't we?

EVA: Yes, Sir.

Action/Plot The officer's severe words and threatening behavior create tension.

Dialogue From this dialogue, we learn that the officer is not just strict but may even be capable of cruelty toward Eva.

Stage Directions The stage directions indicating Eva's silence help capture the terror she feels as the officer questions her.

Independent Practice

About the Selection This excerpt, from Cherie Bennett's play, *Anne Frank & Me,* begins after Nicole, a typical suburban American teenager, bumps her head in an accident. She then wakes up in another time and place—Paris in 1942. Nicole's new family is Jewish. Soon after the Nazis arrest the family, they are put on a train to Auschwitz. This is where Nicole meets Anne Frank, the real writer of *The Diary of a Young Girl.*

Stage Directions
This stage direction describes the action during Nicole's monologue. What does the word *shove* tell you about the experience of being put on the train?

Action/Plot What major event in the plot occurs at this point?

Character What relationship between the girls does this dialogue establish?

from *Anne Frank & Me* by Cherie Bennett

AT RISE: *During the following monologue,* Nazis *shove more people into the cattle car.*

NICOLE *(pre-recorded):* Right now we are in Westerbork, in Holland. Earlier today they opened the door and shoved more people into our car. They speak Dutch. I can't understand them at all. I try to keep track of the dates as best I can. I think it is the 3rd of September, 1944. Surely the war will be over soon.

*(Train sounds. **NICOLE** makes her way to the bucket in the corner which is used as a toilet. A **GIRL** sits in front of the bucket, asleep, her back is to us.)*

NICOLE: *(tapping the **GIRL** on the shoulder).* I'm sorry to disturb you, but I need to use the—

*(The girl turns around. It is **ANNE FRANK,** thin, huge eyes. Their eyes meet. Some memory is instantly triggered in **NICOLE.** She knows this girl, knows things about her. But how?)*

ANNE: *Spreekn U Nederlander?* [Sprek´ ən oo ned´ ər land ər?] *(**NICOLE** just stares.)* So you speak French, then? Is this better?

NICOLE: I . . . I need to use the—

ANNE: It's all right. I'll hold my coat for you to give you some privacy. *(**NICOLE** goes to the bucket, **ANNE** holds her coat open to shield her.)*

NICOLE: Thank you.

ANNE: Just please do the same for me when the time comes. Have you been in here a long time? *(**NICOLE** finishes, fixes her dress.)*

NICOLE: Seventeen days, starting just outside Paris.

ANNE: It smells like it.

NICOLE: Does it? I can't even tell anymore.

ANNE: It's all right. It's not important.

NICOLE: Look, I know this sounds crazy, but . . . I know you.

ANNE: Have you been to Amsterdam?

NICOLE: No, never.

ANNE: Well, I've never been to Paris. Although I will go some day, I can assure you of that.

NICOLE: I do know you. Your name is . . . Anne Frank.

ANNE: *(shocked).* That's right! Who are you?

NICOLE: Nicole Bernhardt. I know so much about you . . . you were in hiding for a long time, in a place you called . . . the Secret Annex[1]—

ANNE: How could you know that?

NICOLE: *(her memory is flooded).* You were with your parents, and your older sister . . . Margot! And . . . some other people . . .

ANNE: Mr. Pfeffer and the Van Pels, they're all back there asleep—

NICOLE: Van Daans!

ANNE: *(shocked).* I only called them that in my diary. How could you know that?

NICOLE: And Peter! Your boyfriend's name was Peter!

ANNE: How could you know that?

NICOLE: You thought your parents would disapprove that you were kissing him—

ANNE: How is this possible?

NICOLE: You kept a diary. I read it.

ANNE: But . . . I left my diary in the Annex when the Gestapo came. You couldn't have read it.

NICOLE: But I did.

Dialogue What is Anne's reaction to Nicole's words? Why?

Character What does the punctuation in these lines help reveal about both characters?

---

1. **Secret Annex** name given to the space in an Amsterdam office building, where in 1942, thirteen-year-old Anne Frank and her family went into hiding.

Practice continued

ANNE: How?

NICOLE: I don't know.

ANNE: *(skeptical)*. This is a very, very strange conversation.

NICOLE: I feel like it was . . . I know this sounds crazy . . . but I feel like it was in the future.

ANNE: This is a joke, right? Peter put you up to this.

NICOLE: No—

ANNE: Daddy, then, to take my mind off—

NICOLE: No.

ANNE: *(cynical)*. Maybe you're a mind reader! *(She closes her eyes.)* What number am I thinking of right now?

NICOLE: I have no idea. Do you believe in time travel?

ANNE: I'm to believe that you're from the future? Really, I'm much more intelligent than I look.

NICOLE: I don't know how I know all this. I just do.

ANNE: Maybe you're an angel.

NICOLE: That would certainly be news to me.

Stage Directions
What do these stage directions tell you about Anne's emotions?

After You Read

from Anne Frank & Me

1. Key Ideas and Details (a) Identify: In what city does the train journey begin? **(b) Generalize:** What are the conditions on the train? **(c) Speculate:** Why are the people treated this way?

2. Key Ideas and Details (a) Make a Judgment: Read the short biography of Anne Frank on page 969 and the excerpts from her diary on pages 970–974. Does Cherie Bennett's Anne Frank seem like the real Anne Frank? Explain. **(b) Discuss:** Compare your answers with a partner's.

3. Key Ideas and Details Analyze: Anne Frank and her family were actually on the transport that left Holland for Auschwitz on September 3, 1944. These details become the setting for Cherie Bennett's play. Why is it important for the play to be historically accurate?

4. Craft and Structure (a) Analyze: Explain how this scene presents an example of dramatic irony. What does the reader understand about the situation that the characters themselves do not know? **(b) Make Connections:** How does the dramatic irony affect your involvement with the story?

5. Craft and Structure Interpret: Based on the scene you just read and on your prior knowledge, is this play best characterized as a comedy or tragedy? Explain.

6. Integration of Knowledge and Ideas (a) Analyze the stage directions and dialogue in this scene to identify details that make Anne and Nicole believable characters. How do these elements help you understand the characters of both the protagonist, Nicole, and Anne? Record your ideas in a chart like the one below.

Character Description	
Anne huge eyes	**Nicole** anxious, confused

(b) Collaborate: Compare charts with a partner. What additional information might you write on your chart?

 **Drama**

Build your skills and improve your comprehension of drama.

Read **The Governess** to find out what motivates a woman to play a cruel joke on her employee.

 Common Core State Standards

Meet these standards with **The Governess** (p. 818).

Reading Literature

1. Cite the textual evidence that most strongly supports an analysis of what the text says explicitly as well as inferences drawn from the text. *(Reading Skill: Draw Conclusions)*

3. Analyze how particular lines of dialogue or incidents in a story or drama propel the action, reveal aspects of a character, or provoke a decision. *(Literary Analysis: Setting and Character)*

Writing

1. Write arguments to support claims with clear reasons and relevant evidence. *(Writing: Public Service Announcement)*

Speaking and Listening

4. Present claims and findings, emphasizing salient points in a focused, coherent manner with relevant evidence; sound, valid reasoning; and well-chosen details. *(Speaking and Listening: Debate)*

Language

1.a. Explain the function of verbals (gerunds, participles, infinitives) in general and their function in particular sentences. *(Conventions: Participial Phrases)*

4.b. Use common, grade-appropriate Greek or Latin affixes and roots as clues to the meaning of a word. *(Vocabulary: Word Study)*

6. Acquire and use accurately grade-appropriate general academic and domain-specific words and phrases; gather vocabulary knowledge when considering a word or phrase important to comprehension or expression. *(Vocabulary: Word Study)*

Reading Skill: Draw Conclusions

Drawing conclusions means reaching decisions or forming opinions after considering details in a text. An author may state information directly or even have a character tell the reader something important. However, meaning in literature is usually suggested through details. To draw conclusions from a play, notice what the characters say and do.

- Look for statements that reveal underlying ideas and attitudes.
- Analyze interactions that show how characters treat each other.
- Notice actions that create a clear pattern of behavior.

Make connections among these items to decide what that pattern tells you about the character.

Using the Strategy: Conclusions Flow Chart

Use a **conclusions flow chart** chart like the one shown to record your observations about characters and draw conclusions from them.

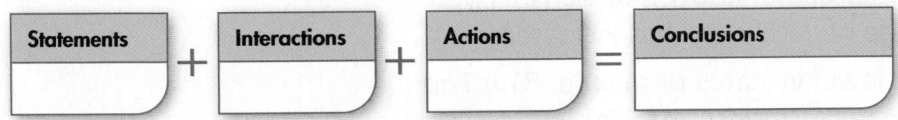

Literary Analysis: Setting and Character

Most characterization in plays is accomplished through dialogue. Setting is largely established through the way the characters react to the onstage world that the playwright has created.

Stage directions, or notes that tell how a play should be performed, also give readers insight into the characters, setting, and action. They describe the scenery, costumes, lighting, and sound and may tell how the characters feel, move, and speak. Stage directions are usually printed in italics and set in brackets.

[*It is late evening. The stage is dark, except for the glow of a small lamp beside the bed.*]

When you read a play, notice key lines of dialogue that help you understand a character, the setting, and the situation. Use the stage directions to develop a mental image of how a stage production would look and sound.

Is it our *differences* or our *similarities* that matter most?

Writing About the Big Question

The characters in *The Governess* come from different levels of society, which affects the way they treat each other. Use this sentence starter to develop your ideas about the Big Question.

An employer might **discriminate** against an employee, or treat her unfairly because _____.

While You Read Think about which differences influence the way the Mistress treats the governess.

Vocabulary

Read each word and its definition. Decide whether you know the word well, know it a little bit, or do not know it at all. After you read, see how your knowledge of each word has increased.

- **inferior** (in fir´ ē ər) *adj.* lower in status or rank (p. 819) *The nobility thought that peasants were inferior. inferiority n.*

- **discrepancies** (di skrep´ ən sēz) *n.* differences; inconsistencies (p. 819) *There were discrepancies between the witnesses' stories of what took place the night of the accident.*

- **discharged** (dis chärjd´) *v.* fired; released (p. 821) *Because she was always late, the manager discharged her. charge n.*

- **satisfactory** (sat´ is fak´ tə rē) *adj.* adequate; sufficient to meet a requirement (p. 822) *The group's final statement was satisfactory to all committee members. satisfaction n. satisfactorily adv. satisfy v.*

- **lax** (laks) *adj.* not strict or exact (p. 822) *Patients who are lax about taking medications risk becoming sicker. laxity n.*

- **guileless** (gīl´ lis) *adj.* not trying to hide anything or trick people; innocent (p. 824) *Jessica was so guileless that people always took advantage of her. guile n. guilelessness n. beguiling adj.*

Word Study

The **Latin suffix -ory** means "of," "relating to," or "characterized by."

In this play, the Mistress thinks Julia's answer to a question is not **satisfactory**. She means that the answer was not satisfying, or that it was not good enough.

Meet
Neil Simon
(b. 1927)

Author of
The
GOVERNESS

Neil Simon has been called the best-loved playwright of the twentieth century. Millions of people have enjoyed his plays and films. He is best known for his comedies—plays that poke gentle fun at people's behavior.

Life in New York Simon grew up in the Washington Heights neighborhood of New York City. He began as a writer for radio and television then moved on to write comedies for the stage. New York is the setting for many of his most popular plays, including *The Odd Couple, Plaza Suite,* and *Barefoot in the Park.* In the 1980s, Simon drew on his own life for three bittersweet plays that made critics view his work more seriously: *Brighton Beach Memoirs, Biloxi Blues,* and *Broadway Bound.*

> ## DID YOU KNOW?
> Simon once had four hit plays running on Broadway at the same time. His 1991 play *Lost in Yonkers* won the Pulitzer Prize.

BACKGROUND FOR THE PLAY

A Governess's Life

In the nineteenth century, when *The Governess* is set, upper-class families in Europe and the United States hired governesses to teach and look after their children. Governesses were often educated single women for whom there were few other ways to make a living. The life of a governess was often lonely because she belonged to neither the servant class nor the upper class.

The Governess

Neil Simon

▲ **Critical Viewing**
Which person in this scene is playing the part of the governess? How can you tell? **[Analyze]**

Draw Conclusions
What conclusion can you draw about the relationship between Julia and the Mistress?

MISTRESS. Julia! [*Calls again*] Julia!

[*A young governess,* JULIA, *comes rushing in. She stops before the desk and curtsies.*]

JULIA. [*Head down*] Yes, madame?

MISTRESS. Look at me, child. Pick your head up. I like to see your eyes when I speak to you.

JULIA. [*Lifts her head up*] Yes, madame. [*But her head has a habit of slowly drifting down again*]

MISTRESS. And how are the children coming along with their French lessons?

JULIA. They're very bright children, madame.

MISTRESS. Eyes up . . . They're bright, you say. Well, why not? And mathematics? They're doing well in mathematics, I assume?

JULIA. Yes, madame. Especially Vanya.

MISTRESS. Certainly. I knew it. I excelled in mathematics. He gets that from his mother, wouldn't you say?

JULIA. Yes, madame.

MISTRESS. Head up . . . [*She lifts head up*] That's it. Don't be afraid to look people in the eyes, my dear. If you think of yourself as inferior, that's exactly how people will treat you.

JULIA. Yes, ma'am.

MISTRESS. A quiet girl, aren't you? . . . Now then, let's settle our accounts. I imagine you must need money, although you never ask me for it yourself. Let's see now, we agreed on thirty rubles[1] a month, did we not?

JULIA. [*Surprised*] Forty, ma'am.

MISTRESS. No, no, thirty. I made a note of it. [*Points to the book*] I always pay my governess thirty . . . Who told you forty?

JULIA. You did, ma'am. I spoke to no one else concerning money . . .

MISTRESS. Impossible. Maybe you *thought* you heard forty when I said thirty. If you kept your head up, that would never happen. Look at me again and I'll say it clearly. *Thirty rubles a month.*

JULIA. If you say so, ma'am.

MISTRESS. Settled. Thirty a month it is . . . Now then, you've been here two months exactly.

JULIA. Two months and five days.

MISTRESS. No, no. Exactly two months. I made a note of it. You should keep books the way I do so there wouldn't be these discrepancies. So—we have two months at thirty rubles a month . . . comes to sixty rubles. Correct?

---

1. **rubles** (rōō′ bəlz) *n.* Russian currency; similar to U.S. dollars.

Vocabulary
inferior (in fir′ ē ər) *adj.* lower in status or rank

Setting and Character
What actions and expressions do the stage directions help you to picture?

Vocabulary
discrepancies (di skrep′ ən sēz) *n.* differences; inconsistencies

Reading Check
What does the Mistress take Julia aside to discuss?

Setting and Character
Which stage directions help you understand the way the characters speak the dialogue?

▼ **Critical Viewing**
If you were Julia, why would you feel intimidated by the Mistress, shown in the picture? Explain. **[Connect]**

JULIA. [*Curtsies*] Yes, ma'am. Thank you, ma'am.

MISTRESS. Subtract nine Sundays . . . We did agree to subtract Sundays, didn't we?

JULIA. No, ma'am.

MISTRESS. Eyes! Eyes! . . . Certainly we did. I've always subtracted Sundays. I didn't bother making a note of it because I always do it. Don't you recall when I said we will subtract Sundays?

JULIA. No, ma'am.

MISTRESS. Think.

JULIA. [*Thinks*] No, ma'am.

MISTRESS. You weren't thinking. Your eyes were wandering. Look straight at my face and look hard . . . Do you remember now?

JULIA. [*Softly*] Yes, ma'am.

MISTRESS. I didn't hear you, Julia.

JULIA. [*Louder*] Yes, ma'am.

MISTRESS. Good. I was sure you'd remember . . . Plus three holidays. Correct?

JULIA. Two, ma'am. Christmas and New Year's.

MISTRESS. And your birthday. That's three.

JULIA. I worked on my birthday, ma'am.

MISTRESS. You did? There was no need to. My governesses never worked on their birthdays . . .

JULIA. But I did work, ma'am.

MISTRESS. But that's not the question, Julia. We're discussing financial matters now. I will, however, only count two holidays if you insist . . . Do you insist?

JULIA. I did work, ma'am.

MISTRESS. Then you *do* insist.

JULIA. No, ma'am.

MISTRESS. Very well. That's three holidays, therefore we take off twelve rubles. Now then, four days little Kolya was sick, and there were no lessons.

JULIA. But I gave lessons to Vanya.

MISTRESS. True. But I engaged you to teach two children, not one. Shall I pay you in full for doing only half the work?

JULIA. No, ma'am.

MISTRESS. So we'll deduct it . . . Now, three days you had a toothache and my husband gave you permission not to work after lunch. Correct?

JULIA. After four. I worked until four.

MISTRESS. [*Looks in the book*] I have here: "Did not work after lunch." We have lunch at one and are finished at two, not at four, correct?

JULIA. Yes, ma'am. But I—

MISTRESS. That's another seven rubles . . . Seven and twelve is nineteen . . . Subtract . . . that leaves . . . forty-one rubles . . . Correct?

JULIA. Yes, ma'am. Thank you, ma'am.

MISTRESS. Now then, on January fourth you broke a teacup and saucer, is that true?

JULIA. Just the saucer, ma'am.

MISTRESS. What good is a teacup without a saucer, eh? . . . That's two rubles. The saucer was an heirloom.[2] It cost much more, but let it go. I'm used to taking losses.

JULIA. Thank you, ma'am.

MISTRESS. Now then, January ninth, Kolya climbed a tree and tore his jacket.

JULIA. I forbid him to do so, ma'am.

MISTRESS. But he didn't listen, did he? . . . Ten rubles . . . January fourteenth, Vanya's shoes were stolen . . .

JULIA. But the maid, ma'am. You **discharged** her yourself.

---

2. **heirloom** (er´ lo͞om´) *n.* treasured possession passed down from generation to generation.

Spiral Review
Conflict How does the difference between the social classes of Julia and the Mistress help create the play's conflict?

Vocabulary
discharged (dis chärjd´)
v. fired; released

Reading Check
How does the Mistress punish Julia for the actions of Kolya?

History Connection

What Is Women's Work?

Throughout the nineteenth century, jobs for women were scarce. Most professions were unavailable to anyone except men. Low-wage factory jobs, such as making clothing, were available to working-class women and girls. A majority of uneducated women, however, were domestic servants.

A middle-class woman with some education could become a teacher or a governess. An unmarried woman who needed to support herself had few other options.

Like domestic workers and factory workers, governesses earned very little. They were viewed as servants.

Connect to the Literature

Would Julia behave differently if she were paid better or if she could pursue other career options? Explain.

Vocabulary

satisfactory (sat´ is fak´ tə rē) *adj.* adequate; sufficient to meet a requirement

lax (laks) *adj.* not strict or exact

MISTRESS. But you get paid good money to watch everything. I explained that in our first meeting. Perhaps you weren't listening. Were you listening that day, Julia, or was your head in the clouds?

JULIA. Yes, ma'am.

MISTRESS. Yes, your head was in the clouds?

JULIA. No, ma'am. I was listening.

MISTRESS. Good girl. So that means another five rubles off [*Looks in the book*] . . . Ah, yes . . . The sixteenth of January I gave you ten rubles.

JULIA. You didn't.

MISTRESS. But I made a note of it. Why would I make a note of it if I didn't give it to you?

JULIA. I don't know, ma'am.

MISTRESS. That's not a satisfactory answer, Julia . . . Why would I make a note of giving you ten rubles if I did not in fact give it to you, eh? . . . No answer? . . . Then I must have given it to you, mustn't I?

JULIA. Yes, ma'am. If you say so, ma'am.

MISTRESS. Well, certainly I say so. That's the point of this little talk. To clear these matters up. Take twenty-seven from forty-one, that leaves . . . fourteen, correct?

JULIA. Yes, ma'am. [*She turns away, softly crying*]

MISTRESS. What's this? Tears? Are you crying? Has something made you unhappy, Julia? Please tell me. It pains me to see you like this. I'm so sensitive to tears. What is it?

JULIA. Only once since I've been here have I ever been given any money and that was by your husband. On my birthday he gave me three rubles.

MISTRESS. Really? There's no note of it in my book. I'll put it down now. [*She writes in the book.*] Three rubles. Thank you for telling me. Sometimes I'm a little lax with my accounts . . . Always shortchanging myself. So then, we take three more from fourteen . . . leaves eleven . . . Do you wish to check my figures?

JULIA. There's no need to, ma'am.

MISTRESS. Then we're all settled. Here's your salary for two months, dear. Eleven rubles. [*She puts the pile of coins on the desk.*] Count it.

JULIA. It's not necessary, ma'am.

MISTRESS. Come, come. Let's keep the records straight. Count it.

JULIA. [*Reluctantly counts it*] One, two, three, four, five, six, seven, eight, nine, ten . . . ? There's only ten, ma'am.

MISTRESS. Are you sure? Possibly you dropped one . . . Look on the floor, see if there's a coin there.

JULIA. I didn't drop any, ma'am. I'm quite sure.

MISTRESS. Well, it's not here on my desk, and I *know* I gave you eleven rubles. Look on the floor.

JULIA. It's all right, ma'am. Ten rubles will be fine.

MISTRESS. Well, keep the ten for now. And if we don't find it on the floor later, we'll discuss it again next month.

JULIA. Yes, ma'am. Thank you, ma'am. You're very kind, ma'am.

[*She curtsies and then starts to leave.*]

MISTRESS. Julia!

[*JULIA stops, turns.*]

Come back here.

[*She goes back to the desk and curtsies again.*]

Why did you thank me?

JULIA. For the money, ma'am.

MISTRESS. For the money? . . . But don't you realize what I've done? I've cheated you . . . *Robbed* you! I have no such notes in my book. I made up whatever came into my mind. Instead of the eighty rubles which I owe you, I gave you only ten. I have actually stolen from you and you still thank me . . . Why?

JULIA. In the other places that I've worked, they didn't give me anything at all.

▼ **Critical Viewing**
Does this photograph accurately capture Julia's personality? Why or why not? **[Make a Judgment]**

Draw Conclusions
Does this speech change your mind about the Mistress's intentions? Explain.

Vocabulary
guileless (gīl´ lis) *adj.* not trying to hide anything or trick people; innocent

MISTRESS. Then they cheated you even worse than I did . . . I was playing a little joke on you. A cruel lesson just to teach you. You're much too trusting, and in this world that's very dangerous . . . I'm going to give you the entire eighty rubles. [*Hands her an envelope*] It's all ready for you. The rest is in this envelope. Here, take it.

JULIA. As you wish, ma'am. [*She curtsies and starts to go again.*]

MISTRESS. Julia! [JULIA *stops.*] Is it possible to be so spineless? Why don't you protest? Why don't you speak up? Why don't you cry out against this cruel and unjust treatment? Is it really possible to be so guileless, so innocent, such a—pardon me for being so blunt—such a simpleton?

JULIA. [*The faintest trace of a smile on her lips*] Yes, ma'am . . . it's possible.

[*She curtsies again and runs off. The* MISTRESS *looks after her a moment, a look of complete bafflement on her face. The lights fade.*]

Critical Thinking

1. **Key Ideas and Details (a)** What does the Mistress want to discuss with Julia? **(b) Connect:** Why does Julia's position make this discussion difficult for her?

2. **Key Ideas and Details (a)** What are the reasons the Mistress gives for cutting Julia's pay? **(b) Infer:** Why does Julia respond the way she does?

3. **Key Ideas and Details (a)** What final action does the Mistress take to try to make Julia fight back? **(b) Analyze:** Is the mistress being kind, cruel, or both? Explain. **(c) Speculate:** Do you think Julia will behave differently in the future? Why or why not?

4. **Integration of Knowledge and Ideas (a)** Beyond class, what differences between the Mistress and Julia help to explain their behavior? **(b)** If Julia had been from the same social class, would the Mistress have acted differently? Explain. *[Connect to the Big Question: Is it our differences or our similarities that matter most?]*

Cite textual evidence to support your responses.

Reading Skill: Draw Conclusions

1. Identify three of the Mistress's lines that demonstrate a particular attitude or behavior. **(a)** Based on these lines, what **conclusions** can you draw about the reasons for the Mistress's behavior? **(b)** Does your opinion of the Mistress change between the middle and the end of the play? Explain.

2. Based on Julia's responses, what can you conclude about the general treatment of governesses at the time of this play?

Literary Analysis: Setting and Character

ⓒ **3. Craft and Structure (a)** List one example of dialogue and two examples of **stage directions** from *The Governess* in a chart like the one shown. **(b)** How does each example help you understand the characters, situation, and setting?

Describing an Action	Showing How a Character Feels

Vocabulary

ⓒ **Acquisition and Use** Use a vocabulary word from page 816 to rewrite each of the following sentences so that it has the opposite meaning.

1. The testimony of the two witnesses was in total agreement.
2. Josie was so clever that no one could play a trick on her.
3. Because he forgot to study, Cy got a poor mark on the test.
4. The debaters treated each other as equals.
5. Ben's work was so outstanding that he was given a raise.
6. No one took a long lunch because the boss watched the clock.

Word Study Use context and what you know about the **Latin suffix -ory** to explain your answer to each question.

1. Why might someone undergo *exploratory* surgery?
2. If Bill acts in a *supervisory* manner, is he showing leadership?

Word Study

The **Latin suffix -ory** means "of," "relating to," or "characterized by."

Apply It Explain how the suffix *-ory* contributes to the meanings of these words. Consult a dictionary, if necessary.

migratory
circulatory
mandatory

Integrated Language Skills

The Governess

Conventions: Participial Phrases

A **participle** is a verb form that is used as an adjective. A **participial phrase** is made up of a participle with its modifiers and complements, such as adverbs or objects.

Participles commonly end in *-ing* (present participle) or *-ed* (past participle). The entire participial phrase is used as an adjective.

Participial Phrases and the Words They Modify

Traveling quickly, we got to the game on time.
(The participial phrase modifies the subject, *we*.)

The tourist, confused by the signs, got lost.
(The participial phrase modifies the subject, *tourist*.)

The hallways are clogged with students going to class.
(The participial phrase modifies the object, *students*.)

Practice A Identify the participial phrase in each sentence below. Then identify the noun that it modifies.

1. Julia, feeling anxious and afraid, knocked on the mistress's door.

2. The mistress's accounts, settled once a month, were always accurate.

3. The children, celebrating the holiday, did not have their lessons today.

4. There are envelopes containing our pay.

© **Writing Application** Write one sentence about a servant and one about an employer. Use a participial phrase in each sentence.

Practice B Use a participial phrase to combine the two sentences into one sentence.

1. Julia carried her suitcase. Julia boarded the carriage.

2. The mistress frowned slightly. The mistress told Julia to count her money carefully.

3. The children ran to their rooms. The children feared the thunder and lightning.

© **Writing Application** Write three sentences, using each of these participial phrases: *walking the dog, amused by the joke, containing good nutrients*. Place one phrase at the start, one in the middle, and one at the end of its sentence.

PH WRITING COACH | Further instruction and practice are available in *Prentice Hall Writing Coach*.

Writing

 **Common Core State Standards**

L.8.4.b, L.8.6, L.8.1.a; W.8.1; SL.8.4
[For the full wording of the standards, see page 814.]

Argumentative Text Write a **public service announcement (PSA)** that persuades listeners to support the fair treatment of workers. Follow these steps:

- Choose a figure from politics, business, or entertainment as your spokesperson. Write your script with this person in mind.
- Summarize the claims you will use to persuade your audience.
- Make a list of specific words, phrases, images, sound effects, or symbols that will help you support your claims.
- Using elements from your notes, write a script for radio or television to be delivered by your celebrity spokesperson.

Grammar Application Make sure your PSA makes use of a variety of phrases and clauses, including adverbial and adjectival forms.

Writing Workshop: *Work in Progress*

Prewriting for Workplace Writing Jot down five careers that interest you. Choose one career and then list the reasons it appeals to you. Save this Career List in your portfolio.

Use this prewriting activity to prepare for the **Writing Workshop** on page 842.

Speaking and Listening

Presentation of Knowledge and Ideas Form two teams to **debate** this proposal: "The minimum working age should be lowered to thirteen for jobs in retail stores."

Choose a moderator to keep time and to see that the debaters follow the rules. Follow these steps to prepare:

- Conduct research to identify evidence and examples that support your position. Differentiate facts from opinions so that you can establish a factual basis for your arguments.
- Jot down thoughts and reasons that will help bolster your argument. Craft a thesis, or statement of your position, from your notes. Present this thesis during your opening statement.
- Prepare for your opponents' arguments by thinking about the topic from their perspective. For example, you might anticipate the argument that working will take time away from schoolwork by countering that it will develop responsibility.
- During the debate, each participant should build on or respond to the arguments presented by the previous speaker. All debaters should use a respectful tone, particularly when pointing out flaws or weaknesses in opponents' arguments.

www.PHLitOnline.com
- Interactive graphic organizers
- Grammar tutorial
- Interactive journals

Test Practice: Reading

Draw Conclusions

Fiction Selection

Directions: *Read the selection. Then, answer the questions.*

As I came into town, I could see that much had changed over the years. The huge trees that had once shaded the streets were gone. The houses looked smaller to my adult eyes. Many stores along High Street were empty, with "For Rent" signs in the windows. There was no workday bustle—nobody going to lunch or rushing to meetings. At the end of the street was a brand-new shopping mall, but its parking lot was only half-full. Feeling hopeless, I wondered what I would do here. I considered turning around and heading straight back to Los Angeles, yet as I neared my parents' street, I remembered the mere six dollars in my bank account.

1. What evidence points to the conclusion that the town is no longer prosperous?
   A. There are "For Rent" signs and empty stores.
   B. There is storm damage and the trees are gone.
   C. There is a new shopping mall and the trees are gone.
   D. People are going to lunch and to meetings.

2. Which conclusion is *most* logical?
   A. The narrator is excited.
   B. The narrator has never visited the town before.
   C. The narrator lived in the town years ago.
   D. The narrator is starting a business.

3. The excerpt "The houses looked smaller to my adult eyes" suggests that—
   A. the narrator has a child
   B. the narrator is thinking about buying a house in the town.
   C. the narrator thinks the houses are big.
   D. the narrator was a child the last time he or she was in the town.

4. You can conclude from the passage that the narrator—
   A. is only passing through town.
   B. is visiting old friends.
   C. has financial trouble.
   D. doesn't drive a car.

Writing for Assessment

Write a few sentences in which you describe the narrator. Use details from the passage to help you draw your conclusions about him or her.

Nonfiction Selection

Directions: *Read the selection. Then, answer the questions.*

In a growing trend often referred to as the "boomerang" effect, young adults are graduating from college and moving back home. Graduation used to signal independence. Now, following the traditional post-college path is not that easy. Jobs are scarce, salaries are low, and rent and other expenses are high. The appeal of traveling the world has also led some recent graduates to live at home and save money until they have enough to travel. More and more older adult children are moving back in with their parents, too. Their reasons range from career changes to the same type of financial concerns that recent college graduates face. Since the 1970s, the number of "boomerangs" has risen from less than 10% of all 20- to 34-year olds to 35%. Some reports even say the number may be as high as 50%!

1. Which conclusion is *most* logical?
   A. Parents hope to support their children.
   B. It costs less to live at home with parents than to live on one's own.
   C. Living at home provides better job opportunities.
   D. Adults look forward to moving home.

2. According to the selection, which *best* describes the "traditional post-college path"?
   A. Students graduate, get jobs, and support themselves.
   B. Students graduate and move home.
   C. Students graduate and buy a house.
   D. Students graduate, get married, and have children.

3. Which conclusion about new college graduates is *most* accurate?
   A. Many of them are too lazy to work.
   B. Many cannot support themselves yet.
   C. Many change jobs often.
   D. Many buy new houses right away.

4. Which detail helps you conclude that some young adults are waiting to start a career?
   A. Young adults want to spend more time with their parents.
   B. Young adults are taking more time to finish school.
   C. Young adults want to start a career, but jobs are scarce.
   D. Young adults want to travel before settling into a job.

Writing for Assessment

Connecting Across Texts
Write a short essay in which you conclude why the narrator of the first selection is moving home. Use information from the second selection to support your ideas.

PHLit
Online!
www.PHLitOnline.com
• Online practice
• Instant feedback

Reading for Information

Analyzing Functional Texts

Public Document

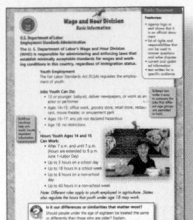

Contract

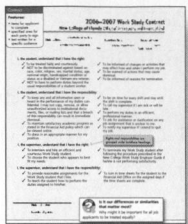

Job Application

Common Core State Standards

Reading Informational Text
1. Cite the textual evidence that most strongly supports an analysis of what the text says explicitly as well as inferences drawn from the text.

Language
6. Acquire and use accurately grade-appropriate general academic and domain-specific words and phrases; gather vocabulary knowledge when considering a word or phrase important to comprehension or expression.

Reading Skill: Compare and Contrast Features and Elements

Functional texts often use a variety of elements and features, such as headings, lists, and type treatments, to convey information clearly and obviously. **Comparing and contrasting these features and elements** will help you better understand the information provided in functional texts. Once you understand the information, you can make generalizations. When you *make generalizations,* you combine specific facts and information stated in the text to draw general conclusions, as in this example.

Information	Information	Generalization
The U.S. Department of Labor permits youth ages 14–15 to work fewer hours on school days than on non-school days.	The contract for the work-study program includes academic requirements.	Employers and the U.S. Department of Labor do not want young people's jobs to interfere with their schoolwork.

(Information **+** Information **=** Generalization)

Content-Area Vocabulary

These words appear in the selections that follow. You may also encounter them in other content-area texts.

- **administering** (ad min´ is tər iŋ) *v.* managing the affairs of
- **termination** (tər´ mə nā´ shən) *n.* the end of something
- **breach** (brēch) *n.* act of breaking or neglect of a law, trust, or duty

Wage and Hour Division
Basic Information

Features:

- agency logo or seal that shows it is an official document
- information published for the benefit of the public
- current and updated information
- text written for a specific audience

U.S. Department of Labor
Employment Standards Administration

The U.S. Department of Labor's Wage and Hour Division (WHD) is responsible for administering and enforcing laws that establish minimally acceptable standards for wages and working conditions in this country, regardless of immigration status.

Youth Employment

The Fair Labor Standards Act (FLSA) regulates the employment of youth.

Jobs Youth Can Do:

- 13 or younger: baby-sit, deliver newspapers, or work as an actor or performer
- Ages 14–15: office work, grocery store, retail store, restaurant, movie theater, or amusement park
- Ages 16–17: any job not declared hazardous
- Age 18: no restrictions

Bulleted lists make it easy to compare the jobs that different age groups are permitted to hold.

Boldface headings help you easily locate important information.

Hours Youth Ages 14 and 15 Can Work:

- After 7 a.m. and until 7 p.m. (Hours are extended to 9 p.m. June 1–Labor Day)
- Up to 3 hours on a school day
- Up to 18 hours in a school week
- Up to 8 hours on a non-school day
- Up to 40 hours in a non-school week

Note: Different rules apply to youth employed in agriculture. States also regulate the hours that youth under age 18 may work.

2006-2007 Work Study Contract

New College of Florida Office of Admissions and Financial Aid

_____ is approved to work for _____ in _____.
Student's Name   **Supervisor's Name**   **Department Name**

He/She has been awarded $_____ in Work Study for the _____ year.
                        Amount   **Academic Year**

I, the student, understand that I have the right:

- ✓ To be treated fairly and courteously.
- ✓ NOT to be discriminated against based on race, color, religion, sex, marital status, age, national origin, handicapped condition or status as a disabled or Vietnam era veteran.
- ✓ NOT to have to perform duties beyond the usual responsibilities of a student worker.
- ✓ To be informed of changes or activities that may affect how and when I perform my job.
- ✓ To be warned of actions that may cause dismissal.
- ✓ To be informed of reasons for **termination**.

I, the student, understand that I have the responsibility:

- ✓ To keep any and all information seen or heard in the performance of my duties confidential. I may not copy, remove, or allow unauthorized access to institutional documents, files, or mailing lists and that a **breach** of this responsibility can result in immediate dismissal.
- ✓ To maintain satisfactory academic progress as stated in the Financial Aid policy which can be viewed online.
- ✓ To dress in an appropriate manner for my position.
- ✓ To be on time for every shift and stay until the shift is complete.
- ✓ To call my supervisor if I am sick or will be late.
- ✓ To perform my duties in an efficient, professional manner.
- ✓ To ask for assistance or clarification on any job assignment that is unclear to me.
- ✓ To notify my supervisor if I intend to quit my job.

> Rights and responsibilities are grouped under boldface headings.

I, the supervisor, understand that I have the right:

- ✓ To interview and hire an efficient and courteous Work Study student.
- ✓ To choose the student who appears to best fit my needs.
- ✓ To terminate my Work Study student after following the procedure prescribed in the New College Work Study Employer Guide if he/she is not performing satisfactorily.

I, the supervisor, understand that I have the responsibility:

- ✓ To provide reasonable assignments for the Work Study student that I hire.
- ✓ To teach the student how to perform the duties assigned to him/her.
- ✓ To turn in time sheets for the student to the Financial Aid Office on the assigned days if the time sheets are complete.

_____   _____
Student's Signature   **Date**

_____   _____
Supervisor's Signature   **Date**

Features:

- descriptions of available positions
- space to fill in contact information, education, and experience
- text written for a specific audience

Tampa Museum of Art

The job title, a key term, is underlined to get the reader's attention.

Be a Museum Volunteer!

Teens

Junior Docents

The text includes a clear description of the duties of a junior docent.

Meet new friends while learning about art and culture. Participate in the Tampa Museum of Art's Junior Docent Program! The Junior Docent program at the Tampa Museum of Art is an exciting experience for teenagers to explore history and culture through art. As a Junior Docent, you will learn about the Museum's collection and assist with family programming including our *Art Spot* classes, Family Day activities, and student and family tours.

A Junior Docent's major responsibilities are to explain art processes and objects to the general public during Saturday afternoon student and family tours, and to assist the art teachers and museum educators with the weekly *Art Spot* classes. Being a Junior Docent requires the ability and desire to engage in on-going learning about the Tampa Museum of Art's collections and exhibitions.

Junior Docent Meetings are held two Wednesday afternoons a month from 3:30 p.m. to 5:30 p.m. In addition to the meetings, Junior Docents will work one Saturday a month from 10:00 to 2:00 p.m. The Junior Docent team will also have an opportunity to attend one off-site event each month to learn more about the art community in Tampa and enjoy some fun!

Refreshments are provided.

Tampa Museum of Art
VOLUNTEER APPLICATION

FOR:

Docent _____   Intern _____   Junior Docent _____   Other _____

Date of Application: _____   Social Security # _____

Name: _____   Home Phone: _____

Address: _____   Zip: _____

Current Employer: _____   Business Phone: _____

Driver's License Number: _____   E-mail address: _____

EDUCATION:

College: _____   Major: _____

Degree: _____   Year: _____   Do you have any art history background? _____

WORK AND VOLUNTEER EXPERIENCE:

List professional and/or volunteer work. Indicate hours of current commitments.

_____

_____

Have you ever worked with the following groups?

Children (ages 3+) _____   Teenagers _____   Senior Citizens _____   Handicapped _____   Disadvantaged? _____

Have you ever been a museum docent? _____   Where? _____

Other (please specify)? _____   Where? _____

Please indicate any other relevant experience or interests (i.e., teaching experience, travel, etc.)

_____

_____

AVAILABILITY:

If you are interested in becoming a docent, are you able to make a one-year commitment (10 hours per week) to the program? _____

Do you prefer to volunteer weekdays? _____   Weekends? _____   Thursday evenings? _____

How did you hear about the program? _____

PLEASE INCLUDE THE FOLLOWING INFORMATION:

In case of emergency please notify: NAME _____

Telephone # _____   Relationship? _____

_____   _____
Date   Volunteer Signature

Features such as write-on lines and boxes allow applicants to provide requested information.

Comparing Functional Texts

© 1. Craft and Structure (a) Compare and contrast the features and elements of the public document with those of the contract. **(b)** How does each text help the reader understand the information presented? **(c)** What **generalizations** can you make about the types of information included in each document? Explain.

Content-Area Vocabulary

2. (a) The words *administering* and *administration* are each formed by adding a suffix to *administer.* In each case, explain how the suffix alters the meaning and part of speech of the base word. **(b)** Use each word in a sentence that shows its meaning.

 Timed Writing

Explanatory Text: Essay

> **Format and Audience**
> The prompt gives specific directions about your audience and the type of information to include in your answer.

> What should you consider when deciding whether or not to volunteer at the Tampa Museum of Art? Using the information given in the job application, write an essay for a school newspaper. Explain how a student should go about making a decision. (30 minutes)

> **Academic Vocabulary**
> When you *explain* something, you make it clear using descriptions, details, and facts.

5-Minute Planner

Complete these steps before you begin to write:

1. Read the prompt carefully and completely. Look for key words like the ones highlighted in color to help you understand the assignment.

2. Reread the volunteer application. As you read, consider what details in the text are most important.

3. Think about your audience—the students reading the school newspaper. Consider the questions they would need to answer before they could decide whether or not to volunteer.

4. Plan the order in which you will place your information.

5. Refer to your notes as you write your essay.

Comparing Adaptations to Originals

A literary **adaptation** is a work that has been changed or adjusted to fit a different form or genre. For example, a novel may be adapted into a play or a movie. When adapting a literary work, an author may change or delete parts of the original to suit the new form and purpose. For instance, since a play depends almost entirely on dialogue to entertain an audience, the narration or description that is included in a story has to be cut or conveyed in a new way.

To compare an adaptation to the original work, remember the differences in the two literary forms. Keep those differences in mind as you analyze the two works.

- First, look for the elements that the writer has kept from the original as well as those he has left out.

- Next, look for new elements the writer has introduced.

- Finally, compare the purposes and styles of the two authors. Determine if one style results in a lighter, more humorous treatment or whether the styles are mostly the same.

"The Ninny" and *The Governess* both borrow plot patterns from traditional fairy tales. In many fairy tales, such as "Cinderella," the main character is a humble young servant who works for a cruel master or mistress. The servant undergoes a series of tests and trials and is eventually rewarded for his or her loyalty and humility. As you read "The Ninny," analyze how Chekhov updates this plot pattern to develop the central idea of the story.

As you read Chekhov's short story "The Ninny," use a Venn diagram like the one shown to analyze the similarities and differences between this work and Neil Simon's dramatic adaptation, *The Governess* (p. 818).

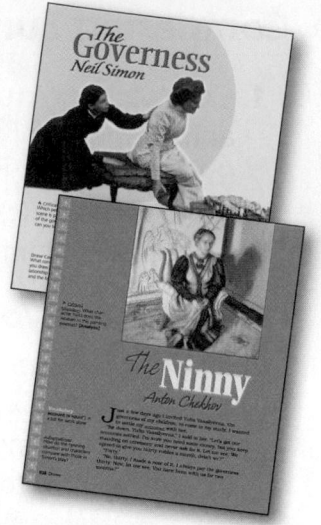

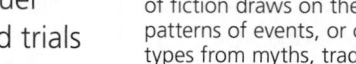
Common Core State Standards

Reading Literature

5. Compare and contrast the structure of two or more texts and analyze how the differing structure of each text contributes to its meaning and style.

9. Analyze how a modern work of fiction draws on themes, patterns of events, or character types from myths, traditional stories, or religious works such as the Bible, including describing how the material is rendered new.

Writing

4. Produce clear and coherent writing in which the development, organization, and style are appropriate to task, purpose, and audience. *(Timed Writing)*

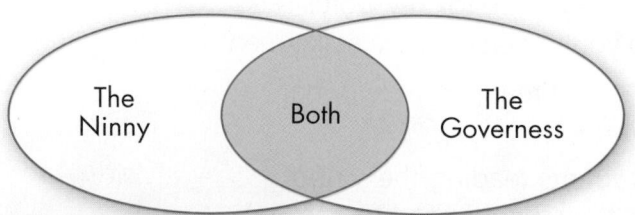

PHLit Online!
www.PHLitOnline.com

- Vocabulary flashcards
- Interactive journals
- More about the authors
- Selection audio
- Interactive graphic organizers

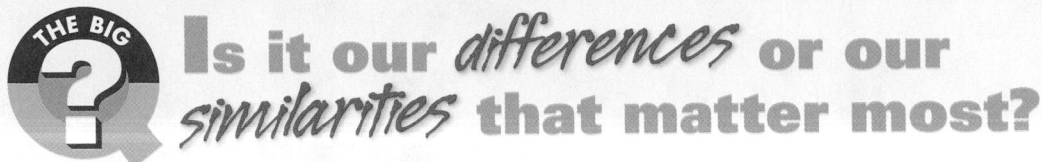

Is it our *differences* or our *similarities* that matter most?

Writing About the Big Question

In "The Ninny" and *The Governess,* two people from very different backgrounds have a disagreement. Use these sentence starters to develop your ideas about the Big Question.

When two people come from different social **classes**, conflicts can arise over issues such as _____ and _____. This is because _____.

Meet the Author

Anton Chekhov (1860–1904)

Author of "The Ninny"

Anton Pavlovich Chekhov originally planned to be a doctor, and studied medicine in Moscow. To pay for medical school and support his family, he began to write humorous articles and stories for journals.

A Master of the Short Story Chekhov wrote more than two hundred short stories. Some are comic, while others show the small tragedies of ordinary life. All show sympathy and understanding for their characters. The stories also paint a realistic and detailed picture of Russian life in both cities and peasant villages.

Despite his success as a writer, Chekhov was surprisingly modest about the writer's role. He wrote: "It is time for writers to admit that nothing in this world makes sense. Only fools . . . think they know and understand everything."

Chekhov was also an accomplished writer of plays. *The Seagull* (1896), *Three Sisters* (1901), and *The Cherry Orchard* (1903) are among his plays that are performed regularly throughout the world. Chekhov died of the lung disease tuberculosis at age forty-four at a health spa in Germany.

Woman in a Chair, John Collier, Courtesy of the artist

▶ **Critical Viewing**
What character traits
does the woman in
this painting seem to
possess? **[Analyze]**

Vocabulary
account (ə kount´) *n.*
a bill for work done

Adaptations
How do the opening
situation and characters
compare with those in
Simon's play (p. 818)?

The Ninny

Anton Chekhov

Translated by Robert Payne

Just a few days ago I invited Yulia Vassilyevna, the
governess of my children, to come to my study. I wanted
to settle my account with her.

"Sit down, Yulia Vassilyevna," I said to her. "Let's get our
accounts settled. I'm sure you need some money, but you keep
standing on ceremony and never ask for it. Let me see. We
agreed to give you thirty rubles a month, didn't we?"

"Forty."

"No, thirty. I made a note of it. I always pay the governess
thirty. Now, let me see. You have been with us for two
months?"

"Two months and five days."

"Two months exactly. I made a note of it. So you have sixty rubles coming to you. Subtract nine Sundays. You know you don't tutor Kolya on Sundays, you just go out for a walk. And then the three holidays . . ."

Yulia Vassilyevna blushed and picked at the trimmings of her dress, but said not a word.

"Three holidays. So we take off twelve rubles. Kolya was sick for four days—those days you didn't look after him. You looked after Vanya, only Vanya. Then there were the three days you had a toothache, when my wife gave you permission to stay away from the children after dinner. Twelve and seven makes nineteen. Subtract. . . . That leaves . . . hm . . . forty-one rubles. Correct?"

Yulia Vassilyevna's left eye reddened and filled with tears. Her chin trembled. She began to cough nervously, blew her nose, and said nothing.

"Then around New Year's Day you broke a cup and saucer. Subtract two rubles. The cup cost more than that—it was an heirloom, but we won't bother about that. We're the ones who pay. Another matter. Due to your carelessness Kolya climbed a tree and tore his coat. Subtract ten. Also, due to your carelessness the chambermaid[1] ran off with Vanya's boots. You ought to have kept your eyes open. You get a good salary. So we dock off five more. . . . On the tenth of January you took ten rubles from me."

"I didn't," Yulia Vassilyevna whispered.

"But I made a note of it."

"Well, yes—perhaps . . ."

"From forty-one we take twenty-seven. That leaves fourteen."

Her eyes filled with tears, and her thin, pretty little nose was shining with perspiration. Poor little child!

"I only took money once," she said in a trembling voice. "I took three rubles from your wife . . . never anything more."

"Did you now? You see, I never made a note of it. Take three from fourteen. That leaves eleven. Here's your money, my dear. Three, three, three . . . one and one. Take it, my dear."

I gave her the eleven rubles. With trembling fingers she took them and slipped them into her pocket.

Vocabulary
carelessness (kār´ləs nəs) *n.* lack of responsibility

Ⓒ Spiral Review
Characterization
Why does Yulia agree so quickly with her employer's assertion that she took ten rubles, when she first insisted she did not?

✓ Reading Check
Why is Yulia crying?

---

1. **chambermaid** female household servant whose main job is to clean and care for bedrooms.

"*Merci*,"[2] she whispered.

I jumped up, and began pacing up and down the room. I was in a furious temper.

"Why did you say '*merci*'?" I asked.

"For the money."

". . . Don't you realize I've been cheating you? I steal your money, and all you can say is '*merci*'!"

"In my other places they gave me nothing."

"They gave you nothing! Well, no wonder! I was playing a trick on you—a dirty trick . . . I'll give you your eighty rubles, they are all here in an envelope made out for you. Is it possible for anyone to be such a nitwit? Why didn't you protest? Why did you keep your mouth shut? Is it possible that there is anyone in this world who is so spineless? Why are you such a ninny?"

She gave me a bitter little smile. On her face I read the words: "Yes, it is possible."

I apologized for having played this cruel trick on her, and to her great surprise gave her the eighty rubles. And then she said "*merci*" again several times, always timidly, and went out. I gazed after her, thinking how very easy it is in this world to be strong.

---

2. *merci* (mer sē´) French for "thank you." In the nineteenth century, many upper-class Russians spoke French.

Vocabulary
spineless (spīn´ ləs)
adj. lacking in courage

timidly (tim´ id lē)
adv. in a shy or fearful manner

Critical Thinking

1. Key Ideas and Details **(a)** Who tells the story of "The Ninny"? **(b) Connect:** What is this person's relationship with Yulia?

2. Key Ideas and Details **(a) Evaluate:** Are any of the reasons the narrator gives for cutting Yulia's pay justifiable? **(b) Infer:** What do Yulia's responses suggest about her personality?

3. Key Ideas and Details **Make a Judgment:** Does the narrator regret or take pleasure in the effect of his "cruel trick" on Yulia? Explain.

4. Integration of Knowledge and Ideas **(a)** What differences separate these characters? **(b)** At the story's conclusion, have they grown more different or more alike? Explain. *[Connect to the Big Question: Is it our differences or our similarities that matter most?]*

Cite textual evidence to support your responses.

Comparing Adaptations to Originals

1. (a) How does Chekhov change the plot pattern of a traditional fairy tale in "The Ninny"? **(b)** What central idea is revealed by this change?

2. Use a chart like the one shown to find similarities and differences between "The Ninny" and *The Governess*.

	Relationships	Events	Endings	Style/Tone
"The Ninny"				
The Governess				

 Timed Writing

Explanatory Text: Essay

In an essay, compare and contrast the characterization, events, style, endings, and tone of Neil Simon's adaptation with the original short story. Use textual evidence to support your ideas. (40 minutes)

5-Minute Planner

1. Read the prompt carefully and completely.

2. Gather your ideas by jotting down answers to these questions:

- Why do you think Chekhov chose to write about Yulia and her employer in a first-person story form rather than as a play?
- What is the biggest change that Simon made?
- What purpose is served by Simon's adaptation as a play? Which message is easier for you to interpret? Why?
- How much do the different elements of drama and short story account for the differences between these specifi c works?
- Which version—the story or the play—is more effective? Why?

3. To organize your essay, use one of your answers to the questions above as your main thesis. Then, draft the body of your essay by using each of the elements listed in the writing prompt as a point of comparison.

4. Reread the prompt, and then draft your essay.

Writing Workshop

 **Common Core State Standards**

Writing

2. Write informative/explanatory texts to examine a topic and convey ideas, concepts, and information through the selection, organization, and analysis of relevant content.

2.a. Introduce a topic clearly, previewing what is to follow; organize ideas, concepts, and information into broader categories; include formatting, graphics, and multimedia when useful to aiding comprehension.

2.d. Use precise language and domain-specific vocabulary to inform about or explain the topic.

2.e. Establish and maintain a formal style.

Write an Informative Text

Workplace Writing: Business Letter

Defining the Form A **business letter** is a document written with a formal tone and with a specific purpose in mind. You might use elements of a business letter when you write a letter of complaint, a letter to an editor, or a cover letter for a job application.

Assignment Write a business letter related to career development with the goal of applying for a job. Include these elements:

✔ *conventional business letter format*, including date, proper salutation, body, closing, and signature

✔ a *clearly stated purpose* for the letter that is connected to the position for which you are applying

✔ content that is clear, concise, and focused

✔ points supported by *facts and details*

✔ a *voice* and style appropriate to your *audience* and *purpose*

✔ error-free grammar, including the use of *gerunds and participles*

To preview the criteria on which your business letter may be judged, see the rubric on page 847.

 Writing Workshop: *Work in Progress*

Review the work you did on page 827.

Prewriting/Planning Strategy

Plan your support. Choose a job for which you think you are qualified. Identify three personal qualities that make you a good candidate for that job. To support your purpose, list examples of past accomplishments that demonstrate these qualities.

Job: Newspaper Delivery	
Qualities	**Accomplishments**
Dependability	Never missed a day of soccer practice
Punctuality	Always on time for school
Honesty	Found a lost wallet and turned it in to the police

Use Appropriate Voice

Voice is the unique tool a writer uses to communicate ideas. Just as a singer adjusts his or her voice to match the material (using a gentle voice for a lullaby and a strong voice for an opera), a writer adjusts his or her voice to match the situation. Since writers cannot adjust their volume, they rely instead on tools such as word choice, tone, and attitude to achieve a purpose. To help ensure that you use an appropriate voice for business purposes, try these methods:

Determining Your Attitude Ask yourself, "What is my attitude toward my audience?" In a business situation, that attitude should include respect for the person you are addressing.

Using a Professional Tone In business correspondence, use a professional tone. This is different from the tone you use when talking to friends and family. It is important that you avoid the following:

- slang or rude comments
- details from your personal life

Instead, use precise language, telling your reader what he or she needs to know and closing in a respectful way.

Adjusting Your Voice All business letters should have a polite, formal tone. However, your voice can vary, depending on your purpose. Consult the chart and these examples for more details:

- When **writing a cover letter** to accompany a job application, your language should convey the impression that you are sincerely interested, qualified, and available for an interview.

- When **writing a letter of complaint,** you should use firm language to express your disappointment and the idea that you expect the reader to take action to correct the situation.

> **PH WRITING COACH**
>
> Further instruction and practice are available in *Prentice Hall Writing Coach*.

	Nonprofessional Tone	Professional Tone
Cover Letter	I think your company is awesome and I would love to work there!	You will notice on my résumé that my education and experience have prepared me well for this job.
Letter of Complaint	Your CD player is a rip-off! It broke and wrecked my party!	This product does not work properly.

Drafting Strategies

Follow the format. A business letter must follow an appropriate format to give your letter a professional look. Include each part of a business letter noted in the chart. (For more on letter formats, see pages R26–R27.)

Make your point. In the first paragraph, state your purpose for writing. In the paragraphs that follow, present a more detailed explanation. Include important supporting information that will help the recipient to fully consider your request. Make sure you address the expectations of your intended audience. For example, if you are writing a cover letter for a job application, communicate how your skills, personality traits, and experience will prove valuable to your employer if you are hired.

Revising Strategies

Revise for businesslike language. Review your draft carefully. Casual language that you might use in a note or a text message to a friend does not belong in a business letter. Circle any instances of language that assume too familiar a tone. Replace items you have circled with serious, polite language that communicates respect and that will reflect positively on you. If you are expecting the recipient to take action or consider you for a job, you want him or her to take you seriously.

Revise for conciseness. Business letters should be brief. Review your letter for wordiness. Condense any passages that are too long, as has been done in the example in the following chart.

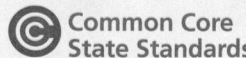

Common Core State Standards

Writing

2.b. Develop the topic with relevant, well-chosen facts, definitions, concrete details, quotations, or other information and examples.

2.e. Establish and maintain a formal style.

Language

1.a. Explain the function of verbals (gerunds, participles, infinitives) in general and their function in particular sentences.

Parts of a Business Letter

Heading: the writer's address and the date

Inside address: the name and address of the recipient

Salutation: The salutation, or greeting to the recipient, is followed by a colon.
Examples: Dear Mr. Davies:
Dear Sir or Madam:
To Whom It May Concern:

Body: The main part of the letter presents the writer's purpose and the information that supports it.

Closing: The closing begins with a capital letter and ends with a comma.
Examples: Yours truly,
With best regards,
Sincerely,

Signature: The writer's name is typed below the closing. Between the closing and the typed name, the writer adds a handwritten signature.

Original	Revised
If you agree that my educational background and experience are qualifications that match your requirements, please call to arrange an interview at your convenience.	If you agree that I am qualified for this job, please call to arrange an interview.

Revising to Combine Sentences
Using Gerunds and Participles

Gerunds and participles are **verbals**, or verb forms that are used as different parts of speech.

Identifying Gerunds A **gerund** is a verb form ending in *-ing* that is used as a noun.

As subject: *Baking* cookies is Heather's hobby.

As direct object: Lucille enjoys *swimming.*

As predicate noun: David's greatest talent is *playing* the piano.

As object of a preposition: Randall never gets tired of *surfing.*

Identifying Participles A **participle** is a verb form that is used as an adjective. There are two kinds of participles: present participles and past participles. The present participle resembles a gerund in that it ends in *-ing*.

Present participle: The *chirping* canary sang sweetly.

Past participle: We hiked off the *beaten* path.

Revising Sentences To combine choppy or short sentences using gerunds and participles, follow these steps:

1. Identify pairs of sentences that sound choppy.

2. Determine whether you can tighten the sentences by revising to include a gerund or a participle.

3. Identify the main idea and insert the less important idea into a gerund or participial phrase.

Choppy Sentences	
The sisters like to draw and paint. They like to play together.	
Combined with Gerunds:	**Combined with Participle:**
The sisters like *drawing* and *painting* together.	*Playing together,* the sisters like to draw and paint.

PH WRITING COACH

Further instruction and practice are available in *Prentice Hall Writing Coach.*

Grammar in Your Writing

Choose three paragraphs in your draft. Find pairs of sentences that deal with the same subject. If they are too choppy or repetitive, combine them using gerunds or participles.

Student Model: Brad Bean, Fernandina Beach, FL

This letter of complaint follows appropriate business writing style.

555 Somestrange Place
Fernandina Beach, FL 32034
September 21, 2010

Customer Service
Ace Software Company
1234 Citrus Parkway #514
Los Angeles, CA 33333

Dear Customer Service Manager:

I recently purchased software from my local Office Supply Superstore. A brightly colored sticker on your box stated that I would receive a free software title if I completed your rebate procedure correctly. Eagerly looking forward to receiving my new computer software, I find myself seriously disappointed with your service instead.

I sent in everything just as you asked, but you sent me a postcard saying the UPC code was invalid. Please explain how this can be true. I am sure that is not true because I carefully cut the code off the box myself. What is even worse is that you cashed the check I sent to pay for shipping without shipping a thing.

I truly would like to receive the software I was promised. At the very least, I would like a refund for the $2.95 check I sent. I am including a copy of each of the following: the completed rebate form, the UPC code from the box, and my receipt.

Mistakes can happen. I am sure this is just a simple error. I hope you will work to resolve this quickly because I would like to continue purchasing your products.

Sincerely,

Brad Bean

Brad Bean

Encl: Copy of completed rebate form
Copy of UPC code
Copy of receipt

Common Core State Standards

Language
2.c. Spell correctly.

Business letters use two-letter abbreviations for states. Those for Florida and California are shown here.

Brad uses a gender-neutral salutation since he does not know if the recipient will be a man or a woman.

Brad describes his purpose for writing in the opening paragraph.

Brad indicates, politely but firmly, how and why the company should resolve his problem.

Two common business letter abbreviations are "Attn:" for Attention and "encl." for *enclosures*.

Editing and Proofreading

Read through your draft, and correct errors in punctuation, spelling, and grammar.

Focus on spelling plurals. Most plural forms of nouns follow basic rules, such as these:

- Add -*s* to most nouns: *effect/effects*.
- Add -*es* to nouns that end in *s*, *ss*, *sh*, *ch*, and *x*: *dress/dresses*.

Publishing and Presenting

Consider one of the following ways to share your writing.

Share your letter. Read your letter to a partner. Ask how he or she would respond to receiving it.

Send your letter. Mail an error-free copy of your letter to the person or group to whom you wrote. Or, find the e-mail address and send your letter electronically. Develop a plan of action or agenda for a written or verbal follow-up after sending your letter.

Reflecting on Your Writing

Writer's Journal Jot down your answers to this question:

Were you confident that your letter made the impression you were trying to make? Why or why not?

Rubric for Self-Assessment

Find evidence in your writing to address each category. Then, use the rating scale to grade your work.

© **Spiral Review**
Earlier in the unit, you learned about **participial phrases** (p. 826). Review your letter to be sure that you have used participial phrases correctly.

Criteria	Rating Scale				
	not very				*very*
Focus: How clearly do you state the purpose of the letter?	1	2	3	4	5
Organization: How effectively is your business-letter format organized?	1	2	3	4	5
Support/Elaboration: How well is each point supported by facts and details?	1	2	3	4	5
Style and Voice: How well have you used language that is appropriate for your audience and purpose?	1	2	3	4	5
Conventions: How correct is your grammar, especially your use of gerunds and participles?	1	2	3	4	5

Drama

Build your skills and improve your comprehension of drama.

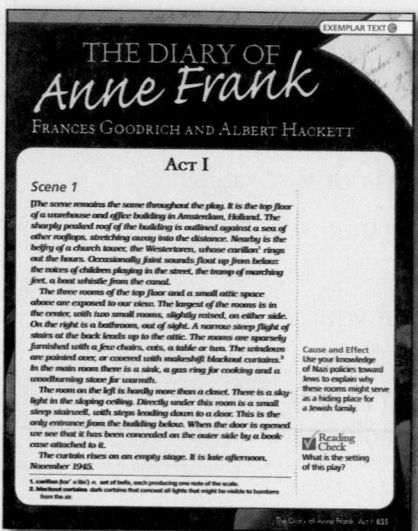

Read ***The Diary of Anne Frank***, Act I
to find out how eight people survive in an attic,
under constant threat of discovery by the Nazis.

Common Core State Standards

Meet these standards with ***The Diary of Anne Frank***, Act I (p. 854).

Reading Literature

3. Analyze how particular lines of dialogue or incidents in a story or drama propel the action, reveal aspects of a character, or provoke a decision. *(Literary Analysis: Dialogue)*

4. Analyze the impact of specific word choices on meaning and tone, including analogies or allusions to other texts. *(Literary Analysis: Dialogue)*

6. Analyze how differences in the points of view of the characters and the audience or reader (e.g., created through the use of dramatic irony) create such effects as suspense or humor. *(Literary Analysis: Dialogue)*

Writing

3. Write narratives to develop real or imagined experiences or events using effective technique, relevant descriptive details, and well-structured event sequences. *(Writing: Diary Entries)*

Speaking and Listening

6. Adapt speech to a variety of contexts and tasks, demonstrating command of formal English when indicated or appropriate. *(Speaking and Listening: Guided Tour)*

Language

1. Demonstrate command of the conventions of standard English grammar and usage when writing or speaking. *(Conventions: Dangling and Misplaced Modifiers)*

4.b. Use common, grade-appropriate Greek or Latin affixes and roots as clues to the meaning of a word. *(Vocabulary: Word Study)*

6. Acquire and use accurately grade-appropriate general academic and domain-specific words and phrases; gather vocabulary knowledge when considering a word or phrase important to comprehension or expression. *(Vocabulary: Word Study)*

Reading Skill: Cause and Effect

A **cause** is an event, action, or feeling that produces a result, or **effect.** When you read a work that is set in a particular time and place, you can **use background information to link historical causes with effects.** Background information may include the introduction to a literary work, information provided in footnotes, facts you learned in other classes, and information you already know. Read the background information that accompanies this play to help you consider how events in the play are linked to history.

Using the Strategy: Connections Chart

Keep track of your analysis in a **connections chart** like this one.

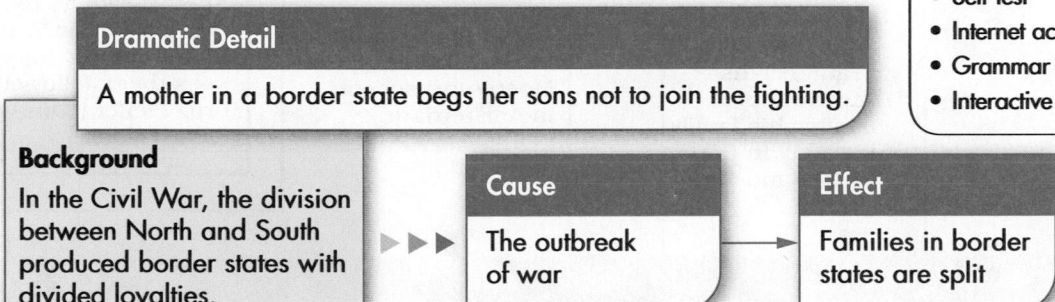

| Dramatic Detail |
| A mother in a border state begs her sons not to join the fighting. |

| Background |
| In the Civil War, the division between North and South produced border states with divided loyalties. |

▶ ▶ ▶

| Cause |
| The outbreak of war |

→

| Effect |
| Families in border states are split |

Literary Analysis: Dialogue

Dialogue is a conversation between or among characters. Through dialogue, we listen in on character's conversations, learning about their unique qualities as well as their hopes and dreams. Playwrights also set the tone of a scene and convey its significance by carefully choosing the words that characters say.

Dialogue serves another key function: to develop a story's **plot** and subplots. Conflicts come to life as characters confide in friends, argue with enemies, and plan their next actions. As you read *The Diary of Anne Frank*, notice how the dialogue develops characters, establishes tone and meaning, and propels the plot. Also, pay attention to what characters and the audience know. Sometimes, that difference in perspective, revealed through dialogue, can result in *dramatic irony,* a situation in which the audience knows more than the characters about events.

Frank Family and World War II Timelines

Shown on these pages is a brief timeline of events in the lives of a single Jewish family, the Frank family. The Franks—Otto and Edith, and their daughters, Anne and Margot—lived in Europe during a period of Nazi terror in which Jews were forced to flee their homes or go into hiding—or face persecution. This period of anti-Jewish violence and mass murder is known as the Holocaust. The major events of the period are shown on the bottom half of the timeline.

Timeline of the Frank Family

1929 Anne Frank is born in Frankfurt, Germany.

Summer 1933 Alarmed by Nazi actions in Germany, Otto Frank begins the process of moving his family to safety in the Netherlands.

1934 Anne starts kindergarten at the Montessori school in Amsterdam.

1941 Growing Nazi restrictions on the daily lives of Dutch Jews force the Frank girls to attend an all-Jewish school.

June 12, 1942 Otto gives Anne a diary for her thirteenth birthday.

July 6, 1942 The Franks go into hiding after receiving an order for Margot to report to a forced labor camp. They hide in the attic rooms above Mr. Frank's workplace with the help of close friends. Another family, the Van Pels (called the "Van Daans" in her diary), joins them, followed by Fritz Pfeffer ("Dussel"), months later.

1925	1930	1935	1940

Timeline of World Events

January 1933 Adolf Hitler comes to power in Germany. Over the next few months, all political parties, except the Nazi Party, are banned. Jews are dismissed from medical, legal, government, and teaching positions.

1935 The Nuremberg Laws are passed in Germany, stripping Jews of their rights as German citizens. Laws passed over the next several years further isolate Jews, including the requirement to wear a yellow Star of David.

September 1, 1939 Germany invades Poland, triggering the beginning of World War II.

May 1940 The Nazis invade the Netherlands. Once in control, they set up a brutal police force, the Gestapo, to administer laws to isolate Dutch Jews from the rest of the Dutch population.

August 4, 1944
The hiding place of the Franks is discovered and the families are arrested.

September 3, 1944
All eight of those who hid in the attic are deported from the Netherlands to the Auschwitz death camp.

March 1945*
Anne and Margot die of the disease typhus in the Bergen-Belsen concentration camp.

1947 Anne's diary is published in Dutch. Over the next few years it is translated and published in France, Germany, the United States, Japan, and Great Britain.

1960 The hiding place of the Franks is converted into a permanent museum that tells the story of Anne and those who hid with her.

1945 **1950** **1955** **1960**

May 1945 The Allies win as the war in Europe ends.

June 1944 The Allies carry out a successful invasion of France. Their success gives many who live under Nazi occupation hope that the end of the war is near.

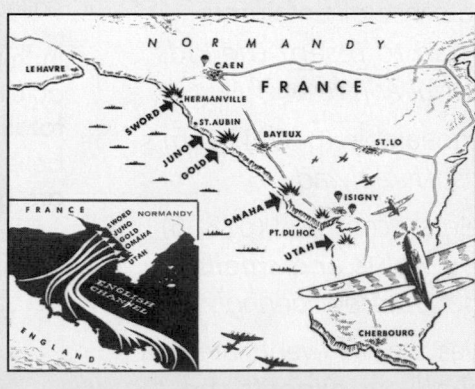

May 1960 Adolf Eichmann, one of the last major Nazi figures to be tried, is captured and put on trial in Israel. He is convicted and executed for his role in arranging the transport of Jews to concentration camps and ghettoes, where an estimated six million Jews died.

January 1943 The Battle of Stalingrad marks the turning of the tide against the Nazis.

*Estimate. Exact date unknown.

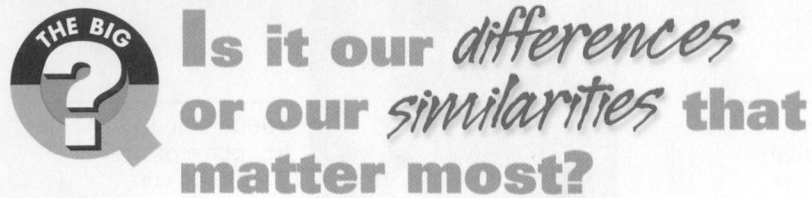

Is it our *differences* or our *similarities* that matter most?

Writing About the Big Question

In this drama, five adults and three teenagers struggle with their differences but face a common danger. To develop your ideas about the Big Question, choose the word in this sentence starter that best matches your opinion. Complete the sentence to support your idea.

Danger tends to **(unify/divide)** people because _____.

While You Read Notice how the characters respond to the multiple stresses of their situation.

Vocabulary

Read each word and its definition. Decide whether you know the word well, know it a little bit, or do not know it at all. After you read, see how your knowledge of each word has increased.

- **conspicuous** (kən spik′ yo͞o əs) *adj.* noticeable (p. 859) *The black stain on the white sofa was <u>conspicuous</u>.* *conspicuously adv. conspicuousness n.*

- **tension** (ten′ shən) *n.* a nervous, worried, or excited state that makes relaxation impossible (p. 863) *After the gas main explosion, there was <u>tension</u> in the neighborhood.* *tense adj.*

- **resent** (ri zent′) *v.* feel angry out of a sense of unfairness (p. 872) *With a report due, she began to <u>resent</u> the kids playing outside.* *resentment n. resentful adj. resentfully adv.*

- **insufferable** (in suf′ ər ə bəl) *adj.* unbearable (p. 874) *Cam's rude behavior was <u>insufferable</u>.* *insufferably adv.*

- **bewildered** (bē wil′ dərd) *adj.* hopelessly confused (p. 886) *The dog seemed <u>bewildered</u> by the sights and smells of the new neighborhood.* *bewilderment n. bewilderingly adv.*

- **fatalist** (fā′ təl ist) *n.* one who believes that all events are determined by fate (p. 898) *A <u>fatalist</u>, Sal always expects the worst.* *fatalism n. fatalistically adv. fatalistic adj.*

Word Study

The **Greek suffix -ist** indicates a noun that means "one who does, makes, practices, is skilled in, or believes in."

In this play, a character claims to be a **fatalist**—someone who believes that our lives are guided by fate and not by our own actions.

Frances Goodrich (1890–1984)
and Albert Hackett (1900–1995)

Author of
THE DIARY OF
Anne Frank

Frances Goodrich (1890–1984) and Albert Hackett (1900–1995) spent two years writing a play based on the world-renowned book *Anne Frank: The Diary of a Young Girl.* As part of their research for the play, they visited with Anne's father, Otto. The play won a Pulitzer Prize, the Drama Critics Circle award, and a Tony Award.

A Successful Partnership Goodrich and Hackett began working together in 1927 and were married in 1931. The couple's writing career included screenplays for such classic films as *The Thin Man* (1934), *It's a Wonderful Life* (1946), and *Father of the Bride* (1950).

BACKGROUND FOR THE PLAY

Nazi Occupation
On September 1, 1939, Nazi Germany launched a sudden attack on Poland that triggered World War II. Over the next several years, the armies of Nazi Germany swept across Europe, conquering and occupying many countries. In each country the Nazis occupied, the Jews were rounded up and sent by train to forced labor camps and death camps. The Nazi occupation of the Netherlands is the background for **The Diary of Anne Frank,** a play based on the actual diary of a young German-Jewish girl whose family chose to hide from the Nazis.

Did You Know?
Before they began writing together, Goodrich and Hackett were actors.

nederland
ANNE FRANK
60c

CHARACTERS

ANNE FRANK	PETER VAN DAAN
OTTO FRANK	MR. KRALER
EDITH FRANK	MRS. VAN DAAN
MARGOT FRANK	MR. VAN DAAN
MIEP GIES	MR. DUSSEL

THE DIARY OF Anne Frank

FRANCES GOODRICH AND ALBERT HACKETT

ACT I

Scene 1

[The scene remains the same throughout the play. It is the top floor of a warehouse and office building in Amsterdam, Holland. The sharply peaked roof of the building is outlined against a sea of other rooftops, stretching away into the distance. Nearby is the belfry of a church tower, the Westertoren, whose carillon[1] rings out the hours. Occasionally faint sounds float up from below: the voices of children playing in the street, the tramp of marching feet, a boat whistle from the canal.

The three rooms of the top floor and a small attic space above are exposed to our view. The largest of the rooms is in the center, with two small rooms, slightly raised, on either side. On the right is a bathroom, out of sight. A narrow steep flight of stairs at the back leads up to the attic. The rooms are sparsely furnished with a few chairs, cots, a table or two. The windows are painted over, or covered with makeshift blackout curtains.[2] In the main room there is a sink, a gas ring for cooking and a woodburning stove for warmth.

The room on the left is hardly more than a closet. There is a skylight in the sloping ceiling. Directly under this room is a small steep stairwell, with steps leading down to a door. This is the only entrance from the building below. When the door is opened we see that it has been concealed on the outer side by a bookcase attached to it.

The curtain rises on an empty stage. It is late afternoon, November 1945.

---

1. carillon (kar´ ə län´) *n.* set of bells, each producing one note of the scale.
2. blackout curtains dark curtains that conceal all lights that might be visible to bombers from the air.

Cause and Effect
Use your knowledge of Nazi policies toward Jews to explain why these rooms might serve as a hiding place for a Jewish family.

✓ Reading Check
What is the setting of this play?

The rooms are dusty, the curtains in rags. Chairs and tables are overturned.

The door at the foot of the small stairwell swings open. MR. FRANK comes up the steps into view. He is a gentle, cultured European in his middle years. There is still a trace of a German accent in his speech.

He stands looking slowly around, making a supreme effort at self-control. He is weak, ill. His clothes are threadbare.

After a second he drops his rucksack on the couch and moves slowly about. He opens the door to one of the smaller rooms, and then abruptly closes it again, turning away. He goes to the window at the back, looking off at the Westertoren as its carillon strikes the hour of six, then he moves restlessly on. From the street below we hear the sound of a barrel organ[3] and children's voices at play. There is a many-colored scarf hanging from a nail. MR. FRANK takes it, putting it around his

---

3. barrel organ *n.* mechanical musical instrument often played by street musicians in past decades.

neck. *As he starts back for his rucksack, his eye is caught by something lying on the floor. It is a woman's white glove. He holds it in his hand and suddenly all of his self-control is gone. He breaks down, crying.*

We hear footsteps on the stairs. MIEP GIES *comes up, looking for* MR. FRANK. MIEP *is a Dutch girl of about twenty-two. She wears a coat and hat, ready to go home. She is pregnant. Her attitude toward* MR. FRANK *is protective, compassionate.*]

MIEP. Are you all right, Mr. Frank?

MR. FRANK. [*Quickly controlling himself*] Yes, Miep, yes.

MIEP. Everyone in the office has gone home . . . It's after six. [*Then pleading*] Don't stay up here, Mr. Frank. What's the use of torturing yourself like this?

MR. FRANK. I've come to say good-bye . . . I'm leaving here, Miep.

MIEP. What do you mean? Where are you going? Where?

MR. FRANK. I don't know yet. I haven't decided.

MIEP. Mr. Frank, you can't leave here! This is your home! Amsterdam is your home. Your business is here, waiting for you . . . You're needed here . . . Now that the war is over, there are things that . . .

MR. FRANK. I can't stay in Amsterdam, Miep. It has too many memories for me. Everywhere there's something . . . the house we lived in . . . the school . . . that street organ playing out there . . . I'm not the person you used to know, Miep. I'm a bitter old man. [*Breaking off*] Forgive me. I shouldn't speak to you like this . . . after all that you did for us . . . the suffering . . .

MIEP. No. No. It wasn't suffering. You can't say we suffered. [*As she speaks, she straightens a chair which is overturned.*]

MR. FRANK. I know what you went through, you and Mr. Kraler. I'll remember it as long as I live. [*He gives one last look around.*] Come, Miep. [*He starts for the steps, then remembers his rucksack, going back to get it.*]

MIEP. [*Hurrying up to a cupboard*] Mr. Frank, did you see? There are some of your papers here. [*She brings a bundle of papers to him.*] We found them in a heap of rubbish on the floor after . . . after you left.

Cause and Effect
The war in Europe ended in May 1945, but many who survived the camps did not return until the fall. What effect has the war had on Mr. Frank?

Dialogue
What do Mr. Frank's words and the hesitation in his speech tell you about his feelings?

Cause and Effect
What events might make it harder for Mr. Frank to think of Amsterdam as home? Explain.

 Reading Check
Why does Miep want Mr. Frank to stay?

MR. FRANK. Burn them. [*He opens his rucksack to put the glove in it.*]

MIEP. But, Mr. Frank, there are letters, notes . . .

MR. FRANK. Burn them. All of them.

MIEP. Burn this? [*She hands him a paper-bound notebook.*]

MR. FRANK. [*quietly*] Anne's diary. [*He opens the diary and begins to read.*] "Monday, the sixth of July, nineteen forty-two." [*To* MIEP] Nineteen forty-two. Is it possible, Miep? . . . Only three years ago. [*As he continues his reading, he sits down on the couch.*] "Dear Diary, since you and I are going to be great friends, I will start by telling you about myself. My name is Anne Frank. I am thirteen years old. I was born in Germany the twelfth of June, nineteen twenty-nine. As my family is Jewish, we emigrated to Holland when Hitler came to power."

[*As* MR. FRANK *reads on, another voice joins his, as if coming from the air. It is* ANNE'S VOICE.]

MR. FRANK AND ANNE. "My father started a business, importing spice and herbs. Things went well for us until nineteen forty. Then the war came, and the Dutch capitulation,[4] followed by the arrival of the Germans. Then things got very bad for the Jews."

[MR. FRANK'S VOICE *dies out.* ANNE'S VOICE *continues alone. The lights dim slowly to darkness. The curtain falls on the scene.*]

ANNE'S VOICE. You could not do this and you could not do that. They forced Father out of his business. We had to wear yellow stars.[5] I had to turn in my bike. I couldn't go to a Dutch school any more. I couldn't go to the movies, or ride in an automobile, or even on a streetcar, and a million other things. But somehow we children still managed to have fun. Yesterday Father told me we were going into hiding. Where, he wouldn't say. At five o'clock this morning Mother woke me and told me to hurry and get dressed. I was to put on as many clothes as I could. It would look too suspicious if we walked along carrying suitcases. It wasn't until we were on our way that I learned where we were going. Our hiding place was to be upstairs in the building where

---

Cause and Effect
Anne is referring to Adolf Hitler, the German dictator who persecuted Jews throughout Europe. What other historical causes and effects do you learn here?

Dialogue
In the play, Anne's lines are often spoken to her diary, as if the diary were another character. What significant plot event is revealed in this speech?

---

4. **capitulation** (kə pich′ ə lā′ shən) *n.* surrender.
5. **yellow stars** Stars of David, the six-pointed stars that are symbols of Judaism. The Nazis ordered all Jews to wear them on their clothing.

Father used to have his business. Three other people were coming in with us . . . the Van Daans and their son Peter . . . Father knew the Van Daans but we had never met them . . .

[*During the last lines the curtain rises on the scene. The lights dim on.* ANNE'S VOICE *fades out.*]

Scene 2

[*It is early morning, July 1942. The rooms are bare, as before, but they are now clean and orderly.*

MR. VAN DAAN, *a tall, portly[6] man in his late forties, is in the main room, pacing up and down, nervously smoking a cigarette. His clothes and overcoat are expensive and well cut.*

MRS. VAN DAAN *sits on the couch, clutching her possessions, a hatbox, bags, etc. She is a pretty woman in her early forties. She wears a fur coat over her other clothes.*

PETER VAN DAAN *is standing at the window of the room on the right, looking down at the street below. He is a shy, awkward boy of sixteen. He wears a cap, a raincoat, and long Dutch trousers, like "plus fours."[7] At his feet is a black case, a carrier for his cat.*

The yellow Star of David is conspicuous *on all of their clothes.*]

---

6. **portly** (pôrt´ lē) *adj.* large and heavy.
7. **plus fours** *n.* loose knickers (short pants) worn for active sports.

▼ **Critical Viewing**
This photograph shows the Frank family with some friends before their years in hiding. How would you describe their mood, judging from their expressions? **[Connect]**

Vocabulary
conspicuous (kən spik´ yōō əs) *adj.* noticeable

Reading Check
How did life change for the Franks after the Germans invaded?

The Diary of Anne Frank, Act I **859**

MRS. VAN DAAN. [*Rising, nervous, excited*] Something's happened to them! I know it!

MR. VAN DAAN. Now, Kerli!

MRS. VAN DAAN. Mr. Frank said they'd be here at seven o'clock. He said . . .

MR. VAN DAAN. They have two miles to walk. You can't expect . . .

MRS. VAN DAAN. They've been picked up. That's what's happened. They've been taken . . .

[MR. VAN DAAN *indicates that he hears someone coming.*]

Dialogue
How do the authors convey a mood of anxiety through the Van Daans' dialogue?

MR. VAN DAAN. You see?

[PETER *takes up his carrier and his schoolbag, etc., and goes into the main room as* MR. FRANK *comes up the stairwell from below.* MR. FRANK *looks much younger now. His movements are brisk, his manner confident. He wears an overcoat and carries his hat and a small cardboard box. He crosses to the* VAN DAANS, *shaking hands with each of them.*]

Cause and Effect
Read the footnote on the "Green Police." Why do the Franks fear this force?

MR. FRANK. Mrs. Van Daan, Mr. Van Daan, Peter. [*Then, in explanation of their lateness*] There were too many of the Green Police[8] on the streets . . . we had to take the long way around.

[*Up the steps come* MARGOT FRANK, MRS. FRANK, MIEP *(not pregnant now) and* MR. KRALER. *All of them carry bags, packages, and so forth. The Star of David is conspicuous on all of the* FRANKS' *clothing.* MARGOT *is eighteen, beautiful, quiet, shy.* MRS. FRANK *is a young mother, gently bred, reserved. She, like* MR. FRANK, *has a slight German accent.* MR. KRALER *is a Dutchman, dependable, kindly.*

    As MR. KRALER *and* MIEP *go upstage to put down their parcels,* MRS. FRANK *turns back to call* ANNE.]

MRS. FRANK. Anne?

[ANNE *comes running up the stairs. She is thirteen, quick in her movements, interested in everything, mercurial[9] in her emotions. She wears a cape, long wool socks and carries a schoolbag.*]

---

8. **Green Police** the Dutch Gestapo, or Nazi police, who wore green uniforms and were known for their brutality. Those in danger of being arrested or deported feared the Gestapo, especially because of their practice of raiding houses to round up victims in the middle of the night—when people are most confused and vulnerable.
9. **mercurial** (mər kyo͞or′ ē əl) *adj.* quick or changeable in behavior.

MR. FRANK. [*Introducing them*] My wife, Edith. Mr. and Mrs. Van Daan . . . their son, Peter . . . my daughters, Margot and Anne.

[MRS. FRANK *hurries over, shaking hands with them.*]

[ANNE *gives a polite little curtsy as she shakes* MR. VAN DAAN'S *hand. Then she immediately starts off on a tour of investigation of her new home, going upstairs to the attic room.*

MIEP *and* MR. KRALER *are putting the various things they have brought on the shelves.*]

MR. KRALER. I'm sorry there is still so much confusion.

MR. FRANK. Please. Don't think of it. After all, we'll have plenty of leisure to arrange everything ourselves.

MIEP. [*To* MRS. FRANK] We put the stores of food you sent in here. Your drugs are here . . . soap, linen here.

MRS. FRANK. Thank you, Miep.

MIEP. I made up the beds . . . the way Mr. Frank and Mr. Kraler said. [*She starts out.*] Forgive me. I have to hurry. I've got to go to the other side of town to get some ration books[10] for you.

MRS. VAN DAAN. Ration books? If they see our names on ration books, they'll know we're here.

MR. KRALER. There isn't anything . . .

MIEP. Don't worry. Your names won't be on them. [*As she hurries out*] I'll be up later.

MR. FRANK. Thank you, Miep.

MRS. FRANK. [*To* MR. KRALER] It's illegal, then, the ration books? We've never done anything illegal.

MR. FRANK. We won't be living here exactly according to regulations.

[*As* MR. KRALER *reassures* MRS. FRANK, *he takes various small things, such as matches, soap, etc., from his pockets, handing them to her.*]

MR. KRALER. This isn't the black market,[11] Mrs. Frank. This is

---

10. **ration** (rash′ ən) **books** *n.* books of stamps given to ensure the equal distribution of scarce items, such as meat or gasoline, in times of shortage.

11. **black market** illegal way of buying scarce items without ration stamps.

▲ **Critical Viewing**
What will having ration books, like the one above, allow the Franks to do? **[Connect]**

Cause and Effect
Why might Mrs. Frank be afraid of doing something illegal? Why is her fear illogical?

Reading Check

How are Miep and Mr. Kraler helping the Franks and Van Daans?

what we call the white market . . . helping all of the hundreds and hundreds who are hiding out in Amsterdam.

[*The carillon is heard playing the quarter-hour before eight.* MR. KRALER *looks at his watch.* ANNE *stops at the window as she comes down the stairs.*]

ANNE. It's the Westertoren!

MR. KRALER. I must go. I must be out of here and downstairs in the office before the workmen get here. [*He starts for the stairs leading out.*] Miep or I, or both of us, will be up each day to bring you food and news and find out what your needs are. Tomorrow I'll get you a better bolt for the door at the foot of the stairs. It needs a bolt that you can throw yourself and open only at our signal. [*To* MR. FRANK] Oh . . . You'll tell them about the noise?

MR. FRANK. I'll tell them.

MR. KRALER. Good-bye then for the moment. I'll come up again, after the workmen leave.

MR. FRANK. Good-bye, Mr. Kraler.

MRS. FRANK. [*Shaking his hand*] How can we thank you?

[*The others murmur their good-byes.*]

MR. KRALER. I never thought I'd live to see the day when a man like Mr. Frank would have to go into hiding. When you think—

[*He breaks off, going out.* MR. FRANK *follows him down the steps, bolting the door after him. In the interval before he returns,* PETER *goes over to* MARGOT, *shaking hands with her. As* MR. FRANK *comes back up the steps,* MRS. FRANK *questions him anxiously.*]

MRS. FRANK. What did he mean, about the noise?

MR. FRANK. First let us take off some of these clothes.

[*They all start to take off garment after garment. On each of their coats, sweaters, blouses, suits, dresses, is another yellow Star of David.* MR. *and* MRS. FRANK *are underdressed quite simply. The others wear several things, sweaters, extra dresses, bathrobes, aprons, nightgowns, etc.*]

MR. VAN DAAN. It's a wonder we weren't arrested, walking along the streets . . . Petronella with a fur coat in July . . . and that cat of Peter's crying all the way.

Cause and Effect
What does the description of the characters' clothing indicate about how long they expect to be in hiding?

ANNE. [*As she is removing a pair of panties*] A cat?

MRS. FRANK. [*Shocked*] Anne, please!

ANNE. It's alright. I've got on three more.

[*She pulls off two more. Finally, as they have all removed their surplus clothes, they look to* MR. FRANK, *waiting for him to speak.*]

MR. FRANK. Now. About the noise. While the men are in the building below, we must have complete quiet. Every sound can be heard down there, not only in the workrooms, but in the offices too. The men come at about eight-thirty, and leave at about five-thirty. So, to be perfectly safe, from eight in the morning until six in the evening we must move only when it is necessary, and then in stockinged feet. We must not speak above a whisper. We must not run any water. We cannot use the sink, or even, forgive me, the w.c.[12] The pipes go down through the workrooms. It would be heard. No trash . . .

[MR. FRANK *stops abruptly as he hears the sound of marching feet from the street below. Everyone is motionless, paralyzed with fear.* MR. FRANK *goes quietly into the room on the right to look down out of the window.* ANNE *runs after him, peering out with him. The tramping feet pass without stopping. The* tension *is relieved.* MR. FRANK, *followed by* ANNE, *returns to the main room and resumes his instructions to the group.*] . . . No trash must ever be thrown out which might reveal that someone is living up here . . . not even a potato paring. We must burn everything in the stove at night. This is the way we must live until it is over, if we are to survive.

[*There is silence for a second.*]

MRS. FRANK. Until it is over.

MR. FRANK. [*Reassuringly*] After six we can move about . . . we can talk and laugh and have our supper and read and play games . . . just as we would at home. [*He looks at his watch.*] And now I think it would be wise if we all went to our rooms, and were settled before eight o'clock. Mrs. Van Daan, you and your husband will be upstairs. I regret that there's no place up there for Peter. But he will be here, near us. This will be our common room, where we'll meet to talk and eat and read, like one family.

---

12. **w.c.** water closet; bathroom.

The Diary of Anne Frank, Act I **863**

Vocabulary
tension (ten´ shən) *n.* a nervous, worried, or excited state that makes relaxation impossible

Cause and Effect
Why is the sound of marching feet alarming to the families?

Cause and Effect
Why must the families maintain different schedules for day and night?

Reading Check
Why is it safe to move around after 6 P.M.?

MR. VAN DAAN. And where do you and Mrs. Frank sleep?

MR. FRANK. This room is also our bedroom.

[*Together*]

> **MRS. VAN DAAN.** That isn't right. We'll sleep here and you take the room upstairs.
>
> **MR. VAN DAAN.** It's your place.

MR. FRANK. Please. I've thought this out for weeks. It's the best arrangement. The only arrangement.

MRS. VAN DAAN. [*To* MR. FRANK] Never, never can we thank you. [*Then to* MRS. FRANK] I don't know what would have happened to us, if it hadn't been for Mr. Frank.

MR. FRANK. You don't know how your husband helped me when I came to this country . . . knowing no one . . . not able to speak the language. I can never repay him for that. [*Going to* VAN DAAN] May I help you with your things?

MR. VAN DAAN. No. No. [*To* MRS. VAN DAAN] Come along, *liefje*.[13]

MRS. VAN DAAN. You'll be all right, Peter? You're not afraid?

PETER. [*Embarrassed*] Please, Mother.

[*They start up the stairs to the attic room above.* MR. FRANK *turns to* MRS. FRANK.]

MR. FRANK. You too must have some rest, Edith. You didn't close your eyes last night. Nor you, Margot.

ANNE. I slept, Father. Wasn't that funny? I knew it was the last night in my own bed, and yet I slept soundly.

MR. FRANK. I'm glad, Anne. Now you'll be able to help me straighten things in here. [*To* MRS. FRANK *and* MARGOT] Come with me . . . You and Margot rest in this room for the time being.

[*He picks up their clothes, starting for the room on the right.*]

MRS. FRANK. You're sure . . .? I could help . . . And Anne hasn't had her milk . . .

MR. FRANK. I'll give it to her. [*To* ANNE *and* PETER] Anne, Peter . . . it's best that you take off your shoes now, before you forget.

[*He leads the way to the room, followed by* MARGOT.]

MRS. FRANK. You're sure you're not tired, Anne?

Dialogue
What does this dialogue reveal about the relationship between Anne and her parents?

---

13. *liefje* (lēf´ hyə) Dutch for "little love."

ANNE. I feel fine. I'm going to help Father.

MRS. FRANK. Peter, I'm glad you are to be with us.

PETER. Yes, Mrs. Frank.

[MRS. FRANK *goes to join* MR. FRANK *and* MARGOT.]

[*During the following scene* MR. FRANK *helps* MARGOT *and* MRS. FRANK *to hang up their clothes. Then he persuades them both to lie down and rest. The* VAN DAANS *in their room above settle themselves. In the main room* ANNE *and* PETER *remove their shoes.* PETER *takes his cat out of the carrier.*]

ANNE. What's your cat's name?

PETER. Mouschi.

ANNE. Mouschi! Mouschi! Mouschi! [*She picks up the cat, walking away with it. To* PETER] I love cats. I have one . . . a darling little cat. But they made me leave her behind. I left some food and a note for the neighbors to take care of her . . . I'm going to miss her terribly. What is yours? A him or a her?

PETER. He's a tom. He doesn't like strangers. [*He takes the cat from her, putting it back in its carrier.*]

ANNE. [*Unabashed*] Then I'll have to stop being a stranger, won't I? Is he fixed?

PETER. [*Startled*] Huh?

ANNE. Did you have him fixed?

PETER. No.

ANNE. Oh, you ought to have him fixed—to keep him from— you know, fighting. Where did you go to school?

PETER. Jewish Secondary.

ANNE. But that's where Margot and I go! I never saw you around.

PETER. I used to see you . . . sometimes . . .

ANNE. You did?

PETER. . . . In the school yard. You were always in the middle of a bunch of kids. [*He takes a penknife from his pocket.*]

ANNE. Why didn't you ever come over?

Dialogue
In what way does this dialogue between Peter and Anne highlight the differences between their personalities?

Reading Check
Where did Peter see Anne before they went into hiding?

PETER. I'm sort of a lone wolf. [*He starts to rip off his Star of David.*]

ANNE. What are you doing?

PETER. Taking it off.

ANNE. But you can't do that. They'll arrest you if you go out without your star.

[*He tosses his knife on the table.*]

PETER. Who's going out?

ANNE. Why, of course! You're right! Of course we don't need them any more. [*She picks up his knife and starts to take her star off.*] I wonder what our friends will think when we don't show up today?

PETER. I didn't have any dates with anyone.

ANNE. Oh, I did. I had a date with Jopie to go and play ping-pong at her house. Do you know Jopie de Waal?

PETER. No.

ANNE. Jopie's my best friend. I wonder what she'll think when she telephones and there's no answer? . . . Probably she'll go over to the house . . . I wonder what she'll think . . . we left everything as if we'd suddenly been called away . . . breakfast dishes in the sink . . . beds not made . . . [*As she pulls off her star, the cloth underneath shows clearly the color and form of the star.*] Look! It's still there! [PETER *goes over to the stove with his star.*] What're you going to do with yours?

PETER. Burn it.

ANNE. [*She starts to throw hers in, and cannot.*] It's funny, I can't throw mine away. I don't know why.

PETER. You can't throw . . .? Something they branded you with . . .? That they made you wear so they could spit on you?

ANNE. I know. I know. But after all, it is the Star of David, isn't it?

[*In the bedroom, right,* MARGOT *and* MRS. FRANK *are lying down.* MR. FRANK *starts quietly out.*]

Cause and Effect
Think about what the yellow star represents in the historical context of World War II. Why is it important to Peter to remove the star?

▼ **Critical Viewing**
Why do you think the Nazis forced Jews to wear yellow stars like this one, bearing the Dutch word for "Jew"? **[Infer]**

PETER. Maybe it's different for a girl.

[MR. FRANK *comes into the main room.*]

MR. FRANK. Forgive me, Peter. Now let me see. We must find a bed for your cat. [*He goes to a cupboard.*] I'm glad you brought your cat. Anne was feeling so badly about hers. [*Getting a used small washtub*] Here we are. Will it be comfortable in that?

PETER. [*Gathering up his things*] Thanks.

MR. FRANK. [*Opening the door of the room on the left*] And here is your room. But I warn you, Peter, you can't grow any more. Not an inch, or you'll have to sleep with your feet out of the skylight. Are you hungry?

PETER. No.

MR. FRANK. We have some bread and butter.

PETER. No, thank you.

MR. FRANK. You can have it for luncheon then. And tonight we will have a real supper . . . our first supper together.

PETER. Thanks. Thanks. [*He goes into his room. During the following scene he arranges his possessions in his new room.*]

MR. FRANK. That's a nice boy, Peter.

ANNE. He's awfully shy, isn't he?

MR. FRANK. You'll like him, I know.

ANNE. I certainly hope so, since he's the only boy I'm likely to see for months and months.

[MR. FRANK *sits down, taking off his shoes.*]

MR. FRANK. Annele,[14] there's a box there. Will you open it?

[*He indicates a carton on the couch.* ANNE *brings it to the center table. In the street below there is the sound of children playing.*]

ANNE. [*As she opens the carton*] You know the way I'm going to think of it here? I'm going to think of it as a boarding house. A very peculiar summer boarding house, like the one that we—[*She breaks off as she pulls out some photographs.*] Father! My movie stars! I was wondering where they were! I was looking for them this morning . . . and Queen Wilhelmina![15] How wonderful!

Dialogue
What does this dialogue tell you about Mr. Frank as a person?

✓ Reading Check
Why had the Franks left their house in a messy state?

---

14. **Annele** (än´ ə lə) nickname for "Anne."
15. **Queen Wilhelmina** (vil´ hel mē´ nä) Queen of the Netherlands from 1890 to 1948.

MR. FRANK. There's something more. Go on. Look further. [*He goes over to the sink, pouring a glass of milk from a thermos bottle.*]

ANNE. [*Pulling out a pasteboard-bound book*] A diary! [*She throws her arms around her father.*] I've never had a diary. And I've always longed for one. [*She looks around the room.*] Pencil, pencil, pencil, pencil. [*She starts down the stairs.*] I'm going down to the office to get a pencil.

MR. FRANK. Anne! No! [*He goes after her, catching her by the arm and pulling her back.*]

ANNE. [*Startled*] But there's no one in the building now.

MR. FRANK. It doesn't matter. I don't want you ever to go beyond that door.

ANNE. [*Sobered*] Never . . .? Not even at nighttime, when everyone is gone? Or on Sundays? Can't I go down to listen to the radio?

MR. FRANK. Never. I am sorry, Anneke.[16] It isn't safe. No, you must never go beyond that door.

[*For the first time* ANNE *realizes what "going into hiding" means.*]

ANNE. I see.

Cause and Effect
Why is Anne forbidden to go downstairs?

MR. FRANK. It'll be hard, I know. But always remember this, Anneke. There are no walls, there are no bolts, no locks that anyone can put on your mind. Miep will bring us books. We will read history, poetry, mythology. [*He gives her the glass of milk.*] Here's your milk. [*With his arm about her, they go over to the couch, sitting down side by side.*] As a matter of fact, between us, Anne, being here has certain advantages for you. For instance, you remember the battle you had with your mother the other day on the subject of overshoes? You said you'd rather die than wear overshoes? But in the end you had to wear them? Well now, you see, for as long as we are here you will never have to wear overshoes! Isn't that good? And the coat that you inherited from Margot, you won't have to wear that any more. And the piano! You won't have to practice on the piano. I tell you, this is going to be a fine life for you!

---

16. **Anneke** (än´ ə kə) nickname for "Anne."

[ANNE'S *panic is gone.* PETER *appears in the doorway of his room, with a saucer in his hand. He is carrying his cat.*]

PETER. I . . . I . . . I thought I'd better get some water for Mouschi before . . .

MR. FRANK. Of course.

[*As he starts toward the sink the carillon begins to chime the hour of eight. He tiptoes to the window at the back and looks down at the street below. He turns to* PETER, *indicating in pantomime that it is too late.* PETER *starts back for his room. He steps on a creaking board. The three of them are frozen for a minute in fear. As* PETER *starts away again,* ANNE *tiptoes over to him and pours some of the milk from her glass into the saucer for the cat.* PETER *squats on the floor, putting the milk before the cat.* MR. FRANK *gives* ANNE *his fountain pen, and then goes into the room at the right. For a second* ANNE *watches the cat, then she goes over to the center table, and opens her diary.*

In the room at the right, MRS. FRANK *has sat up quickly at the sound of the carillon.* MR. FRANK *comes in and sits down beside her on the settee, his arm comfortingly around her.*

Upstairs, in the attic room, MR. *and* MRS. VAN DAAN *have hung their clothes in the closet and are now seated on the iron bed.* MRS. VAN DAAN *leans back exhausted.* MR. VAN DAAN *fans her with a newspaper.*

ANNE *starts to write in her diary. The lights dim out, the curtain falls.*]

Cause and Effect
How does the fear of discovery affect the behavior of the two families?

✓ Reading Check
What positive aspects about living in hiding does Mr. Frank point out to comfort Anne?

◀ The radio was a crucial link to news of the war—especially through non-German stations such as the BBC (British Broadcasting Corporation).

In the darkness ANNE'S VOICE *comes to us again, faintly at first, and then with growing strength.*]

ANNE'S VOICE. I expect I should be describing what it feels like to go into hiding. But I really don't know yet myself. I only know it's funny never to be able to go outdoors . . . never to breathe fresh air . . . never to run and shout and jump. It's the silence in the nights that frightens me most. Every time I hear a creak in the house, or a step on the street outside, I'm sure they're coming for us. The days aren't so bad. At least we know that Miep and Mr. Kraler are down there below us in the office. Our protectors, we call them. I asked Father what would happen to them if the Nazis found out they were hiding us. Pim said that they would suffer the same fate that we would . . . Imagine! They know this, and yet when they come up here, they're always cheerful and gay as if there were nothing in the world to bother them . . . Friday, the twenty-first of August, nineteen forty-two. Today I'm going to tell you our general news. Mother is unbearable. She insists on treating me like a baby, which I loathe. Otherwise things are going better. The weather is . . .

[*As* ANNE'S VOICE *is fading out, the curtain rises on the scene.*]

Scene 3

[*It is a little after six o'clock in the evening, two months later.*

MARGOT *is in the bedroom at the right, studying.* MR. VAN DAAN *is lying down in the attic room above.*

The rest of the "family" is in the main room. ANNE *and* PETER *sit opposite each other at the center table, where they have been doing their lessons.* MRS. FRANK *is on the couch.* MRS. VAN DAAN *is seated with her fur coat, on which she has been sewing, in her lap. None of them are wearing their shoes.*

Their eyes are on MR. FRANK, *waiting for him to give them the signal which will release them from their day-long quiet.* MR. FRANK, *his shoes in his hand, stands looking down out of the window at the back, watching to be sure that all of the workmen have left the building below.*

After a few seconds of motionless silence, MR. FRANK *turns from the window.*]

MR. FRANK. [*Quietly, to the group*] It's safe now. The last workman has left.

[*There is an immediate stir of relief.*]

ANNE. [*Her pent-up energy explodes.*] WHEE!

MR. FRANK. [*Startled, amused*] Anne!

MRS. VAN DAAN. I'm first for the w.c.

[*She hurries off to the bathroom.* MRS. FRANK *puts on her shoes and starts up to the sink to prepare supper.* ANNE *sneaks* PETER'S *shoes from under the table and hides them behind her back.* MR. FRANK *goes in to* MARGOT'S *room.*]

MR. FRANK. [*To* MARGOT] Six o'clock. School's over.

[MARGOT *gets up, stretching.* MR. FRANK *sits down to put on his shoes. In the main room* PETER *tries to find his.*]

PETER. [*To* ANNE] Have you seen my shoes?

ANNE. [*Innocently*] Your shoes?

PETER. You've taken them, haven't you?

ANNE. I don't know what you're talking about.

PETER. You're going to be sorry!

ANNE. Am I?

[PETER *goes after her.* ANNE*, with his shoes in her hand, runs from him, dodging behind her mother.*]

MRS. FRANK. [*Protesting*] Anne, dear!

PETER. Wait till I get you!

ANNE. I'm waiting!
[PETER *makes a lunge for her. They both fall to the floor.* PETER *pins her down, wrestling with her to get the shoes.*]

Don't! Don't! Peter, stop it. Ouch!

MRS. FRANK. Anne! . . . Peter!

[*Suddenly* PETER *becomes self-conscious. He grabs his shoes roughly and starts for his room.*]

ANNE. [*Following him*] Peter, where are you going? Come dance with me.

PETER. I tell you I don't know how.

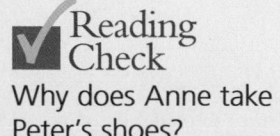

Reading Check

Why does Anne take Peter's shoes?

ANNE. I'll teach you.

PETER. I'm going to give Mouschi his dinner.

ANNE. Can I watch?

PETER. He doesn't like people around while he eats.

ANNE. Peter, please.

PETER. No! [*He goes into his room.* ANNE *slams his door after him.*]

MRS. FRANK. Anne, dear, I think you shouldn't play like that with Peter. It's not dignified.

ANNE. Who cares if it's dignified? I don't want to be dignified.

[MR. FRANK *and* MARGOT *come from the room on the right.* MARGOT *goes to help her mother.* MR. FRANK *starts for the center table to correct* MARGOT'S *school papers.*]

MRS. FRANK. [*To* ANNE] You complain that I don't treat you like a grownup. But when I do, you resent it.

ANNE. I only want some fun . . . someone to laugh and clown with . . . After you've sat still all day and hardly moved, you've got to have some fun. I don't know what's the matter with that boy.

MR. FRANK. He isn't used to girls. Give him a little time.

ANNE. Time? Isn't two months time? I could cry. [*Catching hold of* MARGOT] Come on, Margot . . . dance with me. Come on, please.

MARGOT. I have to help with supper.

ANNE. You know we're going to forget how to dance . . . When we get out we won't remember a thing.

[*She starts to sing and dance by herself.* MR. FRANK *takes her in his arms, waltzing with her.* MRS. VAN DAAN *comes in from the bathroom.*]

MRS. VAN DAAN. Next? [*She looks around as she starts putting on her shoes.*] Where's Peter?

ANNE. [*As they are dancing*] Where would he be!

MRS. VAN DAAN. He hasn't finished his lessons, has he? His father'll kill him if he catches him in there with that cat and his work not done. [MR. FRANK *and* ANNE *finish their dance. They bow to each other with extravagant formality.*]

Cause and Effect
What is the effect of Mrs. Frank's upbringing on the way she expects Anne to act?

Vocabulary
resent (ri zent´) *v.* feel angry out of a sense of unfairness

Dialogue
What subplot does this dialogue develop?

Anne, get him out of there, will you?

ANNE. [*At* PETER'S *door*] Peter? Peter?

PETER. [*Opening the door a crack*] What is it?

ANNE. Your mother says to come out.

PETER. I'm giving Mouschi his dinner.

MRS. VAN DAAN. You know what your father says. [*She sits on the couch, sewing on the lining of her fur coat.*]

PETER. For heaven's sake, I haven't even looked at him since lunch.

MRS. VAN DAAN. I'm just telling you, that's all.

ANNE. I'll feed him.

PETER. I don't want you in there.

MRS. VAN DAAN. Peter!

PETER. [*To* ANNE] Then give him his dinner and come right out, you hear?

[*He comes back to the table.* ANNE *shuts the door of* PETER'S *room after her and disappears behind the curtain covering his closet.*]

MRS. VAN DAAN. [*To* PETER] Now is that any way to talk to your little girl friend?

PETER. Mother . . . for heaven's sake . . . will you please stop saying that?

MRS. VAN DAAN. Look at him blush! Look at him!

PETER. Please! I'm not . . . anyway . . . let me alone, will you?

MRS. VAN DAAN. He acts like it was something to be ashamed of. It's nothing to be ashamed of, to have a little girl friend.

PETER. You're crazy. She's only thirteen.

MRS. VAN DAAN. So what? And you're sixteen. Just perfect. Your father's ten years older than I am. [*To* MR. FRANK I warn you, Mr. Frank, if this war lasts much longer, we're going to be related and then . . .

MR. FRANK. *Mazeltov!*[17]

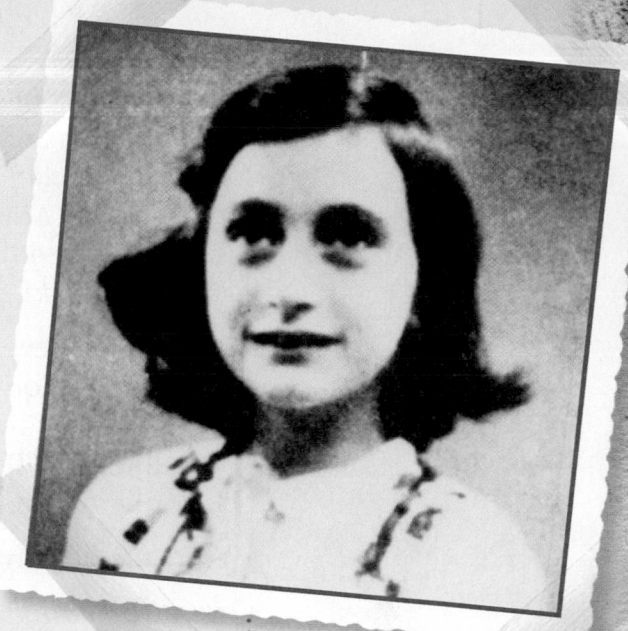

Dialogue
Based on this dialogue, how does Mrs. Van Daan feel about the growing friendship between Anne and Peter?

Reading Check
Why does Peter react negatively in response to his mother's hints about Anne?

---

17. *Mazeltov* (mä´ zəl tōv´) "good luck" in Hebrew and Yiddish.

MRS. FRANK. [*Deliberately changing the conversation*] I wonder where Miep is. She's usually so prompt.

[*Suddenly everything else is forgotten as they hear the sound of an automobile coming to a screeching stop in the street below. They are tense, motionless in their terror. The car starts away. A wave of relief sweeps over them. They pick up their occupations again.* ANNE *flings open the door of* PETER'S *room, making a dramatic entrance. She is dressed in* PETER'S *clothes.* PETER *looks at her in fury. The others are amused.*]

ANNE. Good evening, everyone. Forgive me if I don't stay. [*She jumps up on a chair.*] I have a friend waiting for me in there. My friend Tom. Tom Cat. Some people say that we look alike. But Tom has the most beautiful whiskers, and I have only a little fuzz. I am hoping . . . in time . . .

PETER. All right, Mrs. Quack Quack!

ANNE. [*Outraged—jumping down*] Peter!

PETER. I heard about you . . . How you talked so much in class they called you Mrs. Quack Quack. How Mr. Smitter made you write a composition . . . " 'Quack, Quack,' said Mrs. Quack Quack."

ANNE. Well, go on. Tell them the rest. How it was so good he read it out loud to the class and then read it to all his other classes!

PETER. Quack! Quack! Quack . . . Quack . . . Quack . . .

[ANNE *pulls off the coat and trousers.*]

ANNE. You are the most intolerable, insufferable boy I've ever met!

[*She throws the clothes down the stairwell.* PETER *goes down after them.*]

PETER. Quack, Quack, Quack!

MRS. VAN DAAN. [*To* ANNE] That's right, Anneke! Give it to him!

ANNE. With all the boys in the world . . . Why I had to get locked up with one like you! . . .

PETER. Quack, Quack, Quack, and from now on stay out of my room!

[*As* PETER *passes her,* ANNE *puts out her foot, tripping him. He picks himself up, and goes on into his room.*]

Vocabulary
insufferable
(in suf′ ə rə bəl) *adj.*
unbearable

MRS. FRANK. [*Quietly*] Anne, dear . . . your hair. [*She feels* ANNE'S *forehead.*] You're warm. Are you feeling all right?

ANNE. Please, Mother. [*She goes over to the center table, slipping into her shoes.*]

MRS. FRANK. [*Following her*] You haven't a fever, have you?

ANNE. [*Pulling away*] No. No.

MRS. FRANK. You know we can't call a doctor here, ever. There's only one thing to do . . . watch carefully. Prevent an illness before it comes. Let me see your tongue.

ANNE. Mother, this is perfectly absurd.

MRS. FRANK. Anne, dear, don't be such a baby. Let me see your tongue. [*As* ANNE *refuses,* MRS. FRANK *appeals to* MR. FRANK] Otto . . .?

MR. FRANK. You hear your mother, Anne.

[ANNE *flicks out her tongue for a second, then turns away.*]

MRS. FRANK. Come on—open up! [*As* ANNE *opens her mouth very wide*] You seem all right . . . but perhaps an aspirin . . .

MRS. VAN DAAN. For heaven's sake, don't give that child any pills. I waited for fifteen minutes this morning for her to come out of the w.c.

ANNE. I was washing my hair!

MR. FRANK. I think there's nothing the matter with our Anne that a ride on her bike, or a visit with her friend Jopie de Waal wouldn't cure. Isn't that so, Anne?

[MR. VAN DAAN *comes down into the room. From outside we hear faint sounds of bombers going over and a burst of ack-ack.*][18]

MR. VAN DAAN. Miep not come yet?

MRS. VAN DAAN. The workmen just left, a little while ago.

---

18. **ack-ack** (ak´ ak´) *n.* slang for an anti-aircraft gun's fire.

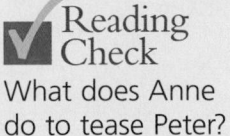

MR. VAN DAAN. What's for dinner tonight?

MRS. VAN DAAN. Beans.

MR. VAN DAAN. Not again!

MRS. VAN DAAN. Poor Putti! I know. But what can we do? That's all that Miep brought us.

[MR. VAN DAAN *starts to pace, his hands behind his back.* ANNE *follows behind him, imitating him.*]

ANNE. We are now in what is known as the "bean cycle." Beans boiled, beans en casserole, beans with strings, beans without strings . . .

[PETER *has come out of his room. He slides into his place at the table, becoming immediately absorbed in his studies.*]

MR. VAN DAAN. [*To* PETER] I saw you . . . in there, playing with your cat.

MRS. VAN DAAN. He just went in for a second, putting his coat away. He's been out here all the time, doing his lessons.

MR. FRANK. [*Looking up from the papers*] Anne, you got an excellent in your history paper today . . . and very good in Latin.

ANNE. [*Sitting beside him*] How about algebra?

MR. FRANK. I'll have to make a confession. Up until now I've managed to stay ahead of you in algebra. Today you caught up with me. We'll leave it to Margot to correct.

ANNE. Isn't algebra *vile*, Pim!

MR. FRANK. Vile!

MARGOT. [*To* MR. FRANK] How did I do?

ANNE. [*Getting up*] Excellent, excellent, excellent, excellent!

MR. FRANK. [*To* MARGOT] You should have used the subjunctive[19] here . . .

MARGOT. Should I? . . . I thought . . . look here . . . I didn't use it here . . .

[*The two become absorbed in the papers.*]

ANNE. Mrs. Van Daan, may I try on your coat?

---

19. subjunctive (səb juŋk´ tiv) *n.* form of a verb that is used to express doubt or uncertainty.

Dialogue
Based on this dialogue, what is Mr. Frank's attitude toward education?

MRS. FRANK. No, Anne.

MRS. VAN DAAN. [*Giving it to* ANNE] It's all right . . . but careful with it. [ANNE *puts it on and struts with it.*] My father gave me that the year before he died. He always bought the best that money could buy.

ANNE. Mrs. Van Daan, did you have a lot of boy friends before you were married?

MRS. FRANK. Anne, that's a personal question. It's not courteous to ask personal questions.

MRS. VAN DAAN. Oh I don't mind. [*To* ANNE] Our house was always swarming with boys. When I was a girl we had . . .

MR. VAN DAAN. Oh, God. Not again!

MRS. VAN DAAN. [*Good-humored*] Shut up! [*Without a pause, to* ANNE, MR. VAN DAAN *mimics* MRS. VAN DAAN, *speaking the first few words in unison with her.*] One summer we had a big house in Hilversum. The boys came buzzing round like bees around a jam pot. And when I was sixteen! . . . We were wearing our skirts very short those days and I had good-looking legs. [*She pulls up her skirt, going to* MR. FRANK.] I still have 'em. I may not be as pretty as I used to be, but I still have my legs. How about it, Mr. Frank?

MR. VAN DAAN. All right. All right. We see them.

MRS. VAN DAAN. I'm not asking you. I'm asking Mr. Frank.

PETER. Mother, for heaven's sake.

MRS. VAN DAAN. Oh, I embarrass you, do I? Well, I just hope the girl you marry has as good. [*Then to* ANNE] My father used to worry about me, with so many boys hanging round. He told me, if any of them gets fresh, you say to him . . . "Remember, Mr. So-and-So, remember I'm a lady."

ANNE. "Remember, Mr. So-and-So, remember I'm a lady." [*She gives* MRS. VAN DAAN *her coat.*]

MR. VAN DAAN. Look at you, talking that way in front of her! Don't you know she puts it all down in that diary?

MRS. VAN DAAN. So, if she does? I'm only telling the truth!

[ANNE *stretches out, putting her ear to the floor, listening to what*

Dialogue
What does Mrs. Van Daan's comment about her father reveal about her values?

Dialogue
What do Mrs. Van Daan's words and actions reveal about her personality?

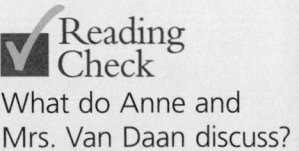
Reading Check
What do Anne and Mrs. Van Daan discuss?

is going on below. The sound of the bombers fades away.]

MRS. FRANK. [*Setting the table*] Would you mind, Peter, if I moved you over to the couch?

ANNE. [*Listening*] Miep must have the radio on.

[PETER *picks up his papers, going over to the couch beside* MRS. VAN DAAN.]

MR. VAN DAAN. [*Accusingly, to* PETER] Haven't you finished yet?

PETER. No.

MR. VAN DAAN. You ought to be ashamed of yourself.

PETER. All right. All right. I'm a dunce. I'm a hopeless case. Why do I go on?

MRS. VAN DAAN. You're not hopeless. Don't talk that way. It's just that you haven't anyone to help you, like the girls have. [*To* MR. FRANK] Maybe you could help him, Mr. Frank?

MR. FRANK. I'm sure that his father . . .?

MR. VAN DAAN. Not me. I can't do anything with him. He won't listen to me. You go ahead . . . if you want.

MR. FRANK. [*Going to* PETER] What about it, Peter? Shall we make our school coeducational?

MRS. VAN DAAN. [*Kissing* MR. FRANK] You're an angel, Mr. Frank. An angel. I don't know why I didn't meet you before I met that one there. Here, sit down, Mr. Frank . . . [*She forces him down on the couch beside* PETER.] Now, Peter, you listen to Mr. Frank.

MR. FRANK. It might be better for us to go into Peter's room.

[PETER *jumps up eagerly, leading the way.*]

MRS. VAN DAAN. That's right. You go in there, Peter. You listen to Mr. Frank. Mr. Frank is a highly educated man.

[*As* MR. FRANK *is about to follow* PETER *into his room*, MRS. FRANK *stops him and wipes the lipstick from his lips. Then she closes the door after them.*]

ANNE. [*On the floor, listening*] Shh! I can hear a man's voice talking.

MR. VAN DAAN. [*To* ANNE] Isn't it bad enough here without your sprawling all over the place?

[ANNE *sits up.*]

MRS. VAN DAAN. [*To* MR. VAN DAAN] If you didn't smoke so much, you wouldn't be so bad-tempered.

MR. VAN DAAN. Am I smoking? Do you see me smoking?

MRS. VAN DAAN. Don't tell me you've used up all those cigarettes.

MR. VAN DAAN. One package. Miep only brought me one package.

MRS. VAN DAAN. It's a filthy habit anyway. It's a good time to break yourself.

MR. VAN DAAN. Oh, stop it, please.

MRS. VAN DAAN. You're smoking up all our money. You know that, don't you?

MR. VAN DAAN. Will you shut up? [*During this,* MRS. FRANK *and* MARGOT *have studiously kept their eyes down. But* ANNE, *seated on the floor, has been following the discussion interestedly.* MR. VAN DAAN *turns to see her staring up at him.*] And what are you staring at?

ANNE. I never heard grownups quarrel before. I thought only children quarreled.

MR. VAN DAAN. This isn't a quarrel! It's a discussion. And I never heard children so rude before.

ANNE. [*Rising, indignantly*] I, rude!

MR. VAN DAAN. Yes!

MRS. FRANK. [*Quickly*] Anne, will you get me my knitting? [ANNE *goes to get it.*] I must remember, when Miep comes, to ask her to bring me some more wool.

MARGOT. [*Going to her room*] I need some hairpins and some soap. I made a list. [*She goes into her bedroom to get the list.*]

MRS. FRANK. [*To* ANNE] Have you some library books for Miep when she comes?

ANNE. It's a wonder that Miep has a life of her own, the way we make her run errands for us. Please, Miep, get me some starch. Please take my hair out and have it cut. Tell me all the latest news, Miep. [*She goes over, kneeling on the couch beside* MRS. VAN DAAN] Did you know she was engaged?

Dialogue
What plot conflict do the lines of dialogue here develop?

I never heard grownups quarrel before. I thought only children quarreled.

✓Reading Check
In what way does Mr. Frank offer to help Peter?

His name is Dirk, and Miep's afraid the Nazis will ship him off to Germany to work in one of their war plants. That's what they're doing with some of the young Dutchmen . . . they pick them up off the streets—

MR. VAN DAAN. [*Interrupting*] Don't you ever get tired of talking? Suppose you try keeping still for five minutes. Just five minutes.

[*He starts to pace again. Again* ANNE *follows him, mimicking him.* MRS. FRANK *jumps up and takes her by the arm up to the sink, and gives her a glass of milk.*]

MRS. FRANK. Come here, Anne. It's time for your glass of milk.

MR. VAN DAAN. Talk, talk, talk. I never heard such a child. Where is my . . .? Every evening it's the same talk, talk, talk. [*He looks around.*] Where is my . . .?

MRS. VAN DAAN. What're you looking for?

MR. VAN DAAN. My pipe. Have you seen my pipe?

MRS. VAN DAAN. What good's a pipe? You haven't got any tobacco.

MR. VAN DAAN. At least I'll have something to hold in my mouth! [*Opening* MARGOT'S *bedroom door*] Margot, have you seen my pipe?

MARGOT. It was on the table last night.

[ANNE *puts her glass of milk on the table and picks up his pipe, hiding it behind her back.*]

MR. VAN DAAN. I know. I know. Anne, did you see my pipe? . . . Anne!

MRS. FRANK. Anne, Mr. Van Daan is speaking to you.

ANNE. Am I allowed to talk now?

MR. VAN DAAN. You're the most aggravating . . . The trouble with you is, you've been spoiled. What you need is a good old-fashioned spanking.

ANNE. [*Mimicking* MRS. VAN DAAN] "Remember, Mr. So-and-So, remember I'm a lady." [*She thrusts the pipe into his mouth, then picks up her glass of milk.*]

MR. VAN DAAN. [*Restraining himself with difficulty*] Why aren't you nice and quiet like your sister Margot? Why do you have to show off all the time? Let me give you a little

Dialogue
What cultural attitudes does Mr. Van Daan show in this dialogue?

advice, young lady. Men don't like that kind of thing in a girl. You know that? A man likes a girl who'll listen to him once in a while . . . a domestic girl, who'll keep her house shining for her husband . . . who loves to cook and sew and . . .

ANNE. I'd cut my throat first! I'd open my veins! I'm going to be remarkable! I'm going to Paris . . .

MR. VAN DAAN. [*Scoffingly*] Paris!

ANNE. . . . to study music and art.

MR. VAN DAAN. Yeah! Yeah!

ANNE. I'm going to be a famous dancer or singer . . . or something wonderful.

[*She makes a wide gesture, spilling the glass of milk on the fur coat in* MRS. VAN DAAN'S *lap.* MARGOT *rushes quickly over with a towel.* ANNE *tries to brush the milk off with her skirt.*]

MRS. VAN DAAN. Now look what you've done . . . you clumsy little fool! My beautiful fur coat my father gave me . . .

ANNE. I'm so sorry.

MRS. VAN DAAN. What do you care? It isn't yours . . . So go on, ruin it! Do you know what that coat cost? Do you? And now look at it! Look at it!

ANNE. I'm very, very sorry.

MRS. VAN DAAN. I could kill you for this. I could just kill you!

[MRS. VAN DAAN *goes up the stairs, clutching the coat.* MR. VAN DAAN *starts after her.*]

MR. VAN DAAN. Petronella . . . *Liefje! Liefje!* . . . Come back . . . the supper . . . come back!

MRS. FRANK. Anne, you must not behave in that way.

ANNE. It was an accident. Anyone can have an accident.

MRS. FRANK. I don't mean that. I mean the answering back. You must not answer back. They are our guests. We must always show the greatest courtesy to them. We're all living under terrible tension. [*She stops as* MARGOT *indicates that* VAN DAAN *can hear. When he is gone, she continues.*]

▼ **Critical Viewing**
Why might the designers of this stamp have chosen such a happy photograph of Anne? **[Speculate]**

Cause and Effect
How is the characters' situation affecting them?

Reading Check
What bothers Mr. Van Daan about Anne?

Cause and Effect
Is Mrs. Frank's advice practical, given the families' situation? Explain.

That's why we must control ourselves . . . You don't hear Margot getting into arguments with them, do you? Watch Margot. She's always courteous with them. Never familiar. She keeps her distance. And they respect her for it. Try to be like Margot.

ANNE. And have them walk all over me, the way they do her? No, thanks!

MRS. FRANK. I'm not afraid that anyone is going to walk all over you, Anne. I'm afraid for other people, that you'll walk on them. I don't know what happens to you, Anne. You are wild, self-willed. If I had ever talked to my mother as you talk to me . . .

ANNE. Things have changed. People aren't like that any more. "Yes, Mother." "No, Mother." "Anything you say, Mother." I've got to fight things out for myself! Make something of myself!

MRS. FRANK. It isn't necessary to fight to do it. Margot doesn't fight, and isn't she . . .?

ANNE. [*Violently rebellious*] Margot! Margot! Margot! That's all I hear from everyone . . . how wonderful Margot is . . . "Why aren't you like Margot?"

MARGOT. [*Protesting*] Oh, come on, Anne, don't be so . . .

ANNE. [*Paying no attention*] Everything she does is right, and everything I do is wrong! I'm the goat around here! . . . You're all against me! . . . And you worst of all!

[*She rushes off into her room and throws herself down on the settee, stifling her sobs.* MRS. FRANK *sighs and starts toward the stove.*]

MRS. FRANK. [*To* MARGOT] Let's put the soup on the stove . . . if there's anyone who cares to eat. Margot, will you take the bread out? [MARGOT *gets the bread from the cupboard.*] I don't know how we can go on living this way . . . I can't say a word to Anne . . . she flies at me . . .

MARGOT. You know Anne. In half an hour she'll be out here, laughing and joking.

Cause and Effect
How does the situation in the outside world force Mrs. Frank to accept conditions she finds unbearable?

MRS. FRANK. And . . . [*She makes a motion upwards, indicating the* VAN DAANS.] . . . I told your father it wouldn't work . . . but no . . . no . . . he had to ask them, he said . . . he owed it to him, he said. Well, he knows now that I was right!

These quarrels! . . . This bickering!

MARGOT. [*With a warning look*] Shush. Shush.

[*The buzzer for the door sounds.* MRS. FRANK *gasps, startled.*]

MRS. FRANK. Every time I hear that sound, my heart stops!

MARGOT. [*Starting for* PETER'S *door*] It's Miep. [*She knocks at the door.*] Father?

[MR. FRANK *comes quickly from* PETER'S *room.*]

MR. FRANK. Thank you, Margot. [*As he goes down the steps to open the outer door*] Has everyone his list?

MARGOT. I'll get my books. [*Giving her mother a list*] Here's your list.
[MARGOT *goes into her and* ANNE'S *bedroom on the right.* ANNE *sits up, hiding her tears, as* MARGOT *comes in.*]
Miep's here.
[MARGOT *picks up her books and goes back.* ANNE *hurries over to the mirror, smoothing her hair.*]

MR. VAN DAAN. [*Coming down the stairs*] Is it Miep?

MARGOT. Yes. Father's gone down to let her in.

MR. VAN DAAN. At last I'll have some cigarettes!

MRS. FRANK. [*To* MR. VAN DAAN] I can't tell you how unhappy I am about Mrs. Van Daan's coat. Anne should never have touched it.

MR. VAN DAAN. She'll be all right.

MRS. FRANK. Is there anything I can do?

MR. VAN DAAN. Don't worry.

[*He turns to meet* MIEP. *But it is not* MIEP *who comes up the steps. It is* MR. KRALER, *followed by* MR. FRANK. *Their faces are grave.* ANNE *comes from the bedroom.* PETER *comes from his room.*]

MRS. FRANK. Mr. Kraler!

MR. VAN DAAN. How are you, Mr. Kraler?

MARGOT. This is a surprise.

MRS. FRANK. When Mr. Kraler comes, the sun begins to shine.

MR. VAN DAAN. Miep is coming?

MR. KRALER. Not tonight.

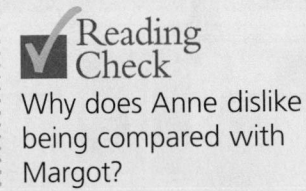

Reading Check

Why does Anne dislike being compared with Margot?

Cause and Effect
Why would a visit from an outside friend be especially welcome to those in hiding?

▼ **Critical Viewing**
This photograph shows the front of the Secret Annex. What are some pros and cons of this hiding place? **[Assess]**

[KRALER *goes to* MARGOT *and* MRS. FRANK *and* ANNE, *shaking hands with them.*]

MRS. FRANK. Wouldn't you like a cup of coffee? . . . Or, better still, will you have supper with us?

MR. FRANK. Mr. Kraler has something to talk over with us. Something has happened, he says, which demands an immediate decision.

MRS. FRANK. [*Fearful*] What is it?

[MR. KRALER *sits down on the couch. As he talks he takes bread, cabbages, milk, etc., from his briefcase, giving them to* MARGOT *and* ANNE *to put away.*]

MR. KRALER. Usually, when I come up here, I try to bring you some bit of good news. What's the use of telling you the bad news when there's nothing that you can do about it? But today something has happened . . . Dirk . . . Miep's Dirk, you know, came to me just now. He tells me that he has a Jewish friend living near him. A dentist. He says he's in trouble. He begged me, could I do anything for this man? Could I find him a hiding place? . . . So I've come to you . . . I know it's a terrible thing to ask of you, living as you are, but would you take him in with you?

MR. FRANK. Of course we will.

MR. KRALER. [*Rising*] It'll be just for a night or two . . . until I find some other place. This happened so suddenly that I didn't know where to turn.

MR. FRANK. Where is he?

MR. KRALER. Downstairs in the office.

MR. FRANK. Good. Bring him up.

MR. KRALER. His name is Dussel . . . Jan Dussel.

MR. FRANK. Dussel . . . I think I know him.

MR. KRALER. I'll get him.

[*He goes quickly down the steps and out.* MR. FRANK *suddenly becomes conscious of the others.*]

MR. FRANK. Forgive me. I spoke without consulting you. But I knew you'd feel as I do.

MR. VAN DAAN. There's no reason for you to consult

anyone. This is your place. You have a right to do exactly as you please. The only thing I feel . . . there's so little food as it is . . . and to take in another person . . .

[PETER *turns away, ashamed of his father.*]

MR. FRANK. We can stretch the food a little. It's only for a few days.

MR. VAN DAAN. You want to make a bet?

MRS. FRANK. I think it's fine to have him. But, Otto, where are you going to put him? Where?

PETER. He can have my bed. I can sleep on the floor. I wouldn't mind.

MR. FRANK. That's good of you, Peter. But your room's too small . . . even for *you.*

ANNE. I have a much better idea. I'll come in here with you and Mother, and Margot can take Peter's room and Peter can go in our room with Mr. Dussel.

MARGOT. That's right. We could do that.

MR. FRANK. No, Margot. You mustn't sleep in that room . . . neither you nor Anne. Mouschi has caught some rats in there. Peter's brave. He doesn't mind.

ANNE. Then how about *this?* I'll come in here with you and Mother, and Mr. Dussel can have my bed.

MRS. FRANK. *No. No. No!* Margot will come in here with us and he can have her bed. It's the only way. Margot, bring your things in here. Help her, Anne.

[MARGOT *hurries into her room to get her things.*]

ANNE. [*To her mother*] Why Margot? Why can't I come in here?

MRS. FRANK. Because it wouldn't be proper for Margot to sleep with a . . . Please, Anne. Don't argue. Please.

[ANNE *starts slowly away.*]

MR. FRANK. [*To* ANNE] You don't mind sharing your room with Mr. Dussel, do you, Anne?

ANNE. No. No, of course not.

MR. FRANK. Good. [ANNE *goes off into her bedroom, helping* MARGOT. MR. FRANK *starts to search in the cupboards.*]

Cause and Effect
What possible effects will Dussel's arrival have on the families' living situation?

Reading Check
What does Mr. Kraler ask of Mr. Frank?

Where's the cognac?

MRS. FRANK. It's there. But, Otto, I was saving it in case of illness.

MR. FRANK. I think we couldn't find a better time to use it. Peter, will you get five glasses for me?

[PETER *goes for the glasses.* MARGOT *comes out of her bedroom, carrying her possessions, which she hangs behind a curtain in the main room.* MR. FRANK *finds the cognac and pours it into the five glasses that* PETER *brings him.* MR. VAN DAAN *stands looking on sourly.* MRS. VAN DAAN *comes downstairs and looks around at all the bustle.*]

MRS. VAN DAAN. What's happening? What's going on?

MR. VAN DAAN. Someone's moving in with us.

MRS. VAN DAAN. In here? You're joking.

MARGOT. It's only for a night or two . . . until Mr. Kraler finds him another place.

MR. VAN DAAN. Yeah! Yeah!

[MR. FRANK *hurries over as* MR. KRALER *and* DUSSEL *come up.* DUSSEL *is a man in his late fifties, meticulous, finicky . . . bewildered now. He wears a raincoat. He carries a briefcase, stuffed full, and a small medicine case.*]

MR. FRANK. Come in, Mr. Dussel.

MR. KRALER. This is Mr. Frank.

DUSSEL. Mr. Otto Frank?

MR. FRANK. Yes. Let me take your things. [*He takes the hat and briefcase, but* DUSSEL *clings to his medicine case.*] This is my wife Edith . . . Mr. and Mrs. Van Daan . . . their son, Peter . . . and my daughters, Margot and Anne.

[DUSSEL *shakes hands with everyone.*]

MR. KRALER. Thank you, Mr. Frank. Thank you all. Mr. Dussel, I leave you in good hands. Oh . . . Dirk's coat.

[DUSSEL *hurriedly takes off the raincoat, giving it to* MR. KRALER. *Underneath is his white dentist's jacket, with a yellow Star of David on it.*]

DUSSEL. [*To* MR. KRALER] What can I say to thank you . . .?

Vocabulary
bewildered
(bē wil´ dərd) *adj.*
hopelessly confused

MRS. FRANK. [*To* DUSSEL] Mr. Kraler and Miep . . . They're our life line. Without them we couldn't live.

MR. KRALER. Please. Please. You make us seem very heroic. It isn't that at all. We simply don't like the Nazis. [*To* MR. FRANK, *who offers him a drink*] No, thanks. [*Then going on*] We don't like their methods. We don't like . . .

MR. FRANK. [*Smiling*] I know. I know. "No one's going to tell us Dutchmen what to do with our damn Jews!"

MR. KRALER. [*To* DUSSEL] Pay no attention to Mr. Frank. I'll be up tomorrow to see that they're treating you right. [*To* MR. FRANK] Don't trouble to come down again. Peter will bolt the door after me, won't you, Peter?

PETER. Yes, sir.

MR. FRANK. Thank you, Peter. I'll do it.

Dialogue
Does Mr. Frank accept Mr. Kraler's explanation of why he is helping the families? Explain.

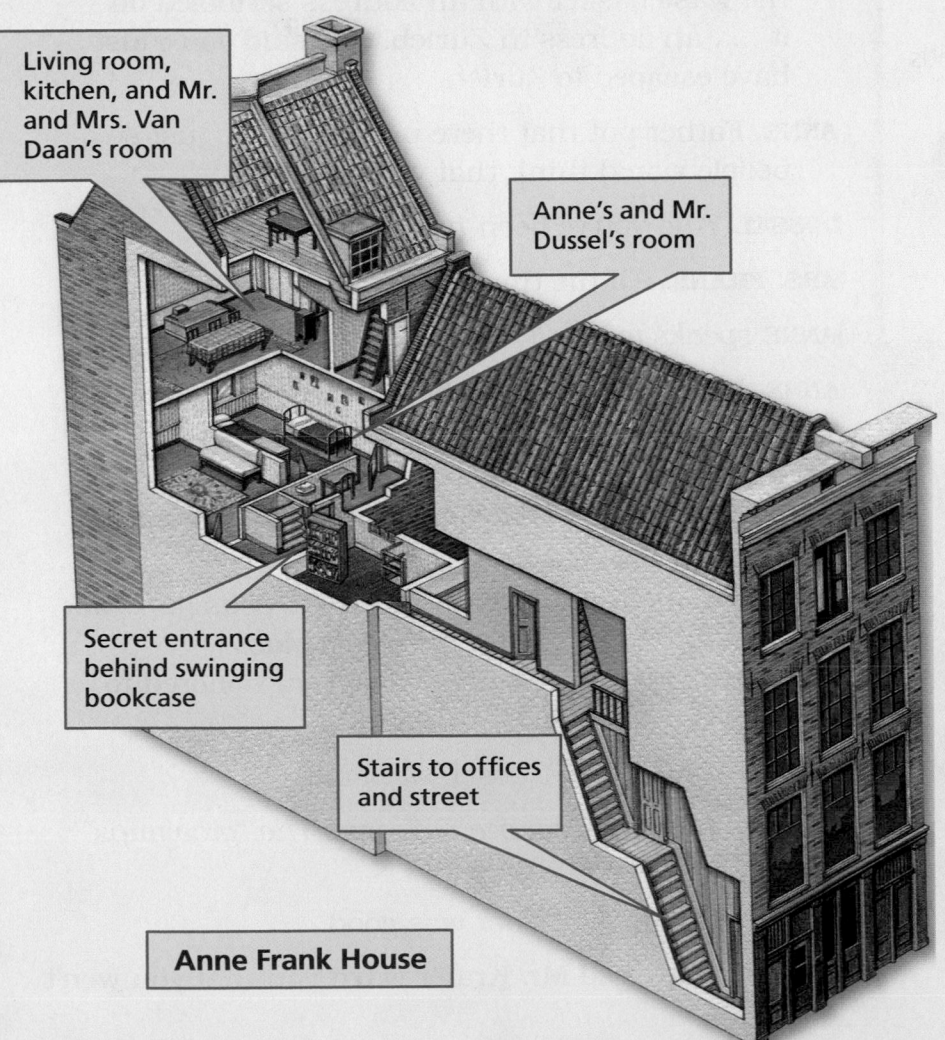

Living room, kitchen, and Mr. and Mrs. Van Daan's room

Anne's and Mr. Dussel's room

Secret entrance behind swinging bookcase

Stairs to offices and street

Anne Frank House

◄ **Critical Viewing**
How does the layout in this diagram help you to imagine what life might have been like for the residents of the Secret Annex? **[Infer]**

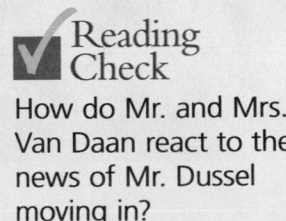

Reading Check
How do Mr. and Mrs. Van Daan react to the news of Mr. Dussel moving in?

The Diary of Anne Frank, Act I **887**

MR. KRALER. Good night. Good night.

GROUP. Good night, Mr. Kraler. We'll see you tomorrow, etc., etc.

[MR. KRALER *goes out with* MR. FRANK, MRS. FRANK *gives each one of the "grownups" a glass of cognac.*]

MRS. FRANK. Please, Mr. Dussel, sit down.

[MR. DUSSEL *sinks into a chair.* MRS. FRANK *gives him a glass of cognac.*]

DUSSEL. I'm dreaming. I know it. I can't believe my eyes. Mr. Otto Frank here! [*To* MRS. FRANK] You're not in Switzerland then? A woman told me . . . She said she'd gone to your house . . . the door was open, everything was in disorder, dishes in the sink. She said she found a piece of paper in the wastebasket with an address scribbled on it . . . an address in Zurich. She said you must have escaped to Zurich.

ANNE. Father put that there purposely . . . just so people would think that very thing!

DUSSEL. And you've been *here* all the time?

MRS. FRANK. All the time . . . ever since July.

[ANNE *speaks to her father as he comes back.*]

ANNE. It worked, Pim . . . the address you left! Mr. Dussel says that people believe we escaped to Switzerland.

MR. FRANK. I'm glad. . . . And now let's have a little drink to welcome Mr. Dussel.
[*Before they can drink,* MR. DUSSEL *bolts his drink.* MR. FRANK *smiles and raises his glass.*]
To Mr. Dussel. Welcome. We're very honored to have you with us.

MRS. FRANK. To Mr. Dussel, welcome.

[*The* VAN DAANS *murmur a welcome. The "grownups" drink.*]

MRS. VAN DAAN. Um. That was good.

MR. VAN DAAN. Did Mr. Kraler warn you that you won't

get much to eat here? You can imagine . . . three ration books among the seven of us . . . and now you make eight.

[PETER *walks away, humiliated. Outside a street organ is heard dimly.*]

DUSSEL. [*Rising*] Mr. Van Daan, you don't realize what is happening outside that you should warn me of a thing like that. You don't realize what's going on . . .

[*as* MR. VAN DAAN *starts his characteristic pacing,* DUSSEL *turns to speak to the others.*]
Right here in Amsterdam every day hundreds of Jews disappear . . . They surround a block and search house by house. Children come home from school to find their parents gone. Hundreds are being deported . . . people that you and I know . . . the Hallensteins . . . the Wessels . . .

MRS. FRANK. [*In tears*] Oh, no. No!

DUSSEL. They get their call-up notice . . . come to the Jewish theater on such and such a day and hour . . . bring only what you can carry in a rucksack. And if you refuse the call-up notice, then they come and drag you from your home and ship you off to Mauthausen.[20] The death camp!

MRS. FRANK. We didn't know that things had got so much worse.

DUSSEL. Forgive me for speaking so.

ANNE. [*Coming to* DUSSEL] Do you know the de Waals? . . . What's become of them? Their daughter Jopie and I are in the same class. Jopie's my best friend.

DUSSEL. They are gone.

ANNE. Gone?

DUSSEL. With all the others.

ANNE. Oh, no. Not Jopie!

[*She turns away, in tears.* MRS. FRANK *motions to* MARGOT *to comfort her.* MARGOT *goes to* ANNE, *putting her arms comfortingly around her.*]

MRS. VAN DAAN. There were some people called Wagner. They lived near us . . .?

---

20. **Mauthausen** (mou′ tou′ zən) village in Austria that was the site of a Nazi concentration camp.

Cause and Effect
How does Dussel's news affect Anne?

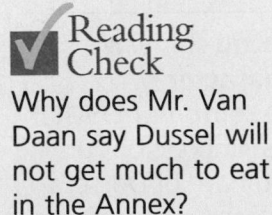
Reading Check
Why does Mr. Van Daan say Dussel will not get much to eat in the Annex?

MR. FRANK. [*Interrupting, with a glance at* ANNE] I think we should put this off until later. We all have many questions we want to ask . . . But I'm sure that Mr. Dussel would like to get settled before supper.

DUSSEL. Thank you. I would. I brought very little with me.

MR. FRANK. [*Giving him his hat and briefcase*] I'm sorry we can't give you a room alone. But I hope you won't be too uncomfortable. We've had to make strict rules here . . . a schedule of hours . . . We'll tell you after supper. Anne, would you like to take Mr. Dussel to his room?

ANNE. [*Controlling her tears*] If you'll come with me, Mr. Dussel? [*She starts for her room.*]

DUSSEL. [*Shaking hands with each in turn*] Forgive me if I haven't really expressed my gratitude to all of you. This has been such a shock to me. I'd always thought of myself as Dutch. I was born in Holland. My father was born in Holland, and my grandfather. And now . . . after all these years . . . [*He breaks off.*] If you'll excuse me.

[DUSSEL *gives a little bow and hurries off after* ANNE. MR. FRANK *and the others are subdued.*]

ANNE. [*Turning on the light*] Well, here we are.

[DUSSEL *looks around the room. In the main room* MARGOT *speaks to her mother.*]

MARGOT. The news sounds pretty bad, doesn't it? It's so different from what Mr. Kraler tells us. Mr. Kraler says things are improving.

MR. VAN DAAN. I like it better the way Kraler tells it.

[*They resume their occupations, quietly.* PETER *goes off into his room. In* ANNE'S *room,* ANNE *turns to* DUSSEL.]

ANNE. You're going to share the room with me.

DUSSEL. I'm a man who's always lived alone. I haven't had to adjust myself to others. I hope you'll bear with me until I learn.

ANNE. Let me help you. [*She takes his briefcase.*] Do you always live all alone? Have you no family at all?

DUSSEL. No one. [*He opens his medicine case and spreads his bottles on the dressing table.*]

ANNE. How dreadful. You must be terribly lonely.

© Spiral Review
Character Development What first impressions do you have of Dussel's character from his dialogue up to this point in the play?

◀ Anne Frank House— The Frank's hiding place is now open to the public. Every year more than 900,000 people from all over the world come to visit.

DUSSEL. I'm used to it.

ANNE. I don't think I could ever get used to it. Didn't you even have a pet? A cat, or a dog?

DUSSEL. I have an allergy for fur-bearing animals. They give me asthma.

ANNE. Oh, dear. Peter has a cat.

DUSSEL. Here? He has it here?

ANNE. Yes. But we hardly ever see it. He keeps it in his room all the time. I'm sure it will be all right.

DUSSEL. Let us hope so. [*He takes some pills to fortify himself.*]

ANNE. That's Margot's bed, where you're going to sleep. I sleep on the sofa there. [*Indicating the clothes hooks on the wall*] We cleared these off for your things. [*She goes over to the window.*] The best part about this room . . . you can look down and see a bit of the street and the canal. There's a

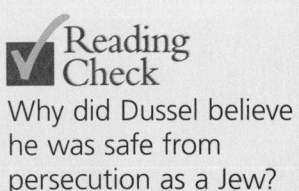

Reading Check

Why did Dussel believe he was safe from persecution as a Jew?

houseboat . . . you can see the end of it . . . a bargeman lives there with his family . . . They have a baby and he's just beginning to walk and I'm so afraid he's going to fall into the canal some day. I watch him. . . .

DUSSEL. [*Interrupting*] Your father spoke of a schedule.

ANNE. [*Coming away from the window*] Oh, yes. It's mostly about the times we have to be quiet. And times for the w.c. You can use it now if you like.

DUSSEL. [*Stiffly*] No, thank you.

ANNE. I suppose you think it's awful, my talking about a thing like that. But you don't know how important it can get to be, especially when you're frightened . . . About this room, the way Margot and I did . . . she had it to herself in the afternoons for studying, reading . . . lessons, you know . . . and I took the mornings. Would that be all right with you?

DUSSEL. I'm not at my best in the morning.

ANNE. You stay here in the mornings then. I'll take the room in the afternoons.

DUSSEL. Tell me, when you're in here, what happens to me? Where am I spending my time? In there, with all the people?

Dialogue
Based on this dialogue, how well do you think Anne and Dussel will get along as the plot develops?

ANNE. Yes.

DUSSEL. I see. I see.

ANNE. We have supper at half past six.

DUSSEL. [*Going over to the sofa*] Then, if you don't mind . . . I like to lie down quietly for ten minutes before eating. I find it helps the digestion.

ANNE. Of course. I hope I'm not going to be too much of a bother to you. I seem to be able to get everyone's back up.

[DUSSEL *lies down on the sofa, curled up, his back to her.*]

DUSSEL. I always get along very well with children. My patients all bring their children to me, because they know I get on well with them. So don't you worry about that.

[ANNE *leans over him, taking his hand and shaking it gratefully.*]

ANNE. Thank you. Thank you, Mr. Dussel.

[*The lights dim to darkness. The curtain falls on the scene.* ANNE'S VOICE *comes to us faintly at first, and then with increasing power.*]

ANNE'S VOICE. . . . And yesterday I finished Cissy Van Marxvelt's latest book. I think she is a first-class writer. I shall definitely let my children read her. Monday the twenty-first of September, nineteen forty-two. Mr. Dussel and I had another battle yesterday. Yes, Mr. Dussel! According to him, nothing, I repeat . . . nothing, is right about me . . . my appearance, my character, my manners. While he was going on at me I thought . . . sometime I'll give you such a smack that you'll fly right up to the ceiling! Why is it that every grownup thinks he knows the way to bring up children? Particularly the grownups that never had any. I keep wishing that Peter was a girl instead of a boy. Then I would have someone to talk to. Margot's a darling, but she takes everything too seriously. To pause for a moment on the subject of Mrs. Van Daan. I must tell you that her attempts to flirt with father are getting her nowhere. Pim, thank goodness, won't play.

[*As she is saying the last lines, the curtain rises on the darkened scene.* ANNE'S VOICE *fades out.*]

Cause and Effect
Are Anne's reactions here a result of her circumstances, or would they occur in any time period? Explain.

> Mr. Dussel and I had another battle yesterday.

Scene 4

[*It is the middle of the night, several months later. The stage is dark except for a little light which comes through the skylight in* PETER'S *room.*

Everyone is in bed. MR. *and* MRS. FRANK *lie on the couch in the main room, which has been pulled out to serve as a makeshift double bed.*

MARGOT *is sleeping on a mattress on the floor in the main room, behind a curtain stretched across for privacy. The others are all in their accustomed rooms.*

From outside we hear two drunken soldiers singing "Lili Marlene." A girl's high giggle is heard. The sound of running feet is heard coming closer and then fading in the distance. Throughout the scene there is the distant sound of airplanes passing overhead.

A match suddenly flares up in the attic. We dimly see MR. VAN DAAN. *He is getting his bearings. He comes quickly down the stairs, and goes to the cupboard where the food is stored. Again the match flares up, and is as quickly blown out.*]

Reading Check
What does Anne explain to Dussel?

The Diary of Anne Frank, Act I **893**

The dim figure is seen to steal back up the stairs.

There is quiet for a second or two, broken only by the sound of airplanes, and running feet on the street below.

Suddenly, out of the silence and the dark, we hear ANNE *scream.*]

ANNE. [*Screaming*] No! No! Don't . . . don't take me!

[*She moans, tossing and crying in her sleep. The other people wake, terrified.* DUSSEL *sits up in bed, furious.*]

DUSSEL. Shush! Anne! Anne, for God's sake, shush!

ANNE. [*Still in her nightmare*] Save me! Save me!

[*She screams and screams.* DUSSEL *gets out of bed, going over to her, trying to wake her.*]

DUSSEL. For God's sake! Quiet! Quiet! You want someone to hear?

[*In the main room* MRS. FRANK *grabs a shawl and pulls it around her. She rushes in to* ANNE, *taking her in her arms.* MR. FRANK *hurriedly gets up, putting on his overcoat.* MARGOT *sits up, terrified.* PETER'S *light goes on in his room.*]

MRS. FRANK. [*To* ANNE, *in her room*] Hush, darling, hush. It's all right. It's all right. [*Over her shoulder to* DUSSEL] Will you be kind enough to turn on the light, Mr. Dussel? [*Back to* ANNE] It's nothing, my darling. It was just a dream.

[DUSSEL *turns on the light in the bedroom.* MRS. FRANK *holds* ANNE *in her arms. Gradually* ANNE *comes out of her nightmare still trembling with horror.* MR. FRANK *comes into the room, and goes quickly to the window, looking out to be sure that no one outside has heard* ANNE'S *screams.* MRS. FRANK *holds* ANNE, *talking softly to her. In the main room* MARGOT *stands on a chair, turning on the center hanging lamp. A light goes on in the* VAN DAANS' *room overhead.* PETER *puts his robe on, coming out of his room.*]

DUSSEL. [*To* MRS. FRANK, *blowing his nose*] Something must be done about that child, Mrs. Frank. Yelling like that! Who knows but there's somebody on the streets? She's endangering all our lives.

MRS. FRANK. Anne, darling.

DUSSEL. Every night she twists and turns. I don't sleep. I spend half my night shushing her. And now it's nightmares!

[MARGOT *comes to the door of* ANNE'S *room, followed by* PETER. MR. FRANK *goes to them, indicating that everything is all right.* PETER *takes* MARGOT *back.*]

MRS. FRANK. [*To* ANNE] You're here, safe, you see? Nothing has happened. [*To* DUSSEL] Please, Mr. Dussel, go back to bed. She'll be herself in a minute or two. Won't you, Anne?

DUSSEL. [*Picking up a book and a pillow*] Thank you, but I'm going to the w.c. The one place where there's peace!

[*He stalks out.* MR. VAN DAAN, *in underwear and trousers, comes down the stairs.*]

MR. VAN DAAN. [*To* DUSSEL] What is it? What happened?

DUSSEL. A nightmare. She was having a nightmare!

MR. VAN DAAN. I thought someone was murdering her.

DUSSEL. Unfortunately, no.

[*He goes into the bathroom.* MR. VAN DAAN *goes back up the stairs.* MR. FRANK, *in the main room, sends* PETER *back to his own bedroom.*]

MR. FRANK. Thank you, Peter. Go back to bed.

[PETER *goes back to his room.* MR. FRANK *follows him, turning out the light and looking out the window. Then he goes back to*

Dialogue
How do the lines delivered by Dussel and Mrs. Frank reveal important differences between them?

Reading
Check
Why does Anne scream in the middle of the night?

the main room, and gets up on a chair, turning out the center hanging lamp.]

MRS. FRANK. [*To* ANNE] Would you like some water? [ANNE *shakes her head.*] Was it a very bad dream? Perhaps if you told me . . . ?

ANNE. I'd rather not talk about it.

MRS. FRANK. Poor darling. Try to sleep then. I'll sit right here beside you until you fall asleep. [*She brings a stool over, sitting there.*]

ANNE. You don't have to.

MRS. FRANK. But I'd like to stay with you . . . very much. Really.

ANNE. I'd rather you didn't.

MRS. FRANK. Good night, then. [*She leans down to kiss* ANNE. ANNE *throws her arm up over her face, turning away.* MRS. FRANK, *hiding her hurt, kisses* ANNE'S *arm.*] You'll be all right? There's nothing that you want?

ANNE. Will you please ask Father to come.

MRS. FRANK. [*After a second*] Of course, Anne dear. [*She hurries out into the other room.* MR. FRANK *comes to her as she comes in.*] *Sie verlangt nach Dir!*[21]

MR. FRANK. [*Sensing her hurt*] Edith, *Liebe, schau . . .*[22]

MRS. FRANK. *Es macht nichts! Ich danke dem lieben Herrgott, dass sie sich wenigstens an Dich wendet, wenn sie Trost braucht! Geh hinein, Otto, sie ist ganz hysterisch vor Angst.*[23] [*As* MR. FRANK *hesitates*] *Geh zu ihr.*[24]
[*He looks at her for a second and then goes to get a cup of water for* ANNE. MRS. FRANK *sinks down on the bed, her face in her hands, trying to keep from sobbing aloud.* MARGOT *comes over to her, putting her arms around her.*] She wants nothing of me. She pulled away when I leaned down to kiss her.

MARGOT. It's a phase . . . You heard Father . . . Most girls go through it . . . they turn to their fathers at this age . . . they give all their love to their fathers.

---

21. *Sie verlangt nach Dir* (sē fer′ laŋt′ nä′ dir′) German for "She is asking for you."
22. *Liebe, schau* (lē′ bə shou′) German for "Dear, look."
23. *Es macht . . . vor Angst* German for "It's all right. I thank dear God that at least she turns to you when she needs comfort. Go in, Otto, she is hysterical because of fear."
24. *Geh zu ihr* (gē′ tsoo′ ēr′) German for "Go to her."

Dialogue
What does this exchange between Anne and her mother reveal about their relationship?

MRS. FRANK. You weren't like this. You didn't shut me out.

MARGOT. She'll get over it . . .

[*She smooths the bed for* MRS. FRANK *and sits beside her a moment as* MRS. FRANK *lies down. In* ANNE'S *room* MR. FRANK *comes in, sitting down by* ANNE. ANNE *flings her arms around him, clinging to him. In the distance we hear the sound of ack-ack.*]

ANNE. Oh, Pim. I dreamed that they came to get us! The Green Police! They broke down the door and grabbed me and started to drag me out the way they did Jopie.

MR. FRANK. I want you to take this pill.

ANNE. What is it?

MR. FRANK. Something to quiet you.

[*She takes it and drinks the water. In the main room* MARGOT *turns out the light and goes back to her bed.*]

MR. FRANK. [*To* ANNE] Do you want me to read to you for a while?

ANNE. No. Just sit with me for a minute. Was I awful? Did I yell terribly loud? Do you think anyone outside could have heard?

MR. FRANK. No. No. Lie quietly now. Try to sleep.

ANNE. I'm a terrible coward. I'm so disappointed in myself. I think I've conquered my fear . . . I think I'm really grown-up . . . and then something happens . . . and I run to you like a baby . . . I love you, Father. I don't love anyone but you.

MR. FRANK. [*Reproachfully*] Annele!

ANNE. It's true. I've been thinking about it for a long time. You're the only one I love.

MR. FRANK. It's fine to hear you tell me that you love me. But I'd be happier if you said you loved your mother as well . . . She needs your help so much . . . your love . . .

ANNE. We have nothing in common. She doesn't understand me. Whenever I try to explain my views on life to her she asks me if I'm constipated.

MR. FRANK. You hurt her very much just now. She's crying. She's in there crying.

ANNE. I can't help it. I only told the truth. I didn't want her

Reading Check

What happens in Anne's nightmare?

here . . . [*Then, with sudden change*] Oh, Pim, I was horrible, wasn't I? And the worst of it is, I can stand off and look at myself doing it and know it's cruel and yet I can't stop doing it. What's the matter with me? Tell me. Don't say it's just a phase! Help me.

MR. FRANK. There is so little that we parents can do to help our children. We can only try to set a good example . . . point the way. The rest you must do yourself. You must build your own character.

ANNE. I'm trying. Really I am. Every night I think back over all of the things I did that day that were wrong . . . like putting the wet mop in Mr. Dussel's bed . . . and this thing now with Mother. I say to myself, that was wrong. I make up my mind, I'm never going to do that again. Never! Of course I may do something worse . . . but at least I'll never do that again! . . . I have a nicer side, Father . . . a sweeter, nicer side. But I'm scared to show it. I'm afraid that people are going to laugh at me if I'm serious. So the mean Anne comes to the outside and the good Anne stays on the inside, and I keep on trying to switch them around and have the good Anne outside and the bad Anne inside and be what I'd like to be . . . and might be . . . if only . . . only . . .

[*She is asleep.* MR. FRANK *watches her for a moment and then turns off the light, and starts out. The lights dim out. The curtain falls on the scene.* ANNE'S VOICE *is heard dimly at first, and then with growing strength.*]

ANNE'S VOICE. . . . The air raids are getting worse. They come over day and night. The noise is terrifying. Pim says it should be music to our ears. The more planes, the sooner will come the end of the war. Mrs. Van Daan pretends to be a fatalist. What will be, will be. But when the planes come over, who is the most frightened? No one else but Petronella! . . . Monday, the ninth of November, nineteen forty-two. Wonderful news! The Allies have landed in Africa. Pim says that we can look for an early finish to the war. Just for fun he asked each of us what was the first thing we wanted to do when we got out of here. Mrs. Van Daan longs to be home with her own things, her needlepoint chairs, the Beckstein piano her father gave her . . . the best that money could buy. Peter would like to go to a movie. Mr. Dussel wants to get back to his dentist's drill.

He's afraid he is losing his touch. For myself, there are so many things . . . to ride a bike again . . . to laugh till my belly aches . . . to have new clothes from the skin out . . . to have a hot tub filled to overflowing and wallow in it for hours . . . to be back in school with my friends . . .

[*As the last lines are being said, the curtain rises on the scene. The lights dim on as* ANNE'S VOICE *fades away.*]

Scene 5

[*It is the first night of the Hanukkah*[25] *celebration.* MR. FRANK *is standing at the head of the table on which is the Menorah.*[26] *He lights the Shamos,*[27] *or servant candle, and holds it as he says the blessing. Seated listening is all of the "family," dressed in their best. The men wear hats,* PETER *wears his cap.*]

MR. FRANK. [*Reading from a prayer book*] "Praised be Thou, oh Lord our God, Ruler of the universe, who has sanctified us with Thy commandments and bidden us kindle the Hanukkah lights. Praised be Thou, oh Lord our God, Ruler of the universe, who has wrought wondrous deliverances for our fathers in days of old. Praised be Thou, oh Lord our God, Ruler of the universe, that Thou has given us life and sustenance and brought us to this happy season." [MR. FRANK *lights the one candle of the Menorah as he continues.*] "We kindle this Hanukkah light to celebrate the great and wonderful deeds wrought through the zeal with which God filled the hearts of the heroic Maccabees, two thousand years ago. They fought against indifference, against tyranny and oppression, and they restored our Temple to us. May these lights remind us that we should ever look to God, whence cometh our help." Amen.

ALL. Amen.

[MR. FRANK *hands* MRS. FRANK *the prayer book.*]

MRS. FRANK. [*Reading*] "I lift up mine eyes unto the mountains, from whence cometh my help. My help cometh from the Lord who made heaven and earth. He will not suffer thy foot to be moved. He that keepeth thee will not slumber. He that keepeth Israel doth neither slumber nor sleep. The Lord is

Cause and Effect
Why might the story of Hanukkah have special meaning for the families in hiding?

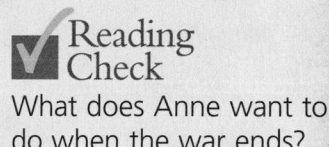
Reading Check

What does Anne want to do when the war ends?

---

25. Hanukkah (khä´ noo kä´) *n.* Jewish celebration that lasts eight days.
26. Menorah (mə nō´ rə) *n.* candle holder with nine candles, used during Hanukkah.
27. Shamos (shä´ məs) *n.* candle used to light the others in a menorah.

▲ **Critical Viewing**
This photo is from
a production of this
play. How well does it
capture the mood of
this scene? **[Assess]**

thy keeper. The Lord is thy shade upon thy right hand. The sun shall not smite thee by day, nor the moon by night. The Lord shall keep thee from all evil. He shall keep thy soul. The Lord shall guard thy going out and thy coming in, from this time forth and forevermore." Amen.

ALL. Amen.

[MRS. FRANK *puts down the prayer book and goes to get the food and wine.* MARGOT *helps her.* MR. FRANK *takes the men's hats and puts them aside.*]

DUSSEL. [*Rising*] That was very moving.

ANNE. [*Pulling him back*] It isn't over yet!

MRS. VAN DAAN. Sit down! Sit down!

ANNE. There's a lot more, songs and presents.

DUSSEL. Presents?

MRS. FRANK. Not this year, unfortunately.

MRS. VAN DAAN. But always on Hanukkah everyone gives presents . . . everyone!

DUSSEL. Like our St. Nicholas' Day.[28]

[*There is a chorus of "no's" from the group.*]

MRS. VAN DAAN. No! Not like St. Nicholas! What kind of a Jew are you that you don't know Hanukkah?

MRS. FRANK. [*As she brings the food*] I remember particularly the candles . . . First one, as we have tonight. Then the second night you light two candles, the next night three . . . and so on until you have eight candles burning. When there are eight candles it is truly beautiful.

MRS. VAN DAAN. And the potato pancakes.

MR. VAN DAAN. Don't talk about them!

MRS. VAN DAAN. I make the best *latkes* you ever tasted!

MRS. FRANK. Invite us all next year . . . in your own home.

MR. FRANK. God willing!

MRS. VAN DAAN. God willing.

Dialogue
What do Dussel's lines reveal about his familiarity with Hanukkah?

Reading Check
What rituals are part of the celebration of Hanukkah?

---

28. **St. Nicholas' Day** December 6, the day Christian children in the Netherlands receive gifts.

Cause and Effect
How do world events make this Hanukkah different from others that the families have celebrated?

MARGOT. What I remember best is the presents we used to get when we were little . . . eight days of presents . . . and each day they got better and better.

MRS. FRANK. [*Sitting down*] We are all here, alive. That is present enough.

ANNE. No, it isn't. I've got something . . . [*She rushes into her room, hurriedly puts on a little hat improvised from the lamp shade, grabs a satchel bulging with parcels and comes running back.*]

MRS. FRANK. What is it?

ANNE. Presents!

MRS. VAN DAAN. Presents!

DUSSEL. Look!

MR. VAN DAAN. What's she got on her head?

PETER. A lamp shade!

ANNE. [*She picks out one at random.*] This is for Margot. [*She hands it to* MARGOT, *pulling her to her feet.*] Read it out loud.

MARGOT. [*Reading*]
"You have never lost your temper.
You never will, I fear,
You are so good.
But if you should,
Put all your cross words here."
[*She tears open the package.*] A new crossword puzzle book! Where did you get it?

Cause and Effect
How do Anne's gifts reflect the reality of the families' situation?

ANNE. It isn't new. It's one that you've done. But I rubbed it all out, and if you wait a little and forget, you can do it all over again.

MARGOT. [*Sitting*] It's wonderful, Anne. Thank you. You'd never know it wasn't new.

[*From outside we hear the sound of a streetcar passing.*]

ANNE. [*With another gift*] Mrs. Van Daan.

MRS. VAN DAAN. [*Taking it*] This is awful . . . I haven't anything for anyone . . . I never thought . . .

MR. FRANK. This is all Anne's idea.

MRS. VAN DAAN. [*Holding up a bottle*] What is it?

ANNE. It's hair shampoo. I took all the odds and ends of soap and mixed them with the last of my toilet water.

MRS. VAN DAAN. Oh, Anneke!

ANNE. I wanted to write a poem for all of them, but I didn't have time. [*Offering a large box to* MR. VAN DAAN] Yours, Mr. Van Daan, is really something . . . something you want more than anything. [*As she waits for him to open it*] Look! Cigarettes!

MR. VAN DAAN. Cigarettes!

ANNE. Two of them! Pim found some old pipe tobacco in the pocket lining of his coat . . . and we made them . . . or rather, Pim did.

MRS. VAN DAAN. Let me see . . . Well, look at that! Light it, Putti! Light it.

[MR. VAN DAAN *hesitates.*]

ANNE. It's tobacco, really it is! There's a little fluff in it, but not much.

[*Everyone watches intently as* MR. VAN DAAN *cautiously lights it. The cigarette flares up. Everyone laughs.*]

PETER. It works!

MRS. VAN DAAN. Look at him.

MR. VAN DAAN. [*Spluttering*] Thank you, Anne. Thank you.

[ANNE *rushes back to her satchel for another present.*]

ANNE. [*Handing her mother a piece of paper*] For Mother, Hanukkah greeting.

[*She pulls her mother to her feet.*]

MRS. FRANK. [*She reads*] "Here's an I.O.U. that I promise to pay. Ten hours of doing whatever you say. Signed, Anne Frank." [MRS. FRANK, *touched, takes* ANNE *in her arms, holding her close.*]

DUSSEL. [*To* ANNE] Ten hours of doing what you're told? Anything you're told?

ANNE. That's right.

DUSSEL. You wouldn't want to sell that, Mrs. Frank?

MRS. FRANK. Never! This is the most precious gift I've ever had!

[*She sits, showing her present to the others.* ANNE *hurries back*

> **Cause and Effect**
> What effect do Anne's gifts have on the group's spirits?

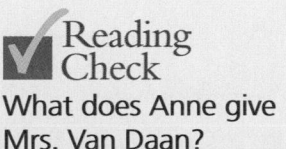
Reading Check
What does Anne give Mrs. Van Daan?

to the satchel and pulls out a scarf, the scarf that MR. FRANK *found in the first scene.*]

ANNE. [*Offering it to her father*] For Pim.

MR. FRANK. Anneke . . . I wasn't supposed to have a present!

[*He takes it, unfolding it and showing it to the others.*]

ANNE. It's a muffler . . . to put round your neck . . . like an ascot, you know. I made it myself out of odds and ends . . . I knitted it in the dark each night, after I'd gone to bed. I'm afraid it looks better in the dark!

MR. FRANK. [*Putting it on*] It's fine. It fits me perfectly. Thank you, Annele.

[ANNE *hands* PETER *a ball of paper with a string attached to it.*]

ANNE. That's for Mouschi.

PETER. [*Rising to bow*] On behalf of Mouschi, I thank you.

ANNE. [*Hesitant, handing him a gift*] And . . . this is yours . . . from Mrs. Quack Quack. [*As he holds it gingerly in his hands*] Well . . . open it . . . Aren't you going to open it?

PETER. I'm scared to. I know something's going to jump out and hit me.

ANNE. No. It's nothing like that, really.

MRS. VAN DAAN. [*As he is opening it*] What is it, Peter? Go on. Show it.

ANNE. [*Excitedly*] It's a safety razor!

DUSSEL. A what?

ANNE. A razor!

MRS. VAN DAAN. [*Looking at it*] You didn't make that out of odds and ends.

ANNE. [*To* PETER] Miep got it for me. It's not new. It's second-hand. But you really do need a razor now.

DUSSEL. For what?

ANNE. Look on his upper lip . . . you can see the beginning of a mustache.

DUSSEL. He wants to get rid of that? Put a little milk on it and let the cat lick it off.

PETER. [*Starting for his room*] Think you're funny, don't you.

DUSSEL. Look! He can't wait! He's going in to try it!

PETER. I'm going to give Mouschi his present!

[*He goes into his room, slamming the door behind him.*]

MR. VAN DAAN. [*Disgustedly*] Mouschi, Mouschi, Mouschi.

[*In the distance we hear a dog persistently barking. ANNE brings a gift to DUSSEL.*]

ANNE. And last but never least, my roommate, Mr. Dussel.

DUSSEL. For me? You have something for me?

[*He opens the small box she gives him.*]

ANNE. I made them myself.

DUSSEL. [*Puzzled*] Capsules! Two capsules!

ANNE. They're ear-plugs!

DUSSEL. Ear-plugs?

ANNE. To put in your ears so you won't hear me when I thrash around at night. I saw them advertised in a magazine. They're not real ones . . . I made them out of cotton and candle wax. Try them . . . See if they don't work . . . see if you can hear me talk . . .

DUSSEL. [*Putting them in his ears*] Wait now until I get them in . . . so.

ANNE. Are you ready?

DUSSEL. Huh?

ANNE. Are you ready?

DUSSEL. Good God! They've gone inside! I can't get them out! [*They laugh as MR. DUSSEL jumps about, trying to shake the plugs out of his ears. Finally he gets them out. Putting them away*] Thank you, Anne! Thank you!

[*Together*] {
MR. VAN DAAN. A real Hanukkah!

MRS. VAN DAAN. Wasn't it cute of her?

MRS. FRANK. I don't know when she did it.

MARGOT. I love my present.
}

ANNE. [*Sitting at the table*] And now let's have the song, Father . . . please . . . [*To DUSSEL*] Have you heard the Hanukkah song, Mr. Dussel? The song is the whole thing!

> I knitted it in the dark each night, after I'd gone to bed. I'm afraid it looks better in the dark!

Dialogue
What subplot does this dialogue develop?

Reading Check
How does Mr. Dussel anger Peter?

[*She sings.*] "Oh, Hanukkah! Oh, Hanukkah! The sweet celebration . . ."

MR. FRANK. [*Quieting her*] I'm afraid, Anne, we shouldn't sing that song tonight. [*To* DUSSEL] It's a song of jubilation, of rejoicing. One is apt to become too enthusiastic.

ANNE. Oh, please, please. Let's sing the song. I promise not to shout!

MR. FRANK. Very well. But quietly now . . . I'll keep an eye on you and when . . .

[*As* ANNE *starts to sing, she is interrupted by* DUSSEL, *who is snorting and wheezing.*]

DUSSEL. [*Pointing to* PETER] You . . . You! [PETER *is coming from his bedroom, ostentatiously holding a bulge in his coat as if he were holding his cat, and dangling* ANNE'S *present before it.*] How many times . . . I told you . . . Out! Out!

MR. VAN DAAN. [*Going to* PETER] What's the matter with you? Haven't you any sense? Get that cat out of here.

PETER. [*Innocently*] Cat?

MR. VAN DAAN. You heard me. Get it out of here!

PETER. I have no cat. [*Delighted with his joke, he opens his coat and pulls out a bath towel. The group at the table laugh, enjoying the joke.*]

DUSSEL. [*Still wheezing*] It doesn't need to be the cat . . . his clothes are enough . . . when he comes out of that room . . .

MR. VAN DAAN. Don't worry. You won't be bothered any more. We're getting rid of it.

DUSSEL. At last you listen to me. [*He goes off into his bedroom.*]

MR. VAN DAAN. [*Calling after him*] I'm not doing it for you. That's all in your mind . . . all of it! [*He starts back to his place at the table.*] I'm doing it because I'm sick of seeing that cat eat all our food.

PETER. That's not true! I only give him bones . . . scraps . . .

MR. VAN DAAN. Don't tell me! He gets fatter every day! Damn cat looks better than any of us. Out he goes tonight!

PETER. No! No!

Dialogue
What does the dialogue between Peter and Mr. Dussel reveal about both their personalities?

ANNE. Mr. Van Daan, you can't do that! That's Peter's cat. Peter loves that cat.

MRS. FRANK. [*Quietly*] Anne.

PETER. [*To* MR. VAN DAAN] If he goes, I go.

MR. VAN DAAN. Go! Go!

MRS. VAN DAAN. You're not going and the cat's not going! Now please . . . this is Hanukkah . . . Hanukkah . . . this is the time to celebrate . . . What's the matter with all of you? Come on, Anne. Let's have the song.

ANNE. [*Singing*]
"Oh, Hanukkah! Oh, Hanukkah! The sweet celebration."

Cause and Effect
How do the families' circumstances influence Mr. Van Daan's opinion about keeping a cat?

Reading Check
Who triggers the argument over the cat?

MR. FRANK. [*Rising*] I think we should first blow out the candle . . . then we'll have something for tomorrow night.

MARGOT. But, Father, you're supposed to let it burn itself out.

MR. FRANK. I'm sure that God understands shortages. [*Before blowing it out*] "Praised be Thou, oh Lord our God, who hast sustained us and permitted us to celebrate this joyous festival."

[*He is about to blow out the candle when suddenly there is a crash of something falling below. They all freeze in horror, motionless. For a few seconds there is complete silence.* MR. FRANK *slips off his shoes. The others noiselessly follow his example.* MR. FRANK *turns out a light near him. He motions to* PETER *to turn off the center lamp.* PETER *tries to reach it, realizes he cannot and gets up on a chair. Just as he is touching the lamp he loses his balance. The chair goes out from under him. He falls. The iron lamp shade crashes to the floor. There is a sound of feet below, running down the stairs.*]

MR. VAN DAAN. [*Under his breath*] God Almighty! [*The only light left comes from the Hanukkah candle.* DUSSEL *comes from his room.* MR. FRANK *creeps over to the stairwell and stands listening. The dog is heard barking excitedly.*] Do you hear anything?

MR. FRANK. [*In a whisper*] No. I think they've gone.

MRS. VAN DAAN. It's the Green Police. They've found us.

MR. FRANK. If they had, they wouldn't have left. They'd be up here by now.

MRS. VAN DAAN. I know it's the Green Police. They've gone to get help. That's all. They'll be back!

MR. VAN DAAN. Or it may have been the Gestapo,[29] looking for papers . . .

MR. FRANK. [*Interrupting*] Or a thief, looking for money.

MRS. VAN DAAN. We've got to do something . . . Quick! Quick! Before they come back.

MR. VAN DAAN. There isn't anything to do. Just wait.

[MR. FRANK *holds up his hand for them to be quiet. He is listening intently. There is complete silence as they all strain to hear any sound from below. Suddenly* ANNE *begins to sway. With a low*

---

29. **Gestapo** (gə stä′ pō) *n.* secret police force of the German Nazi state, known for its terror tactics and brutality.

cry she falls to the floor in a faint. MRS. FRANK *goes to her quickly, sitting beside her on the floor and taking her in her arms.*]

MRS. FRANK. Get some water, please! Get some water!

[MARGOT *starts for the sink.*]

MR. VAN DAAN. [*Grabbing* MARGOT] No! No! No one's going to run water!

MR. FRANK. If they've found us, they've found us. Get the water. [MARGOT *starts again for the sink.* MR. FRANK, *getting a flashlight*] I'm going down.

[MARGOT *rushes to him, clinging to him.* ANNE *struggles to consciousness.*]

MARGOT. No, Father, no! There may be someone there, waiting . . . It may be a trap!

MR. FRANK. This is Saturday. There is no way for us to know what has happened until Miep or Mr. Kraler comes on Monday morning. We cannot live with this uncertainty.

MARGOT. Don't go, Father!

MRS. FRANK. Hush, darling, hush. [MR. FRANK *slips quietly out, down the steps and out through the door below.*] Margot! Stay close to me. [MARGOT *goes to her mother.*]

MR. VAN DAAN. Shush! Shush!

[MRS. FRANK *whispers to* MARGOT *to get the water.* MARGOT *goes for it.*]

MRS. VAN DAAN. Putti, where's our money? Get our money. I hear you can buy the Green Police off, so much a head. Go upstairs quick! Get the money!

MR. VAN DAAN. Keep still!

MRS. VAN DAAN. [*Kneeling before him, pleading*] Do you want to be dragged off to a concentration camp? Are you going to stand there and wait for them to come up and get you? Do something, I tell you!

MR. VAN DAAN. [*Pushing her aside*] Will you keep still!

[*He goes over to the stairwell to listen.* PETER *goes to his mother, helping her up onto the sofa. There is a second of silence, then* ANNE *can stand it no longer.*]

ANNE. Someone go after Father! Make Father come back!

> It's the Green Police. They've found us.

Reading Check

How does Peter fall?

PETER. [*Starting for the door*] I'll go.

MR. VAN DAAN. Haven't you done enough?

[*He pushes* PETER *roughly away. In his anger against his father* PETER *grabs a chair as if to hit him with it, then puts it down, burying his face in his hands.* MRS. FRANK *begins to pray softly.*]

ANNE. Please, please, Mr. Van Daan. Get Father.

MR. VAN DAAN. Quiet! Quiet!

[ANNE *is shocked into silence.* MRS. FRANK *pulls her closer, holding her protectively in her arms.*]

MRS. FRANK. [*Softly, praying*] "I lift up mine eyes unto the mountains, from whence cometh my help. My help cometh from the Lord who made heaven and earth. He will not suffer thy foot to be moved . . . He that keepeth thee will not slumber . . ."

[*She stops as she hears someone coming. They all watch the door tensely.* MR. FRANK *comes quietly in.* ANNE *rushes to him, holding him tight.*]

MR. FRANK. It was a thief. That noise must have scared him away.

MRS. VAN DAAN. Thank God.

MR. FRANK. He took the cash box. And the radio. He ran away in such a hurry that he didn't stop to shut the street door. It was swinging wide open. [*A breath of relief sweeps over them.*] I think it would be good to have some light.

MARGOT. Are you sure it's all right?

MR. FRANK. The danger has passed. [MARGOT *goes to light the small lamp.*] Don't be so terrified, Anne. We're safe.

DUSSEL. Who says the danger has passed? Don't you realize we are in greater danger than ever?

MR. FRANK. Mr. Dussel, will you be still!

[MR. FRANK *takes* ANNE *back to the table, making her sit down with him, trying to calm her.*]

DUSSEL. [*Pointing to* PETER] Thanks to this clumsy fool, there's someone now who knows we're up here! Someone now knows we're up here, hiding!

MRS. VAN DAAN. [*Going to* DUSSEL] Someone knows we're here, yes. But who is the someone? A thief! A thief! You think a thief is going to go to the Green Police and say . . . I was robbing a place the other night and I heard a noise up over my head? You think a thief is going to do that?

DUSSEL. Yes. I think he will.

MRS. VAN DAAN. [*Hysterically*] You're crazy!

[*She stumbles back to her seat at the table.* PETER *follows protectively, pushing* DUSSEL *aside.*]

DUSSEL. I think some day he'll be caught and then he'll make a bargain with the Green Police . . . if they'll let him off, he'll tell them where some Jews are hiding!

[*He goes off into the bedroom. There is a second of appalled silence.*]

MR. VAN DAAN. He's right.

ANNE. Father, let's get out of here! We can't stay here now . . . Let's go . . .

MR. VAN DAAN. Go! Where?

MRS. FRANK. [*Sinking into her chair at the table*] Yes. Where?

MR. FRANK. [*Rising, to them all*] Have we lost all faith? All courage? A moment ago we thought that they'd come for us. We were sure it was the end. But it wasn't the end. We're alive, safe. [MR. VAN DAAN *goes to the table and sits.* MR. FRANK *prays.*] "We thank Thee, oh Lord our God, that in Thy infinite mercy Thou hast again seen fit to spare us." [*He blows out the candle, then turns to* ANNE.] Come on, Anne. The song! Let's have the song! [*He starts to sing.* ANNE *finally starts falteringly to sing, as* MR. FRANK *urges her on. Her voice is hardly audible at first.*]

ANNE. [*Singing*]
"Oh, Hanukkah! Oh, Hanukkah! The sweet . . . celebration . . ."

[*As she goes on singing, the others gradually join in, their voices still shaking with fear.* MRS. VAN DAAN *sobs as she sings.*]

GROUP. Around the feast . . . we . . . gather
In complete . . . jubilation . . .
Happiest of sea . . . sons
Now is here.
Many are the reasons for good cheer.

Cause and Effect
What do Mr. Dussel's lines about the Green Police suggest about their methods for finding Jews?

Reading Check
What is Dussel afraid the thief will do?

[DUSSEL *comes from the bedroom. He comes over to the table, standing beside* MARGOT, *listening to them as they sing.*]

"Together/We'll weather/Whatever tomorrow may bring."

[*As they sing on with growing courage, the lights start to dim.*]

"So hear us rejoicing/And merrily voicing/The Hanukkah song that we sing./Hoy!"

[*The lights are out. The curtain starts slowly to fall.*]

"Hear us rejoicing/And merrily voicing/The Hanukkah song that we sing."

[*They are still singing, as the curtain falls.*]

Dialogue
What is the effect of this song as a finale to the act?

Critical Thinking

1. Key Ideas and Details (a) In Scene 1, what objects does Mr. Frank find in the secret rooms? **(b) Connect:** How are these objects connected with the rest of the act?

2. Key Ideas and Details (a) What special meaning does Hanukkah have for the families? **(b) Deduce:** What do Anne's presents show about her? **(c) Interpret:** Why do the others react with enthusiasm to their presents?

Cite textual evidence to support your responses.

3. Key Ideas and Details (a) Evaluate: With a partner, discuss Mr. Frank's statement, "There are . . . no locks that anyone can put on your mind." How does Anne prove that this is true? **(b) Discuss:** Share your answer with a partner and then with the class.

4. Integration of Knowledge and Ideas (a) What does Mr. Frank's reaction to the crisis involving the thief reveal about his personality, as compared with Mr. Van Daan's? **(b)** In general, what do the stresses faced by the families tend to bring out more—their differences or their similarities? Support your answer with specific examples. *[Connect to the Big Question: Is it our differences or our similarities that matter most?]*

Reading Skill: Cause and Effect

1. (a) What is the historical **cause** that forces the Franks into hiding? **(b)** What **effects** does it have on their daily lives?

2. Anne and Peter discuss the Stars of David. **(a)** What effects do the Nazis intend the stars to have? **(b)** What background information helps you understand the intended effect?

Literary Analysis: Dialogue

3. Craft and Structure Complete an organizer like the one shown with examples of **dialogue** that achieve each purpose.

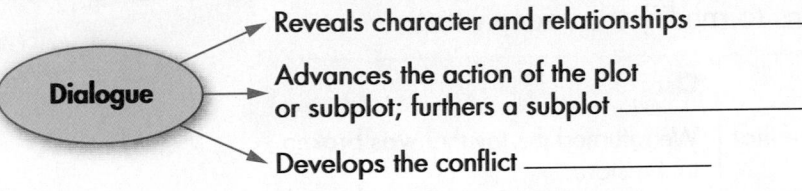

4. Craft and Structure (a) After Mr. Kraler asks if Dussel can join the group, what does the dialogue among the characters reveal about their personalities? **(b)** How does Dussel's dialogue on his arrival affect the scene's tone?

5. Craft and Structure Consider what you know about Anne's eventual fate. How does this knowledge add dramatic irony to the dialogue at the end of the act?

Vocabulary

Acquisition and Use Use a vocabulary word from page 852 to rewrite each sentence to convey the same basic meaning.

1. The summer sun in the desert is difficult to tolerate.

2. The hole in Bryan's sweater is in a noticeable place.

3. Kevin believes that success in life is out of his hands.

4. Jasmine and Carly feel that Alberto gets too much attention.

5. Hostility between the cats has created a stressful situation.

6. Sam was confused by all the buttons on his new camera.

Word Study Use context and what you know about the **Greek suffix -ist** to explain your answer to each question.

1. Is a *violinist* someone who sells violins?

2. If you were a *humorist*, what might you do for a living?

Word Study

The **Greek suffix -ist** means "one who does, makes, practices, is skilled in, or believes in."

Apply It Explain how the suffix *-ist* contributes to the meanings of these words. Consult a dictionary, if necessary.

bicyclist
moralist
artist

Integrated Language Skills

The Diary of Anne Frank, Act I

Conventions:
Dangling and Misplaced Modifiers

A **modifier** is a word, phrase, or clause that clarifies the meaning of a word or group of words in a sentence.

A phrase or clause that acts as a modifier should be placed as close as possible to the word it modifies. If it is placed far away, it might seem to modify the wrong word or no word at all.

A **misplaced modifier** seems to modify the wrong word.

Confusing	Clear
We returned the toy to the store that was broken.	We returned the toy that was broken to the store.

A **dangling modifier** is one that cannot sensibly modify any word in the sentence.

Confusing	Clear
Staring at the ceiling, the idea became clear.	As I was staring at the ceiling, the idea became clear.

Practice A In each sentence, identify the misplaced modifier and the word(s) it modifies.

1. Anne gave gifts to people that were made from recycled items.
2. Writing in her diary things she felt made Anne happy.
3. When she was thirteen years old, Anne's elderly grandmother died.
4. Anne's family joined the Van Daans with a cat.

© **Reading Application** Identify three modifiers in Act I and explain whether each is correctly placed.

Practice B Identify the dangling modifier in each sentence, and indicate the word it seems to modify.

1. Living in the attic rooms, it was lonely.
2. To survive, steady nerves help.
3. When young, adults can seem arbitrary and strange.
4. Getting angrier and angrier, time seemed to stand still.

© **Writing Application** Rewrite each sentence in Practice B so that it makes sense by adding a word for the dangling modifier to modify.

PH WRITING COACH — Further instruction and practice are available in *Prentice Hall Writing Coach.*

Writing

Common Core State Standards

L.8.1; W.8.3; SL.8.6
[For the full wording of the standards, see page 848.]

Narrative Text To explore the perspectives of two characters other than Anne, write two **diary entries** about an event from the play. Follow these steps:

- Choose an event that affects at least two characters. Make a two-column chart to take notes that show how each person might have viewed the event. This chart will help you compare and contrast their perspectives.

- Consider how a single event takes on a different importance depending on the character viewing it.

- Write each diary entry from each character's point of view. Include a description of the event, using carefully chosen details such as remembered dialogue. Show each character's feelings and add details to describe how people looked and acted during the event.

Grammar Application Check your writing. Be sure you have used a variety of complete sentences that include properly placed modifiers.

Writing Workshop: *Work in Progress*

Prewriting for Exposition For a research report that you may write, think of something that you have always wanted to investigate further, such as how World War II ended. Generate a list of questions that could spark your research. Save this Questions List.

Use this prewriting activity to prepare for the **Writing Workshop** on page 982.

Speaking and Listening

Use the photos, descriptions, and major events of the play, along with original research, to present a **guided tour** of daily life in the "Secret Annex." Follow these steps:

- Review the play for details about the layout of the rooms, the food the family ate, and the stresses of life in a cramped attic.

- Keep in mind that the play is a dramatization. The basic facts are true, but some elements have been fictionalized. Check the validity of major events and details in the play by consulting Anne's real diary (a primary source) and reliable secondary sources, such as the Web site of the Anne Frank House.

- For extra impact, include a dramatic soliloquy (solo speech) from the play. Whatever material you choose to present, vary your voice and use dynamic gestures and an appropriate tone to achieve the purpose of conveying the atmosphere of the "Secret Annex" to your audience.

www.PHLitOnline.com
- Interactive graphic organizers
- Grammar tutorial
- Interactive journals

 **Drama**

Build your skills and improve your comprehension of drama.

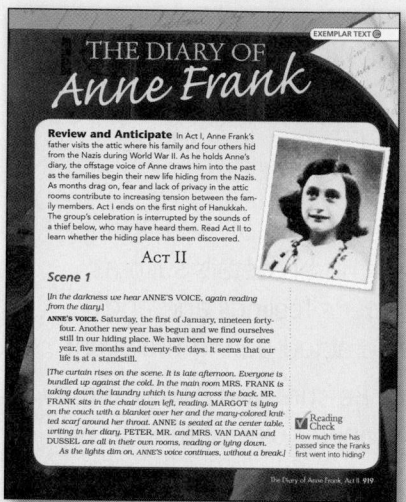

Read ***The Diary of Anne Frank, Act II*** to learn what happens as conditions worsen and tension mounts in the cramped attic rooms.

 Common Core State Standards

Meet these standards with ***The Diary of Anne Frank,*** **Act II** (p. 919).

Reading Literature

3. Analyze how particular lines of dialogue or incidents in a story or drama propel the action, reveal aspects of a character, or provoke a decision. *(Literary Analysis: Character's Motivation)*

7. Analyze the extent to which a filmed or live production of a story or drama stays faithful to or departs from the text or script, evaluating the choices made by the director or actors. *(Writing: Film Review)*

Writing

2. Write informative/explanatory texts to examine a topic and convey ideas, concepts, and information through the selection, organization, and analysis of relevant content. *(Writing: Film Review; Research and Technology: Bulletin Board Display)*

4. Produce clear and coherent writing in which the development, organization, and style are appropriate to task, purpose, and audience. *(Research and Technology: Bulletin Board Display)*

7. Conduct short research projects to answer a question, drawing on several sources and generating additional related, focused questions that allow for multiple avenues of exploration. *(Research and Technology: Bulletin Board Display)*

Speaking and Listening

1. Engage effectively in a range of collaborative discussions with diverse partners, building on others' ideas and expressing their own clearly. *(Research and Technology: Bulletin Board Display)*

Language

1. Demonstrate command of the conventions of standard English grammar and usage when writing or speaking. *(Conventions: Clauses)*

4.b. Use common, grade-appropriate Greek or Latin affixes and roots as clues to the meaning of a word (e.g., *precede, recede, secede*). *(Vocabulary: Word Study)*

Reading Skill: Cause and Effect

Cause-and-effect relationships explain the connections between events, but they do not always follow the simple pattern of a single cause producing a single effect.

To help you discover these patterns in a literary work, **ask questions to analyze cause-and-effect relationships,** such as:

- What other causes might have triggered this event?
- What are all the possible effects—or chains of effects—that might result from this cause?
- Are these events really related? Just because two events occur in order does not mean they have a cause-and-effect relationship. They may be coincidental or random events.

Using the Strategy: Cause-and-Effect Charts

Three relationships are shown in these **cause-and-effect charts**.

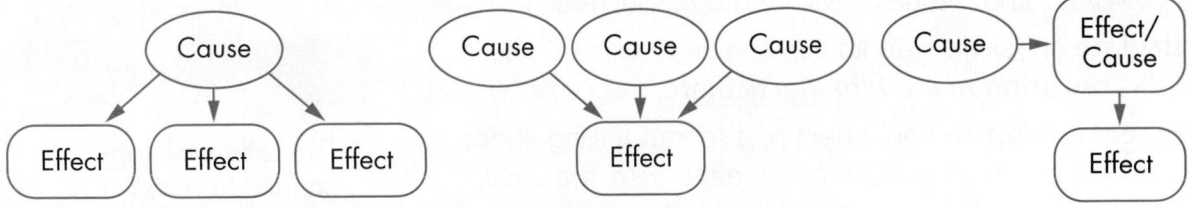

Literary Analysis: Character's Motivation

A **character's motivation** is the reason he or she takes a particular action. This reason may be internal, external, or a mix of both. *Internal motivations* are based on emotions, such as loneliness or jealousy. *External motivations* are sparked by settings, events, or situations, like a war or poverty.

Characters are often affected by their environment. In this play two main **settings** have a major impact on the characters' actions: the raging war being fought across Europe and the confines of the attic in which the characters are forced to hide.

As you read, consider each character's possible motivations for each action he or she takes.

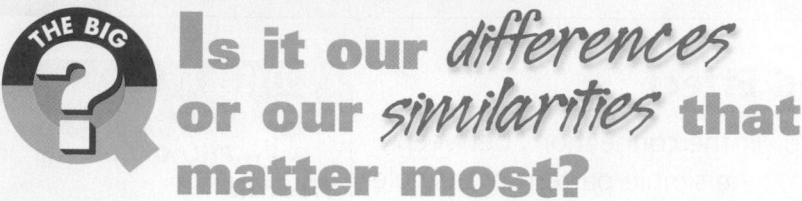

Is it our *differences* or our *similarities* that matter most?

Writing About the Big Question

As the war drags on, conditions worsen in the "Secret Annex" and differences among the residents lead to conflict. Use these sentence starters to develop your ideas about the Big Question.

Superficial differences between people can become magnified when _____. It is difficult to preserve **sympathy** and **tolerance** for others when you are facing _____.

While You Read Look for ways in which the families are or are not able to preserve their human dignity amid their suffering.

Vocabulary

Read each word and its definition. Decide whether you know the word well, know it a little bit, or do not know it at all. After you read, see how your knowledge of each word has increased.

- **inarticulate** (in´ är tik´ yoo lit) *adj.* unable to express oneself (p. 923) *Confusion made him <u>inarticulate</u>. inarticulately adv.*

- **apprehension** (ap´ rē hen´ shən) *n.* a fearful feeling about what will happen next (p. 926) *I squeezed into the cave, despite my <u>apprehension</u>. apprehensive adj.*

- **blackmail** (blak´ māl´) *n.* the practice of making someone do what you want by threatening to reveal his or her secrets (p. 926) *Her fear that her criminal past might be exposed made her vulnerable to <u>blackmail</u>. blackmail v.*

- **forlorn** (fôr lôrn´) *adj.* sad and lonely (p. 931) *The child was <u>forlorn</u> when he was the last to be picked up. forlornly adv.*

- **intuition** (in´ too ish´ ən) *n.* ability to sense immediately, without reasoning (p. 934) *Pat's <u>intuition</u> told her that something was wrong. intuitive adj. intuitively adv.*

- **ineffectually** (in´ e fek´ choo ə lē) *adv.* without producing the desired results (p. 950) *The fan spun <u>ineffectually</u> in the overheated room. ineffectual adj. effect n.*

Word Study

The **Latin prefix** *in-* can mean "into" or "within."

In this play, a character claims to have **intuition**, a feeling within herself that she knows what is going to happen, without having a logical explanation for it.

THE DIARY OF
Anne Frank

Review and Anticipate In Act I, Anne Frank's father visits the attic where his family and four others hid from the Nazis during World War II. As he holds Anne's diary, the offstage voice of Anne draws him into the past as the families begin their new life hiding from the Nazis. As months drag on, fear and lack of privacy in the attic rooms contribute to increasing tension between the family members. Act I ends on the first night of Hanukkah. The group's celebration is interrupted by the sounds of a thief below, who may have heard them. Read Act II to learn whether the hiding place has been discovered.

ACT II

Scene 1

[*In the darkness we hear* ANNE'S VOICE, *again reading from the diary.*]

ANNE'S VOICE. Saturday, the first of January, nineteen forty-four. Another new year has begun and we find ourselves still in our hiding place. We have been here now for one year, five months and twenty-five days. It seems that our life is at a standstill.

[*The curtain rises on the scene. It is late afternoon. Everyone is bundled up against the cold. In the main room MRS. FRANK is taking down the laundry which is hung across the back. MR. FRANK sits in the chair down left, reading. MARGOT is lying on the couch with a blanket over her and the many-colored knitted scarf around her throat. ANNE is seated at the center table, writing in her diary. PETER, MR. and MRS. VAN DAAN and DUSSEL are all in their own rooms, reading or lying down.*

As the lights dim on, ANNE'S voice continues, without a break.]

Reading Check
How much time has passed since the Franks first went into hiding?

Character's Motivation
Why do you think Anne writes about her feelings toward her mother in her diary?

ANNE'S VOICE. We are all a little thinner. The Van Daans' "discussions" are as violent as ever. Mother still does not understand me. But then I don't understand her either. There is one great change, however. A change in myself. I read somewhere that girls of my age don't feel quite certain of themselves. That they become quiet within and begin to think of the miracle that is taking place in their bodies. I think that what is happening to me is so wonderful . . . not only what can be seen, but what is taking place inside. Each time it has happened I have a feeling that I have a sweet secret.

[*We hear the chimes and then a hymn being played on the carillon outside. The buzzer of the door below suddenly sounds. Everyone is startled.* MR. FRANK *tiptoes cautiously to the top of the steps and listens. Again the buzzer sounds, in* MIEP's *V-for-Victory signal.*][1]

MR. FRANK. It's Miep!

[*He goes quickly down the steps to unbolt the door.* MRS. FRANK *calls upstairs to the* VAN DAANS *and then to* PETER.]

MRS. FRANK. Wake up, everyone! Miep is here!

[ANNE *quickly puts her diary away.* MARGOT *sits up, pulling the blanket around her shoulders.* MR. DUSSEL *sits on the edge of his bed, listening, disgruntled.* MIEP *comes up the steps, followed by* MR. KRALER. *They bring flowers, books, newspapers, etc.* ANNE *rushes to* MIEP, *throwing her arms affectionately around her.*]

Miep . . . and Mr. Kraler . . . What a delightful surprise!

MR. KRALER. We came to bring you New Year's greetings.

MRS. FRANK. You shouldn't . . . you should have at least one day to yourselves. [*She goes quickly to the stove and brings down teacups and tea for all of them.*]

ANNE. Don't say that, it's so wonderful to see them! [*Sniffing at* MIEP's *coat*] I can smell the wind and the cold on your clothes.

▼ Critical Viewing
Behind this bookcase are stairs leading to the hiding place. How does this photograph help you understand the tension in the play? **[Assess]**

---

1. **V-for-Victory signal** three short rings and one long one (the letter *V* in Morse code).

MIEP. [*Giving her the flowers*] There you are. [*Then to*
MARGOT, *feeling her forehead*] How are you, Margot? . . .
Feeling any better?

MARGOT. I'm all right.

ANNE. We filled her full of every kind of pill so she won't cough
and make a noise. [*She runs into her room to put the flowers in water.* MR. *and* MRS. VAN DAAN *come from upstairs.
Outside there is the sound of a band playing.*]

MRS. VAN DAAN. Well, hello, Miep.
Mr. Kraler.

MR. KRALER. [*Giving a bouquet of flowers to* MRS. VAN DAAN]
With my hope for peace in the New Year.

PETER. [*Anxiously*] Miep, have you seen Mouschi? Have you
seen him anywhere around?

MIEP. I'm sorry, Peter. I asked everyone in the neighborhood had
they seen a gray cat. But they said no.

[MRS. FRANK *gives* MIEP *a cup of tea.* MR. FRANK *comes up
the steps, carrying a small cake on a plate.*]

MR. FRANK. Look what Miep's brought for us!

MRS. FRANK. [*Taking it*] A cake!

MR. VAN DAAN. A cake! [*He pinches* MIEP'S *cheeks gaily and
hurries up to the cupboard.*] I'll get some plates.

[DUSSEL, *in his room, hastily puts a coat on and starts out to
join the others.*]

MRS. FRANK. Thank you, Miepia. You shouldn't have done
it. You must have used all of your sugar ration for weeks.
[*Giving it to* MRS. VAN DAAN] It's beautiful, isn't it?

MRS. VAN DAAN. It's been ages since I even saw a cake. Not
since you brought us one last year. [*Without looking at the
cake, to* MIEP] Remember? Don't you remember, you gave
us one on New Year's Day? Just this time last year? I'll
never forget it because you had "Peace in nineteen forty-
three" on it. [*She looks at the cake and reads*] "Peace in
nineteen forty-four!"

MIEP. Well, it has to come sometime, you know. [*As DUSSEL
comes from his room*] Hello, Mr. Dussel.

Cause and Effect
What does the dialogue
about the cake reveal
about life under
German occupation?

**Reading
Check**
What occasion are the
families celebrating?

MR. KRALER. How are you?

MR. VAN DAAN. [*Bringing plates and a knife*] Here's the knife, *liefje.* Now, how many of us are there?

MIEP. None for me, thank you.

MR. FRANK. Oh, please. You must.

MIEP. I couldn't.

MR. VAN DAAN. Good! That leaves one . . . two . . . three . . . seven of us.

DUSSEL. Eight! Eight! It's the same number as it always is!

MR. VAN DAAN. I left Margot out. I take it for granted Margot won't eat any.

ANNE. Why wouldn't she!

MRS. FRANK. I think it won't harm her.

MR. VAN DAAN. All right! All right! I just didn't want her to start coughing again, that's all.

DUSSEL. And please, Mrs. Frank should cut the cake.

[*Together*] {
MR. VAN DAAN. What's the difference?

MRS. VAN DAAN. It's not Mrs. Frank's cake, is it, Miep? It's for all of us.
}

DUSSEL. Mrs. Frank divides things better.

[*Together*] {
MRS. VAN DAAN. [*Going to* DUSSEL] What are you trying to say?

MR. VAN DAAN. Oh, come on! Stop wasting time!
}

MRS. VAN DAAN. [*To* DUSSEL] Don't I always give everybody exactly the same? Don't I?

MR. VAN DAAN. Forget it, Kerli.

MRS. VAN DAAN. No. I want an answer! Don't I?

DUSSEL. Yes. Yes. Everybody gets exactly the same . . . except Mr. Van Daan always gets a little bit more.

[VAN DAAN *advances on* DUSSEL, *the knife still in his hand.*]

MR. VAN DAAN. That's a lie!

[DUSSEL *retreats before the onslaught of the* VAN DAANS.]

MR. FRANK. Please, please! [*Then to* MIEP] You see what a little sugar cake does to us? It goes right to our heads!

Character's Motivation
Beyond the excuse he gives, what is another possible reason that Mr. Van Daan leaves out Margot?

Character's Motivation
How do the pressures of life in hiding affect the relationship between Dussel and the Van Daans?

MR. VAN DAAN. [*Handing* MRS. FRANK *the knife*] Here you are, Mrs. Frank.

MRS. FRANK. Thank you. [*Then to* MIEP *as she goes to the table to cut the cake*] Are you sure you won't have some?

MIEP. [*Drinking her tea*] No, really, I have to go in a minute.

[*The sound of the band fades out in the distance.*]

PETER. [*To* MIEP] Maybe Mouschi went back to our house . . . they say that cats . . . Do you ever get over there . . . ? I mean . . . do you suppose you could . . . ?

MIEP. I'll try, Peter. The first minute I get I'll try. But I'm afraid, with him gone a week . . .

DUSSEL. Make up your mind, already someone has had a nice big dinner from that cat!

[PETER *is furious,* *inarticulate.* *He starts toward* DUSSEL *as if to hit him.* MR. FRANK *stops him.* MRS. FRANK *speaks quickly to ease the situation.*]

MRS. FRANK. [*To* MIEP] This is delicious, Miep!

MRS. VAN DAAN. [*Eating hers*] Delicious!

MR. VAN DAAN. [*Finishing it in one gulp*] Dirk's in luck to get a girl who can bake like this!

Vocabulary
inarticulate
(in´ är tik´ yoo lit)
adj. unable to express oneself

Reading Check
What does Peter ask Miep to do?

MIEP. [*Putting down her empty teacup*] I have to run. Dirk's taking me to a party tonight.

ANNE. How heavenly! Remember now what everyone is wearing, and what you have to eat and everything, so you can tell us tomorrow.

MIEP. I'll give you a full report! Good-bye, everyone!

MR. VAN DAAN. [*To* MIEP] Just a minute. There's something I'd like you to do for me.

[*He hurries off up the stairs to his room.*]

MRS. VAN DAAN. [*Sharply*] Putti, where are you going? [*She rushes up the stairs after him, calling hysterically.*] What do you want? Putti, what are you going to do?

MIEP. [*To* PETER] What's wrong?

PETER. [*His sympathy is with his mother.*] Father says he's going to sell her fur coat. She's crazy about that old fur coat.

DUSSEL. Is it possible? Is it possible that anyone is so silly as to worry about a fur coat in times like this?

PETER. It's none of your darn business . . . and if you say one more thing . . . I'll, I'll take you and I'll . . . I mean it . . . I'll . . .

[*There is a piercing scream from* MRS. VAN DAAN *above. She grabs at the fur coat as* MR. VAN DAAN *is starting downstairs with it.*]

MRS. VAN DAAN. No! No! No! Don't you dare take that! You hear? It's mine! [*Downstairs* PETER *turns away, embarrassed, miserable.*] My father gave me that! You didn't give it to me. You have no right. Let go of it . . . you hear?

[MR. VAN DAAN *pulls the coat from her hands and hurries downstairs.* MRS. VAN DAAN *sinks to the floor, sobbing. As* MR. VAN DAAN *comes into the main room the others look away, embarrassed for him.*]

Character's Motivation
Are Mr. Van Daan's reasons for selling his wife's fur coat selfish or unselfish? Explain.

MR. VAN DAAN. [*To* MR. KRALER] Just a little—discussion over the advisability of selling this coat. As I have often reminded Mrs. Van Daan, it's very selfish of her to keep it when people outside are in such desperate need of clothing . . . [*He gives the coat to* MIEP.] So if you will please to sell it for us? It should fetch a good price. And by the way, will you get me cigarettes. I don't care what kind they are . . . get all you can.

MIEP. It's terribly difficult to get them, Mr. Van Daan. But I'll try. Good-bye.

[*She goes.* MR. FRANK *follows her down the steps to bolt the door after her.* MRS. FRANK *gives* MR. KRALER *a cup of tea.*]

MRS. FRANK. Are you sure you won't have some cake, Mr. Kraler?

MR. KRALER. I'd better not.

MR. VAN DAAN. You're still feeling badly? What does your doctor say?

MR. KRALER. I haven't been to him.

MRS. FRANK. Now, Mr. Kraler! . . .

MR. KRALER. [*Sitting at the table*] Oh, I tried. But you can't get near a doctor these days . . . they're so busy. After weeks I finally managed to get one on the telephone. I told him I'd like an appointment . . . I wasn't feeling very well. You know what he answers . . . over the telephone . . . Stick out your tongue! [*They laugh. He turns to* MR. FRANK *as* MR. FRANK *comes back.*] I have some contracts here . . . I wonder if you'd look over them with me . . .

MR. FRANK. [*Putting out his hand*] Of course.

MR. KRALER. [*He rises*] If we could go downstairs . . . [MR. FRANK *starts ahead;* MR. KRALER *speaks to the others.*] Will you forgive us? I won't keep him but a minute. [*He starts to follow* MR. FRANK *down the steps.*]

MARGOT. [*With sudden foreboding*] What's happened? Something's happened! Hasn't it, Mr. Kraler?

[MR. KRALER *stops and comes back, trying to reassure* MARGOT *with a pretense of casualness.*]

MR. KRALER. No, really. I want your father's advice . . .

MARGOT. Something's gone wrong! I know it!

MR. FRANK. [*Coming back, to* MR. KRALER] If it's something that concerns us here, it's better that we all hear it.

MR. KRALER. [*Turning to him, quietly*] But . . . the children . . . ?

MR. FRANK. What they'd imagine would be worse than any reality.

> Is it possible that anyone is so silly as to worry about a fur coat in times like this?

Reading Check

What reason does Mr. Kraler give for wanting to talk with Mr. Frank privately?

Vocabulary
apprehension
(ap′ rē hen′ shən) *n.*
a fearful feeling about
what will happen next

[*As* MR. KRALER *speaks, they all listen with intense* *apprehension.* MRS. VAN DAAN *comes down the stairs and sits on the bottom step.*]

MR. KRALER. It's a man in the storeroom . . . I don't know whether or not you remember him . . . Carl, about fifty, heavy-set, nearsighted . . . He came with us just before you left.

MR. FRANK. He was from Utrecht?

MR. KRALER. That's the man. A couple of weeks ago, when I was in the storeroom, he closed the door and asked me . . . how's Mr. Frank? What do you hear from Mr. Frank? I told him I only knew there was a rumor that you were in Switzerland. He said he'd heard that rumor too, but he thought I might know something more. I didn't pay any attention to it . . . but then a thing happened yesterday . . . He'd brought some invoices to the office for me to sign. As I was going through them, I looked up. He was standing staring at the bookcase . . . your bookcase. He said he thought he remembered a door there . . . Wasn't there a door there that used to go up to the loft? Then he told me he wanted more money. Twenty guilders[2] more a week.

Vocabulary
blackmail (blak′ māl′)
n. the practice of
making someone do
what you want by
threatening to reveal
his or her secrets

MR. VAN DAAN. Blackmail!

MR. FRANK. Twenty guilders? Very modest blackmail.

MR. VAN DAAN. That's just the beginning.

DUSSEL. [*Coming to* MR. FRANK] You know what I think? He was the thief who was down there that night. That's how he knows we're here.

MR. FRANK. [*To* MR. KRALER] How was it left? What did you tell him?

MR. KRALER. I said I had to think about it. What shall I do? Pay him the money? . . . Take a chance on firing him . . . or what? I don't know.

Cause and Effect
How does Dussel's
reaction reflect his fear
about being caught
by the authorities?

DUSSEL. [*Frantic*] Don't fire him! Pay him what he asks . . . keep him here where you can have your eye on him.

MR. FRANK. Is it so much that he's asking? What are they paying nowadays?

MR. KRALER. He could get it in a war plant. But this isn't a

---

2. guilders (gil′ dərz) *n.* monetary unit of the Netherlands.

war plant. Mind you, I don't know if he really knows . . . or if he doesn't know.

MR. FRANK. Offer him half. Then we'll soon find out if it's blackmail or not.

DUSSEL. And if it is? We've got to pay it, haven't we? Anything he asks we've got to pay!

MR. FRANK. Let's decide that when the time comes.

MR. KRALER. This may be all my imagination. You get to a point, these days, where you suspect everyone and everything. Again and again . . . on some simple look or word, I've found myself . . .

[*The telephone rings in the office below.*]

MRS. VAN DAAN. [*Hurrying to* MR. KRALER] There's the telephone! What does that mean, the telephone ringing on a holiday?

MR. KRALER. That's my wife. I told her I had to go over some papers in my office . . . to call me there when she got out of church. [*He starts out.*] I'll offer him half then. Good-bye . . . we'll hope for the best!

[*The group calls their good-byes halfheartedly.* MR. FRANK *follows* MR. KRALER *to bolt the door below. During the following scene,* MR. FRANK *comes back up and stands listening, disturbed.*]

DUSSEL. [*To* MR. VAN DAAN] You can thank your son for this . . . smashing the light! I tell you, it's just a question of time now.

[*He goes to the window at the back and stands looking out.*]

MARGOT. Sometimes I wish the end would come . . . whatever it is.

MRS. FRANK. [*Shocked*] Margot!

[ANNE *goes to* MARGOT, *sitting beside her on the couch with her arms around her.*]

MARGOT. Then at least we'd know where we were.

MRS. FRANK. You should be ashamed of yourself! Talking that way! Think how lucky we are! Think of the thousands dying in the war, every day. Think of the people in concentration camps.

Cause and Effect
Here, Kraler resists a cause-and-effect explanation for events that occurred in order. What else might explain the employee's demand?

Reading Check
What does the employee say to Mr. Kraler?

ANNE. [*Interrupting*] What's the good of that? What's the good of thinking of misery when you're already miserable? That's stupid!

MRS. FRANK. Anne!

[*As ANNE goes on raging at her mother, MRS. FRANK tries to break in, in an effort to quiet her.*]

ANNE. We're young, Margot and Peter and I! You grownups have had your chance! But look at us . . . If we begin thinking of all the horror in the world, we're lost! We're trying to hold onto some kind of ideals . . . when every-thing . . . ideals, hopes . . . everything, are being de-stroyed! It isn't our fault that the world is in such a mess! We weren't around when all this started! So don't try to take it out on us! [*She rushes off to her room, slamming the door after her. She picks up a brush from the chest and hurls it to the floor. Then she sits on the settee, trying to control her anger.*]

MR. VAN DAAN. She talks as if we started the war! Did we start the war?

[*He spots ANNE'S cake. As he starts to take it, PETER anticipates him.*]

Cause and Effect
How does Anne's speech reveal a gap between the adults' and the teenagers' perspectives on the outside world?

PETER. She left her cake. [*He starts for* ANNE'S *room with the cake. There is silence in the main room.* MRS. VAN DAAN *goes up to her room, followed by* VAN DAAN. DUSSEL *stays looking out the window.* MR. FRANK *brings* MRS. FRANK *her cake. She eats it slowly, without relish.* MR. FRANK *takes his cake to* MARGOT *and sits quietly on the sofa beside her.* PETER *stands in the doorway of* ANNE'S *darkened room, looking at her, then makes a little movement to let her know he is there.* ANNE *sits up, quickly, trying to hide the signs of her tears.* PETER *holds out the cake to her.*] You left this.

ANNE. [*Dully*] Thanks.

[PETER *starts to go out, then comes back.*]

PETER. I thought you were fine just now. You know just how to talk to them. You know just how to say it. I'm no good . . . I never can think . . . especially when I'm mad . . . That Dussel . . . when he said that about Mouschi . . . someone eating him . . . all I could think is . . . I wanted to hit him. I wanted to give him such a . . . a . . . that he'd . . . That's what I used to do when there was an argument at school . . . That's the way I . . . but here . . . And an old man like that . . . it wouldn't be so good.

ANNE. You're making a big mistake about me. I do it all wrong. I say too much. I go too far. I hurt people's feelings . . .

[DUSSEL *leaves the window, going to his room.*]

PETER. I think you're just fine . . . What I want to say . . . if it wasn't for you around here, I don't know. What I mean . . .

[PETER *is interrupted by* DUSSEL'S *turning on the light.* DUSSEL *stands in the doorway, startled to see* PETER. PETER *advances toward him forbiddingly.* DUSSEL *backs out of the room.* PETER *closes the door on him.*]

ANNE. Do you mean it, Peter? Do you really mean it?

PETER. I said it, didn't I?

ANNE. Thank you, Peter!

[*In the main room* MR. *and* MRS. FRANK *collect the dishes and take them to the sink, washing them.* MARGOT *lies down again on the couch.* DUSSEL, *lost, wanders into* PETER'S *room and takes up a book, starting to read.*]

Character's Motivation
Why does Peter seek out Anne in her room?

Reading Check
Why does Peter admire Anne?

► **Critical Viewing**
This photograph
shows a museum
re-creation of a wall
in Anne Frank's room.
In what ways does
her room resemble
a typical teenager's
room today? **[Relate]**

PETER. [*Looking at the photographs on the wall*] You've got quite a collection.

ANNE. Wouldn't you like some in your room? I could give you some. Heaven knows you spend enough time in there . . . doing heaven knows what . . .

PETER. It's easier. A fight starts, or an argument . . . I duck in there.

ANNE. You're lucky, having a room to go to. His lordship is always here . . . I hardly ever get a minute alone. When they start in on me, I can't duck away. I have to stand there and take it.

PETER. You gave some of it back just now.

ANNE. I get so mad. They've formed their opinions . . . about everything . . . but we . . . we're still trying to find out . . . We have problems here that no other people our age have ever had. And just as you think you've solved them, something comes along and bang! You have to start all over again.

PETER. At least you've got someone you can talk to.

ANNE. Not really. Mother . . . I never discuss anything serious with her. She doesn't understand. Father's all right. We can talk about everything . . . everything but one thing. Mother. He simply won't talk about her. I don't think you can be really intimate with anyone if he holds something back, do you?

PETER. I think your father's fine.

ANNE. Oh, he is, Peter! He is! He's the only one who's ever given me the feeling that I have any sense. But anyway, nothing can take the place of school and play and friends of your own age . . . or near your age . . . can it?

PETER. I suppose you miss your friends and all.

ANNE. It isn't just . . . [*She breaks off, staring up at him for a second.*] Isn't it funny, you and I? Here we've been seeing each other every minute for almost a year and a half, and this is the first time we've ever really talked. It helps a lot to have someone to talk to, don't you think? It helps you to let off steam.

PETER. [*Going to the door*] Well, any time you want to let off steam, you can come into my room.

ANNE. [*Following him*] I can get up an awful lot of steam.
You'll have to be careful how you say that.

PETER. It's all right with me.

ANNE. Do you mean it?

PETER. I said it, didn't I?

[*He goes out. ANNE stands in her doorway looking after him.
As PETER gets to his door he stands for a minute looking back
at her. Then he goes into his room. DUSSEL rises as he comes
in, and quickly passes him, going out. He starts across for
his room. ANNE sees him coming, and pulls her door shut.
DUSSEL turns back toward PETER'S room. PETER pulls his
door shut. DUSSEL stands there, bewildered,* forlorn.

The scene slowly dims out. The curtain falls on the scene.
ANNE'S VOICE comes over in the darkness . . . faintly at first,
and then with growing strength.*]

Vocabulary
forlorn (fôr lôrn´)
adj. sad and lonely

☑ Reading
  Check
What problems does
Anne describe to Peter?

ANNE'S VOICE. We've had bad news. The people from whom Miep got our ration books have been arrested. So we have had to cut down on our food. Our stomachs are so empty that they rumble and make strange noises, all in different keys. Mr. Van Daan's is deep and low, like a bass fiddle. Mine is high, whistling like a flute. As we all sit around waiting for supper, it's like an orchestra tuning up. It only needs Toscanini[3] to raise his baton and we'd be off in the Ride of the Valkyries.[4] Monday, the sixth of March, nineteen forty-four. Mr. Kraler is in the hospital. It seems he has ulcers. Pim says we are his ulcers. Miep has to run the business and us too. The Americans have landed on the southern tip of Italy. Father looks for a quick finish to the war. Mr. Dussel is waiting every day for the warehouse man to demand more money. Have I been skipping too much from one subject to another? I can't help it. I feel that spring is coming. I feel it in my whole body and soul. I feel utterly confused. I am longing . . . so longing . . . for everything . . . for friends . . . for someone to talk to . . . someone who understands . . . someone young, who feels as I do . . .

[*As these last lines are being said, the curtain rises on the scene. The lights dim on.* ANNE'S VOICE *fades out.*]

Scene 2

[*It is evening, after supper. From outside we hear the sound of children playing. The "grownups," with the exception of* MR. VAN DAAN, *are all in the main room.* MRS. FRANK *is doing some mending,* MRS. VAN DAAN *is reading a fashion magazine.* MR. FRANK *is going over business accounts.* DUSSEL, *in his dentist's jacket, is pacing up and down, impatient to get into his bedroom.* MR. VAN DAAN *is upstairs working on a piece of embroidery in an embroidery frame.*

In his room PETER *is sitting before the mirror, smoothing his hair. As the scene goes on, he puts on his tie, brushes his coat and puts it on, preparing himself meticulously for a visit from* ANNE. *On his wall are now hung some of* ANNE'S *motion picture stars.*

In her room ANNE *too is getting dressed. She stands before*

---

3. **Toscanini** (täs´ kə nē´ nē) Arturo Toscanini, a famous Italian American orchestra conductor.
4. **Ride of the Valkyries** (val kir´ ēz) stirring selection from an opera by Richard Wagner, a German composer.

the mirror in her slip, trying various ways of dressing her hair.
MARGOT *is seated on the sofa, hemming a skirt for* ANNE
to wear.

In the main room DUSSEL *can stand it no longer. He comes over, rapping sharply on the door of his and* ANNE'S *bedroom.*]

ANNE. [*Calling to him*] No, no, Mr. Dussel! I am not dressed yet. [DUSSEL *walks away, furious, sitting down and burying his head in his hands.* ANNE *turns to* MARGOT.]
How is that? How does that look?

MARGOT. [*Glancing at her briefly*] Fine.

ANNE. You didn't even look.

MARGOT. Of course I did. It's fine.

ANNE. Margot, tell me, am I terribly ugly?

MARGOT. Oh, stop fishing.

ANNE. No. No. Tell me.

MARGOT. Of course you're not. You've got nice eyes . . . and a lot of animation, and . . .

ANNE. A little vague, aren't you?

[*She reaches over and takes a brassiére out of Margot's sewing basket. She holds it up to herself, studying the effect in the mirror. Outside,* MRS. FRANK, *feeling sorry for* DUSSEL, *comes over, knocking at the girls' door.*]

MRS. FRANK. [*Outside*] May I come in?

MARGOT. Come in, Mother.

MRS. FRANK. [*Shutting the door behind her*] Mr. Dussel's impatient to get in here.

ANNE. [*Still with the brassière*] Heavens, he takes the room for himself the entire day.

MRS. FRANK. [*Gently*] Anne, dear, you're not going in again tonight to see Peter?

ANNE. [*Dignified*] That is my intention.

MRS. FRANK. But you've already spent a great deal of time in there today.

ANNE. I was in there exactly twice. Once to get the dictionary,

Reading
Check
How does Mrs. Frank
feel about the time Anne
spends with Peter?

Vocabulary
intuition (in´ tōō ish´ ən)
n. ability to sense
immediately, with-
out reasoning

Character's Motivation
What prompts Mrs.
Frank to make these
requests of Anne?

and then three-quarters of an hour before supper.

MRS. FRANK. Aren't you afraid you're disturbing him?

ANNE. Mother, I have some intuition.

MRS. FRANK. Then may I ask you this much, Anne. Please don't shut the door when you go in.

ANNE. You sound like Mrs. Van Daan! [*She throws the brassière back in Margot's sewing basket and picks up her blouse, putting it on.*]

MRS. FRANK. No. No. I don't mean to suggest anything wrong. I only wish that you wouldn't expose yourself to criticism . . . that you wouldn't give Mrs. Van Daan the opportunity to be unpleasant.

ANNE. Mrs. Van Daan doesn't need an opportunity to be unpleasant!

MRS. FRANK. Everyone's on edge, worried about Mr. Kraler. This is one more thing . . .

ANNE. I'm sorry, Mother. I'm going to Peter's room. I'm not going to let Petronella Van Daan spoil our friendship.

[*MRS. FRANK hesitates for a second, then goes out, closing the door after her. She gets a pack of playing cards and sits at the center table, playing solitaire. In ANNE'S room MARGOT hands the finished skirt to ANNE. As ANNE is putting it on, MARGOT takes off her high-heeled shoes and stuffs paper in the toes so that ANNE can wear them.*]

MARGOT. [*To ANNE*] Why don't you two talk in the main room? It'd save a lot of trouble. It's hard on Mother, having to listen to those remarks from Mrs. Van Daan and not say a word.

ANNE. Why doesn't she say a word? I think it's ridiculous to take it and take it.

MARGOT. You don't understand Mother at all, do you? She can't talk back. She's not like you. It's just not in her nature to fight back.

ANNE. Anyway . . . the only one I worry about is you. I feel awfully guilty about you. [*She sits on the stool near MARGOT, putting on MARGOT'S high-heeled shoes.*]

MARGOT. What about?

ANNE. I mean, every time I go into Peter's room, I have a feeling I may be hurting you. [MARGOT *shakes her head.*] I know if it were me, I'd be wild. I'd be desperately jealous, if it were me.

MARGOT. Well, I'm not.

ANNE. You don't feel badly? Really? Truly? You're not jealous?

MARGOT. Of course I'm jealous . . . jealous that you've got something to get up in the morning for . . . But jealous of you and Peter? No.

[ANNE *goes back to the mirror.*]

ANNE. Maybe there's nothing to be jealous of. Maybe he doesn't really like me. Maybe I'm just taking the place of his cat . . . [*She picks up a pair of short white gloves, putting them on.*] Wouldn't you like to come in with us?

MARGOT. I have a book.

[*The sound of the children playing outside fades out. In the main room DUSSEL can stand it no longer. He jumps up, going to the bedroom door and knocking sharply.*]

DUSSEL. Will you please let me in my room!

ANNE. Just a minute, dear, dear Mr. Dussel. [*She picks up her mother's pink stole and adjusts it elegantly over her shoulders, then gives a last look in the mirror.*] Well, here I go . . . to run the gauntlet.[5]

[*She starts out, followed by MARGOT.*]

DUSSEL. [*As she appears—sarcastic*] Thank you so much.

[DUSSEL *goes into his room. ANNE goes toward PETER'S room, passing MRS. VAN DAAN and her parents at the center table.*]

MRS. VAN DAAN. My God, look at her! [ANNE *pays no attention. She knocks at PETER'S door.*] I don't know what good it is to have a son. I never see him. He wouldn't care if I killed myself. [PETER *opens the door and stands aside for ANNE to come in.*] Just a minute, Anne. [*She goes to them at the door.*] I'd like to say a few words to my son. Do you mind? [PETER *and ANNE stand waiting.*] Peter, I don't want you

> Of course I'm jealous... jealous that you've got something to get up in the morning for...

Reading Check
Why does Anne fear she might be hurting Margot?

---

5. **run the gauntlet** (gônt´ lit) formerly, to pass between two rows of men who struck at the offender with clubs as he passed; here, a series of troubles or difficulties.

staying up till all hours tonight. You've got to have your sleep. You're a growing boy. You hear?

MRS. FRANK. Anne won't stay late. She's going to bed promptly at nine. Aren't you, Anne?

ANNE. Yes, Mother . . . [*To* MRS. VAN DAAN] May we go now?

MRS. VAN DAAN. Are you asking me? I didn't know I had anything to say about it.

MRS. FRANK. Listen for the chimes, Anne dear.

[*The two young people go off into* PETER's *room, shutting the door after them.*]

MRS. VAN DAAN. [*To* MRS. FRANK] In my day it was the boys who called on the girls. Not the girls on the boys.

MRS. FRANK. You know how young people like to feel that they have secrets. Peter's room is the only place where they can talk.

MRS. VAN DAAN. Talk! That's not what they called it when I was young.

[MRS. VAN DAAN *goes off to the bathroom.* MARGOT *settles down to read her book.* MR. FRANK *puts his papers away and brings a chess game to the center table. He and* MRS. FRANK *start to play. In* PETER'S *room,* ANNE *speaks to* PETER, *indignant, humiliated.*]

ANNE. Aren't they awful? Aren't they impossible? Treating us as if we were still in the nursery.

[*She sits on the cot.* PETER *gets a bottle of pop and two glasses.*]

PETER. Don't let it bother you. It doesn't bother me.

ANNE. I suppose you can't really blame them . . . they think back to what *they* were like at our age. They don't realize how much more advanced we are . . . When you think what wonderful discussions we've had! . . . Oh, I forgot. I was going to bring you some more pictures.

PETER. Oh, these are fine, thanks.

ANNE. Don't you want some more? Miep just brought me some new ones.

PETER. Maybe later. [*He gives her a glass of pop and, taking some for himself, sits down facing her.*]

Cause and Effect
How might Mrs. Van Daan's beliefs about what is socially acceptable reflect her own upbringing?

ANNE. [*Looking up at one of the photographs*] I remember when I got that . . . I won it. I bet Jopie that I could eat five ice-cream cones. We'd all been playing ping-pong . . . We used to have heavenly times . . . we'd finish up with ice cream at the Delphi, or the Oasis, where Jews were allowed . . . there'd always be a lot of boys . . . we'd laugh and joke . . . I'd like to go back to it for a few days or a week. But after that I know I'd be bored to death. I think more seriously about life now. I want to be a journalist . . . or something. I love to write. What do you want to do?

PETER. I thought I might go off some place . . . work on a farm or something . . . some job that doesn't take much brains.

ANNE. You shouldn't talk that way. You've got the most awful inferiority complex.

PETER. I know I'm not smart.

ANNE. That isn't true. You're much better than I am in dozens of things . . . arithmetic and algebra and . . . well, you're a million times better than I am in algebra. [*With sudden directness*] You like Margot, don't you? Right from the start you liked her, liked her much better than me.

PETER. [*Uncomfortably*] Oh, I don't know.

[*In the main room* MRS. VAN DAAN *comes from the bathroom and goes over to the sink, polishing a coffee pot.*]

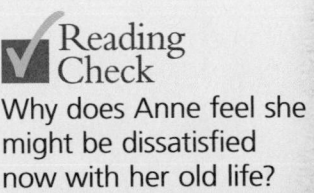

Reading Check

Why does Anne feel she might be dissatisfied now with her old life?

Character's Motivation
What is Anne's possible motivation for asking Peter whether he likes Margot?

ANNE. It's all right. Everyone feels that way. Margot's so good. She's sweet and bright and beautiful and I'm not.

PETER. I wouldn't say that.

ANNE. Oh, no, I'm not. I know that. I know quite well that I'm not a beauty. I never have been and never shall be.

PETER. I don't agree at all. I think you're pretty.

ANNE. That's not true!

PETER. And another thing. You've changed . . . from at first, I mean.

ANNE. I have?

PETER. I used to think you were awful noisy.

ANNE. And what do you think now, Peter? How have I changed?

PETER. Well . . . er . . . you're . . . quieter.

[*In his room* DUSSEL *takes his pajamas and toilet articles and goes into the bathroom to change.*]

ANNE. I'm glad you don't just hate me.

PETER. I never said that.

ANNE. I bet when you get out of here you'll never think of me again.

PETER. That's crazy.

ANNE. When you get back with all of your friends, you're going to say . . . now what did I ever see in that Mrs. Quack Quack.

PETER. I haven't got any friends.

ANNE. Oh, Peter, of course you have. Everyone has friends.

PETER. Not me. I don't want any. I get along all right without them.

ANNE. Does that mean you can get along without me? I think of myself as your friend.

PETER. No. If they were all like you, it'd be different.

[*He takes the glasses and the bottle and puts them away. There is a second's silence and then* ANNE *speaks, hesitantly, shyly.*]

ANNE. Peter, did you ever kiss a girl?

PETER. Yes. Once.

ANNE. [*To cover her feelings*] That picture's crooked.

[PETER *GOES OVER, STRAIGHTENING THE PHOTOGRAPH.*]
Was she pretty?

PETER. Huh?

ANNE. The girl that you kissed.

PETER. I don't know. I was blindfolded. [*He comes back and sits down again.*] It was at a party. One of those kissing games.

ANNE. [*Relieved*] Oh. I don't suppose that really counts, does it?

PETER. It didn't with me.

ANNE. I've been kissed twice. Once a man I'd never seen before kissed me on the cheek when he picked me up off the ice and I was crying. And the other was Mr. Koophuis, a friend of Father's who kissed my hand. You wouldn't say those counted, would you?

PETER. I wouldn't say so.

ANNE. I know almost for certain that Margot would never kiss anyone unless she was engaged to them. And I'm sure too that Mother never touched a man before Pim. But I don't know . . . things are so different now . . . What do you think? Do you think a girl shouldn't kiss anyone except if she's engaged or something? It's so hard to try to think what to do, when here we are with the whole world falling around our ears and you think . . . well . . . you don't know what's going to happen tomorrow and . . . What do you think?

PETER. I suppose it'd depend on the girl. Some girls, anything they do's wrong. But others . . . well . . . it wouldn't necessarily be wrong with them. [*The carillon starts to strike nine o'clock.*] I've always thought that when two people . . .

ANNE. Nine o'clock. I have to go.

PETER. That's right.

ANNE. [*Without moving*] Good night.

[*There is a second's pause, then PETER gets up and moves toward the door.*]

Cause and Effect
Based on Anne's comments, what effect is the war having on prewar attitudes?

Reading Check
How has Peter's view of Anne changed?

Character's Motivation
What causes Anne to want to share her diary with Peter?

PETER. You won't let them stop you coming?

ANNE. No. [*She rises and starts for the door.*] Sometimes I might bring my diary. There are so many things in it that I want to talk over with you. There's a lot about you.

PETER. What kind of things?

ANNE. I wouldn't want you to see some of it. I thought you were a nothing, just the way you thought about me.

PETER. Did you change your mind, the way I changed my mind about you?

ANNE. Well . . . You'll see . . .

[*For a second* ANNE *stands looking up at* PETER, *longing for him to kiss her. As he makes no move she turns away. Then suddenly* PETER *grabs her awkwardly in his arms, kissing her on the cheek.* ANNE *walks out dazed. She stands for a minute, her back to the people in the main room. As she regains her poise she goes to her mother and father and* MARGOT, *silently kissing them. They murmur their good nights to her. As she is about to open her bedroom door, she catches sight of* MRS. VAN DAAN. *She goes quickly to her, taking her face in her hands and kissing her first on one cheek and then on the other. Then she hurries off into her room.* MRS. VAN DAAN *looks after her, and then looks over at* PETER'S *room. Her suspicions are confirmed.*]

MRS. VAN DAAN. [*She knows.*] Ah hah!

[*The lights dim out. The curtain falls on the scene. In the darkness* ANNE'S VOICE *comes faintly at first and then with growing strength.*]

ANNE'S VOICE. By this time we all know each other so well that if anyone starts to tell a story, the rest can finish it for him. We're having to cut down still further on our meals. What makes it worse, the rats have been at work again. They've carried off some of our precious food. Even Mr. Dussel wishes now that Mouschi was here. Thursday, the twentieth of April, nineteen forty-four. Invasion fever is mounting every day. Miep tells us that people outside talk of nothing else. For myself, life has become much more pleasant. I often go to Peter's room after supper. Oh, don't think I'm in love, because I'm not. But it does make life more bearable to have someone with whom you can exchange views. No more tonight. P.S. . . . I must be honest. I must confess that I actually live for the next meeting. Is there anything lovelier than to sit under the skylight and feel the sun on your cheeks and have a darling boy in your arms? I admit now that I'm glad the Van Daans had a son and not a daughter. I've outgrown another dress. That's the third. I'm having to wear Margot's clothes after all. I'm working hard on my French and am now reading *La Belle Nivernaise*.[6]

[*As she is saying the last lines—the curtain rises on the scene. The lights dim on, as ANNE'S VOICE fades out.*]

Scene 3

[*It is night, a few weeks later. Everyone is in bed. There is complete quiet. In the* VAN DAANS' *room a match flares up for a moment and then is quickly put out.* MR. VAN DAAN, *in bare feet, dressed in underwear and trousers, is dimly seen coming stealthily down the stairs and into the main room, where* MR. *and* MRS. FRANK *and* MARGOT *are sleeping. He goes to the food safe and again lights a match. Then he cautiously opens the safe, taking out a half-loaf of bread. As he closes the safe, it creaks. He stands rigid.* MRS. FRANK *sits up in bed. She sees him.*]

MRS. FRANK. [*Screaming*] Otto! Otto! *Komme schnell!*[7]

[*The rest of the people wake, hurriedly getting up.*]

MR. FRANK. *Was ist los? Was ist passiert?*[8]

[DUSSEL, *followed by* ANNE, *comes from his room.*]

MRS. FRANK. [*As she rushes over to* MR. VAN DAAN] *Er stiehlt das Essen!*[9]

DUSSEL. [*Grabbing* MR. VAN DAAN] You! You! Give me that.

MRS. VAN DAAN. [*Coming down the stairs*] Putti . . . Putti . . . what is it?

Character's Motivation
Why is Mr. Van Daan being so cautious about making noise?

✓ Reading Check
Why does Mrs. Frank scream in the middle of the night?

---

6. *La Belle Nivernaise* story by Alphonse Daudet, a French author.
7. *Komme schnell!* (käm´ ə shnel) German for "Come quick!"
8. *Was ist los? Was ist passiert?* (väs ist los väs ist päs´ ērt) German for "What's the matter? What happened?"
9. *Er stiehlt das Essen!* (er stēlt däs es´ ən) German for "He steals food!"

DUSSEL. [*His hands on* VAN DAAN'S *neck*] You dirty thief . . . stealing food . . . you good-for-nothing . . .

MR. FRANK. Mr. Dussel! For God's sake! Help me, Peter!

[PETER *comes over, trying, with* MR. FRANK, *to separate the two struggling men.*]

PETER. Let him go! Let go!

[DUSSEL *drops* MR. VAN DAAN, *pushing him away. He shows them the end of a loaf of bread that he has taken from* VAN DAAN.]

DUSSEL. You greedy, selfish . . . !

[MARGOT *turns on the lights.*]

MRS. VAN DAAN. Putti . . . what is it?

[*All of* MRS. FRANK'S *gentleness, her self-control, is gone. She is outraged, in a frenzy of indignation.*]

MRS. FRANK. The bread! He was stealing the bread!

DUSSEL. It was you, and all the time we thought it was the rats!

MR. FRANK. Mr. Van Daan, how could you!

MR. VAN DAAN. I'm hungry.

MRS. FRANK. We're all of us hungry! I see the children getting thinner and thinner. Your own son Peter . . . I've heard him moan in his sleep, he's so hungry. And you come in the night and steal food that should go to them . . . to the children!

MRS. VAN DAAN. [*Going to* MR. VAN DAAN *protectively*] He needs more food than the rest of us. He's used to more. He's a big man.

[MR. VAN DAAN *breaks away, going over and sitting on the couch.*]

MRS. FRANK. [*Turning on* MRS. VAN DAAN] And you . . . you're worse than he is! You're a mother, and yet you sacrifice your child to this man . . . this . . . this . . .

MR. FRANK. Edith! Edith!

[MARGOT *picks up the pink woolen stole, putting it over her mother's shoulders.*]

MRS. FRANK. [*Paying no attention, going on to* MRS. VAN

ⓒ

Spiral Review

Conflict What long-simmering resentments does Mr. Van Daan's action bring out into the open?

DAAN] Don't think I haven't seen you! Always saving the choicest bits for him! I've watched you day after day and I've held my tongue. But not any longer! Not after this! Now I want him to go! I want him to get out of here!

[*Together*] {
MR. FRANK. Edith!

MR. VAN DAAN. Get out of here?

MRS. VAN DAAN. What do you mean?
}

MRS. FRANK. Just that! Take your things and get out!

MR. FRANK. [*To* MRS. FRANK] You're speaking in anger. You cannot mean what you are saying.

MRS. FRANK. I mean exactly that!

[MRS. VAN DAAN *takes a cover from the* FRANKS' *bed, pulling it about her.*]

MR. FRANK. For two long years we have lived here, side by side. We have respected each other's rights . . . we have managed to live in peace. Are we now going to throw it all away? I know this will never happen again, will it, Mr. Van Daan?

MR. VAN DAAN. No. No.

MRS. FRANK. He steals once! He'll steal again!

[MR. VAN DAAN, *holding his stomach, starts for the bathroom.* ANNE *puts her arms around him, helping him up the step.*]

MR. FRANK. Edith, please. Let us be calm. We'll all go to our rooms . . . and afterwards we'll sit down quietly and talk this out . . . we'll find some way . . .

MRS. FRANK. No! No! No more talk! I want them to leave!

MRS. VAN DAAN. You'd put us out, on the streets?

MRS. FRANK. There are other hiding places.

MRS. VAN DAAN. A cellar . . . a closet. I know. And we have no money left even to pay for that.

MRS. FRANK. I'll give you money. Out of my own pocket I'll give it gladly. [*She gets her purse from a shelf and comes back with it.*]

MRS. VAN DAAN. Mr. Frank, you told Putti you'd never forget what he'd done for you when you came to Amsterdam. You said you could never repay him, that you . . .

Cause and Effect
What causes Mr. Van Daan to steal food, and what is the effect of his actions on the others?

The bread!
He was stealing
the bread!

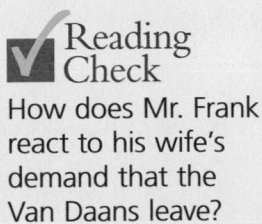

Reading
Check
How does Mr. Frank react to his wife's demand that the Van Daans leave?

The Diary of Anne Frank, Act II **943**

MRS. FRANK. [*Counting out money*] If my husband had any obligation to you, he's paid it, over and over.

MR. FRANK. Edith, I've never seen you like this before. I don't know you.

MRS. FRANK. I should have spoken out long ago.

DUSSEL. You can't be nice to some people.

MRS. VAN DAAN. [*Turning on* DUSSEL] There would have been plenty for all of us, if *you* hadn't come in here!

MR. FRANK. We don't need the Nazis to destroy us. We're destroying ourselves.

[*He sits down, with his head in his hands.* MRS. FRANK *goes to* MRS. VAN DAAN.]

MRS. FRANK. [*Giving* MRS. VAN DAAN *some money*] Give this to Miep. She'll find you a place.

ANNE. Mother, you're not putting Peter out. Peter hasn't done anything.

MRS. FRANK. He'll stay, of course. When I say I must protect the children, I mean Peter too.

[PETER *rises from the steps where he has been sitting.*]

PETER. I'd have to go if Father goes.

[MR. VAN DAAN *comes from the bathroom.* MRS. VAN DAAN *hurries to him and takes him to the couch. Then she gets water from the sink to bathe his face.*]

MRS. FRANK. [*While this is going on*] He's no father to you . . . that man! He doesn't know what it is to be a father!

PETER. [*Starting for his room*] I wouldn't feel right. I couldn't stay.

MRS. FRANK. Very well, then. I'm sorry.

ANNE. [*Rushing over to* PETER] No, Peter! No! [PETER *goes into his room, closing the door after him.* ANNE *turns back to her mother, crying.*] I don't care about the food. They can have mine! I don't want it! Only don't send them away. It'll be daylight soon. They'll be caught . . .

MARGOT. [*Putting her arms comfortingly around* ANNE] Please, Mother!

MRS. FRANK. They're not going now. They'll stay here until

Character's Motivation
What do Mr. Frank's lines show about his character and about what motivates him?

Character's Motivation
What do Peter's words reveal about how he feels about leaving?

Miep finds them a place. [*To* MRS. VAN DAAN] But one thing I insist on! He must never come down here again! He must never come to this room where the food is stored! We'll divide what we have . . . an equal share for each! [DUSSEL *hurries over to get a sack of potatoes from the food safe.* MRS. FRANK *goes on, to* MRS. VAN DAAN] You can cook it here and take it up to him.

[DUSSEL *brings the sack of potatoes back to the center table.*]

MARGOT. Oh, no. No. We haven't sunk so far that we're going to fight over a handful of rotten potatoes.

DUSSEL. [*Dividing the potatoes into piles*] Mrs. Frank, Mr. Frank, Margot, Anne, Peter, Mrs. Van Daan, Mr. Van Daan, myself . . . Mrs. Frank . . .

[*The buzzer sounds in* MIEP's *signal.*]

MR. FRANK. It's Miep! [*He hurries over, getting his overcoat and putting it on.*]

MARGOT. At this hour?

MRS. FRANK. It is trouble.

MR. FRANK. [*As he starts down to unbolt the door*] I beg you, don't let her see a thing like this!

MR. DUSSEL. [*Counting without stopping*] . . . Anne, Peter, Mrs. Van Daan, Mr. Van Daan, myself . . .

MARGOT. [*To* DUSSEL] Stop it! Stop it!

DUSSEL. . . . Mr. Frank, Margot, Anne, Peter, Mrs. Van Daan, Mr. Van Daan, myself, Mrs. Frank . . .

MRS. VAN DAAN. You're keeping the big ones for yourself! All the big ones . . . Look at the size of that! . . . And that! . . .

[DUSSEL *continues on with his dividing.* PETER, *with his shirt and trousers on, comes from his room.*]

MARGOT. Stop it! Stop it!

[*We hear* MIEP'S *excited voice speaking to* MR. FRANK *below.*]

MIEP. Mr. Frank . . . the most wonderful news! . . . The invasion has begun!

MR. FRANK. Go on, tell them! Tell them!

[MIEP *comes running up the steps ahead of* MR. FRANK. *She has a man's raincoat on over her nightclothes and a bunch of orange-colored flowers in her hand.*]

Cause and Effect
What effect does Mr. Van Daan's action have on the tensions among the characters?

Reading Check
Why does Dussel bring the sack of potatoes to the table?

MIEP. Did you hear that, everybody? Did you hear what I said? The invasion has begun! The invasion!

[*They all stare at* MIEP, *unable to grasp what she is telling them.* PETER *is the first to recover his wits.*]

PETER. Where?

MRS. VAN DAAN. When? When, Miep?

MIEP. It began early this morning . . .

[*As she talks on, the realization of what she has said begins to dawn on them. Everyone goes crazy. A wild demonstration takes place.* MRS. FRANK *hugs* MR. VAN DAAN.]

MRS. FRANK. Oh, Mr. Van Daan, did you hear that?

[DUSSEL *embraces* MRS. VAN DAAN. PETER *grabs a frying pan and parades around the room, beating on it, singing the Dutch National Anthem.* ANNE *and* MARGOT *follow him, singing, weaving in and out among the excited grown-ups.* MARGOT *breaks away to take the flowers from* MIEP *and distribute them to everyone. While this pandemonium is going on* MRS. FRANK *tries to make herself heard above the excitement.*]

MRS. FRANK. [*To* MIEP] How do you know?

MIEP. The radio . . . The B.B.C.![10] They said they landed on the coast of Normandy!

PETER. The British?

MIEP. British, Americans, French, Dutch, Poles, Norwegians . . . all of them! More than four thousand ships! Churchill spoke, and General Eisenhower! D-Day they call it!

MR. FRANK. Thank God, it's come!

MRS. VAN DAAN. At last!

MIEP. [*Starting out*] I'm going to tell Mr. Kraler. This'll be better than any blood transfusion.

MR. FRANK. [*Stopping her*] What part of Normandy did they land, did they say?

MIEP. Normandy . . . that's all I know now . . . I'll be up the minute I hear some more! [*She goes hurriedly out.*]

MR. FRANK. [*To* MRS. FRANK] What did I tell you? What did I tell you?

---

10. B.B.C. British Broadcasting System.

[MRS. FRANK *indicates that he has forgotten to bolt the door after* MIEP. *He hurries down the steps.* MR. VAN DAAN, *sitting on the couch, suddenly breaks into a convulsive[11] sob. Everybody looks at him, bewildered.*]

MRS. VAN DAAN. [*Hurrying to him*] Putti! Putti! What is it? What happened?

MR. VAN DAAN. Please, I'm so ashamed.

[MR. FRANK *comes back up the steps.*]

DUSSEL. Oh, for God's sake!

MRS. VAN DAAN. Don't, Putti.

MARGOT. It doesn't matter now!

MR. FRANK. [*Going to* MR. VAN DAAN] Didn't you hear what Miep said? The invasion has come! We're going to

✓ **Reading Check**

What are the details of the news that Miep brings?

---

11. convulsive (kən vul´ siv) *adj.* having an uncontrolled muscular spasm; shuddering.

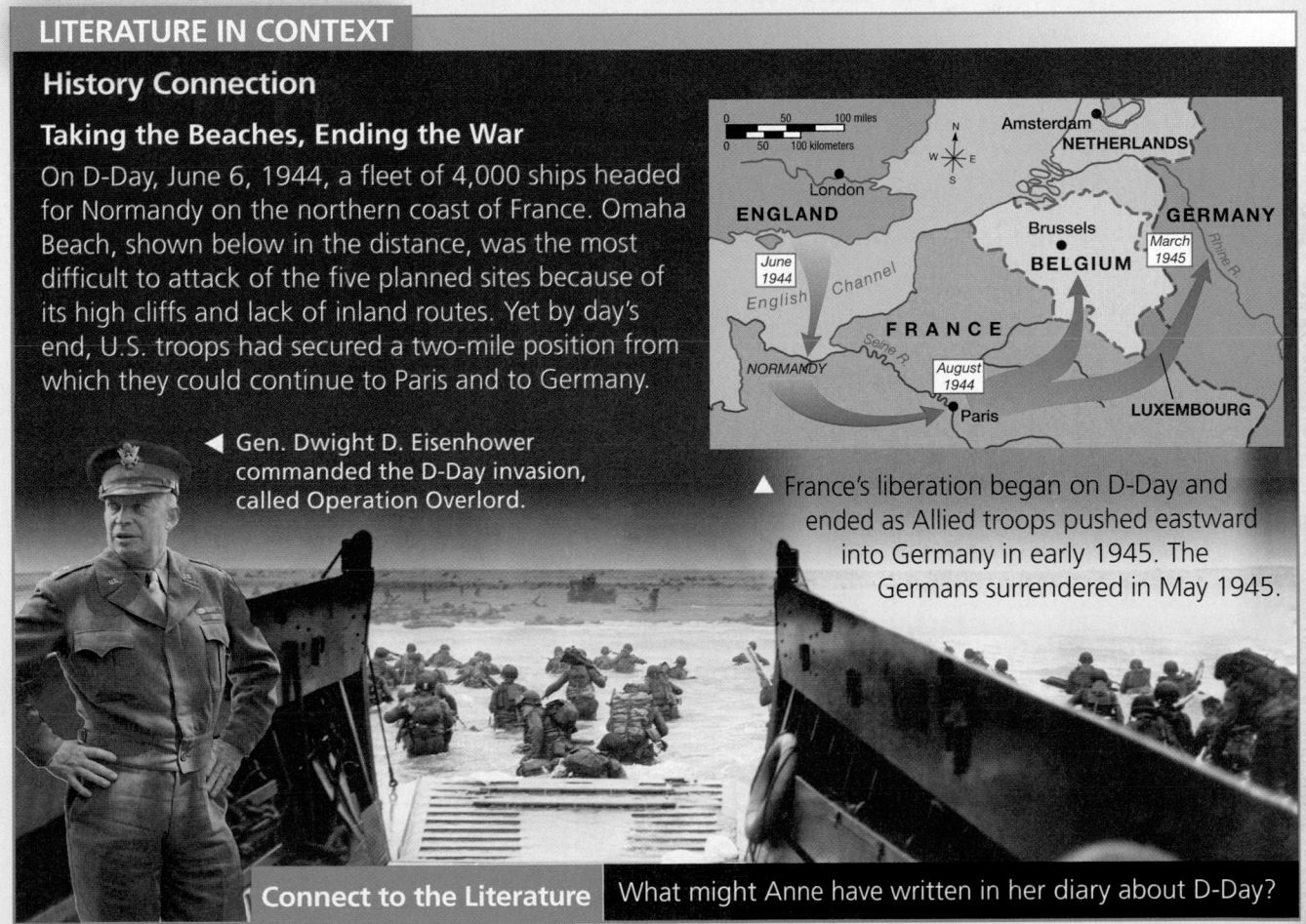

LITERATURE IN CONTEXT

History Connection

Taking the Beaches, Ending the War

On D-Day, June 6, 1944, a fleet of 4,000 ships headed for Normandy on the northern coast of France. Omaha Beach, shown below in the distance, was the most difficult to attack of the five planned sites because of its high cliffs and lack of inland routes. Yet by day's end, U.S. troops had secured a two-mile position from which they could continue to Paris and to Germany.

◄ Gen. Dwight D. Eisenhower commanded the D-Day invasion, called Operation Overlord.

▲ France's liberation began on D-Day and ended as Allied troops pushed eastward into Germany in early 1945. The Germans surrendered in May 1945.

Connect to the Literature What might Anne have written in her diary about D-Day?

The Diary of Anne Frank, Act II **947**

be liberated! This is a time to celebrate! [*He embraces* MRS. FRANK *and then hurries to the cupboard and gets the cognac and a glass.*]

MR. VAN DAAN. To steal bread from children!

MRS. FRANK. We've all done things that we're ashamed of.

ANNE. Look at me, the way I've treated Mother . . . so mean and horrid to her.

MRS. FRANK. No, Anneke, no.

[ANNE *runs to her mother, putting her arms around her.*]

ANNE. Oh, Mother, I was. I was awful.

MR. VAN DAAN. Not like me. No one is as bad as me!

DUSSEL. [*To* MR. VAN DAAN] Stop it now! Let's be happy!

MR. FRANK. [*Giving* MR. VAN DAAN *a glass of cognac*] Here! Here! *Schnapps! L'chaim!*[12]

[VAN DAAN *takes the cognac. They all watch him. He gives them a feeble smile.* ANNE *puts up her fingers in a V-for-Victory sign. As* VAN DAAN *gives an answering V-sign, they are startled to hear a loud sob from behind them. It is* MRS. FRANK, *stricken with remorse. She is sitting on the other side of the room.*]

MRS. FRANK. [*Through her sobs*] When I think of the terrible things I said . . .

[MR. FRANK, ANNE *and* MARGOT *hurry to her, trying to comfort her.* MR. VAN DAAN *brings her his glass of cognac.*]

MR. VAN DAAN. No! No! You were right!

MRS. FRANK. That I should speak that way to you! . . . Our friends! . . . Our guests! [*She starts to cry again.*]

DUSSEL. Stop it, you're spoiling the whole invasion!

[*As they are comforting her, the lights dim out. The curtain falls.*]

ANNE'S VOICE. [*Faintly at first and then with growing strength*] We're all in much better spirits these days. There's still excellent news of the invasion. The best part about it is that I have a feeling that friends are coming. Who knows? Maybe I'll be back in school by fall. Ha, ha! The joke is on us! The warehouse man doesn't know a thing and we are

---

12. *Schnapps!* (shnäps) German for "a drink." *L'chaim!* (lə khä´ yim) Hebrew toast meaning "To life!"

Character's Motivation
What drives Anne to admit that she has treated her mother badly?

paying him all that money! . . . Wednesday, the second of July, nineteen forty-four. The invasion seems temporarily to be bogged down. Mr. Kraler has to have an operation, which looks bad. The Gestapo have found the radio that was stolen. Mr. Dussel says they'll trace it back and back to the thief, and then, it's just a matter of time till they get to us. Everyone is low. Even poor Pim can't raise their spirits. I have often been downcast myself . . . but never in despair. I can shake off everything if I write. But . . . and that is the great question . . . will I ever be able to write well? I want to so much. I want to go on living even after my death. Another birthday has gone by, so now I am fifteen. Already I know what I want. I have a goal, an opinion.

[*As this is being said—the curtain rises on the scene, the lights dim on, and* ANNE'S VOICE *fades out.*]

Scene 4

[*It is an afternoon a few weeks later . . . Everyone but* MARGOT *is in the main room. There is a sense of great tension.*

Both MRS. FRANK *and* MR. VAN DAAN *are nervously pacing back and forth,* DUSSEL *is standing at the window, looking down fixedly at the street below.* PETER *is at the center table, trying to do his lessons.* ANNE *sits opposite him, writing in her diary.* MRS. VAN DAAN *is seated on the couch, her eyes on* MR. FRANK *as he sits reading.*

The sound of a telephone ringing comes from the office below. They all are rigid, listening tensely. DUSSEL *rushes down to* MR. FRANK.]

DUSSEL. There it goes again, the telephone! Mr. Frank, do you hear?

MR. FRANK. [*Quietly*] Yes. I hear.

DUSSEL. [*Pleading, insistent*] But this is the third time, Mr. Frank! The third time in quick succession! It's a signal! I tell you it's Miep, trying to get us! For some reason she can't come to us and she's trying to warn us of something!

MR. FRANK. Please. Please.

MR. VAN DAAN. [*To* DUSSEL] You're wasting your breath.

DUSSEL. Something has happened, Mr. Frank. For three days

> I have often
> been downcast
> myself... but
> never in despair.

Reading Check

What new goal does Anne set for herself?

The Diary of Anne Frank, Act II **949**

now Miep hasn't been to see us! And today not a man has come to work. There hasn't been a sound in the building!

MRS. FRANK. Perhaps it's Sunday. We may have lost track of the days.

MR. VAN DAAN. [*To* ANNE] You with the diary there. What day is it?

DUSSEL. [*Going to* MRS. FRANK] I don't lose track of the days! I know exactly what day it is! It's Friday, the fourth of August. Friday, and not a man at work. [*He rushes back to* MR. FRANK, *pleading with him, almost in tears.*] I tell you Mr. Kraler's dead. That's the only explanation. He's dead and they've closed down the building, and Miep's trying to tell us!

MR. FRANK. She'd never telephone us.

DUSSEL. [*Frantic*] Mr. Frank, answer that! I beg you, answer it!

MR. FRANK. No.

MR. VAN DAAN. Just pick it up and listen. You don't have to speak. Just listen and see if it's Miep.

DUSSEL. [*Speaking at the same time*] For God's sake . . . I ask you.

MR. FRANK. No. I've told you, no. I'll do nothing that might let anyone know we're in the building.

PETER. Mr. Frank's right.

MR. VAN DAAN. There's no need to tell us what side you're on.

MR. FRANK. If we wait patiently, quietly, I believe that help will come.

[*There is silence for a minute as they all listen to the telephone ringing.*]

DUSSEL. I'm going down.
[*He rushes down the steps.* MR. FRANK *tries ineffectually to hold him.* DUSSEL *runs to the lower door, unbolting it. The telephone stops ringing.* DUSSEL *bolts the door and comes slowly back up the steps.*] Too late.

[MR. FRANK *goes to* MARGOT *in* ANNE'S *bedroom.*]

MR. VAN DAAN. So we just wait here until we die.

MRS. VAN DAAN. [*Hysterically*] I can't stand it! I'll kill myself! I'll kill myself!

MR. VAN DAAN. For God's sake, stop it!

Vocabulary
ineffectually
(in´ e fek´ chōō ə lē)
adv. without producing the desired results

[*In the distance, a German military band is heard playing a Viennese waltz.*]

MRS. VAN DAAN. I think you'd be glad if I did! I think you want me to die!

MR. VAN DAAN. Whose fault is it we're here?

[MRS. VAN DAAN *starts for her room. He follows, talking at her.* We could've been safe somewhere . . . in America or Switzerland. But no! No! You wouldn't leave when I wanted to. You couldn't leave your things. You couldn't leave your precious furniture.

MRS. VAN DAAN. Don't touch me!

[*She hurries up the stairs, followed by* MR. VAN DAAN. PETER, *unable to bear it, goes to his room.* ANNE *looks after him, deeply concerned.* DUSSEL *returns to his post at the window.* MR. FRANK *comes back into the main room and takes a book, trying to read.* MRS. FRANK *sits near the sink, starting to peel some potatoes.* ANNE *quietly goes to* PETER'S *room, closing the door after her.* PETER *is lying face down on the cot.* ANNE *leans over him, holding him in her arms, trying to bring him out of his despair.*]

ANNE. Look, Peter, the sky. [*She looks up through the skylight.*] What a lovely, lovely day! Aren't the clouds beautiful? You know what I do when it seems as if I couldn't stand being cooped up for one more minute? I think myself out. I think myself on a walk in the park where I used to go with Pim. Where the jonquils and the crocus and the violets grow down the slopes. You know the most wonderful part about *thinking* yourself out? You can have it any way you like. You can have roses and violets and chrysanthemums all blooming at the same time . . . It's funny . . . I used to take it all for granted . . . and now I've gone crazy about everything to do with nature. Haven't you?

Cause and Effect
What effect has Mrs. Van Daan's love of expensive objects had on the family, according to Mr. Van Daan?

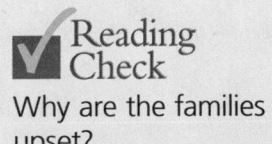

Why are the families upset?

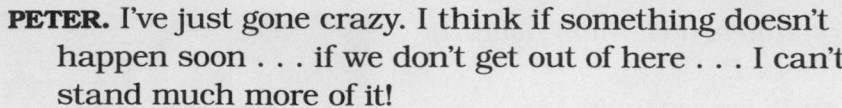

PETER. I've just gone crazy. I think if something doesn't happen soon . . . if we don't get out of here . . . I can't stand much more of it!

ANNE. [*Softly*] I wish you had a religion, Peter.

PETER. No, thanks! Not me!

ANNE. Oh, I don't mean you have to be Orthodox[13] . . . or believe in heaven and hell and purgatory[14] and things . . . I just mean some religion . . . it doesn't matter what. Just to believe in something! When I think of all that's out there . . . the trees . . . and flowers . . . and seagulls . . . when I think of the dearness of you, Peter . . . and the goodness of the people we know . . . Mr. Kraler, Miep, Dirk, the vegetable man, all risking their lives for us every day . . . When I think of these good things, I'm not afraid any more . . . I find myself, and God, and I . . .

[PETER *interrupts, getting up and walking away.*]

PETER. That's fine! But when I begin to think, I get mad! Look at us, hiding out for two years. Not able to move! Caught here like . . . waiting for them to come and get us . . . and all for what?

ANNE. We're not the only people that've had to suffer. There've always been people that've had to . . . sometimes one race . . . sometimes another . . . and yet . . .

PETER. That doesn't make me feel any better!

ANNE. [*Going to him*] I know it's terrible, trying to have any faith . . . when people are doing such horrible . . . But you know what I sometimes think? I think the world may be going through a phase, the way I was with Mother. It'll pass, maybe not for hundreds of years, but some day . . . I still believe, in spite of everything, that people are really good at heart.

PETER. I want to see something now . . . Not a thousand years from now! [*He goes over, sitting down again on the cot.*]

Cause and Effect
How do Anne's religious beliefs affect her ability to cope with a life in hiding?

▼ From the attic window, Anne and Peter could see the rooftops of Amsterdam and the neighboring Westertoren bell tower.

---

13. **Orthodox** (ôr´ thə däks´) *adj.* strictly observing the rites and traditions of Judaism.
14. **purgatory** (pʉr´gə tôr´ ē) *n.* state or place of temporary punishment.

ANNE. But, Peter, if you'd only look at it as part of a great pattern . . . that we're just a little minute in the life . . . [*She breaks off.*] Listen to us, going at each other like a couple of stupid grownups! Look at the sky now. Isn't it lovely?

[*She holds out her hand to him. PETER takes it and rises, standing with her at the window looking out, his arms around her.*]

Some day, when we're outside again, I'm going to . . .

[*She breaks off as she hears the sound of a car, its brakes squealing as it comes to a sudden stop. The people in the other rooms also become aware of the sound. They listen tensely. Another car roars up to a screeching stop. ANNE and PETER come from PETER'S room. MR. and MRS. VAN DAAN creep down the stairs. DUSSEL comes out from his room. Everyone is listening, hardly breathing. A doorbell clangs again and again in the building below. MR. FRANK starts quietly down the steps to the door. DUSSEL and PETER follow him. The others stand rigid, waiting, terrified.*

In a few seconds DUSSEL comes stumbling back up the steps. He shakes off PETER's help and goes to his room. MR. FRANK bolts the door below, and comes slowly back up the steps. Their eyes are all on him as he stands there for a minute. They realize that what they feared has happened. MRS. VAN DAAN starts to whimper. MR. VAN DAAN puts her gently in a chair, and then hurries off up the stairs to their room to collect their things. PETER goes to comfort his mother. There is a sound of violent pounding on a door below.]

Character's Motivations What causes this sudden change in the characters' actions and mood?

MR. FRANK. [*Quietly*] For the past two years we have lived in fear. Now we can live in hope.

[*The pounding below becomes more insistent. There are muffled sounds of voices, shouting commands.*]

MEN'S VOICES. *Auf machen! Da drinnen! Auf machen! Schnell! Schnell! Schnell!*[15] etc., etc.

[*The street door below is forced open. We hear the heavy tread of footsteps coming up. MR. FRANK gets two school bags from the shelves, and gives one to ANNE and the other to MARGOT. He goes to get a bag for MRS. FRANK. The sound of feet coming up grows louder. PETER comes to ANNE, kissing her good-*

Reading Check How does Anne seek to comfort Peter?

---

15. ***Auf machen! . . . Schnell!*** German for "Open up, you in there, open up, quick, quick, quick."

▲ **Critical Viewing**
What does this museum re-creation of her writing space tell you about Anne Frank and her experience in hiding? **[Analyze]**

bye, then he goes to his room to collect his things. The buzzer of their door starts to ring. MR. FRANK *brings* MRS. FRANK *a bag. They stand together, waiting. We hear the thud of gun butts on the door, trying to break it down.*

ANNE *stands, holding her school satchel, looking over at her father and mother with a soft, reassuring smile. She is no longer a child, but a woman with courage to meet whatever lies ahead.*

The lights dim out. The curtain falls on the scene. We hear a mighty crash as the door is shattered. After a second ANNE'S VOICE *is heard.*]

Character's Motivation
Why does Anne leave her diary behind?

ANNE'S VOICE. And so it seems our stay here is over. They are waiting for us now. They've allowed us five minutes to get our things. We can each take a bag and whatever it will hold of clothing. Nothing else. So, dear Diary, that means I must leave you behind. Good-bye for a while. P.S. Please, please, Miep, or Mr. Kraler, or anyone else. If you should find this diary, will you please keep it safe for me, because some day I hope . . .

[*Her voice stops abruptly. There is silence. After a second the curtain rises.*]

Scene 5

[*It is again the afternoon in November, 1945. The rooms are as we saw them in the first scene. MR. KRALER has joined MIEP and MR. FRANK. There are coffee cups on the table. We see a great change in MR. FRANK. He is calm now. His bitterness is gone. He slowly turns a few pages of the diary. They are blank.*]

MR. FRANK. No more. [*He closes the diary and puts it down on the couch beside him.*]

MIEP. I'd gone to the country to find food. When I got back the block was surrounded by police . . .

MR. KRALER. We made it our business to learn how they knew. It was the thief . . . the thief who told them.

[MIEP *goes up to the gas burner, bringing back a pot of coffee.*]

MR. FRANK. [*After a pause*] It seems strange to say this, that anyone could be happy in a concentration camp. But Anne was happy in the camp in Holland where they first took us. After two years of being shut up in these rooms, she could be out . . . out in the sunshine and the fresh air that she loved.

MIEP. [*Offering the coffee to* MR. FRANK] A little more?

MR. FRANK. [*Holding out his cup to her*] The news of the war was good. The British and Americans were sweeping through France. We felt sure that they would get to us in time. In September we were told that we were to be shipped to Poland . . . The men to one camp. The women to another. I was sent to Auschwitz.[16] They went to Belsen.[17] In January we were freed, the few of us who were left. The war wasn't yet over, so it took us a long time to get home. We'd be sent here and there behind the lines where we'd be safe. Each time our train would stop . . . at a siding, or a crossing . . . we'd all get out and go from group to group . . . Where were you? Were you at Belsen? At Buchenwald?[18] At Mauthausen? Is it possible that you knew my wife? Did you ever see my husband? My son? My daughter?

▼ **Critical Viewing**
This is a 1979 German stamp. What changes after the war might make the German government decide to honor Anne? **[Infer]**

DEUTSCHE BUNDESPOST
60
ANNE FRANK · 12.6.1929 · 31.3.1945
1979

✓ Reading Check
Where were the families sent after they were picked up by the police?

---

16. **Auschwitz** (oush′ vits′) Nazi concentration camp in Poland that was well known as a death camp.
17. **Belsen** (bel′ zən) village in Germany that, with the village of Bergen, was the site of Bergen-Belsen, a Nazi concentration camp.

That's how I found out about my wife's death . . . of Margot, the Van Daans . . . Dussel. But Anne . . . I still hoped . . . Yesterday I went to Rotterdam. I'd heard of a woman there . . . She'd been in Belsen with Anne . . . I know now.

[*He picks up the diary again, and turns the pages back to find a certain passage. As he finds it we hear* ANNE'S VOICE.]

ANNE'S VOICE. In spite of everything, I still believe that people are really good at heart. [MR. FRANK *slowly closes the diary.*]

MR. FRANK. She puts me to shame.

[*They are silent.*]

▲ Otto visits children in Dusseldorf where a new school, the Anne Frank School, would be built.

18. **Buchenwald** (bōō′ ken wôld′) Nazi concentration camp in central Germany.

Critical Thinking

© 1. **Key Ideas and Details (a)** What disturbing news does Mr. Kraler bring on New Year's Day? **(b) Connect:** What hint does this give about the ending of the play?

© 2. **Key Ideas and Details (a)** What is the time span of Act II? **(b) Interpret:** How have the characters changed since the end of Act I? **(c) Support:** How do you know that Anne has changed?

© 3. **Integration of Knowledge and Ideas (a)** How was Anne able to preserve her dignity despite her suffering? **(b)** From Anne's statements in Act II, do you think that she believed that differences—or similarities—matter most? Explain, using examples. **(c)** What does Mr. Frank mean when he says of Anne: "She puts me to shame"? [*Connect to the Big Question: Is it our differences or our similarities that matter most?*]

Cite textual evidence to support your responses.

Reading Skill: Cause and Effect

1. For each of these events, identify one **cause** and one **effect**: **(a)** Mr. Van Daan's decision to steal food. **(b)** Mrs. Frank's change of heart about wanting the Van Daans to leave.

2. What are some possible causes of Mrs. Van Daan's attitude toward Anne and Peter's relationship?

3. Living in close quarters has multiple effects on the people in the attic. List three effects that result from this single cause.

Literary Skill: Character's Motivation

4. **Key Ideas and Details** On a chart like the one shown, identify the possible **motivation** behind the actions listed.

Character	Action	Motivation
Miep	Brings flowers and cake	
Mr. Van Daan	Breaks into tears	
Peter Van Daan	Offers to leave	

5. **Key Ideas and Details** What possible motivations might an informer have for telling the authorities about the families in hiding?

6. **Craft and Structure** Give three examples of how the setting affects the characters and their actions.

Vocabulary

Acquisition and Use Write a sentence for each item, using the words correctly.

1. inarticulate, candidate
2. apprehension, unknown
3. intuition, marry
4. ineffectually, weaker
5. blackmail, police
6. forlorn, rescue

Word Study Use the context of the sentences and what you know about the **Latin prefix in-** to explain your answer to each question.

1. What is one effect of an ear *infection*?
2. What happens to your lungs when you *inhale* deeply?

Word Study

The **Latin prefix in-** can mean "into" or "within."

Apply It Explain how the prefix *in-* contributes to the meanings of these words. Consult a dictionary if necessary.

incision
inclusion
inherent

Integrated Language Skills

The Diary of Anne Frank, Act II

Conventions: Clauses

A **clause** is a group of words with its own subject and verb.

There are two basic types of clauses:

- An **independent clause** has a subject and a verb, and it can stand by itself as a complete sentence.

- A **subordinate clause,** or **dependent clause,** has a subject and a verb but cannot stand by itself as a complete sentence. Subordinate clauses begin with subordinating conjunctions such as *although, if, when, while,* and *after*.

This chart shows both types of clauses. Subjects have a single underline; verbs have a double underline.

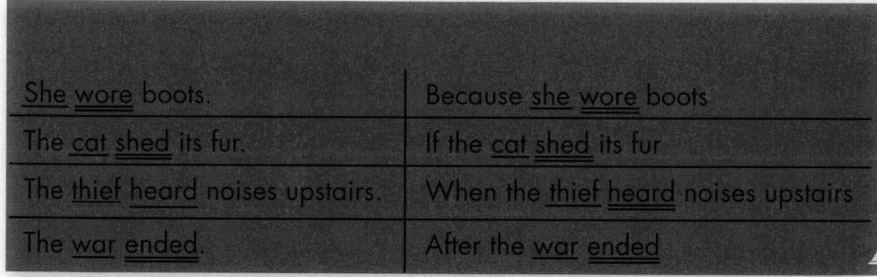

She wore boots.	Because she wore boots
The cat shed its fur.	If the cat shed its fur
The thief heard noises upstairs.	When the thief heard noises upstairs
The war ended.	After the war ended

Practice A Identify the independent clauses and subordinate clauses.

1. When Miep visited, she brought a cake.
2. As the scene continued, Anne and Peter prepared for their date.
3. Anne and Peter closed the door so they could have some privacy.
4. Mr. Frank hoped for liberation after the Allies landed.

© **Reading Application** In *The Diary of Anne Frank,* Act II, find two sentences that have an independent clause and a subordinate clause.

Practice B Identify each clause as independent or subordinate. For subordinate clauses, add independent clauses to make complete sentences.

1. Anne tried various hair styles
2. As Mrs. Van Daan objected
3. Mr. Van Daan was stealing the bread
4. When the car came to a stop

© **Writing Application** Use the following italicized words to write subordinate clauses about *The Diary of Anne Frank,* Act II: *although, after, when, since.* Then, add independent clauses to complete each sentence.

PH WRITING COACH | Further instruction and practice are available in *Prentice Hall Writing Coach.*

Writing

Common Core State Standards

L.8.1; RL.8.7; W.8.2, W.8.4, W.8.7; SL.8.1
[For the full wording of the standards, see page 916.]

Informative Text In preparation for writing a **film review,** watch a film version of *The Diary of Anne Frank.* As you view, use these questions to guide your note-taking:

- How do key scenes in the film compare to those in the written version? If scenes are changed or left out, how do these changes affect the film overall?

- Do the actors make good choices in their portrayals of characters, or do they not live up to your expectations? Why?

- What choices does the director make in sets, music, and camerawork? Do these choices enhance or distract from the mood of each scene?

After viewing, use your notes to draft your review. Be sure to highlight the differences between the filmed and the written versions, and explain which one you thought was more effective.

Grammar Application Your film review should be concise. Edit your writing to eliminate wordiness and repetition.

Writing Workshop: *Work in Progress*

Prewriting for Exposition Refer to the Questions List you generated earlier. Choose one question to develop. Write a *hypothesis*, or educated idea about the answer to this question, as a start to your research. Save this Research Hypothesis in your writing portfolio.

Use this prewriting activity to prepare for the **Writing Workshop** on page 982.

Research and Technology

With a group, create a **bulletin board display** about the experiences of Jewish individuals or communities living under Nazi occupation during World War II. Follow these steps:

- As a group, decide the **audience and purpose** for the display. Use this information to focus your research.

- Begin by drafting a list of specific **research questions.** As you research, refine these questions and ask additional ones.

- Identify **primary sources,** such as photographs, diaries, documents, and letters; and **secondary sources,** such as encyclopedia articles, textbooks, books by historians, and Web pages. Plan to include **attribution** of your sources in captions in your display.

- **Draw conclusions** from the information you have gathered about the experience of living under occupation. Print these as **short summaries** to include in the display, along with **charts, quotations, maps, graphs, drawings, and photographs.**

www.PHLitOnline.com
- Interactive graphic organizers
- Grammar tutorial
- Interactive journals

Test Practice: Reading

Cause and Effect

Fiction Selection

Directions: *Read the selection. Then, answer the questions.*

All over the news, reporters were covering the progress of a storm that was developing just to the east. Weather warnings are usual here, since we are so close to the ocean. Most of the times, they are just that, a warning. But when the reporters' tone grew serious, my parents began to worry. Rain, hail, and strong wind gusts were expected to arrive in only a few hours. The sky was already a dark gray. When the rain started to fall, we expected the winds to follow. Soon, the power went out as strong winds tore through trees. My favorite birch tree in the back yard fell with a deafening crack. The rain fell hard against the windows. Soon all you could hear was the storm and all I could do was try to sleep.

In the morning, when I woke up, I saw what the storm had caused. Our back yard was flooded. Luckily, our house suffered no damage and we were safe.

1. What caused the narrator's parents to worry?
- **A.** the power went out
- **B.** the serious tone of the reporters
- **C.** a tree fell
- **D.** the weather warning

2. What effect did the rain have?
- **A.** the yard flooded
- **B.** a car crashed
- **C.** heavy winds developed
- **D.** the warning sirens sounded

3. What caused the birch tree to fall down?
- **A.** the hail
- **B.** the strong winds
- **C.** the heavy rains
- **D.** the dark gray clouds

4. Which of the following actions is the family likely to take as a result of the storm?
- **A.** They will move to a new home.
- **B.** They will replace broken windows.
- **C.** They will remove the fallen tree.
- **D.** They will waterproof their house.

Writing for Assessment

In a few sentences, explain the effects of the storm on the narrator. Use details from the passage to support each effect.

Nonfiction Selection

Directions: *Read the selection. Then, answer the questions.*

The Great Hurricane of 1938 hit Long Island, New York, surprising the National Weather Service and residents. First rated as a Category 5 hurricane, the highest possible, the storm was supposed to taper off as it traveled north. A hurricane is propelled by warm water, and as soon as it hits land or cooler waters a hurricane should lose speed and strength. But before New England waters could cool the coming storm, the Great Hurricane of 1938 arrived, traveling at an extremely unusual 70 mph. The eye of the storm measured 50 miles across and the hurricane itself was 500 miles wide. The storm hit an unprepared Long Island, leaving in its wake unimaginable damage to homes, businesses, and lives. Surging water destroyed a barrier island, creating Shinnecock Inlet. The hurricane's force even moved large amounts of sand, bridging the gap between the former island of Cedar Point and the mainland.

1. According to the selection, what causes a hurricane to lose speed?
A. when the eye of the storm decreases
B. when the hurricane travels north
C. when it has traveled so many miles
D. when the storm hits cooler waters

2. What effect did the hurricane have on Cedar Point?
A. Cedar Point became an island.
B. Cedar Point became connected to Long Island.
C. Cedar Point was completely destroyed.
D. Cedar Point became submerged under water.

3. Why were so many people in Long Island unprepared for the storm?
A. The storm was expected to slow down and lose strength before it arrived.
B. In 1938, there was little knowledge of hurricanes, so there were no warnings.
C. The storm was expected to move east.
D. The National Weather Service was not tracking the storm.

4. According to the passage, what effect did surging waters have?
A. Surging waters created an island.
B. Surging waters caused the hurricane to speed up.
C. Surging waters sank boats.
D. Surging waters created an inlet.

Writing for Assessment

Connecting Across Texts
In an essay, explain what effects the Great Hurricane of 1938 may have had on the people in Long Island. Use details from both passages to support your response.

www.PHLitOnline.com
- Online practice
- Instant feedback

Reading for Information

Analyzing Expository Texts

Web Site

News Release

 **Common Core State Standards**

Reading Informational Text
5. Analyze in detail the structure of a specific paragraph in a text, including the role of particular sentences in developing and refining a key concept.

Language
4. Determine or clarify the meaning of unknown and multiple-meaning words or phrases, choosing flexibly from a range of strategies.
6. Acquire and use accurately grade-appropriate general academic and domain-specific words and phrases; gather vocabulary knowledge when considering a word or phrase important to comprehension or expression.

Reading Skill: Evaluate Unity and Coherence

When you **evaluate** a text for **unity and coherence,** you examine it for a **consistent** point of view and **logical** structure. Within paragraphs, sentences should build meaning in an organized and logical way. Paragraphs should then build coherent meaning in the work as a whole.

Begin to evaluate unity and coherence by examining details, noting how they are arranged and whether the arrangement makes sense. Next, determine if the details build logically on one another and support the main idea. After evaluating all of the details, consider the text as a whole and decide whether the writer has effectively used the details, sentences, and paragraphs to communicate a clear main idea.

Checklist for Evaluating a Text

- ❑ At every level of the text, do details all relate to the main idea?
- ❑ Do sentences, paragraphs, and graphic elements flow in a logical sequence?
- ❑ Is information clear, consistent, and logical?
- ❑ Does the author provide reliable facts, statistics, or quotations to support main points?

Content-Area Vocabulary

These words appear in the selections that follow. You may also encounter them in other content-area texts.

- **exhibit** (eg zib´ it) *n.* display of art or other objects
- **archive** (är´ kīv) *n.* place where public records or historical documents are kept

EDUCATION EVENTS EXHIBITIONS GET INVOLVED PRESS ROOM VISITOR INFORMATION

VISITOR INFORMATION

The home page provides an organized, logical list of topics covered by the Web site.

The topic of the text is introduced under the first heading and carried throughout the text.

About the Museum

Founders Walter and Edie Loebenberg

Mission

The Florida Holocaust Museum honors the memory of millions of innocent men, women, and children who suffered or died in the Holocaust. The Museum is dedicated to teaching members of all races and cultures to recognize the inherent worth and dignity of human life in order to prevent future genocides.

History

One of the largest Holocaust museums in the country, the Florida Holocaust Museum is the result of St. Petersburg businessman and philanthropist Walter P. Loebenberg's remarkable journey and vision. He escaped Nazi Germany in 1939 and served in the United States Army during WWII. Together, with a group of local businessmen and community leaders, the concept of a living memorial to those who suffered and perished was conceived. Among the participating individuals were survivors of the Holocaust and individuals who lost relatives, as well as those who had no personal investment, other than wanting to ensure that such atrocities could never again happen to any group of people.

To this end, the group enlisted the support of others in the community and were able to involve internationally renowned Holocaust scholars. Thomas Keneally, author of *Schindler's List*, joined the Board of Advisors and Elie Weisel was named Honorary Chairman of this Holocaust Center.

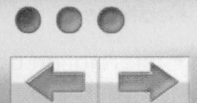

In 1992, the Museum rented a space it could afford, but would soon outgrow, on the grounds of the Jewish Community Center of Pinellas County in Madeira Beach, Florida, tucked away from the main-stream of Tampa Bay life. Starting with only one staff member and a small group of dedicated volunteers, it quickly surpassed all expectations.

Within the first month, over 24,000 visitors came to see *Anne Frank in the World*, the Center's inaugural **exhibit**. The Tampa Bay showing of this exhibition—which traces a young Jewish girl's journey from a complacent child-hood in pre-World War II Holland, through her early teens hiding from the Nazis, to her death at Bergen-Belsen—poignantly touched all visitors.

A painting from the exhibition *The Holocaust Through Czech Children's Eyes*

During the next five years, the new Holocaust Center greeted more than 125,000 visitors to view interna-tionally acclaimed exhibits. Thousands more participated in lectures, seminars and commemorative events at the Center, which now reached directly into schools in an eight county area surrounding Tampa Bay with study guides, teacher training programs, and presen-tations by Center staff and Holocaust survivors.

The Center expanded to encompass a growing print and audio-visual library, a photographic **archive**, a repository for historic artifacts, and a research facility for educators and scholars—all of this crowded into a 4,000 square foot facility that was not designed for museum or educational purposes. . . .

FLORIDA HOLOCAUST MUSEUM

> The main idea of the text is presented here.

Local Holocaust Survivors And Liberators Attend Opening Event For Exhibition

FOR IMMEDIATE RELEASE
July 12, 2006
Contact: Andrea Moore, PR Coordinator

> The facts presented in the opening paragraphs are unified—they answer the questions *Who?*, *What?*, *Where?*, and *When?*

St. Petersburg, FL The Florida Holocaust Museum will honor Holocaust survivors and liberators at the opening event for the photography exhibitions *Fragments: Portraits of Survivors* by Jason Schwartz and *Liberators: Unexpected Outcomes* by Coe Arthur Younger. The reception will take place Thursday, July 13th at 5 pm and will be held at the Museum.

Courtesy of the Florida Holocaust Museum

Both exhibitions will run through October 22. Many of the survivors and liberators featured in the exhibitions, as well as Coe Arthur Younger, photographer of the liberators exhibition, will be in attendance at the event.

Fragments: Portraits of Survivors features one hundred-twelve (112) 16 x 20 black and white photographs of local Holocaust survivors. Accompanying each portrait is a handwritten statement from the survivor in the photo. "I survived . . . I beat Hitler" is just one statement of many that quietly communicates the importance of this exhibition and its power to speak to all generations. The pictures and thoughts tell of the trials and triumphs of these extraordinary men and women survivors who bravely tell their stories as first-hand testimonies of a tragic time during the 20th century. Their memories give a voice to the voiceless.

Courtesy of the Florida Holocaust Museum, copyright Coe Arthur Younger

A photograph from the exhibition *Liberators: Unexpected Outcomes*

This paragraph gives details about the second of the two exhibits, *Liberators: Unexpected Outcomes*.

The black and white photographs of the liberators tell a different story. *Liberators: Unexpected Outcomes* features 18 photographs of local U.S. troops who, as first responders and liberators at the end of WWII, witnessed the horrors behind camp gates. Without preparation or warning, these men happened upon unexpected and unimaginable scenes during regular military operations. Their stories are featured in photography by Coe Arthur Younger, as well as in an accompanying video that highlights the testimonies of several local liberators and survivors.

This paragraph sums up the organization's mission.

The Florida Holocaust Museum honors the memory of millions of innocent men, women, and children who suffered or died in the Holocaust. The Museum is dedicated to teaching members of all races and cultures to recognize the inherent worth and dignity of human life in order to prevent future genocides.

Comparing Expository Texts

© 1. Craft and Structure Compare and contrast the **coherence** of the Web site and news release. **(a)** How would you **evaluate** the **logic** and **consistency** of the texts? **(b)** Does one informational text have a better sense of **unity** than the other? Explain.

Content-Area Vocabulary

2. (a) Review the definitions of *exhibit* and *archive*. **(b)** Then, use both words in a sentence about a school field trip to a museum.

⏱ Timed Writing

Explanatory Text: Evaluation

> **Format**
> The prompt gives clues about what to write and suggests where to look for the information you need.

Write an essay that evaluates the coherence of the news release. Analyze whether details are presented in a logical, consistent order. Then, evaluate the success of the news release in communicating one main idea about the photography exhibits. Use examples from the text to support your evaluation. (45 minutes)

> **Academic Vocabulary**
> When you *analyze* a text, you closely examine its details and organization. When you *evaluate* a text, you judge its effectiveness.

5-Minute Planner

Complete these steps before you begin to write:

1. Read the prompt carefully. Look for key words, such as those that are highlighted, that will help you understand the assignment.

2. Reread the selection carefully. Pay attention to important details.

3. As you read, take notes about the photography exhibits.

4. Think about whether the details are in a logical order and whether the news release communicates its main idea successfully. Jot down notes about your ideas.

5. Refer to your notes as you write your evaluation.

Comparing Sources With a Dramatization

When Anne Frank's diary was published, it inspired Albert Hackett and Frances Goodrich to develop Anne's private thoughts into a play. To do this, they drew on these different types of sources:

- **Primary sources** are firsthand accounts that describe or document events that take place at the time of the writing. Primary sources often directly convey the author's point of view. Primary sources include letters, diaries, and legal documents.

- **Secondary sources** interpret information from primary sources. Secondary sources include biographies, magazine articles, journals, encyclopedias, and textbooks.

The Diary of Anne Frank is a **dramatization,** a play that has been adapted from another work. When playwrights dramatize a primary source, such as a diary, they may also draw on other sources to add information not known by the original author. In addition, they might choose to fictionalize aspects of certain events for dramatic effect.

As you read excerpts from Anne's diary and Miep Gies's memoir, *Anne Frank Remembered,* compare the information they contain with the type of information presented in the play. Look for details in the text that suggest the author's opinions and attitudes. Use a chart like this one to help you compare the two selections.

Common Core State Standards

Reading Informational Text
6. Determine an author's point of view or purpose in a text.

Writing
9. Draw evidence from literary or informational texts to support analysis, reflection, and research. *(Timed Writing)*

Selections	Comparisons
The Diary of Anne Frank (the play)	
Anne Frank: Diary of a Young Girl (diary)	Reveals Anne's thoughts directly
Anne Frank Remembered (memoir)	

www.PHLitOnline.com

- Vocabulary flashcards
- Interactive journals
- More about the authors
- Selection audio
- Interactive graphic organizers

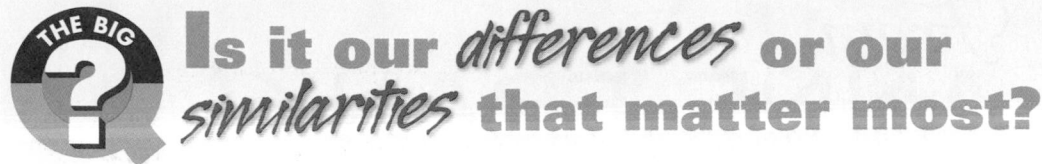

Is it our *differences* or our *similarities* that matter most?

Writing About the Big Question

Both of these selections report the suffering that Anne Frank and her family endured because of their religious background. Use this sentence to develop your ideas about the Big Question:

When authorities try to **discriminate** against others on the basis of race or religion, people can resist by _____.

Meet the Authors

Anne Frank (1929–1945)

Author of *Anne Frank: The Diary of a Young Girl*

More than sixty years after her death, Anne Frank remains the world's best-known victim of the Holocaust. The tragedy of her death is made even more moving by the existence of her diary, a personal and revealing look into a life cut short.

The Diary At first, Anne's father Otto was reluctant to publish Anne's private thoughts, but eventually he overcame his doubts. The book quickly became a best-seller. Anne's diary enabled people to put a human face—the face of an ordinary teenage girl—on a tragedy that had been too enormous to grasp.

Miep Gies (1909–2010)

Author of *Anne Frank Remembered*

Miep Gies was born in Vienna, Austria. In 1922, she moved to Amsterdam and got a job working for Otto Frank. When the Franks were forced into hiding in 1942, Gies immediately offered her support. Despite her efforts, the Franks were discovered and sent to concentration camps after two years in hiding.

An Unsung Hero Miep Gies did not see herself as unusually brave. She said, "I am not a hero. I stand at the end of a long, long line of good Dutch people who did what I did or more—much more—during those dark and terrible times years ago . . ."

From ANNE FRANK: *The* Diary *of a* Young Girl

Saturday, 20 June, 1942

◄ **Critical Viewing**
What value do war-time diaries, such as Anne's, have for readers today? **[Analyze]**

. . . There is a saying that "paper is more patient than man"; it came back to me on one of my slightly melancholy days, while I sat chin in hand, feeling too bored and limp even to make up my mind whether to go out or stay at home. Yes, there is no doubt that paper is patient and as I don't intend to show this cardboard-covered notebook, bearing the proud name of "diary," to anyone, unless I find a real friend, boy or girl, probably nobody cares. And now I come to the root of the matter, the reason for my starting a diary: it is that I have no such real friend.

Let me put it more clearly, since no one will believe that a girl of thirteen feels herself quite alone in the world, nor is it so. I have darling parents and a sister of sixteen. I know about thirty people whom one might call friends—I have strings of boy friends, anxious to catch a glimpse of me and who, failing that, peep at me through mirrors in class. I have relations, aunts and uncles, who are darlings too, a good home, no—I don't seem to lack anything. But it's the same with all my friends, just fun and joking, nothing more. I can never bring myself to talk of anything outside the common round. We don't seem to be able to get any closer, that is the root of the trouble. Perhaps I lack confidence, but anyway, there it is, a stubborn fact and I don't seem to be able to do anything about it.

Sources
What information in this paragraph would be hard to show in a dramatization?

Hence, this diary. In order to enhance in my mind's eye the picture of the friend for whom I have waited so long, I don't want to set down a series of bald facts in a diary like most people do, but I want this diary itself to be my friend, and I shall call my friend Kitty. No one will grasp what I'm talking about if I begin my letters to Kitty just out of the blue, so albeit[1] unwillingly, I will start by sketching in brief the story of my life.

My father was thirty-six when he married my mother, who was then twenty-five. My sister Margot was born in 1926 in Frankfort-on-Main, I followed on June 12, 1929, and, as we are Jewish, we emigrated to Holland in 1933, where my father was appointed Managing Director of Travies N.V. This firm is in close relationship with the firm of Kolen & Co. in the same building, of which my father is a partner.

Vocabulary
enhance (en hans´) v. make greater

emigrated (em´ i grāt´ əd) v. left one place to settle in another

✓ **Reading Check**
Who is Kitty?

---

1. **albeit** (ôl bē´ it) *conj.* although.

▼ An Amsterdam street, labeled "Jewish Street" in German and Dutch, where Jews were permitted to shop.

The rest of our family, however, felt the full impact of Hitler's anti-Jewish laws, so life was filled with anxiety. In 1938 after the pogroms,[2] my two uncles (my mother's brothers) escaped to the U.S.A. My old grandmother came to us, she was then seventy-three. After May 1940 good times rapidly fled: first the war, then the capitulation,[3] followed by the arrival of the Germans, which is when the sufferings of us Jews really began. Anti-Jewish decrees followed each other in quick succession. Jews must wear a yellow star, Jews must hand in their bicycles, Jews are banned from trains and are forbidden to drive. Jews are only allowed to do their shopping between three and five o'clock and then only in shops which bear the placard "Jewish shop." Jews must be indoors by eight o'clock and cannot even sit in their own gardens after that hour. Jews are forbidden to visit theaters, cinemas, and other places of entertainment. Jews may not take part in public sports. Swimming baths, tennis courts, hockey fields, and other sports grounds are all prohibited to them. Jews may not visit Christians. Jews must go to Jewish schools, and many more restrictions of a similar kind.

So we could not do this and were forbidden to do that. But life went on in spite of it all. Jopie[4] used to say to me, "You're scared to do anything, because it may be forbidden." Our freedom was strictly limited. Yet things were still bearable.

Granny died in January 1942; no one will ever know how much she is present in my thoughts and how much I love her still.

In 1934 I went to school at the Montessori Kindergarten and continued there. It was at the end of the school year, I was in form 6B, when I had to say good-by to Mrs. K. We both wept, it was very sad. In 1941 I went, with my sister Margot, to the

Sources
Compare and contrast the presentation of this information with its presentation at the end of Act I Scene I in the play.

Sources
Why do you think the playwrights chose to omit this information about Anne's grandmother from the play?

2. **pogroms** (pō′ grəmz) *n.* organized killings and other persecution of Jews.
3. **capitulation** (kə pich′ yoo lā′ shən) *n.* act of surrendering.
4. **Jopie** (yō′ pē) Jacqueline van Maarsen, Anne's best friend.

Jewish Secondary School, she into the fourth form[5] and I into the first.

So far everything is all right with the four of us and here I come to the present day.

Thursday, 19 November, 1942

Dear Kitty,

Dussel is a very nice man, just as we had all imagined. Of course he thought it was all right to share my little room.

Quite honestly I'm not so keen that a stranger should use my things, but one must be prepared to make some sacrifices for a good cause, so I shall make my little offering with a good will. "If we can save someone, then everything else is of secondary importance," says Daddy, and he's absolutely right.

The first day that Dussel was here, he immediately asked me all sorts of questions: When does the charwoman[6] come? When can one use the bathroom? When is one allowed to use the lavatory?[7] You may laugh, but these things are not so simple in a hiding place. During the day we mustn't make any noise that might be heard downstairs; and if there is some stranger—such as the charwoman for example—then we have to be extra careful. I explained all this carefully to Dussel. But one thing amazed me: he is very slow on the uptake. He asks everything twice over and still doesn't seem to remember. Perhaps that will wear off in time, and it's only that he's thoroughly upset by the sudden change.

Apart from that, all goes well. Dussel has told us a lot about the outside world, which we have missed for so long now. He had very sad news. Countless friends and acquaintances have gone to a terrible fate. Evening after evening the green and gray army lorries trundle past.[8] The Germans ring at every front door to inquire if there are any Jews living in the house. If there are, then the whole family has to go at once. If they don't find any, they go on to the next house. No one has a chance of evading them unless one goes into hiding. Often they go around with lists, and only ring when they know they can get a good haul. Sometimes they let them off for cash—so much per head. It seems like the slave hunts of olden times.

Spiral Review

Conflict Compare Anne's attitude toward Dussel in the diary with the feelings she expresses when she first meets him in the play.

Reading Check

What does Anne notice about Dussel?

---

5. **fourth form** fourth grade.
6. **charwoman** *n.* cleaning woman.
7. **lavatory** *n.* toilet.
8. **lorries trundle past** trucks move along.

Sources
Compare this paragraph with the description on pages 888–889. How does the firsthand account differ from the play's version of similar events?

But it's certainly no joke; it's much too tragic for that. In the evenings when it's dark, I often see rows of good, innocent people accompanied by crying children, walking on and on, in charge of a couple of these chaps, bullied and knocked about until they almost drop. No one is spared—old people, babies, expectant mothers, the sick—each and all join in the march of death.

How fortunate we are here, so well cared for and undisturbed. We wouldn't have to worry about all this misery were it not that we are so anxious about all those dear to us whom we can no longer help.

I feel wicked sleeping in a warm bed, while my dearest friends have been knocked down or have fallen into a gutter somewhere out in the cold night. I get frightened when I think of close friends who have now been delivered into the hands of the cruelest brutes that walk the earth. And all because they are Jews!

Yours, Anne

Critical Thinking

1. **Key Ideas and Details** **(a)** Why does Anne decide to write a diary? **(b) Analyze:** What other reasons might motivate her to write?

2. **Key Ideas and Details** **(a)** As Anne describes in the June 20 entry, how has life changed for Jews since May 1940? **(b) Infer:** What is the purpose of such restrictions?

3. **Key Ideas and Details** **(a) Contrast:** How is Anne's situation different from that of the Jews she sees outside? **(b) Evaluate:** Anne says she is "fortunate" to have a hiding place. Do you agree? Explain.

4. **Integration of Knowledge and Ideas** **(a)** Do the occupying Nazis succeed in creating distinctions between Dutch Jews and Dutch Christians? Explain. **(b)** Why are the Franks limited in their ability to resist the changes Anne describes?
[Connect to the Big Question: Is it our differences or our similarities that matter most?]

Cite textual evidence to support your responses.

From Anne Frank Remembered

Miep Gies

with Alison Leslie Gold

Background Miep Gies helped Anne Frank and her family hide in the attic of an office building during World War II. She was one of the thousands of Dutch citizens who bravely helped Jews hide from the Nazis. In this excerpt from her book, *Anne Frank Remembered*, Miep Gies describes welcoming back Otto Frank as a war refugee, learning of the fate of those who had hidden with him, and giving Anne's diary to him.

Henk flew home that day to tell me. It was June 3, 1945. He ran into the living room and grabbed me. "Miep, Otto Frank is coming back!"

My heart took flight. Deep down I'd always known that he would, that the others would, too.

Just then, my eye caught sight of a figure passing outside our window. My throat closed. I ran outside.

There was Mr. Frank himself, walking toward our door.

We looked at each other. There were no words. He was thin, but he'd always been thin. He carried a little bundle. My eyes swam. My heart melted. Suddenly,

Vocabulary
liberated (lib´ ər āt´ əd)
v. freed; released

I was afraid to know more. I didn't want to know what had happened. I knew I would not ask.

We stood facing each other, speechless. Finally, Frank spoke.

"Miep," he said quietly. "Miep, Edith is not coming back."

My throat was pierced. I tried to hide my reaction to his thunderbolt. "Come inside," I insisted.

He went on. "But I have great hope for Margot and Anne."

"Yes. Great hope," I echoed encouragingly. "Come inside."

He still stood there. "Miep, I came here because you and Henk are the ones closest to me who are still here."

I grabbed his bundle from his hand. "Come, you stay right here with us. Now, some food. You have a room here with us for as long as you want."

He came inside. I made up a bedroom for him, and put everything we had into a fine meal for him. We ate. Mr. Frank told us he had ended up in Auschwitz. That was the last time he'd seen Edith, Margot, and Anne. The men had been separated from the women immediately. When the Russians liberated the camp in January, he had been taken on a very long trip to Odessa. Then from there to Marseille by ship, and at last, by train and truck to Holland.

He told us these few things in his soft voice. He spoke very little, but between us there was no need for words.

▼ **Critical Viewing**
This photo shows Auschwitz survivors liberated by the Soviet Army in January 1945. The Nazi slogan above the entrance reads "Work makes freedom." What details in the photo give you insight into the experiences of concentration camp survivors? **[Analyze]**

Mr. Frank settled in with Henk and me. Right away, he came back to the office and took his place again as the head of the business. I know he was relieved to have something to do each day. Meanwhile, he began exploring the network of information on Jews in the camps—the refugee agencies, the daily lists, the most crucial word-of-mouth information—trying everything to get news about Margot and Anne.

When Auschwitz was liberated, Otto Frank had gone right away to the women's camp to find out about his wife and children. In the chaos and desolation of the camps, he had learned that Edith had died shortly before the liberation.

He had also learned that in all likelihood, Margot and Anne had been transferred to another camp, along with Mrs. van Daan. The camp was called Bergen-Belsen, and was quite a distance from Auschwitz. That was as far as his trail had gone so far, though. Now he was trying to pick up the search.

As to the other men, Mr. Frank had lost track of Albert Dussel. He had no idea what had happened to him after the transit camp of Westerbork. He had seen with his own eyes Mr. van Daan on his way to be gassed. And Peter van Daan had come to visit Frank in the Auschwitz infirmary. Mr. Frank knew that right before the liberation of the camp, the Germans had taken groups of prisoners with them in their retreat. Peter had been in one of these groups.

Otto Frank had begged Peter to try to get into the infirmary himself, but Peter couldn't or wouldn't. He had last been seen going off with the retreating Germans into the snow-covered countryside. There was no further news about him.

Mr. Frank held high hopes for the girls, because Bergen-Belsen was not a death camp. There were no gassings there. It was a work camp—filled with hunger and disease, but with no apparatus for liquidation. Because Margot and Anne had been sent to the camp later than most other inmates they were relatively healthy. I too lived on hope for Margot and Anne. In some deep part of me, like a rock, I counted on their survival and their safe return to Amsterdam.

Mr. Frank had written for news to several Dutch people who he had learned had been in Bergen-Belsen. Through word of mouth people were being reunited every day. Daily, he waited for answers to his letters and for the new lists of survivors to be released and posted. Every time there was a knock at the door or footfalls on the steps, all our hearts would stand still.

Reading Check

How did Mr. Frank and Peter show concern for one another while they were imprisoned in Auschwitz?

from Anne Frank Remembered **977**

Perhaps Margot and Anne had found their way back home, and we could see them with our own eyes at last. Anne's sixteenth birthday was coming on June 12. Perhaps, we hoped, . . . but then the birthday came and went, and still no news.

One morning, Mr. Frank and I were alone in the office, opening mail. He was standing beside me, and I was sitting at my desk. I was vaguely aware of the sound of a letter being slit open. Then, a moment of silence. Something made me look away from my mail. Then, Otto Frank's voice, toneless, totally crushed: "Miep."

My eyes looked up at him, seeking out his eyes.

"Miep." He gripped a sheet of paper in both his hands. "I've gotten a letter from the nurse in Rotterdam. Miep, Margot and Anne are not coming back."

We stayed there like that, both struck by lightning, burnt thoroughly through our hearts, our eyes fixed on each other's. Then Mr. Frank walked toward his office and said in that defeated voice, "I'll be in my office."

I heard him walk across the room and down the hall, and the door closed.

I sat at my desk utterly crushed. Everything that had happened before, I could somehow accept. Like it or not, I had to accept it. But this, I could not accept. It was the one thing I'd been sure would not happen.

I heard the others coming into the office. I heard a door opening and a voice chattering. Then, good-morning greetings and coffee cups. I reached into the drawer on the side of my desk and took out the papers that had been waiting there for Anne for nearly a year now. No one, including me, had

Sources
What do you learn here that only Miep would know?

touched them. Now Anne was not coming back for her diary.

I took out all the papers, placing the little red-orange checkered diary on top, and carried everything into Mr. Frank's office.

Frank was sitting at his desk, his eyes murky with shock. I held out the diary and the papers to him. I said, "Here is your daughter Anne's legacy to you."

I could tell that he recognized the diary. He had given it to her just over three years before, on her thirteenth birthday, right before going into hiding. He touched it with the tips of his fingers. I pressed everything into his hands; then I left his office, closing the door quietly.

Shortly afterward, the phone on my desk rang. It was Mr. Frank's voice. "Miep, please see to it that I'm not disturbed." he said.

"I've already done that," I replied.

The second printing of the diary sold out and another printing was planned. Mr. Frank was approached with the idea of permiting the diary to be translated and published abroad. He was against it at first, but then he succumbed to the pressure on him to allow the diary a more widespread audience.

Again and again, he'd say to me, "Miep, you must read Anne's writing. Who would have imagined what went on in her quick little mind?" Otto was never discouraged by my continuing refusal. He would always wait awhile and then ask me again.

Finally, I gave in to his insistence. I said, "All right, I will read the diary, but only when I'm totally alone."

The next time I was totally alone, on a warm day, I took the second printing of the diary, went to my room, and shut the door.

With awful fear in my heart, I opened the book and turned to the first page.

And so I began to read.

I read the whole diary without stopping. From the first word, I heard Anne's voice come back to speak to me from where she had gone. I lost track of time. Anne's voice tumbled out of the book, so full of life, moods, curiosity, feelings. She was no longer gone and destroyed. She was alive again in my mind.

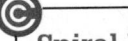

Spiral Review

Conflict Why do you think Miep could not bring herself to read Anne's diary? What might have motivated her to change her mind?

Reading Check

How did Mr. Frank find out that his daughters were not coming back?

Sources

How does Miep's description of her reaction to reading Anne's diary show you she knew Anne Frank well?

I read to the very end. I was surprised by how much had happened in hiding that I'd known nothing about. Immediately, I was thankful that I hadn't read the diary after the arrest, during the final nine months of the occupation, while it had stayed in my desk drawer right beside me every day. Had I read it, I would have had to burn the diary because it would have been too dangerous for people about whom Anne had written.

When I had read the last word, I didn't feel the pain I'd anticipated. I was glad I'd read it at last. The emptiness in my heart was eased. So much had been lost, but now Anne's voice would never be lost. My young friend had left a remarkable legacy to the world.

But always, every day of my life, I've wished that things had been different. That even had Anne's diary been lost to the world, Anne and the others might somehow have been saved.

Not a day goes by that I do not grieve for them.

▲ The author, Miep Gies, with a picture of Anne and her published diary.

Critical Thinking

Cite textual evidence to support your responses.

© 1. Key Ideas and Details (a) When Mr. Frank first returns to Amsterdam, what news does he bring of the other occupants of the Secret Annex? **(b) Infer:** Why is it so difficult for Miep and Otto Frank to find out about the rest of the Frank family?

© 2. Key Ideas and Details (a) Analyze: Why do you think Miep waited so long to read the diary? **(b) Interpret:** What does this selection add to your understanding of Anne Frank's life and legacy?

© 3. Key Ideas and Details (a) Compare and Contrast: How does Miep's attitude toward the diary change after she reads it? **(b) Make a Judgment:** Do you agree with Miep that it would have been better for Anne to have lived, even if her diary had been lost to the world? Explain.

© 4. Integration of Knowledge and Ideas (a) How do Miep and her husband Henk resist the Nazis' attempt to create differences between themselves and the Franks? **(b)** Is their method of resistance ultimately effective? Why or why not? *[Connect to the Big Question: Is it our differences or our similarities that matter most?]*

Comparing Sources With a Dramatization

© **1. Integration of Knowledge and Ideas** Use the chart to compare the diary, the play, and the memoir.

	How Thoughts and Feelings Are Expressed	Whose Perspectives Are Shown	Accuracy of Retelling	How Time Is Represented
Diary				
Play				
Memoir				

© **2. Integration of Knowledge and Ideas (a)** Do you think the playwrights create a fair and accurate portrait of Anne? Support your answer with evidence from the diary. **(b)** Identify two secondary sources you could consult to assess the accuracy of their portrayal.

© **3. Integration of Knowledge and Ideas (a)** Identify the different purposes of the authors of these three works. **(b)** How do the characteristics of each form—play, diary, and memoir—help them meet their goals?

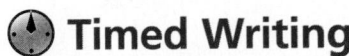 Timed Writing

Explanatory Text: Essay

In an essay, make links across texts to compare the Anne revealed in the diary with the Anne of the later works. **(40 minutes)**

5-Minute Planner

1. Read the prompt carefully and completely.

2. Gather your ideas by jotting down answers to these questions:

   - How might the passage of time affect the retelling of events?

   - How well does the play capture Anne's thoughts and feelings?

   - In the play, what is the effect of other characters on the way we view Anne? Do the other works change that view? Is the portrayal of the others in hiding different among the works?

   - Is one of the three forms more powerful to you? Why?

3. Use the chart you created for question 1 to help you organize the categories in your essay and provide textual evidence.

4. Reread the prompt, and then draft your essay.

Writing Workshop

Write an Informative Text

Exposition: Research Report

Defining the Form **Research writing** brings together information gathered from several sources in order to prove a central point, or thesis. You might use elements of a research report when writing informational articles, historical analyses, or business reports.

Assignment Write a research report based on information from a variety of sources. Your research report should feature the following:

✔ a specific focus, or *main idea,* expressed in a *thesis statement*

✔ supporting evidence collected from a variety of reliable *primary and secondary sources*, with *appropriate citations*

✔ a *clear organization* and *smooth transitions*

✔ a *bibliography* or "Works Cited" list that provides an accurate, complete citation of research sources

✔ error-free writing, including the *correct use of subordinate clauses*

To preview the criteria on which your research report may be judged, see the rubric on page 993.

Writing Workshop: *Work in Progress*

Review the work you did on pages 915 and 959.

WRITE GUY
Jeff Anderson, M.Ed.

What Do You Notice?

Form and Structure

Read the following sentences from Robert MacNeil's "The Trouble with Television."

It is difficult to escape the influence of television. If you fit the statistical averages, by the age of 20 you will have been exposed to at least 20,000 hours of television. You can add 10,000 hours for each decade you have lived after the age of 20. The only things Americans do more than watch television are work and sleep.

With a partner, discuss what you notice about the passage. Then, look at the way MacNeil presents facts and statistics. Think of ways you might structure your own writing to present your ideas effectively.

Writing

2. Write informative/explanatory texts to examine a topic and convey ideas, concepts, and information through the selection, organization, and analysis of relevant content.

2.a. Introduce a topic clearly, previewing what is to follow; organize ideas, concepts, and information into broader categories; include formatting, graphics, tables, and multimedia when useful to aiding comprehension.

7. Conduct short research projects to answer a question, drawing on several sources and generating additional related, focused questions that allow for multiple avenues of exploration.

Prewriting/Planning Strategies

Use the following prewriting strategies before you draft your report:

Browse media. To find topic ideas, flip through recently published magazines or newspapers. Tune in to television and radio broadcasts. Surf the Internet for ideas, creating and organizing bookmarks in your Internet browser to identify possible topics. In a chart like the one shown, list people, places, events, or current issues that you want to investigate.

PHLit
Online!
www.PHLitOnline.com
- Author video: Writing Process
- Author video: Rewards of Writing

People	Places	Events	Current Issues
politicians	Washington, D.C.	mining accident	health care
entertainers	Los Angeles, CA	elections	worldwide hunger
scientists	the Middle East	soccer game	the economy
educators	South America	Hurricane Andrew	school funding

Develop a research plan. Before you finalize your topic, conduct preliminary research to determine how much material is available. Using your general idea as a starting point, search through relevant books, Web sites, magazines, and indexes at a library. Jot down the names, ideas, and events that appear most often. Use this information to narrow a wide subject, such as educational toys, to a narrower one, such as electronic readers.

Ask open-ended questions. Thoughtful, interesting questions can help focus a research topic. To develop these questions, take the following steps:

- Draft a list of broad questions about your topic. These questions will be the starting points for your exploration of the topic and will guide your research.

- As you research, narrow your list by deleting unrelated questions and adding questions that are more specific to your focus.

Use a variety of primary and secondary sources. Use both *primary sources* (firsthand or original accounts, such as interview transcripts and newspaper articles) and *secondary sources* (accounts that are not original, such as encyclopedia entries) in your research. A secondary source often contains a bibliography or list of works cited. You can use these citations to find additional sources.

Prewriting/Planning Strategies *(continued)*

© **Common Core State Standards**

Writing

8. Gather relevant information from multiple print and digital sources, using search terms effectively; assess the credibility and accuracy of each source; and quote or paraphrase the data and conclusions of others while avoiding plagiarism and following a standard format for citation.

Evaluate sources. Just because something is in print or online does not mean it is true or unbiased. Often you will find articles written by unreliable authors, articles with a bias or agenda, or articles that lack factual evidence to support their claims. To ensure that you use the right sources, evaluate their reliability using these questions.

Does the source go into enough depth to cover the subject?	❏ yes ❏ no
Does the publisher have a good reputation?	❏ yes ❏ no
Is the author an authority on the subject?	❏ yes ❏ no
Do at least two other sources agree with this source?	❏ yes ❏ no

To ensure that your information is current, accurate, and balanced, follow these guidelines:

- Check publication dates to make sure the information is current.
- If you note discrepancies in the information given by two sources, check the facts in a third source. If three or more sources disagree, mention the disagreement in your paper.
- Consider the author's perspective. Examine the author's credentials—his or her background—before accepting a conclusion.

Use source cards and note cards. When you find information related to your topic, take detailed notes on index cards.

- Create a *source card* for each book, article, or Web site. For print sources, list the author, title, publisher, and place and date of publication. For each Internet source, list the sponsor, page name, date of last revision, date you accessed it, and address.
- As you take notes, write one idea on each card. When taking notes, be careful to avoid *plagiarism,* the unethical presentation of someone else's ideas as if they were your own. Clearly indicate if your note reflects an author's exact words or a paraphrase of an author's ideas.
- Use quotation marks whenever you copy words exactly. When using cursive, write legibly to avoid misquoting or misspelling.

Alternatively, you can use computer programs, such as database or word processing software, to keep track of source information.

Note Card

Du Bois's Education	Lewis	3

The Academic Council awarded Du Bois a Henry Bromfield Rogers Memorial Fellowship.

p. 103

Lewis, David Levering   3

W. E. B. Du Bois, 1868–1919: Biography of a Race

New York: Henry Holt & Company, 1993

920L Public Library

Source Card

Drafting Strategies

Define your thesis. Sum up the main point you plan to address in your report in a single statement, called a **thesis statement.** Use your thesis statement to direct your writing and include it in the introduction to your report. The arguments and evidence that you present in the body of your report should connect logically to the thesis statement. If they do not connect, you should consider either modifying your original thesis or using other evidence.

Make an outline. Write a formal outline, such as the one shown, for your report before you begin to draft. Use Roman numerals for your most important points and capital letters for the details that support them. Make sure each point in your outline supports your thesis.

Balance research and original ideas. As you write your draft, strive to achieve a balance between research-based information and your own original ideas. The highlighted portion in this example indicates the writer's original words, not research.

Title of Your Report
I. Introduction
Thesis Statement
II. First main point
A. Supporting detail #1
1. Example
2. Example
3. Example
B. Supporting detail #2
C. Supporting detail #3
III. Second main point

Model:

The famous Underground Railroad, which operated from approximately 1780 to 1862 ("The Underground Railroad," PBS.org), was not underground, nor was it a railroad. Rather, it was a system operated by a secret network of courageous people who helped slaves escape from the American South and find their way to freedom. The first slaves had arrived in Jamestown, Virginia, in 1619, a year before the Pilgrims arrived at Plymouth Rock, Massachusetts (Buckmaster 11). By the early 1800s, there were about four million slaves in this country (Siebert 378). It was the Underground Railroad that saved many lives from the hardships of slavery in the American South.

Prepare to credit sources. Any material that is not an original idea should be credited, whether you paraphrase it or quote it directly. As you draft, circle all ideas and phrases that come directly from your research. At this stage, for each circled item, use parentheses to note the author's name and the page number of the source. Internet sources can be identified by Web addresses. You can create formal citations later.

Drafting Strategies

Make direct reference to sources. You can use one of these methods to incorporate the information you have found.

- **Quote directly.** Support your thesis and conclusions with opinions from authorities. When using a source's exact words, enclose the entire statement in quotation marks. However, if the quotation is more than four lines, use a *block quote*. Introduce the quotation with a colon. Then begin on a new line, indenting the entire quotation and leaving out the quotation marks.

- **Paraphrase.** This technique involves restating a writer's specific ideas in your own words. Be sure to properly credit the source.

- **Summarize.** Where appropriate, summarize all major perspectives on the topic. This is especially important when you are describing controversial or complex ideas.

Create visuals. Use visual displays such as charts, graphs, and tables when you want to organize and display information in a way that illustrates your main point and is easy to grasp.

- Pie charts show parts of a whole, so they can be useful in showing any topic with data in percentages.

- Line graphs and bar graphs show information as it changes over time, so they can be useful in showing trends.

Three different ways of visualizing the same general topic—migration—are shown here. Note that important similarities or differences in tables and charts can be emphasized by using different colors and fonts.

Other types of visuals that can help you illustrate your points include photographs, diagrams, and maps. Always make sure the text in your visuals is readable. Add captions to photos so readers can understand what they show. Diagrams and maps should also be clearly labeled. A map requires a legend that tells what the symbols mean, a compass rose indicating where north is, and a scale showing distance.

Create a "Works Cited" list. When you finish drafting, provide full information about your sources in an alphabetical "Works Cited" list or "Bibliography" at the end of your report. Check the format required for your report and follow its style and punctuation guidelines. For more guidance on formats, see the Bibliography on page 992 and pages R34–R35.

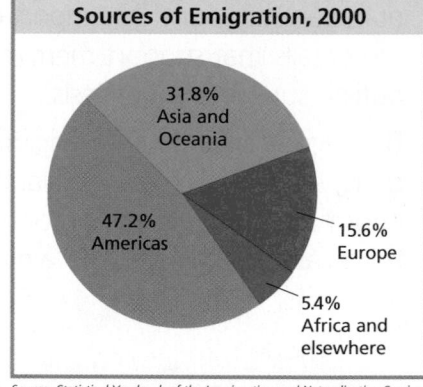

Sources of Emigration, 2000

- 31.8% Asia and Oceania
- 47.2% Americas
- 15.6% Europe
- 5.4% Africa and elsewhere

Source: *Statistical Yearbook of the Immigration and Naturalization Service*

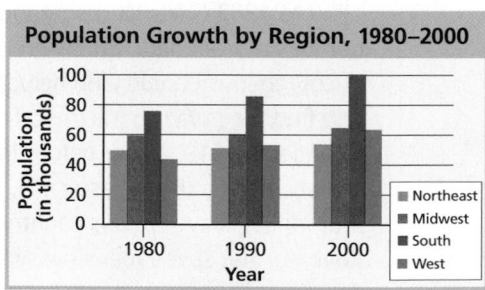

Population Growth by Region, 1980–2000

Population (in thousands) / Year — Northeast, Midwest, South, West

Source: U.S. Bureau of the Census, *The Statistical History of the U.S.* (1976) and 2000 Census of the U.S. www.census.gov

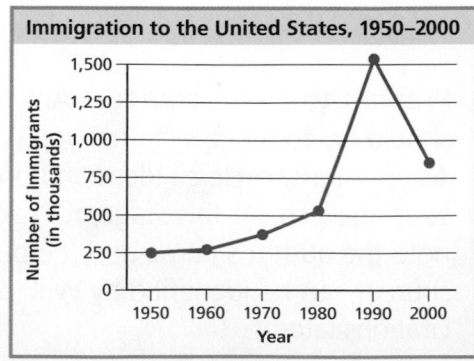

Immigration to the United States, 1950–2000

Number of Immigrants (in thousands) / Year

Source: *Yearbook of Immigration Statistics, 2003*

Writers on Writing

Cherie Bennett On Getting Facts and Words Right

Cherie Bennett is the author of *Anne Frank & Me* (p. 810).

I wrote the play *Anne Frank & Me* first, and then, with my husband, adapted it as a novel. The big difference between the two forms is that a novel gives you so much more freedom. You're not confined by what could go on a stage. But novels require even more research, since they contain so many details. The following selection is from the novel, and it covers part of the same scene as the excerpt from the play you just read.

"We didn't want to get any facts wrong."

— Cherie Bennett

Professional Model:

from *Anne Frank and Me* (novel)

A sudden bump on the track jostled them; they reached to steady each other—Nicole felt as if jolts of electricity were coursing through her. "I remember . . . you thought your parents disapproved that you were kissing him."

Anne's voice became a whisper. "How is this possible?"

"I don't know—" Nicole began, then stopped. Because suddenly, she did know. "You kept a diary. I read it."

"But I left my diary in the Annex when the Gestapo came. You couldn't have read it."

"I did, though."

"How?"

"I don't know," Nicole admitted. "I wish I did."

Anne gave her a ^{n} ~~dubious cock-eyed mischievous~~ arched look. "This is a very strange conversation."

The train lurched violently. People cried out in fear, but Nicole was oblivious, as a new thought surfaced, one so absurd that she was almost too embarrassed to say it. "Anne, I feel like it was—I know this will sound crazy—but I feel like it was in the future."

Research interviews with Holocaust survivors taught us about the rough track bed used by the transports. On stage, the actors synchronized unsteady movements with sound effects of a moving train.

In most plays, characters speak for themselves. But in a novel, you've got to pick a point of view. We wrote this story using a limited third-person point of view, revealing only Nicole's thoughts.

I remember my struggle for the right word to describe the look that Anne gives Nicole. I tried—and tossed out!— curious, cock-eyed, and dubious. Finally, I settled on arched. It conveys both how I imagine Anne raised her eyebrows and her mischievous tone.

Revising Strategies

Common Core State Standards

Writing

2.c. Use appropriate and varied transitions to create cohesion and clarify the relationships among ideas and concepts.

2.f. Provide a concluding statement or section that follows from and supports the information or explanation presented.

Check for unity. All the parts of your report should fit together in a complete, self-contained whole.

1. Check that every paragraph develops your thesis statement. Delete those that do not, or revise to show a connection.

2. Identify the main idea of each paragraph. Often, a topic sentence will directly state that main idea. If a paragraph does not contain a topic sentence, consider adding one.

3. In each paragraph, eliminate any sentences that do not support or explain the topic sentence or main idea.

4. Use transition words and phrases to smooth the flow between paragraphs and between ideas. Examples include *next, finally, although, as a result of, therefore, despite,* and *however.*

5. Check your conclusion to make sure it provides a sense of closure to the writing and that it reinforces your thesis.

Model: Revising for Unity

The Underground Railroad had apparently been in existence toward the end of the 1700s, but it was not named as such until around 1831, when the steam railroads were emerging. Railroad terms were used to describe various aspects of the system. It had "stations" and "depots," the homes and businesses where the runaway slaves could rest and eat. The people who sheltered the fugitives in these stations were called "stationmasters." ~~They would hide people in barns, basements, and back rooms—anywhere they could.~~ People who contributed money or goods were called "stockholders." ~~The money was needed to buy decent clothing for the escaping slaves, for tattered clothing would send an unwanted message about the person's status.~~ The system also had "conductors," whose job was to move fugitives from one station to the next.

> The crossed-out sentences do not belong in a paragraph that deals with the terminology of the Underground Railroad.

Check your citations. You must cite an author's direct quotations as well as his or her ideas, even if you restate the information in your own words. An internal citation appears in parentheses and directly follows the information it references. It includes the author's last name and the page number on which the information appears.

Example: "The Duke of Lancaster, in 1888, controlled more than 163,000 acres of British countryside" (Pool 193).

Peer Review

Ask a partner to read your draft, identifying details that wander too far from your thesis. Together, look for ways to link your information back to the main idea, or consider cutting the text.

Revising to Combine Sentences Using Clauses

To eliminate choppiness and to show connections between ideas, use subordinate clauses to combine sentences.

Identifying Subordinate Clauses A clause is any group of words with a subject and a verb. A subordinate clause cannot stand alone.

> **Subordinate clause:** <u>Although Rosa Parks said she was simply tired,</u> she became a symbol of strength.

Combining Short Sentences Writers often combine two short sentences by converting one into a subordinate clause that establishes a specific relationship between the two ideas.

Time:	*After soccer practice,* we will eat pizza.
Cause and effect:	*If the temperature drops,* winds may pick up.
Contrast:	*Although the sun shone,* it was still raining.

Combining Sentences Using Subordinate Clauses To combine sentences by using subordinate clauses, follow these steps:

1. Identify two sentences whose ideas are connected.
2. Rewrite the less important idea as a subordinate clause.
3. Use punctuation and subordinating conjunctions to combine the two sentences:
   - Use a comma after most introductory clauses. *When he arrived back in Missouri, he visited his family.*
     Do not use a comma if the subordinate clause follows the main clause. *He visited his family when he got to Missouri.*
   - A list of subordinating conjunctions is shown here. Use these conjunctions to join the clause with the rest of the sentence.

Frequently Used Subordinating Conjunctions			
after	as though	in order that	until
although	because	since	when
as long as	before	than	where
as soon as	even though	unless	while

Grammar in Your Writing
Review the sentences in three paragraphs of your draft. Consider whether some of them could be improved by combining them. If so, combine them by using subordinate clauses.

> **PH WRITING COACH**
>
> Further instruction and practice are available in *Prentice Hall Writing Coach.*

Student Model: James Barraclough, Los Alamos, NM

Alexander the Great

Southeastern Europe and western Asia were continually plagued by wars and rebellions in the fourth century B.C. Out of all this strife rose a boy, Alexander III, a hero whose name would be remembered for thousands of years. Alexander became King of Macedonia at the young age of twenty and commenced to conquer the Persian Empire and part of modern-day India using brilliant battle strategy and a quickness to act that kept his enemies guessing. He earned his reputation as 'Alexander the Great' by carving an empire of approximately one million square miles out of a land filled with enemies who were often intent on overthrowing him (Walbank 248).

Alexander was born in July 356 B.C. to King Philip II of Macedonia and Olympias, daughter of the King of Epirus. Throughout his life, Alexander was very close to his mother, Olympias, from whom he learned to pray and to believe deeply in the gods. However, Alexander inherited his military genius and bravery from his father, who conquered all of the Greek city-states and then united them under his rule. Even as a child, Alexander had enough ambition for several men, as shown by his comment after his father had conquered a city: "My father will have everything, and I will have nothing left to conquer." (Wepman)

After uniting Greece, Philip began a campaign to conquer the Persian Empire, but his efforts were cut short when he was assassinated in 336 B.C. Alexander was only twenty years old, though he had been commanding troops with his father for four years. He was not guaranteed power after his father's death, so he quickly claimed the throne with the army's support (Wilcken 61). Picking up where his father left off, Alexander III, King of Macedonia, began a campaign that would change the world.

In the spring of 334 B.C., Alexander led a relatively small army of 30,000 infantry, comprised mostly of soldiers called *hoplites*, who carried 16-foot spears, and 5,000 cavalry, called the Companions, across the Hellespont, a narrow strait. There, he met a force of Persian cavalry and Greek mercenaries, sent by Darius III, King of the Persian Empire, which was intended to throw back the invaders. However, the Macedonians cut them to shreds by employing Alexander's innovative military strategy (Cartledge 28–29). After that battle, Alexander led his army down along the coast of Asia Minor, taking cities for Greece until he met Darius at Issus. There, Alexander's outnumbered soldiers again routed the Persians, but Darius escaped. As the ancient historian Arrian reports, Darius fled in such a panic, he abandoned his royal chariot. "He even left his bow in the chariot; and mounting a horse continued his flight." (Godolphin 450)

James introduces the overall focus— the impressive accomplishments of Alexander—in the first paragraph.

The paper's organization is chronological, following a clear path from Alexander's birth to his death.

James uses a variety of sources—both ancient and modern— for quotations and supporting evidence.

Choosing not to pursue Darius further, Alexander continued along the eastern Mediterranean coast into Egypt, liberating the Egyptians from their hated Persian overlords. In exchange for their liberation, the Egyptians named Alexander pharaoh of Egypt. After his victory, he planned a city called Alexandria to be built on the Mediterranean Sea. As Alexander pressed back into Asia he conquered many cities, but again Darius confronted him—this time better prepared for the man who was such a grave threat to the Persian Empire. However, Alexander employed a cunning ruse to distract the Persians during the battle and crashed back to the middle, crushing the unsuspecting Persians. When Darius fled, the empire was left to Alexander's control (Cartledge 32). At the age of twenty-five, Alexander had become ruler of the Persian Empire and the most powerful man in the world.

After some time in Babylon, the city he made his capital, Alexander decided to head towards India to conquer new land for his empire. Many of the Greek soldiers protested that they wished to go home after years of hard fighting. Even so, Alexander inspired such loyalty that the soldiers reluctantly followed him to India. After fighting their way through modern-day Afghanistan and Pakistan, Alexander crossed into India. Many of his men died when monsoon rains arrived and poisonous snakes, rats, and tropical diseases, such as malaria, became prevalent.

As the army moved deeper into India, King Porus, an Indian ruler, confronted Alexander's troops with approximately two hundred war elephants and an extensive cavalry. Even though the elephants made it difficult for Alexander's cavalry to fight, Alexander once again outsmarted his enemy and defeated the Indian army. Porus surrendered and agreed to be his ally. Following the restoration of Porus to his kingdom, Alexander's men, who were wearied by the intense heat and stricken with homesickness, refused to move on. Alexander sulked in his tent, until he finally relented and set out towards Babylon (Prevas 166–172).

Approximately one year after his return from India, Alexander developed a fever and stomach cramps. These may have been caused by heavy drinking, typhoid, malaria, or poison. The fatal illness kept him in bed until he died on June 11, 323 B.C. at the age of 32. Since Alexander did not appoint a successor to his throne, the mightiest empire of the time, perhaps of all time, fell into disorder and collapsed with his death (Prevas 202–207).

Smooth transitions give the paper a sense of flow.

James credits each source in parentheses—using only author's last name and page number— directly after the information taken from that source. Full citations appear at the end of the paper.

**Common Core
State Standards**

Language
2.b. Use an ellipsis to indicate
an omission.

All in all, Alexander—who was just a boy in some people's eyes when he took the throne—rose to the occasion and conquered the world, forging an empire with his heart and sword. Alexander was a complex man who could be harsh, ruthless, and relentless in battle, but he could also be compassionate and sympathetic towards his wounded soldiers. These characteristics inspired loyalty and unity in thousands of soldiers. They followed Alexander wherever he led, even if they had a fierce desire to go home. The man known as Alexander the Great was a king, an emperor, a pharaoh, a conqueror, and most of all, a leader who could charge into battle, knowing his men would follow.

Bibliography

Alexander, Caroline. "Alexander the Conqueror." *National Geographic*, March 2000: 42–75.

Cartledge, Paul. *Alexander the Great*. New York: Overlook Press, 2004.

Chrisp, Peter. *Alexander the Great The Legend of a Warrior King*. New York: Dorling Kindersley, 2000.

Godolphin, Francis R., ed. and Chinnock, Edward J., translator (Arrian). *The Greek Historians: The Complete and Unabridged Historical Works of Herodotus, Thucydides, Xenophon, Arrian*. New York: Random House, 1942.

Greenblatt, Miriam. *Alexander the Great and Ancient Greece*. New York: Benchmark Books, 2000.

Prevas, John. *Envy of the Gods*. Cambridge, MA: Da Capo Press, 2004.

Stark, Freya. *Alexander's Path*. New York: Harcourt, Brace and Company, 1958.

Walbank, Frank W. "Alexander the Great." *Encyclopedia Britannica*. 1990 ed.

Wepman, Dennis, *Alexander the Great*, book excerpt on <http://www.palmdigitalmedia.com/product/book/excerpt/11250> (14 April 2005).

Wilcken, Ulrich. *Alexander the Great*. New York: W.W. Norton, 1967.

Woodcock, George et al. *Ancient Empires*. New York: Newsweek Books, 1970.

All sources used are listed at the end of the paper in a Bibliography. To see the proper format for different sources, see *Citing Sources and Preparing Manuscript*, pages R34–R35.

You may use a List of Works Cited instead of a Bibliography. Find out which format your teacher prefers.

Editing and Proofreading

Correct errors in grammar, spelling, and punctuation.

Focus on citations. Review your draft against your notes to be sure you have correctly quoted your sources. In addition, check that numbers, dates, and page references are correct.

Focus on ellipses. An ellipsis (. . .) is a punctuation mark that indicates text that is intentionally left out of a quote. Review your report for any long quotes with information that can be safely omitted without changing emphasis or meaning. Substitute an ellipsis for the omitted words to show where you have shortened the text.

Spiral Review
Earlier in this unit, you learned about **dangling and misplaced modifiers** (p. 914) and **clauses** (p. 958). Check your report to make sure that you have used modifiers and clauses correctly.

Publishing and Presenting

Deliver an impromptu speech. Now that you are knowledgeable about your topic, give an impromptu (unrehearsed) speech to your classmates. Describe your initial questions, your thesis, and what you found out as a result of your research. After you finish, answer questions from the audience.

Reflecting on Your Writing

Writer's Journal Jot down your answers to these questions:

What was the most surprising or interesting thing you learned about your topic? Why?

Rubric for Self-Assessment

Find evidence in your writing to address each category. Then, use the rating scale to grade your work.

Criteria	Rating Scale
	not very very
Focus: How clearly do you state your main idea?	1 2 3 4 5
Organization: How clear and logical is your organization?	1 2 3 4 5
Support/Elaboration: How well do you use evidence to support your statements?	1 2 3 4 5
Style: How clearly do you present the sources you used for research?	1 2 3 4 5
Conventions: According to an accepted format, how complete and accurate are your citations? Did you use subordinate clauses effectively?	1 2 3 4 5

Vocabulary Workshop

Borrowed and Foreign Words

A number of English words have been taken directly from other languages. For example, words related to fruit or weather such as *tomato* and *hurricane* are borrowed from Native American languages. Many words borrowed from French relate to art or literature. For example, the word *critique* as a noun means "a critical essay or review." As a verb, *critique* means "to write a critical essay or review." The chart shows some borrowed and foreign words that have become part of the English language.

Common Core State Standards

Language
4.a. Use context as a clue to the meaning of a word or phrase.
4.d. Verify the preliminary determination of the meaning of a word or phrase.

Borrowed Word	Meaning	Example Sentence
café — French	coffee shop	Let's have dessert at a *café*.
balcony — Italian	a porch	The *balcony* overlooked the garden.
canyon — Spanish	a long, narrow valley	Our house has a view of the *canyon*.

Practice A Use a dictionary to find the original language for each of these borrowed English words.

1. pretzel
2. burrito
3. bagel
4. curry
5. waffle
6. barbecue

Recall that context clues are the words and phrases surrounding a word that you may be unfamiliar with. Context clues can help you uncover the meaning of an unfamiliar word.

Practice B Use context clues to help you figure out the meaning of the italicized foreign words and phrases. Check a dictionary if you need help.

1. Darlene was impressed by the colorful *macaw* she saw sitting on the branches of a tree.

2. Bennie called out "*Ciao!*" as he left the party to go home.

3. While in Mexico, Jaime bought a *sombrero* to shade her from the sun's hot rays.

4. Duane told us all the boring details of his vacation, *ad nauseum.*

5. The students in the *anime* club like to illustate their favorite characters.

6. We like living on a street that is a *cul-de-sac* because there isn't much traffic.

7. Keisha had a strong sense of *dèjá vu* when she came to our town, although she had never been here before.

8. Just before parting with his friends at the Tokyo airport, James said, "*Sayonara.*"

Activity Read each of the borrowed words related to music. Then, on a chart like the one shown, write each word next to the language from which it comes.

PHLit
Online!
www.PHLitOnline.com
- Illustrated vocabulary words
- Interactive vocabulary games
- Vocabulary flashcards

suite	tempo	glockenspiel
ensemble	crescendo	piano
waltz	bassoon	violin

Language of Origin	Music Words
Italian	
French	
German	

Comprehension and Collaboration

Some borrowed words come from the names of people or places. With two or three classmates, find the origin of each of these words: *frankfurter, argyle, cologne, manila paper, sandwich, denim, maverick, teddy bear, bloomers,* and *jersey.* Compare your findings with those of another group.

Communications Workshop

Delivering a Narrative Presentation

In a **narrative presentation,** you organize and deliver information to tell a story that will inform or entertain your audience.

Learn the Skills

Consider your audience. To increase the effectiveness of your presentation, take the time to analyze your audience. A profile like the one shown can help you identify the interests, concerns, and knowledge level of your listeners. Use your answers to help you choose the right words and details.

Choose details wisely. The events you choose for your narrative should be ones that help you tell a dramatic or informative story. Choose significant events that have a clear progression and that you can illustrate with specific action, description, and even dialogue.

Practice beforehand. Rehearsing will help you get comfortable with the words and find the right gestures, body movements, and voice modulations.

Use appropriate sentences. Speak in complete sentences, using correct grammar and the active voice. Save slang and sentence fragments for dialogue only. For added impact, vary your sentences by

- mixing short, powerful sentences with longer ones.
- using an interesting assortment of sentence openings.
- using correlatives—word pairs like *either/or*—and subordinate clauses, such as *As a result of the accident,* to indicate relationships between ideas (see pages 570 and 958).

Focus on word choice. Match your vocabulary to your audience and purpose. Use specific nouns and verbs as well as interesting, vivid adjectives. Choose words that help convey the mood of your story and bring it to life for your audience.

Use audience feedback. Gauge your audience's reactions in order to make adjustments to vocabulary level, organization, pacing, tone, and emphasis. If an audience seems confused by unfamiliar terms, define them using appositives (see page 785). If listeners appear bored, pick up the pace and skip unnecessary sections or details.

**Common Core
State Standards**

Speaking and Listening
6. Adapt speech to a variety of contexts and tasks, demonstrating command of formal English when indicated or appropriate.

Audience Profile
- What is the average age of my audience?
- What do they already know about my topic?
- What steps are necessary to understand this subject?
- What details will be most interesting to my audience?
- What background do I need to provide?

Practice the Skills

© **Presentation of Knowledge and Ideas** Use what you've learned in this workshop to perform the following task.

ACTIVITY: Prepare and Deliver a Narrative Presentation

Prepare and deliver a brief narrative presentation about a time that you learned a valuable lesson. For example, you might discuss working hard to achieve a goal, discovering the value of teamwork, or overcoming a setback. In choosing your topic, consider how your audience might benefit from hearing the experience you are relating. To help you construct your presentation, answer the following questions.

- Is my purpose in relating the narrative clear?
- Have I described how others might benefit from hearing my narrative?
- What background information will I need to provide for my presentation to be clear and easy to follow?
- Do I present events in a logical sequence?
- Are the events clearly related to each other and do they build toward the overall point I am trying to make?

As your classmates make their presentations, pay close attention and consider their narratives. Use the Presentation Checklist below to analyze their presentations.

Presentation Checklist

Does the presentation meet all of the requirements of the activity?
Check all that apply.

❑ The subject is appropriate for the audience.
❑ The events of the narrative have a clear progression.
❑ The speaker used action, description, and, if appropriate, dialogue.

Presentation Delivery
Did the speaker deliver the narrative well?
Check all that apply.

❑ The speaker used varied sentences and descriptive word choices.
❑ The speaker used gestures and modulated his or her voice.
❑ The speaker made adjustments as needed, according to audience feedback.

© **Comprehension and Collaboration** After you and your classmates have delivered your presentations, form small discussion groups. Group members should refer to their Presentation Checklists to provide feedback on each person's presentation, noting successes and areas for improvement.

Cumulative Review

**Common Core
State Standards**

RL.8.1, RL.8.3; W.8.2.b; L.8.4.a
[For the full wording of the standards, see the standards chart in the front of your textbook.]

I. Reading Literature

Directions: *Read the scene. Then, answer each question.*

[The setting is a castle room in a mythical land. The KING *sits in a big, plush chair. His 14-year-old daughter,* PRINCESS PRISCILLA, *enters.]*

PRISCILLA. Father, I am troubled. Troubled at heart.

KING. Why, Priscilla, what have you to be troubled with? You are young and care-free—are you burdened by your studies?

PRISCILLA. My studies? No, not at all.

KING. And you are too young to be in love.

PRISCILLA. I disagree with that, but I am not troubled by love.

KING. Then what? You know you can talk to me.

PRISCILLA. Well then, Father, I will come right to the point. [*Like a trial lawyer*] I have learned from the maids and cooks in our kitchen that you pay them one silver coin each month.

KING. That is true.

PRISCILLA. [*Passionately*] And yet you pay the *men* who work in the house and gardens one *gold* coin per month. The women keep house for us, cook, and serve us three meals each day. They work from before sunup to after sundown, inhale all our dust and only know if the sky is bright or cloudy by the light coming through the small windows into the castle. Surely, women deserve the same coin as the men who work outdoors and can breathe the crisp, fall air . . . [*Her voice trails off. Then, in a demanding tone.*] Why do you <u>discriminate</u> by giving the men gold and the women silver?
[*The KING takes a deep breath and gestures, but no words come out. He tries again. PRISCILLA taps her foot impatiently.*]

PRISCILLA. Well?

KING. [*Finally*] Because that is the way we have always done it?

PRISCILLA. Is that an answer or a question?

KING. [*Befuddled*] I do not know.

PRISCILLA. [*With patience and sympathy*] Father, I will leave you to your thoughts, but I would like to discuss this after my studies.

KING. [*Recovering, glad for a change of topic*] Yes, my dear, during lunch. And what are you studying this morning?

PRISCILLA. [*Brightly*] Economics!

KING. Ahhh, well, I'd better rest. [*He slouches and dozes off.*]

1. Which of the following is emphasized in the **stage directions** at the beginning of the play?

A. The setting of the scene

B. The reasons behind characters' speech and actions

C. The development of the characters

D. The characters' emotions

2. Based on their **dialogue**, which statement best describes the relationship between Priscilla and the King?

A. He spoils her and she often takes advantage of him.

B. He does not allow her to question his decisions.

C. They are used to speaking openly with each other.

D. He supervises her with a firm hand.

3. What conflict propels the **plot** of this scene?

A. The King faces a revolt from his servants.

B. The Princess struggles to gain independence.

C. The King refuses to listen to the Princess's ideas.

D. The Princess and her father have different views regarding servants.

4. What is Priscilla's likely **motivation** for challenging her father's payment practices?

A. She believes the women work hard and should be paid the same as the men.

B. She wants to have fun by upsetting her father with challenging questions.

C. She wants to practice leadership skills to prepare herself to be queen.

D. She wants to utilize what she is learning in economics.

5. Which description best fits this **stage direction** about the King: "[*Befuddled*]"?

A. The King is tired and has lost his train of thought.

B. The King is angry about Priscilla talking to the cooks and maids.

C. The King is not sure whether to take Priscilla seriously.

D. The King is surprised and confused by Priscilla's sudden challenge.

6. **Vocabulary** Which word or phrase is closest in meaning to the underlined word <u>discriminate</u>?

A. make unfair choices

B. decide

C. justify

D. make an excuse

7. Which statement *best* describes a **conclusion** that can be drawn about Priscilla, based on her dialogue and actions?

A. She is afraid to confront her father.

B. She stands up for what she believes in.

C. She does not enjoy her studies.

D. She wants only to please her father.

Timed Writing

8. In an essay, describe Priscilla's **character traits. Support** your description with examples from the **dialogue** and **stage directions.**

GO ON

II. Reading Informational Text

Directions: *Read the passage. Then, answer the questions that follow.*

> **Common Core State Standards**
>
> **RI.8.2, RI.8.5; L.8.3**
> [For the full wording of the standards, see the standards chart in the front of your textbook.]

Smithtown Pool Rules

- All children under five must be accompanied by an adult.
- Diving is not permitted in the shallow end or from the pool's sides.
- No glass containers are allowed in the pool area.
- No running, hard shoving, or horseplay will be <u>tolerated</u>.
- Guests must be accompanied by members.
- Above all, keep in mind that the pool is here for everyone's enjoyment. Rowdy behavior ruins the experience for everyone.

Application Process for Lifeguard Positions

1. Check our Web site for open positions, posted weekly.
2. Apply online for the position for which you are interested.
3. We will call you in for an interview, based on your qualifications.
4. Bring your lifeguard certification with you to the interview.
5. After the interview, we will perform a background check.
6. If your application is approved, you will need to complete the appropriate paperwork before your first day of work.

---

1. Which **generalization** could you make about the people who wrote the pool rules?
   - A. They want to keep children out.
   - B. They are interested in making money.
   - C. Safety is their primary concern.
   - D. Their goal is for guests to enjoy themselves.

2. How are the purposes of these materials different?
   - A. one is intended for a wider audience than the other
   - B. one is meant to inform; the other to entertain
   - C. one is meant for adults; the other for children
   - D. one is meant to persuade; the other to entertain

3. Which of the following *best* describes the structural patterns of these two materials?
   - A. The first is organized chronologically; the second is organized step-by-step.
   - B. The first is organized by order of importance; the second is organized chronologically.
   - C. The first is organized randomly; the second is organized step-by-step.
   - D. The first is organized step-by-step; the second is organized chronologically.

III. Writing and Language Conventions

Workplace Writing: Business Letter

Directions: *Read the passage. Then, answer the questions that follow.*

You-Play-It Players
664 South Street
Casaterra, CA 10000

To Whom It May Concern:

(1) I recently bought a faulty MP3 player from your company. (2) I press "play." (3) The unit makes an awful squeal.

(4) I have attempted to solve the problem. (5) I have called the number in the warranty several times. (6) My calls are never answered. (7) Please contact me so that we can arrange to fix the player by telephone. (8) Listening to music is my favorite hobby, so I hope we can take care of this without further delay. (9) You really need to tell your customer service representatives to wake up and do a better job.

(10) Sincerely,

Liz Alvarez

1. What **formatting** change would make this business letter conform to correct style?

A. Move the inside address to the right.
B. Eliminate indents.
C. Combine paragraphs 1 and 2.
D. Remove space after the salutation.

2. Which of the following is the best way to combine sentences 2 and 3, using a **subordinate clause?**

A. I press "play"; the unit squeals.
B. Whenever I press "play," the unit squeals.
C. When I press "play"—the unit squeals.
D. I press "play" and the unit squeals.

3. Which sentence in the letter should be revised to maintain a professional **tone?**

A. Sentence 1
B. Sentence 4
C. Sentence 9
D. Sentence 10

4. How could the writer *best* combine sentences 4 and 5?

A. Attempting to solve the problem, I called the number in the warranty several times.
B. I attempted to solve the problem and called the number in the warranty several times.
C. I called the number in the warranty several times and tried to solve the problem.
D. I called several times and no one answered.

Performance Tasks

**Common Core
State Standards**

RL.8.1, RL.8.2, RL.8.3, RL.8.5; W.8.1,
W.8.2; SL.8.1, SL.8.4, SL.8.6; L.8.1
[For the full wording of the standards,
see the standards chart in the front of
your textbook.]

Directions: *Follow the instructions to complete the tasks
below as required by your teacher.*

*As you work on each task, incorporate both general academic
vocabulary and literary terms you learned in this unit.*

Writing

Task 1: Literature [RL.8.2; W.8.1]
Analyze the Development of Theme
*Write an essay in which you focus on the
impact of character on theme in one of the
drama selections in this unit.*

- Identify the theme of your chosen play.
- Focus on one or more of the main
  characters in the play. Explain how each
  character's words or actions relate to or
  help develop the theme.
- Cite evidence from the drama, including
  dialogue and stage directions, that supports
  your claims.
- Check your writing for correct grammar
  and usage.

Task 2: Literature [RL.8.3; W.8.2]
Analyze Dialogue
*Write an essay in which you analyze how
particular lines of dialogue propel the action
of a drama selection in this unit.*

- Choose a significant passage of dialogue
  from one of the plays in this unit.
- Explain how the passage moves the plot
  forward. Tell how the dialogue provided
  adds to the conflict, shapes the relationship
  between characters, or otherwise affects
  the action.
- Support your ideas with evidence from the
  text.
- Be sure to quote accurately from the text
  and to punctuate your quotations correctly.

Task 3: Literature [RL.8.5; W.8.1]
Analyze Text Structure
*Analyze how the structures of literary works
help to communicate meaning.*

- From this unit, select two works of different
  genres with distinctly different structures,
  such as a drama and a short story.
- Analyze the structure of each. Consider what
  is particular to each genre, such as stage
  directions in drama and a narrator in fiction.
- Compare the ways in which each text
  communicates information to the reader
  about character, plot, and theme.
- Draw logical, well-supported conclusions
  about the ways in which text structure
  contributes to the meaning of a work.
- Make sure you follow standard grammar
  conventions in your writing.

Task 4: Literature [RL.8.3; W.8.2]
Analyze Characterization
Analyze characterization in a play in this unit.

- Select one of the plays in this unit with an
  interesting character. Tell what you found
  interesting about this character.
- Determine your character's function in the
  play—central character, antagonist, and so on.
- Cite specific plot events and dialogue that
  reveal aspects of your character. Explain.
- Review your completed essay for correct
  grammar, punctuation, and spelling.

Speaking and Listening

© Task 5: Literature [RL.8.1; SL.8.4, SL.8.6]
Analyze and Interpret a Speech

Prepare an oral presentation in which you analyze a speech by a character in one of the plays in this unit. As part of your presentation, perform the speech in front of the class.

- Select a significant speech from one of the plays in this unit. Reread it carefully, looking up any unfamiliar words in a dictionary.

- Analyze the message of the speech. It may contain arguments and specific claims. It may reveal something about the character or the plot. It may contribute to the overall theme of the play.

- Present your analysis to the class. Then, perform the speech in front of the class. Make decisions as to how the character should behave; if he or she is angry, upset, or confident, be sure your performance reflects this interpretation.

- Invite questions from the audience and respond with relevant evidence and ideas.

© Task 6: Literature [RL.8.1; SL.8.4]
Critical Review

Prepare and deliver a critical review of a play.

- Select a play from this unit about which you have a definite opinion. The opinion may be either positive or negative.

- Cite your opinion and support it with logic and evidence. Include specific details from the text. Acknowledge both strong and weak points of the play.

- Write your points down on note cards. Put the cards in the most logical order and practice presenting them.

- Present your review to the class. Use appropriate eye contact, adequate volume, and clear pronunciation.

- Conclude your presentation with a question-and-answer period. When possible, make connections between your ideas and new ideas expressed by others.

© Task 7: Literature [RL.8.3; SL.8.1]
Compare and Contrast Characters

Lead a small group discussion in which you compare and contrast two characters in plays from this unit.

- Choose two characters from different plays in this unit who share at least one key trait.

- Determine the similarities and differences of these characters and their effects on the action of the play.

- Come to the discussion prepared with your analysis of both characters. Prepare a list of questions to guide the discussion.

- Follow rules for collegial discussions. Keep the discussion balanced. Based on contributions from the group, pose further questions.

- Wrap up the discussion with a recap of the key points presented.

THE BIG ?

Is it our differences or our similarities that matter most?

At the beginning of Unit 5, you participated in a discussion about the Big Question. Now that you have finished the unit, write a response to the question. Discuss how your views have developed—whether they have changed or been reinforced. Give specific examples from the plays, as well as from other subjects and your personal experiences, to support your ideas. Use Big Question vocabulary words (see p. 803) in your response.

Featured Titles

In this unit, you have read a variety of dramatic works. Continue to read on your own. Select works that you enjoy, but challenge yourself to explore new playwrights and works of increasing depth and complexity. The titles suggested below will help you get started.

Literature

Eight Plays of U.S. History

Learn about important events in United States history in this collection of engaging **plays** that explores freedom, justice, culture, and social themes.

Escape to Freedom: A Play About Young Frederick Douglass
by Ossie Davis

This **play** is an account of Douglass's early life. Douglass secretly taught himself to read in violation of state law, escaped from a brutal master, and became a forceful voice in the movement to abolish slavery.

Nerdlandia
by Gary Soto

Martin and Ceci have crushes on each other. Martin tries to make himself cooler to appeal to Ceci, while Ceci tries to make herself nerdier to appeal to Martin. This unusual situation lays the groundwork for a funny **play** about the superficial differences between people.

The Mousetrap and Other Plays
by Agatha Christie
NAL Trade, 2000

Full of plot twists and potential suspects, these eight **plays** by famed mystery writer Agatha Christie will delight murder-mystery buffs.

Henry Wadsworth Longfellow: Poems and Other Writings
by Henry Wadsworth Longfellow   **EXEMPLAR TEXT** ©

When you enroll in college at age fifteen and become a professor at eighteen, clearly great things are expected of you. Longfellow did not disappoint, as he went on to write such beloved poems as "Paul Revere's Ride," included in this **anthology.**

Anne Frank and Me
by Cherie Bennett and Jeff Gottesfeld

This **novel** presents the Holocaust through the eyes of a modern teenager. Nicole, a bored student, is suddenly jolted back in time. She meets Anne Frank in a cattle car filled with Jews bound for a concentration camp and experiences the horrors of the time firsthand.

Informational Texts

Narrative of the Life of Frederick Douglass
by Frederick Douglass
Signet, 1997   **EXEMPLAR TEXT**

As someone who had personally felt the unimaginable cruelty of slavery, Douglass's was a unique voice for change. Through his powerful **autobiography,** Douglass gave the lie to the common notion that former slaves were incapable of intellectual achievement, and he inspired many readers to question slavery for the first time.

Preparing to Read Complex Texts

Attentive Reading As you read on your own, ask yourself questions about the text. The questions shown below and others that you ask as you read will help you learn and enjoy literature even more.

 **Common Core State Standards**

Reading Literature/Informational Text

10. By the end of the year, read and comprehend literature, including stories, dramas, and poems, and literary nonfiction at the high end of grades 6–8 text complexity band independently and proficiently.

When reading drama, ask yourself...

- Who is the main character? What struggles does this character face?
- What other characters are important? How do these characters relate to the main character?
- Where and when does the play take place? Do the time and place of the setting affect the characters? If so, how?
- Do the characters, settings, and events seem real? Why or why not?
- How does the play end? How does the ending make me feel?
- What theme or insight do I think the playwright is expressing? Do I find that theme to be important and true?

© **Key Ideas and Details**

- Does the play have a narrator? If so, what information does the narrator provide?
- Does the playwright include background information? If so, how does this help me understand what I am reading?
- How many acts are in this play? What happens in each act?
- Does the dialogue sound like real speech? Are there specific passages that seem especially real? Are there any that seem false?
- What do the stage directions tell me about the ways characters move, speak, and feel? In what other ways do I learn about the characters?
- At what point in the play do I feel the most suspense? Why?
- What speech or passage in the play do I like the most? Why?
- Does the playwright seem to have a positive or a negative point of view? How do I think the playwright's point of view affects the story?
- Do I agree with the playwright's point of view? Why or why not?

© **Craft and Structure**

- Does the play remind me of others I have read or seen? If so, how?
- In what ways is the play different from others I have read or seen?
- What new information or ideas have I gained from reading this play?
- What actors would I choose to play each role in this play?
- If I were to be in this play, what role would I want?
- Would I recommend this play to others? Why or why not?

© **Integration of Ideas**

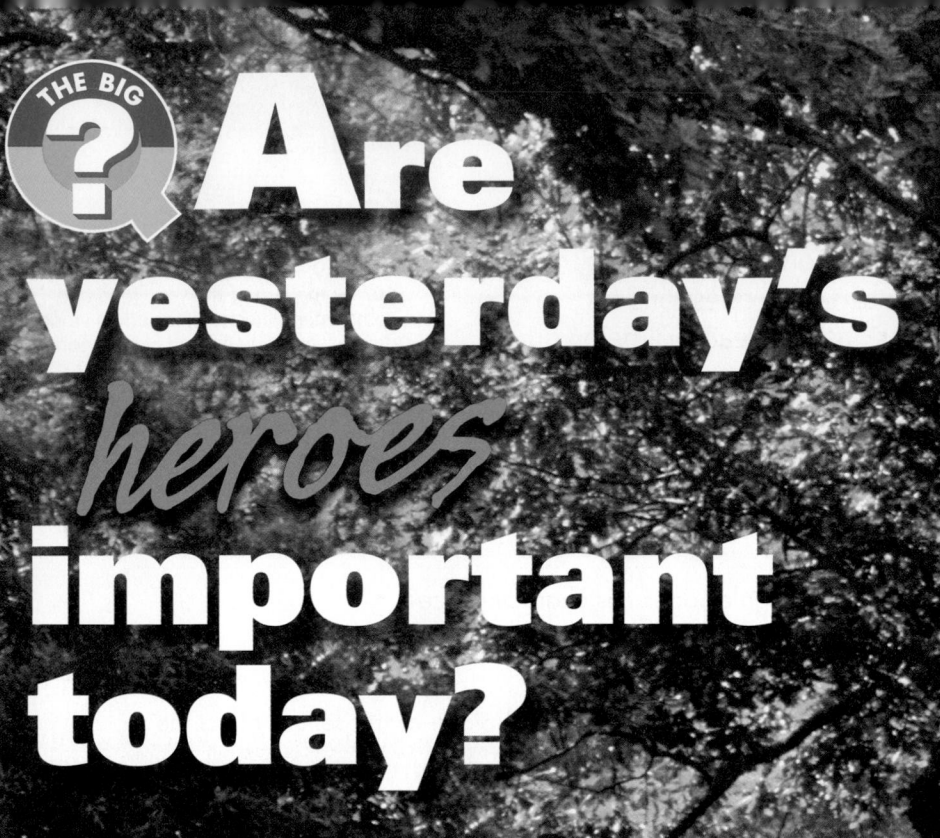

Are yesterday's *heroes* important today?

Themes in American Stories

PHLit Online!
www.PHLitOnline.com

Hear It!
- Selection summary audio
- Selection audio
- BQ Tunes

See It!
- Author videos
- Big Question video
- Get Connected videos
- Background videos
- More about the authors
- Illustrated vocabulary words
- Vocabulary flashcards

Do It!
- Interactive journals
- Interactive graphic organizers
- Grammar tutorials
- Interactive vocabulary games
- Test practice

Are yesterday's *heroes* important today?

Heroes are known for their bravery and their willingness to stand up for what they believe despite opposition. Some heroes become famous for their physical skills; others are admired for their kindness or intelligence. At times, stories about the challenges a hero overcomes are exaggerated to impress an audience.

Stories of all kinds of heroes come from folklore, literature, and real life, and they are passed down from generation to generation. Some heroes endure while others become outdated. Heroes who stand the test of time have the ability to inspire people of different historical periods and cultural backgrounds.

Exploring the Big Question

Collaboration: One-on-One Discussion Start thinking about the Big Question by making a list of people you admire, whether from history, literature, contemporary life, or your personal experience. Make a list of examples of heroic deeds like these:

- rescuing someone from a dangerous situation
- taking an unpopular position to defend a principle
- sacrificing for others so that they might succeed
- preserving dignity despite forces that try to degrade or destroy
- helping people who are in need

Share your examples with a partner. Talk about the aspects of the actions that make them heroic. Build on your partner's ideas, responding to each with related ideas of your own.

Connecting to the Literature Each reading in this unit will give you additional insight into the Big Question.

PHLit Online!
www.PHLitOnline.com
- Big Question video
- Illustrated vocabulary words
- Interactive vocabulary games
- BQ Tunes

Learning Big Question Vocabulary

Acquire and Use Academic Vocabulary Academic vocabulary is the language you encounter in textbooks and on standardized tests. Review the definitions of these academic vocabulary words.

Common Core State Standards

Speaking and Listening
1. Engage effectively in a range of collaborative discussions with diverse partners on *grade 8 topics, texts, and issues,* building on others' ideas and expressing their own clearly.

Language
6. Acquire and use accurately grade-appropriate general academic and domain-specific words and phrases; gather vocabulary knowledge when considering a word or phrase important to comprehension or expression.

aspects (as´ pekts´) *n.* ways an idea or problem may be viewed or seen

cultural (kul´ chər əl) *adj.* relating to the customs and beliefs of a group

emphasize (em´ fə sīz´) *v.* stress; give one idea more importance than others

exaggerate (eg zaj´ ər āt´) *v.* speak of something as being greater or more important than it is

imitate (im´ i tāt´) *v.* copy; follow the example of

influence (in´ floō əns) *v.* affect others' views, habits, plans, and so on

symbolize (sim´ bə līz´) *v.* stand for; take the place of and signify an idea

Use these words as you complete Big Question activities in this unit that involve reading, writing, speaking, and listening.

Gather Vocabulary Knowledge Additional Big Question words are listed below. Categorize the words by deciding whether you know each one well, know it a little bit, or do not know it at all.

accomplishments	courage	overcome
admirably	endure	suffering
bravery	outdated	

Then, do the following:

1. Write the definitions of the words you know.
2. Consult a dictionary to confirm the definitions of the words you know. Revise your definitions if necessary.
3. Using a print or an online dictionary, look up the meanings of the words you do not know. Then, write the meanings.
4. Use all of the words in a brief paragraph about heroes.

Elements of the American Folk Tradition

The American folk tradition includes a rich collection of literature, which grew out of the oral tradition.

Storytelling and the Oral Tradition
People have always enjoyed telling and listening to stories. Long before reading and writing were invented, societies shared information with the next generation through storytelling. This was the origin of the **oral tradition,** in which stories were passed down over time by word of mouth. Eventually, these stories were collected and written down. American folk literature grew out of this same tradition. Told at festivals, around campfires, and at other gatherings, stories from the oral tradition reflect our culture's richness.

Themes and Cultural Context All good stories have a **theme**—a central message or insight about life. Stories in the oral tradition often express universal themes. **Universal themes** recur regularly in stories from many different cultures and time periods. Examples of universal themes include the power of love and the dangers of greed.

In the American folk tradition, universal themes are expressed from an American perspective, or **cultural context.** The stories are inspired by American history, geography, and beliefs. Set against the rugged landscape of America's past, they often celebrate American **heroes** and **heroines.** Some details in the stories are historically true. Others are based on truth but may be greatly exaggerated. This chart shows techniques that are common to the American folk tradition.

Oral Tradition Storytelling Techniques

Technique	Definitions
Hyperbole	An exaggeration, used for comic effect or to express strong emotion
Understatement	A way of expressing something that treats it as smaller or less serious than it actually is, often used for comic effect
Personification	The technique of giving human characteristics to nonhuman subjects
Dialect	The language and grammar of a particular region or group; used to make dialogue sound realistic and to reflect the story's cultural background
Idioms	• Expressions that are not meant to be taken literally, such as "It's raining cats and dogs!" • Developed and understood by people of a certain region or group
Informal Speech	Everyday, conversational language; often includes idioms, slang, and dialect

The American Folk Tradition

American folk stories can be divided into different types.

Myths explain the actions of gods or other supernatural forces and the heroes who interact with them. Ancient peoples often used mythology to explain natural phenomena.

Fables are brief stories that often feature animals that act like humans. The main purpose of a fable is to teach an important life lesson, or **moral.**

Trickster tales tell about tricks or pranks and the characters who play them. Trickster characters are typically clever and mischievous.

Tall tales rely on **hyperbole**— exaggeration for comic effect. The heroes of these tales perform impossible feats.

Legends often originate in fact. Through repeated tellings of a factual story, the real-life characters and events in the story become larger than life, and the story becomes a legend.

Epics are long narrative poems about heroes who engage in dangerous journeys, battles, or quests important to the history of a nation or culture.

The American Folk Hero

American folk literature is a living tradition. Over time, new heroes and subjects appear that reflect the manners, customs, sayings, and stories of our changing culture. For example, American folk heroes of the nineteenth century included patriots, soldiers, farmers, and cowboys. A century later, American folk heroes included sports figures, aviators, civil rights leaders, and astronauts. In the American folk tradition, heroes can be real or fictional. However, they all display traits that Americans admire and strive to imitate.

In This Section

Elements of the American Folk Tradition

Determining Themes in American Stories

Analyzing the Development of Theme

Close Read: Story Elements and Theme
• Model Text
• Practice Text

After You Read

 Common Core State Standards

RL.8.2
[For the full wording of the standards, see the standards chart in the front of your textbook.]

Common Traits of American Folk Heroes				
adventurous determined	honest loyal	strong humble	courageous resourceful	intelligent creative

Fictional	Based to Some Degree on Fact	Real
Paul Bunyan, lumberjack	Johnny "Appleseed" Chapman, farmer	Sacajawea, Native American guide
Pecos Bill, cowboy	John Henry, African American steelworker	Rosa Parks, African American civil rights activist
Little Sal Fink, known for her powerful scream	Davy Crockett, frontiersman	Roberto Clemente, Hispanic baseball player

Determining Themes in American Stories

Themes in the American folk tradition have a distinctly American point of view.

Common Core State Standards

Reading Literature 2. Determine a theme or central idea of a text and analyze its development over the course of the text, including its relationship to the characters, setting, and plot; provide an objective summary of the text.

Themes in American folk stories express ideas about who we are as a people. These stories often present the American landscape as a challenge. Those who triumph over it are considered heroes and heroines.

Social and Cultural Context To recognize the themes in an American folk story, readers should consider the story's **social and cultural context**— the values and customs of the story's original tellers.

America has a rich multicultural heritage shaped by Native Americans, African Americans, Hispanics, Europeans, Asians, and others. All of these groups have contributed stories to the national folk literature. While the themes of these stories are distinctly American, they also reflect the cultures of their tellers.

Factors that can influence a storyteller's view of the world, or **social and cultural perspective,** include the historic events of an era. In America, events such as Westward Expansion, slavery, the Civil War, and the Great Depression deeply influenced those who lived through them. American folk stories often capture how Americans responded to the challenges of such events. The stories emphasize universal American themes such as resourcefulness.

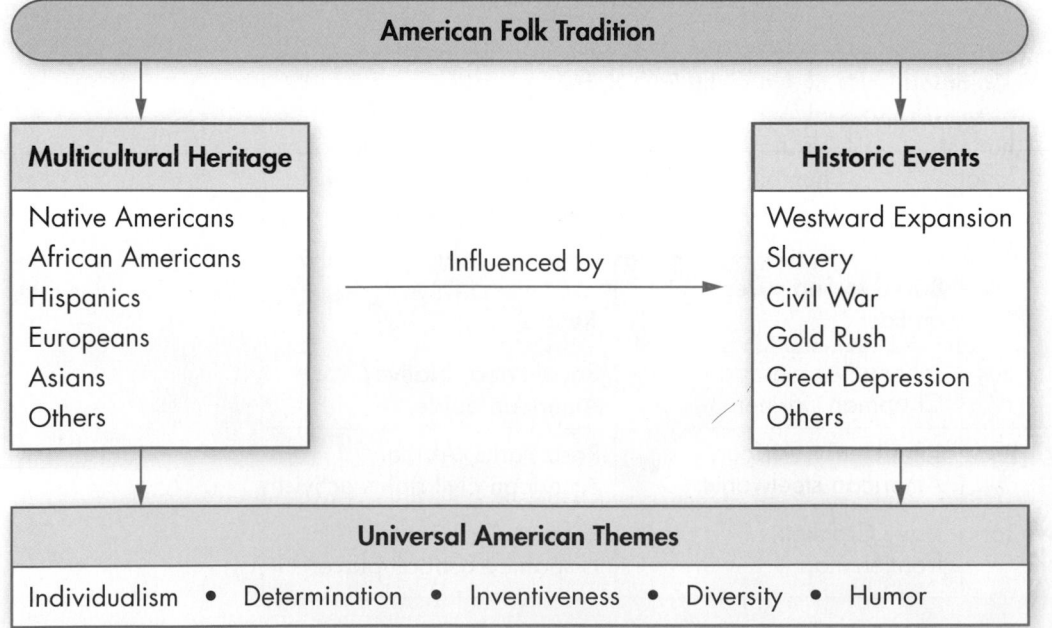

American Folk Tradition

Multicultural Heritage

Native Americans
African Americans
Hispanics
Europeans
Asians
Others

Influenced by

Historic Events

Westward Expansion
Slavery
Civil War
Gold Rush
Great Depression
Others

Universal American Themes

Individualism • Determination • Inventiveness • Diversity • Humor

Analyzing the Development of Theme

As in other literary genres, themes in the American folk tradition are usually developed through details of character, setting, and plot. To determine the theme of a story, read carefully to analyze these details. Think about how the details relate to each other and what underlying message or insight about life they offer.

Character A character is a person, an animal, or an imaginary creature that takes part in the action of a story. In American folk stories, main characters often display remarkable confidence, physical strength, determination, and resourcefulness. These qualities allow them to overcome obstacles, no matter how challenging. The words and actions of these characters, as well as the lessons they learn, help to develop themes such as the value of determination.

Example: Character
Paul Bunyan is an incredibly large, strong, and inventive lumberjack. His deeds illustrate the theme that even the greatest challenge can be overcome through hard work and inventiveness.

Setting The setting is the time and place in which the action of a story occurs. American folk stories are often set in real locations. While the places may be real, the details that describe them are often exaggerated to create greater challenges for characters.

Example: Setting
Paul Bunyan's adventures are set in the logging camps of America's North Woods, in real locations such as Wisconsin and Minnesota.

Plot and Conflict Plot is the sequence of events in a story. The plots of many American folk stories, especially legends, are loosely based on real events.

In all stories, the plot is moved forward by the **conflicts,** or struggles that characters face. In American folk stories, the conflicts are often *external* —they take place between a character and an outside force. Characters may face problems posed by another character, the landscape, economics, or other external obstacles. In some cases, external conflicts may cause characters to deal with *internal* conflicts— struggles within themselves. However, most often the primary conflict in the story is external.

Example: Plot and Conflict
While tales about Paul Bunyan are fictional, the stories often feature activities that actually occurred in logging camps. Paul Bunyan's conflicts reflect the challenges that America's pioneers faced in moving west. These conflicts help to develop themes of determination.

Close Read: Story Elements and Theme

Whether traditional or modern, American folk stories consist of elements that reveal theme.

All story elements work together to express the story's theme, or insight into life. To discover a story's theme, answer the questions in the following chart.

Clues to Theme in American Folk Stories

Setting

The setting in folk stories may or may not be specific. As you read, ask yourself

- Where and when does the story take place?
- Is this a real place or an imaginary place?
- If this is a real place, are any details changed or exaggerated?
- What effect does the setting have on the characters and the plot?

Plot and Conflict

Plot is the sequence of events in a story that show how a conflict develops and is resolved. The main character's response to a conflict can be a key to the theme. As you read, ask yourself

- What conflict, or problem, do the characters face?
- How is the conflict resolved?
- How do the characters feel about the solution?

Characters

Characters in American folk literature demonstrate traits that many Americans find admirable. The details that reveal these traits often relate to theme. As you read, ask yourself

- Is the main character a real person, a made-up person, or an animal?
- What does the main character say or do?
- How do the characters relate to each other?
- What do the characters learn, or how do the characters change?

Statements and Observations

Characters or the narrator may make statements or observations that suggest a theme. As you read, ask yourself

- Does a character or the narrator sum up story events?
- Does a character or the narrator make an observation about how characters feel, how characters change, or what characters learn because of story events?

Model

About the Text This excerpt is from the classic American novel *The Adventures of Tom Sawyer* by Mark Twain. The novel is set in the 1840s, in the small Mississippi River town of St. Petersburg, Missouri. In this excerpt, Tom's Aunt Polly sends him out on a Saturday morning to whitewash a fence as punishment for his mischievous behavior the day before.

---

from *The Adventures of Tom Sawyer* by Mark Twain

. . . But Tom's energy did not last. He began to think of the fun he had planned for this day, and his sorrows multiplied. Soon the free boys would come tripping along on all sorts of delicious expeditions, and they would make a world of fun of him for having to work—the very thought of it burnt him like fire. He got out his worldly wealth and examined it—bits of toys, marbles, and trash; enough to buy an exchange of *work*, maybe, but not half enough to buy so much as half an hour of pure freedom. So he returned his straitened means to his pocket, and gave up the idea of trying to buy the boys. At this dark and hopeless moment an inspiration burst upon him! Nothing less than a great, magnificent inspiration.

He took up his brush and went tranquilly to work. Ben Rogers hove in sight presently—the very boy, of all boys, whose ridicule he had been dreading. Ben's gait was the hop-skip-and-jump—proof enough that his heart was light and his anticipations high. He was eating an apple, and giving a long, melodious whoop, at intervals, followed by a deep-toned ding-dong-dong, ding-dong-dong, for he was personating a steamboat. As he drew near, he slackened speed, took the middle of the street, leaned far over to starboard and rounded to ponderously and with laborious pomp and circumstance—for he was personating the Big Missouri, and considered himself to be drawing nine feet of water. He was boat and captain and engine-bells combined, so he had to imagine himself standing on his own hurricane-deck giving the orders and executing them:

"Stop her, sir! Ting-a-ling-ling!" The headway ran almost out, and he drew up slowly toward the sidewalk.

"Ship up to back! Ting-a-ling-ling!" His arms straightened and stiffened down his sides.

"Set her back on the stabboard! Ting-a-ling-ling! Chow! ch-chow-wow! Chow!" His right hand, meantime, describing stately circles—for it was representing a forty-foot wheel.

Plot and Conflict
Tom's problem is that he has to work while all his friends play. His attempt to solve this problem sets the plot in motion.

Characters Although Tom is unhappy, he works "tranquilly" to trick Ben Rogers into believing he is having fun. Tom's trickery is a key to the story's theme.

 EXEMPLAR TEXT

Model continued

"Let her go back on the labboard! Ting-a-ling-ling! Chow-ch-chow-chow!" The left hand began to describe circles.

"Stop the stabboard! Ting-a-ling-ling! Stop the labboard! Come ahead on the stabboard! Stop her! Let your outside turn over slow! Ting-a-ling-ling! Chow-ow-ow! Get out that head-line! *Lively* now! Come—out with your spring-line—what're you about there! Take a turn round that stump with the bight of it! Stand by that stage, now—let her go! Done with the engines, sir! Ting-a-ling-ling! *Sh't! s'h't! sh't!*" (trying the gauge-cocks).

Tom went on whitewashing—paid no attention to the steamboat. Ben stared a moment and then said: *"Hi-yi! You're* up a stump, ain't you!"

No answer. Tom surveyed his last touch with the eye of an artist, then he gave his brush another gentle sweep and surveyed the result, as before. Ben ranged up alongside of him. Tom's mouth watered for the apple, but he stuck to his work. Ben said:

"Hello, old chap, you got to work, hey?"

Tom wheeled suddenly and said:

"Why, it's you, Ben! I warn't noticing."

"Say—*I'm* going in a-swimming, *I* am. Don't you wish you could? But of course you'd druther *work*—wouldn't you? Course you would!"

Tom contemplated the boy a bit, and said:

"What do you call work?"

"Why, ain't *that* work?"

Tom resumed his whitewashing, and answered carelessly:

"Well, maybe it is, and maybe it ain't. All I know, is, it suits Tom Sawyer."

"Oh come, now, you don't mean to let on that you *like* it?"

The brush continued to move.

"Like it? Well, I don't see why I oughtn't to like it. Does a boy get a chance to whitewash a fence every day?"

That put the thing in a new light. Ben stopped nibbling his apple. Tom swept his brush daintily back and forth—stepped back to note the effect—added a touch here and there—criticised the effect again—Ben watching every move and getting more and more interested, more and more absorbed. Presently he said:

"Say, Tom, let *me* whitewash a little."

Setting The fact that it is a hot summer Saturday plays a key role in the conflict. Tom would rather go swimming than paint the fence.

Tom considered, was about to consent; but he altered his mind:

"No—no—I reckon it wouldn't hardly do, Ben. You see, Aunt Polly's awful particular about this fence—right here on the street, you know—but if it was the back fence I wouldn't mind and *she* wouldn't. Yes, she's awful particular about this fence; it's got to be done very careful; I reckon there ain't one boy in a thousand, maybe two thousand, that can do it the way it's got to be done."

"No—is that so? Oh come, now—lemme just try. Only just a little—I'd let *you,* if you was me, Tom."

"Ben, I'd like to, honest injun; but Aunt Polly—well, Jim wanted to do it, but she wouldn't let him; Sid wanted to do it, and she wouldn't let Sid. Now don't you see how I'm fixed? If you was to tackle this fence and anything was to happen to it—"

"Oh, shucks, I'll be just as careful. Now lemme try. Say—I'll give you the core of my apple."

"Well, here—No, Ben, now don't. I'm afeard —"

"I'll give you *all* of it!"

Tom gave up the brush with reluctance in his face, but alacrity in his heart. And while the late steamer Big Missouri worked and sweated in the sun, the retired artist sat on a barrel in the shade close by, dangled his legs, munched his apple, and planned the slaughter of more innocents. There was no lack of material; boys happened along every little while; they came to jeer, but remained to whitewash. By the time Ben was fagged out, Tom had traded the next chance to Billy Fisher for a kite, in good repair; and when *he* played out, Johnny Miller bought in for a dead rat and a string to swing it with—and so on, and so on, hour after hour. And when the middle of the afternoon came, from being a poor poverty-stricken boy in the morning, Tom was literally rolling in wealth. He had besides the things before mentioned, twelve marbles, part of a jews-harp, a piece of blue bottle-glass to look through, a spool cannon, a key that wouldn't unlock anything, a fragment of chalk, a glass stopper of a decanter, a tin soldier, a couple of tadpoles, six fire-crackers, a kitten with only one eye, a brass doorknob, a dog-collar—but no dog—the handle of a knife, four pieces of orange-peel, and a dilapidated old window sash.

He had had a nice, good, idle time all the while—plenty of company—and the fence had three coats of whitewash on it! If he hadn't run out of whitewash he would have bankrupted every boy in the village.

Tom said to himself that it was not such a hollow world, after all. He had discovered a great law of human action, without knowing it—namely, that in order to make a man or a boy covet a thing, it is only necessary to make the thing difficult to attain.

Characters By cleverly suggesting that Ben cannot do as good a job as he can, Tom makes Ben want to paint even more. This interaction relates to the theme.

Theme Tom tricks the other boys into doing his work for him. The theme might be stated like this: *A person can outwit a fool with cleverness.*

Statements and Observations The narrator states that Tom has discovered you can make people want something just by making it difficult to attain. This observation is closely related to the theme.

Independent Practice

About the Selection Author Lan Samantha Chang grew up in Appleton, Wisconsin. There, she lived with her parents, sisters, and grandmother, Waipuo, who was born in Shanghai, China. This story was inspired by a story Waipuo told Chang and her sisters.

"Water Names" by Lan Samantha Chang

Summertime at dusk we'd gather on the back porch, tired and sticky from another day of fierce encoded quarrels, nursing our mosquito bites and frail dignities, sisters in name only. At first we'd pinch and slap each other, fighting for the best—least ragged—folding chair. Then we'd argue over who would sit next to our grandmother. We were so close together on the tiny porch that we often pulled our own hair by mistake. Forbidden to bite, we planted silent toothmarks on each others' wrists. We ignored the bulk of house behind us, the yard, the fields, the darkening sky. We even forgot about our grandmother. Then suddenly we'd hear her old, dry voice, very close, almost on the backs of our necks.

"*Xiushila!* Shame on you. Fighting like a bunch of chickens."

And Ingrid, the oldest, would freeze with her thumb and forefinger right on the back of Lily's arm. I would slide my hand away from the end of Ingrid's braid. Ashamed, we would shuffle our feet while Waipuo calmly found her chair.

On some nights she sat with us in silence. But on some nights she told us stories, "just to keep up your Chinese," she said.

"In these prairie crickets I often hear the sound of rippling waters, of the Yangtze River," she said. "Granddaughters, you are descended on both sides from people of the water country, near the mouth of the great Chang Jiang, as it is called, where the river is so grand and broad that even on clear days you can scarcely see the other side.

"The Chang Jiang runs four thousand miles, originating in the Himalaya mountains where it crashes, flecked with gold dust, down steep cliffs so perilous and remote that few humans have ever seen them. In central China, the river squeezes through deep gorges, then widens in its last thousand miles to the sea. Our ancestors have lived near the mouth of this river, the ever-changing delta, near a city called Nanjing, for more than a thousand years."

Characters Why might Waipuo want her granddaughters to "keep up" their Chinese?

Setting How does Waipuo form a picture of the Yangtze delta in her granddaughters' minds? Why do you think she does this?

"A thousand years," murmured Lily, who was only ten. When she was younger she had sometimes burst into nervous crying at the thought of so many years. Her small insistent fingers grabbed my fingers in the dark.

"Through your mother and I you are descended from a line of great men and women. We have survived countless floods and seasons of ill-fortune because we have the spirit of the river in us. Unlike mountains, we cannot be powdered down or broken apart. Instead, we run together, like raindrops. Our strength and spirit wear down mountains into sand. But even our people must respect the water."

She paused. "When I was young, my own grandmother once told me the story of Wen Zhiqing's daughter. Twelve hundred years ago the civilized parts of China still lay to the north, and the Yangtze valley lay unspoiled. In those days lived an ancestor named Wen Zhiqing, a resourceful man, and proud. He had been fishing for many years with trained cormorants, which you girls of course have never seen. Cormorants are sleek, black birds with long, bending necks which the fishermen fitted with metal rings so the fish they caught could not be swallowed. The birds would perch on the side of the old wooden boat and dive into the river." We had only known blue swimming pools, but we tried to imagine the sudden shock of cold and the plunge, deep into water.

"Now, Wen Zhiqing had a favorite daughter who was very beautiful and loved the river. She would beg to go out on the boat with him. This daughter was a restless one, never contented with their catch, and often she insisted they stay out until it was almost dark. Even then, she was not satisfied. She had been spoiled by her father, kept protected from the river, so she could not see its danger. To this young woman, the river was as familiar as the sky. It was a bright, broad road stretching out to curious lands. She did not fully understand the river's depths.

"One clear spring evening, as she watched the last bird dive off into the blackening waters, she said, 'If only this catch would bring back something more than another fish!'

"She leaned over the side of the boat and looked at the water. The stars and moon reflected back at her. And it is said that the spirits living underneath the water looked up at her as well. And the spirit of a young man who had drowned in the river many years before saw her lovely face."

We had heard about the ghosts of the drowned, who wait forever in the water for a living person to pull down instead. A faint breeze moved through the mosquito screens and we shivered.

Characters How does Waipuo feel about the Yangtze River? How can you tell?

Plot The river is both familiar and unknown to the daughter. How might this detail influence the plot?

Plot What traditional folk element does this plot event include?

Practice continued

"The cormorant was gone for a very long time," Waipuo said, "so long that the fisherman grew puzzled. Then, suddenly, the bird emerged from the waters, almost invisible in the night. Wen Zhiqing grasped his catch, a very large fish, and guided the boat back to shore. And when Wen reached home, he gutted the fish and discovered, in its stomach, a valuable pearl ring."

"From the man?" said Lily.

"Sshh, she'll tell you."

Waipuo ignored us. "His daughter was delighted that her wish had been fulfilled. What most excited her was the idea of an entire world like this, a world where such a beautiful ring would be only a bauble![1] For part of her had always longed to see faraway things and places. The river had put a spell on her heart. In the evenings she began to sit on the bank, looking at her own reflection in the water. Sometimes she said she saw a handsome young man looking back at her. And her yearning for him filled her heart with sorrow and fear, for she knew that she would soon leave her beloved family.

"'It's just the moon,' said Wen Zhiqing, but his daughter shook her head. 'There's a kingdom under the water,' she said. 'The prince is asking me to marry him. He sent the ring as an offering to you.' 'Nonsense,' said her father, and he forbade her to sit by the water again.

"For a year things went as usual, but the next spring there came a terrible flood that swept away almost everything. In the middle of a torrential rain, the family noticed that the daughter was missing. She had taken advantage of the confusion to hurry to the river and visit her beloved. The family searched for days but they never found her."

Her smoky, rattling voice came to a stop.

"What happened to her?" Lily said.

"It's okay, stupid," I told her. "She was so beautiful that she went to join the kingdom of her beloved. Right?"

"Who knows?" Waipuo said. "They say she was seduced by a water ghost. Or perhaps she lost her mind to desiring."

"What do you mean?" asked Ingrid.

Characters What does the daughter's reaction to the ring reveal about her? What important idea do these details suggest?

Statements and Observations What does Waipuo say happened to the daughter? How might this relate to the story's theme?

1. **bauble** (bô′ bəl) *n.* trinket.

"I'm going inside," Waipuo said, and got out of her chair with a creak. A moment later the light went on in her bedroom window. We knew she stood before the mirror, combing out her long, wavy silver-gray hair, and we imagined that in her youth she too had been beautiful.

We sat together without talking. We had gotten used to Waipuo's abruptness, her habit of creating a question and leaving without answering it, as if she were disappointed in the question itself. We tried to imagine Wen Zhiqing's daughter. What did she look like? How old was she? Why hadn't anyone remembered her name?

While we weren't watching, the stars had emerged. Their brilliant pinpoints mapped the heavens. They glittered over us, over Waipuo in her room, the house, and the small city we lived in, the great waves of grass that ran for miles around us, the ground beneath as dry and hard as bone.

After You Read — Water Names

1. Key Ideas and Details
(a) Summarize: Write an **objective summary** of "Water Names." In your summary, include only central ideas and key details from the story. Do not include your own personal opinions or judgments. **(b) Interpret:** What do you think is the climax, or high point, of the story?

2. Key Ideas and Details
(a) Speculate: Why might the grandmother want to tell Chinese legends to her granddaughters?
(b) Draw Conclusions: Do you think these stories matter to the author and her sisters? Explain.

3. Key Ideas and Details (a) Infer: What is one **theme** in this story?
(b) Analyze: What story details combine to reveal that theme?

4. Craft and Structure Identify: Identify at least two examples of storytelling techniques or details in the story that are part of the **oral tradition.**

5. Integration of Knowledge and Ideas (a) In a chart like the one shown, use the second column to list possible explanations for two unusual events in the story. **(b)** Exchange charts with a partner, and use the third column to explain why you agree or disagree with each explanation.

Event	Explanation	Why You Agree or Disagree
Face in the water		
Ring in the fish		

(c) Collaborate: With your partner, choose the more persuasive explanation of each event to share with the class.

© Leveled Texts

Build your skills and improve your comprehension of literature with texts of increasing complexity.

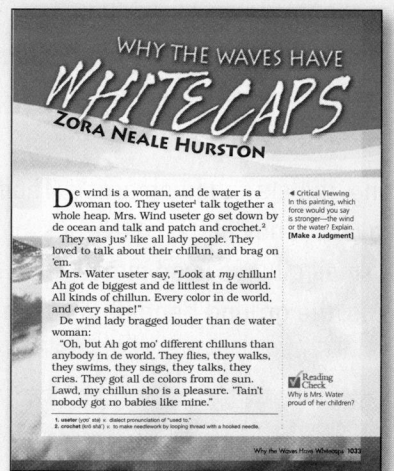

Read **"Coyote Steals the Sun and Moon"** to find out what happens when a wise eagle crosses paths with a mischief-making coyote.

Read **"Why the Waves Have Whitecaps"** to witness the results of an argument between Mrs. Wind and Mrs. Water over who has better children.

© Common Core State Standards

Meet these standards with either **"Coyote Steals the Sun and Moon"** (p. 1026) or **"Why the Waves Have Whitecaps"** (p. 1032).

Reading Literature

2. Determine a theme or central idea of a text and analyze its development over the course of the text, including its relationship to the characters, setting, and plot; provide an objective summary of the text. *(Reading Skill: Summarize; Literary Analysis: Mythology)*

Writing

3. Write narratives to develop real or imagined experiences or events using effective technique, relevant descriptive details, and well-structured event sequences. **3.b.** Use narrative techniques, such as dialogue, pacing, description, and reflection, to develop experiences, events, and/or characters. **3.e.** Provide a conclusion that follows from and reflects on the narrated experiences or events. *(Writing: Myth)*

Speaking and Listening

5. Integrate multimedia and visual displays into presentations to clarify information, strengthen claims and evidence, and add interest.

6. Adapt speech to a variety of contexts and tasks, demonstrating command of formal English when indicated or appropriate. *(Speaking and Listening: Oral Presentation)*

Language

1. Demonstrate command of the conventions of standard English grammar and usage when writing or speaking. *(Conventions: Sentence Structure)*

3. Use knowledge of language and its conventions when writing, speaking, reading, or listening. *(Speaking and Listening: Oral Presentation)*

Reading Skill: Summarize

A **summary** is a short statement that presents the key ideas and main points of a text. Summarizing helps you identify the most important information in a text. Follow these steps to summarize:

- **Reread to identify main events or ideas** in the passage or work. Then, jot them down.

- Organize your notes by putting main events or points in order and crossing off minor details that are not important for an overall understanding of the work.

- Finally, summarize by restating the major events or ideas in as few words as possible. Be sure your summary does not include your personal opinions.

Literary Analysis: Mythology

A **myth** is a traditional tale that presents the beliefs or customs of a culture. Every culture has its own **mythology,** or collection of myths. Myths share the following characteristics:

- They explain events in nature or in a people's history.

- They often describe the actions of gods or other supernatural beings. Many myths also involve animal characters or natural forces that display human qualities.

- They convey *themes,* or insights, expressing the values of the culture that first told them.

To understand myths, it is helpful to understand the culture from which they come. As you read, think about how cultural beliefs might influence the characters and events in the text.

Using the Strategy: Cultural Connection Chart

Record details on a **cultural connection chart** like this one.

Detail	Cultural Connection
Prometheus steals fire from Zeus, king of the gods, and gives it to humans.	To ancient Greeks, fire was essential for cooking, forging weapons, and providing warmth.

Are yesterday's *heroes* important today?

Writing About the Big Question

"Coyote Steals the Sun and Moon" explains a specific event in nature and features Coyote, a popular character in mythology. Use this sentence starter to develop your ideas about the Big Question.

Myths and their heroes have **endured** through the ages because they _____.

While You Read Look for interesting aspects of the myth that might help explain why it has endured for so many years.

Vocabulary

Read each word and its definition. Decide whether you know the word well, know it a little bit, or do not know it at all. After you read, see how your knowledge of each word has increased.

- **sacred** (sā´ krəd) *adj.* considered holy; related to religious cere-monies (p. 1026) *The temple was a <u>sacred</u> space for ancient Greeks.* *sacredly adv. sacredness n.*

- **pestering** (pes´ tər iŋ) *n.* constant bothering (p. 1027) *After ten minutes of <u>pestering</u>, Jan got permission to go to the movies.* *pester v. pestered adj.*

- **lagged** (lagd) *v.* moved slowly (p. 1028) *The turtle <u>lagged</u> far behind the speedy rabbit.* *lag n.*

- **shriveled** (shriv´ əld) *v.* dried up; shrank and wrinkled (p. 1028) *The hot sun <u>shriveled</u> the grass until it was dry and brown.* *shriveled adj.*

- **pursuit** (pər so͞ot´) *n.* chasing in order to catch (p. 1028) *The police sped off in <u>pursuit</u> of the thief.* *pursue v.*

- **curiosity** (kyo͞or´ ē äs ə tē) *n.* the desire to obtain information (p. 1028) *Out of <u>curiosity</u>, she peeked behind the curtain.* *curious adj. curiously adv.*

Word Study

The **Latin root -sacr-** means "holy."

In the myth "Coyote Steals the Sun and Moon," Eagle and Coyote watch the Kachina people per-form their **sacred,** or holy, dances.

"Coyote Steals the Sun and Moon"

A shared love of Native American culture brought together Richard Erdoes and Alfonso Ortiz—two men who grew up worlds apart. They worked together on several collections of Native American stories, some of which "were jotted down at powwows, around campfires, even inside a moving car."

Richard Erdoes (1912–2008)

Richard Erdoes was born in Frankfurt, Germany, and educated in Vienna, Berlin, and Paris. As a young boy, he became fascinated by American Indian culture. In 1940, he moved to the United States to escape Nazi rule and became a well-known author, photographer, and illustrator. He wrote several books on Native Americans and the American West.

Alfonso Ortiz (1939–1997)

Alfonso Ortiz was a Tewa Pueblo, born in New Mexico. He became a professor of anthropology at the University of New Mexico, and a leading expert on Pueblo culture.

BACKGROUND FOR THE MYTH

Zuñi Culture

"Coyote Steals the Moon" is a Zuñi myth. The Zuñi belong to a group of Native American peoples known as the Pueblos. According to Zuñi beliefs, the Great Spirit and other sacred beings guided the people to their homelands, showed them how to plant corn, and taught them to live in peace with each other. Zuñi myths often involve the sun and the moon, with daylight symbolizing life.

DID YOU KNOW?

Coyote is a popular character in Zuñi myths. He is usually depicted as a mischief-maker whose curiosity often gets him into trouble.

ZUÑI MYTH

COYOTE STEALS the SUN and MOON

RETOLD BY RICHARD ERDOES AND ALFONSO ORTIZ

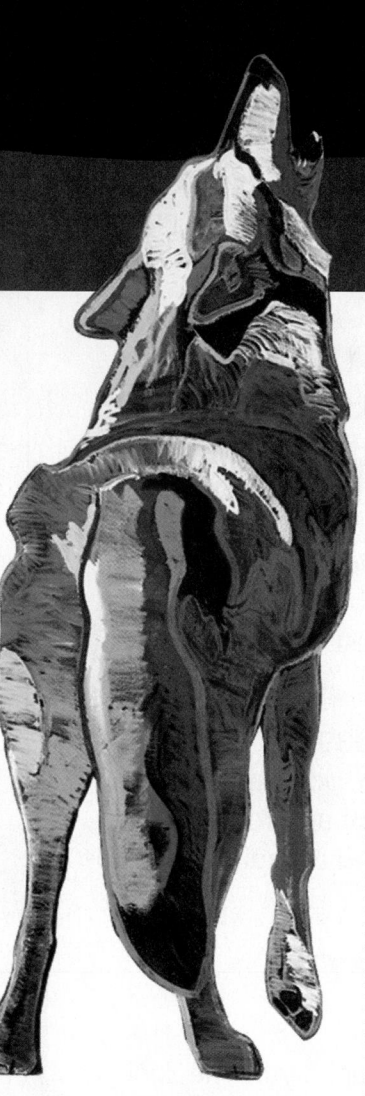

Coyote is a bad hunter who never kills anything. Once he watched Eagle hunting rabbits, catching one after another—more rabbits than he could eat. Coyote thought, "I'll team up with Eagle so I can have enough meat." Coyote is always up to something.

"Friend," Coyote said to Eagle, "we should hunt together. Two can catch more than one."

"Why not?" Eagle said, and so they began to hunt in partnership. Eagle caught many rabbits, but all Coyote caught was some little bugs.

At this time the world was still dark; the sun and moon had not yet been put in the sky. "Friend," Coyote said to Eagle, "no wonder I can't catch anything; I can't see. Do you know where we can get some light?"

"You're right, friend, there should be some light," Eagle said. "I think there's a little toward the west. Let's try and find it."

And so they went looking for the sun and moon. They came to a big river, which Eagle flew over. Coyote swam, and swallowed so much water that he almost drowned. He crawled out with his fur full of mud, and Eagle asked, "Why don't you fly like me?"

"You have wings; I just have hair," Coyote said. "I can't fly without feathers."

At last they came to a pueblo,[1] where the Kachinas happened to be dancing. The people invited Eagle and Coyote to sit down and have something to eat while they watched the sacred dances. Seeing the power of the Kachinas, Eagle said,

Vocabulary
sacred (sā′ krəd) *adj.* considered holy; related to religious ceremonies

---

1. pueblo (pweb′ lō) Native American settlement in the southwestern United States.

"I believe these are the people who have light."

Coyote, who had been looking all around, pointed out two boxes, one large and one small, that the people opened whenever they wanted light. To produce a lot of light, they opened the lid of the big box, which contained the sun. For less light they opened the small box, which held the moon.

Coyote nudged Eagle. "Friend, did you see that? They have all the light we need in the big box. Let's steal it."

"You always want to steal and rob. I say we should just borrow it."

"They won't lend it to us."

"You may be right," said Eagle. "Let's wait till they finish dancing and then steal it."

After a while the Kachinas went home to sleep, and Eagle scooped up the large box and flew off. Coyote ran along trying to keep up, panting, his tongue hanging out. Soon he yelled up to Eagle, "Ho, friend, let me carry the box a little way."

"No, no," said Eagle, "you never do anything right."

He flew on, and Coyote ran after him. After a while Coyote shouted again: "Friend, you're my chief, and it's not right for you to carry the box; people will call me lazy. Let me have it."

"No, no, you always mess everything up." And Eagle flew on and Coyote ran along.

So it went for a stretch, and then Coyote started again. "Ho, friend, it isn't right for you to do this. What will people think of you and me?"

"I don't care what people think. I'm going to carry this box."

Again Eagle flew on and again Coyote ran after him. Finally Coyote begged for the fourth time: "Let me carry it. You're the chief, and I'm just Coyote. Let me carry it."

Eagle couldn't stand any more pestering. Also, Coyote had asked him four times, and if someone asks four times, you'd better give him what he wants. Eagle said, "Since you won't let up on me, go ahead and carry the box for a while. But promise not to open it."

"Oh, sure, oh yes, I promise." They went on as before, but now Coyote had the box. Soon Eagle was far ahead, and Coyote

LITERATURE IN CONTEXT

Culture Connection

Kachinas

The Zuñi and Hopi are Native American nations of the American Southwest. In both of these cultures, the Kachina dancers serve as links between the earthly world and the spirit world. Every year in colorful ceremonies, dancers perform, wearing masks representing various supernatural beings, or Kachinas.

The dancers play a central role in the religions of both cultures, where the blessings of the powerful spirits are sought every year for a good harvest and good fortune.

Connect to the Literature

What details in the story show that the Kachinas are powerful beings?

Vocabulary
pestering (pes´ tər iŋ) *n.* constant bothering

Reading Check
What do Coyote and Eagle team up to do?

Vocabulary
lagged (lagd) *v.*
moved slowly

shriveled (shriv´ əld) *v.*
dried up; shrank
and wrinkled

pursuit (pər soot´) *n.*
chasing in order
to catch

curiosity (kyoor´ ē äs
ə tē) *n.* the desire to
obtain information

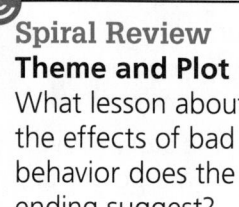

Spiral Review
Theme and Plot
What lesson about
the effects of bad
behavior does the
ending suggest?

lagged behind a hill where Eagle couldn't see him. "I wonder what the light looks like, inside there," he said to himself. "Why shouldn't I take a peek? Probably there's something extra in the box, something good that Eagle wants to keep to himself."

And Coyote opened the lid. Now, not only was the sun inside, but the moon also. Eagle had put them both together, thinking that it would be easier to carry one box than two.

As soon as Coyote opened the lid, the moon escaped, flying high into the sky. At once all the plants shriveled up and turned brown. Just as quickly, all the leaves fell off the trees, and it was winter. Trying to catch the moon and put it back in the box, Coyote ran in pursuit as it skipped away from him. Meanwhile the sun flew out and rose into the sky. It drifted far away, and the peaches, squashes, and melons shriveled up with cold.

Eagle turned and flew back to see what had delayed Coyote. "You fool! Look what you've done!" he said. "You let the sun and moon escape, and now it's cold." Indeed, it began to snow, and Coyote shivered. "Now your teeth are chattering," Eagle said, "and it's your fault that cold has come into the world."

It's true. If it weren't for Coyote's curiosity and mischief making, we wouldn't have winter; we could enjoy summer all the time.

Critical Thinking

Cite textual evidence to support your responses.

1. **Key Ideas and Details (a)** Why does Coyote want to team up with Eagle? **(b) Compare and Contrast:** How do Coyote and Eagle differ in their abilities and attitudes? **(c) Connect:** How do each character's actions reflect his attitude?

2. **Key Ideas and Details (a)** Why do Eagle and Coyote want the Kachinas' box? **(b) Infer:** Why does Eagle agree to steal it?

3. **Key Ideas and Details (a)** How does Coyote finally get the box? **(b) Infer:** What does Coyote's behavior tell you about his character?

4. **Integration of Knowledge and Ideas (a)** What makes myths like this one still appealing in an age of scientific knowledge? **(b)** Could you find these same types of characters and attitudes in any of today's forms of popular entertainment? Explain. *[Connect to the Big Question: Are yesterday's heroes important today?]*

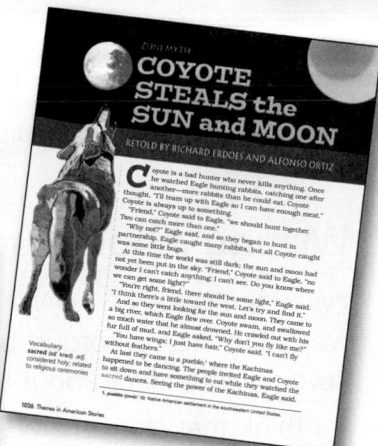

Reading Skill: Summarize

1. The characters' actions in this myth can be divided into four "scenes," or sections. Use a graphic organizer like the one shown to **summarize** the important events in each section.

Section	Summary
The Hunt	
At the Kachinas' Dance	
Running Away	
Coyote's Mistake	

2. Using your chart, summarize the entire story in as few sentences as possible, leaving out minor details.

Literary Analysis: Mythology

©3. Key Ideas and Details (a) What element of nature does this **myth** explain? **(b)** In what ways do its animal characters resemble humans? **(c)** What theme, or message, regarding nature can you infer from the myth? Support your answer with story details.

©4. Key Ideas and Details What does this myth reveal about Zuñi culture and beliefs?

Vocabulary

© Acquisition and Use Write a sentence to answer each question, using a word from the vocabulary list on page 1024.

1. How would you describe a sheriff chasing a fugitive?

2. What made the girl ask so many questions?

3. What happens to garden plants after the first frost?

4. How would you describe an annoying younger child?

5. Where did ancient Greeks worship their gods?

6. Why was the bicycle racer certain he would finish last?

Word Study Use context and what you know about the **Latin root -sacr-** to explain your answer to each question.

1. What might you *sacrifice* to do an extracurricular activity?

2. What would you avoid if you considered free time *sacrosanct*?

Word Study

The **Latin root -sacr-** means "holy."

Apply It Explain how the root -sacr- contributes to the meanings of these words. Consult a dictionary if necessary.

sacrament
sacrilegious
consecrate

Are yesterday's *heroes* important today?

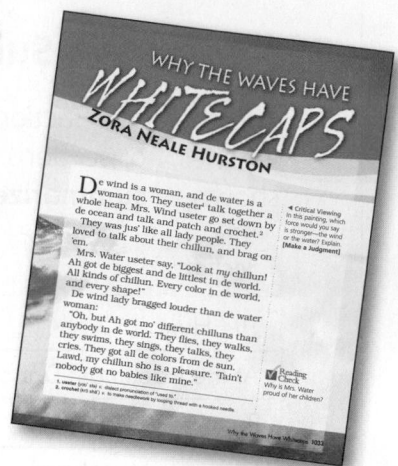

Writing About the Big Question

"Why the Waves Have Whitecaps" is a story whose characters act in ways that are humorous, but unheroic. Use this sentence starter to develop your ideas about the Big Question.

I think that story characters who (do / do not) behave **admirably** have more relevance today because _____.

While You Read Notice the main characters' unheroic behavior.

Vocabulary

Dialect is the form of language spoken in a particular region or by a particular group of people.

- Dialects develop over time. They are usually based on ancestry, geographic location, regional isolation, and economic conditions. For example, people in coastal Georgia traditionally speak a slightly different dialect than people who live in the mountainous Appalachian region, even though they live in the same state. This is due to the historical role the mountains played in keeping people of these regions apart, as well as their different ancestry.

- Dialects of the same language may differ greatly in vocabulary, grammar, and pronunciation. It is not unusual to find that people who speak different dialects of the same language have a hard time understanding one another.

- Dialect is usually written *phonetically*, or the way it sounds when spoken. Letters and syllables may be dropped or altered at the beginning, middle, or end of words. For instance, residents of London's East End say *'ouse* instead of *house*.

When reading stories written in dialect, it helps to read the text aloud. Focus on the sounds of the letters in each word, and try to ignore the odd spellings. Your ear will probably pick out the word it most closely resembles in your own daily speech. If reading aloud does not help, think about the context of the word and what meaning would make the most sense in the sentence.

Word Study

In this myth, the word *chillun* reflects a **dialect** spoken by African Americans in the South in the early nineteenth century. It is derived from the standard English word *children*.

Meet
Zora Neale Hurston
(1891–1960)

Author of
WHY THE WAVES HAVE
WHITECAPS

Zora Neale Hurston was one of the first writers to recognize the richness of African American folk tales. Hurston grew up in Eatonville, Florida. After moving north, she began writing with a group of authors in Harlem, New York, that included Langston Hughes.

Belated Recognition Hurston's talent was recognized by the founder of Barnard College, who arranged for her to study with the anthropologist Franz Boas. Part of Hurston's research involved traveling around the country and collecting folk tales. Without her research, many of these traditional stories might have been lost. Hurston was criticized during her lifetime for featuring local dialect so prominently in her writing style. Only later was her genius recognized and her books widely circulated once again.

BACKGROUND FOR THE MYTH

Waves

"Why the Waves Have Whitecaps" is a myth that explains the natural phenomenon of whitecaps. There is, of course, a scientific explanation for the whitecaps on waves. Waves form when winds blow across the surface of water and transmit their energy to the water. As waves reach shallower water near the shore, the wave height increases until they topple over and break into water droplets. The droplets reflect light and appear as foamy whitecaps.

DID YOU KNOW?

Hurston's most popular book is the novel *Their Eyes Were Watching God* (1937). She also wrote a play, *Mule Bone*, with Langston Hughes.

WHY THE WAVES HAVE

WHITECAPS

ZORA NEALE HURSTON

De wind is a woman, and de water is a woman too. They useter[1] talk together a whole heap. Mrs. Wind useter go set down by de ocean and talk and patch and crochet.[2]

They was jus' like all lady people. They loved to talk about their chillun, and brag on 'em.

Mrs. Water useter say, "Look at *my* chillun! Ah got de biggest and de littlest in de world. All kinds of chillun. Every color in de world, and every shape!"

De wind lady bragged louder than de water woman:

"Oh, but Ah got mo' different chilluns than anybody in de world. They flies, they walks, they swims, they sings, they talks, they cries. They got all de colors from de sun. Lawd, my chillun sho is a pleasure. 'Tain't nobody got no babies like mine."

---

1. useter (yoo´ stə) *v.* dialect pronunciation of "used to."
2. crochet (krō shā´) *v.* make needlework by looping thread with a hooked needle.

◀ **Critical Viewing**
In this painting, which force would you say is stronger—the wind or the water? Explain. **[Make a Judgment]**

Spiral Review
Theme and Character What theme might the characters' bragging suggest?

Reading Check
Why is Mrs. Water proud of her children?

Summarize
What causes the argument between Mrs. Wind and Mrs. Water?

Mythology
What human qualities does Mrs. Wind possess?

Mrs. Water got tired of hearin' 'bout Mrs. Wind's chillun so she got so she hated 'em.

One day a whole passle of her chillun come to Mrs. Wind and says: "Mama, wese thirsty. Kin we go git us a cool drink of water?"

She says, "Yeah chillun. Run on over to Mrs. Water and hurry right back soon."

When them chillun went to squinch they thirst Mrs. Water grabbed 'em all and drowned 'em.

When her chillun didn't come home, de wind woman got worried. So she went on down to de water and ast for her babies.

"Good evenin' Mis' Water, you see my chillun today?"

De water woman tole her, "No-oo-oo."

Mrs. Wind knew her chillun had come down to Mrs. Water's house, so she passed over de ocean callin' her chillun, and every time she call de white feathers would come up on top of de water. And dat's how come we got white caps on waves. It's de feathers comin' up when de wind woman calls her lost babies.

When you see a storm on de water, it's de wind and de water fightin' over dem chillun.

Critical Thinking

1. **Key Ideas and Details** **(a)** What is Mrs. Wind's and Mrs. Water's relationship as the story begins? **(b) Infer:** What changes their relationship?

2. **Key Ideas and Details** **(a)** What qualities of their children do Mrs. Wind and Mrs. Water brag about? **(b) Connect:** How do these qualities relate to the behavior of wind and water in the natural world?

3. **Key Ideas and Details** **(a)** What happens to Mrs. Wind's children? **(b) Deduce:** What does this event reveal about Mrs. Water?

4. **Craft and Structure** **(a) Cause and Effect:** What are the results of the quarrel? **(b) Speculate:** Given the nature of the characters, could this story have ended differently?

5. **Integration of Knowledge and Ideas** **(a)** What qualities make Mrs. Water and Mrs. Wind unheroic? **(b)** Does a traditional story with antiheroes have as much relevance as a story featuring heroes? Explain. *[Connect to the Big Question: Are yesterday's heroes important today?]*

Cite textual evidence to support your responses.

Reading Skill: Summarize

1. The characters' actions in this myth can be divided into three "scenes," or sections. Use a graphic organizer like the one shown to **summarize** the important events of each section.

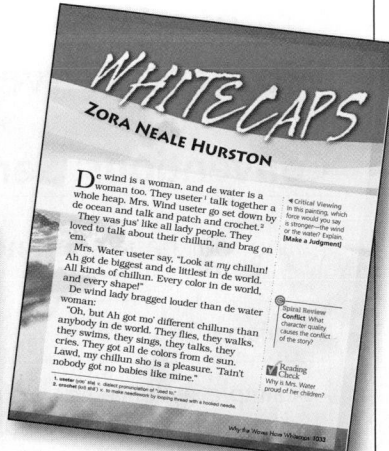

Section	Summary
Mrs. Water and Mrs. Wind Compete	
Mrs. Water's Revenge	
Whitecaps and Storms	

2. Using your chart, summarize the entire story in as few sentences as possible, leaving out minor details.

Literary Analysis: Mythology

3. Key Ideas and Details How does this **myth** explain the phenomenon of whitecaps?

4. Key Ideas and Details (a) In what ways do the myth's characters act like humans? **(b)** How might the experiences of enslaved Africans have contributed to this myth? **(c)** What theme, or message, does the myth convey about human behavior?

Vocabulary

Acquisition and Use Rewrite each sentence in Standard English.

1. Mrs. Wind <u>useter</u> go <u>set</u> down by <u>de</u> ocean.

2. <u>Ah</u> got <u>mo'</u> different <u>chilluns</u> than anybody in <u>de</u> world.

3. Mrs. Water got tired of <u>hearin'</u> 'bout Mrs. Wind's <u>chilluns</u>.

4. When <u>them chillun</u> went to <u>squinch they</u> thirst Mrs. Water grabbed <u>'em</u> all.

5. When you see a storm on <u>de</u> water, it's <u>de</u> wind and <u>de</u> water <u>fightin'</u> over <u>dem chillun</u>.

Word Study An important part of Zora Neale Hurston's style is her use of authentic **dialect.** Would this myth have the same appeal if it were written in Standard English? Why or why not?

Word Study

Keep in mind that **dialects** arise from the regional influences and isolation of a group of people.

Apply It What impact do you think television, radio, and other mass media have on the survival of specific regional dialects and on the rise of new dialects?

Integrated Language Skills

Coyote Steals the Sun and Moon • Why the Waves Have Whitecaps

Conventions: Sentence Structure

The four basic **sentence structures** are shown below.

Sentence Structures	Examples
A **simple sentence** has a single independent clause with at least one subject and verb.	**The cat sleeps on the chair.**
A **compound sentence** consists of two or more independent clauses usually joined by a comma and a conjunction.	**The cat sleeps on the chair,** and **the dog sleeps on the floor.**
A **complex sentence** consists of one independent clause and one or more subordinate clauses.	**Jack,** who is my cousin, **raises golden retrievers,** which he exhibits at dog shows.
A **compound-complex sentence** consists of two or more independent clauses and one or more subordinate clauses.	After she took her exam, **Sue remembered she had to pick up her sister,** but **she wanted to finish writing first.**

Practice A Identify the structure of each of the following sentences.

1. When the world was still dark, Coyote and Eagle went in search of light.

2. Eagle could fly, but Coyote, who did not have feathers or wings, could not.

3. Eagle swooped and scooped up the box.

4. Although he promised not to, Coyote opened the box, and when he did, the sun and moon escaped.

ⓒ **Reading Application** In "Coyote . . .," find one example of each of the four basic sentence structures.

Practice B Change each of the following simple sentences into either a compound or a complex sentence. Then, identify its structure.

1. Mrs. Wind sat by the ocean and talked with Mrs. Water.

2. Mrs. Wind bragged about her children.

3. Mrs. Water developed a hatred for Mrs. Wind's children.

4. One day, Mrs. Wind's children didn't come home.

ⓒ **Writing Application** Write four sentences about either myth using each of the four sentence types.

PH WRITING COACH Further instruction and practice are available in *Prentice Hall Writing Coach*.

Writing

**Common Core
State Standards**

**L.8.1, L.8.3; W.8.3; W.8.3.b,
W.8.3.e; SL.8.5, SL.8.6**
[For the full wording of the
standards, see page 1022.]

Narrative Text Create a **myth** to explain a natural phenomenon.

- First, choose a natural feature or event—for example, a rainbow, the seasons, or certain animal behaviors.
- Think of yourself as a storyteller. Entertain your audience with informal elements such as dialect, idioms, and humor.
- Develop the personalities of each character through their actions, expressions, physical description, and dialogue.
- Make sure your myth has a central problem that comes to a reasonable and satisfactory conclusion during the resolution of the plot. The resolution should be the basis for the myth.
- Edit to check that your resolution explains the natural event.

Grammar Application In your myth, use each of the four sentence structures at least once.

Writing Workshop: *Work in Progress*

Prewriting for Exposition For a multimedia report you may develop, choose two subjects that you think will lend themselves to interesting visuals. Use the Internet to search for images. Then, print them out, along with source information. Save this Image Research in your writing portfolio.

Use this prewriting activity to prepare for the **Writing Workshop** on page 1084.

Speaking and Listening

Comprehension and Collaboration With a group, use the Internet and print sources to gather information for an **oral presentation** about the myth you read.

- If you read "Coyote . . .," look for ways in which history and traditional beliefs influence Zuñi life and culture today.
- If you read "Why the Waves . . .," look for ways in which the history and traditional folklore of African Americans have influenced modern culture.

Keep these tips in mind while completing the assignment:

- Display information with visuals—charts, maps, and graphs.
- Use appropriate digital tools to create your presentation. For example, you could use multimedia software to create a slide-show of images related to the culture, accompanied by music.
- As you present, choose language that shows sensitivity and respect when you discuss another culture's traditions.

PHLit Online!
www.PHLitOnline.com

- Interactive graphic organizers
- Grammar tutorial
- Interactive journals

Ⓒ Leveled Texts

Build your skills and improve your comprehension of literature with
texts of increasing complexity.

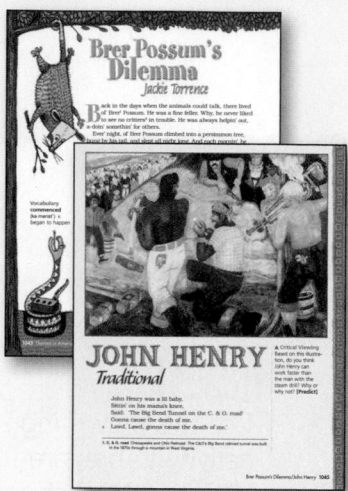

Read **"Brer Possum's Dilemma"**
to see whether kindness is
always repaid. Read **"John
Henry"** to see the outcome
when a man challenges a
machine.

Read **"Chicoria"** for a lesson in
good manners. Read the excerpt
from ***The People, Yes*** to chuckle
over absurd characters from
American folklore.

Ⓒ Common Core State Standards

Meet these standards with **"Brer Possum's Dilemma"** (p. 1042) and **"John Henry"** (p. 1045) or
"Chicoria" (p. 1052) and the excerpt from ***The People, Yes*** (p. 1055).

Reading Literature
4. Determine the meaning of words and phrases as they
are used in a text, including figurative and connotative
meanings; analyze the impact of specific word choices on
meaning and tone, including analogies or allusions to
other texts. *(Literary Analysis: Oral Tradition; Writing:
Critical Analysis)*

7. Analyze the extent to which a filmed or live production
of a story or drama stays faithful to or departs from the
text or script, evaluating the choices made by the director
or actors. *(Speaking and Listening: Storytelling Workshop)*

Writing
2. Write informative/explanatory texts to examine a
topic and convey ideas, concepts, and information

through the selection, organization, and analysis of
relevant content.

9. Draw evidence from literary or informational texts to
support analysis, reflection, and research. *(Writing:
Critical Analysis)*

Speaking and Listening
6. Adapt speech to a variety of contexts and tasks,
demonstrating command of formal English when
indicated or appropriate. *(Speaking and Listening:
Storytelling Workshop)*

Language
2.a. Use punctuation to indicate a pause or break.
(Conventions: Commas)

Reading Skill: Summarize

A **summary** is a short restatement of the main points of a text or the main events of a plot. Summaries leave out minor details, providing a quick way to preview or review a longer work.

Before you summarize a work of literature, follow these steps:

- First, read the selection, and identify the main idea or main event. Consider details to determine whether each event or idea is important enough to be included in your summary.
- Then, **use graphics** to help organize the major events or ideas. For example, if you are summarizing an essay or a poem, you might use a cluster diagram with the main idea in the center and supporting details in attached circles.

Literary Analysis: Oral Tradition

In the **oral tradition,** storytellers pass on legends, songs, folk tales, tall tales, and stories from generation to generation by word of mouth. Here are some key features of the oral tradition:

- As stories and songs are written down, they are often written in **dialect**—the language and grammar of a particular region.
- Stories and songs in the oral tradition frequently contain **idioms**—expressions that are not meant to be understood literally, such as "strictly for the birds" and "spoiling for a fight."

As you read, identify the tone, or attitude, created by the author's use of dialect and idioms.

Using the Strategy: Oral Tradition Chart

Record story details on an **oral tradition chart** like this one.

Oral Tradition	Story Detail
repetition and exaggeration (hyperbole)	
heroes who are brave, clever, or strong	
animal characters that act like humans	
dialect, idioms, and informal speech	
traditions of a culture	

Are yesterday's *heroes* important today?

Writing About the Big Question

The human-like animals in "Brer Possum's Dilemma" and the larger-than-life hero "John Henry" are typical one-dimensional folk tale characters. Use this sentence starter to develop your ideas about the Big Question.

Although the **accomplishments** of folk heroes are **exaggerated,** these stories have value today because _____.

While You Read Look for story details that show qualities that we might admire or recognize in ourselves.

Vocabulary

Read each word and its definition. Decide whether you know the word well, know it a little bit, or do not know it at all. After you read, see how your knowledge of each word has increased.

- **commenced** (kə menst´) *v.* began to happen (p. 1042) *The meeting <u>commenced</u> quietly, but then became noisy.* *commencement n.*

- **pitiful** (pit´ i fəl) *adj.* arousing sympathy (p. 1044) *The wet, lost puppy was a <u>pitiful</u> sight. pitifully adv. pity n. or v.*

- **coiled** (kɔild) *v.* twisted around and around (p. 1044) *The cat <u>coiled</u> up into a tight ball to take a nap on the sunny window ledge. coil n. recoil v.*

- **flagged** (flagd) *v.* gave a sign to stop, often with a flag or another object (p. 1047) *The stranded travelers <u>flagged</u> a passing motorist to ask for help. flag n. flagging adj.*

Word Study

The **Old English suffix -ful** means "full of" or "having the qualities of." It can indicate a word is an adjective.

In "Brer Possum's Dilemma," one of the characters looks and acts in a way that is **pitiful,** or full of sadness and misfortune.

Meet
Jackie Torrence
(1944–2004)

Author of
Brer Possum's Dilemma

Starting in the 1970s, Jackie Torrence became one of America's best-known and best-loved storytellers. Born in Chicago, she spent her childhood with her grandparents in a North Carolina farming settlement. From them, she learned the "Brer Rabbit" fables and other African American tales that had been passed along to the descendants of enslaved Africans in the South.

A Lively Presenter Torrence told classic ghost stories and her own tales, along with traditional folk tales. She animated her storytelling with humor, engaging language, hisses, shrieks, and facial expressions. Torrence collected stories in *The Accidental Angel, My Grandmother's Treasure*, and other books. She also recorded stories on compact discs, videos, and DVDs.

DID YOU KNOW?
Jackie Torrence began telling stories in the public library, and soon large audiences were coming to hear "the Story Lady."

BACKGROUND FOR THE TALES

Folk Heroes

The main characters in many folk tales are folk heroes—larger-than-life characters who are sometimes based on real people. Typically, though, folk tales exaggerate these characters, making them bigger, faster, stronger, smarter, or braver. Animal characters with human traits are also common in folk tales.

Brer Possum's Dilemma

Jackie Torrence

Back in the days when the animals could talk, there lived ol' Brer[1] Possum. He was a fine feller. Why, he never liked to see no critters[2] in trouble. He was always helpin' out, a-doin' somethin' for others.

Ever' night, ol' Brer Possum climbed into a persimmon tree, hung by his tail, and slept all night long. And each mornin', he climbed outa the tree and walked down the road to sun 'imself.

One mornin', as he walked, he come to a big hole in the middle of the road. Now, ol' Brer Possum was kind and gentle, but he was also nosy, so he went over to the hole and looked in. All at once, he stepped back, 'cause layin' in the bottom of that hole was ol' Brer Snake with a brick on his back.

Brer Possum said to 'imself, "I best git on outa here, 'cause ol' Brer Snake is mean and evil and lowdown, and if I git to stayin' around 'im, he jist might git to bitin' me."

So Brer Possum went on down the road.

But Brer Snake had seen Brer Possum, and he commenced to callin' for 'im.

"Help me, Brer Possum."

Brer Possum stopped and turned around. He said to 'imself, "That's ol' Brer Snake a-callin' me. What do you reckon he wants?"

Well, ol' Brer Possum was kindhearted, so he went back down the road to the hole, stood at the edge, and looked down at Brer Snake.

"Was that you a-callin' me? What do you want?"

Vocabulary
commenced
(kə menst´) *v.*
began to happen

---

1. **Brer** (brür) dialect for "brother," used before a name.
2. **critters** dialect for "creatures"; animals.

Brer Snake looked up and said, "I've been down here in this hole for a mighty long time with this brick on my back. Won't you help git it offa me?"

Brer Possum thought.

"Now listen here, Brer Snake. I knows you. You's mean and evil and lowdown, and if'n I was to git down in that hole and git to liftin' that brick offa your back, you wouldn't do nothin' but bite me."

Ol' Brer Snake just hissed.

"Maybe not. Maybe not. Maaaaaaaybe not."

Brer Possum said, "I ain't sure 'bout you at all. I jist don't know. You're a-goin' to have to let me think about it."

So ol' Brer Possum thought—he thought high, and he thought low—and jist as he was thinkin', he looked up into a tree and saw a dead limb a-hangin' down. He climbed into the tree, broke off the limb, and with that ol' stick, pushed that brick offa Brer Snake's back. Then he took off down the road.

Brer Possum thought he was away from ol' Brer Snake when all at once he heard somethin'.

"Help me, Brer Possum."

Brer Possum said, "Oh, no, that's him agin."

But bein' so kindhearted, Brer Possum turned around, went back to the hole, and stood at the edge.

"Brer Snake, was that you a-callin' me? What do you want now?"

Ol' Brer Snake looked up outa the hole and hissed.

"I've been down here for a mighty long time, and I've gotten a little weak, and the sides of this ol' hole are too slick for me to climb. Do you think you can lift me outa here?"

Brer Possum thought.

"Now, you jist wait a minute. If'n I was to git down into that hole and lift you outa there, you wouldn't do nothin' but bite me."

Brer Snake hissed.

"Maybe not. Maybe not. Maaaaaaaybe not."

Brer Possum said, "I jist don't know. You're a-goin' to have to give me time to think about this."

So ol' Brer Possum thought.

And as he thought, he jist happened to look down there in that hole and see that ol' dead limb. So he pushed the limb underneath ol' Brer Snake and he lifted 'im outa the hole, way up into the air, and throwed 'im into the high grass.

◄ **Critical Viewing**
What characteristics of Brer Possum and Brer Snake does this illustration show? **[Analyze]**

Oral Tradition
What examples of dialect here reflect the story's origins as an oral tale?

Reading Check
Why does Brer Snake first call for help?

Oral Tradition
What role does repetition play in building suspense in this story?

Vocabulary
pitiful (pit´ i fəl) *adj.* arousing sympathy

coiled (koild) *v.* twisted around and around

Summarize
What are the consequences of Brer Possum's kindness?

Brer Possum took off a-runnin' down the road.

Well, he thought he was away from ol' Brer Snake when all at once he heard somethin'.

"Help me, Brer Possum."

Brer Possum thought, "That's him agin."

But bein' so kindhearted, he turned around, went back to the hole, and stood there a-lookin' for Brer Snake. Brer Snake crawled outa the high grass just as slow as he could, stretched 'imself out across the road, rared up, and looked at ol' Brer Possum.

Then he hissed. "I've been down there in that ol' hole for a mighty long time, and I've gotten a little cold 'cause the sun didn't shine. Do you think you could put me in your pocket and git me warm?"

Brer Possum said, "Now you listen here, Brer Snake. I knows you. You's mean and evil and lowdown, and if'n I put you in my pocket you wouldn't do nothin' but bite me."

Brer Snake hissed.

"Maybe not. Maybe not. Maaaaaaaybe not."

"No sireee. Brer Snake. I knows you. I jist ain't a-goin' to do it."

But jist as Brer Possum was talkin' to Brer Snake, he happened to git a real good look at 'im. He was a-layin' there lookin' so *pitiful*, and Brer Possum's great big heart began to feel sorry for ol' Brer Snake.

"All right," said Brer Possum. "You must be cold. So jist this once I'm a-goin' to put you in my pocket."

So ol' Brer Snake *coiled* up jist as little as he could, and Brer Possum picked 'im up and put 'im in his pocket.

Brer Snake laid quiet and still—so quiet and still that Brer Possum even forgot that he was a-carryin' 'im around. But all of a sudden, Brer Snake commenced to crawlin' out, and he turned and faced Brer Possum and hissed.

"I'm a-goin' to bite you."

But Brer Possum said, "Now wait a minute. Why are you a-goin' to bite me? I done took that brick offa your back, I got you outa that hole, and I put you in my pocket to git you warm. Why are you a-goin' to bite me?"

Brer Snake hissed.

"You knowed I was a snake before you put me in you pocket."

And when you're mindin' your own business and you spot trouble, don't never trouble trouble 'til trouble troubles you.

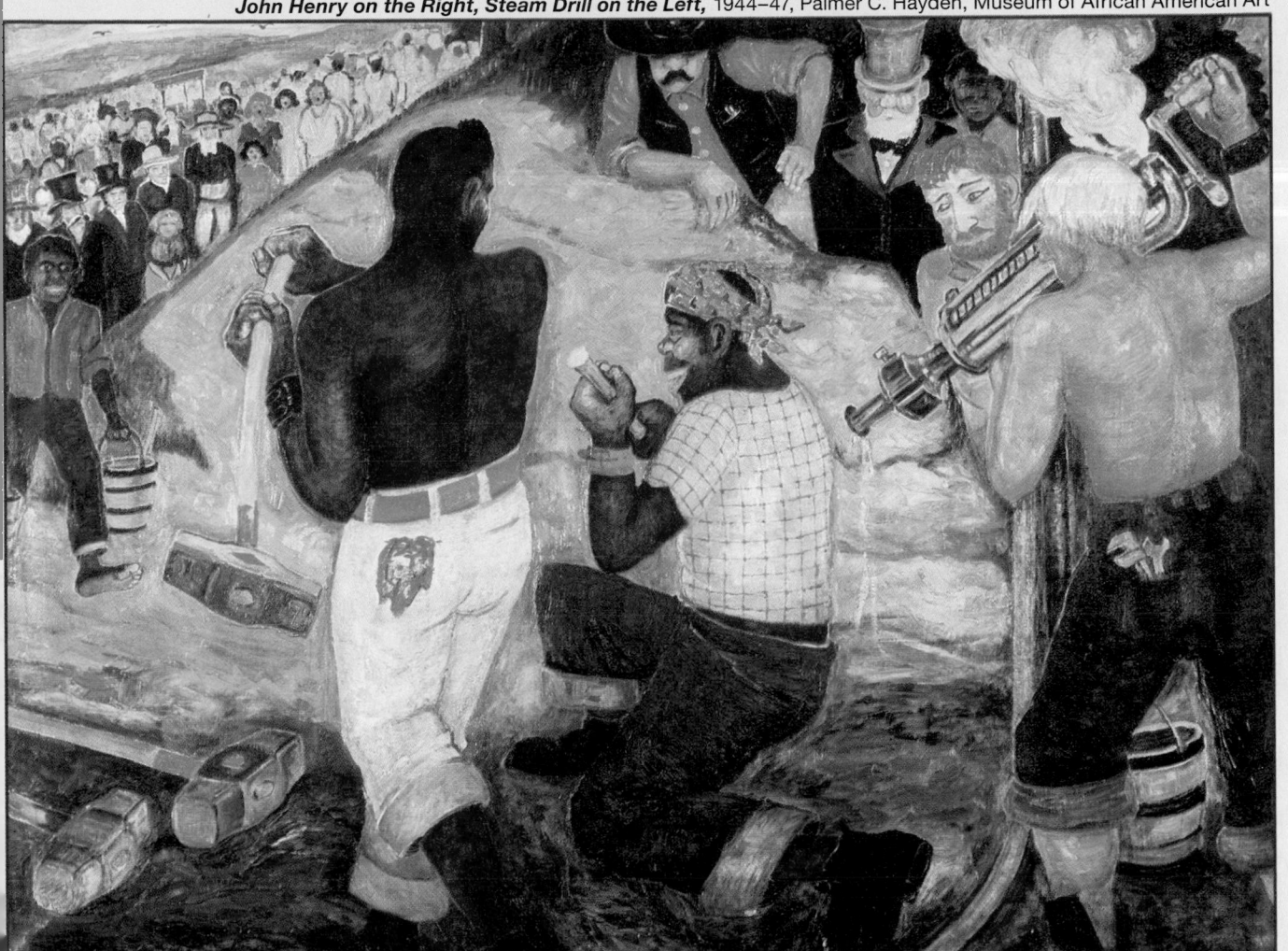

John Henry on the Right, Steam Drill on the Left, 1944–47, Palmer C. Hayden, Museum of African American Art

JOHN HENRY
Traditional

▲ **Critical Viewing**
Based on this illustration, do you think John Henry can work faster than the man with the steam drill? Why or why not? **[Predict]**

John Henry was a lil baby,
Sittin' on his mama's knee,
Said: 'The Big Bend Tunnel on the C. & O. road[1]
Gonna cause the death of me,
5   Lawd, Lawd, gonna cause the death of me.'

---

1. **C. & O. road** Chesapeake and Ohio Railroad. The C & O's Big Bend railroad tunnel was built in the 1870s through a mountain in West Virginia.

Summarize
What key events happen
in lines 11–20?

LITERATURE IN CONTEXT

Social Studies Connection

Machine Age
Enormous steam engines, like
the Corliss engines shown
below, helped transform work
in the nineteenth century.
Steam engines were used
to power everything from
locomotives to woolen mills.
Goods could now be mass
produced in sprawling factories by far fewer workers in far
less time.

   With this tremendous rise in
machine power, many people
feared that machines would
eventually replace workers.
In England, this gave rise to
unions, labor laws, and in a
few cases, even the smashing of machinery. In America,
where labor laws and unions
were weaker, people cel-
ebrated heroes over lifeless
machines in stories and songs.

Connect to the Literature

Why would people in a
machine age look up to John
Henry as a folk hero?

Cap'n says to John Henry,
'Gonna bring me a steam drill 'round,
Gonna take that steam drill out on the job,
Gonna whop that steel on down,
10   Lawd, Lawd, gonna whop that steel on down.'

John Henry tol' his cap'n,
Lightnin' was in his eye:
'Cap'n, bet yo' las, red cent on me,
Fo' I'll beat it to the bottom or I'll die,
15   Lawd, Lawd, I'll beat it to the bottom or I'll die.'

Sun shine hot an' burnin',
Wer'n't no breeze a-tall,
Sweat ran down like water down a hill,
That day John Henry let his hammer fall,
20   Lawd, Lawd, that day John Henry let his hammer fall.

John Henry went to the tunnel,
An' they put him in the lead to drive,
The rock so tall an' John Henry so small,
That he lied down his hammer an' he cried,
25   Lawd, Lawd, that he lied down his hammer an' he cried.

John Henry started on the right hand,
The steam drill started on the lef'—
'Before I'd let this steam drill beat me down,
I'd hammer my fool self to death,
30   Lawd, Lawd, I'd hammer my fool self to death.'

John Henry had a lil woman,
Her name were Polly Ann,
John Henry took sick an' had to go to bed,
Polly Ann drove steel like a man,
35   Lawd, Lawd, Polly Ann drove steel like a man.

John Henry said to his shaker,[2]
'Shaker, why don' you sing?
I'm throwin' twelve poun's from my hips on down,
Jes' listen to the col' steel ring,
40   Lawd, Lawd, jes' listen to the col' steel ring.'

---

2. **shaker** (shā´ kər) *n.* person who sets the spikes and places the drills for a steel-
driver to hammer.

Oh, the captain said to John Henry,
'I b'lieve this mountain's sinkin' in.'
John Henry said to his captain, oh my!
'Ain' nothin' but my hammer suckin' win',
45 Lawd, Lawd, ain' nothin' but my hammer
   suckin' win'.'

John Henry tol' his shaker,
'Shaker, you better pray,
For, if I miss this six-foot steel,
Tomorrow'll be yo' buryin' day,
50 Lawd, Lawd, tomorrow'll be yo' buryin' day.'

John Henry tol' his captain,
'Look yonder what I see—
Yo' drill's done broke an' yo' hole's done choke,
An' you cain' drive steel like me,
55 Lawd, Lawd, an' you cain' drive steel like me.'

The man that invented the steam drill,
Thought he was mighty fine.
John Henry drove his fifteen feet,
An' the steam drill only made nine,
60 Lawd, Lawd, an' the steam drill only made
   nine.

The hammer that John Henry swung,
It weighed over nine pound;
He broke a rib in his lef'-han' side,
An' his intrels[3] fell on the groun',
65 Lawd, Lawd, an' his intrels fell on the
   groun'.

All the womens in the Wes',
When they heared of John Henry's death,
Stood in the rain, flagged the eas'-boun'
   train,
Goin' where John Henry fell dead,
70 Lawd, Lawd, goin' where John Henry fell
   dead.

He Laid Down his Hammer and Cried,
1944–1947, Palmer C. Hayden, Museum of
African American Art, Los Angeles, CA

Oral Tradition
Read the repeated lines
at the end of each
stanza. What is the
effect of this repetition?

Spiral Review
Theme What
possible theme is
suggested in lines
51–60?

Vocabulary
flagged (flagd) *v.*
gave a sign to stop,
often with a flag or
another object

Reading
Check
What challenge does
John Henry accept?

_____
3. **intrels** (en ´ trālz) *n.* dialect for *entrails*—internal organs.

Oral Tradition
This ballad was meant to be sung. What makes a song more likely to be passed down than a story?

John Henry's lil mother,
She was all dressed in red,
She jumped in bed, covered up her head,
Said she didn' know her son was dead,
75 Lawd, Lawd, didn' know her son was dead.

Dey took John Henry to the graveyard,
An' they buried him in the san',
An' every locomotive come roarin' by,
Says, 'There lays a steel-drivin' man,
80 Lawd, Lawd, there lays a steel-drivin' man.'

Critical Thinking

Cite textual evidence to support your responses.

© **1. Key Ideas and Details (a)** What words does Torrence use to describe Brer Possum? **(b) Infer:** Is Brer Possum meant to look foolish or simply big-hearted? **(c) Compare and Contrast:** How are Brer Possum and Brer Snake different?

© **2. Key Ideas and Details (a) Deduce:** Why might Brer Possum think it is safe to trust Brer Snake? **(b) Apply:** What is the lesson of this story?

© **3. Key Ideas and Details (a)** Why does John Henry challenge the steam drill? **(b) Connect:** How do his actions contribute to his legend? **(c) Discuss:** Would the story of John Henry be remembered if he had beaten the machine but still survived? Share your answer with the class.

© **4. Craft and Structure Forms of Poetry:** A *ballad* is a song or poem that tells a story, often involving adventure or romance. Ballads are divided into short rhyming stanzas. They generally repeat certain lines, as in a refrain. How does the form of "John Henry" match the purpose and characteristics of a ballad?

© **5. Integration of Knowledge and Ideas (a)** What common human qualities do John Henry and Brer Possum possess? **(b)** What might cause a folk hero like John Henry to transform over time from a local hero into a national folk hero? *[Connect to the Big Question: Are yesterday's heroes important today?]*

Reading Skill: Summarize

1. (a) To help you **summarize** "John Henry," complete a timeline like the one shown. **(b)** Use your timeline to write a brief summary.

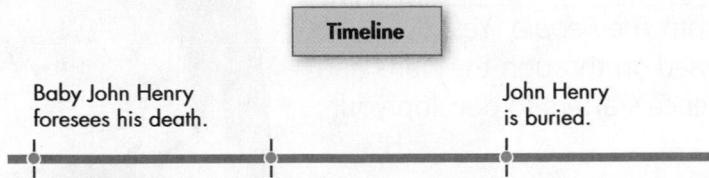

Timeline

Baby John Henry foresees his death.

John Henry is buried.

2. (a) What type of graphic organizer would be most helpful in writing a summary of "Brer Possum's Dilemma"? Explain. **(b)** Use that organizer and write a summary of the story.

Literary Analysis: Oral Tradition

© 3. Key Ideas and Details (a) How is John Henry both typical and *not* typical of a hero of the **oral tradition**? **(b)** What story elements might explain why the story has endured?

© 4. Craft and Structure (a) Review the chart on page 1039. For each feature listed, give one example from "Brer Possum's Dilemma." Explain the effects of each. **(b)** Give the meaning of the example you list for "dialect, idioms, or informal speech." Explain the tone it helps to create.

Vocabulary

© Acquisition and Use Use a word from page 1040 to form an **analogy** that matches the relationship of the other word pair given.

1. *Curl* is to _____ as *rod* is to *straight*.
2. *Opened* is to *closed* as *stopped* is to _____.
3. *Halted* is to _____ as *called* is to *shouted*.
4. *Champion* is to *strong* as *victim* is to _____.

Word Study Use context and what you know about the **Old English suffix -*ful*** to explain your answer to each question.

1. Would a ballerina want critics to describe her as *graceful*?
2. Is a well-written mystery likely to be *suspenseful*?

Are yesterday's *heroes* important today?

Writing About the Big Question

In both "Chicoria" and the excerpt from *The People, Yes,* the values and beliefs of a culture are passed on through the traits and qualities of its heroes. Use these sentence starters to develop your ideas about the Big Question.

In today's stories, qualities such as _____ may be considered **outdated** for a heroic character.

On the other hand, in movies and in books, characters with heroic qualities such as _____ are still relevant because _____.

While You Read Look for details that provide a window into the values a culture considers important.

Vocabulary

Read each word and its definition. Decide whether you know the word well, know it a little bit, or do not know it at all. After you read, see how your knowledge of each word has increased.

- **self-confident** (self kän´ fə dənt) *adj.* certain of one's ability (p. 1054) *She is so <u>self-confident</u> that she does not worry about what others think.* self-confidently *adv.* self-confidence *n.*

- **cordially** (kôr´ jə lē) *adv.* warmly (p. 1054) *The gracious host welcomed his guests <u>cordially</u>.* cordiality *n.* cordial *adj.*

- **haughty** (hôt´ ē) *adj.* scornfully superior (p. 1054) *They thought the <u>haughty</u> prince was rude.* haughtily *adv.* haughtiness *n.*

- **straddling** (strad´ ´liŋ) *v.* standing or sitting with a leg on either side of something (p. 1056) *The cowboy sat high in the saddle, <u>straddling</u> his horse.* straddle *v.*

- **cyclone** (sī´ klōn´) *n.* violent, rotating windstorm; tornado (p. 1056) *The <u>cyclone</u> tore off the roofs.* cycle *n.* or *v.*

- **mutineers** (myo͞ot´ ´n irz´) *n.* rebels (p. 1056) *The <u>mutineers</u> plotted to take over the ship.* mutiny *n.* or *v.*

Word Study

The **suffix -eer** means "one who does something." It is usually a noun ending.

In the excerpt from *The People, Yes,* the narrator describes a group of **mutineers**, or sailors who rebel against their ship's captain.

José Griego y Maestas
(b. 1949)

Rudolfo A. Anaya
(b. 1937)

Authors of "Chicoria" (p. 1052)

José Griego y Maestas and Rudolfo A. Anaya share a common love of old New Mexican folktales, or *cuentos*. It is a true partnership. Griego y Maestas finds and collects the tales, and Anaya translates them into English.

José Griego y Maestas is an expert in bilingual education and is the dean of instruction at Northern New Mexico Community College. He also loves telling stories.

Rudolfo Anaya, author of novels, poetry, and stories, is a celebrated figure in Hispanic literature. His novel *Bless Me, Ultima* is a well-loved classic. Anaya says, "I am an oral storyteller, but now I do it on the printed page."

Carl Sandburg
(1878–1967)

Author of *The People, Yes* (p. 1055)

Carl Sandburg was a journalist and historian as well as a poet and folklorist. In the early 1900s, he was part of a writers' movement in Chicago, a city that inspired some of his best-known poems. Sandburg won the Pulitzer Prize twice—once in 1940 for a biography of Abraham Lincoln and again in 1951 for his *Complete Poems*.

DID YOU KNOW?

As a young man, Sandburg worked as a truck driver and as a ranchhand. These jobs acquainted him with the rhythms of everyday speech.

▲ **Critical Viewing**
What features of this painting indicate the start of a festive occasion, such as the feast in the story? **[Analyze]**

Chicoria

Retold in English by Rudolfo A. Anaya | **Adapted in Spanish by José Griego y Maestas**

There were once many big ranches in California, and many New Mexicans went to work there. One day one of the big ranch owners asked his workers if there were any poets in New Mexico.

"Of course, we have many fine poets," they replied. "We have old Vilmas, Chicoria, Cinfuegos, to say nothing of the poets of Cebolleta and the Black Poet."

"Well, when you return next season, why don't you bring one of your poets to compete with Gracia—here none can compare with him!"

When the harvest was done the New Mexicans returned home. The following season when they returned to California they took with them the poet Chicoria, knowing well that in spinning a rhyme or in weaving wit there was no *Californio*[1] who could beat him.

As soon as the rancher found out that the workers had brought Chicoria with them, he sent his servants to invite his good neighbor and friend to come and hear the new poet. Meanwhile, the cooks set about preparing a big meal. When the maids began to dish up the plates of food, Chicoria turned to one of the servers and said, "Ah, my friends, it looks like they are going to feed us well tonight!"

The servant was surprised. "No, my friend," he explained, "the food is for *them*. We don't eat at the master's table. It is not permitted. We eat in the kitchen."

"Well, I'll bet I can sit down and eat with them," Chicoria boasted.

"If you beg or if you ask, perhaps, but if you don't ask they won't invite you," replied the servant.

"I never beg," the New Mexican answered. "The master will invite me of his own accord, and I'll bet you twenty dollars he will!"

Oral Tradition
What ability of Chicoria's could be considered admirable in his culture?

Reading Check
What request did the ranch owner make of the New Mexicans?

---

1. **Californio** (kä´ lē fôr´ nyō) term for the Spanish-speaking colonists who established ranches in California under Spanish and Mexican rule.

self-confident (self kän´ fə dənt) *adj.* certain of one's ability

cordially (kôr´ jə lē) *adv.* warmly

haughty (hôt´ ē) *adj.* scornfully superior

Oral Tradition
Do you think the teller of this story is a New Mexican or a *Californio*? Why?

ⓒ

Spiral Review
Theme What possible theme is suggested by the conclusion of the story?

Summarize
Would you consider the winning of the bet important enough to include in a summary? Why or why not?

So they made a twenty-dollar bet and they instructed the serving maid to watch if this **self-confident** New Mexican had to ask the master for a place at the table. Then the maid took Chicoria into the dining room. Chicoria greeted the rancher **cordially**, but the rancher appeared **haughty** and did not invite Chicoria to sit with him and his guest at the table. Instead, he asked that a chair be brought and placed by the wall where Chicoria was to sit. The rich ranchers began to eat without inviting Chicoria.

So it is just as the servant predicted, Chicoria thought. The poor are not invited to share the rich man's food!

Then the master spoke: "Tell us about the country where you live. What are some of the customs of New Mexico?"

"Well, in New Mexico when a family sits down to eat each member uses one spoon for each biteful of food," Chicoria said with a twinkle in his eyes.

The ranchers were amazed that the New Mexicans ate in that manner, but what Chicoria hadn't told them was that each spoon was a piece of tortilla:[2] one fold and it became a spoon with which to scoop up the meal.

"Furthermore," he continued, "our goats are not like yours."

"How are they different?" the rancher asked.

"Here your nannies[3] give birth to two kids, in New Mexico they give birth to three!"

"What a strange thing!" the master said. "But tell us, how can the female nurse three kids?"

"Well, they do it exactly as you're doing it now: While two of them are eating the third one looks on."

The rancher then realized his lack of manners and took Chicoria's hint. He apologized and invited his New Mexico guest to dine at the table. After dinner, Chicoria sang and recited his poetry, putting Gracia to shame. And he won his bet as well.

---

2. tortilla (tôr tē´ yə) *n.* thin, round pancake of cornmeal or flour.
3. nannies (nan´ ēz) *n.* female goats.

from The People, Yes
Carl Sandburg

They have yarns[1]
Of a skyscraper so tall they had to put hinges
On the two top stories so to let the moon go by,
Of one corn crop in Missouri when the roots
5 Went so deep and drew off so much water

---

1. yarns (yärnz) *n.* tall tales that depend on humor and exaggeration.

▼ **Critical Viewing**
What type of mood does this illustration create? **[Analyze]**

Vocabulary

straddling (strad´ ´lin)
v. standing or sitting
with a leg on either
side of something

cyclone (sī´ klon´) *n.*
violent, rotating wind-
storm; tornado

mutineers (myoōt´
´n irz´) *n.* rebels

Oral Tradition
Does Sandburg's use
of exaggeration and
repetition portray a
country at rest or on
the move? Explain.

The Mississippi riverbed that year was dry,
Of pancakes so thin they had only one side,
Of "a fog so thick we shingled the barn and six feet out
    on the fog,"
Of Pecos Pete straddling a cyclone in Texas and riding it
    to the west coast where "it rained out under him,"
10 Of the man who drove a swarm of bees across the Rocky
    Mountains and the Desert "and didn't lose a bee,"
Of a mountain railroad curve where the engineer in his
    cab can touch the caboose and spit in the conductor's eye,
Of the boy who climbed a cornstalk growing so fast he
    would have starved to death if they hadn't shot
    biscuits up to him,
Of the old man's whiskers: "When the wind was with
    him his whiskers arrived a day before he did,"
Of the hen laying a square egg and cackling, "Ouch!"
    and of hens laying eggs with the dates printed on them,
15 Of the ship captain's shadow: it froze to the deck one
    cold winter night,
Of mutineers on that same ship put to chipping rust
    with rubber hammers,
Of the sheep counter who was fast and accurate: "I just
    count their feet and divide by four,"
Of the man so tall he must climb a ladder to shave
    himself,

Of the runt so teeny-weeny it takes two men and a boy to
    see him,
20 Of mosquitoes: one can kill a dog, two of them a man,
Of a cyclone that sucked cookstoves out of the kitchen,
    up the chimney flue, and on to the next town,
Of the same cyclone picking up wagontracks in Nebraska
    and dropping them over in the Dakotas,
Of the hook-and-eye snake unlocking itself into forty
    pieces, each piece two inches long, then in nine seconds
    flat snapping itself together again,
Of the watch swallowed by the cow—when they butchered
    her a year later the watch was running and had the
    correct time,
25 Of horned snakes, hoop snakes that roll themselves
    where they want to go, and rattlesnakes carrying bells
    instead of rattles on their tails,
Of the herd of cattle in California getting lost in a giant
    redwood tree that had hollowed out,
Of the man who killed a snake by putting its tail in its
    mouth so it swallowed itself,
Of railroad trains whizzing along so fast they reach the
    station before the whistle,
Of pigs so thin the farmer had to tie knots in their tails
    to keep them from crawling through the cracks in their
    pens,

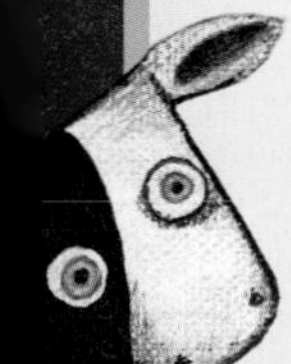

Summarize
Would it be essential to
list all of the characters
and animals in a sum-
mary of this poem?
Why or why not?

Reading
Check
What tall tales from the
poem do the illustra-
tions on pages 1056
and 1057 show?

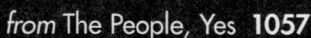

BM-17—Paul Bunyan and Babe, his Blue Ox, Bemidji, Minn.

PAUL BUNYAN

8B-H10S2

Oral Tradition
What characteristics are shared by the folk heroes mentioned at the end of the poem?

30 Of Paul Bunyan's big blue ox, Babe, measuring between
    the eyes forty-two ax-handles and a plug of Star tobacco
    exactly,
   Of John Henry's hammer and the curve of its swing and
    his singing of it as "a rainbow round my shoulder."

Critical Thinking

Cite textual evidence to support your responses.

1. **Key Ideas and Details (a)** In "Chicoria," how does the server respond when Chicoria says he expects to be fed well? **(b) Analyze:** Why does Chicoria assume that he will eat at the rancher's table?

2. **Key Ideas and Details Analyze:** Why does Chicoria tell the story about the goats?

3. **Key Ideas and Details (a)** Identify three people mentioned in the excerpt from *The People, Yes* who have amazing abilities or skills. **(b) Evaluate:** In what way does each character's ability contribute to survival in a wild, new country?

4. **Integration of Knowledge and Ideas (a) Interpret:** With a partner, interpret the meaning of the title *The People, Yes*. **(b) Discuss:** Are the heroes of these tales inspirational in today's world? Share your answers with the class.

5. **Integration of Knowledge and Ideas (a)** What traits do you think are valued by the cultures that developed these tales? **(b)** What aspects of these tales are most relevant to modern readers? *[Connect to the Big Question: Are yesterday's heroes important today?]*

Reading Skill: Summarize

1. **(a)** To help you **summarize** "Chicoria," construct a timeline of events. **(b)** Use your timeline to write a brief summary.

2. **(a)** Fill in a cluster diagram like the one shown with images from *The People, Yes.* **(b)** Summarize the poem by stating the main idea behind the images.

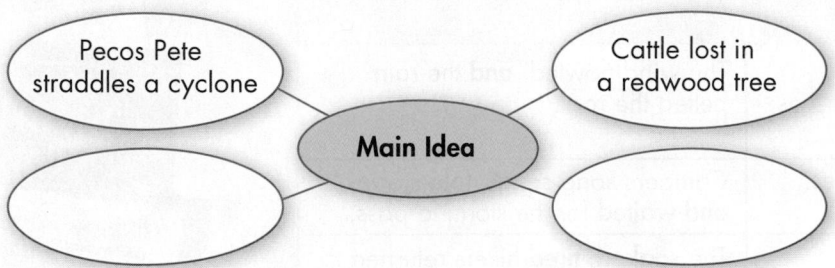

Literary Analysis: Oral Tradition

©3. **Integration of Knowledge and Ideas** How is Chicoria both typical and *not* typical of a hero of the **oral tradition**?

©4. **Craft and Structure (a)** What features of the oral tradition are contained in lines 8–21 of Sandburg's poem? **(b)** Explain the meanings of *runt* and *teeny-weeny* (line 19) and the tone they create.

Vocabulary

© **Acquisition and Use** Use a word from page 1050 to form an **analogy** that matches the relationship of the other word pair.

1. *Rain* is to *cloudburst* as *wind* is to _____.
2. *Rudely* is to *enemy* as _____ is to *friend*.
3. *Rebel* is to _____ as *hike* is to *mountaineers*.
4. *Arms* are to *hugging* as *legs* are to _____.
5. *Insecure* is to _____ as *talkative* is to *silent*.
6. *Gentle* is to *rough* as *humble* is to _____.

Word Study Use the context of the sentences and what you know about the **suffix -eer** to explain your answer to each question.

1. Does an *auctioneer* want responses from an audience?
2. Would it be helpful for a *balladeer* to have a pleasant voice?

Word Study

The **suffix -eer** means "one who does."

Apply It Explain how the suffix -eer contributes to the meanings of these words. Consult a dictionary if necessary.

mountaineer
profiteer
rocketeer

Integrated Language Skills

Brer Possum's Dilemma • John Henry • Chicoria • from The People, Yes •

Conventions: Commas

A **comma** is a punctuation mark that signals a brief pause.

Use a Comma...	
1) ...before a conjunction to separate two independent clauses in a compound sentence.	The wind howled, **and** the rain pelted the roof.
2) ...between items in a series.	Campers sang **songs, told stories, and waited** for the storm to pass.
3) ...between adjectives.	The **soaked, tired** hikers returned to the cabin.
4) ...after introductory material.	**The next day,** the sun shined brightly.
5) ...with parenthetical expressions.	Everyone was, **without a doubt,** eager to go outside.
6) ...to set off appositives, participial phrases, or adjective clauses.	The water level at the lake, **where we swam every morning,** had risen slightly.

Practice A Identify where commas are needed in each of the following sentences.

1. According to Sandburg's poem folk literature has preserved many tall tales.

2. The long thirsty roots of one corn crop in Missouri drained the Mississippi River dry.

3. The eggs of some hens were square and the eggs of others had dates on them.

4. A herd of cattle got lost inside the cavity of a redwood a giant tree.

◉ **Reading Application** In "Chicoria," find a sentence modeling each of the following uses of a comma listed in the chart above: Rules 1, 4, and 6.

Practice B Use the chart to explain where commas are needed in each sentence and why.

1. Brer Possum a kind critter never liked to see anyone in trouble.

2. One morning Brer Possum discovered Brer Snake at the bottom of a hole.

3. Brer Possum wanted to help but he didn't trust Brer Snake.

4. That mean evil lowdown snake was likely to bite him.

◉ **Writing Application** Include commas in three sentences you write about folk tales. Use a different comma rule from the chart above in each sentence.

PH WRITING COACH Further instruction and practice are available in *Prentice Hall Writing Coach*.

Writing

 **Common Core State Standards**

L.8.2; RL.8.4; W.8.2, W.8.9; SL.8.1, SL.8.6
[For the full wording of the standards, see page 1038.]

Explanatory Text Write a **critical analysis** to explain how language affects the tone, meaning, and mood in folk literature. Use these tips:

- Draw on specific examples from the stories and poems you read here, or find examples in other sources.

- Analyze the literal and figurative meanings of idioms, analogies, metaphors, and similes in the stories you choose. Then, explain how these word choices evoke an emotional response. For example, in "Chicoria," a goat analogy draws a comparison and helps the reader appreciate Chicoria's cleverness. The analogy also may entertain readers.

- Point out examples of comic techniques, such as *hyperbole* (exaggeration) or understatement.

Grammar Application Check your draft to make sure you used commas correctly, particularly with introductory structures.

Writing Workshop: *Work in Progress*

Prewriting for Exposition To prepare for a multimedia report, review your Image Research. In a rough outline, write facts and examples you could use to build a narrative with the visuals you have identified. Save this Multimedia Outline in your writing portfolio.

Use this prewriting activity to prepare for the **Writing Workshop** on page 1084.

Speaking and Listening

Comprehension and Collaboration Working with a group, conduct a **storytelling workshop.**

- Choose a folk tale that the class has read, and discuss ways of presenting it.

- Each group member should then make his or her own determinations about the most effective way to interpret the story, including the use of voice and gestures to dramatize the action, the inclusion of props, and the addition of new descriptions using appropriate language.

- If there is dialect in the original, performers may choose to translate it for clarity or retain it for faithfulness to the original.

- In your group, take turns retelling the story for the class.

- Audience members should determine ways in which each retelling is faithful to or departs from the original. Then, they should evaluate the choices each performer has made, based on criteria such as dramatic impact, clarity of meaning, and consistency of approach.

www.PHLitOnline.com
- Interactive graphic organizers
- Grammar tutorial
- Interactive journals

Test Practice: Reading

Summarize

Fiction Selection

Directions: *Read the selection. Then, answer the questions.*

Ms. Kline was fed up with kids riding through her driveway. Mrs. Kim was tired of dodging skateboarders in the supermarket parking lot while she tried to wheel her grocery cart out to her car. Mr. Perez was just worried that someone would get hurt. Members of the Elm Street Association wanted the situation to change.

So they met at City Hall to talk and create slogans addressing the problem with the skateboarders. Signs with slogans were posted on lawns and the local newspaper featured editorials and cartoons addressing the issue. The community was frustrated, and skateboarders were getting restless. Something had to be done. Finally, a proposal was written and a vote was scheduled. If approved, the new law would ban skating in all public spaces, including streets, sidewalks, and parking lots. However, the law also provides funding for a skate-park where kids could skateboard safely without bothering people.

1. Which detail is unnecessary in a summary of this selection?
   A. Mrs. Kim has trouble getting her shopping cart to her car.
   B. The new law would provide funding for a skate park.
   C. The neighbors want to protect their property.
   D. The association wanted to make a positive solution.

2. Which detail is *most* important in a summary of this selection?
   A. Kids are allowed to skate wherever they choose.
   B. The new law bans skating on public property.
   C. Kids are irresponsible on skateboards.
   D. Angry citizens punish kids for skateboarding.

3. What is the topic of this selection?
   A. Kids who skateboard cause trouble in the community.
   B. The town finds creative ways to advertise their problems.
   C. Citizens ban skateboarding in the community.
   D. Citizens meet to solve the problem of skateboarding in the community.

Writing for Assessment

Summarize the selection in a few sentences. Include only the most important main ideas and key details.

Nonfiction Selection

Directions: *Read the selection. Then, answer the questions.*

Political cartoons that often appear in print media present a particular point of view. These cartoons often focus on pressing and current issues that a community may be facing, such as banning skateboarding on public property. Political cartoonists emphasize an issue and try to persuade the reader to think a certain way. Cartoons usually focus on one image accompanied by a memorable and humorous slogan. Using exaggeration and humor, cartoonists make powerful statements.

Most political cartoons use symbols rather than a lot of words. A symbol is a concrete object that represents something else. Uncle Sam, for example, is often used to represent the United States. In analyzing a political cartoon, look at all the images and words. They are the keys to understanding the cartoonist's point of view.

1. Which of the following details could be left out of a summary of this passage?
  A. Political cartoons emphasize an issue.
  B. Political cartoons often appear in print media.
  C. Most political cartoons use symbols rather than a lot of words.
  D. A symbol is a concrete object that represents something else.

2. Which of the following forms would a summary of this selection *best* utilize?
  A. a timeline
  B. a chart
  C. an outline
  D. a Venn diagram

3. Which of the following statements is the *best* summary of this selection?
  A. A political cartoon uses humor to present a point of view and to influence readers.
  B. A political cartoon uses symbols to promote ideas, such as patriotism.
  C. To understand a political cartoon, you would need sufficient knowledge of the subject matter.
  D. Political cartoons make fun of society

Writing for Assessment

Connecting Across Texts
In a paragraph, compare the signs with slogans discussed in the first selection with the political cartoons discussed in the second selection. What is similar and different about them?

PHLit Online!
www.PHLitOnline.com
• Online practice
• Instant feedback

Reading for Information

Analyzing Argumentative and Functional Texts

Book Review

Book Features

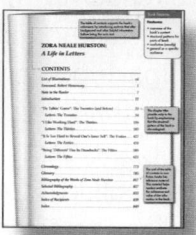

Common Core State Standards

Reading Informational Text
3. Analyze how a text makes connections among and distinctions between individuals, ideas, or events (e.g., through comparisons, analogies, or categories).

Language
4. Determine or clarify the meaning of unknown and multiple-meaning words or phrases based on *grade 8 reading and content,* choosing flexibly from a range of strategies.

6. Acquire and use accurately grade-appropriate general academic and domain-specific words and phrases; gather vocabulary knowledge when considering a word or phrase important to comprehension or expression.

Reading Skill: Evaluate Structural Patterns

Structural patterns in texts organize information. Articles, such as book reviews, and books typically include **text features** that reinforce the structural patterns of a text. The chart shows examples of features that keep text unified and coherent. As you examine the book review and the excerpt of features from a book, **evaluate** whether the author has successfully used structural patterns.

Structural Features of Books	Structural Features of Book Reviews
• **table of contents:** an opening section that provides information to help the reader locate sections of a book • **chapters:** sections that organize information by topic or by time period • **index:** a listing of key words and phrases that helps readers to locate specific information in a book	• **heading:** large, bold text that identifies the book being reviewed • **byline:** a line that shows who wrote the review • **introduction:** an opening section that briefly describes the book being reviewed or provides information that is useful for context • **conclusion:** a closing section that sums up the book's contents and the reviewer's opinion of it

Content-Area Vocabulary

These words appear in the selections that follow. You may also encounter them in other content-area texts.

- **annotated** (an´ ə tā´ id) *adj.* containing notes or comments
- **scholarship** (skäl´ ər ship) *n.* knowledge gained by study
- **acknowledgments** (ak näl´ ij mənts) *n.* a section of a book expressing gratitude or giving credit to those who have helped the author with the work

Book Review

Features:
- name of reviewer
- summary of book
- evaluation of the work

A Life in Letters

Book Review by Zakia Carter

This structural feature of the review gives information about the book being reviewed, including title, author, publisher, and publication date.

Zora Neale Hurston: A Life in Letters.
Edited by Carla Kaplan
Doubleday; October 2002; 896 pages

Within days of having *Zora Neale Hurston: A Life in Letters* in my possession, I was inspired to devote the total of my lunch hour to selecting beautiful blank cards and stationery, a fine ink pen and a book of stamps. By the end of the day, I had penned six letters, the old-fashioned way, to friends and relatives—something I haven't done since summer camp. In our haste to save time, we check our inboxes with an eagerness that was once reserved for that moment before pushing a tiny silver key into a mailbox door. E-mail has replaced paper and pen, so much so that the U.S. Postal Service is losing business. But the truth of the matter is, folks will neither salvage nor cherish e-mail as they might a handwritten letter.

And so *A Life in Letters* is a gift. It includes more than 500 letters and postcards written by Zora Neale Hurston over four decades. The 800-plus-page collection reveals more about this brilliant and complex woman than perhaps the entire body of her published works combined, including her notoriously unrevealing autobiography, *Dust Tracks on the Road*. Amazingly, the urgency and immediacy (typos and all) we associate with e-mail can also be found in Zora's letters. She writes to a veritable who's who in American history and society, including Langston Hughes, Carl Van Vechten, Charlotte Osgood Mason, Franz Boas, Dorothy West and

"An astonishingly brilliant artist. . . . In these letters we encounter Zora Neale Hurston as if for the first time." —Henry Louis Gates, Jr.

ZORA NEALE
HURSTON
A Life in Letters
Collected and Edited by
CARLA KAPLAN

The cover photograph from the book is consistent with the information covered in the review.

Book Review

The details provided here create coherence; the details give reasons that the book is worth reading.

A brief summary of the book's contents adds unity to a book review.

W.E.B. Du Bois among others, sometimes more than once or twice a day. In these, her most intimate writings, Zora comes to life.

While we are familiar with Zora the novelist, essayist, playwright and anthropologist, *A Life in Letters* introduces us to Zora the filmmaker; Zora the Barnard College undergrad and Columbia University student; Zora the two-time Guggenheim fellow; Zora the chicken specialist; Zora the thrice-married wife; and Zora the political pundit. Zora's letters are at times flip, ironic, heartbreaking and humorous. They are insightful, biting and candid as journal entries. One can only wish for responses to Zora's words, but the work is not incomplete without them.

A treasure trove of information, in addition to the **annotated** letters, a chronology of Zora's life, a glossary of the people, events, and institutions to which she refers in her letters, and a thorough bibliographical listing are generously included by editor Carla Kaplan. Each decade of writing is introduced by an essay on the social, political, and personal points of significance in Zora's life. Kaplan's is a fine, well edited and utterly revealing work of **scholarship** into the life of one of the greatest and often most misunderstood American writers. In many ways, *A Life in Letters* is, in fact, a long love letter for Zora. It is a reminder to salvage and cherish what should not be forgotten and an admonishment to write what you love on paper.

—Zakia Carter is an editor at Africana.com.

This structural feature provides information about the reviewer. Reviewers are often experts on the subjects of the books they review.

ZORA NEALE HURSTON:
A Life in Letters

CONTENTS

INDEX

The index provides an alphabetical listing of details provided in the book, along with page numbers that show where the information is located.

Comparing Argumentative and Functional Texts

1. Craft and Structure (a) Explain how the book review distinguishes and connects different aspects of Zora Neale Hurston's life. **(b)** Compare the purpose of a book review to that of a table of contents and an index. **(c)** Explain how the **structural patterns** of each of these texts help you understand what a book is about.

Content-Area Vocabulary

2. (a) Use a print or an online dictionary to identify and explain the meaning of the root *scholar* in the words *scholarship* and *scholarly*. **(b)** Then, use the words *scholar, scholarship,* and *scholarly* in a paragraph about students who achieve academic success.

⏱ Timed Writing

Explanatory Text: Explanation

> **Format**
> The prompt gives specific directions about the topic to discuss and the details to include in your writing.

> Examine the table of contents and index, noting the ways in which they present the information. Then, write an explanation of the purpose of those book features and give tips for using them as reference tools. Use examples from the text to make your points clear. (40 minutes)

> **Academic Vocabulary**
> When you *examine* something, you study the details in order to come to a conclusion.

5-Minute Planner

Complete these steps before you begin to write:

1. Read the prompt carefully, noting the key highlighted terms.

2. Examine the table of contents and index. Look for details that help explain their function and purpose.

3. List the types of information found in the two features.

4. Jot down two ways you would use each book feature.

5. Consult your notes as you draft your explanation.

Comparing Literary Works

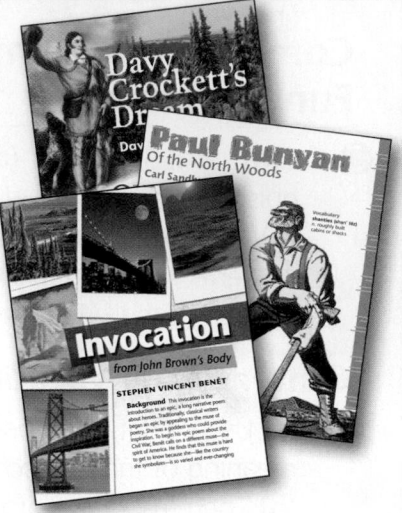

Comparing Heroic Characters

Heroic characters are men and women who show great courage and overcome difficult challenges. A hero in a literary work may be real, fictional, or even based in myth. Often, the hero in a tall tale or legend is a mixture of both—a real historical figure whose actions have become so exaggerated that he or she becomes a legend.

As these selections show, the **theme** of heroism runs across time periods and appears in different literary forms. Carl Sandburg and Stephen Vincent Benét wrote in the period between the world wars—a time when many Americans were looking back fondly at the heroes and values of the western frontier. In contrast, Davy Crockett wrote his own heroic story of the frontier as he lived it— except that he added a few creative touches to fuel his legend.

"Davy Crockett's Dream" and "Paul Bunyan of the North Woods" portray traditional heroes. The hero of "Invocation" is the American muse, who personifies the American spirit. As you read, look for instances in which the hero overcomes larger-than-life challenges. Identify the heroic traits, such as bravery and endurance, that help the hero to master each challenge. Then, fill in a character web like this one to compare the characters' heroic traits.

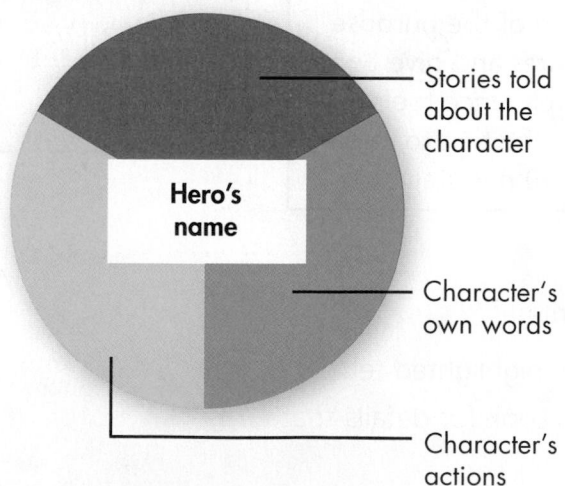

Stories told about the character

Character's own words

Character's actions

Common Core State Standards

Reading Literature

3. Analyze how a particular line of dialogue or incidents in a story propel the action, reveal aspects of a character, or provoke a decision.

9. Analyze how a modern work of fiction draws on themes, patterns of events, or character types from myths, traditional stories, or religious works such as the Bible, including describing how the material is rendered new. *(Literature in Context)*

Writing

2. Write informative/explanatory texts to examine a topic and convey ideas, concepts, and information through the selection, organization, and analysis of relevant content.

9. Draw evidence from literary or informational texts to support analysis, reflection, and research. *(Timed Writing)*

www.PHLitOnline.com

- Vocabulary flashcards
- Interactive journals
- More about the authors
- Selection audio
- Interactive graphic organizers

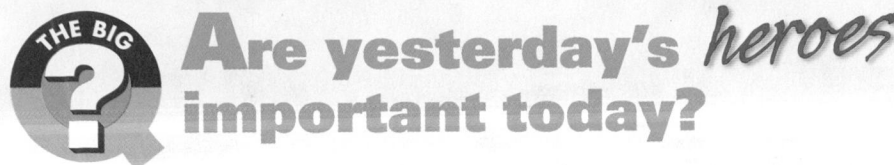

Are yesterday's *heroes* important today?

Writing About the Big Question

In different ways, these selections look back to the heroes of an earlier America. Use this sentence starter to develop your ideas.

To be a hero today, a person can win **admiration** through such actions as _____ and _____.

Meet the Authors

Davy Crockett (1786–1836)
Author of "Davy Crockett's Dream"

Davy Crockett was a genuine frontiersman, but the colorful tall tales in his autobiography helped make him a legend. Crockett was also a politician, representing Tennessee in Congress. He joined the fight for Texas independence and was killed at the battle of the Alamo in 1836. The legends surrounding Crockett took on new form with the airing of the 1950's television show *Davy Crockett*. Millions tuned in, sparking a nationwide fad for Crockett-style coonskin caps.

Carl Sandburg (1878–1967)
Author of "Paul Bunyan of the North Woods"

Carl Sandburg had a lifelong interest in American history and folklore, especially the nation's myths and tall tales. These stories influenced much of his poetry in works such as *The People, Yes* (p. 1055). Sandburg was also a journalist and historian who wrote a widely admired biography of Abraham Lincoln that was six volumes long.

Stephen Vincent Benét (1898–1943)
Author of "Invocation" from *John Brown's Body*

A poet, novelist, and short-story writer, Stephen Vincent Benét often wrote about American history and its heroes. With his wife, Rosemary Carr, Benét wrote *A Book of Americans,* a collection of lively poems for young people about characters in American history. Benét's widely read Civil War epic, *John Brown's Body,* won him the Pulitzer Prize in 1929.

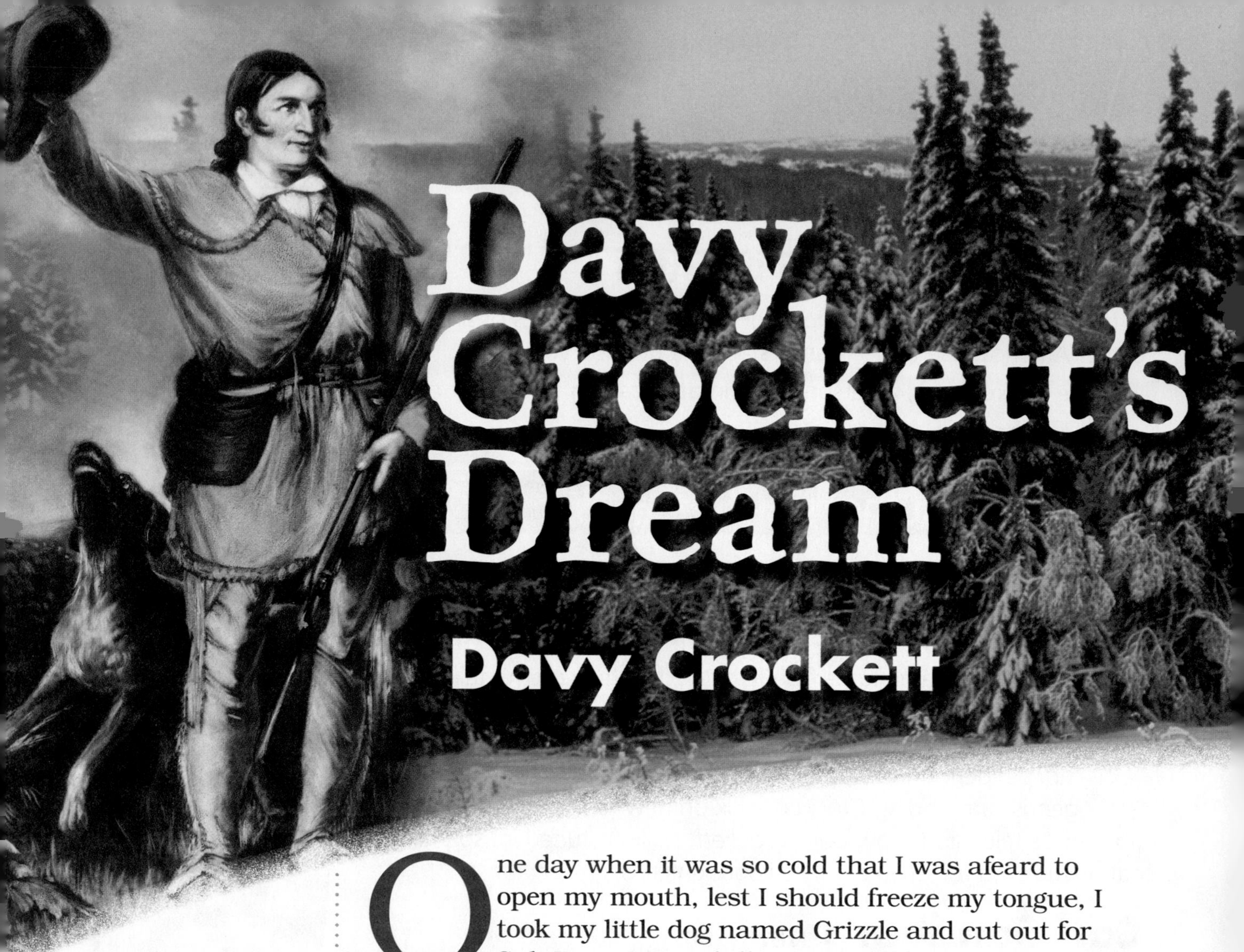

Davy Crockett's Dream

Davy Crockett

Vocabulary
kindled (kind´ əld) *v.*
built or lit a fire

Heroic Characters
What elements of comic exaggeration do you notice here?

One day when it was so cold that I was afeard to open my mouth, lest I should freeze my tongue, I took my little dog named Grizzle and cut out for Salt River Bay to kill something for dinner. I got a good ways from home afore I knowed where I was, and as I had swetted some before I left the house my hat froze fast to my head, and I like to have put my neck out of joint in trying to pull it off. When I sneezed the icicles crackled all up and down the inside of my nose, like when you walk over a bog in winter time. The varmints was so scarce that I couldn't find one, and so when I come to an old log hut that had belonged to some squatter that had ben reformed out by the nabors, I stood my rifle up agin one of the door posts and went in. I kindled up a little fire and told Grizzle I was going to take a nap. I piled up a heap of chestnut burs for a pillow and straitened myself out on the ground, for I can curl closer than a rattlesnake and lay straiter than a log. I laid with the back of my head agin the hearth, and my eyes looking up chimney so that I could see when it was noon by the sun, for

Mrs. Crockett was always rantankerous[1] when I staid out over the time. I got to sleep before Grizzle had done warming the eend of his nose, and I had swallowed so much cold wind that it laid hard on my stomach, and as I laid gulping and belching the wind went out of me and roared up chimney like a young whirlwind. So I had a pesky dream, and kinder thought, till I waked up, that I was floating down the Massassippy in a holler tree, and I hadn't room to stir my legs and arms no more than they were withed together with young saplings. While I was there and want able to help myself a feller called Oak Wing that lived about twenty miles off, and that I had give a most almighty licking once, cum and looked in with his blind eye that I had gouged out five years before, and I saw him looking in one end of the hollow log, and he axed me if I wanted to get out. I told him to tie a rope to one of my legs and draw me out as soon as God would let him and as

◄ **Critical Viewing**
Does Davy Crockett, pictured here, look like he might use "a heap of chestnut burs" for a pillow? Explain. **[Assess]**

Reading Check

Why does Crockett fall asleep looking up a chimney?

---

1. **rantankerous** (ran taŋ′ kər əs) *adj.* dialect for *cantankerous*, meaning "bad-tempered and quarrelsome."

much sooner as he was a mind to. But he said he wouldn't do it that way, he would ram me out with a pole. So he took a long pole and rammed it down agin my head as if he was ramming home the cattridge in a cannon. This didn't make me budge an inch, but it pounded my head down in between my shoulders till I look'd like a turcle with his head drawn in. This started my temper a trifle, and I ript and swore till the breath boiled out of the end of the log like the steam out of the funnel pipe of a steemboat. Jest then I woke up, and seed my wife pulling my leg, for it was enermost sundown and she had cum arter me. There was a long icicle hanging to her nose, and when she tried to kiss me, she run it right into my eye. I told her my dreem, and sed I would have revenge on Oak Wing for pounding my head. She said it was all a dreem and that Oak was not to blame; but I had a very diffrent idee of the matter. So I went and talked to him, and told him what he had done to me in a dreem, and it was settled that he should make me an apology in his next dreem, and that wood make us square,[2] for I don't like to be run upon when I'm asleep, any more than I do when I'm awake.

Heroic Characters
What examples of exaggeration and understatement can you find in this passage?

---

2. **square** even.

Critical Thinking

Cite textual evidence to support your responses.

1. **Key Ideas and Details (a)** Why does Davy Crockett go out in the woods? **(b) Infer:** What can you infer about his home life?

2. **Key Ideas and Details (a)** What happens in Davy Crockett's dream, and how does he react? **(b) Analyze Cause and Effect:** How does he actually settle the matter with Oak Wing? **(c) Analyze:** How does this outcome show that this narrative is a "tall tale"?

3. **Craft and Structure (a) Analyze:** How do the dialect, spelling, and grammar of the writing affect the tone of the tale? **(b) Infer:** From the way he tells this tale, how would you describe Davy Crockett?

4. **Integration of Knowledge and Ideas (a)** Could an adventurer like Crockett become a hero today? Why or why not? **(b)** Do we expect today's heroes to have a sense of humor? Explain. *[Connect to the Big Question: Are yesterday's heroes important today?]*

Paul Bunyan
Of the North Woods

Carl Sandburg

Who made Paul Bunyan, who gave him birth as a myth, who joked him into life as the Master Lumberjack, who fashioned him forth as an apparition[1] easing the hours of men amid axes and trees, saws and lumber? The people, the bookless people, they made Paul and had him alive long before he got into the books for those who read. He grew up in shanties, around the hot stoves of winter, among socks and mittens drying, in the smell of tobacco smoke and the roar of laughter mocking the outside weather. And some of Paul came overseas in wooden bunks below decks in sailing vessels. And some of Paul is old as the hills, young as the alphabet.

---

1. **apparition** (ap´ ə rish´ ən) *n.* sudden or unusual sight.

▶ **Critical Viewing**
What characteristics in this picture fit Paul Bunyan's role as a legendary hero? **[Analyze]**

Heroic Characters
What qualities of
Paul Bunyan and
his men does this
anecdote illustrate?

The Pacific Ocean froze over in the winter of the Blue Snow and Paul Bunyan had long teams of oxen hauling regular white snow over from China. This was the winter Paul gave a party to the Seven Axmen. Paul fixed a granite floor sunk two hundred feet deep for them to dance on. Still, it tipped and tilted as the dance went on. And because the Seven Axmen refused to take off their hobnailed boots, the sparks from the nails of their dancing feet lit up the place so that Paul didn't light the kerosene lamps. No women being on the Big Onion river at that time the Seven Axmen had to dance with each other, the one left over in each set taking Paul as a partner. The **commotion** of the dancing that night brought on an earthquake and the Big Onion river moved over three counties to the east.

Vocabulary
commotion
(kə mō´ shən) *n.* noisy
movement

One year when it rained from St. Patrick's Day till the Fourth of July, Paul Bunyan got disgusted because his celebration on the Fourth was spoiled. He dived into Lake Superior and swam to where a solid pillar of water was coming down. He dived under this pillar, swam up into it and climbed with powerful swimming strokes, was gone about an hour, came splashing down, and as the rain stopped, he explained, "I turned the darn thing off." This is told in the Big North Woods and on the Great Lakes, with many particulars.

Two mosquitoes lighted on one of Paul Bunyan's oxen, killed it, ate it, cleaned the bones, and sat on a grub shanty picking their teeth as Paul came along. Paul sent to Australia for two special bumblebees to kill these mosquitoes. But the bees and the mosquitoes intermarried; their children had stingers on both ends. And things kept getting worse till Paul brought a big boatload of sorghum[2] up from Louisiana and while all the bee-mosquitoes were eating at the sweet sorghum he floated them down to the Gulf of Mexico. They got so fat that it was easy to drown them all between New Orleans and Galveston.

---

2. sorghum (sôr´ gəm) *n.* tropical grasses bearing flowers and seeds, grown for use as grain or syrup.

Paul logged on the Little Gimlet in Oregon one winter. The cookstove at that camp covered an acre of ground. They fastened the side of a hog on each snowshoe and four men used to skate on the griddle while the cook flipped the pancakes. The eating table was three miles long; elevators carried the cakes to the ends of the table where boys on bicycles rode back and forth on a path down the center of the table dropping the cakes where called for.

Benny, the Little Blue Ox of Paul Bunyan, grew two feet every time Paul looked at him, when a youngster. The barn was gone one morning and they found it on Benny's back; he grew out of it in a night. One night he kept pawing and bellowing for more pancakes, till there were two hundred men at the cookshanty stove trying to keep him fed. About breakfast time Benny broke loose, tore down the cookshanty, ate all the pancakes piled up for the loggers' breakfast. And after that Benny made his mistake; he ate the red hot stove; and that finished him. This is only one of the hot-stove stories told in the North Woods.

Critical Thinking

1. **Key Ideas and Details** **(a)** According to Sandburg, what is the origin of the Paul Bunyan stories? **(b) Interpret:** What does Sandburg mean by saying that "some of Paul is old as the hills, young as the alphabet"?

Cite textual evidence to support your responses.

2. **Key Ideas and Details** **(a) Classify:** Identify two actions that show that Paul Bunyan is clever as well as strong. **(b) Connect:** How do these qualities relate to the myth of the heroic character?

3. **Key Ideas and Details** **(a)** How does Paul Bunyan stop the rain? **(b) Generalize:** What do this anecdote and other details in the selection tell you about life in the Midwest in the early nineteenth century?

4. **Integration of Knowledge and Ideas** **(a) Speculate:** Do you think the Paul Bunyan stories might have been based on a real person? **(b) Hypothesize:** What type of person in today's world might inspire this kind of story?

5. **Integration of Knowledge and Ideas** **(a)** Why would a lumberjack have been a hero in frontier America? **(b)** What qualities does Paul Bunyan share with today's heroes? *[Connect to the Big Question: Are yesterday's heroes important today?]*

Invocation

from John Brown's Body

STEPHEN VINCENT BENÉT

Background This invocation is the introduction to an **epic,** a long narrative poem about heroes. Traditionally, classical writers began an epic by appealing to the muse of poetry, a goddess who could provide inspiration. To begin his epic poem about the Civil War, Benét calls on a different muse—the spirit of America. He finds that this muse is hard to get to know because she—like the country she symbolizes—is so varied and ever-changing.

American *muse,* whose strong and diverse heart
So many men have tried to understand
But only made it smaller with their art,
Because you are as various as your land,

5   As mountainous-deep, as flowered with blue rivers,
Thirsty with deserts, buried under snows,
As native as the shape of Navajo quivers.
And native, too, as the sea-voyaged rose.

Swift runner, never captured or subdued,
10 Seven-branched elk[1] beside the mountain stream,
That half a hundred hunters have pursued
But never matched their bullets with the dream,

Where the great huntsmen failed, I set my sorry
And mortal snare for your immortal quarry.[2]

15 You are the buffalo-ghost, the broncho-ghost
With dollar-silver in your saddle-horn,
The cowboys riding in from Painted Post,
The Indian arrow in the Indian corn,

And you are the clipped velvet of the lawns
20 Where Shropshire grows from Massachusetts sods,
The grey Maine rocks—and the war-painted dawns
That break above the Garden of the Gods.

The prairie-schooners crawling toward the ore
And the cheap car, parked by the station-door.

25 Where the skyscrapers lift their foggy plumes
Of stranded smoke out of a stony mouth,
You are that high stone and its arrogant fumes,
And you are ruined gardens in the South

---

1. **seven-branched elk** *n.* large American deer with wide antlers that divide into several branches.
2. **mortal snare for your immortal quarry** The poet is only human and so cannot set a trap (snare) that can catch the muse, who is immortal.

LITERATURE IN CONTEXT

Cultural Connection

Allusions This poem uses allusions, references to places and events, in order to capture the varied and changeable nature of the American spirit.

- **Navajo quivers** Cases for holding arrows used by Native Americans of the Southwest
- **buffalo-ghost, broncho-ghost** The buffalo and bronco (wild pony), symbols of the western frontier
- **Shropshire** English county known for its green countryside
- **prairie-schooners** Covered wagons used by pioneers moving westward
- **medicine-bag** Small leather bag containing herbs and other sacred objects used by Indian shamans, or healers
- **"Thames and all the rivers of the kings"** England's main river, and those of other Old World powers

Vocabulary
subdued (səb dood´) *adj.* beaten; brought under control

arrogant (ar´ ə gənt) *adj.* self-important

Reading
Check
What is the speaker trying to understand?

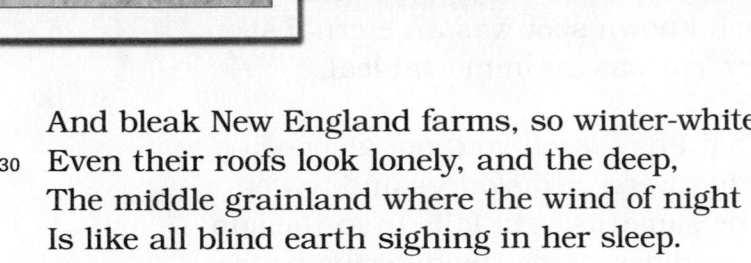

And bleak New England farms, so winter-white
30   Even their roofs look lonely, and the deep,
The middle grainland where the wind of night
Is like all blind earth sighing in her sleep.

A friend, an enemy, a sacred hag³
With two tied oceans in her medicine-bag.

35   They tried to fit you with an English song
And clip your speech into the English tale.
But, even from the first, the words went wrong,
The catbird pecked away the nightingale.⁴

The homesick men begot high-cheekboned things
40   Whose wit was whittled with a different sound,
And Thames and all the rivers of the kings
Ran into Mississippi and were drowned . . .

. . . All these you are, and each is partly you,
And none is false, and none is wholly true.

45   So how to see you as you really are,
So how to suck the pure, distillate,⁵ stored
Essence of essence from the hidden star
And make it pierce like a riposting⁶ sword.

---

3. **hag** (hag) *n.* a witch; also an ugly, old woman.
4. **catbird . . . nightingale** The catbird is an American bird; the nightingale a European one.
5. **distillate** (dis´ tə lāt´) *n.* a substance that has been reduced to its purest form, or essence.
6. **riposting** (ri pōst´ iŋ) *v.* in swordplay, thrusting to counter an opponent's blow.

Heroic Characters
How does the imagery in lines 35–42 emphasize the young country's break with its past?

◄ **Critical Viewing**
How do you think this Colorado landscape came to be called the "Garden of the Gods"? **[Speculate]**

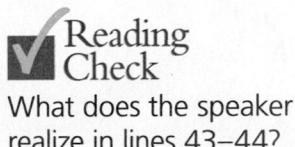

✔ Reading Check
What does the speaker realize in lines 43–44?

For, as we hunt you down, you must escape
50 And we pursue a shadow of our own
That can be caught in a magician's cape
But has the flatness of a painted stone.

Never the running stag, the gull at wing,
The pure elixir[7], the American thing.

55 And yet, at moments when the mind was hot
With something fierier than joy or grief,
When each known spot was an eternal spot
And every leaf was an immortal leaf,

I think that I have seen you, not as one,
60 But clad in diverse *semblances* and powers,
Always the same, as light falls from the sun,
And always different, as the differing hours. . . .

---

7. elixir (i lik´ sər) *n.* a magic potion; or the essential quality of something.

Critical Thinking

Cite textual evidence to support your responses.

© **1. Key Ideas and Details** **(a)** To whom does Benét address this "Invocation"? **(b) Analyze:** What qualities does he first note about this subject? **(c) Connect:** How does this observation influence the rest of the poem?

© **2. Craft and Structure** **(a) Forms of Poetry:** Review the Background note on page 1078. How does this poem fit the purpose and characteristics of an epic? **(b) Assess:** How does its subject suit an epic treatment?

© **3. Integration of Knowledge and Ideas** **(a)** In what lines does Benét emphasize conflicts between England and America? **(b) Infer:** Why are those differences important to his vision of America? **(c) Assess:** Does Benét succeed in capturing the American spirit? Why or why not?

© **4. Integration of Knowledge and Ideas** **(a)** What does Benét find heroic about the American muse? **(b)** Are the many "faces" of this muse still present today? **(c)** What places or figures would you add to Benét's list? *[Connect to the Big Question: Are yesterday's heroes important today?]*

After You Read

Davy Crockett's Dream • Paul
Bunyan of the North Woods •
Invocation *from* John Brown's Body

Comparing Heroic Characters

1. Key Ideas and Details (a) Identify examples of exaggeration in "Paul Bunyan of the North Woods." **(b)** Why would exaggeration be typical in stories about heroes?

2. Key Ideas and Details What heroic traits does Benét's American muse share with Paul Bunyan and Davy Crockett?

3. Integration of Knowledge and Ideas (a) Complete a chart like this one to compare heroic characters. **(b)** Choose two story incidents from your chart. Explain how each develops the heroism of the main character.

	Davy Crockett's Dream	Paul Bunyan of the North Woods
Real or Legend?		
Challenges		
Heroic Actions		
Exaggeration		
Tone: Humorous or Serious?		

⏱ Timed Writing

Explanatory Text: Essay

Write an essay comparing how heroic characters are presented in these three works. Consider how each writer has explored the theme of American heroism. **(40 minutes)**

5-Minute Planner

1. Read the prompt carefully and completely.

2. Gather your ideas by jotting down answers to these questions:
- What do these American heroes have in common?
- How does each hero reflect the values of a time period?
- How important are humor and exaggeration in each work?

3. Use the chart you filled in above to help you compare Davy Crockett and Paul Bunyan. Since Benét's American muse is a special, unusual type of hero, consider that work separately.

4. Reread the prompt, and then draft your essay.

Writing Workshop

 **Common Core State Standards**

Reading Informational Text
7. Evaluate the advantages and disadvantages of using different mediums to present a particular topic or idea.

Writing
2. Write informative/explanatory texts to examine a topic and convey ideas, concepts, and information through the selection, organization, and analysis of relevant content.
6. Use technology, including the Internet, to produce and publish writing and present the relationships between information and ideas efficiently as well as to interact and collaborate with others.
7. Conduct short research projects to answer a question, drawing on several sources and generating additional related, focused questions that allow for multiple avenues of exploration.

Write an Informative Text

Research: Multimedia Report

Defining the Form A **multimedia report** presents information about a topic using a variety of delivery methods, such as audio and video. You might use elements of this form to produce documentaries, present scientific findings, or deliver news reports.

Assignment Write a report about a topic that interests you, using audio and visual media as support. Include these elements:

✔ a *focused topic* that you can cover adequately within the given time frame

✔ a *coherent thesis*, ending with a *well-supported conclusion*

✔ well-integrated and *appropriate audio* and *visual* materials from a variety of primary and secondary sources

✔ use of formatting and *presentation techniques* for *visual appeal*

✔ a presentation tailored to your specific *audience* and *purpose*

✔ *smooth transitions* between passages and ideas

✔ a *command of oral and written standard English conventions*

To preview the criteria on which your multimedia report may be judged, see the rubric on page 1089.

 Writing Workshop: *Work in Progress*

Review the work you did on pages 1037 and 1061.

Prewriting/Planning Strategy

Research your topic. Choose a topic that interests you. To find creative ways of presenting the topic, conduct a multiple-step search using a variety of sources. While you collect basic information, also look for audio clips, video footage, photographs, charts, maps, and graphs. Take notes on what you find. Then, in a chart like the one below, list the media you plan to use.

	Interviews	Music	Art	Informational graphics
Audio				
Video/Photos/Visuals				

Setting Off an Explosion of Ideas

Ideas are the starting points a writer uses to launch an interesting and effective presentation. When preparing an oral multimedia report, begin with creative ideas and a workable plan that fits your purpose, format, and audience. Ask yourself these questions:

- How will my audience react to the topic?
- What are the pros and cons of presenting my topic in a digital presentation rather than in a written work?
- What information, audio and visual aids, and digital tools should I use to keep the audience interested?

To address these questions, use a sunburst chart like this one.

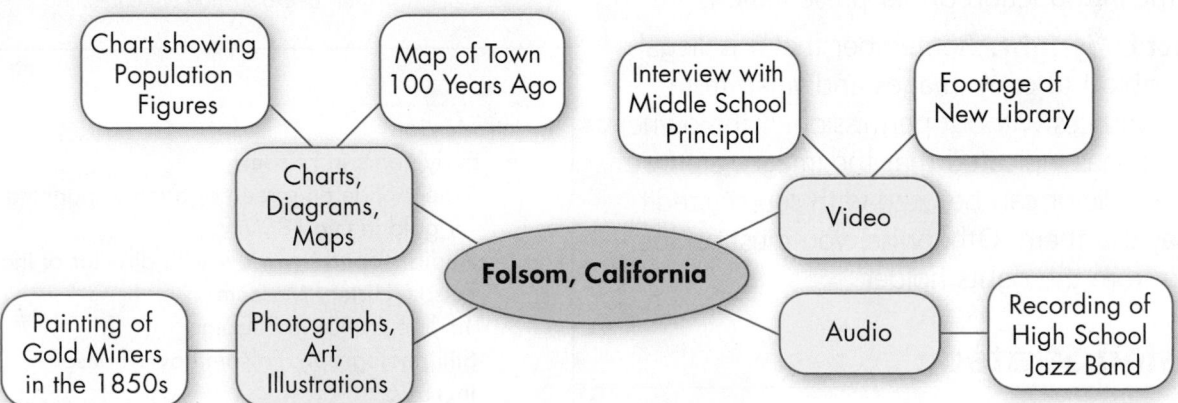

For further ways to generate ideas, consider these techniques:

Borrowing from TV Shows or Movies Think about television shows or movies that use media well. Evaluate the media techniques they use to see if those techniques would be appropriate and practical for your own audience and purpose.

Using Computer Software Various software programs can be used to pump up the excitement in your presentation. For instance, you might present a slideshow that combines a dramatic narrative with photographs, music, and sound effects.

Creating a Web Site Use web tools to create a Web site that provides information about your topic. Show your site to the class as part of your presentation.

Drafting Strategies

Sketch an outline. Before you begin writing, develop an outline to shape the sequence of your presentation. Organize the outline to begin with an introduction that identifies your topic and *thesis*, or main idea. Next, in the body of the report, support and develop your main idea. Finally, in a conclusion, sum up your research and key points. Your outline will also help you to do the following:

- Decide how long to spend on each topic
- Maintain a balance between spoken, audio, and visual elements of your presentation
- Include information about how and when you will use media
- Create variety that will keep your audience engaged

The example outline shows how one writer plans to use multimedia in the introduction of her presentation.

Respect copyright. Remember that it is illegal and unethical to copy images and video from Internet sources without permission. If the owner of the site has indicated that the images are free for the public or can be used with source credit, you may use them. Otherwise, you must ask permission from the rights holder.

Revising Strategy

Revise to address your audience. Consider the level of knowledge that your audience will bring to your topic.

- If the audience is well informed, delete facts that are too basic.
- If the group does not know a lot about your topic, add more background information and define any unfamiliar terms.

The chart shows how to help an audience that might be unfamiliar with a key term by using an *appositive phrase*.

Common Core State Standards

Writing

2.a. Introduce a topic clearly, previewing what is to follow; organize ideas, concepts, and information into broader categories; include formatting, graphics, and multimedia when useful to aiding comprehension.

2.b. Develop the topic with relevant, well-chosen facts, definitions, concrete details, quotations, or other information and examples.

2.c. Use appropriate and varied transitions to create cohesion and clarify the relationships among ideas and concepts.

2.f. Provide a concluding statement or section that follows from and supports the information or explanation presented.

I. Introduction
   A. Early years in Folsom
      Video: Slide on screen of a miner panning for gold in mid-1800s
      Audio: Taped interview with director of the Folsom History Museum
   B. The late 1800s in Folsom
      Still photograph: Folsom Powerhouse in 1896
      Map: Historic map of Folsom

Original	Revised
City planners are thinking about removing the median from historic Sutter Street in Folsom.	City planners are thinking about removing the median, **the raised center divider,** from historic Sutter Street in Folsom.

Using Language to Maintain Interest

One way a multimedia presentation differs from a written one is that your audience cannot go back and review sections that are difficult to understand. For this reason, you must keep the audience actively engaged so that they can follow what you are saying.

Engaging the Audience Remember that the one key element in any presentation is variation. If you are overly repetitive, your audience will lose interest. Just as you should vary the media you show, work to vary the sentences you use to make your points.

- **Vary sentence length.** If you use one long sentence after another, your audience will have trouble following your speech. If you use one short sentence after another, your audience will start to feel jumpy. The key is to vary sentence length, alternating short sentences with long ones in a pleasing rhythm.

- **Vary sentence type.** Hearing the same type of sentence over and over can be boring. Add interest to your report by weaving together simple, compound, complex, and compound-complex sentences (see p. 1036) in an unpredictable pattern.

> **PH WRITING COACH**
>
> Further instruction and practice are available in *Prentice Hall Writing Coach.*

Compound
Harlem in the 1920s was an exciting place to be, and the arts flourished.
Simple　　　　　　　　**Complex**
Creativity was everywhere. From the earthy folk tales of Zora Neale Hurston to the powerful poetry of Langston Hughes, artists and writers were shattering barriers.

Using Transitions To smooth sudden shifts in topic or changes in media, use transitions. The chart shows common transitions that indicate different types of relationships between ideas.

Sequence	Comparison	Contrast	Examples	Summarizing
again, also, and then, finally, further, last	in the same way, likewise, similarly, in like manner	although, and yet, but, despite, even so, however	an illustration of, for example, for instance	all in all, altogether, as has been said, in brief, in conclusion

Grammar in Your Writing

Read your draft. Revise it by adding variation in sentence structure and using appropriate transitions.

Student Model: Jessica Leanore Adamson, Boise, ID

The Attack on Pearl Harbor

Slide 1
Visual: Image of Pearl Harbor ca. 1940
Sound: Airplane/explosion
Script: Pearl Harbor was one of the principal naval bases of WWII. It is located approximately six miles west of Honolulu in Oahu, Hawaii. Early in the morning on December 7, 1941, Japanese submarines and carrier-based planes attacked the U.S. Pacific fleet at Pearl Harbor.

Jessica chose a title that reflects her topic.

The writer has chosen a topic that can be covered in the brief time allotted to her report.

Slide 2
Visual: Image of American battleship U.S.S. *Arizona.*
Sound: Bugle playing Taps
Script: Eight American battleships, including the U.S.S. *Arizona* shown here, and ten other navy vessels were sunk or badly damaged, almost 200 American aircraft were destroyed, and approximately 3,000 naval and military personnel were killed or wounded.

The sound effects and images are dramatic and appropriate to the topic, audience, and purpose.

Slide 8
Visual: Blank screen (black). Words "dereliction of duty" and "errors of judgment" appear letter by letter.
Sound: Typewriter
Script: Shortly after the attack, U.S. President Franklin D. Roosevelt appointed a commission to determine whether negligence had contributed to the raid. The commission found the naval and army commanders of the area guilty of "dereliction of duty" and "errors of judgment."

The writer uses bold-faced heads and other appropriate formatting to present the organization of the report clearly.

This model represents the introductory and concluding slides of a multimedia report. Slides 3–7 are not shown. In the full report they present more information along with supporting audio and visual materials to develop the presentation's main idea.

Editing and Proofreading

Focus on conventional English. Look over the written version of your oral presentation, and correct all errors in grammar. Make sure your report demonstrates a command of standard English conventions. Eliminate any slang or incomplete sentences, unless you are quoting directly from your sources.

Publishing and Presenting

Consider one of the following ways to share your writing:

Deliver an oral presentation. Give a practice performance and try to keep to a strict time limit. Do a final check of your equipment before presenting the report to your classmates.

Post your presentation. Using authoring software, post your presentation to a class Web site. If possible, link to related online sites and invite comments from classmates.

Reflecting on Your Writing

Writer's Journal Jot down your answers to this question:

If you had to create another multimedia report, what would you do differently?

Rubric for Self-Assessment

Find evidence in your writing to address each category. Then, use the rating scale to grade your work.

© **Spiral Review**

Earlier in this unit, you learned about **sentence structure** (p. 1036) and **commas** (p. 1060). Check any written material you plan to present as part of your multimedia report for errors in comma usage and make sure that you vary your sentence structures.

Criteria	Rating Scale
	not very *very*
Focus: How clearly do you identify and cover your topic?	1 2 3 4 5
Organization: How well focused is your presentation, considering your specific audience?	1 2 3 4 5
Support/Elaboration: How well do you integrate audio and visual support for your topic?	1 2 3 4 5
Style: How well do you use formatting and presentation techniques for visual appeal?	1 2 3 4 5
Conventions: How well do you demonstrate a command of standard English conventions such as using transitions and varying sentence types?	1 2 3 4 5

Leveled Texts

Build your skills and improve your comprehension of literature with texts of increasing complexity.

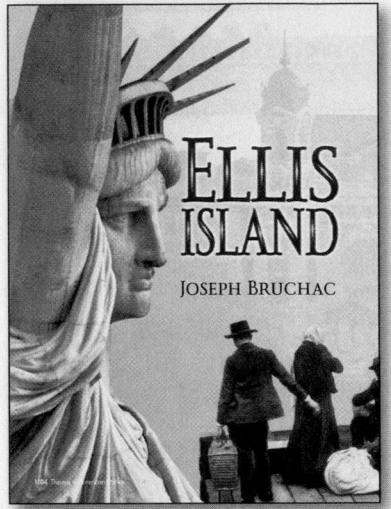

Read the excerpt from ***Out of the Dust*** to learn how a farm family coped with the drought and Great Depression of the 1930s.

Read **"Ellis Island"** to encounter a unique perspective on Ellis Island and what it means to be an American.

Common Core State Standards

Meet these standards with either the excerpt from ***Out of the Dust*** (p. 1094) or **"Ellis Island"** (p. 1104).

Reading Literature
1. Cite the textual evidence that most strongly supports an analysis of what the text says explicitly as well as inferences drawn from the text. *(Literary Analysis: Cultural Context)*

Spiral Review: RL.8.2

Writing
3. Write narratives to develop real or imagined experiences or events using effective technique, relevant descriptive details, and well-structured event sequences. **3.a.** Engage and orient the reader by establishing a context and point of view and introducing a narrator and/or characters; organize an event sequence that unfolds naturally and logically. **3.d.** Use precise words and phrases, relevant descriptive details, and sensory language to capture the action and convey experiences and events. *(Research and Technology: Letter)*

7. Conduct short research projects to answer a question (including a self-generated question), drawing on several sources. *(Writing: Research Proposal)*

Language
2. Demonstrate command of the conventions of standard English capitalization, punctuation, and spelling when writing. *(Conventions: Semicolons and Colons)*

4.b. Use common, grade-appropriate Greek or Latin affixes and roots as clues to the meaning of a word (e.g., *precede, recede, secede*). *(Vocabulary: Word Study)*

Reading Skill: Purpose for Reading

Just as a writer might write for a variety of purposes, there are many reasons you might read. **Setting a purpose for reading** helps focus your attention. You might read for these purposes:

- To learn something new or seek out additional information
- To amuse or challenge yourself
- To seek out another person's point of view

When you read about people from a different time and place, a likely purpose is to learn about their views of the world and the problems they face. An effective way to achieve this purpose is to use a "K-W-L" chart to **ask questions** about the work.

Using the Strategy: "K-W-L" Chart

Use this **"K-W-L" chart** to set a purpose for reading. Fill in the "K" and "W" columns before you read. If you can successfully fill in the "L" column after reading, you have achieved your purpose.

K-W-L Chart		
What I **K**now	What I **W**ant to Know	What I **L**earned

Literary Analysis: Cultural Context

The **cultural context** of a literary work is the social and historical environment in which the characters live. Major historical events, such as bad economic times or the outbreak of war, can shape people's lives in important ways. Understanding the effects of such events can give you insight into characters' attitudes and actions.

To understand the cultural context of a literary work, prepare by reading information about the subject. Use the background before the story, an encyclopedia article, or a reliable Internet site to add to the knowledge you might already have from other classes. Then, as you read, look for and make inferences from textual evidence that shows how characters respond to the larger events that you researched.

Are yesterday's *heroes* important today?

Writing About the Big Question

In these three poems from *Out of the Dust*, Hesse explores how an ordinary farm family responds to the drought and economic depression that destroy their livelihood. Use this sentence starter to develop your ideas about the Big Question.

> Acts of **courage** can come from unexpected places. One person that others might not consider heroic, but I do, is _____ because _____.

While You Read Decide whether the characters in the poem are heroic. Consider how they respond to the series of negative events that confront them.

Vocabulary

Read each word and its definition. Decide whether you know the word well, know it a little bit, or do not know it at all. After you read, see how your knowledge of each word has increased.

- **feuding** (fyōōd´ iŋ) *v.* quarreling; fighting (p. 1095) *The two families were <u>feuding</u> over a piece of property.* feud *n.*

- **spindly** (spind´ lē) *adj.* long and thin (p. 1097) *The <u>spindly</u> legs of the table could not support much weight.* spindliness *n.* spindle *n.*

- **drought** (drout) *n.* lack of rain; long period of dry weather (p. 1098) *The plants dried out and died during the <u>drought</u>.* drought-stricken *adj.*

- **grateful** (grāt´ fəl) *adj.* thankful (p. 1098) *Sue was <u>grateful</u> her sister did not tell her parents about the broken lamp.* gratitude *n.* gratefully *adv.* gratify *v.* ungrateful *adj.*

- **sparse** (spärs) *adj.* thinly spread and small in amount (p. 1099) *The hair on the old man's head was <u>sparse</u>.* sparseness *n.* sparsely *adv.*

- **rickety** (rik´ it ē) *adj.* weak; likely to break (p. 1100) *The <u>rickety</u> old shed fell down during a storm.*

Word Study

The **Latin root -grat-** means "thankful" or "pleased."

In *Out of the Dust*, characters are **grateful**, or thankful, when a change in the weather provides a break from destructive dust storms.

Meet
Karen Hesse

(b. 1952)

Author of
Out of the Dust

In her fiction, Karen Hesse shows a deep understanding of outsiders—characters who do not quite fit in—because that is how she felt as she was growing up in Baltimore, Maryland. A shy girl who lived in her imagination, Hesse loved curling up in an apple tree in her backyard and reading for hours at a time.

Giving a Face to History Hesse's imagination and powers of understanding enable her to create vivid characters who struggle to survive during difficult times in history. Characters in her historical novels include a Russian immigrant in 1919, a woman caught up in the drama of the Civil War, and a boy who stows away on an explorer's ship during the 1700s. "I love research, love dipping into another time and place, and asking questions," Hesse says.

BACKGROUND FOR THE POEMS

The Dust Bowl

Out of the Dust is the story of a farm family's struggles during the 1930s. From 1931 to 1939, farmers in the southern Great Plains suffered from the worst drought in American history. Their crops dried up and died, and powerful dust storms blew away millions of tons of soil. By 1935, many farmers gave up and moved west to California. Meanwhile, the nation was also suffering from the effects of the Great Depression. Banks and other businesses failed, workers lost their jobs, and many Americans were left hungry and homeless.

DID YOU KNOW?

Hesse spent weeks in her local library reading Depression-era newspapers on microfilm to prepare for writing *Out of the Dust*.

from Out of the Dust **1093**

from
OUT of the DUST
Karen Hesse

Debts

Purpose for Reading
What is a purpose you
could set for reading
historical fiction, such as
this poem?

Daddy is thinking
of taking a loan from Mr. Roosevelt and his men,[1]
to get some new wheat planted
where the winter crop has spindled out and died.
5   Mr. Roosevelt promises
Daddy won't have to pay a dime
till the crop comes in.

---

1. **a loan from Mr. Roosevelt and his men** In 1933, President Franklin D. Roosevelt began
a series of government programs, called the New Deal, to help Americans suffering from
the effects of the Great Depression. Among these programs were government loans to
help Dust Bowl farmers.

Daddy says,
"I can turn the fields over,
10 start again.
It's sure to rain soon.
Wheat's sure to grow."

Ma says, "What if it doesn't?"

Daddy takes off his hat,
15 roughs up his hair,
puts the hat back on.
"Course it'll rain," he says.

Ma says, "Bay,
it hasn't rained enough to grow wheat in
20 three years."

Daddy looks like a fight brewing.

He takes that red face of his out to the barn,
to keep from feuding with my pregnant ma.

I ask Ma
25 how,
after all this time,
Daddy still believes in rain.

"Well, it rains enough," Ma says,
"now and again,
30 to keep a person hoping.
But even if it didn't
your daddy would have to believe.
It's coming on spring,
and he's a farmer."

March 1934

◄ **Critical Viewing**
Why does a dust storm
like this one pose a
danger to farms and
farmers? **[Connect]**

Cultural Context
What does this con-
versation indicate
about the effect of
dry weather on farm
families?

Vocabulary
feuding (fyo͞od´ iŋ) *v.*
quarreling; fighting

Purpose for Reading
What can you learn
from the poem about
farmers' reactions to the
lack of rainfall in 1934?

Social Studies Connection

The Great Depression

The stock market crashed October 29, 1929—"Black Tuesday"—ushering in the worst economic collapse the United States ever experienced. More than 15 million Americans lost their jobs. The Depression lasted through the early 1940s. Making matters worse, a drought spread through 75 percent of the country during the 1930s, causing devastating dust storms.

BROOKLYN DAILY EAGLE
And Complete Long Island News

89th YEAR—No. 295.   ★ NEW YORK CITY, THURSDAY, OCTOBER 24, 1929. ★   32 PAGES   THREE CENTS

LATE NEWS
WALL STREET
1:15 PRICES ★★

WALL ST. IN PANIC AS STOCKS CRASH

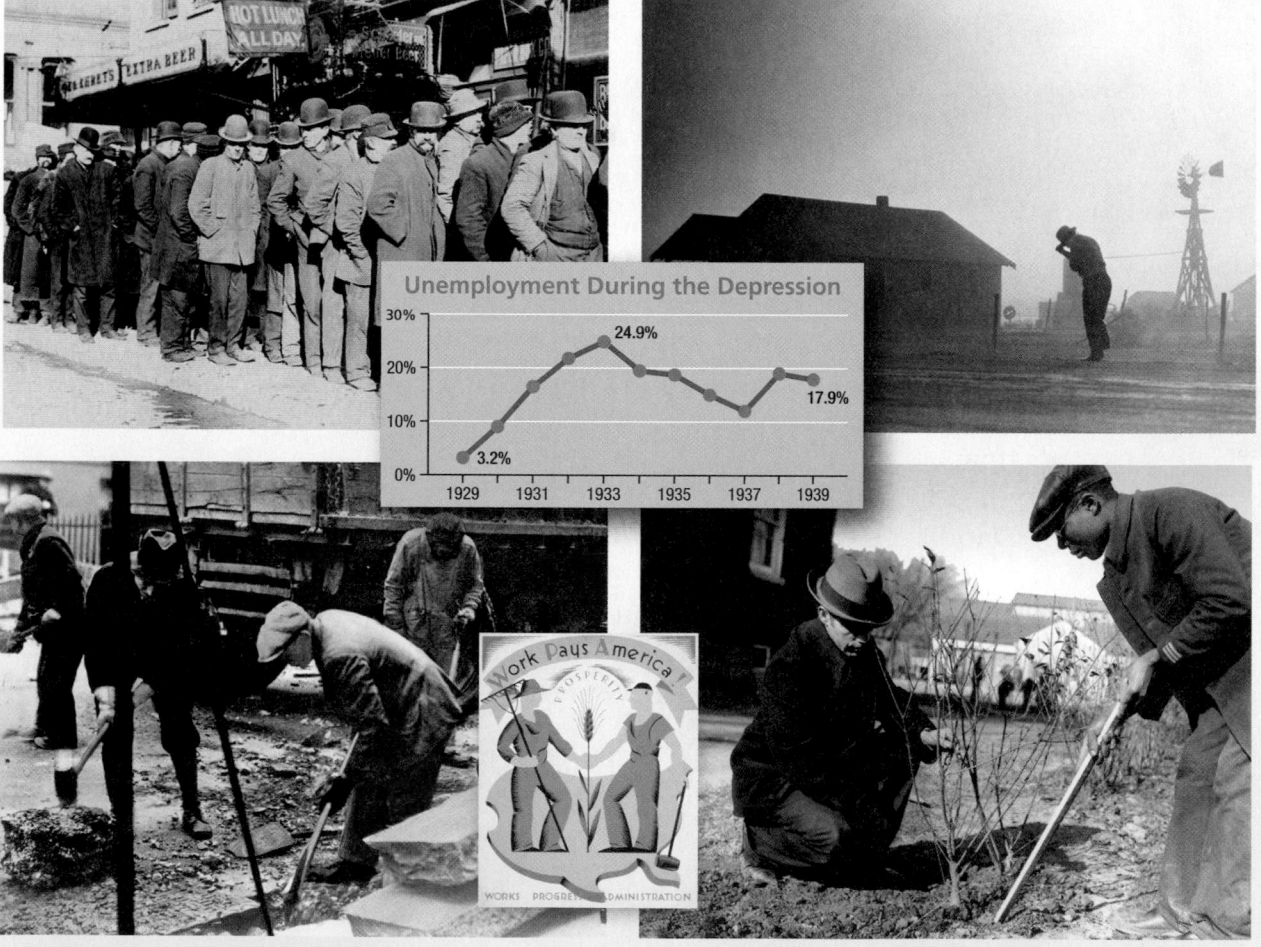

Bread lines were common city sights during ▼ the Depression.

President Franklin D. Roosevelt offered assistance to people in rural areas who were ▼ affected by the drought.

Unemployment During the Depression

3.2% (1929) ... 24.9% (1933) ... 17.9% (1939)

▲ In cities, the WPA (Works Progress Administration) put people to work repairing roads.

▲ Restoring drought-damaged land by planting new trees was another WPA goal.

Connect to the Literature How could government programs have helped Ma and Daddy?

Fields of Flashing Light

I heard the wind rise,
and stumbled from my bed,
down the stairs,
out the front door,
5 into the yard.
The night sky kept flashing,
lightning danced down on its spindly legs.

I sensed it before I knew it was coming.
I heard it,
10 smelled it,
tasted it.
Dust.

While Ma and Daddy slept,
the dust came,
15 tearing up fields where the winter wheat,
set for harvest in June,
stood helpless.

Purpose for Reading
What would you want to know after reading this poem's title?

Vocabulary
spindly (spind´ lē)
adj. long and thin

Reading Check
What noise wakes the speaker from her bed?

I watched the plants,
surviving after so much **drought** and so much wind,
20 I watched them fry,
or
flatten,
or blow away,
like bits of cast-off rags.
25 It wasn't until the dust turned toward the house,
like a fired locomotive,
and I fled,
barefoot and breathless, back inside,
it wasn't until the dust
30 hissed against the windows,
until it ratcheted the roof,
that Daddy woke.

He ran into the storm,
his overalls half-hooked over his union suit.[2]
35 "Daddy!" I called. "You can't stop dust."

Ma told me to
cover the beds,
push the scatter rugs against the doors,
dampen the rags around the windows.
40 Wiping dust out of everything,
she made coffee and biscuits,
waiting for Daddy to come in.

Sometime after four,
rubbing low on her back,
45 Ma sank down into a chair at the kitchen table
and covered her face.
Daddy didn't come back for hours,
not
until the temperature dropped so low,
50 it brought snow.

Ma and I sighed, **grateful**,
staring out at the dirty flakes,
but our relief didn't last.
The wind snatched that snow right off the fields,

---

2. union suit type of long underwear, common in the 1930s, that combines a shirt and leggings in one garment.

55 leaving behind a sea of dust,
waves and
waves and
waves of
dust,
60 rippling across our yard.

Daddy came in,
he sat across from Ma and blew his nose.
Mud streamed out.
He coughed and spit out
65 mud.
If he had cried,
his tears would have been mud too,
but he didn't cry.
And neither did Ma.

March 1934

Migrants

We'll be back when the rain comes,
they say,
pulling away with all they own,
straining the springs of their motor cars.
5 Don't forget us.

And so they go,
fleeing the blowing dust,
fleeing the fields of brown-tipped wheat
barely ankle high,
10 and **sparse** as the hair on a dog's belly.

We'll be back, they say,
pulling away toward Texas,
Arkansas,
where they can rent a farm,
15 pull in enough cash,
maybe start again.

Purpose for Reading
What information does the poem provide about the Dust Bowl that you could not get from a history textbook?

Cultural Context
What economic forces drive away the migrants?

Vocabulary
sparse (spärs) *adj.*
thinly spread and small in amount

▶ **Critical Viewing** What details in this historic photograph indicate that this family is moving? **[Analyze]**

We'll be back when it rains,
they say,
setting out with their bedsprings and mattresses,
20 their cookstoves and dishes,
their kitchen tables,
and their milk goats
tied to their running boards[3]
in **rickety** cages,
25 setting out for
California,
where even though they say they'll come back,
they just might stay
if what they hear about that place is true.

30 Don't forget us, they say.
But there are so many leaving,
how can I remember them all?

April 1935

Vocabulary
rickety (rik´ it ē) *adj.*
weak; likely to break

---

3. **running boards** steps, or footboards, that ran along the lower part of each side of a car, as shown in the photograph (p. 1099). Running boards were common on cars of the 1930s.

Critical Thinking

Cite textual evidence to support your responses.

1. Key Ideas and Details (a) In "Debts," what is the subject of the discussion between Ma and Daddy? **(b)** How does Ma explain Daddy's point of view? **(c) Infer:** What is Ma's point of view?

2. Key Ideas and Details (a) In "Fields of Flashing Light," what does the narrator do during the dust storm? **(b) Infer:** What is the purpose of these actions? **(c) Draw Conclusions:** How do you know that these actions are not very effective?

3. Key Ideas and Details (a) Analyze Causes and Effects: In "Migrants," why do the family's neighbors move? **(b) Speculate:** What effects might their decision have on the people who stay behind?

4. Integration of Knowledge and Ideas (a) Do the family members in these poems act in ways that you consider heroic? Why or why not? **(b)** What can we learn today from the struggles of Depression-era families like the one in *Out of the Dust?* *[Connect to the Big Question: Are yesterday's heroes important today?]*

Reading Skill: Purpose for Reading

1. (a) What **purpose** did you set for reading the three poems?
(b) What questions did you ask to help you set a purpose?

2. (a) What details from the poems helped you answer your questions? **(b)** Where could you look to find more information to answer your questions?

Literary Analysis: Cultural Context

ⓒ **3. Key Ideas and Details** Fill in the chart by explaining what each detail from *Out of the Dust* reveals about the poem's **cultural context**—the living conditions and attitudes of farmers during the Dust Bowl.

Detail	Cultural Conditions and Attitudes
Dust blew away and covered crops.	
Ma and Daddy do not cry when their wheat crop is destroyed.	
Daddy decides to plant again, but other families decide to move away.	

Vocabulary

ⓒ **Acquisition and Use** Write a word from page 1092 that matches the meaning of each pair of **synonyms.** Explain why its meaning is similar.

1. weak, shaky, _____

2. long, thin, _____

3. quarreling, fighting, _____

4. scanty, scattered, _____

5. dryness, aridness, _____

6. thankful, appreciative, _____

Word Study Use context and what you know about the **Latin root -*grat*-** to explain your answer to each question.

1. Why is *ingratitude* a poor reaction to receiving a gift?

2. Why might someone *congratulate* you?

Word Study

The **Latin root -*grat*-** means "thankful" or "pleased."

Apply It Explain how the root -*grat*- contributes to the meaning of each word. Consult a dictionary, if necessary.

ingrate
gratitude
ingratiate

Are yesterday's *heroes* important today?

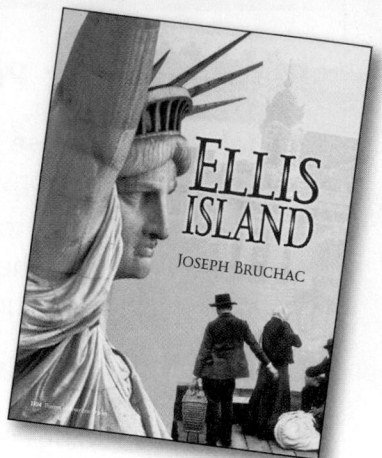

Writing About the Big Question

In "Ellis Island," Joseph Bruchac writes of the conflicting feelings the famous immigrant processing station awakes in him. Use this sentence starter to develop your ideas about the Big Question:

Many people view the **accomplishments** of their immigrant ancestors with pride because _____.

While You Read Look for the ways that Bruchac describes the two branches of his ancestry.

Vocabulary

Read each word and its definition. Decide whether you know the word well, know it a little bit, or do not know it at all. After you read, see how your knowledge of each word has increased.

- **quarantine** (kwôr´ ən tēn) *n.* period of separation from others to stop the spread of disease (p. 1105) *The passengers were kept in quarantine after one of them became sick.* *quarantine v.*

- **empires** (em´ pīrz´) *n.* powerful nations; countries ruled by emperors or empresses (p. 1105) *The Western Roman and the Byzantine Empires were governed by ancient Rome.* *emperor n. empress n.*

- **native** (nāt´ iv) *adj.* related to the place of one's birth (p. 1106) *He traveled far from his native land. native n. natively adv.*

- **invaded** (in vād´ əd) *adj.* forcibly entered in order to conquer (p. 1106) *In the science-fiction film, Earth is invaded by aliens from another galaxy. invasion n. invader n.*

Word Study

The **Latin root -nat-** means "born."

The author of this poem speaks of **native** lands in America, referring to lands inhabited by people whose ancestors were the continent's first inhabitants.

Meet
Joseph Bruchac
(b. 1942)

Author of
ELLIS ISLAND

"Ellis Island" describes Joseph Bruchac's heritage as the son of an Abenaki Indian mother and a Slovak father. Bruchac grew up in a small town in the Adirondack Mountains of New York State, where he still lives today.

A Passion for Tradition and Diversity When he became a father, Bruchac began telling traditional stories to his two young sons. Before long, he had established a career as a storyteller, sharing his stories with schoolchildren. He is also an award-winning author who has published more than three dozen books. Of his motivation to tell stories that bridge cultures, Bruchac says, "We learn about ourselves by understanding others."

DID YOU KNOW?
Bruchac was chosen to write informational panels for the National Museum of the American Indian in Washington, D.C.

BACKGROUND FOR THE POEM

Immigrants and Native Americans

The speaker of "Ellis Island" pays tribute to his two sets of ancestors—European immigrants and Native Americans. These groups had very different experiences. From 1892 to 1924, about seventeen million European immigrants passed through government buildings on Ellis Island in New York Harbor. There, they received official permission to enter the United States. Meanwhile, from the 1600s through the 1800s, Native Americans had been pushed farther and farther west to make room for new settlers. By the 1890s, most Native American tribes had been moved onto reservations.

ELLIS ISLAND

JOSEPH BRUCHAC

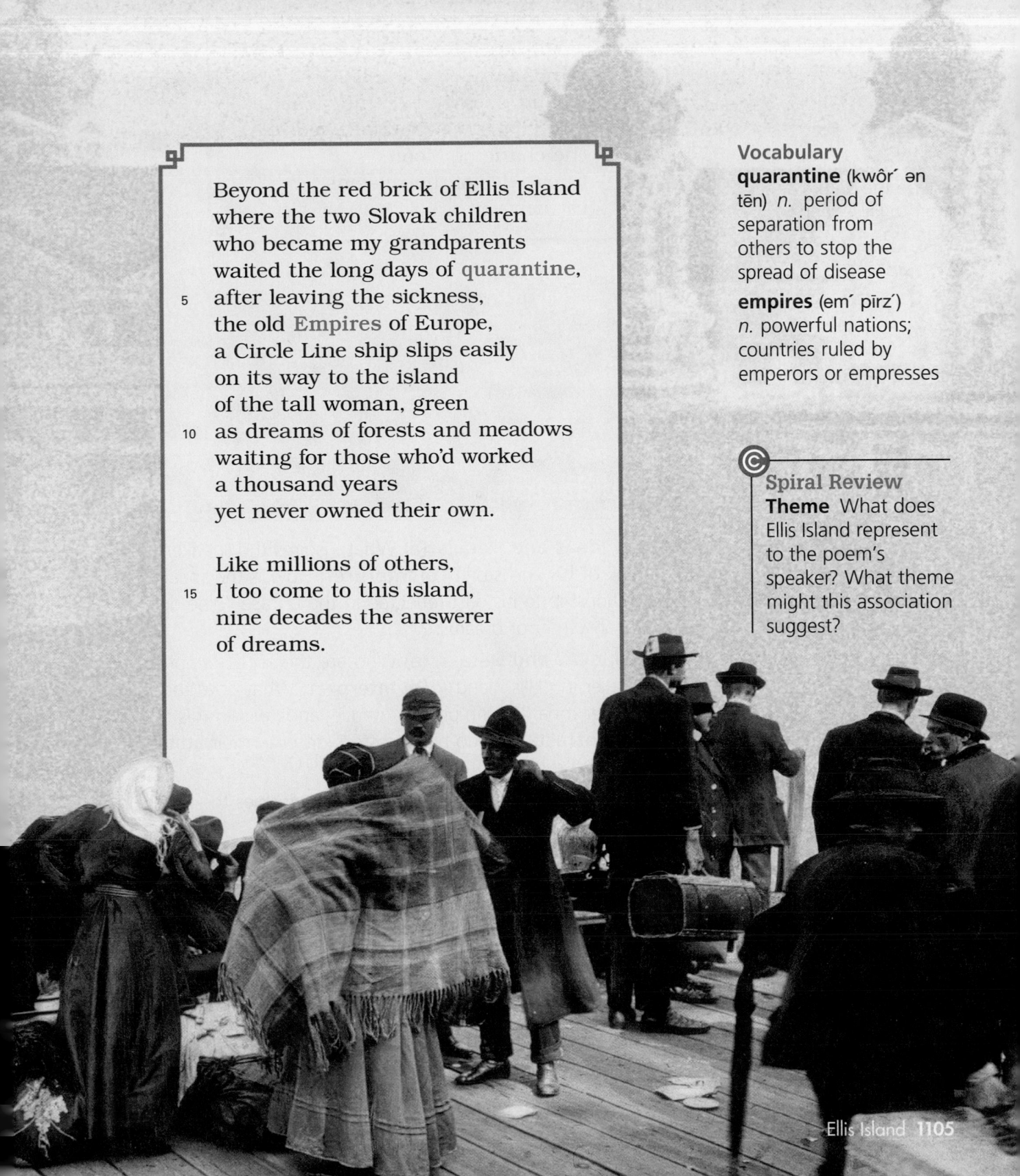

Beyond the red brick of Ellis Island
where the two Slovak children
who became my grandparents
waited the long days of quarantine,
5   after leaving the sickness,
the old Empires of Europe,
a Circle Line ship slips easily
on its way to the island
of the tall woman, green
10   as dreams of forests and meadows
waiting for those who'd worked
a thousand years
yet never owned their own.

Like millions of others,
15   I too come to this island,
nine decades the answerer
of dreams.

Vocabulary
quarantine (kwôr´ ən
tēn) *n.* period of
separation from
others to stop the
spread of disease

empires (em´ pīrz´)
n. powerful nations;
countries ruled by
emperors or empresses

Ⓒ

Spiral Review
Theme What does
Ellis Island represent
to the poem's
speaker? What theme
might this association
suggest?

Vocabulary

native (nāt´ iv) *adj.* related to the place of one's birth

invaded (in vād´ əd) *adj.* forcibly entered in order to conquer

Cultural Context

What historical events shape the author's reaction to Ellis Island?

Yet only one part of my blood
  loves that memory.
Another voice speaks
20 of native lands
within this nation.
Lands invaded
when the earth became owned.
Lands of those who followed
25 the changing Moon,
knowledge of the seasons
in their veins.

Critical Thinking

Cite textual evidence to support your responses.

1. **Key Ideas and Details** **(a)** What inspires the speaker to think of his ancestors? **(b) Interpret:** How is the speaker's relationship to his past reflected in the phrase "nine decades the answerer of dreams"?

2. **Key Ideas and Details** **(a)** Who are the ancestors of the speaker in "Ellis Island"? **(b) Interpret:** What does the speaker mean by the phrase "native lands within this nation"? **(c) Contrast:** How do his ancestors differ in their attitudes toward the land?

3. **Key Ideas and Details** **(a) Apply:** Why does the speaker see the United States as "lands invaded"?

4. **Integration of Knowledge and Ideas** **(a)** How does the speaker's dual ancestry influence his feelings toward Ellis Island? **(b)** What people from the past might Bruchac consider to be heroes in his life? **(c)** Can the same people who are viewed as heroes by some be viewed as unheroic by others? Explain, using an example. *[Connect to the Big Question: Are yesterday's heroes important today?]*

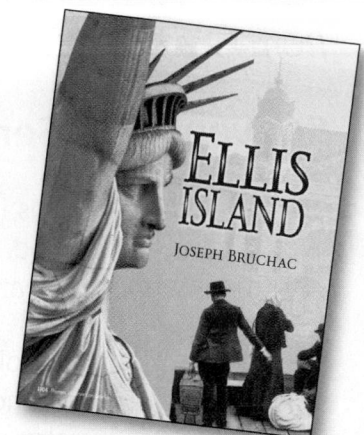

Reading Skill: Purpose for Reading

1. **(a)** What **purpose** did you set for reading "Ellis Island"?
   (b) What questions did you ask to help you set a purpose?

2. **(a)** What details in "Ellis Island" helped you to answer your questions? **(b)** Where could you look for more information?

Literary Analysis: Cultural Context

3. Key Ideas and Details Fill in the chart by explaining what each detail from "Ellis Island" reveals about the poem's **cultural context**—the living conditions and attitudes of immigrants and Native Americans in the late 1800s.

Detail	Cultural Conditions and Attitudes
Immigrants were kept in quarantine.	
Immigrants dreamed of owning land.	
Native American lands were invaded.	
Native Americans had "knowledge of the seasons in their veins."	

Vocabulary

Acquisition and Use Write a word from page 1102 that matches the meaning of each pair of **synonyms**. Explain why its meaning is similar.

1. isolation, detention, _____
2. original, belonging, _____
3. kingdoms, realms, _____
4. assailed, infringed, _____

Word Study Use context and what you know about the **Latin word root -nat-** to explain your answer to each question.

1. Does a bird with an *innate* sense of direction get lost?
2. What might you expect to find in a hospital's *neonatal* room?

Word Study

The **Latin word root -nat-** means "born."

Apply It Explain how the root *-nat-* contributes to the meanings of these words. Consult a dictionary, if necessary.

nationality
denatured
natural

Integrated Language Skills

from **Out of the Dust • Ellis Island**

Conventions: Semicolons and Colons

A **semicolon (;)** joins independent clauses and takes the place of a comma or period. A **colon (:)** directs the reader's attention to the information that follows it.

- Use semicolons to join independent clauses that are not already joined by the conjunctions *and, but, or, nor, for, so,* or *yet.* Semicolons are also used to separate independent clauses that are joined by adverbs such as *however* and *therefore.*

- Use colons before lists of items that follow an independent clause.

Incorrect	Correct
The car ran out of gas we had to call a tow truck.	The car ran out of gas; we had to call a tow truck.
We walked in the rain, however, our umbrellas kept us dry.	We walked in the rain; however, our umbrellas kept us dry.
Please bring the following supplies; a notebook, two pencils, and a pen.	Please bring the following supplies: a notebook, two pencils, and a pen.

Practice A Rewrite each sentence, replacing the blank underline with the correct mark— a colon or a semicolon.

1. Two of Bruchac's grandparents were immigrants_ he was born in America.

2. Immigrants from many nations were processed at Ellis Island_ Ireland, England, Poland, Italy, Spain, France, and others.

3. Bruchac tells many stories from his Abenaki background_ however, he is in favor of learning from many cultures.

Ⓒ **Reading Application** Write two sentences about the difficulties of farming. One should use a colon; the other, a semicolon.

Practice B Rewrite each sentence, adding a semicolon or a colon where it is needed.

1. Before the wind began, she sensed it in several ways hearing, smell, and taste.

2. Daddy decided they would stay on their farm however, many others had left.

3. The car was loaded with every sort of thing they even took their milk goats and kitchen tables.

Ⓒ **Writing Application** Using each correct sentence in the chart as a model, write three more sentences about the immigrant experience.

PH WRITING COACH Further instruction and practice are available in *Prentice Hall Writing Coach.*

Writing

 **Common Core State Standards**

L.8.2; W.8.3, W.8.3.a, W.8.3.d, W.8.7
[For the full wording of the standards, see page 1090.]

© Explanatory Text Write a brief **research proposal** on how the Dust Bowl affected farmers in the 1930s or on immigrants' experiences as they passed through Ellis Island in the 1890s and early 1900s.

- First, generate three specific questions you would like to answer. In a chart, identify the type of source that might provide the information you need to answer each question.

- Find at least three sources, including both *primary sources* (first-hand accounts) and *secondary sources* (secondhand analyses). Use an approved format for a preliminary bibliography.

- In a paragraph, present and explain your thesis statement, the main idea that you would use to begin your research.

Grammar Application Check your research proposal to make sure you use semicolons and colons correctly.

Writing Workshop: *Work in Progress*

Prewriting for Exposition For a cause-and-effect essay you may write, list ideas from science or history that have causes and effects. For each cause, jot down possible effects. For each effect, jot down potential causes. Save this Causes-Effects List in your writing portfolio.

Use this prewriting activity to prepare for the **Writing Workshop** on page 1156.

Research and Technology

© Build and Present Knowledge Write a **letter** that describes the experience of a migrant. If you read the poems from *Out of the Dust,* write a letter from California to a friend who stayed in the Midwest. If you read "Ellis Island," write a letter to a friend back in Europe. Use these steps:

- Research the experiences of Dust Bowl migrants to California or European immigrants who entered through Ellis Island. Use the Internet and a key word search to find and print a historic photograph related to your topic.

- Imagine that you are the person in the photograph you chose, and write a letter to your friend back in Europe or the Midwest.

- Establish context by giving details that indicate your situation. Using vivid sensory details, describe your thoughts, emotions, and experiences on the trip and then upon your arrival.

- Write your letter by hand, and use the proper format for a friendly letter. Be sure that your letter is neat and legible and has correct spelling and capitalization for place names.

PHLit Online!
www.PHLitOnline.com
- Interactive graphic organizers
- Grammar tutorial
- Interactive journals

© **Leveled Texts**

Build your skills and improve your comprehension of literature or literary nonfiction with texts of increasing complexity.

Read **"Choice: A Tribute to Martin Luther King, Jr."** to learn about the inspirational effect Dr. King had on a young African American woman.

Read **"An Episode of War"** to see how a wounded soldier—and those around him—respond to his plight.

© **Common Core State Standards**

Meet these standards with either **"Choice: A Tribute to Martin Luther King, Jr."** (p. 1114) or **"An Episode of War"** (p. 1122).

Reading Literature/Informational Text
1. Cite the textual evidence that most strongly supports an analysis of what the text says explicitly as well as inferences drawn from the text. (*Literary Analysis: Author's Influences*)
Spiral Review: RL.8.2
Writing
1. Write arguments to support claims with clear reasons and relevant evidence. **1.a.** Introduce claim(s), acknowledge and distinguish the claim(s) from alternate or opposing claims, and organize the reasons and evidence logically. **1.d.** Establish and maintain a formal style. **1.e.** Provide a concluding statement or section that follows from and supports the argument presented. (*Writing: Persuasive Speech*)

2. Write informative/explanatory texts to examine a topic and convey ideas, concepts, and information through the selection, organization, and analysis of relevant content. (*Research and Technology: Newspaper Article*)
Language
2. Demonstrate command of the conventions of standard English capitalization. (*Conventions: Capitalization*)
4.b. Use common, grade-appropriate Greek or Latin affixes and roots as clues to the meaning of a word.
6. Acquire and use accurately grade-appropriate general academic and domain-specific words and phrases; gather vocabulary knowledge when considering a word or phrase important to comprehension or expression. (*Vocabulary: Word Study*)

Reading Skill: Purpose for Reading

When you **set a purpose for reading,** you determine your focus before reading. Once you have set a purpose, you can **adjust your reading rate** to best meet that goal.

- For information: read *slowly* and *carefully.* After completing a difficult or important passage, take time to think about what you have read. If necessary, read it again.

- For entertainment: read more *quickly.* You may reread or linger over certain passages, but studying the text is less important.

Whatever your reading rate, check regularly to make sure you are meeting your purpose. If not, you may need to consult another source or work in order to better understand the first one.

Using the Strategy: Reading Rate Chart

Complete a **reading rate chart** like the one shown to determine how to approach a specific source or literary work.

Source	Purpose	Reading Rate
Magazine article on rock star	Entertainment	Read quickly to find interesting details.
Biography of John F. Kennedy	Research	Read slowly, selecting facts for a report.

Literary Analysis: Author's Influences

An **author's influences** are the cultural and historical factors that affect his or her writing. Take these steps to connect a literary work with its author's heritage, attitudes, and beliefs:

- Read biographical information to learn about an author's important life experiences and cultural background.

- When reading, note any details in the work that show cultural values or attitudes. In addition, note references to historical events and figures or cultural influences that might have shaped the author's outlook and values. Make inferences from these references to determine the effect of culture and history on the author's views.

Are yesterday's *heroes* important today?

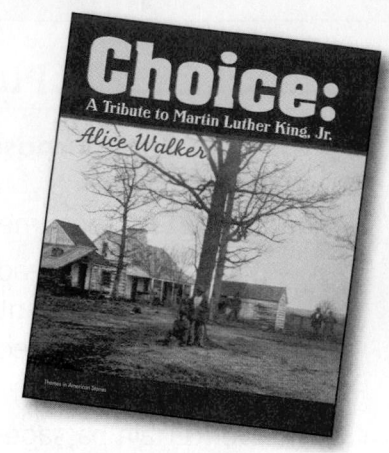

Writing About the Big Question

In "Choice," Alice Walker recalls the tremendous influence of Martin Luther King, Jr., on herself and her community. Use the following sentence starters to develop your ideas about the Big Question.

A figure from the past, besides King, who continues to **influence** people today is _____ because _____.

People who have **overcome** difficult challenges, such as _____ can show us _____.

While You Read Look for the ways that King has influenced Walker's life — both while he was alive and after his death.

Vocabulary

Read each word and its definition. Decide whether you know the word well, know it a little bit, or do not know it at all. After you read, see how your knowledge of each word has increased.

- **ancestral** (an ses′ trəl) *adj.* related to a family (p. 1115) *Since 1801, her relatives have lived on the ancestral estate.* ancestor *n.* ancestry *n.*

- **brutal** (broot′ ′l) *adj.* harsh; demanding (p. 1115) *The brutal cold destroyed the farmers' crops.* brutally *adv.* brutality *n.* brute *n.*

- **integrate** (in′ tə grāt′) *v.* make equally available to all members of society (p. 1116) *The Brown decision in 1954 ordered schools to racially integrate.* integration *n.* integral *adj.*

- **disinherit** (dis′ in her′ it) *v.* deprive a person or people of a right or privilege (p. 1116) *In his will, he chose to disinherit his son and left his money to charity.* inherit *v.* inheritance *n.*

- **revolutionary** (rev′ ə loo′ shə ner′ ē) *adj.* favoring or bringing about sweeping change (p. 1117) *Einstein's revolutionary ideas changed how people viewed the universe.* revolution *n.* revolt *v.*

Word Study

The **Latin root -her-** means "heir" or "one who receives."

The author writes of King's concern for the **disinherited**, those who have been stripped of the rights they receive as citizens or members of a community.

Alice Walker

(b. 1944)

Author of

Choice:
A Tribute to Martin Luther King, Jr.

Alice Walker's childhood in rural Georgia had a lasting impact on her writing. Walker's parents loved to tell her stories—so much so, that she later referred to her mother as "a walking history of our community."

An Author's Influences Walker's love of stories and learning inspired her to go to college, where she became involved in the civil rights movement. After meeting Martin Luther King, Jr., she participated in marches and registered African Americans to vote in Georgia, at a time when it was dangerous to do so. By the end of the 1960s, Walker had launched a writing career that included essays, novels, and poems.

BACKGROUND FOR THE SPEECH

The Great Migration

In "Choice . . . ," Alice Walker describes how her brothers and sisters wanted to leave the South. Beginning in the 1890s, millions of African Americans left the South and journeyed to northern cities. Economic need, racial violence, and inequality were all factors in what became known as "The Great Migration." In the 1970s, after the successes of the civil rights movement, this migration slowed and actually reversed course.

DID YOU KNOW?

Walker's 1982 novel *The Color Purple* won the Pulitzer Prize and the National Book Award. It was adapted as a motion picture, directed by Steven Spielberg.

Choice:
A Tribute to Martin Luther King, Jr.

Alice Walker

Background

This address was made in 1972 at a Jackson, Mississippi, restaurant that had refused to serve people of color until forced to do so by the civil rights movement a few years before.

My great-great-great-grandmother walked as a slave from Virginia to Eatonton, Georgia—which passes for the Walker ancestral home—with two babies on her hips. She lived to be a hundred and twenty-five years old and my own father knew her as a boy. (It is in memory of this walk that I choose to keep and to embrace my "maiden" name, Walker.)

There is a cemetery near our family church where she is buried; but because her marker was made of wood and rotted years ago, it is impossible to tell exactly where her body lies. In the same cemetery are most of my mother's people, who have lived in Georgia for so long nobody even remembers when they came. And all of my great-aunts and -uncles are there, and my grandfather and grandmother, and, very recently, my own father.

If it is true that land does not belong to anyone until they have buried a body in it, then the land of my birthplace belongs to me, dozens of times over. Yet the history of my family, like that of all black Southerners, is a history of dispossession. We loved the land and worked the land, but we never owned it; and even if we bought land, as my great-grandfather did after the Civil War, it was always in danger of being taken away, as his was, during the period following Reconstruction.[1]

My father inherited nothing of material value from his father, and when I came of age in the early sixties I awoke to the bitter knowledge that in order just to continue to love the land of my birth, I was expected to leave it. For black people—including my parents—had learned a long time ago that to stay willingly in a beloved but brutal place is to risk losing the love and being forced to acknowledge only the brutality.

---

1. **Reconstruction** (1865–1877) period following the American Civil War when the South was rebuilt and reestablished as part of the Union.

▼ **Critical Viewing**
How do the faces of these former slaves reflect the same types of hardships that Walker's grandmother experienced? **[Connect]**

Vocabulary
ancestral (an ses´ trəl) *adj.* related to a family

brutal (broot´'l) *adj.* harsh; demanding

Author's Influences
What attachment does the author feel to her ancestors and their land?

Reading Check
How does Alice Walker's last name honor her ancestors?

Vocabulary

integrate (in´ tə
grāt´) v. make equally
available to all mem-
bers of society

disinherit (dis´ in
her´ it) v. deprive a
person or people of
a right or privilege

▼ **Critical Viewing**
Why might Walker use
the word *fearless* to
describe King, shown
here in jail? **[Connect]**

It is a part of the black Southern sensibility that we treasure memories; for such a long time, that is all of our homeland those of us who at one time or another were forced away from it have been allowed to have.

I watched my brothers, one by one, leave our home and leave the South. I watched my sisters do the same. This was not unusual; abandonment, except for memories, was the common thing, except for those who "could not do any better," or those whose strength or stubbornness was so colossal they took the risk that others could not bear. •

In 1960, my mother bought a television set, and each day after school I watched Hamilton Holmes and Charlayne Hunter[2] as they struggled to integrate—fair-skinned as they were—the University of Georgia. And then, one day, there appeared the face of Dr. Martin Luther King, Jr. What a funny name, I thought. At the moment I first saw him, he was being handcuffed and shoved into a police truck. He had dared to claim his rights as a native son, and had been arrested. He displayed no fear, but seemed calm and serene, unaware of his own extraordinary courage. His whole body, like his conscience, was at peace.

At the moment I saw his resistance I knew I would never be able to live in this country without resisting everything that sought to disinherit me, and I would never be forced away from the land of my birth without a fight.

He was The One, The Hero, The One Fearless Person for whom we had waited. I hadn't even realized before that we *had* been waiting for Martin Luther King, Jr., but we had. And I knew it for sure when my mother added his name to the list of people she prayed for every night.

---

2. **Hamilton Holmes and Charlayne Hunter** the first two African American students to attend the University of Georgia.

I sometimes think that it was literally the prayers of people like my mother and father, who had bowed down in the struggle for such a long time, that kept Dr. King alive until five years ago.[3] For years we went to bed praying for his life, and awoke with the question "Is the 'Lord' still here?"

The public acts of Dr. King you know. They are visible all around you. His voice you would recognize sooner than any other voice you have heard in this century—this in spite of the fact that certain municipal libraries, like the one in downtown Jackson, do not carry recordings of his speeches, and the librarians chuckle cruelly when asked why they do not.

You know, if you have read his books, that his is a complex and **revolutionary** philosophy that few people are capable of understanding fully or have the patience to embody in themselves. Which is our weakness, which is our loss.

And if you know anything about good Baptist preaching, you can imagine what you missed if you never had a chance to hear Martin Luther King, Jr., preach at Ebeneezer Baptist Church.

You know of the prizes and awards that he tended to think very little of. And you know of his concern for the think disinherited: the American Indian, the Mexican-American, and the poor American white—for whom he cared much.

You know that this very room, in this very restaurant, was closed to people of color not more than five years ago. And that we eat here together tonight largely through his efforts and his blood. We accept the common pleasures of life, assuredly, in his name.

But add to all of these things the one thing that seems to me second to none in importance: He gave us back our heritage. He gave us back our homeland; the bones and dust of our ancestors, who may now sleep within our caring *and* our hearing. He gave us the blueness of the Georgia sky in autumn as in summer; the colors of the Southern winter as

3. until five years ago Dr. Martin Luther King, Jr., was assassinated on April 4, 1968.

LITERATURE IN CONTEXT

History Connection

Marching for Freedom
In March 1965, Martin Luther King, Jr., organized a march from Selma to Montgomery, Alabama, to protest restrictions on African Americans' right to vote. The peaceful protest was turned back by police using tear gas and clubs.

After this incident, some people advised King to abandon nonviolence. King ignored these voices and tried again. He set out from Selma with 3,200 marchers. Four days and fifty miles later they arrived in Montgomery, 25,000-strong. Five months later, President Johnson signed the Voting Rights Act of 1965.

Connect to the Literature

What qualities enabled King to become a voice for change?

Vocabulary
revolutionary (rev´ ə l$\overline{oo}$´ shə ner´ ē) *adj.* favoring or bringing about sweeping change

well as glimpses of the green of vacation-time spring. Those of our relatives we used to invite for a visit we now can ask to stay. . . . He gave us full-time use of our woods, and restored our memories to those of us who were forced to run away, as realities we might each day enjoy and leave for our children.

He gave us continuity of place, without which community is ephemeral.[4] He gave us home. *1973*

---

4. **ephemeral** (e fem´ ər əl) *adj.* short-lived; fleeting.

Critical Thinking

1. **Key Ideas and Details (a)** Where is Walker making this speech? **(b) Connect:** What is significant about the location?

2. **Key Ideas and Details (a)** What impressed Walker when she first saw Martin Luther King, Jr.? **(b) Interpret:** What did she realize about King's significance for her own life?

3. **Integration of Knowledge and Ideas (a)** Before the civil rights movement, why did African Americans in the South feel left out of American society? **(b) Evaluate:** According to Walker, what was King's most important gift to African Americans?

4. **Integration of Knowledge and Ideas (a)** What aspects of Walker's life in Georgia prepared her to be so receptive to the actions of King? **(b)** Changes have occurred in the decades since Walker's speech. Do you think she would say that King continues to have an influence today? Why or why not? *[Connect to the Big Question: Are yesterday's heroes important today?]*

Cite textual evidence to support your responses.

Reading Skill: Purpose for Reading

1. (a) What **purpose** might you set for reading Walker's speech? **(b)** How does this purpose affect your reading rate?

2. If you were writing a research report on King's accomplishments as a civil rights leader, would this be an appropriate text to read for information? Why or why not?

Literary Analysis: Author's Influences

3. Integration of Knowledge and Ideas Complete a chart like the one shown to evaluate the effect of the author's influences on her writing.

	Influences	Effect on Her Portrayal of Dr. King
Time and place of Walker's birth		
Walker's cultural background		
Major news events		

4. Integration of Knowledge and Ideas (a) How did King's influence change Alice Walker's perspective toward Georgia? **(b)** How did the historic events in which King played a leading role influence her beliefs and values?

Vocabulary

Acquisition and Use Determine whether the following statements are true or false. Then, explain your answers.

1. If you *disinherit* someone, you will probably be thanked.

2. A *revolutionary* concept is one that is familiar to most people.

3. An *ancestral* background can be illustrated with a family tree.

4. If a race is *brutal*, it can be completed without much effort.

5. When schools *integrate*, no single group is excluded.

Word Study Use content and what you know about the **Latin root -her-** to explain your answer to each question.

1. Why might an *heirloom* have special meaning to a person?

2. Why might somone want to preserve his or her *heritage*?

Word Study

The **Latin root -her-** means "heir" or "one who receives."

Apply It Explain how the root -her- contributes to the meanings of these words. You may consult a dictionary, if necessary.

inheritance

hereditary

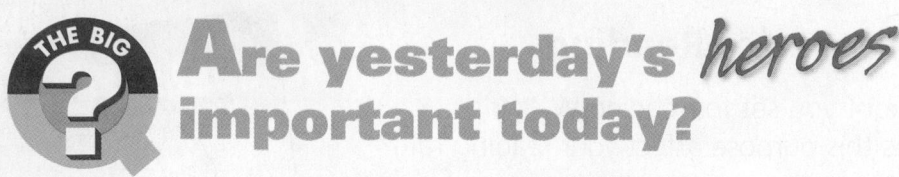

Are yesterday's *heroes* important today?

Writing About the Big Question

"An Episode of War" explores various reactions to the wounding of a Civil War soldier, including those of the soldier himself. Use this sentence starter to develop your ideas about the Big Question.

The concept of heroism (is/is not) **outdated** in our times because _____.

While You Read Notice the behavior of the wounded soldier and those around him to decide if he acts heroically or not.

Vocabulary

Read each word and its definition. Decide whether you know the word well, know it a little bit, or do not know it at all. After you read, see how your knowledge of each word has increased.

- **winced** (winst) *v.* shrank or drew back slightly, usually with a grimace, as in pain (p. 1123) *The boy <u>winced</u> when the doctor touched his injured arm.* wince *n.*

- **audible** (ôʹ də bəl) *adj.* able to be heard (p. 1123) *The child spoke in a whisper that was barely <u>audible</u>.* audibly *adv.*

- **compelled** (kəm peldʹ) *v.* forced (p. 1123) *He felt <u>compelled</u> to defend himself against the unfair attack.* compelling *adj.* compulsive *adj.* compulsory *adj.*

- **tumultuous** (t
oo mulʹ ch
oo əs) *adj.* wild; chaotic (p. 1126) *The wind whipped the waves on the <u>tumultuous</u> sea.*

- **contempt** (kən temptʹ) *n.* scorn; disrespect (p. 1127) *He felt only <u>contempt</u> for his enemy.* contemptuous *adj.* contemptuously *adv.*

- **disdainfully** (dis dānʹ fə lē) *adv.* scornfully (p. 1127) *Convinced he was superior to his coworkers, he treated them <u>disdainfully</u>.* disdain *n.* disdainful *adj.*

Word Study

The **Latin root -aud-** means "hear."

In this story, a soldier's silent breathing becomes **audible,** or able to be heard, when he is suddenly wounded during a peaceful moment in camp.

Stephen Crane
(1871–1900)

Author of
An Episode *of* War

When Stephen Crane wrote *The Red Badge of Courage,* he set out to change the way people viewed war novels. As a journalist who was largely unknown outside of New York City, Crane created a novel about a young Civil War soldier. The book made him a household name.

Stories of War Although he was born years after the Civil War had ended, Crane was fascinated by the war. He interviewed Civil War veterans and pored over photographs, battlefield maps, and firsthand accounts of the fighting. All this research paid off in Crane's realistic portrait of Henry Fleming, the hero of *The Red Badge of Courage.*

DID YOU KNOW?

Crane was an influential writer despite his short life. He died of tuberculosis at age twenty-eight.

BACKGROUND FOR THE STORY

Civil War Wounded

Like the lieutenant in "An Episode of War," soldiers who were wounded in the Civil War faced very long odds. Field hospitals were unsanitary and crowded with wounded soldiers. Medical practices of the time, such as not sterilizing surgical instruments, encouraged the spread of disease and infection. To save soldiers' lives from deadly infections, doctors were often forced to amputate limbs.

An Episode of War

Stephen Crane

▲ **Critical Viewing**
What does the picture suggest about the setting of the story? **[Analyze]**

T he lieutenant's rubber blanket lay on the ground, and upon it he had poured the company's supply of coffee. Corporals and other representatives of the grimy and hot-throated men who lined the breast-work[1] had come for each squad's portion.

---

1. breast-work *n.* low wall put up quickly as a defense in battle.

The lieutenant was frowning and serious at this task of division. His lips pursed as he drew with his sword various crevices in the heap, until brown squares of coffee, astoundingly equal in size, appeared on the blanket. He was on the verge of a great triumph in mathematics, and the corporals were thronging forward, each to reap a little square, when suddenly the lieutenant cried out and looked quickly at a man near him as if he suspected it was a case of personal assault. The others cried out also when they saw blood upon the lieutenant's sleeve.

He had **winced** like a man stung, swayed dangerously, and then straightened. The sound of his hoarse breathing was plainly **audible**. He looked sadly, mystically, over the breast-work at the green face of a wood, where now were many little puffs of white smoke. During this moment the men about him gazed statuelike and silent, astonished and awed by this catastrophe which happened when catastrophes were not expected—when they had leisure to observe it.

As the lieutenant stared at the wood, they too swung their heads, so that for another instant all hands, still silent, contemplated the distant forest as if their minds were fixed upon the mystery of a bullet's journey.

The officer had, of course, been **compelled** to take his sword into his left hand. He did not hold it by the hilt. He gripped it at the middle of the blade, awkwardly. Turning his eyes from the hostile wood, he looked at the sword as he held it there, and seemed puzzled as to what to do with it, where to put it. In short, this weapon had of a sudden become a strange thing to him. He looked at it in a kind of stupefaction, as if he had been endowed with a trident, a sceptre, or a spade.[2]

Finally he tried to sheathe it. To sheathe a sword held by the left hand, at the middle of the blade, in a scabbard hung

Vocabulary
winced (winst) *v.* shrank or drew back slightly, usually with a grimace, as in pain
audible (ô´ də bəl) *adj.* able to be heard
compelled (kəm peld´) *v.* forced

Reading Check

What happens to the lieutenant while he is distributing coffee?

---

2. a trident, a sceptre, or a spade *n.* symbols of royal power.

at the left hip, is a feat worthy of a sawdust ring.[3] This wounded officer engaged in a desperate struggle with the sword and the wobbling scabbard, and during the time of it breathed like a wrestler.

But at this instant the men, the spectators, awoke from their stone-like poses and crowded forward sympathetically. The orderly-sergeant took the sword and tenderly placed it in the scabbard. At the time, he leaned nervously backward, and did not allow even his finger to brush the body of the lieutenant. A wound gives strange dignity to him who bears it. Well men shy from his new and terrible majesty. It is as if the wounded man's hand is upon the curtain which hangs before the revelations of all existence—the meaning of ants, potentates,[4] wars, cities, sunshine, snow, a feather dropped from a bird's wing; and the power of it sheds radiance upon a bloody form, and makes the other men understand sometimes that they are little. His comrades look at him with large eyes thoughtfully. Moreover, they fear vaguely that the weight of a finger upon him might send him headlong, precipitate the tragedy, hurl him at once into the dim, grey unknown. And so the orderly-sergeant, while sheathing the sword, leaned nervously backward.

There were others who proffered assistance. One timidly presented his shoulder and asked the lieutenant if he cared to lean upon it, but the latter waved him away mournfully. He wore the look of one who knows he is the victim of a terrible disease and understands his helplessness. He again stared over the breast-work at the forest, and then, turning, went slowly rearward. He held his right wrist tenderly in his left hand as if the wounded arm was made of very brittle glass.

And the men in silence stared at the wood, then at the departing lieutenant; then at the wood, then at the lieutenant.

As the wounded officer passed from the line of battle, he was enabled to see many things which as a participant

Author's Influences
What realistic details in this paragraph suggest the influence of first-hand accounts on the author's writing?

---

3. **sawdust ring** *n.* ring in which circus acts are performed.
4. **potentates** (pōt´ ən tāts´) *n.* rulers; powerful people.

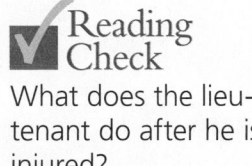

in the fight were unknown to him. He saw a general on a black horse gazing over the lines of blue infantry at the green woods which veiled his problems. An aide galloped furiously, dragged his horse suddenly to a halt, saluted, and presented a paper. It was, for a wonder, precisely like a historical painting.

To the rear of the general and his staff a group, composed of a bugler, two or three orderlies, and the bearer of the corps standard,[5] all upon maniacal horses, were working like slaves to hold their ground, preserve their respectful interval, while the shells boomed in the air about them, and caused their chargers to make furious quivering leaps.

5. corps (kôr) standard n. flag or banner representing a military unit.

▲ **Critical Viewing**
How does this painting of a Civil War battle capture the confusion of the battlefield? **[Analyze]**

Reading
Check
What does the lieutenant do after he is injured?

A battery, a **tumultuous** and shining mass, was swirling toward the right. The wild thud of hoofs, the cries of the riders shouting blame and praise, menace and encouragement, and, last, the roar of the wheels, the slant of the glistening guns, brought the lieutenant to an intent pause. The battery[6] swept in curves that stirred the heart; it made halts as dramatic as the crash of a wave on the rocks, and when it fled onward this aggregation of wheels, levers, motors had a beautiful unity, as if it were a missile. The sound of it was a war-chorus that reached into the depths of man's emotion.

The lieutenant, still holding his arm as if it were of glass, stood watching this battery until all detail of it was lost, save the figures of the riders, which rose and fell and waved lashes over the black mass.

Later, he turned his eyes toward the battle, where the shooting sometimes crackled like bush-fires, sometimes sputtered with exasperating irregularity, and sometimes reverberated like the thunder. He saw the smoke rolling upward and saw crowds of men who ran and cheered, or stood and blazed away at the inscrutable distance.

He came upon some stragglers, and they told him how to find the field hospital. They described its exact location. In fact, these men, no longer having part in the battle, knew more of it than others. They told the performance of every corps, every division, the opinion of every general. The lieutenant, carrying his wounded arm rearward, looked upon them with wonder.

At the roadside a brigade was making coffee and buzzing with talk like a girls' boarding-school. Several officers came

Vocabulary
tumultuous (to͞o mul´ cho͞o əs) *adj.* wild; chaotic

Purpose for Reading
For what purpose might you read this story slowly?

▲ **Critical Viewing**
How do Crane's descriptions reflect the influence of Civil War photographs like the one shown here of an 1862 Virginia field hospital? **[Connect]**

---

6. battery (bat´ ər ē) *n.* military unit of men and cannons.

out to him and inquired concerning things of which he knew nothing. One, seeing his arm, began to scold. "Why, man, that's no way to do. You want to fix that thing." He appropriated the lieutenant and the lieutenant's wound. He cut the sleeve and laid bare the arm, every nerve of which softly fluttered under his touch. He bound his handkerchief over the wound, scolding away in the meantime. His tone allowed one to think that he was in the habit of being wounded every day. The lieutenant hung his head, feeling, in this presence, that he did not know how to be correctly wounded. •

The low white tents of the hospital were grouped around an old schoolhouse. There was here a singular commotion. In the foreground two ambulances interlocked wheels in the deep mud. The drivers were tossing the blame of it back and forth, gesticulating and berating,[7] while from the ambulances, both crammed with wounded, there came an occasional groan. An interminable crowd of bandaged men were coming and going. Great numbers sat under the trees nursing heads or arms or legs. There was a dispute of some kind raging on the steps of the schoolhouse. Sitting with his back against a tree a man with a face as grey as a new army blanket was serenely smoking a corncob pipe. The lieutenant wished to rush forward and inform him that he was dying.

A busy surgeon was passing near the lieutenant. "Good-morning," he said, with a friendly smile. Then he caught sight of the lieutenant's arm, and his face at once changed. "Well, let's have a look at it." He seemed possessed suddenly of a great contempt for the lieutenant. This wound evidently placed the latter on a very low social plane. The doctor cried out impatiently, "What mutton-head had tied it up that way anyhow?" The lieutenant answered, "Oh, a man."

When the wound was disclosed the doctor fingered it disdainfully. "Humph," he said. "You come along with me and I'll 'tend to you." His voice contained the same scorn as if he were saying: "You will have to go to jail."

The lieutenant had been very meek, but now his face flushed, and he looked into the doctor's eyes. "I guess I won't have it amputated," he said.

"Nonsense, man! Nonsense! Nonsense!" cried the doctor.

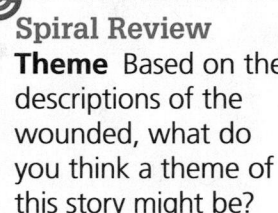

Spiral Review
Theme Based on the descriptions of the wounded, what do you think a theme of this story might be?

Vocabulary
contempt (kən tempt´) *n.* scorn; disrespect
disdainfully (dis dān´ fə lē) *adv.* scornfully

Reading Check
How was the lieutenant made to feel by the first officer who bandaged his arm?

---

7. **gesticulating** (jes tik´ yoo lāt´ iŋ) **and berating** (bē rāt´ iŋ) *v.* waving arms about wildly and scolding.

► **Critical Viewing**
What do these sur-
geons' tools reveal
about the state of
medicine at the time of
the Civil War? **[Infer]**

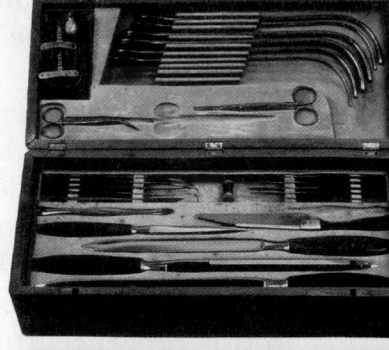

Purpose for Reading
What insight does the
ending give you into
attitudes toward
wounded soldiers at
the time of this story?

"Come along, now. I won't amputate it.
Come along. Don't be a baby."

"Let go of me," said the lieutenant,
holding back wrathfully, his glance fixed
upon the door of the old schoolhouse, as
sinister to him as the portals of death.

And this is the story of how the
lieutenant lost his arm. When he
reached home, his sisters, his mother,
his wife, sobbed for a long time at the
sight of the flat sleeve. "Oh, well," he
said, standing shamefaced amid these
tears, "I don't suppose it matters so
much as all that."

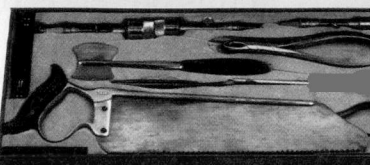

Critical Thinking

Cite textual evidence to support your responses.

© 1. **Key Ideas and Details** **(a)** After he is hit, what does the
lieutenant attempt to do with his sword? **(b) Infer:** Why
does he feel the need to do this? **(c) Analyze:** How does
his action expose the absurd nature of warfare?

© 2. **Key Ideas and Details** **(a)** How do the lieutenant's men
behave toward him when he is wounded? **(b) Compare
and Contrast:** How does this treatment compare with the
way the lieutenant is treated after he leaves his men?
(c) Analyze: In what ways does this interaction seem to
strip him of his individuality?

© 3. **Key Ideas and Details** **Interpret:** Why do you think the
lieutenant tells his family "I don't suppose it matters so
much as all that"?

© 4. **Integration of Knowledge and Ideas** **(a)** Do the
circumstances in which the lieutenant is wounded seem
heroic to you? Why or why not? **(b)** Are his reactions to his
wounds heroic? Explain. **(c)** Do you think the concept of
heroism changes over time or that certain people and
actions are always considered heroic? Support your answer
with reasons. *[Connect to the Big Question: Are
yesterday's heroes important today?]*

Reading Skill: Purpose for Reading

1. (a) What **purpose** might you set for reading "An Episode of War"? **(b)** How would this purpose affect your reading rate?

2. Would this be an appropriate text to read for information for a research report on Civil War leadership? Why or why not?

Literary Analysis: Author's Influences

3. Integration of Knowledge and Ideas Complete a chart like the one shown to evaluate the effect of the **author's influences** on his writing. Refer to the author's biography on page 1121 to help you.

	Influences	Effect on "An Episode of War"
Crane's interests		
Crane's research		

4. Integration of Knowledge and Ideas Crane's writing was unique because it captured the effect of war on the individual soldier. What values are reflected in this approach to writing and in Crane's portrayal of the lieutenant?

Vocabulary

Acquisition and Use Determine whether the following statements are true or false. Then, explain your answers.

1. A neat person would feel *compelled* to pick up litter.

2. Someone who gets seasick prefers a *tumultuous* ocean.

3. If a man *winced* while lifting a box, it was probably heavy.

4. If planes are *audible* from homes, residents often complain.

5. People who feel *contempt* for each other make great friends.

6. If I respect someone, I will respond to him or her *disdainfully*.

Word Study Use context and what you know about the **Latin root -aud-** to explain your answer to each question.

1. What should an *audience* expect to experience at a play?

2. If the music at a concert is *inaudible*, can you enjoy it?

Word Study

The **Latin root -aud-** means "hear."

Apply It Explain how the root -aud- contributes to the meaning of each word. Consult a dictionary, if necessary.

auditorium
audio
audition

Integrated Language Skills

Choice: A Tribute to Martin Luther King, Jr. • An Episode of War

Conventions: Capitalization

Capital letters are used at the beginnings of the first words of sentences and for the pronoun *I*. Proper nouns and proper adjectives are also capitalized.

The chart shows examples of how **capitalization** is used.

Capitalize	Examples
the first word in a sentence	The blue jay is a very aggressive bird. Wait! Can you give me back my pen?
the first word in a quotation that is a complete sentence	Einstein said, "Anyone who has never made a mistake has never tried anything new."
the pronoun *I*	After swimming, I felt tired.
proper nouns, geographical names, and organizations	Elsa went sailing down the Hudson River with her Girl Scout troop.
titles of people	Mr. Donohue was not amused.

Practice A Identify the capital letter or letters in each sentence. Then, give the reason for each use of capitalization.

1. The state of Georgia had been the Walker family's home for generations.

2. King is famous for saying, "Injustice anywhere is a threat to justice everywhere."

3. The American government now supports civil rights for all citizens.

4. When I go to the library, I will look for other books by Alice Walker.

Reading Application In "Choice . . . ," find examples of three types of capitalization, and explain why each word is capitalized.

Practice B Rewrite each sentence to correct errors in capitalization. Substitute capital or lowercase letters where appropriate.

1. the Lieutenant approached and said, "captain, a Man has been wounded."

2. soldiers wounded in the civil war did not have the benefit of Modern Medicine.

3. life on the Battlefield was dangerous for soldiers from the north and the South.

4. When the War ended, my fellow soldiers and i felt great relief.

Writing Application Write a paragraph about the American Civil War. In your writing, use each capitalization rule identified in the chart.

PH WRITING COACH   Further instruction and practice are available in *Prentice Hall Writing Coach*.

Writing

Common Core State Standards

L.8.2; W.8.1, W.8.1.a, W.8.1.d, W.8.1.e, W.8.2
[For the full wording of the standards, see page 1110.]

Argumentative Text Write a **persuasive speech** in favor of building a memorial in honor of either Dr. King or Civil War soldiers.

- Reread the selection to find details about the goals your subject set and the sacrifices and emotions your subject experienced.

- Prepare a speech outline with an introduction, a body, and a conclusion. The introduction should provide a preview of your proposal. The body should offer reasons, and your conclusion should summarize these reasons.

- As you draft your speech, use a reasonable and appropriate tone to present evidence that supports your opinion.

- To make the speech more powerful when it is read aloud, add repetition, dramatic pauses, and vivid language.

Grammar Application Check your speech to make sure you capitalized place names and names of people.

Writing Workshop: *Work in Progress*

Prewriting for Exposition Use the Causes-Effects List from your writing portfolio to diagram a cause-effect chain. Each cause can lead to an effect, and each effect in turn can become a cause of other effects, and so on. Save your Cause-and-Effect Diagram in your writing portfolio.

Use this prewriting activity to prepare for the **Writing Workshop** on page 1156.

Research and Technology

Build and Present Knowledge Write a **newspaper article** on one of the following topics:

- If you read "Choice . . . ," write an article for Martin Luther King Day that looks at King's career as a whole. Research his role in the civil rights movement and the hardships he faced.

- If you read "An Episode of War," write an article about the experience and cost of fighting in the Civil War. You can use information from modern sources, but write the article from the perspective of someone during, or shortly after, the war.

Follow these guidelines to complete the assignment.

- Start your article with an effective and attention-grabbing lead.

- Use quotations from individuals such as Alice Walker on civil rights, or Civil War soldiers on battle conditions, to provide first-hand accounts of the events you describe. Add comparisons to help readers understand your main idea.

PHLit Online!
www.PHLitOnline.com
- Interactive graphic organizers
- Grammar tutorial
- Interactive journals

Test Practice: Reading

Purpose for Reading

Fiction Selection

Directions: *Read the selection. Then, answer the questions.*

Class Clown Strikes Again

Our class had just finished a unit on famous African Americans, and Ms. Wilson had planned a field trip to the Tuskegee Institute National Historic Site. She was very excited about taking us to a "living history" museum to learn more about the people in the unit.

Pete Keegan had been the class clown since he moved to town in third grade. Pete decided to dress in honor of George Washington Carver who is remembered for such scientific achievements as inventing more than 300 uses for the peanut. When he arrived that morning of the trip, he was plastered with peanuts, from neck to ankles. We all burst out laughing. "You *said* "living" history, Ms. Wilson." Pete said with a big grin.

"Good thing we're going to a museum and not a zoo! You'd be elephant food!" someone called from the back of the room.

Ms. Wilson looked at Pete with a perfectly straight face and said, "Good morning, Peter. I see you brought snacks for the bus ride."

1. What is the most likely purpose for reading this story?
   A. to be entertained
   B. to find statistics
   C. to be persuaded
   D. to learn a new skill

2. What would be a good question to focus your reading purpose?
   A. What does Ms. Wilson want the students to learn?
   B. How does Pete reinforce his reputation as the class clown?
   C. What happens during the field trip?
   D. Who was George Washington Carver, and what made him famous?

3. What reading rate is most appropriate for this selection?
   A. quickly, to find facts
   B. quickly, to find out what happens
   C. slowly, to learn about history
   D. slowly, to critically analyze the text

Writing for Assessment

What details in the story helped you determine your purpose for reading this selection? In a few sentences, explain how that determined your reading rate for the selection.

Nonfiction Selection

Directions: *Read the selection. Then, answer the questions.*

George Washington Carver: Plant Genius

Early Years The son of African American slaves in Missouri, George Washington Carver grew up on a farm and began studying plants when he was only a child. By the time he was a teenager, his neighbors called on him as a "plant doctor" to help with their failing crops. He eventually became a national expert on breeding plants.

An Aid to Farmers As a professor in Alabama, Carver saw that farmers were destroying the soil by growing only plants that drain the ground of nitrogen—an important plant nutrient. He persuaded them to alternate their crops. One of those crops was the peanut, something that farmers could eat and sell. To persuade farmers to plant peanuts, Carver listed more than 300 of its uses, such as dyes, oils, and cooking.

1. What is the most likely purpose for reading this article?
   A. to be entertained
   B. to take action
   C. to get information
   D. to confirm predictions

2. What question is answered by this selection?
   A. What is a genius?
   B. How did Carver get involved with plants?
   C. How many types of plants are there?
   D. Why did Carver want to study plants?

3. How should you adjust your reading rate for this selection?
   A. Read quickly looking for details that entertain.
   B. Skim the selection focusing on the subheads.
   C. Scan the selection for difficult words.
   D. Read slowly to understand the facts.

4. Which of the following research questions would *not* be satisfied by reading this article?
   A. What obstacles did Carver face?
   B. What was Carver an expert on?
   C. How did Carver change agriculture?
   D. Where did Carver grow up?

Writing for Assessment

Connecting Across Texts

Write a paragraph in which you compare the types of information provided in these selections. Then, explain how your purpose for reading differs for each.

PHLit Online!
www.PHLitOnline.com
- Online practice
- Instant feedback

Reading for Information

Analyzing Expository Texts

Radio Transcript

Photo Essay

Political Cartoon

Common Core State Standards

Reading Informational Text
7. Evaluate the advantages and disadvantages of using different mediums to present a particular topic or idea.

Language
6. Acquire and use accurately grade-appropriate general academic and domain-specific words and phrases; gather vocabulary knowledge when considering a word or phrase important to comprehension or expression.

Reading Skill: Evaluate the Treatment, Scope, and Organization of Ideas

When doing research, always **evaluate the treatment, scope, and organization** of the ideas presented. *Treatment* refers to the manner in which a writer presents a topic. *Scope* is the range of information discussed. The *organization* of a text is its structure. When you evaluate these elements, you judge the quality, reliability, and appropriateness of the text you are considering. Use this checklist to evaluate the way a similar subject—readjustment to life after World War II—is presented in three different texts.

Checklist for Evaluating Treatment, Scope, and Organization

❏ Has the author addressed the topic in a way that is neutral or biased?

❏ Does the author cover different sides of an issue or only one?

❏ Does the author present ideas in a logical sequence?

❏ Are details organized in a way that enhances the author's points?

Content-Area Vocabulary

These words appear in the selections that follow. You may also encounter them in other content-area texts.

- **paraplegia** (par′ ə plē′ jē ə) *n.* paralysis of the legs and the lower part of the body

- **disabled** (dis ā′ bəld) *adj.* not able to perform certain actions that most people can perform

- **antibiotics** (an′ ti bī ät′ iks) *n.* substances produced by living things, especially bacteria or molds, that destroy or weaken germs

Morning Edition,
NATIONAL PUBLIC RADIO
November 11, 2003

Features:
- speakers' exact words
- comments that are not interpreted
- text written for a general or a specific audience

PROFILE: World War II veterans who founded the Paralyzed Veterans of America.

BOB EDWARDS, host: This is MORNING EDITION from NPR News. I'm Bob Edwards.

In February of 1947, a small group of World War II veterans gathered at Hines VA Hospital near Chicago. The fact that they were there at all was considered extraordinary. The men were paralyzed, living at a time when **paraplegia** was still an unfamiliar word and most people with spinal cord injuries were told they would die within a few years. But these wounded veterans had other ideas, so they came from hospital wards across the country to start a national organization to represent veterans with spinal cord injuries. Today on Veterans Day, NPR's Joseph Shapiro tells their story.

> The reporter presents factual information in a neutral way, suggesting his reporting is unbiased.

JOSEPH SHAPIRO reporting: The logo of the Paralyzed Veterans of America looks a bit like the American flag, except that it's got 16 stars, one for each of the men who started the PVA when they gathered at that first convention nearly 57 years ago. Today only one of those 16 paralyzed veterans is still alive. His name is Ken Seaquist. He lives in a gated community in Florida. . . . It's there that Seaquist sits in his wheelchair and flips through some yellowed newspaper clippings . . .

PARALYZED VETERANS OF AMERICA
PVA

Mr. KEN SEAQUIST: Oh, here it is. OK.

SHAPIRO: . . . until he finds a photo. . . . The picture shows that convention. It was held in a veterans hospital just outside Chicago. A large room is filled with scores of young men in wheelchairs. Others are in their pajamas and hospital beds, propped up on white pillows.

Mr. SEAQUIST: There's Bill Dake. He came with us and then Mark Orr. Three of us came in the car from Memphis. Mark had one good leg, his right leg, and he was the driver of the car.

> Ken Seaquist, a PVA founder, is personally involved in the issue being discussed. That gives him a unique perspective.

SHAPIRO: Ken Seaquist was a tall, lanky 20-year-old in an Army mountain ski division when he was wounded in Italy. He was flown back to the United

States to a veterans hospital in Memphis. He came back to a society that was not ready for paraplegics.

Mr. SEAQUIST: Before the war, people in our condition were in the closet. They never went out hardly. They didn't take them out.

SHAPIRO: Few people had ever survived for more than a few years with a spinal cord injury. Infections were common and deadly. But that was about to change. David Gerber is a historian at the University at Buffalo. He's written about **disabled** veterans.

Mr. DAVID GERBER (University at Buffalo): With the development of **antibiotics**, which came into general use in World War II, there were many healthy spinal cord-injured veterans who were able to survive and begin to aspire to have a normalized life.

SHAPIRO: Gerber says neither the wounded veterans, nor the world around them at that time knew what to make of men who were seen as having gone from manly warriors to dependent invalids.

Mr. GERBER: The society is emphatically not ready for them, and nor is the medical profession. To this extent, it was often the paralyzed veterans themselves who were pioneers in the development of a new way of life for themselves.

SHAPIRO: Seaquist and the others set out to overcome the fear and pity of others. After Seaquist was injured, he never heard from his girlfriend. His mother's hair turned white in a matter of months. People stared when he went out in public. It was a time when a president with polio felt he had to hide the fact that he used a wheelchair. Beyond attitudes, there was a physical world that had to change. When Seaquist arrived at the Memphis hospital, he could not get off the ward. There were steps in the way.

Mr. SEAQUIST: They had no idea of what they had to do for wheelchairs. So when we got there, they had to put in all these long ramps and this is what we were talking about. The ramping and just to get around the hospital and get out ourselves, you know; not having somebody help us all the time. We were an independent bunch.

SHAPIRO: There were about 2,500 soldiers with spinal cord injuries, most of them living in military hospitals around the country. Pat Grissom lived at Birmingham Hospital in California. He would become one of the first presidents of the PVA, but he was unable to travel from California to Chicago for that first convention. Grissom, too, had come back from war with little hope for his future.

Comments are presented in chronological order, according to the order of the events being discussed.

Mr. PAT GRISSOM: I just suppose that we were going to live the rest of our lives either in the hospital or go to an old soldiers' home. We were just going to be there taking medicine and if you got sick, they would try to take care of you and you'd have your meals provided and your future was the hospital or the old soldiers' home.

SHAPIRO: At Birmingham Hospital, Grissom met a doctor who was about to become a pioneer in the new field of spinal cord medicine. Dr. Ernst Bors did a lot to improve the physical care of paraplegics. He also pushed the men at Birmingham to set goals for their lives, to go back to school, get jobs and marry. Bors and the veterans at Birmingham Hospital were the subject of a Hollywood film, *The Men*. The realistic and sympathetic portrayal helped the American public better understand paralyzed veterans. In the film, the kindly doctor in a lab coat is based on Bors. He urges on a wounded soldier in a white T-shirt, played by a young Marlon Brando.

(Soundbite of *The Men*)

> Mr. MARLON BRANDO: Well, what am I going to do? Where am I going to go?
>
> Unidentified Actor: Into the world.
>
> Mr. BRANDO: I can't go out there anymore.
>
> Unidentified Actor: You still can't accept it, can you?
>
> Mr. BRANDO: No. What did I do? Why'd it have to be me?
>
> Unidentified Actor: Is there an answer? I haven't got it. Somebody always gets hurt in the war.

Marlon Brando in *The Men*

SHAPIRO: For Grissom and the other paralyzed veterans, there was something else that helped them go out into the world, a new technology. The introduction of automatic transmission meant that a car could be modified with hand controls for the gas and brakes. Pat Grissom.

Mr. GRISSOM: Oldsmobile came up with the hydromatic drive and they put on hand controls and they sent people out to start giving driving lessons to us and we started having visions of saving up enough money to get a car and then things were looking better all the time.

Here, Pat Grissom is expressing the facts from his personal point of view.

SHAPIRO: Ken Seaquist says driving opened up all kinds of possibilities, from going out to a restaurant with a bunch of friends to romance.

Mr. SEAQUIST: In Memphis, we had—our favorite place was called the Silver Slipper and they welcomed us with open arms and we had maybe 10, 12 wheelchairs going with our dates. Generally it was our nurses that we dated, 'cause, you know, we couldn't get out anywhere. We took the girls with us, you know. Eventually I married one of them.

SHAPIRO: Seaquist and his wife quickly had two daughters. And with a young family, he had to find work. He went to school and became a landscape architect. Ken Seaquist stopped seeing himself as an invalid and became a man with a future. So in 1947, he and the other founders of the PVA met in Chicago to put together a collective voice to express their dreams and what they needed to accomplish them. They came up with a slogan to get others to join, "Awaken, gentlemen, lest we decay." Ken Seaquist explains what it meant.

Car modified with hand controls

Mr. SEAQUIST: If they forget us, we're going to decay. We're going to be left in the closet. We've got to get out there and speak out, getting things done so we can roll around this country and have access to the whole country.

SHAPIRO: The PVA quickly won some important legislative victories in Washington: money for paralyzed veterans to modify automobiles and houses, money for medical care. Later they would help push for laws that would make buildings and streets accessible to wheelchair users. The PVA has continued to advocate for veterans with spinal cord injuries through every war since World War II.

Joseph Shapiro, NPR News.

> The reporter concludes by summing up the PVA's activities to date.

Readjustment

VETERANS AND EX-WARWORKERS HAVE DIFFICULTY IN PEACETIME LIFE

Photo Essay

Features:

- images that tell a story
- human-interest issue
- text for a general or specific audience

The boys were pouring home from the Army and Navy. Their presence gladdened homes all over the city—on the middle-class South Side, on swank Kessler Boulevard, in . . . homes along North Illinois Street. But the men were coming home to a community not altogether ready for them emotionally, or industrially. There were family tensions, misunderstandings between veterans and old civilian friends. Often the men could find no place to live. Sometimes they could not get jobs, not because there was no work in the city but because available jobs were low-paid or highly technical. Neither the veterans nor the warworkers, laid off from the Allison engine or Curtiss-Wright propeller plants, were willing enough in some cases or skilled enough in others to take them.

Together the veterans and the warworkers formed a restless, still-prosperous group of unemployed. Daily they journeyed to the Indianapolis office of the USES [United States Employment Service] . . . to shop for the work they wanted.

But the people worried little about the situation. Probably they were right in assuming that it would clear up as soon as reconversion, lagging badly, got under way in earnest. Meanwhile many a citizen of Indianapolis with a son or husband or friend in the service tried to get him out. They bombarded their congressmen with letters, telegrams, and personal calls. Said General Marshall, "Demobilization has become disintegration" because of a "widespread emotional crisis of the American people."

> The scope of this photo essay is small, focusing on a specific place in Indianapolis.

> These images and captions give the photo essay a sympathetic tone and make it more personal.

THE RESTLESS UNEMPLOYED appear at USES. Still prosperous, most of them are shopping for jobs, seeing what is available. From left to right: Cpl. Ralph Garbett, 38, who wants a job as a diesel mechanic; Carl A. Seherb, former worker at Allison, who wants precision-inspector work; Leah H. Blow, who wants a job as a pie baker.

CLOSED TIGHT is the Curtiss-Wright plant in Indianapolis. It made propellers during the war. Once 6,200 people worked there. A city of diversified industries, Indianapolis should be able to reconvert very successfully.

Features:

- text and illustrations that comment on society
- familiar and easy-to-follow comic strip format
- text for a general or specific audience

Political cartoons treat serious subjects in a humorous way.

The Sad Sack® is a Registered Trademark and ©Sad Sack, Inc. Created by George Baker.

Finally discharged after 3½ years in the Army, Sad Sack meets his final disillusionment when he approaches the complexities of human reconversion.

This cartoon presents events chronologically, showing a day in the life of an army veteran.

Comparing Expository Texts

1. Craft and Structure (a) Compare and contrast the **treatment, scope, and organization of ideas** in the three texts.
(b) Suppose you are writing an informational report on challenges soldiers faced when rejoining civilian life after World War II. Evaluate the texts, explaining which would be the most appropriate source for such a report and why.

Content-Area Vocabulary

2. (a) Explain the meaning of the prefixes *para-*, *dis-*, and *anti-*, as in *paraplegia, disabled,* and *antibiotics.* Consult a dictionary as needed. **(b)** Use each word in a sentence that shows its meaning.

⏱ Timed Writing

Explanatory Text: Essay

> **Format and Details**
> The prompt gives specific directions about what to write and the types of details to include.

Write a brief essay that compares the effect produced by the photo essay with the impact of the political cartoon. Give examples to illustrate similarities and differences between your impressions of each. (30 minutes)

> **Academic Vocabulary**
> When you *illustrate* an idea, you give details and examples that help readers understand it.

5-Minute Planner

Complete these steps before you begin to write:

1. Read the prompt carefully and completely.

2. Review the text and images in the photo essay and the political cartoon. Jot down your impressions.

3. Compare your notes on the two texts, looking for similarities and differences. To help clarify your thoughts, take notes on the advantages and disadvantages of each type of media in addressing a topic as complex and emotional as readjustment.

4. Use your notes to make an outline before you begin writing.

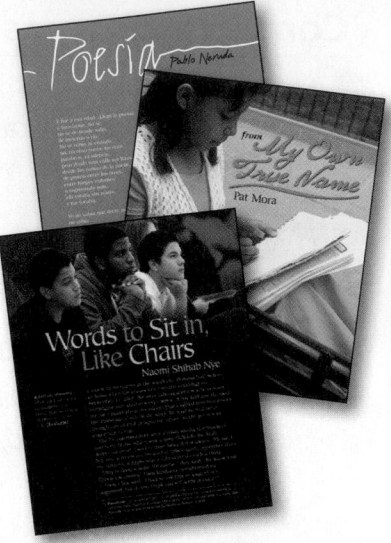

Comparing Works on a Similar Theme

The **theme** of a literary work is its central idea or underlying message. A **universal theme** is an insight or lesson that appears in literature across cultures and throughout different periods in history. Universal themes include the power of love and the desire for freedom.

These three selections represent very different forms—a poem, an open letter, and a personal essay. Each author comes from a different cultural background. However, all of the works focus on a similar universal theme: the need for self-expression.

Even when writers choose to focus on the same theme, they often produce contrasting results. This is because they have different purposes, or reasons for writing. One may write to reflect, another to entertain, and yet another to persuade or inform. In addition, writers may draw on different life experiences and cultural backgrounds, and they may explore different aspects of the same theme in their works.

Use a chart like this to analyze the way the theme is presented in these selections. Refer to page 1143 to find information about each author's cultural background.

	Neruda	Mora	Nye
Literary Form	Poem	Open Letter	Essay
Details About Culture			
Details That Reveal Theme			
Statement of Theme			

**Common Core
State Standards**

Reading Literature

2. Determine a theme or central idea of a text and analyze its development over the course of the text, including its relationship to the characters, setting, and plot; provide an objective summary of the text.

5. Compare and contrast the structure of two or more texts and analyze how the differing structure of each text contributes to its meaning and style.

Writing

9. Draw evidence from literary or informational texts to support analysis, reflection, and research. *(Timed Writing)*

**PHLit
Online!**
www.PHLitOnline.com

- Vocabulary flashcards
- Interactive journals
- More about the authors
- Selection audio
- Interactive graphic organizers

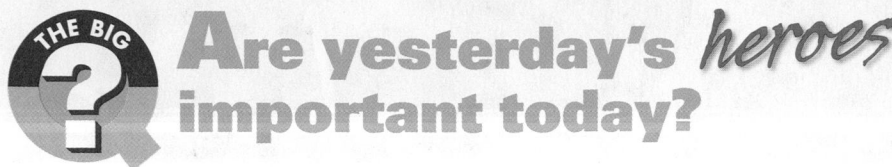

Are yesterday's *heroes* important today?

Writing About the Big Question

Many heroes are ordinary people who face challenges in their everyday lives. Use these sentence starters to develop your ideas.

Writing about one's feelings takes **courage** because _____.

Writers, past or present, could become personal heroes for me if they _____.

Meet the Authors

Pablo Neruda (1904–1973)

Author of "Poetry" (La Poesía)

"Pablo Neruda" was the pen name taken by a young Chilean poet who was afraid his father would not approve of his writing. Eventually Neruda became one of the most popular poets writing in Spanish, and his pen name became his official name. In addition to his writing, Neruda also had a long political career as a diplomat.

Pat Mora (b. 1942)

Author of "My Own True Name"

In her work, Pat Mora explores cultural diversity and her own life experiences as a Mexican-American woman. Born in El Paso, Texas, she was raised partly by her grandmother and her Aunt "Lobo." Her writings include volumes of poetry and essays, children's books, and a memoir.

Naomi Shihab Nye (b. 1952)

Author of "Words to Sit in, Like Chairs"

Arab American writer Naomi Shihab Nye is widely admired for the keen observations and insights she brings to her poetry and short stories. Nye writes that "the primary source of poetry has always been local life, random characters met on the streets, our own ancestry sifting down to us through small essential daily tasks."

La

Poesía

Pablo Neruda

Poetry

translation by Alastair Reid

Y fue a esa edad...Llegó la poesía	And it was at the age...poetry
a buscarme. No sé,	arrived in search of me. I don't know,
no sé de dónde salió,	I don't know where it came from, from
de invierno o río.	winter or a river.
No sé cómo ni cuándo,	5 I don't know how or when,
no, no eran voces, no eran	no, they were not voices, they were
palabras, ni silencio,	not words, not silence,
pero desde una calle me llamaba,	but from a street it called me,
desde las ramas de la noche,	from the branches of night,
de pronto entre los otros,	10 abruptly from the others,
entre fuegos violentos	among raging fires
o regresando solo,	or returning alone,
allí estaba sin rostro	there it was, without a face,
y me tocaba.	and it touched me.
Yo no sabía qué decir, mi boca	15 I didn't know what to say, my mouth
no sabía	had no way
nombrar,	with names,
mis ojos eran ciegos,	my eyes were blind.
y algo golpeaba en mi alma,	Something knocked in my soul,
fiebre o alas perdidas,	20 fever or forgotten wings,
y me fui haciendo solo,	and I made my own way,
descifrando	deciphering
aquella quemadura,	that fire,
y escribí la primera línea vaga,	and I wrote the first, faint line,
vaga, sin cuerpo, pura	25 faint, without substance, pure
tontería,	nonsense,
pura sabiduría	pure wisdom
del que no sabe nada,	of someone who knows nothing;

y vi de pronto
el cielo
desgranado
y abierto,
planetas,
plantaciones palpitantes,
la sombra perforada,
acribillada
por flechas, fuego y flores,
la noche arrolladora, el universo.

Y yo, mínimo ser,
ebrio del gran vacío
constelado,
a semejanza, a imagen
del misterio,
me sentí parte pura
del abismo,
rodé con las estrellas,
mi corazón se desató en el viento.

and suddenly I saw
30 the heavens
unfastened
and open,
planets,
palpitating plantations,
35 the darkness perforated,
riddled
with arrows, fire, and flowers,
the overpowering night, the universe.

And I, tiny being,
40 drunk with the great starry
void,
likeness, image of
mystery,
felt myself a pure part
of the abyss.
45 I wheeled with the stars.
My heart broke loose with the wind.

Theme
What happens after the poem's speaker writes his first lines?

Vocabulary
abyss (ə bis´)
n. an immeasurable space

Critical Thinking

© **1. Key Ideas and Details** **(a)** How does the writer's first experience with poetry occur? **(b) Support**: What lines or phrases describe this? **(c) Infer:** How difficult does he find writing, at first? Why?

© **2. Key Ideas and Details** **(a)** Identify at least two images that describe what happens once the poet begins to write. **(b) Connect:** What are his feelings about this experience? **(c) Speculate:** Do you think that this poem reflects Neruda's true experiences? Explain.

© **3. Integration of Knowledge and Ideas** **(a)** Are the obstacles Neruda overcomes real or imagined? **(b)** Do you think today's writers would see Neruda as a hero? Why or why not? *[Connect to the Big Question: Are yesterday's heroes important today?]*

Cite textual evidence to support your responses.

from **My Own True Name**

Pat Mora

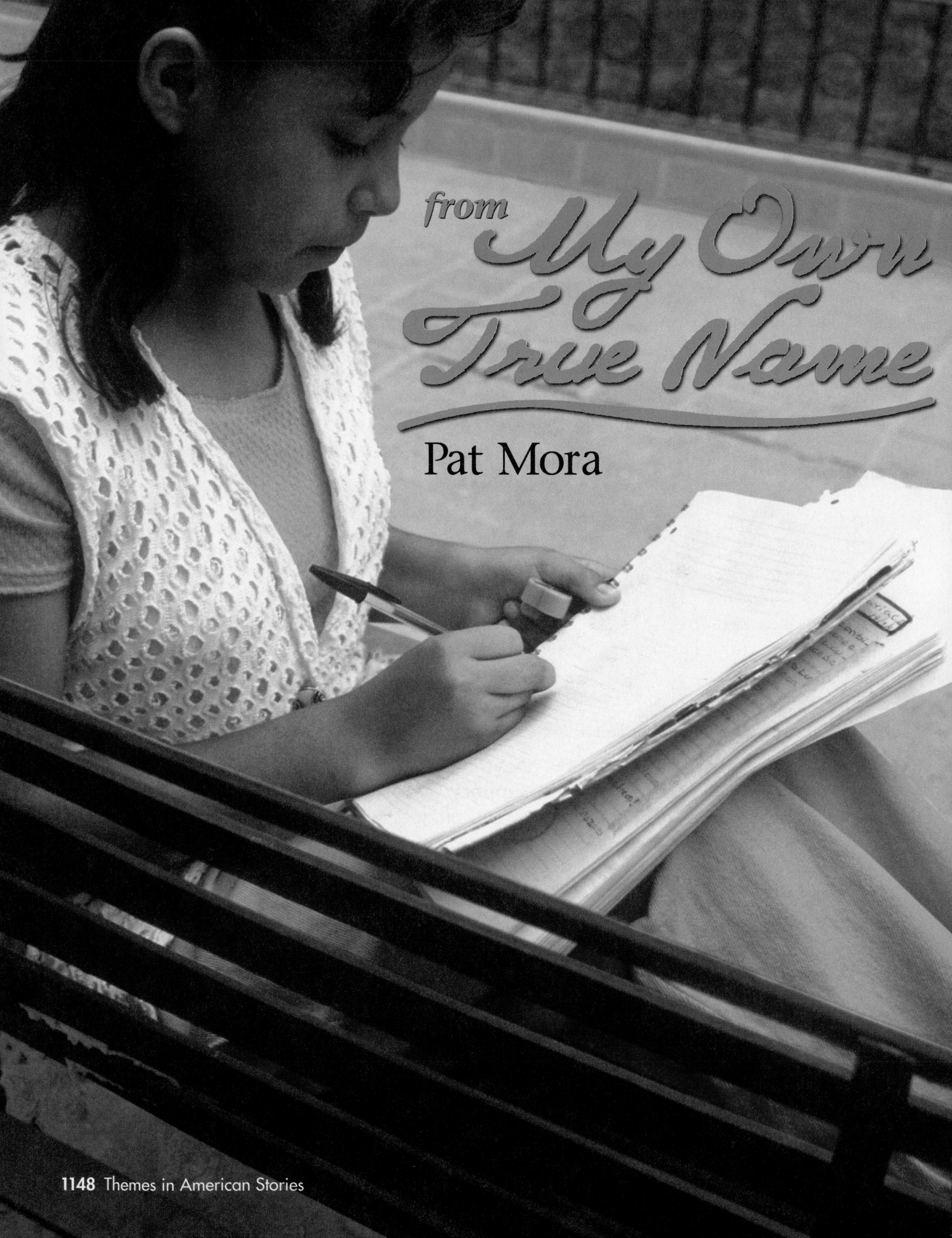

Dear Fellow Writer,

A blank piece of paper can be exciting and intimidating. Probably every writer knows both reactions well. I know I do. I wanted to include a letter to you in this book because I wish I could talk to you individually. I'd say: Listen to your inside self, your private voice. Respect your thoughts and feelings and ideas. You—yes, you—play with sounds. With language(s), explore the wonder of being alive.

Living hurts, so sometimes we write about a miserable date, a friend who betrayed us, the death of a parent. Some days, though, we're so full of joy we feel like a kite. We can fly! Whether we write for ourselves or to share our words, we discover ourselves when we truly write: when we dive below the surface. It's never easy to really reveal ourselves in school, but remember that writing is practice. Without practice, you will never learn to hear and sing your own unique song.

I have always been a reader, which is the best preparation for becoming a writer. When I was in grade school in El Paso, Texas (where I was born), I read comic books and mysteries and magazines and library books. I was soaking up language.

I've always liked to write, too—but I was a mother before I began to create regular time for my writing. Was it that I didn't think that I had anything important to say? Was it that I didn't believe that I could say anything that well? Was it that when I was in school we never studied a writer who was like me—bilingual, a Mexican American—and so somehow I decided that "people like me" couldn't be writers?

I have a large poster of an American Indian storyteller right above my desk. Children are climbing all over her, just as my sisters and my brother and I climbed over *nuestra tía*, our aunt, Ignacia Delgado, the aunt we called Lobo. She was our storyteller. Who is yours? Would you like to be a storyteller? Would you like to write or paint or draw or sing your stories?

I became a writer because words give me so much pleasure that I have always wanted to sink my hands and heart into them, to see what I can create, what will rise up, what will appear on the page. I've learned that some writers are quiet and shy, others noisy, others just plain obnoxious. Some like

Vocabulary
intimidating (in tim´ ə dā´ tiŋ) *adj.* frightening

Theme
What two reasons does Mora give for writing?

Vocabulary
bilingual (bī liŋ´ gwəl) *adj.* able to speak two languages

Reading Check
What helped Mora prepare to become a writer?

◄ **Critical Viewing** What feelings and ideas in the essay's first paragraph does this photograph best illustrate? Explain. **[Connect]**

enchiladas and others like sushi; some like rap and others like *rancheras*.[1] Some write quickly, and some are as slow as an elderly man struggling up a steep hill on a windy day. I'll tell you a few of our secrets.

The first is that we all read. Some of us like mysteries and some of us like memoirs, but writers are readers. We're curious to see what others are doing with words, but—what is more important—we like what happens to us when we open a book, how we journey into the pages.

Another secret is that we write often. We don't just talk about writing. We sit by ourselves inside or outside, writing at airports or on kitchen tables, even on napkins.

We're usually nosy and very good at eavesdropping. Just ask my three children! And writers are collectors. We collect facts and phrases and stories: the names of cacti,[2] the word for cheese in many languages.

In the last twenty years, I've spent more and more time writing my own books for children and adults. I have received many rejections and will probably receive many more, darn it. I just keep writing—and revising. Revising is now one of my favorite parts of being a writer, though I didn't always feel that way. I enjoy taking what I've written—a picture or a book or a poem—and trying to make the writing better, by changing words or rhythm. Sometimes by starting over!

Writing is my way of knowing myself better, of hearing myself, of discovering what is important to me and what makes me sad, what makes me different, what makes me me—of discovering my own true name. And writing makes me less lonely. I have all these words in English and Spanish whispering or sometimes shouting at me, just waiting for me to put them to work, to combine them so that they leap over mountains on small hooves or slip down to the sandy bottom of the silent sea.

And you? Maybe these poems—taken from my collections *Chants, Borders,* and *Communion,* along with some new poems written for this book, for you—will tempt you to write your

▲ **Critical Viewing**
Why might a writer keep an object such as this one in the place he or she writes? **[Connect]**

Theme
How does Mora use personification and imagery to explain her need to express herself?

---

1. *rancheras* (rän che´ räs) *n.* type of popular Latino music.
2. *cacti* (kak´ tī) *n.* plural form of cactus, a type of desert plant.

own poems about a special person or a special place, about a gray fear or a green hope. What are your blooms, your thorns, your roots?

Remember, my friend, never speak badly of your writing. Never make fun of it. Bring your inside voice out and let us hear you on the page. Come, join the serious and sassy family of writers.

◄ **Critical Viewing** Why might Pat Mora approve of this scene? **[Connect]**

Critical Thinking

© **1. Key Ideas and Details (a)** Does Mora think it is easy or difficult for most students to reveal their thoughts and feelings in papers written as school assignments? **(b) Draw Conclusions:** Why does Mora address this issue?

© **2. Key Ideas and Details (a)** According to Mora, what is the most important reason for writing? **(b) Evaluate:** Do you agree with her? Why or why not?

© **3. Integration of Knowledge and Ideas (a)** What feelings or limitations did Mora have to challenge to start writing? **(b)** How does she use her experience to help other aspiring writers overcome their fears? *[Connect to the Big Question: Are yesterday's heroes important today?]*

Cite textual evidence to support your responses.

Words to Sit in, Like Chairs

Naomi Shihab Nye

▲ **Critical Viewing**
What does their body language tell you about how well these students are listening? **[Evaluate]**

I was with teenagers at the wonderful Holland Hall School in Tulsa when the planes flew into the buildings on September 11, 2001. We were talking about words as ways to imagine one another's experience. A boy had just thanked me for a poem about Jerusalem that enabled him to consider the Palestinian[1] side of the story. He said he had never thought about that perspective before, so the poem was important to him.

The TV commentators were already saying the hijackers had been Arabs, which sent a deep chill into my Arab-American blood. I said to those beautiful students, "Please, I beg you, if Arabs are involved in this tragedy, remember there are millions of Arabs who would never do such a thing."

They nodded soberly. "Of course," they said. "We know that. This is Oklahoma." Their kindness overwhelmed me.

Then a boy said, "I hate to ask this so soon after it happened, but do you think you will write about it?"

---

1. **Palestinian** (pal' es tin'ē en) *adj.* of the people of Palestine, a region bounded by Lebanon, Syria, Egypt, and Jordan. Many Arabs living in this area were displaced when the state of Israel was established by the United Nations in 1948.

"It would not be my choice of topic," I said, feeling sick, my head spinning, "but as writers, we are always exploring what happens, what comes next, turning it over, finding words to sit in like chairs, even in terrible scenery, so maybe I will have to write about it; maybe we all will. Because words shape the things that we live, whether beautiful or sorrowful, and help us connect to one another, this will be part of our history now."

Then a boy gave me a "Collapse-It" laundry basket that his parents had invented. Made of some kind of modern, waterproof, heavy-duty cardboard, it folded flat when not in use. He seemed mournful, handing it over.

"I brought this for you as a small gift," he said, "but after what happened today, it almost seems inappropriate."

Collapse-It. All Fall Down.

I clutched it to my chest and carried it with me on the long bus ride (since the planes were not flying) home to south Texas.

I have used the neat little white basket every time I've washed clothes since then. What came to me on a day of horror and tragedy and terrible mess, accompanied by kind words, continues as a helpful friend in daily life. Just the way words help us all not to be frozen in horror and fear.

USE WORDS. It is the most helpful thing I have learned in my life. We find words, we select and arrange them, to help shape our experiences of things. Whether we write them down for ourselves or send them into the air as connective lifelines between us, they help us live, and breathe, and see.

When I felt the worst after September 11, I called people. How is it for you? What are you thinking about? Have you heard anything helpful lately? Many of you probably did that, too. Sometimes it seemed good, and important, to call unexpected people—people who were not, in any way, expecting to hear from us right then. Hello, I'm thinking of you. Do you have any good news? If I had heard a useful quote or story recently myself, I shared it. Talking with friends felt like a connected chain. We passed things on down the wire.

It was very helpful for me to talk with Arab-American friends who automatically shared the doubled sense of sorrow. A poet friend of mine in New York City, just blocks from the disaster, said his wife saw him staring at a wall in their apartment one day, and said, "Don't withdraw! Speak!"

Sometimes we have to remind one another.

Theme
According to Nye, what is the value of words in our everyday lives?

Reading Check
What does a boy give Nye on the day she visits his school?

Vocabulary
turmoil (tʉr´ moil´) *n.*
condition of great
confusion or agitation

I also wrote sentences and phrases down in small notebooks, as I have done almost every day of my life since I was six. It is the best clue I know for how to stay balanced as we live. Bits and pieces of lines started fitting together again, offering small scraps of sense, ways out of the turmoil-of-mind, shining as miniature beacons, from under heaps of leaves.

Very rarely did I hang up from speaking with anyone or close my notebook feeling worse. Usually, that simple sharing of feelings, whether with another person, or with a patient page, helped ease the enormous feeling that the sorrow was too big to get one's mind around.

War is too big to get one's mind around too.

I keep thinking—if people who are angry, or frustrated, could use words instead of violence, how would our world be different? Maybe if enough of us keep in practice using our own honest words, that basic human act can help balance bigger things in the world.

▲ **Critical Viewing**
Based on her essay, what advice might Nye offer this young woman? **[Speculate]**

Cite textual evidence to support your responses.

Critical Thinking

© **1. Key Ideas and Details (a)** How did Nye deal with her emotions after the events of September 11, 2001? **(b) Evaluate:** Do you think this is an effective way to ease sorrow? Explain.

© **2. Key Ideas and Details (a)** What does Nye propose as a solution to the problem of violence in our world? **(b) Take a Position:** Do you think Nye's ideas could help change the world? Explain.

© **3. Integration of Knowledge and Ideas (a)** Did it take special courage for Nye to write about the events of September 11, 2001? Explain. **(b)** Do you think her words and the actions of other ordinary people on that day are still important today? Why or why not? *[Connect to the Big Question: Are yesterday's heroes important today?]*

Comparing Works on a Similar Theme

© **1. Key Ideas and Details (a)** What reasons does Mora give to discuss the value of expressing oneself in writing? **(b)** What reasons does Nye give?

© **2. Integration of Knowledge and Ideas (a)** How does Neruda's description of his approach to writing differ from the other selections? **(b)** Are similar themes and ideas expressed differently in poetry than in prose? Explain.

© **3. Integration of Knowledge and Ideas** How does the form each writer chose work to achieve a different purpose, despite their similarities in theme? Give specific examples of ways the structure of the works affect their meaning.

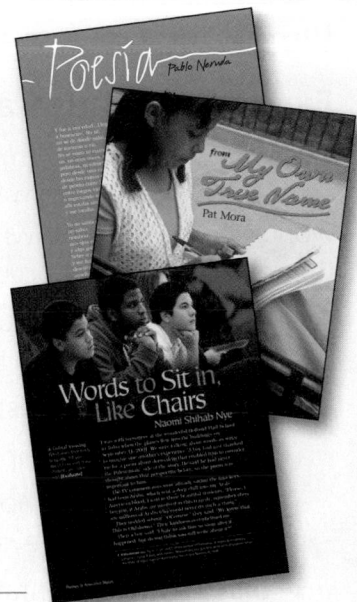

⏱ Timed Writing

Explanatory Text: Essay

Write an essay to compare the three works. In your essay, discuss how each writer approaches the universal theme of self-expression. Provide details and quotations from the texts as support. **(40 minutes)**

5-Minute Planner

1. Read the prompt carefully and completely.

2. Gather your ideas by completing a chart like the one shown.

Category	Poetry (La Poesía)	My Own True Name	Words to Sit In . . .
Topic/Situation			
Use of Personal Experience			
Influence of Form on Theme			
Influence of Cultural Background			
Tone/Style			

3. Choose an organizational strategy. To use the block method, give your analysis of one work, then the next, focusing on the same categories each time. To use the point-by-point method, examine one category at a time, discussing all three works.

4. Reread the prompt, and then draft your essay.

Writing Workshop

Write an Explanatory Text

Exposition: Cause-and-Effect Essay

Defining the Form Almost everything that happens involves causes and effects, from local events to those that impact people worldwide. When you write a **cause-and-effect essay,** you analyze the reasons an event occured or you consider its results.

Assignment Write a cause-and-effect essay about a question that interests you. Your essay should feature the following elements:

✔ a clear thesis that establishes a *controlling idea*

✔ a consistent and appropriate *organization*

✔ an explanation of how one or more events or situations results in another event or situation

✔ a thorough presentation of *facts*, *quotations*, and other *details* that *support* the explanation presented

✔ an *effective and well-supported conclusion*

✔ error-free grammar, including the avoidance of *run-on sentences and sentence fragments*

To preview the criteria on which your research report may be judged, see the rubric on page 1163.

 **Writing Workshop:** *Work in Progress*

Review the work you did on pages 1109 and 1131.

WRITE GUY
Jeff Anderson, M.Ed.

What Do You Notice?

Structural Elements

Read the following sentences from Anaïs Nin's "Forest Fire."

In Sierra Madre, following the fire, the January rains brought floods. People are sandbagging their homes. At four A.M. the streets are covered with mud. The bare, burnt, naked mountains cannot hold the rains and slide down bringing rocks and mud. One of the rangers must now take photographs and movies of the disaster.

Discuss what you notice about the passage with a partner. Take note of how Nin presents cause-and-effect relationships, and think of ways you can do the same in your essay.

 **Common Core State Standards**

Writing

2. Write informative/explanatory texts to examine a topic and convey ideas, concepts, and information through the selection, organization, and analysis of relevant content.

2.a. Introduce a topic clearly, previewing what is to follow; organize ideas, concepts, and information into broader categories; include formatting, graphics, and multimedia when useful to aiding comprehension.

2.b. Develop the topic with relevant, well-chosen facts, definitions, concrete details, quotations, or other information and examples.

Reading-Writing Connection

To get the feel for a cause-and-effect essay, read "Why Leaves Turn Color in the Fall," by Diane Ackerman, on page 540.

Prewriting/Planning Strategies

Discuss with a classmate. To determine topics that interest you, pair up with a classmate and take turns asking these questions:

- What are your favorite books? What natural or historical events are crucial to those books' subjects or plots?

- What is a science topic that you find interesting?

- Which political leader do you admire most? With which national or world events is he or she most closely associated?

- For what invention are you most grateful? Why?

Review your answers in order to choose a broad topic.

Narrow your topic. Make sure you develop a topic narrow enough for you to cover in depth. First, take time to jot down subtopics of your broader topic. Continue this process until you pinpoint a well-defined subject for your writing. The chart shows how one topic is narrowed.

Conduct research. Gather the facts, statistics, examples, and other details you need to thoroughly illustrate cause-and-effect relationships. A K-W-L chart like the one shown is an excellent tool for planning and guiding your research.

Natural Disasters
Earthquakes
North American Earthquakes
Earthquakes in the last decade

K-W-L Chart		
What I Know	**What I Want to Know**	**What I Learned**
• Air pollution is increasing and dangerous. • Pollution smells bad. • Cars and factories cause it. • It hurts people and animals.	• How can it be reduced? • What causes it besides cars and factories? • Which countries or cities are the worst? • How can we stop it? • What does it do to people? • To animals?	

Plan your support. Now that have you gathered information, think through the cause-and-effect relationship you will explain. Determine which details are needed to clearly show a reader the connections between cause and effect. These supporting details can take the form of facts, expert opinions, or comparisons to similar cause-and-effect relationships.

Drafting Strategies

Common Core State Standards

Writing
2.a. Introduce a topic clearly, previewing what is to follow; organize ideas, concepts, and information into broader categories; include formatting, graphics, and multimedia when useful to aiding comprehension.

Focus and organize your ideas. Review your research, and circle the main causes and effects. Identify which description below best fits your topic. Then, organize your essay accordingly.

- **Many Causes/Single Effect:** If your topic has several causes of a single event, develop a paragraph to discuss each cause.

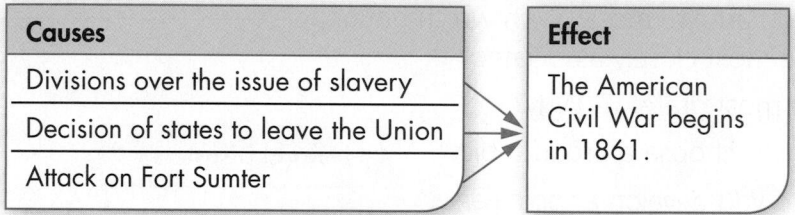

- **Single Cause/Many Effects:** For one cause with several effects, devote a paragraph to each effect.

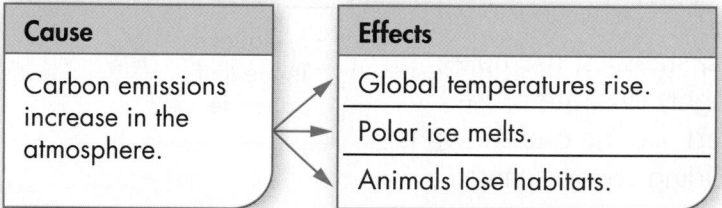

- **Chain of Causes and Effects:** If you are presenting a chain of causes and effects, present them in chronological order with transitions to show the connections.

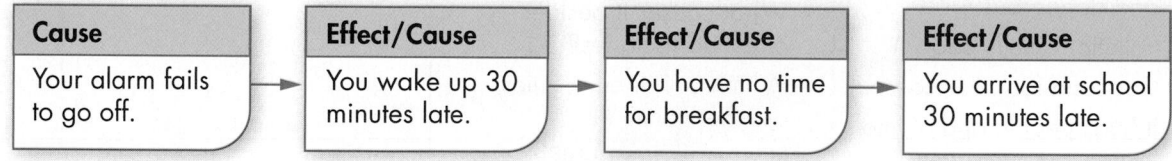

Prove the connection. To convince your audience that the causes and effects you connect are not just coincidental, add details to elaborate on the link you are showing.

- **Weak connection:** The local hardware store is losing business because another hardware store opened.

- **Cause-and-effect connection:** The local hardware store is losing business because a larger hardware store *with a bigger inventory opened a few miles away.*

Writers on Writing

Lan Samantha Chang On Using Specific Details

Lan Samantha Chang is the author of "Water Names" (p. 1018).

At the heart of my story "San" is the idea that every child is a detective, searching for clues about her parents' mysterious past lives. In this passage, I tried to show the development of this obsession by describing the way that Caroline, the 13-year-old narrator, hunts through the closets in her own house. I tried to reveal this information through action and specific details, rather than summary.

"I want to show, not tell . . ."
—Lan Samantha Chang

Professional Model:

from "San"

At the back of the foyer closet, inside the faded red suitcase my mother had brought from China, I discovered a cache of little silk purses wrapped in a cotton shirt. When I heard her footsteps I instinctively closed the suitcase and pretended I was looking for a pair of mittens. Then I went to my room and shut the door, slightly dizzy with anticipation and guilt.

A few days later when my mother was out, I opened one purse. Inside was a swirling gold pin with pearl and coral flowers. I made many secret visits to the closet, a series of small sins. Each time I opened one more treasure. There were bright green, milky white, and ~~blood-red~~ *carmine* bracelets. Some of the bracelets were so small I could not fit them over my hand. There was a ring with a pearl as big as a marble. . . .

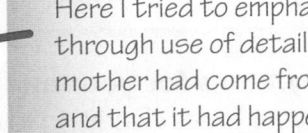

Here I tried to emphasize, through use of detail, that the mother had come from China and that it had happened years ago (the suitcase is "faded").

I don't use adverbs very often and when I do I want them to reveal character. In this case I wanted to reveal Caroline's instinctive need for secrecy, her desire to hide her private explorations from her mother.

I kept "blood-red" for many drafts because I liked the idea of blood (family) secrets being excavated. Later I crossed out the words, because they are a cliché.

Revising Strategies

Fill in gaps in support. Read through your draft to determine if you clearly and persuasively connect causes with effects. One way to do this is to label your support (for example, "F" for fact). If it looks like you have too much of one type of support or there is no support at all for one of your main points, consider including additional information.

Use transitions to show connections. Your goal is to prove the link between cause and effect. Transition words can help you make sure the relationship between cause and effect is obvious to your readers. Use transitional words and phrases like the ones shown here to clarify connections.

Cause-and-Effect Transitions	
Introducing Causes	since, if, because, as soon as, until
Introducing Effects	consequently, as a result, subsequently, then

Define key terms for your audience. To make sure you have expressed your ideas clearly, follow these steps:

1. Reread your essay, circling any terms that your audience may not know.

2. Provide more background information or definitions where necessary. You may have to consult your research notes or other reference materials for this information. The example below uses an *appositive phrase* to provide the additional information.

Original	Revision With Key Terms Defined
Henry's kitten had to get a shot to prevent feline leukemia.	Henry's kitten had to get a shot to prevent feline leukemia, an incurable disease in cats that is caused by a virus.

Peer Review

Ask a classmate to review your draft to help you identify places in your draft where adding transitions would improve the writing. Consider these suggestions while you are revising to clarify cause-and-effect relationships.

Revising Run-on Sentences and Sentence Fragments

Sentence errors such as run-on sentences and sentence fragments can make writing difficult to understand.

Identifying Sentence Errors A **run-on sentence** is two or more complete sentences that are not properly joined or separated. This sentence error can be corrected by breaking the sentence into two, or by adding punctuation or words to clarify the meaning of a single sentence.

PH WRITING COACH

Further instruction and practice are available in *Prentice Hall Writing Coach.*

Run-On	Revision Tips
Charles is an avid reader he also is a dedicated athlete.	**Separate sentences:** Charles is an avid reader. He also is a dedicated athlete. *or* **Add comma and coordinating conjunction:** Charles is an avid reader, but he also is a dedicated athlete. *or* **Use a semicolon:** Charles is an avid reader; he also is a dedicated athlete.

A **sentence fragment** is a group of words that does not express a complete thought. To fix fragments, add more information to complete the idea.

Fragment: By the next day.

Corrected: By the next day, she felt better.

Fixing Errors Follow these steps to fix sentence errors.

1. To fix a run-on, rewrite it using one of these methods:
   - Break the clauses into separate sentences.
   - Join the clauses using a comma and a coordinating conjunction, such as *and, or, but, yet, so.*
   - Join the clauses using a semicolon.
2. Fix a fragment by either adding it to a nearby sentence or adding the necessary words to turn it into a sentence.

Grammar in Your Writing

Read through your draft to see if you have used run-on sentences or fragments. Correct them by adding the necessary words and punctuation.

Student Model: Max Norowzi, Raleigh, NC

Sleep—It's Healthy

Since the beginning of time, sleep has been an important factor in maintaining good health. While people sleep, they refuel their bodies and minds to help them through the next day. Many people do not get the proper amount of sleep, however, and this has a negative effect on their health.

During the day, our bodies and minds consume a great deal of energy. Sleep recharges our bodies and minds, giving our bodies and minds a chance to recover the energy that we have lost. We wake up feeling refreshed because, while we sleep, our brains do not need to focus and our muscles can relax.

Sleep deprivation occurs when someone receives fewer hours of sleep than his or her body needs. Many different things can cause sleep deprivation. A few of the main causes are drinking caffeine, living in a noisy environment, and working long hours. The effect on a person who does not get enough sleep can be devastating. Some effects of sleep deprivation are stress, anxiety, inability to concentrate, and loss of coping skills. Another effect is weight gain, which is very unhealthy for most people. Mood shifts, including depression, increased irritability, and loss of a sense of humor all result from not getting enough sleep.

I have observed some of these sleep deprivation effects in people I know. My friend Tim had to stay up late several nights in a row in order to finish a term paper on time. Here is how Tim describes how the loss of sleep affected him: "The first thing I noticed was that I couldn't concentrate in class. My attention would wander and I couldn't understand ideas that would ordinarily be very easy for me to grasp. My body was achy, my head was cloudy, and I was snapping at everyone about everything. The sleep that I did get wasn't very good because my dreams were bad ones about things like forgetting to turn my paper in."

People often dream when they have been thinking hard about something right before they go to sleep. Dreams can be good or bad for us. A good dream is relaxing and does not disturb the sleeper. A bad dream causes stress, anxiety, and restlessness. To avoid bad dreams, people should do something relaxing, like reading, before going to bed.

In conclusion, adequate sleep promotes good health and helps us feel better about ourselves. Sleep deprivation can seriously harm our minds and bodies. To counter these harmful effects, the answer is to simply get more sleep. Sleeping well can guarantee us better health and a better life.

Max clearly outlines the cause-and-effect relationship he will address.

This paragraph identifies the causes of sleep deprivation.

To support his explanation, Max offers detailed descriptions of sleep deprivation's effects.

Max concludes his essay effectively by summarizing the health benefits of sleep.

Editing and Proofreading

Make corrections in grammar, usage, and mechanics to ensure that your final draft is error-free.

Focus on prepositions. Whenever possible, avoid ending sentences with a preposition.

> **Draft Sentence:** Which friend are you traveling **with**?
>
> **Revised Sentence: With** which friend are you traveling? Who is traveling with you?

Publishing and Presenting

Consider one of the following ways to share your writing:

Present a speech. If your essay addresses a situation that others face, offer to speak to classes that can benefit from your work.

Publish a feature article. Submit your essay to your local or school newspaper. In a letter accompanying your essay, explain to the editor why the issue you address is important to readers.

Reflecting on Your Writing

Writer's Journal Jot down your answer to this question:

Did learning about the causes and effects of your topic motivate you to take any action?

Rubric for Self-Assessment

Find evidence in your writing to address each category. Then, use the rating scale to grade your work.

Spiral Review
Earlier in this unit, you learned about **colons and semicolons** (p. 1108) and **capitalization** (p. 1130). Check your essay to make sure that you have used semicolons and colons correctly and that you have correctly capitalized names of people, places, and things.

Criteria	Rating Scale				
	not very				*very*
Focus: How clearly do you explain the cause-and-effect relationship?	1	2	3	4	5
Organization: How clear and consistent is your organization?	1	2	3	4	5
Support/Elaboration: How convincing are the facts and statistics that support your explanations?	1	2	3	4	5
Style: How clearly does your language convey your conclusion?	1	2	3	4	5
Conventions: How correct is your grammar, especially your avoidance of fragments and run-on sentences?	1	2	3	4	5

Vocabulary Workshop

Figurative Language

Figurative language is writing that is imaginative and not meant to be taken literally. Writers use figurative language for its descriptive impact and to vividly convey emotions or ideas. The chart shows some examples of figurative language.

**Common Core
State Standards**

Language
5. Demonstrate understanding of figurative language, word relationships, and nuances in word meanings.

Type of Figurative Language	Example
Simile: a comparison of two apparently unlike things using *like, as, than,* or *resembles.*	Her eyes are <u>like</u> diamonds.
Metaphor: a description of one thing as if it were another.	You <u>are</u> my sunshine.
Analogy: an extended comparison of relationships. An analogy shows how the relationship between one pair of things is like the relationship between another pair.	<u>Juggling</u> is like <u>riding a bicycle</u>. Once you learn how to do it, you never forget.
Personification: giving human characteristics to a nonhuman subject.	The <u>willow trees sang</u> a sad song as the wind blew through their branches.
Hyperbole: an intentional (and sometimes outrageous) overstatement, or exaggeration.	It is so hot outside that <u>you could fry an egg on the sidewalk</u>.
Idiom: an expression whose meaning differs from the meanings of its individual words.	Your description of the situation really <u>hit the nail on the head</u>.

Practice A Identify the type of figurative language used in each of these sentences. Use the chart to help you.

1. This book weighs a ton.
2. Justine is as graceful as a swan when she dances.
3. My Aunt Nina's favorite photos are squirreled away in the attic.
4. His smile lights up the room.
5. The waves murmured their sleepy good-nights.
6. My brother is in the doghouse because he broke his curfew.

Practice B Identify the figurative language in each item as an example of simile, metaphor, personification, or hyperbole.

1. Jamie was as quiet as a mouse, hardly making a sound when she entered the room.

2. Moving quickly from one spot on the ground to another, the tumbleweed danced merrily over the prairie.

3. Jonah's little sister is as cute as a button when she giggles at her own made-up jokes.

4. Tyrone learned to swim like a fish at summer camp, perfectly mastering every stroke.

5. The school collected enough donations to sink a ship.

6. My mother is a whirlwind of activity; she never seems to rest.

7. The water cradled and rocked the young boy as he peacefully floated.

8. Her singing is so pleasant—a soft, sweet breeze that carries a lovely tune.

Activity Write a message that you might put in a postcard, describing an activity that you enjoy. Gather ideas for using figurative language in your message by completing a note card like the one shown. Use ideas from the note card to vividly convey your message with similes, metaphors, personification, or hyperbole.

Similes:
Metaphors:
Personification:
Hyperbole:

PHLit Online!
www.PHLitOnline.com
- Illustrated vocabulary words
- Interactive vocabulary games
- Vocabulary flashcards

Comprehension and Collaboration
Working in a small group, create a poster for a school event. Do your best to use one example each of simile, metaphor, personification, and hyperbole in your poster. When the poster is completed, discuss what impact the use of figurative language has on the finished product.

Communications Workshop

Delivering a Persuasive Speech Using Multimedia

A persuasive multimedia presentation uses visuals, sound, speech, and text to persuade an audience.

Learn the Skills

Use these strategies to complete the activity on p. 1167.

Advocate a position. Your presentation should flow from a sound, well-stated position, and every detail should relate to and advocate for this position. Write a statement, or *thesis*, to express your main idea.

Use primary and secondary sources. Support your ideas using firsthand accounts, as well as expert analysis or observation.

Decide which media to use. Choose media that emphasize your points. You might use a film with sound or even a still photo and silence.

Choose an organization. Use a structure suited to your purpose, such as point-by-point or block method (see p. 782).

Make an outline. Use an outline to organize your speech into sections, noting where you will use evidence and examples to support your arguments. Include an introduction, a body, and a conclusion.

Be prepared. If possible, practice the speech using the equipment. Have a backup plan in case a piece of equipment does not function.

Be dramatic. Use creative language, such as similes, idioms, and extended comparisons (analogies) to make your points. To add persuasive appeal, choose words for their emotional associations (connotations), as well as for their precise, literal meanings (denotations).

Use verb voice and mood. Be aware of the different ways you can use verb voice and mood to enhance your presentation.

Active voice (emphasizes actor): Sherman ordered his troops into battle.

Passive voice (emphasizes action): The proclamation was signed by Lincoln on January 1, 1863.

Conditional/subjunctive (contrary to fact): Were he to have run for another term, it's not certain he would have won.

Be clear. When presenting, use transitions, such as *because, next,* or *as a result,* to show connections between ideas. Also, be sure to clearly differentiate between facts and your own opinions.

Common Core State Standards

Reading Informational Text
7. Evaluate the advantages of using different mediums to present a particular topic or idea.

Speaking and Listening
5. Integrate multimedia and visual displays into presentations to clarify information, strengthen claims and evidence, and add interest.

Language
3.a. Use verbs in the active and passive voice and in the conditional and subjunctive mood to achieve particular effects.

Practice the Skills

© **Presentation of Knowledge and Ideas** Use what you've learned in this workshop to perform the following task.

> ### ACTIVITY: Delivering a Persuasive Presentation
>
> Prepare and deliver a persuasive presentation with multimedia.
>
> Follow the steps below:
>
> • Advocate a position on a school- or community-related issue.
> • Include similes, idioms, analogies, and multimedia (text, graphics, images, and sound).
> • Use speaking techniques to effectively deliver your presentation.
> • Refer to the Model Outline to help you organize your presentation.

Construct an outline for your presentation similar to the model below. Draft your speech and rehearse with a partner, paying special attention to the smooth integration of media. In your presentation, remember to make eye contact, use natural gestures, vary your speaking rate and volume, and enunciate. Follow language conventions correctly to communicate your ideas effectively.

> ### Model Outline
>
> **My Position**
>   I. **Introduction:**
>   A. Introduce the position for which I am advocating.
>   B. Give background, accompanied by multimedia #1: slideshow.
>
>   II. **Body of Presentation:**
>   A. Discuss supporting example/evidence #1.
>   B. Discuss supporting example/evidence #2.
>   (include an analogy to help listeners understand)
>   C. Discuss supporting example/evidence #3.
>   i. Present multimedia #2: short video clip.
>   ii. Explain implications of clip, using a simile.
>
>   III. **Conclusion:**
>   Use multimedia, along with a simile or an analogy, to create a strong ending to my persuasive message.

© **Comprehension and Collaboration** At the end of your presentation, discuss it with your audience, eliciting and responding to questions and comments. Ask your audience if you were successful in advocating for your position.

Cumulative Review

I. Reading Literature

Directions: *Read the story. Then, answer the questions that follow.*

Common Core
State Standards

RL.8.2, RL.8.3; W.8.2.b; L.8.4.a
[For the full wording of the standards, see the standards chart in the front of your textbook.]

The Ojibwa people have always lived in the northern United States and southern Canada, near Lake Superior. Winters here are long, cold, and snowy. Surviving the winter was hard, and the Ojibwa <u>eagerly</u> waited for warm weather, when they could plant crops and make maple sugar. But one year, spring and summer almost never came. Ojibwa elders told this story.

Once there was an evil giant who lived in the far south. When the summer birds flew south in the fall, the giant captured them. He locked them up in big cages—the robins and larks, the wrens and finches and warblers, and the cardinals and woodpeckers. He set two large, mean crows to guard them. (Crows have never gotten along with other birds!)

When it was time for winter to end, the summer birds could not fly north. Without them, spring could not arrive in the Ojibwa's lands. Rivers and lakes stayed frozen. Trees were bare of leaves. It was far too cold to hunt, and crops did not grow. People shivered and wondered what to do. Animals were cold and miserable, too.

In those days, animals and humans could talk to each other. So they all met together to think about what to do. They chattered and argued, but no one had a plan. Finally, one creature came forward with a plan. It was the kingfisher, a blue-gray and white bird with a tuft of feathers on his head.

Kingfisher flew south to look for the missing birds. He took only one weapon, a ball of wax. At last he spotted the cages full of birds, with the giant asleep nearby. Quickly he took the ball of wax and used it to seal the crows' bills shut so they could not wake the giant. Then he used his strong beak to break the locks on the cages.

"Quiet! Don't wake the giant," Kingfisher warned the birds. Silently, they stretched their wings and took to the air. As the summer birds flew north, the air got warmer. Ice and snow melted; leaves and blossoms grew on the trees. Spring returned to the Ojibwa.

1. What natural event does this **myth** explain?
   A. why spring returns
   B. why winters are cold
   C. why birds fly south
   D. why crows are mean

2. What is the **cultural context** of this story?
   A. a crowded city environment
   B. a society made up only of animals
   C. a culture of farming and hunting
   D. a culture of brave warriors

3. Which sentence is the *best* indicator that this story comes from the **oral tradition?**
   A. But one year spring and summer never came.
   B. In those days, animals and humans could talk to each other.
   C. Spring returned to the Ojibwa.
   D. Ojibwa elders told this story.

4. Which feature of the **oral tradition** does this story contain?
   A. An animal character is the hero.
   B. The story is told in dialect.
   C. The story ends with a moral, or lesson.
   D. The story is in the form of an epic poem.

5. What traits of a **heroic character** does Kingfisher show?
   A. He brags about his deeds.
   B. He is brave and clever.
   C. He can speak to human characters.
   D. He can fly.

6. What does the myth reveal about the **heritage,** or culture, of the Ojibwa people?
   A. They are not in touch with their natural environment.
   B. They celebrate the coming of spring so farming can begin.
   C. They prefer living in warmer climates.
   D. They dislike kingfishers and crows.

7. How does this story differ from a **legend?**
   A. It does not have a hero.
   B. It does not contain impossible or exaggerated incidents.
   C. It is not based on a real person or fact.
   D. It features both humans and animals.

8. **Vocabulary** Which word is closest in meaning to the underlined word <u>eagerly</u>?
   A. scarcely
   B. calmly
   C. willingly
   D. excitedly

 Timed Writing

9. In two paragraphs, **explain** how Kingfisher's trip to rescue the summer birds is like and unlike the quest of the hero of an **epic poem** to find or rescue something or someone. Use **details** from the story to **support** your answer.

 GO ON

II. Reading Informational Text

Directions: *Read these two examples of media types. Then, answer the questions that follow.*

Common Core State Standards

RI.8.2, RI.8.5; L.8.1, L.8.2, L.8.4.a
[For the full wording of the standards, see the standards chart in the front of your textbook.]

Interview

Reporter ("TV News at 5"): So, Coach Collins, how do you feel now that the soccer team has won its third state championship?

Coach Collins: We've had a great season, and we can all be proud! I especially want to thank our team captain, Sofia. We're sorry to lose her, as she's graduating, but I'm happy to honor her as our MVP!

Reporter: I didn't realize she was a senior. What's next for her?

Coach Collins: She hasn't decided. But we are more focused on next year's young stars, for now.

Movie Review

His new comedy, *Morning Coffee,* may <u>astonish</u> fans of actor Ian Browne, who is best known for his roles in Shakespeare tragedies. In this clever film, however, Browne shows an unexpected skill for comedy as the host of a failing early-morning TV show. While some long-time fans may be disappointed, the film should win new fans for the actor. This reviewer gives it four stars.

1. What main **structural pattern** is evident in the interview?
   A. order of importance
   B. question and answer
   C. cause and effect organization
   D. chronological organization

2. What main **structural pattern** is evident in the movie review?
   A. increasing order of importance
   B. descending order of importance
   C. chronological organization
   D. cause and effect organization

3. In what way does the review show **unity?**
   A. the details all support its topic
   B. there is only one author
   C. the conclusion comes last
   D. two points of view are given

4. **Vocabulary** Which word is closest in meaning to the underlined word <u>astonish</u>?
   A. surprise
   B. scare
   C. horrify
   D. disappoint

III. Writing and Language Conventions

Directions: *Read the sample multimedia report. Then, answer all the questions that follow.*

> (1) In the 1800s, many nations dreamed of creating a channel through Central America. (2) The map shows how ships could then sail directly between the Atlantic and Pacific Oceans. (3) President Theodore Roosevelt was determined to make this dream real. (4) Roosevelt said "I took the Canal Zone and let Congress debate. (5) The canal cut across an isthmus in Panama. (6) Although the terrain was challenging, work moved quickly. (7) As this photograph shows, the first ship passed through the canal locks in 1914. (8) Now, instead of circumnavigating the southernmost promontory of South America to sail between oceans, ships could traverse the new Panama Canal.

1. How could the writer *best* **organize** the report so the multimedia prompts are easier to use and follow?
   A. Use more than one paragraph.
   B. List the details of the report on one page and the multimedia aids on another.
   C. Create an outline, noting when and how each multimedia aid is used.
   D. Use different symbols to show each multimedia aid.

2. An isthmus is a narrow strip of land. How could the writer use an **appositive** to clarify this term in sentence 5?
   A. The canal cut across an isthmus in Panama, a narrow strip of land.
   B. The canal cut across an isthmus which is a narrow strip of land in Panama.
   C. The canal cut across a narrow strip of land in Panama.
   D. The canal cut across an isthmus, a narrow strip of land, in Panama.

3. What is the correct way to **punctuate** the direct quotation in sentence 4?
   A. Roosevelt said, "I took the Canal Zone and let Congress debate."
   B. Roosevelt said I took the Canal Zone and let Congress debate.
   C. Roosevelt said "I took the Canal Zone, and let Congress debate.
   D. The quotation is punctuated correctly.

4. How should the writer revise sentence 8 to make it more suitable for an **audience** of classmates?
   A. Add more information.
   B. Choose different, less difficult words.
   C. Split the sentence in two and use a semicolon.
   D. Use a graph to explain meaning.

Performance Tasks

Directions: *Follow the instructions to complete the tasks below as required by your teacher.*

As you work on each task, incorporate both general academic vocabulary and literary terms you learned in this unit.

 **Common Core State Standards**

RL.8.1, RL.8.2, RL.8.3, RL.8.4, RL.8.9; W.8.2, W.8.9.a; SL.8.1, SL.8.4; L.8.1, L.8.2, L.8.5
[For the full wording of the standards, see the standards chart in the front of your textbook.]

Writing

Task 1: Literature [RL.8.1, RL.8.3; W.8.2]
Analyze Characterization in a Story

Write an essay in which you analyze how the events in a story reveal aspects of character.

- Choose a story from this unit that has clearly defined characters. Write a brief description of the character or characters you are analyzing.

- List several examples in which characters' reactions to a story event show something important about their personalities. The characters' responses may take the form of actions or dialogue.

- Analyze how these responses reveal key personality traits such as bravery, cleverness, or arrogance.

- Correct any run-on sentences or sentence fragments in your essay.

Task 2: Literature [RL.8.2; W.8.9; L.8.2]
Compare Themes in Two Works

Write an essay in which you analyze the themes in two works in this unit.

- Select two stories in this unit that have identifiable themes.

- First, provide a summary of each story's plot. Explain how the story events you have summarized are connected to the theme, or message, of each story.

- Next, explain the theme's relationship to characters' attitudes and actions and the setting in each story.

- Finally, describe how the two themes are similar and note ways in which they differ. For example, you might explain how one or both stories have universal themes by showing how the same theme occurs in stories from other cultures or time periods.

- As you write, be sure to capitalize characters' names and place names correctly.

Task 3: Literature [RL.8.4; W.8.2]
Analyze Word Choice

Write an essay in which you analyze the use of figurative language in a story or poem.

- Select a work in this unit that features figurative language, such as similes, metaphors, personification, or hyperbole.

- Give specific examples of figurative language in the text and explain the meaning of each example as well as its impact on the work's meaning and tone.

- Note the overall impact figurative language has on the story or poem. State whether or not you think the writer's use of figurative language is effective, and explain why.

- Choose language that expresses your ideas precisely, eliminating vague words.

Speaking and Listening

Task 4: Literature [RL.8.2; SL.8.4; L.8.1]

Present a Speech on a Hero

Present a speech about a hero from one of the texts in this unit.

- Choose a heroic character from one of the texts in this unit.

- Describe the traits, qualities, and accomplishments that make this person a hero.

- Identify quotations and descriptions from the text that will help you characterize certain actions and behavior as heroic. Record these examples as evidence to present in your speech.

- Arrange your notes in logical order.

- Present your speech to the class, observing standard English grammar and usage.

Task 5: Literature [RL.8.9; SL.8.1]

Compare Legends and Retellings

Moderate a group discussion in which you compare the heroes presented in the two Carl Sandburg pieces in this unit with the traditional legends from which they come.

- As a group, list the heroes mentioned in the two Sandburg selections in this unit. Then, identify the original legends from which these heroes are drawn. (Obtain and read copies of the original stories as needed.)

- Ask participants to compare and contrast the way the heroes are represented in the traditional legends with the way that Sandburg represents them.

- Participants should base their responses on evidence from the texts, such as plot events, descriptions, and dialogue.

- Finally, ask participants to evaluate the effects that Sandburg's retellings produce and to judge whether his changes improve on or detract from the original tales.

Task 6: Literature [RL.8.4; L.8.5]

Analyze Word Choice

Analyze how figurative language and idioms affect the tone, meaning, and mood of a work in this unit.

- Identify a work in this unit that has strong examples of idioms and figurative language.

- Analyze the meaning of the idioms and figurative language in the text, and discuss the impact this language has on the tone, meaning, and mood of the work. For example, you could note when the use of idioms gives the work a humorous tone.

- Present your analysis and invite follow-up questions from the audience.

THE BIG ?

Are yesterday's heroes important today?

At the beginning of Unit 6, you participated in a discussion about the Big Question. Now that you have finished the unit, write a response to the question. Discuss how and why the views you shared about the relevance of yesterday's heroes have either changed or been reinforced. Give examples from the stories, as well as from other subjects and your personal experiences, to support your ideas. Use Big Question vocabulary words (see p. 1009) in your response.

Featured Titles

In this unit, you have read a variety of literary works that originated in the oral tradition. Continue to read on your own. Select works that you enjoy, but challenge yourself to explore new writers and works of increasing depth and complexity. The titles suggested below will help you get started.

Literature

The Adventures of Tom Sawyer

by Mark Twain   EXEMPLAR TEXT

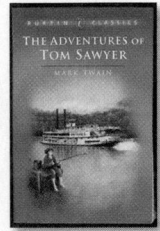
Read about the escapades of mischievous Tom Sawyer and his best friend, Huck Finn, in this classic nineteenth-century American **novel.**

Fast Sam, Cool Clyde, and Stuff

by Walter Dean Myers

Stuff is new to Harlem when he meets Fast Sam, Cool Clyde, and Gloria. Watch Harlem come alive in this funny, sad, and realistic **novel** about city life in the 1970s.

The American Songbag

Edited by Carl Sandburg
Mariner Books, 1990

Carl Sandburg is best known as a poet, but he was also a collector of American **folk music.** This book includes 290 songs and their lyrics that give voice to many uniquely American experiences.

Cut From the Same Cloth: American Women of Myth, Legend, and Tall Tale

by Robert San Souci

San Souci explores larger-than-life adventures in these often humorous **folktales** featuring clever, brave, and strong women.

Informational Texts

John F. Kennedy

by Howard S. Kaplan

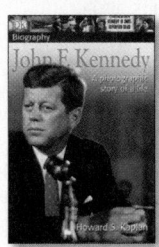
Read about our thirty-fifth president, John F. Kennedy, in this **biography.** Kennedy was an inspirational leader whose promising term in office was cut short by his shocking assassination.

Freedom Walkers

by Russell Freedman
Holiday House, 2006   EXEMPLAR TEXT

This **historical account** tells the story of the Montgomery Bus Boycott, which gave rise to the Civil Rights movement in the United States. Learn about famous figures such as Rosa Parks, as well as many other people who fought for justice and equality.

Preparing to Read Complex Texts

Attentive Reading As you read on your own, ask yourself questions about the text. The questions shown below and others that you ask as you read will help you learn and enjoy literature even more.

 **Common Core State Standards**

Reading Literature/Informational Text
10. By the end of the year, read and comprehend literature, including stories, dramas, and poems, and literary nonfiction at the high end of the grades 6–8 text complexity band independently and proficiently.

When reading texts from the oral tradition, ask yourself...

- From what culture does this text come? What do I know about that culture?

- What type of text am I reading? For example, is it a myth, a legend, or a tall tale? What characters and events do I expect to find in this type of text?

- Does the text include the elements I expected? If not, how does it differ from what I expected?

- What elements of the culture do I see in the text? For example, do I notice beliefs, foods, or settings that have meaning for the people of this culture?

- Does the text teach a lesson or a moral? If so, is this a valuable lesson?

© **Key Ideas and Details**

- Who is retelling or presenting this text? Do I think the author has changed the text from the original? If so, how?

- Does the text include characters and tell a story? If so, are the characters and plot interesting?

- What do I notice about the language used in the text? Which aspects seem similar to or different from the language used in modern texts?

- Does the text include symbols? If so, do they have a special meaning in the original culture of the text? Do they also have meaning in modern life?

© **Craft and Structure**

- What does this text teach me about the culture from which it comes?

- What, if anything, does this text teach me about people in general?

- Does this text seem like others I have read or heard? Why or why not?

- Do I know of any modern versions of this text? How are they similar to or different from this one?

- If I were researching this culture for a report, would I include passages from this text? If so, what would those passages show?

- Do I enjoy reading this text and others like it? Why or why not?

© **Integration of Ideas**

Resources

Glossary

Big Question vocabulary appears in **blue type**. High-utility Academic vocabulary is <u>underlined</u>.

A

abyss (uh BIHS) *n.* immeasurable space, such as a bottomless gulf

accomplishments (uh KOM plihsh muhnts) *n.* things done successfully or completed

account (uh KOWNT) *n.* bill for work done

<u>accumulate</u> (uh KYOO myuh layt) *v.* collect or gather

acquire (uh KWYR) *v.* get; obtain

admirably (AD muhr uh blee) *adv.* in a manner deserving praise

affectionate (uh FEHK shuhn niht) *adj.* loving

affluence (AF loo uhns) *n.* wealth

alibi (AL uh by) *n.* believable reason why a suspect could not have been at the scene of a crime

alienate (AYL yuh nayt) *v.* make unfriendly

alliance (uh LY uhns) *n.* group united for a common goal

ancestral (an SEHS truhl) *adj.* related to a family

anguish (ANG gwihsh) *n.* distress

anonymously (uh NON uh muhs lee) *adv.* without a name or any identification

antithesis (an TIHTH uh sihs) *n.* direct opposite

apprehension (ap rih HEHN shuhn) *n.* fearful feeling about what will happen

<u>argument</u> (AHR gyuh muhnt) *n.* claim; persuasive reasoning

aromas (uh ROH muhz) *n.* smells

arrogant (AR uh guhnt) *adj.* feeling or showing proud self-importance and disregard for others

ascent (uh SEHNT) *n.* act of climbing or rising

<u>aspects</u> (AS pehkts) *n.* ways in which an idea or problem may be viewed

aspirations (as puh RAY shuhnz) *n.* strong desires or ambitions

assail (uh SAYL) *v.* attack with arguments, questions, doubts, etc.

assumption (uh SUHMP shuhn) *n.* act of taking for granted

audacity (aw DAS uh tee) *n.* bold courage; nerve

audible (AW duh buhl) *adj.* able to be heard

authentic (aw THEHN tihk) *adj.* genuine; real

authorized (AW thuh ryzd) *v.* approved

avert (uh VURT) *v.* avoid

awed (awd) *v.* filled with wonder

B

barren (BAR uhn) *adj.* empty; bare

beacons (BEE kuhnz) *n.* signals meant to warn or guide, as a light or fire

beckoning (BEHK uhn ihng) *adj.* summoning

bellow (BEHL oh) *v.* make a deep, loud sound like a bull

<u>benefit</u> (BEHN uh fiht) *n.* advantage or positive result

benign (bih NYN) *adj.* kindly

bewildered (bih WIHL duhrd) *adj.* hopelessly confused

<u>bias</u> (BY uhs) *n.* tendency to see things from a slanted or prejudiced viewpoint

bilingual (by LIHNG gwuhl) *adj.* able to speak two languages

blackmail (BLAK mayl) *n.* forcing people to give you money by threatening to tell secrets about them

bleak (bleek) *adj.* bare and windswept; cold

boulevard (BUL uh vahrd) *n.* wide road

bravery (BRAY vuhr ee) *n.* courage or valor

brutal (BROO tuhl) *adj.* cruel

burrow (BUR oh) *n.* passage or hole for shelter

C

capricious (kuh PRIHSH uhs) *adj.* tending to change abruptly, without apparent reason

carelessness (KAIR luhs nuhs) *n.* lack of responsibility

cataclysm (KAT uh klihz uhm) *n.* sudden, violent event that causes change

ceaseless (SEES lihs) *adj.* never stopping; continual

<u>challenge</u> (CHAL uhnj) *v.* calling into question; demanding of proof

cicada (suh KAY duh) *n.* large insect that resembles a fly; the male makes a loud high-pitched noise

<u>class</u> (klas) *n.* group of people or objects

coiled (koyld) *v.* twisted around and around

commenced (kuh MEHNST) *v.* began to happen

common (KOM uhn) *adj.* ordinary or expected

commotion (kuh MOH shuhn) *n.* noisy movement

compassionate (kuhm PASH uh niht) *adj.* deeply sympathetic

compelled (kuhm PEHLD) *v.* forced

compensate (KOM puhn sayt) *v.* pay

compromise (KOM pruh myz) *n.* settling of differences in a way that allows both sides to feel satisfied

compulsory (kuhm PUHL suhr ee) *adj.* required

conceivable (kuhn SEE vuh buhl) *adj.* able to be imagined

conceivably (kuhn SEE vuh blee) *adv.* in an imaginable or believable way

confirm (kuhn FURM) *v.* prove or establish as true

confronted (kuhn FRUHNT uhd) *v.* brought face to face

connection (kuh NEHK shuhn) *n.* joining or linking

consoling (kuhn SOH lihng) *adj.* comforting

conspicuous (kuhn SPIHK yoo uhs) *adj.* noticeable

constructive (kuhn STRUHK tihv) *adj.* leading to improvement

contact (KON takt) *n.* touching; communication

contemplation (KON tuhm PLAY shuhn) *n.* act of thinking about something

contempt (kuhn TEMPT) *n.* scorn; disrespect

contemptuously (kuhn TEHMP choo uhs lee) *adv.* scornfully

contraction (kuhn TRAK shuhn) *n.* act of becoming smaller

contradict (kon truh DIHKT) *v.* deny or go against a viewpoint

conviction (kuhn VIHK shuhn) *n.* strong belief; certainty

cordially (KAWR juhl lee) *adv.* warmly

courage (KUR ihj) *n.* valor or bravery

credibility (krehd uh BIHL uh tee) *n.* believability

criteria (kry TIHR ee uh) *n.* standards or tests by which something can be judged

cultural (KUHL chuhr uhl) *adj.* having to do with the collected customs and beliefs of a group or community

cunningly (KUHN ihng lee) *adv.* skillful in deception; crafty

curiosity (kyur ee OS uh tee) *n.* desire to get information

cyclone (SY klohn) *n.* violent, rotating windstorm; tornado

cynically (SIHN uh kuhl lee) *adv.* doubtfully; skeptically

D

debates (dih BAYTS) *v.* tries to decide

debris (duh BREE) *n.* rough, broken bits of stone, concrete, or glass left after something is destroyed

decadent (dih KAY duhnt) *adj.* marked by decay or decline

deceive (dih SEEV) *v.* make someone believe what is not true; mislead

deciphering (dih SY fuhr ihng) *v.* working out the meaning of; decoding

decision (dih SIHZH uhn) *n.* choice; act of making up one's mind

decrees (dih KREEZ) *n.* orders with the force of law

deductions (dih DUHK shuhnz) *n.* judgments about something, based on available information

deed (deed) *n.* document which, when signed, transfers ownership of property

deferred (dih FURD) *adj.* delayed

defiance (dih FY uhns) *n.* refusal to obey authority

deficiency (dih FIHSH uhn see) *n.* lack of something that is necessary

degrading (dih GRAY dihng) *adj.* insulting; dishonorable

deliberating (dih LIHB uhr iht ihng) *v.* thinking carefully

deprived (dih PRYVD) *v.* not permitted to have

derision (dih RIHZH uhn) *n.* statements or actions that show you have no respect for someone or something

derived (dih RYVD) *v.* received or taken from a source

descendants (dih SEHN duhnts) *n.* children, grandchildren, and continuing generations

descent (dih SEHNT) *n.* act of climbing down

desolate (DEHS uh liht) *adj.* sad; lonely

deterioration (dih tihr ee uh RAY shuhn) *n.* the process of becoming worse

development (dih VEHL uhp muhnt) *n.* event or happening; outcome

devoid (dih VOYD) *adj.* completely without

dew (doo) *n.* tiny drops of moisture that condense on cooled objects at night

diffused (dih FYOOZD) *v.* spread out widely in different directions

diplomatic (dihp luh MAT ihk) *adj.* showing skill in dealing with people

discharged (dihs CHAHRJD) *v.* fired; released

discreet (dihs KREET) *adj.* careful with words or actions

discrepancies (dihs KREHP uhn seez) *n.* differences; inconsistencies

discriminate (dihs KRIHM uh nayt) *v.* see the difference between; tell apart

discrimination (dihs krihm uh NAY shuhn) *n.* ability to see differences between objects or ideas

disdainfully (dihs DAYN fuhl lee) *adv.* scornfully

disinherit (dihs ihn HEHR iht) *v.* deprive people of their rights as citizens

dispel (dihs PEHL) *v.* cause something to go away

distinction (dihs TIHNGK shuhn) *n.* difference

distinguish (dihs TIHNG gwihsh) *v.* mark as different; set apart

diverged (duh VURJD) *v.* branched off

diverts (duh VURTS) *v.* distracts; amuses

divide (duh VYD) *v.* separate

dock (dok) *v.* deduct part of one's salary or wages

doubtful (DOWT fuhl) *adj.* not likely; open to challenge

drought (drowt) *n.* lack of rain; long period of dry weather

E

eavesdropping (EEVZ drop ihng) *n.* secretly listening to the private conversation of others

eloquent (EHL uh kwuhnt) *adj.* vividly expressive

emancipated (ih MAN suh payt uhd) *adj.* freed

emigrated (EHM uh grayt uhd) *v.* left one place to settle in another

emphasize (EHM fuh syz) *v.* stress; show the importance of

empires (EHM pyrz) *n.* powerful nations; countries ruled by emperors or empresses

enchantment (ehn CHANT muhnt) *n.* feeling of delight

endure (ehn DUR) *v.* hold up under; last

enhance (ehn HANS) *v.* make greater

erosion (ih ROH zhuhn) *n.* wearing away by action of wind or water

evacuees (ih VAK yoo eez) *n.* people who leave a dangerous area

evaded (ih VAYD uhd) *v.* avoided

evidence (EHV uh duhns) *n.* proof

exaggerate (ehg ZAJ uh rayt) *v.* magnify beyond fact

exertion (ehg ZUR shuhn) *n.* energetic activity; effort

exiles (EHG zylz) *n.* people who are forced to live in another country

expansive (ehk SPAN sihv) *adj.* characterized by a free and generous nature

experience (ehk SPIHR ee uhns) *n.* act of living through an event

explanation (ehks pluh NAY shuhn) *n.* act of giving meaning to an idea or concept

exploitation (ehks ploy TAY shuhn) *n.* act of using another person for selfish purposes

exploration (ehks pluh RAY shuhn) *n.* act of looking into closely or examining carefully

express (ehk SPREHS) *v.* put into words

exquisite (EHKS kwih ziht) *adj.* very beautiful

extinction (ehk STIHNGK shuhn) *n.* dying out of a species

extinguished (ehk STIHNG gwihsht) *v.* put out; ended

exultantly (ehg ZUHL tuhnt lee) *adv.* triumphantly

exulting (ehg ZUHLT ihng) *v.* rejoicing

F

factor (FAK tuhr) *n.* any of the circumstances or conditions that lead to a result

factual (FAK choo uhl) *adj.* based on or limited to fact

fantasy (FAN tuh see) *n.* product of the imagination or make-believe

fatalist (FAY tuh lihst) *n.* one who believes that all events are determined by fate

feedback (FEED bak) *n.* response that sets a process in motion

feuding (fyood ihng) *v.* quarreling

fiscal (FIHS kuhl) *adj.* having to do with finances

flagged (flagd) *v.* gave a sign to stop, often with a flag or flag-like object

flatterer (FLAT uhr uhr) *n.* one who praises insincerely to win approval

foreboding (fawr BOH dihng) *n.* feeling that something bad will happen

forlorn (fawr LAWRN) *adj.* sad and lonely

frail (frayl) *adj.* slender and delicate

fugitives (FYOO juh tihvz) *n.* people fleeing from danger

G

generalization (jehn uhr uh luh ZAY shuhn) *n.* statement that captures the broad idea

gesture (JEHS chuhr) *n.* something said or done merely as a formality

global (GLOH buhl) *adj.* complete, covering a large class of cases

grateful (GRAYT fuhl) *adj.* thankful

guileless (GYL lihs) *adj.* not trying to hide anything or trick people; innocent

H

haggard (HAG uhrd) *adj.* having a wasted, worn look

harmonious (hahr MOH nee uhs) *adj.* combined in a pleasing arrangement

haughty (HAW tee) *adj.* scornfully superior

horizon (huh RY zuhn) *n.* imaginary line where the sky and earth appear to meet

hostile (HOS tuhl) *adj.* related to the enemy; unfriendly

humiliating (hyoo MIHL ee ayt ihng) *adj.* embarrassing

I

identify (y DEHN tuh fy) *v.* recognize as being

ignorance (IHG nuhr uhns) *n.* lack of knowledge or awareness

illogical (ih LOJ uh kuhl) *adj.* contrary or opposed to fact

imitate (IHM uh tayt) *v.* copy or follow the example of

immensely (ih MEHNS lee) *adv.* greatly

immensity (ih MEHN suh tee) *n.* vastness; hugeness

immortality (ihm awr TAL uh tee) *n.* endless life

immunities (ih MYOO nuh teez) *n.* freedoms; protections

impertinently (ihm PUR tuh nuhnt lee) *adv.* disrespectfully

imprint (IHM prihnt) *v.* make a lasting mark

inarticulate (ihn ahr TIHK yuh liht) *adj.* unable to express oneself

incentive (ihn SEHN tihv) *n.* motivation

indiscreetly (ihn dihs KREET lee) *adv.* carelessly

individuality (ihn duh vihj oo AL uh tee) *n.* way in which a person or thing stands apart or is different

ineffectually (ihn uh FEHK chu uhl lee) *adv.* without producing the desired results

inequality (ihn ih KWOL uh tee) *n.* state of being unfair or not being treated equally

inevitable (ihn EHV uh tuh buhl) *adj.* certain to happen

inexplicable (ihn EHK spluh kuh buhl) *adj.* impossible to explain

inexpressible (ihn ihk SPREHS uh buhl) *adj.* not able to be described

inferior (ihn FIHR ee uhr) *adj.* lower in status or rank

influence (IHN floo uhns) *v.* sway or affect in some other way

inform (ihn fuhr MAY shuhn) *v.* tell; give information or knowledge

ingratitude (ihn GRAT uh tood) *n.* lack of appreciation

injury (IHN juhr ee) *n.* harm or damage to a person

insecurity (ihn sih KYUR uh tee) *n.* lack of confidence; self-doubt

insolently (IHN suh luhnt lee) *adv.* in an impolite manner

insufferable (ihn SUHF uhr uh buhl) *adj.* unbearable

integrate (IHN tuh grayt) *v.* make equally available to all members of society

intellectual (ihn tuh LEHK choo uhl) *adj.* relating to the ability to think intelligently

interact (ihn tuhr AKT) *v.* relate with others

intimidating (ihn TIHM uh dayt ihng) *adj.* frightening

intolerant (ihn TOL uhr uhnt) *adj.* not able or willing to accept

introspective (ihn truh SPEHK tihv) *adj.* inward looking; thoughtful

intuition (ihn too IHSH uhn) *n.* ability to sense immediately, without reasoning

invaded (ihn VAYD uhd) *v.* entered in order to conquer

invaluable (ihn VAL yu uh buhl) *adj.* extremely useful

invariably (ihn VAIR ee uh blee) *adv.* almost all the time

investigate (ihn VEHS tuh gayt) *v.* search; look for ·

irritate (IHR uh tayt) *v.* anger or annoy

J

jostling (JOS uhl ihng) *n.* knocking into, often on purpose

judge (juhj) *v.* form an opinion about

judicious (joo DIHSH uhs) *adj.* showing sound judgment; wise

K

kindled (KIHN duhld) *v.* built or lit

L

lagged (lagd) *v.* moved slowly

lax (laks) *adj.* not strict or exact

legacy (LEHG uh see) *n.* something physical or spiritual handed down from an ancestor

legitimately (luh JIHT uh miht lee) *adv.* legally

liable (LY uh buhl) *adj.* likely

liberated (LIHB uh rayt uhd) *v.* freed; released from slavery, enemy occupation, etc.

luminous (LOO muh nuhs) *adj.* giving off light

M

malicious (muh LIHSH uhs) *adj.* mean; spiteful

maneuver (muh NOO vuhr) *n.* series of planned steps

meadows (MEHD ohz) *n.* areas of grassy land

meager (MEE guhr) *adj.* small amount

meaningful (MEE nihng fuhl) *adj.* having significance or purpose

media (MEE dee uh) *n.* collected sources of information, including newspapers, television, and the Internet

melancholy (MEHL uhn kol ee) *adj.* sad; depressed

mislead (mihs LEED) *v.* give a wrong idea; deceive

mistrusted (mihs TRUHST uhd) *v.* be suspicious of or lack confidence in

misunderstand (mihs uhn duhr STAND) *v.* misinterpret; fail to understand

mockery (MOK uhr ee) *n.* false, insulting action or statement

modes (mohdz) *n.* ways of doing or behaving

mutineers (myoo tuh NIHRZ) *n.* rebels

mutinous (MYOO tuh nuhs) *adj.* rebellious

N

naïveté (nah eev TAY) *n.* state of being simple or childlike

native (NAY tihv) *adj.* related to the place of one's birth

negotiate (nih GOH shee ayt) *v.* bargain or deal with another party to reach a settlement

negotiation (nih goh shee AY shuhn) *n.* bargaining; discussing; deal making

ninny (NIHN ee) *n.* simple or foolish person

O

objective (uhb JEHK tihv) *adj.* open-minded; not influenced by personal feelings or prejudice

obscure (uhb SKYUR) *adj.* little known

observation (ob zuhr VAY shuhn) *n.* statement; point of view

omens (OH muhnz) *n.* sign of a bad or good event in the future

opinion (uh PIHN yuhn) *n.* personal view or attitude

oppose (uh POHZ) *v.* go against; stand in the way of

oppressed (uh PREHST) *v.* kept down

option (OP shuhn) *n.* choice

outdated (owt DAYT uhd) *adj.* behind the times; no longer popular

overcome (oh vuhr KUHM) *v.* conquer or get beyond a setback

overwhelming (oh vuhr HWEHL mihng) *adj.* emotionally overpowering

P

pageant (PAJ uhnt) *n.* an elaborate play

paradoxes (PAR uh doks uhz) *n.* two things that seem directly at odds

partition (pahr TIHSH uhn) *n.* interior dividing wall

passively (PAS ihv lee) *adv.* without resistance

perceived (puhr SEEVD) *v.* grasped mentally; saw

peril (PEHR uhl) *n.* danger

periscope (PEHR uh skohp) *n.* tube on a submarine that raises and lowers to show objects on the water's surface

perish (PEHR ihsh) *v.* to be destroyed or wiped out

persistent (puhr SIHS tuhnt) *adj.* continuing to happen, especially for longer than is usual or desirable

persuade (puhr SWAYD) *v.* to convince; bring around to one's way of thinking

pervading (puhr VAYD ihng) *adj.* spreading throughout

pestering (PEHS tuhr ihng) *n.* constant bothering

pitiful (PIHT ih fuhl) *adj.* arousing sympathy

pollen (POL uhn) *n.* powdery grains on male plants

ponderous (PON duhr uhs) *adj.* very heavy

possession (puh ZEHSH uhn) *n.* ownership

posterity (pos TEHR uh tee) *n.* future generations

predisposed (pree dihs POHZD) *adj.* inclined

predominantly (prih DOM uh nuhnt lee) *adv.* mainly

preliminary (prih LIHM uh nehr ee) *adj.* introductory; preparatory

presentable (prih ZEHN tuh buhl) *adj.* neat enough to be seen by others

pretext (PREE tehkst) *n.* excuse; reason that hides one's real motives

procession (pruh SEHSH uhn) *n.* group moving forward, as in a parade

prodigy (PROD uh jee) *n.* an unusually talented person

prove (proov) *v.* show or demonstrate

pursuit (puhr SOOT) *n.* the act of chasing in order to catch

Q

quaint (kwaynt) *adj.* unusual or old-fashioned in a pleasing way

quality (KWOL uh tee) *n.* characteristic or feature

quantity (KWON tuh tee) *n.* amount

quarantine (KWAWR uhn teen) *n.* period of separation from others to stop the spreading of a disease

R

radiation (ray dee AY shuhn) *n.* the sending of waves of energy through space

radical (RAD uh kuhl) *adj.* favoring major change in the social structure

rapture (RAP chuhr) *n.* ecstasy

ravaged (RAV ihj) *v.* devastated

reaction (ree AK shuhn) *n.* response to an influence, action, or statement

rebellion (rih BEHL yuhn) *n.* open resistance to authority or dominance

recede (rih SEED) *v.* move away

recoiled (rih KOYLD) *v.* draw back in disgust

reeds (reedz) *n.* tall slender grasses that grow in wetland areas

refugees (rehf yuh JEEZ) *n.* people who flee from their homes in time of trouble

refute (rih FYOOT) *v.* give evidence to prove an argument or statement false

rehabilitate (ree huh BIHL uh tayt) *v.* restore the reputation of

relentless (rih LEHNT lihs) *adj.* persistent; unending

relevant (REHL uh vuhnt) *adj.* to the point; relating to the matter at hand

reluctance (ri LUK tuhns) *n.* hesitation; unwillingness

remote (rih MOHT) *adj.* aloof; cold; distant

renounced (rih NOWNST) *v.* gave up

represent (rehp rih ZEHNT) *v.* stand for or symbolize

reputation (rehp yuh TAY shuhn) *n.* widely held opinion about someone, whether good or bad

resent (rih ZEHNT) *v.* feel angry or upset out of a sense of unfairness

resolute (REHZ uh loot) *adj.* showing a firm purpose

resolved (rih ZOLVD) *v.* decided

resounding (rih ZOWND ihng) *adj.* sounding loudly

respectively (rih SPEHK tihv lee) *adv.* in the order previously named

resurgence (rih SUR juhns) *n.* reappearance; revival

retribution (reht ruh BYOO shuhn) *n.* punishment for wrongdoing

reveal (rih VEEL) *v.* make known; uncover

revelation (REHV uh LAY shuhn) *n.* something that suddenly becomes known

revolutionary (rehv uh LOO shuh nehr ee) *adj.* favoring sweeping change

rickety (RIHK uh tee) *adj.* weak; likely to break

rituals (RIHCH u uhlz) *n.* practices done at regular times

roam (rohm) *v.* go aimlessly; wander

rotate (ROH tayt) *v.* switch

rut (ruht) *n.* a groove in the ground made by a wheeled vehicle or natural causes

S

sacred (SAY krihd) *adj.* considered holy; related to religious ceremonies

sacrifices (SAK rih fy sez) *n.* the act of deciding not to have or do something valuable or important in order to get something that is more important, often for someone else

satisfactory (sat ihs FAK tuhr ee) *adj.* adequate; sufficient to meet a requirement

scampering (SKAM puhr ihng) *v.* running quickly

scarce (skairs) *adj.* few in number; not common

scheme (skeem) *n.* organized way of doing something

self-confident (sehlf KON fuh duhnt) *adj.* assured of one's ability

sensibility (sehn suh BIHL uh tee) *n.* moral, artistic, or intellectual outlook

sensory (SEHN suhr ee) *adj.* having to do with the senses

separate (SEHP uh rayt) *v.* set apart

serene (suh REEN) *adj.* calm; undisturbed

shackles (SHAK uhlz) *n.* metal bonds used to restrain prisoners

shanties (SHAN teez) *n.* roughly built cabins or shacks

shiftless (SHIHFT lihs) *adj.* without ambition

shriveled (SHRIHV uhld) *v.* dried up; shrank; wrinkled

sidling (sy duh lihng) *v.* moving sideways in a sly manner

significance (sihg NIHF uh kuhns) *n.* importance

simultaneously (sy muhl TAY nee uhs lee) *adv.* at the same time

singularity (sihng gyuh LAR uh tee) *n.* unique or distinct feature

sinister (SIHN uh stuhr) *adj.* threatening harm or evil

skeptically (SKEHP tuh kuhl lee) *adv.* with doubt and distrust

slung (sluhng) *v.* hung loosely

solution (suh LOO shuhn) *n.* act of solving a problem or answering a question

somber (SOM buhr) *adj.* dark; gloomy

sparse (spahrs) *adj.* thinly spread and small in amount

spindly (SPIHN dlee) *adj.* long and thin

spineless (SPYN lihs) *adj.* lacking in courage or willpower

spite (spyt) *n.* nastiness

squatter (SKWOT uhr) *n.* someone who settles illegally on land or in a building

stalemate (STAYL mayt) *n.* standoff; outcome of a conflict where no one wins

statistics (stuh TIHS tihks) *n.* numerical facts or data

stealthily (stehlth uh lee) *adv.* in a secret or sly way

straddling (STRAD uhl ihng) *v.* standing or sitting with a leg on either side of something

strife (stryf) *n.* conflict

studious (STOO dee uhs) *adj.* devoted to learning

subdued (suhb DOOD) *adj.* beaten down; conquered

succumbed (suh KUHMD) *v.* gave way to; yielded

suffering (SUHF uhr ihng) *n.* undergoing of pain or injury

superficial (soo puhr FIHSH uhl) *adj.* limited to the surface; lacking depth

supple (SUHP uhl) *adj.* yielding; soft

suppressed (suh PREHST) *v.* yielding; soft

surrogate (SUR uh gayt) *n.* substitute

sustain (suh STAYN) *v.* keep up

symbolize (SIHM buh lyz) *v.* stand for

sympathy (SIHM puh thee) *n.* sameness of feeling; act of feeling for another person

T

tangible (TAN juh buhl) *adj.* easy to see or notice, so there is no doubt

tantalized (TAN tuh lyzd) *v.* tormented by something just out of reach

tedious (TEE dee uhs) *adj.* boring; tiresome

tenacious (tih NAY shuhs) *adj.* holding on firmly; stubborn

tension (TEHN shuhn) *n.* nervous, worried, or excited state that makes relaxation impossible

theory (THEE uhr ee) *n.* idea based on gathered information or evidence

thrives (thryvz) *v.* does well; prospers

timidly (TIHM ihd lee) *adv.* in a shy or fearful manner

tolerance (TOL uhr uhns) *n.* freedom from prejudice; acceptance of the views of others

tongue (tuhng) *n.* language

transfigured (tranz FIHG yuhrd) *adj.* transformed in a glorious way

trivial (TRIHV ee uhl) *adj.* of little importance

tumultuous (too MUHL choo uhs) *adj.* wild; chaotic

turbulent (TUR byuh luhnt) *adj.* marked by wild, irregular motion

turmoil (TUR moyl) *n.* condition of great confusion or agitation

U

unanimous (yoo NAN uh muhs) *adj.* in complete agreement

undulation (uhn juh LAY shuhn) *n.* curvy, wavy form

uneasily (uhn EE zuh lee) *adv.* restlessly

unequivocal (uhn ih KWIHV uh kuhl) *adj.* clear; plainly understood

unify (YOO nuh fy) *v.* bring together; to make united

unobtrusively (uhn uhb TROO sihv lee) *adv.* without calling attention to oneself

unresponsive (uhn rih SPON sihv) *adj.* not reacting

unseemly (uhn SEEM lee) *adj.* inappropriate

urban (UR buhn) *adj.* having to do with the city

V

valid (VAL ihd) *adj.* backed by evidence

valuable (VAL yu uh buhl) *adj.* having worth or importance

vertical (VUR tuh kuhl) *adj.* straight up and down; upright

vex (vehks) *v.* annoy; distress

victorious (vihk TAWR ee uhs) *adj.* having won; triumphant

viewpoint (VYOO poynt) *n.* position regarding an idea or statement

violation (vy uh LAY shuhn) *n.* the breaking or ignoring of rules, laws, or rights

violence (VY uh luhns) *n.* result of the use of physical force, often causing injury

virtue (VUR choo) *n.* a quality that gives value

vulnerable (VUHL nuhr uh buhl) *adj.* likely to be hurt

W

wearisome (WIHR ee suhm) *adj.* tiresome

willingly (WIHL ihng lee) *adv.* voluntarily; without needing to be forced

winced (wihnst) *v.* showed pain

Y

yearning (YURN ihng) *v.* filled with the feeling of wanting something

Spanish Glossary

El vocabulario de Gran Pregunta aparece en **azul**. El vocabulario académico de alta utilidad está **subrayado**.

A

abyss / abismo *s.* espacio que no se puede medir, como un golfo sin fondo

accomplishments / logros *s.* lo que se hace o completa con éxito

account / cuenta *s.* factura por servicios prestados

accumulate / acumular *v.* coleccionar; juntar

acquire / adquirir *v.* conseguir; obtener

admirably / admirablemente *adv.* de tal manera que se merece ser elogiado

affectionate / afectuoso *adj.* cariñoso

affluence / opulencia *s.* riqueza

alibi / coartada *s.* argumento que explica por qué un sospechoso no pudo estar presente en la escena de un crimen

alienate / enajenar *v.* alejarse de una relación de amistad

alliance / alianza *s.* grupo unido con una meta en común

ancestral / ancestral *adj.* relacionado a la familia

anguish / angustia *s.* intranquilidad, ansiedad

anonymously / en anonimato *adv.* sin nombre o identificación

antithesis / antítesis *s.* oposición o contrariedad

apprehension / aprensión *s.* sentimiento temoroso de lo que ocurrirá

argument / argumento *s.* debate; reclamación; perspectiva en un asunto controversial

aromas / aromas *s.* olores

arrogant / arrogante *adj.* persona engreída e indiferente a otros

ascent / ascenso *s.* acto de escalar o subir

aspects / aspectos *s.* maneras en que se ve o asimila una idea o problema

aspirations / aspiraciones *s.* deseos fuertes o ambiciones

B

assail / asediar *v.* atacar a alguien con argumentos, preguntas, dudas, etc.

assumption / suposición *s.* acto de asumir

audacity / audacia *s.* gran valor; osadía

audible / audible *adj.* que se puede oír

authentic / auténtico *adj.* genuino; real

authorized / autorizó *v.* aprobó

avert / evitar *v.* apartar algo

awed / sobrecoger *v.* asombrar

B

barren / baldío *adj.* vacío; yermo

beacons / faros *s.* señales para advertir o guiar, como la luz o el fuego

beckoning / convocar *v.* llamar

bellow / bramar *v.* rugir profundamente, como el sonido que hace un toro

benefit / beneficio *s.* ventaja o resultado positivo

benign / benigno *adj.* bondadoso

bewildered /desconcertado *adj.* completamente confundido

bias / parcialidad *s.* tendencia a interpretar las cosas de manera sesgada o prejuiciosa

blackmail / chantaje *s.* amenaza de divulgar secretos de una persona, a cambio de dinero

bleak / inhóspito *adj.* desapacible y desértico; frío

boulevard / bulevar *s.* camino ancho

bravery/ valentía *s.* coraje; valor

brutal / brutal *adj.* cruel

burrow / madriguera *s.* espacio o hueco que sirve de refugio

C

capricious / caprichoso *adj.* que tiende a cambiar abruptamente, sin razón aparente

cataclysm / cataclismo *s.* suceso súbito y violento que causa gran cambio

ceaseless / incesante *adj.* que no para; continuo

challenge / desafío *v.* cuestionar; exigencia de pruebas

cicada / cigarra *s.* insecto grande parecido a una mosca; el macho emite un sonido de tono alto

class /clase *s.* grupo de personas u objetos

coiled / enroscarse *v.* torcerse y ponerse en forma de espiral

commenced / comenzó *v.* empezó

common / común *adj.* ordinario; esperado

commotion / conmoción *s.* movimiento ruidoso y desordenado

compassionate / compasivo *adj.* de gran bondad

compelled / obligó *v.* forzó

compensate / compensar *v.* pagar

compromise / solución *s.* convenio satisfactorio entre dos partes

compulsory / obligatorio *adj.* requerido

conceivable / concebible *adj.* que se puede imaginar

conceivably / posiblemente *adv.* imaginable o creíble

concise / conciso *adj.* que incluye sólo los detalles necesarios; claro; breve

confirm / confirmar *v.* probar; establecer como cierto

confronted / enfrentó *v.* se puso frente a frente

connection / conección *s.* enlace o vínculo

consoling / consolador *adj.* confortador

conspicuous / conspicuo *adj.* notable

constructive / constructivo *adj.* que conduce al progreso

contact / contacto *s.* relación entre dos cosas; comunicación

contemplation / contemplación *s.* acto de pensar en algo o prestarle atencióna algo

contemptuously / despectivamente *adv.* con desprecio

contraction / contracción *s.* acto de hacerse mas pequeño

contradict / contradecir *v.* negar; oponerse a un punto de vista

conviction / convicción *s.* creencia fuertemente arraigada; certeza

cordially / cordialmente *adv.* calurosamente

courage / coraje *s.* valor; valentía

credibility / credibilidad *s.* característica de lo que es aceptable o creíble

criteria / criterio *s.* estándares o pruebas que se usan para juzgar algo

cultural / cultural *adj.* que es pertinente al conjunto de modos de vida y costumbres de un grupo o una comunidad

cunningly / astutamente *adv.* con facilidad para engañar; con ingenio

curiosity / curiosidad *s.* deseo de obtener información

cyclone / ciclón *s.* tormenta de viento rotativa y violenta; tornado

cynically / cínicamente *adv.* dudosamente; de modo escéptico

D

debates / debatir *v.* tratar de decidir

debris / escombro *s.* desecho de piedra, concreto o vidrio que resulta de la destrucción de algo

decadent / decadente *adj.* marcado por descomposición o deterioro

deceive / engañar *v.* hacer a alguien creer lo que no es cierto; malinformar

deciphering / decifrar *v.* encontrar el significado de algo; decodificar

decision / decisión *s.* elección; el resultado de un juicio

decrees / decretos *s.* órdenes que se hacen cumplir, como la ley

deductions / deducciones *s.* juicios basados en información disponible

deed / escritura *s.* documento que al ser firmado transfiere posesión de propiedad

deferred / diferido *adj.* retrasado

defiance / desafío *s.* oposición a obedecer la autoridad

deficiency / deficiencia *s.* carencia, o falta, de algo necesario

degrading / denigrante *adj.* insultante; deshonroso; ofensivo

deliberating / deliberar *v.* pensar cuidadosamente

deprived / privar *v.* no permitirle a alguien tener algo

derision / escarnio *s.* declaraciones o acciones irrespetuosas

derived / derivado *v.* generado u obtenido de una fuente

descendants / descendientes *s.* hijos, nietos y las generaciones que siguen a una persona

descent / descenso *s.* acto de bajar de un lugar

desolate / desolado *adj.* triste; solitario

deterioration / deterioro *s.* proceso por el que algo se daña o empeora

development / desarrollo *s.* evento o suceso; resultado

devoid / desprovisto *adj.* que carece completamente

dew / rocío *s.* pequeñas gotas que se forman con el frío de la noche a raíz del vapor en el ambiente

diffused / difuso *v.* esparcido en diferentes direcciones

diplomatic / diplomático *adj.* que muestra elegancia y destreza al relacionarse con otras personas

discharged / liberar *v.* eximir a alguien de una obligación; poner en libertad

discreet / discreto *adj.* cuidadoso con sus palabras y acciones

discrepancies / discrepancias *s.* diferencias; inconsistencias

discriminate / discriminante *v.* notar la diferencia; distinguir

discrimination / discriminación *s.* trato injusto de una persona o grupo a causa de prejuicios

disdainfully / desdeñoso *adv.* con indiferencia

disinherit / desheredar *v.* privar a las personas de sus derechos como ciudadanos

dispel / disipar *v.* hacer que algo desaparezca

distinction / distinción *s.* diferencia

distinguish / distinguir *v.* tildar como diferente; considerar por separado

diverged / divergir *v.* separarse; tener diferencias

diverts / desvía *v.* distrae; entretiene

divide / dividir *v.* separar

dock / descontar *v.* quitar parte del sueldo de una persona

doubtful / dudoso *adj.* de baja probabilidad; dispuesto a ser desafiado

drought / sequía *s.* falta de lluvia; períodos largos de clima seco

E

eavesdropping / escuchar a escondidas *v.* escuchar las conversaciones de otros de manera discreta

eloquent / elocuente *adj.* que se expresa de manera vívida

emancipated / emancipado *adj.* liberado

emigrated / emigró *v.* dejó un sitio para establecerse en otro

emphasize / enfatizar *v.* estresar; dar importancia a algo

empires / imperios *s.* naciones poderosas; países gobernados por emperadores o emperatrices

enchantment / encanto *s.* sentimiento de fascinación

endure / aguantar *v.* mantener guardado; que perdura

enhance / mejorar *v.* aumentar las cualidades buenas de algo; incrementar

erosion / erosión *s.* desgaste del terreno a causa del viento o del agua

evacuees / evacuados *s.* personas que se marchan de una zona peligrosa

evaded / evadió *v.* evitó

evidence / evidencia *s.* prueba

exaggerate / exagerar v. magnificar más allá de la realidad

exertion / esfuerzo s. ánimo, vigor

exiles / exiliados s. personas que se ven obligadas a vivir en otro país

expansive / expansivo adj. generoso; que se extiende y abarca gran espacio

experience / experiencia s. participación en una actividad que lleva a obtener conocimiento, sabiduría o destrezas

explanation / explicación s. dar a conocer razones, causas o motivos; aclaración

exploitation / explotación s. acto de usar a otra persona con intenciones egoístas

exploration / exploración s. acto de observar de cerca; examinar detenidamente

express / expresar v. poner en palabras

exquisite / exquisito adj. muy bello

extinction / extinción n. desaparición de una especie

extinguished / extinguir v. apagar; finalizar

exultantly / de forma exultante adv. con gran alegría y satisfacción

exulting / exultar v. mostrar gran alegría

F

factor / factor s. circunstancias o condiciones que dan un resultado

factual / basado en hechos adj. basado en o limitado a lo real o que puede ser probado

fantasy / fantasía s. producto de la imaginación; ficción

fatalist / fatalista s. el que cree que todo lo que sucede lo determina el destino

feedback / reacción s. respuesta que provoca una sucesión de acontecimientos

feuding / pelear v. discutir

fiscal / fiscal adj. relacionado con las finanzas

flagged / marcar v. señalar para parar, usualmente con una bandera o un objeto semejante

flatterer / adulador s. el que prodiga alabanzas interesadas

foreboding / premonición s. presentimiento de que algo va a ocurrir

forlorn / desolado adj. triste y solitario

frail / frágil adj. débil y delicado

fugitives / fugitivos s. personas que huyen o se esconden

G

generalization / generalización s. afirmación que refleja una idea amplia

gesture / gesto s. algo que se dice o hace como formalidad

global / global adj. completo; que cubre un tipo amplio de casos

grateful / agradecido adj. que siente gratitud

guileless / sincero adj. sin intención de ocultar o engañar a alguien; inocente

H

haggard / demacrado adj. de mala apariencia

harmonious / armonioso adj. que combina de manera agradable

haughty / arrogante adj. altanero

horizon / horizonte s. línea imaginaria donde se unen el cielo y la tierra

hostile / hostil adj. relacionado con el enemigo

humiliating / humillante adj. embarazoso

I

identify / identificar v. reconocer como existente

ignorance / ignorancia s. falta de conocimiento o conciencia

illogical / ilógico adj. contrario; que se opone a los hechos

imitate / imitar v. copiar; seguir el ejemplo de algo

immensely / inmensamente adv. de gran manera; en gran medida

immensity / inmensidad s. extensión grande; enormidad

immortality / inmortalidad s. vida eterna

immunities / inmunidad s. libertad; protección

impaired / perjudicar v. debilitar, hacer menos útil; dañar

impertinently / de manera impertinente adv. con irrespeto

imprint / impresionar v. dejar una marca

inarticulate / inarticulado adj. que se expresa con dificultad

incentive / incentivo s. motivación

indiscreetly / indiscretamente adv. sin cuidado

individuality / individualidad s. cualidad por la que una persona o cosa se da a conocer o se diferencia de otra

ineffectually / ineficazmente adv. sin producir el resultado deseado

inequality / desigualdad s. estado injusto o en el que no se da un tratamiento equitativo

inevitable / inevitable adj. que pasará con seguridad

inexplicable / inexplicable adj. que no se puede explicar o describir

inexpressible / indescriptible adj. que no se puede describir

inferior / inferior adj. de calidad, nivel o rango más bajos

influence / influencia v. poder o efecto sobre algo

inform / informar v. decir; dar información o conocimiento de algo

ingratitude / ingratitud s. falta de apreciación

injury / lesión s. daño o detrimento físico

insecurity / inseguridad s. falta de confianza en sí mismo

insolently / insolentemente adv. de manera descortés

insufferable / insufrible adj. insoportable

integrate / integrar *v.* hacer disponible de manera equitativa para todos los miembros de la sociedad

intellectual / intelectual *adj.* relativo a la habilidad de pensar de manera inteligente

interact / interactuar *v.* actuar junto con otros

intimidating / intimidante *adj.* atemorizante

intolerant / intolerante *adj.* que no puede o logra aceptar

introspective / introspectivo *adj.* que observa internamente; atento

intuition / intuición *s.* habilidad para sentir de inmediato, sin razonamiento

invaded / invadió *v.* entró con el propósito de conquistar

invaluable / invaluable *adj.* de gran valor

invariably / invariablemente *adv.* constante

investigate / investigar *v.* examinar detenidamente

irritate / irritar *v.* molestar; fastidiar

J

jostling / empujón *s.* golpe, generalmente intencional

judge / juzgar *v.* formar una opinión o pronunciar juicio

judicious / sensato *adj.* que demuestra prudencia y honestidad

K

kindled / encender *v.* prender

L

lagged / demorarse *v.* moverse lentamente

lax / laxo *adj.* poco estricto o exacto, relajado

legacy / herencia *s.* algo físico o espiritual que se transmite de un ancestro

legitimately / legítimamente *adv.* legalmente

liable / probable *s.* factible, que puede ocurrir

liberated / emancipó *v.* liberó; libró de la esclavitud o de una ocupación

luminous / luminoso *adj.* que irradia luz

M

malicious / malicioso *adj.* de malas intenciones

maneuver / maniobra *s.* serie de pasos planeados

meadows / prados *s.* áreas cubiertas de hierba

meager / exiguo *adj.* pequeña cantidad

meaningful / significante *adj.* que tiene importancia o propósito

media / medios de comunicación *s.* conjunto de fuentes de información incluyendo periódicos, televisión y la Internet

melancholy / melancólico *adj.* triste; deprimido

mislead / despistar *v.* inducir a creer lo que no es por medio de ideas fingidas; engañar

mistrusted / desconfiar *v.* sospechar de las acciones de alguien; no tener confianza en alguien

misunderstand / malentender *v.* malinterpretar; equivocación en el entendimiento de algo

mockery / burla *s.* farsa; acción o declaración ofensiva o falsa

modes / modos *s.* maneras de hacer cosas o de comportarse

mutineers / amotinadores *s.* rebeldes

mutinous / amotinado *adj.* rebelde

N

naïveté / ingenuidad *s.* sencillez o carácter infantil

native / nativo *adj.* relacionado al lugar de nacimiento

negotiate / negociar *v.* decidir; llegar a un acuerdo

negotiation / negociación *s.* regateo; discusión; acuerdo

ninny / tonto *s.* persona que carece de razonamiento

O

objective / objetivo *adj.* sin prejuicios; donde no influyen sentimientos personales o prejuicios

obscure / críptico *adj.* poco conocido

observation / observación *s.* aseveración; punto de vista

omens / presagio *s.* señal de algo bueno o malo en el porvenir

opinion / opinión *s.* visión personal o actitud

oppose / oponer *v.* ir en contra; ser un obstáculo

oppressed / oprimido *v.* comprimido o restringido

option / opción *s.* curso o decisión que se puede tomar

outdated / anticuado *adj.* propio de otra época; pasado de moda

overcome / superar *v.* vencer; salir adelante después de sufrir un cotratiempo

overwhelming / abrumador *adj.* emocionalmente fuerte

P

pageant / desfile *s.* presentación o espectáculo elaborado

paradoxes / paradoja *s.* dos cosas que parecen completamente opuestas

partition / mampara *s.* pared que divide el interior de una edificación

passively / pasivamente *adv.* sin resistencia

perceived / percibido *v.* entendido; observado

peril / riesgo *s.* peligro

periscope / periscopio *s.* tubo de un submarino que se mueve para poder observar la superficie del agua

perish / perecer *v.* ser destruido o aniquilado

persistent / persistente *adj.* que continua, especialmente por más tiempo de lo usual o de lo debido

persuade / persuadir *v.* convencer; incitar a otro a pensar de la misma manera

pervading / invasor *adj.* que se extiende por todas partes

pestering / molestia *s.* fastidio constante

pitiful / lastimoso *adj.* que causa compasión

pollen / polen *s.* granos polvorosos de las plantas masculinas

ponderous / ponderoso *adj.* muy pesado

possession / posesión *s.* pertenencia

posterity / posteridad *s.* generaciones futuras

predisposed / predispuesto *adj.* de cierta tendencia

predominantly / predominantemente *adv.* principalmente

preliminary / preliminar *adj.* introductorio; preparatorio

presentable / presentable *adj.* lo suficientemente ordenado o limpio para que otros lo vean

pretext / pretexto *s.* excusa; razón que oculta los motivos reales

procession / procesión *s.* personas que se movilizan en grupo, como en un desfile

prodigy / prodigio *s.* persona con un talento extraordinario

prove / probar *v.* exponer; demostrar

pursuit / persecución *s.* seguimiento con la intención de capturar

Q

quaint / pintoresco *adj.* curiosamente inusual o antiguo

quality / calidad *s.* característica o elemento

quantity / cantidad *s.* cuantía

quarantine / cuarentena *s.* período en que las personas permanecen separadas para detener la propagación de una enfermedad contagiosa

R

radiation / radiación *s.* emisión de energía a través del espacio

radical / radical *adj.* que favorece un gran cambio de la estructura social

rapture / embeleso *s.* éxtasis

ravaged / arruinó *v.* devastó, destruyó

reaction / reacción *s.* respuesta a una influencia, acción o aseveración

rebellion / rebelión *s.* resistencia ante la autoridad o ante el dominio

recede / alejarse *v.* distanciarse

recoiled / recular *v.* retroceder con repugnancia

reeds / caña *s.* hierba de tallo alto que crece en pantanos

refugees / refugiados *s.* personas que han tenido que huir de su país en tiempos difíciles

refute / refutar *v.* evidencia que prueba la verosimilitud de un argumento

rehabilitate / rehabilitar *v.* restablecer la reputación de alguien o algo

relentless / implacable *adj.* persistente; sin fin

relevant / relevante *adj.* directo al punto; relativo al asunto del momento

remote / remoto *adj.* apartado; frío; distante

renounced / renunció *v.* abandonó; desistió

represent / representar *v.* figurar; simbolizar

reputation / reputación *s.* opinión, buena o mala, que comparte un grupo de personas sobre alguien

resent / resentir *v.* sentirse bravo o disgustado por una injusticia

resolute / determinado *adj.* que demuestra un propósito fijo

resolved / resolvió *v.* decidió

resounding / resonante *adj.* que suena muy duro

respectively / respectivamente *adv.* en el orden en que se nombró previamente

resurgence / resurgimiento *s.* reaparición; renacimiento

retribution / sanción *s.* castigo por haber cometido una falta

reveal / revelar *v.* exponer; descubrir

revelation / revelación *s.* algo que sale al descubierto

revolutionary / revolucionario *adj.* que favorece un cambio radical

rickety / deteriorado *adj.* débil; con aspecto frágil

rituals / rituales *s.* prácticas que se hacen en momentos específicos y con regularidad

roam / vagar *v.* andar sin rumbo fijo; merodear

rotate / rotar *v.* cambiar

rut / surco *s.* hendidura que se hace en la tierra con el arado

S

sacred / sagrado *adj.* bendito; relacionado con ceremonias religiosas

sacrifices / sacrificio *s.* decisión de dejar de tener o hacer algo importante para obtener algo aún más importante, generalmente para otra persona

satisfactory / satisfactorio *adj.* adecuado; lo suficiente para cumplir con los requisitos

scampering / corretear *v.* correr apresuradamente

scarce / escaso *adj.* en poca cantidad; poco común

scheme / esquema *s.* manera organizada de hacer las cosas

self-confident / seguro de sí mismo *adj.* que confía en su propia habilidad

sensibility / sensibilidad *s.* actitud moral, artística, intelectual

sensory / sensorial *adj.* relativo a los sentidos de la vista, el oido, el gusto, el olfato y el tacto

separate / separar *v.* cosiderar aparte

serene / sereno *adj.* tranquilo

shackles / grilletes *s.* arco de hierro que se usa para restringir a prisioneros

shanties / barracas s. algergue o vivienda rústica construida toscamente

shiftless / holgazán adj. sin ambición

shriveled / marchito adj. seco; encogido, arrugado

sidling / movimiento furtivo v. moverse de manera astute, con cautela

significance / significado s. importancia

simultaneously / simultáneamente adv. al mismo tiempo

singularity / singularidad s. único o de rasgos distintos

sinister / siniestro adj. que amenaza con causar daño; malicioso

skeptically / de modo escéptico adv. con duda y desconfianza

slung / colgar v. suspender algo sin apretar

solution / solución s. acto de resolver un problema o responder a una pregunta

somber / sombrio adj. oscuro; lúgubre

sparse / escaso adj. en poca cantidad

spindly / escuálido adj. delgado, flaco

spineless / débil adj. que carece que corage y voluntad

spite / rencor s. resentimiento y hostilidad

squatter / ocupante ilegal s. alguien que se establece ilegalmente en un terreno o edificación

stalemate / estancamiento s. punto muerto; resultado de un conflicto en el que no hay ganador

statistics / estadísticas s. datos numéricos

stealthily / a hurtadillas adv. a escondidas o con disimulo

straddling / horcajadas adv. con las piernas a cada lado de un objeto

strife / disputa s. conflicto

studious / estudioso adj. devoto al aprendizaje

subdued / dominado adj. oprimido; conquistado

succumbed / sucumbir v. desistir; rendirse; ceder

suffering / sufrimiento s. padecer de dolor o de una lesión corporal

superficial / superficial adj. limitado a la superficie, que carece de profundidad

supple / flexible adj. que cede; suave

suppressed / suprimido v. reprimido

surrogate / sustituto s. de remplazo, suplente

sustain / sostener v. mantener

symbolize / simbolizar v. figurar

sympathy / compasión s. el acto de compartir un sentimiento o de sentir conmiseración por otra persona

T

tangible / tangible adj. que se puede ver y notar con facilidad, sin duda alguna

tantalized / tentar v. atraer la atención intensamente con algo que está fuera del alcance

tedious / tedioso adj. aburrido; cansón

tenacious / tenaz adj. adherido firmemente, con fuerza; terco

tension / tensión s. estado nervioso, preocupado o exaltación que dificulta la relajación

theory / teoría s. idea basada en información recaudada o evidencia

timidly / tímidamente adv. de manera reservada o con inseguridad

tolerance / tolerancia s. libertad de prejuicios; aceptación de los puntos de vista de otros

tongue / lengua s. idioma

transfigured / transfigurado adj. que se transforma de manera gloriosa

trivial / trivial adj. de poca importancia

tumultuous / tumultuoso adj. salvaje; caótico

turbulent / turbulento adj. con movimientos irregulares y abruptos

turmoil / confusión s. condición de gran inquietud, desorden y falta de claridad

U

unanimous / unánime adj. en acuerdo absoluto

undulation / ondulación s. curvatura

uneasily / con intranquilidad adv. con inquietud

unequivocal / inequívoco adj. claro; obvio

unify / unificar v. juntar; unir

unobtrusively / discretamente adv. sin llamar la atención

unresponsive / indiferente adj. que no reacciona; que no se ve afectado por algo

unseemly / inecoroso adj. inapropiado

urban / urbano adj. de la ciudad o relativo a ella

V

valid / válido adj. convincente; contundente

valid / válido adj. que es apoyado por evidencia; digno

valuable / valioso adj. que tiene valor o importancia

vertical / vertical adj. que se extiende de arriba abajo en línea recta

vex / irritar v. molestar; disgustar

victorious / victorioso adj. que ha ganado; triumfador

viewpoint / punto de vista s. posición ante una idea o aseveración

violation / violación s. incumplimiento o ignorancia de la ley o los derechos

violence / violencia s. el resultado del uso de fuerza física, que con frecuencia es causante de lesión corporal

virtue / virtud s. cualidad que agrega valor

vulnerable / vulnerable adj. que puede ser herido

W

wearisome / pesado adj. que fatiga, aburre o exhausta

willingly / por voluntad propia adv. con gusto; sin necesidad de ser forzado

winced / estremecerse v. demostrar dolor

Y

yearning / anhelar v. desear o ansiar con vehemencia

Literary Terms

ALLITERATION *Alliteration* is the repetition of initial consonant sounds. Writers use alliteration to draw attention to certain words or ideas, to imitate sounds, and to create musical effects.

ALLUSION An *allusion* is a reference to a well-known person, event, place, literary work, or work of art. Allusions connect literary works to a larger cultural heritage. They allow the writer to express complex ideas without spelling them out. Understanding what a literary work is saying often depends on recognizing its allusions and the meanings they suggest.

ANALOGY An *analogy* makes a comparison between two or more things that are similar in some ways but otherwise unalike.

ANECDOTE An *anecdote* is a brief story about an interesting, amusing, or strange event. Writers tell anecdotes to entertain or to make a point.

ANTAGONIST An *antagonist* is a character or a force in conflict with a main character, or protagonist.

See *Conflict* and *Protagonist.*

ARGUMENT See *Persuasion.*

ATMOSPHERE *Atmosphere,* or *mood,* is the feeling created in the reader by a literary work or passage.

AUTHOR'S INFLUENCES An *author's influences* include his or her heritage, culture, and personal beliefs.

AUTHOR'S STYLE *Style* is an author's typical way of writing. Many factors determine a writer's style, including diction; tone; use of characteristic elements such as figurative language, dialect, rhyme, meter, or rhythmic devices; typical grammatical structures and patterns, typical sentence length, and typical methods of organization. Style comprises every feature of a writer's use of language.

AUTOBIOGRAPHY An *autobiography* is the story of the writer's own life, told by the writer. Autobiographical writing may tell about the person's whole life or only a part of it.

Because autobiographies are about real people and events, they are a form of nonfiction. Most autobiographies are written in the first person.

See *Biography, Nonfiction,* and *Point of View.*

BIOGRAPHY A *biography* is a form of nonfiction in which a writer tells the life story of another person. Most biographies are written about famous or admirable people. Although biographies are nonfiction, the most effective ones share the qualities of good narrative writing.

See *Autobiography* and *Nonfiction.*

CHARACTER A *character* is a person or an animal that takes part in the action of a literary work. The main, or *major,* character is the most important character in a story, poem, or play. A *minor* character is one who takes part in the action but is not the focus of attention.

Characters are sometimes classified as flat or round. A *flat character* is one-sided and often stereotypical. A *round character,* on the other hand, is fully developed and exhibits many traits—often both faults and virtues. Characters can also be classified as dynamic or static. A *dynamic character* is one who changes or grows during the course of the work. A *static character* is one who does not change.

See *Characterization, Hero/Heroine,* and *Motive.*

CHARACTERIZATION *Characterization* is the act of creating and developing a character. Authors use two major methods of characterization—*direct* and *indirect.* When using *direct* characterization, a writer states the *character's traits,* or characteristics.

When describing a character *indirectly,* a writer depends on the reader to draw conclusions about the character's traits. Sometimes the writer tells what other participants in the story say and think about the character.

See *Character* and *Motive.*

CHARACTER TRAITS *Character traits* are the qualities, attitudes, and values that a character has or displays—such as dependability, intelligence, selfishness, or stubbornness.

CLIMAX The *climax,* also called the turning point, is the high point in the action of the plot. It is the moment of greatest tension, when the outcome of the plot hangs in the balance.

See *Plot.*

COMEDY A *comedy* is a literary work, especially a play, that is light, often humorous or satirical, and ends happily. Comedies frequently depict ordinary characters faced with temporary difficulties and conflicts. Types of comedy include *romantic comedy,* which involves problems between lovers, and the *comedy of manners,* which satirically challenges social customs of a society.

CONCRETE POEM A *concrete poem* is one with a shape that suggests its subject. The poet arranges the letters, punctuation, and lines to create an image, or picture, on the page.

CONFLICT A *conflict* is a struggle between opposing forces. Conflict is one of the most important elements of stories, novels, and plays because it causes the action. There are two kinds of conflict: external and internal. An *external conflict* is one in which a character struggles against some outside force, such as another person. Another kind of external conflict may occur between a character and some force in nature.

An *internal conflict* takes place within the mind of a character. The character struggles to make a decision, take an action, or overcome a feeling.

See *Plot.*

CONNOTATIONS The *connotation* of a word is the set of ideas associated with it in addition to its explicit meaning. The connotation of a word can be personal, based on individual experiences. More often, cultural connotations—those recognizable by most people in a group—determine a writer's word choices.

See also *Denotation.*

DENOTATION The *denotation* of a word is its dictionary meaning, independent of other associations that the word may have. The denotation of the word *lake,* for example, is "an inland body of water." "Vacation spot" and "place where the fishing is good" are connotations of the word *lake.*

See also *Connotation.*

DESCRIPTION A *description* is a portrait, in words, of a person, place, or object. Descriptive writing uses images that appeal to the five senses—sight, hearing, touch, taste, and smell.

See *Images.*

DEVELOPMENT See *Plot.*

DIALECT *Dialect* is the form of a language spoken by people in a particular region or group. Dialects differ in pronunciation, grammar, and word choice. The English language is divided into many dialects. British English differs from American English.

DIALOGUE A *dialogue* is a conversation between characters. In poems, novels, and short stories, dialogue is usually set off by quotation marks to indicate a speaker's exact words.

In a play, dialogue follows the names of the characters, and no quotation marks are used.

DICTION *Diction* is a writer's or speaker's word choice. Diction is part of a writer's style and may be described as formal or informal, plain or fancy, ordinary or technical, sophisticated or down-to-earth, old-fashioned or modern.

DRAMA A *drama* is a story written to be performed by actors. Although a drama is meant to be performed, one can also read the script, or written version, and imagine the action. The *script* of a drama is made up of dialogue and stage directions. The *dialogue* is the words spoken by the actors. The *stage directions,* usually printed in italics, tell how the actors should look, move, and speak. They also describe the setting, sound effects, and lighting.

Dramas are often divided into parts called *acts.*

The acts are often divided into smaller parts called *scenes.*

DYNAMIC CHARACTER See *Character.*

ESSAY An *essay* is a short nonfiction work about a particular subject. Most essays have a single major focus and a clear introduction, body, and conclusion.

There are many types of essays. An *informal essay* uses casual, conversational language. A *historical essay* gives facts, explanations, and insights about historical events. An *expository essay* explains an idea by breaking it down. A *narrative essay* tells a story about a real-life experience. An *informational essay* explains a process. A *persuasive essay* offers an opinion and supports it.
See *Exposition, Narration,* and *Persuasion.*

EXPOSITION In the plot of a story or a drama, the *exposition,* or introduction, is the part of the work that introduces the characters, setting, and basic situation.
See *Plot.*

EXPOSITORY WRITING *Expository writing* is writing that explains or informs.

EXTENDED METAPHOR In an *extended metaphor,* as in a regular metaphor, a subject is spoken or written of as though it were something else. However, extended metaphor differs from regular metaphor in that several connected comparisons are made.

See *Metaphor.*

EXTERNAL CONFLICT See *Conflict.*

FABLE A *fable* is a brief story or poem, usually with animal characters, that teaches a lesson, or moral. The moral is usually stated at the end of the fable.

See *Irony* and *Moral.*

FANTASY A *fantasy* is highly imaginative writing that contains elements not found in real life. Examples of fantasy include stories that involve supernatural elements, stories that resemble fairy tales, stories that deal with imaginary places and creatures, and science-fiction stories.

See *Science Fiction.*

FICTION *Fiction* is prose writing that tells about imaginary characters and events. Short stories and novels are works of fiction. Some writers base their fiction on actual events and people, adding invented characters, dialogue, settings, and plots. Other writers rely on imagination alone.

See *Narration, Nonfiction,* and *Prose.*

FIGURATIVE LANGUAGE *Figurative language* is writing or speech that is not meant to be taken literally. The many types of figurative language are known as *figures of speech.* Common figures of speech include metaphor, personification, and simile. Writers use figurative language to state ideas in vivid and imaginative ways.

See *Metaphor, Personification, Simile,* and *Symbol.*

FIGURE OF SPEECH See *Figurative Language.*

FLASHBACK A *flashback* is a scene within a story that interrupts the sequence of events to relate events that occurred in the past.

FLAT CHARACTER See *Character.*

FOLK TALE A *folk tale* is a story composed orally and then passed from person to person by word of mouth. Folk tales originated among people who could neither read nor write. These people entertained one another by telling stories aloud—often dealing with heroes, adventure, magic, or romance. Eventually, modern scholars collected these stories and wrote them down.

Folk tales reflect the cultural beliefs and environments from which they come.

See *Fable, Legend, Myth,* and *Oral Tradition.*

FOOT See *Meter.*

FORESHADOWING *Foreshadowing* is the author's use of clues to hint at what might happen later in the story. Writers use foreshadowing to build their readers' expectations and to create suspense.

FREE VERSE *Free verse* is poetry not written in a regular, rhythmical pattern, or meter. The poet is free to write lines of any length or with any number of stresses, or beats. Free verse is therefore less constraining than *metrical verse,* in which every line must have a certain length and a certain number of stresses.

See *Meter.*

GENRE A *genre* is a division or type of literature. Literature is commonly divided into three major genres: poetry, prose, and drama. Each major genre is, in turn, divided into lesser genres, as follows:

1. *Poetry:* lyric poetry, concrete poetry, dramatic poetry, narrative poetry, epic poetry

2. *Prose:* fiction (novels and short stories) and nonfiction (biography, autobiography, letters, essays, and reports)

3. *Drama:* serious drama and tragedy, comic drama, melodrama, and farce

See *Drama, Poetry,* and *Prose.*

HAIKU The *haiku* is a three-line Japanese verse form. The first and third lines of a haiku each have five syllables. The second line has seven syllables. A writer of haiku uses images to create a single, vivid picture, generally of a scene from nature.

HERO/HEROINE A *hero* or *heroine* is a character whose actions are inspiring, or noble. Often heroes and heroines struggle to overcome the obstacles and problems that stand in their way. Note that the term *hero* was originally used only for male characters, while heroic female characters were always called *heroines.* However, it is now acceptable to use *hero* to refer to females as well as to males.

HISTORICAL FICTION In *historical fiction,* real events, places, or people are incorporated into a fictional, or made-up, story.

HUMOR *Humor* is writing intended to evoke laughter. While most humorists are trying to entertain, humor can also be used to convey a serious theme.

IMAGERY See *Images.*

IMAGES *Images* are words or phrases that appeal to one or more of the five senses. Writers use images to describe how their subjects look, sound, feel, taste, and smell. Poets often paint images, or word pictures, that appeal to your senses. These pictures help you to experience the poem fully.

INTERNAL CONFLICT See *Conflict.*

IRONY *Irony* is a contradiction between what happens and what is expected. There are three main types of irony. *Situational irony* occurs when something happens that directly contradicts the expectations of the characters or the audience. *Verbal irony* is something contradictory that is said. In *dramatic irony,* the audience is aware of something that the character or speaker is not.

JOURNAL A *journal* is a daily, or periodic, account of events and the writer's thoughts and feelings about those events. Personal journals are not normally written for publication, but sometimes they do get published later with permission from the author or the author's family.

LEGEND A *legend* is a widely told story about the past—one that may or may not have a foundation in fact. Every culture has its own legends—its familiar, traditional stories.

See *Folk Tale, Myth,* and *Oral Tradition.*

LETTERS A *letter* is a written communication from one person to another. In personal letters, the writer shares information and his or her thoughts and feelings with one other person or group. Although letters are not normally written for publication, they sometimes do get published later with the permission of the author or the author's family.

LIMERICK A *limerick* is a humorous, rhyming, five-line poem with a specific meter and rhyme scheme. Most limericks have three strong stresses in lines 1, 2, and 5 and two strong stresses in lines 3 and 4. Most follow the rhyme scheme *aabba.*

LYRIC POEM A *lyric poem* is a highly musical verse that expresses the observations and feelings of a single speaker. It creates a single, unified impression.

MAIN CHARACTER See *Character.*

MEDIA ACCOUNTS *Media accounts* are reports, explanations, opinions, or descriptions written for television, radio, newspapers, and magazines. While some media accounts report only facts, others include the writer's thoughts and reflections.

METAPHOR A *metaphor* is a figure of speech in which something is described as though it were something else. A metaphor, like a simile, works by pointing out a similarity between two unlike things.

See *Extended Metaphor* and *Simile.*

METER The *meter* of a poem is its rhythmical pattern. This pattern is determined by the number of *stresses,* or beats, in each line. To describe the meter of a poem, read it while emphasizing the beats in each line. Then, mark the stressed and unstressed syllables, as follows:

M̆y fáth | ĕr wás | thĕ fírst | tŏ héar |

As you can see, each strong stress is marked with a slanted line (´) and each unstressed syllable with a horseshoe symbol (˘). The weak and strong stresses are then divided by vertical lines (|) into groups called feet.

MINOR CHARACTER See *Character.*

MOOD See *Atmosphere.*

MORAL A *moral* is a lesson taught by a literary work. A fable usually ends with a moral that is directly stated. A poem, novel, short story, or essay often suggests a moral that is not directly stated. The moral must be drawn by the reader, based on other elements in the work.

See *Fable.*

MOTIVATION See *Motive.*

MOTIVE A *motive* is a reason that explains or partially explains a character's thoughts, feelings, actions, or speech. Writers try to make their characters' motives, or motivations, as clear as possible. If the motives of a main character are not clear, then the character will not be well understood.

Characters are often motivated by needs, such as food and shelter. They are also motivated by feelings, such as fear, love, and pride. Motives may be obvious or hidden.

MYTH A *myth* is a fictional tale that explains the actions of gods or heroes or the origins of elements of nature. Myths are part of the oral tradition. They are composed orally and then passed from generation to generation by word of mouth. Every ancient culture has its own mythology, or collection of myths. Greek and Roman myths are known collectively as *classical mythology.*

See *Oral Tradition.*

NARRATION *Narration* is writing that tells a story. The act of telling a story is also called narration. A story told in fiction, nonfiction, poetry, or even in drama is called a *narrative.*

See *Narrative, Narrative Poem,* and *Narrator.*

NARRATIVE A *narrative* is a story. A narrative can be either fiction or nonfiction. Novels and short stories are types of fictional narratives. Biographies and autobiographies are nonfiction narratives. Poems that tell stories are also narratives.

See *Narration* and *Narrative Poem.*

NARRATIVE POEM A *narrative poem* is a story told in verse. Narrative poems often have all the elements of short stories, including characters, conflict, and plot.

NARRATOR A *narrator* is a speaker or a character who tells a story. The narrator's perspective is the way he or she sees things. A *third-person narrator* is one who stands outside the action and speaks about it. A *first-person narrator* is one who tells a story and participates in its action.

See *Point of View.*

NONFICTION *Nonfiction* is prose writing that presents and explains ideas or that tells about real people, places, objects, or events. Autobiographies, biographies, essays, reports, letters, memos, and newspaper articles are all types of nonfiction.

See *Fiction.*

NOVEL A *novel* is a long work of fiction. Novels contain such elements as characters, plot, conflict, and setting. The writer of novels, or novelist, develops these elements. In addition to its main plot, a novel may contain one or more subplots, or independent, related stories. A novel may also have several themes.

See *Fiction* and *Short Story.*

NOVELLA A *novella* is a fiction work that is longer than a short story but shorter than a novel.

ONOMATOPOEIA *Onomatopoeia* is the use of words that imitate sounds. *Crash, buzz, screech, hiss, neigh, jingle,* and *cluck* are examples of onomatopoeia. *Chickadee, towhee,* and *whippoorwill* are onomatopoeic names of birds.

Onomatopoeia can help put the reader in the action of a poem.

ORAL TRADITION *Oral tradition* is the passing of songs, stories, and poems from generation to generation by word of mouth. Folk songs, folk tales, legends, and myths all come from the oral tradition. No one knows who first created these stories and poems.

See *Folk Tale, Legend,* and *Myth.*

OXYMORON An *oxymoron* (pl. *oxymora*) is a figure of speech that links two opposite or contradictory words, to point out an idea or situation that seems contradictory or inconsistent but on closer inspection turns out to be somehow true.

PERSONIFICATION *Personification* is a type of figurative language in which a nonhuman subject is given human characteristics.

PERSPECTIVE See *Narrator* and *Point of View.*

PERSUASION *Persuasion* is used in writing or speech that attempts to convince the reader or listener to adopt a particular opinion or course of action. Newspaper editorials and letters to the editor use persuasion. So do advertisements and campaign speeches given by political candidates. An *argument* is a logical way of presenting a belief, conclusion, or stance. A good argument is supported with reasoning and evidence.

See *Essay.*

PLAYWRIGHT A *playwright* is a person who writes plays. William Shakespeare is regarded as the greatest playwright in English literature.

PLOT *Plot* is the sequence of events in a story. In most novels, dramas, short stories, and narrative poems, the plot involves both characters and a central conflict. The plot usually begins with an exposition that introduces the setting, the characters, and the basic situation. This is followed by the *inciting incident,* which introduces the central conflict. The conflict then increases during the *development* until it reaches a high point of interest or suspense, the *climax.* The climax is followed by the *falling action,* or end, of the central conflict. Any events that occur during the *falling action* make up the *resolution* or *denouement.*

Some plots do not have all of these parts. For example, some stories begin with the inciting incident and end with the resolution.

See *Conflict.*

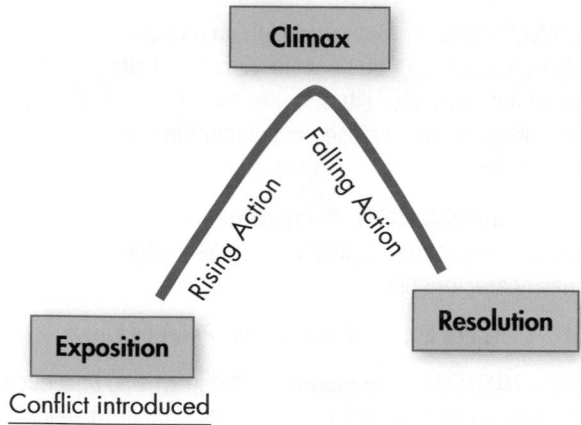

POETRY *Poetry* is one of the three major types of literature, the others being prose and drama. Most poems make use of highly concise, musical, and emotionally charged language. Many also make use of imagery, figurative language, and special devices of sound such as rhyme. Major types of poetry include *lyric poetry, narrative poetry,* and *concrete poetry.*

See *Concrete Poem, Genre, Lyric Poem,* and *Narrative Poem.*

POINT OF VIEW *Point of view* is the perspective, or vantage point, from which a story is told. It is either a narrator outside the story or a character in the story. *First-person point of view* is told by a character who uses the first-person pronoun "I."

The two kinds of *third-person point of view,* limited and omniscient, are called "third person" because the narrator uses third-person pronouns such as "he" and "she" to refer to the characters. There is no "I" telling the story.

In stories told from the *omniscient third-person point of view,* the narrator knows and tells about what each character feels and thinks.

In stories told from the *limited third-person point of view,* the narrator relates the inner thoughts and feelings of only one character, and everything is viewed from this character's perspective.

See *Narrator.*

PROBLEM See *Conflict.*

PROSE *Prose* is the ordinary form of written language. Most writing that is not poetry, drama, or song is considered prose. Prose is one of the major genres of literature and occurs in two forms—fiction and nonfiction.

See *Fiction, Genre,* and *Nonfiction.*

PROTAGONIST The *protagonist* is the main character in a literary work. Often, the protagonist is a person, but sometimes it can be an animal.

See *Antagonist* and *Character.*

REFRAIN A *refrain* is a regularly repeated line or group of lines in a poem or a song.

REPETITION *Repetition* is the use, more than once, of any element of language—a sound, word, phrase, clause, or sentence. Repetition is used in both prose and poetry.

See *Alliteration, Meter, Plot, Rhyme,* and *Rhyme Scheme.*

RESOLUTION The *resolution* is the outcome of the conflict in a plot.

See *Plot.*

RHYME *Rhyme* is the repetition of sounds at the ends of words. Poets use rhyme to lend a songlike quality to their verses and to emphasize certain words and ideas. Many traditional poems contain *end rhymes,* or rhyming words at the ends of lines.

Another common device is the use of *internal rhymes,* or rhyming words within lines. Internal rhyme also emphasizes the flowing nature of a poem.

See *Rhyme Scheme.*

RHYME SCHEME A *rhyme scheme* is a regular pattern of rhyming words in a poem. To indicate the rhyme scheme of a poem, one uses lowercase letters. Each rhyme is assigned a different letter, as follows in the first stanza of "Dust of Snow," by Robert Frost:

The way a crow	*a*
Shook down on me	*b*
The dust of snow	*a*
From a hemlock tree	*b*

Thus, this stanza has the rhyme scheme *abab.*

RHYTHM *Rhythm* is the pattern of stressed and unstressed syllables in spoken or written language.

See *Meter.*

ROUND CHARACTER See *Character.*

SCENE A *scene* is a section of uninterrupted action in the act of a drama.

See *Drama.*

SCIENCE FICTION *Science fiction* combines elements of fiction and fantasy with scientific fact. Many science-fiction stories are set in the future.

SENSORY LANGUAGE *Sensory language* is writing or speech that appeals to one or more of the five senses.

See *Images.*

SETTING The *setting* of a literary work is the time and place of the action. The setting includes all the details of a place and time—the year, the time of day, even the weather. The place may be a specific country, state, region, community, neighborhood, building, institution, or home. Details such as dialects, clothing, customs, and modes of transportation are often used to establish setting. In most stories, the setting serves as a backdrop—a context in which the characters interact. Setting can also help to create a feeling, or atmosphere.

See *Atmosphere.*

SHORT STORY A *short story* is a brief work of fiction. Like a novel, a short story presents a sequence of events, or plot. The plot usually deals with a central conflict faced by a main character, or protagonist. The events in a short story usually communicate a message about life or human nature. This message, or central idea, is the story's theme.

See *Conflict, Plot,* and *Theme.*

SIMILE A *simile* is a figure of speech that uses *like* or *as* to make a direct comparison between two unlike ideas. Everyday speech often contains similes, such as "pale as a ghost," "good as gold," "spread like wildfire," and "clever as a fox."

SPEAKER The *speaker* is the imaginary voice a poet uses when writing a poem. The speaker is the character who tells the poem. This character, or voice, often is not identified by name. There can be important differences between the poet and the poem's speaker.

See *Narrator.*

STAGE DIRECTIONS *Stage directions* are notes included in a drama to describe how the work is to be performed or staged. Stage directions are usually printed in italics and enclosed within parentheses or brackets. Some stage directions describe the movements, costumes, emotional states, and ways of speaking of the characters.

STAGING *Staging* includes the setting, lighting, costumes, special effects, music, dance, and so on that go into putting on a stage performance of a drama.

See *Drama.*

STANZA A *stanza* is a group of lines of poetry that are usually similar in length and pattern and are separated by spaces. A stanza is like a paragraph of poetry—it states and develops a single main idea.

STATIC CHARACTER See *Character.*

SURPRISE ENDING A *surprise ending* is a conclusion that is unexpected. The reader has certain expectations about the ending based on details in the story. Often, a surprise ending is *foreshadowed,* or subtly hinted at, in the course of the work.

See *Foreshadowing* and *Plot.*

SUSPENSE *Suspense* is a feeling of anxious uncertainty about the outcome of events in a literary work. Writers create suspense by raising questions in the minds of their readers.

SYMBOL A *symbol* is anything that stands for or represents something else. Symbols are common in everyday life. A dove with an olive branch in its beak is a symbol of peace. A blindfolded woman holding a balanced scale is a symbol of justice. A crown is a symbol of a king's status and authority.

SYMBOLISM *Symbolism* is the use of symbols. Symbolism plays an important role in many different types of literature. It can highlight certain elements the author wishes to emphasize and also add levels of meaning.

THEME The *theme* is a central message, concern, or purpose in a literary work. A theme can usually be expressed as a generalization, or a general statement, about human beings or about life. The theme of a work is not a summary of its plot. The theme is the writer's central idea.

Although a theme may be stated directly in the text, it is more often presented indirectly. When the theme is stated indirectly, or implied, the reader must figure out what the theme is by looking carefully at what the work reveals about people or about life.

TONE The *tone* of a literary work is the writer's attitude toward his or her audience and subject. The tone can often be described by a single adjective, such as *formal* or *informal, serious* or *playful, bitter,* or *ironic.* Factors that contribute to the tone are word choice, sentence structure, line length, rhyme, rhythm, and repetition.

TRAGEDY A *tragedy* is a work of literature, especially a play, that results in a catastrophe for the main character. In ancient Greek drama, the main character is always a significant person—a king or a hero—and the cause of the tragedy is a tragic flaw, or weakness, in his or her character. In modern drama, the main character can be an ordinary person, and the cause of the tragedy can be some evil in society itself. The purpose of tragedy is not only to arouse fear and pity in the audience, but also, in some cases, to convey a sense of the grandeur and nobility of the human spirit.

TURNING POINT See *Climax.*

UNIVERSAL THEME A *universal theme* is a message about life that is expressed regularly in many different cultures and time periods. Folk tales, epics, and romances often address universal themes like the importance of courage, the power of love, or the danger of greed.

WORD CHOICE An author's *word choice*—sometimes referred to as *diction*—is an important factor in creating the tone or mood of a literary work. Authors choose words based on the intended audience and the work's purpose.

Tips for Literature Circles

As you read and study literature, discussions with other readers can help you understand and enjoy what you have read. Use the following tips.

- ## Understand the purpose of your discussion

  Your purpose when you discuss literature is to broaden your understanding of a work by testing your own ideas and hearing the ideas of others. Keep your comments focused on the literature you are discussing. Starting with one focus question will help to keep your discussion on track.

- ## Communicate effectively

  Effective communication requires thinking before speaking. Plan the points that you want to make and decide how you will express them. Organize these points in logical order and use details from the work to support your ideas. Jot down informal notes to help keep your ideas focused.

  Remember to speak clearly, pronouncing words slowly and carefully. Also, listen attentively when others are speaking, and avoid interrupting.

- ## Consider other ideas and interpretations

  A work of literature can generate a wide variety of responses in different readers. Be open to the idea that many interpretations can be valid. To support your own ideas, point to the events, descriptions, characters, or other literary elements in the work that led to your interpretation. To consider someone else's ideas, decide whether details in the work support the interpretation he or she presents. Be sure to convey your criticism of the ideas of others in a respectful and supportive manner.

- ## Ask questions

  Ask questions to clarify your understanding of another reader's ideas. You can also use questions to call attention to possible areas of confusion, to points that are open to debate, or to errors in the speaker's points. To move a discussion forward, summarize and evaluate conclusions reached by the group members.

  When you meet with a group to discuss literature, use a chart like the one shown to analyze the discussion.

Work Being Discussed:	
Focus Question:	
Your Response:	Another Student's Response:
Supporting Evidence:	Supporting Evidence:

Tips for Improving Reading Fluency

When you were younger, you learned to read. Then, you read to expand your experiences or for pure enjoyment. Now, you are expected to read to learn. As you progress in school, you are given more and more material to read. The tips on these pages will help you improve your reading fluency, or your ability to read easily, smoothly, and expressively.

Keeping Your Concentration

One common problem that readers face is the loss of concentration. When you are reading an assignment, you might find yourself rereading the same sentence several times without really understanding it. The first step in changing this behavior is to notice that you do it. Becoming an active, aware reader will help you get the most from your assignments. Practice using these strategies:

- Cover what you have already read with a note card as you go along. Then, you will not be able to reread without noticing that you are doing it.

- Set a purpose for reading beyond just completing the assignment. Then, read actively by pausing to ask yourself questions about the material as you read.

- Use the Reading Strategy instruction and notes that appear with each selection in this textbook.

- Stop reading after a specified period of time (for example, 5 minutes) and summarize what you have read. To help you with this strategy, use the Reading Check questions that appear with each selection in this textbook. Reread to find any answers you do not know.

Reading Phrases

Fluent readers read phrases rather than individual words. Reading this way will speed up your reading and improve your comprehension. Here are some useful ideas:

- Experts recommend rereading as a strategy to increase fluency. Choose a passage of text that is neither too hard nor too easy. Read the same passage aloud several times until you can read it smoothly. When you can read the passage fluently, pick another passage and keep practicing.

- Read aloud into a tape recorder. Then, listen to the recording, noting your accuracy, pacing, and expression. You can also read aloud and share feedback with a partner.

- Use the *Prentice Hall Listening to Literature* audiotapes or CDs to hear the selections read aloud. Read along silently in your textbook, noticing how the reader uses his or her voice and emphasizes certain words and phrases.

Understanding Key Vocabulary

If you do not understand some of the words in an assignment, you may miss out on important concepts. Therefore, it is helpful to keep a dictionary nearby when you are reading. Follow these steps:

- Before you begin reading, scan the text for unfamiliar words or terms. Find out what those words mean before you begin reading.

- Use context—the surrounding words, phrases, and sentences—to help you determine the meanings of unfamiliar words.
- If you are unable to understand the meaning through context, refer to the dictionary.

Paying Attention to Punctuation

When you read, pay attention to punctuation. Commas, periods, exclamation points, semicolons, and colons tell you when to pause or stop. They also indicate relationships between groups of words. When you recognize these relationships you will read with greater understanding and expression. Look at the chart below.

Punctuation Mark	Meaning
comma	brief pause
period	pause at the end of a thought
exclamation point	pause that indicates emphasis
semicolon	pause between related but distinct thoughts
colon	pause before giving explanation or examples

Using the Reading Fluency Checklist

Use the checklist below each time you read a selection in this textbook. In your Language Arts journal or notebook, note which skills you need to work on and chart your progress each week.

Reading Fluency Checklist
❏ Preview the text to check for difficult or unfamiliar words.
❏ Practice reading aloud.
❏ Read according to punctuation.
❏ Break down long sentences into the subject and its meaning.
❏ Read groups of words for meaning rather than reading single words.
❏ Read with expression (change your tone of voice to add meaning to the word).

Reading is a skill that can be improved with practice. The key to improving your fluency is to read. The more you read, the better your reading will become.

Types of Writing

Good writing can be a powerful tool used for many purposes. Writing can allow you to defend something you believe in or show how much you know about a subject. Writing can also help you share what you have experienced, imagined, thought, and felt. The three main types of writing are argument, informative/explanatory, and narrative.

Argument

When you think of the word *argument,* you might think of a disagreement between two people, but an argument is more than that. An argument is a logical way of presenting a belief, conclusion, or stance. A good argument is supported with reasoning and evidence.

Argument writing can be used for many purposes, such as to change a reader's point of view or opinion or to bring about an action or a response from a reader.

There are three main purposes for writing a formal argument:

- to change the reader's mind

- to convince the reader to accept what is written

- to motivate the reader to take action, based on what is written

The following are some types of argument writing:

Advertisements An advertisement is a planned message meant to be seen, heard, or read. It attempts to persuade an audience to buy a product or service, accept an idea, or support a cause. Advertisements may appear in print, online, or in broadcast form.

Several common types of advertisements are public service announcements, billboards, merchandise ads, service ads, and political campaign literature.

Persuasive Essay A persuasive essay presents a position on an issue, urges readers to accept that position, and may encourage a specific action. An effective persuasive essay

- Explores an issue of importance to the writer

- Addresses an issue that is arguable

- Uses facts, examples, statistics, or personal experiences to support a position

- Tries to influence the audience through appeals to the readers' knowledge, experiences, or emotions

- Uses clear organization to present a logical argument

Forms of persuasion include editorials, position papers, persuasive speeches, grant proposals, advertisements, and debates.

Informative/Explanatory

Informative/explanatory writing should rely on facts to inform or explain. Informative/explanatory writing serves some closely related purposes: to increase readers' knowledge of a subject, to help readers better understand a procedure or process, or to provide readers with an enhanced comprehension of a concept. It should also feature a clear introduction, body, and conclusion. The following are some examples of informative/explanatory writing:

Cause-and-Effect Essay A cause-and-effect essay examines the relationship between events, explaining how one event or situation causes another. A successful cause-and-effect essay includes

- A discussion of a cause, event, or condition that produces a specific result

- An explanation of an effect, outcome, or result

- Evidence and examples to support the relationship between cause and effect

- A logical organization that makes the explanation clear

Comparison-and-Contrast Essay A comparison-and-contrast essay analyzes the similarities and differences between or among two or more things. An effective comparison-and-contrast essay

- Identifies a purpose for comparison and contrast

- Identifies similarities and differences between or among two or more things, people, places, or ideas

- Gives factual details about the subjects

- Uses an organizational plan suited to the topic and purpose

Descriptive Writing Descriptive writing creates a vivid picture of a person, place, thing, or event. Most descriptive writing includes

- Sensory details—sights, sounds, smells, tastes, and physical sensations

- Vivid, precise language

- Figurative language or comparisons

- Adjectives and adverbs that paint a word picture
- An organization suited to the subject

Types of descriptive writing include descriptions of ideas, observations, travel brochures, physical descriptions, functional descriptions, remembrances, and character sketches.

Problem-and-Solution Essay A problem-and-solution essay describes a problem and offers one or more solutions to it. It describes a clear set of steps to achieve a result. An effective problem-and-solution essay includes

- A clear statement of the problem, with its causes and effects summarized for the reader
- The most important aspects of the problem
- A proposal for at least one realistic solution
- Facts, statistics, data, or expert testimony to support the solution
- A clear organization that makes the relationship between problem and solution obvious

Research Writing Research writing is based on information gathered from outside sources. A research paper—a focused study of a topic—helps writers explore and connect ideas, make discoveries, and share their findings with an audience. An effective research paper

- Focuses on a specific, narrow topic, which is usually summarized in a thesis statement
- Presents relevant information from a wide variety of sources
- Uses a clear organization that includes an introduction, body, and conclusion
- Includes a bibliography or works-cited list that identifies the sources from which the information was drawn

Other types of writing that depend on accurate and insightful research include multimedia presentations, statistical reports, annotated bibliographies, and experiment journals.

Workplace Writing Workplace writing is probably the format you will use most after you finish school. In general, workplace writing is fact-based and meant to communicate specific information in a structured format. Effective workplace writing

- Communicates information concisely
- Includes details that provide necessary information and anticipate potential questions

- Is error-free and neatly presented

Common types of workplace writing include business letters, memorandums, résumés, forms, and applications.

Narrative

Narrative writing conveys experience, either real or imaginary, and uses time to provide structure. It can be used to inform, instruct, persuade, or entertain. Whenever writers tell a story, they are using narrative writing. Most types of narrative writing share certain elements, such as characters, a setting, a sequence of events, and, often, a theme. The following are some types of narration:

Autobiographical Writing Autobiographical writing tells a true story about an important period, experience, or relationship in the writer's life. Effective autobiographical writing includes

- A series of events that involve the writer as the main character
- Details, thoughts, feelings, and insights from the writer's perspective
- A conflict or an event that affects the writer
- A logical organization that tells the story clearly
- Insights that the writer gained from the experience

Types of autobiographical writing include personal narratives, autobiographical sketches, reflective essays, eyewitness accounts, and memoirs.

Short Story A short story is a brief, creative narrative. Most short stories include

- Details that establish the setting in time and place
- A main character who undergoes a change or learns something during the course of the story
- A conflict or a problem to be introduced, developed, and resolved
- A plot, the series of events that make up the action of the story
- A theme or message about life

Types of short stories include realistic stories, fantasies, historical narratives, mysteries, thrillers, science-fiction stories, and adventure stories.

Writing Friendly Letters

Writing Friendly Letters

A friendly letter is much less formal than a business letter. It is a letter to a friend, a family member, or anyone with whom the writer wants to communicate in a personal, friendly way. Most friendly letters are made up of five parts:

- ✔ the heading
- ✔ the salutation, or greeting
- ✔ the body
- ✔ the closing
- ✔ the signature

The purpose of a friendly letter is often one of the following:

- ✔ to share personal news and feelings
- ✔ to send or to answer an invitation
- ✔ to express thanks

Model Friendly Letter

In this friendly letter, Betsy thanks her grandparents for a birthday present and gives them some news about her life.

11 Old Farm Road
Topsham, Maine 04011

April 14, 20—

Dear Grandma and Grandpa,

Thank you for the sweater you sent me for my birthday. It fits perfectly, and I love the color. I wore my new sweater to the carnival at school last weekend and got lots of compliments.

The weather here has been cool but sunny. Mom thinks that "real" spring will never come. I can't wait until it's warm enough to go swimming.

School is going fairly well. I really like my Social Studies class. We are learning about the U.S. Constitution, and I think it's very interesting. Maybe I will be a lawyer when I grow up.

When are you coming out to visit us? We haven't seen you since Thanksgiving. You can stay in my room when you come. I'll be happy to sleep on the couch. (The TV is in that room!!)

Well, thanks again and hope all is well with you.

Love,

Betsy

The **heading** includes the writer's address and the date on which he or she wrote the letter.

The **body** is the main part of the letter and contains the basic message.

Some common **closings** for personal letters include "Best wishes," "Love," "Sincerely," and "Yours truly."

Writing Business Letters

Formatting Business Letters

Business letters follow one of several acceptable formats. In **block format,** each part of the letter begins at the left margin. A double space is used between paragraphs. In **modified block format,** some parts of the letter are indented to the center of the page. No matter which format is used, all letters in business format have a heading, an inside address, a salutation or greeting, a body, a closing, and a signature. These parts are shown and annotated on the model business letter below, formatted in modified block style.

Model Business Letter

In this letter, Yolanda Dodson uses modified block format to request information.

Students for a Cleaner Planet
c/o Memorial High School
333 Veteran's Drive
Denver, CO 80211

January 25, 20—

Steven Wilson, Director
Resource Recovery Really Works
300 Oak Street
Denver, CO 80216

Dear Mr. Wilson:

Memorial High School would like to start a branch of your successful recycling program. We share your commitment to reclaiming as much reusable material as we can. Because your program has been successful in other neighborhoods, we're sure that it can work in our community. Our school includes grades 9–12 and has about 800 students.

Would you send us some information about your community recycling program? For example, we need to know what materials can be recycled and how we can implement the program.

At least fifty students have already expressed an interest in getting involved, so I know we'll have the people power to make the program work. Please help us get started.

Thank you in advance for your time and consideration.

Sincerely,

Yolanda Dodson

Yolanda Dodson

The **heading** shows the writer's address and organization (if any) and the date.

The **inside address** indicates where the letter will be sent.

A **salutation** is punctuated by a colon. When the specific addressee is not known, use a general greeting such as "To whom it may concern:"

The **body** of the letter states the writer's purpose. In this case, the writer requests information.

The **closing** "Sincerely" is common, but "Yours truly" or "Respectfully yours" are also acceptable. To end the letter, the writer types her name and provides a **signature**.

21st-Century Skills

New technology has created many new ways to communicate. Today, it is easy to contribute information to the Internet and send a variety of messages to friends far and near. You can also share your ideas through photos, illustrations, video, and sound recordings. *21st Century Skills* gives you an overview of some ways you can use today's technology to create, share, and find information. Here are the topics you will find in this section.

- ✔ Blogs
- ✔ Social Networking
- ✔ Widgets and Feeds
- ✔ Multimedia Elements
- ✔ Podcasts
- ✔ Wikis

BLOGS

A **blog** is a common form of online writing. The word *blog* is a contraction of *Web log*. Most blogs include a series of entries known as *posts*. The posts appear in a single column and are displayed in reverse chronological order. That means that the most recent post is at the top of the page. As you scroll down, you will find earlier posts.

Blogs have become increasingly popular. Researchers estimate that 75,000 new blogs are launched every day. Blog authors are often called *bloggers*. They can use their personal sites to share ideas, songs, videos, photos, and other media. People who read blogs can often post their responses with a comments feature found in each new post.

Because blogs are designed so that they are easy to update, bloggers can post new messages as often as they like, often daily. For some people blogs become a public journal or diary, in which they share their thoughts about daily events.

Types of Blogs

Not all blogs are the same. Many blogs have a single author, but others are group projects. These are some common types of blog:

- ✔ Personal blogs often have a general focus. Bloggers post their thoughts on any topic they find interesting in their daily lives.

- ✔ Topical blogs focus on a specific theme, such as movie reviews, political news, class assignments, or health-care opportunities.

Web Safety

Always be aware that information you post on the Internet can be read by everyone with access to that page. Once you post a picture or text, it can be saved on someone else's computer, even if you later remove it.

Using the Internet safely means keeping personal information personal. Never include your address (e-mail or real), last name, or telephone numbers. Avoid mentioning places you can be frequently found. Never give out passwords you use to access other Web sites and do not respond to e-mails from people you do not know.

Anatomy of a Blog

Here are some of the features you can include in a blog.

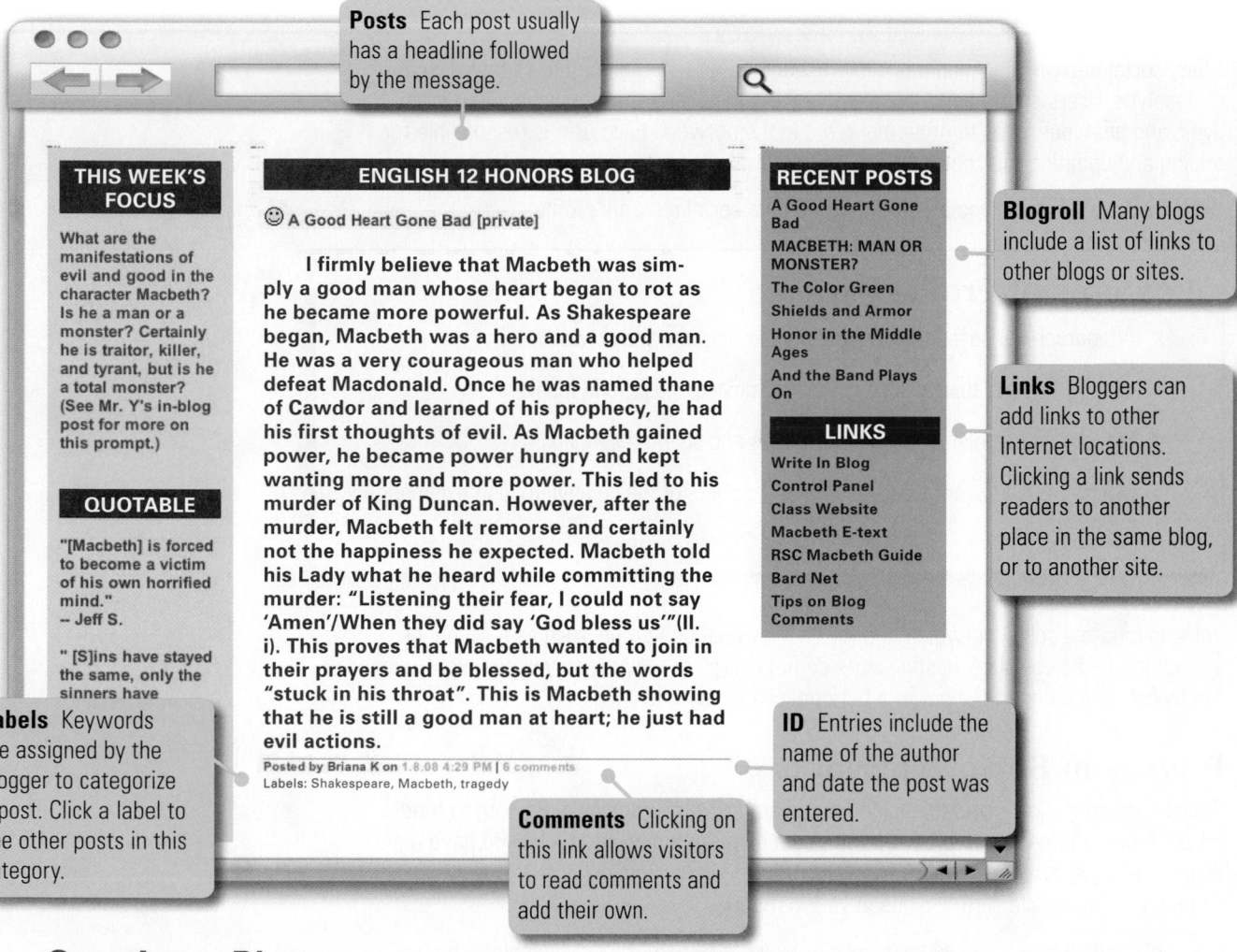

Posts Each post usually has a headline followed by the message.

THIS WEEK'S FOCUS

What are the manifestations of evil and good in the character Macbeth? Is he a man or a monster? Certainly he is traitor, killer, and tyrant, but is he a total monster? (See Mr. Y's in-blog post for more on this prompt.)

QUOTABLE

"[Macbeth] is forced to become a victim of his own horrified mind."
-- Jeff S.

" [S]ins have stayed the same, only the sinners have

ENGLISH 12 HONORS BLOG

☺ A Good Heart Gone Bad [private]

I firmly believe that Macbeth was simply a good man whose heart began to rot as he became more powerful. As Shakespeare began, Macbeth was a hero and a good man. He was a very courageous man who helped defeat Macdonald. Once he was named thane of Cawdor and learned of his prophecy, he had his first thoughts of evil. As Macbeth gained power, he became power hungry and kept wanting more and more power. This led to his murder of King Duncan. However, after the murder, Macbeth felt remorse and certainly not the happiness he expected. Macbeth told his Lady what he heard while committing the murder: "Listening their fear, I could not say 'Amen'/When they did say 'God bless us'"(II. i). This proves that Macbeth wanted to join in their prayers and be blessed, but the words "stuck in his throat". This is Macbeth showing that he is still a good man at heart; he just had evil actions.

Posted by Briana K on 1.8.08 4:29 PM | 6 comments
Labels: Shakespeare, Macbeth, tragedy

RECENT POSTS

A Good Heart Gone Bad
MACBETH: MAN OR MONSTER?
The Color Green
Shields and Armor
Honor in the Middle Ages
And the Band Plays On

LINKS

Write In Blog
Control Panel
Class Website
Macbeth E-text
RSC Macbeth Guide
Bard Net
Tips on Blog Comments

Blogroll Many blogs include a list of links to other blogs or sites.

Links Bloggers can add links to other Internet locations. Clicking a link sends readers to another place in the same blog, or to another site.

ID Entries include the name of the author and date the post was entered.

Labels Keywords are assigned by the blogger to categorize a post. Click a label to see other posts in this category.

Comments Clicking on this link allows visitors to read comments and add their own.

Creating a Blog

Keep these hints and strategies in mind to help you create an interesting and fair blog:

- ✔ Focus each blog entry on a single topic.

- ✔ Vary the length of your posts. Sometimes, all you need is a line or two to share a quick thought. Other posts will be much longer.

- ✔ Choose font colors and styles that can be read easily.

- ✔ Many people scan blogs rather than read them closely. You can make your main ideas pop out by using clear or clever headlines and boldfacing key terms.

- ✔ Give credit to other people's work and ideas. State the names of people whose ideas you are quoting or add a link to take readers to that person's blog or site.

- ✔ If you post comments, try to make them brief and polite.

SOCIAL NETWORKING

Social networking means any interaction between members of an online community. People can exchange many different kinds of information, from text and voice messages to video images.

Many social network communities allow users to create permanent pages that describe themselves. Users create home pages to express themselves, share ideas about their lives, and post messages to other members in the network. Each user is responsible for adding and updating the content on his or her profile page.

Here are some features you are likely to find on a social network profile:

Features of Profile Pages

- A biographical description, including photographs and artwork.

- Lists of favorite things, such as books, movies, music, and fashions.

- Playable media elements such as videos and sound recordings.

- Message boards, or "walls" in which members of the community can exchange messages.

You can create a social network page for an individual or a group, such as a school or special interest club. Many hosting sites do not charge to register, so you can also have fun by creating a page for a pet or a fictional character.

Privacy in Social Networks

Social networks allow users to decide how open their profiles will be. Be sure to read introductory information carefully before you register at a new site. Once you have a personal profile page, monitor your privacy settings regularly. Remember that any information you post will be available to anyone in your network.

Users often post messages anonymously or using false names, or *pseudonyms*. People can also post using someone else's name. Judge all information on the net critically. Do not assume that you know who posted some information simply because you recognize the name of the post author. The rapid speed of communication on the Internet can make it easy to jump to conclusions—be careful to avoid this trap.

Tips for Sending Effective Messages

Technology makes it easy to share ideas quickly, but writing for the Internet poses some special challenges as well. The writing style for blogs and social networks is often very conversational. In blog posts and comments, instant messages, and e-mails, writers often express themselves very quickly, using relaxed language, short sentences, and abbreviations. However, in a conversation, we get a lot of information from a speaker's tone of voice and body language. On the Internet, those clues are missing. As a result, Internet writers often use italics or bracketed labels to indicate emotions. Another alternative is using *emoticons*—strings of characters that give visual clues to indicate emotion:

:-) smile (happy)	:-(frown (unhappy)	;-) wink (light sarcasm)

Use these strategies to communicate effectively when using technology:

✔ Reread your messages. Before you click *Send,* read your message through and make sure that your tone will be clear to the reader.

✔ Do not jump to conclusions—ask for clarification first. Make sure you really understand what someone is saying before you respond.

✔ Use abbreviations your reader will understand.

WIDGETS AND FEEDS

A **widget** is a small application that performs a specific task. You might find widgets that give weather predictions, offer dictionary definitions or translations, provide entertainment such as games, or present a daily word, photograph, or quotation.

A **feed** is a special kind of widget. It displays headlines taken from the latest content on a specific media source. Clicking on the headline will take you to the full article.

Many social network communities and other Web sites allow you to personalize your home page by adding widgets and feeds.

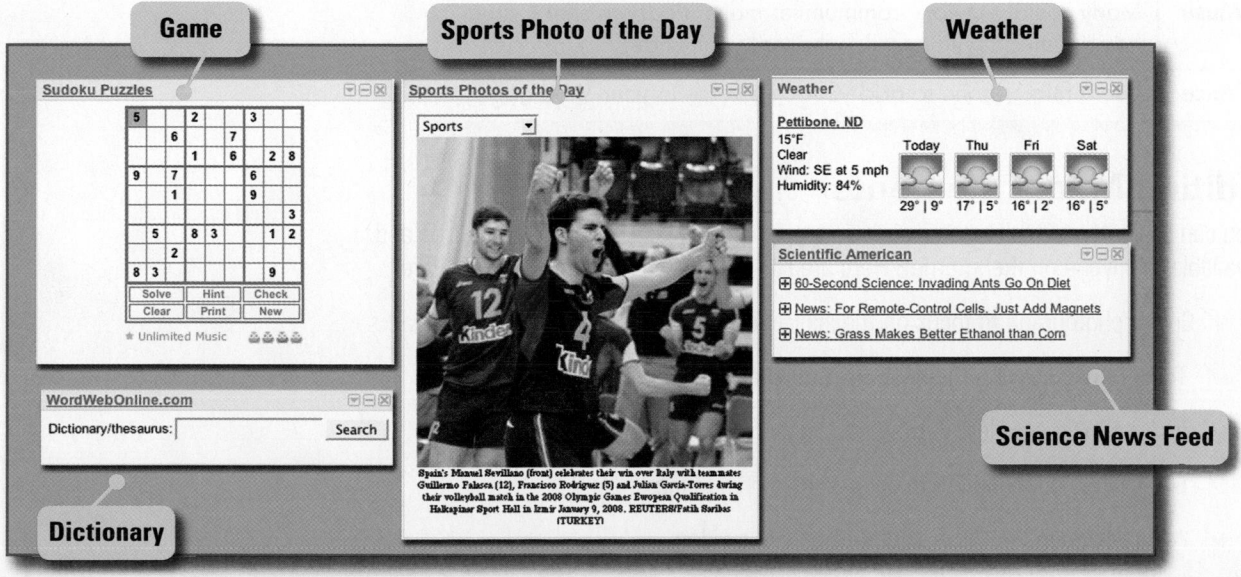

MULTIMEDIA ELEMENTS

One of the great advantages of communicating on the Internet is that you are not limited to using text only. When you create a Web profile or blog, you can share your ideas using a wide variety of media. In addition to widgets and feeds (see page R31), these media elements can make your Internet communication more entertaining and useful.

Graphics

Graphics	
Photographs	You can post photos taken by digital cameras.
Illustrations	Artwork can be created using computer software. You can also use a scanner to post a digital image of a drawing or sketch.
Charts, Graphs, and Maps	Charts and graphs can make statistical information clear. Use spreadsheet software to create these elements. Use Internet sites to find maps of specific places.

Video

Video	
Live Action	Digital video can be recorded by a camera or recorded from another media source.
Animation	Animated videos can also be created using software.

Sound

Sound	
Music	Many social network communities make it easy to share your favorite music with people who visit your page.
Voice	Use a microphone to add your own voice to your Web page.

Editing Media Elements

You can use software to customize media elements. Open source software is free and available to anyone on the Internet. Here are some things you can do with software:

- ✔ Crop a photograph to focus on the subject or brighten an image that is too dark.

- ✔ Transform a drawing's appearance from flat to three-dimensional.

- ✔ Insert a "You Are Here" arrow on a map.

- ✔ Edit a video or sound file to shorten its running time.

- ✔ Add background music or sound effects to a video.

PODCASTS

A **podcast** is a digital audio or video recording of a program that is made available on the Internet. Users can replay the podcast on a computer, or download it and replay it on a personal audio player. You might think of podcasts as radio or television programs that you create yourself. They can be embedded on a Web site or fed to a Web page through a podcast widget.

Creating an Effective Podcast

To make a podcast, you will need a recording device, such as a microphone or digital video camera, as well as editing software. Open source editing software is widely available and free of charge. Most audio podcasts are converted into the MP3 format. Here are some tips for creating a podcast that is clear and entertaining:

✔ Listen to several podcasts by different authors to get a feeling for the medium. Make a list of features and styles you like and also those you want to avoid.

✔ Test your microphone to find the best recording distance. Stand close enough to the microphone so that your voice sounds full, but not so close that you create an echo.

✔ Create an outline that shows your estimated timing for each element.

✔ Be prepared before you record. Rehearse, but do not create a script. Podcasts are best when they have a natural, easy flow.

✔ Talk directly to your listeners. Slow down enough so they can understand you.

✔ Use software to edit your podcast before publishing it. You can edit out mistakes or add additional elements.

WIKIS

A **wiki** is a collaborative Web site that lets visitors create, add, remove, and edit content. The term comes from the Hawaiian phrase *wiki wiki,* which means "quick." Web users at a wiki are both the readers and the writers of the site. Some wikis are open to contributions from anyone. Others require visitors to register before they can edit the content.

All of the text in these collaborative Web sites was written by people who use the site. Articles are constantly changing, as visitors find and correct errors and improve texts.

Wikis have both advantages and disadvantages as sources of information. They are valuable open forums for the exchange of ideas. The unique collaborative writing process allows entries to change over time. However, entries can also be modified incorrectly. Careless or malicious users can delete good content and add inappropriate or inaccurate information.

You can change the information on a wiki, but be sure your information is correct and clear before you add it. Wikis keep track of all changes, so your work will be recorded and can be evaluated by other users.

Citing Sources and Preparing Manuscript

Proofreading and Preparing Manuscript

Before preparing a final copy, proofread your manuscript. The chart shows the standard symbols for marking corrections to be made.

Proofreading Symbols	
insert	$\wedge$
delete	✄
close space	⌒
new paragraph	¶
add comma	⌄
add period	⊙
transpose (switch)	∾
change to cap	a̲
change to lowercase	ℓ

- Choose a standard, easy-to-read font.

- Type or print on one side of unlined 8 1/2" x 11" paper.

- Set the margins for the side, top, and bottom of your paper at approximately one inch. Most word-processing programs have a default setting that is appropriate.

- Double-space the document.

- Indent the first line of each paragraph.

- Number the pages in the upper right corner.

Follow your teacher's directions for formatting formal research papers. Most papers will have the following features:

- Title page

- Table of Contents or Outline

- Works-Cited List

Avoiding Plagiarism

Whether you are presenting a formal research paper or an opinion paper on a current event, you must be careful to give credit for any ideas or opinions that are not your own. Presenting someone else's ideas, research, or opinion as your own—even if you have phrased it in different words—is *plagiarism,* the equivalent of academic stealing, or fraud.

Do not use the ideas or research of others in place of your own. Read from several sources to draw your own conclusions and form your own opinions. Incorporate the ideas and research of others to support your points. Credit the source of the following types of support:

- Statistics

- Direct quotations

- Indirectly quoted statements of opinions

- Conclusions presented by an expert

- Facts available in only one or two sources

Crediting Sources

When you credit a source, you acknowledge where you found your information and you give your readers the details necessary for locating the source themselves. Within the body of the paper, you provide a short citation, a footnote number linked to a footnote, or an endnote number linked to an endnote reference. These brief references show the page numbers on which you found the information. Prepare a reference list at the end of the paper to provide full bibliographic information on your sources. These are two common types of reference lists:

- A bibliography provides a listing of all the resources you consulted during your research.

- A works-cited list indicates the works you have referenced in your paper.

The chart on the next page shows the Modern Language Association format for crediting sources. This is the most common format for papers written in the content areas in middle school and high school. Unless instructed otherwise by your teacher, use this format for crediting sources.

MLA Style for Listing Sources

Book with one author	Pyles, Thomas. *The Origins and Development of the English Language.* 2nd ed. New York: Harcourt, 1971. Print.
Book with two or three authors	McCrum, Robert, William Cran, and Robert MacNeil. *The Story of English.* New York: Penguin, 1987. Print.
Book with an editor	Truth, Sojourner. *Narrative of Sojourner Truth.* Ed. Margaret Washington. New York: Vintage, 1993. Print.
Book with more than three authors or editors	Donald, Robert B., et al. *Writing Clear Essays.* Upper Saddle River: Prentice, 1996. Print.
Single work in an anthology	Hawthorne, Nathaniel. "Young Goodman Brown." *Literature: An Introduction to Reading and Writing.* Ed. Edgar V. Roberts and H. E. Jacobs. Upper Saddle River: Prentice, 1998. 376–385. Print. [Indicate pages for the entire selection.]
Introduction to a work in a published edition	Washington, Margaret. Introduction. *Narrative of Sojourner Truth.* By Sojourner Truth. Ed. Washington. New York: Vintage, 1993. v–xi. Print.
Signed article from an encyclopedia	Askeland, Donald R. "Welding." *World Book Encyclopedia.* 1991 ed. Print.
Signed article in a weekly magazine	Wallace, Charles. "A Vodacious Deal." *Time* 14 Feb. 2000: 63. Print.
Signed article in a monthly magazine	Gustaitis, Joseph. "The Sticky History of Chewing Gum." *American History* Oct. 1998: 30–38. Print.
Newspaper	Thurow, Roger. "South Africans Who Fought for Sanctions Now Scrap for Investors." *Wall Street Journal* 11 Feb. 2000: A1+. Print. [For a multipage article that does not appear on consecutive pages, write only the first page number on which it appears, followed by the plus sign.]
Unsigned editorial or story	"Selective Silence." Editorial. *Wall Street Journal* 11 Feb. 2000: A14. Print. [If the editorial or story is signed, begin with the author's name.]
Signed pamphlet or brochure	[Treat the pamphlet as though it were a book.]
Work from a library subscription service	Ertman, Earl L. "Nefertiti's Eyes." *Archaeology* Mar.–Apr. 2008: 28–32. *Kids Search.* EBSCO. New York Public Library. Web. 18 June 2008 [Indicate the date you accessed the information.]
Filmstrips, slide programs, videocassettes, DVDs, and other audiovisual media	*The Diary of Anne Frank.* Dir. George Stevens. Perf. Millie Perkins, Shelley Winters, Joseph Schildkraut, Lou Jacobi, and Richard Beymer. 1959. Twentieth Century Fox, 2004. DVD.
CD-ROM (with multiple publishers)	Simms, James, ed. *Romeo and Juliet.* By William Shakespeare. Oxford: Attica Cybernetics; London: BBC Education; London: Harper, 1995. CD-ROM.
Radio or television program transcript	"Washington's Crossing of the Delaware." *Weekend Edition Sunday.* Natl. Public Radio. WNYC, New York. 23 Dec. 2003. Television transcript.
Internet Web page	"Fun Facts About Gum." NACGM site. 1999. National Association of Chewing Gum Manufacturers. Web. 19 Dec. 1999 [Indicate the date you accessed the information.]
Personal interview	Smith, Jane. Personal interview. 10 Feb. 2000.

All examples follow the style given in the *MLA Handbook for Writers of Research Papers,* seventh edition, by Joseph Gibaldi.

Guide to Rubrics

What is a rubric?

A rubric is a tool, often in the form of a chart or a grid, that helps you assess your work. Rubrics are particularly helpful for writing and speaking assignments.

To help you or others assess, or evaluate, your work, a rubric offers several specific criteria to be applied to your work. Then the rubric helps you or an evaluator indicate your range of success or failure according to those specific criteria. Rubrics are often used to evaluate writing for standardized tests.

Using a rubric will save you time, focus your learning, and improve the work you do. When you know what the rubric will be before you begin writing a persuasive essay, for example, as you write you will be aware of specific criteria that are important in that kind of an essay. As you evaluate the essay before giving it to your teacher, you will focus on the specific areas that your teacher wants you to master—or on areas that you know present challenges for you. Instead of searching through your work randomly for any way to improve it or correct its errors, you will have a clear and helpful focus on specific criteria.

How are rubrics constructed?

Rubrics can be constructed in several different ways.

- Your teacher may assign a rubric for a specific assignment.

- Your teacher may direct you to a rubric in your textbook.

- Your teacher and your class may construct a rubric for a particular assignment together.

- You and your classmates may construct a rubric together.

- You may create your own rubric with criteria you want to evaluate in your work.

How will a rubric help me?

A rubric will help you assess your work on a scale. Scales vary from rubric to rubric but usually range from 6 to 1, 5 to 1, or 4 to 1, with 6, 5, or 4 being the highest score and 1 being the lowest. If someone else is using the rubric to assess your work, the rubric will give your evaluator a clear range within which to place your work. If you are using the rubric yourself, it will help you make improvements to your work.

What are the types of rubrics?

- A **holistic rubric** has general criteria that can apply to a variety of assignments. See p. R38 for an example of a holistic rubric.

- An **analytic rubric** is specific to a particular assignment. The criteria for evaluation address the specific issues important in that assignment. See p. R37 for examples of analytic rubrics.

Sample Analytic Rubrics

Rubric With a 4-point Scale

The following analytic rubric is an example of a rubric to assess a persuasive essay. It will help you evaluate focus, organization, support/elaboration, and style/convention.

	Focus	Organization	Support/Elaboration	Style/Convention
4	Demonstrates highly effective word choice; clearly focused on task.	Uses clear, consistent organizational strategy.	Provides convincing, well-elaborated reasons to support the position.	Incorporates transitions; includes very few mechanical errors.
3	Demonstrates good word choice; stays focused on persuasive task.	Uses clear organizational strategy with occasional inconsistencies.	Provides two or more moderately elaborated reasons to support the position.	Incorporates some transitions; includes few mechanical errors.
2	Shows some good word choices; minimally stays focused on persuasive task.	Uses inconsistent organizational strategy; presentation is not logical.	Provides several reasons, but few are elaborated; only one elaborated reason.	Incorporates few transitions; includes many mechanical errors.
1	Shows lack of attention to persuasive task.	Demonstrates lack of organizational strategy.	Provides no specific reasons or does not elaborate.	Does not connect ideas; includes many mechanical errors.

Rubric With a 6-point Scale

The following analytic rubric is an example of a rubric to assess a persuasive essay. It will help you evaluate presentation, position, evidence, and arguments.

	Presentation	Position	Evidence	Arguments
6	Essay clearly and effectively addresses an issue with more than one side.	Essay clearly states a supportable position on the issue.	All evidence is logically organized, well presented, and supports the position.	All reader concerns and counterarguments are effectively addressed.
5	Most of essay addresses an issue that has more than one side.	Essay clearly states a position on the issue.	Most evidence is logically organized, well presented, and supports the position.	Most reader concerns and counterarguments are effectively addressed.
4	Essay adequately addresses issue that has more than one side.	Essay adequately states a position on the issue.	Many parts of evidence support the position; some evidence is out of order.	Many reader concerns and counterarguments are adequately addressed.
3	Essay addresses issue with two sides but does not present second side clearly.	Essay states a position on the issue, but the position is difficult to support.	Some evidence supports the position, but some evidence is out of order.	Some reader concerns and counterarguments are addressed.
2	Essay addresses issue with two sides but does not present second side.	Essay states a position on the issue, but the position is not supportable.	Not much evidence supports the position, and what is included is out of order.	A few reader concerns and counterarguments are addressed.
1	Essay does not address issue with more than one side.	Essay does not state a position on the issue.	No evidence supports the position.	No reader concerns or counterarguments are addressed.

Sample Holistic Rubric

Holistic rubrics such as this one are sometimes used to assess writing assignments on standardized tests. Notice that the criteria for evaluation are focus, organization, support, and use of conventions.

Points	Criteria
6 Points	• The writing is strongly focused and shows fresh insight into the writing task. • The writing is marked by a sense of completeness and coherence and is organized with a logical progression of ideas. • A main idea is fully developed, and support is specific and substantial. • A mature command of the language is evident, and the writing may employ characteristic creative writing strategies. • Sentence structure is varied, and writing is free of all but purposefully used fragments. • Virtually no errors in writing conventions appear.
5 Points	• The writing is clearly focused on the task. • The writing is well organized and has a logical progression of ideas, though there may be occasional lapses. • A main idea is well developed and supported with relevant detail. • Sentence structure is varied, and the writing is free of fragments, except when used purposefully. • Writing conventions are followed correctly.
4 Points	• The writing is clearly focused on the task, but extraneous material may intrude at times. • Clear organizational pattern is present, though lapses may occur. • A main idea is adequately supported, but development may be uneven. • Sentence structure is generally fragment free but shows little variation. • Writing conventions are generally followed correctly.
3 Points	• Writing is generally focused on the task, but extraneous material may intrude at times. • An organizational pattern is evident, but writing may lack a logical progression of ideas. • Support for the main idea is generally present but is sometimes illogical. • Sentence structure is generally free of fragments, but there is almost no variation. • The work generally demonstrates a knowledge of writing conventions, with occasional misspellings.
2 Points	• The writing is related to the task but generally lacks focus. • There is little evidence of organizational pattern, and there is little sense of cohesion. • Support for the main idea is generally inadequate, illogical, or absent. • Sentence structure is unvaried, and serious errors may occur. • Errors in writing conventions and spellings are frequent.
1 Point	• The writing may have little connection to the task and is generally unfocused. • There has been little attempt at organization or development. • The paper seems fragmented, with no clear main idea. • Sentence structure is unvaried, and serious errors appear. • Poor word choice and poor command of the language obscure meaning. • Errors in writing conventions and spelling are frequent.
Unscorable	The paper is considered unscorable if: • The response is unrelated to the task or is simply a rewording of the prompt. • The response has been copied from a published work. • The student did not write a response. • The response is illegible. • The words in the response are arranged with no meaning. • There is an insufficient amount of writing to score.

Student Model

Persuasive Writing

This persuasive essay, which would receive a top score according to a persuasive rubric, is a response to the following writing prompt, or assignment:

Most young people today spend more than 5 hours a day watching television. Many adults worry about the effects on youth of seeing too much television violence. Write a persuasive piece in which you argue against or defend the effects of television watching on young people. Be sure to include examples to support your views.

Until the television was invented, families spent their time doing different activities. Now most families stay home and watch TV. Watching TV risks the family's health, reduces the children's study time, and is a bad influence on young minds. Watching television can be harmful.

> The writer clearly states a position in the first paragraph.

The most important reason why watching TV is bad is that the viewers get less exercise. For example, instead of watching their favorite show, people could get exercise for 30 minutes. If people spent less time watching TV and more time exercising, then they could have healthier bodies. My mother told me a story about a man who died of a heart attack because he was out of shape from watching television all the time. Obviously, watching TV put a person's health in danger.

> Each paragraph provides details that support the writer's main point.

Furthermore, watching television reduces childern's study time. For example, children would spend more time studying if they didn't watch television. If students spent more time studying at home, then they would make better grades at school. Last week I had a major test in science, but I didn't study because I started watching a movie. I was not prepared for the test and my grade reflected my lack of studying. Indeed, watching television is bad because it can hurt a student's grades.

Finally, watching TV can be a bad influence on children. For example, some TV shows have inappropriate language and too much violence. If children watch programs that use bad language and show violence, then they may start repeating these actions because they think the behavior is "cool." In fact, it has been proven that children copy what they see on TV. Clearly, watching TV is bad for children and its affects children's behavior.

In conclusion, watching television is a bad influence for these reasons: It reduces people's exercise time and students' study time and it shows children inappropriate behavior. Therefore, people should take control of their lives and stop allowing television to harm them.

> The conclusion restates the writer's position.

Grammar, Usage, and Mechanics Handbook

Parts of Speech

Nouns A **noun** is the name of a person, place, or thing. A **common noun** names any one of a class of people, places, or things. A **proper noun** names a specific person, place, or thing.

A collective noun is a noun that names a group of individual people or things.

A compound noun is a noun made up of two or more words.

Pronouns A **pronoun** is a word that stands for a noun or for a word that takes the place of a noun.

A **personal pronoun** refers to (1) the person speaking, (2) the person spoken to, or (3) the person, place, or thing spoken about.

	Singular	*Plural*
First Person	I, me, my, mine	we, us, our, ours
Second Person	you, your, yours	you, your, yours
Third Person	he, him, his, she, her, hers, it, its	they, them, their, theirs

A **demonstrative pronoun** directs attention to a specific person, place, or thing.

> *These* are the juiciest pears I have ever tasted.

An **interrogative pronoun** is used to begin a question.

> *Who* is the author of "Jeremiah's Song"?

An **indefinite pronoun** refers to a person, place, or thing, often without specifying which one.

> *Everyone* bought something.

A relative pronoun begins a subordinate clause and connects it to another idea in the same sentence. There are five relative pronouns: *that, which, who, whom, whose.*

Verbs A **verb** is a word that expresses time while showing an action, a condition, or the fact that something exists. An **action verb** indicates the action of someone or something. A **linking verb** connects the subject of a sentence with a noun or a pronoun that renames or describes the subject. A **helping verb** can be added to another verb to make a single verb phrase. An **action verb** is transitive if the receiver of the action is named in the sentence. The receiver of the action is called the object of the verb.

Adjectives An **adjective** describes a noun or a pronoun or gives a noun or a pronoun a more specific meaning. Adjectives answer the questions *what kind, which one, how many,* or *how much.*

The articles *the, a,* and *an* are adjectives. *An* is used before a word beginning with a vowel sound.

A noun may sometimes be used as an adjective.

> *family* home   *science* fiction

Adverbs An **adverb** modifies a verb, an adjective, or another adverb. Adverbs answer the questions *where, when, in what way,* or *to what extent.*

Prepositions A **preposition** relates a noun or a pronoun following it to another word in the sentence.

Conjunctions A **conjunction** connects other words or groups of words. A **coordinating conjunction** connects similar kinds or groups of words. **Correlative conjunctions** are used in pairs to connect similar words or groups of words.

> *both* Grandpa *and* Dad   *neither* they *nor* I

Interjections An **interjection** is a word that expresses feeling or emotion and functions independently of a sentence.

Phrases, Clauses, and Sentences

Sentences A **sentence** is a group of words with two main parts: a complete subject and a complete predicate. Together, these parts express a complete thought.

A **fragment** is a group of words that does not express a complete thought.

Subject The **subject** of a sentence is the word or group of words that tells whom or what the sentence is about. The **simple subject** is the essential noun, pronoun, or group of words acting as a noun that cannot be left out of the complete subject. A **complete subject** is the simple subject plus any modifiers.

A **compound subject** is two or more subjects that have the same verb and are joined by a conjunction.

> Neither the *horse nor the driver* looked tired.

Predicate The **predicate** of a sentence is the verb or verb phrase that tells what the complete subject of the sentence does or is. The **simple predicate** is the essential verb or verb phrase that cannot be left out of the complete predicate. A **complete predicate** is the simple predicate plus any modifiers or complements.

A **compound predicate** is two or more verbs that have the same subject and are joined by a conjunction.

> She *sneezed and coughed* throughout the trip.

Complement A **complement** is a word or group of words that completes the meaning of the predicate of a sentence. Five different kinds of complements can be found in English sentences: *direct objects, indirect objects, objective complements, predicate nominatives,* and *predicate adjectives.*

A **direct object** is a noun, pronoun, or group of words acting as a noun that receives the action of a transitive verb.

We watched the *liftoff.*

An **indirect object** is a noun, pronoun, or group of words that appears with a direct object and names the person or thing that something is given to or done for.

He sold the *family* a mirror.

An **objective complement** is an adjective or noun that appears with a direct object and describes or renames it.

I called Meg my *friend.*

A **subject complement** is a noun, pronoun, or adjective that appears with a linking verb and tells something about the subject. A subject complement may be a *predicate nominative* or a *predicate adjective.*

A **predicate nominative** is a noun or pronoun that appears with a linking verb and renames, identifies, or explains the subject.

Kiglo was the *leader.*

A **predicate adjective** is an adjective that appears with a linking verb and describes the subject of a sentence.

Roko became *tired.*

Sentence Types A **simple sentence** consists of a single independent clause.

A **compound sentence** consists of two or more independent clauses joined by a comma and a coordinating conjunction or by a semicolon.

A **complex sentence** consists of one independent clause and one or more subordinate clauses.

A **compound-complex sentence** consists of two or more independent clauses and one or more subordinate clauses.

A **declarative sentence** states an idea and ends with a period.

An **interrogative sentence** asks a question and ends with a question mark.

An **imperative sentence** gives an order or a direction and ends with either a period or an exclamation mark.

An **exclamatory sentence** conveys a strong emotion and ends with an exclamation mark.

Phrases A **phrase** is a group of words, without a subject and a verb, that functions in a sentence as one part of speech.

A **prepositional phrase** is a group of words that includes a preposition and a noun or a pronoun that is the object of the preposition.

An **adjective phrase** is a prepositional phrase that modifies a noun or a pronoun by telling *what kind* or *which one.*

An **adverb phrase** is a prepositional phrase that modifies a verb, an adjective, or an adverb by pointing out *where, when, in what manner,* or *to what extent.*

An **appositive phrase** is a noun or a pronoun with modifiers, placed next to a noun or a pronoun to add information and details.

A **participial phrase** is a participle modified by an adjective or an adverb phrase or accompanied by a complement. The entire phrase acts as an adjective.

Running at top speed, he soon caught up with them.

An **infinitive phrase** is an infinitive with modifiers, complements, or a subject, all acting together as a single part of speech.

At first I was too busy enjoying my food *to notice how the guests were doing.*

Gerunds A **gerund** is a noun formed from the present participle of a verb by adding *–ing.* Like other nouns, gerunds can be used as subjects, direct objects, predicate nouns, and objects of prepositions.

Gerund Phrases A **gerund phrase** is a gerund with modifiers or a complement, all acting together as a noun.

Clauses A **clause** is a group of words with its own subject and verb.

An **independent clause** can stand by itself as a complete sentence.

A **subordinate clause** has a subject and a verb but cannot stand by itself as a complete sentence; it can only be part of a sentence.

Using Verbs, Pronouns, and Modifiers

Principal Parts A **verb** has four **principal parts:** the *present,* the *present participle,* the *past,* and the *past participle.*

Regular verbs form the past and past participle by adding *-ed* to the present form.

Irregular verbs form the past and past participle by changing form rather than by adding *-ed.*

Verb Tense A **verb tense** tells whether the time of an action or condition is in the past, the present, or the future. Every verb has six tenses: *present, past, future, present perfect, past perfect,* and *future perfect.*

The **present tense** shows actions that happen in the present. The **past tense** shows actions that have already happened. The **future tense** shows actions that will happen. The **present perfect tense** shows actions that begin in the past and continue to the present. The **past perfect tense** shows a past action or condition that ended before another past action. The **future perfect tense** shows a future action or condition that will have ended before another begins.

Pronoun Case The **case** of a pronoun is the form it takes to show its use in a sentence. There are three pronoun cases: *nominative, objective,* and *possessive.*

The **nominative case** is used to name or rename the subject of the sentence. The nominative case pronouns are *I, you, he, she, it, we, you, they.*

The **objective case** is used as the direct object, indirect object, or object of a preposition. The objective case pronouns are *me, you, him, her, it, us, you, them.*

The **possessive case** is used to show ownership. The possessive pronouns are *my, your, his, her, its, our, their, mine, yours, his, hers, its, ours, theirs.*

Subject-Verb Agreement To make a subject and a verb agree, make sure that both are singular or both are plural. Two or more singular subjects joined by *or* or *nor* must have a singular verb. When singular and plural subjects are joined by *or* or *nor,* the verb must agree with the closest subject.

Pronoun-Antecedent Agreement Pronouns must agree with their antecedents in number and gender. Use singular pronouns with singular antecedents and plural pronouns with plural antecedents. Many errors in pronoun-antecedent agreement occur when a plural pronoun is used to refer to a singular antecedent for which the gender is not specified.

Incorrect: Everyone did their best.

Correct: Everyone did his or her best.

The following indefinite pronouns are singular: *anybody, anyone, each, either, everybody, everyone, neither, nobody, no one, one, somebody, someone.*

The following indefinite pronouns are plural: *both, few, many, several.*

The following indefinite pronouns may be either singular or plural: *all, any, most, none, some.*

Modifiers The **comparative** and **superlative** degrees of most adjectives and adverbs of one or two syllables can be formed in either of two ways: Use *–er* or *more* to form a comparative degree and *–est* or *most* to form the superlative degree of most one- and two-syllable modifiers. These endings are added to the *positive,* or base, form of the word.

More and *most* can also be used to form the comparative and superlative degrees of most one- and two-syllable modifiers. These words should not be used when the result sounds awkward, as in "A greyhound is *more fast* than a beagle."

Glossary of Common Usage

accept, except: *Accept* is a verb that means "to receive" or "to agree to." *Except* is usually used as a preposition that means "other than" or "leaving out." Do not confuse these two words.

affect, effect: *Affect* is normally a verb meaning "to influence" or "to bring about a change in." *Effect* is usually a noun, meaning "result."

among, between: *Among* is usually used with three or more items. *Between* is generally used with only two items.

bad, badly: Use the predicate adjective *bad* after linking verbs such as *feel, look,* and *seem.* Use *badly* whenever an adverb is required.

beside, besides: *Beside* means "at the side of" or "close to." *Besides* means "in addition to."

can, may: The verb *can* generally refers to the ability to do something. The verb *may* generally refers to permission to do something.

different from, different than: *Different from* is generally preferred over *different than.*

farther, further: Use *farther* when you refer to distance. Use *further* when you mean "to a greater degree or extent" or "additional."

fewer, less: Use *fewer* for things that can be counted. Use *less* for amounts or quantities that cannot be counted.

good, well: Use the predicate adjective *good* after linking verbs such as *feel, look, smell, taste,* and *seem.* Use *well* whenever you need an adverb.

its, it's: The word *its* with no apostrophe is a possessive pronoun. The word *it's* is a contraction for *it is.* Do not confuse the possessive pronoun *its* with the contraction *it's,* standing for "it is" or "it has."

lay, lie: Do not confuse these verbs. *Lay* is a transitive verb meaning "to set or put something down." Its principal parts are *lay, laying, laid, laid. Lie* is an intransitive verb meaning "to recline." Its principal parts are *lie, lying, lay, lain.*

like, as: *Like* is a preposition that usually means "similar to" or "in the same way as." *Like* should always be followed by an object. Do not use *like* before a subject and a verb. Use *as* or *that* instead.

of, have: Do not use *of* in place of *have* after auxiliary verbs like *would, could, should, may, might,* or *must.*

raise, rise: *Raise* is a transitive verb that usually takes a direct object. *Rise* is intransitive and never takes a direct object.

set, sit: *Set* is a transitive verb meaning "to put (something) in a certain place." Its principal parts are *set, setting, set, set. Sit* is an intransitive verb meaning "to be seated." Its principal parts are *sit, sitting, sat, sat.*

than, then: The conjunction *than* is used to connect the two parts of a comparison. Do not confuse *than* with the adverb *then,* which usually refers to time.

that, which, who: Use the relative pronoun *that* to refer to things or people. Use *which* only for things and *who* only for people.

when, where, why: Do not use *when, where,* or *why* directly after a linking verb such as *is.* Reword the sentence.

Faulty: Suspense is *when* an author increases the reader's tension.

Revised: An author uses suspense to increase the reader's tension.

who, whom: In formal writing, remember to use *who* only as a subject in clauses and sentences and *whom* only as an object.

Capitalization and Punctuation

Capitalization

1. Capitalize the first word of a sentence.
2. Capitalize all proper nouns and adjectives.
3. Capitalize a person's title when it is followed by the person's name or when it is used in direct address.
4. Capitalize titles showing family relationships when they refer to a specific person, unless they are preceded by a possessive noun or pronoun.
5. Capitalize the first word and all other key words in the titles of books, periodicals, poems, stories, plays, paintings, and other works of art.
6. Capitalize the first word and all nouns in letter salutations and the first word in letter closings.

Punctuation

End Marks

1. Use a **period** to end a declarative sentence, an imperative sentence, and most abbreviations.
2. Use a **question mark** to end a direct question or an incomplete question in which the rest of the question is understood.
3. Use an **exclamation mark** after a statement showing strong emotion, an urgent imperative sentence, or an interjection expressing strong emotion.

Commas

1. Use a comma before the conjunction to separate two independent clauses in a compound sentence.
2. Use commas to separate three or more words, phrases, or clauses in a series.
3. Use commas to separate adjectives of equal rank. Do not use commas to separate adjectives that must stay in a specific order.
4. Use a comma after an introductory word, phrase, or clause.
5. Use commas to set off parenthetical and nonessential expressions.

6. Use commas with places and dates made up of two or more parts.
7. Use commas after items in addresses, after the salutation in a personal letter, after the closing in all letters, and in numbers of more than three digits.

Semicolons

1. Use a semicolon to join independent clauses that are not already joined by a conjunction.
2. Use a semicolon to join independent clauses or items in a series that already contain commas.

Colons

1. Use a colon before a list of items following an independent clause.
2. Use a colon in numbers giving the time, in salutations in business letters, and in labels used to signal important ideas.

Quotation Marks

1. A **direct quotation** represents a person's exact speech or thoughts and is enclosed in quotation marks.
2. An **indirect quotation** reports only the general meaning of what a person said or thought and does not require quotation marks.
3. Always place a comma or a period inside the final quotation mark of a direct quotation.
4. Place a question mark or an exclamation mark inside the final quotation mark if the end mark is part of the quotation; if it is not part of the quotation, place it outside the final quotation mark.

Titles

1. Underline or italicize the titles of long written works, movies, television and radio shows, lengthy works of music, paintings, and sculptures.
2. Use quotation marks around the titles of short written works, episodes in a series, songs, and titles of works mentioned as parts of collections.

Hyphens Use a **hyphen** with certain numbers, after certain prefixes, with two or more words used as one word, and with a compound modifier that comes before a noun.

Apostrophes

1. Add an **apostrophe** and *s* to show the possessive case of most singular nouns.
2. Add an apostrophe to show the possessive case of plural nouns ending in *s* and *es.*
3. Add an apostrophe and *s* to show the possessive case of plural nouns that do not end in *s* or *es.*
4. Use an apostrophe in a contraction to indicate the position of the missing letter or letters.

Index of Skills

Note: Page numbers in **boldface** refer to pages where terms are defined.

Literary Analysis

Action, **806, 808**
   drama, 809, 810
   rising/falling, **25,** 39, 51, **R18**

Adaptation, **836,** 838, 841

Advertisement, R24

Alliteration, **641, 651,** 659, 667, **R13**

Allusion, **640, 715,** 725, 737, **R13**

American folk hero, **1011**

Analogy, **17, 640, 772,** 779, **1166, R13**
   autobiography, 19
   nonfiction book, 20

Analytic rubric, **R36, R37**

Anecdote , **17,** 22, **105, R13**

Antagonist, **R13**

Appeals, types, **555**

Argument, lxxii, lxxiii, 3, 82, 182, 461, 500,
   525, 528, 554, 571, 572, 592, 614, 616,
   618, 626, 630
   elements, lxviii
   rhetorical devices and persuasive
   techniques, lxx
   types of, R24

Assonance, **641**

Atmosphere, **R13**

Attitudes, 157, 168, 177

Author's influences, **1111,** 1115, 1119,
   1124, 1129, **R13**

Author's point of view, 462, **464, 466**

Author's purpose, **7, 111,** 462
   journal, 472

Author's style, **R13**
   fiction/nonfiction, 116, **157,** 161, 163,
   164, 165, 169, 173, 175, 177
   poetry, **741**

Autobiographical writing, **R25**

Autobiography, 5, **501,** 516, 519, 521, 523,
   R13

Ballad, **639,** 1048

Bandwagon/anti-bandwagon approach, **lxx**

Beliefs, 157, 168, 177

Bibliography, **R34**

Biography, **501,** 507, 509, 511, **R13**

Bloggers, **R28**

Blogs, **R28, R29**

Book reviews, **R25**

Business letter, **842, 844, R25, R27**

Cause-and-effect essay, **1156, R24**

Cause-and-effect organization, **534,** 547
   drama, 807

Central idea, **4,** 7, 462, **464**
   autobiography, 19
   journal, 472
   nonfiction book, 22, 467
   stated and implied, 17

Chain of events, **234**

Character, 4, 8, **232,** 235, 236, 1013, 1014,
   R13
   development, 5
   of different eras, 190, 194, 196, 198,
   199, 201, 202, 203, 204, 206, 207
   drama, 804, 806, 807, 808, 810, 811,
   815, 819, 820, 825
   fiction, 4, 5, 6, 14
   folk literature, 1013, 1014
   heroic, 1070, 1072, 1074, 1076, 1081,
   1082, 1083
   narrative, 312
   novel, 1015, 1017
   short story, 232, 235, **236,** 237, 239,
   241, 242, 300, 1018, 1019, 1020

Characterization, **5, 232,** 234, **R13**
   direct, **234**
   indirect, **234**

Character's motivation, **R16**
   drama, **806,** 807, 808, **917,** 920, 922,
   924, 929, 934, 938, 940, 941, 944, 948,
   953, 954, 957
   short story, 232

Character traits, 232, **277,** 282, 285, 286,
   289, 291, 296, 298, 301, 302, 303, **R13**

Charged or loaded words. *See* Loaded words

Chronological order/organization, **86,** 103,
   234, **462, 534,** 547, **549**

Claim (assertion), lxviii

Climax, **25,** 39, 51, 233, 804, **R13**
   plot, **233, R18**

Comedy, **R14**
   drama, **805**

Comic relief, **805**

Comparison-and-contrast essay, **780, R24**

Comparison-and-contrast organization,
   534, 547

Comparison of works, **R25**

Complex character
   drama, 807

Concrete poem, **R14**

Conflict, 4, 8, 232, 236, 1013, 1014, **R14**
   Can all conflicts be resolved?, **230,** 446
   drama, 804, 806
   fiction, 4, **25,** 39, 51, **55,** 61, 63, 68, 73,
   74, 77
   folk literature, 1013, 1014
   internal/external, **232,** 804, **806, R14**
   novel, 9, 10, 1015
   plot, **R18**
   short story, 13, 14, 16, **232, 235, 236,** 237,
   238, 241, 242

Connotation, 464, **573,** 579, 587, 641, 642, **R14**
   poetry, 642, 645, 648

Consonance, **641**

Context, **624**

Craft and structure, lxvi, 23, 243, 473,
   643, 813, 1021

Creative writing, **R25**

Critical review, **326**

Cultural connection chart, 1023

Cultural context, 1010, 1012, **1091,** 1095,
   1098, 1099, 1101, 1106, 1107

Denotation, 464, **573,** 641, **R14**

Description, **R14, R24**
   poetry, **772,** 775, 777, 778, 779

Descriptive essay, **104**

Descriptive writing, 463, **772, R24**

Dialect, **1010,** 1011, **1039, R14**

Dialogue, 234, 236, 462, **804,** 806, 808,
   849, 857, 858, 860, 864, 865, 867, 872,
   873, 876, 877, 879, 880, 887, 893, 895,
   896, 898, 899, 901, 905, 906, 909, 912,
   913, **R14**
   drama, 808, 809, 811
   short story, 237, 238, 239, 240, 241

Diction, **R14, R20**

Direct characterization, **234**

Directions, **5**

Drama, **804, R14, R25**
   analyzing, 806–807
   elements/types, **804, 805,** 806

Dramatic irony, 807

Dramatic poetry, **639**

Reading for Information

Reading Skills

Writing Strategies

Prewriting:

Emotional appeals, use, 616
Emotions, describe, 155, 179, 210
Events, order, 210
Evidence, present supporting, 155, 1131
Examples, organize, 106
Flashbacks, use, 440
Focus, find/define, 328
Foreshadowing, use, 440
Format, use appropriate, 79, 550, 710, 782, 844, 1109
Formatting techniques, use, 550
Graphs, create, 986
Ideas
    balance research with, 985
    focus/organize, 1158
    include important, 155
    show progression, 499
Inferences, make, 328
Interest, develop, 210
Libel, avoid, 616
Main idea
    apply to own experience, 589
    develop/support, 179, 499, 525, 985
Many causes/single effect, use, 1158
Maps, create/label, 986
MLA style, use, **R35**
Modified block format, use, **R27**
Mood, create appropriate, 1037
Notes, use, 739
Opinion, state/support, 571, 763
Organization, select/use consistent, 328, 782
Outcome, explain, 155
Outline, make, 985, 1086
Parallelism, use, 616, 782
Paraphrase, 986
Persuasive techniques, use, 616, 959
Photographs, add captions, 986
Plot devices, use, 440
Point, make your, 844
Point-by-point organization, use, 782
Point of view, use consistent, 210
Problem, identify/resolve, 155, 210, 1037
Purpose, state, 79
Quotations, use, 106, 499, 984
References, support with, 763
Repetition, add, 616, 1131
Research, balance with ideas, 985
Response, identify, 328
SEE method, use, 782
Single cause/many effects, use, 1158
Solution, discuss evidence and steps, 155
Solution, promote your, 710
Sources, credit, 985, 986, **R34, R35**
Summarize, 986
Support, offer, 710
Tables, create, 986
Theme, state/restate, 405
Thesis, define/outline, 985, 1086

Thesis statement, write, 525, 615, 985, 1109
Tone, use appropriate, 79, 1131
Transitions, use, 499
Visuals, create, 986
Word choice, consider, 669, 1037
Works cited list, create, 986

Revising:
Action verbs, include, 442
Analogy, support with, 618
Appeals, strengthen, 618
Appositive phrases, use, 1086, 1160
Arguments, strengthen/support, 618
Audience, consider, 618, 710, 1086, 1087, 1160
Characters, add detail, 442
Citations, check, 988
Coherence, improve, 618
Comparatives, fix faulty, 551
Completeness, check for, 328
Conciseness, improve, 844
Conclusion, modify/check, 550, 988
Conjunctions, join with, 619
Connections, show, 1160
Consistency, check, 328
Description, replace dull, 739
Details, add/delete, 442, 784
Dialogue, add rhythm/emotion, 442
Ideas, develop, 710
Information, look for missing, 550
Interjections, include, 442
Introduction, add interest with, 550
Key terms, define, 1160
Language devices, use creative, 275
Main idea, identify, 988
Nouns, fix/replace, 107, 212
Organization/structure, check, 784
Parallelism, include, 784
Peer review, use, 212, 442, 618, 784, 988, 1160
Pronoun-antecedent agreement, fix, 213
Proofread, use symbols, **R34**
Questions, answer, 328
Reader concerns, anticipate, 710
Sentences
    check for variety, 212
    combine, 619, 845, 989
    eliminate unnecessary, 988
    fix fragment/run-on, 1161
    fix repetitive, 785
    vary length/type, 1087
Subject/verb agreement, fix faulty, 443
Superlatives, fix faulty, 551
Support, fill gaps in, 1160
Thesaurus, use, 275
Thesis statement, check, 988
Topic sentence, add, 988
Transitions, use, 618, 988, 1087, 1160
Troubleshooting guide, add, 550

Unity, check, 988
Verbs, fix/replace, 212, 329
Voice, evaluate, 106, 711
Word choice, evaluate/fix, 618, 739, 844, 1087

Editing/Proofreading:
Adjectives, focus on, 109, 553
Citations, focus on, 993
Colons/commas, use in series, 787
Dialogue, punctuate, 215
Double negatives, focus on, 621
Homophones, spell, 713
Plurals, spell, 847
Point of view, maintain consistent, 445
Prepositions, focus on, 1163
Semicolons, use in series, 787
Sentences, focus on, 445
Series, focus on items in, 787
Standard English, use, 1089
Subject/verb agreement, review for, 445
Words, check commonly misspelled, 109, 331

Publishing/Presenting:
Audience, share report with, 993
Book talk, present, 331
Column, publish, 787
Comic strip, make, 215
Demonstration day, plan, 553
Family tradition, start, 787
Feature article, publish, 1163
Forum, organize, 621
Ideas, post, 713
Letter, share/send, 847
Newspaper, publish in, 621
Photo scrapbook, make, 109
Presentation
    deliver, 1089
    offer to organization, 1089
    prepare, 109
Short story, submit/tell aloud, 445
Solution, implement, 713
Speech, present, 215, 993, 1163
Storytelling, present, 215
"Teens Review" column, publish, 331
Web page, make, 553

Reflecting on Writing (Writer's journal):
Autobiographical essay, 215
Business letter, 847
Cause-and-effect essay, 1163
Comparison-and-contrast essay, 787
Critical review, 331
Descriptive essay, 109
Editorial, 621
How-to essay, 553
Multimedia report, 1089
Problem-and-solution essay, 713
Research report, 993
Short story, 445

More Skills...
Critical Thinking

Critical Viewing

Listening And Speaking

Index of Features

Notes: Page numbers in *italics* refer to biographical information. Nonfiction appears in red.

Grateful acknowledgment is made to the following for copyrighted material:

English—Language Arts Content Standards for California Public Schools reproduced by permission, California Department of Education, CD Press, 1430 N Street, Suite 3207, Sacramento, CA 95814.

Arte Publico Press From *My Own True Name* by Pat Mora. Copyright © 2000 Arte Publico Press-University of Houston. Published by Arte Publico Press. "Baseball" by Lionel G. Garcia from *I Can Hear the Cowbells Ring* (Houston: Arte Publico Press - University of Houston, 1994). Used by permission.

Ashabranner, Brent "Always to Remember: The Vision of Maya Ying Lin" by Brent Ashabranner from *Always to Remember*. Copyright © 1988. Used by permission of Brent Ashabranner.

The Bancroft Library, Administrative Offices "Tears of Autumn" from *The Forbidden Stitch: An Asian American Women's Anthology* by Yoshiko Uchida. Copyright © 1989 by Yoshiko Uchida. Used by permission of the Bancroft Library, University of California, Berkeley.

Bantam Doubleday Dell Publishing Group, Inc. "A Wrinkle in Time" by Madeleine L'Engle Franklin from *Dell Publishing*. Copyright © 1962 by Madeleine L'Engle Franklin. All rights reserved.

Berkley Books From *A Small Enough Team to Do the Job* by Andrew Mishkin from *Sojourner*. Copyright © 2003 by Andrew Mishkin.

Black Issues Book Review "Zora Neale Hurston: A Life in Letters, Book Review" by Zakia Carter from *Black Issues Book Review, Nov-Dec 2002;* www.bibookreview.com. Used by permission.

Brandt & Hochman Literary Agents, Inc. "Invocation" from John Brown's Body by Stephen Vincent Benet Copyright © 1927, 1928 by Stephen Vincent Benet. Copyright renewed © 1955 by Rosemary Carr Benet. Any electronic copying or redistribution of the text is expressly forbidden. Used by permission of Brandt & Hochman Literary Agents, Inc.

Curtis Brown London "Who Can Replace a Man" by Brian Aldiss from *Masterpieces: The Best Science Fiction of the Century*. Copyright © 1966 by Brian Aldiss. Reproduced with permission of Curtis Brown Group Ltd, London on behalf of Brian Aldiss.

Charlotte Observer "The Season's Curmudgeon Sees the Light" by Mary C. Curtis *www.charlotte.com*. © Copyright 2004 Knight Ridder. All Rights Reserved. Used by permission.

Child Health Association of Sewickley, Inc. "Thumbprint Cookies" from *Three Rivers Cookbook*. Copyright © Child Health Association of Sewickley, Inc. Used by permission.

Clarion Books, a division of Houghton Mifflin Excerpt from "Emancipation" from *Lincoln: A Photobiography*. Copyright © 1987 by Russell Freedman. Reproduced by permission of Clarion Books, an imprint of Houghton Mifflin Company.

Jonathan Clowes Ltd. "The Adventure of the Speckled Band" from *The Adventure Of The Speckled Band*. Copyright © 1996 Sir Arthur Conan Doyle Copyright Holders. Used with kind permission of Jonathan Clowes Ltd., London, on behalf of Andrea Plunket, the Administrator of the Conan Doyle Copyrights.

Ruth Cohen Literary Agency, Inc. "Fox Hunt" by Lensey Namioka, copyright © 1993 from *Join In: Multi-Ethnic Short Stories by Outstanding Writers for Young Adults*, edited by Donald R. Gallo. Used by permission of Lensey Namioka. All rights are reserved by the Author.

Don Congdon Associates, Inc. "The Drummer Boy of Shiloh" by Ray Bradbury published in *Saturday Evening Post April 30, 1960*. Copyright © 1960 by the Curtis Publishing Company, renewed © 1988 by Ray Bradbury.

Copper Canyon Press c/o The Permissions Company "Snake on the Etowah" by David Bottoms from *Armored Hearts: Selected and New Poems*. Copyright © 1995 by David Bottoms. Used by the permission of Copper Canyon Press, www.copppercanyonpress.org. All rights reserved.

Gary N. DaSilva for Neil Simon "The Governess" from *The Good Doctor* © 1974 by Neil Simon. Copyright renewed © 2002 by Neil Simon. Used by permission. CAUTION: Professionals and amateurs are hereby warned that *The Good Doctor* is fully protected under the Berne Convention and the Universal Copyright Convention and is subject to royalty. All rights, including without limitation professional, amateur, motion picture, television, radio, recitation, lecturing, public reading and foreign translation rights, computer media rights and the right of reproduction, and electronic storage or retrieval, in whole or in part and in any form, are strictly reserved and none of these rights can be exercised or used without written permission from the copyright owner. Inquiries for stock and amateur performances should be addressed to Samuel French, Inc., 45 West 25th Street, New York, NY 10010. All other inquiries should be addressed to Gary N. DaSilva, 111 N. Sepulveda Blvd., Suite 250, Manhattan Beach, CA 90266-6850.

Disney-Hyperion Books for Children "Words We Live By: Your Annotated Guide to the Constitution" by Linda R. Monk from *The Stonesong Press*. Copyright © 2003 Linda R. Monk and The Stonesong Press, Inc. All rights reserved.

Doubleday "Table of Contents and Index Page" from *Zora Neale Hurston: A Life In Letters* Carla Kaplan. From *The Diary of a Young Girl: The Definitive Edition* by Anne Frank, edited by Otto H. Frank and Mirjam Pressler. Translated by Susan Massotty. Copyright © 1995 by Doubleday, a division of Random House, Inc. Used by permission of Doubleday, a division of Random House, Inc.

Dramatic Publishing From *Anne Frank & Me* by Cherie Bennett with Jeff Gottesfeld. Copyright © 1997 by Cherie Bennett. Printed in the United States of America. Used by permission. CAUTION: Professionals and amateurs are hereby warned that *Anne Frank & Me*, being fully protected under the copyright Laws of the United States of America, the British Empire, including the Dominion of Canada, and all other countries of the Universal Copyright and Berne Conventions, are subject to royalty. All rights, including professional, amateur, motion picture, recitation, lecturing, public reading, radio and television broadcasting, and the rights of translation into foreign languages, are strictly reserved. All inquiries regarding performance rights should be addressed to Dramatic Publishing, 311 Washington St., Woodstock, IL 60098. Phone: (815) 338-7170. All rights reserved. Used by permission.

Farrar, Straus & Giroux, LLC "Little Exercise" from *The Complete Poems 1927-1979* by Elizabeth Bishop. Copyright © 1979, 1983 by Alice Helen Methfessel. "Charles" by Shirley Jackson from *The Lottery*. Copyright © 1948, 1949 by Shirley Jackson and copyright renewed © 1976, 1977 by Laurence Hyman, Barry Hyman, Mrs. Sarah Webster and Mrs. Joanne Schnurer. "La Poesia" from *Isla Negra* by Pablo Neruda, translated by Alastair Reid. Translation copyright © 1981 by Alastair Reid. CAUTION: Users are warned that this work is protected under copyright laws and downloading is strictly prohibited. The right to reproduce or transfer the work via any medium must be secured with Farrar, Straus and Giroux, LLC. Used by permission of Farrar, Straus and Giroux, LLC.

Florida Holocaust Museum Florida Holocaust Museum Press Release from *www.flholocaustmuseum.org*. Copyright © Florida Holocaust Museum, 2001, 2005; All rights reserved. Used by permission.

Florida Senate Office Building "Senator Michael S. Bennett: Be a Sport: Professional Teams Should Pay Their Own Way and FL Senate Logo" from *http://www.flsenate.gov/cgi-bin/view_page*. Copyright © 2000-2006 State of Florida. Used by permission.

Katherine Froman "Easy Diver" by Robert Froman from *A Poke In The I*. Edited by Paul B. Janeczko. Used by permission of Katherine Froman on behalf of Robert Froman.

Richard Garcia "The City is So Big" by Richard Garcia from *The City Is So Big*.

Maxine Groffsky Literary Agency "The White Umbrella" by Gish Jen © 1984 by Gish Jen first published in *The Yale Review*. From the collection *Who's Irish?* by Gish Jen published in 1999 by Alfred A. Knopf. Used by permission of Maxine Groffsky Literary Agency, on behalf of the author.

Gutenberg Website Excerpt from "Narrative of the Life of Frederick Douglass: An American Slave" by Frederick Douglass. Copyright © 2011 *gutenberg.org*. All rights reserved.

Harcourt, Inc. "Choice: A Tribute to Martin Luther King, Jr." by Alice Walker from *In Search Of Our Mothers' Gardens: Womanist Prose*. Copyright © 1983 by Alice Walker. "For My Sister Molly Who in the Fifties" from *Revolutionary Petunias & Other Poems*, copyright © 1972 and renewed 2000 by Alice Walker. "Forest Fire" from *The Diary of Anais Nin 1947-1955, Volume V*. Copyright © 1974 by Anais Nin. Excerpt from *The People, Yes* by Carl Sandburg, copyright © 1936 by Harcourt, Inc. and renewed 1964 by Carl Sandburg. "Paul Bunyan of the North Woods" is excerpted from *The People, Yes* by Carl Sandburg, copyright © 1936 by Harcourt, Inc. and renewed 1964 by Carl Sandburg. This material may not be reproduced in any form or by any means without the prior written permission of the publisher. Used by permission of Harcourt, Inc.

HarperCollins Publishers "Brown vs. Board of Education" from *Now is Your Time: The African-American Struggle for Freedom* by Walter Dean Myers. Copyright © 1991 by Walter Dean Myers. From *An American Childhood* by Annie Dillard. Copyright © 1987 by Annie Dillard. "Why the Waves Have Whitecaps" from *Mules and Men* by Zora Neale Hurston. Copyright © 1935 by Zora Neale Hurston. Copyright renewed 1963 by John C. Hurston and Joel Hurston. Used by permission of HarperCollins Publishers. "A Poem for My Librarian, Mrs. Long" by Nikki Giovanni from Acolytes. Copyright © 2007 by Nikki Giovanni. All rights reserved.

Hill and Wang, a division of Farrar, Straus & Giroux "Thank You, M'am" from *Short Stories* by Langston Hughes. Copyright © 1996 by Ramona Bass and Arnold Rampersad. Used by permission of Hill and Wang, a division of Farrar, Straus and Giroux, LLC.

Gelston Hinds, Jr. o/b/o Amy Ling "Grandma Ling" by Amy Ling from *Bridge: An Asian American Perspective, Vol. 7, No. 3*. Copyright © 1980 by Amy Ling. Used by permission of the author's husband.

Holiday House "January" from *A Child's Calendar* by John Updike. Text copyright © 1965, 1999 by John Updike. All rights reserved. Used by permission of Holiday House, Inc.

Georgia Douglas Johnson "Your World" by Georgia Douglas Johnson from *American Negro Poetry*.

The Estate of Dr. Martin Luther King, Jr. c/o Writer's House LLC "The American Dream" by Dr. Martin Luther King, Jr. from *A Testament Of Hope: The Essential Writings Of Martin Luther King, Jr.* Copyright © 1961 Martin Luther King Jr.; Copyright © renewed 1989 Coretta Scott King. Used by arrangement with The Heirs to the Estate of Martin Luther King Jr., c/o Writers House as agent for the proprietor New York, N.Y.

Alfred A. Knopf, Inc. "Harlem Night Song" from *The Collected Poems of Langston Hughes* by Langston Hughes, edited by Arnold Rampersad with David Roessel, Associate Editor, copyright © 1994 by The Estate of Langston Hughes. From *Author's Note* by Patricia C. McKissack from *The Dark-Thirty*. Text copyright © 1992 by Patricia C. McKissack. "The Ninny" from *Image Of Chekhov* by Anton Chekhov, translated by Robert Payne, copyright © 1963 and renewed © 1991 by Alfred A. Knopf, Inc. "The 11:59" by Patricia C. McKissack from *The Dark Thirty* by Patricia McKissack illustrated by Brian Pinkney, copyright © 1992 by Patricia C. McKissack. Illustrations copyright © 1992 by Brian Pinkney. Used by permission of Alfred A. Knopf, a division of Random House, Inc.

Barbara S. Kouts Literary Agency "Ellis Island" by Joseph Bruchac from *The Remembered Earth*.

Life Magazine "Readjustment: A Life Photoessay" from *LIFE Magazine Vol. 19, No. 23 December 3, 1945*. Copyright © 1945 Life, Inc. Used by permission. All rights reserved.

Little, Brown and Company, Inc. "Ode to Enchanted Light" from *Odes to Opposites* by Pablo Neruda. Copyright © 1995 by Pablo Neruda and Fundacion Pablo Neruda (Odes in Spanish). Copyright © 1995 by Ken Krabbenhoft (Odes in English); Copyright © 1995 by Ferris Cook (Illustrations and Compilation). Used by permission of Little, Brown and Company. All rights reserved.

Liveright Publishing Corporation "your little voice/Over the wires came leaping" copyright © 1923, 1951, 1991 by the Trustees for the E. E. Cummings Trust. Copyright © 1976 by George James Firmage, from *Complete Poems: 1904-1962* by E. E. Cummings, edited by George J. Firmage. "Runagate Runagate" Copyright © 1966 by Robert Hayden, from *Collected Poems of Robert Hayden*, edited by Frederick Glaysher. This selection may not be reproduced, stored in a retrieval system, or transmitted in any form or by any means without prior written permission of the publisher. Used by permission of Liveright Publishing Corporation.

Robert MacNeil "The Trouble with Television" by Robert MacNeil condensed from a speech, *November 1984 at President Leadership Forum, SUNY*. Copyright © 1985 by Reader's Digest and Robert MacNeil. Used by permission of Robert MacNeil.

Eve Merriam c/o Marian Reiner "Thumbprint" from *A Sky Full of Poems* by Eve Merriam. Copyright © 1964, 1970, 1973, 1986 by Eve Merriam. Used by permission of Marian Reiner.

The Miami Herald Miami Herald Editorial: *Don't Refuse This Deal* from *Miami Herald Online Tuesday, March 29, 2005 http://capefish. blogspot.com/2005/03/miami-herald-editorial-dont-refuse.html*. Copyright © 2005 by McClatchy Interactive West. Used by permission of McClatchy Interactive West via Copyright Clearance Center.

N. Scott Momaday "New World" by N. Scott Momaday from *The Gourd Dancers*. Used with the permission of Navarre Scott Momaday.

William Morris Agency "Flowers for Algernon" (short story version edited for this edition) by Daniel Keyes. Copyright © 1959 & 1987 by Daniel Keyes. Expanded story published in paperback by Bantam Books. Used by permission of William Morris Agency, LLC on behalf of the author.

Scholastic Inc. From *Out of the Dust* ("Debts", "Fields of Flashing Light" and "Migrants") by Karen Hesse. Published by Scholastic Press/Scholastic Inc. Copyright © 1997 by Karen Hesse. "An Hour with Abuelo" from *An Island Like You: Stories of the Barrio* by Judith Ortiz Cofer. Published by Orchard Books/Scholastic Inc. Copyright © 1995 by Judith Ortiz Cofer. Used by permission of Scholastic Inc.

Argelia Sedillo "Gentleman of Rio en Medio" by Juan A.A. Sedillo from *The New Mexico Quarterly, A Regional Review, Volume IX, August, 1939, Number 3.*

Simon & Schuster, Inc. From *Anne Frank Remembered: The Story Of The Woman Who Helped To Hide The Frank Family* by Miep Gies with Alison Leslie Gold. Copyright © 1987 by Miep Gies and Alison Leslie Gold. Used and edited with the permission of Simon & Schuster Adult Publishing Group. All Rights Reserved. CAUTION:Professionals and amateurs are hereby warned that *Anne Frank Remembered: The Story Of The Woman Who Helped To Hide The Frank Family*, being fully protected under the copyright Laws of the United States of America, the British Empire, including the Dominion of Canada, and all other countries of the Universal Copyright and Berne Conventions, are subject to royalty. All rights, including professional, amateur, motion picture, recitation, lecturing, public reading, radio and television broadcasting, and the rights of translation into foreign languages, are strictly reserved. All inquiries should be addressed to Simon & Schuster, Inc.

Simon & Schuster Books for Young Readers "A Glow in the Dark" from *Woodsong* by Gary Paulsen. Text copyright © 1990 by Gary Paulsen. Used by permission.

Virginia Driving Hawk Sneve "The Medicine Bag" by Virginia Driving Hawk Sneve from *Boy's Life.* Copyright © 1975 by Virginia Driving Hawk Sneve. Used by permission.

The Society of Authors "Silver" by Walter de la Mare from *The Complete Poems of Walter de la Mare 1901-1918.* Used by permission of The Literary Trustees of Walter de la Mare and the Society of Authors as their representative.

The Jesse Stuart Foundation c/o Marian Reiner "Old Ben" by Jesse Stuart from *Dawn of Remembered Spring.* Copyright © 1955, 1972 Jesse Stuart. Copyright © renewed 1983 by The Jesse Stuart Foundation. Used by permission of Marian Reiner, Literary Agent. on behalf of the Jesse Stuart Foundation, P.O. Box 669, Ashland, KY 41105.

Tampa Museum of Art Tampa Museum of Art Job Description and Application from *http://www.tampagov.net/dept_tampa_museum_ of_art/index.asp.* Copyright © 1996-2007 City of Tampa. Used by permission.

Thomson Higher Education "Summary of The Tell-Tale Heart" from *Short Story Criticism: Criticism Of The Works Of Short Fiction Writers, Short Story Criticism Vol 34 34th Edition* by Anna Sheets Nesbitt (Editor). Copyright © 1999. Used with permission of Gale, a division of Thomson Learning: www.thomsonrights.com.

Thomson, Inc. Answering Machine Warranty from *http://www. home-electronics.net/en-us/gelimitedwarranty.html.* Copyright © 2007 Thomson. All Rights Reserved.

Estate of Jackie Torrence "Brer Possum's Dilemma" retold by Jackie Torrence from *Homespun: Tales From America's Favorite Storytellers.* Copyright © 1988 by Jackie Torrence, published in *Homespun: Tales from America's Favorite Storytellers* by Jimmy Neil Smith. Used by permission of author.

University Press of Virginia "Harriet Beecher Stowe" edited by Joanne M. Braxton from *The Collected Poetry of Paul Laurence Dunbar.* Copyright © 1993. Used by permission of University of Virginia Press.

Vallejo Baylink Baylink Ferry Schedule and Logo from *http://www. baylinkferry.com.* Copyright © 2007. Used by permission.

Ralph M. Vicinanza, Ltd. "Science and the Sense of Wonder" by Isaac Asimov from *Patterns Of Reflection: A Reader.* Copyright © 1998, 1995 by Allyn & Bacon. Copyright © 1992 by Macmillan Publishing Company. Used by permission of The Estate of Isaac Asimov c/o Ralph M. Vicinanza, Ltd.

Viking Penguin, Inc. Excerpt from *Travels with Charley* by John Steinbeck, copyright © 1961, 1962 by The Curtis Publishing Co., © 1962 by John Steinbeck, renewed © 1990 by Elaine Steinbeck, Thom Steinbeck and John Steinbeck IV. Used by permission of Viking Penguin, a division of Penguin Group (USA) Inc. "Letters from John Steinbeck to Elaine Steinbeck (9/29/1960 and 10/11/1960)" by John Steinbeck, Edited by Elaine Steinbeck and Robert Wallsten from *Steinbeck: A Life In Letters.* Copyright © 1975 by Elaine A. Steinbeck and Robert Wallsten, Copyright © 1954 by John Steinback, Copyright © 1969 by the Executors of the Estate of John Steinbeck. All rights reserved.

Vital Speeches of the Day From *Sharing in the American Dream* by Colin Powell from *Vital Speeches, June 1, 1997, V63 N16, P484(2).* Used by permission of Vital Speeches of the Day.

W. W. Norton & Company, Inc. "Water Names" from *Hunger* by Lan Samantha Chang. Copyright © 1998 by Lan Samantha Chang. Used by permission of W. W. Norton & Company, Inc. (From San by Lan Samantha Chang from *Hunger.* Copyright © 1998 by Lan Samantha Chang.)

Walker & Company "The Baker Heater League" by Patricia and Frederick McKissack from *A Long Hard Journey: The Story of the Pullman Porter.* Copyright © 1989 by Patricia and Frederick McKissack. Used with permission of Walker & Company.

Water Taxi, Inc. Fort Lauderdale Water Taxi™ Map and Schedule from *http://www.watertaxi.com.* Copyright © 2002 - 2007 Water Taxi, Inc. All Rights Reserved. Used by permission.

Richard & Joyce Wolkomir "Sun Suckers and Moon Cursers" by Richarad and Joyce Wolkomir. Copyright © 2002 by Richard & Joyce Wolkomir. Used with the authors' permission.

Note: Every effort has been made to locate the copyright owner of material reproduced on this component. Omissions brought to our attention will be corrected in subsequent editions.

Credits

Photo Credits

xlviii Yaro/Shutterstock **Grade 8 Unit 1 11:** r. Hulton Archive/Getty Images Inc.; **11:** b. The Granger Collection, New York; **12:** b. Wolfgang Kaehler/CORBIS; **12:** t. Lake County Museum/CORBIS; **12:** b. AP/Wide World Photos; **15:** Swim Ink/CORBIS; **16:** Vintage Books; **18:** *The Ministries of Silence,* 2000 (oil on canvas) by Bob Lescaux (b.1928) Private Collection/The Bridgeman Art Library. French/in copyright; **20:** *The Ministries of Silence,* 2000 (oil on canvas) by Bob Lescaux (b.1928) Private Collection/The Bridgeman Art Library. French/in copyright; **22:** Courtesy of Diane Alimena; **22:** © David Fokos/CORBIS; **27:** Nikky Finney; **36:** Tony Freeman/PhotoEdit; **41:** Bettmann/CORBIS; **41:** b. Mary Evans Picture Library; **42:** Inset. New York State Historical Association, Cooperstown, New York; **46:** Images.com/CORBIS; **48:** I. Mary Evans Picture Library; **57:** t. Courtesy Raul Sedillo; **57:** b. "The Parker Family Collection, Fort Worth, TX"; **61:** "The Parker Family Collection, Fort Worth, TX"; **65:** t. Bettmann/CORBIS; **68:** Courtesy US Army Corp of Engineers; **69:** *The Champions of the Mississippi,* Currier & Ives, Scala/Art Resource, New York; **83:** © Charles E. Rotkin/CORBIS; **87:** b. Courtesy of the author. Photo by Don Perkins.; **87:** t. Jesse Stuart Foundation; **88:** M.P. Kahl/Photo Researchers, Inc.; **88-93:** border. istockphoto.com/; **90-91:** border. istockphoto.com/; **92:** National Geographic/Getty Images; **92-93:** border. istockphoto.com/; **99:** Portrait of a Mandarin, Chinese School, 19th century/The Bridgeman Art Library, London/New York; **113:** © Rosalie Thorne McKenna Foundation. Courtesy Center for Creative Photography, University of Arizona Foundation; **114:** Joe Squillante/Photonica; **117:** Edward Holub/Getty Images; **121:** Hulton Archive/Getty Images Inc.; **124:** from *The Complete Adventures of Sherlock Holmes,* illustration by Sidney Paget; **127:** from *The Complete Adventures of Sherlock Holmes,* illustration by Sidney Paget; **128:** from *The Complete Adventures of Sherlock Holmes,* illustration by Sidney Paget; **130:** from *The Complete Adventures of Sherlock Holmes,* illustration by Sidney Paget; **135:** from *The Complete Adventures of Sherlock Holmes,* illustration by Sidney Paget; **138:** from *The Complete Adventures of Sherlock Holmes,* illustration by Sidney Paget; **146:** t. Tek Image/Photo Researchers, Inc.; **146:** m. Getty Images; **146:** r. © Leonard Lessin/Peter Arnold, Inc.; **149:** from *The Complete Adventures of Sherlock Holmes,* illustration by Sidney Paget; **159:** t. Bettmann/CORBIS; **160:** Connie Ricca/CORBIS; **161-168:** border. Silver Burdett Ginn; **162:** Bettmann/CORBIS; **166-167:** b. Morey Milbradt/Brand X/CORBIS; **167:** t. Lake County Museum/CORBIS; **171:** t. Time Life Pictures/Getty Images; **171:** b. Reuters//Mannie Garcia/CORBIS; **172:** b. Flip Schulke/CORBIS; **172:** t. Corel Professional Photos CD-ROM™; **174:** t. Joseph Sohm/Visions of America/CORBIS; **174:** b. Michale Ventura/PhotoEdit; **175:** Martin Takigawa/Getty Images, Inc.; **181:** b. Thomas Victor; **183:** Charles Krebs/CORBIS; **184:** ©Daryl Benson/Masterfile; **186:** The Granger Collection, New York; **186:** Prentice Hall; **187:** Prentice Hall; **200:** *Drummer Boy,* Julian Scott, N.S. Mayer; **202:** Courtesy National Archives; **203:** Inset. Bettmann/CORBIS; **204:** David; **205:** Bkgrnd. Jackie DesJariais/istockphoto.com; **205:** The Granger Collection, New York; **206:** *Drummer Boy,* Julian Scott, N.S. Mayer; **208:** Index Stock Imagery, Inc.; **324:** ©2001 Mitchell, C.E./Stockphoto.com; **325: 326:** Steve Kraseman/DRK Photo

Grade 8 Unit 2 191: t. Courtesy of Ohio State Historical Society; **192:** © Skip Dickstein/NewSport/CORBIS; **193:** *Farm Boy,* 1941, Charles Alston, Courtesy of Clark Atlanta University; **196:** Alan D. Carey/Photo Researchers, Inc.; **198:** © Kevin R. Morris/CORBIS; **237:** Franco Vogt/CORBIS; **241:** Courtesy National Archives, photo no. (542390); **242:** Myrleen Ferguson Cate/PhotoEdit; **247:** t. Bassouls Sophie/CORBIS; **248:** Bkgrnd. Bruce Stoddard/Getty Images; **253:** Franco Brambilla/Airstudio; **256:** Dawid Michalczyk/Eon Works; **258:** Franco Brambilla/Airstudio; **263:** NO CREDIT NECESSARY; **267:** *Enoshima.* Island at left

with cluster of buildings among trees. Fuji in distance at right, c. 1823. (detail), Katsusika Hokusai, The Newark Museum/Art Resource, NY; **271:** br. Brown Brothers; **271:** bl. Courtesy of State Museum Resource Center, California State Parks; **271:** tr. Michael Moran/© Dorling Kindersley; **271:** tl. Courtesy of the Library of Congress; **279:** ©1998 James McGoon; **282:** David Turnley/CORBIS; **283:** b. Bettmann/CORBIS; **283:** t. Major Keith Hamilton Maxwell/The Mariners' Museum/CORBIS; **284:** *Jubayl,* 1997 (oil on canvas) by Private Collection/The Bridgeman Art Library Nationality/copyright status: French/in copyright; **285:** Pearson Education; **286:** Image Source Black/Getty Images, Inc; **293:** t. Bettmann/CORBIS; **294:** © Thomas Paschke / istockphoto.com; **294:** Bkgrnd. © Ufuk Zivana / istockphoto.com; **294:** border. © Blackred / istockphoto.com; **294:** Inset. © Clint Spencer / istockphoto.com; **296:** Culver Pictures, Inc.; **297:** Culver Pictures, Inc.; **298:** Inset. © Duncan Walker / istockphoto.com; **298:** © Clint Spencer / istockphoto.com; **300:** © Zmajdoo / istockphoto.com; **301:** © Dylan Hewitt / istockphoto.com; **302:** © Janne Ahvo / istockphoto.com; **309:** Courtesy of the Library of Congress; **313:** t. Bettmann/CORBIS; **314:** © Bettmann/CORBIS; **315:** The Granger Collection, New York; **318:** Paul Nicklen/National Geographic Image Collection; **320:** Paul Nicklen/National Geographic Image Collection; **322:** Shutterstock, Inc.; **335:** t. AP/Wide World Photos; **345:** Miriam Berkley/Authorpix **347:** b. istockphoto.com/ GlobalP; **348-380:** istockphoto.com/Sharon Shimoni; **350:** m. © Dorling Kindersley; **350:** br. © Dorling Kindersley; **350:** tm. © Dorling Kindersley; **352:** t. Tim Flach/Getty Images; **354:** ©Cinerama/Archive Photos; **355:** Photofest; **358:** Photofest; **364:** Photofest; **371:** Will & Deni McIntyre/Getty Images; **373:** istockphoto.com/dra_schwartz; **378:** Photofest; **387:** t. New York Public Library, (Rare Book Division or Print Collection. Miriam and Ira D. Wallach Division of Art, Prints and Photographs); Astor, Lenox and Tilden Foundations); **387:** b. *Empire State,* Tom Christopher, Courtesy of the artist.;**388:** *Empire State,* Tom Christopher, Courtesy of the artist.; **391:** *Minnie,* 1930, William Johnson, National Museum of American Art, Washington, DC/Art Resource, NY; **395:** t. E.O. Hoppe/Stringer/Time Life Pictures/Getty Images; **395:** b. *Stirling Station,* 1887, William Kennedy, Collection of Andrew McIntosh Patrick, UK/The Bridgeman Art Library International Ltd., London/New York; **396:** *Stirling Station,* 1887, William Kennedy, Collection of Andrew McIntosh Patrick, UK/The Bridgeman Art Library International Ltd., London/New York; **399:** George Marks; **400:** *Pure Pleasure,* Pat Scott/The Bridgeman Art Library, London/New York; **401:** istockphoto.com; **410:** Courtesy of Amtrak; **411:** Jumpstart for Young Children, Inc.; **412:** © courtesy of City Harvest -http://www.cityharvest. org/; Photo by Timothy White; **415:** b. Courtesy of the author; **415:** AP/Wide World Photos; **416:** *Girl in Car Window,* Winson Trang, Courtesy of the artist; **420:** Will Faller; **422:** Arjan de Jager; **425:** Matt Wilson/istockphoto.com; **426:** Courtesy of Diane Alimena; **427:** LOOK Die Bildagentur der Fotografen mbH/Alamy; **428:** CORBIS; **430:** Pamela Moore/istockphoto.com; **431:** Werner Forman/Art Resource, NY; **433:** © Marilyn Angel Wynn/Nativestock.com; **434:** ©Tom Bean/CORBIS; **436:** Pamela Moore/istockphoto.com; **456:** (TR) James McGoon Photography

Grade 8 Unit 3 467: NASA Jet Propulsion Laboratory (NASA-JPL); **469:** Spots on the Spot; **470:** NASA; **472:** bl. NASA/JPL; **477:** t. ©HOUSTON CHRONICLE; **477:** b. Craig Barhorst; **478:** Craig Barhorst; **479:** Michael Newman/PhotoEdit; **481:** Cultura/CORBIS; **482:** Mike Ehrmann/Stringer/Getty Images, Inc.; **485:** t. AP/Wide World Photos; **490:** Tom Uhlman/Alamy; **492:** Bettmann/CORBIS; **503:** t. Courtesy Brent Ashabranner; **503:** b. Paul Conklin/PhotoEdit; **504:** Catherine Ursillo/Photo Researchers, Inc.; **506:** Paul Conklin/PhotoEdit; **508:** AP/Wide World Photos; **508:** Catherine Ursillo/Photo Researchers, Inc.; **510:** Richard Howard/Black Star; **513:** t. Getty Images; **515:** ©FPG International LLC; **520:** tr. ©2004 JupiterImages and its Licensors. All Rights Reserved.; **520:** br. Pearson Education/PH School Division; **520:** m. Pearson Education/PH School Division; **520:** bl. Pearson Education/PH School

Anne Frank House - Amsterdam/Getty Images; **978:** t. Allard Bovenberg/ Anne Frank Fonds - Basel/Anne Frank House/Hulton Archive/Getty Images; **979:** b. AP/Wide World Photos; **1004** (TR) Getty Images

Grade 8 Unit 6 1012: m. Reprinted with the permission of Bob Thaves and the Cartoonist Group. All rights reserved.; **1015:** t. Liu Liqun/CORBIS; **1016:** ©Qinetiq Ltd//Peter Arnold, Inc.; **1016:** Bettmann/CORBIS; **1016:** PictureQuest/Stock Connection/Peter Samp; Georgina Bowater; **1016:** Michael S. Yamashita/CORBIS; **1017:** r. Kevin Schafer/CORBIS; **1018:** b. China Span, LLC/CORBIS; **1020:** b. © Rainer Holz/ zefa/ CORBIS; **1025:** b. AP/Wide World Photos; **1025:** t. ©Bassouls Sophie/CORBIS Sygma; **1026:** l. Cosmic Canine, John Nieto, Courtesy of the artist; **1027:** Bob Rowan, Progressive Image/CORBIS; **1031:** t. The Granger Collection, New York; **1032-1033:** b. © Artkey/CORBIS; **1045:** t. Irene Young; **1049:** t. *John Henry on the Right, Steam Drill on the Left,* 1944-47, Palmer C. Hayden, Museum of African American Art; **1050:** b. Courtesy of the Library of Congress; **1051:** t. *He Laid Down his Hammer and Cried,* 1944-47, Palmer C. Hayden, Museum of African American Art, Los Angeles, CA; **1051:** border. artville/ getty images; **1055:** m. Courtesy of the author; **1055:** b. Time Life Pictures/Getty Images; **1055:** t. Chuck Slade; **1056:** t. *Invitation to the Dance (el convite),* Theodore Gentilz, Gift, Yanaguana Society in memory of Frederick C. Chabot, Daughters of the Republic of Texas Library; **1057:** t. **1062:** t. Lake County Museum/ CORBIS; **1065:** Random House Inc.; **1073:** b. The Granger Collection, New York; **1073:** t. Burstein Collection/CORBIS; **1073:** m. Time Life Pictures/ Getty Images; **1074:** tl. Bettmann/CORBIS; **1074-1075:** t. © Anders Ryman/ CORBIS; **1075:** Courtesy of Plattsburgh State Art Museum, Rockwell Kent Collection, Gift of Sally Kent Gorton; **1078:** t. Blank Archives/Getty Images; **1079:** t. © Patrick Hattori/ epa/CORBIS; **1079:** t. istockphoto. com; **1080:** tl. James Randklev/ Photodisc/ Getty Images; **1080:** tm. Andrea Salcioli/ Photodisc/ Getty Images; **1080:** bl. Peter Adams/ Digital Vision/ Getty Images; **1080:** tr. Connie Coleman/ Getty Images; **1080:** ml. John Wang/ Photodisc/ Getty Images; **1080:** m. © Fototeca Storica Nazionale/ Photodisc/ Getty Images; **1082:** r. istockphoto.com; **1082:** © David Muench/ CORBIS; **1083:** tl. istockphoto.com; **1083:** rm. istockphoto. com; **1083:** tr. istockphoto.com; **1093:** t. AP/Wide World Photos; **1093:** b. Bettmann/CORBIS; **1094:** t. Courtesy National Archives; **1096:** Getty Images; **1096:** bm. Bettmann/CORBIS; **1096:** br. Courtesy National Archives, photo no. (19425); **1096:** bl. Bettmann/CORBIS; **1096:** ml. Courtesy of the Library of Congress; **1097:** t. AP/Wide World Photos; **1099:** b. Bettmann/ CORBIS; **1103:** t. Prentice Hall; **1104-1105:** Joseph McNally/Getty Images; **1104-1105:** Felix Zaska/CORBIS; **1104-1105:** b. The Granger Collection, New York; **1106:** Blue Line Pictures; **1113:** t. AP/Wide World Photos; **1114:** © CORBIS; **1115:** b. Courtesy of the Library of Congress; **1116:** b. Bettmann/ CORBIS; **1117:** b. Bettmann/CORBIS; **1118:** t. ©altrendo nature/ Getty Images; **1121:** t. Bettmann/CORBIS; **1122-1123:** t. Art Resource, NY; **1125:** t. The Granger Collection, New York; **1126:** t. Bettmann/CORBIS; **1128:** tr. The Museum of the Confederacy, Richmond, Virginia, Photography by Katerine Wetzel; **1137:** Bettmann/CORBIS; **1138:** Frank Scherschel//Time Life Pictures/Getty Images; **1139:** L Frank Scherschel// Time Life Pictures/Getty Images; **1139 :** m. Frank Scherschel//Time Life Pictures/Getty Images; **1139:** r. Frank Scherschel//Time Life Pictures/ Getty Images; **1140:** The Sad Sack® is a Registered Trademark and © Sad Sack, Inc. Created by George Baker; **1145:** m. Cheron Bayna; **1145:** b. ©1998 James McGoon; **1150:** ©Robert Fried; **1153:** m. Royalty-Free/CORBIS; **1154:** t. Tony Freeman/PhotoEdit; **1156:** l. Esbin/Anderson/ Omni-Photo Communications, Inc.; **1159:** t. Prentice Hall; **1174:** (BL) Time & Life Pictures/Getty Images

Staff Credits

The people who made up the Pearson Prentice Hall Literature team— representing design, editorial, editorial services, education technology, manufacturing and inventory planning, market research, marketing services, planning and budgeting, product planning, production services, project office, publishing processes, and rights and permissions—are listed below. Boldface type denotes the core team members.

Tobey Antao, Margaret Antonini, Rosalyn Arcilla, Penny Baker, James Ryan Bannon, Stephan Barth, **Tricia Battipede,** Krista Baudo, Rachel Beckman, Julie Berger, Lawrence Berkowitz, Melissa Biezin, **Suzanne Biron,** Rick Blount, **Marcela Boos, Betsy Bostwick,** Kay Bosworth, Jeff Bradley, Andrea Brescia, Susan Brorein, Lois Brown, **Pam Carey,** Lisa Carrillo, **Geoffrey Cassar,** Patty Cavuoto, Doria Ceraso, Jennifer Ciccone, Jaime Cohen, Rebecca Cottingham, Joe Cucchiara, Jason Cuoco, **Alan Dalgleish, Karen Edmonds, Irene Ehrmann,** Stephen Eldridge, Amy Fleming, Dorothea Fox, Steve Frankel, Cindy Frederick, Phil Fried, Diane Fristachi, Phillip Gagler, **Pamela Gallo,** Husain Gatlin, **Elaine Goldman,** Elizabeth Good, John Guild, Phil Hadad, Patricia Hade, Monduane Harris, Brian Hawkes, Jennifer B. Heart, Martha Heller, John Hill, Beth Hyslip, Mary Jean Jones, Grace Kang, Nathan Kinney, Roxanne Knoll, **Kate Krimsky,** Monisha Kumar, Jill Kushner, Sue Langan, Melisa Leong, Susan Levine, Dave Liston, **Mary Luthi, George Lychock, Gregory Lynch, Joan Mazzeo, Sandra McGloster,** Salita Mehta, Eve Melnechuk, Kathleen Mercandetti, Artur Mkrtchyan, Karyn Mueller, Alison Muff, Christine Mulcahy, Kenneth Myett, Elizabeth Nemeth, Stefano Nese, Carrie O'Connor, April Okano, Kim Ortell, Sonia Pap, Raymond Parenteau, Dominique Pickens, Linda Punskovsky, **Sheila Ramsay,** Maureen Raymond, Mairead Reddin, **Erin Rehill-Seker, Renee Roberts, Laura Ross,** Bryan Salacki, Sharon Schultz, Jennifer Serra, **Melissa Shustyk,** Rose Sievers, Christy Singer, Yvonne Stecky, **Cynthia Summers,** Steve Thomas, Merle Uuesoo, Roberta Warshaw, Patricia Williams, Daniela Velez

Additional Credits

Lydie Bemba, Victoria Blades, Denise Data, Rachel Drice, Eleanor Kostyk, Jill Little, Loraine Machlin, Evan Marx, Marilyn McCarthy, Patrick O'Keefe, Shelia M. Smith, Lucia Tirondola, Laura Vivenzio, Linda Waldman, Angel Weyant